Unified Transfer Tax Rates

For Gifts Made and for Deaths after 2012

If the Amount with Respect to Which the Tentative Tax to Be Computed Is:	The Tentative Tax Is:
Not over $10,000	18 percent of such amount.
Over $10,000 but not over $20,000	$1,800, plus 20 percent of the excess of such amount over $10,000.
Over $20,000 but not over $40,000	$3,800, plus 22 percent of the excess of such amount over $20,000.
Over $40,000 but not over $60,000	$8,200, plus 24 percent of the excess of such amount over $40,000.
Over $60,000 but not over $80,000	$13,000, plus 26 percent of the excess of such amount over $60,000.
Over $80,000 but not over $100,000	$18,200, plus 28 percent of the excess of such amount over $80,000.
Over $100,000 but not over $150,000	$23,800, plus 30 percent of the excess of such amount over $100,000.
Over $150,000 but not over $250,000	$38,800, plus 32 percent of the excess of such amount over $150,000.
Over $250,000 but not over $500,000	$70,800, plus 34 percent of the excess of such amount over $250,000.
Over $500,000 but not over $750,000	$155,800, plus 37 percent of the excess of such amount over $500,000.
Over $750,000 but not over $1,000,000	$248,300, plus 39 percent of the excess of such amount over $750,000.
Over $1,000,000	$345,800, plus 40 percent of the excess of such amount over $1,000,000.

BECKER
PROFESSIONAL EDUCATION®

Powerful preparation.
Maximum confidence.

The right tools to help prepare you for the Exam

With Becker Professional Education, you get a fully integrated
CPA Exam Review course that helps you:

MOVE BEYOND MEMORIZATION TO APPLICATION

Interactive simulations and videos move you beyond memorization,
helping you apply concepts — a critical component of the CPA Exam.

CPA SkillMaster Videos

Tackle Task-Based Simulations
with confidence. Our
expert instructors take you
through the most complex
questions step-by-step.

*It's like having your
own CPA coach!*

STUDY SMART

Adapt2U pre-assessment provides you a recommended study path.

TRACK PROGRESS AND BUILD CONFIDENCE

Mock exams, progress tests and a study planner help you focus on where you need the most help.

LEARN WHAT'S NEEDED

Study with a course that replicates the CPA Exam.

CHOOSE FROM 3 FLEXIBLE COURSE FORMATS

Choose from Self-Study, LiveOnline or Live Classroom formats.

the **CPA** *review*

Learn more at **becker.com**

THOMSON REUTERS

CHECKPOINT™

3 Simple Ways Checkpoint Helps You Make Sense of All Those Taxes.

- Find what you are looking for quickly and easily online with Thomson Reuters Checkpoint™
- A comprehensive collection of primary tax law, cases and rulings, along with analytical insight you simply can't find anywhere else
- Checkpoint has built-in productivity tools to make research more efficient — a resource more tax pros use than any other

Titles that include Checkpoint Student Edition:

- **Young/Nellen/Hoffman/Raabe/Maloney,** *South-Western Federal Taxation: Individual Income Taxes, 2020 Edition*

- **Raabe/Young/Hoffman/Nellen/Maloney,** *South-Western Federal Taxation: Corporations, Partnerships, Estates & Trusts, 2020 Edition*

- **Maloney/Raabe/Young/Nellen/Hoffman,** *South-Western Federal Taxation: Comprehensive Volume, 2020 Edition*

- **Nellen/Young/Raabe/Maloney,** *South-Western Federal Taxation: Essentials of Taxation: Individuals and Business Entities, 2020 Edition*

- **Murphy/Higgins,** *Concepts in Federal Taxation, 2020 Edition*

I M P O R T A N T   I N F O R M A T I O N

The purchase of this textbook includes access to Thomson Reuters Checkpoint™ Student Edition for a 6-month duration.

To log in visit **checkpoint.tr.com**
You will be asked to supply a User ID and Password. Please use the following:

USER ID: CEN19-12279

PASSWORD: CEN19-12279

PLEASE NOTE: If you have purchased a used copy of this text, the User ID and Password may have already been used. A new User ID and Password may be obtained by purchasing a new copy of this text.

 THOMSON REUTERS®

ISBN-13: 978-0-357-10968-7 • ISBN-10: 0-357-10968-6

For technical support please visit
cengage.com/support

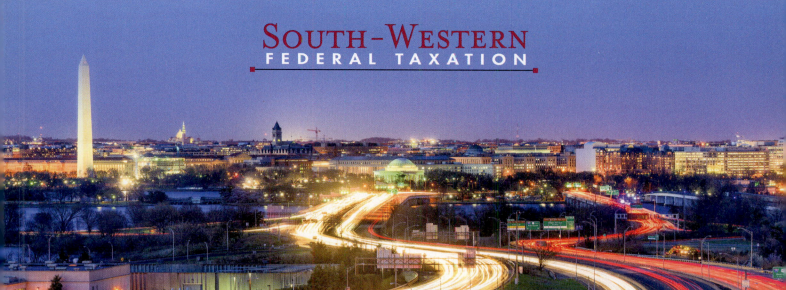

SOUTH-WESTERN
FEDERAL TAXATION

CORPORATIONS, PARTNERSHIPS, ESTATES & TRUSTS

2020

General Editors

William A. Raabe
Ph.D., CPA

James C. Young
Ph.D., CPA

William H. Hoffman, Jr.
J.D., Ph.D., CPA

Annette Nellen
J.D., CPA, CGMA

David M. Maloney
Ph.D., CPA

Contributing Authors

James H. Boyd
Ph.D., CPA
Arizona State University

Gregory Carnes
Ph.D., CPA
University of North Alabama

D. Larry Crumbley
Ph.D., CPA
Louisiana State University

Andrew Cuccia
Ph.D., CPA
University of Oklahoma

Steven C. Dilley
J.D., Ph.D., CPA
Michigan State University

Steven L. Gill
Ph.D., CPA
San Diego State University

William H. Hoffman, Jr.
J.D., Ph.D., CPA
University of Houston

David M. Maloney
Ph.D., CPA
University of Virginia

Annette Nellen
J.D., CPA, CGMA
San Jose State University

Mark B. Persellin
Ph.D., CPA, CFP
St. Mary's University

William A. Raabe
Ph.D., CPA
Madison, Wisconsin

Debra L. Sanders
Ph.D., CPA
Washington State
University, Vancouver

Toby Stock
Ph.D., CPA
Ohio University

James C. Young
Ph.D., CPA
Northern Illinois University

Kristina Zvinakis
Ph.D.
The University of Texas
at Austin

CENGAGE

Australia • Brazil • Mexico • Singapore • United Kingdom • United States

South-Western Federal Taxation: Corporations, Partnerships, Estates & Trusts, 2020 Edition

William A. Raabe, James C. Young, William H. Hoffman, Jr., Annette Nellen, David M. Maloney

Senior Vice President, Higher Ed Product, Content, and Market Development: Erin Joyner

Product Director: Jason Fremder

Assoc. Product Manager: Jonathan Gross

Sr. Content Manager: Nadia Saloom

Learning Designer: Natasha Allen

Marketing Manager: Chris Walz

Sr. Digital Delivery Lead: Tim Richison

Production Service: SPi Global

Designer: Chris A. Doughman

Text Designer: Red Hangar Design

Cover Designer: Bethany Bourgeois

Cover Image: iStock.com/Sean Pavone

Intellectual Property:
    Analyst: Reba Frederics
    Project Manager: Carly Belcher

Design Images:
    Concept Summary: iStock.com/enot-poloskun
    Global Tax Issues: enot-poloskun/ E+/Getty Images
    Ethics & Equity: iStock.com/LdF
    Comprehensive Tax Return Problems: iStock.com/peepo
    Financial Disclosure Insights: Vyaseleva Elena/Shutterstock.com

For product information and technology assistance, contact us at **Cengage Customer & Sales Support, 1-800-354-9706** or **support.cengage.com.**

For permission to use material from this text or product, submit all requests online at **cengage.com/permissions**.

All tax forms within the text are: Source: Internal Revenue Service
Tax software: Source: Intuit Proconnect
Becker CPA Review: Source: Becker CPA
Excel screenshots ©Microsoft Corporation.

ISSN: 0270-5265
2020 Annual Edition

Student Edition ISBN: 978-0-357-10920-5
Student Edition with Intuit Proconnect + RIA Checkpoint
ISBN: 978-0-357-10916-8

Cengage
20 Channel Center Street
Boston, MA 02210
USA

Cengage is a leading provider of customized learning solutions with employees residing in nearly 40 different countries and sales in more than 125 countries around the world. Find your local representative at **cengage.com**.

Cengage products are represented in Canada by Nelson Education, Ltd.

To learn more about Cengage platforms and services, register or access your online learning solution, or purchase materials for your course, visit **cengage.com**.

Printed in the United States of America
Print Number: 01   Print Year: 2019

Preface

COMMITTED TO EDUCATIONAL SUCCESS

South-Western Federal Taxation (SWFT) is the most trusted and best-selling series in college taxation. We are focused exclusively on providing the most useful, comprehensive, and up-to-date tax texts, online study aids, tax preparation tools, and research tools to help instructors and students succeed in their tax courses and beyond.

SWFT is a comprehensive package of teaching and learning materials, significantly enhanced with each edition to meet instructor and student needs and to add overall value to learning taxation.

Corporations, Partnerships, Estates & Trusts, 2020 Edition provides a dynamic learning experience inside and outside of the classroom. Built with resources and tools that have been identified as the most important, our complete learning system provides options for students to achieve success.

Corporations, Partnerships, Estates & Trusts, 2020 Edition covers tax concepts as they affect corporations, partnerships, estates, and trusts. The authors provide accessible, comprehensive, and authoritative coverage of relevant tax code and regulations, as well as all major developments in Federal income taxation. This market-leading text is intended for students who have had a previous course in taxation.

In revising the 2020 Edition, we focused on:

- *Accessibility. Clarity. Substance.* The text authors and editors made this their mantra as they revised the 2020 edition. Coverage has been streamlined to make it more accessible to students, and difficult concepts have been clarified, all without losing the substance that makes up the *South-Western Federal Taxation series*.

- *Developing professional skills.* SWFT excels in bringing students to a professional level in their tax knowledge and skills, to prepare them for immediate success in their careers. In this regard, we include development of speaking and writing communications skills, the use of tax preparation and tax research software, orientation toward success on the CPA Exam, consideration of the time value of money in the tax planning process, and facility with advanced spreadsheet applications and data analytics.

- *CengageNOWv2 as a complete learning system.* Cengage Learning understands that digital learning solutions are central to the classroom. Through sustained research, we continually refine our learning solutions in CengageNOWv2 to meet evolving student and instructor needs. CengageNOWv2 fulfills learning and course management needs by offering a personalized study plan, video lectures, auto-graded homework, auto-graded tests, and a full eBook with features and advantages that address common challenges.

FULL-COLOR DESIGN: We understand that students struggle with learning difficult tax code concepts and applying them to real-world scenarios. The 2020 edition uses color to bring the text to life, capture student attention, and present the tax code in an understandable and logical format.

❏ Selected **content is streamlined** to guide students in focusing on the most important concepts for the CPA Exam while still providing in-depth coverage of topics.

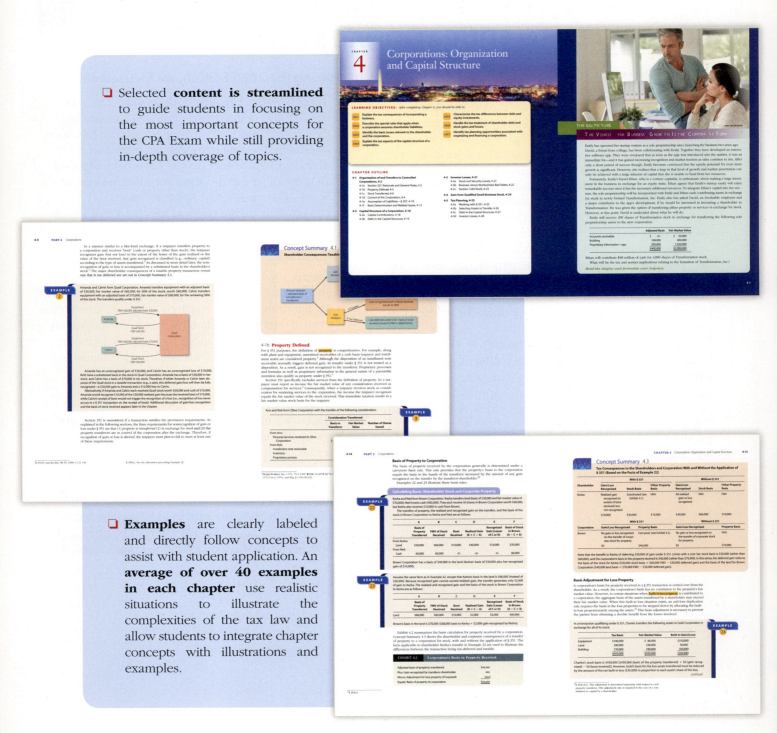

❏ **Examples** are clearly labeled and directly follow concepts to assist with student application. An **average of over 40 examples in each chapter** use realistic situations to illustrate the complexities of the tax law and allow students to integrate chapter concepts with illustrations and examples.

COMPUTATIONAL EXERCISES: Students need lots of practice in areas such as computing tax return problems and adjusting rates. We have developed these exercises to give students practice in calculating the solutions they need to make business decisions.

- ❏ Found in end-of-chapter section of the textbook

- ❏ CengageNOWv2 provides algorithmic versions of these problems

Computational Exercises

19. **LO.1** Marie and Ethan form Roundtree Corporation with the transfer of the following. Marie performs personal services for the corporation with a fair market value of $80,000 in exchange for 400 shares of stock. Ethan contributes an installment note receivable (basis $25,000; fair market value $30,000), land (basis $50,000; fair market value $170,000), and inventory (basis $100,000; fair market value $120,000) in exchange for 1,600 shares. Determine Marie and Ethan's current income, gain, or loss; calculate the basis that each takes in the Roundtree stock.

20. **LO.1** Grady exchanges qualified property, basis of $12,000 and fair market value of $18,000, for 60% of the stock of Eadie Corporation. The other 40% of the stock is owned by Pedro, who acquired it five years ago. Calculate Grady's current income, gain, or loss and the basis he takes in his shares of Eadie stock as a result of this transaction.

DATA ANALYTICS

- ❏ Research Problems provide students with vital practice in an increasingly demanded skill area. These end-of-chapter items task students with the analysis of important tax data, with a focus on helping them understand the application of this information in various scenarios. This essential feature will better prepare students for professional tax environments.

BECKER PROFESSIONAL EDUCATION REVIEW QUESTIONS: End-of-Chapter CPA Review Questions from Becker PREPARE STUDENTS FOR SUCCESS. Students review key concepts using proven questions from Becker Professional Education®—one of the industry's most effective tools to prepare for the CPA Exam.

- ❏ Located in select end-of-chapter sections

- ❏ Tagged by concept in CengageNOWv2

- ❏ Questions similar to what students would actually find on the CPA Exam

Becker CPA Review Question

1. Paula has sales that qualify to be reported on the installment basis. In year 2, installment sales were $40,000 with a cost of $30,000. In year 3, installment sales were $50,000 with a cost of $25,000. Collections in year 2 were in the amount of $30,000. Collections in year 3 were $10,000 on the year 2 sales and $30,000 on the year 3 sales. How much deferred gross profit exists as of the end of year 2?

   a. $2,500   c. $7,500

   b. $5,000   d. $10,000

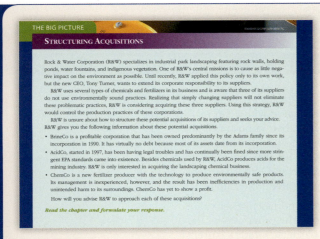

THE BIG PICTURE: Tax Solutions for the Real World. Taxation comes alive at the start of each chapter as The Big Picture examples give a glimpse into the lives, families, careers, and tax situations of typical filers. Students will follow this one family, individual, or other taxpayer throughout the chapter showing students how the concepts they are learning play out in the real world.

Finally, to solidify student comprehension, each chapter concludes with a **Refocus on the Big Picture** summary and tax planning scenario. These scenarios apply the concepts and topics from the chapter in a reasonable and professional way.

FINANCIAL DISCLOSURE INSIGHTS:

Tax professionals need to understand how taxes affect the GAAP financial statements. **Financial Disclosure Insights**, appearing throughout the text, use current data about existing taxpayers to highlight book-tax reporting differences, effective tax rates, and trends in reporting conventions.

ETHICS & EQUITY The Costs of Good Tax Planning

High Tech Tops (HTT), a C corporation based in California, manufactures resilient cases and covers for laptops, smartphones, and tablets. Its sales and profits have more than doubled in each of the last five years (i.e., the company is growth-oriented and recession-proof). Its employees and contractors make above-average wages, so they make important contributions to the local individual income, sales, and property tax collections.

But the Federal and state corporate income tax is another story. Using legal and effective transfer pricing techniques, HTT shifts most of its operating profits to low-tax subsidiaries in Ireland and Singapore. Most of the firm's executives, engineers, and designers are based in the United States, but almost all of the sales operations are run from overseas. HTT's customers live around the world, but its tax liabilities are concentrated in the low-tax jurisdictions.

You are the president of State University, across town from HTT's headquarters. The company sends hundreds of its employees to take graduate and professional courses on your campus, and several of the corporate leaders are frequent guest speakers and adjunct lecturers in classes.

Still, the state income tax the company avoids through its transfer pricing plans would fund millions of dollars of campus growth and improvements for State University.

Should you become involved in the politics of the matter and lobby at your statehouse for tighter rules on transfer pricing? Such an action might result in tax increases that would improve your university's situation, but it also might force HTT to consider moving its headquarters to another location.

ETHICS & EQUITY: Some tax issues do not have just one correct answer. **Ethics & Equity** features will spark critical thinking and invite classroom discussion, enticing students to evaluate their own value system. Suggested answers to Ethics & Equity scenarios appear in the Solutions Manual.

9-8 TAX PLANNING

Return to the timeline of Exhibit 9.6, and consider the decision to operate a multi-national business entity as a branch and when to convert the structure of the business to an overseas subsidiary. Exhibit 9.9 identifies the major advantages and disadvantages for each of these decisions from a Federal income tax standpoint.

Additional tax planning opportunities and considerations are discussed below.

9-8a The Foreign Tax Credit Limitation and Sourcing Provisions

The FTC limitation is partially based on the amount of foreign-source taxable income in the numerator of the limitation formula. Consequently, the sourcing of income is extremely important. Generally, in this regard, the U.S. taxpayer benefits when the sourcing rules work to:

- Generate *income* items that are *foreign-source*, to maximize net foreign-source income (the numerator of the FTC fraction). Alternatively, a branch or flow-through entity might want overseas income to be U.S.-source, to increase its 20 percent deduction for qualified business income.[57]

- Realize *deduction* items as *U.S.-source*, to minimize any reduction in net foreign-source income (the numerator of the FTC fraction).

TAX PLANNING: Chapters include a separate section calling attention to how taxpayers can use the law to reach financial and other goals. Tax planning applications and suggestions also appear throughout each chapter.

GLOBAL TAX ISSUES Tax Reform Adds a New Wrinkle to the Choice of Organizational Form When Operating Overseas

When the management of a corporation decides to expand its business by establishing a presence in a foreign market, the new business venture may take one of several organizational forms. As each form comes with its respective advantages and disadvantages, making the best choice can be difficult. And the choice is even more difficult now since a new set of rules applies to the taxation of international operations beginning in 2018.

Nonetheless, one common approach is to conduct the foreign activity as a *branch* operation of the U.S. corporation. The foreign branch is not a separate legal entity, but a division of the U.S. corporation established overseas. As a result, any gains and losses produced by the foreign unit are included in the corporation's overall financial results.

Another possibility is to organize the foreign operations as a *subsidiary* of the U.S. parent corporation. If this route is chosen, the subsidiary may be either a *domestic* subsidiary (i.e., organized in the United States) or a *foreign* subsidiary (organized under the laws of a foreign country).

One fundamental tax difference between these two approaches is that the gains and losses of a domestic subsidiary may be consolidated with the operations of the U.S. parent, but the operations of a foreign subsidiary cannot. Thus, the use of a domestic subsidiary to conduct foreign operations generally yields the same final result as the use of a branch. With both approaches, the financial statements of the U.S. parent reflect the results of its worldwide operations.

As noted, the tax rules associated with international operations and their impact on organizational forms have changed with the passage of the Tax Cuts and Jobs Act (TCJA) of 2017. Now the United States uses a "territorial system" when taxing foreign earnings, which, generally, requires U.S. corporations to pay U.S. tax only on their domestic income. Given the complexity of the organizational form decisions and the significance of the changes to international taxation rules in the TCJA of 2017, it will take time for tax professionals to determine the most tax-effective ways of structuring foreign operations of U.S. corporations. See Chapter 9 for additional discussion of the taxation of international operations.

GLOBAL TAX ISSUES: The **Global Tax Issues** feature gives insight into the ways in which taxation is affected by international concerns and illustrates the effects of various events on tax liabilities across the globe.

Take your students from Motivation to Mastery with CengageNOWv2

MASTERY
APPLICATION
MOTIVATION

CengageNOWv2 is a powerful course management tool and online homework resource that elevates student thinking by providing superior content designed with the entire student workflow in mind.

❏ **MOTIVATION:** engage students and better prepare them for class

❏ **APPLICATION:** help students learn problem-solving behavior and skills to guide them to complete taxation problems on their own

❏ **MASTERY:** help students make the leap from memorizing concepts to actual critical thinking

Motivation —

Many instructors find that students come to class unmotivated and unprepared. To help with engagement and preparedness, CengageNOWv2 for SWFT offers:

❏ **"Tax Drills" test students on key concepts and applications.** With three to five questions per learning objective, these "quick-hit" questions help students prepare for class lectures or review prior to an exam.

Application —

Students need to learn problem-solving behavior and skills, to guide them to complete taxation problems on their own. However, as students try to work through homework problems, sometimes they become stuck and need extra help. To reinforce concepts and keep students on the right track, CengageNOWv2 for SWFT offers the following.

❏ **End-of-chapter homework from the text** is expanded and enhanced to follow the workflow a professional would use to solve various client scenarios. These enhancements better engage students and encourage them to think like a tax professional.

- ❏ **Algorithmic versions** of end-of-chapter homework are available for computational exercises and at least 15 problems per chapter.

- ❏ **"Check My Work" Feedback.** Homework questions include immediate feedback so students can learn as they go. Levels of feedback include an option for "check my work" prior to submission of an assignment.

- ❏ **Post-Submission Feedback.** After submitting an assignment, students receive even more extensive feedback explaining why their answers were incorrect. Instructors can decide how much feedback their students receive and when, including the full solution.

- ❏ **Built-in Test Bank** for online assessment.

Mastery —

- ❏ **Tax Form Problems** give students the option to complete the Cumulative Intuit ProConnect Problems and other homework items found in the end-of-chapter manually or in a digital environment.

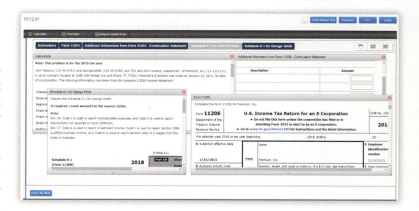

- ❏ **"What-If" Questions** allow students to develop a deeper understanding of the material as they are challenged to use their prior knowledge of the tax situations and critically think through new attributes to determine how the outcome will change.

- ❏ **An Adaptive Study Plan** comes complete with an eBook, practice quizzes, crossword puzzle, glossary, and flashcards. It is designed to help give students additional support and prepare them for the exam.

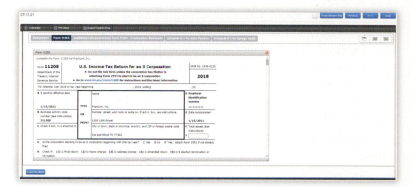

CengageNOWv2 Instant Access Code ISBN:
978-0-357-10952-6

Contact your Cengage Learning Consultant about different bundle options.

EXTENSIVELY REVISED. DEFINITIVELY UP TO DATE.

Each year the *South-Western Federal Taxation* series is updated with thousands of changes to each text. Some of these changes result from the feedback we receive from instructors and students in the form of reviews, focus groups, web surveys, and personal e-mail correspondence to our authors and team members. Other changes come from our careful analysis of the evolving tax environment. **We make sure that every tax law change relevant to the introductory taxation course was considered, summarized, and fully integrated into the revision of text and supplementary materials.**

The *South-Western Federal Taxation* authors have made every effort to keep all materials up to date and accurate. All chapters contain the following general changes for the 2020 Edition.

- Updated materials to reflect changes made by Congress through legislative action.
- Streamlined chapter content (where applicable) to clarify material and make it easier for students to understand.
- Revised numerous materials as the result of changes caused by indexing of statutory amounts.
- Revised Problem Materials, Computational Exercises, and CPA Exam problems.
- Updated Chapter Outlines to provide an overview of the material and to make it easier to locate specific topics.
- Revised *Financial Disclosure Insights* and *Global Tax Issues* as to current developments.

In addition, the following materials are available online.

- An appendix that helps instructors broaden and customize coverage of important tax provisions of the Affordable Care Act. (Instructor Companion Website at **cengage.com/login**)
- The Depreciation and the Accelerated Cost Recovery System (ACRS) appendix. (Instructor Companion Website at **cengage.com/login**)
- The *Taxation in the Real World* weekly blog posts for instructors. (**tinyurl.com/swft-blog**)

Chapter 1

- Updated references and citations throughout the chapter.
- Modified discussion of the Small Claims Division of the U.S. Tax Court.

- Updated discussion on changes to the CPA Exam.
- Updated end-of-chapter materials as needed.

Chapter 2

- Revised and updated chapter materials based on Final § 199A Regulations released in January 2019. Added materials on (1) the definition of a qualified trade or business and the new rental real estate safe harbor, (2) rules on the aggregation of qualified trades and businesses, (3) implications of losses (and netting requirements), and (4) a new exhibit summarizing specified services businesses.
- Updated chapter materials to reflect inflation adjustments to threshold limits.
- Revised and clarified materials based on feedback from adopters.
- Added new end-of-chapter materials based on the Final § 199A Regulations.

Chapter 3

- Updated chapter materials as needed for new rulings and inflation adjustments.
- Restructured the chapter "Tax Planning" section and added three new topics regarding planning for the business interest expense limitation, executive compensation, and avoiding the accumulated earnings tax.
- Updated end-of-chapter materials as needed.
- Included completed forms (in Solutions Manual) for Tax Return Problems.

Chapter 4

- Combined investor loss and gain provisions into one section.
- Added an example of § 1202 Qualified Small Business Stock exclusion.
- Streamlined and enhanced chapter materials.
- Added an end-of-chapter problem on § 1202 Qualified Small Business Stock exclusion.

Chapter 5

- Revised and updated chapter materials as needed; clarified chapter materials.
- Updated end-of-chapter materials as needed.
- Revised and expanded a Research Problem to include Data Analytics.

Chapter 6

- Added new text material in "Tax Planning—Stock Redemptions" regarding the advantages to corporation and shareholder of debt-financed redemptions.
- Updated and revised end-of-chapter materials as needed.

Chapter 7

- Added an assignment item about post-merger E & P.
- Created one new Research Problem.
- Added a graphics component to one Research Problem.

Chapter 8

- Updated statistics regarding consolidated returns.
- Revised material about advantages and disadvantages of the consolidation election.
- Streamlined material about controlled groups.
- Added one new Microsoft Excel problem.
- Added two Data Analytics Research Problems.

Chapter 9

- Streamlined text Section 9-4 (Foreign Currency Gain/Loss).
- Updated statistics about worldwide tax rates and the global economy.
- Revised overview language and Exhibit 9.2.
- Clarified materials on transfer pricing.
- Added a comment about the FASB treatment of the BEAT tax rate in deriving the deferred tax amounts.
- Reduced discussion of foreign currency gain/loss; added a reference to Bitcoin (and related) currencies.
- Added comments about the application of § 199A and the GILTI computation for flow-through entities.
- Added a Microsoft Excel feature to one problem.
- Added a new Research Problem concerning the international tax implications of the 2017 tax reform provisions.

Chapter 10

- Updated and clarified Global Tax Issues item "Withholding Requirements for non-U.S. Partners."
- Updated Schedule K–1 to reflect partnership reporting requirements for the qualified business income deduction, per Form 1065, Schedule K–1.
- Updated Concept Summary 10.3 (Tax Reporting of Partnership Items) to reflect IRS guidance in Regulations and Form 1065 and Schedule K–1.
- Updated and clarified Concept Summary 10.4 (Major Advantages and Disadvantages of the Partnership Form).
- Modified introduction to text Section 10-1b, "Key Concepts in Taxation of Partnership Income."
- Streamlined discussion of terms such as *inside basis*, *outside basis*, and *separately stated items*.
- Streamlined discussion of gain or loss recognition on formation of a partnership.
- Streamlined discussion of disguised sales.
- Streamlined discussion of carried interests and partnership interests received in exchange for services.
- Streamlined discussion of organization and startup costs.
- Clarified that the $26 million "average annual gross receipts" test now applies only to the most immediately preceding three-tax-year period rather than all prior three-tax-year periods.
- Streamlined the discussion of "Other Items Reported on Schedule K."
- Updated and substantially modified discussion of qualified business income to reflect Regulations.
- Updated and clarified discussion in text Section 10-5a, "Choosing Partnership Taxation."
- Slightly modified fact pattern in Computational Exercise 26 to reflect different profit- and loss-sharing ratios to illustrate differences in recourse and nonrecourse debt allocations.
- Added concept of § 704(b) book capital accounts in Problem 29 to illustrate accounting for precontribution gains.
- Added requirement in Problem 31 to address built-in gain on contribution of assets to partnership.
- Replaced Research Problems 2 and 6.

Chapter 11

- Reorganized text Section 11-2 (§ 736) into three new categories.
  - 11-2a, General Partners in Service-Providing Partnerships
  - 11-2b, Limited Partners or Capital-Intensive Partnerships
  - 11-2c, Tax Treatment of § 736 Payments

- Clarified Concept Summary 11.1 and Concept Summary 11.2.
- Streamlined discussions of disguised sales, marketable securities, and disproportionate distributions.
- Refocused and simplified the discussion of § 736 payments.
- Streamlined the discussion related to death of a partner.
- Added requirement to Computational Exercise 11 to calculate partner's basis.
- Added a requirement to Problem 42 to illustrate using a § 754 election to bring inside and outside basis into balance, as shown in Example 34.

Chapter 12

- Updated statistics about S corporations and partnerships/LLCs.
- Clarified materials concerning the QBI regime.
- Added two new Microsoft Excel problems.
- Added two new Research Problems.

Chapter 13

- Converted data about the tax forms of doing business into a graphic.
- Added § 1202 benefit to Concept Summary 13.1 that compares entity types.
- Added a problem about bonus depreciation for various business forms.
- Revised Research Problem about entity taxable receipts.
- Added new Research Problem asking students to look at initial coin offering (ICO) for entity financing.

Chapter 14

- Highlighted the recognition and measurement steps in disclosing tax uncertainties in the financial statements.
- Elaborated the financial accounting income effects of the 2017 corporate tax rate cut.
- Emphasized the effects on a valuation allowance from the changes to the treatment of post-2017 NOLs, and of AMT repeal.
- Noted the different deadlines under tax and financial accounting rules and the need for tax and reporting professionals to work together to meet these requirements.
- Expanded the discussion of planning ideas for releasing a valuation allowance.

- Added a new Critical Thinking Research Problem.
- Replaced one Research Problem.

Chapter 15

- Clarified the purpose of a tax exemption and of Federal taxes on exempt entities in the introductory comments.
- Updated statistics about the charitable sector of the U.S. economy.
- Reorganized the introduction to the discussion of taxes that fall on exempt entities.
- Revised discussion of the taxation of lobbying expenses by a public charity.
- Updated and added to statistics about private foundations and the UBIT.
- Added an additional Microsoft Excel problem.
- Identified two problems as Data Analytics items.

Chapter 16

- Updated statistics as to state and local government tax collections.
- Updated financial statement data for state/local taxes for selected corporations.
- Updated material relative to sales/use tax nexus, in light of the Supreme Court's *Wayfair* decision.
- Identified two Research Problems as Data Analytics items.
- Created two additional Microsoft Excel problems.

Chapter 17

- Updated statistics about IRS budget and personnel, and about tax audits, refunds, and penalties.
- Updated results concerning whistleblowers and informants.
- Updated results of the Taxpayer Attitude Survey.
- Updated user fees for various programs and IRS interest rates on underpayments and overpayments.
- Adjusted various penalty amounts for indexing.
- Added one new Microsoft Excel problem.
- Replaced one Research Problem with another requiring internet research.

Chapter 18

- Updated statistics about Federal estate and gift tax filings and payments.
- Clarified that the chapter uses a flat 40 percent tax rate only as a simplifying assumption; added reference to § 2001 Tax Rate Schedule as reproduced on the inside front cover of the book.

- Added text example illustrating the determination of generations for the GSTT.
- Added another Microsoft Excel problem.
- Designated one problem as a Data Analytics item.

Chapter 19

- Emphasized the importance of planning for the income tax basis consequences of the survivors, given a high exemption equivalent amount.
- Clarified content throughout the chapter, including language regarding special use valuation and the deceased spouse's unused exclusion amount.
- Streamlined Concept Summary 19.1.

- Added two new Microsoft Excel problems.
- Added two new Research Problems, one of which is a Data Analytics exercise.

Chapter 20

- Added references to the NOL deduction limitation, and the deduction for QBI, where the entity operates a trade or business.
- Added item about the fiduciary entity claiming a QBI deduction.
- Added another Microsoft Excel item.
- Designated one Research Problem as a Data Analytics item.

TAX LAW OUTLOOK

From your SWFT Series Editors:

Treasury and the IRS will continue to issue guidance on the Tax Cuts and Jobs Act of 2017 throughout 2019 and beyond. With over 100 changes, this is a time-consuming process. Much of the initial guidance was proposed or transitional. As a result, what applied for one year, might apply the same way in the next year. Whether the 116th Congress will enact any of the over 70 technical corrections identified by the Joint Committee on Taxation in the Bluebook (JCS-1-18; 12/20/18) is unknown due both to challenges of obtaining the necessary 60 votes in the Senate and that the House is controlled by Democrats. The technical corrections are a mix of taxpayer favorable and unfavorable items. States will continue to analyze the effects of the TCJA as they make or revisit conformity considerations.

With respect to sales and use tax, many states have adopted the South Dakota law that was analyzed in the 2018 *Wayfair* decision. Litigation could surface as the 200 or more transactions threshold causes very small sellers to collect use tax. More states are likely to consider enacting marketplace facilitator collection obligations.

Finally, as candidates prepare for the 2020 presidential election, many tax ideas will be suggested. They present opportunities for students and researchers to analyze how they work and how they measure up against principles of good tax policy.

SUPPLEMENTS SUPPORT STUDENTS AND INSTRUCTORS

Built around the areas students and instructors have identified as the most important, our integrated supplements package offers more flexibility than ever before to suit the way instructors teach and students learn.

Online and Digital Resources for Students

CengageNOWv2 is a powerful course management and online homework tool that provides robust instructor control and customization to optimize the student learning experience and meet desired outcomes.

CengageNOWv2 Instant Access Code ISBN:
978-0-357-10952-6

Contact your Cengage Learning Consultant about different bundle options.

THOMSON REUTERS
CHECKPOINT™ **Thomson Reuters Checkpoint**™ is the leading online tax research database used by professionals. There are three simple ways Checkpoint™ helps introduce students to tax research:

- Intuitive web-based design makes it fast and simple to find what you need.
- Checkpoint™ provides a comprehensive collection of primary tax law, cases, and rulings along with analytical insight you simply can't find anywhere else.
- Checkpoint™ has built-in productivity tools such as calculators to make research more efficient—a resource more tax pros use than any other.

Six months' access to Checkpoint™ (after activation) is packaged automatically with every NEW copy of the textbook.*

 More than software: Put the experience of ProConnect™ Tax Online on your side.

- Get returns done right the first time with access to all the forms you need, backed by industry-leading calculations and diagnostics.
- Save time with logical data-entry worksheets instead of traditional forms-based methods.
- It's all online, so there's nothing to install or maintain.

Online access to ProConnect™ Tax Online is offered with each NEW copy of the textbook—at no additional cost to students.*

cengage.com Students can use **cengage.com** to select this textbook and access Cengage Learning content, empowering them to choose the most suitable format and giving them a better chance of success in the course. Buy printed materials, eBooks, and digital resources directly through Cengage Learning and save at **cengage.com.**

Online Student Resources

Students can go to **cengage.com** for free resources to help them study as well as the opportunity to purchase additional study aids. These valuable free study resources will help students earn a better grade:

- Flashcards use chapter terms and definitions to aid students in learning tax terminology for each chapter.
- Online glossary for each chapter provides terms and definitions from the text in alphabetical order for easy reference.
- Learning objectives can be downloaded for each chapter to help keep students on track.
- Tax tables used in the textbook are downloadable for reference.

 The first-of-its-kind digital subscription designed specially to lower costs.

Students get total access to everything Cengage has to offer on demand—in one place. That's 20,000 eBooks, 2,300 digital learning products, and dozens of study tools across 70 disciplines and over 675 courses. **cengage.com/unlimited**

Printed Resources for Students

Looseleaf Edition (978-0-357-10925-0)

This version provides all the pages of the text in an unbound, three-hole punched format for portability and ease of use. Online access to ProConnect™ Tax Online software is included with every NEW textbook as well as Checkpoint™ from Thomson Reuters.*

*NEW printed copies of the textbook are automatically packaged with access to Checkpoint™ and ProConnect™ Tax Online tax software. If students purchase the eBook, they will not automatically receive access to Checkpoint™ and ProConnect™ Tax Online software.

Comprehensive Supplements Support Instructors' Needs

CengageNOWv2 is a powerful course management and online homework tool that provides robust instructor control and customization to optimize the student learning experience and meet desired outcomes. In addition to the features and benefits mentioned earlier for students, CengageNOWv2 includes these features for instructors:

- **Learning Outcomes Reporting** and the ability to analyze student work from the gradebook. Each exercise and problem is tagged by topic, learning objective, level of difficulty, estimated completion time, and business program standards to allow greater guidance in developing assessments and evaluating student progress.

- **Built-in Test Bank for online assessment.** The Test Bank files are included in CengageNOWv2 so that they may be used as additional homework or tests.

Solutions Manual

Written by the **South-Western Federal Taxation** editors and authors, the Solutions Manual features solutions arranged in accordance with the sequence of chapter material.

Solutions to all homework items are tagged with their Estimated Time to Complete, Level of Difficulty, and Learning Objective(s), as well as the AACSB's and AICPA's core competencies—giving instructors more control than ever in selecting homework to match the topics covered. The Solutions Manual also contains the solutions to the Tax Return Problems and the lettered answers (only) to the end-of-chapter Becker CPA Review Questions. **Available on the Instructor Companion Website at cengage.com/login.**

PowerPoint® Lectures with Notes

The Instructor PowerPoint® Lectures contain more than 30 slides per chapter, including outlines and instructor guides, concept definitions, and key points. Available on **Instructor Companion Website at cengage.com/login.**

Test Bank

Written by the **South-Western Federal Taxation** editors and authors, the Test Bank contains approximately 2,200 items and solutions arranged in accordance with the sequence of chapter material.

Each test item is tagged with its Estimated Time to Complete, Level of Difficulty, and Learning Objective(s), as well as the AACSB's and AICPA's core competencies—for easier instructor planning and test item selection. The 2020 Test Bank is available in Cengage's test generator software, Cognero.

Cengage Learning Testing Powered by Cognero is a flexible, online system that allows you to:

- author, edit, and manage Test Bank content from multiple Cengage Learning solutions
- create multiple test versions in an instant
- deliver tests from your LMS, your classroom, or wherever you want
- create tests from school, home, the coffee shop—anywhere with internet access (No special installs or downloads needed.)

Test Bank files in Word format as well as versions to import into your LMS are available on the Instructor Companion Website. **Cognero Test Banks available via single sign-on (SSO) account at cengage.com/login.**

Other Instructor Resources

All of the following instructor course materials are available online at cengage.com/login. Once logged into the site, instructors should select this textbook to access the online Instructor Resources.

- Instructor Guide
- Edition-to-edition correlation grids by chapter
- Detailed answer feedback for the end-of-chapter Becker CPA Review Questions in Word format. (Lettered answers only are available in the Solutions Manual.)
- An appendix that helps instructors broaden and customize coverage of important tax provisions of the Affordable Care Act
- The Depreciation and the Accelerated Cost Recovery System (ACRS) appendix
- Comprehensive Tax Return Problems appendix

Custom Solutions

Cengage Learning Custom Solutions develops personalized solutions to meet your taxation education needs. Consider the following for your adoption of **South-Western Federal Taxation 2020 Edition.**

- Remove chapters you do not cover or rearrange their order to create a streamlined and efficient text.
- Add your own material to cover additional topics or information.
- Add relevance by including sections from Sawyers/Gill's *Federal Tax Research* or your state's tax laws and regulations.

ACKNOWLEDGMENTS

We want to thank all the adopters and others who participated in numerous online surveys as well as the following individuals who provided content reviews and feedback in the development of the ***South-Western Federal Taxation*** 2020 titles.

William A. Raabe / James C. Young / William H. Hoffman, Jr. / Annette Nellen / David M. Maloney

Lindsay G. Acker, *University of Wisconsin-Madison*

Deborah S. Adkins, *Nperspective, LLC*

Mark P. Altieri, *Kent State University*

Amy An, *University of Iowa*

Susan E. Anderson, *Elon University*

Henry M. Anding, *Woodbury University*

Jennifer A. Bagwell, *Ohio University*

George Barbi, *Lanier Technical College*

Terry W. Bechtel, *Texas A&M University – Texarkana*

Chris Becker, *LeMoyne College*

John G. Bell

Tamara Berges, *UCLA*

Ellen Best, *University of North Georgia*

Tim Biggart, *Berry College*

Rachel Birkey, *Illinois State University*

Patrick M. Borja, *Citrus College / California State University, Los Angeles*

Dianne H. Boseman, *Nash Community College*

Cathalene Bowler, *University of Northern Iowa*

Madeline Brogan, *Lone Star College – Montgomery*

Darryl L. Brown, *Illinois Wesleyan University*

Timothy G. Bryan, *University of Southern Indiana*

Robert S. Burdette, *Salt Lake Community College*

Ryan L. Burger, *Concordia University Nebraska*

Lisa Busto, *William Rainey Harper College*

Julia M. Camp, *Providence College*

Al Case, *Southern Oregon University*

Machiavelli W. Chao, *Merage School of Business University of California, Irvine*

Eric Chen, *University of Saint Joseph*

Christine Cheng, *Louisiana State University*

James Milton Christianson, *Southwestern University and Austin Community College*

Wayne Clark, *Southwest Baptist University*

Ann Burstein Cohen, *University at Buffalo, The State University of New York*

Ciril Cohen, *Fairleigh Dickinson University*

Dixon H. Cooper, *University of Arkansas*

Rick L. Crosser, *Metropolitan State University of Denver*

John P. Crowley, *Castleton University*

Susan E. M. Davis, *South University*

Dwight E. Denman, *Newman University*

James M. DeSimpelare, *Ross School of Business at the University of Michigan*

John Dexter, *Northwood University*

James Doering, *University of Wisconsin – Green Bay*

Michael P. Donohoe, *University of Illinois at Urbana Champaign*

Deborah A. Doonan, *Johnson & Wales University*

Monique O. Durant, *Central Connecticut State University*

Wayne L. Edmunds, *Virginia Commonwealth University*

Rafi Efrat, *California State University, Northridge*

Charles R. Enis, *The Pennsylvania State University*

Frank J. Faber, *St. Joseph's College*

A. Anthony Falgiani, *University of South Carolina, Beaufort*

Jason Fiske, *Thomas Jefferson School of Law*

John Forsythe, *Eagle Gate College*

Alexander L. Frazin, *University of Redlands*

Carl J. Gabrini, *College of Coastal Georgia*

Kenneth W. Gaines, *East-West University, Chicago, Illinois*

Carolyn Galantine, *Pepperdine University*

Sheri Geddes, *Hope College*

Alexander Gelardi, *University of St. Thomas*

Daniel J. Gibbons, *Waubonsee Community College*

Martie Gillen, *University of Florida*

Charles Gnizak, *Fort Hays State University*

J. David Golub, *Northeastern University*

George G. Goodrich, *John Carroll University*

Marina Grau, *Houston Community College – Houston, TX*

Vicki Greshik, *University of Jamestown College*

Jeffrey S. Haig, *Santa Monica College*

Marcye S. Hampton, *University of Central Florida*

June Hanson, *Upper Iowa University*

Donald Henschel, *Benedictine University*

Susanne Holloway, *Salisbury University*

Susan A. Honig, *Herbert H. Lehman College*

Jeffrey L. Hoopes, University of North Carolina

Christopher R. Hoyt, *University of Missouri (Kansas City) School of Law*

Marsha M. Huber, *Youngstown State University*

Carol Hughes, *Asheville-Buncombe Technical Community College*

Helen Hurwitz, *Saint Louis University*

Richard R. Hutaff, *Wingate University*

Zite Hutton, *Western Washington University*

Steven L. Jager, *Cal State Northridge*

Janeé M. Johnson, *University of Arizona*

Brad Van Kalsbeek, *University of Sioux Falls*

John E. Karayan, *Woodbury University*

Carl Keller, *Missouri State University*

Cynthia Khanlarian, *Concord University*

Bob G. Kilpatrick, *Northern Arizona University*

Gordon Klein, Lecturer, *UCLA Anderson School*

Taylor Klett, *Sam Houston State University*

Aaron P. Knape, *Peru State College*

Cedric Knott, *Colorado State University – Global Campus*

Ausher M. B. Kofsky, *Western New England University*

Emil Koren, *Saint Leo University*

Jack Lachman, *Brooklyn College – CUNY*

Richard S. Leaman, *University of Denver*

Adena LeJeune, *Louisiana College*

Gene Levitt, *Mayville State University*

Teresa Lightner, *University of North Texas*

Sara Linton, *Roosevelt University*

Roger Lirely, *The University of Texas at Tyler*

Jane Livingstone, *Western Carolina University*

Heather Lynch, *Northeast Iowa Community College*

Michael J. MacDonald, *University of Wisconsin-Whitewater*

Mabel Machin, *Florida Institute of Technology*

Maria Alaina Mackin, *ECPI University*

Anne M. Magro, *George Mason University*

Richard B. Malamud, *California State University, Dominguez Hills*

Harold J. Manasa, *Winthrop University*

Barry R. Marks, *University of Houston – Clear Lake*

Dewey Martin, *Husson University*

Anthony Masino, *East Tennessee State University*

Norman Massel, *Louisiana State University*

Bruce W. McClain, *Cleveland State University*

Allison M. McLeod, *University of North Texas*

Meredith A. Menden, *Southern New Hampshire University*

Robert H. Meyers, *University of Wisconsin-Whitewater*

John G. Miller, *Skyline College*

Tracie L. Miller-Nobles, *Austin Community College*
Jonathan G. Mitchell, *Stark State College*
Richard Mole, *Hiram College*
David Morack, *Lakeland University*
Lisa Nash, *University of North Georgia*
Mary E. Netzler, *Eastern Florida State College*
Joseph Malino Nicassio, *Westmoreland County Community College*
Mark R. Nixon, *Bentley University*
Garth Novack, *Pantheon Heavy Industries & Foundry*
Claude R. Oakley, *DeVry University, Georgia*
Al Oddo, *Niagara University*
Sandra Owen, *Indiana University – Bloomington*
Vivian J. Paige, *Old Dominion University*
Carolyn Payne, *University of La Verne*
Ronald Pearson, *Bay College*
Thomas Pearson, *University of Hawaii at Manoa*
Nichole L. Pendleton, *Friends University*
Chuck Pier, *Angelo State University*
Lincoln M. Pinto, *DeVry University*
Sonja Pippin, *University of Nevada – Reno*
Steve Platau, *The University of Tampa*
Walfyette Powell, *Strayer University*
Dennis Price, *Samford University*
Darlene Pulliam, *West Texas A&M University*
John S. Repsis, *University of Texas at Arlington*
John D. Rice, *Trinity University*

Jennifer Hardwick Robinson, *Trident Technical College*
Shani N. Robinson, *Sam Houston State University*
Donald Roth, *Dordt College*
Richard L. Russell, *Jackson State University*
Robert L. Salyer, *Northern Kentucky University*
Rhoda Sautner, *University of Mary*
Bunney L. Schmidt, *Keiser University*
Allen Schuldenfrei, *University of Baltimore*
Eric D. Schwartz, *LaRoche College*
Tony L. Scott, *Norwalk Community College*
Randy Serrett, *University of Houston – Downtown*
Wayne Shaw, *Southern Methodist University*
Paul A. Shoemaker, *University of Nebraska – Lincoln*
Kimberly Sipes, *Kentucky State University*
Georgi Smatrakalev, *Florida Atlantic University*
Randy Smit, *Dordt College*
Leslie S. Sobol, *California State University Northridge*
Marc Spiegel, *University of California, Irvine*
Teresa Stephenson, *University of Wyoming*
Beth Stetson, *Oklahoma City University*
Debra Stone, *Eastern New Mexico University*
Frances A. Stott, *Bowling Green State University*
Todd S. Stowe, *Southwest Florida College*
Julie Straus, *Culver-Stockton College*
Martin Stub, *DeVry University*

James Sundberg, *Eastern Michigan University*
Kent Swift, *University of Montana*
Robert L. Taylor, *Lees-McRae College*
Francis C. Thomas, *Richard Stockton College of New Jersey*
Randall R. Thomas, *Upper Iowa University*
Ronald R. Tidd, *Central Washington University*
MaryBeth Tobin, *Bridgewater State University*
James P. Trebby, *Marquette University*
James M. Turner, *Georgia Institute of Technology*
Anthony W. Varnon, *Southeast Missouri State University*
Adria Palacios Vasquez, *Texas A&M University – Kingsville*
Terri Walsh, *Seminole State College of Florida Marie Wang*
Natasha R. Ware, *Southeastern University*
Mark Washburn, *Sam Houston State University*
Bill Weispfenning, *University of Jamestown (ND)*
Andrew L. Whitehair
Kent Williams, *Indiana Wesleyan University*
Candace Witherspoon, *Valdosta State University*
Sheila Woods, *DeVry University, Houston, TX*
Xinmei Xie, *Woodbury University*
Thomas Young, *Lone Star College – Tomball*

SPECIAL THANKS

We are grateful to the faculty members who have diligently worked through the problems and test questions to ensure the accuracy of the **South-Western Federal Taxation** homework, solutions manuals, test banks, and comprehensive tax form problems. Their comments and corrections helped us focus on clarity as well as accuracy and tax law currency. We also thank Thomson Reuters for its permission to use Checkpoint™ with the text.

Sandra A. Augustine, *Hilbert College*
Machiavelli Chao, *University of California Irvine*
Bradrick M. Cripe, *Northern Illinois University*
Felicia Farrar, *Houston Community College*
Robyn Dawn Jarnagin, *University of Arkansas*
Stephanie Lewis, *The Ohio State University*

Kate Mantzke, *Northern Illinois University*
Ray Rodriguez, *Murray State University*
Miles Romney, *Florida State University*
George R. Starbuck, *McMurry University*
Lisa Swallow, *Missoula College University of Montana*
Donald R. Trippeer, *State University of New York College at Oneonta*

Raymond Wacker, *Southern Illinois University, Carbondale*
Michael Weissenfluh, *Tillamook Bay Community College*
Marvin Williams, *University of Houston-Downtown*

The South-Western Federal Taxation Series

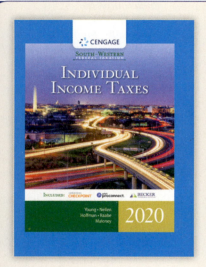

INDIVIDUAL INCOME TAXES, 2020 EDITION

(YOUNG, NELLEN, HOFFMAN, RAABE, MALONEY, Editors) provides accessible, comprehensive, and authoritative coverage of the relevant tax code and regulations as they pertain to the individual taxpayer, as well as coverage of all major developments in Federal taxation.

(ISBN 978-0-357-10915-1)

CORPORATIONS, PARTNERSHIPS, ESTATES & TRUSTS 2020 EDITION

(RAABE, YOUNG, HOFFMAN, NELLEN, MALONEY, Editors) covers tax concepts as they affect corporations, partnerships, estates, and trusts. The authors provide accessible, comprehensive, and authoritative coverage of relevant tax code and regulations, as well as all major developments in Federal income taxation. This market-leading text is intended for students who have had a previous course in tax.

(ISBN 978-0-357-10916-8)

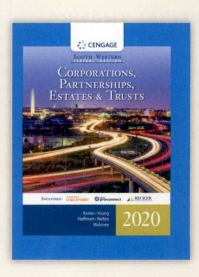

To find out more about these books, go to cengage.com.

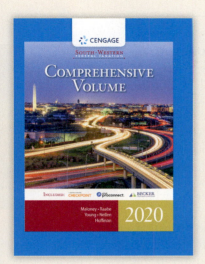

COMPREHENSIVE VOLUME, 2020 EDITION

(MALONEY, RAABE, YOUNG, NELLEN, HOFFMAN, Editors)
Combining the number one individual tax text with the number one corporations text, *Comprehensive Volume, 2020 Edition* is a true winner. An edited version of the first two **South-Western Federal Taxation** textbooks, this book is ideal for undergraduate or graduate levels. This text works for either a one-semester course in which an instructor wants to integrate coverage of individual and corporate taxation or for a two-semester sequence in which the use of only one book is desired.

(ISBN 978-0-357-10914-4)

ESSENTIALS OF TAXATION: INDIVIDUALS & BUSINESS ENTITIES, 2020 EDITION

(NELLEN, YOUNG, RAABE, MALONEY, Editors)
emphasizes tax planning and the multidisciplinary aspects of taxation. This text is designed with the AICPA Model Tax Curriculum in mind, presenting the introductory Federal taxation course from a business entity perspective. Its **Tax Planning Framework** helps users fit tax planning strategies into an innovative pedagogical framework. The text is an ideal fit for programs that offer only one course in taxation where users need to be exposed to individual taxation, as well as corporate and other business entity taxation. This text assumes no prior course in taxation has been taken.

(ISBN 978-0-357-10917-5)

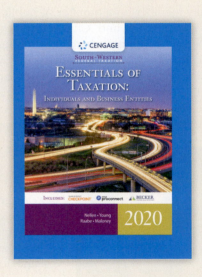

FEDERAL TAX RESEARCH, 11E

(SAWYERS AND GILL) *Federal Tax Research*, Eleventh Edition, offers hands-on tax research analysis and fully covers computer-oriented tax research tools. Also included in this edition is coverage on international tax research, a review of tax ethics, and many new real-life cases to help foster a true understanding of Federal tax law.

(ISBN 978-1-337-28298-7)

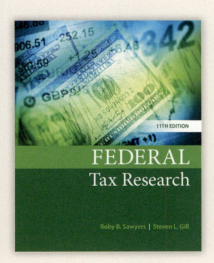

ABOUT THE EDITORS

William A. Raabe, Ph.D., CPA, was the Wisconsin Distinguished Professor of Taxation. He taught at Ohio State, Arizona State, the Capital University (OH) Law School, and the Universities of Wisconsin – Milwaukee and Whitewater. A graduate of Carroll University (Wisconsin) and the University of Illinois, Dr. Raabe's teaching and research interests include international and multistate taxation, technology in tax education, and personal financial planning. Dr. Raabe was a visiting tax faculty member for a number of public accounting firms, bar associations, and CPA societies. He has received numerous teaching awards, including the Accounting Educator of the Year award from the Wisconsin Institute of CPAs. He was the faculty adviser for student teams in the Deloitte Tax Case Competition (national finalists at three different schools) and the PricewaterhouseCoopers Extreme Tax policy competition (national finalist).

James C. Young is the PwC Professor of Accountancy at Northern Illinois University. A graduate of Ferris State University (B.S.) and Michigan State University (M.B.A. and Ph.D.), Jim's research focuses on taxpayer responses to the income tax using archival data. His dissertation received the PricewaterhouseCoopers/ American Taxation Association Dissertation Award, and his subsequent research has received funding from a number of organizations, including the Ernst & Young Foundation Tax Research Grant Program. His work has been published in a variety of academic and professional journals, including the *National Tax Journal, The Journal of the American Taxation Association*, and *Tax Notes*. Jim is a Northern Illinois University Distinguished Professor, received the Illinois CPA Society Outstanding Accounting Educator Award in 2012, and has received university teaching awards from Northern Illinois University, George Mason University, and Michigan State University.

William H. Hoffman, Jr. earned both his undergraduate (B.A.) and law (J.D.) degrees from the University of Michigan. He completed both an M.B.A. and a Ph.D. at The University of Texas at Austin. Bill began his academic career at Louisiana State University, where he served as a professor of accounting and taxation, before moving to the University of Houston in 1967. Bill remained at Houston for the rest of his academic career, retiring in 1999. Bill published extensively in academic and professional journals. His articles appeared in *The Journal of Taxation, The Tax Adviser, Taxes—The Tax Magazine, The Journal of Accountancy, The Accounting Review*, and *Taxation for Accountants*.

Annette Nellen, CPA, CGMA, Esquire, directs San José State University's graduate tax program (MST) and teaches courses in tax research, tax fundamentals, accounting methods, property transactions, employment tax, ethics, leadership, and tax policy. Professor Nellen is a graduate of CSU Northridge, Pepperdine (MBA), and Loyola Law School. Prior to joining SJSU in 1990, she was with a Big 4 firm and the IRS. At SJSU, Professor Nellen is a recipient of the Outstanding Professor and Distinguished Service Awards. Professor Nellen is an active member of the tax sections of the AICPA and American Bar Association. In 2013, she received the AICPA Arthur J. Dixon Memorial Award, the highest award given by the accounting profession in the area of taxation. Professor Nellen is the author of Bloomberg-BNA Tax Portfolio, *Amortization of Intangibles*, and the Bloomberg BNA Internet Law Resource Center, *Overview of Internet Taxation Issues*. She has published numerous articles in the *AICPA Tax Insider, Tax Adviser, State Tax Notes*, and *The Journal of Accountancy*. She has testified before the House Ways & Means and Senate Finance Committees and other committees on Federal and state tax reform. Professor Nellen maintains the 21st Century Taxation website and blog (21stcenturytaxation .com) as well as websites on tax policy and reform, virtual currency, and state tax issues (sjsu.edu/people/ annette.nellen/).

David M. Maloney, Ph.D., CPA, is the Carman G. Blough Professor of Accounting Emeritus at the University of Virginia's McIntire School of Commerce. He completed his undergraduate work at the University of Richmond and his graduate work at the University of Illinois at Urbana-Champaign. Upon joining the Virginia faculty in January 1984, Dr. Maloney taught Federal taxation in the graduate and undergraduate programs and was a recipient of major research grants from the Ernst & Young and KPMG Foundations. Dr. Maloney has published work in numerous professional journals, including *Journal of Taxation, The Tax Adviser, Tax Notes, Corporate Taxation, Accounting Horizons, Journal of Taxation of Investments*, and *Journal of Accountancy*.

Brief Contents

PART 4: ADVANCED TAX PRACTICE CONSIDERATIONS

PART 5: FAMILY TAX PLANNING

Contents

Part 2: Corporations

Part 3: Flow-Through Entities

Part 4: Advanced Tax Practice Considerations

CHAPTER 13
COMPARATIVE FORMS OF DOING BUSINESS

CHAPTER 14
TAXES ON THE FINANCIAL STATEMENTS

APPENDICES

Online Appendices

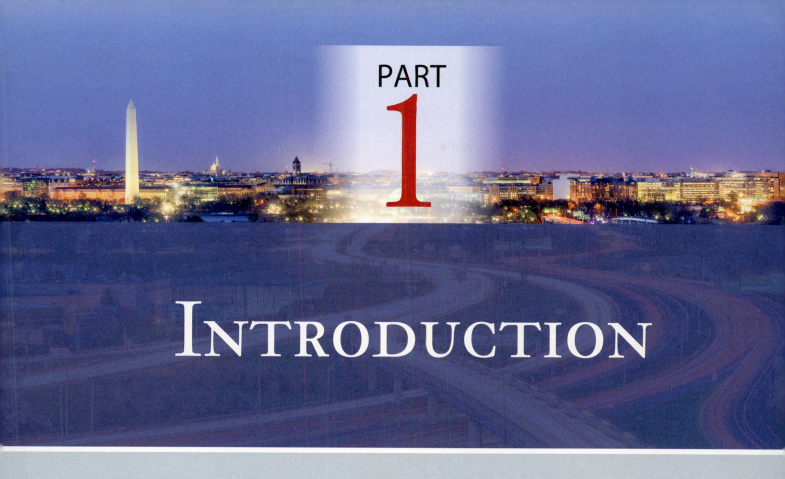

PART 1

INTRODUCTION

CHAPTER **1**

Understanding and Working with the Federal Tax Law

CHAPTER **2**

The Deduction for Qualified Business Income for Pass-Through Entities

The opening chapter of the text is devoted to the "whys and hows" of the tax law, and to the tax research process as it is used by the tax professional. Chapter 2 begins by discussing the distinctions between various taxpayer entities, including sole proprietorships, partnerships, and corporations. Then the chapter explores the deduction for qualified business income available to *noncorporate* taxpayers.

Understanding and Working with the Federal Tax Law

LEARNING OBJECTIVES: *After completing Chapter 1, you should be able to:*

LO.1 Stress the importance of revenue needs as an objective of Federal tax law.

LO.2 Demonstrate the influence of economic, social, equity, and political considerations on the development of the tax law.

LO.3 Illustrate how the IRS, as the protector of the revenue, has affected tax law.

LO.4 Recognize the role of the courts in interpreting and shaping tax law.

LO.5 Identify tax law sources—statutory, administrative, and judicial.

LO.6 List and assess tax law sources.

LO.7 Demonstrate tax research.

LO.8 Assess the validity and weight of tax law sources.

LO.9 Describe various tax planning procedures.

LO.10 Explain the role of taxation on the CPA examination.

CHAPTER OUTLINE

THE BIG PICTURE

IMPORTANCE OF TAX RESEARCH

Dana Andrews advanced $93,000 to her nephew in 2012 to enable him to attend a private university. Over the next few years, the nephew repays Dana $16,000 on the loan. However, seven years later Dana comes to you to determine whether she can claim a bad debt deduction for the $77,000 the nephew has not repaid. What planning tips might you give to Dana? Were any mistakes made?

Read the chapter and formulate your response.

The Federal tax law reflects the three branches of our Federal government. It is a mixture of laws passed by Congress, explanations provided by the Treasury Department and the Internal Revenue Service (IRS), and court decisions. Anyone who has attempted to work with this vast amount of information is familiar with its complexity. Commenting on his 48-page tax return, author James Michener said, "It is unimaginable in that I graduated from one of America's better colleges, yet I am totally incapable of understanding tax returns." For the person who must sift through this information to find the solution to a tax problem, he or she should recognize that there are reasons behind the law. Knowing these reasons is a first step toward understanding the Federal tax law.

1-1   THE WHYS OF THE TAX LAW

The primary objective of Federal tax law is the raising of revenue. Despite the importance of the fiscal needs of the government, however, other considerations (e.g., economic, social, equity, and political factors) play a significant role. The Treasury Department, the IRS, and the courts also have significant impacts on the evolution of Federal tax law. The first part of this chapter focuses on these topics.

1-1a Revenue Needs

Stress the importance of revenue needs as an objective of Federal tax law.

Raising revenues to fund the cost of government operations is the key factor in structuring a tax system. In a perfect world, taxes raised by the government would equal the expenses incurred by government operations. However, this goal has not been the case in the United States. Over the past century, the national debt has been increasing significantly, reaching more than $21.7 trillion, or more than $178,000 per taxpayer, in November 2018. According to the U.S. National Debt Clock, the U.S. total unfunded liabilities (including Social Security, Medicare, and Federal employee and veterans benefits) could be as much as $115 trillion, or almost $946,000 per taxpayer.

When enacting tax legislation, Congress is often guided by the concept of revenue neutrality so that any changes neither increase nor decrease the net revenues received by the government. With revenue neutral legislation, there are likely to be both "winners" (taxpayers who see a reduction in taxes paid) and "losers" (taxpayers who see an increase in taxes paid).

1-1b Economic Considerations

Demonstrate the influence of economic, social, equity, and political considerations on the development of the tax law.

Using the tax system to attempt to accomplish economic objectives generally involves changing the Internal Revenue Code[1] to help control the economy or encourage certain activities and businesses.

Control of the Economy

Congress has used the tax depreciation system as one means of controlling the economy. Theoretically, shorter asset lives and accelerated methods should encourage additional investments in depreciable business property. On the other hand, longer asset lives and the use of straight-line depreciation should discourage capital outlays. Congress also uses incentives like immediate expensing (§ 179) and bonus depreciation to stimulate the economy when needed.

A change in tax rates has a more immediate impact on the economy. When tax rates are lowered, taxpayers retain money that can be used for other purposes (e.g., purchases or savings). If, however, Congress is using the concept of revenue neutrality, these rate

---

[1]The Internal Revenue Code is a compilation of Federal tax legislation that appears in Title 26 of the U.S. Code.

reductions may be offset by a reduction or elimination of deductions or credits. As a result, lower rates do not always mean lower taxes.

Encouragement of Certain Activities

Congress uses the tax law to encourage certain types of economic activity or segments of the economy. For example, research and development expenditures can be deducted in the year incurred or, alternatively, capitalized and amortized over a period of 60 months or more.[2]

Inventions also are encouraged under tax law. Patents can qualify as capital assets, and under certain conditions, their disposition automatically carries long-term capital gain treatment.[3]

Are ecological considerations a desirable objective? This objective explains why pollution control facilities can be amortized over a 60-month period (rather than over the 39-year period required for most business buildings).

Is saving desirable for the economy? Saving leads to capital formation and thus makes funds available to finance home construction and industrial expansion. The tax law provides incentives to encourage saving by giving private retirement plans preferential treatment. Contributions to certain Individual Retirement Accounts (IRAs) and Keogh (H.R. 10 plans) are deductible, and income from these contributions accumulates on a tax-free basis.

Encouragement of Certain Industries

Historically, agricultural activities have been favored under Federal tax law. Among the benefits are the election to expense rather than capitalize certain expenditures for soil and water conservation and fertilizers and the election to defer the recognition of gain on the receipt of crop insurance proceeds.

The tax law favors the development of natural resources by permitting the use of percentage depletion and a write-off (rather than a capitalization) of certain exploration costs. The railroad and banking industries also receive special tax treatment.

Encouragement of Small Business

Small business development is also encouraged under the tax law. For example, a shareholder in a small business corporation can take an ordinary deduction (rather than a capital loss) for any loss recognized on a stock investment.[4] Another provision permits the shareholders of a small business corporation to make a special election that allows the profits (or losses) of the corporation to flow through to its shareholders (avoiding the corporate income tax).[5]

1-1c Social Considerations

Some of the tax laws, especially those related to the Federal income tax of individuals, can be explained by social considerations. Here are some notable examples:

- Certain benefits provided to employees through accident and health plans financed by employers are nontaxable. It is socially desirable to encourage these plans because they provide medical benefits in the event of an employee's illness or injury. Further, insurance companies are paying for these benefits (rather than the government).

- Most premiums paid by an employer for group term insurance covering the life of the employee are nontaxable. These funds help the family unit adjust to the loss of wages caused by the employee's death.

---

[2]If the asset developed has no estimated useful life, no write-off would be available without the two options allowed by the tax law.

[3]A long-term capital gain has a favorable tax advantage for individuals.

[4]Known as § 1244 stock, this subject is covered in Chapter 4.

[5]Known as the S corporation election, this subject is discussed extensively in Chapter 12.

- A deduction is allowed for contributions to qualified charities. The deduction shifts some of the financial and administrative burden of socially desirable programs from the public (the government) to the private sector.

- Various tax credits, deductions, and exclusions are designed to encourage taxpayers to obtain additional education.[6]

- Certain expenses are deemed to be contrary to public policy and therefore are disallowed. These expenses include items like fines, penalties, illegal kickbacks, and bribes to government officials.

1-1d Equity Considerations

The concept of equity is relative. Reasonable persons can, and often do, disagree about what is fair or unfair. Compare the tax treatment of a corporation with that of a partnership. The corporation is subject to a separate Federal income tax; the partnership is not. The tax law can and does make a distinction between these business forms.

Equity, then, is not what appears fair or unfair to any one taxpayer or group of taxpayers. It is, instead, what the tax law recognizes. The concept of equity appears in tax provisions that alleviate the effect of multiple taxation and postpone the recognition of gain when the taxpayer lacks the ability or wherewithal to pay the tax. Equity also helps mitigate the effect of the application of the annual accounting period concept and helps taxpayers cope with the eroding result of inflation.

Alleviating the Effect of Multiple Taxation

The same income earned by a taxpayer may be subject to taxes imposed by different taxing authorities. If, for example, the taxpayer is situated in New York City, income might generate Federal, New York state, and New York City income taxes. To compensate for this inequity, the Federal tax law allows a taxpayer to claim a deduction for some state and local income taxes. The deduction, however, does not eliminate the effect of multiple taxation; the benefit derived from the deduction depends on the taxpayer's Federal income tax rate.[7]

Equity considerations can explain the Federal tax treatment of income from foreign sources. Because double taxation results when the same income is subject to both foreign and U.S. income taxes, the tax law permits the taxpayer to choose either a credit or a deduction for the foreign taxes paid.

Another example is the corporate income tax, which can lead to multiple taxation of the same income.

EXAMPLE 1

During the current year, Gray Corporation has net income of $100,000, of which $5,000 was received as dividends from stock it owns in IBM Corporation. Assume that Gray Corporation distributes its after-tax income to its shareholders (all individuals).

The shareholder distribution will be subject to two income taxes: the corporate income tax when the income is earned by Gray Corporation and the individual income tax when it is distributed to the shareholders as a dividend.[8]

The $5,000 that Gray receives from IBM Corporation fares even worse. Because it is paid from income earned by IBM, it has been subjected to a third income tax (the corporate income tax imposed on IBM).[9]

---

[6]These provisions also can be justified under the category of economic considerations since a better educated workforce carries a positive economic impact.

[7]A tax credit rather than a deduction would eliminate the effects of multiple taxation on the same income.

[8]An additional 3.8% Medicare tax also applies to certain high-income shareholders.

[9]This result materializes because under the tax law, a corporation is not allowed a deduction for the dividend distributions it makes.

Congress has moved to mitigate the multiple taxation of corporate profits in several ways. For corporate shareholders, for whom triple taxation is possible, the law provides a deduction for dividends received from certain domestic corporations. The deduction, usually 50 percent of the dividends, would be allowed to Gray Corporation for the $5,000 it received from IBM Corporation (see the discussion in Chapter 3). For the individual shareholder, the law taxes qualified dividends at lower rates (from 0 percent for lower tax bracket shareholders to 20 percent for certain high-income shareholders). By allowing a lower tax rate, this approach *mitigates* (not *eliminates*) the effect of multiple taxation (see the discussion in Chapter 5).

In the area of the Federal estate tax, several provisions reflect attempts to mitigate the effect of multiple taxation. For example, a limited credit against the estate tax for foreign death taxes imposed is allowed. Other estate tax credits are available and can be explained on the same grounds.[10]

The Wherewithal to Pay Concept

The **wherewithal to pay** concept recognizes the inequity of taxing a transaction when the taxpayer lacks the means (i.e., funds) to pay the tax. This concept is typically applied to transactions where the taxpayer's economic position has not changed significantly. The following examples illustrate this concept.

Wherewithal to Pay Concept Illustrations

White Corporation holds unimproved land to build a new warehouse. The land has a basis to White of $60,000 and a fair market value of $100,000. The land is exchanged for a building (worth $100,000) that White will use in its business.[11]

EXAMPLE 2

White Corporation owns a warehouse that it uses in its business. At a time when the warehouse has an adjusted basis of $60,000, it is destroyed by fire. White collects the insurance proceeds of $100,000, and within two years of the end of the year in which the fire occurred, White uses all of the proceeds to purchase a new warehouse.[12]

EXAMPLE 3

Tom, a sole proprietor, decides to incorporate his business. In exchange for the business's assets (adjusted basis of $60,000 and a fair market value of $100,000), Tom receives all of the stock of Azure Corporation, a newly created corporation.[13] The Azure stock is worth $100,000.

EXAMPLE 4

Rose, Sam, and Tom want to develop unimproved land owned by Tom. The land has a basis to Tom of $60,000 and a fair market value of $100,000. The RST Partnership is formed with the following investments: land worth $100,000 transferred by Tom, $100,000 cash by Rose, and $100,000 cash by Sam. Each party receives a one-third interest in the RST Partnership.[14]

EXAMPLE 5

Amber Corporation and Crimson Corporation decide to consolidate to form Aqua Corporation.[15] Pursuant to the plan of reorganization, Tera exchanges her stock in Amber Corporation (basis of $60,000 and fair market value of $100,000) for stock in Aqua Corporation worth $100,000.

EXAMPLE 6

---

[10]See Chapter 18.

[11]The nontaxability of like-kind exchanges applies to the exchange of real property held for investment or used in a trade or business for property to be similarly held or used (not held for sale).

[12]The nontaxability of gains realized from involuntary conversions applies when the proceeds received by the taxpayer are reinvested within a prescribed period of time in property similar or related in service or use to that converted. Involuntary conversions take place as a result of casualty losses, theft losses, or condemnations by a public authority.

[13]Transfers of property to controlled corporations are discussed in Chapter 4.

[14]The formation of a partnership is discussed in Chapter 10.

[15]Corporate reorganizations are discussed in Chapter 7.

In all of the preceding examples, White Corporation, Tom, or Tera had a realized gain of $40,000 [$100,000 (fair market value of the property received) − $60,000 (basis of the property given up)].[16] It would be inequitable to force the taxpayer to recognize any of this gain for two reasons. First, the taxpayer did not end the transaction with any cash in hand (i.e., the taxpayer does not have the means to pay the tax).[17] Second, in each case, the taxpayer's economic situation has not changed significantly. In Example 2, White Corporation owned land before the exchange and owns land after the exchange. In Example 4, Tom owns a business both before and after the transaction (just in a different business form).

In these examples, recognized gain is merely postponed and not necessarily avoided. Because basis carries over to the new property or interest acquired in these nontaxable transactions, the gain element is still present and might be recognized on a subsequent taxable disposition. In Example 4, suppose Tom later sells his Azure Corporation stock for $100,000. Tom's basis in the stock is $60,000 (the same basis as in the assets transferred), and the sale results in a recognized gain of $40,000. Tom now has the funds to pay the related tax.

Many of these provisions also prevent the recognition of realized losses.

The wherewithal to pay concept, however, is not followed in every situation. The concept is only applied when the tax law specifically allows it.

EXAMPLE 7

Mary Jo exchanges stock in Green Corporation (basis of $60,000 and fair market value of $100,000) for stock in Purple Corporation (fair market value of $100,000). If the exchange is not pursuant to a reorganization, Mary Jo's realized gain of $40,000 is recognized for Federal income tax purposes.[18]

The result reached in Example 7 seems harsh in that the exchange does not place Mary Jo in a position to pay the tax on the $40,000 gain. Why does the tax law apply the wherewithal to pay concept to the exchange of stock pursuant to a corporate reorganization (Example 6) but not to certain other stock exchanges (Example 7)?

The wherewithal to pay concept is typically applied to situations in which the taxpayer's economic position has not changed significantly. In Example 6, Tera's stock investment in Amber Corporation really continues in the form of the Aqua Corporation stock because Aqua was formed through a consolidation of Amber and Crimson Corporations.[19] In Example 7, however, the investment has not continued. Here, Mary Jo's ownership in Green Corporation has ceased, and an investment in an entirely different corporation has been substituted.

Mitigating the Effect of the Annual Accounting Period Concept

All taxpayers must report their taxable income to the Federal government at regular intervals. The annual accounting period for the reporting of taxable income (and the settlement of any tax liability) is one year. Referred to as the annual accounting period concept, the effect is to divide each taxpayer's life into equal annual intervals for tax purposes.

---

[16]Realized gain can be likened to economic gain. However, the Federal income tax is imposed only on that portion of realized gain considered to be recognized under the law. Generally, recognized (or taxable) gain can never exceed realized gain.

[17]If the taxpayer ends up with other property (boot) as part of the transfer, gain may be recognized to this extent. The presence of boot, however, helps solve the wherewithal to pay problem because it provides property (other than the property or interest central to the transaction) with which to pay the tax.

[18]The exchange of stock does not qualify for nontaxable treatment as a like-kind exchange (refer to Example 2).

[19]This continuation is known as the continuity of interest concept, which forms the foundation for all nontaxable corporate reorganizations. The concept is discussed at length in Chapter 7.

This annual accounting period concept sometimes leads to different tax treatment for taxpayers who are in the same economic position. Consider the following example.

EXAMPLE 8

Rena and Samuel are both sole proprietors and show the following results during the past three years:

	Profit (or Loss)	
Year	Rena	Samuel
2017	$50,000	$150,000
2018	60,000	60,000
2019	60,000	(40,000)

Although Rena and Samuel have the same total profit of $170,000 over the three-year period, the annual accounting period concept places Samuel at a definite disadvantage for tax purposes. The net operating loss procedure offers Samuel some relief by allowing him to carry forward some or all of his 2019 loss to any profitable years in the future. With a net operating loss carryforward, Samuel may obtain a reduction in future taxes. Beginning in 2018, the ability to carry back losses was eliminated.

The reasoning used to support the net operating loss deduction helps explain the special treatment that excess capital losses and excess charitable contributions receive. Carryback and carryover procedures help mitigate the effect of limiting a loss or a deduction to the accounting period in which it is realized. Using these procedures, a taxpayer can salvage a loss or a deduction that might otherwise be wasted.

Example 9 illustrates how the installment method of recognizing gain on the sale of property allows a taxpayer to spread tax consequences over the payout period.[20] The installment method is supported by the wherewithal to pay concept; recognition of gain corresponds to the collection of cash received from the sale of the property. Tax consequences match the seller's ability to pay the tax.

EXAMPLE 9

In 2017, Tim sold unimproved real estate (cost of $40,000) for $100,000. Under the terms of the sale, Tim receives two notes from the purchaser, each for $50,000 (plus interest). One note is payable in 2018; the other, in 2019.

Without the installment method Tim would have to recognize and pay a tax on the gain of $60,000 for the year of the sale (2017). This result is harsh because none of the sale proceeds will be received until 2018 and 2019.

Using the installment method and presuming the notes are paid when each comes due, Tim recognizes half of the gain ($30,000) in 2018 and the remaining half in 2019.

The annual accounting period concept has been modified to apply to situations where taxpayers may have difficulty accurately assessing their tax positions by year-end. Here, the law permits taxpayers to treat transactions taking place in the next year as having occurred in the prior year.

EXAMPLE 10

Monica, a calendar year taxpayer, is a participant in an H.R. 10 (Keogh) retirement plan (see Appendix C for a definition of a Keogh plan). Under the plan, Monica contributes 20% of her net self-employment income, and this amount is deductible for Federal income tax purposes. On April 9, 2019, Monica

continued

---

[20]Under the installment method, each payment received by the seller represents a return of basis (the nontaxable portion) and profit from the sale (the taxable portion).

determines that her net self-employment income for calendar year 2018 was $80,000. Consequently, she contributes $16,000 (20% × $80,000) to the plan.

Even though the $16,000 contribution is made in 2019, the law permits Monica to claim this contribution as a deduction in the 2018 tax year. Requiring Monica to make the contribution by December 31, 2018, to obtain the deduction for that year would force her to arrive at an accurate determination of net self-employment income before her income tax return must be prepared and filed.

Similar exceptions to the annual accounting period concept cover certain charitable contributions by accrual basis corporations (Chapter 3) and the dividend distributions by S corporations (Chapter 12).

Coping with Inflation

During periods of inflation, *bracket creep* can plague a working person. Because of the progressive nature of the Federal individual income tax, a wage adjustment that merely compensates for inflation could place the employee in a higher income tax bracket, and this erodes the taxpayer's purchasing power. Congress recognized this problem and began to adjust various income tax components through an **indexation** procedure. Indexation, which began in 1985, is based on the rise in the consumer price index over the prior year.

1-1e   Political Considerations

The Federal tax laws are composed of statutory provisions. Because these statutes are enacted by Congress, political considerations often influence tax law. The effect of politics on the tax law includes special interest legislation, political expediency, and state and local influences.

Special Interest Legislation

Certain provisions of the tax law can be explained largely by the political influence some pressure groups exerted on Congress. For example, prepaid subscription and dues income is not taxed until earned, but prepaid rents are taxed to the landlord in the year received. The subscription and dues exception was created because certain organizations (e.g., the American Automobile Association) convinced Congress that special tax treatment was needed to cover income received from multiyear dues and subscriptions. Another provision, sponsored by a senator from Georgia, suspended the import duties on ceiling fans. The nation's largest seller of ceiling fans is Atlanta-based Home Depot.

Although some special interest legislation can be justified on economic or social grounds, other special interest legislation cannot. This type of legislation is, however, an inevitable product of our political system.

Political Expediency

Various tax changes can be tied to the shifting moods of the American public. That Congress is sensitive to popular feeling is an accepted fact. As a result, certain provisions of the tax law can be explained by the political climate at the time they were enacted. Measures that deter more affluent taxpayers from obtaining so-called preferential tax treatment have always had popular appeal and, consequently, the support of Congress. Provisions like the imputed interest rules and the limitation on the deductibility of interest on investment indebtedness can be explained on this basis.

State and Local Government Influences

Political considerations played a major role in providing an exclusion from gross income for interest received on state and local obligations. Somewhat less apparent has been the influence state law has had in shaping our present Federal tax law. Of major importance has been the effect of the community property system used by some states.[21] At one time, the tax position of the residents of these states was so advantageous that a number of common law states adopted the community property systems.[22] The political pressure placed on Congress to correct the disparity in tax treatment was considerable. To a large extent, this disparity was eliminated by the Revenue Act of 1948, which extended many of the community property tax advantages to residents of common law jurisdictions.[23] The impact of community property law on the Federal estate and gift taxes is discussed in Chapters 18 and 19.

1-1f Influence of the Internal Revenue Service

LO.3

Illustrate how the IRS, as the protector of the revenue, has affected tax law.

The IRS has exerted its influence on many areas of the tax law. As the protector of the national revenue, the IRS has been instrumental in securing the passage of legislation designed to curtail aggressive tax avoidance practices (i.e., closing tax loopholes). In addition, the IRS has sought and obtained law changes to make its job easier (administrative feasibility).

The IRS as Protector of the Revenue

There are many provisions in the tax law that have resulted from the direct efforts of the IRS to prevent taxpayers from exploiting a tax loophole. Working within the letter of existing laws, ingenious taxpayers and their advisers devise techniques that accomplish indirectly what cannot be accomplished directly. As a result, Congress passes laws to close the loopholes that taxpayers locate and exploit. Here are some examples (and where they are discussed in the text):

- The use of a fiscal year by personal service corporations, partnerships, S corporations, and trusts to defer income recognition to the owners (see Chapters 3, 10, 12, and 20).
- The use of the cash basis method of accounting by certain large corporations (see Chapter 3).
- The deduction of passive investment losses and expenses against other income (see Chapters 3 and 10).
- The shifting of income to lower-bracket taxpayers through the use of reversionary trusts (see Chapter 20).

In addition, Congress has passed laws that enable the IRS to make adjustments based on the substance of a transaction (rather than the form used by the taxpayer). One provision, for example, authorizes the IRS to establish guidelines on "thinly capitalized" corporations. Here, the question is whether corporate debt is recognized as debt for tax purposes or reclassified as equity (see the discussion in Chapter 4). Another provision allows the IRS to make adjustments to a taxpayer's method of accounting when the method used by the taxpayer does not clearly reflect income. The IRS also has the authority to allocate income and deductions among taxpayers (or businesses owned or

---

[21]The states with community property systems are Louisiana, Texas, New Mexico, Arizona, California, Washington, Idaho, Nevada, Wisconsin, and (if elected by the spouses) Alaska. The rest of the states are classified as common law jurisdictions. The difference between common law and community property systems centers around the property rights possessed by married persons. In a common law system, each spouse owns whatever he or she earns. Under a community property system, one-half of the earnings of each spouse is considered owned by the other spouse. For example, assume that Harold and Ruth are husband and wife and that their only income is the $80,000 annual salary Harold receives. If they live in Oklahoma (a common law state), the $80,000 salary belongs to Harold.

If, however, they live in Texas (a community property state), the $80,000 salary is divided equally, in terms of ownership, between Harold and Ruth.

[22]Such states included Michigan, Oklahoma, and Pennsylvania.

[23]The major advantage extended was the provision allowing married taxpayers to file joint returns and compute the tax liability as if each spouse had earned one-half of the income. This result is automatic in a community property state because half of the income earned by one spouse belongs to the other spouse. The income-splitting benefits of a joint return are now incorporated as part of the tax rates applicable to married taxpayers.

controlled by the same interests) when the allocation is necessary to prevent the evasion of taxes or to correctly reflect the income of each taxpayer.

Gold Corporation is owned entirely by Justin Gold (a single taxpayer), and both use the calendar year for tax purposes. For the current tax year, Gold Corporation has taxable income of $335,000; Justin Gold has taxable income of $175,000. Not included in Justin Gold's taxable income, however, is $10,000 of rent income usually charged Gold Corporation for the use of some property owned by Justin.

Because the parties have not clearly reflected their taxable income, the IRS can allocate $10,000 of rent income to Justin Gold. After the allocation, Gold Corporation has taxable income of $325,000 and Justin Gold has taxable income of $185,000.[24]

The IRS also has the authority to prevent taxpayers from acquiring corporations to obtain a tax advantage when the principal purpose of the acquisition is the evasion or avoidance of the Federal income tax (this rule is discussed briefly in Chapter 7).

Administrative Feasibility

Some tax laws are created in order to simplify the task of the IRS in collecting the revenue and administering the law. As to collecting revenue, the IRS long ago realized the importance of placing taxpayers on a pay-as-you-go basis. Withholding procedures apply to wages, while the tax on other types of income may have to be paid via quarterly estimated tax payments. The IRS has been instrumental in convincing the courts that accrual basis taxpayers should pay taxes on prepaid income in the year received and not when earned. This approach may be contrary to generally accepted accounting principles, but prepayment is consistent with the wherewithal to pay concept.

To help the IRS collect revenues when due, Congress has passed many provisions that impose interest and penalties on taxpayers if they don't comply with the tax law. These provisions include penalties for failure to pay a tax or to file a return that is due and the negligence penalty for intentional disregard of rules and regulations. Various penalties for civil and criminal fraud are intended to encourage taxpayers to comply with tax laws. This aspect of the tax law is discussed in Chapter 17.

The IRS audit process is essential to an effective administration of our tax system. To carry out this function, the IRS is aided by provisions that reduce the chance of taxpayer error or manipulation, thus simplifying the audit effort. For example, by increasing the individual standard deduction amount, the audit function is simplified because there are fewer returns with itemized deductions needing to be checked.[25] The $15,000 annual gift tax exclusion has the same objective (see Chapter 18). This provision decreases the number of gift tax returns that must be filed (and also reduces the taxes paid), making the job of the IRS easier.[26]

The Big Picture

Return to the facts of *The Big Picture* on p. 1–1. The advance of $93,000 to her nephew might be considered a taxable gift. If so, Dana would have been allowed a $13,000 gift tax exclusion in 2012. Further, if Dana were married, she and her husband would have been allowed a $26,000 gift tax exclusion (this is called "gift splitting"). Finally, Dana also could use her lifetime exemption to eliminate any gift tax, depending on her previous gift history (see Chapter 18).

---

[24]By shifting $10,000 of income to Justin (who is in the 32% bracket), the IRS gains $3,200 in taxes. Allowing the $10,000 deduction to Gold Corporation (which is in the 21% bracket) costs the IRS only $2,100. See Chapter 3 for further discussion of corporate taxable income and taxes.

[25]The IRS gave the same administrative justification when it proposed to Congress the $100 per event limitation on personal casualty and theft losses. Imposition of the limitation eliminated many casualty and theft loss deductions and, as a consequence, saved the IRS considerable audit

time. Also, an additional limitation equal to 10% of adjusted gross income applies to the total of nonbusiness losses after reduction by the floor of $100 for each loss.

[26]Particularly in the case of nominal gifts among family members, taxpayer compliance in reporting and paying a tax on such transfers would be questionable. The absence of the $15,000 gift tax exclusion would create a serious enforcement problem for the IRS.

1-1g **Influence of the Courts**

LO.4

Recognize the role of the courts in interpreting and shaping tax law.

In addition to interpreting statutory provisions and the administrative pronouncements issued by the Treasury Department and the IRS, the Federal courts have influenced tax law in two other ways.[27] First, the courts have developed a number of judicial concepts that help guide how tax provisions are applied. Second, certain key decisions have led to changes in the Internal Revenue Code.

Judicial Concepts Relating to Tax Law

Although ranking the tax concepts developed by the courts in order of importance is difficult, the concept of ==substance over form== is certainly near the top of any list. Variously described as the "telescoping" or "collapsing" process or the "step transaction approach," it involves determining the true substance of what happened. In a transaction involving many steps, any one step may be collapsed (or disregarded) as part of determining the substance of the event.

In 2019, Mrs. Greer, a widow, wants to give $30,000 to Jean without incurring any gift tax liability.[28] She knows that the law permits her to give up to $15,000 each year per person without any tax consequences (the annual exclusion). With this limitation in mind, the following steps are taken: a gift by Mrs. Greer to Jean of $15,000 (nontaxable because of the $15,000 annual exclusion), a gift by Mrs. Greer to Ben of $15,000 (also nontaxable), and a gift by Ben to Jean of $15,000 (nontaxable because of Ben's annual exclusion). Considering only the form of what Mrs. Greer and Ben have done, all appears well from a tax standpoint. In substance, however, what has happened?

By collapsing the steps involving Ben, Mrs. Greer has made a gift of $30,000 to Jean and, therefore, has not avoided the Federal gift tax.

EXAMPLE 13

The substance over form concept plays an important role in transactions involving corporations.

Another tax concept developed by the courts deals with the interpretation of statutory tax provisions that operate to benefit taxpayers. The courts have decided that these relief provisions are to be applied narrowly. If a taxpayer wants a relief provision to apply, the taxpayer has the responsibility to meet the provision's requirements (i.e., no exceptions).

The ==arm's length== concept is important in the area of corporate-shareholder dealings (see the discussion of constructive dividends in Chapter 5) and in the resolution of valuation problems for estate and gift tax purposes (see Chapters 18 and 19). Particularly in dealings between related parties, transactions can be tested by asking the question: Would unrelated parties have handled the transaction in the same way?

The sole shareholder of a corporation leases property to the corporation for a monthly rental of $50,000. To test whether the corporation should be allowed a rent deduction for this amount, the IRS and the courts will apply the arm's length concept. Would the corporation have paid $50,000 a month in rent if the same property had been leased from an unrelated party (rather than from the sole shareholder)?

EXAMPLE 14

Although the ==continuity of interest== concept originated with the courts, it has, in many situations, been incorporated into the Internal Revenue Code. If property is transferred and the taxpayer retains an interest in the property in some form ("continuity of interest"), then the taxpayer should not be subject to tax, since the taxpayer's position has not changed. A like-kind exchange (land for land) is an example of a transaction where this concept applies. This concept also applies to transfers to controlled corporations

---

[27]A great deal of case law is devoted to ascertaining congressional intent. The courts, in effect, ask: What did Congress have in mind when it enacted a particular tax provision?

[28]The example assumes that Mrs. Greer has exhausted her unified tax credit. See Chapter 18.

(see Chapter 4), corporate reorganizations (see Chapter 7), and transfers to partnerships (see Chapter 10).[29]

The court-developed **business purpose** concept, discussed in Chapter 7, principally applies to corporate transactions. Under this concept, there must be a sound business reason motivating a transaction in order for the tax treatment to result. The avoidance of taxation is *not* considered a sound business purpose.

EXAMPLE 15

Beth and Charles are equal shareholders in Brown Corporation. They have recently disagreed about the company's operations, and they are at an impasse about the future of Brown Corporation. This shareholder disagreement on corporate policy constitutes a sound business purpose and would justify a division of Brown Corporation that will permit Beth and Charles to go their separate ways.

Whether the division of Brown would be nontaxable to the parties depends on their compliance with the statutory provisions dealing with corporate reorganizations. The point is that compliance with statutory provisions is not enough to ensure nontaxability without a business purpose for the transaction.

Judicial Influence on Statutory Provisions

Some court decisions have been so important that Congress has incorporated them into the Internal Revenue Code. Example 16 illustrates this influence.

EXAMPLE 16

In 1983, Brad claimed a capital loss of $100,000 for Tan Corporation stock that became worthless during the year. In the absence of any offsetting gains, the capital loss deduction produced no income tax savings for Brad either in 1983 or in future years. Brad instituted a lawsuit against the former officers of Tan Corporation for their misconduct that resulted in the corporation's failure and thereby led to Brad's $100,000 loss. In settlement of the suit, the officers paid $50,000 to Brad in 1986. The IRS argued that the full $50,000 should be taxed as gain to Brad. The Tan stock was written off in 1983 and had a zero basis for tax purposes. The $50,000 recovery that Brad received on the stock was, therefore, all gain.

The IRS's position was logical but not equitable. The court stated that Brad should not be taxed on the recovery of an amount previously deducted unless the deduction produced a tax savings. Because the $100,000 capital loss deduction in 1983 produced no tax benefit, none of the $50,000 received in 1986 resulted in gain.

The decision reached by the courts in Example 16, known as the **tax benefit rule**, is now part of the Internal Revenue Code.

Court decisions sometimes create uncertainty about the tax law. These decisions may reach the right result, but they do not produce the guidelines necessary to enable taxpayers to comply. In many situations, Congress may be compelled to add certainty to the law by revising the Internal Revenue Code. The following are examples of this type of judicial "cause" and the statutory "effect":

- When a stock redemption will be treated as an exchange or as a dividend (see Chapter 6).

- What basis a parent corporation will have in the assets received from a subsidiary that is liquidated shortly after its acquisition (see Chapter 6).

Some statutory provisions can be explained by congressional reactions to a particular court decision. One decision, for example, held that the transfer of a liability to a controlled corporation should be treated as boot received by the transferor, creating a taxable gain (see Chapter 4). Congress disagreed with this treatment and promptly enacted legislation to change the result.

---

[29]Also see Examples 4 (forming a corporation), 5 (forming a partnership), and 6 (reorganizing corporations) of this chapter.

1-2 SUMMARY

In addition to raising revenues, other factors have influenced the development of Federal tax law:

- *Economic considerations.* Using tax law to help regulate the economy and encourage certain activities and types of businesses.
- *Social considerations.* Using tax law to encourage or discourage certain socially desirable or undesirable practices.
- *Equity considerations.* Using tax law to alleviate the effect of multiple taxation, recognize the wherewithal to pay concept, mitigate the effect of the annual accounting period concept, and recognize the eroding effect of inflation.
- *Political considerations.* Some tax law represents special interest legislation, reflects political expediency, and illustrates the effect of state law.
- *Influence of the IRS.* Laws are enacted to aid the IRS in collecting revenue and administering the tax law.
- *Influence of the courts.* Court decisions have established a body of judicial concepts relating to tax law and have, on occasion, led Congress to enact laws that either clarify or negate their effect.

These factors help us understand how tax law develops (and why some provisions exist). We also must learn to work with the tax law.

1-3 RECONCILING ACCOUNTING CONCEPTS

The vast majority of an entity's business transactions receive the same treatment for financial accounting purposes as they do under Federal and state tax law. But "book-tax differences" exist. When there are differences between **Generally Accepted Accounting Principles (GAAP)** or **International Financial Reporting Standards (IFRS)** and tax rules, they are highlighted and discussed in a special feature used throughout the text titled *Financial Disclosure Insights*.

1-4 WORKING WITH THE TAX LAW— TAX SOURCES

Understanding taxation requires a mastery of the sources of tax law. These sources include laws passed by Congress, which are contained in the Internal Revenue Code and also congressional Committee Reports, Regulations, Treasury Department and IRS pronouncements, and court decisions. Thus, the *primary sources* of tax law include information from all three branches of government: legislative (or statutory), executive, and judicial.[30]

The law is of little significance, however, until it is applied to a set of facts and circumstances. A tax researcher not only must be able to read and interpret the sources of the law but also must understand the relative *weight of authority* that each source carries. Learning to work with the tax law involves three basic steps:

1. Familiarity with the sources of the law
2. Application of research techniques
3. Effective use of planning procedures

---

[30]*Secondary sources* also are used by tax practitioners. These sources are not part of the tax law and include items like tax articles from professional tax journals, newsletters, and textbooks. Commentary contained in various tax research services (like Thomson Reuters *Checkpoint*) also are secondary sources.

The remainder of this chapter introduces the sources of tax law and explains how the law is applied to problems and conditions of individual and business transactions. Statutory, administrative, and judicial sources of the tax law are considered first.

1-4a **Statutory Sources of the Tax Law**

LO.5

Identify tax law sources—statutory, administrative, and judicial.

Statutory sources of law include the Constitution (Article I, Sections 7, 8, and 10), the Internal Revenue Code, and tax treaties (agreements between countries to mitigate the double taxation of taxpayers subject to the tax laws of those countries). The Constitution grants Congress the power to impose and collect taxes and also authorizes the creation of treaties with other countries. The power of Congress to implement and collect taxes is summarized in the Internal Revenue Code, the official title of U.S. tax law, and the Code is the basis for arriving at solutions to all tax questions.

Origin of the Internal Revenue Code

Before 1939, the statutory provisions relating to taxation were contained in the individual revenue acts enacted by Congress. The inconvenience and confusion that resulted from dealing with many separate acts led Congress to codify all of the Federal tax laws. Known as the Internal Revenue Code of 1939, the codification arranged all Federal tax provisions in a logical sequence and placed them in a separate part of the Federal statutes. A further rearrangement took place in 1954 and resulted in the Internal Revenue Code of 1954.

Perhaps to emphasize the magnitude of the changes made by the Tax Reform Act (TRA) of 1986, Congress redesignated the Internal Revenue Code of 1954 as the Internal Revenue Code of 1986.[31]

The Legislative Process

Exhibit 1.1 illustrates the legislative process for enacting changes to the Internal Revenue Code of 1986. Federal tax legislation generally originates in the House of Representatives, where it is first considered by the House Ways and Means Committee.[32] Once approved by the House Ways and Means Committee, the proposed bill is referred to the entire House of Representatives for approval or disapproval. Approved bills are sent to the Senate, where they are considered by the Senate Finance Committee.

After approval by the Senate Finance Committee, the bill is sent to the entire Senate. Assuming no disagreement between the House and the Senate, a bill passed by the Senate is referred to the President for approval or veto. If the bill is approved or if the President's veto is overridden by a two-thirds vote, the bill becomes law and part of the Internal Revenue Code.

When the Senate version of the bill differs from that passed by the House, the Joint Conference Committee resolves these differences. The Joint Conference Committee includes members of the House Ways and Means Committee and the Senate Finance Committee.

The House Ways and Means Committee, the Senate Finance Committee, and the Joint Conference Committee each produce a Committee Report. These Committee Reports explain the provisions of the proposed legislation and are therefore a valuable source in ascertaining the *intent* of Congress. What Congress has in mind when it considers and enacts tax legislation is, of course, the key to interpreting that legislation. Because it takes time to develop other primary authority (e.g., from the Treasury Department, the IRS, and the courts), tax researchers rely heavily on Committee Reports to interpret and apply new tax laws.

---

[31]Congress enacts tax legislation virtually every year, and each piece of legislation contains changes to the Internal Revenue Code of 1986.

[32]Although rare, a tax bill can originate in the Senate when it is attached as a rider to a different legislative proposal. The Tax Equity and Fiscal Responsibility Act of 1982 originated in the Senate; its constitutionality was upheld by the courts.

EXHIBIT 1.1	Legislative Process for Tax Bills

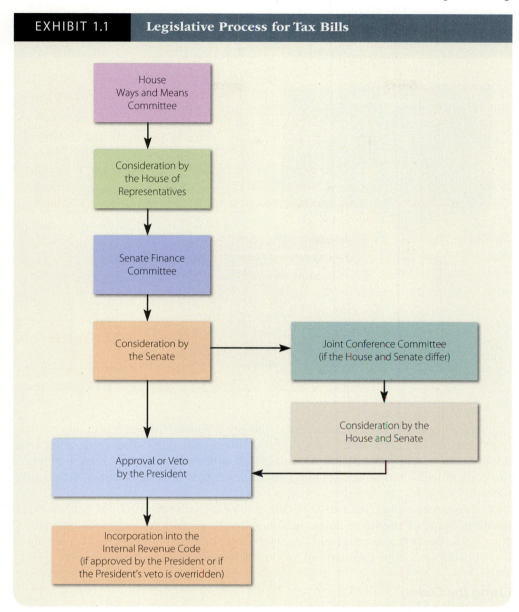

The role of the Joint Conference Committee indicates the importance of compromise in the legislative process. Exhibit 1.2 illustrates what happened in the Tax Cuts and Jobs Act (TCJA) of 2017 regarding corporate tax rates and a new qualified business income deduction for noncorporate taxpayers.

Arrangement of the Internal Revenue Code

In working with the Internal Revenue Code, it helps to understand the format. Here is a partial table of contents:

Subtitle A. Income Taxes
  Chapter 1. Normal Taxes and Surtaxes
    Subchapter A. Determination of Tax Liability
      Part I. Tax on Individuals
        Sections 1–5
      Part II. Tax on Corporations
        Sections 11–12

* * *

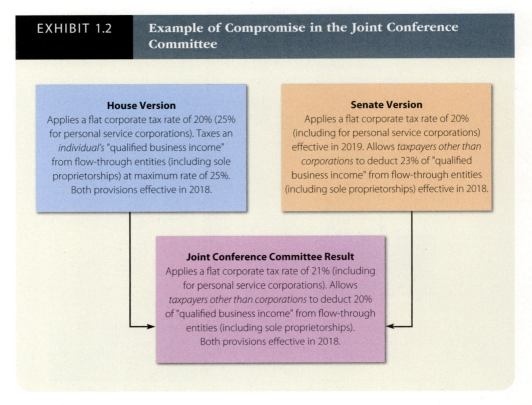

| EXHIBIT 1.2 | Example of Compromise in the Joint Conference Committee |

House Version
Applies a flat corporate tax rate of 20% (25% for personal service corporations). Taxes an *individual's* "qualified business income" from flow-through entities (including sole proprietorships) at maximum rate of 25%. Both provisions effective in 2018.

Senate Version
Applies a flat corporate tax rate of 20% (including for personal service corporations) effective in 2019. Allows *taxpayers other than corporations* to deduct 23% of "qualified business income" from flow-through entities (including sole proprietorships) effective in 2018.

Joint Conference Committee Result
Applies a flat corporate tax rate of 21% (including for personal service corporations). Allows *taxpayers other than corporations* to deduct 20% of "qualified business income" from flow-through entities (including sole proprietorships). Both provisions effective in 2018.

In referring to a provision of the Code, the *key* is usually the Section number. In citing a Section number, identifying the related Subtitle, Chapter, Subchapter, and Part is not necessary. Merely mentioning Section 2(a) is sufficient because the Section numbers run consecutively and do not begin again with each new Subtitle, Chapter, Subchapter, or Part.[33]

Tax researchers often refer to a specific area of income taxation by Subchapter designation. Some of the more common Subchapter designations include Subchapter C (Corporate Distributions and Adjustments), Subchapter K (Partners and Partnerships), and Subchapter S (Tax Treatment of S Corporations and Their Shareholders).

Citing the Code

Code Sections often are broken down into subparts.[34] Section 2(a)(1)(A) serves as an example.

| § | 2 | (a) | (1) | (A) |

- Abbreviation for "Section"
- Section number
- Subsection designation[35]
- Paragraph designation
- Subparagraph designation

---

[33]When the 1954 Code was drafted, some section numbers were intentionally omitted. This omission provided flexibility to incorporate later changes into the Code without disrupting its organization. When Congress does not leave enough space, subsequent Code Sections are given A, B, C, etc., designations. A good example is the treatment of §§ 280A through 280H.

[34]Some Code Sections do not have subparts. See, for example, § 482.

[35]Some Code Sections omit the subsection designation and use, instead, the paragraph designation as the first subpart. See, for example, §§ 212(1) and 1222(1).

Broken down as to content, § 2(a)(1)(A) becomes:

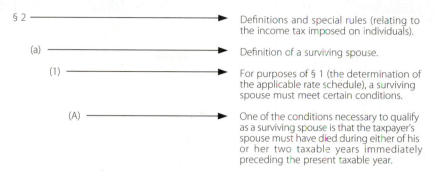

§ 2	→	Definitions and special rules (relating to the income tax imposed on individuals).
(a)	→	Definition of a surviving spouse.
(1)	→	For purposes of § 1 (the determination of the applicable rate schedule), a surviving spouse must meet certain conditions.
(A)	→	One of the conditions necessary to qualify as a surviving spouse is that the taxpayer's spouse must have died during either of his or her two taxable years immediately preceding the present taxable year.

Throughout this text, references to Code Sections are in the form just given. The symbols "§" and "§§" are used in place of "Section" and "Sections," respectively. The following table summarizes the format that we use:

Complete Reference	Text Reference
Section 2(a)(1)(A) of the Internal Revenue Code of 1986	§ 2(a)(1)(A)
Sections 1 and 2 of the Internal Revenue Code of 1986	§§ 1 and 2
Section 2 of the Internal Revenue Code of 1954	§ 2 of the Internal Revenue Code of 1954
Section 12(d) of the Internal Revenue Code of 1939[36]	§ 12(d) of the Internal Revenue Code of 1939

1-4b Administrative Sources of the Tax Law

The administrative sources of the Federal tax law include Treasury Department Regulations, Revenue Rulings and Procedures, and various other administrative pronouncements (see Exhibit 1.3). All are issued by either the U.S. Treasury Department or the IRS. The role played by the IRS in this process is considered in greater depth in Chapter 17.

Treasury Department Regulations

Regulations are issued by the U.S. Treasury Department under authority granted by Congress (§ 7805). Interpretive by nature, they provide taxpayers with considerable guidance on the meaning and application of the Code. Regulations, which carry considerable authority as the official interpretation of tax law, may be issued in *proposed*, *temporary*, or *final* form.

Because Regulations interpret the Code, they are arranged in the same sequence. Regulations are, however, prefixed by a number that indicates the type of tax or administrative, procedural, or definitional matter to which they relate.[37] For example, the prefix 1 designates the Regulations under the income tax law. Thus, the Regulations under Code § 2 would be cited as Reg. § 1.2, with subparts added for further identification. The numbering pattern of these subparts often has no correlation with the Code subsections.

New Regulations and changes in existing Regulations usually are issued in proposed form before they are finalized. The time interval between the proposal of a Regulation and its finalization permits taxpayers and other interested parties to comment on the propriety of the proposal. **Proposed Regulations** under Code § 2, for example, would be cited as Prop.Reg. § 1.2.

---

[36]Section 12(d) of the Internal Revenue Code of 1939 is the predecessor to § 2 of the Internal Revenue Code of 1954. Keep in mind that the 1954 Code superseded the 1939 Code.

[37]The prefix 20 designates estate tax Regulations, 25 covers gift tax Regulations, 31 relates to employment taxes, and 301 refers to procedure and administration.

EXHIBIT 1.3	Administrative Sources

Source	Location	Authority
Regulations	*Federal Register*	Force and effect of law.
Temporary Regulations	*Federal Register*	May be cited as a precedent.
	Internal Revenue Bulletin	
	*Cumulative Bulletin**	
Proposed Regulations	*Federal Register*	Preview of final Regulations.
	Internal Revenue Bulletin	
	*Cumulative Bulletin**	
Revenue Rulings	*Internal Revenue Bulletin*	Do not have the force and effect of law.
Revenue Procedures	*Cumulative Bulletin**	
Treasury Decisions		
Actions on Decisions		
General Counsel Memoranda	Tax Analysts' *Tax Notes;*	May not be cited as a precedent.
Technical Advice Memoranda	Thomson Reuters *Checkpoint***;	
	Commerce Clearing House *IntelliConnect*	
Letter Rulings	Thomson Reuters and Commerce Clearing House tax services	Applicable only to taxpayer addressed. No precedential force.

*Through 2008, the contents of Internal Revenue Bulletins were consolidated semiannually into a Cumulative Bulletin. Beginning in 2009, the IRS decided to stop producing a Cumulative Bulletin because all Internal Revenue Bulletins are available electronically on the IRS website.

**Thomson Reuters *Checkpoint* includes a wide variety of tax resources. The most significant are materials produced by the Research Institute of America (RIA), including the *Federal Tax Coordinator 2d*.

Sometimes the Treasury Department issues **Temporary Regulations** relating to elections and other matters where immediate guidance is critical. These Regulations often are needed for recent legislation that takes effect immediately. Temporary Regulations, cited as Temp.Reg. §, have the same authoritative value as final Regulations and may be cited as precedent for three years. However, Temporary Regulations also must be issued as Proposed Regulations and automatically expire within three years after the date of issuance.[38] The Tax Court indicates that Proposed Regulations carry little weight.[39]

Proposed, final, and Temporary Regulations are published in the *Federal Register* (now online) and are reproduced in major tax services. **Final Regulations** are issued as Treasury Decisions (TDs) and carry the force and effect of law.

Revenue Rulings and Revenue Procedures

Revenue Rulings are official pronouncements of the National Office of the IRS. Like Regulations, Revenue Rulings are designed to provide interpretation of the tax law. Although they do not carry the same legal force and effect as Regulations, because they are focused on a specific fact pattern, they provide a more detailed analysis of the law.

A Revenue Ruling often results from a specific taxpayer's request for a letter ruling (as discussed below). If the IRS believes that a letter ruling request has widespread impact, the letter ruling will be converted into a Revenue Ruling and issued. Revenue Rulings also can be issued in response to technical advice to District Offices of the IRS, court decisions, and suggestions from tax practitioner groups.

Revenue Procedures deal with the internal management practices and procedures of the IRS. For example, Rev.Proc. 2019–1 (2019–1 I.R.B. 1) provides general instructions for taxpayers requesting letter rulings or determination letters from the IRS.

---

[38]§ 7805(e).

[39]*F. W. Woolworth Co.*, 54 T.C. 1233 (1970); *Harris M. Miller*, 70 T.C. 448 (1978); and *James O. Tomerlin Trust*, 87 T.C. 876 (1986).

Both Revenue Rulings and Revenue Procedures serve an important function in that they provide *guidance* to both IRS personnel and taxpayers in handling routine tax matters. Revenue Rulings and Revenue Procedures generally apply retroactively and are binding on the IRS until revoked or modified by subsequent rulings or procedures, Regulations, legislation, or court decisions.

Revenue Rulings and Revenue Procedures are published weekly by the U.S. Government in the *Internal Revenue Bulletin* (I.R.B.).

The proper form for citing Revenue Rulings follows. Revenue Procedures are cited in the same manner, except that "Rev.Proc." is substituted for "Rev.Rul."

> Rev.Rul. 2018–5, 2018–6 I.R.B. 341.
> *Explanation*: Revenue Ruling Number 5, appearing on page 341 of the 6th weekly issue of the *Internal Revenue Bulletin* for 2018.

Revenue Rulings and other tax resources may be found at the IRS website: **irs.gov**.[40]

Other Administrative Pronouncements

Letter rulings are issued for a fee by the National Office of the IRS upon a taxpayer's request and describe how the IRS will treat a proposed transaction for tax purposes. Issued by the National Office of the IRS, they apply only to the taxpayer who asks for and obtains the ruling.[41] Letter rulings can be useful to taxpayers who want to be certain of how a transaction will be taxed before proceeding with it. Letter rulings also allow taxpayers to avoid unexpected tax costs and may be the most effective way to carry out tax planning. However, the IRS limits the issuance of letter rulings to restricted, pre-announced areas of taxation.[42]

The IRS must make letter rulings available for public inspection after identifying details are deleted.[43] Published digests of private letter rulings can be found in a variety of sources, including *IRS Private Letter Rulings Reports* (published by CCH), Bloomberg BNA *Daily Tax Reports*, and Tax Analysts' *Tax Notes*, and in electronic (online) tax research services (like Thomson Reuters *Checkpoint*).

The National Office of the IRS releases Technical Advice Memoranda (TAMs) weekly. TAMs resemble letter rulings in that they give the IRS's determination of an issue. However, they differ in several respects. Letter rulings deal with proposed transactions and are issued to taxpayers at their request. In contrast, TAMs deal with completed (rather than proposed) transactions. TAMs are issued by the National Office of the IRS in response to questions raised by taxpayers or IRS field personnel during audits. TAMs are not officially published and may not be cited or used as precedent.[44]

Both letter rulings and TAMs are issued with multi-digit file numbers. Consider, for example, Ltr.Rul. 201833018, requesting tax-exempt status under § 501(c)(3) by a class reunion organization. Broken down by digits, the file number reveals the following information:

2018	33	018
Year 2018	Issued during the 33rd week of 2018	18th ruling issued during the 33rd week

Letter rulings and TAMs issued before 2000 are often cited with only two-digit years (e.g., Ltr.Rul. 9933108).

---

[40]Commercial sources for Revenue Rulings and Procedures are available, usually requiring a subscription fee. Older Revenue Rulings and Procedures often are cited as being published in the *Cumulative Bulletin* (C.B.) rather than the *Internal Revenue Bulletin* (I.R.B.).

[41]Post-1984 letter rulings may be substantial authority for purposes of the accuracy-related penalty; see Notice 90–20, 1990–1 C.B. 328, part V (A).

[42]Rev.Proc. 2019–3, 2019–1 I.R.B. 130, contains a list of areas in which the IRS will not issue advance rulings. According to the IRS, the main reason they will not rule in certain areas is that specific fact-oriented situations are involved. Thus, a ruling may not be obtained on many of the problems that are particularly troublesome for taxpayers.

[43]§ 6110.

[44]§ 6110(k)(3). Post-1984 TAMs may be substantial authority for purposes of avoiding the accuracy-related penalty. Notice 90–20, 1990–1 C.B. 328.

Like letter rulings, **determination letters** are issued at the request of taxpayers and provide guidance concerning the application of the tax law. They differ from individual rulings in that the issuing source is an IRS Area Director (rather than the National Office of the IRS). Also, determination letters usually involve completed (as opposed to proposed) transactions. Determination letters are not published by the government and are made known only to the party making the request.

The following examples illustrate the distinction between individual rulings and determination letters.

Difference between Letter Rulings and Determination Letters

The shareholders of Black Corporation and White Corporation want assurance that the consolidation of the corporations into Gray Corporation will be a nontaxable reorganization (see Chapter 7). The proper approach is to request from the National Office of the IRS an individual ruling concerning the income tax effect of the proposed transaction.

Gilbert operates a barbershop in which he employs eight barbers. To comply with the rules governing income tax and payroll tax withholdings, Gilbert wants to know whether the barbers working for him are employees or independent contractors. The proper procedure is to request a determination letter on the status of the barbers from the Area Director in Holtsville, New York, or Newport, Vermont, depending on the location of the requesting firm.

1-4c Judicial Sources of the Tax Law

Five Federal courts have jurisdiction over tax disputes between the IRS and taxpayers: the U.S. Tax Court, the U.S. District Court, the U.S. Court of Federal Claims, the U.S. Court of Appeals, and the U.S. Supreme Court.

The Judicial Process in General

Once a taxpayer has exhausted the remedies available within the IRS (i.e., no satisfactory settlement has been reached at the agent or at the Appeals Division), the dispute can be taken to the Federal courts. The trial and appellate court system for Federal tax litigation is illustrated in Exhibit 1.4.

A trial court, also known as a **court of original jurisdiction**, initially hears the case. Appeals (either by the taxpayer or the IRS) are heard by the appropriate appellate court. A taxpayer has a choice of *three trial courts*: a U.S. District Court, the U.S. Court of Federal Claims, or the U.S. Tax Court.

The U.S. Tax Court contains a Small Cases Division that only hears cases involving amounts of $50,000 or less. The ruling of the judge is final (no appeal is available), and these rulings are not precedent for any other cases (i.e., they are not primary authority and are not citable as substantial authority). Proceedings of the Small Cases Division are informal, and because there is no requirement that a taxpayer be represented by an attorney, they can be less costly for a taxpayer. The typical small case lasts one to two hours, and the taxpayer only needs to tell the judge his or her story and present any supporting evidence. Special trial judges, rather than Tax Court judges, often preside over these hearings. Some of these cases can be found on the U.S. Tax Court website.

American law, following English law, is frequently *created* by judicial decisions. Under the doctrine of *stare decisis* ("let the decision stand"), each case has precedential value for future cases with the same controlling set of facts.

Judges are not required to follow judicial precedent beyond their own jurisdiction. For example, the decisions of an appellate court are binding only on the trial courts within its jurisdiction and not on other trial courts. Different appellate courts may reach different opinions about the same issue. Further, the doctrine of precedential authority requires a court to follow prior cases only when the issues and material facts of the current case are essentially the same as those involved in the prior decisions.

EXHIBIT 1.4	Federal Judicial Tax Process

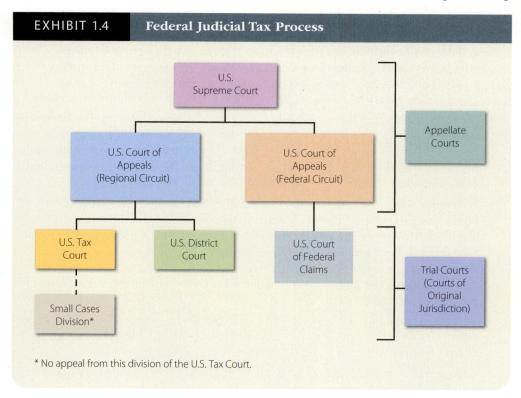

* No appeal from this division of the U.S. Tax Court.

Most Federal and state appellate court decisions and some decisions of trial courts are published. Published court decisions are organized by jurisdiction (Federal or state) and level of court (appellate or trial).

Trial Courts

Here are some differences between the various trial courts (courts of original jurisdiction):

- *Number of courts*. There is only one Court of Federal Claims and only one Tax Court, but there are many U.S. District Courts. District Courts hear cases based on where the taxpayer lives (so a taxpayer in Atlanta would have her case heard by the Atlanta U.S. District Court).

- *Number of judges*. District Courts have a number of judges, but only one judge hears a case. The Court of Federal Claims has 16 judges, and the Tax Court has 19 regular judges. Typically, Tax Court cases are heard and decided by only one of the 19 regular judges. However, if the case is viewed as important, or novel tax issues are raised, the entire Tax Court might hear the case. If a case is reviewed by the full Tax Court, such an *en banc* decision has compelling authority.

- *Location*. The Court of Federal Claims meets most often in Washington, D.C. Each state has at least one District Court, and many of the populous states have more. The Tax Court is officially based in Washington, D.C., but the various judges travel to different parts of the country and hear cases at predetermined locations and dates.

- *Jurisdiction of the Tax Court and District Courts*. The Tax Court hears only tax cases and is the most popular forum for tax cases since its judges have more tax expertise; many had careers in the IRS or Treasury Department before being appointed to the Tax Court. The District Courts hear nontax cases as well. As a result, these judges are viewed as generalists (rather than specialists) in tax law.

- *Jurisdiction of the Court of Federal Claims.* The U.S. Court of Federal Claims has jurisdiction over any claim against the United States. As a result, the Court of Federal Claims hears nontax litigation as well as tax cases. Court of Federal Claims judges are tax law generalists. This court is viewed as a stronger option when equity is an issue (as opposed to purely technical issues) or when the case requires extensive discovery of evidence. In addition, it has a pro-business orientation.[45]

- *Jury trial.* A jury trial is only available in a District Court. However, because juries can decide only questions of fact (and not questions of law), taxpayers who choose a District Court often do not request a jury trial. In that event, the judge decides all issues in a bench trial. A District Court decision carries precedential value only in its district.

- *Payment of deficiency.* Before the Court of Federal Claims or a District Court will hear a case, the taxpayer must pay any taxes assessed by the IRS and then sue for a refund. This is not the case with the Tax Court. Here, a taxpayer may request a hearing without making any payments to the IRS. As a result, whether to pay the tax in advance (and limit further interest and penalties) or wait to pay the tax (and risk additional interest and penalties) becomes part of the decision-making process of selecting a venue.

- *Appeals.* Appeals from a District Court or a Tax Court decision are to the appropriate U.S. Court of Appeals. Appeals from the Court of Federal Claims go to the Court of Appeals for the Federal Circuit.

- *Gray areas.* Because there are "gray areas" in the tax laws, courts may disagree as to the proper tax treatment of an item. With these differences in judicial authority, a taxpayer may have some flexibility to choose the most favorable forum to hear the case.

Some of the characteristics of the judicial system just described are summarized in Concept Summary 1.1.

Concept Summary 1.1

Federal Judicial System

Issue	U.S. Tax Court	U.S. District Court	U.S. Court of Federal Claims
Number of judges per court	19*	1	16
Payment of deficiency before trial	No	Yes	Yes
Jury trial available	No	Yes	No
Types of disputes	Tax cases only	Most criminal/civil cases	Claims against the United States
Jurisdiction	Nationwide	Location of taxpayer	Nationwide
IRS acquiescence policy	Yes	Yes	Yes
Appeal route	U.S. Court of Appeals	U.S. Court of Appeals	U.S. Court of Appeals for the Federal Circuit

*Currently, there are only 15 regular judges. They are assisted by 10 senior judges (whose terms have ended but return to hear cases as needed) and 5 special trial judges (who are appointed by the Senior Judge of the U.S. Tax Court rather than by the President) (November 2018).

Appellate Courts

A trial court can be appealed to the appropriate U.S. Court of Appeals. The 11 geographic circuits, the circuit for the District of Columbia, and the Federal Circuit[46] appear

---

[45]T.D. Peyser, "The Case for Selecting the Claims Court to Litigate a Federal Tax Liability," *The Tax Executive* (Winter 1988): 149.

[46]The Court of Appeals for the Federal Circuit was created, effective October 1, 1982, by P.L. 97–64 (4/2/82) to hear decisions appealed from the Claims Court (now the Court of Federal Claims).

EXHIBIT 1.5   The Federal Courts of Appeals

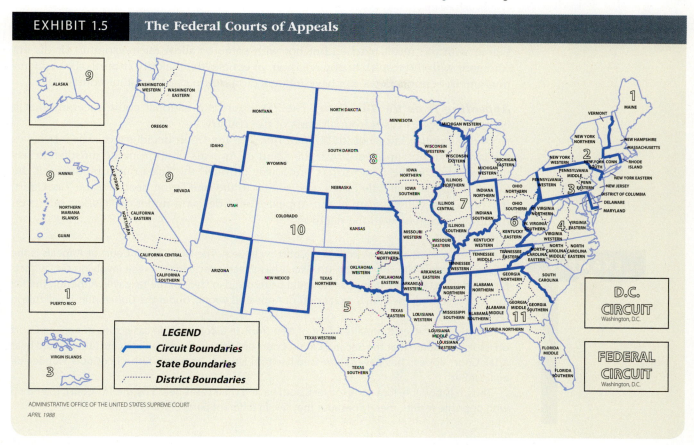

ADMINISTRATIVE OFFICE OF THE UNITED STATES SUPREME COURT
APRIL 1988

in Exhibit 1.5. Generally, a three-judge panel hears a Court of Appeals case, but occasionally the *full* court decides more controversial cases.

If the Government loses at the trial court level (District Court, Tax Court, or Court of Federal Claims), it may decide not to appeal. However, the fact that the IRS does not appeal does not mean that the IRS agrees with the result (and it may litigate similar issues in the future).

The IRS may decide not to appeal for a number of reasons. First, the IRS may decide that available personnel should be assigned to other more important cases. Second, the IRS may decide that the taxpayer has a sympathetic position or the facts may be particularly strong in his or her favor. In this event, the IRS may wait to test the legal issues with a different taxpayer (who might have a weaker case). Third, the Court of Appeals of jurisdiction might matter. Based on past experience and precedent, the IRS may decide that the chance for success on a particular issue might be more promising in a different Court of Appeals.

District Courts, the Tax Court, and the Court of Federal Claims must abide by the precedents set by a Court of Appeals of jurisdiction. A particular Court of Appeals need not follow the decisions of another Court of Appeals. All courts, however, must follow the decisions of the U.S. Supreme Court.

The role of appellate courts is usually limited to a review of whether the trial court applied the proper law in arriving at its decision. Rarely does an appellate court question a lower court's fact-finding determination.

An appeal can have a number of possible outcomes. The appellate court may approve (affirm) or disapprove (reverse) the lower court's finding, or it may send the case back to the trial court for further consideration (remand). When many issues are involved, a taxpayer may encounter a mixed result. Thus, the lower court may be affirmed (*aff'd*) on Issue A and reversed (*rev'd*) on Issue B, while Issue C is remanded (*rem'd*) for additional fact finding.

When more than one judge is involved in the decision-making process, disagreements are common. In addition to the majority view, one or more judges may concur (agree with the result reached but not with some or all of the reasoning) or dissent (disagree with the result). In any decision, of course, the majority controls. But concurring and dissenting views can have influence on future cases or other courts.

Appealing from the Tax Court   The Tax Court is a national court, meaning that it hears and decides cases from all parts of the country.

Under a policy known as the *Golsen* rule, the Tax Court decides a case as it believes the law should be applied *only* if the Court of Appeals of appropriate jurisdiction has not yet ruled on the issue or has previously affirmed the Tax Court's rationale. If the Court of Appeals has ruled on a case similar to the one being heard by the Tax Court, the Tax Court will conform to the Appeals Court decision under the *Golsen* rule even though it disagrees with the decision.[47]

EXAMPLE

19

Gene lives in Texas and sues in the Tax Court on Issue A. The Fifth Circuit Court of Appeals is the appropriate appellate court. The Fifth Circuit has already decided, in a case involving similar facts but a different taxpayer, that Issue A should be resolved in favor of the taxpayer. Although the Tax Court believes that the Fifth Circuit Court of Appeals is wrong, under the *Golsen* rule, it will rule in favor of Gene.

Shortly thereafter, Beth, a resident of New York, in a comparable case, sues in the Tax Court on Issue A. Assume that the Second Circuit Court of Appeals, the appellate court that would hear a Tax Court appeal, has never expressed itself on Issue A. As a result, the Tax Court will decide against Beth.

Thus, it is possible for two taxpayers, both having their cases heard by the Tax Court, to end up with opposite results, merely because they live in different parts of the country.

Appeal to the U.S. Supreme Court   Appeal to the U.S. Supreme Court is by <mark>Writ of Certiorari</mark>. If the Court agrees to hear the case, it will grant the Writ (*cert. granted*). Since the Supreme Court rarely hears tax cases, most often it denies jurisdiction (*cert. denied*). The Court usually grants certiorari when it must resolve a conflict among the Courts of Appeals (e.g., two or more appellate courts have assumed opposing positions on a particular issue) or when the tax issue is extremely important. The granting of a Writ of Certiorari indicates that at least four of the nine members of the Supreme Court believe that the issue is of sufficient importance to be heard by the full Court.

Judicial Citations

Court decisions are an important source of tax law, and the ability to cite and locate a case is a critical skill when working with the tax law. Judicial citations usually follow a standard pattern: case name, volume number, reporter series, page or paragraph number, court (where necessary), and year of the decision (see Concept Summary 1.2).

Judicial Citations—The U.S. Tax Court   The U.S. Tax Court issues two types of decisions: Regular decisions and Memorandum decisions based on the Chief Judge's determination. They differ in both substance and form. In terms of substance, *Memorandum* decisions deal with cases that involve only the application of established principles of law. *Regular* decisions involve novel issues not previously resolved by the Tax Court. In actual practice, however, both *Regular* and *Memorandum* decisions represent the position of the Tax Court and, as such, can be relied upon.[48]

The Regular and Summary decisions issued by the Tax Court also differ in form. Regular decisions are published by the U.S. Government in a series called *Tax Court of the United States Reports* (T.C.). Each volume of these reports covers a six-month period (January 1 through June 30 and July 1 through December 31) and is given a succeeding

---

[47] *Jack E. Golsen*, 54 T.C. 742 (1970); see also *John A. Lardas*, 99 T.C. 490 (1992).

[48] U.S. Tax Court Small Cases Division Summary Opinions carry no precedential value. Summary Opinions issued after January 9, 2001, are available on the U.S. Tax Court website.

Concept Summary 1.2

Judicial Sources

Court	Location	Authority
U.S. Supreme Court	S.Ct. Series (West)	Highest authority
	U.S. Series (U.S. Gov't.)	
	L.Ed.2d (Lawyer's Co-op.)	
	AFTR (RIA)	
	USTC (CCH)	
U.S. Courts of Appeal	Federal 3d (West)	Next highest appellate court
	AFTR (RIA)	
	USTC (CCH)	
Tax Court (Regular decisions)	U.S. Gov't. Printing Office	Highest trial court*
	RIA/CCH separate services	
Tax Court (Memorandum decisions)	RIA T.C.Memo. (RIA)	Less authority than Regular T.C. decision
	TCM (CCH)	
U.S. Court of Federal Claims**	Federal Claims Reporter (West)	Similar authority as Tax Court
	AFTR (RIA)	
	USTC (CCH)	
U.S. District Courts	F.Supp.2d Series (West)	Lowest trial court
	AFTR (RIA)	
	USTC (CCH)	
Small Cases Division of Tax Court	U.S. Tax Court website***	No precedent value

*Theoretically, the Tax Court, Court of Federal Claims, and District Courts are on the same level of authority. But some people believe that because the Tax Court hears and decides tax cases from all parts of the country (i.e., it is a national court), its decisions may be more authoritative than a Court of Federal Claims or District Court decision.
**Before October 29, 1992, the U.S. Claims Court.
***Starting in 2001.

volume number. Usually there is a time lag between the date a decision is rendered and the date it is published. A temporary citation may be necessary to help the researcher locate a recent Regular decision. Consider, for example, the temporary and permanent citations for *Mehrdad Rafizadeh*, a decision filed on January 2, 2018:

Temporary Citation
{ *Mehrdad Rafizadeh*, 150 T.C. _____, No. 1 (2018).
Explanation: Page number left blank because not yet known.

Permanent Citation
{ *Mehrdad Rafizadeh*, 150 T.C. 1 (2018).
Explanation: Page number now available.

Both citations tell us that the case ultimately will appear in Volume 150 of the *Tax Court of the United States Reports*. But until this volume is made available, the page number must be left blank. Instead, the temporary citation identifies the decision as being the 1st Regular decision issued by the Tax Court since Volume 149 ended. With this information, the decision can be easily located in the special Tax Court services published by Commerce Clearing House (CCH) and Research Institute of America (RIA). Once Volume 150 is released, the permanent citation can be substituted and the number of the case dropped. Starting in 1995, both Regular and Memorandum decisions are issued on the U.S. Tax Court website (**ustaxcourt.gov**). Memorandum decisions, although available on the U.S. Tax Court website, are not published by the U.S. Government.

Before 1943, the Tax Court was called the Board of Tax Appeals, and its decisions were published as the *United States Board of Tax Appeals Reports* (B.T.A.). These 47 volumes cover the period from 1924 to 1942. For example, the citation *Karl Pauli*, 11 B.T.A. 784 (1928) refers to the 11th volume of the *Board of Tax Appeals Reports*, page 784, issued in 1928.

Memorandum decisions are published by both CCH and RIA. Consider, for example, the three different ways the *Nick R. Hughes* case can be cited:

> *Nick R. Hughes*, T.C.Memo. 2009–94.
> > *Explanation:* The 94th Memorandum decision issued by the Tax Court in 2009.

> *Nick R. Hughes*, 97 TCM 1488.
> > *Explanation:* Page 1488 of Vol. 97 of the CCH *Tax Court Memorandum Decisions*.

> *Nick R. Hughes*, 2009 RIA T.C.Memo. ¶2009,094.
> > *Explanation:* Paragraph 2009,094 of the RIA T.C. *Memorandum Decisions*.

Note that the third citation contains the same information as the first. As a result, ¶2009,094 indicates both the year and decision number of the case.[49]

U.S. Tax Court Summary Opinions relate to decisions of the Tax Court's Small Cases Division and may not be treated as precedent. For example, *John A. Garcia*, filed on August 7, 2018, is cited as follows:

> *John A. Garcia*, T.C. Summary 2018–38.

If the IRS loses a decision, it may indicate whether it agrees or disagrees with the results reached by the court by publishing an **acquiescence** ("A" or "*Acq.*") or **nonacquiescence** ("NA" or "*Nonacq.*"), respectively. The acquiescence or nonacquiescence is published in the *Internal Revenue Bulletin* as an *Action on Decision*. The IRS can retroactively revoke an acquiescence or nonacquiescence. Originally, acquiescences and nonacquiescences were published only for Regular U.S. Tax Court decisions, but since 1991, the IRS has expanded its acquiescence program to include other civil tax cases where guidance is helpful.

Judicial Citations—The U.S. District Courts, Court of Federal Claims, and Courts of Appeals

District Court, Court of Federal Claims, Court of Appeals, and Supreme Court decisions dealing with Federal tax matters are reported in both the CCH *U.S. Tax Cases* (USTC) and the RIA *American Federal Tax Reports* (AFTR) series.

U.S. District Court decisions, dealing with both tax and nontax issues, also are published by West in its *Federal Supplement* (F.Supp.) series. The following examples illustrate three different ways to cite a District Court case:

> *Turner v. U.S.*, 2004–1 USTC ¶60,478 (D.Ct. Tex., 2004).
> > *Explanation:* Reported in the first volume of the *U.S. Tax Cases*, published by Commerce Clearing House for calendar year 2004 (2004–1) and located at paragraph 60,478 (¶60,478).

> *Turner v. U.S.*, 93 AFTR 2d 2004–686 (D.Ct. Tex., 2004).
> > *Explanation:* Reported in the 93rd volume of the second series of the *American Federal Tax Reports* (AFTR 2d), published by RIA and beginning on page 686.

> *Turner v. U.S.*, 306 F.Supp.2d 668 (D.Ct. Tex., 2004).
> > *Explanation:* Reported in the 306th volume of the second series of the *Federal Supplement* (F.Supp.2d), published by West and beginning on page 668.

The case name, the reference to the U.S. District Court of Texas (D.Ct. Tex.), and the year the decision was rendered (2004) appear in each of the citations.[50]

---

[49] In this text, the Research Institute of America (RIA) citation for Memorandum decisions of the U.S. Tax Court is omitted. Thus, *Nick R. Hughes* is cited as 97 TCM 1488, T.C.Memo. 2009–94.

[50] In the text, the case is cited in the following form: *Turner v. U.S.*, 2004–1 USTC ¶60,478, 93 AFTR 2d 2004–686, 306 F.Supp.2d 668 (D.Ct.Tex., 2004).

Decisions of the Court of Federal Claims are published in the USTCs, the AFTRs, and in a West reporter, the *Federal Claims Reporter*, abbreviated as Fed.Cl.

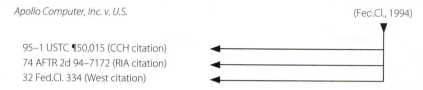

Apollo Computer, Inc. v. U.S.   (Fec.Cl., 1994)

95–1 USTC ¶50,015 (CCH citation)
74 AFTR 2d 94–7172 (RIA citation)
32 Fed.Cl. 334 (West citation)

Decisions of the Courts of Appeals are published in a West reporter designated as the *Federal Third* (F.3d) series, which began in October 1993, in addition to USTCs and AFTRs. Illustrations of the different forms follow:

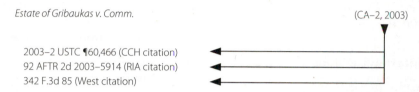

Estate of Gribaukas v. Comm.   (CA–2, 2003)

2003–2 USTC ¶60,466 (CCH citation)
92 AFTR 2d 2003–5914 (RIA citation)
342 F.3d 85 (West citation)

Judicial Citations—The U.S. Supreme Court Supreme Court decisions are published by CCH in the USTCs and by RIA in the AFTRs. The U.S. Government Printing Office also publishes these decisions in the *United States Supreme Court Reports* (U.S.), as does West in its *Supreme Court Reporter* (S.Ct.), and the Lawyer's Co-operative Publishing Company in its *United States Reports, Lawyer's Edition* (L.Ed.). The following illustrates the different ways the same decision can be cited:

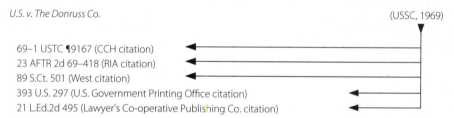

U.S. v. The Donruss Co.   (USSC, 1969)

69–1 USTC ¶9167 (CCH citation)
23 AFTR 2d 69–418 (RIA citation)
89 S.Ct. 501 (West citation)
393 U.S. 297 (U.S. Government Printing Office citation)
21 L.Ed.2d 495 (Lawyer's Co-operative Publishing Co. citation)

The parenthetical reference (USSC, 1969) identifies the decision as having been rendered by the U.S. Supreme Court in 1969. In this text, Supreme Court decision citations are limited to the CCH (USTC), the RIA (AFTR), and the West (S.Ct.) versions.

1-4d **Other Sources of the Tax Law**

Other sources of the tax law include tax treaties and tax periodicals.

Tax Treaties

The United States signs certain tax treaties (sometimes called tax conventions) with foreign countries to assist in tax enforcement and to avoid double taxation. Since 1988, when there is a direct conflict between a treaty and the Code, the most recent item takes precedence. A taxpayer must disclose on the tax return any position where a treaty overrides a tax law.[51]

Tax Periodicals

The use of tax periodicals can often shorten the research time needed to resolve a tax problem. An article relevant to the issue at hand may provide the references needed to locate the primary sources of the tax that apply (e.g., citations to judicial decisions, Regulations, and other IRS pronouncements).

Several indexes are available for locating tax articles, including *Federal Tax Articles* (published by CCH) and *Index to Federal Tax Articles* (published by Thomson Reuters). Both of these indexes are available by subscription.

---

[51]§ 7852(d).

Here are some of the more useful tax periodicals:

Journal of Taxation	*The ATA Journal of Legal Tax*
Journal of International Taxation	*Research*
Practical Tax Strategies	**aaajournals.org/loi/jltr**
Estate Planning	
Corporate Taxation	*Oil, Gas & Energy Quarterly*
Business Entities	**bus.lsu.edu/accounting/faculty/**
Taxation of Exempts	**lcrumbley/oilgas.html**
Real Estate Taxation	
ria.thomsonreuters.com/journals	*Trusts and Estates*
	wealthmanagement.com/te-home
The Tax Executive	
tei.org	*Journal of Passthrough Entities*
	TAXES—The Tax Magazine
The Tax Adviser	**tax.cchgroup.com/books**
thetaxadviser.com	
	Tax Notes
Journal of the American Taxation	**taxnotes.com**
Association	
aaajournals.org/loi/atax	*Tax Law Review*
	law.nyu.edu/tax/
	taxlawreview/index.htm

LO.6

List and assess tax law sources.

1-5 WORKING WITH THE TAX LAW—LOCATING AND USING TAX SOURCES

Tax law consists of a body of legislative (e.g., Code Sections and tax treaties), administrative (e.g., Regulations and Rulings), and judicial (e.g., court cases) pronouncements. Working with the tax law requires being able to locate and effectively use these sources. A major consideration is the time required to find relevant information related to the issues identified.

Unless the problem is simple (e.g., the Code Section is known and there is a Regulation on point), the research process begins with a tax service.

1-5a Commercial Tax Services

In the past, commercial tax services could be classified as *annotated* (i.e., organized by Internal Revenue Code) or *topical* (i.e., organized by major topics). However, as tax research has become electronic, this classification system is no longer appropriate. For example, Thomson Reuters *Checkpoint* includes both the *Federal Tax Coordinator 2d* (topical) and the *United States Tax Reporter* (annotated).

Here is a partial list of the available commercial tax services:

- *Standard Federal Tax Reporter*, Commerce Clearing House.
- CCH *IntelliConnect*, Commerce Clearing House—the online version of the *Standard Federal Tax Reporter* (along with other CCH materials).
- *United States Tax Reporter*, Research Institute of America, Thomson Reuters.
- Thomson Reuters *Checkpoint*, Research Institute of America—the online version of RIA's *Federal Tax Coordinator 2d* and *United States Tax Reporter*.
- *Practical Tax Expert*, CCH/Wolters Kluwer.
- *Tax Management Portfolios*, Bloomberg BNA.
- *Mertens Law of Federal Income Taxation*, Thomson Reuters.
- Thomson Reuters *Westlaw* and *WestlawNext*—compilations include access to *Tax Management Portfolios*, *Federal Tax Coordinator 2d*, and *Mertens*.
- LexisNexis *Tax Center*—a compilation of primary sources and various materials taken from CCH, Matthew Bender, Kleinrock, and Bloomberg BNA.

FINANCIAL DISCLOSURE INSIGHTS   Where Does GAAP Come From?

Tax law has many sources, including Congress and the legislators of other countries, the courts, and the IRS. Similarly, accounting principles also have many sources. In reconciling the tax and financial accounting reporting of a transaction, the tax professional needs to know the hierarchy of authority of accounting principles so that the proper level of importance can be assigned to a specific GAAP document. The diagram shown below presents the sources of GAAP listed in general order of authority from highest to lowest.

Professional research is conducted to find and analyze the sources of accounting reporting standards in much the same way tax professionals conduct research into open tax questions. In fact, many of the publishers that provide tax research materials also can be used to find GAAP and IFRS documents. The Financial Accounting Standards Board (FASB) also makes its standards and interpretations available by subscription.

Highest Authority
- Financial Accounting Standards and Interpretations of the FASB.
- Pronouncements of bodies that preceded the FASB, such as the Accounting Principles Board (APB).

- FASB Technical Bulletins.
- Audit and Accounting Guides, prepared by the American Institute of CPAs (AICPA) and cleared by the FASB.
- Practice Bulletins, prepared by the AICPA and cleared by the FASB.

- Interpretation Guides of the FASB Staff.
- Accounting Interpretations of the AICPA.
- IASB Accounting Standards.
- FASB Concepts Standards.
- Widely accepted accounting practices, professional journals, accounting textbooks, and treatises.

1-5b Using Electronic (Online) Tax Services

A competent tax professional must become familiar and proficient with electronic research services and be able to use them to complete research projects efficiently. Following certain general procedures, however, can simplify the research process. The following suggestions may be helpful:[52]

- Carefully choose keywords for the search. Words with a broad usage, such as *income*, are of limited value. If the researcher is interested in a specific type of dividend income, the search phrase *dividend income* is too broad because it finds a variety of topics including stock dividends, constructive dividends, and liquidating dividends (drawing about 2,000 hits in Thomson Reuters *Checkpoint*). Searching for *qualified dividend income* obtains 793 items, while *stock dividend income* obtains 59 items, *cash dividend income* finds 44 items, and *property dividend income* finds 20 items.

- Take advantage of *connectors* to place parameters on the search and further restrict the output. Although each tax service has its own set of connectors, many are similar. Thus, enclosing words in quotation marks (e.g., "personal service

---

[52] For a more complete discussion of the use of Thomson Reuters *Checkpoint* and CCH *IntelliConnect*, as well as internet research in taxation in general, see Sawyers and Gill, *Federal Tax Research*, 11th ed. (Cengage Learning, 2018), Chapters 6 and 7.

corporation") means "exact phrase" in both Thomson Reuters *Checkpoint* and CCH *IntelliConnect*.

- Be selective in choosing the data to search. For example, if the research project does not involve case law, do not include judicial decisions in the search.

- Use a table of contents, an index, or a citation when appropriate. Although the keyword approach is most frequently used, there are other ways to search tax databases. Using the table of contents or index may narrow the information that needs to be examined. Citations may be used to search for statutory (e.g., Code Section), administrative (e.g., Rev.Rul.), or judicial (e.g., Tax Court) sources and also can provide access to the tax service's annotations.

1-5c Noncommercial Electronic (Online) Tax Sources

The internet provides a wealth of tax information in several popular forms, sometimes at no cost to the researcher. A tax professional can access a significant amount of information that can aid the research process.

- *Websites* are provided by accounting and consulting firms, publishers, tax academics, libraries, and governmental bodies as a means of making information widely available. One of the best sites available to the tax professional is the Internal Revenue Service's home page, illustrated in Exhibit 1.6. This site offers

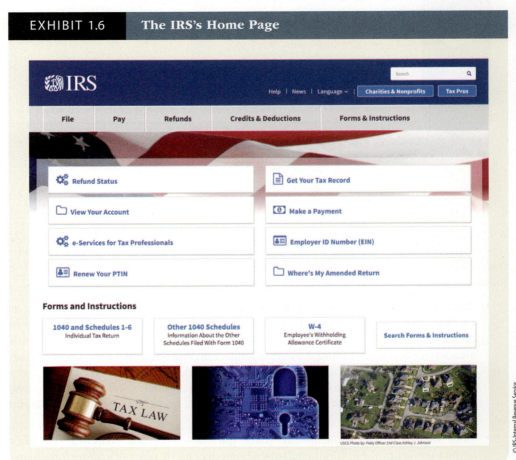

EXHIBIT 1.6   **The IRS's Home Page**

downloadable forms and instructions, interpretations of Regulations, and news update items. Exhibit 1.7 lists some of the websites that may be most useful to tax researchers. Particularly useful is the directory at **taxsites.com**, which provides links to accounting and tax sources (including international, state, and payroll tax sources).

- *Blogs and RSS sites* provide a means by which information related to the tax law can be exchanged among taxpayers, tax professionals, and others who subscribe to the group's services. Individuals can read the exchanges and offer replies and suggestions to inquiries. Discussions address the interpretation and application of existing law, analysis of proposals and new pronouncements, and reviews of tax software.

Although tax information on the internet is plentiful, information in the public domain should not be relied upon without referring to other sources. Anyone can set up a website, and the quality of the information can be difficult for a tax professional to ascertain.

EXHIBIT 1.7	Tax-Related Websites	
Website	**Web Address**	**Description**
Accounting firms and professional organizations	For instance, the AICPA's page is at **aicpa.org**, Ernst & Young is at **ey.com**, and KPMG is at **kpmg.com**	Tax planning newsletters, descriptions of services offered and career opportunities, and exchange of data with clients and subscribers
Cengage Learning	**cengage.com**	Informational updates, newsletters, support materials for students and adopters, and continuing education
Commercial tax publishers	For instance, **taxnotes.com**, **cchgroup.com**, **tax.thomsonreuters.com**, and **bna.com**	Information about products and services available for subscription and newsletter excerpts
Court opinions	The site at **law.justia.com** covers state, Federal, and Supreme Court decisions (but not Tax Court)	A synopsis of result reached by the court
Federal Register	**federalregister.gov**	Releases from the IRS (e.g., Regulations)
Internal Revenue Service	**irs.gov**	News releases, downloadable forms and instructions, tables, Circular 230, and e-mail
Tax Almanac	**taxalmanac.org**	Smorgasbord of tax research resources
Tax Analysts	**taxanalysts.org**	Policy-oriented readings on the tax law and proposals to change it and moderated bulletins on various tax subjects
Tax Foundation	**taxfoundation.org**	Nonprofit educational organization that promotes sound tax policy and measures tax burdens
Tax laws online	Regulations are at **law.cornell.edu/cfr**, and the Code is at **uscode.house.gov**	
Tax Sites Directory	**taxsites.com**	References and links to tax sites on the internet, including state and Federal tax sites, academic and professional pages, tax forms, and software
U.S. Tax Court decisions	**ustaxcourt.gov**	Recent U.S. Tax Court decisions

Caution: Web addresses change frequently.

LO.7

Demonstrate tax research.

1-6 WORKING WITH THE TAX LAW— TAX RESEARCH

Tax research is the process of finding a competent and professional conclusion to a tax problem. The problem may originate from either completed or proposed transactions. In the case of a completed transaction, the objective of the research is to determine the tax result of what has already taken place. For example, is a taxpayer expense deductible? When dealing with proposed transactions, tax research has a different objective: effective tax planning by determining the tax consequences of various alternatives. A large part of a tax professional's career is spent on this type of tax research.

Tax research involves the following steps:

- Identifying and refining the problem.
- Locating the appropriate tax law sources.
- Assessing the validity of the tax law sources.
- Arriving at the solution or at alternative solutions (including consideration of nontax factors).
- Effectively communicating the solution to the taxpayer.
- Updating the solution (where appropriate) in light of new developments.

The tax research process is illustrated in Exhibit 1.8. The broken lines indicate steps of particular interest when tax research is directed toward proposed rather than completed transactions.

1-6a Identifying the Problem

Problem identification starts by documenting the relevant facts involved with the issue. *All* of the facts that might have a bearing on the problem must be gathered; if any facts are omitted, the solution provided will likely change. To illustrate, refer to the facts of *The Big Picture* on p. 1-1. Is Dana entitled to a bad debt deduction?

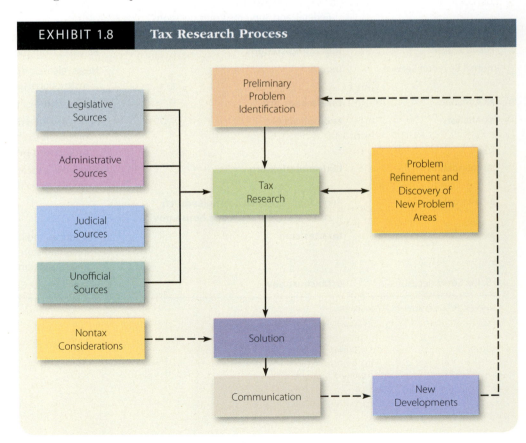

EXHIBIT 1.8   Tax Research Process

Refining the Problem

Before a bad debt deduction is allowed, it must be proven that a debt really existed. In a related-party setting (e.g., aunt and nephew), the IRS may argue that the original advance was not a loan but was, in reality, a gift. A key factor is whether the lender (the aunt) had an honest and real expectation of payment by the borrower (the nephew).[53] An expectation of repayment could be established by the following:

- The borrower issued a written instrument evidencing the obligation.
- The loan arrangement provided for interest.
- The note specified a set due date.
- Collateral was available to the lender in the event of default by the borrower.[54]

The presence of some (or all) of these items does not, however, guarantee that a loan exists. And the absence of some or all of these items does not make the advance a gift. Although *The Big Picture* on p. 1-1 does not provide all of the facts (e.g., was a written note created and signed?), several items appear to indicate that a loan was created:

- It appears that the nephew has repaid $16,000 of the $93,000 that he borrowed. If both parties intended the advance to be a gift, why was a partial repayment made?
- Although a nephew on his way to college would likely have limited assets to serve as collateral for a loan, the fact that he was obtaining additional education could reinforce an expectation of repayment. In general, the earning potential of an individual increases as a result of a college education. By obtaining the education, the nephew will increase earning power and his financial ability to repay the loan.

Further Refinement of the Problem

Without additional facts, it may be impossible to conclude whether the advance was a loan or a gift. However, it is possible to document the tax consequences of each outcome.

If the advance is determined to be a gift, it is subject to the Federal gift tax.[55] Whether a gift tax results depends on the aunt's available unified tax credit. Absent a unified credit, there will be a gift tax on $80,000 [$93,000 (total gift) − $13,000 (annual exclusion in 2012)].[56] Whether the transfer results in a gift tax, it must be reported on Form 709 (United States Gift Tax Return) because the amount of the gift exceeds the annual exclusion.

Even if it is assumed that Dana made a gift to her nephew in 2012, will the intervening seven years preclude the IRS from assessing any gift tax that might be due as a result of the transfer?[57] Further research indicates that the statute of limitations on assessments does not begin to run when a tax return is not filed.[58]

What are the tax consequences if the advance is treated as a loan? Aside from the bad debt deduction aspects (covered later in the chapter), the tax law identifies several immediate implications:[59]

- If the loan did not provide for interest (or if the interest was at a below-market rate), interest will be imputed (i.e., "created").
  a. The lender (the aunt) will be required to include any imputed interest in her income.

---

[53]*William F. Mercil*, 24 T.C. 1150 (1955), and *Evans Clark*, 18 T.C. 780 (1952), *aff'd* 53–2 USTC ¶9452, 44 AFTR 70, 205 F.2d 353 (CA–2, 1953).

[54]*Arthur T. Davidson*, 37 TCM 725, T.C.Memo. 1978–167.

[55]The transfer does not come within the unlimited gift tax exclusion of § 2503(e)(2)(A) because the aunt did not pay the amount directly to an educational institution. Besides, the exclusion covers only tuition payments and not other costs attendant on going to college (e.g., room and board).

[56]The tax, in turn, depends upon the amount of taxable gifts the aunt has made in the past. For a discussion of the mechanics of the Federal gift tax, see Chapter 18.

[57]Throughout the discussion of *The Big Picture* on p. 1-1, the assumption has been made that if a gift occurred, it took place in 2012. That assumption need not be the case. Depending upon the aunt's intent, she could have decided to make a gift of the unpaid balance anytime after the loan was made (e.g., 2013 or 2014).

[58]See § 6501(c)(3) and the discussion of the statute of limitations in Chapter 17.

[59]§ 7872.

b. She also is deemed to have made a gift of the interest to the borrower.

c. The borrower (nephew) may be entitled to deduct (as an itemized deduction) a portion of the interest deemed paid to the lender (aunt).

- If the stated interest is at a below-market rate, the difference is treated as noted above.

- For gift loans of $100,000 or less, the imputed element cannot exceed the net investment income of the borrower.

1-6b Locating the Appropriate Tax Law Sources

Once a problem is clearly defined, what is the next step? Although the next step is a matter of individual judgment, most tax research begins with a keyword search using an electronic tax service. If the problem is not complex, the researcher may turn directly to the Internal Revenue Code and the Treasury Regulations. The Code and Regulations are available in print form (and accessible electronically).

1-6c Assessing the Validity of Tax Law Sources

LO.8

Assess the validity and weight of tax law sources.

After a source has been located, the next step is to assess the source in light of the problem at hand. Proper assessment involves careful interpretation of the tax law and consideration of the law's relevance and validity.

Interpreting the Internal Revenue Code

The language of the Code can be extremely difficult to comprehend. Some of this difficulty is due to its structure (the Code follows the structure of all U.S. law), so getting used to reading (and interpreting) the Code can take time.

The Code must be read carefully for restrictive language such as "*at least* 80 percent" and "*more than* 80 percent" or "*less than* 50 percent" and "*exceeds* 50 percent." Whether two or more clauses are connected by "*or*" or by "*and*" makes a great deal of difference.

Sometimes the Code directs the researcher elsewhere for the answer. For example, § 162(c) refers to the Foreign Corrupt Practices Act for purposes of determining when payments to foreign officials are deductible.

Definitions vary from one Code Section to another. For example, § 267 disallows losses between related parties. Brothers and sisters are included in this definition of related parties. This is not the case with § 318, which deals with the definition of related parties for certain stock redemptions. Research has shown that in one-third of the conflicts reaching the Tax Court, the court could not discern the intent of Congress by simply reading the statute (the Court had to look to Committee Reports to understand intent).[60]

If an answer is not in the Code, it may be necessary to look to other tax law, including Regulations and judicial decisions.

Assessing the Validity of a Treasury Regulation

Treasury Regulations are the official interpretation of the Code and have the force and effect of law. Occasionally, however, a court invalidates a Regulation (or a portion of it) because the Regulation is contrary to the intent of Congress.

Keep the following things in mind when you assess the validity of a Regulation:

- IRS agents must give the Code and any related Regulations equal weight when dealing with taxpayers and their representatives.

- Taxpayers have the burden of proof to show that a Regulation varies from the language of the statute and is not supported by the related Committee Reports.

- If the taxpayer challenges a Regulation and loses, a 20 percent negligence penalty may apply. This accuracy-related provision deals with the "intentional disregard of rules and regulations" discussed in Chapter 17.

---

[60]T. L. Kirkpatrick and W. B. Pollard, "Reliance by the Tax Court on the Legislative Intent of Congress," *The Tax Executive* (Summer 1986): 358–359.

- Some Regulations merely rephrase what Congress has stated in its Committee Reports issued when the tax legislation was enacted. These Regulations are almost impossible to overturn because they clearly reflect the intent of Congress.

- In some Code Sections, Congress has given to the "[Treasury] Secretary or his delegate" the authority to prescribe Regulations to carry out the details of administration or to otherwise complete the operating rules. In these cases, Congress is delegating its legislative powers to the Treasury Department. Regulations issued under this type of authority truly possess the force and effect of law and are often called "legislative" Regulations. They are to be distinguished from "interpretative" Regulations, which are issued to explain the meaning of a particular Code Section.[61]

- Courts tend to apply a legislative reenactment doctrine. A particular interpretive Regulation is assumed to have achieved congressional approval if the Regulation was finalized many years earlier and Congress has not amended the related Code Section.

ETHICS & EQUITY Choosing Cases for Appeal

The U.S. Government loses a tax case against a prominent citizen in the U.S. District Court of Iowa. The taxpayer, a minister, had set up three separate trusts for each of his three children (i.e., a total of nine trusts). The Government argued that these trusts should be consolidated and treated as three trusts (one for each child) to stop the taxpayer from mitigating the progressive individual tax rate structure.

The IRS has decided to appeal a case in this multiple trust area. As one of the attorneys for the Government, you must choose between the Iowa case and a similar multiple trust case decided by the U.S. District Court of Virginia, also in favor of the taxpayer. In this case, the taxpayer is a CPA who established four separate trusts for her two children (i.e., a total of eight trusts).

Factors you are considering are the potential sympathy associated with the minister's profession (and a lack thereof associated with the CPA), the facts indicating that the attempt at tax avoidance is more egregious in the Iowa case, and a colleague's opinion that the Virginia case is winnable. Which case will you select? Comment on the fairness of the Government's ability and willingness to select a case to appeal in this fashion.

Assessing the Validity of Other Administrative Sources of the Tax Law

Revenue Rulings issued by the IRS carry less weight than Treasury Department Regulations. Rulings are important, however, in that they reflect the position of the IRS on tax matters. IRS agents will follow the results reached in a Revenue Ruling.

Actions on Decisions document the IRS's reaction to certain court decisions. The IRS follows a practice of either acquiescing (agreeing) or nonacquiescing (not agreeing) with selected court decisions.

Assessing the Validity of Judicial Sources of the Tax Law

The judicial process as it relates to the formulation of tax law has been described. How much reliance can be placed on a particular decision depends on the following variables:

- *The level of the court.* A decision rendered by a trial court carries less weight than one issued by an appellate court. Unless Congress changes the Code, decisions by the U.S. Supreme Court represent the last word on any tax issue.

- *Residence of the taxpayer.* A decision of the appellate court in the taxpayer's circuit carries more weight than one rendered by an appellate court in a different circuit. If, for example, a taxpayer lives in Texas, a decision of the Fifth Circuit Court of

---

[61]However, see *Mayo Foundation for Medical Education and Research*, 2011–1 USTC ¶50,143, where the Supreme Court provided greater deference to interpretive regulations (and appeared to blur the line between legislative and interpretive regulations).

Appeals (which would hear an appeal from a Texas trial court) means more than one rendered by the Second Circuit Court of Appeals.

- *Whether the decision represents the weight of authority on the issue.* In other words, is it supported by the results reached by other courts?

- *The outcome or status of the decision on appeal.* That is, if the decision was appealed, what was the result?

In connection with the last two variables, the use of a citator is invaluable to tax research. A citator provides the history of a case, including the authority relied on (e.g., other judicial decisions) in reaching the result. Reviewing the references listed in the citator discloses whether the decision was appealed and, if so, with what result (e.g., affirmed, reversed, or remanded). It also shows other cases with the same or similar issues and explains how they were decided. Thus, a citator reflects on the validity of a case and may lead to other relevant judicial material.[62] If one intends to rely on a judicial decision, "citating" the case is imperative.

Assessing the Validity of Other Sources

Primary sources of tax law include the Constitution, legislative history materials, statutes, treaties, Treasury Regulations, IRS pronouncements, and judicial decisions. The IRS regards only primary sources to constitute substantial authority. However, reference to *secondary sources* such as legal periodicals, treatises, legal opinions, General Counsel Memoranda, IRS publications, and other sources can be useful. In general, secondary sources are not authority.

Although the statement that the IRS regards only primary sources as substantial authority generally is true, there is one exception. For purposes of the accuracy-related penalty in § 6662, the IRS expands the list of substantial authority to include a number of secondary sources (e.g., letter rulings, General Counsel and Technical Advice Memoranda, and a Bluebook).[63] A "Bluebook" is the general explanation of tax legislation prepared by the Joint Committee on Taxation of the U.S. Congress. "Authority" does not include conclusions reached in treatises, legal periodicals, or opinions rendered by tax professionals.

1-6d Arriving at the Solution or at Alternative Solutions

Returning to *The Big Picture* on p. 1-1, assume that everyone agrees that treating the advance as a loan is justified based on the facts. As a result, will a bad debt deduction be allowed for the aunt? To answer this question, the loan must be classified as either a business or nonbusiness debt. Knowing this classification is important because a nonbusiness bad debt cannot be deducted until it becomes entirely worthless. Unlike a business debt, no deduction for partial worthlessness is allowed.[64]

Given the facts, it is very likely that the aunt made a nonbusiness loan in 2012. Almost always, loans made in a related-party setting are treated as nonbusiness.

The aunt has the burden of proving that the remaining unpaid balance of $77,000 is *entirely* worthless.[65] Some additional questions will need to be answered: Has the aunt tried to collect on the loan? Has the nephew told her he cannot repay the loan (maybe due to insolvency)? Maybe the aunt has lost touch with her nephew and does not know where he is.

If the debt *is* entirely worthless, we need to determine the year it became worthless. It could be, for example, that worthlessness took place in a year before it was claimed.[66]

Without additional information, a definitive answer may not be possible. The value of the research in this case was to raise additional questions. With answers to these questions (or some of the questions), a specific answer can be given to the aunt. Sometimes guarded judgment is the best possible solution to a tax problem.

---

[62]The major citators are published by CCH, RIA, Westlaw, and Shepard's. The CCH and RIA citators are available electronically through the CCH *IntelliConnect* service and Thomson Reuters *Checkpoint*, respectively. Westlaw's citator (KeyCite) is part of its online service. Shepard's citator is part of LexisNexis.

[63]Notice 90–20, 1990–1 C.B. 328, part V (A).

[64]See § 166 and the discussion of investor losses in Chapter 4.

[65]Compare *John K. Sexton*, 48 TCM 512, T.C.Memo. 1984–360, with *Stewart T. Oatman*, 45 TCM 214, T.C.Memo. 1982–684.

[66]*Ruth Wertheim Smith*, 34 TCM 1474, T.C.Memo. 1975–339.

1-6e Communicating Tax Research

Once the research process has been completed, the researcher will need to prepare a memo, letter, or spoken presentation. The form of communication depends on a number of factors. For example, most firms document the results of a tax research project in a memorandum. Although the format of this memorandum can vary, certain elements will appear in all memos. In addition, virtually all memos are reviewed by senior tax professionals to ensure accuracy.

How are results communicated to the client (does the client receive the tax research memo, a letter, or some other form of communication)? If an oral presentation is required, who will be the audience?[67] Whatever form it takes, the following elements will be part of the communication:

- A clear statement of the issue.
- In more complex situations, a short review of the facts that raised the issue.
- A review of the relevant tax law sources (e.g., Code, Regulations, rulings, and judicial authority).
- Any assumptions made in arriving at the solution.
- The solution recommended and the logic or reasoning supporting it.
- The references consulted in the research process.

Exhibits 1.9, 1.10, and 1.11 present a sample client letter and memoranda for the tax files based on the facts of *The Big Picture*.

EXHIBIT 1.9	Client Letter

Raabe, Young, Hoffman, Nellen, & Maloney, CPAs
5191 Natorp Boulevard
Mason, OH 45040

August 23, 2019

Dana Andrews
111 Avenue G
Lakeway, OH 45232

Dear Ms. Andrews:

This letter is in response to your question with respect to your $93,000 advance to your nephew in 2012. In order to advise you correctly, I need the following additional information:

1. Is there a written instrument evidencing this obligation, and is an interest rate specified?
2. When and how much has your nephew paid on the loan?
3. What factors exist to indicate whether the remaining debt will be repaid (for example, does he live within his means)?
4. Does he have a job?
5. Does he owe money to other people?
6. What is his credit rating?
7. How much credit card debt does he have?
8. What collection efforts, if any, have you made to collect the remaining $77,000?

Any other information or material you can provide would be greatly appreciated.

Sincerely,

James Hicks, CPA
Partner

---

[67]For more on crafting oral presentations, see W. A. Raabe and G. E. Whittenburg, "Talking Tax: How to Make a Tax Presentation," *Tax Adviser,* March 1997, pp. 179–182.

EXHIBIT 1.10	**Tax File Memorandum**

August 20, 2019

TAX FILE MEMORANDUM

FROM: James Hicks

SUBJECT: Dana Andrews
              Engagement Issues

Today I talked to Dana Andrews with regard to her letter of August 14, 2019.

Dana Andrews advanced $93,000 to her nephew in 2012 to enable him to attend a private college. Seven years later she claims a bad debt deduction for $77,000 that the nephew has not repaid.

ISSUE: Is Dana entitled to a bad debt deduction?

EXHIBIT 1.11	**Tax File Memorandum**

August 27, 2019

TAX FILE MEMORANDUM

FROM: James Hicks

SUBJECT: Dana Andrews

Tentative Conclusions

The initial advance could have been a gift rather than a loan and possibly subject to the gift tax. In any case, if the advance was a gift, it should have been reported on Form 709. Further, the statute of limitations does not begin to run when a tax return is not filed.

If the advance is treated as a loan, the probability is high that the aunt would receive nonbusiness bad debt status. This classification means that Ms. Andrews has the burden of proving that the $77,000 unpaid balance is entirely worthless.

<table>
<tr><td>LO.9</td></tr>
</table>

Describe various tax planning procedures.

1-7 WORKING WITH THE TAX LAW— TAX PLANNING

Tax research and tax planning are inseparable. The primary purpose of effective tax planning is to maximize the taxpayer's after-tax wealth. The course of action selected might not produce the lowest possible tax under the circumstances. The minimization of tax liability must be considered in context with the nontax goals of the taxpayer.

1-7a Nontax Considerations

There is a danger that tax considerations may impair the exercise of sound financial planning or business judgment by the taxpayer. Thus, the tax planning process can lead to ends that are economically (or socially) incorrect. Unfortunately, a tendency exists for planning to move toward the opposing extremes of either not enough or too much emphasis on tax considerations. The goal should be a balance that recognizes the significance of taxes, but not beyond the point at which planning detracts from the exercise of good business judgment. In general, if the only reason for pursuing a specific course of action is because of the tax benefits, then one should rethink that decision.

1-7b Components of Tax Planning

Popular perception of tax planning often is restricted to the adage "defer income and accelerate deductions." Although this timing approach does hold true and is important, meaningful tax planning involves considerably more.

Preferable to deferring taxable income is complete *avoidance* of taxation. Consider, for example, the employee who chooses nontaxable fringe benefits over a fully taxable future pay increase.[68] Complete avoidance of gain recognition also occurs when the owner of appreciated property transfers it by death. Here, the "step-up" (appreciation) in basis to fair market value completely escapes the income tax.[69]

If the recognition of income cannot be avoided, its deferral will postpone income tax consequences. A tax paid in the future costs less than a tax paid today because of the time value of money. *Deferral* of income can take many forms. Besides like-kind exchanges and involuntary conversions, most retirement plans postpone income tax consequences until benefits are paid. Deferral of gain recognition also can occur when appreciated property is transferred to a newly formed corporation or partnership.[70]

A corollary to the deferral of income is the acceleration of deductions. For example, if an accrual basis, calendar year corporation authorizes a charitable contribution in 2019 and pays it on or before the due date of its tax return in 2020, the deduction can be claimed for 2019.[71] Taxes also can be saved by *shifting* income to lower-bracket taxpayers. Gifts of appreciated property to lower-bracket family members can reduce the related capital gain tax rate on a later sale by up to 20 percentage points (from 20 percent to 0 percent).[72]

If income cannot be avoided, deferred, or shifted, the nature of the gain can be *converted*. By changing the classification of property, income taxes can be reduced. Thus, the taxpayer who transfers appreciated inventory to a controlled corporation has converted ordinary income property (the inventory) to a capital asset (stock in the corporation). When the stock is later sold, preferential capital gain rates apply.

The conversion approach also can work in tax planning for losses. Properly structured, a loan to a corporation that becomes worthless can be an ordinary loss rather than a capital loss. Likewise, via § 1244, an investor in qualified small business stock can convert what would be a capital loss into an ordinary loss.[73]

Effective tax planning requires that careful consideration be given to the *choice of entity* used for conducting a business. The corporate form results in double taxation but permits shareholder-employees to be covered by fringe benefit programs. Partnerships and S corporations allow a pass-through of losses and other tax attributes, but transferring ownership interests as gifts to family members may be difficult.[74]

Although the substance of a transaction rather than its form generally controls, this rule is not always the case with tax planning. *Preserving formalities*, with particularly clear documentation, often is crucial to the result. Is an advance to a corporation a loan or a contribution to capital? The answer may depend on the existence of a note.

Along with preserving formalities, the taxpayer should keep records that support how a transaction is treated. Returning to the issue of loan versus contribution to capital, how is the advance listed on the books of the borrower? What do the corporate minutes say about the advance?

Finally, effective tax planning requires *consistency* on the part of taxpayers. A shareholder who treats a corporate distribution as a return of capital cannot later avoid a stock basis adjustment by contending that the distribution was really a dividend.

In summary, the key components of tax planning include the following:

- *Avoid* the recognition of income (usually by resorting to a nontaxable source or nontaxable event).

- *Defer* the recognition of income (or accelerate deductions).

- *Convert* the classification of income (or deductions) to a more advantageous form (e.g., ordinary income into capital gain).

---

[68]See Example 9 (and related discussion) in Chapter 13.

[69]See Example 17 in Chapter 19.

[70]See Example 1 in Chapter 4 and Example 5 in Chapter 10.

[71]See Example 11 in Chapter 3.

[72]See Example 25 in Chapter 19. A 3.8% Medicare tax also might be avoided.

[73]See Examples 33 and 34 in Chapter 4.

[74]See Example 37 in Chapter 11 and Example 41 in Chapter 12.

- *Choose* the business *entity* with the desired tax attributes.
- Preserve *formalities* by generating and maintaining supporting documentation.
- Act in a manner *consistent* with the intended objective.

1-7c **Follow-Up Procedures**

Because tax planning usually involves a proposed (rather than a completed) transaction, being aware of if or when the law changes is critical to the tax planning process. A change in the tax law (legislative, administrative, or judicial) could alter the original conclusion. Additional research may be necessary to test the solution in light of current developments.

Under what circumstances does a tax professional have an obligation to inform a client as to changes in the tax law? The legal and ethical aspects of this question are discussed in Chapter 17.

1-7d **Tax Planning—A Practical Application**

Returning to the facts in *The Big Picture* on p. 1-1, what should be done to help protect the aunt's bad debt deduction?

- All formalities of a loan should be present (e.g., written instrument and definite and realistic due date).
- Upon default, the lender (aunt) should make a reasonable effort to collect from the borrower (nephew). If not, the aunt should be in a position to explain why any such effort would be to no avail.
- If interest is provided for, it should be paid.
- Any interest paid (or imputed under § 7872) should be recognized as income by the aunt.
- Because of the annual exclusion of $13,000 in 2012 (it is currently $15,000), it appears doubtful that actual (or imputed) interest would necessitate the filing of a Federal gift tax return by the aunt. But should a return be due, it should be filed.
- If § 7872 applies (not enough or no interest is provided for), the nephew should keep track of his net investment income. This record keeping is important because the income the aunt must recognize may be limited by this amount.

In terms of the components of tax planning (see discussion beginning on p. 1-38), what do these suggestions entail? Note the emphasis on the formalities—written instrument and definite and realistic due date. Also, much is done to provide the needed documentation—gift tax returns, if necessary, are filed, and the nephew keeps track of his investment income. Most important, however, is that the aunt will have been *consistent* in her actions—recognizing actual (or imputed) interest income and making a reasonable effort to collect on the loan.

Throughout this text, each chapter concludes with observations on Tax Planning. Such observations are not all-inclusive, but they are intended to illustrate some of the ways in which the material covered in the chapter can be effectively used to minimize taxes.

LO.10

Explain the role of taxation on the CPA examination.

1-8 **TAXATION ON THE CPA EXAMINATION**

The revised CPA exam continues to test in the familiar four sections—Auditing and Attestation (AUD), Business Environment and Concepts (BEC), Financial Accounting and Reporting (FAR), and Regulation (REG). However, the exam places less emphasis on remembering-and-understanding skills, enabling higher-level analysis and evaluation skills to be tested.

- The number of task-based simulations, a highly effective way to assess higher-order skills, increased. Task-based simulations are part of the BEC section for the first time, and the AUD, FAR, and REG sections each have eight or nine task-based simulations.

- Total testing time is now 16 hours (up from 14 hours). Both the BEC and REG sections increased by one hour, partly because of the increase in task-based simulations. Testing time remains the same for the AUD and FAR sections.

- Multiple-choice questions and task-based simulations each contribute about 50 percent toward the candidate's score in the AUD, FAR, and REG sections. In the BEC section, multiple-choice questions contribute about 50 percent of the scoring, with 35 percent coming from task-based simulations and 15 percent from written communication.

- The revised CPA exam places less emphasis on multiple-choice questions, with about 50 percent of the total points (down from about 60 percent of the total points).

- The revised CPA exam tests remembering and understanding, application, analysis, and evaluation (from Bloom's taxonomy). The previous CPA exam only tested for the first two of these items.

1-8a Preparation Blueprints

To prepare for the revised CPA exam, candidates are able to use AICPA-developed blueprints that replaced the Content Specification Outline (CSO) and Skill Specification Outline (SSO).[75]

The blueprints provide candidates with more detail about what to expect on the exam. They contain about 600 representative tasks, which are aligned with the skills required of newly licensed CPAs, across the four exam sections. The blueprints are designed to provide candidates with clearer information on the material the exam tests and show educators what knowledge and skills candidates need as newly licensed CPAs. In addition, the blueprints provide candidates with sample tasks that align with both the content and the skill level at which the content will be tested.

1-8b Regulation Section

Taxation continues to be tested within the REG section of the CPA exam. Testing within REG is administered in five blocks called testlets, which feature multiple-choice questions (MCQs) and task-based simulations (TBSs). Candidates receive at least one research question (research-oriented TBS) that requires the candidate to search the applicable authoritative literature and find an appropriate reference.

Each of the five topics in REG includes one or more representative tasks that are not necessarily questions on the exam. For example, the exam does not specifically ask a candidate to "Calculate taxpayer penalties relating to Federal tax returns." However, identifying *situations* where a taxpayer penalty might apply would be appropriate. In addition, tasks are to be inclusive, not exclusive, of exam content. For example, the task "Calculate tax depreciation for a tangible business property…" could include the calculation of additional first-year (bonus) depreciation.

Task-based simulations are case studies that allow candidates to demonstrate their knowledge and skills by generating responses to questions rather than simply selecting an answer. They typically require candidates to use spreadsheets and/or research authoritative literature provided in the CPA exam (e.g., Internal Revenue Code, Regulations, IRS publications, and tax forms).

---

[75]The blueprints can be accessed at **aicpa.org/becomeacpa/cpaexam/examinationcontent/downloadabledocuments/cpa-exam-blueprints-effective-20180101.pdf**; a summary of changes made to the previous blueprints can be accessed at **aicpa.org/becomeacpa/cpaexam/examinationcontent/downloadabledocuments/cpa-exam-blueprints-20180101-summary-changes.pdf**.

There are five content areas in the REG section of the CPA exam:

- Area 1: Ethics, professional responsibilities, and Federal tax procedures (weight 10–20 percent).
- Area 2: Business law (weight 10–20 percent).
- Area 3: Federal taxation of property transactions (weight 12–22 percent).
- Area 4: Federal taxation of individuals (weight 15–25 percent).
- Area 5: Federal taxation of entities (weight 28–38 percent).

Area 1 covers ethics and responsibilities in tax practice, licensing and disciplinary systems, Federal tax procedures, and legal duties and responsibilities of a CPA.

Area 3 covers Federal taxation of property transactions and Federal estate and gift taxation.

Area 4 covers the Federal income taxation of individuals from both a tax preparation and tax planning perspective (e.g., income, exclusions, deductions, and retirement plans).

Area 5 covers the Federal income taxation of entities including sole proprietorships, partnerships, limited liability companies, C corporations, S corporations, joint ventures, trusts, estates, and tax-exempt organizations from both a tax preparation and tax planning perspective.

Accounting methods and periods and tax elections are included in Areas 3, 4, and 5. Only Area 2 does not involve taxation.

Remembering-and-understanding skills are mainly tested in Areas 1 and 2. Application and analysis skills are primarily tested in Areas 3, 4, and 5. These three areas contain more of the day-to-day tasks that newly licensed CPAs are expected to perform. As a result, they are tested at the higher end of the skill level continuum. Overall, the REG section tests skills in the following way: remembering and learning (25 to 35 percent), application (35 to 45 percent), and analysis (25 to 35 percent). The REG section does not test any content at the Evaluation skill level since newly licensed CPAs are not expected to demonstrate that level of skill in regards to the REG content.

The REG section has 76 multiple-choice questions and eight to nine task-based simulations (TBSs); the key increase is in TBSs (up from six in the previous CPA exam). This change allows the AICPA to assess the candidate's higher-order skills. In addition, TBSs on the CPA exam provide increased background material and data that require candidates to determine what information is or is not relevant to the question. The scoring weight of multiple-choice questions and TBSs is about 50 percent each on the REG section of the CPA exam.

Depending on the skill level being assessed, well-prepared candidates likely will spend 15 to 20 minutes for each TBS. Certain analysis and/or evaluation level TBSs could take a well-prepared candidate up to 30 minutes to complete. Several examples of task-based simulations follow.

CPA Exam Simulation Examples

EXAMPLE 20

The *tax citation type* simulation requires the candidate to research the Internal Revenue Code and enter a Code Section and subsection.

For example, Amber Company is considering using the simplified dollar-value method of pricing its inventory for purposes of the LIFO method that is available to certain small businesses. What Code Section is the relevant authority in the Internal Revenue Code to which you should refer to determine whether the taxpayer is eligible to use this method? To be successful, the candidate must find § 474.

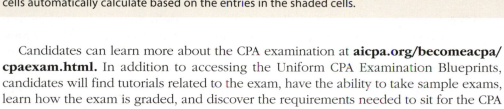

A *tax form completion* simulation requires the candidate to fill out a portion of a tax form. For example, Blue Company is a limited liability company (LLC) for tax purposes. Complete the income section of Form 1065 for Blue Company using the values found and calculated on previous tabs along with the following data:

Ordinary income from other partnerships	$ 5,200
Net gain (loss) from Form 4797	2,400
Management fee income	12,000

The candidate is provided with page 1 of Form 1065 on which to record the appropriate amounts. Any field that requires an entry is a shaded rectangular cell. Some white rectangular cells automatically calculate based on the entries in the shaded cells.

Candidates can learn more about the CPA examination at **aicpa.org/becomeacpa/cpaexam.html.** In addition to accessing the Uniform CPA Examination Blueprints, candidates will find tutorials related to the exam, have the ability to take sample exams, learn how the exam is graded, and discover the requirements needed to sit for the CPA exam in each licensing jurisdiction.

Content related to the TCJA of 2017 is eligible for testing on the CPA exam starting January 1, 2019. Beginning in 2019, there will be a simultaneous introduction of content related to the TCJA of 2017 and removal of content related to the previous tax law.

Key Terms

Acquiescence, 1-26

Arm's length, 1-11

Business purpose, 1-12

Continuity of interest, 1-11

Court of original jurisdiction, 1-20

Determination letters, 1-20

Final Regulations, 1-18

Generally Accepted Accounting Principles (GAAP), 1-13

Indexation, 1-8

International Financial Reporting Standards (IFRS), 1-13

Letter rulings, 1-19

Nonacquiescence, 1-26

Proposed Regulations, 1-17

Revenue neutrality, 1-2

Revenue Procedures, 1-18

Revenue Rulings, 1-18

Substance over form, 1-11

Tax benefit rule, 1-12

Technical Advice Memoranda (TAMs), 1-19

Temporary Regulations, 1-18

Wherewithal to pay, 1-5

Writ of Certiorari, 1-24

Discussion Questions

1. **LO.1** What is meant by *revenue neutrality*?

2. **LO.2** Have nonrevenue factors had any impact upon the development of our taxation system? If so, how?

3. **LO.2** How does the tax law encourage technological progress?

4. **LO.2** Why is personal saving desirable for the U.S. economy?

5. **LO.2** Explain how the following tax provisions encourage small businesses.
   a. The nature of a shareholder's loss on a stock investment.
   b. The S corporation election.

6. **LO.2** The concept of equity is relative. Explain.

7. **LO.2** What purpose is served by allowing a deduction for contributions to qualified charitable organizations?

8. **LO.2** Savings leads to capital formation and thus makes funds available to finance home construction and industrial expansion. What is a major tax law incentive to encourage savings?

9. **LO.2** How does the tax law encourage the development of natural resources?

10. **LO.2** What is the justification for the favorable treatment of corporate reorganizations?

11. **LO.2** Other than raising revenue, what considerations explain various provisions in our tax laws?

Critical Thinking   12. **LO.2** A provision of the Code allows a taxpayer a deduction for Federal income tax purposes for some state and local income taxes paid. Does this provision eliminate the effect of multiple taxation of the same income? Why or why not? In this connection, consider the following:

    a. Taxpayer, an individual, has itemized deductions that are less than the standard deduction.

    b. Taxpayer is in the 10% tax bracket for Federal income tax purposes. The 32% tax bracket.

13. **LO.2** Heather and her partners operate a profitable partnership. Because the business is expanding, the partners would like to transfer it to a newly created corporation. Heather is concerned, however, over the possible tax consequences that would result from incorporating. Please comment.

Critical Thinking   14. **LO.2** Assume the same facts as in Question 13. Heather is also worried that once the partnership incorporates, the business will be subject to the Federal corporate income tax. What suggestions do you have?

15. **LO.2** Give some examples of the wherewithal to pay concept.

16. **LO.2** Can recognized gain exceed the realized gain? Explain.

17. **LO.2** In a like-kind exchange, recognized gain is postponed and not avoided. Explain.

18. **LO.2** Under the annual accounting period concept, what time period is normally selected for final settlement of most tax liabilities?

19. **LO.2** How does the installment method overcome the harsh treatment of the annual accounting treatment concept?

20. **LO.2** Why is there a grace period for contributions to a Keogh retirement plan?

21. **LO.2** Contrast the tax treatment between a community property state and a common law state.

22. **LO.2** List some tax provisions used to deter affluent taxpayers from obtaining preferential tax treatment.

23. **LO.4** Explain the continuity of interest concept.

Critical Thinking   24. **LO.3** White Corporation lends $425,000 to Blue Corporation with no provision for interest. White Corporation and Blue Corporation are owned by the same shareholders. How might the IRS restructure this transaction with adverse tax consequences?

25. **LO.5** Federal tax legislation generally originates in the Senate Finance Committee. Comment on the validity of this statement.

26. **LO.5** If a tax bill is vetoed by the President, the provisions cannot become law. Evaluate this statement.

27. **LO.5** Determine the subparts of § 1563(a)(1)(A).

28. **LO.5** Is § 212(1) a proper Code Section citation? Why or why not?

29. **LO.5** Why are certain Code Section numbers missing from the Internal Revenue Code (e.g., §§ 6, 7, 8, 9, 10)?

30. **LO.6** Where can a researcher find newly issued Proposed, final, and Temporary Regulations?

31. **LO.6** Interpret each of the following citations:
    a. Temp.Reg. § 1.707–5T(a)(2).
    b. Rev.Rul. 60–11, 1960–1 C.B. 174.
    c. TAM 8837003.

32. **LO.5** Jennifer Olde calls you requesting an explanation of the fact-finding determi-   *Communications*
    nation of a Federal Court of Appeals. Prepare a letter to be sent to Jennifer
    answering this query. Her address is 3246 Highland Drive, Clifton, VA 20124.

33. **LO.5** Will Thomas calls you with respect to a tax issue. He has found a tax case   *Communications*
    in the U.S. District Court of South Carolina that is in favor of his position.
    The IRS lost and did not appeal the case. Over the phone, you explain to Will the
    significance of the failure to appeal. Prepare a tax file memorandum outlining your
    remarks to Will.

34. **LO.5, 8** In assessing the validity of a court decision, discuss the significance of the
    following:
    a. The decision was rendered by the U.S. District Court of Utah. Taxpayer lives
        in Utah.
    b. The decision was rendered by the U.S. Court of Federal Claims. Taxpayer lives
        in Utah.
    c. The decision was rendered by the Second Circuit Court of Appeals. Taxpayer
        lives in California.
    d. The decision was rendered by the U.S. Supreme Court.
    e. The decision was rendered by the U.S. Tax Court. The IRS has acquiesced in
        the result.
    f. Same as part (e), except that the IRS has issued a nonacquiescence as to
        the result.

35. **LO.6, 7** Aleshia needs to learn quickly about § 351 transfers to a controlled corpora-   *Decision Making*
    tion. How should Aleshia approach her research?

36. **LO.7** Where does most tax research begin when someone is searching for an
    answer about a tax dispute?

37. **LO.8** Determine whether the following items are primary sources or secondary
    sources for the purpose of substantial authority.
    a. Revenue Procedure.
    b. Article written by a judge in *Journal of Taxation*.
    c. U.S. District Court decision.
    d. The "Bluebook."
    e. A general counsel memorandum.

38. **LO.9** What are the key components of effective tax planning?

39. **LO.10** Discuss task-based simulations that are part of the CPA examination.

Problems

40. **LO.2** Juniper, Inc., exchanges some real estate (basis of $800,000 and fair market value of $1,000,000) for other real estate owned by Birch, Inc., (basis of $1,200,000 and fair market value of $900,000) and $100,000 in cash. The real estate involved is unimproved and is held by Juniper and Birch, before and after the exchange, as non-investment property.

    a. What is Juniper's realized gain on the exchange? Recognized gain?

    b. What is Birch's realized loss? Recognized loss?

    c. Support your results in parts (a) and (b) under the wherewithal to pay concept as applied to like-kind exchanges (§ 1031).

41. **LO.2, 3** Using the legend provided, classify the overall objective of the particular tax provision.

Legend	
CE = Control of the economy	W = Wherewithal to pay concept
EA = Encouragement of certain activities	AF = Administrative feasibility
EI = Encouragement of certain industries	ESB = Encouragement of small business
SC = Social considerations	

    a. Like-kind exchange treatment.

    b. An increase in the individual tax rate.

    c. The S corporation election.

    d. Adoption expense credit.

    e. Percentage depletion.

    f. Unified estate tax credit.

    g. Charitable contribution deduction.

42. **LO.2** Determine whether the following states are community property or common law states.

    a. Louisiana.

    b. Virginia.

    c. Arizona.

    d. Rhode Island.

    e. Alaska.

    f. California.

Communications
43. **LO.4** Benny sells property (basis of $70,000) to Jet Corporation for $100,000. Based on the following conditions, how could the IRS challenge this transaction?

    a. Benny is the sole shareholder of Jet Corporation.

    b. Benny is the son of the sole shareholder of Jet Corporation.

    c. Benny is neither a shareholder in Jet Corporation nor related to any of Jet's shareholders.

    d. Summarize your conclusions in an e-mail to your instructor.

44. **LO.5** Answer the following questions:

    a. What are letter rulings?

    b. What are technical advice memoranda (TAMs)?

45. **LO.5** Explain what is meant by the following citations:

    a. Rev.Proc. 2001–10, 2001–1 C.B. 272.

    b. Rev.Rul. 2011–14, 2011–27 I.R.B. 31.

    c. Ltr.Rul. 201125030.

46. **LO.6** Using the legend provided, classify each of the following citations as to the location. A citation may have more than one answer.

Legend

IRC = Internal Revenue Code	FR = *Federal Register*
IRB = *Internal Revenue Bulletin*	NA = Not applicable
CB = *Cumulative Bulletin*	
---

  a. § 61(a)(13).
  b. Prop.Reg. § 1.368–2(b)(1).
  c. Rev.Proc. 77–37, 1977–2 C.B. 568.
  d. Temp.Reg. § 1.163–9T(b)(2)(I)(A).
  e. Rev.Rul. 64–56, 1964–1 C.B. 133.
  f. *Jack E. Golsen*, 54 T.C. 742 (1970).
  g. Ltr.Rul. 9802018.

47. **LO.5** To which U.S. Court of Appeals would a person living in each of the following states appeal from the U.S. Tax Court?

  a. Texas.
  b. Colorado.
  c. Georgia.
  d. Montana.
  e. New York.

48. **LO.5** Using the legend provided, classify each of the following citations as to the court.

Legend

T = U.S. Tax Court	D = U.S. District Court
C = U.S. Court of Federal Claims	A = U.S. Court of Appeals
U = U.S. Supreme Court	N = None of the above
---

  a. 388 F.2d 420 (CA–7, 1968).
  b. 79 T.C. 7 (1982).
  c. 54 S.Ct. 8 (USSC, 1933).
  d. 3 B.T.A. 1042 (1926).
  e. T.C.Memo 1954–141.
  f. 597 F.2d 760 (Ct.Cl., 1979).
  g. Ltr.Rul. 9414051.
  h. 465 F.Supp. 341 (D.Ct. Okla., 1978).

49. **LO.6** Identify the name of the publisher for the following tax services:

  a. *United States Tax Reporter.*
  b. *Standard Federal Tax Reporter.*
  c. *Federal Tax Coordinator 2d.*
  d. *Mertens Law of Federal Income Taxation.*
  e. *Tax Management Portfolios.*
  f. CCH's *Tax Research Consultant.*

50. **LO.5, 8** Using the legend provided, classify each of the following tax sources:

Legend	
P = Primary tax source	B = Both
S = Secondary tax source	N = Neither

a. Sixteenth Amendment to the Constitution.
b. Tax treaty between the United States and China.
c. Temporary Regulations (issued 2015).
d. Revenue Procedure.
e. An IRS publication.
f. Tax Court Memorandum decision.
g. *Harvard Law Review* article.
h. Legislative Regulations.
i. Letter ruling (before 1991).
j. Fifth Circuit Court of Appeals decision.
k. Small Cases Division of U.S. Tax Court decision.
l. Senate Finance Committee Report.
m. Technical advice memorandum (1993).
n. Proposed Regulations.

51. **LO.5** Interpret each of the following citations:
a. 54 T.C. 1514 (1970).
b. 408 F.2d 1117 (CA–2, 1969).
c. 69–1 USTC ¶ 9319 (CA–2, 1969).
d. 23 AFTR 2d 69–1090 (CA–2, 1969).
e. 293 F.Supp. 1129 (D.Ct. Miss., 1967).
f. 67–1 USTC ¶ 9253 (D.Ct. Miss., 1967).
g. 19 AFTR 2d 647 (D.Ct. Miss., 1967).
h. 56 S.Ct. 289 (USSC, 1935).
i. 36–1 USTC ¶ 9020 (USSC, 1935).
j. 16 AFTR 1274 (USSC, 1935).
k. 422 F.2d 1336 (Ct.Cl., 1970).

Research Problems

THOMSON REUTERS
CHECKPOINT™

Note: Solutions to the Research Problems can be prepared by using the Thomson Reuters Checkpoint™ online tax research database, which accompanies this textbook. Solutions can also be prepared by using research materials found in a typical tax library.

Research Problem 1. Locate the following cited items, and give a brief description of the topic or opinion in the item.

a. § 6694(a).
b. Reg. § 1.6694–1(b).
c. Rev.Rul. 86–55, 1986–1 C.B. 373.
d. PLR 8022027.

Research Problem 2. Determine the disposition of the following decisions at the appellate level.

   a. *Gary A. Sargent*, 93 T.C. 572 (1989).

   b. *Charles Johnson*, 78 T.C. 882 (1982).

   c. *Smith & Wiggins Gin, Inc.*, 37 T.C. 861 (1962).

   d. *George W. Wiebusch*, 59 T.C. 777 (1973).

   e. *Zanesville Inv. Co.*, 38 T.C. 406 (1962).

Research Problem 3. The TV show TMZ spoke with Larry Edema from Michigan, who was selected to be in the audience for Oprah's big giveaway: a free trip to Australia. Supposedly, Winfrey had a certified public accountant on hand to address the tax issue right after the taping. Edema said that the CPA assured the group that all taxes associated with the trip would be "handled by the Oprah show," so the trip would truly be 100% free. The CPA also explained that Oprah would cover all sightseeing costs and travel-related expenses, including passport costs for people who could not afford them. It was a big change from Oprah's 2004 controversy when she famously gave away brand-new cars but saddled audience members with as much as $7,000 in income taxes.

   Discuss any tax aspects or problems with this statement. E-mail a response to your instructor.

Communications

Use internet tax resources to address the following questions. Look for reliable web-sites and blogs of the IRS and other government agencies, media outlets, businesses, tax professionals, academics, think tanks, and political outlets.

Research Problem 4. Locate the following on the internet:
   a. Several primary sources of the tax law, including the U.S. Supreme Court, a Court of Appeals, the Internal Revenue Service, the U.S. Tax Court, and final Regulations.
   b. Sources of proposed Federal tax legislation.
   c. A collection of tax rules for your state.

Research Problem 5. Using the internet, find a definition for each of these terms.

   a. Rule 155.

   b. *En banc*.

   c. *Pro se*.

   d. Dicta.

   e. Parallel cite.

   f. Sunset provisions.

   g. Work product.

   h. Remanded.

CHAPTER

2

The Deduction for Qualified Business Income for Pass-Through Entities

LEARNING OBJECTIVES: *After completing Chapter 2, you should be able to:*

LO.1 Summarize the tax treatment of various forms of conducting a business.

LO.2 Explain the rationale for the deduction for qualified business income.

LO.3 Describe the types of taxpayers and activities that potentially generate a deduction for qualified business income.

LO.4 Determine a taxpayer's deduction for qualified business income.

LO.5 List and evaluate tax planning ideas for choice of entity and the deduction for qualified business income.

CHAPTER OUTLINE

ASPEN PHOTO/SHUTTERSTOCK.COM

ENTREPRENEURIAL PURSUITS

Amy plans to start at least two different business activities after she graduates from college. She will apply the knowledge gained in her business courses to use various forms of social media to promote her skills and experience as a volleyball player to help younger players develop their skills. She plans to generate income from advertising on her social media sites. She also will use her artistic and marketing talents to find work using several web platforms, like Upwork and Freelancer.

Based on what she has read on websites and heard from friends, Amy is wondering if she should form a corporation or a limited liability company for these pursuits or just be a sole proprietor. She is also curious whether, for tax and legal purposes, she has one business or two.

After reading this chapter, you can help Amy with her questions, including aiding her in better framing the questions should she decide to seek assistance from an attorney on business entity formation matters or a CPA for tax and accounting assistance.

Read the chapter and formulate your response.

For Federal income tax purposes, the distinctions among forms of business organization are important. This chapter begins by discussing the distinctions between sole proprietorships, partnerships, S corporations, and regular corporations. Limited liability companies, which generally are taxed as one of these entity forms, are also introduced.

A key piece of the TCJA of 2017 was to lower the corporate income tax rate from a progressive tax rate structure (with rates from 15 percent to 35 percent) to a flat tax of 21 percent. To also provide a tax reduction for businesses that do *not* operate as regular corporations, the TCJA of 2017 created a special deduction for noncorporate taxpayers with business income. These changes affect tax liabilities as well as planning, such as for the form of business organization, that taxpayers should consider.

2-1 TAX TREATMENT OF VARIOUS BUSINESS FORMS

LO.1

Summarize the tax treatment of various forms of conducting a business.

Business operations can be conducted in a number of different forms including:

- Sole proprietorships.
- Partnerships.
- Trusts and estates.
- S corporations.
- Regular corporations.
- Limited liability companies.

2-1a Sole Proprietorships

A sole proprietorship is not a separate taxable entity. Rather, its operations are reported as part of the sole proprietor's individual income tax return. The owner of a sole proprietorship reports all business income and expenses of the proprietorship on Schedule C of Form 1040, with the net profit or loss from the proprietorship included in the taxable income of the individual proprietor. The proprietor reports all of the net profit from the business, regardless of any amounts actually withdrawn during the year.

Income and expenses of the proprietorship retain their character when reported by the proprietor. For example, ordinary income of the proprietorship is treated as ordinary income when reported by the proprietor, and capital gain is treated as capital gain. In addition, a deduction for qualified business income (§ 199A) is available for sole proprietors. In general, this deduction is 20 percent of proprietorship net income (or, if less, taxable income before the qualified business income deduction less any net capital gain) and is claimed on the proprietor's Form 1040 in determining taxable income.[1]

The Big Picture

EXAMPLE

1

Return to the facts of *The Big Picture* on p. 2-1. The easiest business entity for Amy to form is a sole proprietorship. She need not create any legal documents for the proprietorship, although she may need to obtain a business license in her county or city (and pay a tax or fee for it), including filing a statement of business purpose.

She should also set up accounting records (e.g., using QuickBooks) and make her accounting and tax record keeping simpler by having a separate bank account and credit card for business purposes (accounts that are *not* used for personal purchases).

---

[1]There are limitations on this deduction for higher-income taxpayers. This chapter includes a detailed discussion of the deduction for qualified business income. For treatment of the qualified business income deduction by partnerships and S corporations, see Chapters 10 and 12, respectively.

2-1b **Partnerships**

Partnerships are not subject to a Federal income tax. However, a partnership is required to file Form 1065, which reports the results of the partnership's activities. Business income and expense items are aggregated in computing the ordinary business income (loss) of the partnership on Form 1065. Any remaining income and expense items are reported separately to the partners.[2] Partnerships are discussed in detail in Chapters 10 and 11.

The partnership ordinary business income (loss) and the separately reported items are allocated to the partners according to the partnership's profit and loss sharing agreement. Each partner receives a Schedule K–1 that reports this information. Each partner then reports these items on his or her own tax return. In addition, individual partners can claim the deduction for qualified business income (to the extent available) on his or her Form 1040.

EXAMPLE 2

Sundra and Patel are equal partners in Canary Enterprises, a calendar year partnership. During the year, Canary Enterprises had $500,000 gross income and $350,000 operating expenses. In addition, the partnership sold land that had been held for investment purposes for a long-term capital gain of $60,000. During the year, Sundra withdrew $40,000 from the partnership, and Patel withdrew $45,000.

The partnership's Form 1065 reports ordinary business income of $150,000 ($500,000 income − $350,000 expenses) and long-term capital gain of $60,000 as a separately stated item.

Sundra and Patel each receive a Schedule K–1 reporting ordinary business income of $75,000 and separately stated long-term capital gain of $30,000. Each partner reports ordinary business income of $75,000 and long-term capital gain of $30,000 on his own return. Likewise, Sundra and Patel would claim any related deduction for qualified business income on their individual tax returns.

2-1c **Corporations**

Corporations are governed by Subchapter C or Subchapter S of the Internal Revenue Code. Those governed by Subchapter C are referred to as **C corporations** or **regular corporations**. Corporations governed by Subchapter S are referred to as **S corporations**.

S corporations, which generally do not pay Federal income tax, are similar to partnerships in that ordinary business income (loss) flows through to the shareholders to be reported on the shareholder's separate returns. Also like partnerships, certain items flow through from the S corporation to the shareholders and retain their separate character when reported on the shareholders' returns. The S corporation ordinary business income (loss) and the separately reported items are allocated to the shareholders according to their stock ownership interests. S corporations are discussed in detail in Chapter 12.

Unlike proprietorships, partnerships, and S corporations, C corporations are subject to an entity-level Federal income tax. This results in what is known as *double taxation*. A C corporation reports its income and expenses on Form 1120 and then computes tax on its taxable income using a flat 21 percent rate.[3] When a corporation distributes its income, the corporation's shareholders report dividend income on their own tax returns; further, no corporate deduction is allowed for the dividends paid (discussed next). As a result, income that has already been taxed at the corporate level is also taxed at the shareholder level.

Taxation of Dividends

Double taxation stems, in part, from the fact that dividend distributions are not deductible by a C corporation. To avoid this, closely held corporation shareholders try to convert dividend distributions into tax-deductible expenses. A common way to do this

---

[2]Some examples of separately reported income items are interest income, dividend income, and long-term capital gain. Examples of separately reported expenses include charitable contributions and expenses related to investment income.

[3]For taxable years prior to 2018, corporations faced tax rates that varied from 15% to 39%. Corporations with taxable income of $18,333,333 or more paid a flat 35% tax rate.

is to increase compensation to shareholder-employees. However, the IRS scrutinizes compensation and other economic transactions (e.g., loans, leases, and sales) between shareholders and closely held corporations to ensure that payments are reasonable in amount.[4]

For individual shareholders, some of the double taxation effect is alleviated because dividends are generally taxed at lower tax rates. Qualified dividend income is taxed at a rate of 15 percent (20 percent for high-income taxpayers; 0 percent for lower-income taxpayers).[5] These rates also apply to long-term capital gains.[6]

The effects of double taxation are illustrated in Examples 3 and 4.

Double Taxation Illustrated

EXAMPLE 3

Lavender Corporation has taxable income of $100,000 in 2019. It pays corporate tax of $21,000. This leaves $79,000, all of which is distributed as a dividend to Ashley, a 43-year-old single individual and the corporation's sole shareholder. Ashley has no income sources other than Lavender Corporation.

Ashley has taxable income of $66,800 ($79,000 − $12,200 standard deduction). She pays tax at the preferential rate applicable to qualified dividends received by individuals. Her tax is $4,111 [($39,375 × 0%) + ($100 × 12%) + ($27,325 × 15%)].

The combined tax on the corporation's net profit is $25,111 ($21,000 paid by the corporation + $4,111 paid by the shareholder).

EXAMPLE 4

Assume the same facts as in Example 3, except that the business is organized as a sole proprietorship. Ashley reports the $100,000 profit from the business on her tax return. She has taxable income of $70,240 [$100,000 − $12,200 standard deduction − $17,560 deduction for qualified business income [($100,000 − $12,200) × 20%)] and pays tax of $11,311.

As a result, operating the business as a sole proprietorship results in a tax *savings* of $13,800 in 2019 [$25,111 (from Example 3) − $11,311].

Comparison of Corporations and Other Forms of Doing Business

When comparing C corporations to other business forms, there are a number of factors to consider including:

- Tax rates,
- Character of business income,
- Business losses,
- Employment taxes, and
- State taxes.

Each of these is discussed below.

Tax Rates As noted earlier, a flat rate of 21 percent applies to corporate taxable income. The marginal rates for individuals range from 10 percent to 37 percent. In many cases, taxes will be greater in the corporate form (as in Example 3). However, the corporate form of doing business presents tax savings opportunities when the applicable corporate marginal rate is *lower* than the applicable individual marginal rate. The flat 21 percent corporate rate that now applies could significantly increase these tax savings opportunities.

---

[4]See Chapter 5 for a discussion of constructive dividends.

[5]The 0% (20%) rate applies if taxable income, including the net capital gain, is below (above) specific thresholds based on filing status. In 2019, below $78,750 (or above $488,850) for married taxpayers filing a joint return; below $39,375 (or above $434,550) for single taxpayers.

[6]A 3.8% Medicare surtax applies to net investment income in excess of modified adjusted gross income of $200,000 ($250,000 if married filing jointly), thus increasing the double taxation of dividend income for high-income taxpayers.

Susanna, an individual taxpayer in the 37% marginal tax rate bracket, can generate $100,000 of additional taxable income in the current year. If the income is taxed to Susanna, the associated tax is $37,000 ($100,000 × 37%).

If, however, Susanna is able to shift the income to a newly created corporation, the corporate tax is $21,000 ($100,000 × 21%). Thus, by taking advantage of the lower corporate marginal tax rates, a tax *savings* of $16,000 ($37,000 − $21,000) is achieved.

Any attempt to take advantage of the difference between the corporate and individual marginal tax rates also must consider the effect of double taxation. When the preferential rate for dividend income is considered, however, tax savings opportunities still exist.

Assume in Example 5 that the corporation distributes all of its after-tax earnings to Susanna as a dividend. The dividend results in income tax of $15,800 [($100,000 − $21,000) × 20%] to Susanna.

Thus, even when the double taxation effect is considered, the combined tax burden of $36,800 ($21,000 paid by the corporation + $15,800 paid by the shareholder) represents an income tax *savings* of $200 when compared to the $37,000 of tax that results when the $100,000 of income is subject to Susanna's 37% marginal rate.

Examples 5 and 6 ignore other tax issues that also must be considered in selecting the proper form of doing business (e.g., the availability of the deduction for qualified business income), but they illustrate the tax savings that can be achieved by taking advantage of rate differentials.

Character of Business Income Unlike other forms of business, the tax attributes of income and expense items of a C corporation do not pass through the corporate entity to the shareholders. As a result, if the business is expected to generate tax-favored income (e.g., tax-exempt income or long-term capital gains), it may be better to choose a different business form.

Pass-Through of Losses C corporation losses are treated differently than losses of other business forms. A loss incurred by a proprietorship may be deductible by the owner, because all income and expense items are reported by the proprietor. Partnership and S corporation losses are passed through the entity and may be deductible by the partners or S corporation shareholders. C corporation losses, however, are retained at the corporate level. If losses are anticipated, it may be better to choose a business form other than a C corporation.

Franco plans to start a business this year. He expects that the business will incur operating losses for the first three years and then become highly profitable. Franco decides to operate as an S corporation during the loss period, because the losses will flow through and be deductible on his personal return. When the business becomes profitable, he intends to switch to C corporation status.

Employment Taxes The net income of a proprietorship is subject to the self-employment tax (15.3 percent), as are some partnership allocations of income to partners. Alternatively, wages paid to a shareholder-employee of a corporation (C or S) are subject to payroll taxes. The combined corporation-employee payroll tax burden must be compared with the self-employment tax in the proprietorship and partnership business forms. This analysis should include the benefit of the deduction available to a corporation for payroll taxes paid, as well as the deduction available to an individual for one-half of the self-employment taxes paid.

State Taxes At the entity level, state corporate income taxes and/or franchise taxes apply to corporations. Some states impose a franchise tax on all business forms (including partnerships and S corporations). If a business will be operating in multiple states, state taxes become more important (Chapter 16 discusses the taxation of multistate corporations). At the owner level, the income of sole proprietorships, S corporations, and partnerships (along with dividend distributions) is subject to state individual income taxation.

The tax attributes of the various forms of business entities are compared in Concept Summary 2.1.[7]

Concept Summary 2.1

Tax Treatment of Business Forms Compared

	Sole Proprietorships	Partnerships	S Corporations	Regular (C) Corporations
Entity tax return	None	Form 1065	Form 1120S	Form 1120
Taxation of entity income	No separate entity-level income tax. Proprietorship's income and expenses are reported on owner's Form 1040 (Schedule C). Character of entity income and expenses retained at owner level. Proprietor eligible for deduction for qualified business income.	No separate entity-level income tax. Partnership's income and expenses are allocated and reported (on Schedule K–1) to partners who report these items on their returns (e.g., Form 1040 for individual partners). Character of entity income and expenses retained at partner level. Individual partners eligible for deduction for qualified business income.	Generally, no separate entity-level income tax. S corporation's income and expenses are allocated and reported (on Schedule K–1) to shareholders who report these items on their returns (e.g., Form 1040 for individual shareholders). Character of entity income and expenses retained at shareholder level. Shareholders eligible for deduction for qualified business income.	Corporate income tax applies. Flat rate of 21% on corporate taxable income.
Taxation of withdrawals/ distributions from entity	Withdrawals by owner are not subject to separate tax.	Distributions to partners are generally not subject to separate tax.	Distributions to shareholders are generally not subject to separate tax.	Character of entity income and expenses not retained at shareholder level. Instead, distributions to shareholders are generally taxed as dividend income. Preferential tax rates (0%/15%/20%) apply to qualified dividends.
Employment taxes	Schedule C income subject to self-employment tax.	Some partnership allocations subject to self-employment tax.	Compensation paid to shareholder/employees subject to payroll taxes. Shareholder's allocated portion of entity income not subject to self-employment tax.	Compensation paid to shareholder/employees subject to payroll taxes.

---

[7]Chapter 13 presents a detailed comparison of sole proprietorships, partnerships, S corporations, and C corporations as forms of doing business.

GLOBAL TAX ISSUES | **U.S. Corporate Taxes and International Business Competitiveness**

In a 2017 study, the Tax Foundation examined the impact of national tax systems on international business competitiveness. In its report, the Tax Foundation ranked the international tax competitiveness of the 35 members of the Organization for Economic Co-operation and Development (OECD) by examining each country's tax policies. The rankings were based on many tax policy factors, including corporate and individual tax rates, consumption taxes, payroll and property taxes, and international tax rules.

The United States ranked 30th out of the 35 OECD countries in overall international tax competitiveness, largely due to its comparative rankings on corporate taxes (35th) and international tax rules (33rd). Estonia claimed the top ranking in the report, followed by New Zealand, Switzerland, and Latvia.

One of the primary goals underlying the enactment of the TCJA of 2017 was to increase the international competitiveness of U.S. businesses. The reduction in the corporate tax rate to 21 percent was the centerpiece of that legislation. It will be interesting to see how the United States ranks in future studies on international tax competitiveness.

Source: taxfoundation.org/2017-international-tax-competitiveness-index.

Nontax Considerations

Nontax considerations may override tax considerations and lead owners to conclude that a business should be operated as a corporation. Here are some of the more important *nontax considerations*.

- Sole proprietors and general partners in partnerships face the danger of *unlimited liability*. That is, business creditors can file claims against the assets of the business *and* the personal assets of proprietors or general partners. State corporate law protects the personal assets of shareholders.

- The corporate form of business provides a vehicle for *raising capital* through widespread stock ownership. Most major businesses in the United States are operated as corporations.

- Shares of stock in a corporation are *freely transferable*; a partner's sale of his or her partnership interest must be approved by the other partners.

- A corporation continues to exist even when a shareholder dies. Death or withdrawal of a partner, on the other hand, may terminate the existing partnership and cause financial difficulties that result in dissolution of the entity. This *continuity of life* is a distinct advantage of the corporate form.

- Corporations have *centralized management*. All management responsibility is assigned to a board of directors, who appoint officers to carry out the corporation's business. Partnerships often have decentralized management, in which every partner has a right to participate in the organization's business decisions. Limited partnerships, though, may have centralized management.

2-1d Limited Liability Companies

The limited liability company (LLC) is a business form that blends some corporate form advantages into a flow-through entity. All 50 states and the District of Columbia have passed laws that allow LLCs, and thousands of companies have chosen LLC status. As with a corporation, operating as an LLC allows its owners (called "members") to avoid unlimited liability exposure, which is a primary *nontax* consideration in choosing a business form. The tax advantage of LLCs is that qualifying businesses may be treated as proprietorships or partnerships for tax purposes, thereby avoiding the problem of double taxation associated with regular corporations.[8]

---

[8]Some states allow an LLC to have centralized management, but not continuity of life or free transferability of interests. Other states allow LLCs to adopt any or all of the corporate characteristics of centralized management, continuity of life, and free transferability of interests. The comparison of business entities in Chapter 13 includes a discussion of LLCs.

Entity Classification

Can an organization that is *not* a corporation under state law still be treated as one for Federal income tax purposes? The tax law defines a corporation as including "associations, joint stock companies, and insurance companies."[9] Unfortunately, the Code contains no definition of what constitutes an *association*, and the issue became the subject of frequent litigation.

It was finally determined that an entity would be treated as a corporation if it had a majority of characteristics common to corporations.

- Continuity of life.
- Centralized management.
- Limited liability.
- Free transferability of interests.

These criteria did not resolve all of the problems that continued to arise over corporate classification. And when the states allowed the creation of LLCs, the IRS was deluged with inquiries regarding its tax status. The Code does not identify LLCs as a business form. And state LLC laws differed (e.g., some allowed centralized management, but others did not). So the question was how these entities would be treated under Federal tax law.

To ease this problem, the **check-the-box Regulations** were issued by the Treasury Department.[10] The Regulations enable taxpayers to choose the tax status of a business entity without regard to its corporate (or noncorporate) characteristics. These rules simplified tax administration considerably and eliminated much of the litigation related to association (i.e., corporation) status.

Under the check-the-box Regulations, an unincorporated entity with *more than one* owner is, by default, classified as a partnership. An unincorporated entity with *only one* owner is, by default, classified as a **disregarded entity** (or DRE). A DRE is treated as a sole proprietorship if it is owned by an individual or as a branch or a division of a corporate owner. If the entity wants to use its default status, it simply files the appropriate tax return. If it wants to use a different status or change its status, it does so by "checking a box" on Form 8832. Thus, an LLC (single or multi-member) can choose to be taxed as a C corporation and, if it otherwise qualifies, even elect S corporation status.[11] Although an LLC does not typically pay Federal income taxes, LLCs are required to report and pay employment and excise taxes.

2-2   THE TAX CUTS AND JOBS ACT (TCJA) OF 2017 AND ENTITY TAX RATES

A primary goal for tax reform in 2017 was to lower the Federal income tax rate for C corporations, improving the international competitiveness of U.S. corporations and attracting investment in the United States from non-U.S. multinational corporations. As described below, lowering tax rates is a challenging task.

2-2a   Challenges of Lowering Tax Rates

The Tax Reform Act of 1986 lowered the Federal corporate income tax rate from a maximum of 46 percent to 34 percent. This led many other industrialized countries also to lower their corporate tax rate. After many years, most of these countries had

---

[9]§ 7701(a)(3).

[10]Reg. §§ 301.7701–1 through –4, and –7.

[11]The "check-the-box" option is not available to entities that are incorporated under state law or to entities that are required to be taxed as corporations under Federal law (e.g., certain publicly traded partnerships). LLCs are not treated as being incorporated under state law, so they default to either partnership or DRE status.

lowered their rate below 34 percent, but the United States *raised* the top corporate rate to 35 percent. With U.S. companies facing increasing global competition, most members of Congress and U.S. Presidents favored lowering the corporate tax rate. Such a task, though, is easier said than done.

One obstacle in lowering tax rates is the related reduction in revenues for the Federal government. Alternatively, tax rates can be lowered and the tax base can be expanded (or broadened; recall that tax liability equals tax base times tax rate). Broadening the tax base for the corporate tax system is difficult because virtually all business expenses are allowed as deductions in determining taxable income. Lengthening the lives of depreciable assets can help reduce loss of government revenues in the short run but does not help U.S. businesses be more globally competitive.

Another obstacle to lowering the Federal corporate income tax rate is that most businesses in the United States operate as sole proprietorships, partnerships, or S corporations, rather than as C corporations. These non-C corporation entities are pass-through entities, where the business income is taxed to owners (rather than being subject to double taxation). In addition, the owners of these businesses are likely to have other forms of income. For example, a sole proprietor is likely also to have investment income and wages. As a result, determining how to tax the business income of pass-through entities in a manner comparable to that of a C corporation is challenging, as explained next. Text Section 2-3 then explains how Congress met this challenge in the TCJA of 2017 with a special deduction for qualified business income for owners of pass-through entities.

2-2b Lowering Tax Rates for Different Business Forms

There is more than one way to lower the tax rate on the business income that noncorporate taxpayers earn from their businesses. For example, similar to the lower income tax rates that apply to the net capital gains and qualified dividends received by noncorporate taxpayers, an alternative rate structure could be applied to business income. Or noncorporate taxpayers could be allowed a special deduction to reduce the income from their business activities, thereby lowering the tax base (and lowering the taxes due).

> **LO.2**
>
> **Explain the rationale for the deduction for qualified business income.**

Challenges exist in both of these approaches, as well as in determining what rate is comparable to the corporate tax rate given the double taxation of corporate income. These challenges include entity differences (e.g., sole proprietors and partnerships do not pay wages to their owners, but S corporations generally do).

Ultimately, the business deduction approach was selected and § 199A (Qualified Business Income; QBI) was added to the Internal Revenue Code. The QBI deduction allows up to a 20 percent deduction on the qualified business income of *noncorporate* taxpayers. As a result, this deduction is potentially available to individuals, trusts, and estates. Owners of partnerships and S corporations use relevant information provided to them from the entity (on their Schedule K–1 and related attachments) to calculate the deduction on their tax return (e.g., an individual's Form 1040).

As with most of the noncorporate changes made by the TCJA of 2017, the deduction for qualified business income is temporary; it is in effect from 2018 through 2025. At some point, Congress will need to revisit § 199A, deciding whether to extend, make permanent, modify, or repeal this deduction. The balance of this chapter explains the deduction for qualified business income. The QBI deduction includes numerous definitions, limitations, and special rules. Appreciating the purpose of the deduction—to reduce the tax on business income derived outside of the C corporate form—will help in understanding this provision.

LO.3

Describe the types of taxpayers and activities that potentially generate a deduction for qualified business income.

2-3 THE DEDUCTION FOR QUALIFIED BUSINESS INCOME

With the reduction in the corporate income tax rate to 21 percent in 2018, Congress needed to provide a means of reducing the taxes on businesses that operate in different business forms (e.g., sole proprietors, partnerships, and S corporations). Congress accomplished this with the creation of the <mark>deduction for qualified business income</mark> (§ 199A), which applies to *noncorporate taxpayers*.[12]

In general, the deduction for qualified business income is 20 percent of qualified business income (QBI). As you would suspect, however, the deduction is subject to a variety of limitations. We begin by discussing the general rules, defining key terms, and providing some basic examples. Then we turn our attention to the various limitations that apply to higher-income taxpayers, discuss the Treasury Department's § 199A Regulations, and conclude with some other implications of the qualified business income deduction (<mark>QBI deduction</mark>).

LO.4

Determine a taxpayer's deduction for qualified business income.

2-3a **General Rule**

At its most basic level, § 199A permits an individual to deduct 20 percent of the qualified business income generated through a sole proprietorship, a partnership, or an S corporation.[13] As will quickly become apparent, § 199A uses the word *qualified* to modify many phrases. For example, to determine the "qualified business income deduction," one has to understand the definition of a "qualified trade or business" and "qualified business income." But let's begin with the basics. In general, the deduction for qualified business income is the *lesser of*:[14]

1. 20 percent of qualified business income (QBI),[15] or
2. 20 percent of modified taxable income.[16]

Effectively, the QBI deduction—a *from* AGI deduction—is the last deduction taken in determining taxable income.[17] Further, the deduction is available whether a taxpayer uses the standard deduction or itemizes deductions.[18]

There are *three limitations* on the QBI deduction: an overall limitation (based on modified taxable income), another that applies to high-income taxpayers, and a third that applies to certain types of services businesses. The second and third limitations only apply when taxable income before the QBI deduction exceeds, in 2019, $321,400 (married taxpayers filing a joint return) or $160,700 (single and head-of-household taxpayers).[19] We'll discuss these two limitations later.

2-3b **The Overall Limitation: Modified Taxable Income**

In all cases, the § 199A deduction may not exceed 20 percent of the taxpayer's modified taxable income. Modified taxable income is taxable income *before* the deduction for qualified business income[20] reduced by any net capital gain.[21] In computing modified taxable income, the term *net capital gain* includes both a net capital gain [the excess of a long-term capital gain over a short-term capital loss; § 1222(11)] plus any qualified dividend income.[22]

---

[12]§ 199A(a).

[13]§§ 199A(a)(1)(A), (b)(1)(A), and (b)(2)(A).

[14]§ 199A(a)(1).

[15]If the taxpayer has more than one qualified trade or business, the qualified business income deduction is determined for each business independently [§ 199A(b)(1)(A)]. These are then combined [into the "combined qualified business income amount" of §199A(a)(1)(A)] and compared to the modified taxable income limitation.

[16]In addition, taxpayers are allowed a deduction for 20% of qualified REIT dividends and 20% of qualified publicly traded partnership income [§ 199A(b)(1)(B)].

[17]See TCJA § 11011(b), the last sentence of § 62(a), and § 63(b)(3).

[18]§ 63(d)(3).

[19]In 2019, married taxpayers filing separately (MFS) have a threshold amount of $160,725 (see Rev.Proc. 2018–57, 2018–49 I.R.B. 827, Section 3.27). We have not included MFS in the text discussion. In 2018, the threshold amounts were $315,000 (married taxpayers filing a joint return) and $157,500 (all other taxpayers).

[20]§ 199A(e)(1).

[21]§ 199A(a)(1)(B).

[22]§ 199A(a)(1)(B)(ii) and Reg. § 1.199A–1(b)(3); § 199A relies on the definition of "net capital gain" in § 1(h).

2-3c Definition of Qualified Business Income

Qualified business income[23] (QBI) is defined as the ordinary income less ordinary deductions a taxpayer earns from a "qualified trade or business" conducted in the United States by the taxpayer (e.g., from a sole proprietorship).[24] It also includes the distributive share of these amounts from each partnership or S corporation interest held by the taxpayer.

In determining QBI, all deductions attributable to a trade or business are taken into account.[25] As a result, a taxpayer must reduce QBI by the self-employment tax deduction [§ 164(f)], the self-employed health insurance deduction [§ 162(l)], and any deduction for contributions to qualified retirement plans [§ 404].[26]

**EXAMPLE
8**

Vicki Howard's sole proprietorship reports $54,000 of net income [on Schedule C (Form 1040)]. As a result, Vicki's self-employment tax liability is $7,630 ($54,000 × 0.9235 × 15.3%). She is allowed a *for* AGI deduction for one-half of her self-employment tax liability ($3,815; $7,630 × ½). Vicki's QBI is $50,185 ($54,000 − $3,815).

Qualified business income does not include certain types of investment income, such as:[27]

- Capital gains or capital losses (including any net § 1231 gain included in capital gain and loss computations),[28]
- Dividends,
- Interest income (unless "properly allocable" to a trade or business, such as lending), or
- Certain other investment items.

Nor does qualified business income include:[29]

- The "reasonable compensation" paid to the taxpayer with respect to any qualified trade or business, or
- Guaranteed payments made to a partner for services rendered.

As noted above, the § 199A Regulations indicate that a net § 1231 gain for a taxable year that is treated as a long-term capital gain is *excluded* from the computation of qualified business income. The Regulations also note that if the result of § 1231 netting is a *loss*, the ordinary loss will *reduce* qualified business income for that year. The Regulations are silent regarding what to do if there are multiple qualified trades or businesses, and each have § 1231 gains and losses.

2-3d Definition of a Qualified Trade or Business

For taxpayers who fall below critical taxable income thresholds established under § 199A (in 2019, $321,400 for married taxpayers filing jointly; $160,700 for single and head-of-household taxpayers), the scope of a **qualified trade or business** (QTB) is broad. In general, it includes any trade or business other than providing services as an employee.[30]

As a result, the deduction is available to sole proprietors, independent contractors, and noncorporate owners of S corporations, partnerships, and LLCs. But as discussed below, this otherwise broad application has some considerable restrictions

---

[23]§ 199A(c).

[24]§ 199A(c)(3)(A). As a result, foreign trade or business income does not qualify for the deduction. Certain Puerto Rico activities qualify for the deduction.

[25]§ 199A(c)(3)(A).

[26]Reg. § 1.199A-3(b)(1)(vi).

[27]§ 199A(c)(3)(B).

[28]Reg. § 1.199A–3(b)(2)(ii).

[29]§ 199A(c)(4).

[30]§ 199A(d)(1)(B).

for high-income taxpayers who are engaged in businesses involving the performance of services in certain "specified" fields.

Basic QBI Deduction Computation

EXAMPLE 9

Sanjay, a married taxpayer, operates a candy store as a sole proprietor. The business has no employees (Sanjay provides all services to customers). During 2019, Sanjay's qualified business income is $210,000 [this is his Schedule C (Form 1040) net income reduced by his self-employment tax deduction]. Sanjay's AGI is $274,400, which includes wages earned by his spouse, but no other income. He and his spouse claim the standard deduction ($24,400). Sanjay's modified taxable income is $250,000 ($274,400 − $24,400).

Sanjay's QBI deduction is $42,000, the *lesser of:*

1. 20% of qualified business income ($42,000; $210,000 × 20%), or
2. 20% of modified taxable income ($50,000; $250,000 × 20%).

Sanjay's taxable income is $208,000 ($250,000 of taxable income before the QBI deduction less his $42,000 QBI deduction).

EXAMPLE 10

Assume that Abby is a single taxpayer who does not itemize deductions and operates a sole proprietorship. Over the year, her business generates $140,000 of business income, $40,000 of deductible business expenses (including her self-employment tax deduction), and $2,200 of interest income from her business deposits. She has no other sources of income. Abby's AGI is $102,200.

Abby has $100,000 of qualified business income ($140,000 − $40,000). The interest income does not qualify for the QBI deduction. Her modified taxable income is $90,000 ($102,200 AGI − $12,200 standard deduction).

Abby's QBI deduction is $18,000, the *lesser of:*

1. 20% of qualified business income ($20,000; $100,000 × 20%), or
2. 20% of modified taxable income ($18,000; $90,000 × 20%).

Abby's taxable income is $72,000 ($90,000 of taxable income before the QBI deduction less her $18,000 QBI deduction).

EXAMPLE 11

Assume the same facts as in Example 10, except that Abby has no interest income, but $2,200 of qualified dividend income. Abby's AGI remains $102,200, and her taxable income before the QBI deduction remains $90,000 ($102,200 AGI − $12,200 standard deduction).

However, Abby's modified taxable income is now $87,800 [$90,000 taxable income before the QBI deduction less $2,200 of "net capital gain" (the qualified dividend income)].

Abby's QBI deduction is $17,560, the *lesser of:*

1. 20% of qualified business income ($20,000; $100,000 × 20%), or
2. 20% of modified taxable income ($17,560; $87,800 × 20%).

Abby's taxable income is $72,440 ($90,000 of taxable income before the QBI deduction less her $17,560 QBI deduction).

"Trade or Business" Under § 199A

What is a "trade or business" for purposes of § 199A? Reg. § 1.199A–1(b)(14) interprets the term *trade or business* by looking at the meaning of this phrase under § 162(a). With no formal definition of that phrase in § 162, the Supreme Court[31] has determined that to be "engaged in a trade or business, the taxpayer must be involved in the activity

---

[31]*Groetzinger v. Comm.*, 85–2 USTC ¶9622, 56 AFTR 2d 85–5683, 771 F.2d 269 (CA–7, 1985), *aff'd* in 87–1 USTC ¶9191, 59 AFTR 2d 87–532, 107 S.Ct. 980 (USSC, 1987). Performing services as an employee is *not* a "trade or business."

with continuity and regularity and that the taxpayer's primary purpose for engaging in the activity must be for income or profit." Ultimately, this is a "facts and circumstances" test.[32] The § 199A Regulations acknowledge that multiple businesses might be contained in a single entity, but emphasize that this determination depends on "all the facts and circumstances." At a minimum, for § 199A to apply to each business, separate books and records must be maintained for each business.

Does a rental activity qualify as a "trade or business"? Only if its activities rise to the level of those seen in a non-rental business. Here, the courts have based their decisions on a variety of factors including the type of property (commercial real property versus a residential condominium versus personal property), the number of properties rented, the nature of the owner's involvement [handling matters directly (or through an agent) versus a triple net lease arrangement], and the rental period (short term versus long term).[33]

Rental Real Estate Safe Harbor A rental real estate activity (or multiple rentals if the taxpayer chooses to combine them) will be treated as a trade or business for purposes of § 199A if the following conditions are met:[34]

- Separate books and records are maintained for each rental activity (or the combined enterprise if grouped together).
- At least 250 hours of "rental services" are performed per year for the activity (or combined enterprise). Rental services include time spent on maintenance, repairs, collection of rent, paying bills, providing services to tenants, supervising contractors and employees, and efforts to rent the property (including advertising and negotiating and executing a lease).
- The taxpayer maintains contemporaneous records, including time reports or similar documents, supporting the services performed (including hours, dates, description of services, and who performed the services).

A taxpayer can't use the safe harbor for the rental of any residence that the taxpayer uses as a personal residence for more than 14 days during the year (e.g., a vacation home). In addition, the taxpayer must own the rental property directly (rather than, for example, as a partner in a partnership). Finally, triple net leases are excluded from the safe harbor (these are leases where the landlord passes on the responsibility for paying real estate taxes, insurance, and maintenance to the tenant).

If property owners do not satisfy the safe harbor conditions, they still might find that their real estate rental is a trade or business under § 162 as defined in case law and the specific court cases that have considered whether rental properties constitute a trade or business.

Taxpayers with Multiple Businesses

The deduction for qualified business income must be determined separately for each qualified trade or business.[35] These independent calculations are then aggregated [becoming the "combined qualified business income amount" identified in § 199A(a)(1)(A)]. This combined amount is then compared to the overall modified taxable income limit.

2-3e **Limitations on the QBI Deduction**

The basic application of § 199A becomes more complex once a taxpayer reaches certain taxable income thresholds. These taxable income thresholds—determined without regard to the QBI deduction—are $321,400 for married taxpayers filing jointly and $160,700 for single and head-of-household taxpayers in 2019.[36] In 2018, these amounts were $315,000 and $157,500.

---

[32]*Higgins v. Comm.*, 41–1 USTC ¶9233, 25 AFTR 1160, 61 S.Ct. 475 (USSC, 1941).

[33]See, for example, *Alvary v. United States*, 302 F.2d 790 (2d Cir. 1962), *Curphey v. Comm'r.*, 73 T.C. 766 (1980), *Gilford v. Comm'r.*, 201 F.2d 735 (2d Cir. 1953), *Murtaugh v. Comm'r.*, T.C. Memo. 1997–319, and *Balsamo v. Comm'r.*, T.C. Memo. 1987–477.

[34]Notice 2019-7, 2019-9 I.R.B. 740.

[35]§ 199A(b)(2).

[36]§ 199A(e)(2). Married taxpayers filing separately have a taxable income threshold of $160,725 in 2019.

Once these thresholds are reached, § 199A imposes two *independent* limitations.

1. The QBI deduction is capped based on the percentage of the W–2 wages paid by the business (i.e., wages paid to its employees) *or* based on a smaller percentage of W–2 wages paid by the business and a percentage of the cost of its depreciable property used to produce QBI.[37]

2. The QBI deduction generally is *not available* for income earned from "specified service" businesses.[38] "Specified service" businesses include doctors, dentists, lawyers, accountants, consultants, investment advisers, entertainers, and athletes (among others), but not engineers and architects.

These limitations, discussed in more detail below, are fully phased in once taxable income (before the QBI deduction) exceeds $421,400 for married taxpayers filing jointly and $210,700 for single and head-of-household taxpayers. Within the phase-in ranges ($100,000 for married taxpayers filing jointly; $50,000 for all other taxpayers), the limitations are each applied by comparing the amount of taxable income that exceeds the threshold amount to the appropriate phase-in range.[39]

Because the "specified services" limitation can be more complex (due to incorporating the "wages and capital investment" limitation after the "specified services" limitation), the wages and capital investment limitation is discussed first, followed by the "specified services" limitation.

Remember that in all cases, the QBI deduction can never exceed 20 percent of the taxpayer's modified taxable income (taxable income before the QBI deduction reduced by any net capital gain, including qualified dividend income). To help navigate this "thicket," Concept Summary 2.2 provides a flowchart to assist in applying these rules.

2-3f Limitation Based on Wages and Capital Investment

The W–2 Wages/Capital Investment Limit, which does not apply to taxpayers below the taxable income thresholds mentioned previously and is phased in as a taxpayer's income exceeds those thresholds, limits the 20 percent QBI deduction to the *greater of*:

1. 50 percent of the "W–2 wages" paid by the QTB, or
2. 25 percent of the "W–2 wages" paid by the QTB *plus* 2.5 percent of the taxpayer's share of the unadjusted basis immediately after acquisition of all tangible depreciable property (including real estate) used in the QTB that has not been fully depreciated prior to the close of the taxable year.

W–2 Wages Limit

"W–2 wages" includes the total amount of wages subject to income tax withholding, compensation paid into qualified retirement accounts, and certain other forms of deferred compensation paid to the employees of the business.[40] For labor-intensive businesses, 50 percent of the W–2 wages paid by the business will likely be the relevant limit on the QBI deduction.

W–2 Wages/Capital Investment Limit

For capital-intensive businesses (e.g., real estate), an alternate limit exists. It begins with 25 percent of W–2 wages paid by the QTB and adds to this amount 2.5 percent of the unadjusted basis (immediately after acquisition) of "qualified property."

---

[37]§ 199A(b)(2)(B).

[38]§ 199A(d)(2).

[39]§§ 199A(b)(3)(B) and (d)(3).

[40]§ 199A(b)(4).

Concept Summary 2.2

An Overview of the 2019 Qualified Business Income Deduction

<u>How to Use the Concept Summary:</u> ***First,*** identify all qualified trades or businesses (QTB) of the taxpayer and the related qualified business income (QBI). ***Then*** for each QTB, move through the flowchart to determine the QBI amount for each QTB. Once this process is complete, combine all of the QBI amounts (this is the "combined qualified business income amount"). ***Finally,*** apply the *overall limitation* (based on modified taxable income). The QBI deduction is the *lesser of:*

1. The combined "qualified business income (QBI) amount," or
2. 20% of modified taxable income.*

* Modified taxable income is taxable income *before* the QBI deduction less any "net capital gain" (including any qualified dividend income).

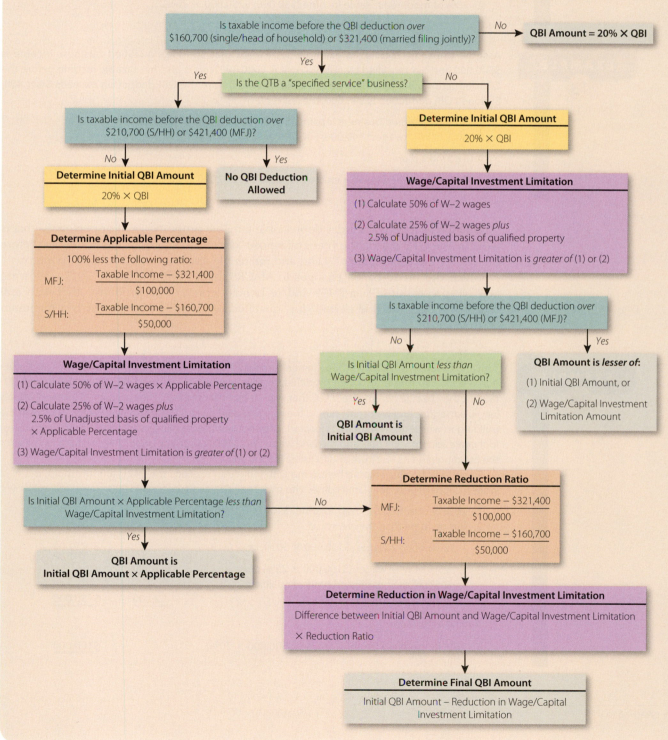

W–2 Wages Limit

EXAMPLE 12

Simone, a married taxpayer, operates a business as a sole proprietor. The business has one employee, who is paid $80,000 during 2019. Assume that the business has no significant assets. During 2019, Simone's qualified business income is $230,000, and her modified taxable income is $250,000 (this is also her taxable income before the QBI deduction).

Since Simone's taxable income before the QBI deduction is below the income threshold for married taxpayers filing a joint return ($321,400), the W–2/Capital Investment Limitation does not apply. As a result, Simone's QBI deduction is $46,000, the *lesser of*:

1. 20% of qualified business income ($46,000; $230,000 × 20%), or
2. 20% of modified taxable income ($50,000; $250,000 × 20%).

EXAMPLE 13

Assume the same facts as in Example 12, except that Simone's qualified business income is $500,000 and her modified taxable income is $600,000 (this is also her taxable income before the QBI deduction). Because Simone's taxable income before the QBI deduction exceeds $421,400, Simone's QBI deduction is $40,000, the *lesser of*:

1. 20% of qualified business income ($100,000; $500,000 × 20%), or
2. 50% of W–2 wages ($40,000; $80,000 × 50%).

And *no more than*:

3. 20% of modified taxable income ($120,000; $600,000 × 20%).

Qualified property includes depreciable tangible property—real or personal—that is used by the QTB during the year and whose "depreciable period" has not ended before the end of the taxable year.[41] Land and intangible assets are *not* qualified property.

Given the broad-based changes to MACRS made by the TCJA of 2017—allowing taxpayers to expense (via § 179 and/or bonus depreciation) property other than real estate—the "depreciable period" for "qualified property" under § 199A is a minimum of 10 years.[42]

EXAMPLE 14

Tom and Eileen are married and file a joint return for 2019. Their taxable income before the QBI deduction is $500,000 (this is also their modified taxable income). They have $400,000 in QBI from a restaurant they own (a two-member LLC that reports as a partnership). They employed four individuals (cook, bartender, and wait staff) during the year and paid them $150,000 in W–2 wages. They own the building in which the restaurant is located. They bought the building (and its furniture and fixtures) four years ago for $600,000, and the land was worth $100,000, so the unadjusted acquisition basis of the building (and its furniture and fixtures) is $500,000.

Since their taxable income before the QBI deduction exceeds the $421,400 threshold, the W–2 Wages/Capital Investment Limit comes into play. Their QBI deduction is $75,000, computed as follows:

1. 20% of qualified business income ($400,000 × 20%) $ 80,000
2. But no more than the *greater of*:

   • 50% of W–2 wages ($150,000 × 50%), or $ 75,000

   • 25% of W–2 wages ($150,000 × 25%) *plus* $37,500
   • 2.5% of the unadjusted basis of qualified
     property ($500,000 × 2.5%)   12,500 $ 50,000

And *no more than*:

3. 20% of modified taxable income ($500,000 × 20%) $100,000

---

[41]§ 199A(b)(6)(A).   [42]§ 199A(b)(6)(B).

Many owners of pass-through businesses, especially landlords, have no employees. As a result, the 25 percent of W–2 wages plus 2.5 percent of the unadjusted basis of qualified property is most likely to affect them.

EXAMPLE

15

Jiaxiu, a single taxpayer, owns a five-unit apartment building that he purchased five years ago. His unadjusted basis in the building (purchase price minus the value of the land) is $500,000. He has taxable income before the QBI deduction of $250,000 during 2019 (this is also his modified taxable income). He has no employees in his business, and his QBI is $220,000.

Since his taxable income before the QBI deduction exceeds the $210,700 threshold, the W–2 Wages/Capital Investment Limit comes into play. His QBI deduction is $12,500, computed as follows:

1. 20% of qualified business income ($220,000 × 20%) $44,000
2. But no more than the *greater of*:

   • 50% of W–2 wages ($0 × 50%), or $ –0–

   • 25% of W–2 wages ($0 × 25%) *plus* $ –0–
   • 2.5% of the unadjusted basis of qualified
      property ($500,000 × 2.5%)   12,500 $12,500

And *no more than*:

3. 20% of modified taxable income ($250,000 × 20%) $50,000

Phase-In of W–2 Wages/Capital Investment Limit

The W–2 Wages/Capital Investment Limit does not apply to taxpayers with taxable income before the QBI deduction less than the threshold amount ($321,400 for married taxpayers filing jointly; $160,700 for singles and heads of household). And if taxable income before the QBI deduction exceeds the threshold amount by more than $100,000 (married filing jointly) or $50,000 (all other taxpayers), the W–2 Wages/Capital Investment Limit must be used.

If, however, the taxpayer's taxable income before the QBI deduction is between these two amounts *and the W–2 Wages/Capital Investment portion of the QBI deduction is capping the deduction*, then the general 20 percent QBI amount is used, but reduced as follows:

1. Determine difference between the general 20 percent QBI deduction amount and the W–2 Wages/Capital Investment amount.[43]

2. Determine the Reduction Ratio:[44]

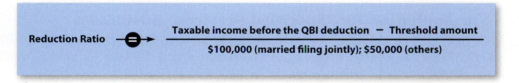

$$\text{Reduction Ratio} = \frac{\text{Taxable income before the QBI deduction} - \text{Threshold amount}}{\$100,000 \text{ (married filing jointly); } \$50,000 \text{ (others)}}$$

3. Determine the Reduction in the W–2 Wages/Capital Investment Limit:

   Reduction = Difference [from (1)] × Reduction ratio [from (2)]

4. Determine QBI amount:

   20% QBI deduction − Reduction [from (3)]

---

[43]This is the "excess amount" in § 199A(b)(3)(B)(iii).   [44]§ 199A(b)(3)(B)(ii).

EXAMPLE 16

Return to the facts of Example 14, but assume that Tom and Eileen's taxable income before the QBI deduction is $361,400 (this is also their modified taxable income), QBI is $320,000, and W–2 wages are $100,000. Their unadjusted property basis remains at $500,000. Tom and Eileen's initial calculation yields a qualified business income amount of $50,000, computed as follows:

1. 20% of qualified business income ($320,000 × 20%)		$ 64,000
2. But no more than the *greater of*:		
• 50% of W–2 wages ($100,000 × 50%), or		$ 50,000
• 25% of W–2 wages ($100,000 × 25%) *plus*	$25,000	
2.5% of the unadjusted basis of qualified property ($500,000 × 2.5%)	12,500	$ 37,500

And *no more than*:

3. 20% of modified taxable income ($361,400 × 20%)		$ 72,280

Since Tom and Eileen's taxable income before the QBI deduction exceeds $321,400 but is less than $421,400 and *the W–2 Wages/Capital Investment portion of the computation is capping the deduction*, the general 20% QBI amount is used, but reduced as follows:

1. Determine the difference between the general 20% QBI deduction amount and the W–2 Wages/Capital Investment amount:

General 20% QBI deduction amount	$ 64,000
Less: The W–2 Wages/Capital Investment Limit	(50,000)
Excess	$ 14,000

2. Determine the Reduction Ratio:

$$\text{Reduction Ratio} = \frac{\$40,000 \ (\$361,400 - \$321,400)}{\$100,000} = 40\%$$

3. Determine the Reduction in the W–2 Wages/Capital Investment Limit:

$$\text{Excess (\$14,000)} \times \text{Reduction ratio (40\%)} = \underline{\$5,600}$$

4. Determine Final QBI Amount:

General 20% QBI deduction amount	$64,000
Less: Reduction in the W–2 Wages/Capital Investment Limit	(5,600)
Final QBI amount	$58,400

Since the QBI amount ($58,400) is less than 20% of their modified taxable income ($72,280; $361,400 × 20%), they will be allowed a $58,400 deduction for qualified business income.

2-3g Limitation for "Specified Services" Businesses

For high-income taxpayers (in 2019, $421,400 for married taxpayers filing jointly; $210,700 for single and head-of-household taxpayers), § 199A excludes any "specified service trade or business" from the definition of a qualified trade or business.[45] A specified service trade or business includes those involving:[46]

- The performance of services in certain fields, including health, law, accounting, actuarial science, performing arts, consulting, athletics, financial services, and brokerage services;

- Services consisting of investing and investment management, trading or dealing in securities, partnership interests, or commodities; and

- Any trade or business where the business's principal asset is the reputation of one or more of its employees or owners.

Architects and engineers are specifically excluded from this definition.[47]

[45]§§ 199A(d)(1)(A) and (d)(2).

[46]§ 199A(d)(2); see also § 1202(e)(3)(A).

[47]§ 199A(d)(2)(A).

According to the legislative history of the TCJA of 2017, the taxable income thresholds where the QBI deduction is phased out for "specified service" businesses were set by Congress "to deter high-income taxpayers from attempting to convert wages or other compensation for personal services to income eligible for the 20 percent deduction under the provision." However, the phaseout rules operate without regard to the taxpayer's specific motivation.

In Example 9, Sanjay operated a sole proprietorship that generated QBI of $210,000 and he was able to claim a QBI deduction of $42,000.

But if his spouse had a salary of $300,000 (instead of $64,000), Sanjay would not be able to claim a QBI deduction since their taxable income before the QBI deduction exceeds $421,400 [$210,000 (QBI) + $300,000 (spouse's wages) − $24,400 (standard deduction) = $485,600]. Sanjay did not attempt to "convert wages to . . . income eligible for the (QBI) deduction." The *income of his spouse* triggered the limitation.

Example 17 illustrates a crucial fact. The QBI deduction phaseout for a "specified services" business is based on *taxable income* before the QBI deduction (*not* on QBI). *Any* income that contributes to taxable income can cause the "specified services" QBI deduction to be reduced.

"Specified Services" Under the § 199A Regulations

The § 199A Regulations provide specific guidance for each of the "specified services" fields identified in § 199A.[48] Exhibit 2.1 provides an overview of this guidance.

A series of examples in the Regulations illustrate these concepts.[49]

"Specified Services" Businesses

Surgery Centers LLC (SC) operates specialty surgical centers that provide outpatient medical procedures (none of which require the patient to stay overnight). The company owns a number of facilities throughout the country. For each facility, SC ensures compliance with Federal and state laws and manages each facility's operations and performs all administrative functions. SC does not employ physicians, nurses, and medical assistants. Rather, it enters into agreements with medical professionals and other medical organizations to perform the procedures and provide all needed medical care. Patients are billed by SC for the facility costs related to their procedure; they are separately billed by the health care professional (or the medical organization) for the costs of the procedure performed by the physician and medical support team.

SC is *not* engaged in a "specified services" business (health) because it is not providing the medical services (the medical professionals using the centers are operating businesses in the field of health).

Abby, a singer, records a song. Abby is paid a mechanical royalty when the song is licensed or streamed. She is also paid a performance royalty when the recorded song is played publicly.

Abby is engaged in a "specified services" business (performing arts).

Roger is a partner in RoundballSports (RS), which owns and operates a professional basketball team. RS employs athletes and sells tickets to the public to attend games in which its basketball team competes.

RS is engaged in a "specified services" business (athletics).

---

[48]Reg. § 1.199A–5(b)(2).   [49]Reg. § 1.199A–5(b)(3).

EXHIBIT 2.1	"Specified Services"	

Field	"Specified Services"	Not "Specified Services"
Health	Doctors, pharmacists, nurses, dentists, veterinarians, physical therapists, psychologists, and other similar health care professionals.	Those who provide services that may improve the health of the recipient (e.g., the operator of a health club or spa) or the research, testing, and sale of pharmaceuticals or medical devices.
Law	Lawyers, paralegals, legal arbitrators, and mediators.	Those who provide services not unique to law, like printing, stenography, or delivery services.
Accounting	Accountants, enrolled agents, return preparers, financial auditors, bookkeepers, and similar professionals (whether licensed by a state or not).	Businesses that provide payment processing and billing analysis.
Actuarial Science	Actuaries and similar professionals.	Services provided by analysts, economists, mathematicians, and statisticians not engaged in analyzing or assessing the financial costs of risk or uncertainty of events.
Performing Arts	Actors, singers, musicians, entertainers, directors, and similar professionals (including screenwriters and composers) who provide services that lead to the creation of performing arts.	Those who broadcast or disseminate video or audio to the public and those who maintain or operate equipment or facilities used in the performing arts.
Consulting	Those who provide professional advice and counsel to clients to assist in achieving goals and solving problems, including government lobbyists.	Salespeople and those who provide training or educational courses. Services provided in the fields of architecture or engineering.
Athletics	Athletes, coaches, and team managers.	Broadcasters or those who maintain or operate equipment used in an athletic event; services related to the maintenance and operation of equipment or facilities for use in athletic events.
Financial Services	Those who provide financial services to clients, including managing wealth, developing retirement or transition plans, providing advisory services related to mergers and acquisitions (including restructurings, raising capital, underwriting, and other valuation services). In summary, financial advisers, investment bankers, wealth planners, and retirement advisers.	Banking services (e.g., taking deposits or making loans).
Brokerage Services	A broker who arranges *securities* transactions.	Real estate agents and brokers.
Investment Management	Persons who receive fees for providing investing, asset management, or investment management services.	Real estate managers.
Trading	Persons who trade in securities, commodities, or partnership interests.	A farmer or manufacturer who engages in hedging transactions as part of his or her trade or business.
Reputation of One or More Employees or Owners	Any trade or business that consists of any of the following (or any combination of them): (1) Receiving fees, compensation, or other income for endorsing products or services; (2) Licensing or receiving fees, compensation, or other income for the use of an individual's image, likeness, name, signature, voice, trademark, or any other symbols associated with the individual's identity; and (3) Receiving fees, compensation, or other income for appearing at an event or on radio, television, or another media format.	Persons not covered by this narrowly crafted definition (and not in another "specified services" field). Examples include authors and personal trainers.

"Specified Services" Businesses

Christian is in the business of providing services that assist unrelated entities in making their personnel structures more efficient. Christian studies a variety of client organizations and structures and compares each to peers in its industry. He then makes recommendations and provides advice to clients regarding possible changes to their personnel structure, including the use of temporary workers.

Christian is engaged in a "specified services" business (consulting).

EXAMPLE 21

Danielle is in the business of licensing software to customers. As part of her business, she evaluates a customer's software needs and discusses alternatives with her customers. She advises the customer on the particular software products her business licenses. Danielle is paid a flat price for the software license. After a customer licenses the software, Danielle helps to implement it.

Danielle is engaged in the trade or business of licensing software and is *not* engaged in a "specified services" business.

EXAMPLE 22

Sarah is in the business of providing services to assist clients with their finances. Sarah generally studies a particular client's financial situation, including the client's present income, savings, and investments, and anticipated future economic and financial needs. Based on this study, she then assists the client in making decisions and plans regarding the client's financial activities. This planning includes the design of a personal budget to assist the client in monitoring the client's financial situation, the adoption of investment strategies tailored to the client's needs, and other similar services.

Sarah is engaged in a "specified services" business (financial services).

EXAMPLE 23

Emeril is a well-known chef and the sole owner of multiple restaurants, each of which is an LLC. Due to his skill and reputation as a chef, Emeril receives an endorsement fee of $5 million for the use of his name on a line of cooking utensils and cookware.

Emeril is in the trade or business of being a chef and owning restaurants—*neither* is a "specified services" business. However, he is also in the trade or business of receiving endorsement income. This business—consisting of endorsement fees for Emeril's skill and/or reputation—is a "specified services" business.

EXAMPLE 24

Jennifer is a well-known actor. Jennifer entered into a partnership with Shoe Company, in which she contributed her likeness and the use of her name to the partnership in exchange for a 50% interest in the partnership and a guaranteed payment.

Jennifer's trade or business consisting of the receipt of the partnership interest and guaranteed payment for use of her likeness and name is a "specified services" business.

EXAMPLE 25

De Minimis Rule

The § 199A Regulations contain a *de minimis* rule providing that a trade or business will *not* be considered a "specified services" business merely because it provides a small amount of services in a "specified service" activity.[50]

- If a business has gross receipts of $25 million or less and *less than 10 percent* of its receipts relates to a "specified service," the business will *not* be a "specified services" business.

- If the business has gross receipts greater than $25 million, then the test is *less than 5 percent* (rather than less than 10 percent).

Computer Company has annual revenue of $20 million ($18.5 million of the revenue is related to the sale of computers and peripheral equipment; the remaining $1.5 million relates to consulting, installation, and training services).

Because its consulting services revenues are less than 10% of Computer Company's total revenues, those services are ignored for purposes of determining whether Computer Company is a "specified services" business. As a result, Computer Company is *not* a "specified services" business.

EXAMPLE 26

---

[50]Reg. § 1.199A–5(c)(1).

Although the *de minimis* rules offer relief to a business with both service and non-service income, what happens if the "specified services" income is more than *de minimis*? Is the entire business tainted (or just the "specified services" portion of the business)? The § 199A Regulations provide two examples to illustrate the consequences.

"Specified Services" *De Minimis* Rule

EXAMPLE 27

Landscape LLC sells lawn care and landscaping equipment. It also provides advice and counsel on landscape design for large office parks and residential buildings. The landscape design services include advice on the selection and placement of trees, shrubs, and flowers (these are "consulting services" under § 199A).

Landscape LLC separately invoices for its landscape design services and does not sell the trees, shrubs, or flowers it recommends for use in the landscape design. Landscape LLC maintains one set of books and records and treats the equipment sales and design services as a *single trade or business*. Landscape LLC has gross receipts of $2,000,000; $250,000 of the gross receipts relates to the landscape design services.

Because the gross receipts from the consulting services exceed 10% of Landscape LLC's total gross receipts, the entirety of Landscape LLC's business is considered a "specified services" business.

EXAMPLE 28

Animal Care LLC provides veterinary services performed by licensed staff. It also develops and sells its own line of organic dog food at its veterinarian clinic and online. The veterinary services are in the field of health (a "specified service"). Animal Care LLC separately invoices for its veterinarian services and the sale of its organic dog food. Animal Care LLC maintains separate books and records for its veterinarian clinic and its development and sale of its dog food. Animal Care LLC also has separate employees who are unaffiliated with the veterinary clinic and who only work on the formulation, marketing, sales, and distribution of the organic dog food products.

Animal Care LLC treats its veterinary practice and the dog food development and sales as *separate trades or businesses*. Animal Care LLC has gross receipts of $3,000,000; $1,000,000 of the gross receipts relates to the veterinary services. Although the gross receipts from the veterinary services exceed 10% of Animal Care LLC's total gross receipts, the dog food development and sales business is *not* considered a "specified services" business. Animal Care LLC has chosen to treat each business separately, so the veterinarian services business is a "specified services" business, while the dog food business is not.

As you can see, two factors led to the favorable result in Example 28. First, the taxpayer keeps separate books and records for each business. Second, each business has separate employees. As discussed previously, it is possible for a single entity to have multiple trades or businesses. However, whether multiple businesses exist depends on "all the facts and circumstances." At a minimum, separate books and records must be maintained; the § 199A Regulations imply (via the outcome in Example 28) that separate employees with separate books and records means separate businesses. But the differing outcomes of Examples 27 and 28 do mean that without separate books and records, multiple businesses in a single entity are not possible. And, in that case, if the "specified services" revenue becomes more than *de minimis*, the entire entity is tainted.

Phase-In of the "Specified Services" Limit

In computing the qualified business income with respect to a "specified services" business, the taxpayer takes into account only the "applicable percentage" of QBI *and* the components of the W–2 Wages/Capital Investment Limit.[51]

$$\text{Applicable percentage} = 100\% - \frac{\text{Taxable income before the QBI deduction} - \text{Threshold amount}}{\$100,000 \text{ (married filing jointly); } \$50,000 \text{ (others)}}$$

---

[51]§ 199A(d)(3)(B).

EXAMPLE
29

In 2019, a single taxpayer has modified taxable income of $190,700, of which $150,000 is attributable to an accounting sole proprietorship that pays wages of $100,000 to employees.

The taxpayer has an applicable percentage of 40%, computed as follows:

$$\text{Applicable percentage} = 100\% - \frac{\$190,700 - \$160,700}{\$50,000} = 40\%$$

In determining includible qualified business income, the taxpayer takes into account 40% of $150,000, or $60,000. In determining the includible W–2 wages, the taxpayer takes into account 40% of $100,000, or $40,000.

A second complication exists if a taxpayer has a "specified services" business with taxable income before the QBI deduction in the phaseout range. Here, in addition to the amount of QBI, W–2 wages, and unadjusted basis of property being subject to a limitation, the W–2 Wages/Capital Investment Limitation might also apply (provided the 20 percent QBI deduction is greater than the W–2 Wages/Capital Investment Limit). The following example illustrates the complexity.

"Specified Services" Limit

EXAMPLE
30

In 2019, Jenna and Paul have taxable income before the QBI deduction (and modified taxable income) of $361,400, and Jenna is a part-time financial adviser (a "specified service trade or business") with QBI of $75,000. Jenna pays $20,000 in wages to employees and has qualified business property of $90,000.

Normally, Jenna and Paul would be entitled to a QBI deduction of $15,000 ($75,000 × 20%). But since their taxable income exceeds the threshold for married taxpayers ($321,400), their QBI deduction is limited to $7,800, computed as follows:

1. Determine Applicable Percentage:

$$\text{Applicable percentage} = 100\% - \frac{\$40,000\ (\$361,400 - \$321,400)}{\$100,000} = 60\%$$

2. Determine QBI deduction:

a. 20% of qualified business income ($75,000 × 20%)		$15,000
× Applicable percentage		× 60%
		$ 9,000
b. But no more than the *greater of*:		
• 50% of W–2 wages ($20,000 × 50% × 60%), or		$ 6,000
• 25% of W–2 wages ($20,000 × 25% × 60%) *plus*	$3,000	
2.5% of the unadjusted basis of qualified property ($90,000 × 2.5% × 60%)	1,350	$ 4,350

Since Jenna and Paul's taxable income before the QBI deduction exceeds $321,400 but is less than $421,400 and *the W–2 Wages/Capital Investment portion of the computation is capping the deduction*, the general 20% QBI amount is used, but reduced as follows:

1. Determine the difference between the general 20% QBI deduction amount and the W–2 Wages/Capital Investment amount:

General 20% QBI deduction amount	$ 9,000
Less: The W–2 Wages/Capital Investment Limit	(6,000)
Excess	$ 3,000

2. Determine the Reduction Ratio:

$$\text{Reduction Ratio} = \frac{\$40,000\ (\$361,400 - \$321,400)}{\$100,000} = 40\%$$

continued

3. Determine the Reduction in the W–2 Wages/Capital Investment Limit:

$$\text{Excess (\$3,000)} \times \text{Reduction Ratio (40\%)} = \underline{\$1,200}$$

4. Determine Final QBI Amount:

General 20% QBI deduction amount	$ 9,000
Less: Reduction in the W–2 Wages/Capital Investment Limit	(1,200)
Final QBI amount	$ 7,800

Since the QBI amount ($7,800) is less than 20% of their modified taxable income ($72,280; $361,400 × 20%), they will be allowed a $7,800 deduction for qualified business income.

Assume the same facts as Example 30, except that Jenna and Paul's taxable income before the QBI deduction is $450,000.

Because their modified taxable income exceeds the $421,400 threshold for married taxpayers, and their only QBI is from a "specified services" business, Jenna and Paul are not allowed a QBI deduction.

Now assume the same facts as Example 30, except that Jenna's business is a flower and gift shop (*not* a "specified services" business). As before, Jenna and Paul have modified taxable income of $361,400 and Jenna has QBI of $75,000, pays $20,000 in wages to employees, and has qualified business property of $90,000.

1. 20% of qualified business income ($75,000 × 20%)		$15,000
2. But no more than the *greater of*:		
• 50% of W–2 wages ($20,000 × 50%), or		$10,000
• 25% of W–2 wages ($20,000 × 25%) *plus*	$5,000	
• 2.5% of the unadjusted basis of qualified property ($90,000 × 2.5%)	2,250	$ 7,250

And *no more than*:

3. 20% of modified taxable income ($361,400 × 20%)	$72,280

Since Jenna and Paul's modified taxable income exceeds $321,400 but is less than $421,400 and *the W–2 Wages/Capital Investment portion of the computation is capping the deduction*, the general 20% QBI amount is used, but reduced as follows:

1. Determine the difference between the general 20% QBI deduction amount and the W–2 Wages/Capital Investment amount:

General 20% QBI deduction amount	$ 15,000
Less: The W–2 Wages/Capital Investment Limit	(10,000)
Excess	$ 5,000

2. Determine the Reduction Ratio:

$$\text{Reduction Ratio} = \frac{\$40,000\ (\$361,400 - \$321,400)}{\$100,000} = 40\%$$

3. Determine the Reduction in the W–2 Wages/Capital Investment Limit:

$$\text{Excess (\$5,000)} \times \text{Reduction Ratio (40\%)} = \underline{\$2,000}$$

4. Determine Final QBI Amount:

General 20% QBI deduction amount	$ 15,000
Less: Reduction in the W–2 Wages/Capital Investment Limit	(2,000)
Final QBI amount	$ 13,000

Since the QBI amount ($13,000) is less than 20% of their modified taxable income ($72,280; $361,400 × 20%), they will be allowed a $13,000 deduction for qualified business income.

A comparison of Examples 30 and 32 demonstrates the implications (and disadvantages) of having a "specified services" business.

An even more complex setting is having multiple businesses—some "specified services" and others not. Here, a QBI deduction is determined for each business and then combined. This "combined qualified business income amount" is then compared to the overall modified taxable income limitation.

> **EXAMPLE**
>
> **33**
>
> Chaz is a management consultant. Chaz and his wife, Abby, also own and operate rental properties. Chaz's consulting business is an LLC (and a "specified services" business), which he reports as a sole proprietor. The proprietorship generates qualified business income of $230,000, Chaz pays W–2 wages of $50,000 to an employee, and he has $100,000 of qualified property. The couple report $140,800 of net income from their real estate business (three rental properties that they manage; they meet the rental real estate safe harbor requirements for this business). They pay no wages in this business and have $450,000 of qualified property. They have no other income or deductions (and will use the standard deduction).
>
> Their modified taxable income is $346,400 (AGI of $370,800 less their $24,400 standard deduction); this is also taxable income before the QBI deduction. The maximum QBI deduction they can claim is $69,280 ($346,400 × 20%). Because their modified taxable income is more than $321,400 and less than $421,400, both of the QBI deduction limitations apply.
>
> **Consulting ("Specified Services") Business**
>
> 1. Determine Applicable Percentage:
>
> $$\text{Applicable percentage} = 100\% - \frac{\$25,000\ (\$346,400 - \$321,400)}{\$100,000} = 75\%$$
>
> 2. Determine QBI deduction:
>
> | | | |
> |---|---|---:|
> | a. | 20% of qualified business income ($230,000 × 20%) | $46,000 |
> | | × Applicable percentage | × 75% |
> | | | $34,500 |
>
> b. But no more than the *greater of*:
>
> | | | |
> |---|--:|--:|
> | • 50% of W–2 wages ($50,000 × 50% × 75%), or | | $18,750 |
> | • 25% of W–2 wages ($50,000 × 25% × 75%) *plus* | $9,375 | |
> | • 2.5% of the unadjusted basis of qualified property ($100,000 × 2.5% × 75%) | 1,875 | $11,250 |
>
> Since their taxable income before the QBI deduction exceeds $321,400 but is less than $421,400 and *the W–2 Wages/Capital Investment portion of the computation is capping the deduction*, the general 20% QBI amount is used, but reduced as follows:
>
> 1. Determine the difference between the general 20% QBI deduction amount and the W–2 Wages/Capital Investment amount:
>
> | | |
> |---|---:|
> | General 20% QBI deduction amount | $ 34,500 |
> | Less: The W–2 Wages/Capital Investment Limit | (18,750) |
> | Excess | $ 15,750 |
>
> 2. Determine the Reduction Ratio:
>
> $$\text{Reduction Ratio} = \frac{\$25,000\ (\$346,400 - \$321,400)}{\$100,000} = 25\%$$
>
> 3. Determine the Reduction in the W–2 Wages/Capital Investment Limit:
>
> $$\text{Excess (\$15,750)} \times \text{Reduction Ratio (25\%)} = \underline{\$3,938}$$
>
> 4. Determine Final QBI Amount:
>
> | | |
> |---|---:|
> | General 20% QBI deduction amount | $ 34,500 |
> | Less: Reduction in the W–2 Wages/Capital Investment Limit | (3,938) |
> | Final QBI amount | $ 30,562 |
>
> *continued*

Rental Business

1. General QBI Deduction Computation:

   a. 20% of qualified business income ($140,800 × 20%) $28,160
   b. But no more than the *greater of*:

   • 50% of W–2 wages ($0 × 50%), or $ –0–

   • 25% of W–2 wages ($0 × 25%) *plus* $ –0–
   • 2.5% of the unadjusted basis of qualified
     property ($450,000 × 2.5%)   11,250 $11,250

Since their taxable income before the QBI deduction exceeds $321,400 but is less than $421,400 and *the W–2 Wages/Capital Investment portion of the computation is capping the deduction*, the general 20% QBI amount is used, but reduced as follows:

1. Determine the difference between the general 20% QBI deduction amount and the W–2 Wages/Capital Investment amount:

   General 20% QBI deduction amount $ 28,160
   Less: The W–2 Wages/Capital Investment Limit   (11,250)
   Excess $ 16,910

2. Determine the Reduction Ratio:

$$\text{Reduction Ratio} = \frac{\$25,000\ (\$346,400 - \$321,400)}{\$100,000} = 25\%$$

3. Determine the Reduction in the W–2 Wages/Capital Investment Limit:

   Excess ($16,910) × Reduction Ratio (25%) = $4,228

4. Determine Final QBI Amount:

   General 20% QBI deduction amount $28,160
   Less: Reduction in the W–2 Wages/Capital Investment Limit   (4,228)
   Final QBI amount $23,932

So for Chaz and Abby, the "combined qualified income amount" is $54,494, computed as follows:

   QBI amount from consulting business $30,562
   + QBI amount from rental business   23,932
   Combined qualified business income amount $54,494

Since the combined QBI amount ($54,494) is *less than* 20% of their modified taxable income ($69,280; $346,400 × 20%), they will be allowed a $54,494 deduction for qualified business income. Their final taxable income is $291,906 ($346,400 − $54,494).

2-3h Aggregation of Qualified Trades and Businesses Under the § 199A Regulations

In general, each trade or business conducted by an individual or a "relevant pass-through entity" (e.g., a partnership or an S corporation; RPE) is a separate trade or business under § 199A. However, under the § 199A Regulations, taxpayers may aggregate businesses if the following requirements are met:[52]

1. There must be control. The same person or a group of persons must own, directly or indirectly, *50 percent or more* of each business to be aggregated.[53]

   • For S corporations, ownership is measured by reference to the outstanding stock.

   • For partnerships, ownership is measured by reference to the interest in capital or profits in the partnership.

2. Control is met for the "majority" of the tax year (which must include the last day of the tax year).

3. The businesses share the same tax year.

[52]Reg. § 1.199A–4(b).   [53]The § 267(b) or § 707(b) attribution rules are used for this purpose.

4. None of the businesses are "specified services" businesses.

5. The businesses to be aggregated must satisfy two of the following three factors:

   • They must provide products or services that are the same or customarily offered together.

   • They must share facilities or significant centralized business elements, such as personnel, accounting, legal, manufacturing, purchasing, human resources, or information technology resources.

   • The businesses are operated in coordination with, or reliance upon, one or more of the businesses in the aggregated group.

Aggregation can be done by either an owner or an RPE.[54] If an RPE chooses to aggregate, the owners of the RPE are bound by that aggregation.[55] If an RPE does not aggregate, the RPE owners need not aggregate in the same manner. As a result, one owner may choose to aggregate that business with another business while a second owner may not choose to do so.

Aggregation is optional and generally cannot be changed once businesses are aggregated.[56] An individual (or RPE) may add a newly created (or acquired) business to the aggregation provided all of the requirements (above) are met.[57] If, in a subsequent year, there is a change in facts and circumstances indicating that a prior aggregation is no longer allowed, the aggregation is terminated and the taxpayer must reapply the aggregation rules to see if aggregation is allowed.

If businesses are aggregated, the taxpayer determines his or her share of qualified business income, W–2 wages, and property basis for the aggregated businesses before computing the QBI deduction.

Aggregating QTBs

EXAMPLE 34

Anita wholly owns and operates a catering business and a restaurant through separate entities. The catering business and the restaurant share centralized purchasing to obtain volume discounts and a centralized accounting office that performs all of the bookkeeping, tracks and issues statements on all of the receivables, and prepares the payroll for each business. Anita maintains a website and print advertising materials that reference both the catering business and the restaurant. She uses the restaurant kitchen to prepare food for the catering business. The catering business employs its own staff and owns equipment and trucks that are not used by the restaurant.

Because the restaurant and catering business are held in separate entities, Anita will be treated as operating each of these businesses directly. Both businesses offer prepared food to customers. The two businesses share the same kitchen facilities in addition to centralized purchasing, marketing, and accounting. As a result, Anita may choose to treat the catering business and restaurant as a single trade or business in determining her QBI deduction.

EXAMPLE 35

Assume the same facts as in the previous example. However, the catering and restaurant businesses are operated in separate partnerships with Anita, Ben, Carole, and David each owning a 25% interest in the capital and profits of each partnership. The partners are unrelated.

Because Anita, Ben, Carole, and David together own more than 50% of the capital and profits in each of the partnerships, *each* may choose to treat the catering business and the restaurant as a single trade or business in determining their QBI deduction. Further, if Anita chooses to aggregate the businesses, her decision has no effect on what Ben, Carole, and David may (independently) choose to do.

EXAMPLE 36

Wanda owns a 75% interest in Sunshine, Inc., (a clothing manufacturer operating as an S corporation) and a 75% interest in PetFriendly (a retail pet food store operating as a partnership). Wanda manages both businesses, but they operate in separate facilities, with no overlap of business operations, and do not coordinate or rely on each other.

As a result, Wanda must treat the two businesses separately for purposes of determining the QBI deduction.

---

[54]Reg. §1.199A–4(b)(2).

[55]Reg. §1.199A–4(b)(2)(ii).

[56]Reg. § 1.199A–4(a). According to Reg. §§ 1.199A–4(c)(2) and (4), if aggregation occurs, an individual must attach a statement to his or her income tax return *each year* identifying each aggregated trade or business (an RPE must attach this statement to each owner's Schedule K–1). Failure to disclose this information may result in the IRS not permitting the aggregation.

[57]Reg. §§ 1.199A–4(c)(1) and (3).

Here is a key point: The owner does *not* have to own more than 50 percent of each business directly; rather, he or she must simply establish that a group of persons owns 50 percent or more of all of the entities the owner wants to aggregate.

Frank owns a 75% interest and Geoff owns a 5% interest in each of five partnerships. Helen owns a 10% interest in only two of the partnerships. Each partnership operates a restaurant, each restaurant is a trade or business, and there is centralized management across the restaurants (Geoff is the executive chef of all of the restaurants, and he creates the menus and orders all of the food and related supplies).

Frank may choose to aggregate all five partnerships. Geoff may do the same even though he only owns a 5% interest in each partnership (Geoff can show that Frank owns 50% or more of each of the partnerships; as a result, they are "commonly controlled"). Helen may only aggregate the two partnerships in which she has an interest.

In order to include a business within an aggregated group, the activity must rise to the level of a trade or business under § 162.

Jennifer owns a majority interest in a sailboat racing team; she also owns an interest in JB Marina (a partnership that operates a marina). JB Marina is a trade or business under § 162, but the operations of the sailboat racing team are not sufficient to establish a trade or business under § 162.

As a result, Jennifer has only one trade or business for purposes of § 199A and cannot aggregate her interest in the sailboat racing team with her interest in JB Marina.

2-3i Treatment of Losses

If a taxpayer has a qualified business loss in one year, no QBI deduction is allowed, and the loss is carried over to the next year to reduce QBI (but not below zero).[58] Further, the statute indicates that if a taxpayer has more than one QTB and the net results of all businesses create a loss, the net loss is carried forward to the following year. Here is an example from the TCJA of 2017 Conference Report.

A taxpayer has QBI of $20,000 from qualified business A and a qualified business loss of $50,000 from qualified business B in 2018. The taxpayer is not permitted a deduction for year 1 and has a carryover qualified business loss of $30,000 to 2019.

In 2019, the taxpayer has QBI of $20,000 from qualified business A and QBI of $50,000 from qualified business B. To determine the deduction for 2019, the taxpayer reduces the 20% deductible amount determined for the QBI of $70,000 from qualified businesses A and B by 20% of the $30,000 carryover qualified business loss.

The result is that the taxpayer has a QBI deduction in 2019 of $8,000 [($20,000 + $50,000) − $30,000 = $40,000 × 20% = $8,000].

The statute and Conference Report provided no guidance, however, on what happens when there is a loss from one QTB and net income from another QTB that nets to a *positive amount*. Fortunately, the § 199A Regulations provide the guidance needed.[59] The Regulations begin by restating the general rule of § 199A(c)(2): if the net amount of all positive and negative QBI is a loss, no § 199A deduction is allowed in the current year and the net loss is carried forward to the next year. The Regulations also indicate that the § 199A loss limitation has no effect on the availability of the loss for other purposes (e.g., reducing taxable income and/or creating a net operating loss). The Regulations make clear, however, that no W–2 wages or capital investment amounts carry forward—only the loss.

---

[58]§ 199A(c)(2).   [59]Reg. § 1.199A–1(d)(iii).

Where a taxpayer's netting of all positive and negative QBI is positive, and at least one business produces negative QBI, an "adjusted QBI" is determined by allocating the negative QBI among all of the businesses that produce QBI in proportion to their respective amounts of QBI. Only *after* this allocation and netting takes place are the W–2 wages and capital investment limitations applied, and no part of the W–2 wages or capital investment amounts related to the loss business are used by the businesses with positive QBI.[60] By requiring the allocation of the loss across all of the businesses that generate QBI, the § 199A Regulations prevent taxpayers from selectively allocating the loss to businesses that will have limited (or no) QBI deduction (e.g., taxpayers above the threshold amount with businesses that pay no W–2 wages).

Multiple Businesses and Negative QBI

EXAMPLE 40

Erica, who is single, operates three sole proprietorships that generate the following information in 2019 (none are "specified services" businesses):

Business	QBI	W–2 Wages	Capital Investment
A	$200,000	$60,000	$ –0–
B	100,000	–0–	–0–
C	20,000	40,000	–0–

Erica chooses not to aggregate the businesses. She also earns $250,000 of wages from an unrelated business, and her modified taxable income (before any QBI deduction) is $520,000.

Because Erica's taxable income is above the threshold amount, her QBI deduction is subject to the W–2 Wages/Capital Investment limitations. These limitations must be applied on a business-by-business basis. None of the businesses own "qualified property." As a result, only the "W–2 Wages" limitation applies.

Because QBI from each business is positive, Erica applies the limitation by determining the lesser of 20% of QBI and 50% of W–2 wages for each business.

Business	QBI × 20%	W–2 Wages × 50%	Lesser
A	$40,000	$30,000	$30,000
B	20,000	–0–	–0–
C	4,000	20,000	4,000

Erica's "combined qualified business income amount" is $34,000 ($30,000 + $0 + $4,000). Since this amount is less than 20% of Erica's modified taxable income ($84,000; $420,000 × 20%), Erica's QBI deduction is $34,000 and her taxable income is $486,000.

EXAMPLE 41

Assume the same facts as in Example 40, except that Business C generates a loss that results in ($90,000) of negative QBI.

Business	QBI	W–2 Wages	Capital Investment
A	$200,000	$60,000	$ –0–
B	100,000	–0–	–0–
C	(90,000)	40,000	–0–

Erica chooses not to aggregate the businesses. Erica also earns $250,000 of wages from an unrelated business, and her modified taxable income (before any QBI deduction) is $410,000.

Absent the rules provided by the § 199A Regulations, Erica would allocate the Business C negative QBI to Business B. Why? Since Erica's income is over the threshold amount and Business B pays no wages, Business B will not generate a QBI deduction. By offsetting the Business C negative QBI against Business B's positive QBI, Erica maximizes her QBI deduction on Business A.

continued

---

[60]Reg. § 1.199A–1(d)(iii)(A).

However, under the § 199A Regulations, Erica is not allowed to choose where to allocate Business C's negative QBI. Erica must allocate Business C's negative QBI to Business A and Business B in proportion to their positive QBI amounts ($200,000 for Business A and $100,000 for Business B). As a result, the negative QBI from Business C is apportioned 66.66% to Business A and 33.33% to Business B. So ($60,000) is apportioned to Business A and ($30,000) to Business B.

Business	Adjusted QBI	W–2 Wages	Capital Investment
A	$140,000 ($200,000 − $60,000)	$60,000	$ –0–
B	$70,000 ($100,000 − $30,000)	–0–	–0–
C	$–0– [($90,000) + $90,000]	40,000	–0–

Erica now applies the "W–2 Wages" limitation by determining the lesser of 20% of QBI and 50% of W–2 wages for each business.

Business	QBI × 20%	W–2 Wages × 50%	Lesser
A	$28,000 ($140,000 × 20%)	$30,000	$28,000
B	$14,000 ($70,000 × 20%)	–0–	–0–
C	$ –0–	20,000	–0–

Erica's "combined qualified business income amount" is $28,000 ($28,000 + $0 + $0). Since this amount is less than 20% of Erica's modified taxable income ($82,000; $410,000 × 20%), her QBI deduction is $28,000, and her taxable income is $382,000. There is no carryover of any loss into the following taxable year for purposes of § 199A (the Business C negative QBI was completely used).

EXAMPLE 42

Assume the same facts as in Example 41, except that Businesses A, B, and C meet the aggregation requirements of Reg. § 1.199A–4, and Erica chooses to aggregate the three businesses.

Because Erica's taxable income is above the threshold amount, her QBI deduction is subject to the W–2 wages and capital investment limitations. Because the businesses are aggregated, these limitations are applied on an *aggregated* basis.

Business	QBI	W–2 Wages	Capital Investment
A	$200,000	$ 60,000	$ –0–
B	100,000	–0–	–0–
C	(90,000)	40,000	–0–
Total	$210,000	$100,000	$ –0–

None of the businesses own "qualified property." As a result, only the "W–2 Wages" limitation applies. Erica's "combined qualified income amount" is $42,000, the lesser of 20% of the QBI from the aggregated businesses ($42,000; $210,000 × 20%), or 50% of W–2 wages from the aggregated businesses ($50,000; $100,000 × 50%).

Erica then applies the overall limitation, comparing her "combined qualified income amount" ($42,000) to 20% of her modified taxable income ($82,000; $410,000 × 20%). Erica's QBI deduction is $42,000 (the lesser of $42,000 or $82,000).

Note that by aggregating her businesses, Erica has increased the amount of her QBI deduction.

2-3j Coordination with Other Rules

The deduction for qualified business income operates along with other rules (e.g., how to determine business income). In other cases, Congress specified the treatment. For example, § 199A(f)(3) provides that the QBI deduction is allowed only for *income* taxes. As a result, the QBI deduction does not reduce the tax bases for self-employment taxes or the net investment income tax (NIIT).

Also, in computing an individual's alternative minimum taxable income (AMTI), qualified business income is not changed by any of the AMT's preferences or adjustments (like depreciation) that usually apply in determining AMTI.[61]

---

[61]For an explanation of alternative minimum tax, see Chapter 12 of South-Western Federal Taxation, *Individual Income Taxes.*

2-3k **Considerations for Partnerships and S Corporations**

The deduction for qualified business income applies to taxpayers other than corporations. As a result, the QBI deduction is available to individuals, trusts, and estates. As explained earlier, C corporations received a tax benefit via the reduction in income tax rates to 21 percent.

Although the earlier examples involved sole proprietors, the same result would occur if the business income was instead generated by a partnership or an S corporation. These entities will need to report information to their owners (on the Schedule K–1) to enable the owners to compute their QBI deduction. The QBI deduction will vary among owners even if they share equally in the net earnings of the partnership or S corporation because the taxable income of owners will vary.

EXAMPLE
43

AB Partnership operates an accounting practice and is equally owned by two CPAs, Amy and Barbara. In 2019, partnership income is $340,000 and no guaranteed payments are made to the partners. Both Amy and Barbara are married and file jointly with their spouses. Amy's spouse has wage income of $80,000, and Barbara's spouse has wage income of $300,000. Assume that each couple has other income equal to their standard deduction amount.

The CPA practice is a "specified services" trade or business. Limitations on the QBI deduction will apply if the taxpayer's taxable income exceeds $321,400 if married filing jointly, and no deduction will be available if the couple's taxable income exceeds $421,400.

Amy and her spouse have taxable income of $250,000 ($170,000 partnership income + $80,000 of wage income). They may claim a QBI deduction. In contrast, Barbara and her spouse have taxable income of $470,000 ($170,000 partnership income + $300,000 of wage income). This couple may *not* claim a QBI deduction.

Unlike sole proprietors, partnerships and S corporations might use a tax year other than a calendar year. Because the QBI deduction is claimed by the individual owner rather than the entity, the information needed for the owner to compute the QBI deduction on his or her calendar year tax return follows the same protocol as all other entity items reported on the Schedule K–1 (see text Section 10-2g).

EXAMPLE
44

Grover Partnership is owned by two individuals and a C corporation. The individuals, James and Sarah, each own 20%, and Elmer, Inc., owns 60%. Elmer uses a June 30 fiscal year, which also requires Grover to use a June 30 fiscal year (because Elmer is the majority interest partner).

When James and Sarah received their Schedule K–1s from Grover for the partnership ended June 30, 2018, all of the information was reported on their 2018 tax returns. And all of this information was included in the calculation of their 2018 QBI deduction even though this partnership information includes six months of activity from 2017 before the QBI deduction was effective.

The QBI deduction is in effect for 2018 through 2025 (eight years). Assuming that there is no change in the tax year of Grover Partnership and James and Sarah remain partners, they will obtain eight years of QBI deductions consisting of information from the partnership years ending in 2018 through 2025. They will not receive a QBI deduction for Grover's activity for the year ended June 30, 2026, even though it includes six months of 2025.

2-3l **Other Items in the § 199A Regulations**

Employee Turned Independent Contractor

The § 199A Regulations indicate that the status of an individual as an employee or independent contractor is determined by common law and statutory rules.[62] However, under the Regulations, an individual who was an employee of an employer and becomes an independent contractor while providing substantially the same services (either directly or indirectly through another entity) is presumed, for a three-year period, still to be an employee.[63] This presumption may be overturned if it can be demonstrated—using common law and statutory rules—that the individual is *not* an employee.

---

[62]See, for example, Rev.Rul. 87–41 (1987–1 C.B. 296) and Reg. §§ 31.3121(d)–1, 31.3306(i)–1, and 31.3401(c)–1.

[63]Reg. § 1.199A–5(d)(3).

EXAMPLE
45

Corbin is an attorney employed as an associate with LegalEagles LLP (LE). Corbin and the other associates in LE have taxable income below the threshold amount. LE terminates its employment relationship with Corbin and its other associates, allowing Corbin and the other former associates to form a new partnership, LegalBeagles LLP (LB). LB then contracts to perform services to LE. Corbin continues to provide substantially the same services to LE and its clients through LB.

The goal, obviously, is for Corbin (and the other associates) to convert wage income into pass-through income from LB that is eligible for the QBI deduction (even though LB is a "specified services" business, Corbin is below the taxable income threshold).

Because Corbin was formerly an employee of LE and continues to provide substantially the same services to LE, Corbin is presumed to be an employee of LE. Unless the presumption is rebutted, Corbin's distributive share of income from LB will be treated like wages for purposes of § 199A for a period of three years, and will not be treated as qualified business income.

What if LB, instead, provides contractual services to a *different* law firm? Now the QBI deduction is available (again assuming that Corbin is below the taxable income threshold).

Determination of "W–2 Wages"

In general, the term *W–2 wages* includes the total amount of wages [as defined in § 3401(a)] plus the total amount of elective compensation deferrals (under § 457) plus the amount of designated Roth contributions (§ 402A).[64]

A business can take into account any W–2 wages paid by another business provided that the W–2 wages were paid to "common law employees or officers" of that business.[65] This means that a business using a professional employer organization (PEO) to manage parts of its business (e.g., human resources) or to lease employees can use an allocable portion of the PEO's W–2 wages in determining its total W–2 wages. Of course, this also means that the business that actually paid and reported the W–2 wages must reduce its § 199A wages by the same amount.

Determination of Unadjusted Basis Immediately After Acquisition (UBIA)

For purchased or produced property, UBIA generally will be the property's cost (under § 1012) when the property is placed in service. An addition or improvement to qualified property already placed in service is treated as *separate qualified property* on the date the addition or improvement is placed in service.[66] For purposes of the QBI deduction, property is not qualified property if it is acquired within 60 days of the end of the tax year and disposed of within 120 days without having been used in a trade or business for at least 45 days prior to disposition, unless the taxpayer demonstrates that the principal purpose of the acquisition and disposition was a purpose other than increasing the QBI deduction.[67]

2-4 TAX PLANNING

LO.5

List and evaluate tax planning ideas for choice of entity and the deduction for qualified business income.

2-4a Corporate versus Noncorporate Forms of Business Organization

The form of business organization is an important tax planning consideration. It affects the application of various tax rules including tax rates, deductions, tax accounting methods, and tax years. The decision on what form to use can change as a business grows. For example, in the early years of a business (when it is more likely to generate losses), a pass-through entity is usually desired so that individual owners can utilize the losses

---

[64]Reg. § 1.199A–2(b)(2).

[65]Reg. § 1.199A–2(b)(2)(ii).

[66]Reg. § 1.199A–2(c)(1)(ii).

[67]Reg. § 1.199A–2(c)(1)(iv). Notice 2018–84 (2018–34 I.R.B. 347) and Rev.Proc. 2019–11 (2019–9 I.R.B. 742) provide detailed guidance about calculating "W–2 wages" for purposes of the QBI deduction.

generated by the business. If instead the entity was a C corporation from the beginning, it would not be able to use the losses until later years when it generates taxable income.

See text Section 3-4a and Chapter 13 for additional information on the differences between business forms and planning considerations.

2-4b Optimizing the Deduction for Qualified Business Income

As noted in a few of the QBI deduction examples, some planning is possible to increase the deduction or perhaps to avoid losing the deduction.

- For taxpayers with taxable income above the thresholds ($321,400 if married filing jointly and $160,700 for other taxpayers in 2019), consider converting any contractor payments to employee wages to increase the 50 percent of W–2 wages limitation.

- For a married couple who does not reside in a community property state and has "specified services" business income above the thresholds that allow a QBI deduction, determine whether it might be better to file separate tax returns, enabling the spouse with QBI to qualify for the QBI deduction.

- Given the § 199A Regulations, consider how businesses can be combined or separated, including perhaps placing one or more in separate legal entities, to increase the QBI deduction.

- Employees might consider whether they can become self-employed in their field (which would enable the QBI deduction). As part of this consideration, the employee will need to consider whether it is possible to generate greater income tax savings via the QBI deduction (and other business deductions). Also important will be considering the effect of self-employment taxes and the need to provide health insurance and other benefits, as well as potentially incurring additional business expenses.

REFOCUS ON THE BIG PICTURE

ENTREPRENEURIAL PURSUITS

The simplest entity for Amy to use is a sole proprietorship. If she generates losses, they can be used to offset other income she might have (e.g., if she also takes on a part-time job until her businesses generate sufficient income to enable Amy to support herself).

If the risks for her business, such as injury to customers, are minimal, she will likely find that forming an LLC or a corporation to reduce her personal risk is not warranted. The additional formation costs, continuing fees, and possible business taxes she might owe in her state of residence can be avoided. And Amy can purchase insurance to reduce the costs of any personal risk.

If Amy wants a more formal structure or a legal structure to reduce her personal risk, an S corporation should work well since it allows her income and losses to flow through to her individual tax return. As Amy's income grows, she might consider converting to a C corporation due to the 21 percent maximum rate, although she must also consider the effect of double taxation.

Amy must also consider the QBI deduction (assuming that she does not operate as a C corporation). Until her income reaches the thresholds for the specified service trade or business, she should obtain a deduction even though both of her pursuits might be a "specified services" business (i.e., consulting or where the principal business asset is Amy's reputation or skill).

Finally, Amy should consider state and local taxes. She will need to check these laws to determine, for example, if a business license tax is owed at the local level and if she is considered to have one business or two.

Key Terms

C corporations, 2-3

Check-the-box Regulations, 2-8

Deduction for qualified business income, 2-10

Disregarded entity, 2-8

Limited liability company (LLC), 2-7

Limited partnerships, 2-7

QBI deduction, 2-10

Qualified business income, 2-11

Qualified trade or business, 2-11

Regular corporations, 2-3

S corporations, 2-3

Specified service trade or business, 2-18

W–2 Wages/Capital Investment Limit, 2-14

Discussion Questions

1. **LO.1** Jennifer and Jamie are starting a business and have asked you for advice about whether they should form a partnership, a corporation, or some other type of entity. Prepare a list of questions you would ask in helping them decide which type of entity they should choose. Explain your reasons for asking each of the questions.

2. **LO.1** Barbara owns 40% of the stock of Cassowary Corporation (a C corporation) and 40% of the stock of Emu Corporation (an S corporation). In the current year, each corporation has operating income of $120,000 and tax-exempt interest income of $8,000. Neither corporation pays any dividends during the year. Discuss how this information will be reported by the corporations and Barbara for the year.

3. **LO.1, 5** Art, an executive with Azure Corporation, plans to start a part-time business selling products on the internet. He will devote about 15 hours each week to running the business. Art's salary from Azure places him in the 35% tax bracket. He projects substantial losses from the new business in each of the first three years and expects sizable profits thereafter. Art plans to leave the profits in the business for several years, sell the business, and then retire. Would you advise Art to incorporate the business or operate it as a sole proprietorship? Why?

4. **LO.1** Can a sole proprietor form as a single member limited liability company (LLC)? If so, how would such an LLC be taxed?

5. **LO.1** In the current year, Juanita and Joseph form a two-member LLC and do not file Form 8832 (Entity Classification Election). As a result, the LLC will be treated as a partnership for Federal income tax purposes. Assess the validity of this statement.

6. **LO.2** Why did the TCJA of 2017 include a deduction for qualified business income?

7. **LO.3, 4** Who can claim the qualified business income (QBI) deduction?

8. **LO.3, 4** What are the general rules surrounding the QBI deduction? How is it computed?

9. **LO.3, 4** Define each of the following terms, and explain how each is used in determining the QBI deduction.
   a. Modified taxable income.
   b. Qualified business income.
   c. Qualified trade or business.
   d. "Specified services" business.

10. **LO.3, 4, 5** Jane and Ben are married and usually file a joint return. They live in a separate property state (rather than a community property state). Jane is a partner in a law firm and typically generates income of $158,000. Ben is a grade school teacher with wage income of $75,000. The couple has investment income that

is less than their standard deduction. With enactment of the deduction for qualified business income, the couple is wondering if they should continue to file as married filing jointly or instead use the married filing separately status. Why do they wonder this, and what advice would you offer them and why?

11. **LO.3** Which of the following taxpayers may claim a deduction for qualified business income?

   a.   A driver for Uber or Lyft.
   b.   A veterinarian operating as an S corporation. In addition to veterinary services, revenues are also derived from the sale of pet food and supplies and from the boarding of animals.
   c.   A CPA operating as an LLC taxed as a sole proprietorship. The CPA is single and has taxable income of $150,000.
   d.   Same as part (c), except that the CPA has taxable income of $200,000.
   e.   A real estate salesperson.
   f.   A pet sitter/dog walker.
   g.   A sole proprietor software developer.
   h.   An individual wage earner who derives $60,000 of rental income from a duplex she owns.

12. **LO.3, 4** Identify the requirements that must be met in order to aggregate businesses for purposes of the QBI deduction.

13. **LO.3, 4** Paul wholly owns and operates an office supplies business and a printing/shipping business through separate entities. The office supplies business and printing/shipping business share centralized purchasing to obtain volume discounts and also share a centralized accounting office that performs all necessary accounting for both businesses (including preparing financial statements, paying bills, collecting receivables, and preparing payrolls for both businesses). Paul maintains a website that promotes both businesses. The businesses operate in separate spaces in the same building (next to each other) but share an office and a shipping/receiving space at the rear of the building and an opening in the shared inside wall that allows customers to move between the businesses without going outside. Each business owns its own equipment and employs its own staff. May Paul aggregate these businesses for purposes of the QBI deduction? Explain.

14. **LO.2,4** Why do you think the QBI deduction is limited to earnings from a business conducted in the United States and doesn't also include business income from a foreign business activity?

Computational Exercises

15. **LO.3, 4** In 2019, Meghann Carlson, a single taxpayer, has QBI of $110,000 and modified taxable income of $78,000 (this is also her taxable income before the QBI deduction). Given this information, what is Meghann's QBI deduction?

16. **LO.3,4** Charlotte is a partner in, and sales manager for, CD Partners, a domestic business that is not a "specified services" business. During the tax year, she receives guaranteed payments of $250,000 from CD Partners for her services to the partnership as its sales manager. In addition, her distributive share of CD Partners' ordinary income (its only item of income or loss) was $175,000. What is Charlotte's qualified business income?

17. **LO.3, 4** Robert is the sole shareholder and CEO of ABC, Inc., an S corporation that is a qualified trade or business. During the current year, ABC has net income of $325,000 after deducting Robert's $100,000 salary. In addition to his compensation, ABC pays Robert dividends of $250,000.

    a. What is Robert's qualified business income?

    b. Would your answer to part (a) change if you determined that reasonable compensation for someone with Robert's experience and responsibilities is $200,000? Why or why not?

18. **LO.3, 4** Maria and Javier are the equal partners in MarJa, a partnership that is a qualfied trade or business. In the current year, MarJa had $350,000 of ordinary income after reporting $500,000 in guaranteed payments to Maria and Javier for their services to MarJa ($250,000 each).

    a. What is Maria's and Javier's qualified business income?

    b. How would your answer to part (a) change if MarJa had $550,000 of ordinary income after reporting $300,000 in guaranteed payments to Maria and Javier ($150,000 each)?

19. **LO.3, 4** Thad, a single taxpayer, has taxable income before the QBI deduction of $190,700. Thad, a CPA, operates an accounting practice as a single member LLC (which he reports as a sole proprietorship). During 2019, his proprietorship generates qualified business income of $150,000, W–2 wages of $125,000, and $10,000 of qualified property. What is Thad's qualified business income deduction?

20. **LO.3, 4** Jason and Paula are married. They file a joint return for 2019 on which they report taxable income before the QBI deduction of $200,000. Jason operates a sole proprietorship, and Paula is a partner in the PQRS Partnership. Both are a qualified trade or business, and neither is a "specified services" business. Jason's sole proprietorship generates $150,000 of qualified business income and W–2 wages of $45,000 and has qualified property of $50,000. Paula's partnership reports a loss for the year, and her allocable share of the loss is $40,000. The partnership reports no W–2 wages, and Paula's share of the partnership's qualified property is $20,000. What is their QBI deduction for the year?

21. **LO.3, 4** Henry, a freelance driver, finds passengers using various platforms such as Uber and Grubhub. He is single and has no other sources of income. In 2019, Henry's qualified business income from driving is $61,200. Compute Henry's QBI deduction and his tax liability.

Problems

22. **LO.1** Ellie and Linda are equal owners in Otter Enterprises, a calendar year business. During the current year, Otter Enterprises has $320,000 of gross income and $210,000 of operating expenses. In addition, Otter has a long-term capital gain of $15,000 and makes distributions to Ellie and Linda of $25,000 each. Discuss the impact of this information on the taxable income of Otter, Ellie, and Linda if Otter is:

    a. A partnership.

    b. An S corporation.

    c. A C corporation.

23. **LO.1** Purple Company has $200,000 in net income for 2019 before deducting any compensation or other payment to its sole owner, Kirsten. Kirsten is single, and she claims the $12,200 standard deduction for 2019. Purple Company is Kirsten's only source of income. Ignoring any employment tax considerations, compute Kirsten's after-tax income if:

a. Purple Company is a proprietorship and Kirsten withdraws $50,000 from the business during the year; Kirsten claims a $37,560 deduction for qualified business income.

b. Purple Company is a C corporation and the corporation pays out all of its after-tax income as a dividend to Kirsten.

c. Purple Company is a C corporation and the corporation pays Kirsten a salary of $158,000.

24. **LO.3, 4** Shelly has $200,000 of QBI from her local jewelry store (a sole proprietorship). Shelly's proprietorship paid $30,000 in W–2 wages and has $20,000 of qualified property. Shelly's spouse earned $74,400 of wages as an employee, they earned $20,000 of interest income during the year, and they will be filing jointly and using the standard deduction. What is their QBI deduction for 2019?

25. **LO.3, 4** Peter Samuels owns and manages his single member LLC that provides a wide variety of financial services to his clients. He is married and will file a joint tax return with his spouse, Amy. His LLC reports $300,000 of qualified business income, W–2 wages of $120,000, and assets with an unadjusted basis of $75,000. Their taxable income before the QBI deduction is $285,000 (this is also their modified taxable income). Determine their QBI deduction for 2019.

26. **LO.3, 4** Ashley (a single taxpayer) is the owner of ABC LLC. The LLC (which reports as a sole proprietorship) generates QBI of $900,000 and is not a "specified services" business. ABC paid total W–2 wages of $300,000, and the total unadjusted basis of property held by ABC is $30,000. Ashley's taxable income before the QBI deduction is $740,000 (this is also her modified taxable income). What is Ashley's QBI deduction for 2019?

27. **LO.3, 4** Donald (a married taxpayer filing jointly) owns a wide variety of commercial rental properties held in a single member LLC. Donald's LLC reports rental income of $1.5 million. The LLC pays no W–2 wages; rather, it pays a management fee to an S corporation Donald controls. The management company pays W–2 wages but reports no income (or loss). Donald's total unadjusted basis of the commercial rental property is $10 million. Donald's taxable income before the QBI deduction (and his modified taxable income) is $2 million. What is Donald's QBI deduction for 2019?

28. **LO.3, 4** Scott and Laura are married and will file a joint tax return. Laura has a sole proprietorship (not a "specified services" business) that generates qualified business income of $300,000. The proprietorship pays W–2 wages of $40,000 and holds property with an unadjusted basis of $10,000. Scott is employed by a local school district. Their taxable income before the QBI deduction is $381,400 (this is also their modified taxable income). Determine their QBI deduction for 2019.

29. **LO.3, 4** Stella Watters is a CPA and operates her own accounting firm (Watters CPA LLC). As a single member LLC, Stella reports her accounting firm operations as a sole proprietor. Stella has QBI from her accounting firm of $540,000, she reports W–2 wages of $156,000, and the unadjusted basis of property used in the LLC is $425,000. Stella is married and will file a joint tax return with her spouse. Their taxable income before the QBI deduction is $475,000, and their modified taxable income is $448,000. Determine Stella's QBI deduction for 2019.

30. **LO.3, 4** Ben and Molly are married and will file jointly. Ben generates $300,000 of qualified business income from his single member LLC (a law firm). He reports his business as a sole proprietorship. Wages paid by the law firm amount to $40,000; the law firm has no significant property. Molly is employed as a tax manager by a local CPA firm. Their modified taxable income is $381,400 (this is also their taxable income before the deduction for qualified business income). Determine their QBI deduction for 2019.

31. **LO.3, 4** Tammy, a single taxpayer, has a part-time job at BigCo, a company in which she has no ownership interest. In addition, she owns and operates LittleCo, a sole proprietorship that is a qualified trade or business. Tammy is paid wages of $40,000 by BigCo and has $100,000 in qualified business income from LittleCo. She has no other items of income or loss and $25,000 of itemized deductions. What is her qualified business income deduction for 2019?

32. **LO.3, 4** Assume the same facts as in Problem 31, except that Tammy does not have a part-time job at BigCo. How does this affect her qualified business income deduction?

33. **LO.3, 4** Susan, a single taxpayer, owns and operates a bakery (as a sole proprietorship). The business is *not* a "specified services" business. In 2019, the business pays $100,000 in W–2 wages, has $150,000 of qualified property, and generates $350,000 of qualified business income. Susan has no other items of income or loss and will take the standard deduction. What is Susan's qualified business income deduction?

34. **LO.3, 4** Assume the same facts as in Problem 33, except that Susan's business generates $150,000 of qualified business income. What is Susan's QBI deduction?

35. **LO.3, 4** Assume the same facts as in Problem 33, except that Susan's business pays $60,000 of W–2 wages and generates $200,000 of qualified business income. Susan also has a part-time job earning wages of $11,000 and receives $3,200 of interest income. What is Susan's QBI deduction?

36. **LO.3, 4** Jennifer is a CPA and a single taxpayer using the standard deduction. In 2019, her CPA practice generates qualified business income of $162,200 and she has no other income or losses. Jennifer's taxable income before the QBI deduction is $150,000 ($162,200 – $12,200 standard deduction). Jennifer employs an administrative assistant in her practice and pays him $75,000 in wages. The unadjusted basis of depreciable assets employed in the practice total $30,000.
    a.   What is Jennifer's qualified business income deduction?
    b.   Determine Jennifer's qualified business income deduction if her CPA practice generates qualified business income of $312,200.

37. **LO.3, 4** Elliot operates his clothing store as a single member LLC (which he reports as a sole proprietorship). In 2019, his proprietorship generates qualified business income of $280,000, he pays W–2 wages of $170,000, and he has qualified business property of $140,000. Elliot's wife, Julie, is an attorney who works for a local law firm and receives wages of $90,000. They will file a joint tax return and use the standard deduction. What is Elliot's qualified business income deduction?

38. **LO.3, 4** Assume the same facts as in Problem 37, except that the business is a "specified services" business (e.g., a consulting firm) owned equally by Elliot and Conrad (an unrelated individual) in a two-member LLC. Assume that each member's share of qualified business income, W–2 wages, and qualified business property is one-half of the information provided in Problem 37. Conrad's wife, Rachel, earned wages during the year of $350,000, and Conrad and Rachel have itemized deductions of $62,000.
    a.   What is Elliot's qualified business income deduction?
    b.   What is Conrad's qualified business income deduction?

39. **LO.4** Tristan, who is single, operates three sole proprietorships that generate the following information in 2019 (none are "specified services" businesses).

Business	QBI	W–2 Wages	Capital Investment
A	$300,000	$90,000	$ –0–
B	(135,000)	60,000	–0–
C	150,000	–0–	–0–

Tristan chooses not to aggregate the businesses. She also earns $150,000 of wages from an unrelated business, and her modified taxable income (before any QBI deduction) is $380,000.

a. What is Tristan's QBI deduction?

b. Assume that Tristan can aggregate these businesses. Determine her QBI deduction if she decides to aggregate the businesses.

Research Problems

Note: Solutions to the Research Problems can be prepared by using the Thomson Reuters Checkpoint™ online tax research database, which accompanies this textbook. Solutions can also be prepared by using research materials found in a typical tax library.

THOMSON REUTERS
CHECKPOINT™

Research Problem 1. A client has asked you for guidance on selecting the best type of entity for her new business. Using the internet as your sole research source, prepare an outline detailing the advantages and disadvantages of the entity forms available to a sole owner. Include both tax and nontax issues in your analysis.

Research Problem 2. Starting with the website for the Secretary of State's office in your state, find out how to create an LLC and whether your state has any restrictions on the type of business or size. Present your findings using slides suitable for a presentation to your classmates.

Research Problem 3. The deduction for qualified business income received considerable praise and criticism in the press from the time it was introduced in November 2017 to the present. Find reliable articles that explain at least two arguments for and against the QBI deduction. Explain whether you agree with these positions and why.

Research Problem 4. Some states automatically conform to any Federal tax changes, but others require special legislation to conform. Generally, states do not conform to rate changes because state income tax systems have their own rate structure (generally at rates well below the Federal tax rates). Find out if your state conformed to the deduction for qualified business income. Explain why the state did or did not conform. Do you agree? Explain.

Becker CPA Review Questions

1. Which of the following is considered a specified service trade or business (SSTB) for purposes of the qualifying business income deduction?

    a. Accounting firm

    b. Manufacturing company

    c. Engineering firm

    d. Architectural services

BECKER
PROFESSIONAL EDUCATION®

2. What is the basic deduction calculation for the qualifying business income deduction?

    a. 30% × Qualifying business income (QBI)

    b. 20% × W–2 wages

    c. 20% × Qualifying business income (QBI)

    d. 30% × W–2 wages

3. Which of the following statements is true regarding taxpayers with taxable income below the taxable income limitations for the qualifying business income (QBI) deduction?

   a. QBI deduction is only allowed if a qualified trade or business (QTB).

   b. QBI deduction is a phased-out deduction if a specified service trade or business (SSTB).

   c. QBI deduction is limited to 50 percent of W–2 wages.

   d. A qualified trade or business (QTB) and specified trade or business (SSTB) are treated the same.

4. Which of the following is true about the qualifying business income (QBI) deduction for taxpayers with taxable income above the taxable income limitations?

   a. If the taxpayer is a specified service trade or business (SSTB), no QBI deduction is allowed.

   b. If the taxpayer is a qualified trade or business (QTB), W–2 wage and property limitations do not apply.

   c. If the taxpayer is a qualified trade or business (QTB), W–2 wage and property limitations are phased in.

   d. If the taxpayer is a specified service trade or business (SSTB), W–2 wage and property limitations apply.

5. Which of the following is the overall limitation to the qualifying business income (QBI) deduction?

   a. Lesser of: 50 percent of combined QBI or 20 percent of the taxpayer's taxable income in excess of net capital gain

   b. Lesser of: combined QBI or 20 percent of the taxpayer's taxable income in excess of net capital gain

   c. Lesser of: 50 percent of W–2 wages or 25 percent of W–2 wages plus 2.5 percent of the unadjusted basis of qualified property

   d. Taxable income limitations based on filing status

6. Calculate the taxpayer's qualifying business income deduction for a qualified trade or business:

   Filing status: Single
   Taxable income: $100,000
   Net capital gains: $0
   Qualified business income (QBI): $30,000
   W–2 wages: $10,000

   a. $5,000   c. $20,000

   b. $70,000   d. $6,000

7. Calculate the taxpayer's 2019 qualifying business income deduction for a qualified trade or business:

   Filing status: Single
   Taxable income: $180,000
   Net capital gains: $0
   Qualified business income (QBI): $80,000
   W–2 wages: $20,000

   a. $16,000   c. $2,700

   b. $10,000   d. $13,684

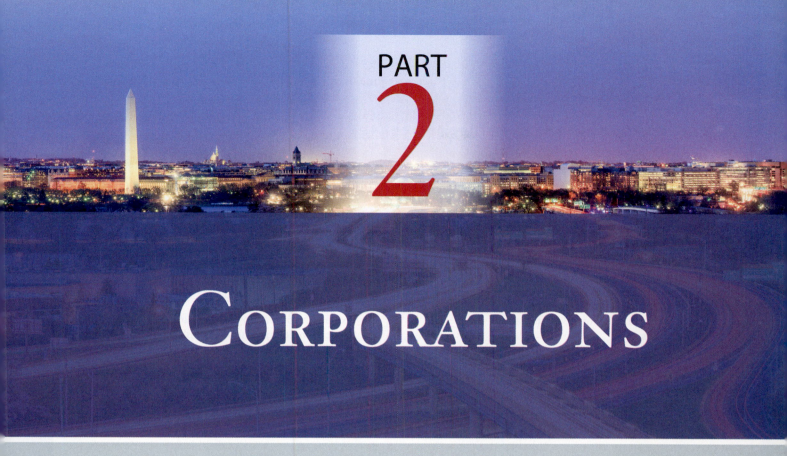

PART 2

CORPORATIONS

A business must choose the legal and tax form in which it will operate. Part 2 of this text examines the operating rules that apply to C corporations and the effects of various capital transactions on the entity and its shareholders. Part 2 also discusses the Federal income tax effects of changes in the corporation's capital structure, the taxation of corporate conglomerates, and additional rules that apply when a U.S. taxpayer does business outside the United States.

CHAPTER

3

Corporations: Introduction and Operating Rules

LEARNING OBJECTIVES: *After completing Chapter 3, you should be able to:*

LO.1 Compare the taxation of individuals and corporations.

LO.2 List and apply the tax rules unique to corporations.

LO.3 Compute the corporate income tax.

LO.4 Explain the operation of the accumulated earnings and personal holding company taxes.

LO.5 Describe and illustrate the reporting process for corporations.

LO.6 Evaluate corporations as an entity form for minimizing income taxes on businesses.

CHAPTER OUTLINE

THE BIG PICTURE

A HALF-BAKED IDEA?

Samantha Johnson owns Skylark Bakery. Currently, the bakery is operated as a sole proprietorship and generates an annual operating profit of $100,000. In addition, the bakery earns annual dividends of $5,000 from investing excess working capital in the stock of publicly traded corporations. These stock investments typically are held for a minimum of three to four months before funds are required for the business. As a result of earning income from other business ventures and investments, Samantha is in the 37 percent marginal tax rate bracket before considering bakery operations. In the past, Samantha has withdrawn $50,000 annually from the bakery, which she regards as reasonable payment for her services.

Samantha has asked you about the tax consequences of conducting the business as a regular (C) corporation. Based on the given information, what would be the annual income tax savings (or cost) of operating the bakery as a corporation? For purposes of this analysis, use the 2019 tax rates and ignore any employment tax or state tax considerations.

Read the chapter and formulate your response.

As discussed in Chapter 2, the distinctions among forms of business organizations are important. Chapter 3 begins a sequence of chapters focusing on corporations. Subchapter C of the Internal Revenue Code is devoted to the tax treatment of regular corporations (or C corporations). The chapter begins with an introduction to the income taxation of corporations, including the determination of taxable income. We then discuss calculating the tax liability of a corporation and special rules designed to prevent corporations and their shareholders from avoiding the double tax on dividend distributions. Finally, we discuss various procedural matters that a corporate taxpayer faces, including tax return filing requirements, estimated tax payments, reconciling book income to taxable income, and special disclosure schedules on the tax return.

LO.1

Compare the taxation of individuals and corporations.

3-1 AN INTRODUCTION TO THE INCOME TAXATION OF CORPORATIONS

When examining how corporations are treated under the Federal income tax, a useful approach is to compare their treatment with that applicable to individual taxpayers. In addition, tax provisions that are unique to corporations must be addressed.

3-1a An Overview of Corporate versus Individual Income Tax Treatment

The corporate and individual tax formulas appear in Exhibit 3.1, and the following discussion highlights similarities and differences between the two formulas.

Similarities

Gross income of a corporation is determined in much the same manner as it is for individuals. As a result, gross income includes compensation for services rendered, business income, gains from selling property, interest, rents, royalties, and dividends. Although both individuals and corporations are entitled to exclusions from gross income, corporate taxpayers are allowed fewer. Interest on municipal bonds and life insurance proceeds are exclusions that apply to both individual and corporate taxpayers.

EXHIBIT 3.1	Tax Formulas

Corporations	Individuals
Income (broadly conceived)	Income (broadly conceived)
(Exclusions)	(Exclusions)
Gross income	Gross income
(Deductions except for NOL and DRD)*	(Deductions *for* AGI)**
Taxable income before NOL and DRD	Adjusted gross income
(Net operating loss deduction)	(Greater of itemized or standard deductions)
(Dividends received deduction)	(Deduction for qualified business income)
Taxable income	Taxable income
Tax on taxable income	Tax on taxable income
(Tax credits)	(Tax credits)
Tax due (or refund)	Tax due (or refund)

*NOL = net operating loss; DRD = dividends received deduction.
**AGI = adjusted gross income.

Gains and losses from property transactions are handled similarly. For example, whether a gain or loss is capital or ordinary depends on the nature of the asset in the hands of the taxpayer. In defining what is *not* a capital asset, § 1221 makes no distinction between corporate and noncorporate taxpayers.

In the area of nontaxable exchanges, both corporations and individuals do not recognize gain or loss on a like-kind exchange and may defer recognized gain on an involuntary conversion. The disallowance of losses on property sales to related parties (e.g., a corporation and a more-than-50-percent shareholder) and on wash sales of securities apply to both individual and corporate taxpayers. The exclusion of gain from the sale of a personal residence does not apply to corporations.

Business deductions are allowed for both corporations and individuals. Business deductions include interest (subject to the limitations discussed in text Section 3-1f), certain taxes, losses (including casualty and theft losses), bad debts, accelerated cost recovery, charitable contributions, net operating losses, research and experimental expenditures, and some other less common deductions. In the corporate form, there is no distinction between business and nonbusiness bad debts. Like individuals, corporations are not allowed an interest expense deduction if tax-exempt securities are purchased with borrowed funds. The same holds true for entertainment expenses, expenses contrary to public policy, certain accrued expenses between related parties, and lobbying expenses.

Some of the tax credits available to individuals, such as the foreign tax credit, can also be claimed by corporations. Not available to corporations are certain credits that are personal in nature, such as the child tax credit, the credit for elderly or disabled taxpayers, and the earned income credit.

Dissimilarities

The income taxation of corporations and individuals also differs significantly. Individuals are subject to a progressive tax rate structure; a flat tax rate applies to corporations. The corporate tax rate is discussed in more detail later in the chapter (see Examples 27 and 28). Further, individuals are subject to an alternative minimum tax while the corporate AMT was repealed by the Tax Cuts and Jobs Act (TCJA) of 2017.

All allowable corporate deductions are treated as business deductions. As a result, the determination of adjusted gross income (AGI), so essential for individual taxpayers, has no relevance to corporations. Taxable income is computed simply by subtracting all allowable deductions from gross income. Itemized deductions (and the related limitations), the standard deduction, and the deduction for qualified business income do not apply to corporations. In addition, individuals are subject to a limitation on "excess business losses" (which does not apply to corporations).[1]

3-1b Specific Provisions Compared

A comparison of the income taxation of individuals and corporations appears in Concept Summary 3.2 (located at the end of text Section 3-1). Some of the key differences include:

- Accounting periods and methods.
- Capital gains and losses.
- Recapture of depreciation.
- Business interest expense limitation.
- Passive activity losses.
- Charitable contributions.
- Executive compensation.

---

[1]§ 461(l).

- Net operating losses.
- Special deductions available only to corporations.

3-1c Accounting Periods and Methods

Accounting Periods

Corporations generally have the same choices of accounting periods as do individual taxpayers. A corporation may choose a calendar year or a fiscal year for reporting purposes, but corporations normally can have different tax years from those of their shareholders. Newly formed corporations (as new taxpayers) usually can choose an accounting period (IRS consent is not needed). Personal service corporations (PSCs) and S corporations, however, are restricted in the use of a fiscal year. The rules applicable to S corporations are discussed in Chapter 12.

A PSC is a corporation:[2]

- Formed to provide "personal services" (services in the fields of health, law, engineering, architecture, accounting, actuarial science, performing arts, or consulting);
- Where the services are substantially performed by shareholder-employees; and
- Where more than 10 percent of the stock (in value) is held by shareholder-employees.

To limit deferral of income possibilities, a PSC must generally use a calendar year.[3] However, a PSC can *elect* a fiscal year under either of the following conditions:

- A business purpose (e.g., natural business cycle) for the year can be demonstrated.
- The PSC year results in a deferral of not more than three months' income. An election under § 444 is required, and the PSC's deduction for shareholder-employee salaries will be limited if payment of those salaries is disproportionately postponed beyond December 31 (§ 280H; see Example 2).

Fiscal Year Exceptions

Valdez & Vance is a professional association of public accountants that receives over 40% of its gross receipts in March and April of each year from the preparation of tax returns. Under these circumstances, the IRS might permit Valdez & Vance to use a May 1 to April 30 fiscal year because it reflects a natural business cycle (the end of the tax season).

Sentinel Corporation, a PSC, has made an election under § 444 to use a fiscal year ending September 30. For its fiscal year ending September 30, 2019, Sentinel paid Burke, its sole shareholder, $120,000 in salary. Under § 280H, Burke must receive at least $30,000 [(3 months ÷ 12 months) × $120,000] as salary during the period October 1 through December 31, 2019.

Accounting Methods

As a general rule, the cash method of accounting is unavailable to corporations.[4] However, several important exceptions apply in the case of the following types of corporations:

- S corporations.
- Corporations engaged in the trade or business of farming or timber.
- Qualified PSCs.
- Corporations with average annual gross receipts of $26 million or less for the most recent three-year period (for taxable years beginning in 2019).

---

[2]§ 448(d)(2)(A) and Reg. § 1.441–3(d)(1). Any stock held by an employee on any *one day* causes the employee to be a shareholder-employee.

[3]§ 441(i). In some cases, a PSC was able to retain the same year as its fiscal year ending in 1987. See § 444(b)(3).

[4]§ 448.

In general, entities that maintain inventory for sale to customers are required to use the accrual method of accounting for determining sales and cost of goods sold. However, for 2019, entities with average annual gross receipts of $26 million or less for the most recent three-year period can use the cash method to account for inventories.[5]

A corporation using the accrual method of accounting must observe a special rule in dealing with cash basis related parties. If the corporation has an accrual outstanding at the end of any taxable year with a related party, it cannot claim a deduction until the related party reports the amount as income.[6] This rule is most often encountered when an accrual method corporation deals with a cash method individual who owns (directly or indirectly) more than 50 percent of the corporation's stock. However, in the case of a personal service corporation, *any* shareholder-employee is treated as a related party for purposes of this limitation.

The Big Picture

EXAMPLE 3

Return to the facts of *The Big Picture* on p. 3-1. Assume that Samantha incorporates her business as Skylark Bakery, Inc., a calendar year, accrual method C corporation. Samantha, a cash method taxpayer, owns 100% of the corporation's stock at the end of 2019. On December 31, 2019, Skylark Bakery has accrued a $10,000 bonus to Samantha. Samantha receives the bonus in 2020 and reports it on her 2020 tax return. Skylark Bakery cannot claim a deduction for the $10,000 until 2020.

For tax years beginning after 2017, *accrual basis taxpayers* generally must recognize gross income no later than the tax year in which the income is included as income for financial statement purposes. In addition, accrual taxpayers can elect to defer income inclusion of advance payments for goods and services to the end of the tax year following the tax year of receipt.[7]

3-1d Capital Gains and Losses

Capital gains and losses result from the taxable sales or exchanges of capital assets.[8] These gains and losses are classified as long-term or short-term depending on the holding period. Each year, a taxpayer's short-term gains and losses are combined, and long-term gains and losses are combined. The result is a net short-term capital gain or loss and a net long-term capital gain or loss. If gains *and* losses result (e.g., net short-term capital gain and net long-term capital loss), these amounts are further netted against each other. If instead the results are *all* gains or *all* losses (e.g., net short-term capital loss and net long-term capital loss), no further combination is necessary.

Capital Gains

Individuals generally pay a preferential tax rate of 15 or 20 percent on net capital gains (i.e., excess of net long-term capital gain over net short-term capital loss).[9] Corporations, however, receive no favorable tax rate on long-term capital gains; this income is taxed at the normal corporate tax rates.

---

[5]Such an entity can account for inventory as non-incidental materials and supplies or as conforms to its financial accounting for inventories. The $26 million average annual gross receipts test was $25 million for taxable years beginning in 2018.

[6]§ 267(a)(2).

[7]This deferral applies only if the advance payment is similarly deferred for financial statement purposes. See Chapter 18 of *South-Western Federal Taxation: Individual Income Taxes* for a detailed discussion of accounting periods and methods.

[8]See Chapter 16 of *South-Western Federal Taxation: Individual Income Taxes* for a detailed discussion of capital gains and losses.

[9]A 0% rate applies to individual taxpayers with lower income levels.

Capital Losses

Net capital losses of corporate and individual taxpayers receive different income tax treatment. Generally, individual taxpayers can deduct up to $3,000 of net capital losses against other income. Any remaining capital losses are carried forward to future years until offset by capital gains or by the $3,000 annual deduction. Loss carryovers retain their identity as either long term or short term.[10]

EXAMPLE 4

Robin, an individual, incurs a net long-term capital loss of $7,500 for calendar year 2019. Assuming adequate taxable income, Robin may deduct $3,000 of this loss on her 2019 return. The remaining $4,500 ($7,500 − $3,000) of the loss is carried to 2020 and years thereafter until completely deducted. The $4,500 will be carried forward as a long-term capital loss.

Unlike individuals, corporate taxpayers are not permitted to deduct any net capital losses against ordinary income. Capital losses, therefore, can be used only as an offset against capital gains. Corporations, however, carry back net capital losses three years, applying them first to the earliest year. Carryforwards then are allowed for a period of five years from the year of the loss. When carried back or forward, a long-term capital loss is treated as a short-term capital loss.[11]

EXAMPLE 5

Assume the same facts as in Example 4, except that Robin is a corporation. None of the $7,500 long-term capital loss incurred in 2019 can be deducted in that year. Robin Corporation may, however, carry back the loss to 2016, 2017, and 2018 (in this order) and offset it against any capital gains recognized in these years.

If the carryback does not exhaust the loss, it may be carried forward to 2020, 2021, 2022, 2023, and 2024 (in this order). The long-term capital loss is treated as short term in any carryover year.

3-1e **Recapture of Depreciation**

In general, the §§ 1245 and 1250 depreciation recapture rules apply to both individual and corporate taxpayers. However, corporations may have more depreciation recapture (ordinary income) on the disposition of § 1250 property than individuals because of § 291 recapture.

Under § 291, a corporation has additional ordinary income equal to 20 percent of the excess of (1) the amount of depreciation recapture that would be required *if* § 1245 applied to the disposition (i.e., § 1245 recapture potential) over (2) the amount of depreciation recapture computed under § 1250 (without regard to § 291). As a result, the § 1231 portion of the corporation's gain on the disposition is reduced by the additional recapture.

Under § 1250, recapture is limited to the excess of accelerated depreciation over straight-line depreciation. In general, only straight-line depreciation is allowed for real property placed in service after 1986; thus, there will usually be no § 1250 depreciation recapture. In contrast, all depreciation taken on § 1245 property is subject to recapture.

EXAMPLE 6

Red Corporation purchases nonresidential real property on May 1, 2004, for $800,000. Straight-line depreciation is taken in the amount of $316,239 before the property is sold on October 7, 2019, for $1,200,000.

First, determine the recognized gain.

Sales price		$1,200,000
Less: Adjusted basis—		
Cost of property	$ 800,000	
Less: Cost recovery	(316,239)	(483,761)
Recognized gain		$ 716,239

continued

---

[10]§§ 1211(b) and 1212(b).   [11]§§ 1211(a) and 1212(a).

Second, determine the § 1245 recapture potential. This is the lesser of $716,239 (recognized gain) or $316,239 (cost recovery claimed).

Third, determine the normal § 1250 recapture amount.

Cost recovery taken	$ 316,239
Less: Straight-line cost recovery	(316,239)
§ 1250 ordinary income	$ –0–

Fourth, because the taxpayer is a corporation, determine the additional § 291 amount.

§ 1245 recapture potential	$ 316,239
Less: § 1250 recapture amount	(–0–)
Excess § 1245 recapture potential	$ 316,239
Apply § 291 percentage	× 20%
Additional ordinary income under § 291	$ 63,248

Red Corporation's recognized gain of $716,239 is accounted for as follows:

Ordinary income under § 1250	$ –0–
Ordinary income under § 291	63,248
§ 1231 gain	652,991
Total recognized gain	$ 716,239

3-1f Business Interest Expense Limitation

A limitation on the deduction for business interest applies to all taxpayers for tax years beginning after 2017.[12] Business interest is interest paid or accrued on trade or business debt. Although the limitation applies to *any* business, the rules are most likely to affect large corporations and flow-through entities due to a small business exception.

Under § 163(j), the deduction for business interest for any year is limited to the sum of:

1. The taxpayer's *business interest income* for the year,
2. 30 percent of the taxpayer's *adjusted taxable income* for the year, and
3. The taxpayer's *floor plan financing interest* for the year.

Any business interest deduction disallowed by reason of the limitation is treated as business interest paid or accrued in the succeeding tax year. The carryforward period is unlimited.

The business interest deduction limitation does not apply to certain small businesses. In general, the small business exception applies to taxpayers with average gross receipts for the prior three-year period of $26 million or less (taxable years beginning in 2019).[13]

Business Interest Income

"Business interest income" is the amount of interest income includible in gross income for the year that is related to a trade or business. Congress believes that a corporation typically will have neither investment interest income nor investment interest expense; instead, all interest income and interest expense of a corporation is assumed to be part of the corporation's trade or business.[14]

---

[12]§ 163(j).

[13]§ 163(j)(3). The $26 million average annual gross receipts test was $25 million for taxable years beginning in 2018.

[14]TCJA of 2017 Joint Explanatory Statement, p. 288. The Joint Explanatory Statement relies on the rationale that since § 163(d)—the investment

interest expense limitation—does not apply to corporations, then any interest income and interest expense should be related to the corporation's trade or business activities (not investment activities).

Adjusted Taxable Income

"Adjusted taxable income"[15] is taxable income computed without regard to any:

1. Nonbusiness income, gain, deduction, or loss;
2. Business interest or business interest income;
3. Net operating loss (NOL) deduction;
4. Deduction for qualified business income (§ 199A); and
5. Deduction allowable for depreciation, amortization, or depletion.[16]

The Treasury Department and the IRS are authorized to provide other adjustments to the computation of adjusted taxable income.[17] The 30 percent of adjusted taxable income amount cannot be less than zero.[18]

Floor Plan Financing Interest

Virtually all auto dealers acquire their inventory via debt (known as "floor plan" financing), with the debt being secured by the inventory. Interest on this debt ("floor plan financing interest") is deductible without limitation.

Business Interest Expense Limitation

EXAMPLE 7

In 2019, Tangerine Corporation, a calendar year C corporation, has $5,000,000 of adjusted taxable income, $75,000 of business interest income, zero floor plan financing interest, and $600,000 of business interest expense.

Tangerine's business interest deduction limitation is $1,575,000 [$75,000 (business interest income) + $1,500,000 (30% × $5,000,000 adjusted taxable income)]. As a result, Tangerine can deduct all $600,000 of its business interest expense.

EXAMPLE 8

Assume the same facts as in Example 7, except that Tangerine has $2,000,000 of business interest expense. Here, the deduction for business interest is limited to $1,575,000, and the disallowed amount of $425,000 ($2,000,000 − $1,575,000) is carried forward to next year and treated as business interest in that year.

If Tangerine satisfies the small business exception (i.e., had average gross receipts for the prior three-year period of $26,000,000 or less), the limitation on business interest does not apply and the entire $2,000,000 of business interest is deductible in the current year.

EXAMPLE 9

In 2019, Eagle Corporation, a calendar year C corporation, has ($1,000,000) of adjusted taxable income, $40,000 of business interest income, zero floor plan financing interest, and $100,000 of business interest expense.

Eagle's business interest deduction limitation is $40,000 [$40,000 (business interest income) + $0 (30% × adjusted taxable income amount, but not less than zero)]. As a result, Eagle's current year deduction for business interest is limited to $40,000, and the disallowed amount of $60,000 ($100,000 − $40,000) is carried forward to next year and treated as business interest in that year.

If Eagle satisfies the small business exception (i.e., had average gross receipts for the prior three-year period of $26,000,000 or less), the limitation on business interest does not apply and the entire $100,000 of business interest is deductible in the current year.

---

[15]§ 163(j)(8)(A).

[16]The depreciation, amortization, and depletion adjustment only applies to taxable years beginning before January 1, 2022; § 163(j)(8)(A)(v).

[17]§ 163(j)(8)(B).

[18]§ 163(j)(1), flush language.

Other Rules

Flow-Through Entities In the case of a partnership or an S corporation, the business interest deduction limitation applies at the entity level. The general carryforward rule for disallowed business interest does not apply to partnerships (or S corporations); rather, a partner (or S corporation shareholder) can deduct the disallowed interest under a special carryforward rule. A partner's (or S corporation shareholder's) adjusted taxable income is determined without regard to the partner's (or shareholder's) distributive share of the partnership's (or S corporation's) items of income, gain, deduction, or loss.[19]

Trade or Business. The term *trade or business* does not include performing services as an employee.[20] As a result, an individual cannot include W–2 wages in adjusted taxable income for purposes of computing the interest deduction limitation. The term also does not include certain real property trades or businesses and certain farming businesses.

3-1g Passive Activity Losses

The passive activity loss rules apply to individual taxpayers, closely held C corporations, and personal service corporations (PSCs; see definition in text Section 3-1c).[21] These rules prevent taxpayers from incorporating to avoid the passive activity loss limitation. A corporation is *closely held* if, at any time during the last half of the taxable year, more than 50 percent of the value of the corporation's outstanding stock is owned, directly or indirectly, by five or fewer individuals.

PSCs generally cannot deduct passive activity losses against either active income or portfolio income. However, the application of the passive activity loss rules is not as harsh for closely held C corporations (that are not PSCs). They may offset passive activity losses against *net active income*, but not against portfolio income. The special rules applicable to PSCs are recapped in Concept Summary 3.1.

EXAMPLE 10

Brown, a closely held C corporation that is *not* a PSC, has $300,000 of passive activity losses from a rental activity, $200,000 of net active income, and $100,000 of portfolio income. The corporation may offset $200,000 of the $300,000 passive activity loss against the $200,000 net active income but may not offset the remainder against the $100,000 of portfolio income.

If Brown is a PSC, then none of the $300,000 of passive activity losses is deductible in the current year.

Concept Summary 3.1

Special Rules Applicable to Personal Service Corporations (PSCs)

Item	PSC Treatment
Accounting periods	Calendar year is generally required. Fiscal year exceptions are available for a business purpose or under a § 444 election.
Accounting methods	Both cash and accrual methods are generally available. Any PSC shareholder-employee is treated as a related party for purposes of the accrued expenditure limitation.
Passive activity losses	Passive activity loss rules apply.

---

[19] § 163(j)(4).

[20] § 163(j)(7).

[21] § 469(a). For S corporations and partnerships, passive activity income or loss flows through to the owners, and the passive activity loss rules are applied at the owner level. For definitions, see § 469(j)(1) (closely held) and § 469(j)(2) (PSC).

3-1h Charitable Contributions

Both corporate and individual taxpayers may deduct charitable contributions for the year in which the payment is made. However, an *accrual basis corporation* may claim the deduction in the year preceding payment if two requirements are met. First, the contribution must be authorized by the board of directors by the end of that year. Second, it must be paid on or before the due date of the corporation's tax return (i.e., the fifteenth day of the fourth month following the close of its taxable year).[22]

On December 27, 2019, Peach Company, a calendar year, accrual basis taxpayer, authorizes a $5,000 donation to the Atlanta Symphony Association (a qualified charitable organization). The donation is made on April 10, 2020.

If Peach Company is a corporation and the December 27, 2019 authorization was made by its board of directors, Peach may claim the $5,000 donation as a deduction for calendar year 2019.

However, if Peach Company is a partnership, the contribution can be deducted only in 2020.[23]

Property Contributions

Generally, a charitable contribution of property results in a deduction equal to the property's fair market value at the date of the gift. As a result, a contribution of loss property (fair market value less than basis) should be avoided. Instead, the loss property should be sold (allowing the loss to be recognized) and the proceeds contributed to the charity.

Heron Corporation owns inventory with a basis of $10,000 and a fair market value of $8,000. A charitable contribution of the inventory results in a deductible amount of $8,000, the inventory's fair market value.

However, a sale of the inventory, for a recognized loss of $2,000 ($8,000 amount realized − $10,000 basis), and donation of the sale proceeds, for a charitable deduction of $8,000, results in a combined deduction of $10,000.

Fair market value also is the valuation amount for most charitable contributions of capital gain property. *Capital gain property* is property that, if sold, would result in long-term capital gain or § 1231 gain for the taxpayer.

During the current year, Mallard Corporation donates a parcel of land (a capital asset) to Oakland Community College. Mallard acquired the land five years ago for $60,000, and the fair market value on the date of the contribution is $100,000.

The corporation's charitable contribution deduction (subject to a percentage limitation discussed later) is measured by the asset's fair market value of $100,000, even though the $40,000 appreciation on the land has never been included in income.

In two situations, a charitable contribution of capital gain property is measured by the basis of the property, rather than fair market value. First, if the taxpayer contributes *tangible personal property* and the charitable organization puts the property to an *unrelated use*, the deduction is limited to the basis of the property. If the use is related to the charity's exempt purpose, the contribution deduction will be based on the property's fair market value. Second, the deduction for charitable contributions of capital gain property to certain private foundations is also limited to the basis of the property.

---

[22]§ 170(a)(2).

[23]Each calendar year partner will report an allocable portion of the charitable contribution deduction as of December 31, 2020 (the end of the partnership's tax year). See Chapter 10.

Contributions of Tangible Personal Property

During the current year, White Corporation donates a painting worth $200,000 to Western States Art Museum (a qualified organization), which exhibits the painting. White had acquired the painting in 2000 for $90,000. Because the museum put the painting to a related use, White is allowed to deduct $200,000, the fair market value of the painting.

EXAMPLE 14

Assume the same facts as in the previous example, except that White Corporation donates the painting to the American Cancer Society, which sells the painting and deposits the $200,000 proceeds in the organization's general fund.

Here, White's deduction is limited to the $90,000 basis because it contributed tangible personal property that was put to an unrelated use by the charitable organization.

EXAMPLE 15

As a general rule, the deduction for a contribution of ordinary income property is also limited to the *basis* of the property. *Ordinary income property* is appreciated property that, if sold, would not result in long-term capital gain (inventory and stock held for 12 months or less are common examples).[24] On certain contributions of inventory by *corporations*, however, the amount of the deduction is equal to the *lesser of* (1) the sum of the property's basis plus 50 percent of the appreciation on the property or (2) twice the property's basis. The following inventory contributions qualify for this increased contribution amount:

- A contribution of property to a charitable organization whose exempt purpose includes the care of the ill, needy, or infants.

- A contribution of tangible personal research property constructed by the corporation to a qualified educational or scientific organization that uses the property for research or experimentation or for research training.[25]

Lark Corporation, a clothing retailer, donates children's clothing to the Salvation Army to be used to clothe homeless children. Lark's basis in the clothes is $2,000, and the fair market value is $3,000. Lark's deduction is $2,500 [$2,000 basis + 50%($3,000 − $2,000)].

If, instead, the fair market value is $7,000, Lark's deduction is $4,000 (2 × $2,000 basis).

EXAMPLE 16

Limitations Imposed on Charitable Contribution Deductions

Like individuals, corporations are subject to percentage limits on the charitable contribution deduction.[26] For any tax year, a corporate taxpayer's contribution deduction is limited to 10 percent of taxable income. For this purpose, taxable income is computed without regard to the charitable contribution deduction, any net operating loss carryback or capital loss carryback, and dividends received deduction.

Any contributions in excess of the 10 percent limitation may be carried forward to the five succeeding tax years. Any carryforward is combined with contributions in those years and then subject to the 10 percent limitation. The current year's contributions are always deducted first, with carryover amounts from previous years deducted in order of time.[27]

---

[24]In addition, § 1231 property (depreciable property used in a trade or business) is treated as ordinary income property to the extent of any depreciation recaptured under § 1245 or § 1250 (as adjusted under § 291).

[25]The property must be contributed within two years from the date of its construction by the donor, and its original use must begin with the donee. S corporations do not qualify for the increased contribution amount for inventory. These conditions are identified in §§ 170(e)(3) and (4).

[26]The percentage limitations applicable to individuals and corporations are identified in § 170(b).

[27]The carryover rules relating to all taxpayers are in § 170(d).

Annual Limitation and Carryover Rules Illustrated

EXAMPLE 17

During 2019, Orange Corporation (a calendar year taxpayer) had the following income and expenses:

Income from operations	$140,000
Expenses from operations	110,000
Dividends received	10,000
Charitable contributions made in May 2019	6,000

For purposes of the 10% limitation *only*, Orange Corporation's taxable income is $40,000 ($140,000 − $110,000 + $10,000). Consequently, the allowable charitable deduction for 2019 is $4,000 (10% × $40,000). The $2,000 unused portion of the contribution can be carried forward to 2020, 2021, 2022, 2023, and 2024 (in that order) until exhausted.

EXAMPLE 18

Assume the same facts as in Example 17. In 2020, Orange Corporation has taxable income (for purposes of the 10% limitation) of $50,000 and makes a charitable contribution of $4,500. The maximum deduction allowed for 2020 is $5,000 (10% × $50,000).

The $5,000 allowed deduction is made up of the 2020 $4,500 contribution and $500 of the carryforward from 2019. Current year contributions are always used first. The remaining $1,500 of the 2019 contribution may be carried over until it is used (or until the five-year carryforward period ends).

3-1i **Excessive Executive Compensation**

A closely held corporation's deduction for shareholder-employee compensation is subject to the reasonableness standard of § 162(a)(1). A second limitation applies to *publicly held corporations*. In general, § 162(m) limits the deductible amount of a publicly held corporation's compensation to any covered employee to $1 million annually. Covered employees are the principal executive officer, the principal financial officer, and the three other most highly compensated officers.[28]

In general, the $1 million maximum applies to compensation, commissions based on individual performance, and performance-based compensation tied to overall company performance. Before 2018, the $1 million limit *excluded* commissions and performance-based compensation. Contracts in place on November 2, 2017, are grandfathered under pre-2018 law as long as there are no material changes to the contract. The limitation also does not apply to retirement plan contributions or employer-provided benefits that are excludible from gross income by the employee (e.g., health care benefits).

EXAMPLE 19

Dora is the newly hired Chief Executive Officer of White Corporation, a publicly traded corporation. For the current year, her compensation package consists of:

Cash compensation	$2,700,000
Taxable fringe benefits	200,000
Bonus tied to company performance	5,000,000
Nontaxable fringe benefits	100,000

White Corporation can deduct $1,100,000 of Dora's compensation package ($1,000,000 of the cash compensation, taxable fringe benefits, and bonus) plus the nontaxable fringe benefits of $100,000.

---

[28]An individual is a covered employee if the individual holds one of the principal officer positions at any time during the taxable year. Further, an individual who is a covered employee for any tax year beginning after 2016 remains a covered employee for all future years, including years during which the individual is no longer employed by the corporation and years after the individual has died. For example, the limitation would apply to deferred compensation payments to a covered employee after the individual's departure from the corporation.

3-1j Net Operating Losses

Like the net operating loss (NOL) of an individual, the NOL of a corporation may be carried forward indefinitely to offset taxable income for those future years. The NOL deduction for any carryover year is limited to 80 percent of taxable income (determined without regard to the NOL deduction) for both individuals and corporations.[29]

Unlike individual taxpayers, however, a corporation:[30]

- Does not adjust its tax loss for the year for any capital losses (since a corporation cannot deduct net capital losses),

- Does not make adjustments for any nonbusiness deductions (as individual taxpayers do), and

- Is allowed to include the dividends received deduction (discussed below) in computing its NOL.

EXAMPLE

20

In 2019, Green Corporation has gross income (including dividends) of $200,000 and deductions of $300,000 excluding the dividends received deduction. Green Corporation had received $100,000 of dividends from Fox, Inc., in which Green holds a 5% stock interest. Green has an NOL computed as follows:

Gross income (including dividends)		$200,000
Less:		
Business deductions	$300,000	
Dividends received deduction (50% of $100,000)	50,000	(350,000)
Taxable income (or loss)		($150,000)

The NOL is carried forward to 2020 and future years until it is used up. In addition, the NOL can offset no more than 80% of taxable income (computed without regard to the NOL) in those years.

3-1k Deductions Available Only to Corporations

LO.2

List and apply the tax rules unique to corporations.

Certain deductions are specific to corporate taxpayers, including the dividends received deduction and the organizational expenditures deduction.

Dividends Received Deduction

The purpose of the **dividends received deduction** is to mitigate multiple taxation of corporate income. Without the deduction, dividend income paid to a corporation would be taxed to the recipient corporation, with no corresponding deduction to the distributing corporation. Later, when the recipient corporation distributed the income to its shareholders, the income would *again* be subject to taxation, with no corresponding deduction to the corporation. The dividends received deduction alleviates this inequity.

As Exhibit 3.2 illustrates, the amount of the dividends received deduction depends on the percentage of ownership (voting power and value) the recipient corporate shareholder holds in a *domestic corporation* making the dividend distribution.[31]

The dividends received deduction cannot exceed the taxable income limitation. This limitation is equal to the corporation's taxable income multiplied by the same percentage used to compute the deduction. As a result, if a corporate shareholder owns less than 20 percent of the stock in the distributing corporation, the dividends received deduction is limited to 50 percent of taxable income. For this purpose, taxable income

---

[29]These rules apply for NOLs arising in tax years ending after 2017. For NOLs arising in prior years, a 2-year carryback and 20-year carryforward apply, and there is no taxable income limitation on the deductibility of the NOL carryovers.

[30]The modifications required to arrive at the amount of NOL that can be carried forward are in § 172(d).

[31]§ 243(a). Dividends from foreign corporations generally do not qualify for a dividends received deduction. But see §§ 245 and 245A. These rules apply for tax years beginning after 2017.

EXHIBIT 3.2	Dividends Received Deduction

Percentage of Ownership by Corporate Shareholder	Deduction Percentage
Less than 20%	50%
20% or more (but less than 80%)	65%
80% or more*	100%

*The payor corporation must be a member of an affiliated group with the recipient corporation.

is computed without regard to the NOL deduction, the dividends received deduction, and any capital loss carryback. However, the taxable income limitation does not apply if the corporation has an NOL for the current taxable year.[32]

The following steps are useful in applying these rules:

1. Multiply the dividends received by the deduction percentage.
2. Multiply the taxable income by the deduction percentage.
3. The deduction is limited to the lesser of Step 1 or Step 2, unless deducting the amount derived in Step 1 results in an NOL. If so, the amount derived in Step 1 is used. This is sometimes referred to as the *NOL rule*.

EXAMPLE 21

Red, White, and Blue Corporations, three unrelated calendar year corporations, have the following information for the year:

	Red Corporation	White Corporation	Blue Corporation
Gross income from operations	$ 400,000	$ 320,000	$ 230,000
Expenses from operations	(340,000)	(340,000)	(340,000)
Dividends received from domestic corporations (less than 20% ownership)	200,000	200,000	200,000
Taxable income before the dividends received deduction	$ 260,000	$ 180,000	$ 90,000

In determining the dividends received deduction, use the three-step procedure described above.

Step 1 (50% × $200,000)	$ 100,000	$ 100,000	$ 100,000
Step 2			
50% × $260,000 (taxable income)	$ 130,000		
50% × $180,000 (taxable income)		$ 90,000	
50% × $90,000 (taxable income)			$ 45,000
Step 3			
Lesser of Step 1 or Step 2	$ 100,000	$ 90,000	
Deduction results in an NOL (use Step 1)			$ 100,000

White Corporation is subject to the 50% of taxable income limitation (Step 2). The NOL rule does not apply because subtracting $100,000 (Step 1) from $180,000 (taxable income before the DRD) does not yield a negative figure. Blue Corporation does qualify for NOL rule treatment because subtracting $100,000 (Step 1) from $90,000 (taxable income before the DRD) yields a negative figure.

In summary, each corporation has a dividends received deduction for the year as follows: $100,000 for Red Corporation, $90,000 for White Corporation, and $100,000 for Blue Corporation.

---

[32]Further, the limitation does not apply in the case of the 100% deduction available to members of an affiliated group. § 246(b).

In those cases where the taxable income limitation applies, the taxpayer should consider the proper timing of income and deductions to bring the NOL rule into play. This can result in a significant increase in the amount of a corporation's dividends received deduction.

EXAMPLE 22

Pearl Corporation, a calendar year C corporation, has the following information for the year:

Gross income from operations	$ 200,000
Expenses from operations	(245,000)
Dividends received from domestic corporations (less than 20% ownership)	100,000
Taxable income before dividends received deduction	$ 55,000

Pearl's dividends received deduction is $27,500 [50% × $55,000 (taxable income limitation)].

If, however, Pearl incurs additional expenses of $5,001 (or defers $5,001 of income), its taxable income before the dividends received deduction will be reduced to $49,999. If this occurs, the NOL rule applies and Pearl's dividends received deduction is $50,000 [50% × $100,000 (dividends received)].

No dividends received deduction is allowed unless the corporation has held the stock for more than 45 days.[33] This restriction was enacted to close a tax loophole involving dividends on stock that is held only briefly. When stock is purchased shortly before a dividend record date and soon thereafter sold ex-dividend, a capital loss corresponding to the amount of the dividend often results (ignoring other market valuation changes). If the dividends received deduction was allowed in such cases, the capital loss resulting from the stock sale would exceed the taxable portion of the related dividend income.

EXAMPLE 23

On October 1, 2019, Pink Corporation declares a $1 per share dividend for shareholders of record as of November 1, 2019, and payable on December 1, 2019. Black Corporation purchases 10,000 shares of Pink stock on October 30, 2019, for $25,000 and sells those 10,000 shares ex-dividend on November 6, 2019, for $15,000. (It is assumed that there is no fluctuation in the market price of the Pink stock other than the dividend element.) The sale results in a short-term capital loss of $10,000 ($15,000 amount realized − $25,000 basis). On December 1, Black receives a $10,000 dividend from Pink.

Without the holding period restriction, Black Corporation would recognize a $10,000 deduction (subject to the capital loss limitation) but only $5,000 of income [$10,000 dividend − $5,000 dividends received deduction ($10,000 × 50%)], or a $5,000 net loss. However, because Black did not hold the Pink stock for more than 45 days, no dividends received deduction is allowed.

ETHICS & EQUITY   Pushing the Envelope on Year-End Planning

As of December 30, 2019, Larson Corporation (a calendar year taxpayer) has gross income from operations of $497,000, expenses from operations of $596,000, and dividends received from domestic corporations (less than 20 percent ownership) of $200,000.

Currently, Larson does not expect any more income or expenses to be realized by year-end. However, Larson's tax department has suggested that the corporation incur another $1,001 of deductible expenditures before year-end. What is the motivation behind the tax department's recommendation, and is such year-end planning ethical?

---

[33]The stock must be held more than 45 days during the 91-day period beginning on the date that is 45 days before the ex-dividend date (or in the case of preferred stock, more than 90 days during the 181-day period beginning on the date that is 90 days before the ex-dividend date). § 246(c).

Organizational Expenditures Deduction

Expenses incurred in connection with the organization of a corporation normally are capitalized. That they benefit the corporation during its existence seems clear. But how can they be amortized when most corporations possess unlimited life? If a useful life cannot be determined, no deduction is allowed. Section 248 was enacted to solve this problem.

Under § 248, a corporation may *elect* to amortize **organizational expenditures** over the 180-month period beginning with the month in which the corporation begins business.[34] Organizational expenditures include the following:

- Legal services related to organization (e.g., drafting the corporate charter, bylaws, minutes of organizational meetings, and terms of original stock certificates).
- Necessary accounting services.
- Expenses of temporary directors and of organizational meetings of directors or shareholders.
- Fees paid to the state of incorporation.

Expenses that *do not qualify* as organizational expenditures include those connected with issuing or selling shares of stock or other securities (e.g., commissions, professional fees, and printing costs) or with transferring assets to a corporation. These expenses must be capitalized.

The first $5,000 of organizational costs is immediately expensed, with any remaining costs amortized over a 180-month period. However, the $5,000 expensing amount is phased out on a dollar-for-dollar basis when these costs exceed $50,000.

EXAMPLE 24

Stork Corporation (a calendar year C corporation) began business on July 1 of the current year and incurred $52,000 of organizational expenditures. Stork wants to expense as much of these expenditures as possible, electing to amortize any amount it cannot expense. Stork's current year deduction is $4,633, determined as follows:

Immediate expense [$5,000 − ($52,000 − $50,000)]	$3,000
Amortization [($52,000 − $3,000) ÷ 180] × 6 months in tax year	1,633
Total	$4,633

To qualify for the election, the expenditure must be *incurred* before the end of the taxable year in which the corporation begins business. The corporation's method of accounting is of no consequence; an expense incurred by a cash basis corporation in its first tax year qualifies even though it is not paid until a subsequent year. However, this rule could prove to be an unfortunate trap for corporations formed late in the first taxable year. Consider the following example.

EXAMPLE 25

Thrush Corporation is formed in December 2019. Qualified organizational expenditures are incurred as follows: $62,000 in December 2019 and $30,000 in January 2020. If Thrush uses the calendar year for tax purposes, only $62,000 of the organizational expenditures can be written off over a period of 180 months.

Being aware of the rule and planning appropriately can solve this problem. One option is to make sure that all of the expenditures are incurred in December. Another option is to adopt a different year-end. If Thrush Corporation adopts a fiscal year that ends on or beyond January 31, all organizational expenditures will then have been incurred before the close of the first taxable year. With either of these options, $92,000 ($62,000 + $30,000) of organizational expenditures can be amortized over 180 months.

---

[34]The month in which a corporation begins business may not be immediately apparent. Ordinarily, a corporation begins business when it starts the business operations for which it was organized. Reg. § 1.248–1(d). For a similar problem in the Subchapter S area, see Chapter 12.

A corporation is deemed to have made the election to amortize organizational expenditures for the taxable year in which it begins business. A corporation can elect to forgo the election by capitalizing organizational expenditures on its first tax return.

EXAMPLE
26

Black Corporation (an accrual method, calendar year, C corporation) was formed and began operations on April 1, 2019. The following expenses were incurred during its first year of operations (April 1–December 31, 2019):

Expenses of temporary directors and of organizational meetings	$15,500
Fee paid to the state of incorporation	2,000
Accounting services incident to organization	18,000
Legal services for drafting the corporate charter and bylaws	32,000
Expenses incident to the printing and sale of stock certificates	48,000

Black Corporation elects to amortize organizational costs under § 248. Because of the dollar cap (i.e., dollar-for-dollar reduction for amounts in excess of $50,000), none of the $5,000 expensing allowance is available. The monthly amortization is $375 [($15,500 + $2,000 + $18,000 + $32,000) ÷ 180 months], and $3,375 ($375 × 9 months) is deductible for tax year 2019.

Note that the $48,000 of expenses incident to the printing and sale of stock certificates does not qualify for the election. These expenses must be capitalized.

Organizational expenditures are different from *startup expenditures*.[35] Startup expenditures include various investigation expenses involved in entering a new business (e.g., travel, market surveys, financial audits, and legal fees) and operating expenses such as rent and payroll that are incurred by a corporation before it actually begins to produce any gross income. In general, startup expenditures must be capitalized. However, at the election of the taxpayer, startup expenditures are deductible in the same manner as organizational expenditures. So up to $5,000 can be immediately expensed (subject to the phaseout) and any remaining amounts amortized over a period of 180 months. The same rules that apply to the deemed election (and election to forgo the election) for organizational expenditures also apply to startup expenditures.

Concept Summary 3.2

Income Taxation of Individuals and Corporations Compared

	Individuals	Corporations
Computation of gross income	§ 61.	§ 61.
Computation of taxable income	§§ 62, 63(b) through (g).	§ 63(a). Concept of AGI has no relevance.
Deductions	Trade or business (§ 162); nonbusiness (§ 212); deduction for qualified business income (§ 199A); reimbursed employee business expenses; some personal expenses (generally deductible as itemized deductions).	Trade or business (§ 162).
Charitable contributions	Limited in any tax year to 50% of AGI (60% of AGI for cash contributions); 30% for capital gain property unless election is made to reduce fair market value of gift.	Limited in any tax year to 10% of taxable income computed without regard to the charitable contribution deduction, net operating loss carryback, capital loss carryback, and dividends received deduction.
	Excess charitable contributions carried over for five years.	Same as for individuals.

continued

---

[35]§ 195. The deduction for startup expenditures is also available to noncorporate taxpayers.

Income Taxation of Individuals and Corporations Compared—(Continued)

	Individuals	Corporations
Charitable contributions (*continued*)	Amount of contribution is the fair market value of capital gain property; ordinary income property is limited to adjusted basis; capital gain property is treated as ordinary income property if tangible personalty is donated to a nonuse charity or the donation is to certain private foundations.	Same as for individuals, but exceptions allowed for certain inventory and for research property where one-half of the appreciation is allowed as a deduction.
	Time of deduction—year in which payment is made.	Time of deduction—year in which payment is made unless accrual basis taxpayer. Accrual basis corporation can take deduction in year preceding payment if contribution was authorized by board of directors by end of year and contribution is paid by fifteenth day of fourth month of following year.
Casualty losses	Personal casualty losses limited to losses attributable to a Federally declared disaster; $100 floor on losses; total personal casualty losses deductible only to extent losses exceed 10% of AGI.	Deductible in full.
Net operating loss	Adjusted for several items, including nonbusiness deductions over nonbusiness income.	Generally no adjustments.
	Indefinite carryforward; carryforward deduction limited to 80% of taxable income.	Same as for individuals.
Dividends received deduction	None.	50%, 65%, or 100% of dividends received depending on percentage of ownership by corporate shareholder.
Net capital gains	Taxed in full. Tax rate generally 15% or 20% on net capital gains.	Taxed in full. No preferential tax rate.
Capital losses	Only $3,000 of capital loss per year can offset ordinary income; unused loss is carried forward indefinitely to offset capital gains or ordinary income up to $3,000; short-term and long-term carryovers retain their character.	Can offset only capital gains; unused loss is carried back three years and forward five; carryovers and carrybacks are characterized as short-term losses.
Passive activity losses	In general, passive activity losses cannot offset either active income or portfolio income.	Passive activity loss rules apply to closely held C corporations and personal service corporations.
		For personal service corporations, passive activity losses cannot offset either active income or portfolio income.
		For closely held C corporations, passive activity losses may offset active income but not portfolio income.
Tax rates	Progressive with seven rates (10%, 12%, 22%, 24%, 32%, 35%, and 37%).	Flat rate of 21%.
Alternative minimum tax	Applied at a graduated rate schedule of 26% and 28%. Exemption allowed depending on filing status (e.g., $111,700 in 2019 for married filing jointly); phaseout begins when AMTI reaches a certain amount (e.g., $1,020,600 in 2019 for married filing jointly).	None.

EXHIBIT 3.3	Corporate Income Tax Rates for Taxable Years Beginning Before 2018

Taxable Income		Tax Is:	
Over—	But Not Over—		Of the Amount Over—
$ 0	$ 50,000	15%	$ 0
50,000	75,000	$ 7,500 + 25%	50,000
75,000	100,000	13,750 + 34%	75,000
100,000	335,000	22,250 + 39%	100,000
335,000	10,000,000	113,900 + 34%	335,000
10,000,000	15,000,000	3,400,000 + 35%	10,000,000
15,000,000	18,333,333	5,150,000 + 38%	15,000,000
18,333,333	—	35%	0

Note: PSCs are taxed at a flat rate of 35%.

3-2 DETERMINING THE CORPORATE INCOME TAX LIABILITY

LO.3

Compute the corporate income tax.

3-2a Corporate Income Tax Rates

Corporate income tax rates have fluctuated over the years. The top corporate income tax rate was reduced from 46 percent to 34 percent in 1986 and then raised to a top rate of 35 percent a few years later (see Exhibit 3.3). This rate was the highest of all the OECD countries prior to the enactment of the TCJA of 2017. The TCJA of 2017 reduced the corporate tax rate to a flat rate of 21 percent for tax years beginning after 2017 (including for PSCs).[36]

EXAMPLE 27

Agile Corporation, a calendar year C corporation, has taxable income of $1,000,000. For 2019, Agile Corporation's tax liability is $210,000 ($1,000,000 × 21%).

If, instead, the tax year is 2017, Agile's tax liability is $340,000 {$113,900 + [($1,000,000 − $335,000) × 34%]} (see Exhibit 3.3).

The Big Picture

EXAMPLE 28

Return to the facts of *The Big Picture* on p. 3-1. Assume that Samantha incorporates her business as Skylark Bakery, Inc., a calendar year C corporation. The corporation pays Samantha a salary of $50,000 for the current year. For the year, Skylark Bakery has taxable income of $52,500 [$100,000 operating profit + $5,000 dividends − $50,000 salary expense − $2,500 dividends received deduction ($5,000 × 50%)]. Its income tax liability is $11,025 ($52,500 × 21%).

3-2b Alternative Minimum Tax

Prior to the enactment of the TCJA of 2017, corporations were subject to an alternative minimum tax (AMT) that was similar to the individual AMT. However, the TCJA of 2017 repealed the corporate AMT for tax years beginning after 2017.

[36]Section 15 requires fiscal year corporations with taxable years ending in 2018 to use a blended rate calculation (based on the number of days in the taxable year under the old tax rate structure and the new tax rate structure).

LO.4

Explain the operation of the accumulated earnings and personal holding company taxes.

3-2c Restrictions on Corporate Accumulations

Over the past several decades, there has been little difference between the top individual and corporate marginal tax rates. For instance, prior to the TCJA of 2017, there was less than a 5 percent difference between those rates (39.6 percent individual rate versus 35 percent corporate rate). This nominal differential in top rates limited the tax savings opportunities that could be achieved by individuals shifting income to a corporation. However, beginning in 2018, this landscape changed dramatically with the enactment of the corporate 21 percent flat tax rate. Consequently, a high-income individual now can achieve up to a 16 percent reduction in tax rate by shifting income to a corporation (37 percent individual rate versus 21 percent corporate rate). As a result, high-income individuals might consider the corporate entity form as a means to reduce their tax burdens.

The taxation of dividend distributions to shareholders will reduce the tax savings that can be achieved through the shifting of income to a corporation and the arbitraging of tax rates. However, what if the double taxation of corporate earnings could be deferred or possibly avoided entirely? Double taxation is deferred to the extent earnings are accumulated within the corporation instead of distributed to shareholders. The present value of any tax liability on dividends is reduced the longer distributions are deferred. Also, a corporation's accumulation of earnings should cause its stock to appreciate in value. If a shareholder dies with such appreciated stock, all of the appreciation would avoid income taxation due to the step-up in basis under § 1014 (see Chapter 19). In addition, for most taxpayers, no estate tax would be assessed on the appreciated stock due to the high estate exclusion amount. Thus, double taxation could be avoided entirely by accumulating earnings within the corporation and a subsequent transfer of the stock by death.

Two provisions of the Code are designed to prevent corporations and their shareholders from avoiding the double tax on dividend distributions. Both provisions impose a penalty tax on undistributed income retained by the corporation. The rules underlying these provisions are complex and beyond the scope of this text. However, a brief description is provided as an introduction.

Accumulated Earnings Tax

The accumulated earnings tax (described in §§ 531–537) imposes a 20 percent tax on the current year's corporate earnings that have been accumulated without a reasonable business need. The burden of proving what constitutes a reasonable need is borne by the taxpayer. In determining accumulated income, businesses are allowed a $250,000 ($150,000 for service corporations) minimum credit. As a result, most corporations can accumulate $250,000 in earnings over a series of years without fear of an accumulated earnings tax. Beyond the minimum credit, earnings can be accumulated for reasonable needs of the business, such as expansion of the business, replacement of plant and equipment, working capital needs, product liability losses, debt retirement, self-insurance, and loans to suppliers and customers. Reasonable needs do *not* include loans to shareholders, investments in unrelated properties or businesses, and unrealistic hazards and contingencies. Finally, the accumulated earnings tax can be further reduced or eliminated by distributing dividends.

Personal Holding Company Tax

20%

The personal holding company (PHC) tax (described in §§ 541–547) was enacted to discourage the sheltering of certain kinds of passive income in corporations owned by individuals with high marginal tax rates. Historically, the tax was aimed at "incorporated pocketbooks" that were frequently found in the entertainment and construction industries. For example, a taxpayer could shelter income from securities in a corporation, which would pay no dividends, and allow the corporation's stock to increase in value. Like the accumulated earnings tax, the PHC tax employs a 20 percent rate and is designed to force a corporation to distribute earnings to shareholders.

In any single year, the IRS cannot impose both the PHC tax and the accumulated earnings tax. Generally, a company is considered a PHC and may be subject to the tax if:

- More than 50 percent of the value of the outstanding stock is owned by five or fewer individuals at any time during the last half of the year, and
- A substantial portion (60 percent or more) of the corporation's income is comprised of passive types of income including dividends, interest, rents, royalties, or certain personal service income.

Similar to the accumulated earnings tax, the PHC tax can be further reduced or eliminated by distributing dividends.

3-3 PROCEDURAL MATTERS

LO.5

Describe and illustrate the reporting process for corporations.

This section covers various aspects of the corporate income tax return, including filing requirements, estimated tax payments, and special disclosure schedules on the return.

3-3a Filing Requirements for Corporations

A corporation must file a Federal income tax return whether or not it has taxable income. If a corporation began (or ceased) operations during a year, a short-period return (less than 12 months) must be filed for that year.[37]

The corporate income tax return is Form 1120. Corporations electing under Subchapter S (see Chapter 12) use Form 1120S. Forms 1120 and 1120S are reproduced in Appendix B. Corporations with assets of $10 million or more generally are required to file returns electronically.[38]

A Form 1120 must be filed on or before the fifteenth day of the fourth month following the close of a corporation's tax year.[39] A regular corporation, other than a PSC, can use either a calendar year or a fiscal year to report its taxable income. A Form 1120S must be filed on or before the fifteenth day of the third month following the close of an S corporation's tax year.[40]

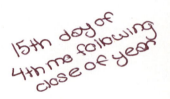
15th day of 4th mo following close of year

A corporation that needs more time to prepare and file its tax return can receive an automatic six-month extension of its tax return due date if it files Form 7004 (and pays the related tax liability) by the due date of its return.[41] The IRS may terminate an extension by mailing a 10-day notice to the corporation.

3-3b Estimated Tax Payments

A corporation must make estimated tax payments unless its tax liability can reasonably be expected to be less than $500. The required annual payment is the *lesser* of:

1. 100 percent of the corporation's tax for the current year, or
2. 100 percent of the tax for the preceding year (if that was a 12-month tax year and the return filed showed a tax liability).

Estimated payments can be made in four installments due on or before the fifteenth day of the fourth month, the sixth month, the ninth month, and the twelfth month of the corporate taxable year.[42] For a calendar year corporation, the payment dates are:

April 15
June 15
September 15
December 15

---

[37] § 6012(a)(2) and Reg. § 1.6012–2(a). A corporation must file a return even though it has ceased to do business if it has valuable claims for which it will bring suit. A corporation is relieved of filing income tax returns only when it ceases to do business and retains no assets.

[38] Reg. §§ 1.6012–2(a)(3) (Form 1120), 1.6012–2(h) (Form 1120S), and 301.6011–5 (electronic filing).

[39] § 6072(a). A corporation with a June 30 year-end must file a Form 1120 by the fifteenth day of the *third* month following the close of its fiscal year through 2025 [P.L. 114–41, § 2006(a)(3)(B)]. If the due date falls on a Saturday, Sunday, or legal holiday, the due date is the next business day.

[40] § 6072(b).

[41] Reg. § 1.6081–3. An extension of seven months applies for C corporations with a June 30 year-end through 2025 [§ 6081(b)].

[42] § 6655. If the due date falls on a Saturday, Sunday, or legal holiday, the due date is the next business day.

A *large* corporation cannot base its installment payments on its previous year's tax liability except for its first installment payment. A corporation is considered large if it had taxable income of $1 million or more in any of its three preceding years.

EXAMPLE

29

Condor Corporation, a calendar year C corporation, has taxable income of $1,500,000 and $2,000,000 for 2019 and 2020, respectively. The required 2020 estimated tax installment payments for Condor, a "large corporation," are computed as follows:

Payment	Amount
April 15, 2020	$ 78,750*
June 15, 2020	131,250**
September 15, 2020	105,000
December 15, 2020	105,000
Total	$420,000

*Based on preceding year's tax, for first installment only:
($1,500,000 taxable income × 21%) = $315,000 ÷ 4 = $78,750.
**Based on current year's tax, for remaining installments:
($2,000,000 taxable income × 21%) = $420,000 ÷ 4 = $105,000.
Second installment must include shortfall from first installment:
[$105,000 + ($105,000 − $78,750)] = $131,250.

A corporation that fails to pay its required estimated tax payments (or underestimates those payments) can be assessed a nondeductible penalty. In general, a penalty will not be assessed if the corporation pays its required annual payment (discussed above) on a quarterly basis.

3-3c Schedule M–1—Reconciliation of Income (Loss) per Books with Income per Return

Schedule M–1 of Form 1120 is used to *reconcile* net income as computed for financial accounting purposes with taxable income reported on the corporation's income tax return (commonly referred to as book-tax differences). Schedule M–1 is required of corporations with less than $10 million of total assets.

The starting point on Schedule M–1 is net income (or loss) per books. Additions and subtractions are entered for items that affect financial accounting net income and taxable income differently. The following items are entered as additions (see lines 2 through 5 of Schedule M–1):

- Federal income tax per books (deducted in computing net income per books but not deductible in computing taxable income).

- The excess of capital losses over capital gains (deducted for financial accounting purposes but not deductible by corporations for income tax purposes).

- Income that is reported in the current year for tax purposes but is not reported in computing net income per books (e.g., prepaid income).

- Various expenses that are deducted in computing net income per books but are not allowed in computing taxable income (e.g., charitable contributions in excess of the 10 percent ceiling applicable to corporations).

The following subtractions are entered on lines 7 and 8 of Schedule M–1:

- Income reported for financial accounting purposes but not included in taxable income (e.g., tax-exempt interest).

- Deductions taken on the tax return but not expensed in computing net income per books (e.g., tax depreciation in excess of financial accounting depreciation).

The result is taxable income (before the NOL deduction and the dividends received deduction). Concept Summary 3.3 provides a conceptual diagram of Schedule M–1.

During the current year, Tern Corporation had the following transactions:

Net income per books (after tax)	$89,400
Taxable income	50,000
Federal income tax per books (21% × $50,000)	10,500
Interest income from tax-exempt bonds	5,000
Interest paid on loan, the proceeds of which were used to purchase the tax-exempt bonds	500
Life insurance proceeds received as a result of the death of a key employee	50,000
Premiums paid on key employee life insurance policy	2,600
Excess of capital losses over capital gains	2,000

EXAMPLE 30

For book and tax purposes, Tern Corporation determines depreciation under the straight-line method. Tern's Schedule M–1 for the current year is constructed as follows:

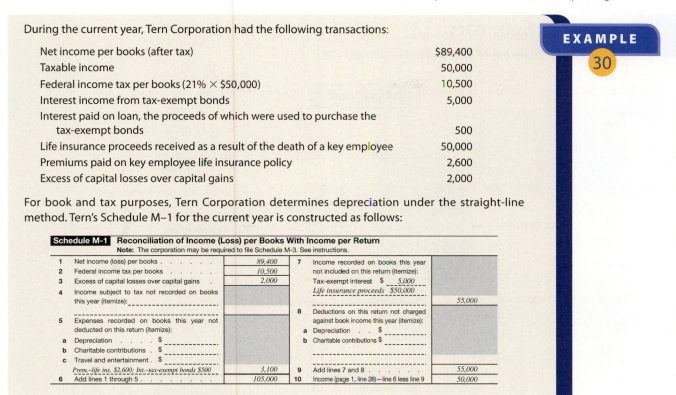

Schedule M-1	**Reconciliation of Income (Loss) per Books With Income per Return**					
	Note: The corporation may be required to file Schedule M-3. See instructions.					
1	Net income (loss) per books	89,400	7	Income recorded on books this year not included on this return (itemize):		
2	Federal income tax per books	10,500		Tax-exempt interest $ ___5,000___		
3	Excess of capital losses over capital gains .	2,000		*Life insurance proceeds $50,000*		
4	Income subject to tax not recorded on books this year (itemize): _____					55,000
	_____		8	Deductions on this return not charged against book income this year (itemize):		
5	Expenses recorded on books this year not deducted on this return (itemize):		a	Depreciation . . $ _____		
a	Depreciation . . . $ _____		b	Charitable contributions $ _____		
b	Charitable contributions . $ _____			_____		
c	Travel and entertainment . $ _____					
	Prem.–life ins. $2,600; Int.–tax-exempt bonds $500	3,100	9	Add lines 7 and 8		55,000
6	Add lines 1 through 5	105,000	10	Income (page 1, line 28)—line 6 less line 9		50,000

3-3d Schedule M–2—Analysis of Unappropriated Retained Earnings per Books

Schedule M–2 reconciles unappropriated retained earnings at the beginning of the year with unappropriated retained earnings at year-end. In general, this *financial statement* reconciliation is done by adding net income per books to the beginning balance of retained earnings and subtracting distributions made during the year. Other sources of increases or decreases in retained earnings are also listed on Schedule M–2.

Assume the same facts as in Example 30. Tern Corporation's beginning balance in unappropriated retained earnings is $125,000. During the year, Tern distributed a cash dividend of $30,000 to its shareholders. Based on this additional information, Tern's Schedule M–2 for the current year is constructed as follows:

EXAMPLE 31

Schedule M-2	**Analysis of Unappropriated Retained Earnings per Books (Line 25, Schedule L)**				
1	Balance at beginning of year	125,000	5	Distributions: a Cash	30,000
2	Net income (loss) per books	89,400		b Stock	
3	Other increases (itemize): _____			c Property . . .	
	_____		6	Other decreases (itemize): _____	
	_____		7	Add lines 5 and 6	30,000
4	Add lines 1, 2, and 3	214,400	8	Balance at end of year (line 4 less line 7)	184,400

Corporations with less than $250,000 of gross receipts and less than $250,000 in assets do not have to complete Schedule L (balance sheet) and Schedules M–1 and M–2 of Form 1120. Similar rules apply to Form 1120S. These rules are intended to ease the compliance burden on small business.

3-3e Schedule M–3—Net Income (Loss) Reconciliation for Corporations with Total Assets of $10 Million or More

Corporate taxpayers with total assets of $10 million or more are required to report much greater detail relative to differences between income (loss) reported for financial purposes and income (loss) reported for tax purposes. This expanded reconciliation

Concept Summary 3.3

Conceptual Diagram of Schedule M–1 (Form 1120)

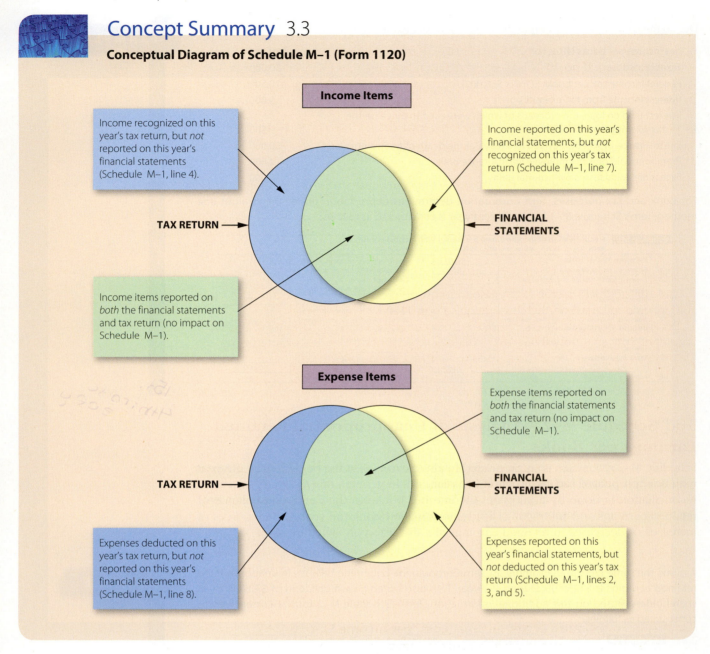

Income Items

Income recognized on this year's tax return, but *not* reported on this year's financial statements (Schedule M–1, line 4).

Income reported on this year's financial statements, but *not* recognized on this year's tax return (Schedule M–1, line 7).

TAX RETURN ⟶

⟵ FINANCIAL STATEMENTS

Income items reported on *both* the financial statements and tax return (no impact on Schedule M–1).

Expense Items

Expense items reported on *both* the financial statements and tax return (no impact on Schedule M–1).

TAX RETURN ⟶

⟵ FINANCIAL STATEMENTS

Expenses deducted on this year's tax return, but *not* reported on this year's financial statements (Schedule M–1, line 8).

Expenses reported on this year's financial statements, but *not* deducted on this year's tax return (Schedule M–1, lines 2, 3, and 5).

of book and taxable income (loss) is reported on **Schedule M–3**.[43] Schedule M–3 is reproduced in Appendix B.

Schedule M–3 is a response, at least in part, to a variety of financial reporting scandals. One objective of Schedule M–3 is to create greater transparency between corporate financial statements and tax returns. Another objective is to identify corporations that engage in aggressive tax practices by requiring that transactions that create book-tax differences be disclosed on corporate tax returns.

---

[43]Corporations that are not required to file Schedule M–3 may do so voluntarily. Any corporation that files Schedule M–3 is not allowed to file Schedule M–1. Corporations (and partnerships) with $10 million to $50 million of total assets may elect to file Schedule M–1 in lieu of Schedule M–3, Parts II and III. Electing entities must still file Schedule M–3, Part I (lines 1–12). Entities with less than $10 million of assets that voluntarily file Schedule M–3 also may elect the reduced Schedule M–3 filing requirements.

Total assets for purposes of the $10 million test and the income and expense amounts required by Schedule M–3 are determined from the taxpayer's financial reports. If the taxpayer files Form 10–K with the Securities and Exchange Commission (SEC), that statement is used. If no 10–K is filed, information from another financial source is used, in the following order: certified (audited) financial statements, prepared income statements, or the taxpayer's books and records.

Part I—Financial Information and Net Income (Loss) Reconciliation

Part I requires the following financial information about the corporation:

- The source of the financial net income (loss) amount used in the reconciliation— SEC Form 10–K, audited financial statements, prepared financial statements, or the corporation's books and records.
- Any restatements of the corporation's income statement for the filing period, as well as any restatements for the past five filing periods.
- Any required adjustments to the net income (loss) amount referred to above (see Part I, lines 5 through 10).

The adjusted net income (loss) amount must be reconciled with the amount of taxable income reported on the corporation's Form 1120.

Because of Schedule M–3's complexity, our coverage is limited to some of the more important concepts underlying the schedule. A series of examples adapted from the instructions for Schedule M–3 are used to illustrate these concepts.

EXAMPLE 32

Southwest Sportsman's Corporation (SSC) sells hunting and fishing equipment to sportsmen. SSC has several stores in Texas, New Mexico, and Arizona. It also has a subsidiary in Mexico, which is organized as a Mexican corporation.

SSC, which does not file a Form 10–K with the SEC, reports income from its Mexican subsidiary on its audited financial statements, which show net income of $45 million in the current year. The Mexican corporation, which is not consolidated by SSC for tax purposes (and, as a result, is not an includible corporation), had net income of $7 million.

SSC will enter $7 million on Part I, line 5a of Schedule M–3, resulting in "net income per income statement of includible corporations" of $38 million (Part I, line 11).

A situation similar to that described in Example 32 could result in additional entries in Part I of Schedule M–3. For example, if SSC engaged in transactions with its non-includible Mexican subsidiary, an entry would be required on line 8 (adjustment to eliminations of transactions between includible corporations and nonincludible entities).

Part II—Reconciliation of Net Income (Loss) per Income Statement of Includible Corporations with Taxable Income per Return

Part II reconciles income and loss items of includible corporations (Part III reconciles expenses and deductions). As indicated in Example 32, corporations included in a financial reporting group may differ from corporations in a tax reporting group. Corporations may also be partners in a partnership, which is a flow-through entity. The following example illustrates the adjustments that are required in this situation.

EXAMPLE 33

Southwest Sportsman's Corporation also owns an interest in a U.S. partnership, Southwest Hunting Lodges (SHL). On its audited financial statements, SSC treats the difference between financial statement net income and taxable income from its investment in SHL as a permanent difference. During the year, SSC reported net income of $10,000,000 as its distributive share from SHL. SSC's Schedule K–1 from SHL reports the following amounts:

Ordinary income	$5,000,000
Long-term capital gain	7,000,000
Charitable contributions	4,000,000
Section 179 expense	100,000

continued

To adjust for the flow-through items from the partnership, SSC must report these items on Schedule M–3, Part II, line 9 [Income (loss) from U.S. partnerships]. The corporation reports $10,000,000 (book income) on line 9, column (a). SSC reports income per tax return of $7,900,000 ($5,000,000 + $7,000,000 − $4,000,000 − $100,000) in column (d) of line 9 and a permanent difference of $2,100,000 in column (c).

Part III—Reconciliation of Expense/Deduction Items

Part III lists 37 reconciling items relating to expenses and deductions. For these items, taxpayers must reconcile differences between income statement amounts (column a) and tax return amounts (column d), and then classify these differences as temporary (column b) or permanent (column c) differences. The totals of the reconciling items from Part III are transferred to Part II, line 27, and are included with other items required to reconcile financial statement net income (loss) to tax return net income (loss).

Book-Tax Differences Reconciled

EXAMPLE 34

Southwest Sportsman's Corporation acquired intellectual property in the current year and expensed amortization of $20,000 on its financial statements, which were prepared according to GAAP. For Federal income tax purposes, SSC deducted $30,000.

The corporation must report the amortization on line 28, Part III as follows: $20,000 book amortization in column (a), $10,000 temporary difference in column (b), and $30,000 tax return amortization in column (d).

EXAMPLE 35

In January of the current year, Southwest Sportsman's Corporation established an allowance for uncollectible accounts (bad debt reserve) of $35,000 on its books and increased the allowance by $65,000 during the year. As a result of a client's bankruptcy, SSC decreased the allowance by $25,000 later in the year. The corporation deducted the $100,000 of increases to the allowance on its income statement but was not allowed to deduct that amount on its tax return. On its tax return, the corporation was allowed to deduct the $25,000 actual loss sustained because of its client's bankruptcy.

These amounts must be reported on line 32, Part III as follows: $100,000 book bad debt expense in column (a), $75,000 temporary difference in column (b), and $25,000 tax return bad debt expense in column (d).

Example 34 illustrates the Schedule M–3 reporting when book expenses are less than tax return deductions. Example 35 illustrates reporting procedures when book expenses are greater than tax return deductions. Both examples illustrate the reporting of temporary differences. The amounts from both examples are included in the totals derived in Part III and are carried to Part II, line 27. The reconciliation of book income and taxable income occurs in lines 26 through 30. The reconciled amount on Part II, line 30, column (a) must be equal to the net income per income statement of includible corporations on Part I, line 11. The reconciled amount on Part II, line 30, column (d) must be equal to the taxable income reported on Form 1120.

3-3f Effect of Taxes on the Financial Statements

Because differences exist between taxable income and net income per books, what effect do these differences have on an entity's financial statements? How are income tax accruals arrived at and reported for accounting purposes? What other types of disclosures regarding present and potential tax liabilities are required to satisfy accounting standards? These and other questions are answered and discussed at length in Chapter 14.

A corporation with total assets of $10 million or more must file Schedule UTP (Uncertain Tax Position Statement) with its Form 1120. In general, a corporation is required to report tax positions taken on a current or prior year's Federal income tax return and for which the corporation recorded a reserve for Federal income tax in its audited financial statements (or for which no reserve was recorded because of an expectation to litigate). Financial reporting of tax positions is discussed in Chapter 14.

3-3g Form 1120 Illustrated

To provide an illustration of the corporate income tax return, a Form 1120 has been completed for Swift Corporation. Due to the $10 million test, Swift Corporation does not need to complete Schedule M–3.

Swift Corporation was formed on January 10, 1985, by James Brown and Martha Swift to sell men's clothing. Pertinent information regarding Swift is summarized as follows:

- The business address is 6210 Norman Street, Buffalo, TX 75831.
- The employer identification number is 11-1111111; the principal business activity code is 448110.
- James Brown and Martha Swift each own one-half of the outstanding common stock; no other class of stock is authorized. James Brown is president of the company, and Martha Swift is secretary-treasurer. Both are full-time employees of the corporation, and each receives a salary of $70,000. James's Social Security number is 123-45-6789; Martha's Social Security number is 987-65-4321.
- The corporation uses the accrual method of accounting and reports on a calendar basis. The specific chargeoff method is used in handling bad debt losses, and inventories are determined using the lower of cost or market method. For book and tax purposes, the straight-line method of depreciation is used.
- During 2018, the corporation distributed a cash dividend of $35,000. Swift's profit and loss statement reflect the following information:

Account	Debit	Credit
Gross sales		$1,045,000
Sales returns and allowances	$ 50,000	
Purchases	506,000	
Dividends received from stock investments in less-than-20%-owned U.S. corporations		60,000
Interest income		
State bonds	$ 4,000	
Certificates of deposit	6,000	10,000
Premiums on term life insurance policies on the lives of James Brown and Martha Swift; Swift Corporation is the designated beneficiary	8,000	
Salaries—officers	140,000	
Salaries—clerical and sales	100,000	
Taxes (state, local, and payroll)	35,000	
Repairs	20,000	
Interest expense		
Loan to purchase state bonds	$ 2,000	
Other business loans	10,000	12,000
Advertising	8,000	
Rental expense	24,000	
Depreciation	16,000	
Other deductions	21,000	

A comparative balance sheet for Swift Corporation reveals the following information:

Assets	January 1, 2018	December 31, 2018
Cash	$ 240,000	$ 178,850
Trade notes and accounts receivable	104,200	142,300
Inventories	200,000	256,000
Certificates of deposit	150,000	150,000
State bonds	100,000	100,000
Prepaid Federal tax	—	2,530
Stock investment	300,000	400,000
Buildings and other depreciable assets	120,000	120,000
Accumulated depreciation	(44,400)	(60,400)
Land	10,000	10,000
Other assets	1,800	1,000
Total assets	$1,181,600	$1,300,280

Liabilities and Equity	January 1, 2018	December 31, 2018
Accounts payable	$ 150,000	$ 125,000
Other current liabilities	40,150	36,300
Mortgages	105,000	100,000
Capital stock	250,000	250,000
Retained earnings	636,450	788,980
Total liabilities and equity	$1,181,600	$1,300,280

Net income per books (before any income tax accrual) is $231,000. During 2018, Swift Corporation made estimated tax payments to the IRS of $46,000. Swift Corporation's Form 1120 for 2018 is reproduced on the following pages.

Although most of the entries on Form 1120 for Swift Corporation are self-explanatory, the following comments may be helpful:

- To arrive at the cost of goods sold amount (line 2 on page 1), Form 1125–A must be completed.

- Reporting of dividends requires the completion of Schedule C (page 2). Total dividends are shown on line 4 (page 1), and the dividends received deduction appears on line 29b (page 1). Separating the dividend from the deduction facilitates the application of any taxable income limitations (which did not apply in Swift's case).

- Income tax liability is $43,470 ($207,000 × 21%).

- The computed tax liability is placed on line 2 of Schedule J and ultimately is listed on line 31 (page 1). Because the estimated tax payments of $46,000 are more than the tax liability of $43,470, Swift will receive a tax refund of $2,530.

- Schedule K, line 4b, requires a Schedule G (Form 1120) to be completed; the schedule has not been completed for this illustrated example.

- In completing Schedule M–1 (page 6), the net income per books (line 1) is net of the Federal income tax ($231,000 − $43,470). The left side of Schedule M–1 (lines 2–5) represents positive adjustments to net income per books. After the negative adjustments are made (line 9), the result is taxable income before NOLs and special deductions (line 28, page 1).

- In completing Schedule M–2 (page 6), net income per books of $187,530 is added to the beginning retained earnings figure of $636,450. The dividends distributed in the amount of $35,000 are entered on line 5 and subtracted to arrive at the ending balance in unappropriated retained earnings of $788,980.

- Because this example lacks certain details, supporting schedules that would be attached to Form 1120 have not been included. For example, a Form 1125–E would be included to support the officer compensation deduction (page 1, line 12), a Form 4562 would be included to verify the depreciation deduction (page 1, line 20), and other deductions (page 1, line 26) would be supported by a schedule.

Form **1120**

Department of the Treasury
Internal Revenue Service

U.S. Corporation Income Tax Return

For calendar year 2018 or tax year beginning _____ , 2018, ending _____ , 20 _____

▶ Go to *www.irs.gov/Form1120* for instructions and the latest information.

OMB No. 1545-0123

2018

A Check if:		
1a Consolidated return (attach Form 851) . . ☐	**TYPE OR PRINT**	Name: *Swift Corporation*
b Life/nonlife consolidated return . . ☐		Number, street, and room or suite no. If a P.O. box, see instructions. *6210 Norman Street*
2 Personal holding co. (attach Sch. PH) . . ☐		City or town, state or province, country, and ZIP or foreign postal code *Buffalo, TX 75831*
3 Personal service corp. (see instructions) . . ☐		

B Employer identification number: *11–1111111*
C Date incorporated: *1-10-85*
D Total assets (see instructions): $ *1,300,280*

4 Schedule M-3 attached ☐   **E** Check if: **(1)** ☐ Initial return   **(2)** ☐ Final return   **(3)** ☐ Name change   **(4)** ☐ Address change

Income

1a	Gross receipts or sales	1a	1,045,000	
b	Returns and allowances	1b	50,000	
c	Balance. Subtract line 1b from line 1a	**1c**		995,000
2	Cost of goods sold (attach Form 1125-A)	**2**		450,000
3	Gross profit. Subtract line 2 from line 1c	**3**		545,000
4	Dividends and inclusions (Schedule C, line 23, column (a))	**4**		60,000
5	Interest	**5**		6,000
6	Gross rents	**6**		
7	Gross royalties	**7**		
8	Capital gain net income (attach Schedule D (Form 1120))	**8**		
9	Net gain or (loss) from Form 4797, Part II, line 17 (attach Form 4797)	**9**		
10	Other income (see instructions—attach statement)	**10**		
11	**Total income.** Add lines 3 through 10 ▶	**11**		611,000

Deductions (See instructions for limitations on deductions.)

12	Compensation of officers (see instructions—attach Form 1125-E) ▶	**12**		140,000
13	Salaries and wages (less employment credits)	**13**		100,000
14	Repairs and maintenance	**14**		20,000
15	Bad debts	**15**		
16	Rents	**16**		24,000
17	Taxes and licenses	**17**		35,000
18	Interest (see instructions)	**18**		10,000
19	Charitable contributions	**19**		
20	Depreciation from Form 4562 not claimed on Form 1125-A or elsewhere on return (attach Form 4562)	**20**		16,000
21	Depletion	**21**		
22	Advertising	**22**		8,000
23	Pension, profit-sharing, etc., plans	**23**		
24	Employee benefit programs	**24**		
25	Reserved for future use	**25**		
26	Other deductions (attach statement)	**26**		21,000
27	**Total deductions.** Add lines 12 through 26 ▶	**27**		374,000
28	Taxable income before net operating loss deduction and special deductions. Subtract line 27 from line 11.	**28**		237,000
29a	Net operating loss deduction (see instructions)	29a		
b	Special deductions (Schedule C, line 24, column (c))	29b	30,000	
c	Add lines 29a and 29b	**29c**		30,000

Tax, Refundable Credits, and Payments

30	**Taxable income.** Subtract line 29c from line 28. See instructions	**30**	207,000
31	Total tax (Schedule J, Part I, line 11)	**31**	43,470
32	2018 net 965 tax liability paid (Schedule J, Part II, line 12)	**32**	
33	Total payments, credits, and section 965 net tax liability (Schedule J, Part III, line 23)	**33**	46,000
34	Estimated tax penalty. See instructions. Check if Form 2220 is attached ▶ ☐	**34**	
35	**Amount owed.** If line 33 is smaller than the total of lines 31, 32, and 34, enter amount owed	**35**	
36	**Overpayment.** If line 33 is larger than the total of lines 31, 32, and 34, enter amount overpaid	**36**	2,530
37	Enter amount from line 36 you want: **Credited to 2019 estimated tax** ▶ **Refunded** ▶	**37**	2,530

Sign Here

Under penalties of perjury, I declare that I have examined this return, including accompanying schedules and statements, and to the best of my knowledge and belief, it is true, correct, and complete. Declaration of preparer (other than taxpayer) is based on all information of which preparer has any knowledge.

▶ _____ Signature of officer   Date _____   ▶ _____ Title

May the IRS discuss this return with the preparer shown below? See instructions. ☐ Yes ☐ No

Paid Preparer Use Only

Print/Type preparer's name	Preparer's signature	Date	Check ☐ if self-employed	PTIN
Firm's name ▶			Firm's EIN ▶	
Firm's address ▶			Phone no.	

For Paperwork Reduction Act Notice, see separate instructions.   Cat. No. 11450Q   Form **1120** (2018)

Form 1120 (2018)   Page **2**

Schedule C	**Dividends, Inclusions, and Special Deductions** (see instructions)	(a) Dividends and inclusions	(b) %	(c) Special deductions (a) × (b)
1	Dividends from less-than-20%-owned domestic corporations (other than debt-financed stock)	60,000	50	30,000
2	Dividends from 20%-or-more-owned domestic corporations (other than debt-financed stock)		65	
3	Dividends on certain debt-financed stock of domestic and foreign corporations . .		see instructions	
4	Dividends on certain preferred stock of less-than-20%-owned public utilities . . .		23.3	
5	Dividends on certain preferred stock of 20%-or-more-owned public utilities		26.7	
6	Dividends from less-than-20%-owned foreign corporations and certain FSCs . . .		50	
7	Dividends from 20%-or-more-owned foreign corporations and certain FSCs . . .		65	
8	Dividends from wholly owned foreign subsidiaries		100	
9	**Subtotal.** Add lines 1 through 8. See instructions for limitations	60,000	see instructions	30,000
10	Dividends from domestic corporations received by a small business investment company operating under the Small Business Investment Act of 1958		100	
11	Dividends from affiliated group members		100	
12	Dividends from certain FSCs		100	
13	Foreign-source portion of dividends received from a specified 10%-owned foreign corporation (excluding hybrid dividends) (see instructions)		100	
14	Dividends from foreign corporations not included on line 3, 6, 7, 8, 11, 12, or 13 (including any hybrid dividends)			
15	Section 965(a) inclusion		see instructions	
16a	Subpart F inclusions derived from the sale by a controlled foreign corporation (CFC) of the stock of a lower-tier foreign corporation treated as a dividend (attach Form(s) 5471) (see instructions)		100	
b	Subpart F inclusions derived from hybrid dividends of tiered corporations (attach Form(s) 5471) (see instructions)			
c	Other inclusions from CFCs under subpart F not included on line 15, 16a, 16b, or 17 (attach Form(s) 5471) (see instructions).			
17	Global Intangible Low-Taxed Income (GILTI) (attach Form(s) 5471 and Form 8992) . .			
18	Gross-up for foreign taxes deemed paid			
19	IC-DISC and former DISC dividends not included on line 1, 2, or 3			
20	Other dividends			
21	Deduction for dividends paid on certain preferred stock of public utilities			
22	Section 250 deduction (attach Form 8993)			
23	**Total dividends and inclusions.** Add lines 9 through 20. Enter here and on page 1, line 4	60,000		
24	**Total special deductions.** Add lines 9 through 22, column (c). Enter here and on page 1, line 29b			30,000

Form **1120** (2018)

Form 1120 (2018) Page **3**

Schedule J	Tax Computation and Payment (see instructions)

Part I–Tax Computation

1	Check if the corporation is a member of a controlled group (attach Schedule O (Form 1120)). See instructions ▶ ☐				
2	Income tax. See instructions			**2**	43,470
3	Base erosion minimum tax (attach Form 8991)			**3**	
4	Add lines 2 and 3			**4**	43,470
5a	Foreign tax credit (attach Form 1118)	**5a**			
b	Credit from Form 8834 (see instructions)	**5b**			
c	General business credit (attach Form 3800)	**5c**			
d	Credit for prior year minimum tax (attach Form 8827)	**5d**			
e	Bond credits from Form 8912	**5e**			
6	**Total credits.** Add lines 5a through 5e			**6**	
7	Subtract line 6 from line 4			**7**	43,470
8	Personal holding company tax (attach Schedule PH (Form 1120))			**8**	
9a	Recapture of investment credit (attach Form 4255)	**9a**			
b	Recapture of low-income housing credit (attach Form 8611)	**9b**			
c	Interest due under the look-back method—completed long-term contracts (attach Form 8697)	**9c**			
d	Interest due under the look-back method—income forecast method (attach Form 8866)	**9d**			
e	Alternative tax on qualifying shipping activities (attach Form 8902)	**9e**			
f	Other (see instructions—attach statement)	**9f**			
10	**Total.** Add lines 9a through 9f			**10**	
11	**Total tax.** Add lines 7, 8, and 10. Enter here and on page 1, line 31			**11**	43,470

Part II–Section 965 Payments (see instructions)

12	2018 net 965 tax liability paid from Form 965-B, Part II, column (k), line 2. Enter here and on page 1, line 32 .	**12**	

Part III–Payments, Refundable Credits, and Section 965 Net Tax Liability

13	2017 overpayment credited to 2018			**13**	
14	2018 estimated tax payments			**14**	46,000
15	2018 refund applied for on Form 4466			**15**	( )
16	Combine lines 13, 14, and 15			**16**	46,000
17	Tax deposited with Form 7004			**17**	
18	Withholding (see instructions)			**18**	
19	**Total payments.** Add lines 16, 17, and 18			**19**	46,000
20	Refundable credits from:				
a	Form 2439	**20a**			
b	Form 4136	**20b**			
c	Form 8827, line 8c	**20c**			
d	Other (attach statement—see instructions)	**20d**			
21	**Total credits.** Add lines 20a through 20d			**21**	
22	2018 net 965 tax liability from Form 965-B, Part I, column (d), line 2. See instructions			**22**	
23	**Total payments, credits, and section 965 net tax liability.** Add lines 19, 21, and 22. Enter here and on page 1, line 33			**23**	46,000

Form **1120** (2018)

Form 1120 (2018)   Page **4**

Schedule K	Other Information (see instructions)		Yes	No

1 Check accounting method: **a** ☐ Cash   **b** ☑ Accrual   **c** ☐ Other (specify) ▶ _____

2 See the instructions and enter the:

a Business activity code no. ▶   *448110*

b Business activity ▶   *Retail sales*

c Product or service ▶   *Men's clothing*

3 Is the corporation a subsidiary in an affiliated group or a parent-subsidiary controlled group? . . . . | | ✓

If "Yes," enter name and EIN of the parent corporation ▶ _____

_____

4 At the end of the tax year:

a Did any foreign or domestic corporation, partnership (including any entity treated as a partnership), trust, or tax-exempt organization own directly 20% or more, or own, directly or indirectly, 50% or more of the total voting power of all classes of the corporation's stock entitled to vote? If "Yes," complete Part I of Schedule G (Form 1120) (attach Schedule G) . . . . . . | | ✓

b Did any individual or estate own directly 20% or more, or own, directly or indirectly, 50% or more of the total voting power of all classes of the corporation's stock entitled to vote? If "Yes," complete Part II of Schedule G (Form 1120) (attach Schedule G) . | ✓ |

5 At the end of the tax year, did the corporation:

a Own directly 20% or more, or own, directly or indirectly, 50% or more of the total voting power of all classes of stock entitled to vote of any foreign or domestic corporation not included on **Form 851,** Affiliations Schedule? For rules of constructive ownership, see instructions. | | ✓

If "Yes," complete (i) through (iv) below.

(i) Name of Corporation	(ii) Employer Identification Number (if any)	(iii) Country of Incorporation	(iv) Percentage Owned in Voting Stock

b Own directly an interest of 20% or more, or own, directly or indirectly, an interest of 50% or more in any foreign or domestic partnership (including an entity treated as a partnership) or in the beneficial interest of a trust? For rules of constructive ownership, see instructions. | | ✓

If "Yes," complete (i) through (iv) below.

(i) Name of Entity	(ii) Employer Identification Number (if any)	(iii) Country of Organization	(iv) Maximum Percentage Owned in Profit, Loss, or Capital

6 During this tax year, did the corporation pay dividends (other than stock dividends and distributions in exchange for stock) in excess of the corporation's current and accumulated earnings and profits? See sections 301 and 316 . . . . | | ✓

If "Yes," file **Form 5452,** Corporate Report of Nondividend Distributions. See the instructions for Form 5452.

If this is a consolidated return, answer here for the parent corporation and on Form 851 for each subsidiary.

7 At any time during the tax year, did one foreign person own, directly or indirectly, at least 25% of the total voting power of all classes of the corporation's stock entitled to vote or at least 25% of the total value of all classes of the corporation's stock? . | | ✓

For rules of attribution, see section 318. If "Yes," enter:

(a) Percentage owned ▶ _____ and **(b)** Owner's country ▶ _____

(c) The corporation may have to file **Form 5472,** Information Return of a 25% Foreign-Owned U.S. Corporation or a Foreign Corporation Engaged in a U.S. Trade or Business. Enter the number of Forms 5472 attached ▶ _____

8 Check this box if the corporation issued publicly offered debt instruments with original issue discount . . . . . . ▶☐

If checked, the corporation may have to file **Form 8281,** Information Return for Publicly Offered Original Issue Discount Instruments.

9 Enter the amount of tax-exempt interest received or accrued during the tax year ▶ $ _____*4,000*_____

10 Enter the number of shareholders at the end of the tax year (if 100 or fewer) ▶ _____*2*_____

11 If the corporation has an NOL for the tax year and is electing to forego the carryback period, check here (see instructions) ▶ ☐

If the corporation is filing a consolidated return, the statement required by Regulations section 1.1502-21(b)(3) must be attached or the election will not be valid.

12 Enter the available NOL carryover from prior tax years (do not reduce it by any deduction reported on page 1, line 29a.) . . . . ▶ $ _____

Form **1120** (2018)

Form 1120 (2018)   Page **5**

Schedule K	**Other Information** *(continued from page 4)*		

		Yes	**No**
13	Are the corporation's total receipts (page 1, line 1a, plus lines 4 through 10) for the tax year **and** its total assets at the end of the tax year less than $250,000?		✓
	If "Yes," the corporation is not required to complete Schedules L, M-1, and M-2. Instead, enter the total amount of cash distributions and the book value of property distributions (other than cash) made during the tax year ▶ $ _____		
14	Is the corporation required to file Schedule UTP (Form 1120), Uncertain Tax Position Statement? See instructions		✓
	If "Yes," complete and attach Schedule UTP.		
15a	Did the corporation make any payments in 2018 that would require it to file Form(s) 1099?	✓	
b	If "Yes," did or will the corporation file required Forms 1099?	✓	
16	During this tax year, did the corporation have an 80% or more change in ownership, including a change due to redemption of its own stock?		✓
17	During or subsequent to this tax year, but before the filing of this return, did the corporation dispose of more than 65% (by value) of its assets in a taxable, non-taxable, or tax deferred transaction?		✓
18	Did the corporation receive assets in a section 351 transfer in which any of the transferred assets had a fair market basis or fair market value of more than $1 million?		✓
19	During the corporation's tax year, did the corporation make any payments that would require it to file Forms 1042 and 1042-S under chapter 3 (sections 1441 through 1464) or chapter 4 (sections 1471 through 1474) of the Code?		✓
20	Is the corporation operating on a cooperative basis?.		✓
21	During the tax year, did the corporation pay or accrue any interest or royalty for which the deduction is not allowed under section 267A? See instructions		✓
	If "Yes," enter the total amount of the disallowed deductions ▶ $ _____		
22	Does the corporation have gross receipts of at least $500 million in any of the 3 preceding tax years? (See sections 59A(e)(2) and (3))		✓
	If "Yes," complete and attach Form 8991.		
23	Did the corporation have an election under section 163(j) for any real property trade or business or any farming business in effect during the tax year? See instructions		✓
24	Does the corporation satisfy **one** of the following conditions and the corporation does not own a pass-through entity with current year, or prior year carryover, excess business interest expense? See instructions	✓	
a	The corporation's aggregate average annual gross receipts (determined under section 448(c)) for the 3 tax years preceding the current tax year do not exceed $25 million, and the corporation is not a tax shelter, or		
b	The corporation only has business interest expense from (1) an electing real property trade or business, (2) an electing farming business, or (3) certain utility businesses under section 163(j)(7).		
	If "No," complete and attach Form 8990.		
25	Is the corporation attaching Form 8996 to certify as a Qualified Opportunity Fund?		✓
	If "Yes," enter amount from Form 8996, line 13 . . . . . ▶ $		

Form **1120** (2018)

Form 1120 (2018)

Schedule L	Balance Sheets per Books	Beginning of tax year		End of tax year	
	Assets	**(a)**	**(b)**	**(c)**	**(d)**
1	Cash		240,000		178,850
2a	Trade notes and accounts receivable	104,200		142,300	
b	Less allowance for bad debts	( )	104,200	( )	142,300
3	Inventories		200,000		256,000
4	U.S. government obligations				
5	Tax-exempt securities (see instructions)		100,000		100,000
6	Other current assets (attach statement)		150,000		152,530
7	Loans to shareholders				
8	Mortgage and real estate loans				
9	Other investments (attach statement)		300,000		400,000
10a	Buildings and other depreciable assets	120,000		120,000	
b	Less accumulated depreciation	(44,400)	75,600	(60,400)	59,600
11a	Depletable assets				
b	Less accumulated depletion	( )		( )	
12	Land (net of any amortization)		10,000		10,000
13a	Intangible assets (amortizable only)				
b	Less accumulated amortization	( )		( )	
14	Other assets (attach statement)		1,800		1,000
15	Total assets		1,181,600		1,300,280
	Liabilities and Shareholders' Equity				
16	Accounts payable		150,000		125,000
17	Mortgages, notes, bonds payable in less than 1 year				
18	Other current liabilities (attach statement)		40,150		36,300
19	Loans from shareholders				
20	Mortgages, notes, bonds payable in 1 year or more		105,000		100,000
21	Other liabilities (attach statement)				
22	Capital stock: **a** Preferred stock				
	b Common stock	250,000	250,000	250,000	250,000
23	Additional paid-in capital				
24	Retained earnings—Appropriated (attach statement)				
25	Retained earnings—Unappropriated		636,450		788,980
26	Adjustments to shareholders' equity (attach statement)				
27	Less cost of treasury stock		( )		( )
28	Total liabilities and shareholders' equity		1,181,600		1,300,280

Schedule M-1	Reconciliation of Income (Loss) per Books With Income per Return

Note: The corporation may be required to file Schedule M-3. See instructions.

1	Net income (loss) per books	187,530	7	Income recorded on books this year not included on this return (itemize): Tax-exempt interest $ 4,000	
2	Federal income tax per books	43,470			
3	Excess of capital losses over capital gains				
4	Income subject to tax not recorded on books this year (itemize):				4,000
5	Expenses recorded on books this year not deducted on this return (itemize):		8	Deductions on this return not charged against book income this year (itemize):	
a	Depreciation $		a	Depreciation $	
b	Charitable contributions $		b	Charitable contributions $	
c	Travel and entertainment $				
	Life insurance premiums $8,000; State bond interest $2,000	10,000	9	Add lines 7 and 8	4,000
6	Add lines 1 through 5	241,000	10	Income (page 1, line 28)—line 6 less line 9	237,000

Schedule M-2	Analysis of Unappropriated Retained Earnings per Books (Line 25, Schedule L)

1	Balance at beginning of year	636,450	5	Distributions: **a** Cash	35,000
2	Net income (loss) per books	187,530		**b** Stock	
3	Other increases (itemize):			**c** Property	
			6	Other decreases (itemize):	
			7	Add lines 5 and 6	35,000
4	Add lines 1, 2, and 3	823,980	8	Balance at end of year (line 4 less line 7)	788,980

Form **1120** (2018)

Form **1125-A**

(Rev. November 2018)

Department of the Treasury
Internal Revenue Service

Cost of Goods Sold

▶ Attach to Form 1120, 1120-C, 1120-F, 1120S, or 1065.
▶ Go to *www.irs.gov/Form1125A* for the latest information.

OMB No. 1545-0123

Name

Swift Corporation

Employer identification number

11-1111111

1	Inventory at beginning of year	**1**	*200,000*
2	Purchases	**2**	*506,000*
3	Cost of labor	**3**	
4	Additional section 263A costs (attach schedule)	**4**	
5	Other costs (attach schedule)	**5**	
6	**Total.** Add lines 1 through 5	**6**	*706,000*
7	Inventory at end of year	**7**	*256,000*
8	**Cost of goods sold.** Subtract line 7 from line 6. Enter here and on Form 1120, page 1, line 2 or the appropriate line of your tax return. See instructions	**8**	*450,000*

9a Check all methods used for valuing closing inventory:

   (i) ☐ Cost

   (ii) ☑ Lower of cost or market

   (iii) ☐ Other (Specify method used and attach explanation.) ▶ --

b Check if there was a writedown of subnormal goods ▶ ☐

c Check if the LIFO inventory method was adopted this tax year for any goods (if checked, attach Form 970) ▶ ☐

d If the LIFO inventory method was used for this tax year, enter amount of closing inventory computed under LIFO   **9d** |

e If property is produced or acquired for resale, do the rules of section 263A apply to the entity? See instructions   ☐ Yes ☑ No

f Was there any change in determining quantities, cost, or valuations between opening and closing inventory? If "Yes," attach explanation   ☐ Yes ☑ No

---

Section references are to the Internal Revenue Code unless otherwise noted.

What's New

Small business taxpayers. For tax years beginning after December 31, 2017, the following apply.

• A small business taxpayer (defined below), may use a method of accounting for inventories that either: (1) treats inventories as nonincidental materials and supplies, or (2) conforms to the taxpayer's financial accounting treatment of inventories.

• A small business taxpayer is not required to capitalize costs under section 263A.

General Instructions

Purpose of Form

Use Form 1125-A to calculate and deduct cost of goods sold for certain entities.

Who Must File

Filers of Form 1120, 1120-C, 1120-F, 1120S, or 1065, must complete and attach Form 1125-A if the applicable entity reports a deduction for cost of goods sold.

Inventories

Generally, inventories are required at the beginning and end of each tax year if the production, purchase, or sale of

merchandise is an income-producing factor. See Regulations section 1.471-1. If inventories are required, you generally must use an accrual method of accounting for sales and purchases of inventory items.

Exception for certain taxpayers. A small business taxpayer (defined below), can adopt or change its accounting method to account for inventories in the same manner as material and supplies that are non-incidental, or conform to its treatment of inventories in an applicable financial statement (as defined in section 451(b)(3)), or if it does not have an applicable financial statement, the method of accounting used in its books and records prepared in accordance with its accounting procedures. See section 471(c)(3).

A small business taxpayer claiming exemption from the requirement to keep inventories is changing its method of accounting for purposes of section 481. For additional guidance on this method of accounting, see Pub. 538, Accounting Periods and Methods. For guidance on changing to this method of accounting, see Form 3115 and the Instructions for Form 3115.

Small business taxpayer. A small business taxpayer is a taxpayer that (a) has average annual gross receipts of $25 million or less (indexed for inflation) for the 3 prior tax years, and (b) is not a tax shelter (as defined in section 448(d)(3)). See Pub. 538.

Uniform capitalization rules. The uniform capitalization rules of section 263A generally require you to capitalize, or include in inventory, certain costs incurred in connection with the following.

• The production of real property and tangible personal property held in inventory or held for sale in the ordinary course of business.

• Real property or personal property (tangible and intangible) acquired for resale.

• The production of real property and tangible personal property for use in its trade or business or in an activity engaged in for profit.

A small business taxpayer (defined above) is not required to capitalize costs under section 263A. See section 263A(i).

See the discussion on section 263A uniform capitalization rules in the instructions for your tax return before completing Form 1125-A. Also see Regulations sections 1.263A-1 through 1.263A-3. See Regulations section 1.263A-4 for rules for property produced in a farming business.

For Paperwork Reduction Act Notice, see instructions.

Cat. No. 55988R

Form **1125-A** (Rev. 11-2018)

3-3h **Consolidated Returns**

Corporations that are members of a parent-subsidiary affiliated group may be able to file a consolidated income tax return for a taxable year. Consolidated returns are discussed in Chapter 8.

3-4 **TAX PLANNING**

LO.6

Evaluate corporations as an entity form for minimizing income taxes on businesses.

3-4a **Corporate versus Noncorporate Forms of Business Organization**

The decision to use the corporate form in conducting a trade or business must be weighed carefully. Besides the nontax considerations of the corporate form (limited liability, continuity of life, free transferability of interests, and centralized management), tax ramifications will play an important role in any such decision. Close attention should be paid to the following:

1. Operating as a regular corporate entity (C corporation) results in the imposition of the corporate income tax. Corporate taxable income will be taxed twice—once as earned by the corporation and again when distributed to the shareholders. Because dividends are not deductible, a closely held corporation may have a strong incentive to structure corporate distributions in a deductible form. With the preferential rates on qualified dividends, shareholders may save taxes by having the corporation pay dividends rather than salaries, rent, or interest, which could be taxed at an individual marginal rate as high as 37 percent. The decision should be made only after comparing the tax cost of the two alternatives. The 3.8 percent Medicare surtax on net investment income (including dividend and net capital gain income) must be considered in this analysis.

2. The differences in Federal tax brackets between an individual and a corporation can be substantial. The potential for a 16 percent difference between the top individual rate and the corporate rate (i.e., 37 percent less 21 percent) presents opportunities for significant tax savings. However, several state and local governments impose higher taxes on corporations than on individuals. In these jurisdictions, the combined Federal, state, and local tax rates on the two types of taxpayers must be evaluated. In addition, the deduction for qualified business income must be considered in any tax savings determination. The savings associated with incorporating is enhanced to the extent double taxation of corporate earnings can be deferred or avoided completely. The TCJA of 2017 significantly increased the estate exemption ($11.4 million for 2019), thus creating greater opportunities for the complete avoidance of double taxation. This complete tax avoidance can be achieved by never distributing corporate earnings and obtaining a stepped-up basis for the corporate stock upon a shareholder's death. However, the accumulated earnings tax and the personal holding company tax may limit opportunities for corporate accumulations and must be factored into any analysis. Consequently, the tax ramifications of incorporating can be determined *only* on a case-by-case basis.

3. Corporate-source income loses its identity as it passes through the corporation to the shareholders. Thus, items that normally receive preferential tax treatment (e.g., interest on municipal bonds) are not taxed as such to the shareholders.

4. As noted in Chapter 5, it may be difficult for shareholders to recover some or all of their investment in the corporation without an ordinary income result. Most corporate distributions are treated as dividends to the extent of the corporation's earnings and profits. However, the preferential rate on qualified dividends reduces the impact of such a result.

5. Corporate losses cannot be passed through to the shareholders.[44]

---

[44]Points 1, 2, and 5 could be resolved through a Subchapter S election (see Chapter 12), assuming that the corporation qualifies for such an election. In part, the same can be said for point 3.

6. The liquidation of a corporation will normally generate tax consequences to both the corporation and its shareholders (see Chapter 6).
7. The corporate form provides shareholders with the opportunity to be treated as employees for tax purposes if the shareholders render services to the corporation. Such status makes a number of attractive tax-sheltered fringe benefits available. They include, but are not limited to, group term life insurance and excludible meals and lodging. One of the most attractive benefits of incorporation is the ability of the business to provide accident and health insurance to its employees, including shareholder-employees. Such benefits are not included in the employee's gross income. Similar rules apply to other medical costs paid by the employer. These benefits are not available to partners, sole proprietors, and more-than-2-percent shareholder-employees of S corporations.

3-4b Operating the Corporation

Tax planning to reduce corporate income taxes should occur before the end of the tax year. Effective planning can cause income to be shifted to the next tax year and can produce large deductions by incurring expenses before year-end. Particular attention should be focused on the following.

Timing of Capital Gains and Losses

A corporation should consider offsetting gains on the sale of capital assets by selling some of the depreciated securities in the corporate portfolio. In addition, any already realized capital losses should be carefully monitored. Recall that corporate taxpayers are not permitted to claim any net capital losses as deductions against ordinary income. Capital losses can be used only as an offset against capital gains. Further, net capital losses can only be carried back three years and forward five. Gains from the sales of capital assets should be timed to offset any capital losses. The expiration of the carryover period for any net capital losses should be watched carefully so that sales of appreciated capital assets occur before that date.

Planning for the Business Interest Expense Limitation

Some business sectors (e.g., health care) are currently more exposed to the limitation than others due to a greater reliance on debt financing, but the limitation's reach is expected to expand significantly in 2022. Beginning in 2022, depreciation, amortization, and depletion will be deducted in arriving at "adjusted taxable income," thus reducing the allowable business interest deduction. The clearest path for reducing the limitation's impact is to pay down debt, such as issuing stock to replace debt. Other alternatives might include forgoing stock buybacks and/or dividends in favor of debt reduction and issuing new debt to replace existing higher interest rate debt.

Charitable Contributions

Recall that accrual basis corporations may claim a deduction for charitable contributions in the year preceding payment. The contribution must be authorized by the board of directors by the end of the tax year and paid on or before the fifteenth day of the fourth month of the following year. It might be useful to authorize a contribution even though it may not ultimately be made. A deduction cannot be thrown back to the previous year (even if paid within the three and one-half months) if it has not been authorized.

   The enhanced deduction amount for contributions of qualified inventory can produce significant tax savings. Gifts of inventory should be designed to take advantage of this provision whenever feasible. Effort should be taken to properly document the type of inventory donated and each recipient charitable organization, since the statutory provisions that allow for an enhanced deduction have very specific requirements for qualification. Further, a corporation's cost of goods sold must be reduced to reflect any charitable contribution of inventory.

The five-year carryover period for excess charitable contributions, coupled with the requirement that a current year's contribution be applied against the 10%-of-taxable-income limitation before the utilization of any carryover amount, may require some tax planning. Under these rules, a charitable contribution in the current year could preclude any deduction for an amount in its fifth year of the carryover period. For a corporation with an annual gift-giving plan, this dilemma may require the deferral of a current year's contribution to obtain a deduction for the expiring carryover amount.

Executive Compensation

A written binding contract in effect on November 2, 2017, is grandfathered under the old executive compensation rules, but only if the contract is not "materially modified" after such date. The renewal of a contract in effect on November 2, 2017, will be treated as a new contract that is not grandfathered. Since performance-based compensation is excluded from the $1 million limitation under prior law, material modifications of grandfathered contracts with such incentives should be avoided. For example, a material modification generally results if a contract is amended to increase or accelerate payment of an employee's compensation.[45]

Net Operating Losses

The 80 percent of taxable income limitation applies to NOLs arising after 2017. NOLs arising in earlier years and carried over to years after 2017 are not subject to the taxable income limitation.

EXAMPLE 36

Ruby Corporation has a $10 million carryover of an NOL that originated in 2017. In 2019, Ruby has taxable income (before the NOL deduction) of $11 million. Since the $10 million NOL carryover arose prior to 2018, the taxable income limitation does not apply and the full amount is deductible in 2019.

For a tax year in which the taxable income limitation is applicable, a corporation might consider taking steps to increase the deductible amount. These steps might include accelerating income into the current tax year or deferring deductions to a subsequent tax year.

Shareholder-Employee Payment of Corporate Expenses

In a closely held corporate setting, shareholder-employees often pay corporate expenses (e.g., office supplies) for which they are not reimbursed by the corporation. Prior to 2018, unreimbursed employee expenses were deductible by an employee (subject to certain limitations). However, the TCJA of 2017 repealed the deduction for miscellaneous itemized deductions (which includes unreimbursed employee expenses) for tax years after 2017. Thus, under current law, neither the corporation nor the employee would be able to deduct such expenses. To preserve the deduction of corporate expenses incurred by shareholder-employees, corporate policy should provide for the reimbursement of these items. The issue can be avoided entirely by having the corporation directly incur the related expenses (e.g., providing a corporate credit card to the shareholder-employee for corporate expenditures).

Personal Service Corporations

The fiscal year limitation, coupled with the treatment of every PSC shareholder-employee as a related party for purposes of the accrued expenditure limitation, severely limit income deferral opportunities. Absent a business purpose, a fiscal year is available only with a § 444 election and the accompanying § 280H deduction limitations for shareholder-employee compensation. The minimum payments under § 280H are based on prior year's compensation, so some deferral may be obtained with a § 444 election for a cash basis PSC when shareholder-employee compensation is anticipated to increase

---

[45]See Notice 2018–68 (2018–36 I.R.B. 418).

yearly. Maximizing shareholder-employee compensation is a way to avoid double taxation on PSC taxable income, but such compensation must pass the reasonableness standard to avoid dividend recharacterization.

Avoiding the Accumulated Earnings Tax

The 21 percent flat corporate tax rate will encourage high-income individual taxpayers to shift income to C corporations to obtain a potential 16 percent reduction in their current tax rate (a maximum 37 percent individual tax rate). This tax savings is enhanced the longer dividend distributions can be deferred, thus increasing the possible imposition of the accumulated earnings tax (AET). However, $250,000 ($150,000 for service corporations) of earnings can be accumulated without imposition of the penalty tax.

Accumulations for reasonable needs of the business in excess of the minimum credit amount should be specific, definite, and feasible (see Reg. § 1.537 for further insight into what constitutes reasonable needs of the business). Dividends reduce the impact of the AET, and if the corporation lacks liquidity to make a distribution, a consent dividend (under § 565) should be considered (here, a dividend is deemed distributed by the corporation to the shareholder, then an equal amount is deemed contributed to the capital of the corporation by the shareholder). The lack of liquidity to make dividend distributions is not a defense against the imposition of the AET.

REFOCUS ON THE BIG PICTURE

COOKED TO PERFECTION

Conducting Skylark Bakery as a corporation would save Samantha $8,475 ($38,000 − $29,525) in income taxes annually, computed as follows:

Bakery Operated as Sole Proprietorship

Operating profit of $100,000:	
Tax on $100,000 × 37%	$37,000
Dividends of $5,000:	
Tax on $5,000 × 20%	1,000
Withdrawals of $50,000:	
No tax	–0–
Total income tax when operated as sole proprietorship	$38,000

Bakery Operated as Regular Corporation

Corporate taxable income of $52,500* (see below):	
Tax on $52,500 × 21%	$11,025
Samantha's salary of $50,000:	
Tax on $50,000 × 37%	18,500
Total income tax when operated as C corporation	$29,525

*Computation of corporate taxable income:

Operating profit	$100,000
Dividends	5,000
Less: Salary to Samantha	(50,000)
Dividends received deduction (50%)	(2,500)
Taxable income	$ 52,500

Note: If available, the deduction for qualified business income would reduce Samantha's $100,000 proprietorship operating profit and, thereby, reduce the tax savings of incorporating.

continued

The example illustrates the tax savings available when a high-income individual taxpayer takes advantage of the lower corporate tax rate. However, other issues, such as employment tax considerations and the taxation of dividend distributions (income taxes and the additional Medicare taxes on net investment income), also should be considered. Further, other potential entity options, such as the LLC and S corporation, also should be evaluated.

What If?

What if the bakery in the first year it becomes a corporation generates a $10,000 short-term capital loss (STCL) on the disposition of some of its stock investments? Regular corporations can only deduct capital losses against capital gains; thus, the $10,000 STCL would not be deductible currently by the corporation and, instead, would be carried forward for up to five years. If the bakery is operated as a sole proprietorship, Samantha would report the capital loss on her individual return. She could use the $10,000 STCL to offset any capital gains she may have and deduct up to $3,000 of the loss against ordinary income.

Key Terms

Accumulated earnings tax, 3-20

C corporations, 3-2

Dividends received deduction, 3-13

Organizational expenditures, 3-16

Passive activity loss, 3-9

Personal holding company (PHC) tax, 3-20

Personal service corporations (PSCs), 3-4

Reasonable needs of the business, 3-20

Regular corporations, 3-2

Schedule M–1, 3-22

Schedule M–3, 3-24

Discussion Questions

1. **LO.1** Janice is the sole owner of Catbird Company. In the current year, Catbird had operating income of $100,000, a long-term capital gain of $15,000, and a charitable contribution of $5,000. Janice withdrew $70,000 of profit from Catbird. How should Janice report this information on her individual tax return if Catbird Company is:

   a. An LLC?

   b. An S corporation?

   c. A C corporation?

Critical Thinking 2. **LO.1** Joel is the sole shareholder of Manatee Corporation, a C corporation. Because Manatee's sales have increased significantly over the last several years, Joel has determined that the corporation needs a new distribution warehouse. Joel has asked your advice as to whether (1) Manatee should purchase the warehouse or (2) he should purchase the warehouse and lease it to Manatee. What relevant tax issues will you discuss with Joel?

3. **LO.1** Ann is the sole shareholder of Salmon Corporation, a newly formed C corporation. Fran is the sole shareholder of Scarlet Corporation, a newly formed C corporation that is a personal service corporation. Both Ann and Fran plan to have their corporations elect a March 31 fiscal year-end. Will the IRS treat both corporations alike with respect to the fiscal year election? Why or why not?

4. **LO.1** Which of the following C corporations will be allowed to use the cash method of accounting for 2019? Explain your answers.

   a. Jade Corporation, which had gross receipts of $26.3 million in 2016, $25.1 million in 2017, and $26 million in 2018.

   b. Lime Corporation, a personal service corporation, which had gross receipts of $26.8 million in 2016, $26.2 million in 2017, and $25.4 million in 2018.

5. **LO.1** Lupe, a cash basis taxpayer, owns 55% of the stock of Jasper Corporation, a calendar year accrual basis C corporation. On December 31, 2019, Jasper accrues a performance bonus of $100,000 to Lupe that it pays to him on January 15, 2020. In which year can Jasper deduct the bonus? In which year must Lupe include the bonus in gross income?

6. **LO.1** In the current year, Jeanette, an individual in the 24% marginal tax bracket, recognized a $20,000 long-term capital gain. Also in the current year, Parrot Corporation, a calendar year C corporation, recognized a $20,000 long-term capital gain. Neither taxpayer had any other property transactions in the year. What tax rates are applicable to these capital gains?

7. **LO.1** John (a sole proprietor) and Eagle Corporation (a C corporation) each recognize a long-term capital gain of $10,000 and a short-term capital loss of $18,000 on the sale of capital assets. Neither taxpayer had any other property transactions during the year. Describe the tax consequences of these gains and losses for John and for Eagle.

8. **LO.1** A taxpayer sells a warehouse for a recognized gain. Depreciation had been properly claimed on the property based on the straight-line method over a 39-year recovery period. Will the same amount of depreciation recapture result whether the taxpayer is an individual or a C corporation? Explain.

9. **LO.1** In general, what is the limitation on the deductibility of business interest expense? What happens to any business interest deduction disallowed under the limitation?

10. **LO.1** Osprey Corporation, a closely held corporation, has $100,000 of net active income, $25,000 of portfolio income, and a $120,000 loss from a passive activity.

    a. How much of the passive activity loss can Osprey deduct in the current year if it is a PSC?

    b. If it is not a PSC?

11. **LO.1** On December 27, 2019, the directors of Partridge Corporation, an accrual basis calendar year taxpayer, authorized a cash contribution of $10,000 to the American Cancer Association. The payment is made on April 13, 2020. Can Partridge deduct the charitable contribution in 2019? Explain.

12. **LO.1, 6** The board of directors of Orange Corporation, a calendar year taxpayer, is holding its year-end meeting on December 27, 2019. One topic on the board's agenda is the approval of a $25,000 gift to a qualified charitable organization. Orange has a $20,000 charitable contribution carryover to 2019 from a prior year. Identify the tax issues the board should consider regarding the proposed contribution. Critical Thinking

13. **LO.1** In general, what is the limitation on the deductibility of executive compensation that applies to publicly traded corporations?

14. **LO.1, 2, 6** Gold Corporation, a calendar year C corporation, was formed in 2012 and has been profitable until the current year. In 2019, Gold incurs a net operating loss. Identify the issues that Gold Corporation should consider regarding its NOL. Critical Thinking

15. **LO.1, 2** Marmot Corporation pays a dividend of $100,000 in the current year. Otter Corporation, a calendar year C corporation, owns 15% of Marmot's stock. Gerald, an individual taxpayer in the 24% marginal bracket, also owns 15% of Marmot's stock. Compare and contrast the treatment of the dividend by Otter Corporation and Gerald.

16. **LO.2** Mustard Corporation (a C corporation) owns 15% of the stock of Burgundy Corporation (a C corporation), which pays an annual dividend to its shareholders. Mustard is considering the purchase of additional shares of Burgundy stock. Would this stock purchase affect the amount of dividends received deduction that Mustard can claim? Explain.

17. **LO.2** Determine whether the following expenditures by Cuckoo Corporation are organizational expenditures, startup expenditures, or neither.
    a. Legal expenses incurred for drafting the corporate charter and bylaws.
    b. Accounting fees incurred in organization.
    c. Expenses of temporary board of directors' organizational meetings.
    d. Employee salaries incurred during the training period before opening for business.
    e. Brokerage fees incurred in initial stock sales.

18. **LO.4** Omar, an individual in the 37% tax bracket, wants to shift some of his income to a new corporation in order to take advantage of the 21% corporate tax rate. Omar plans to avoid any tax on dividends by retaining all earnings within the corporation. Will Omar's plan work? Discuss.

19. **LO.5** When are C corporations required to make estimated tax payments? How are these payments calculated?

20. **LO.5** Schedule M–1 of Form 1120 is used to reconcile financial net income with taxable income reported on the corporation's income tax return as follows: Net income per books + Additions − Subtractions = Taxable income. Classify the following items as additions or subtractions in the Schedule M–1 reconciliation.
    a. Life insurance proceeds received upon death of covered executive.
    b. Tax depreciation in excess of book depreciation.
    c. Federal income tax per books.
    d. Capital loss in excess of capital gain.
    e. Charitable contributions in excess of taxable income limitation.
    f. Premiums paid on life insurance policies covering executives (corporation is beneficiary).

21. **LO.5** In the current year, Woodpecker, Inc., a C corporation with $8,500,000 in assets, deducted amortization of $40,000 on its financial statements and $55,000 on its Federal tax return. Is Woodpecker required to file Schedule M–3? If a Schedule M–3 is filed by Woodpecker, how is the difference in amortization amounts treated on that schedule?

Computational Exercises

22. **LO.1** Goose Corporation, a C corporation, incurs a net capital loss of $12,000 for 2019. It also has ordinary income of $10,000 in 2019. Goose had net capital gains of $2,500 in 2015 and $5,000 in 2018.
    a. Determine the amount, if any, of the net capital loss of $12,000 that is deductible in 2019.
    b. Determine the amount, if any, of the net capital loss of $12,000 that is carried forward to 2020.

23. **LO.1** Aqua Corporation purchases nonresidential real property on May 8, 2016, for $1,000,000. Straight-line cost recovery is taken in the amount of $89,765 before the property is sold on November 27, 2019, for $1,500,000.

    a. Compute the amount of Aqua's recognized gain on the sale of the realty.

    b. Determine the amount of the recognized gain that is treated as § 1231 gain and the amount that is treated as § 1250 recapture (ordinary income).

24. **LO.1** In 2019, Nighthawk Corporation, a calendar year C corporation, has $3,700,000 of adjusted taxable income, $125,000 of business interest income, zero floor plan financing interest, and $1,400,000 of business interest expense.

    a. Assume that Nighthawk has average gross receipts for the prior three-year period of $33,000,000. Determine Nighthawk's current year deduction for business interest.

    b. Assume that Nighthawk has average gross receipts for the prior three-year period of $23,000,000. Determine Nighthawk's current year deduction for business interest.

25. **LO.1** Hummingbird Corporation, a closely held C corporation that is not a PSC, has $40,000 of net active income, $15,000 of portfolio income, and a $45,000 loss from a passive activity. Compute Hummingbird's taxable income for the year.

26. **LO.1** Compute the charitable contribution deduction (ignoring the percentage limitation) for each of the following C corporations.

    a. Amber Corporation donated inventory of clothing (basis of $24,000, fair market value of $30,000) to a qualified charitable organization that operates homeless shelters.

    b. Brass Corporation donated stock held as an investment to Western College (a qualified organization). Brass acquired the stock three years ago for $18,000, and the fair market value on the date of the contribution is $32,000. Western College plans on selling the stock.

    c. Ruby Corporation donates a sculpture held as an investment and worth $130,000 to a local museum (a qualified organization), which exhibits the sculpture. Ruby acquired the sculpture four years ago for $55,000.

27. **LO.2** Crane and Loon Corporations, two unrelated calendar year C corporations, have the following transactions for the current year:

	Crane	Loon
Gross income from operations	$180,000	$300,000
Expenses from operations	255,000	310,000
Dividends received from domestic corporations (15% ownership)	100,000	230,000

    a. Compute the dividends received deduction for Crane Corporation.

    b. Compute the dividends received deduction for Loon Corporation.

28. **LO.2** Cherry Corporation, a calendar year C corporation, is formed and begins business on April 1, 2019. In connection with its formation, Cherry incurs organizational expenditures of $54,000. Determine Cherry Corporation's deduction for organizational expenditures for 2019.

29. **LO.3** Compute the current-year income tax liability for each of the following unrelated calendar year C corporations.

    a. Darter Corporation has taxable income of $68,000.

    b. Owl Corporation has taxable income of $10,800,000.

    c. Toucan Corporation, a personal service corporation, has taxable income of $170,000.

Problems

30. **LO.1** In the current year, Riflebird Company had operating income of $220,000, operating expenses of $175,000, and a long-term capital loss of $10,000. How do Riflebird Company and Roger, the sole owner of Riflebird, report this information on their respective Federal income tax returns for the current year under the following assumptions?

    a.   Riflebird Company is a proprietorship (Roger did not make any withdrawals from the business).

    b.   Riflebird Company is a C corporation (no dividends were paid during the year).

31. **LO.1** In the current year, Azure Company has $350,000 of net operating income before deducting any compensation or other payment to its sole owner, Sasha. In addition, Azure has interest on municipal bonds of $25,000. Sasha has significant income from other sources and is in the 37% marginal tax bracket. Based on this information, determine the income tax consequences to Azure Company and to Sasha during the year for each of the following independent situations. (Ignore the deduction for qualified business income and the 3.8% Medicare surtax on net investment income.)

    a.   Azure is a C corporation and pays no dividends or salary to Sasha.

    b.   Azure is a C corporation and distributes $75,000 of dividends to Sasha.

    c.   Azure is a C corporation and pays $75,000 of salary to Sasha.

    d.   Azure is a sole proprietorship, and Sasha withdraws $0.

    e.   Azure is a sole proprietorship, and Sasha withdraws $75,000.

32. **LO.1** Torsten owns 100% of Taupe Corporation (a calendar year corporation), which had net operating income of $420,000 and long-term capital gain of $30,000 in the current year. Torsten has significant income from other sources and is in the 37% marginal tax bracket without regard to the results of Taupe Corporation. The corporation makes no distributions to Torsten during the year. Ignoring the deduction for qualified business income and the 3.8% Medicare surtax on net investment income, explain the tax treatment if Taupe Corporation is:

    a.   An S corporation.

    b.   A C corporation.

33. **LO.1** In the current year, Wilson Enterprises, a calendar year taxpayer, suffers a casualty loss of $90,000. The casualty was attributable to a Federally declared disaster. How much of the casualty loss will be deductible by Wilson under the following circumstances?

    a.   Wilson is an individual proprietor and has AGI of $225,000. The casualty loss was a personal loss, and the insurance recovered was $50,000.

    b.   Wilson is a corporation, and the insurance recovered was $50,000.

Decision Making

Critical Thinking

Communications

34. **LO.1, 3, 6** Benton Company (BC), a calendar year entity, has one owner, who is in the 37% Federal income tax bracket (any net capital gains or dividends would be taxed at a 20% rate). BC's gross income is $395,000, and its ordinary trade or business deductions are $245,000. Compute the Federal income tax liability on BC's income for the current year under the following assumptions. Ignore the standard deduction (or itemized deductions) and the deduction for qualified business income.

    a.   BC is operated as a proprietorship, and the owner withdraws $100,000 for personal use.

    b.   BC is operated as a corporation, pays out $100,000 as salary, and pays no dividends to its shareholder.

    c.   BC is operated as a corporation and pays out no salary or dividends to its shareholder.

d.   BC is operated as a corporation, pays out $100,000 as salary, and pays out the remainder of its earnings as dividends.

e.   Assume that Robert Benton of 1121 Monroe Street, Ironton, OH 45638 is the owner of BC, which was operated as a proprietorship. Robert is thinking about incorporating the business for next year and asks your advice. He expects about the same amounts of income and expenses and plans to take $100,000 per year out of the company whether he incorporates or not. Based on your analysis in parts (a) and (b), write a letter to Robert containing your recommendations.

35.   **LO.1, 3** Juan, an attorney, is the sole shareholder of Carmine Corporation, a C corporation and professional association. The corporation paid Juan a salary of $336,000 during its fiscal year ending September 30, 2019.

a.   How much salary must Carmine pay Juan during the period October 1 through December 31, 2019, to permit the corporation to continue to use its fiscal year without negative tax effects?

b.   Carmine Corporation had taxable income of $95,000 for the year ending September 30, 2019. Compute the corporation's income tax liability for the year.

36.   **LO.1** Broadbill Corporation, a calendar year C corporation, has two unrelated cash method shareholders: Marcia owns 51% of the stock, and Zack owns the remaining 49%. Each shareholder is employed by the corporation at an annual salary of $240,000. During 2019, Broadbill paid each shareholder-employee $220,000 of his or her annual salary, with the remaining $20,000 paid in January 2020. How much of the 2019 salaries for Marcia and Zack is deductible by Broadbill in 2019 if the corporation is:

a.   A cash method taxpayer?

b.   An accrual method taxpayer?

37.   **LO.1, 3** Jonathan owns 100% of Lemon Company (a calendar year entity). In the current year, Lemon recognizes a long-term capital gain of $70,000 and no other income (or loss). Jonathan is in the 37% tax bracket (and 20% tax bracket for any net capital gains or dividends) and has no recognized capital gains (or losses) before considering his ownership interest in Lemon Company. What is the income tax result from the $70,000 if Lemon is:

a.   An LLC? (No election has been filed under the check-the-box Regulations.)

b.   A C corporation?

38.   **LO.1, 3** In the current year, Tanager Corporation (a calendar year C corporation) had operating income of $480,000 and operating expenses of $390,000. In addition, Tanager had a long-term capital gain of $55,000 and a short-term capital loss of $40,000.

a.   Compute Tanager's taxable income and tax for the year.

b.   Assume, instead, that Tanager's long-term capital gain was $15,000 (not $55,000). Compute Tanager's taxable income and tax for the year.

39.   **LO.1** Virginia owns 100% of Goshawk Company. In the current year, Goshawk Company sells a capital asset (held for three years) at a loss of $40,000. In addition, Goshawk has a short-term capital gain of $18,000 and net operating income of $90,000 during the year. Virginia has no recognized capital gain (or loss) before considering her ownership in Goshawk. How much of the capital loss may be deducted for the year, and how much is carried back or forward if Goshawk is:

a.   A proprietorship?

b.   A C corporation?

Critical Thinking   40. **LO.1** During 2019, Gorilla Corporation, a calendar year C corporation, has net short-term capital gains of $15,000, net long-term capital losses of $105,000, and taxable income from other sources of $460,000. Prior years' transactions included the following:

2015 net short-term capital gains	$40,000
2016 net long-term capital gains	18,000
2017 net short-term capital gains	25,000
2018 net long-term capital gains	20,000

a. How are the capital gains and losses treated on Gorilla's 2019 tax return?

b. Determine the amount of the 2019 capital loss that is carried back to each of the previous years.

c. Compute the amount of capital loss carryforward, if any, and indicate the years to which the loss may be carried.

d. If Gorilla is a sole proprietorship rather than a corporation, how would the owner report these transactions on her 2019 tax return?

e. Assume that Gorilla Corporation's capital loss carryfoward in part (c) is $27,000 and that Gorilla will be able to use $11,000 of the carryover to offset capital gains in 2020 and the remaining $16,000 to offset capital gains in 2021. In present value terms, determine the tax savings of the $105,000 long-term capital loss recognized in 2019. Assume a discount rate of 5% (present value factors are in Appendix F). Further, assume that Gorilla Corporation's marginal income tax rate is 34% for all tax years prior to 2018. Create a spreadsheet using Microsoft Excel (or a similar software program) that summarizes your analysis.

41. **LO.1** Heron Company purchases commercial realty on November 13, 2001, for $650,000. Straight-line depreciation of $287,492 is claimed before the property is sold on February 22, 2019, for $850,000. What are the tax consequences of the sale of realty if Heron is:

a. A C corporation?

b. A sole proprietorship?

42. **LO.1** In the current year, Plum, Inc., a closely held C corporation, has $410,000 of net active income, $20,000 of portfolio income, and a $75,000 passive activity loss. What is Plum's taxable income for the current year under the following circumstances?

a. Plum is a personal service corporation.

b. Plum is not a personal service corporation.

43. **LO.1** Aquamarine Corporation, a calendar year C corporation, makes the following donations to qualified charitable organizations during the current year:

	Adjusted Basis	Fair Market Value
Painting held four years as an investment, to a church, which sold it immediately	$15,000	$25,000
Apple stock held two years as an investment, to United Way, which sold it immediately	40,000	90,000
Canned groceries held one month as inventory, to Catholic Meals for the Poor	10,000	17,000

Determine the amount of Aquamarine Corporation's charitable deduction for the current year. (Ignore the taxable income limitation.)

Decision Making   44. **LO.1, 6** Joseph Thompson is president and sole shareholder of Jay Corporation (a
Critical Thinking   cash method, calendar year C corporation). In December 2019, Joe asks
Communications   your advice regarding a charitable contribution he plans to have the corporation make to the University of Maine, a qualified public charity. Joe is considering the following alternatives as charitable contributions in December 2019:

	Fair Market Value
(1) Cash donation	$200,000
(2) Unimproved land held for six years ($110,000 basis)	200,000
(3) Maize Corporation stock held for eight months ($140,000 basis)	200,000
(4) Brown Corporation stock held for nine years ($360,000 basis)	200,000

Joe has asked you to help him decide which of these potential contributions will be most advantageous taxwise. Jay's taxable income is $3,500,000 before considering the contribution. Rank the four alternatives, and write a letter to Joe communicating your advice. The corporation's address is 1442 Main Street, Freeport, ME 04032.

45. **LO.1, 6** In 2019, Gray Corporation, a calendar year C corporation, has a $75,000 charitable contribution carryover from a gift made in 2014. Gray is contemplating a gift of land to a qualified charity in either 2019 or 2020. Gray purchased the land as an investment five years ago for $100,000 (current fair market value is $250,000). Before considering any charitable deduction, Gray projects taxable income of $1,000,000 for 2019 and $1,200,000 for 2020. Should Gray make the gift of the land to charity in 2019 or in 2020? Provide support for your answer.

Decision Making
Critical Thinking

46. **LO.1, 6** Julieta Simms is the president and sole shareholder of Simms Corporation (a cash method, calendar year C corporation), 1121 Madison Street, Seattle, WA 98121. Julieta plans for the corporation to make a charitable contribution to the University of Washington, a qualified public charity. She will have the corporation donate Jaybird Corporation stock, held for five years, with a basis of $11,000 and a fair market value of $25,000. Julieta projects a $310,000 net profit for Simms Corporation in 2019 and a $100,000 net profit in 2020. Julieta calls you on December 12, 2019, and asks whether she should make the contribution in 2019 or 2020. Write a letter advising Julieta about the timing of the contribution.

Decision Making
Critical Thinking
Communications

47. **LO.1** Florence is the Chief Financial Officer of Hazel Corporation, a publicly traded, calendar year C corporation. For the current year, her compensation package consists of:

Cash compensation	$1,500,000
Bonus tied to company performance	700,000
Taxable fringe benefits	250,000
Nontaxable fringe benefits	75,000

How much of Florence's compensation is deductible by Hazel Corporation?

48. **LO.1, 2** During the current year, Swallow Corporation, a calendar year C corporation, has the following transactions:

Income from operations	$660,000
Expenses from operations	760,000
Dividends received from Brown Corporation	240,000

a. Swallow Corporation owns 12% of Brown Corporation's stock. How much is Swallow's taxable income or NOL for the year?

b. Assume instead that Swallow Corporation owns 26% of Brown Corporation's stock. How much is Swallow's taxable income or NOL for the year?

49. **LO.2** In each of the following independent situations, determine the dividends received deduction for the calendar year C corporation. Assume that none of the corporate shareholders owns 20% or more of the stock in the corporations paying the dividends.

	Almond Corporation	Banana Corporation	Cherry Corporation
Income from operations	$ 700,000	$ 800,000	$ 900,000
Expenses from operation	(600,000)	(860,000)	(910,000)
Qualifying dividends	100,000	100,000	100,000

50. **LO.2** Gull Corporation, a cash method, calendar year C corporation, was formed and began business on November 1, 2019. Gull incurred the following expenses during its first year of operations (November 1, 2019–December 31, 2019):

Expenses of temporary directors and organizational meetings	$21,000
Fee paid to state of incorporation	3,000
Expenses for printing and sale of stock certificates	11,000
Legal services for drafting the corporate charter and bylaws (not paid until January 2020)	19,000

   a. Assuming that Gull Corporation elects under § 248 to expense and amortize organizational expenditures, what amount may be deducted in 2019?

   b. Assume the same facts as above, except that the amount paid for the legal services was $28,000 (instead of $19,000). What amount may be deducted as organizational expenditures in 2019?

51. **LO.2** Egret Corporation, a calendar year C corporation, was formed on March 6, 2019, and opened for business on July 1, 2019. After its formation but prior to opening for business, Egret incurred the following expenditures:

Accounting	$ 7,000
Advertising	14,500
Employee payroll	11,000
Rent	8,000
Utilities	1,000

   What is the maximum amount of these expenditures that Egret can deduct in 2019?

52. **LO.3** In each of the following independent situations, determine the corporation's income tax liability. Assume that all corporations use a calendar year for tax purposes and that the tax year involved is 2019.

	Taxable Income
Purple Corporation	$ 65,000
Azul Corporation	290,000
Pink Corporation	12,350,000
Turquoise Corporation	19,000,000
Teal Corporation (a personal service corporation)	130,000

53. **LO.5** Grouse Corporation, a calendar year C corporation, had taxable income of $1,400,000, $1,200,000, and $700,000 for 2017, 2018, and 2019, respectively. Grouse has taxable income of $1,600,000 for 2020. What are Grouse Corporation's minimum required estimated tax payments for 2020?

54. **LO.5** Emerald Corporation, a calendar year and accrual method taxpayer, provides the following information and asks you to prepare Schedule M–1 for 2019:

Net income per books (after-tax)	$268,200
Federal income tax per books	31,500
Tax-exempt interest income	15,000
Life insurance proceeds received as a result of death of corporate president	150,000
Interest on loan to purchase tax-exempt bonds	1,500
Excess of capital loss over capital gains	6,000
Premiums paid on life insurance policy on life of Emerald's president	7,800

55. **LO.5** The following information for 2019 relates to Sparrow Corporation, a calendar year, accrual method taxpayer:

Net income per books (after-tax)	$205,050
Federal income tax per books	55,650
Tax-exempt interest income	4,500
MACRS depreciation in excess of straight-line depreciation used for financial purposes	7,200
Excess of capital loss over capital gains	9,400
Nondeductible meals and entertainment	5,500
Interest on loan to purchase tax-exempt bonds	1,100

Based on the above information, use Schedule M–1 of Form 1120, which is available on the IRS website, to determine Sparrow's taxable income for 2019.

56. **LO.5** Dove Corporation, a calendar year C corporation, had the following information for 2019:

Net income per books (after-tax)	$386,250
Taxable income	120,000
Federal income tax per books	25,200
Cash dividend distributions	150,000
Unappropriated retained earnings, as of January 1, 2019	796,010

Based on the above information, use Schedule M–2 of Form 1120 (see Example 31 in the text) to determine Dove's unappropriated retained earnings balance as of December 31, 2019.

57. **LO.5** In the current year, Pelican, Inc., a calendar year C corporation, incurs $10,000 of meals and entertainment expenses that it deducts in computing net income per the corporation's financial statements. All of the meals and entertainment expenditures are subject to the 100% disallowance rule applicable to such expenditures. How is this information reported on Schedule M–3?

58. **LO.5** In the current year, Pelican, Inc., incurs $50,000 of nondeductible fines and penalties. Its depreciation expense is $245,000 for financial statement purposes and $310,000 for tax purposes. How is this information reported on Schedule M–3?

59. **LO.5** In January 2019, Pelican, Inc., established an allowance for uncollectible accounts (bad debt reserve) of $70,000 on its books and increased the allowance by $120,000 during the year. As a result of a client's bankruptcy, Pelican, Inc., decreased the allowance by $60,000 in November 2019. Pelican, Inc., deducted the $190,000 of increases to the allowance on its 2019 income statement but was not allowed to deduct that amount on its tax return. On its 2019 tax return, the corporation was allowed to deduct the $60,000 actual loss sustained because of its client's bankruptcy. On its financial statements, Pelican, Inc., treated the $190,000 increase in the bad debt reserve as an expense that gave rise to a temporary difference. On its 2019 tax return, Pelican, Inc., took a $60,000 deduction for bad debt expense. How is this information reported on Schedule M–3?

60. **LO.1, 2, 6** In January 2019, Don and Steve each invested $100,000 cash to form a corporation to conduct business as a retail golf equipment store. On January 5, they paid Bill, an attorney, to draft the corporate charter, file the necessary forms with the state, and write the bylaws. They leased a store building and began to acquire inventory, furniture, display equipment, and office equipment in February. They hired a sales staff and clerical personnel in March and conducted

Critical Thinking

training sessions during the month. They had a successful opening on April 1, and sales increased steadily throughout the summer. The weather turned cold in October, and all local golf courses closed by October 15, which resulted in a drastic decline in sales. Don and Steve expect business to be very good during the Christmas season and then to taper off significantly from January 1 through the end of February. The corporation accrued bonuses to Don and Steve on December 31, payable on April 15 of the following year. The corporation made timely estimated tax payments throughout the year. The corporation hired a bookkeeper in February, but he does not know much about taxation. Don and Steve have retained you as a tax consultant and have asked you to identify the tax issues they should consider.

Tax Return Problems

1. On November 1, 2008, Janet Morton and Kim Wong formed Pet Kingdom, Inc., to sell pets and pet supplies. Pertinent information regarding Pet Kingdom is summarized as follows:

   - Pet Kingdom's business address is 1010 Northwest Parkway, Dallas, TX 75225; its telephone number is (214) 555-2211; and its e-mail address is petkingdom@pki.com.
   - The employer identification number is 11-1111112, and the principal business activity code is 453910.
   - Janet and Kim each own 50% of the common stock; Janet is president and Kim is vice president of the company. No other class of stock is authorized.
   - Both Janet and Kim are full-time employees of Pet Kingdom. Janet's Social Security number is 123-45-6788, and Kim's Social Security number is 123-45-6787.
   - Pet Kingdom is an accrual method, calendar year taxpayer. Inventories are determined using FIFO and the lower of cost or market method. Pet Kingdom uses the straight-line method of depreciation for book purposes and accelerated depreciation (MACRS) for tax purposes.
   - During 2018, the corporation distributed cash dividends of $250,000.

   Pet Kingdom's financial statements for 2018 are shown below.

Income Statement

Income		
Gross sales		$ 5,750,000
Sales returns and allowances		(200,000)
Net sales		$ 5,550,000
Cost of goods sold		(2,300,000)
Gross profit		$ 3,250,000
Dividends received from stock investments in less-than-20%-owned U.S. corporations		43,750
Interest income:		
State bonds	$ 15,000	
Certificates of deposit	20,000	35,000
Total income		$ 3,328,750

continued

Expenses

Salaries—officers:		
Janet Morton	$262,500	
Kim Wong	262,500	$525,000
Salaries—clerical and sales		725,000
Taxes (state, local, and payroll)		238,000
Repairs and maintenance		140,000
Interest expense:		
Loan to purchase state bonds	$ 9,000	
Other business loans	207,000	216,000
Advertising		58,000
Rental expense		109,000
Depreciation*		106,000
Charitable contributions		38,000
Employee benefit programs		60,000
Premiums on term life insurance policies on lives of Janet Morton and Kim Wong; Pet Kingdom is the designated beneficiary		40,000
Total expenses		(2,255,000)
Net income before taxes		$ 1,073,750
Federal income tax		(221,734)
Net income per books		$ 852,016

*Depreciation for tax purposes is $136,000. You are not provided enough detailed data to complete a Form 4562 (depreciation). If you solve this problem using Intuit ProConnect, enter the amount of depreciation on line 20 of Form 1120.

Balance Sheet

Assets	January 1, 2018	December 31, 2018
Cash	$ 1,200,000	$ 1,039,461
Trade notes and accounts receivable	2,062,500	2,147,000
Inventories	2,750,000	3,030,000
Stock investment	1,125,000	1,125,000
State bonds	375,000	375,000
Certificates of deposit	400,000	400,000
Prepaid Federal tax	–0–	2,266
Buildings and other depreciable assets	5,455,000	5,455,000
Accumulated depreciation	(606,000)	(712,000)
Land	812,500	812,500
Other assets	140,000	128,500
Total assets	$13,714,000	$13,802,727

Liabilities and Equity	January 1, 2018	December 31, 2018
Accounts payable	$ 2,284,000	$ 1,840,711
Other current liabilities	175,000	155,000
Mortgages	4,625,000	4,575,000
Capital stock	2,500,000	2,500,000
Retained earnings	4,130,000	4,732,016
Total liabilities and equity	$13,714,000	$13,802,727

During 2018, Pet Kingdom made estimated tax payments of $56,000 each quarter to the IRS. Prepare a Form 1120 for Pet Kingdom for tax year 2018. Suggested software: ProConnect Tax Online.

2. On February 12, 2005, Nancy Trout and Delores Lake formed Kingfisher Corporation to sell fishing tackle. Pertinent information regarding Kingfisher is summarized as follows:

- Kingfisher's business address is 1717 Main Street, Ely, MN 55731; its telephone number is (218) 555-2211; and its e-mail address is kingfisher@kf.com.
- The employer identification number is 11-1111113, and the principal business activity code is 451110.
- Nancy owns 50% of the common stock and is president of the company, and Delores owns 50% of the common stock and is vice president of the company. No other class of stock is authorized.
- Both Nancy and Delores are full-time employees of Kingfisher. Nancy's Social Security number is 123-45-6788, and Delores's Social Security number is 123-45-6787.
- Kingfisher is an accrual method, calendar year taxpayer. Inventories are determined using FIFO and the lower of cost or market method. Kingfisher uses the straight-line method of deprecation for book purposes and accelerated depreciation (MACRS) for tax purposes.
- During 2018, the corporation distributed cash dividends of $80,000.

Kingfisher's financial statements for 2018 are shown below and on the next page.

Income Statement

Income

Gross sales		$2,408,000
Sales returns and allowances		(80,000)
Net sales		$2,328,000
Cost of goods sold		(920,000)
Gross profit		$1,408,000
Dividends received from stock investments in less-than-20%-owned U.S. corporations		12,000
Interest income:		
State bonds	$ 14,000	
Certificates of deposit	10,000	24,000
Total income		$1,444,000

Expenses

Salaries—officers:			
Nancy Trout	$160,000		
Delores Lake	160,000	$320,000	
Salaries—clerical and sales		290,000	
Taxes (state, local, and payroll)		85,000	
Repairs and maintenance		56,000	
Interest expense:			
Business loans	$ 12,000		
Loan to purchase state bonds	8,000	20,000	
Advertising		6,000	
Rental expense		68,000	
Depreciation*		40,000	
Charitable contributions		15,000	
Employee benefit programs		24,000	
Premiums on term life insurance policies on lives of Nancy Trout and Delores Lake; Kingfisher is the designated beneficiary		16,000	
Total expenses			(940,000)
Net income before taxes			$ 504,000
Federal income tax			(106,680)
Net income per books			$ 397,320

*You are not provided enough detailed information to complete a Form 4562 (depreciation). If you solve this problem using Intuit ProConnect, enter the amount of deprecation on line 20 of Form 1120.

Balance Sheet

Assets	January 1, 2018	December 31, 2018
Cash	$ 380,000	$ 337,300
Trade notes and accounts receivable	308,400	480,280
Inventories	900,000	1,012,000
State bonds	160,000	160,000
Federal income tax refund	–0–	1,320
Certificates of deposit	140,000	140,000
Stock investments	300,000	300,000
Building and other depreciable assets	240,000	240,000
Accumulated depreciation	(88,800)	(128,800)
Land	20,000	20,000
Other assets	3,600	2,000
Total assets	$2,363,200	$2,564,100

Liabilities and Equity	January 1, 2018	December 31, 2018
Accounts payable	$ 300,000	$ 233,880
Other current liabilities	80,300	40,000
Mortgages	210,000	200,000
Capital stock	500,000	500,000
Retained earnings	1,272,900	1,590,220
Total liabilities and equity	$2,363,200	$2,564,100

During 2018, Kingfisher made estimated tax payments of $27,000 each quarter to the IRS. Prepare a Form 1120 for Kingfisher for tax year 2018. Suggested software: ProConnect Tax Online.

Research Problems

Note: Solutions to the Research Problems can be prepared by using the Thomson Reuters Checkpoint™ online tax research database, which accompanies this textbook. Solutions can also be prepared by using research materials found in a typical tax library.

Research Problem 1. A personal service corporation (PSC) generally is limited to the calendar year for reporting purposes. One exception to this rule is when the PSC can demonstrate a business purpose for a fiscal year-end. Discuss the business purpose exception, including examples of when the standard is and is not satisfied. Support your research with proper citations of tax authority.

Partial list of research aids:
§ 441(i).
Reg. § 1.441–3.

Research Problem 2. A new client, John Dobson, recently formed John's Premium Steakhouse, Inc., to operate a new restaurant. The restaurant will be a first-time business venture for John, who recently retired after 30 years of military service. John transferred cash to the corporation in exchange for 100% of its stock, and the corporation has leased a building and restaurant equipment. John has asked you for guidance on the tax treatment of various expenses (e.g., licensing, training, advertising) he expects the corporation to incur during the restaurant's preopening period. Research the tax treatment of startup expenditures, including the point at which a business begins for purposes of determining what expenses are included. Prepare a memo for the client files describing the results of your research.

Communications

Partial list of research aids:
§ 195.
Reg. § 1.195–1.

Communications
Critical Thinking

Research Problem 3. Tern Corporation, a calendar year C corporation, is solely owned by Jessica Ramirez. Tern's only business since its incorporation in 2016 has been land surveying services. In Tern's state of incorporation, land surveying can be performed only by a licensed surveyor. Jessica, Tern's only employee, is a licensed surveyor but is not a licensed engineer. Upon audit of Tern's 2016 and 2017 tax returns, the IRS assessed tax deficiencies stemming from its conclusion that the corporation was a personal service corporation subject to the flat tax rate of 35%. Jessica believes that the IRS's determination is incorrect, and she has asked you for advice on how to proceed. Evaluate the IRS's position regarding the treatment of Tern Corporation as a personal service corporation, and prepare a memo for the client files describing the results of your research.

Use internet tax resources to address the following questions. Look for reliable websites and blogs of the IRS and other government agencies, media outlets, businesses, tax professionals, academics, think tanks, and political outlets.

Communications

Research Problem 4. A significant percentage of U.S. corporations are closely held corporations, with the stock of such corporations often owned predominately or exclusively by family members. Using the internet as your sole research source, prepare an outline describing the tax implications and planning opportunities unique to family-owned, closely held corporations.

Research Problem 5. Download Schedule M–3 and the accompanying instructions from the IRS website. The instructions provide several examples of adjustments that are reported on Schedule M–3. Select three of these examples, and make the required entries to the appropriate parts and lines of Schedule M–3.

Data Analytics
Communications

Research Problem 6. Find the most recent *IRS Tax Statistics* (**irs.gov/statistics**) report for Corporation Income Tax Returns. Based solely on this report, prepare an outline highlighting the top three industries based on corporate pretax profits reported (Figure B), the three most common corporate tax reporting year-ends (Figure D), and the three most common types of corporate returns filed (Figure E).

Becker CPA Review Questions

1. In the current year, Acorn, Inc., had the following items of income and expense:

Sales	$500,000
Cost of sales	250,000
Dividends received	25,000

   The dividends were received from a corporation of which Acorn owns 30%. In Acorn's current-year corporate income tax return, what amount should be reported as income before special deductions?

   a. $525,000   c. $275,000
   b. $505,000   d. $250,000

2. Before the provision for Federal income tax, Karas Corporation had book income of $400,000 for the current year. The book income included $100,000 of dividends received from a 15% owned domestic corporation. What was Karas Corporation's taxable income for the current year?

   a. $300,000   c. $350,000
   b. $335,000   d. $400,000

3. In year 6, Garland Corp. contributed $40,000 to a qualified charitable organization. Garland's year 6 taxable income before the deduction for charitable contributions was $410,000. Included in that amount is a $20,000 dividends received deduction. Garland also had carryover contributions of $5,000 from the prior year. In year 6, what amount can Garland deduct as charitable contributions?

   a. $40,000
   b. $41,000
   c. $43,000
   d. $45,000

4. Tapper Corp., an accrual basis calendar year corporation, was organized on January 2, year 1. During year 1, revenue was exclusively from sales proceeds and interest income. The following information pertains to Tapper:

Taxable income before charitable contributions for the year ended December 31, year 1	$500,000
Tapper's matching contribution to employee-designated qualified universities made during year 1	10,000
Board of Directors' authorized contribution to a qualified charity (authorized December 1, year 1, made February 1, year 2)	30,000

   What is the maximum allowable deduction that Tapper may take as a charitable contribution on its tax return for the year ended December 31, year 1?

   a. $0
   b. $10,000
   c. $30,000
   d. $40,000

5. Campbell Corporation, an accrual basis calendar year corporation, had income of $450,000 for financial statement purposes in year 7. This amount included book depreciation of $50,000. The related tax depreciation was $65,000. Further, the financial statements reported $100,000 of municipal bond interest income, an expense of $2,000 for life insurance premiums on the corporation's president, charitable contributions of $5,000, excess capital losses over capital gains of $3,000, income tax penalties of $10,000, state income tax of $40,000, and Federal income tax expense of $175,000. What is the amount of Campbell's taxable income for year 7?

   a. $522,000
   b. $525,000
   c. $530,000
   d. $565,000

6. Hirsch, Incorporated, is a calendar year corporation that has had revenues of less than $500,000 since inception. In 2017, Hirsch had a net operating loss that was able to be used in full via a carryback to 2016. For 2018, Hirsch expects to have taxable income of $100,000. How will Hirsch avoid a penalty for underpayment of estimated Federal taxes in the current year?

   a. Hirsch must pay 100% of the tax shown on its 2018 return via estimated taxes to avoid an underpayment penalty.

   b. Hirsch must pay the amount of taxes owed on its 2017 return via estimated taxes to avoid an underpayment penalty.

   c. Hirsch must pay 90% of the tax shown on its 2018 return via estimated taxes to avoid an underpayment penalty.

   d. Hirsch may pay the lower of the amount of taxes owed in 2017 or 100% of the tax shown on the return for 2018 via estimated taxes to avoid an underpayment penalty.

7. The dividends received deduction (DRD) is a tax deduction that may be taken by which of the following?

   a. An individual
   b. An S corporation
   c. A partnership
   d. A C corporation

8. Which of the following statements is *not* true for tax years beginning after 2017?

   a. Affiliated corporations that file consolidated returns can take a 100% dividends received deduction.

   b. The dividends received deduction for a small investment in an unrelated corporation is 50%.

   c. The dividends received deduction for a large investment in a corporation is 65%.

   d. There is no income limitation on the dividends received deduction.

9. Parent Corp. owns 40% of Sub Corp. In the current year, Parent has gross income of $43,000 and allowable deductions of $30,000 before considering any dividends received deduction (DRD). Included in the $43,000 gross income is $8,000 of dividends from Sub. What is the maximum DRD available to Parent?

   a. $4,000   c. $8,000

   b. $5,200   d. $8,450

10. Parent Corp. owns 15% of Sub Corp. Parent has gross income of $43,000 and allowable deductions of $40,000 before considering any dividends received deduction (DRD). Included in the $43,000 gross income is $8,000 in dividends from Sub. What is the maximum DRD available to Parent?

    a. $1,500   c. $4,000

    b. $1,950   d. $8,000

Corporations: Organization and Capital Structure

LEARNING OBJECTIVES: *After completing Chapter 4, you should be able to:*

LO.1 Explain the tax consequences of incorporating a business.

LO.2 Describe the special rules that apply when a corporation assumes shareholder liabilities.

LO.3 Identify the basis issues relevant to the shareholder and the corporation.

LO.4 Explain the tax aspects of the capital structure of a corporation.

LO.5 Characterize the tax differences between debt and equity investments.

LO.6 Handle the tax treatment of shareholder debt and stock gains and losses.

LO.7 Identify tax planning opportunities associated with organizing and financing a corporation.

CHAPTER OUTLINE

GOODLUZ/SHUTTERSTOCK.COM

THE VEHICLE FOR BUSINESS GROWTH IS THE CORPORATE FORM

Emily has operated her startup venture as a sole proprietorship since launching the business two years ago. David, a friend from college, has been collaborating with Emily. Together they have developed an innovative software app. They were overjoyed that as soon as the app was introduced into the market, it was an immediate hit—and it has gained increasing recognition and market traction as sales continue to rise. After only a short period of success though, Emily becomes convinced that the upside potential for even more growth is significant. However, she realizes that a leap to that level of growth and market penetration can only be achieved with a large infusion of capital that she is unable to fund from her resources.

Fortunately, Emily's friend Ethan, who is a venture capitalist, is enthusiastic about making a large investment in the business in exchange for an equity stake. Ethan agrees that Emily's startup easily will enjoy remarkable success once it has the necessary additional resources. To integrate Ethan's capital into the venture, the sole proprietorship will be incorporated with Emily and Ethan each contributing assets in exchange for stock in newly formed Transformation, Inc. Emily also has asked David, an invaluable employee and a major contributor to the app's development, if he would be interested in becoming a shareholder in Transformation. He was given the option of transferring either property or services in exchange for stock. However, at this point, David is undecided about what he will do.

Emily will receive 200 shares of Transformation stock in exchange for transferring the following sole proprietorship assets to the new corporation:

	Adjusted Basis	Fair Market Value
Accounts receivable	$ –0–	$ 50,000
Building	100,000	400,000
Proprietary information—app	300,000	1,550,000
	$400,000	$2,000,000

Ethan will contribute $48 million of cash for 4,800 shares of Transformation stock.

What will be the tax and nontax implications relating to the formation of Transformation, Inc.?

Read the chapter and formulate your response.

Chapters 2 and 3 dealt with four principal areas fundamental to working with corporations: (1) understanding the unique treatment that applies to entities treated as corporations for Federal income tax purposes, (2) recognizing specific income tax rules that apply only to corporations, (3) identifying filing and reporting procedures, and (4) considering special situations involving corporations.

Chapter 4 addresses more sophisticated issues involving corporations:

- The tax consequences to the shareholders and the corporation when transferring property to form a new corporation.
- The tax result from shareholders transferring property to an already-existing corporation.
- The capital structure of a corporation, including equity and debt financing.
- The special tax treatment of investor losses.
- The special treatment given to gain realized from the disposition of qualified small business stock.

LO.1

Explain the tax consequences of incorporating a business.

4-1 ORGANIZATION OF AND TRANSFERS TO CONTROLLED CORPORATIONS

Property transactions normally produce tax consequences if a gain or loss is realized. As a result, unless special provisions in the Code apply, a transfer of property to a corporation in exchange for stock is a taxable transaction. The amount of gain or loss equals the difference between the fair market value of the stock received and the tax basis of the property transferred.

4-1a Section 351 Rationale and General Rules

In contrast to the typical result of full gain or loss recognition, the Code permits nonrecognition of gain or loss in limited circumstances. For example, with both § 1031 (like-kind exchanges) and § 351 (transfers of property to controlled corporations), recognition of gain or loss is postponed until a substantive change in the taxpayer's investment occurs (e.g., a sale of property or ownership shares to outsiders). Section 1031 provides for gain or loss deferral when a taxpayer exchanges certain property for "like-kind property." The rules accomplish this deferral by reducing the basis for deferred gain or increasing the basis for deferred loss. This substituted basis results in the taxpayer recognizing the gain or loss when the taxpayer sells the new property for cash or non-like-kind property.[1]

Similarly, Example 1 below illustrates that § 351 defers gain or loss when transferring property to a controlled corporation (defined in text Section 4-1d) in exchange for the corporation's own stock. There are at least two reasons for this tax deferral treatment. First, an owner's economic status is unchanged when incorporating business assets; only the *form* of the investment has changed. The investment in the business assets carries over to an investment in corporate stock. When only stock in the corporation is received, the shareholder is hardly in a position to pay a tax on any realized gain. Thus, this approach is justified under the *wherewithal to pay concept* discussed in Chapter 1. As noted later, however, when the taxpayer receives property other than stock (i.e., cash or other "boot") from the corporation, the shareholder recognizes some or all of the realized gain.

A second justification for the nonrecognition of gain or loss provisions under § 351 is that Congress believes tax rules should not impede a taxpayer's judgment about the best choice of entity form for conducting business.

---

[1]For a complete discussion of the rationale and rules pertaining to like-kind exchanges under § 1031, see Chapter 15 in *Individual Income Taxes*, 2019 Edition.

GLOBAL TAX ISSUES — Tax Reform Adds a New Wrinkle to the Choice of Organizational Form When Operating Overseas

When the management of a corporation decides to expand its business by establishing a presence in a foreign market, the new business venture may take one of several organizational forms. As each form comes with its respective advantages and disadvantages, making the best choice can be difficult. And the choice is even more difficult now since a new set of rules applies to the taxation of international operations beginning in 2018.

Nonetheless, one common approach is to conduct the foreign activity as a *branch* operation of the U.S. corporation. The foreign branch is not a separate legal entity, but a division of the U.S. corporation established overseas. As a result, any gains and losses produced by the foreign unit are included in the corporation's overall financial results.

Another possibility is to organize the foreign operations as a *subsidiary* of the U.S. parent corporation. If this route is chosen, the subsidiary may be either a *domestic* subsidiary (i.e., organized in the United States) or a *foreign* subsidiary (organized under the laws of a foreign country).

One fundamental tax difference between these two approaches is that the gains and losses of a domestic subsidiary may be consolidated with the operations of the U.S. parent, but the operations of a foreign subsidiary cannot. Thus, the use of a domestic subsidiary to conduct foreign operations generally yields the same final result as the use of a branch. With both approaches, the financial statements of the U.S. parent reflect the results of its worldwide operations.

As noted, the tax rules associated with international operations and their impact on organizational forms have changed with the passage of the Tax Cuts and Jobs Act (TCJA) of 2017. Now the United States uses a "territorial system" when taxing foreign earnings, which, generally, requires U.S. corporations to pay U.S. tax only on their domestic income. Given the complexity of the organizational form decisions and the significance of the changes to international taxation rules in the TCJA of 2017, it will take time for tax professionals to determine the most tax-effective ways of structuring foreign operations of U.S. corporations. See Chapter 9 for additional discussion of the taxation of international operations.

EXAMPLE 1

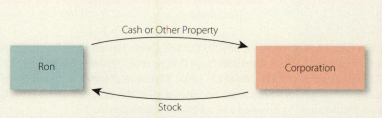

Ron is considering incorporating his sole proprietorship to obtain the limited liability of the corporate form. Ron realizes that if he incorporates, depending on state law, he will be personally liable only for the debts of the business that he has guaranteed.

If Ron incorporates his business, he will transfer the following assets to the corporation:

	Tax Basis	Fair Market Value
Cash	$ 10,000	$ 10,000
Furniture and fixtures	20,000	60,000
Land and building	240,000	300,000
	$270,000	$370,000

In this change of business form, Ron will receive the corporation's stock worth $370,000 in exchange for the assets he transfers. Without the deferral provisions of § 351, Ron would recognize a taxable gain of $100,000 on the transfer ($370,000 value of the stock received − $270,000 basis of the assets transferred).

Under § 351, however, Ron does not recognize any gain because his economic status has not really changed. Ron's investment in the assets of his sole proprietorship is now represented by his ownership of stock in the corporation. Ron will take a $270,000 basis in his stock and *not* a $370,000 cost basis. This adjustment to his stock basis results in a $100,000 gain *deferral* and not gain *exemption*. As a result, § 351 provides for tax neutrality on the incorporation decision because there is no tax cost of incorporating his business.

In a manner similar to a like-kind exchange, if a taxpayer transfers property to a corporation and receives "boot" (cash or property other than stock), the taxpayer recognizes gain (but not loss) to the extent of the lesser of the gain realized or the value of the boot received. Any gain recognized is classified (e.g., ordinary, capital) according to the type of assets transferred.[2] As discussed in more detail later, the non-recognition of gain or loss is accompanied by a substituted basis in the shareholder's stock.[3] The major shareholder consequences of a taxable property transaction versus one that is tax deferred are set out in Concept Summary 4.1.

EXAMPLE 2

Amanda and Calvin form Quail Corporation. Amanda transfers equipment with an adjusted basis of $30,000, fair market value of $60,000, for 50% of the stock, worth $60,000. Calvin transfers equipment with an adjusted basis of $70,000, fair market value of $60,000, for the remaining 50% of the stock. The transfers qualify under § 351.

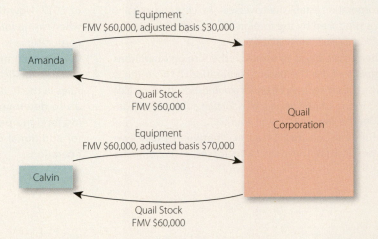

Amanda has an unrecognized gain of $30,000, and Calvin has an unrecognized loss of $10,000. Both have a substituted basis in the stock in Quail Corporation. Amanda has a basis of $30,000 in her stock, and Calvin has a basis of $70,000 in his stock. Therefore, if either Amanda or Calvin later disposes of the Quail stock in a taxable transaction (e.g., a sale), this deferred gain/loss will then be fully recognized—a $30,000 gain to Amanda and a $10,000 loss to Calvin.

Alternatively, if Amanda and Calvin each received Quail stock worth $50,000 and cash of $10,000, Amanda would recognize $10,000 of the $30,000 realized gain because she received boot of $10,000, while Calvin's receipt of boot would not trigger the recognition of a loss (i.e., recognition of loss never occurs in a § 351 transaction on the receipt of boot). Additional discussion of gain/loss recognition and the basis of stock received appears later in the chapter.

Section 351 is *mandatory* if a transaction satisfies the provision's requirements. As explained in the following sections, the three requirements for nonrecognition of gain or loss under § 351 are that (1) *property is transferred* (2) in exchange for *stock* and (3) the property transferors are in *control* of the corporation after the exchange. Therefore, if recognition of gain or loss is *desired*, the taxpayer must plan to fail to meet at least one of these requirements.

---

[2]§ 351(b) and Rev.Rul. 68–55, 1968–1 C.B. 140.

[3]§ 358(a). See the discussion preceding Example 22.

Concept Summary 4.1

Shareholder Consequences: Taxable Corporate Formation versus Tax-Deferred § 351 Transaction

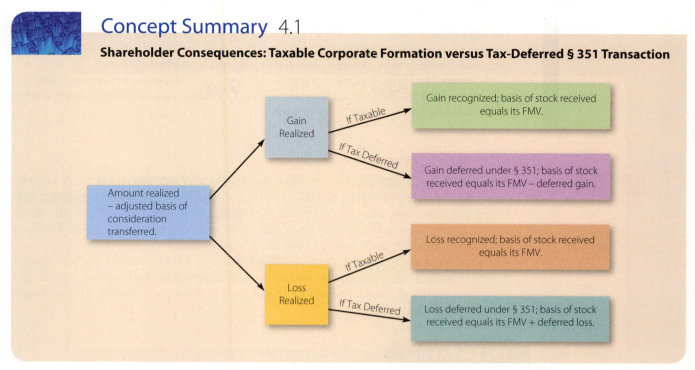

4-1b **Property Defined**

For § 351 purposes, the definition of **property** is comprehensive. For example, along with plant and equipment, unrealized receivables of a cash basis taxpayer and install-ment notes are considered property.[4] Although the disposition of an installment note receivable normally triggers deferred gain, its transfer under § 351 is not treated as a disposition. As a result, gain is not recognized to the transferor. Proprietary processes and formulas as well as proprietary information in the general nature of a patentable invention also qualify as property under § 351.[5]

Section 351 specifically excludes services from the definition of property. So a tax-payer must report as income the fair market value of any consideration received as compensation for services.[6] Consequently, when a taxpayer receives stock as consid-eration for rendering services to the corporation, the income the taxpayer recognizes equals the fair market value of the stock received. This immediate taxation results in a fair market value stock basis for the taxpayer.

EXAMPLE 3

Ann and Bob form Olive Corporation with the transfer of the following consideration:

| | Consideration Transferred | | |
	Basis to Transferor	Fair Market Value	Number of Shares Issued
From Ann:			
Personal services rendered to Olive Corporation	$ –0–	$20,000	200
From Bob:			
Installment note receivable	5,000	40,000	
Inventory	10,000	30,000	800
Proprietary process	–0–	10,000	

continued

---

[4]*Hempt Brothers, Inc. v. U.S.,* 74–1 USTC ¶9188, 33 AFTR 2d 74–570, 490 F.2d 1172 (CA–3, 1974), and Reg. § 1.453–9(c)(2).

[5]Rev.Rul. 64–56, 1964–1 C.B. 133; Rev.Rul. 71–564, 1971–2 C.B. 179.
[6]§§ 61 and 83.

The value of each share in Olive Corporation is $100.[7] Ann has income of $20,000 on the transfer because services do not qualify as "property." She has a basis of $20,000 in her 200 shares of Olive (i.e., Ann is treated as having bought some of the Olive stock by rendering services).

In contrast, Bob has no recognized gain on the receipt of stock because he transfers "property" and he has "control" of Olive after the transfer; see the discussion concerning control that follows. Bob has a substituted basis of $15,000 in the Olive stock.

4-1c Stock Transferred

Nonrecognition of gain occurs only when the shareholder receives stock. Stock includes common and most preferred shares. However, it does not include "nonqualified preferred stock," which possesses many of the attributes of debt. In addition, the Regulations state that the term *stock* does not include stock rights and stock warrants. Otherwise, the term *stock* generally needs no clarification.[8]

As a result, any corporate debt or securities (e.g., long-term debt such as bonds) received are treated as boot because they are not shares of stock. Therefore, the receipt of debt in exchange for the transfer of appreciated property to a controlled corporation causes recognition of gain.

The Big Picture

EXAMPLE 4

Return to the facts of *The Big Picture* on p. 4-1. Assume that the proposed transaction involving Emily and Ethan qualifies under § 351, but Emily decides to receive some corporate debt along with the stock.

If she receives Transformation stock worth $1,900,000 and Transformation debt of $100,000 in exchange for the property transferred, Emily realizes gain of $1,600,000 [$2,000,000 (value of consideration received) − $400,000 (basis in the transferred property)]. However, because the transaction qualifies under § 351, only $100,000 of gain is recognized—the $100,000 of Transformation debt is treated as boot. The remaining realized gain of $1,500,000 is deferred.

4-1d Control of the Corporation

For the transaction to qualify as nontaxable under § 351, the property transferors must be in control of the corporation immediately after the exchange. That is, the person or persons transferring the property must have at least an 80 percent stock ownership in the corporation, resulting in the entity being a controlled corporation. More specifically, the property transferors must own stock possessing at least 80 percent of the total combined *voting power* of all classes of stock entitled to vote *and* at least 80 percent of the total *number of shares* of all other classes of stock.[9]

Control Immediately after the Transfer

Control after the exchange can apply to a single person or to several taxpayers if they are all parties to an integrated transaction. To satisfy the timing requirement, when more than one person is involved, the exchange does not necessarily require simultaneous exchanges by those persons. However, the rights of those transferring property to the corporation must be previously set out and determined. Also, the agreement to transfer property should be executed "with an expedition consistent with orderly procedure," and the transfers should occur close together in time.[10]

---

[7]The value of closely held stock normally is presumed to equal the value of the property transferred.

[8]§ 351(g). Examples of nonqualified preferred stock include preferred stock that is redeemable within 20 years of issuance and whose dividend rate is based on factors other than corporate performance. See also Reg. § 1.351–1(a)(1)(ii).

[9]§ 368(c). Nonqualified preferred stock is treated as stock, not boot, for purposes of this control test.

[10]Reg. § 1.351–1(a)(1).

The Point at Which Control Is Determined

Jack exchanges property with a basis of $60,000 and fair market value of $100,000 for 70% of the stock of Gray Corporation. The other 30% of the stock is owned by Jane, who acquired it several years ago. The fair market value of Jack's stock is $100,000.

Jack recognizes a taxable gain of $40,000 on the transfer because he does not control the corporation after his transfer and his transaction cannot be integrated with Jane's for purposes of the control requirement.

EXAMPLE
5

The Big Picture

Return to the facts of *The Big Picture* on p. 4-1. Assume that the proposed transaction involving Emily and Ethan occurs as described. However, in addition, David decides to contribute property to the new corporation in exchange for an equity interest.

As a result, Emily exchanges her property for 200 shares of Transformation, Inc. stock on January 7, 2018, David exchanges his property for 10 shares of Transformation stock on January 14, 2018, and Ethan exchanges his property for 4,800 shares in Transformation on March 5, 2018.

Because the three exchanges are part of a prearranged plan and the control test is met, the nonrecognition provisions of § 351 apply to all of the exchanges.

EXAMPLE
6

Stock need not be issued to the property transferors in the same proportion as the relative value of the property transferred by each. However, when stock received is not proportionate to the value of the property transferred, the actual effect of the transactions must be properly characterized. For example, in such situations, one transferor may actually be making a gift to another transferor.

Noah and Shelia, father and daughter, form Oak Corporation. Noah transfers property worth $50,000 in exchange for 100 shares of stock, and Shelia transfers property worth $50,000 for 400 shares of stock.

The transfers qualify under § 351 because Noah and Shelia have control of the Oak stock immediately after the transfers of property. However, the implicit gift of 150 shares by Noah to Shelia must be recognized and appropriately characterized. As such, the value of the gift might be subject to the gift tax (see Chapter 18).

EXAMPLE
7

Once control has been achieved, it is not necessarily lost if, shortly after the transaction, stock received by shareholders is sold or given to persons who are not parties to the exchange.[11]

Naomi and Eric form Eagle Corporation. They transfer appreciated property to the corporation with each receiving 50 shares of Eagle stock. Shortly after the formation, Naomi gives 25 shares to her son.

Because Naomi was not committed to making the gift, she met the control test "immediately after the exchange." Therefore, the requirements of § 351 are met, and neither Naomi nor Eric is taxed on the exchange.

EXAMPLE
8

The following two examples show that a different result might materialize if a plan for the ultimate disposition of the stock existed *before* the exchange. In other words, mere momentary control on the part of the transferor may not suffice if loss of control is compelled by a prearranged agreement.[12]

---

[11]*Wilgard Realty Co. v. Comm.*, 42–1 USTC ¶9452, 29 AFTR 325, 127 F.2d 514 (CA–2, 1942).   [12]Rev.Rul. 54–96, 1954–1 C.B. 111.

The Impact of a Preconceived Plan on the Control Requirement

EXAMPLE 9

Assume the same facts as in Example 8, except that Naomi immediately gives 25 shares to a business associate pursuant to a plan to satisfy an outstanding obligation.

In this case, the formation of Eagle would be taxable to Naomi and Eric because they jointly owned only 75% of the stock.

EXAMPLE 10

For many years, Paula operated a business as a sole proprietor employing Brooke as manager. To dissuade Brooke from quitting and going out on her own, Paula promised her a 30% interest in the business. To fulfill this promise, Paula transfers the business to newly formed Green Corporation in return for all of its stock. Immediately thereafter, Paula transfers 30% of the stock to Brooke.

Section 351 probably does not apply to Paula's transfer to Green Corporation because it appears that Paula was under an obligation to relinquish control. If this preexisting obligation exists, § 351 will not be available to Paula because, as the sole property transferor, she does not have 80% control of Green Corporation.

However, if there is no obligation and the loss of control was voluntary on Paula's part, momentary control would suffice.[13]

Transfers for Property and Services

Examples 5, 9, and 10 show that taxpayers can lose § 351 treatment if persons who do not transfer property own "too much" stock. Example 11 shows how a service contributor can cause a property contributor to fail the control test and thus have to recognize gain.

EXAMPLE 11

Sarah transfers property with a basis of $400,000 and fair market value of $1,000,000 to Garden, Inc., and receives 50% of its stock. Tiffany receives the other 50% of the stock for services rendered (worth $1,000,000).

Tiffany has ordinary income of $1,000,000 because she contributes only services. She must recognize compensation income for services rendered.

Sarah contributes property, but she receives only 50% of Garden's stock. Because Sarah does not own at least 80% of Garden's stock, she has a taxable gain of $600,000 [$1,000,000 (fair market value of the stock in Garden) − $400,000 (basis in the transferred property)].

As noted earlier, a person receiving stock in exchange for services and for property transferred is taxed on the stock value related to those services but not on the stock issued for property, assuming the property transferors control the corporation. In addition, such a person can still be treated as a "property transferor," and in this case, all stock received by the person transferring both property and services is counted in determining whether the transferors acquired control of the corporation.[14]

EXAMPLE 12

Assume the same facts as in Example 11, except that Tiffany transfers property worth $800,000 (basis of $260,000) in addition to services rendered to Garden, Inc. (valued at $200,000).

Now Tiffany becomes a part of the control group. Sarah and Tiffany, as property transferors, together receive 100% of the corporation's stock. Consequently, § 351 applies to the exchanges.

As a result, Sarah recognizes no gain. Tiffany does not recognize gain on the transfer of the property, but she recognizes ordinary income to the extent of the value of the shares issued for services rendered. Thus, Tiffany recognizes $200,000 of ordinary income currently.

---

[13]Compare *Fabs v. Florida Machine and Foundry Co.*, 48–2 USTC ¶9329, 36 AFTR 1161, 168 F.2d 957 (CA–5, 1948), with *John C. O'Connor*, 16 TCM 213, T.C.Memo. 1957–50, *aff'd* in 58-2 USTC ¶9913, 2 AFTR 2d 6011, 260 F.2d 358 (CA–6, 1958).

[14]Reg. § 1.351–1(a)(2), Ex. 3.

Transfers for Services and Nominal Property

Note that to be part of the group meeting the 80 percent control test, the person contributing services must transfer property having more than a "relatively small value" compared with the services performed. When the primary purpose of the transfer is to qualify the transaction under § 351 for concurrent transferors, the Regulations provide that stock issued for property whose value is relatively small compared with the value of the stock already owned (or to be received for services rendered) will not be treated as issued in return for property.[15]

Exactly when a taxpayer who renders services and transfers property is included in the control group is often subject to question. However, the IRS has stated that such a transferor can be included in the control group if the value of the property transferred is at least 10 percent of the value of the services provided. If the value of the property transferred is less than this amount, the IRS is likely to treat the property contributed as having a relatively small value and disregard it in applying the control test.[16]

Determining Control Group Membership When Services Are Rendered

Ava and Rick form Grouse Corporation. Ava transfers land worth $100,000 with a basis of $20,000. Rick transfers equipment worth $50,000 with an adjusted basis of $10,000 and provides services worth $50,000. Ava and Rick each receive 50% of the Grouse stock.

Because the value of the property Rick transfers is not small relative to the value of the services he renders, his stock in Grouse Corporation is counted in determining control for purposes of § 351; thus, Ava and Rick jointly own 100% of the stock in Grouse. In addition, all of Rick's stock, not just the shares received for the equipment, counts in determining control.

As a result, Ava does not recognize gain on the transfer of the land. Rick similarly does not recognize the gain on his equipment; however, he must recognize income of $50,000 on the transfer of services. Even though the transfer of the equipment qualifies Rick as a property contributor under § 351, his transfer of services for stock is still taxable compensation income.

EXAMPLE 13

Assume the same facts as in Example 13, except that the value of Rick's property is $2,000 and the value of his services is $98,000.

In this situation, the value of the property is small relative to the value of the services (and well below the 10% IRS threshold); therefore, Rick will not be considered a property transferor. Consequently, the transaction will be fully taxable to both Ava and Rick. In this situation, Ava, the sole property transferor, lacks at least 80% control of Grouse Corporation following the transfer.

As a result, she will fully recognize her realized gain. Further, because Rick is not treated as having transferred property, the § 351 deferral is not available to him. As a result, he will recognize income of $98,000 relating to the services provided along with any realized gain or loss on the transfer of the additional $2,000 of consideration.

EXAMPLE 14

Transfers to Existing Corporations

Once a corporation is in operation, § 351 also applies to any later transfers of property for stock by either new or existing shareholders. That is, § 351 does not apply solely at the time of corporate formation.

Tyrone and Andrew formed Blue Corporation three years ago. Both Tyrone and Andrew transferred appreciated property to Blue in exchange for 50 shares each in the corporation. The original transfers qualified under § 351, and neither Tyrone nor Andrew was taxed on the exchange. In the current year, Tyrone transfers property (worth $90,000, adjusted basis of $5,000) for 50 additional Blue shares.

Tyrone has a taxable gain of $85,000 on the transfer. The exchange does not qualify under § 351 because Tyrone does not have 80% control of Blue Corporation immediately after the transfer—he owns 100 shares of the 150 shares outstanding, or a 66⅔% interest.

EXAMPLE 15

---

[15]Reg. § 1.351–1(a)(1)(ii).

[16]Rev.Proc. 77–37, 1977–2 C.B. 568.

LO.2

Describe the special rules that apply when a corporation assumes shareholder liabilities.

4-1e Assumption of Liabilities—§ 357

It is not uncommon to form a corporation by transferring assets *and* liabilities of an unincorporated business. Generally, the party that enjoys the debt relief treats it as cash received equal to the debt relief. Without a provision to the contrary, the transfer of mortgaged property to a controlled corporation could trigger gain to the property transferor if the corporation took over the mortgage. Section 357(a) provides, however, that when the acquiring corporation assumes a liability in a § 351 transaction, the liability is not treated as boot received for gain recognition purposes. (However, liabilities assumed by the corporation are treated as boot in determining the basis of the stock received by the shareholder.) As a result, the basis of the stock received is reduced by the amount of the liabilities assumed by the corporation. See the more complete discussion of basis computations in text Section 4-1f.

The Big Picture

EXAMPLE 16

Return to the facts of *The Big Picture* on p. 4-1. Assume that you learn that David is not interested in becoming a stockholder in Transformation, Inc., and that Emily and Ethan will transfer their property for 100% of the stock. In addition, you learn that Emily's building is subject to a liability of $70,000 that Transformation assumes. Consequently, Emily receives her Transformation stock and is relieved of the $70,000 liability in exchange for property with an adjusted basis of $400,000 and fair market value of $2,000,000.

The exchange is tax-free to Emily under § 351 because the release of a liability is not treated as boot under § 357(a). However, the basis to Emily of the Transformation stock is $330,000 [$400,000 (basis of property transferred) − $70,000 (amount of the liability assumed by Transformation)]. This basis reduction reflects the economic benefit that Emily enjoys by transferring her mortgage to the corporation.

The general rule of § 357(a) has two exceptions: (1) § 357(b) provides that if the principal purpose of the assumption of the liabilities is to avoid tax *or* if there is no bona fide business purpose behind the exchange, the liabilities are treated as boot; (2) § 357(c) provides that if the sum of the liabilities exceeds the adjusted basis of the properties transferred, the excess is taxable gain.

Exception (1): Tax Avoidance or No Bona Fide Business Purpose

Satisfying the bona fide business purpose under § 357(b) is not difficult if the liabilities are incurred in connection with the transferor's normal course of conducting a trade or business. But this requirement can cause difficulty if the liability is taken out shortly before the property is transferred and the proceeds are utilized for personal purposes.[17] This type of situation is analogous to the corporation transferring both stock and cash to the shareholder, resulting in boot treatment for the liabilities assumed.

EXAMPLE 17

Dan transfers real estate with a basis of $140,000 and fair market value of $190,000 to a controlled corporation in return for stock in the corporation. However, shortly before the transfer, Dan mortgages the real estate and uses the $20,000 of proceeds to meet personal obligations.

In this case, the assumption of the mortgage lacks a bona fide business purpose. Consequently, § 357(b) treats the debt relief as boot received, and Dan has a taxable gain on the transfer of $20,000.[18]

Amount realized:	
Stock	$ 170,000
Release of liability—treated as boot	20,000
Total amount realized	$ 190,000
Less: Basis of real estate	(140,000)
Realized gain	$ 50,000
Recognized gain	$ 20,000

---

[17]See, for example, *Campbell, Jr. v. Wheeler*, 65–1 USTC ¶9294, 15 AFTR 2d 578, 342 F.2d 837 (CA–5, 1965).   [18]§ 351(b).

The effect of the application of § 357(b) is to taint *all* liabilities transferred even if *some* are supported by a bona fide business purpose.

Tim, an accrual basis taxpayer, incorporates his sole proprietorship. Among the liabilities transferred to the new corporation are trade accounts payable of $100,000 and a credit card bill of $5,000. Tim had used the credit card to purchase an anniversary gift for his spouse.

Under these circumstances, *all* of the $105,000 of liabilities are treated as boot and trigger the recognition of gain to the extent gain is realized.

Exception (2): Liabilities in Excess of Basis

The second exception in § 357(c) provides that if the amount of a shareholder's liabilities assumed exceeds the total of the adjusted bases of the properties transferred by that shareholder, the excess is taxable gain. Without this provision, when there are **liabilities in excess of basis** in a property exchange, a taxpayer would have a negative basis in the stock received in the controlled corporation.[19] Section 357(c) precludes the negative basis possibility by treating the excess over basis as gain to the transferor.

Andre transfers land and equipment with adjusted bases of $350,000 and $50,000, respectively, to a newly formed corporation in exchange for 100% of the stock. The corporation assumes a $500,000 liability on the transferred land.

Without § 357(c), Andre's basis in the stock of the new corporation would be negative $100,000 [$400,000 (bases of properties transferred) + $0 (gain recognized) − $0 (boot received) − $500,000 (liability assumed)]. Section 357(c), however, requires Andre to recognize gain of $100,000 ($500,000 liability assumed − $400,000 total bases of assets transferred).

As a result, the stock has a zero basis in Andre's hands, determined as follows:

Bases in the properties transferred ($350,000 + $50,000)	$ 400,000
Plus: Gain recognized	100,000
Less: Boot received	–0–
Less: Liability assumed	(500,000)
Basis in the stock received	$ –0–

Consequently, Andre recognizes $100,000 of gain and avoids a negative stock basis.

The definition of liabilities under § 357(c) excludes obligations that would have been deductible to the transferor had those obligations been paid before the transfer. Therefore, accounts payable of a cash basis taxpayer are not considered liabilities for purposes of § 357(c). In addition, they are not considered in the computation of the shareholder's stock basis.

Tina, a cash basis taxpayer, incorporates her sole proprietorship. In return for all of the stock of the new corporation, she transfers the following items:

	Adjusted Basis	Fair Market Value
Cash	$10,000	$10,000
Unrealized accounts receivable (amounts due to Tina but not yet received by her)	–0–	40,000
Trade accounts payable	–0–	30,000
Note payable	5,000	5,000

continued

---

[19] *Jack L. Easson,* 33 T.C. 963 (1960), *rev'd* in 61–2 USTC ¶9654, 8 AFTR 2d 5448, 294 F.2d 653 (CA–9, 1961).

> Because the unrealized accounts receivable and trade accounts payable have a zero basis under the cash method of accounting, no income is recognized until the receivables are collected and no deduction materializes until the payables are satisfied. The note payable has a basis because it was issued for consideration received.
>
> In this situation, the trade accounts payable are disregarded for gain recognition purposes and in determining Tina's stock basis. Thus, for purposes of § 357(c), because the balance of the note payable does not exceed the basis of the assets transferred, Tina does not face the situation of liabilities in excess of basis (i.e., the note payable of $5,000 does not exceed the aggregate basis in the cash and accounts receivable of $10,000).

Conceivably, a situation could arise where both §§ 357(b) and (c) apply in the same transfer. In such a situation, § 357(b) predominates.[20] This could be significant because § 357(b) does not automatically create gain on the transfer, as does § 357(c), but merely converts the liability to boot. Thus, the realized gain limitation continues to apply to § 357(b) transactions.

EXAMPLE

21

Chris forms Robin Corporation by transferring land with a basis of $100,000 and a fair market value of $1,000,000. The land is subject to a mortgage of $300,000. One month before incorporating Robin, Chris borrows $200,000 for personal purposes and gives the lender a second mortgage on the land. Therefore, on the incorporation, Robin issues stock worth $500,000 to Chris and assumes the two mortgages on the land.

Section 357(c) seems to apply to the transfer, given that the mortgages on the property exceed the basis of the property. As a result, Chris would have a gain of $400,000 under § 357(c).

Section 357(b), however, also applies to the transfer because Chris borrowed $200,000 just prior to the transfer and used the loan proceeds for personal purposes. Thus, under § 357(b), Chris has boot of $500,000 in the amount of the liabilities, which triggers $500,000 of recognized gain. Note that *all* of the liabilities are treated as boot, not just the tainted $200,000 liability.

	§ 357(b) Result	§ 357(c) Result
Amount realized:		
Robin Corporation stock	$ 500,000	$ 500,000
Release of mortgage on land	300,000	300,000
Release of second mortgage—personal purposes	200,000	200,000
Total amount realized	$1,000,000	$1,000,000
Basis of land	(100,000)	(100,000)
Realized gain	$ 900,000	$ 900,000
Gain recognized under § 357(b) ($300,000 + $200,000)	$ 500,000	
Gain recognized under § 357(c)		
[($300,000 + $200,000) − $100,000]		$ 400,000

Unfortunately for Chris, the relatively more onerous rule of § 357(b) predominates over § 357(c), requiring the recognition of $500,000 of gain.

Concept Summary 4.2 summarizes the tax rules that apply when liabilities are transferred in property transactions, including the special rules that apply in § 351 transactions.

LO.3

Identify the basis issues relevant to the shareholder and the corporation.

4-1f Basis Determination and Related Issues

Recall that § 351(a) postpones gain or loss until the transferor-shareholder disposes of the stock in a taxable transaction. The postponement of shareholder gain or loss has a corollary effect on the basis of the stock received by the shareholder and the basis of the property received by the corporation. This procedure ensures that any gain or loss postponed under § 351 ultimately will be recognized when the affected asset is disposed of in a taxable transaction.

---

[20]§ 357(c)(2)(A).

Concept Summary 4.2

Tax Consequences of Liability Assumption

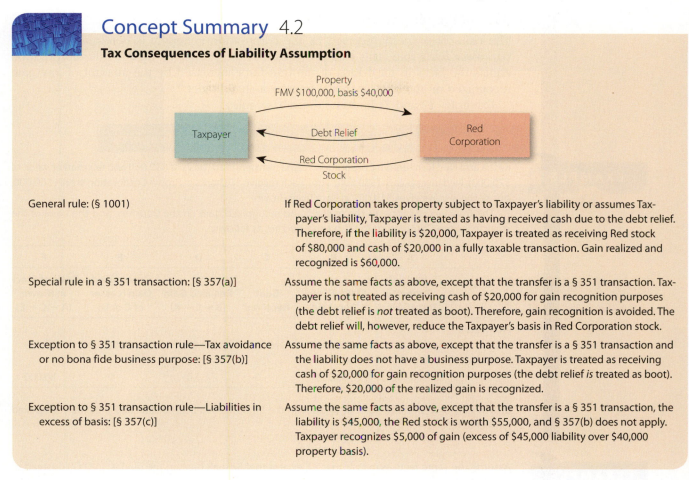

Property
FMV $100,000, basis $40,000

Taxpayer ← Debt Relief → Red Corporation

Red Corporation Stock

General rule: (§ 1001)	If Red Corporation takes property subject to Taxpayer's liability or assumes Taxpayer's liability, Taxpayer is treated as having received cash due to the debt relief. Therefore, if the liability is $20,000, Taxpayer is treated as receiving Red stock of $80,000 and cash of $20,000 in a fully taxable transaction. Gain realized and recognized is $60,000.
Special rule in a § 351 transaction: [§ 357(a)]	Assume the same facts as above, except that the transfer is a § 351 transaction. Taxpayer is not treated as receiving cash of $20,000 for gain recognition purposes (the debt relief is *not* treated as boot). Therefore, gain recognition is avoided. The debt relief will, however, reduce the Taxpayer's basis in Red Corporation stock.
Exception to § 351 transaction rule—Tax avoidance or no bona fide business purpose: [§ 357(b)]	Assume the same facts as above, except that the transfer is a § 351 transaction and the liability does not have a business purpose. Taxpayer is treated as receiving cash of $20,000 for gain recognition purposes (the debt relief *is* treated as boot). Therefore, $20,000 of the realized gain is recognized.
Exception to § 351 transaction rule—Liabilities in excess of basis: [§ 357(c)]	Assume the same facts as above, except that the transfer is a § 351 transaction, the liability is $45,000, the Red stock is worth $55,000, and § 357(b) does not apply. Taxpayer recognizes $5,000 of gain (excess of $45,000 liability over $40,000 property basis).

Basis of Stock to Shareholder

For a taxpayer transferring property to a corporation in a § 351 transaction, the *stock received* in the transaction is given a *substituted basis*. Essentially, the stock's basis is the same as the basis the taxpayer had in the property transferred, increased by any gain recognized on the exchange of property and decreased by boot received (see Exhibit 4.1). Recall that for basis purposes, boot received always includes liabilities transferred by the shareholder to the corporation. Also note that if the shareholder receives *other property* (i.e., boot) along with the stock, that property takes a basis equal to its fair market value.[21] See the discussion below relating to an elective stock basis reduction that may be made when a shareholder contributes property with a net built-in loss.

EXHIBIT 4.1	Shareholder's Basis of Stock Received in Exchange for Property
Adjusted basis of property transferred	$xx,xxx
Plus: Gain recognized	xxx
Minus: Boot received (including any liabilities transferred)	(xxx)
Minus: Adjustment for loss property (if elected)	(xxx)
Equals: Basis of stock received	$xx,xxx

---

[21]§ 358(a). Recall from earlier discussions that the basis of stock received for services rendered equals its fair market value.

Basis of Property to Corporation

The basis of *property* received by the corporation generally is determined under a *carryover basis* rule. This rule provides that the property's basis to the corporation equals the basis in the hands of the transferor increased by the amount of any gain recognized on the transfer by the transferor-shareholder.[22]

Examples 22 and 23 illustrate these basis rules.

Calculating Basis: Shareholder Stock and Corporate Property

EXAMPLE 22

Kesha and Ned form Brown Corporation. Kesha transfers land (basis of $30,000 and fair market value of $70,000); Ned invests cash ($60,000). They each receive 50 shares in Brown Corporation worth $60,000, but Kesha also receives $10,000 in cash from Brown.

The transfers of property, the realized and recognized gain on the transfers, and the basis of the stock in Brown Corporation to Kesha and Ned are as follows:

	A	B	C	D	E	F
	Basis of Property Transferred	FMV of Stock Received	Boot Received	Realized Gain (B + C − A)	Recognized Gain (Lesser of C or D)	Basis of Stock in Brown (A − C + E)
From Kesha:						
Land	$30,000	$60,000	$10,000	$40,000	$10,000	$30,000
From Ned:						
Cash	60,000	60,000	–0–	–0–	–0–	60,000

Brown Corporation has a basis of $40,000 in the land (Kesha's basis of $30,000 plus her recognized gain of $10,000).

EXAMPLE 23

Assume the same facts as in Example 22, except that Kesha's basis in the land is $68,000 (instead of $30,000). Because recognized gain cannot exceed realized gain, the transfer generates only $2,000 of gain to Kesha. The realized and recognized gain and the basis of the stock in Brown Corporation to Kesha are as follows:

	A	B	C	D	E	F
	Basis of Property Transferred	FMV of Stock Received	Boot Received	Realized Gain (B + C − A)	Recognized Gain (Lesser of C or D)	Basis of Stock in Brown (A − C + E)
Land	$68,000	$60,000	$10,000	$2,000	$2,000	$60,000

Brown's basis in the land is $70,000 ($68,000 basis to Kesha + $2,000 gain recognized by Kesha).

Exhibit 4.2 summarizes the basis calculation for property received by a corporation. Concept Summary 4.3 shows the shareholder and corporate consequences of a transfer of property to a corporation for stock, with and without the application of § 351. The facts applicable to shareholder Kesha's transfer in Example 22 are used to illustrate the differences between the transaction being tax-deferred and taxable.

EXHIBIT 4.2	Corporation's Basis in Property Received
Adjusted basis of property transferred	$xx,xxx
Plus: Gain recognized by transferor-shareholder	xxx
Minus: Adjustment for loss property (if required)	(xxx)
Equals: Basis of property to corporation	$xx,xxx

[22]§ 362(a).

Concept Summary 4.3

Tax Consequences to the Shareholders and Corporation: With and Without the Application of § 351 (Based on the Facts of Example 22)

Shareholder	With § 351			Without § 351		
	Gain/Loss Recognized	Stock Basis	Other Property Basis	Gain/Loss Recognized	Stock Basis	Other Property Basis
Kesha	Realized gain recognized to extent of boot received; loss not recognized.	Substituted (see Exhibit 4.1).	FMV	All realized gain or loss recognized.	FMV	FMV
	$10,000	$30,000	$10,000	$40,000	$60,000	$10,000

Corporation	With § 351		Without § 351	
	Gain/Loss Recognized	Property Basis	Gain/Loss Recognized	Property Basis
Brown	No gain or loss recognized on the transfer of corporate stock for property.	Carryover (see Exhibit 4.2).	No gain or loss recognized on the transfer of corporate stock for property.	FMV
	$0	$40,000	$0	$70,000

Note that the benefit to Kesha of deferring $30,000 of gain under § 351 comes with a cost: her stock basis is $30,000 (rather than $60,000), and the corporation's basis in the property received is $40,000 (rather than $70,000). In this sense, the deferred gain reduces the basis of the stock for Kesha ($30,000 stock basis = $60,000 FMV − $30,000 deferred gain) and the basis of the land for Brown Corporation ($40,000 land basis = $70,000 FMV − $30,000 deferred gain).

Basis Adjustment for Loss Property

A corporation's basis for property received in a § 351 transaction is carried over from the shareholder. As a result, the corporation's basis has no correlation to the property's fair market value. However, in certain situations when built-in loss property is contributed to a corporation, the aggregate basis of the assets transferred by a shareholder may exceed their fair market value. When this built-in loss situation exists, an anti-loss duplication rule requires the basis in the loss properties to be stepped down by allocating the built-in loss proportionately among the assets.[23] This basis adjustment is necessary to prevent the parties from obtaining a double benefit from the losses involved.

In a transaction qualifying under § 351, Charles transfers the following assets to Gold Corporation in exchange for all of its stock:

EXAMPLE 24

	Tax Basis	Fair Market Value	Built-In Gain/(Loss)
Equipment	$100,000	$ 90,000	($10,000)
Land	200,000	230,000	30,000
Building	150,000	100,000	(50,000)
	$450,000	$420,000	($30,000)

Charles's stock basis is $450,000 [$450,000 (basis of the property transferred) + $0 (gain recognized) − $0 (boot received)]. However, Gold's basis for the loss assets transferred must be reduced by the amount of the net built-in loss ($30,000) in proportion to each asset's share of the loss.

continued

---

[23]§ 362(e)(2). This adjustment is determined separately with respect to each property transferor. This adjustment also is required in the case of a contribution to capital by a shareholder.

	Unadjusted Tax Basis	Adjustment	Adjusted Tax Basis
Equipment	$100,000	($ 5,000)*	$ 95,000
Land	200,000		200,000
Building	150,000	(25,000)**	125,000
	$450,000	($30,000)	$420,000

* $\dfrac{\$10,000 \ (\text{loss attributable to equipment})}{\$60,000 \ (\textit{total} \ \text{built-in loss})} \times \$30,000 \ (\textit{net} \ \text{built-in loss})$

$= \$5,000 \ (\text{adjustment to basis in equipment})$

** $\dfrac{\$50,000 \ (\text{loss attributable to building})}{\$60,000 \ (\textit{total} \ \text{built-in loss})} \times \$30,000 \ (\textit{net} \ \text{built-in loss})$

$= \$25,000 \ (\text{adjustment to basis in building})$

Note the end result of Example 24:

- Charles still has a built-in loss in his stock basis. As a result, if he sells the Gold Corporation stock, he will recognize a loss of $30,000 [$420,000 (selling price based on presumed value of the stock) − $450,000 (basis in the stock)].

- Gold Corporation can no longer recognize a loss on the sale of *all* of its assets [$420,000 (selling price based on value of assets) − $420,000 (adjusted basis in assets) = $0 (gain or loss)].

In the event a corporation is subject to the built-in loss adjustment, an alternative approach is available. If *both* the shareholder and the corporation elect, the basis reduction can be made to the shareholder's stock rather than to the corporation's property.

EXAMPLE 25

Assume the same facts as in the previous example. If Charles and Gold elect, Charles can reduce his stock basis to $420,000 ($450,000 − $30,000). As a result, Gold's aggregate basis in the assets is $450,000.

If Charles has no intention of selling his stock, this election could be desirable since it benefits Gold by giving the corporation a higher depreciable basis in the equipment and building.

Note the end result of Example 25:

- Charles has no built-in loss. As a result, if he sells the Gold Corporation stock, he will recognize no gain or loss [$420,000 (presumed value of the stock) − $420,000 (basis in the stock)].

- Gold Corporation has a built-in loss. As a result, if it sells *all* of its assets [$420,000 (selling price based on value of assets) − $450,000 (basis in assets)], it recognizes a loss of $30,000.

Consequently, as shown in the two previous examples, the built-in loss adjustment places the loss with *either* the shareholder or the corporation but not both.

Stock Issued for Services Rendered

A corporation's transfer of its stock for property is not a taxable exchange. A transfer of shares for services is also not a taxable transaction to a corporation.[24] But another issue arises: Can a corporation deduct as a business expense the fair market value of the stock it issues in consideration of services? Yes, unless the services are a capital expenditure.[25]

---

[24]Reg. § 1.1032–1(a).

[25]Rev.Rul. 62–217, 1962–2 C.B. 59, modified by Rev.Rul. 74–503, 1974–2 C.B. 117.

The Big Picture

EXAMPLE 26

Return to the facts of *The Big Picture* on p. 4-1. Emily transfers her $2,000,000 of property to Transformation, Inc., and receives 200 shares of stock, and Ethan transfers $48,000,000 of cash for 4,800 shares of stock. In the same transaction, David transfers property worth $800,000 (basis of $260,000) and agrees to serve as manager of the corporation for one year (services worth $200,000) for 100 shares of the stock.

Emily's, Ethan's, and David's transfers qualify under § 351. None of them is taxed on the transfer of his or her property. However, David has income of $200,000, the value of the stock received for the services he will render to Transformation, Inc.

Transformation has a basis of $260,000 in the property it acquired from David, and it may claim a compensation expense deduction under § 162 for $200,000. David's stock basis is $460,000 [$260,000 (basis of property transferred) + $200,000 (income recognized for services rendered)].

The Big Picture

EXAMPLE 27

Assume the same facts as in Example 26, except that David provides legal services (instead of management services) in organizing the corporation. The value of David's legal services is $200,000.

David has no gain on the transfer of the property but has income of $200,000 for the value of the stock received for the services rendered. Transformation, Inc., has a basis of $260,000 in the property it acquired from David and must capitalize the $200,000 as an organizational expenditure. David's stock basis is $460,000 [$260,000 (basis of property transferred) + $200,000 (income recognized for services rendered)].

Holding Period for Shareholder and Transferee Corporation

In a § 351 transfer, the shareholder's holding period for stock received in exchange for a capital asset or § 1231 property includes the holding period of the property transferred to the corporation. That is, the holding period of the property is "tacked on" to the holding period of the stock. The holding period for stock received for any other property (e.g., cash or inventory) begins on the day after the exchange.

The corporation's holding period for property acquired in a § 351 transfer is the holding period of the transferor-shareholder regardless of the character of the property in the transferor's hands. For instance, whether the property transferred is an ordinary asset (e.g., inventory), a § 1231 asset, or a capital asset, the corporation's holding period is the same as the transferor's.[26]

Recapture Considerations

Sales of depreciable assets with a value that exceeds their basis result in ordinary gain up to the accumulated depreciation deducted. The rest of the gain usually is § 1231 gain. Because § 351 defers the gain when a shareholder contributes depreciable property to a corporation, the depreciation recapture potential also transfers to the corporation.[27] That is, any recapture potential associated with the property carries over to the corporation. This rule prevents taxpayers from converting ordinary income into § 1231 gain by transferring the property to a controlled corporation.

EXAMPLE 28

Paul transfers equipment (adjusted basis of $30,000, original cost of $120,000, and fair market value of $100,000) to a controlled corporation in return for stock. If Paul had sold the equipment, it would have yielded a gain of $70,000, all of which would have been treated as ordinary income under the § 1245 depreciation recapture rules.

Because the transfer comes within § 351, Paul has no recognized gain and no depreciation to recapture. However, if the corporation later disposes of the equipment in a taxable transaction, it must take into account the § 1245 recapture potential originating with Paul.

So, for example, if the corporation were to sell the asset shortly after incorporation for $100,000, all of the $70,000 gain recognized would be given ordinary treatment because of the depreciation recapture rules.

---

[26]§§ 1223(1) and (2).

[27]§§ 1245(b)(3) and 1250(d)(3).

4-2 **CAPITAL STRUCTURE OF A CORPORATION**

When forming or expanding a corporation, the transaction can be financed with capital contributions or debt proceeds, or a combination of the two. Evaluating the relative tax and non-tax advantages and disadvantages of these two basic elements in the capital structure of a corporation can help the corporation decide how to finance its activities.

4-2a **Capital Contributions**

Corporations recognize no gain or loss when they issue shares of stock (including treasury stock) for money or property.[28] This is also true for shareholder contributions of money or property through voluntary or required contributions when the corporation issues no shares in return for the contributions. The contributions represent an additional price paid for the shares held by the shareholders and are treated as additions to the capital of the corporation.[29]

Corporations sometimes receive assets from *nonshareholders*. If a civic or government entity contributes property to a corporation to induce the corporation to locate in a particular community, the contributions are not considered tax-free capital contributions. As a result, the corporation includes these contributions in the corporation's gross income and takes a fair market value basis in the assets contributed.[30] However, a governmental tax abatement granted to a corporation for locating in the jurisdiction is not taxable. The abatement just reduces future payments and related deductions for state and local taxes and is therefore ignored when granted.

EXAMPLE 29

A city donates land worth $400,000 to Teal Corporation as an inducement for Teal to locate in the city. In addition, the city has agreed to reduce the standard real estate tax rate for Teal by 50% on newly constructed property in the city.

The receipt of the land produces $400,000 of gross income to Teal, and as a result, the land's basis to the corporation is $400,000. However, the real estate tax abatement is not considered a contribution and it is not taxable to Teal.

In addition, a corporation recognizes income if a nonshareholder (a customer or potential customer) contributes assets to a corporation, even if the corporation labels these as contributions to aid construction or other capital expenditures.[31] Further, if the property is transferred to a corporation by a nonshareholder in exchange for goods or services, the corporation must recognize income.

EXAMPLE 30

A cable television company charges its customers an initial fee to hook up to a new cable system installed in the area. These payments are used to finance the total cost of constructing the cable company's infrastructure. In addition, the customers will make monthly payments for the cable service.

The initial payments are used for capital expenditures, but they represent payments for services to be rendered by the cable company. As such, they are taxable income to the cable company and not contributions to capital.

---

[28]§ 1032.

[29]§ 118(a) and Reg. § 1.118–1.

[30]§ 118(b)(2). However, under the law in effect on and before December 22, 2017, such contributions *were* excluded from gross income.

[31]§ 118(b)(1).

The basis of property received by a corporation from a shareholder as a **capital contribution** equals the basis of the shareholder's basis in the property on the contribution date. However, there is a reduction in basis if the entire contribution has a built-in loss on the contribution date. This reduction is the same as illustrated in Example 24.[32] The basis of property transferred to a corporation that is not a capital contribution (e.g., by a governmental entity) equals the property's fair market value.

4-2b Debt in the Capital Structure

Various tax and nontax considerations are relevant when developing the capital structure of a corporation. The relative amounts of debt and equity and their characteristics are of primary importance.

LO.5

Characterize the tax differences between debt and equity investments.

Advantages of Debt

Significant tax differences exist between debt and equity in the capital structure. The advantages of issuing long-term debt instead of stock are numerous. Interest on debt is deductible by the corporation, but dividend payments are not. Further, loan repayments are not taxable to investors unless the repayments exceed basis. A shareholder's receipt of property from a corporation, however, cannot be tax-free as long as the corporation has earnings and profits (see Chapter 5). Such distributions will be taxed as dividends to the extent of earnings and profits of the distributing corporation.

Another distinction between debt and equity relates to the taxation of dividend and interest income. Dividend income on equity holdings is taxed to individual investors at low capital gains rates, while interest income on debt is taxed at higher ordinary income rates.

EXAMPLE

31

Wade transfers cash of $100,000 to a newly formed corporation for 100% of the stock. In its initial year, the corporation has net income of $40,000. The income is credited to the earnings and profits account of the corporation. If the corporation distributes $7,500 to Wade, the distribution is a taxable dividend to Wade with no corresponding deduction to the corporation.

Assume, instead, that Wade transfers to the corporation cash of $50,000 for stock and cash of $50,000 for a note of the same amount. The note is payable in equal annual installments of $5,000 and bears interest at the rate of 5%. At the end of the year, the corporation pays Wade interest of $2,500 ($50,000 × 5%) and a note repayment of $5,000. The interest payment is a deductible expense to the corporation and taxable to Wade. The $5,000 principal repayment on the note is neither deducted by the corporation nor taxed to Wade.

Based on the tax rates as noted, the after-tax impact to Wade and the corporation under each alternative is illustrated below. For both Wade and the corporation, the better outcome occurs when the distribution is comprised of a note repayment and interest.

	If the Distribution Is	
	$7,500 Dividend	**$5,000 Note Repayment and $2,500 Interest**
*After-tax benefit to Wade**		
[$7,500 × (1 − 15%)]	$6,375	
{$5,000 + [$2,500 × (1 − 35%)]}		$6,625
After-tax cost to corporation		
No deduction to corporation	$7,500	
{$5,000 + [$2,500 × (1 − 21%)]}		$6,975

*Assumes that Wade's dividend income is taxed at the 15% capital gains rate and that his interest income is taxed at the 35% ordinary income rate.

---

[32]§§ 362(a) and 362(e).

Reclassification of Debt as Equity (Thin Capitalization Problem)

In situations where the corporation is said to be thinly capitalized, the IRS contends that debt is an equity interest and denies the corporation the tax advantages of debt financing. **Thin capitalization** occurs when shareholder debt is high relative to shareholder equity. If the debt instrument has too many features of stock, it may be treated for tax purposes as if it were stock. In that case, the principal and interest payments are treated as dividends. Now that individual rates are higher (up to 37 percent) than corporate rates (21 percent), however, the IRS may be less inclined to raise the thin capitalization issue because the conversion of interest income to dividend income would produce a tax benefit to individual investors.

Section 385 lists several factors that *may* be used to determine whether a debtor-creditor relationship or a shareholder-corporation relationship exists. Also, the section authorizes the Treasury to prescribe Regulations that provide more definitive guidelines. For years, however, definitive Treasury Regulations have not been available to provide guidance in this area. As a result, taxpayers have had to rely on numerous judicial decisions to determine whether a true debtor-creditor relationship exists.

In late 2016, the Treasury Department released final and temporary Regulations under § 385, which target certain "earnings stripping" transactions and related-party loans.[33] However, portions of the Regulations apply only to debt instruments issued on or after January 1, 2018. According to some tax professionals, these rules have left other important questions unanswered. As a result, the long line of judicial decisions establishing key guidelines and principles are likely to have continuing relevance.

For the most part, the principles used to classify debt as equity developed in connection with closely held corporations. Here the holders of the debt are also shareholders. Consequently, the rules have often proved inadequate for dealing with such problems in large, publicly traded corporations.

Together, Congress, through § 385, and the courts have identified the following factors to be considered in resolving the thin capitalization issue:

- Whether the debt instrument is in proper form. The IRS is more likely to treat a verbal, unwritten debt agreement as a contribution to capital than a loan evidenced by a properly written note.[34]

- Whether the debt instrument bears a reasonable rate of interest and has a definite maturity date. When a shareholder advance does not provide for interest, the return expected may appear to be a share of the profits or an increase in the value of the shares.[35] Likewise, a lender unrelated to the corporation will usually be unwilling to commit funds to the corporation without a definite due date.

- Whether the corporation repays the debt on a timely basis. A lender's failure to insist upon timely repayment or satisfactory renegotiation indicates that the return sought does not depend upon interest income and the repayment of principal.

- Whether payment is contingent upon earnings. A lender ordinarily will not advance funds that are likely to be repaid only if the venture is successful.

- Whether the debt is subordinated to other liabilities. Subordination tends to eliminate a significant characteristic of the creditor-debtor relationship. Creditors should have the right to share with other general creditors in the event of the corporation's dissolution or liquidation. Subordination also weakens another basic attribute of creditor status—the power to demand payment at a fixed maturity date.[36]

- Whether holdings of debt and stock are proportionate to shares owned (e.g., each shareholder owns the same percentage of debt as stock). When debt and equity obligations are held in the same proportion, shareholders are, apart from

[33]See final and temporary Reg. §§ 1.385–1 to –4T (T.D. 9790).

[34]*Estate of Mixon, Jr. v. U.S.,* 72–2 USTC ¶9537, 30 AFTR 2d 72–5094, 464 F.2d 394 (CA–5, 1972).

[35]*Slappey Drive Industrial Park v. U.S.,* 77–2 USTC ¶9696, 40 AFTR 2d 77–5940, 561 F.2d 572 (CA–5, 1977).

[36]*Fin Hay Realty Co. v. U.S.,* 68-2 USTC ¶9438, 22 AFTR 2d 5004, 398 F.2d 694 (CA–3, 1968).

tax considerations, indifferent as to whether corporate distributions are in the form of interest or dividends.

- Whether funds loaned to the corporation are used to finance initial operations or capital asset acquisitions. Funds used to finance initial operations or to acquire capital assets the corporation needs are generally obtained through equity investments.

- Whether the corporation has a high ratio of shareholder debt to shareholder equity. Thin capitalization indicates that the corporation lacks reserves to pay interest and principal on debt when corporate income is insufficient to meet current needs.[37] In determining a corporation's debt-equity ratio, courts look at the relation of the debt both to the book value of the corporation's assets and to their actual fair market value.[38]

Under § 385, the IRS also has the authority to classify an instrument either as *wholly* debt or equity or as *part* debt and *part* equity. This flexible approach is important because some instruments cannot readily be classified either wholly as stock or wholly as debt. It may also provide an avenue for the IRS to address problems in publicly traded corporations.

4-3 INVESTOR LOSSES

LO.6

Handle the tax treatment of shareholder debt and stock gains and losses.

The difference between equity and debt financing involves a consideration of the tax treatment of worthless stock and securities versus that applicable to bad debts.

4-3a Stock and Security Losses

If stocks and bonds are capital assets in their owner's hands, losses from their worthlessness are governed by § 165(g)(1). Under this provision, a capital loss materializes as of the last day of the taxable year in which the stocks or bonds become worthless. No deduction is allowed for a mere decline in value. The burden of proving complete worthlessness is on the taxpayer claiming the loss. One way to recognize partial worthlessness is to dispose of the stocks or bonds in a taxable sale or exchange.[39] But even then, the **investor loss** is disallowed if the sale or exchange is to a related party as defined under § 267(b) (e.g., parents and children are related, but aunts, uncles, and cousins are not considered related).

ETHICS & EQUITY   Can a Loss Produce a Double Benefit?

In late 2007, Sally invested $100,000 in TechCo, a startup high-tech venture. Although she had great expectations of financial gain, TechCo's efforts were not well received in the market, and the value of its stock plummeted. Four years ago when TechCo declared bankruptcy, Sally wrote off her $100,000 stock investment as worthless securities.

To Sally's surprise, this year she receives $40,000 from the bankruptcy trustee as a final settlement for her TechCo stock.

Sally now realizes that she probably should not have claimed the loss four years ago because the stock was not *completely* worthless.

However, since the statute of limitations has passed, she does not plan to amend her tax return from four years ago. She also decides that the $40,000 is not income but is merely a recovery of some of her original investment. How do you react to Sally's plans?

---

[37]A court held that a debt-equity ratio of approximately 14.6:1 was not excessive. See *Tomlinson v. 1661 Corp.*, 67–1 USTC ¶9438, 19 AFTR 2d 1413, 377 F.2d 291 (CA–5, 1967). A 26:1 ratio was found acceptable in *Delta Plastics, Inc.*, 85 TCM 940, T.C.Memo. 2003–54.

[38]In *Bauer v. Comm.*, 84–2 USTC ¶9996, 55 AFTR 2d 85–433, 748 F.2d 1365 (CA–9, 1984), a debt-equity ratio of 92:1 resulted when book value was used. But the ratio ranged from 2:1 to 8:1 when equity included both paid-in capital and accumulated earnings.

[39]Reg. § 1.165–4(a).

Stocks and bonds are usually held as investments and, as a result, are capital assets. However, when they are not capital assets, such as when they are held by a broker for resale to customers, worthlessness yields an ordinary loss.[40]

Under certain circumstances involving stocks and bonds of affiliated corporations, an ordinary loss is allowed upon worthlessness.[41] A corporation is an affiliate of another corporation if the corporate shareholder owns at least 80 percent of the voting power of all classes of stock entitled to vote and 80 percent of each class of nonvoting stock. Further, to be considered affiliated, the corporation must have derived more than 90 percent of its aggregate gross receipts for all taxable years from sources other than passive income. Passive income for this purpose includes items such as rents, royalties, dividends, and interest. The reason for this latter requirement is to prevent a corporation from creating a subsidiary corporation by contributing capital assets and then taking an ordinary loss instead of capital losses from the capital assets.

4-3b   Business versus Nonbusiness Bad Debts

In addition to worthlessness of stocks and bonds, the financial demise of a corporation can result in bad debt deductions to those who have extended credit to the corporation. These deductions can be either business bad debts or **nonbusiness bad debts**. The distinction between the two types of deductions is important for tax purposes in the following respects:

- Business bad debts result in ordinary losses, while nonbusiness bad debts result in short-term capital losses.[42] A business bad debt can also result in (or increase) a net operating loss, but a nonbusiness bad debt cannot.[43]

- A deduction is allowed for the partial worthlessness of a business debt, but nonbusiness debts can be written off only when they become entirely worthless.[44]

- Because corporations do not engage in personal transactions, all of their bad debts qualify as business bad debts and are never given nonbusiness bad debt treatment.[45]

When is a debt business or nonbusiness? Unfortunately, because the Code sheds little light on the matter, the distinction has been left to the courts.[46] In a leading decision, the Supreme Court somewhat clarified the picture when it held that if individual shareholders lend money to a corporation in their capacity as investors, any resulting bad debt is classified as nonbusiness.[47] Nevertheless, the Court did not preclude the possibility of a shareholder-creditor incurring a business bad debt.

If a loan is made in some capacity that qualifies as a trade or business, nonbusiness bad debt treatment is avoided. For example, if an employee who is also a shareholder makes a loan to preserve employment status, the loan qualifies for business bad debt treatment.[48] Shareholders also receive business bad debt treatment if they are in the trade or business of lending money or of buying, promoting, and selling corporations. If the shareholder has multiple motives for making the loan, according to the Supreme Court, the "dominant" or "primary" motive for making the loan controls the classification of the loss.[49]

[40]§ 165(a) and Reg. § 1.165–5(b).

[41]§ 165(g)(3).

[42]Compare § 166(a) with § 166(d)(1)(B).

[43]Note the modification required by § 172(d)(2).

[44]Compare § 166(a)(2) with § 166(d)(1)(A).

[45]§ 166(d)(1).

[46]For definitional purposes, § 166(d)(2) is almost as worthless as the debt it purports to describe.

[47]*Whipple v. Comm.,* 63–1 USTC ¶9466, 11 AFTR 2d 1454, 83 S.Ct. 1168 (USSC, 1963).

[48]*Trent v. Comm.,* 61–2 USTC ¶9506, 7 AFTR 2d 1599, 291 F.2d 669 (CA–2, 1961).

[49]*U.S. v. Generes,* 72–1 USTC ¶9259, 29 AFTR 2d 72–609, 92 S.Ct. 827 (USSC, 1972).

EXAMPLE 32

Juwon owns 48% of the stock of Lark Corporation, which he acquired several years ago at a cost of $600,000. Juwon is also employed by the corporation at an annual salary of $240,000.

At a time when Lark Corporation is experiencing financial problems, Juwon lends it $300,000. Subsequently, the corporation becomes bankrupt, and both Juwon's stock investment and his loan become worthless.

Juwon's stock investment is treated as a long-term capital loss (assuming that § 1244 does not apply, as discussed below). But how is the bad debt classified? If Juwon can prove that his dominant or primary reason for making the loan was to protect his salary, a business bad debt deduction results. If not, it is assumed that Juwon was trying to protect his stock investment, and nonbusiness bad debt treatment results.

Factors in resolving the matter of business versus nonbusiness bad debts include the following:

- A comparison of the amount of the stock investment with the trade or business benefit derived. In Example 32, the stock investment of $600,000 is compared with the annual salary of $240,000. In this regard, the salary should be considered as a recurring item and not viewed in isolation. A salary of $240,000 each year means a great deal to a person who has no other means of support and may have difficulty obtaining similar employment elsewhere.

- A comparison of the amount of the loan with the stock investment and the trade or business benefit derived.

- The percentage of ownership held by the shareholder. A minority shareholder, for example, is under more compulsion to lend the corporation money to protect a job than a person who is in control of corporate policy.

In summary, without additional facts, it is impossible to conclude whether Juwon in Example 32 suffered a business or nonbusiness bad debt. Even with such facts, the guidelines are vague. Recall that a taxpayer's intent or motivation is at issue. For this reason, the problem is frequently the subject of litigation.[50]

4-3c Section 1244 Stock

In an exception to the capital treatment that generally results, § 1244 permits ordinary loss treatment for losses on the sale or worthlessness of stock of so-called small business corporations. By placing shareholders on a more nearly equal basis with proprietors and partners in terms of the tax treatment of losses, the provision encourages investment of capital in small corporations. Gain on the sale of § 1244 stock remains capital. Consequently, the shareholder has nothing to lose and everything to gain by complying with § 1244.

Qualification for § 1244

The ordinary loss treatment for **§ 1244 stock** applies to the first $1 million of capitalized value of the corporation's stock. If more than $1 million of the corporation's stock is issued, the entity designates which of the shares qualify for § 1244 treatment.[51] In measuring the capitalization of the newly issued stock, property received in exchange for stock is valued at its adjusted basis, reduced by any liabilities assumed by the corporation or to which the property is subject. The fair market value of the property is not considered, presumably because determining fair market value is costly and sometimes difficult, especially for small businesses. The $1 million limitation is determined on the date the stock is issued. Consequently, even though a corporation fails to meet these requirements when the stock is disposed of later by the shareholder, the stock can still qualify as § 1244 stock if the requirements were met on the date the stock was issued.

[50]See, for example, *Kelson v. U.S.*, 74–2 USTC ¶9714, 34 AFTR 2d 74–6007, 503 F.2d 1291 (CA–10, 1974), *Kenneth W. Graves*, 87 TCM 1409, T.C.Memo. 2004–140, and *Harry Robert Haury*, 104 TCM 121, T.C.Memo. 2012–215.

[51]Reg. § 1.1244(c)–2(b)(2).

Mechanics of the Loss Deduction

The ordinary loss deduction limit in any one year from the disposition of § 1244 stock is $50,000 (or $100,000 for spouses filing a joint return). Any loss sustained in the taxable year exceeding the limit is considered a capital loss.

Several years ago, Chao acquired § 1244 stock at a cost of $100,000. He sells the stock for $10,000 in the current year. He has an ordinary loss of $50,000 and a capital loss of $40,000. Alternatively, on a joint return, the entire $90,000 loss is ordinary.

Only the original holder of § 1244 stock, whether an individual or a partnership, qualifies for ordinary loss treatment. If the stock is sold or donated, it loses its § 1244 status.

Special treatment applies if § 1244 stock is issued by a corporation in exchange for property that has an adjusted basis above its fair market value immediately before the exchange. For purposes of determining ordinary loss upon a subsequent sale, the stock basis is reduced to the fair market value of the property on the date of the exchange. This rule is another effort to prevent taxpayers from converting capital losses into ordinary losses. Note, however, that this rule applies even if shareholders contribute ordinary income property to the corporation.

Dana transfers property with a basis of $10,000 and a fair market value of $5,000 to a corporation in exchange for shares of § 1244 stock. Assuming that the transfer qualifies under § 351, the basis of the stock under the general rule is $10,000, the same as Dana's basis in the property.

However, for purposes of § 1244 and measuring the amount of ordinary loss, the stock basis is only $5,000. If the stock is later sold for $3,000, the total loss sustained is $7,000 ($3,000 − $10,000); however, only $2,000 of the loss is ordinary ($3,000 − $5,000). The remaining portion of the loss, $5,000, is a capital loss.

Recall the advantages of issuing some debt to shareholders in exchange for cash contributions to a corporation. A disadvantage of issuing debt is that it does not qualify under § 1244. Should the debt become worthless, the taxpayer generally has a short-term capital loss rather than the ordinary loss for § 1244 stock.

4-4   GAIN FROM QUALIFIED SMALL BUSINESS STOCK

To encourage corporate formations by small businesses, § 1202 gives shareholders special tax relief for gains recognized on the sale or exchange of stock acquired in a qualified small business corporation. The holder of qualified small business stock may exclude a portion of any gain from the sale or exchange of such stock. The exclusion percentage varies, depending on when the shareholder acquired the qualified small business stock. For example, 100 percent of the gain is excluded for qualified stock acquired after September 27, 2010. However, for earlier acquisitions of qualified stock, either 75 percent or 50 percent is excluded.[52]

To qualify for the exclusion, the taxpayer must have held the stock for more than five years and must have acquired the stock as part of an original issue.[53] Only noncorporate shareholders qualify for the exclusion.

A qualified small business corporation is a C corporation whose aggregate gross assets did not exceed $50 million on the date the stock was issued.[54] The corporation must be actively involved in a trade or business. This means that at least 80 percent of the corporation's assets must be used in the active conduct of one or more qualified trades or businesses.

A shareholder can apply the exclusion to the greater of (1) $10 million or (2) 10 times the shareholder's aggregate adjusted basis in the qualified stock disposed of during a taxable year.[55]

---

[52]§ 1202(a).

[53]The stock must have been issued after August 10, 1993, which is the effective date of § 1202 as originally enacted.

[54]§ 1202(d). Its aggregate assets may not exceed this amount at any time between August 10, 1993, and the date the stock was issued.

[55]§ 1202(b). The amount is $5 million for married taxpayers filing separately.

EXAMPLE
35

Star Corporation originally issued stock in January 2012 to Jenna and Hao for capital contributions of $3 million each. Star manufactures pipe fittings and other plumbing materials that are much less prone to failure and require much less maintenance than standard fittings. All Star assets contribute to the production and distribution of its products. The corporation performed extremely well, rising in value to $100 million. Unfortunately, Hao resigned from the corporation after several heated and unpleasant arguments with Jenna over the future direction of the company. In the middle of the current year, Hao sold his investment in Star to a private equity investment firm for $50 million.

Hao's sale qualifies for a 100% § 1202 gain exclusion. Hao is an original individual investor, he has held the stock for over 5 years, Star's initial assets amounted to far less than $50 million, and Star uses all of its assets in a business. The resulting computations are:

- Realized gain = $50 million amount realized − $3 million basis = $47 million.
- § 1202 exclusion = greater of $10 million or ($3 million × 10) = $30 million.
- Long-term capital gain = $47 million − $30 million = $17 million.
- Hao's expected tax cost = $17 million × 23.8% = $4 million (rounded).

The tax rate applied to this gain equals the top 20% net long-term capital gain rate plus the 3.8% net investment income tax rate. Note that if § 1202 did not exist, Hao's expected tax liability would be $11.2 million (rounded) ($47 million × 23.8%). Thus, the § 1202 gain exclusion resulted in a tax savings to Hao of over $7 million.

4-5 TAX PLANNING

LO.7
Identify tax planning opportunities associated with organizing and financing a corporation.

With any provision in the tax law affording special treatment, taxpayers must consider whether they *qualify* or *could* qualify for the special treatment and whether they *should* take advantage of the treatment. Section 351 provides one such provision that requires careful planning.

4-5a Working with § 351

Effective tax planning with transfers of property to corporations requires a clear understanding of § 351 and its related Code provisions. The most important question in planning is simply this: Does the desired tax result come from complying with § 351 or from avoiding it? The following discussion reviews key requirements to meet as well as traps to avoid when planning a § 351 transaction.

Using § 351

If the tax-free treatment of § 351 is desired, ensure that the parties transferring property (which includes cash) receive control of the corporation. Simultaneous transfers are not necessary, but a long period of time between transfers can trigger problems if the transfers are not properly documented as part of a single plan. The parties should document and preserve written evidence of their intentions. Also, it is helpful to have some reasonable explanation for any delay in the transfers.

The control requirement can be especially difficult to meet for exchanges of property for stock of a mature corporation. In these situations, gain deferral might require a larger contribution of assets than the new shareholders can afford. This provides an incentive to convince existing shareholders to make an "accommodation transfer" so that their shares count toward the control requirement. However, the Regulations make clear that an existing shareholder's previously acquired shares do not count toward meeting the control test if (a) the primary purpose of the transfer is to qualify other transferors for § 351 treatment and (b) the value of the "new stock" received is relatively small compared to the value of stock already owned.[56] Therefore, if a transferring shareholder who does not meet the 80 percent control test desires tax-deferred treatment of § 351, then the other shareholders should contribute property that equals at least 10 percent of the fair market value of the stock already owned.[57]

[56]Reg. § 1.351–1(a)(1)(ii).   [57]Rev.Proc. 77–37, 1977–2 C.B. 568.

For contributions of property by a partner to a partnership, at formation or subsequent to formation, § 721 is available to provide nonrecognition treatment. This partnership provision generally resembles § 351. However, in such situations, any partner can make a tax-deferred contribution without regard to a control test. Thus, the 80 percent control requirement, which serves as a high threshold to be met if tax-deferred treatment is desired in a corporate setting, contrasts to the treatment given in partnership taxation where no such control test applies. See Chapters 10 and 13 for additional discussion.

Avoiding § 351

Because § 351 provides for the nonrecognition of gain on transfers to controlled corporations, it is often regarded as a favorable relief provision. In some situations, however, avoiding § 351 may produce a more advantageous tax result. The transferors might prefer to recognize gain on the transfer of property if the tax cost from the gain is low. For example, they may be in low tax brackets, or they could have capital losses available to offset capital gains. The corporation will then have a stepped-up basis in the transferred property.

A transferor might also prefer to avoid § 351 to allow for immediate recognition of a loss. Recall that § 351 provides for the nonrecognition of both gains and losses. A transferor who wants to recognize loss has several alternatives:

- Sell the property to the corporation for its stock. The IRS could attempt to collapse the "sale," however, by taking the approach that the transfer really falls under § 351.[58] If the sale is disregarded, the transferor ends up with a realized but unrecognized loss.

- Sell the property to the corporation for other property or boot. Because the transferor receives no stock, § 351 is inapplicable.

- Transfer the property to the corporation in return for securities or nonqualified preferred stock. Recall that § 351 does not apply to a transferor who receives securities or nonqualified preferred stock. In both this and the previous alternatives, watch for the possible disallowance of the loss under the related-party rules.

The deferral provisions in § 351 effectively transfer gains and losses from shareholders to the corporation. This can increase or decrease future corporate tax liabilities. That is, transferring a gain asset creates a deferred tax liability for the corporation, but transferring a loss asset creates a deferred tax asset. The shareholders would be justified in considering this in establishing the number of shares granted, even if the properties transferred have the same fair market value.

> **EXAMPLE 36**
>
> Iris and Lamont form Wren Corporation with the following investments: property by Iris (basis of $40,000 and fair market value of $50,000) and property by Lamont (basis of $60,000 and fair market value of $50,000). Each receives 50% of the Wren stock. Has Lamont acted wisely in settling for only 50% of the stock?
>
> At first, it would appear so because Iris and Lamont each invested property of the same value ($50,000). But what about tax considerations? By applying the general carryover basis rules, the corporation now has a basis of $40,000 in Iris's property and $60,000 in Lamont's property. In essence, Iris has shifted a possible $10,000 gain to the corporation, while Lamont has transferred a $10,000 potential loss. Thus, an equitable allocation of the Wren stock would call for Lamont to receive a greater percentage interest than Iris would receive.
>
> This issue is further complicated by the special basis adjustment required when a shareholder such as Lamont contributes property with a built-in loss to a corporation. In this situation, if Wren is to take a carryover basis in Lamont's property, Lamont must reduce his stock basis by the $10,000 built-in loss. This reduced stock basis, of course, could lead to a greater tax burden on Lamont when he sells the Wren stock. This may suggest additional support for Lamont having a greater percentage interest than Iris has.

4-5b Selecting Assets to Transfer

To obtain an optimal result when planning to incorporate a business, the organizers must determine which assets and liabilities shareholders should transfer to the corporation. A transfer of assets that produce passive income (rents, royalties, dividends, and interest)

---

[58]*U.S. v. Hertwig,* 68–2 USTC ¶9495, 22 AFTR 2d 5249, 398 F.2d 452 (CA–5, 1968).

can cause the corporation to be a personal holding company in a tax year when operating income is low. Thus, the corporation could be subject to the personal holding company penalty tax (imposed by § 541) in addition to the regular income tax.

Leasing property to the corporation sometimes is a more attractive alternative than transferring ownership. Leasing provides the taxpayer with the opportunity to withdraw money from the corporation in a deductible form instead of receiving a nondeductible dividend. If the property is given to a family member in a lower tax bracket, the lease income can be shifted as well. If the depreciation and other deductions available in connection with the property are larger than the lease income, the taxpayer would retain the property until the income exceeds the deductions.

When an existing cash basis business is incorporated, an important issue to consider is whether the business's accounts receivable and accounts payable will be transferred to the new corporation or be retained by the owner of the unincorporated business. Depending on the approach taken, either the new corporation or the owner of the old unincorporated business will recognize the income associated with the cash basis receivables when they are collected. The cash basis accounts payable raise the corresponding issue of who will claim the deduction.

The Big Picture

EXAMPLE 37

Return to the facts of *The Big Picture* on p. 4-1. If Emily decides to retain the $50,000 of cash basis accounts receivable rather than transfer them to the newly formed Transformation, Inc., she will recognize $50,000 of ordinary income upon their collection.

Alternatively, if she contributes the receivables to Transformation as the facts suggest, the corporation will recognize the ordinary income when they are collected. However, a subsequent corporate distribution to Emily of the cash collected could be subject to double taxation as a dividend (see Chapter 5 for further discussion). Given the alternatives available, Emily needs to evaluate which approach is better for the parties involved.

Another way to shift income to other taxpayers is by the use of corporate debt. Shareholder debt in a corporation can be given to family members in a lower tax bracket. This technique also causes income to be shifted without a loss of control by the corporation.

4-5c **Debt in the Capital Structure**

The advantages and disadvantages of debt as opposed to equity have previously been noted. To increase debt without incurring the thin capitalization problem, consider the following tax planning strategies:

- Preserve the formalities of the debt. This includes providing for written instruments, realistic interest rates, and specified due dates.

- If possible, have the corporation repay the debt when it comes due. If this is not possible, have the parties renegotiate the arrangement. Try to proceed as a nonshareholder creditor would. It is not unusual, for example, for bondholders of publicly held corporations to extend due dates when default occurs. The alternative is to foreclose and perhaps seriously impair the amount the creditors will recover.

- Avoid provisions in the debt instrument that make the debt convertible to equity in the event of default. These provisions are standard practice when nonshareholder creditors are involved. They serve no purpose if the shareholders are also the creditors and hold debt in proportion to ownership shares.

EXAMPLE 38

Gail, Cliff, and Ruth are equal shareholders in Magenta Corporation. Each transfers cash of $100,000 to Magenta in return for its bonds. The bond agreement provides that the holders will receive additional voting rights in the event Magenta Corporation defaults on its bonds.

The voting rights provision is worthless and merely raises the issue of thin capitalization. Gail, Cliff, and Ruth already control Magenta Corporation, so what purpose is served by increasing their voting rights? The parties probably used a boilerplate bond agreement that was designed for third-party lenders (e.g., banks and other financial institutions).

- Pro rata holding of debt is difficult to avoid. For example, if each of the shareholders owns one-third of the stock, each will want one-third of the debt. Nevertheless, some variation is possible.

EXAMPLE 39

Assume the same facts as Example 38, except that only Gail and Cliff acquire the bonds. Ruth leases property to Magenta Corporation at an annual rent that approximates the yield on the bonds.

Presuming the rent passes the arm's length test (i.e., what unrelated parties would charge), all parties reach the desired result. Gail and Cliff withdraw corporate profits in the form of interest income, and Ruth is provided for with rent income. Magenta Corporation can deduct both the interest and the rent payments.

- Try to keep the debt-equity ratio within reasonable proportions. A problem frequently arises when the parties form the corporation. Often, the amount invested in capital stock is the minimum required by state law. For example, if the state of incorporation permits a minimum of $1,000, limiting the investment to this amount does not provide much safety for later debt financing by the shareholders.

EXAMPLE 40

Emily, Josh, and Jun form Black Corporation with the following capital investments: cash of $200,000 from Emily, land worth $200,000 (basis of $20,000) from Josh, and a patent worth $200,000 (basis of $0) from Jun. To state that the equity of Black Corporation is $220,000 (the tax basis to the corporation) does not reflect reality. The equity account is more properly stated at $600,000 ($200,000 + $200,000 + $200,000).

- The nature of the business can have an effect on what is an acceptable debt-equity ratio. Capital-intensive industries (e.g., manufacturing and transportation) characteristically rely heavily on debt financing. Consequently, larger debt should be tolerated.

What if a corporation's efforts to avoid the thin capitalization problem fail and the IRS raises the issue in a tax audit? What steps should the shareholders take? They should hedge their position by filing a protective claim for refund, claiming dividend treatment on the previously reported interest income. In such an event, ordinary income would be converted to preferential dividend income treatment. Otherwise, the IRS could ultimately invoke the statute of limitations and achieve the best of all possible worlds—the shareholders would have been taxed on the interest income at the ordinary income rates, and the corporation would receive no deduction for what is now reclassified as a dividend. By filing the claim for refund, the shareholders have kept the statute of limitations from running until the thin capitalization issue is resolved at the corporate level.

4-5d Investor Losses

Section 1244 can provide beneficial treatment to qualifying taxpayers. However, careful planning may be necessary to avoid the risk of losing the attributes of the provision. Only the original holder of § 1244 stock is entitled to ordinary loss treatment. If after a corporation is formed the owner transfers shares of stock to family members to shift income within the family group, the benefits of § 1244 are lost.

EXAMPLE 41

Norm incorporates his business by transferring property with a basis of $100,000 for 100 shares of stock. The stock qualifies as § 1244 stock. Norm later gives 50 shares each to his children, Susan and Paul. Eventually, the business fails, and the shares of stock become worthless.

If Norm had retained the stock, he would have had an ordinary loss deduction of $100,000 (assuming that he filed a joint return). Susan and Paul, however, have a capital loss of $50,000 each because the § 1244 attributes are lost as a result of the gift (i.e., neither Susan nor Paul was an original holder of the stock).

A similar result occurs with § 1202 small business stock. The exclusion of capital gain is available only to the original shareholder, not later holders of the stock.

THE VEHICLE FOR BUSINESS GROWTH IS THE CORPORATE FORM

Emily and Ethan, the sole property transferors, must acquire at least 80 percent of the stock issued by Transformation, Inc., for the transaction to receive tax-deferred treatment under § 351. This stock ownership threshold is easily achieved under the facts as presented. Otherwise, Emily would recognize a tremendous amount of gain (up to $1,600,000). Because Ethan transfers cash, he would not recognize gain even if the transaction fails to qualify under § 351 (i.e., the fair market value and basis of the cash are identical). However, even if § 351 is available, any debt issued by the corporation will be treated as boot and will trigger gain recognition to Emily (see Example 4). Therefore, Emily must evaluate the cost of recognizing gain now versus the benefit of Transformation obtaining an interest deduction later.

If David decides to transfer property to Transformation in exchange for stock, § 351 also is available to him as long as his transfer is considered part of a prearranged plan that involves Emily, Ethan, and himself (see Example 6). In addition, if David's transaction involves transferring property *and* services in return for stock, § 351 shelters gain recognition only for the property—he will recognize ordinary income for the value of the services rendered (see Examples 26 and 27).

As a result of the incorporation, in addition to being able to raise significant capital with Ethan's equity investment, Emily also benefits from another significant corporate nontax advantage: state law protects her personal assets from unlimited liability exposure.

Another benefit of Transformation operating as a corporation is that if Emily and Ethan desire, David easily could be brought in later as a shareholder (assuming he does not participate at the time of incorporation). They could offer him outright stock ownership in exchange for services rendered or establish a stock incentive plan as a reward for his outstanding service and longevity with the business. Further, similar strategies could be used to entice into the business new employees who may possess unique talents needed to support future expansion.

What If?

Can the § 351 transaction be modified to further reduce personal and business tax costs, both at the time of formation and in future years? Several strategies may be worth considering.

- Instead of having Transformation issue debt on formation (see Example 4), Emily might withhold certain assets. If the building is not transferred, for example, it can be leased to the corporation. The resulting rent payment would mitigate the double tax problem by producing a tax deduction for Transformation.

- An additional benefit results if Emily does not transfer the cash basis receivables to Transformation. This approach avoids an income tax at the corporate level and a further income tax when the receipts are distributed in the form of a dividend. If the receivables are withheld, their collection is taxed only to Emily (see Example 37). Double taxation can be mitigated in certain situations with a modest amount of foresight.

- The Transformation case facts do not mention any accounts payable outstanding at the time of corporate formation. If they do exist, which is likely, it might be wise for Emily to transfer them to Transformation. The subsequent corporate payment of the liability produces a corporate deduction that will reduce any corporate income tax.

Key Terms

Built-in loss property, 4-15

Capital contribution, 4-19

Control, 4-6

Investor loss, 4-21

Liabilities in excess of basis, 4-11

Nonbusiness bad debts, 4-22

Property, 4-5

Qualified small business corporation, 4-24

Qualified small business stock, 4-24

Section 1244 stock, 4-23

Securities, 4-6

Thin capitalization, 4-20

Discussion Questions

1. **LO.1** In terms of justification and effect, § 351 (transfers to a controlled corporation) and § 1031 (like-kind exchanges) are much alike. Explain.

2. **LO.1** Under what circumstances will a realized gain and/or loss be recognized on a § 351 transfer?

3. **LO.1** What does "property" include for purposes of § 351?

4. **LO.1** Can gain ever be recognized in a § 351 transfer if boot is not received? Explain.

5. **LO.1** Does the receipt of securities in exchange for the transfer of appreciated property to a controlled corporation cause recognition of gain? Explain.

6. **LO.1** What is the control requirement of § 351? Describe the effect of the following in satisfying this requirement:
   a. A shareholder renders only services to the corporation for stock.
   b. A shareholder renders services and transfers property to the corporation for stock.
   c. A shareholder has only momentary control after the transfer.
   d. A long period of time elapses between the transfers of property by different shareholders.

Critical Thinking 7. **LO.1** Nancy and her daughter, Kathleen, have been working together in a cattery called "The Perfect Cat." Nancy formed the business several years ago as a sole proprietorship, and it has been very successful. Assets currently have a fair market value of $450,000 and a basis of $180,000. On the advice of their tax accountant, Nancy decides to incorporate "The Perfect Cat." Because of Kathleen's participation, Nancy would like her to receive shares in the corporation. What are the relevant tax issues?

Decision Making 8. **LO.1, 2, 7** Four friends plan to form a corporation for purposes of constructing a
Critical Thinking shopping center. Charlie will be contributing the land for the project and wants more security than shareholder status provides. He is contemplating two possibilities: receive corporate bonds for his land or take out a mortgage on the land before transferring it to the corporation. Comment on the choices Charlie is considering. What alternatives can you suggest?

Critical Thinking 9. **LO.1** At a point when Robin Corporation has been in existence for six years, shareholder Ted transfers real estate (adjusted basis of $20,000 and fair market value of $100,000) to the corporation for additional stock. At the same time, Peggy, the other shareholder, acquires one share of stock for cash. After the two transfers, the percentages of stock ownership are as follows: 79% by Ted and 21% by Peggy.
   a. What were the parties trying to accomplish?
   b. Will it work? Explain.

10. **LO.2** How does the transfer of mortgaged property to a controlled corporation affect the transferor-shareholder's basis in stock received? Assume that no gain is recognized on the transfer.

11. **LO.3** Discuss how each of the following affects the calculation of the basis of stock received by a shareholder in a § 351 transfer.
    a. The transfer of a liability to the corporation along with property.
    b. The basis in the property transferred to the corporation.
    c. Property that has been transferred to the corporation has built-in losses.
    d. The receipt of "other property" (i.e., boot) in addition to stock.

12. **LO.3** In a § 351 transfer, Grebe Corporation receives property in exchange for stock. Will Grebe's holding period for the property be the same as the shareholder's holding period for the stock? Explain.

13. **LO.4** A corporation acquires property as a contribution to capital from a shareholder. Describe the rules pertaining to the property's basis.

14. **LO.5** In structuring the capitalization of a corporation, what are the advantages and disadvantages of utilizing debt rather than equity?

15. **LO.6** Hai, a single taxpayer, invested $75,000 in the stock of Penguin Corporation, which recently declared bankruptcy. Although distressed over the loss of her investment, Hai is relieved that she can claim a $75,000 ordinary (rather than capital) loss deduction. Comment on Hai's expectations.

16. **LO.6** Under what circumstances, if any, may a shareholder deduct a business bad debt on a loan made to the corporation?

17. **LO.1, 7** Keith's sole proprietorship holds assets that, if sold, would yield a gain of $100,000. It also owns assets that would yield a loss of $30,000. Keith incorporates his business using only the gain assets. Two days later, Keith sells the loss assets to the newly formed corporation. What is Keith trying to accomplish? Will he be successful? Explain.   *Critical Thinking*

18. **LO.1, 7** Sarah incorporates her small business but does not transfer the machinery and equipment the business uses to the corporation. Subsequently, the machinery and equipment are leased to the corporation for an annual rent. What tax reasons might Sarah have for not transferring the machinery and equipment to the corporation when the business was incorporated?   *Critical Thinking*

Computational Exercises

19. **LO.1** Marie and Ethan form Roundtree Corporation with the transfer of the following. Marie performs personal services for the corporation with a fair market value of $80,000 in exchange for 400 shares of stock. Ethan contributes an installment note receivable (basis $25,000; fair market value $30,000), land (basis $50,000; fair market value $170,000), and inventory (basis $100,000; fair market value $120,000) in exchange for 1,600 shares. Determine Marie and Ethan's current income, gain, or loss; calculate the basis that each takes in the Roundtree stock.

20. **LO.1** Grady exchanges qualified property, basis of $12,000 and fair market value of $18,000, for 60% of the stock of Eadie Corporation. The other 40% of the stock is owned by Pedro, who acquired it five years ago. Calculate Grady's current income, gain, or loss and the basis he takes in his shares of Eadie stock as a result of this transaction.

21. **LO.1, 2** Jocelyn contributes land with a basis of $60,000 and fair market value of $90,000 and inventory with a basis of $5,000 and fair market value of $8,000 in exchange for 100% of Zion Corporation stock. The land is subject to a $15,000 mortgage. Determine Jocelyn's recognized gain or loss and the basis in the Zion stock received.

22. **LO.1, 2, 3** Diego transfers real estate with an adjusted basis of $260,000 and fair market value of $350,000 to a newly formed corporation in exchange for 100% of the stock. The corporation assumes the liability on the transferred real estate in the amount of $300,000. Determine Diego's recognized gain on the transfer and the basis for his stock.

23. **LO.1, 3** Yvonne and Simon form Ion Corporation. Yvonne transfers equipment (basis of $110,000 and fair market value of $165,000). Simon invests $130,000 of cash. They each receive 100 shares in Ion Corporation, worth $130,000, but Yvonne also receives $35,000 in cash from Ion. Calculate Ion Corporation's basis in the equipment. In addition, determine Yvonne and Simon's basis in the Ion stock.

24. **LO.5** Chaz transfers cash of $60,000 to a newly formed corporation for 100% of the stock. In its initial year, the corporation has net income of $15,000. The income is credited to its earnings and profits account. The corporation distributes $5,000 to Chaz.

   a. How do Chaz and the corporation treat the $5,000 distribution?

   b. Assume instead that Chaz transfers to the corporation cash of $30,000 for stock and cash of $30,000 for a note of the same amount. The note is payable in equal annual installments of $3,000 each (beginning at the end of the corporation's initial year of operations) and bears interest at the rate of 6%. At the end of the year, the corporation pays an amount to meet this obligation (i.e., the annual $3,000 principal payment plus the interest due). Determine the total amount of the payment and its tax treatment to Chaz and the corporation.

25. **LO.6** Several years ago, Minjun, who is single, acquired § 1244 stock in Blue Corporation at a cost of $60,000. He sells the Blue stock for $5,000 in the current year. Determine the amount and nature of Minjun's gain or loss recognized this year.

Problems

26. **LO.1, 3** Seth, Pete, Cara, and Jen form Kingfisher Corporation with the following consideration:

	Consideration Transferred		
	Basis to Transferor	Fair Market Value	Number of Shares Issued
From Seth—			
Inventory	$30,000	$96,000	30*
From Pete—			
Equipment ($30,000 of depreciation taken by Pete in prior years)	45,000	99,000	30**
From Cara—			
Proprietary process	15,000	90,000	30
From Jen—			
Cash	30,000	30,000	10

*Seth receives $6,000 in cash in addition to the 30 shares.
**Pete receives $9,000 in cash in addition to the 30 shares.

Assume that the value of each share of Kingfisher stock is $3,000. As to these transactions, provide the following information:

   a. Seth's recognized gain or loss. Identify the nature of any such gain or loss.

   b. Seth's basis in the Kingfisher Corporation stock.

c.   Kingfisher Corporation's basis in the inventory.

d.   Pete's recognized gain or loss. Identify the nature of any such gain or loss.

e.   Pete's basis in the Kingfisher Corporation stock.

f.   Kingfisher Corporation's basis in the equipment.

g.   Cara's recognized gain or loss.

h.   Cara's basis in the Kingfisher Corporation stock.

i.   Kingfisher Corporation's basis in the proprietary process.

j.   Jen's recognized gain or loss.

k.   Jen's basis in the Kingfisher stock.

l.   During discussions relating to the formation of Kingfisher, Seth mentions that he may be interested in either (1) just selling all of his inventory in the current year for its fair market value of $96,000 or (2) proceeding with his involvement in Kingfisher's formation as shown above but followed by a sale of his stock five years later for $90,000. What would be the tax cost of these alternative plans stated in present value terms? Referring to Appendix F, assume a discount rate of 6%. Further, assume Seth's marginal income tax rate is 35% and his capital gains rate is 15%.

m.   Prepare your solution to part (l) using spreadsheet software such as Microsoft Excel.

27. **LO.1, 3** Tom and Gail form Owl Corporation with the following consideration:

| | Consideration Transferred | | |
	Basis to Transferor	Fair Market Value	Number of Shares Issued
From Tom—			
Cash	$ 50,000	$ 50,000	
Installment note	240,000	350,000	40
From Gail—			
Inventory	60,000	50,000	
Equipment	125,000	250,000	
Patentable invention	15,000	300,000	60

The installment note has a face amount of $350,000 and was acquired last year from the sale of land held for investment purposes (adjusted basis of $240,000). As to these transactions, provide the following information:

a.   Tom's recognized gain or loss.

b.   Tom's basis in the Owl Corporation stock.

c.   Owl Corporation's basis in the installment note.

d.   Gail's recognized gain or loss.

e.   Gail's basis in the Owl Corporation stock.

f.   Owl Corporation's basis in the inventory, equipment, and patentable invention.

g.   How would your answers to the preceding questions change if Tom received common stock and Gail received preferred stock?

h.   How would your answers change if Gail was a partnership?

i.   Gail is considering an alternative to the plan as presented above. She is considering selling the inventory to an unrelated third party for $50,000 in the current year instead of contributing it to Owl. After the sale, she will transfer the $50,000 sales proceeds along with the equipment and patentable invention to Owl for 60 shares of Owl stock. Whether or not she pursues the alternative, she plans to sell her Owl stock in six years for an anticipated sales price of $700,000. In present value terms and assuming she later sells her Owl stock, determine the tax cost of (1) contributing the property as originally planned or (2) pursuing the alternative she has identified. Referring to Appendix F, assume a discount rate of 6%. Further, assume Gail's marginal income tax rate is 32% and her capital gains rate is 15%.

j. Prepare your solution to part (i) using spreadsheet software such as Microsoft Excel.

Decision Making 28. **LO.1, 7** Luciana, Jon, and Clyde incorporate their respective businesses and form Starling Corporation. On March 1 of the current year, Luciana exchanges her property (basis of $50,000 and value of $150,000) for 150 shares in Starling Corporation. On April 15, Jon exchanges his property (basis of $70,000 and value of $500,000) for 500 shares in Starling. On May 10, Clyde transfers his property (basis of $90,000 and value of $350,000) for 350 shares in Starling.

a. If the three exchanges are part of a prearranged plan, what gain will each of the parties recognize on the exchanges?

b. Assume that Luciana and Jon exchanged their property for stock four years ago, while Clyde transfers his property for 350 shares in the current year. Clyde's transfer is not part of a prearranged plan with Luciana and Jon to incorporate their businesses. What gain will Clyde recognize on the transfer?

c. Returning to the original facts, if the property that Clyde contributes has a basis of $490,000 (instead of $90,000), how might the parties otherwise structure the transaction?

Communications 29. **LO.1** Troy Kennedy (1635 Maple Street, Syracuse, NY 13201) exchanges property (basis of $200,000 and fair market value of $850,000) for 75% of the stock of Red Corporation. The other 25% is owned by Sarah Mitchell, who acquired her stock several years ago. You represent Troy, who asks whether he must report gain on the transfer. Prepare a letter to Troy and a memorandum for the tax files documenting your response.

30. **LO.1** Dan Knight and Patricia Chen, who are good friends, form Crane Corporation. Dan transfers land (worth $200,000, basis of $60,000) for 50% of the stock in Crane. Patricia transfers machinery (worth $150,000, adjusted basis of $30,000) and provides services worth $50,000 for 50% of the stock.

a. Will the transfers qualify under § 351? Explain.

b. What are the tax consequences to Dan and Patricia?

c. What is Crane Corporation's basis in the land and the machinery?

d. Enter the results of this transaction to Patricia on her Form 1040 (use the most current form available). Assume Patricia is single, has no other income, and claims the standard deduction ($12,000 for 2018; $12,200 for 2019). Complete the Form 1040 to the taxable income line.

31. **LO.1** John organized Toucan Corporation 10 years ago. He contributed property worth $1,000,000 (basis of $200,000) for 2,000 shares of stock in Toucan (representing 100% ownership). John later gave each of his children, Julie and Rachel, 500 shares of the stock. In the current year, John transfers property worth $350,000 (basis of $170,000) to Toucan for 1,000 more of its shares. What gain, if any, will John recognize on the transfer?

32. **LO.1, 3** Ann and Bob form Robin Corporation. Ann transfers property worth $420,000 (basis of $150,000) for 70 shares in Robin Corporation. Bob receives 30 shares for property worth $165,000 (basis of $30,000) and for legal services (worth $15,000) in organizing the corporation.

a. What gain or income, if any, will the parties recognize on the transfer?

b. What basis do Ann and Bob have in the Robin Corporation stock?

c. What is Robin Corporation's basis in the property and services it received from Ann and Bob?

33. **LO.1, 3** Assume in Problem 32 that the property Bob transfers to Robin Corporation is worth $15,000 (basis of $3,000) and that his services in organizing the corporation are worth $165,000. What are the tax consequences to Ann, Bob, and Robin Corporation?

34. **LO.1, 3** Kim is an employee of Azure Corporation. In the current year, she receives a cash salary of $30,000 and also is given 10 shares of Azure stock for services she renders to the corporation. The shares in Azure Corporation are worth $1,000 each. For tax purposes, how will Kim treat the receipt of the 10 shares? What is Azure Corporation's total compensation deduction for Kim's services?

35. **LO.1, 7** Rhonda owns 50% of the stock of Peach Corporation. She and the other 50% shareholder, Rachel, have decided that additional contributions of capital are needed if Peach is to remain successful in its competitive industry. The two shareholders have agreed that Rhonda will contribute assets having a value of $200,000 (adjusted basis of $15,000) in exchange for additional shares of stock. After the transaction, Rhonda will hold 75% of Peach Corporation and Rachel's interest will fall to 25%.

    Decision Making

    Communications

    a. What gain is realized on the transaction? How much of the gain will be recognized?

    b. Rhonda is not satisfied with the transaction as proposed. How will the consequences change if Rachel agrees to transfer $1,000 of cash in exchange for additional stock? In this case, Rhonda will own slightly less than 75% of Peach and Rachel's interest will be slightly more than 25%.

    c. If Rhonda still is not satisfied with the result, what should be done to avoid any gain recognition?

    d. Summarize your solution in an e-mail, and send it to your instructor.

36. **LO.1, 2, 3** Adam transfers property with an adjusted basis of $50,000 (fair market value of $400,000) to Swift Corporation for 90% of the stock. The property is subject to a liability of $60,000, which Swift assumes.

    a. What is the basis of the Swift stock to Adam?

    b. What is the basis of the property to Swift Corporation?

37. **LO.1, 2, 3** Cynthia, a sole proprietor, was engaged in a service business and reported her income on the cash basis. In February of the current year, she incorporates her business as Dove Corporation and transfers the assets of the business to the corporation in return for all of the stock in addition to the corporation's assumption of her proprietorship's liabilities. All of the receivables and the unpaid trade payables are transferred to the newly formed corporation. The balance sheet of the corporation immediately after its formation is as follows:

Assets		
	Basis to Dove	**Fair Market Value**
Cash	$ 80,000	$ 80,000
Accounts receivable	–0–	240,000
Equipment (cost $180,000; depreciation previously claimed $60,000)	120,000	320,000
Building (straight-line depreciation)	160,000	400,000
Land	40,000	160,000
Total	$400,000	$1,200,000

Liabilities and Stockholders' Equity	
Liabilities:	
Accounts payable—trade	$ 120,000
Notes payable—bank	360,000
Stockholders' equity:	
Common stock	720,000
Total	$1,200,000

Discuss the tax consequences of the incorporation of the business to Cynthia and to Dove Corporation.

38. **LO.1, 2, 3** Allie forms Broadbill Corporation by transferring land (basis of $125,000, fair market value of $775,000), which is subject to a mortgage of $375,000. One month prior to incorporating Broadbill, Allie borrows $100,000 for personal reasons and gives the lender a second mortgage on the land. Broadbill Corporation issues stock worth $300,000 to Allie and assumes the mortgages on the land.

    a.   What are the tax consequences to Allie and to Broadbill Corporation?

    b.   How would the tax consequences to Allie differ if she had not borrowed the $100,000?

Decision Making   39. **LO.1, 3** Rafael transfers the following assets to Crane Corporation in exchange for all of its stock. (Assume that neither Rafael nor Crane plans to make any special tax elections at the time of incorporation.)

Assets	Rafael's Adjusted Basis	Fair Market Value
Inventory	$ 60,000	$100,000
Equipment	150,000	105,000
Shelving	80,000	65,000

    a.   What is Rafael's recognized gain or loss?

    b.   What is Rafael's basis in the stock?

    c.   What is Crane's basis in the inventory, equipment, and shelving?

    d.   If Rafael has no intentions of selling his Crane stock for at least 15 years, what action would you recommend that Rafael and Crane Corporation consider? How does this change the previous answers?

40. **LO.1, 2, 3** Kesha, a sole proprietor, is engaged in a cash basis service business. In the current year, she incorporates the business to form Kiwi Corporation. She transfers assets with a basis of $500,000 (fair market value of $1,200,000), a bank loan of $450,000 (which Kiwi assumes), and $80,000 in trade payables in return for all of Kiwi's stock. What are the tax consequences of the incorporation of the business?

41. **LO.1, 3** Alice and Jane form Osprey Corporation. Alice transfers property, basis of $25,000 and value of $200,000, for 50 shares in Osprey Corporation. Jane transfers property, basis of $50,000 and value of $165,000, and agrees to serve as manager of Osprey for one year; in return, Jane receives 50 shares in Osprey. The value of Jane's services to Osprey is $35,000.

    a.   What gain or income do Alice and Jane recognize on the exchange?

    b.   What is Osprey Corporation's basis in the property transferred by Alice and Jane? How does Osprey treat the value of the services that Jane renders?

42. **LO.1, 3** Assume in Problem 41 that Jane receives the 50 shares of Osprey Corporation stock in consideration for the appreciated property and for the provision of accounting services in organizing the corporation. The value of Jane's services is $35,000.

    a.   What gain or income does Jane recognize?

    b.   What is Osprey Corporation's basis in the property transferred by Jane? How does Osprey treat the value of the services that Jane renders?

Critical Thinking   43. **LO.1, 3** In January of the current year, Wanda transferred machinery worth $200,000 (basis of $30,000) to a controlled corporation, Oriole, Inc., in a transfer that qualified under § 351. Wanda had deducted depreciation on the machinery in the amount of $165,000 when she held the machinery for use in her proprietorship. Later during the year, Oriole sells the machinery for $190,000. What are the tax consequences to Wanda and to Oriole on the sale of the machinery?

44. **LO.4** Red Corporation wants to set up a manufacturing facility in a midwestern state. After considerable negotiations with a small town in Ohio, Red accepts the following offer: land (fair market value of $3 million) and cash of $1 million.

    a. How much income, if any, must Red Corporation recognize?

    b. What basis will Red Corporation have in the land?

    c. Assume that in addition to the facts given, the small town offers to reduce the established property tax rate by 40% on new assets acquired by Red during the two-year period after locating in the town. What are the Federal income tax consequences of the property tax abatement?

45. **LO.5, 6** Emily Patrick (36 Paradise Road, Northampton, MA 01060) formed Teal Corporation a number of years ago with an investment of $200,000 cash, for which she received $20,000 in stock and $180,000 in bonds bearing interest of 8% and maturing in nine years. Several years later Emily lent the corporation an additional $50,000 on open account. In the current year, Teal Corporation becomes insolvent and is declared bankrupt. During the corporation's existence, Emily was paid an annual salary of $60,000. Write a letter to Emily in which you explain how she would treat her losses for tax purposes. *Critical Thinking* *Communications*

46. **LO.5, 6** Stock in Jaybird Corporation (555 Industry Lane, Pueblo, CO 81001) is held equally by Vera, Wade, and Wes. Jaybird seeks additional capital in the amount of $900,000 to construct a building. Vera, Wade, and Wes each propose to lend Jaybird Corporation $300,000, taking from Jaybird a $300,000 four-year note with interest payable annually at two points below the prime rate. Jaybird Corporation has current taxable income of $2,000,000. You represent Jaybird Corporation. Jaybird's president, Steve Ferguson, asks you how the payments on the notes might be treated for tax purposes. Prepare a letter to Ferguson and a memo for your tax files in which you document your conclusions. *Critical Thinking* *Communications*

47. **LO.6** Sam Upchurch, a single taxpayer, acquired stock in Hummer Corporation that qualified as a small business corporation under § 1244 at a cost of $100,000 three years ago. He sells the stock for $10,000 in the current tax year. *Critical Thinking*

    a. How will the loss be treated for tax purposes?

    b. Assume instead that Sam sold the stock to his sister, Kara Upchurch, a few months after it was acquired for $100,000 (its fair market value). If Kara sells the Hummer stock for $60,000 in the current year, how should she treat the loss for tax purposes?

    c. Enter the results of this transacton to Kara on Form 1040, Schedule D (p. 1) (use the most current form available). Her Social Security number is 123-45-6789. Assume that relevant facts from the transaction initially had been shown on Form 8949 with Box F checked.

48. **LO.6, 7** Three years ago at a cost of $40,000, Paul Sanders acquired stock in a corporation that qualified as a small business corporation under § 1244. A few months after he acquired the stock, when it was still worth $40,000, he gave it to his brother, Mike Sanders. Mike, who is married and files a joint return, sells the stock for $25,000 in the current tax year. Mike asks you, his tax adviser, how the sale will be treated for tax purposes. Prepare a letter to your client and a memo for the file. Mike's address is 10 Hunt Wood Drive, Hadley, PA 16130. *Communications*

49. **LO.6** Gigi transfers real estate (basis of $60,000 and fair market value of $40,000) to Monarch Corporation in exchange for shares of § 1244 stock. (Assume that the transfer qualifies under § 351.) *Critical Thinking*

    a. What is the basis of the stock to Gigi? (Gigi and Monarch do not make an election to reduce her stock basis.)

    b. What is the basis of the stock to Gigi for purposes of § 1244?

    c. If Gigi sells the stock for $38,000 two years later, how will the loss be treated for tax purposes?

Decision Making   50.   **LO.5, 7** Frank, Cora, and Mitch are equal shareholders in Purple Corporation. The corporation's assets have a tax basis of $50,000 and a fair market value of $600,000. In the current year, Frank and Cora each loan Purple Corporation $150,000. The notes to Frank and Cora bear interest of 8% per annum. Mitch leases equipment to Purple Corporation for an annual rental of $12,000. Discuss whether the shareholder loans from Frank and Cora might be reclassified as equity. Consider in your discussion whether Purple Corporation has an acceptable debt-equity ratio.

51.   **LO.6, 7** Julio sold his corporation to a competitor, Exeter LLC, for $100,000,000. Julio incorporated his business 17 years ago by investing $500,000 plus his proprietary know-how. There have been no other corporate shareholders. Compute Julio's after-tax cash flow from the sale, assuming he is in the 35% tax bracket and has no other property sales during the year.

Research Problems

THOMSON REUTERS
CHECKPOINT™

Note: Solutions to the Research Problems can be prepared by using the Thomson Reuters Checkpoint™ online tax research database, which accompanies this textbook. Solutions can also be prepared by using research materials found in a typical tax library.

Decision Making

Communications

Research Problem 1. Lynn Jones, along with Shawn, Walt, and Donna, are deciding whether they should organize a corporation and transfer their shares of stock in several corporations to this new corporation. All of their shares are listed on the New York Stock Exchange and are readily marketable. Lynn would transfer shares in Brown Corporation, Shawn would transfer stock in Rust Corporation, Walt would transfer stock in White Corporation, and Donna would transfer stock in several corporations. The stock would be held by the newly formed corporation for investment purposes. Lynn asks you, her tax adviser, whether she would have gain on the transfer of her substantially appreciated shares in Brown Corporation if she transferred the shares to a newly formed corporation. Your input will be critical as they make their decision. Prepare a letter to your client, Lynn Jones, and a memo for the firm's files. Lynn's address is 1540 Maxwell Avenue, Highland, KY 41099.

Research Problem 2. Tim is a real estate broker who specializes in commercial real estate. Although he usually buys and sells on behalf of others, he also maintains a portfolio of property of his own. He holds this property, mainly unimproved land, either as an investment or for sale to others.

In early 2016, Irene and Al contact Tim regarding a tract of land located just outside the city limits. Tim bought the property, which is known as the Moore farm, several years ago for $600,000. At that time, no one knew that it was located on a geological fault line. Irene, a well-known architect, and Al, a building contractor, want Tim to join them in developing the property for residential use. They are aware of the fault line but believe that they can circumvent the problem by using newly developed design and construction technology. Because of the geological flaw, however, they regard the Moore farm as being worth only $450,000. Their intent is to organize a corporation to build the housing project, and each party will receive stock commensurate to the property or services contributed.

After consulting his tax adviser, Tim agrees to join the venture if certain modifications to the proposed arrangement are made. The transfer of the land would be structured as a sale to the corporation. Instead of receiving stock, Tim would receive a note from the corporation. The note would be interest-bearing and be due in five years. The maturity value of the note would be $450,000—the amount that even Tim concedes is the fair market value of the Moore farm.

What income tax consequences ensue from Tim's suggested approach? Compare this result with what would happen if Tim merely transferred the Moore farm in return for stock in the new corporation.

Research Problem 3. Sarah is the sole owner of Bluegrass Corporation. The basis and value of her stock investment in Bluegrass are approximately $100,000. In addition, she manages Bluegrass's operations on a full-time basis and pays herself an annual salary of $40,000. Because of a recent downturn in business, she needs to put an additional $80,000 into her corporation to help meet short-term cash-flow needs (e.g., inventory costs, salaries, and administrative expenses). Sarah believes that the $80,000 transfer can be structured in one of three ways: as a capital contribution, as a loan made to protect her stock investment, or as a loan intended to protect her job. From a tax perspective, which alternative would be preferable in the event that Bluegrass's economic slide worsens and bankruptcy results? Explain your answer.

Partial list of research aids:
Kenneth W. Graves, 87 TCM 1409, T.C.Memo. 2004–140.

Use internet tax resources to address the following questions. Look for reliable web-sites and blogs of the IRS and other government agencies, media outlets, businesses, tax professionals, academics, think tanks, and political outlets.

Research Problem 4. Find an SEC offering that involves a corporation that originally was established as other than a C corporation (e.g., an S corporation). Describe the particular circumstances that justified the original non-C status and the rationale for subsequently converting to a C corporation.

Research Problem 5. Limited liability company (LLC) status has become a popular form of operating a business in the United States. Investigate how the growth of LLC status has affected the relative number of new businesses that have chosen to operate as corporations.

Research Problem 6. Has § 1202, which relates to qualified small business stock, been widely used since its enactment? What leads you to this conclusion? What rationale did Congress provide as a justification for the provision's enactment? Do you believe that such rationale still is valid in today's environment?

Research Problem 7. Many newly created businesses are established using a tax status that avoids the double tax that applies to C corporations and their owners. Calculate the percentage of entities that filed income tax returns as C corporations (Form 1120), S corporations (Form 1120S), and partnerships and other flow-through entities (Form 706) for the most recent year for which data are available. Use data from the *IRS Tax Statistics* as the basis for your calculations. Compare your findings with comparable percentages for the third and fifth prior years. Using Microsoft Excel, create graphs that illustrate the results of your research. Be sure the graphs have proper labels and explanations.   *Data Analytics*

Becker CPA Review Questions

1. Gearty and Olinto organized The Worthington Corp., which issued voting com-mon stock with a fair market value of $240,000. They each transferred property in exchange for stock as follows:

Property		Adjusted Basis	Fair Market Value	Percentage of The Worthington Corp. Stock Acquired
Gearty	Building	$80,000	$164,000	60%
Olinto	Land	10,000	96,000	40%

The building was subject to a $20,000 mortgage that was assumed by The Worthington Corp. What was The Worthington Corp.'s basis in the building?

a. $60,000   c. $144,000

b. $80,000   d. $104,000

2. Angie and Brad form Cats Are Us, Inc. Angie contributes $120,000 cash for 60% of the stock. Brad contributes an asset with an FMV of $90,000 and an adjusted basis of $30,000 for 40% of the stock. Brad also receives $10,000 cash from the corporation. What is the corporation's basis in the asset received from Brad?

    a. $10,000   c. $40,000

    b. $30,000   d. $90,000

3. Gearty and Olinto organized The Worthington Corp., which issued voting common stock with a fair market value of $240,000. They each transferred property in exchange for stock as follows:

Property		Adjusted Basis	Fair Market Value	Percentage of The Worthington Corp. Stock Acquired
Gearty	Building	$80,000	$164,000	60%
Olinto	Land	10,000	96,000	40%

The building was subject to a $20,000 mortgage that was assumed by The Worthington Corp. What was Gearty's basis in The Worthington Corp. stock?

    a. $164,000   c. $60,000

    b. $80,000   d. $0

4. Gearty and Olinto organized The Worthington Corp., which issued voting common stock with a fair market value of $240,000. They each transferred property in exchange for stock as follows:

Property		Adjusted Basis	Fair Market Value	Percentage of The Worthington Corp. Stock Acquired
Gearty	Building	$80,000	$164,000	60%
Olinto	Land	10,000	96,000	40%

The building was subject to a $20,000 mortgage that was assumed by The Worthington Corp. What amount of gain did Gearty recognize on the exchange?

    a. $0   c. $84,000

    b. $20,000   d. $104,000

5. Ron, David, and Mary formed Widget, Inc. Ron and David each received 40% of the stock, and Mary received the remaining 20%. Ron contributed land with an FMV of $70,000 and an adjusted basis of $20,000. The corporation also assumed a $30,000 liability on the property. David contributed land with an FMV of $30,000 and an adjusted basis of $15,000. David also contributed $10,000 in cash. Mary received her stock for services rendered. She would normally bill $20,000 for these services. What is Ron's basis in the corporate stock received?

    a. $0   c. $40,000

    b. $20,000   d. $70,000

6. Ron, David, and Mary formed Widget, Inc. Ron and David each received 40% of the stock, and Mary received the remaining 20%. Ron contributed land with an FMV of $70,000 and an adjusted basis of $20,000. The corporation also assumed a $30,000 liability on the property. David contributed land with an FMV of $30,000 and an adjusted basis of $15,000. David also contributed $10,000 in cash. Mary received her stock for services rendered. She normally would bill $20,000 for these services. What is Mary's basis in the corporate stock received?

    a. $0   c. $15,000

    b. $10,000   d. $20,000

7. Ron, David, and Mary formed Widget, Inc. Ron and David each received 40% of the stock, and Mary received the remaining 20%. Ron contributed land with an FMV of $70,000 and an adjusted basis of $20,000. The corporation also assumed a $30,000

liability on the property. David contributed land with an FMV of $30,000 and an adjusted basis of $15,000. David also contributed $10,000 in cash. Mary received her stock for services rendered. She normally would bill $20,000 for these services. What is Ron's taxable gain as a result of this transaction?

a. $0

b. $10,000

c. $20,000

d. $30,000

8. In year 1, Stone, a cash basis taxpayer, incorporated her CPA practice. No liabilities were transferred. The following assets were transferred to the corporation:

Cash (checking account)	$ 500
Computer equipment:	
Adjusted basis	30,000
Fair market value	34,000
Cost	40,000

Immediately after the transfer, Stone owned 100% of the corporation's stock. The corporation's total basis for the transferred assets is:

a. $30,000

b. $30,500

c. $34,500

d. $40,500

9. Adams, Beck, and Carr organized Flexo Corp. with authorized voting common stock of $100,000. Adams received 10% of the capital stock in payment for the organizational services that he rendered for the benefit of the newly formed corporation. Adams did not contribute property to Flexo and was under no obligation to be paid by Beck or Carr. Beck and Carr transferred property in exchange for stock as follows:

	Adjusted Basis	Fair Market Value	Percentage of Flexo Stock Acquired
Beck	$ 5,000	$20,000	20%
Carr	60,000	70,000	70%

What amount of gain did Carr recognize from this transaction?

a. $40,000

b. $15,000

c. $10,000

d. $0

10. Clark and Hunt organized Jet Corp. with authorized voting common stock of $400,000. Clark contributed $60,000 cash. Both Clark and Hunt transferred other property in exchange for Jet stock as follows:

	Adjusted Basis	Fair Market Value	Percentage of Jet Stock Acquired
Clark	$ 50,000	$100,000	40%
Hunt	120,000	240,000	60%

What was Clark's basis in Jet stock?

a. $0

b. $100,000

c. $110,000

d. $160,000

11. Ron, David, and Mary formed Widget, Inc. Ron and David each received 40% of the stock, and Mary received the remaining 20%. Ron contributed land with an FMV of $70,000 and an adjusted basis of $20,000. The corporation also assumed a $30,000 liability on the property. David contributed land with an FMV of $30,000 and an adjusted basis of $15,000. David also contributed $10,000 in cash. Mary received her stock for services rendered. She normally would bill $20,000 for these services. What is David's basis in the corporate stock received?

a. $0

b. $10,000

c. $25,000

d. $40,000

CHAPTER

5

Corporations: Earnings & Profits and Dividend Distributions

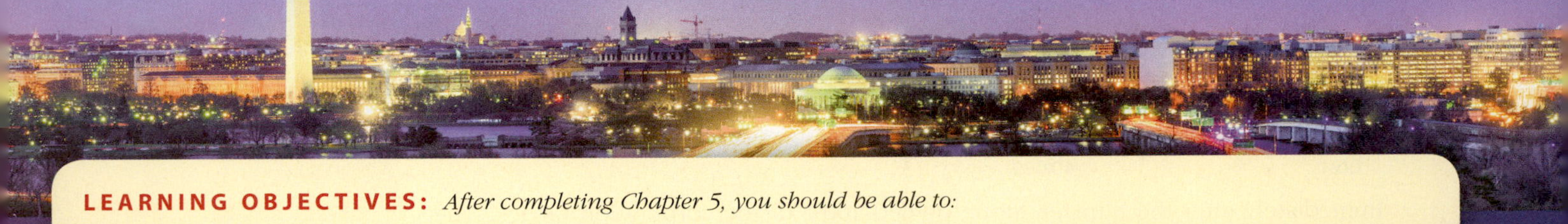

LEARNING OBJECTIVES: *After completing Chapter 5, you should be able to:*

LO.1 Explain the role that earnings and profits play in determining the tax treatment of distributions.

LO.2 Compute a corporation's earnings and profits (E & P).

LO.3 Determine taxable dividends paid during the year by correctly allocating current and accumulated E & P to corporate distributions.

LO.4 Describe the tax treatment of dividends for individual shareholders.

LO.5 Evaluate the tax impact of property dividends by computing the shareholder's dividend income, basis in the property received, and the effect on the distributing corporation's E & P and taxable income.

LO.6 Recognize situations when constructive dividends exist and compute the tax resulting from such dividends.

LO.7 Determine the tax implications arising from receipt of stock dividends and stock rights and the shareholder's basis in the stock and stock rights received.

LO.8 Structure corporate distributions in a manner that minimizes the tax consequences to the parties involved.

CHAPTER OUTLINE

ALEXANDER RATHS/SHUTTERSTOCK.COM

TAXING CORPORATE DISTRIBUTIONS

Plainwell Ice Cream Corporation (Plainwell), a premium ice cream manufacturer, has had a very profitable year. To share its profits with its two shareholders, Waffle Cone Corporation and Luis, it distributes cash of $200,000 to Waffle Cone and real estate worth $300,000 (adjusted basis of $20,000) to Luis (a married taxpayer filing a joint return). The real estate is subject to a mortgage of $100,000, which Luis assumes. The distribution is made on December 31, Plainwell's year-end.

Plainwell has had both good and bad years in the past. More often than not, however, it has lost money. Despite this year's record profits, the GAAP-based balance sheet for Plainwell indicates a year-end deficit in retained earnings. Consequently, the distribution of cash and land is treated as a liquidating distribution for financial reporting purposes, resulting in a reduction of Plainwell's paid-in capital account.

The tax consequences of the distributions to the corporation and its shareholders depend on a variety of factors that are not directly related to the financial reporting treatment. Identify these factors, and explain the tax effects of the distributions to both Plainwell Ice Cream Corporation and its two shareholders.

Read the chapter and formulate your response.

Chapter 4 examines the tax consequences of corporate formation. In Chapters 5 and 6, the focus shifts to the tax treatment of corporate distributions, a topic that plays a leading role in tax planning. The importance of corporate distributions comes from the variety of tax treatments that may apply.

From the *shareholder's perspective*, distributions received from the corporation may be treated as ordinary income, preferentially taxed dividend income, capital gain, or a nontaxable return of capital.

From the *corporation's perspective*, distributions made to shareholders are generally not deductible. However, a corporation may recognize losses in liquidating distributions (see Chapter 6), and gains may be recognized at the corporate level on distributions of appreciated property.

In the most common scenario, a corporate distribution is dividend income to the shareholder and provides no deduction to the corporation, resulting in a double tax (at both the corporate and shareholder levels). The effects of this double tax may be reduced by the corporate dividends received deduction and preferential tax rates on qualified dividends paid to individuals.

The tax treatment of corporate distributions can be affected by a number of items:

- The availability of earnings to be distributed.
- The basis of the shareholder's stock.
- The character of the property being distributed.
- Whether the distribution is a "qualified dividend."
- Whether the distribution is nonliquidating or liquidating.
- Whether the shareholder gives up ownership in return for the distribution.
- Whether the shareholder is an individual or another kind of taxpaying entity.

This chapter discusses the tax rules related to nonliquidating distributions of cash and property. Distributions of stock and stock rights are also addressed. Chapter 6 extends the discussion to the tax treatment of stock redemptions (a nonliquidating distribution where the shareholder gives up stock) and corporate liquidations.

5-1 CORPORATE DISTRIBUTIONS—OVERVIEW

LO.1

Explain the role that earnings and profits play in determining the tax treatment of distributions.

When a distribution is made from corporate earnings and profits (E & P), the shareholder is deemed to receive a dividend, which is taxed either as ordinary income or as preferentially taxed dividend income.[1] Generally, corporate distributions are presumed to be paid out of E & P (discussed in text Section 5-2) and are treated as dividends *unless* the parties to the transaction can show otherwise. Distributions not treated as dividends (because of insufficient E & P) are treated as a nontaxable return of capital to the extent of the shareholder's stock basis, which is reduced accordingly. If the distribution exceeds the shareholder's basis, the excess is treated as a gain from sale or exchange of the stock.[2]

EXAMPLE 1

At the beginning of the year, Amber Corporation (a calendar year taxpayer) has E & P of $15,000. The corporation generates no additional E & P during the year. On July 1, the corporation distributes $20,000 to its sole shareholder, Bonnie, whose stock basis is $4,000.

In this situation, Bonnie recognizes dividend income of $15,000 (the amount of E & P distributed). Of the remaining $5,000 distributed, $4,000 reduces her stock basis to zero and Bonnie recognizes a taxable gain of $1,000.

---

[1] §§ 301(c)(1), 316, and 1(h)(11).

[2] §§ 301(c)(2) and (3).

5-2 EARNINGS AND PROFITS (E & P)—§ 312

The notion of **earnings and profits (E & P)** is similar in many respects to the accounting concept of retained earnings. Both are measures of the firm's accumulated capital. E & P includes both the accumulated E & P of the corporation since its incorporation date (or February 28, 1913, if later) and the current year's E & P. A difference exists, however, in the way these figures are calculated. The computation of retained earnings is based on financial accounting rules, while E & P is determined using rules specified in the tax law.

Congress has not provided a specific calculation of *earnings and profits* in the Internal Revenue Code. Rather, in § 312, it has provided adjustments that must be made to a corporation's taxable income to arrive at E & P. The Treasury Department (through regulations), the IRS (through rulings), and the courts (through case law) have provided additional guidance. All these must be taken into account when calculating E & P.

E & P is a measure of the dividend-paying capacity of a corporation (i.e., a measure of *economic income*). As a result, when a corporation makes a distribution to a shareholder, E & P identifies the maximum amount of dividend income that shareholders must recognize. As a result, the effect of a specific transaction on E & P can often be determined by assessing whether the transaction increases or decreases the corporation's ability to pay a dividend.

5-2a Computation of E & P

The Code, regulations, rulings, and court cases provide a series of adjustments to taxable income that result in a measure of the corporation's dividend-paying capacity (or economic income). Both cash basis and accrual basis corporations use the same approach when determining E & P.[3]

Additions to Taxable Income

To determine current E & P, *all* excluded income items are added back to taxable income. These positive adjustments include tax-exempt interest, life insurance proceeds (in excess of cash surrender value), and Federal income tax refunds from tax paid in prior years.

The dividends received deduction is also added back to taxable income to determine E & P since it does not impair a corporation's ability to pay dividends. Effectively, the dividends received deduction is a partial *exclusion* for a specific type of income (dividend income).

Subtractions from Taxable Income

When calculating current E & P, certain nondeductible expenses are subtracted from taxable income. These negative adjustments include the nondeductible portion of meals, entertainment expenses, related-party losses, expenses incurred to produce tax-exempt income, Federal income taxes paid, nondeductible key employee life insurance premiums (net of increases in cash surrender value), and nondeductible fines, penalties, and lobbying expenses.

LO.2

Compute a corporation's earnings and profits (E & P).

E & P Calculations

Eagle Corporation paid $120,000 of Federal income taxes this year. Eagle also received $6,000 of tax-exempt interest on State of Pennsylvania bonds.

In calculating taxable income for Eagle, the $120,000 is not deductible and the $6,000 is not taxable. The Federal taxes are subtracted from taxable income to compute Eagle's E & P because this is an amount not available for distribution to shareholders. In contrast, the tax-exempt interest is added to taxable income to compute Eagle's E & P because it represents funds available for distribution.

EXAMPLE 2

---

[3]Section 312 describes many of the adjustments to taxable income necessary to determine E & P. Regulation § 1.312–6 addresses the effect of accounting methods on E & P.

E & P Calculations

EXAMPLE 3

Herron Corporation sells property with a basis of $10,000 to its sole shareholder for $8,000. Because of § 267 (disallowance of losses on sales between related parties), Herron cannot deduct the $2,000 loss when calculating its taxable income.

However, because the overall economic effect of the transaction is a decrease in its assets by $2,000, the loss reduces Herron's current E & P for the year of sale.

EXAMPLE 4

Crane Corporation pays a $10,000 premium on a key employee life insurance policy covering the life of its president. As a result of the payment, the cash surrender value of the policy is increased by $7,000.

Although none of the $10,000 premium is deductible for tax purposes, current E & P is reduced by $3,000. The $7,000 increase in cash surrender value is not subtracted because it does not represent a decrease in Crane's ability to pay a dividend. Instead, it represents a shift in Crane's assets from cash to life insurance.

Timing Adjustments

Some E & P adjustments shift the effect of a transaction from the year of its inclusion in the computation of taxable income to the year in which it has an economic effect on the corporation. Charitable contributions, net operating losses, and capital losses all necessitate this kind of adjustment.

EXAMPLE 5

During 2019, Hawk Corporation makes charitable contributions, $12,000 of which cannot be deducted when calculating its taxable income for the year because of the 10% of taxable income limitation. Consequently, the $12,000 is carried forward to 2020 and fully deducted in that year.

The excess charitable contribution reduces Hawk's current E & P for 2019 by $12,000 and increases its current E & P for 2020 (when the deduction is allowed) by the same amount. The increase in E & P in 2020 is necessary because the charitable contribution carryover reduces the taxable income for that year (the starting point for computing E & P) but already has been taken into account in determining its E & P for 2019.

Gains and losses from property transactions generally affect the determination of E & P only to the extent they are recognized for tax purposes. As a result, gains and losses deferred under the like-kind exchange provision and gains deferred under the involuntary conversion provision do not affect E & P until recognized.

Accounting Method Adjustments

In addition to the above adjustments, accounting methods used for determining E & P generally are more conservative than those allowed for calculating taxable income. For example, the installment method is not permitted for E & P purposes.[4] As a result, an adjustment is required for the deferred gain from property sales made during the year under the installment method. All principal payments are treated as having been received in the year of sale.

EXAMPLE 6

In 2019, Cardinal Corporation, a calendar year taxpayer, sells unimproved real estate for $100,000; its basis in the land is $20,000. Under the terms of the sale, Cardinal will receive two payments, $60,000 in 2020 and $40,000 in 2021, along with interest of 4%. Cardinal Corporation does not elect out of the installment method.

Because Cardinal's taxable income for 2019 will not reflect any of the gain from the sale, the corporation must make an $80,000 positive adjustment for 2019 (the deferred gain from the sale). Then negative adjustments of $48,000 in 2020 and $32,000 in 2021 will be required when the deferred gain is recognized under the installment method.

continued

---

[4]§ 312(n)(5).

Treatment of the gain for regular tax and E & P purposes is summarized as follows:

Tax Year	Regular Tax Treatment	E & P Treatment	E & P Adjustment
2019	$ –0–	$80,000	$ 80,000
2020	48,000	–0–	(48,000)
2021	32,000	–0–	(32,000)

A similar analysis can be used for most of the timing and accounting method adjustments.

The alternative depreciation system (ADS) must be used for purposes of computing E & P.[5] This method requires straight-line depreciation with a half-year convention over a recovery period equal to the Asset Depreciation Range (ADR) midpoint life of an asset.[6] Also, ADS prohibits additional first-year (bonus) depreciation.[7] If MACRS cost recovery is used for income tax purposes, a positive or negative adjustment equal to the difference between MACRS and ADS must be made each year. Likewise, when assets are sold, an additional adjustment to taxable income is required to account for the difference in gain or loss between income tax basis and E & P basis.[8] The adjustments arising from depreciation are illustrated in the following example.

EXAMPLE 7

On January 2, 2017, White Corporation paid $30,000 to purchase equipment with an ADR midpoint life of 10 years and a MACRS class life of 7 years. The equipment was depreciated under MACRS. The asset was sold on July 2, 2019, for $27,000. For purposes of determining taxable income and E & P, cost recovery claimed on the equipment is summarized below. Assume that White elected not to claim § 179 expense or additional first-year depreciation on the property.

Year	Cost Recovery Computation	MACRS	ADS	E & P Adjustment
2017	$30,000 × 14.29%	$ 4,287		
	$30,000 ÷ 10-year ADR recovery period × ½ (half-year for first year of service)		$1,500	$2,787
2018	$30,000 × 24.49%	7,347		
	$30,000 ÷ 10-year ADR recovery period		3,000	4,347
2019	$30,000 × 17.49% × ½ (half-year for year of disposal)	2,624		
	$30,000 ÷ 10-year ADR recovery period × ½ (half-year for year of disposal)		1,500	1,124
Total cost recovery		$14,258	$6,000	$8,258

Each year, White Corporation will increase taxable income by the adjustment amount indicated above to determine E & P. In addition, when computing E & P for 2019, White will reduce taxable income by $8,258 to account for the excess gain recognized for income tax purposes.

	Income Tax	E & P
Amount realized	$27,000	$ 27,000
Adjusted basis for income tax ($30,000 cost − $14,258 MACRS)	(15,742)	
Adjusted basis for E & P ($30,000 cost − $6,000 ADS)		(24,000)
Gain on sale	$11,258	$ 3,000
E & P adjustment ($3,000 − $11,258)	($ 8,258)	

---

[5]§ 312(k)(3)(A).

[6]See § 168(g)(2). The ADR midpoint lives for most assets are set out in Rev.Proc. 87–56, 1987–2 C.B. 674. The recovery period is 5 years for automobiles and light-duty trucks and 40 years for real property. For assets with no class life, the recovery period is 12 years.

[7]§ 168(k). In general, additional first-year depreciation (also called "bonus depreciation") is allowed for qualified property placed in service after 2011 and before 2027. No bonus depreciation is scheduled for tax years after 2026. Different rules applied between 2008 and 2011 and prior to 2005.

[8]§ 312(f)(1).

In addition to more conservative depreciation methods, the E & P rules impose limitations on the deductibility of § 179 expense. Specifically, any § 179 expense must be deducted over a period of five years (20 percent per year).[9] As a result, in any year that § 179 is elected, 80 percent of the resulting expense must be added back to taxable income to determine current E & P. In each of the following four years, a subtraction from taxable income equal to 20 percent of the § 179 expense must be made.

EXAMPLE 8

On January 2, 2018, Blue Corporation placed in service a five-year depreciable asset. The acquisition price of the asset was $25,000, and Blue Corporation claimed a § 179 deduction for the full amount. Treatment of the § 179 deduction for regular tax and E & P purposes is summarized as follows:

Tax Year	Regular Tax Treatment	E & P Treatment	E & P Adjustment
2018	($25,000)	($5,000)	$20,000
2019	–0–	(5,000)	(5,000)
2020	–0–	(5,000)	(5,000)
2021	–0–	(5,000)	(5,000)
2022	–0–	(5,000)	(5,000)

The E & P rules also require specific accounting methods in various situations. For example:

- E & P requires cost depletion rather than percentage depletion.[10]
- When accounting for long-term contracts, E & P requires the percentage of completion method rather than the completed contract method.[11]
- E & P does not allow for the amortization of organizational expenses. As a result, any expense deducted when computing taxable income must be added back to determine E & P.[12]
- If a corporation is using the LIFO inventory method, E & P requires an adjustment for changes in the LIFO recapture amount (the excess of FIFO over LIFO inventory value) during the year. Increases in LIFO recapture are added to taxable income, and decreases are subtracted.[13]
- E & P requires that intangible drilling costs and mine exploration and development costs be amortized over a period of 60 months and 120 months, respectively.[14]

5-2b Summary of E & P Adjustments

E & P serves as a measure of a corporation's dividend-paying capacity. Concept Summary 5.1 summarizes the required adjustments to the corporation's taxable income to arrive at current E & P. Other items that affect E & P, such as property dividends, are covered later in the chapter. The effect of stock redemptions on E & P is covered in Chapter 6.

---

[9]§ 312(k)(3)(B).
[10]Reg. § 1.316–2(e).
[11]§ 312(n)(6).

[12]§ 312(n)(3).
[13]§ 312(n)(4).
[14]§ 312(n)(2).

Concept Summary 5.1

E & P Adjustments

Nature of the Transaction	Addition	Subtraction
	Adjustment to Taxable Income to Determine Current E & P	
Tax-exempt income	X	
Dividends received deduction	X	
Collection of proceeds from insurance policy on life of corporate employee (in excess of cash surrender value)	X	
Deferred gain on installment sale (all gain is added to E & P in year of sale)	X	
Future recognition of installment sale gross profit		X
Excess charitable contribution (over 10% limitation) and excess capital loss in year incurred		X
Deduction of charitable contribution, NOL, or capital loss carryovers in succeeding taxable year (increase E & P because deduction reduces taxable income while E & P was reduced in a prior year)	X	
Federal income taxes paid		X
Federal income tax refund	X	
Loss on sale between related parties		X
Nondeductible fines, penalties, entertainment, and lobbying expenses		X
Nondeductible portion of meal expenses		X
Payment of premiums on insurance policy on life of corporate employee (in excess of increase in cash surrender value of policy)		X
Realized gain (not recognized) on an involuntary conversion	No effect	
Realized gain or loss (not recognized) on a like-kind exchange	No effect	
Excess percentage depletion (only cost depletion can reduce E & P)	X	
Accelerated depreciation (E & P is reduced only by straight-line, units-of-production, or machine hours depreciation)	X	X
Additional first-year (bonus) depreciation	X	
Section 179 expense in year elected (80%)	X	
Section 179 expense in four years following election (20% each year)		X
Increase (decrease) in LIFO recapture amount	X	X
Intangible drilling costs deducted currently (reduce E & P in future years by amortizing costs over 60 months)	X	
Mine exploration and development costs (reduce E & P in future years by amortizing costs over 120 months)	X	

EXAMPLE

9

Crimson Corporation (a calendar year, accrual basis taxpayer) reports taxable income of $429,000 in 2019. In addition, it provides the following information:

Federal income tax liability paid	$ 90,090
Tax-exempt interest income	6,250
Meal expenses (total)	10,000
Entertainment expenses	3,000
Premiums paid on key employee life insurance*	8,500
Life insurance proceeds from key employee life insurance policy*	250,000
Excess of capital losses over capital gains	22,000
MACRS cost recovery deduction	82,000
E & P depreciation (straight-line depreciation using ADS)	64,000
Section 179 expense elected and deducted during 2016 for regular tax purposes	120,000
Dividends received from domestic corporations (less than 20% owned)	35,000

*Term policy; no cash surrender value.

continued

Crimson sold property on installment during 2017. The property was sold for $120,000 and had an $84,000 adjusted basis when sold. During 2019, Crimson received a $30,000 payment on the installment sale. Finally, assume that Crimson did not claim any § 179 expense or bonus depreciation in 2019. What is Crimson's current E & P?

Taxable income	$429,000
Federal income tax liability paid	(90,090)
Tax-exempt interest income	6,250
Disallowed portion of meal expenses	(5,000)
Entertainment expenses	(3,000)
Life insurance premiums paid	(8,500)
Proceeds from life insurance policy	250,000
Excess capital losses	(22,000)
Excess of MACRS cost recovery over E & P (ADS) depreciation	18,000**
Allowable portion of 2016 § 179 expenses (20% × $120,000)	(24,000)
Dividends received deduction (50% × $35,000)	17,500
Installment sale gain	(9,000)***
Current E & P	$559,160

**$82,000 − $64,000
***[($120,000 sales price − $84,000 adjusted basis) ÷ $120,000 sales price] × $30,000

How would your answer change if Crimson told you that the $82,000 MACRS cost recovery deduction was entirely a § 179 expense election?

For E & P purposes, the $82,000 § 179 expense must be deducted over five years (20% per year). So 80% of the $82,000 would be an addition to taxable income in 2019, and there would be no need to compute E & P depreciation on these items (so the $18,000 E & P depreciation add-back would be eliminated). As a result, Crimson's current E & P would be $606,760 ($559,160 + $65,600 − $18,000). Over each of the next four taxable years, Crimson would have a $16,400 current E & P deduction to account for the § 179 expense taken in 2019 for regular tax purposes ($82,000 × 20%).

5-2c Current versus Accumulated E & P

Accumulated E & P is the total of all previous years' current E & P (since February 28, 1913) reduced by distributions made from E & P in previous years. It is important to distinguish between <mark>current E & P</mark> and <mark>accumulated E & P</mark> because the taxability of corporate distributions depends on how these two accounts are allocated to each distribution made during the year. A complex set of rules governs the allocation process.[15] These rules are described in the following section and summarized in Concept Summary 5.2.

5-2d Allocating E & P to Distributions

LO.3

Determine taxable dividends paid during the year by correctly allocating current and accumulated E & P to corporate distributions.

When a positive balance exists in both the current and accumulated E & P accounts, corporate distributions are deemed to be made first from current E & P and then from accumulated E & P. If there is only one distribution during the year and the distribution is less than total E & P (both current and accumulated), the distribution will be classified as a dividend.

When there are multiple distributions and total distributions exceed the amount of current E & P, it becomes necessary to allocate current and accumulated E & P to each distribution made during the year. First, current E & P is prorated among the distributions using the following formula:[16]

$$\text{Current E \& P} \times \frac{\text{Amount of distribution}}{\text{Total distributions}} = \text{Current E \& P allocated to a distribution}$$

---

[15]Regulations relating to the source of a distribution are at Reg. § 1.316–2.   [16]Reg. § 1.316–2(b), (c) Example.

Concept Summary 5.2

Allocating E & P to Distributions

Current E & P at Time of Distribution	Accumulated E & P at Time of Distribution	Outcome	Illustration
Positive	Positive	Current E & P is applied first to distributions on a pro rata basis; then accumulated E & P is applied (as necessary) in chronological order beginning with the earliest distribution.	Example 10
		Unless the parties can show otherwise, it is presumed that current E & P covers all distributions.	Example 11
Positive	Deficit	Current and accumulated E & P are *not* netted. Distributions are dividends to the extent of current E & P. If the distribution exceeds the current E & P, the excess first reduces the stock basis to zero and then generates a taxable gain.	Example 12
Deficit	Positive	Current and accumulated E & P are netted. Any loss in current E & P is deemed to accrue ratably throughout the year unless the corporation can show otherwise.	
		(1) If net amount is *positive:* Distribution is a dividend to the extent of the balance. If the distribution exceeds the net E & P, the excess first reduces the stock basis to zero and then generates a taxable gain.	Example 13
		(2) If net amount is *negative:* Distribution is treated as a return of capital, first reducing the stock basis to zero, then generating taxable gain.	Example 14
Deficit	Deficit	Distribution is treated as a return of capital, first reducing the basis of the stock to zero, then generating taxable gain.	Example 15

Then accumulated E & P is applied in chronological order, beginning with the earliest distribution (i.e., on a "first-come, first-served" basis).[17] As shown in the following example, this allocation is important if any shareholder sells stock during the year.

EXAMPLE 10

On January 1 of the current year, Black Corporation has accumulated E & P of $10,000. Current E & P for the year amounts to $30,000, earned evenly throughout the year. Megan and Matt are sole *equal* shareholders of Black from January 1 to July 31.

On August 1, Megan sells all of her stock to Sundra. Black makes two distributions to shareholders during the year: $40,000 to Megan and Matt ($20,000 to each) on July 1 and $40,000 to Matt and Sundra ($20,000 to each) on December 1. Current and accumulated E & P are applied to the two distributions as follows:

	Source of Distribution		
	Current E & P	Accumulated E & P	Return of Capital
July 1 distribution ($40,000)	$15,000	$10,000	$15,000
December 1 distribution ($40,000)	15,000	—	25,000

Because 50% of the total distributions are made on July 1 and December 1, respectively, one-half of current E & P is applied to each of the two distributions. Accumulated E & P is applied in chronological order, so the entire amount attaches to the July 1 distribution. The tax consequences to the shareholders are presented on the next page.

continued

---

[17]Ibid.

	Shareholder		
	Megan	**Matt**	**Sundra**
July distribution ($40,000)			
Dividend income—			
From current E & P ($15,000)	$ 7,500	$ 7,500	$ –0–
From accumulated E & P ($10,000)	5,000	5,000	–0–
Return of capital ($15,000)	7,500	7,500	–0–
December distribution ($40,000)			
Dividend income—			
From current E & P ($15,000)	–0–	7,500	7,500
From accumulated E & P ($0)	–0–	–0–	–0–
Return of capital ($25,000)	–0–	12,500	12,500
Total distribution	$20,000	$40,000	$20,000
Total dividend income	$12,500	$20,000	$ 7,500
Nontaxable return of capital (assuming sufficient basis in the stock investment)	$ 7,500	$20,000	$12,500

Because the balance in the accumulated E & P account is exhausted when it is applied to the July 1 distribution, Megan has more dividend income than Sundra, even though both receive equal distributions during the year. In addition, each shareholder's basis is reduced by the nontaxable return of capital; any excess over basis results in taxable gain.

==When the tax years of the corporation and its shareholders are not the same, it may be impossible to determine the amount of current E & P on a timely basis.== For example, if shareholders use a calendar year and the corporation uses a fiscal year, then current E & P may not be known until after the shareholders' returns have been filed. To address this timing issue, the allocation rules presume that current E & P is sufficient to cover every distribution made during the year until the parties can show otherwise.

EXAMPLE 11

Green Corporation uses a June 30 fiscal year for tax purposes. Carol, Green's only shareholder, uses a calendar year. On July 1, 2019, Green Corporation has a zero balance in its accumulated E & P account. On August 1, 2019, Green distributes $10,000 to Carol. For fiscal year 2019–2020, the corporation determines that it has a $5,000 deficit in current E & P.

Because Carol cannot prove until June 30, 2020, that the corporation has a current E & P deficit for the 2019–2020 fiscal year, she must assume that current E & P is sufficient to cover the $10,000 distribution. As a result, the distribution will be dividend income to Carol and reported as such when she files her tax return for the 2019 calendar year. When Carol learns of the deficit, she can file an amended return for 2019 showing the $10,000 as a return of capital.

Additional difficulties arise when either the current or the accumulated E & P account has a deficit balance. When current E & P is positive and accumulated E & P has a deficit balance, accumulated E & P is *not* netted against current E & P. Instead, the distribution is deemed to be a taxable dividend to the extent of the positive current E & P balance.

The Big Picture

EXAMPLE 12

Return to the facts of *The Big Picture* on p. 5-1. Recall that Plainwell Ice Cream Corporation had a deficit in GAAP-based retained earnings at the start of the year and record profits during the year. Assume that these financial results translate into an $800,000 deficit in accumulated E & P at the start of the year and current E & P of $600,000.

In this case, current E & P would exceed the total cash and property distributed to the shareholders. The distributions are treated as taxable dividends; they are deemed to be paid from current E & P even though Plainwell still has a deficit in accumulated E & P at the end of the year.

Alternatively, when a deficit exists in current E & P and a positive balance exists in accumulated E & P, the accounts are *netted* at the date of distribution. If the resulting balance is zero or negative, the distribution is a return of capital to the extent of basis; any excess over basis results in a taxable gain. If a positive balance results, the distribution is a dividend to the extent of the balance. A deficit in current E & P is deemed to accrue ratably throughout the year unless the parties can show otherwise.

Distributions with E & P Deficits

EXAMPLE 13

At the beginning of the current year, Gray Corporation (a calendar year taxpayer) has accumulated E & P of $10,000. During the year, the corporation incurs a $15,000 deficit in current E & P that accrues ratably. On July 1, Gray Corporation distributes $6,000 in cash to Jennifer, its sole shareholder. Jennifer has a $7,500 basis in her Gray Corporation stock.

To determine how much of the $6,000 cash distribution represents dividend income to Jennifer, the balances of both accumulated and current E & P as of July 1 are determined and netted. This is necessary because of the deficit in current E & P.

	Source of Distribution	
	Current E & P	**Accumulated E & P**
January 1		$10,000
July 1 (½ of $15,000 current E & P deficit)	($7,500)	2,500
Outcome: July 1 distribution of $6,000:		
Dividend:	$2,500	
Return of capital:	$3,500	

The balance in E & P just before the July 1 distribution is $2,500. As a result, of the $6,000 distribution, $2,500 is taxed as a dividend and $3,500 represents a return of capital. After the distribution, Jennifer's stock basis is $4,000 ($7,500 − $3,500).

EXAMPLE 14

Assume the same facts as Example 13, except that Gray Corporation's current E & P deficit amounts to $30,000 and Jennifer's stock basis is $5,000.

	Source of Distribution	
	Current E & P	**Accumulated E & P**
January 1		$10,000
July 1 (½ of $30,000 current E & P deficit)	($15,000)	(5,000)
Outcome: July 1 distribution of $6,000:		
Return of capital:	$5,000	
Taxable gain:	$1,000	

The balance in E & P just before the July 1 distribution is ($5,000). As a result, the distribution is first treated as a return of capital (to the extent of Jennifer's stock basis) and then as a taxable gain. Here, Jennifer's basis is reduced to zero and she has a taxable (capital) gain of $1,000.

EXAMPLE 15

Assume the same facts as Example 14, except that Gray Corporation began the year with an accumulated E & P deficit of $10,000.

Because Gray has deficits in both accumulated and current E & P, the outcome is the same as in Example 14: a $5,000 return of capital and a $1,000 taxable (capital) gain.

ETHICS & EQUITY   Shifting E & P

Ten years ago, Spencer began a new business venture with Robert. Spencer owns 70 percent of the outstanding stock, and Robert owns 30 percent. The business has had some difficult times, but current prospects are favorable.

On November 15, Robert decides to quit the venture and plans to sell all of his stock to Spencer's sister, Heidi, a long-time employee of the business. Robert will sell his stock to Heidi after the company pays out the current-year shareholder distribution of about $100,000. Spencer is looking forward to working with his sister, but he now faces a terrible dilemma.

The corporation has a $300,000 deficit in accumulated E & P and only about $20,000 of current E & P to date. Within the next two months, however, Spencer expects to sign a major deal with a large client. If Spencer signs the contract before the end of the year, the corporation will have a large increase in current E & P, causing the upcoming distribution to be fully taxable to Robert as a dividend.

Since a similar contract is not expected next year, most of next year's distribution will be treated as a tax-free return of capital for Heidi. Alternatively, if Spencer waits until January, both he and Robert will receive a nontaxable distribution this year. However, next year's annual distribution will be fully taxable to his sister as a dividend. What should Spencer do?

LO.4

Describe the tax treatment of dividends for individual shareholders.

5-3 DIVIDENDS

Distributions by a corporation from its E & P are treated as dividends. The tax treatment of dividends varies, depending on whether the shareholder receiving them is a corporation or an individual. All corporations treat dividends as ordinary income and are permitted a dividends received deduction (see Chapter 3). Qualified dividend income received by individuals is taxed at reduced tax rates.

5-3a Rationale for Reduced Tax Rates on Dividends

The double tax on corporate income has always been controversial. Arguably, taxing dividends twice creates several undesirable economic distortions, including:

- An incentive to invest in noncorporate rather than corporate entities.

- An incentive for corporations to finance operations with debt rather than with equity because interest payments are deductible. Notably, this behavior increases the vulnerability of corporations in economic downturns because of higher leverage.

- An incentive for corporations to retain earnings and structure distributions of profits to avoid the double tax.

Collectively, these distortions raise the cost of capital for corporate investments. Estimates are that eliminating the double tax would increase capital stock in the corporate sector by as much as $500 billion.[18] In addition, some argue that elimination of the double tax would make the United States more competitive globally since a majority of our trading partners assess only one tax on corporate income.

Although many support a reduced or no tax rate on dividends, others contend that the double tax should remain in place because of the concentration of economic power held by publicly traded corporations. And many of the distortions noted above can be avoided through the use of deductible payments by C corporations (e.g., by employing, renting property from, or borrowing money from shareholders) or by using other entity types (e.g., partnerships, limited liability companies, and Subchapter S corporations). Those favoring retention of the double tax also note that the benefits of reduced tax rates on dividends flow disproportionately to the wealthy.[19]

---

[18]Integration of Individual and Corporate Tax Systems, Report of the Department of the Treasury (January 1992); "Eliminating Double Taxation Through Corporate Integration," Tax Foundation, February 23, 2015.

[19]The Urban Institute–Brookings Institution Tax Policy Center estimates that more than half of the benefits from the reduced tax rate on dividends go to the 0.2% of households with incomes over $1 million.

Because of these differing opinions, the taxation of dividends in the United States has varied through the years. The reduced tax rate on **qualified dividends** for individuals reflects a compromise between the complete elimination of tax on dividends and the treatment of dividends as ordinary income.

5-3b Qualified Dividends

Qualified Dividends—Application and Effect

For most individual taxpayers, dividends that meet certain requirements (called "qualified dividends") are subject to a 15 percent tax rate. High-income taxpayers are subject to a 20 percent rate; a zero percent rate applies to lower-income taxpayers.[20]

Qualified Dividends—Requirements

To be taxed at the lower rates, dividends must be paid by either domestic or certain qualified foreign corporations. Qualified foreign corporations include those traded on a U.S. stock exchange or any corporation located in a country that (1) has a comprehensive income tax treaty with the United States, (2) has an information-sharing agreement with the United States, and (3) is approved by the Treasury.[21]

Two other requirements must be met for dividends to qualify for the favorable rates. First, dividends paid to shareholders who hold both long and short positions in the stock do not qualify. Second, the stock on which the dividend is paid must be held for more than 60 days during the 121-day period beginning 60 days before the ex-dividend date.[22] To allow for settlement delays, the ex-dividend date is typically two days before the date of record on a dividend. This holding period rule parallels the rule applied to corporations that claim the dividends received deduction.[23]

> **EXAMPLE 16**
>
> In June of the current year, Green Corporation announces that a dividend of $1.50 will be paid on each share of its common stock to shareholders of record on July 15. The ex-dividend date is July 13. Amy and Caleb, two unrelated shareholders, own 1,000 shares of the stock on the record date (July 15). Consequently, each receives $1,500 (1,000 shares × $1.50). Assume that Amy purchased her stock on January 15 of this year and that Caleb purchased his stock on July 1. Both shareholders sell their stock on July 20.
>
> To qualify for the lower dividend rate, stock must be held for more than 60 days during the 121-day period beginning 60 days prior to July 13 (the ex-dividend date). In this case, the 121-day period runs from May 14 to September 11. The $1,500 Amy receives is subject to preferential tax treatment since she held the stock for more than 60 days during this 121-day period. The $1,500 Caleb receives, however, is not. Caleb did not meet the 60-day holding requirement, so his dividend will be taxed as ordinary income.

Qualified dividends are *not* considered investment income when determining the investment interest expense deduction. Taxpayers can, however, elect to treat qualified dividends as ordinary income (taxed at regular rates) and include them in investment interest income. As a result, taxpayers subject to an investment interest expense limitation must evaluate the relative benefits of taxing qualified dividends at reduced rates versus using the dividends as investment income to increase the amount of deductible investment interest expense.

---

[20]See §§ 1(h)(1) and (11). In 2019, the 20% rate applies to married taxpayers filing jointly with taxable income greater than $488,850 ($434,550 for single taxpayers); the 0% rate applies to married taxpayers filing jointly with taxable income of $78,750 or less ($39,375 for single taxpayers). In 2018, these amounts were $479,000, $425,800, $77,200, and $38,600, respectively.

[21]In Notice 2011–64, 2011–37 I.R.B 231, the Treasury identified 57 qualifying countries (among those included in the list are the members of the European Union, the Russian Federation, Canada, and Mexico). Nonqualifying countries not on the list include most of the former Soviet republics (except Kazakhstan), Bermuda, and the Netherlands Antilles.

[22]§ 1(h)(11)(B)(iii)(I).

[23]See § 246(c) and Chapter 3.

LO.5

Evaluate the tax impact of property dividends by computing the shareholder's dividend income, basis in the property received, and the effect on the distributing corporation's E & P and taxable income.

5-3c Property Dividends

Although most corporate distributions are cash, a corporation may distribute a **property dividend** for various reasons. For example, shareholders might want a particular property that is held by the corporation. Similarly, a corporation with low cash reserves may still want to distribute a dividend to its shareholders.

Property distributions have the same impact as cash distributions except for effects related to any difference between the basis and the fair market value of the distributed property. In most situations, distributed property is appreciated, so its sale would result in a gain to the corporation. Distributions of property with a basis that differs from fair market value raise several tax questions.

- *For the shareholder:*
  - ➤ What is the amount of the distribution?
  - ➤ What is the basis of the property in the shareholder's hands?

- *For the corporation:*
  - ➤ Is a gain or loss recognized as a result of the distribution?
  - ➤ What is the effect of the distribution on E & P?

Property Dividends—Effect on the Shareholder

When a corporation distributes property rather than cash to a shareholder, the amount distributed is measured by the fair market value of the property on the date of distribution.[24] As with a cash distribution, the portion of a property distribution covered by existing E & P is a dividend, with any excess treated as a return of capital. If the fair market value of the property distributed exceeds *both* the corporation's E & P and the shareholder's stock basis, a taxable (capital) gain usually results.

If, as part of the distribution, the shareholder assumes a liability of the corporation or if the property the shareholder receives is subject to a liability (both immediately before and immediately after the distribution), the amount of the distribution is reduced by the liability, but not below zero. The basis of the distributed property for the shareholder is the fair market value of the property on the date of the distribution.

The Big Picture

EXAMPLE 17

Return to the facts of *The Big Picture* on p. 5-1. Plainwell Ice Cream Corporation distributed property with a $300,000 fair market value and $20,000 adjusted basis to Luis, one of its shareholders. The property was subject to a $100,000 mortgage, which Luis assumed.

As a result, Luis has a distribution of $200,000 [$300,000 (fair market value) − $100,000 (liability)] that is treated as a taxable dividend. The basis of the property to Luis is $300,000.

EXAMPLE 18

Red Corporation owns 10% of Tan Corporation. Tan has ample E & P to cover any distributions made during the year. One distribution made to Red Corporation consists of a vacant lot with an adjusted basis of $80,000 and a fair market value of $50,000. Red has a taxable dividend of $50,000 (before the dividends received deduction), and its basis in the lot becomes $50,000.

As discussed in the following section, distributing depreciated property is not wise from a tax perspective.

Property Dividends—Effect on the Corporation

All distributions of appreciated property generate gain to the distributing corporation.[25] In effect, a corporation that distributes gain property is treated as if it had sold the property to the shareholder for its fair market value. However, the distributing corporation does *not* recognize loss on distributions of property.

---

[24]Section 301 describes the tax treatment of corporate distributions to shareholders.

[25]Section 311 describes how corporations are taxed on distributions.

Refer back to the facts of Example 18. Tan Corporation is not allowed to recognize the $30,000 loss on the property distribution. The $30,000 basis disappears ($50,000 fair market value less $80,000 adjusted basis).

As an alternative, Tan Corporation could sell the vacant lot for $50,000 and use the related $30,000 loss to reduce its taxes. Then Tan could distribute the $50,000 of sales proceeds to its shareholders. Either way, the shareholders end up with property worth $50,000. But by selling the vacant lot and distributing the cash, Tan Corporation benefits by being able to use the $30,000 loss.

The Big Picture

Return to the facts of *The Big Picture* on p. 5-1. Plainwell Ice Cream Corporation distributed property with a fair market value of $300,000 and an adjusted basis of $20,000 to Luis, one of its shareholders. As a result, Plainwell recognizes a $280,000 gain on the distribution.

If the distributed property is subject to a liability in excess of basis or the shareholder assumes the liability, a special rule applies. For purposes of determining gain on the distribution, the fair market value of the property is treated as being at least the amount of the liability.[26]

Assume that the land in Example 18 is subject to a liability of $85,000. Tan Corporation recognizes gain of $5,000 on the distribution [$85,000 (liability) − $80,000 (basis of the land)]. Red Corporation has no dividend income (the liability assumed exceeds the fair market value of the land), and its basis in the land is $85,000 (the land's deemed fair market value based on the liability assumed).

Corporate distributions reduce E & P by the amount of money distributed or by the greater of the fair market value or the adjusted basis of property distributed, less the amount of any liability on the property.[27] E & P is increased by gain recognized on appreciated property distributed as a property dividend.

Property Distributions—E & P Impacts

Crimson Corporation distributes property (basis of $10,000 and fair market value of $20,000) to Brenda, its shareholder. Crimson Corporation recognizes a gain of $10,000. Crimson's E & P is increased by the $10,000 gain and decreased by the $20,000 fair market value of the distribution. Brenda has dividend income of $20,000 (presuming sufficient E & P).

Assume the same facts as in Example 22, except that Crimson's adjusted basis of the property is $25,000. Because loss is not recognized and the adjusted basis is greater than fair market value, E & P is reduced by $25,000, which is greater than the property's fair market value. Brenda reports dividend income of $20,000.

Assume the same facts as in Example 23, except that the property is subject to a liability of $6,000, which Brenda assumes. E & P is now reduced by $19,000 [$25,000 (adjusted basis) − $6,000 (liability)]. Brenda has a dividend of $14,000 [$20,000 (amount of the distribution) − $6,000 (liability)], and her basis in the property is $20,000.

---

[26]§ 311(b)(2).

[27]§§ 312(a), (b), and (c).

Under no circumstances can a distribution, whether cash or property, either generate a deficit in E & P or add to a deficit in E & P. Deficits can arise only through corporate operations.

EXAMPLE 25

Teal Corporation has accumulated E & P of $10,000 at the beginning of the current tax year. During the year, it has current E & P of $15,000. At the end of the year, it distributes cash of $30,000 to Walter, its sole shareholder. Walter's basis in his Teal stock is $18,000.

Teal's E & P at the end of the year is reduced to zero in the following manner: first, the accumulated E & P of $10,000 is increased by current E & P of $15,000, and then this amount is reduced by $25,000 (the amount of the distribution treated as a dividend).

The remaining $5,000 of the distribution to Walter does not reduce E & P because a distribution cannot generate a deficit in E & P. It is treated as a return of capital and reduces Walt's stock basis to $13,000 ($18,000 − $5,000).

The noncash property distribution rules are summarized in Concept Summary 5.3.

Concept Summary 5.3

Noncash Property Distributions

Appreciated Property	Depreciated Property
1. **Regular Tax:** Increase regular taxable income by regular tax gain (difference between FMV and regular tax adjusted basis).	1. **Regular Tax:** No impact on regular taxable income (regular tax loss not recognized).
2. **Current E & P:** Increase current earnings and profits by E & P gain (difference between FMV and E & P adjusted basis).	2. **Current E & P:** Generally, no change in current earnings and profits.
3. **Shareholder(s):** Determine impact of distribution on the shareholder(s).	3. **Shareholder(s):** Determine impact of distribution on the shareholder(s).
4. **End-of-Year E & P:** Decrease earnings and profits by the *fair market value* of property (net of liabilities assumed by the shareholder). As with cash distributions, property distributions cannot create an E & P deficit.	4. **End-of-Year E & P:** Decrease earnings and profits by the *E & P adjusted basis* of property (net of liabilities assumed by the shareholder). As with cash distributions, property distributions cannot create an E & P deficit.
Note: The Internal Revenue Code puts the corporation in the same position as if it had sold the property and distributed the cash.	**Note:** Earnings and profits will reflect the "loss" on the distribution of depreciated property (via the adjusted basis decrease to E & P), but the regular tax loss vanishes.

LO.6

Recognize situations when constructive dividends exist and compute the tax resulting from such dividends.

5-3d Constructive Dividends

An economic benefit provided by a corporation to a shareholder can be treated as a dividend for Federal income tax purposes even though it is not formally declared or identified as a dividend. **Constructive dividends** need not be issued pro rata to all shareholders[28] or satisfy the legal requirements of a dividend.

For tax purposes, constructive distributions are treated the same as actual distributions.[29] As a result, the corporation providing the constructive dividend is not allowed a deduction, corporate shareholders can use the dividends received deduction (see Chapter 3), and noncorporate shareholders receive preferential tax rates (0, 15, or 20 percent) on qualified constructive dividends. The constructive distribution is taxable as a dividend only to the extent of the corporation's current and accumulated E & P; constructive distributions in excess of E & P are treated as a return of capital and then a taxable (capital) gain.

Constructive dividend situations usually arise in closely held corporations. Here, the dealings between the parties are less structured and may not be well documented. The constructive dividend often is intended to convert a nondeductible dividend into some

---

[28]See *Lengsfield v. Comm.*, 57–1 USTC ¶9437, 50 AFTR 1683, 241 F.2d 508 (CA–5, 1957).

[29]*Simon v. Comm.*, 57–2 USTC ¶9989, 52 AFTR 698, 248 F.2d 869 (CA–8, 1957).

type of corporate deduction.[30] Alternatively, the shareholders may be seeking benefits for themselves while avoiding the recognition of income.

Although some constructive dividends are disguised dividends, not all are deliberate attempts to avoid dividends; many are inadvertent. As a result, being aware of the most common types of constructive dividends is important; these are briefly summarized below.

Shareholder Use of Corporate-Owned Property

A constructive dividend can occur when a shareholder uses corporation property for personal purposes at no cost. Personal use of corporate-owned automobiles, airplanes, yachts, and facilities used for entertainment (e.g., a lake house that is used for entertaining clients) is commonplace in some closely held corporations. In these situations, the shareholder has dividend income equal to the fair rental value of the property for the period of its personal use.[31]

Bargain Sale of Corporate Property to a Shareholder

Shareholders often purchase property from a corporation at a cost below the fair market value. These bargain sales produce dividend income equal to the difference between the property's fair market value on the date of sale and the amount the shareholder paid for the property.[32]

Bargain Rental of Corporate Property

A bargain rental of corporate property by a shareholder also produces dividend income. Here, the measure of the constructive dividend is the excess of the property's fair rental value over the rent actually paid.

Payments for the Benefit of a Shareholder

If a corporation pays a shareholder's personal expenses (or obligations), these payments are treated as a constructive dividend. Forgiveness of shareholder debt by the corporation also results in a constructive dividend.[33] Excessive rentals paid by a corporation for the use of shareholder property are treated as constructive dividends.

Constructive Dividends—Shareholder Benefit

EXAMPLE 26

Libby, the president and sole shareholder of Taylor Corporation, is paid an annual salary of $400,000 by the corporation. She is always looking for ways to receive additional benefits from the corporation. However, Libby wants to avoid dividends (because of the effects of double taxation) and has no desire to increase her compensation because she is concerned that additional salary payments might cause the IRS to contend that her salary is unreasonable (see discussion that follows).

Libby has been considering donating $50,000 to her alma mater to establish scholarships for needy students. Taylor Corporation could make the contribution instead of Libby. The payment clearly benefits Libby, but the amount of the contribution is not taxed to her.[34] Taylor Corporation claims a charitable contribution deduction for the payment.

EXAMPLE 27

Assume in Example 26 that Libby has made an individual pledge to the university to provide $50,000 for scholarships for needy students. Taylor Corporation satisfies Libby's obligation by paying the $50,000 to the university. The $50,000 will be taxed to Libby.[35] In this context, the $50,000 payment to the university may be treated as indirect compensation to Libby.

continued

---

[30]Recall that dividend distributions do not provide the distributing corporation with an income tax deduction, although they do reduce E & P.

[31]See *Daniel L. Reeves*, 94 TCM 287, T.C.Memo. 2007–273.

[32]Reg. § 1.301–1(j).

[33]Reg. § 1.301–1(m).

[34]*Henry J. Knott*, 67 T.C. 681 (1977).

[35]*Schalk Chemical Co. v. Comm.*, 62–1 USTC ¶9496, 9 AFTR 2d 1579, 304 F.2d 48 (CA–9, 1962).

In determining whether Libby's salary is unreasonable, both the *direct* salary payment of $400,000 and the *indirect* $50,000 payment are considered. Libby's total compensation package is $450,000. Libby may be eligible for a charitable contribution deduction of up to 50% of her adjusted gross income.

Unreasonable Compensation

A salary payment to a shareholder-employee that is determined to be **unreasonable compensation** is frequently treated as a constructive dividend and, as a result, is not deductible by the corporation. Whether compensation is reasonable or not depends on all the facts and circumstances. In determining the reasonableness of salary payments, the following factors have been used by courts:[36]

- The employee's qualifications.
- A comparison of salaries with dividend distributions.
- The prevailing rates of compensation for comparable positions in comparable business concerns.
- The nature and scope of the employee's work.
- The size and complexity of the business.
- A comparison of salaries paid with both gross and net income.
- The taxpayer's salary policy toward all employees.
- For small corporations with a limited number of officers, the amount of compensation paid to the employee in question in previous years.
- Whether a shareholder, acting in the best interests of the corporation, would have agreed to the level of compensation paid.

The last factor above, known as the "reasonable investor test," has been used in different ways by different courts.[37] In some cases, the Seventh Circuit Court of Appeals has relied solely on the reasonable investor test in determining reasonableness. On the other hand, the Tenth Circuit Court of Appeals has largely ignored this factor. Other Federal circuits have used an approach that considers all of the factors in the list.[38]

Ultimately, this is a challenging area. Taxpayers, the IRS, and the courts apply these factors in different ways to support conclusions that often differ. Taxpayers should keep good records and be prepared to defend their conclusions.

Loans to Shareholders

Advances to shareholders that are not bona fide loans usually are reclassified as constructive dividends. As with the reasonableness of compensation, whether an advance qualifies as a bona fide loan depends on all the facts and circumstances. Factors considered in determining whether an advance is a bona fide loan include the following:[39]

- Whether the advance is on open account or is evidenced by a written instrument.
- Whether the shareholder furnished collateral or other security for the advance.
- How long the advance has been outstanding.
- Whether any repayments have been made.
- The shareholder's ability to repay the advance.
- The shareholder's use of the funds (e.g., payment of routine bills versus nonrecurring, extraordinary expenses).

---

[36]All but the final factor in this list are identified in *Mayson Manufacturing Co. v. Comm.*, 49–2 USTC ¶9467, 38 AFTR 1028, 178 F.2d 115 (CA–6, 1949).

[37]For example, see *Alpha Medical, Inc. v. Comm.*, 99–1 USTC ¶50,461, 83 AFTR 2d 99–697, 172 F.3d 942 (CA–6, 1999).

[38]See *Vitamin Village, Inc.*, 94 TCM 277, T.C.Memo. 2007–272, for an example of a case that uses the reasonable investor test and other factors.

[39]*Fin Hay Realty Co. v. U.S.*, 68–2 USTC ¶9438, 22 AFTR 2d 5004, 398 F.2d 694 (CA–3, 1968). But see *Nariman Teymourian*, 90 TCM 352, T.C.Memo. 2005–302, for an example of how good planning can avoid constructive dividends in the shareholder loan context.

- The regularity of the advances.
- The dividend-paying history of the corporation.

Even when a corporation makes a bona fide loan to a shareholder, a constructive dividend may be triggered if the loan is interest-free (or carries a very low rate of interest). In this case, the constructive dividend is equal to the amount of imputed (forgone) interest on the loan.[40] Imputed interest equals the amount by which the interest paid by the Federal government on new borrowings, compounded semiannually, exceeds the interest charged on the loan.

When the imputed interest provision applies, the shareholder is deemed to have made an interest payment to the corporation equal to the amount of imputed interest and the corporation is deemed to have repaid the imputed interest to the shareholder through a constructive dividend. As a result, the corporation receives interest income and makes a nondeductible dividend payment, and the shareholder has taxable dividend income that might be offset with an interest deduction.

EXAMPLE

28

Mallard Corporation lends its principal shareholder, Henry, $100,000 on January 2 of the current year. The loan is interest-free and payable on demand. On December 31, the imputed interest rules are applied. Assuming that the Federal rate is 3%, compounded semiannually, the amount of imputed interest is $3,045. This amount is deemed paid by Henry to Mallard in the form of interest. Mallard then is deemed to return the amount to Henry as a constructive dividend.

As a result, Henry has dividend income of $3,045, which might be offset with a deduction for the interest paid to Mallard. Mallard has interest income of $3,045 for the interest received, with no offsetting deduction for the dividend payment.

Loans to a Corporation by Shareholders

Shareholder loans to a corporation may be reclassified as equity because the debt has too many features of stock. Any interest and principal payments made by the corporation to the shareholder are then treated as constructive dividends. This topic is covered more thoroughly in Chapter 4 (see text Section 4-2b and the discussion of "thin capitalization").

5-3e **Stock Dividends and Stock Rights**

LO.7

Determine the tax implications arising from receipt of stock dividends and stock rights and the shareholder's basis in the stock and stock rights received.

Stock Dividends—§ 305

In general, **stock dividends** are excluded from income on the theory that the ownership interest of the shareholder is unchanged as a result of the distribution.[41]

When a stock dividend is declared, the shareholder ends up with additional shares of stock but retains the same total stock basis. As a result, the shareholder's basis is reallocated across both the original shares and the new shares.[42] In total, the basis remains the same, but the *per share* basis decreases.

EXAMPLE

29

Green Corporation declares a 10% stock dividend when its stock is selling for $100 per share. As a result of the stock dividend, the per share stock value declines to $90.91 (Green's market capitalization remains the same, but it is spread over 10% more shares). Jennifer owns 100 shares of Green and has a basis of $1,100 for those shares. Jennifer receives 10 shares as a result of the stock dividend. How does the stock dividend affect Jennifer?

1. The stock dividend does not generate gross income to Jennifer (and has no impact on Green Corporation's taxable income or E & P).
2. Before the stock dividend, Jennifer had 100 shares and a basis of $11 per share ($1,100/100).
3. After the stock dividend, Jennifer has the same total basis ($1,100), but it is now allocated over the original shares plus the shares received in the stock dividend.
4. Each share of Jennifer's stock now has a basis of $10 ($1,100/110 shares).

---

[40]See § 7872.

[41]§ 305(a). See *Eisner v. Macomber*, 1 USTC ¶32, 3 AFTR 3020, 40 S.Ct. 189 (USSC, 1920).

[42]§ 307(a).

Stock splits—a more common occurrence—are treated in the same way as a stock dividend. So a 4-for-1 stock split provides a shareholder with three additional shares for each share held before the split. Total basis of the original shares is reallocated across all shares after the split. This means that each share carries one-quarter the per share basis of the original shares.

Assume the same information as in Example 29, except that Green Corporation declares a 4-for-1 stock split. After the split, Jennifer will own 400 shares, but her total basis remains $1,100. So her per share basis is $2.75 ($1,100 ÷ 400 shares).

If the dividend stock is not identical to the underlying shares (e.g., a stock dividend of preferred on common), basis is determined by allocating the basis of the formerly held shares between the old and new stock according to the fair market value of each. The holding period includes the holding period of the formerly held stock.[43]

Gail bought 1,000 shares of common stock two years ago for $10,000. In the current tax year, Gail receives a nontaxable preferred stock dividend of 100 shares. The preferred stock has a fair market value of $1,000, and the common stock, on which the preferred is distributed, has a fair market value of $19,000.

After the receipt of the stock dividend, the basis of the common stock is $9,500 and the basis of the preferred is $500, computed as follows:

Fair market value of common	$19,000
Fair market value of preferred	1,000
	$20,000
Basis of common: $^{19}\!/_{20} \times \$10,000$	$ 9,500
Basis of preferred: $^{1}\!/_{20} \times \$10,000$	$ 500

Recognizing that some distributions of stock could affect ownership interests, Congress added rules that tax stock dividends in certain situations.[44] The § 305 rules are based on the proportionate interest concept. Under the general rule, illustrated above, stock dividends are excluded from income if they are pro rata stock distributions paid on common stock.

If the stock dividend is a disproportionate distribution, the stock dividend is taxable. For example, a stock dividend where some common shareholders receive common stock and other common shareholders receive preferred stock would be a disproportionate distribution. The same is true if preferred shareholders received a common stock dividend.

If a stock dividend is determined to be taxable, the fair market value of the shares received is included in the shareholder's gross income. The shareholder's basis for the newly received shares is fair market value, and the holding period starts on the date of receipt. Since taxable stock dividends are rarely encountered in practice, we have chosen not to discuss the technical intricacies of § 305(b).

If stock dividends are not taxable, the corporation's E & P is not reduced.[45] If the stock dividends are taxable, the distributing corporation treats the distribution in the same manner as any other taxable property dividend.

Stock Rights

The rules for determining taxability of stock rights are identical to those for determining taxability of stock dividends. If the rights are taxable, the recipient has income equal to the fair market value of the rights. The fair market value then becomes the shareholder-distributee's basis in the rights.[46] If the rights are exercised, the holding period for the new stock begins on the date the rights (whether taxable or nontaxable) are exercised.

---

[43]§ 1223(5).

[44]§ 305(b); see "Stock Dividends," Senate Report 91–552, 1969–3 C.B. 519.

[45]§ 312(d)(1).

[46]Reg. § 1.305–1(b).

The basis of the new stock is the basis of the rights plus the amount of any other consideration given.

If stock rights are not taxable and the value of the rights is less than 15 percent of the value of the old stock, the basis of the rights is zero. However, the shareholder may elect to have some of the basis in the formerly held stock allocated to the rights.[47] The election is made by attaching a statement to the shareholder's return for the year in which the rights are received.[48] If the fair market value of the rights is 15 percent or more of the value of the old stock and the rights are exercised or sold, the shareholder *must* allocate some of the basis in the formerly held stock to the rights.

EXAMPLE

32

A corporation with common stock outstanding declares a nontaxable dividend payable in rights to subscribe to common stock. Each right entitles the holder to purchase one share of stock for $90. One right is issued for every two shares of stock owned. Fred owns 400 shares of stock purchased two years ago for $15,000. At the time of the distribution of the rights, the market value of the common stock is $100 per share, and the market value of the rights is $8 per right. Fred receives 200 rights. He exercises 100 rights and sells the remaining 100 rights three months later for $9 per right.

Fred need not allocate the cost of the original stock to the rights because the value of the rights is less than 15% of the value of the stock ($1,600 ÷ $40,000 = 4%). If Fred does not allocate his original stock basis to the rights, the tax consequences are as follows:

- Basis of the new stock is $9,000 [$90 (exercise price) × 100 (shares)]. The holding period of the new stock begins on the date the stock was purchased.

- Sale of the rights produces long-term capital gain of $900 [$9 (sales price) × 100 (rights)]. The holding period of the rights starts with the date the original 400 shares of stock were acquired.

If Fred elects to allocate basis to the rights, the tax consequences are as follows:

- Basis of the stock is $14,423 [$40,000 (value of stock) ÷ $41,600 (value of rights and stock) × $15,000 (cost of stock)].

- Basis of the rights is $577 [$1,600 (value of rights) ÷ $41,600 (value of rights and stock) × $15,000 (cost of stock)].

- When Fred exercises the rights, his basis for the new stock will be $9,288.50 [$9,000 (cost) + $288.50 (basis for 100 rights)].

- Sale of the rights would produce a long-term capital gain of $611.50 [$900 (sales price) − $288.50 (basis in the remaining 100 rights)].

5-4 TAX PLANNING

5-4a Corporate Distributions

The following points are especially important when planning for corporate distributions.

- Because E & P is the pool of funds from which dividends may be distributed, its computation is essential to corporate planning. However, many corporations do not calculate E & P on a regular basis. Some firms view the financial accounting concept of "retained earnings" as a surrogate; if there are sufficient retained earnings, they assume there is sufficient E & P. And in many instances, this is a fairly safe assumption. But if retained earnings is reduced (or low), the corporation may be at risk for making a distribution that is not a dividend for tax purposes (and, instead, a return of capital). Thus, an E & P account should be established and maintained.

- Accumulated E & P is the sum of all past years' current E & P. Because there is no statute of limitations on the computation of E & P, the IRS can redetermine a corporation's current E & P for a tax year long since passed. Any changes made

LO.8

Structure corporate distributions in a manner that minimizes the tax consequences to the parties involved.

---

[47]§ 307(b)(1).   [48]Reg. § 1.307–2.

will affect accumulated E & P and have a direct impact on the taxability of current distributions to shareholders.

- Distributions can be planned to avoid or minimize dividend exposure.

Corporate Distributions—Tax Planning

EXAMPLE 33

Flicker Corporation has accumulated E & P of $100,000 as of January 1 of the current year. During the year, it expects to have earnings from operations of $80,000 and to sell an asset for a loss of $100,000. As a result, it anticipates a current E & P deficit of $20,000. Flicker Corporation also expects to make a cash distribution of $60,000.

If the shareholders would prefer *not* to have dividend income, the best approach is to recognize the loss as soon as possible and, immediately thereafter, make the cash distribution to the shareholders. Suppose these two steps take place on January 1. Because there is a $100,000 deficit in current E & P at the time of the distribution, the accumulated E & P account comes into play (refer to Example 13 in this chapter).

As a result, at the time of the distribution, the combined E & P balance is zero [$100,000 (beginning balance in accumulated E & P) − $100,000 (existing deficit in current E & P)] and the $60,000 distribution to the shareholders constitutes a return of capital. Current deficits are deemed to accrue pro rata throughout the year unless the parties can prove otherwise; here, they can.

EXAMPLE 34

After several unprofitable years, Darter Corporation has a deficit in accumulated E & P of $100,000 as of January 1, 2019. Starting in 2019, Darter expects to generate annual E & P of $50,000 for the next four years and would like to distribute this amount to its shareholders. The corporation's cash position (for dividend purposes) will correspond to the current E & P generated. Consider the following two distribution schedules:

1. On December 31 of 2019, 2020, 2021, and 2022, Darter Corporation distributes cash of $50,000.
2. On December 31 of 2020 and 2022, Darter Corporation distributes cash of $100,000.

The two alternatives are illustrated below.

Year	Accumulated E & P (First of Year)	Current E & P	Distribution	Amount of Dividend
Alternative 1				
2019	($100,000)	$50,000	$ 50,000	$50,000
2020	(100,000)	50,000	50,000	50,000
2021	(100,000)	50,000	50,000	50,000
2022	(100,000)	50,000	50,000	50,000
Alternative 2				
2019	($100,000)	$50,000	$ –0–	$ –0–
2020	(50,000)	50,000	100,000	50,000
2021	(50,000)	50,000	–0–	–0–
2022	–0–	50,000	100,000	50,000

Alternative 1 produces $200,000 of dividend income because each $50,000 distribution is fully covered by current E & P. Alternative 2, however, produces only $100,000 of dividend income for the shareholders. The remaining $100,000 is a return of capital. Why?

At the time Darter Corporation made its first distribution of $100,000 on December 31, 2020, it had a deficit of $50,000 in accumulated E & P (the original deficit of $100,000 is reduced by the $50,000 of current E & P from 2019). Consequently, the $100,000 distribution yields a $50,000 dividend (the current E & P for 2020), and $50,000 is treated as a return of capital.

As of January 1, 2021, Darter's accumulated E & P now has a deficit balance of $50,000 because a distribution cannot increase a deficit in E & P. After adding the remaining $50,000 of current E & P from 2021, the balance on January 1, 2022, is zero. As a result, the second distribution of $100,000, made on December 31, 2022, also yields $50,000 of dividends (the current E & P for 2022) and a $50,000 return of capital.

5-4b Planning for Qualified Dividends

Retirement Plans

The reduced tax rates available to individual taxpayers on net capital gain and qualified dividend income are not available when stock is held in retirement accounts. Because income in § 401(k) plans and IRAs is not taxed when earned, the benefits of the lower tax rates on these forms of income are lost. Instead, distributions from these plans (other than Roth IRAs) are taxed at ordinary income tax rates.

Individual Alternative Minimum Tax

The lower rates on dividends and long-term capital gains apply under both the regular income tax and the alternative minimum tax. This increases the exposure of many individuals to the alternative minimum tax, particularly those with significant income from dividends or long-term capital gain. As a result, individual taxpayers who pay the alternative minimum tax should consider modifying their investment strategies. Appropriately managing the mix of ordinary income, dividend income, and capital gain can minimize the alternative minimum tax.

Closely Held Corporations

Closely held corporations have considerable discretion regarding their dividend policies. In the past, the double tax result provided strong motivation to avoid the payment of dividends. Instead, the incentive was to bail out corporate profits in a manner that provided tax benefits to the corporation. As a result, liberal use was made of compensation, loan, and lease arrangements because salaries, interest, and rent are deductible. Under current law, however, shareholders might prefer dividends because salaries, interest, and rent are taxed at ordinary rates while dividends receive preferential treatment. As a result, the question becomes this: *Should the corporation or the shareholders benefit?* In general, the best strategy considers the tax consequences to *both parties*.

Consider a corporation paying tax at the 21% rate and an individual shareholder in the 32% tax bracket. A deductible $10,000 payment to the shareholder will *save* the corporation $2,100 in tax, resulting in an after-tax cost of $7,900. The shareholder will pay $3,200 in tax, resulting in after-tax income of $6,800. This creates a joint tax burden of $1,100 ($3,200 tax paid by the shareholder − $2,100 tax saved by the corporation).

If, instead, the corporation paid a $10,000 qualified dividend (subject to a 15% tax rate) to the shareholder, no tax savings would be realized by the corporation, resulting in an after-tax cost of $10,000. The shareholder would owe $1,500 in taxes, leaving $8,500 of income. Considering both the corporation and the shareholder, a dividend creates $400 more tax liability than a deductible payment, so the deductible payment is more tax-efficient.

EXAMPLE 35

In Example 35, when the deductible payment is made, the shareholder bears an increased tax burden of $1,700 ($3,200 tax due from the deductible payment − $1,500 tax due from the dividend) while the corporation saves $2,100 ($2,100 tax saved because of the deductible payment − $0 tax saved because of the dividend). Both parties could actually benefit if the corporation transfers part of its benefit to the shareholder through a larger deductible payment.

Assume the same facts as in Example 35, except that the corporation pays a $12,600 deductible payment to the shareholder. In this case, the corporation will save $2,646 ($12,600 × 21%) in tax, resulting in an after-tax cost of $9,954.

From the corporation's perspective, this is preferable to a $10,000 dividend because it costs $46 less after tax ($10,000 dividend cost − $9,954 after-tax cost of a $12,600 deductible payment). The shareholder will pay taxes of $4,032 on the deductible payment, resulting in after-tax income of $8,568. The shareholder will also prefer this payment to a $10,000 dividend because it generates $68 more after-tax income ($8,568 − $8,500 from a dividend).

EXAMPLE 36

As a result, if properly structured, deductible payments by the corporation to the shareholder can be preferable to dividends in many situations. The benefit of this strategy will be even greater if the shareholder is paying alternative minimum tax.

5-4c **Constructive Dividends**

Tax planning can be particularly effective in avoiding constructive dividend situations. Shareholders should try to structure their dealings with the corporation on an arm's length basis. For example, reasonable rent should be paid for the use of corporate property, and a fair price should be paid by a shareholder for its purchase. The parties should support the amount involved with appraisal data or market information obtained from reliable sources at or near the time of the transaction. In the case of loans to shareholders, the parties should provide for an adequate rate of interest and written evidence of the debt. Shareholders also should establish and follow a realistic repayment schedule.

If shareholders want to bail out corporate profits in a form deductible to the corporation, a balanced mix of the possible alternatives lessens the risk of constructive dividend treatment. Rent for the use of shareholder property, interest on amounts borrowed from shareholders, or salaries for services rendered by shareholders are all feasible substitutes for dividend distributions. Overdoing any one approach, however, may attract the attention of the IRS. Too much interest, for example, may mean that the corporation is thinly capitalized, and some of the debt may be reclassified as equity investment.

Much can be done to protect against the disallowance of unreasonable compensation. Example 37 is an illustration, all too common in a family corporation, of what *not* to do.

EXAMPLE

37

Rebecca Cole wholly owns Eagle Corporation. Corporate employees and annual salaries include Bob, Rebecca's husband ($120,000); Sam, Rebecca's son ($80,000); Rebecca ($640,000); and Tanuja, Rebecca's longtime friend who is unrelated to the Cole family ($320,000). The operation of Eagle Corporation is shared about equally between Rebecca and Tanuja.

Bob performed significant services for Eagle during its formative years, but now merely attends the annual meeting of the board of directors. Sam is a full-time student and occasionally signs papers for the corporation in his capacity as treasurer. Eagle Corporation has not distributed a dividend for 10 years although it has accumulated substantial E & P. Bob, Sam, and Rebecca run the risk of a finding of unreasonable compensation, based on the following factors:

- Bob's salary is vulnerable unless proof is available that some or all of his $120,000 annual salary is payment for services rendered to the corporation in prior years and that he was underpaid for those years.[49]

- Sam's salary is also vulnerable; he does not appear to earn the $80,000 paid to him by the corporation. Neither Sam nor Bob is a shareholder, but each one's relationship to Rebecca is enough of a tie-in to raise the unreasonable compensation issue.

- Rebecca's salary could be challenged by the IRS. Why is Rebecca receiving $320,000 more than Tanuja when they share equally in the operation of the corporation?

- The fact that Eagle Corporation has not distributed dividends over the past 10 years, even though it is capable of doing so, also increases the likelihood of a constructive dividend.

What could have been done to improve the tax position of the parties in Example 37? Bob and Sam are not entitled to a salary since neither seems to be performing any services for the corporation. Paying them a salary simply aggravates the problem. The IRS is more apt to consider *all* the family members' salaries excessive under the circumstances. Rebecca should probably reduce her compensation to correspond with that paid to Tanuja. She can then attempt to distribute corporate earnings to herself in some other form.

Paying some dividends to Rebecca would also help alleviate the problem raised in Example 37. The IRS has been successful in denying a deduction for salary paid to a

---

[49]See, for example, *R.J. Nicoll* Co., 59 T.C. 37 (1972).

shareholder-employee, even when the payment was reasonable, in a situation where the corporation had not distributed any dividends.[50] Most courts, however, have not denied deductions for compensation solely because a dividend was not paid. A better approach is to compare an employee's compensation with the level of compensation prevalent in the particular industry.

The corporation can provide *indirect* compensation to Rebecca by paying expenses that benefit her personally but are nevertheless deductible to the corporation. For example, premiums paid by the corporation for sickness, accident, and hospitalization insurance for Rebecca are deductible to the corporation and nontaxable to her.[51] Any payments under the policy are not taxable to Rebecca unless they exceed her medical expenses.[52] The corporation can also pay for travel and entertainment expenses incurred by Rebecca on behalf of the corporation. If these expenses are primarily for the benefit of the corporation, Rebecca will not recognize any taxable income and the corporation will receive a deduction.[53] However, when testing for reasonableness, the IRS looks at the total compensation package, including indirect compensation payments to a shareholder-employee.

Here are some examples of indirect compensation:

- Corporate payment of the shareholder's personal expenses that are not related to the business (e.g., vacations, rent, medical bills, legal fees, country club dues, and/or other living expenses).
- Corporate reimbursements (e.g., excessive expense allowances and moving allowances).
- Shareholder use of company-owned property for personal purposes without fair payment by the shareholder (e.g., automobiles, boats, and office space).
- Purchase (or rental) of shareholder property in excess of fair market (rental) value.
- Shareholder purchase (or lease) of corporate property at a bargain price (rental).
- Corporate payment of a shareholder's debt or obligation.
- Corporate loan to a shareholder where there is no expectation or demand for repayment (or with a below-market interest rate).
- Corporate loans to finance a shareholder's purchase of personal items (e.g., a house, a vacation, and/or personal investments).
- Shareholder loans to the corporation at an interest rate in excess of market rate.

As with many things in life, indirect compensation is a "gray area" with no single set of standards to be applied. Certain activities can combine both business and personal dimensions (e.g., a business trip to Hawaii). A country club membership can generate both business and personal use. Disentangling the business and personal use of business assets can also be a challenge. In fact, many companies have policies that allow for the "limited personal use" of certain corporate assets (such as computers, mobile devices, copy machines, conference rooms, and vehicles). This "limited personal use" exception is normally provided as long as the use is occasional, is not for outside employment, does not result in excessive costs, and does not interfere with work responsibilities. Ultimately, whether there is "indirect compensation" (and a constructive dividend) will depend on taxpayer policies and related documentation substantiating business justification for the usage.

---

[50]*McCandless Tile Service v. U.S.*, 70–1 USTC ¶9284, 25 AFTR 2d 70–870, 422 F.2d 1336 (Ct.Cls., 1970). The court in *McCandless* concluded that a return on equity of 15% of net profits was reasonable.
[51]Reg. § 1.162–10.

[52]The medical reimbursement plan must meet certain nondiscrimination requirements of § 105(h)(2).
[53]Reg. § 1.62–2(c)(4).

REFOCUS ON THE BIG PICTURE

TAXING CORPORATE DISTRIBUTIONS

A number of factors affect the tax treatment of Plainwell Ice Cream Corporation's distributions. The amount of current and accumulated E & P (which differ from the financial reporting concept of retained earnings) partially determines the tax effect on the shareholders. Given that Plainwell Ice Cream Corporation has had a highly profitable year (see Example 12), it is likely that there is sufficient current E & P to cover the distributions. If so, they are dividends to the shareholders rather than a return of capital. Waffle Cone Corporation receives $200,000 of dividend income that is offset by the dividends received deduction.* Luis has $200,000 of dividend income (i.e., $300,000 value of the land less the $100,000 mortgage). Assuming that Plainwell is a domestic corporation and that Luis has held his stock for the entire year, the land is a qualified dividend. As a result, the tax depends on Luis's taxable income.** Luis's basis in the land is its fair market value at distribution, or $300,000 (see Example 17).

From Plainwell Ice Cream Corporation's perspective, the distribution of appreciated property creates a deemed gain (see Example 20). As a result, a $280,000 gain results ($300,000 fair market value of the land less its adjusted basis of $20,000). Although the gain increases Plainwell's E & P, the distributions to the shareholders reduce it by $200,000 for the cash and $200,000 for the land ($300,000 fair market value reduced by the $100,000 mortgage).

What If?

What if current E & P is less than the cash and land distributed to the shareholders? Current E & P is applied pro rata to the cash and the land. Because the amounts received by the two shareholders are equal ($200,000 each), the current E & P applied is taxed as a dividend and is treated as described above. To the extent the distributions are not covered by current E & P, accumulated E & P is then applied in a pro rata fashion (because both distributions were made on December 31). However, Plainwell probably has a deficit in accumulated E & P. As a result, the remaining amounts distributed to the two shareholders are first a tax-free recovery of stock basis, and any excess is taxed as a sale of the stock (likely classified as capital gain).

* Because both shareholders received equal distributions ($200,000), it would appear that each is a 50% shareholder. As a result, Waffle Cone's dividends would be offset by a 65% dividends received deduction.

** Because Luis is married filing jointly in 2019, there will be no tax on the dividend if his taxable income is $78,750 or less; a 20% tax if his taxable income is greater than $488,850; a 15% tax if his taxable income is between these two figures.

Key Terms

Discussion Questions

1. **LO.2** In determining Blue Corporation's current E & P for 2019, how should taxable income be adjusted as a result of the following transactions?

   a. A capital loss carryover from 2018, fully used in 2019.

   b. Nondeductible meal expenses in 2019.

    c.   Interest on municipal bonds received in 2019.

    d.   Nondeductible lobbying expenses in 2019.

    e.   Loss on a sale between related parties in 2019.

    f.   Federal income tax refund received in 2019.

2. **LO.3** Describe the effect of a distribution in a year when the distributing corporation has:

    a.   A deficit in accumulated E & P and a positive amount in current E & P.

    b.   A positive amount in accumulated E & P and a deficit in current E & P.

    c.   A deficit in both current and accumulated E & P.

    d.   A positive amount in both current and accumulated E & P.

3. **LO.3** A calendar year corporation has substantial accumulated E & P, but it expects to incur a deficit in current E & P for the year due to significant losses in the last half of the year. A cash distribution to its shareholders on January 1 should result in a return of capital. Comment on the validity of this statement.

4. **LO.4** Discuss the rationale for the reduced tax rates on dividends paid to individuals.

5. **LO.5** Discuss the impact each of the following has on generating or adding to a deficit in E & P.

    a.   The distribution of a property dividend, where the basis of the property exceeds its fair market value.

    b.   An operating loss of the corporation.

6. **LO.1, 2, 3, 4, 5** Orange Corporation distributes $200,000 in cash to each of its three shareholders: Sandy, Byron, and Fuchsia Corporation. What factors must be considered when determining how the distribution is treated for tax purposes by the shareholders?   *Critical Thinking*

7. **LO.5** Assume the same facts as in Question 6, except that property is distributed. What factors must be considered when determining how the distribution is treated for tax purposes by Orange Corporation?   *Critical Thinking*

8. **LO.5** Orion Corporation's board of directors decides to distribute property to its shareholders rather than pay a cash dividend. Why might Orion's board make this decision?

9. **LO.5** Raven Corporation owns three machines that it uses in its business. It no longer needs two of these machines and is considering distributing them to its two shareholders as a property dividend. All three machines have a fair market value of $20,000 each. The basis of each machine is as follows: Machine A, $27,000; Machine B, $20,000; and Machine C, $12,000. The corporation has asked you for advice. What do you recommend?   *Decision Making*

10. **LO.5** Tangerine Corporation is considering a property distribution to its shareholders. If appreciated property is to be used, does it matter to Tangerine whether the property distributed is a long-term capital asset or depreciable property subject to recapture? Would your answer differ if the property distributed has a fair market value less than the adjusted basis? Explain.   *Critical Thinking*

11. **LO.6** Samantha is the president and sole shareholder of Toucan Corporation. She is paid an annual salary of $500,000, and her son, Aaron, the company's chief financial officer, is paid a salary of $290,000. Aaron works for Toucan on a part-time basis and spends most of his time training for triathlons. Toucan advances $85,000 to Samantha as an interest-free loan. What are the tax issues?   *Critical Thinking*

12. **LO.6** Whether compensation paid to a corporate employee is reasonable is a question of fact to be determined from the surrounding circumstances. How would the resolution of this problem be affected by each of the following factors?

a. The employee owns no stock but is the mother-in-law of the sole shareholder.

b. The shareholder-employee does not have a college degree.

c. The shareholder-employee works 40 hours per week for another unrelated employer.

d. The shareholder-employee was underpaid for services during the formative period of the corporation.

e. The corporation has never paid a dividend.

f. Year-end bonuses are paid to all employees, but officer-shareholders receive disproportionately larger bonuses.

13. **LO.6, 8** Pink Corporation has several employees. Their names and salaries are listed below.

Judy	$470,000
Holly (Judy's daughter)	100,000
Terry (Judy's son)	100,000
John (an unrelated third party)	320,000

Holly and Terry are the only shareholders of Pink Corporation. Judy and John share equally in the management of the company's operations. Holly and Terry are both full-time college students at a university 200 miles away. Pink has substantial E & P and has never distributed a dividend. Discuss any problems related to Pink's salary arrangement.

Communications   14. **LO.7** Your client, Raptor Corporation, declares a dividend permitting its common shareholders to elect to receive 9 shares of cumulative preferred stock or 3 additional shares of Raptor common stock for every 10 shares of common stock held. Raptor has only common stock outstanding (fair market value of $45 per share). One shareholder elects to receive preferred stock, while the remaining shareholders choose the common stock. Raptor asks you whether the shareholders have any taxable income on the receipt of the stock. Prepare a letter to Raptor's president (Sarah Thomas) and a memo for the file regarding this matter. Raptor's address is 1812 S. Camino Seco, Tucson, AZ 85710.

Computational Exercises

15. **LO.1** At the beginning of the year, Myrna Corporation (a calendar year taxpayer) has E & P of $32,000. The corporation generates no additional E & P during the year. On December 31, the corporation distributes $50,000 to its sole shareholder, Abby, whose stock basis is $10,000. How is the distribution treated for tax purposes?

16. **LO.3** On January 1 of the current year, Rhondell Corporation has accumulated E & P of $13,000. Current E & P for the year is $84,000, earned evenly throughout the year. Elizabeth and Jonathan are sole equal shareholders of Rhondell from January 1 to April 30. On May 1, Elizabeth sells all of her stock to Marshall. Rhondell makes two distributions to shareholders during the year: a total of $42,000 ($21,000 to Elizabeth and $21,000 to Jonathan) on April 30 and a total of $58,000 ($29,000 to Jonathan and $29,000 to Marshall) on December 31.

Determine the allocation of the distributions by completing the table below. Assume that the shareholders have sufficient basis in their stock for any amount that is treated as return of capital.

	From Current E & P	From Accumulated E & P	Treated as Return of Capital
April 30 distribution of $42,000	_____	_____	_____
December 31 distribution of $58,000	_____	_____	_____

17. **LO.4, 8** Rover Corporation would like to transfer excess cash to its sole shareholder,   Decision Making
    Aleshia, who is also an employee. Aleshia is in the 24% tax bracket, and
    Rover is subject to a 21% rate. Because Aleshia's contribution to the business is
    substantial, Rover believes that a $25,000 bonus in the current year is reasonable
    compensation and should be deductible by the corporation. However, Rover is
    considering paying Aleshia a $25,000 dividend because the tax rate on dividends is
    lower than the tax rate on compensation. Is Rover correct in believing that a divi-
    dend is the better choice? Why or why not?

18. **LO.5** Global Corporation distributed property with an $850,000 fair market value
    and a $415,000 adjusted basis to one of its shareholders. The property was
    subject to a $230,000 mortgage, which the shareholder assumed. Global has ample
    E & P to cover any distribution made during the year. What is the amount of the
    shareholder's dividend income on the distribution? What is the shareholder's basis
    in the property received?

19. **LO.5** Quinlan has ample E & P to cover any distributions made during the year.
    One distribution made to a shareholder consists of property with an adjusted
    basis of $150,000 and a fair market value of $90,000. What are the tax consequences
    of this distribution to Quinlan?

20. **LO.5** Fargo Corporation distributes property (basis of $260,000 and fair market
    value of $310,000) to a shareholder. Fargo Corporation has sufficient E & P
    for its distributions. What are the tax consequences of this distribution to Fargo?

21. **LO.6** Deerwood Corporation lends its principal shareholder, Lafayette, $500,000 on
    July 1 of the current year. The loan is interest-free and payable on demand.
    On December 31, the imputed interest rules are applied. Assume that the Federal
    rate is 3%, compounded semiannually. What are the tax consequences of this loan
    to Lafayette?

22. **LO.7** What are the tax consequences to Euclid from the following independent
    events?
    a. Euclid bought 500 shares of common stock five years ago for $50,000. This year,
       Euclid receives 20 shares of common stock as a nontaxable stock dividend.
       What is Euclid's basis per share after this event?
    b. Assume instead that Euclid received a nontaxable preferred stock dividend of
       20 shares. The preferred stock has a fair market value of $5,000, and the common
       stock, on which the preferred is distributed, has a fair market value of $75,000.

23. **LO.7** A corporation with common stock outstanding declares a nontaxable dividend
    payable in rights to subscribe to common stock on June 30 of the current year.
    Each right entitles the holder to purchase one share of stock for $25. One right is
    issued for every share of stock owned. Thomas owns 100 shares of stock purchased
    10 years ago for $1,000. At the time of the distribution of the rights, the market value
    of the common stock is $40 per share and the market value of the rights is $5 per
    right. Thomas receives 100 rights. On September 30, he exercises 75 of the rights
    and sells the remaining 25 rights for $6 per right.
    a. Assuming that Thomas does not allocate his original stock basis to the rights,
       what is his basis in the new stock?
    b. When does his holding period begin?
    c. What are the tax consequences of the sale of the rights?

Problems

24. **LO.1, 4** At the start of the current year, Blue Corporation (a calendar year taxpayer) has accumulated E & P of $100,000. Blue's current E & P is $60,000, and at the end of the year, it distributes $200,000 ($100,000 each) to its equal shareholders, Pam and Jon. Pam's stock basis is $11,000; Jon's stock basis is $26,000. How is the distribution treated for tax purposes?

25. **LO.1, 2** Cardinal Corporation, a calendar year taxpayer, receives dividend income of $250,000 from a corporation in which it holds a 10% interest. Cardinal also receives interest income of $35,000 from municipal bonds. (The municipality used the proceeds from the bond issue to construct a library.) Cardinal borrowed funds to purchase the municipal bonds and pays $20,000 of interest on the loan. Excluding these three items, Cardinal's taxable income is $500,000. Cardinal has $150,000 of accumulated E & P at the end of the prior year, and it paid Federal income taxes of $131,250 during the year.

    a.   What is Cardinal Corporation's taxable income after these three items are taken into account?

    b.   What is Cardinal Corporation's accumulated E & P at the start of next year?

26. **LO.1, 2, 3** On September 30, Silver Corporation, a calendar year taxpayer, sold a parcel of land (basis of $400,000) for a $1,000,000 note. The note is payable in five installments, with the first payment due next year. Because Silver did not elect out of the installment method, none of the $600,000 gain is taxed this year.

    Silver Corporation had a $300,000 deficit in accumulated E & P at the beginning of the year. Before considering the effect of the land sale, Silver had a deficit in current E & P of $50,000.

    Javiera, the sole shareholder of Silver, has a basis of $200,000 in her stock. If Silver distributes $900,000 to Javiera on December 31, how much income must she report for tax purposes?

27. **LO.2** Sparrow Corporation (a calendar year, accrual basis taxpayer) had the following transactions in 2019, its second year of operation:

Taxable income	$330,000
Federal income tax liability paid	69,300
Tax-exempt interest income	5,000
Meals expense (total)	3,000
Premiums paid on key employee life insurance	3,500
Increase in cash surrender value attributable to life insurance premiums	700
Proceeds from key employee life insurance policy	130,000
Cash surrender value of life insurance policy at distribution	20,000
Excess of capital losses over capital gains	13,000
MACRS deduction	26,000
Straight-line depreciation using ADS lives	16,000
Section 179 expense elected during 2018	25,000
Dividends received from domestic corporations (less than 20% owned)	35,000

Sparrow uses the LIFO inventory method, and its LIFO recapture amount increased by $10,000 during 2019. In addition, Sparrow sold property on installment during 2018. The property was sold for $40,000 and had an adjusted basis at sale of $32,000. During 2019, Sparrow received a $15,000 payment on the installment sale. Finally, assume that no additional first-year depreciation was claimed. Compute Sparrow's current E & P.

28. **LO.1, 2** In each of the following independent situations, indicate the effect on tax-   Critical Thinking
able income and E & P, stating the amount of any increase (or decrease)
in each as a result of the transaction. Assume that E & P has already been increased
by taxable income.

Transaction	Taxable Income Increase (Decrease)	E & P Increase (Decrease)
a. Realized gain of $80,000 on involuntary conversion of building ($10,000 of gain is recognized).	_____	_____
b. Mining exploration costs incurred on May 1 of current year; $24,000 is deductible from current-year taxable income.	_____	_____
c. Sale of equipment to unrelated third party for $240,000; basis is $120,000 (no election out of installment method; no payments are received in current year).	_____	_____
d. Dividends of $20,000 received from 5% owned corporation, together with dividends received deduction (assume that taxable income limit does not apply).	_____	_____
e. Additional first-year (bonus) depreciation of $45,000 claimed in current year.	_____	_____
f. Section 179 expense deduction of $25,000 in current year.	_____	_____
g. Impact of current-year § 179 expense deduction in succeeding year.	_____	_____
h. MACRS depreciation of $80,000. ADS depreciation would have been $90,000.	_____	_____
i. Federal income taxes of $80,000 paid in current year.	_____	_____

29. **LO.2** Yellow Corporation, a calendar year taxpayer, made estimated   Critical Thinking
tax payments of $40,000 for 2019 ($10,000 per quarter). Yellow filed its Federal
income tax return for 2019 reflecting a tax liability of $15,000. Due to its overpay-
ments, Yellow received a $25,000 refund in 2020. What is the impact on Yellow's E & P
of the payment of estimated taxes and the receipt of the Federal income tax refund?

30. **LO.1, 3** Sparrow Corporation is a calendar year taxpayer. At the beginning of the   Critical Thinking
current year, Sparrow has accumulated E & P of $33,000. The corporation
incurs a deficit in current E & P of $46,000 that accrues ratably throughout the year.
On June 30, Sparrow distributes $20,000 to its sole shareholder, Libby. If Libby's
stock has a basis of $4,000, how is she taxed on the distribution?

31. **LO.1, 3** At the beginning of the year, Teal Corporation had accumulated E & P of
$210,000. On March 30, Teal sold an asset at a loss of $200,000. For the
calendar year, Teal incurred a deficit in current E & P of $305,000, which includes
the $200,000 loss on the sale of the asset. If Teal made a distribution of $50,000 to its
sole shareholder on April 1 and the shareholder had a basis in her stock of $72,000,
how will the shareholder be taxed?

32. **LO.1, 3** Green Corporation (a calendar year taxpayer) had a deficit in accumulated
E & P of $250,000 at the beginning of the current year. Its net profit for the
period January 1 through July 30 was $300,000, but its E & P for the entire taxable
year was only $40,000. If Green made a distribution of $60,000 to its sole shareholder on August 1, how will the shareholder be taxed?

33. **LO.1, 3** Black Corporation and Tom each own 50% of Tan Corporation's common
stock. On January 1, Tan has a deficit in accumulated E & P of $200,000. Its

current E & P is $90,000. During the year, Tan makes cash distributions of $40,000 each to Black and Tom.

a.   How are the two shareholders taxed on the distribution?

b.   What is Tan Corporation's accumulated E & P at the end of the year?

34.   **LO.1, 3** Complete the following schedule for each case. Unless otherwise indicated, assume that the shareholders have ample basis in the stock investment.

	Accumulated E & P Beginning of Year	Current E & P	Cash Distributions (All on Last Day of Year)	Dividend Income	Return of Capital
a.	($200,000)	$ 70,000	$130,000	_____	_____
b.	150,000	(120,000)	210,000	_____	_____
c.	90,000	70,000	150,000	_____	_____
d.	120,000	(60,000)	130,000	_____	_____
e.	Same as part (d), except that the distribution of $130,000 is made on June 30 and the corporation uses the calendar year for tax purposes.			_____	_____

35.   **LO.1, 3** Larry, the sole shareholder of Brown Corporation, sold his Brown stock to Ed on July 30 for $270,000. Larry's basis in the stock was $200,000 at the beginning of the year. Brown had accumulated E & P of $120,000 on January 1 and has current E & P of $240,000. During the year, Brown made the following distributions: $450,000 cash to Larry on July 1 and $150,000 cash to Ed on December 30. How will Larry and Ed be taxed on the distributions? How much gain will Larry recognize on the sale of his stock to Ed?

Decision Making

Critical Thinking

36.   **LO.4** Sean, a shareholder of Crimson Corporation, is single and in the 35% tax bracket. This year, he receives a $7,000 qualified dividend from Crimson. Sean has investment interest expense of $16,000 and net investment income of $9,000 (not including the qualified dividend). Assume that Sean does not expect to have any investment income in the foreseeable future. Should Sean treat the distribution as a qualified dividend (subject to a 15% tax rate) or classify it as net investment income?

37.   **LO.4** In November of the current year, Emerald Corporation declared a dividend of $2 per share (the shareholder record date is December 15). Assume that Emerald has sufficient current E & P to cover the dividend payment. If Judy purchases 500 shares of Emerald stock on December 5 and sells the stock on December 25, how is she taxed on the $1,000 dividend?

Critical Thinking

38.   **LO.1, 5** Heather, an individual, owns all of the outstanding stock in Silver Corporation. Heather purchased her stock in Silver nine years ago, and her basis is $56,000. At the beginning of this year, the corporation has $76,000 of accumulated E & P and no current E & P (before considering the effect of the distributions as noted below). What are the tax consequences to Heather (amount and type of income and basis in property received) and Silver Corporation (gain or loss and effect on E & P) in each of the following situations?

a.   Silver distributes land to Heather. The land was held as an investment and has a fair market value of $54,000 and an adjusted basis of $42,000.

b.   Assume that Silver Corporation has no current or accumulated E & P prior to the distribution. How would your answer to part (a) change?

c.   Assume that the land distributed in part (a) is subject to a $46,000 mortgage (which Heather assumes). How would your answer change?

d. Assume that the land has a fair market value of $54,000 and an adjusted basis of $62,000 on the date of the distribution. How would your answer to part (a) change?

e. Instead of distributing land in part (a), assume that Silver decides to distribute equipment used in its business. The equipment has a $14,000 market value, a $1,200 adjusted basis for income tax purposes, and a $5,200 adjusted basis for E & P purposes. When the equipment was purchased four years ago, its original fair market value was $18,000.

39. **LO.1, 5** Apricot Corporation distributes property ($125,000 basis and $150,000 fair market value) to its sole shareholder, Ellie. The property is subject to a liability of $200,000, which Ellie assumes. Apricot has E & P of $325,000 prior to the distribution.

a. What gain, if any, does Apricot recognize on the distribution? What is Apricot's accumulated E & P at the start of the following year?

b. What is the amount of Ellie's dividend income on the distribution? What is her basis in the property received?

40. **LO.1, 5** Lime Corporation, with E & P of $500,000, distributes land (worth $300,000, adjusted basis of $350,000) to Harry, its sole shareholder. The land is subject to a liability of $120,000, which Harry assumes. What are the tax consequences to Lime and to Harry?

41. **LO.1, 3** At the beginning of the year, Penguin Corporation (a calendar year taxpayer) has accumulated E & P of $55,000. During the year, Penguin incurs a $36,000 loss from operations that accrues ratably. On October 1, Penguin distributes $40,000 in cash to Holly, its sole shareholder. How is Holly taxed on the distribution?

42. **LO.1, 5** Cornflower Corporation distributes equipment (adjusted basis of $70,000, fair market value of $55,000) to its shareholder, Roy. Assume that Cornflower has more than $100,000 of current E & P. What are the tax consequences to Cornflower Corporation and to Roy?

43. **LO.1, 2, 3, 4, 5** Cerulean Corporation has two equal shareholders, Marco and Avery. Critical Thinking Marco acquired his Cerulean stock three years ago by transferring property worth $700,000, basis of $300,000, for 70 shares of the stock. Avery acquired 70 shares in Cerulean Corporation two years ago by transferring property worth $660,000, basis of $110,000. Cerulean Corporation's accumulated E & P as of January 1 of the current year is $350,000. On March 1 of the current year, the corporation distributed to Marco property worth $120,000, basis to Cerulean of $50,000. It distributed cash of $220,000 to Avery. On July 1 of the current year, Avery sold her stock to Harpreet for $820,000. On December 1 of the current year, Cerulean distributed cash of $90,000 each to Harpreet and Marco. What are the tax issues?

44. **LO.1, 2, 5** Petrel Corporation has accumulated E & P of $85,000 at the beginning of Decision Making the year. Its current-year taxable income is $320,000. On December 31, Critical Thinking Petrel distributed business property (land: fair market value of $140,000, adjusted basis of $290,000) to Juan, its sole shareholder. Juan assumes a $70,000 liability on the property. Included in the determination of Petrel's current taxable income is $16,000 of income recognized from an installment sale in a previous year. In addition, the corporation incurred a Federal income tax liability of $67,200, paid life insurance premiums of $4,500, and received term life insurance proceeds of $150,000 on the death of an officer.

a. What is Juan's gross income from the distribution?

b. What is the E & P of Petrel Corporation after the property distribution?

c. What is Juan's tax basis in the property received?

d. How would your answers to parts (a) and (b) change if Petrel had sold the property at its fair market value, used $70,000 of the proceeds to pay off the liability, and distributed the remaining cash and any tax savings to Juan?

45. **LO.5** Iris Corporation owns 30% of Fresia Corporation's stock. On November 15, Fresia Corporation, with current E & P of $320,000, distributes land (fair market value of $100,000; basis of $160,000) to Iris. The land is subject to a liability of $80,000, which Iris assumes.

a. How is Iris Corporation taxed on the distribution?

b. What is Fresia Corporation's E & P after the distribution?

Critical Thinking

46. **LO.6** Parrot Corporation is a closely held company with accumulated E & P of $300,000 and current E & P of $350,000. Tom and Jerry are brothers; each owns a 50% share in Parrot, and they share management responsibilities equally. What are the tax consequences of each of the following independent transactions involving Parrot, Tom, and Jerry? How does each transaction affect Parrot's E & P?

a. Parrot sells an office building (adjusted basis of $350,000; fair market value of $300,000) to Tom for $275,000.

b. Parrot lends Jerry $250,000 on March 31 of this year. The loan is evidenced by a note and is payable on demand. No interest is charged on the loan (the current applicable Federal interest rate is 3%).

c. Parrot owns an airplane that it leases to others for a specified rental rate. Tom and Jerry also use the airplane for personal use and pay no rent. During the year, Tom used the airplane for 120 hours and Jerry used it for 160 hours. The rental value of the airplane is $350 per hour, and its maintenance costs average $80 per hour.

d. Tom leases equipment to Parrot for $20,000 per year. The same equipment can be leased from another company for $9,000 per year.

47. **LO.7** Ken purchased 10,000 shares of Gold Corporation common stock six years ago for $160,000. In the current year, Ken received a preferred stock dividend of 800 shares, while the other holders of common stock received a common stock dividend. The preferred stock Ken received has a fair market value of $80,000, and his common stock has a fair market value of $240,000. Assume that Gold has ample E & P to cover any distributions made during the year. What is Ken's basis in the preferred and common stock after the dividend is received? When does his holding period commence for the preferred stock?

Communications

48. **LO.7** Jacob Corcoran bought 10,000 shares of Grebe Corporation stock two years ago for $24,000. Last year, Jacob received a nontaxable stock dividend of 2,000 shares in Grebe Corporation. In the current tax year, Jacob sold all of the stock received as a dividend for $18,000. Prepare a letter to Jacob and a memo for the file describing the tax consequences of the stock sale. Jacob's address is 925 Arapahoe Street, Boulder, CO 80304.

49. **LO.7** Denim Corporation declares a nontaxable dividend payable in rights to subscribe to common stock. One right and $60 entitle the holder to subscribe to one share of stock. One right is issued for every two shares of stock owned. At the date of distribution of the rights, the market value of the stock is $110 per share and the market value of the rights is $55 per right. Lauren owns 300 shares of stock that she purchased two years ago for $9,000. Lauren receives 150 rights, of which she exercises 105 to purchase 105 additional shares. She sells the remaining 45 rights for $2,475. What are the tax consequences of this transaction to Lauren?

50. **LO.4, 8** Kristen, the president and sole shareholder of Egret Corporation, has earned a salary bonus of $30,000 for the current year. Because of the lower tax rates on qualifying dividends, Kristen is considering substituting a dividend for the bonus. Assume that the tax rates are 24% for Kristen and 21% for Egret Corporation.

    a.   How much better off would Kristen be if she were paid a dividend rather than salary?

    b.   How much better off would Egret Corporation be if it paid Kristen a salary rather than a dividend?

    c.   If Egret Corporation paid Kristen a salary bonus of $35,000 instead of a $30,000 dividend, how would your answers to parts (a) and (b) change?

    d.   What should Kristen do? Summarize your conclusion in a two- to three-paragraph e-mail to your instructor.

Decision Making
Critical Thinking
Communications

51. **LO.1, 3, 8** Your client, Heron Corporation, has a deficit in accumulated E & P of $300,000. Starting this year, it expects to generate annual E & P of $150,000 for the next four years and would like to distribute this amount to its shareholders. How should Heron Corporation distribute the $600,000 over the four-year period to provide the least amount of dividend income to its shareholders (all individuals)? In a letter to your client, make appropriate suggestions on how this should be done. Also prepare a memo for your firm's file. Heron Corporation's address is 12 Nature Trail Way, Daytona Beach, FL 32114.

Critical Thinking
Communications

Research Problems

Note: Solutions to the Research Problems can be prepared by using the Thomson Reuters Checkpoint™ online tax research database, which accompanies this textbook. Solutions can also be prepared by using research materials found in a typical tax library.

THOMSON REUTERS
CHECKPOINT™

Research Problem 1. Kenny Merinoff and his son, John, own all outstanding stock of Flamingo Corporation. Both John and Kenny are officers in the corporation and, together with their uncle, Ira, comprise the entire board of directors. Flamingo uses the cash method of accounting and has a calendar year-end. In late 2011, the board of directors adopted the following legally enforceable resolution (agreed to in writing by each of the officers):

Communications

> Salary payments made to an officer of the corporation that shall be disallowed in whole or in part as a deductible expense for Federal income tax purposes shall be reimbursed by such officer to the corporation to the full extent of the disallowance. It shall be the duty of the board of directors to enforce payment of each such amount.

In 2017, Flamingo paid Kenny $800,000 in compensation. John received $650,000. On an audit in late 2018, the IRS found the compensation of both officers to be excessive. It disallowed deductions for $400,000 of the payment to Kenny and $350,000 of the payment to John. The IRS recharacterized the disallowed payments as constructive dividends. Complying with the resolution by the board of directors, both Kenny and John repaid the disallowed compensation to Flamingo Corporation in 2019. John and Kenny have asked you to determine how their repayments should be treated for tax purposes. John is still working as a highly compensated executive for Flamingo, while Kenny is retired and living off his savings. Prepare a memo for your firm's client files describing the results of your research.

Partial list of research aids:
§ 1341.
Vincent E. Oswald, 49 T.C. 645 (1968).

Research Problem 2. Your client, White Corporation, has done well since its formation 20 years ago. This year, it recognized a $50 million capital gain from the sale of a subsidiary. White's CEO has contacted you to discuss a proposed transaction to reduce the tax on the capital gain. Under the proposal, White will purchase all of the common stock in Purple Corporation for $200 million. Purple is a profitable corporation that has $63 million in cash and marketable securities, $137 million in operating assets, and approximately $280 million in E & P. After its acquisition, Purple will distribute $50 million in cash and marketable securities to White. Due to the 100% dividends received deduction, no taxable income results to White from the dividend. White will then resell Purple for $150 million. The subsequent sale of Purple generates a $50 million capital loss [$200 million (stock basis) − $150 million (sales price)]. The loss from the stock sale can then be used to offset the preexisting $50 million capital gain. Will the proposed plan work? Why or why not?

Partial list of research aids:
§ 1059.

Communications   **Research Problem 3.** Emerald Corporation is required to change its method of accounting for Federal income tax purposes. The change will require an adjustment to income to be made over three tax periods. Jonas, the sole shareholder of Emerald Corporation, wants to better understand the implications of this adjustment for E & P purposes, because he anticipates a distribution from Emerald in the current year. Prepare a memo for your firm's client files describing the results of your research.

Partial list of research aids:
§ 481(a).
Rev.Proc. 97–27, 1997–1 C.B. 680.

Use internet tax resources to address the following questions. Look for reliable websites and blogs of the IRS and other government agencies, media outlets, businesses, tax professionals, academics, think tanks, and political outlets.

Research Problem 4. In July 2014, Windstream Corp. (Nasdaq: WIN), a Fortune 500 and S&P 500 company, made an announcement regarding the taxation of a recent distribution. It also made a projection regarding the anticipated tax consequences of future distributions. Locate articles or press releases regarding Windstream's announcement and related distribution. What might have led Windstream to make the announcement? What implications might the information contained in the announcement have for investors' expectations regarding the company's future earnings? On what might the predictions regarding the taxation of future distributions be based?

Data Analytics   **Research Problem 5.** Just how common are dividend distributions? Are dividends con-
Communications   centrated in the companies traded on the New York Stock Exchange, or do closely held corporations pay dividends in a similar manner? Did dividends decrease during the Great Recession of 2008 and 2009? Search for answers to these questions on the internet and/or in academic journal articles.

In addition, using data from the IRS Tax Statistics website (**irs.gov/statistics**), find and analyze corporate balance sheet data (overall and by size of total assets) to provide answers to the questions above. Summarize the data you find in a Microsoft Excel spreadsheet, and report your findings to your instructor in a three-paragraph e-mail.

Becker CPA Review Questions

1. On January 1, year 5, Olinto Corp., an accrual basis, calendar year C corporation, had $35,000 in accumulated earnings and profits. For year 5, Olinto had current earnings and profits of $15,000 and made two $40,000 cash distributions to its shareholders, one in April and one in September of year 5. What amount of the year 5 distributions is classified as dividend income to Olinto's shareholders?

    a. $15,000   c. $50,000

    b. $35,000   d. $80,000

2. Fox Corp. owned 2,000 shares of Duffy Corp. stock that it bought in year 0 for $9 per share. In year 8, when the fair market value of the Duffy stock was $20 per share, Fox distributed this stock to a noncorporate shareholder. Fox's recognized gain on this distribution was:

   a. $40,000   c. $18,000

   b. $22,000   d. $0

3. Ridge Corp., a calendar year C corporation, made a nonliquidating cash distribution to its shareholders of $1,000,000 with respect to its stock. At that time, Ridge's current and accumulated earnings and profits totaled $750,000 and its total paid-in capital for tax purposes was $10,000,000. Ridge had no corporate shareholders. Ridge's cash distribution:

   I.   Was taxable as $750,000 in dividend income to its shareholders.

   II. Reduced its shareholders' adjusted bases in Ridge stock by $250,000.

   a. I only   c. Both I and II

   b. II only   d. Neither I nor II

4. Which of the following statements is *not* true?

   a. Affiliated corporations that file consolidated returns can take a 100% dividends received deduction.

   b. The dividends received deduction for a small investment in an unrelated corporation is 50%.

   c. The dividends received deduction for a large investment in a corporation is 65%.

   d. There is no income limitation on the dividends received deduction.

5. Jane is the sole shareholder of Buttons, Inc. Buttons has a deficit of $60,000 in accumulated earnings and profits (E & P) at the beginning of the current year. Current E & P is $35,000. If Buttons pays out a cash distribution to Jane during the current year of $50,000, how much is a taxable dividend to Jane?

   a. $0   c. $50,000

   b. $35,000   d. $85,000

6. Jane is the sole shareholder of Buttons, Inc. Buttons has accumulated earnings and profits (E & P) of $65,000 at the beginning of the current year. The current E & P is $35,000. Buttons pays out a property distribution to Jane during the current year with an FMV of $150,000 and an adjusted basis of $130,000. How much is a taxable dividend to Jane?

   a. $35,000   c. $120,000

   b. $100,000   d. $150,000

7. ABC Corp. paid two cash distributions during year 5. The first was $42,000, and the second was $33,000. Accumulated earnings and profits (E & P) at the end of year 4 were $80,000. Current E & P for year 5 is $30,000. How will the second distribution be allocated between current E & P and accumulated E & P?

	Current E & P	Accumulated E & P
a.	$13,200	$19,800
b.	$16,500	$16,500
c.	$19,800	$13,200
d.	$30,000	$30,000

8. ABC Corp. paid two cash distributions during year 5. The first was $42,000, and the second was $33,000. Accumulated earnings and profits (E & P) at the end of year 4 were $10,000. Current E & P for year 5 is $30,000. How will the first distribution be allocated between current E & P and accumulated E & P?

	Current E & P	Accumulated E & P
a.	$16,800	$25,200
b.	$16,800	$10,000
c.	$25,200	$16,800
d.	$30,000	$10,000

Corporations: Redemptions and Liquidations

LEARNING OBJECTIVES: *After completing Chapter 6, you should be able to:*

LO.1 Identify the stock redemptions that qualify for sale or exchange treatment.

LO.2 Determine the tax impact of stock redemptions on the distributing corporation.

LO.3 Determine the tax consequences of § 306 stock dispositions.

LO.4 Determine the tax consequences of complete liquidations for both the corporation and its shareholders.

LO.5 Determine the tax consequences of subsidiary liquidations for both the parent and the subsidiary corporations.

LO.6 Identify planning opportunities available to minimize the tax impacts of stock redemptions and complete liquidations.

CHAPTER OUTLINE

FAMILY CORPORATIONS AND STOCK REDEMPTIONS

Christina Flores formed Orange Corporation 15 years ago, and she continues to own all 10,000 shares of Orange stock outstanding (basis of $800,000). Christina has been employed full-time with Orange since its inception, handling all of the corporation's management and strategy decisions during that time. Christina receives an annual salary of $250,000 from Orange for this work.

Within the next five to seven years, Christina would like to retire and transfer ownership in Orange to her two children, who are currently ages 24 and 22. The children have worked full-time with Orange over the last two years and have demonstrated both the capacity and the willingness to take over the business after their mother's retirement.

Currently, the Orange stock is worth $12,000,000, and it is expected to be worth $16,000,000 by the time of Christina's retirement. The stock represents approximately 80 percent of Christina's net worth. Orange Corporation (E & P of $4,000,000) generates strong positive cash flow, but a significant investment in property, plant, and equipment will be required over the next several years. The children are not expected to have the financial wherewithal to purchase the Orange stock from their mother at the time of her retirement, although Christina would be receptive to taking promissory notes in exchange for her Orange stock.

How could a stock redemption be used to assist Christina in achieving her goal of transferring control of Orange to the children upon her retirement?

Read the chapter and formulate your response.

When a shareholder sells stock to an unrelated third party, the transaction typically is treated as a sale or exchange. Here, the amount realized is offset by the shareholder's stock basis and a capital gain (or loss) results. Effectively, the Code treats the proceeds as a return *of* the shareholder's stock investment.

The Big Picture

EXAMPLE 1

Return to the facts of *The Big Picture* on p. 6-1. Assume that Christina sells 2,000 shares of Orange Corporation stock to a third party for $2,400,000. If the transaction is treated as a sale or exchange (a return *of* the owner's stock investment), Christina has a long-term capital gain of $2,240,000 [$2,400,000 (amount realized) − $160,000 (stock basis)].

In a *stock redemption*, where a shareholder sells stock back to the issuing corporation, the transaction can have the *effect* of a dividend distribution (rather than a sale or exchange). This is particularly the case when the stock of the corporation is closely held. For instance, consider a redemption of stock from a sole shareholder. Here, the shareholder's ownership interest is not affected by the stock redemption (the shareholder owns 100 percent of the corporation's outstanding shares before *and* after the transaction). If these redemptions were granted sale or exchange treatment, dividend distributions could be avoided entirely. Instead of formally distributing dividends, the corporation could redeem stock whenever corporate cash was desired by shareholders. Nontaxable stock dividends then could be used to replenish shares as needed.

The key distinction between a sale of stock to an unrelated third party and some stock redemptions is the effect of the transaction on the shareholder's ownership interest in the corporation. In a sale of stock to an unrelated third party, the shareholder's ownership interest in the corporation is reduced ("diminished"). In the case of many stock redemptions, however, there is little or no change to the shareholder's ownership interest. In general, if a shareholder's ownership interest is *not* reduced as a result of a stock redemption, the Code will treat the transaction as a dividend distribution (a return *from* the shareholder's stock investment).

The Big Picture

EXAMPLE 2

Return to the facts of *The Big Picture* on p. 6-1. Assume that Orange Corporation redeems 2,000 of its shares from Christina for $2.4 million.

If the transaction is treated as a dividend distribution (a return *from* the owner's stock investment), Christina has $2.4 million of dividend income. After the redemption, Christina continues to own 100% of the Orange shares outstanding (8,000 shares owned ÷ 8,000 shares outstanding).

The Code does allow sale or exchange treatment for *certain* kinds of stock redemptions. In these transactions, as a general rule, the shareholder's ownership interest is reduced as a result of the redemption. In addition, a disposition of stock in a complete liquidation of a corporation generally produces sale or exchange treatment to the shareholder. This chapter examines the tax implications of corporate distributions that are stock redemptions and complete liquidations.

LO.1

Identify the stock redemptions that qualify for sale or exchange treatment.

6-1 STOCK REDEMPTIONS—IN GENERAL

Under § 317(b), a **stock redemption** occurs when a corporation acquires its stock from a shareholder in exchange for cash or other property. Although a sale of stock to an outsider normally results in sale or exchange treatment, only a *qualifying* stock redemption is treated as a sale for tax purposes. Nonqualified stock redemptions are denied sale or exchange treatment because they are deemed to have the same effect as dividend distributions. (The requirements for qualifying stock redemptions are provided later in this chapter.)

Stock redemptions occur for a variety of reasons. Publicly traded corporations often reacquire their shares in order to increase shareholder value. For corporations where the stock is closely held, redemptions frequently occur to achieve shareholder objectives. For instance, a closely held corporation might use a redemption to acquire the stock of a deceased shareholder. Using corporate funds to purchase the stock from the decedent's estate means that the remaining shareholders do not need to use their own money to acquire the stock. Stock redemptions also occur as a result of property settlements when a divorce occurs. When spouses jointly own 100 percent of a corporation's shares, a divorce decree may require that the stock interest of one spouse be bought out. A redemption accomplishes this without using the other spouse's personal assets. Stock redemptions are also frequently incorporated into buy-sell agreements between shareholders. This allows a corporation to redeem (purchase) the stock of a shareholder who wants to end his or her ownership in the corporation.

6-2 STOCK REDEMPTIONS—SALE OR EXCHANGE TREATMENT

Noncorporate shareholders generally prefer to have a stock redemption treated as a sale or exchange rather than as a dividend distribution. As Examples 3 and 4 illustrate, a stock redemption that qualifies for sale or exchange treatment is preferred because it results in *both* the tax-free recovery of the redeemed stock's basis and the ability to offset any capital gain against capital losses. In a nonqualified stock redemption, the *entire* distribution (assuming adequate E & P) is taxed as dividend income and cannot be offset by capital losses. For individual taxpayers, the tax rate for long-term capital gains and qualified dividend income is 0, 15, or 20 percent depending on the taxpayer's taxable income.[1]

Qualifying and Nonqualified Redemptions Compared

EXAMPLE 3

Abby, an individual in the 32% tax bracket, acquired stock in Quail Corporation four years ago for $80,000. In the current year, Quail Corporation (E & P of $1,000,000) redeems her shares for $170,000. If the redemption qualifies for sale or exchange treatment, Abby will have a long-term capital gain of $90,000 [$170,000 (redemption amount) − $80,000 (basis)]. Her income tax liability on the $90,000 gain will be $13,500 ($90,000 × 15%).

If the stock redemption does not qualify as a sale or exchange, the entire distribution will be treated as a dividend, and her income tax liability will be $25,500 ($170,000 × 15%). Thus, Abby will save $12,000 ($25,500 − $13,500) in income taxes if the transaction is a qualifying stock redemption.

EXAMPLE 4

Assume in Example 3 that Abby has a capital loss carryover of $60,000 in the current tax year. If the transaction is a qualifying stock redemption, Abby can offset the entire $60,000 capital loss carryover against her $90,000 long-term capital gain. As a result, only $30,000 of the gain will be taxed and her income tax liability will be only $4,500 ($30,000 × 15%).

On the other hand, if the transaction does not qualify for sale or exchange treatment, the entire $170,000 will be taxed as a dividend at 15%. In addition, assuming that she has no capital gains in the current year, Abby will be able to deduct only $3,000 of the $60,000 capital loss carryover to offset her ordinary income.

In contrast, *corporate* shareholders normally receive more favorable tax treatment from a dividend distribution. As a result, most corporations would prefer a *nonqualifying* stock redemption. Corporate taxpayers typically report only a portion of a dividend distribution as taxable income because of the dividends received deduction

---

[1]A 3.8 percent additional tax on net investment income of certain high-income taxpayers applies to capital gains and dividend income.

GLOBAL TAX ISSUES   Foreign Shareholders Prefer Sale or Exchange Treatment in Stock Redemptions

As a general rule, foreign shareholders are subject to U.S. tax on dividend income from U.S. corporations but not on capital gains from the sale of U.S. stock.

In some situations, a nonresident alien is taxed on a capital gain from the disposition of stock in a U.S. corporation, but only if the stock was effectively connected with the conduct of a U.S. trade or business of the individual. Foreign corporations are similarly taxed on gains from the sale of U.S. stock investments.

Whether a stock redemption qualifies for sale or exchange treatment therefore takes on added significance for foreign shareholders. If one of the qualifying stock redemption rules can be satisfied, the foreign shareholder typically will avoid U.S. tax on the transaction. If, instead, dividend income is the result, a 30 percent withholding tax typically applies. For further details, see Chapter 9.

(see Chapter 3). In addition, corporations do not have a preferential tax rate on dividend and long-term capital gain income. As a result, tax planning for stock redemptions must consider the different preferences of corporate and noncorporate shareholders.

EXAMPLE 5

Assume in Example 3 that Abby is a calendar year C corporation, that the stock represents a 40% ownership interest in Quail Corporation, and that in the current year Abby has corporate taxable income of $850,000 before the redemption transaction. If the transaction is a qualifying stock redemption, Abby will have a long-term capital gain of $90,000 that will be subject to tax at 21%, or $18,900.

On the other hand, if the $170,000 distribution is treated as a dividend, Abby will have a dividends received deduction of $110,500 ($170,000 × 65%); so only $59,500 of the payment will be taxed. Consequently, Abby's tax liability on the transaction will be only $12,495 ($59,500 × 21%).

When a qualifying stock redemption results in a *loss* to a shareholder rather than a gain, § 267 disallows loss recognition if the shareholder owns (directly or indirectly) more than 50 percent of the corporation's stock.

A shareholder's basis in any property received in a stock redemption, qualifying or nonqualified, generally will be the property's fair market value on the date of the redemption. The holding period of the property also begins on that date. Concept Summary 6.1 reviews the major tax consequences of stock redemptions to shareholders.

Concept Summary 6.1

Tax Consequences of Stock Redemptions to Shareholders

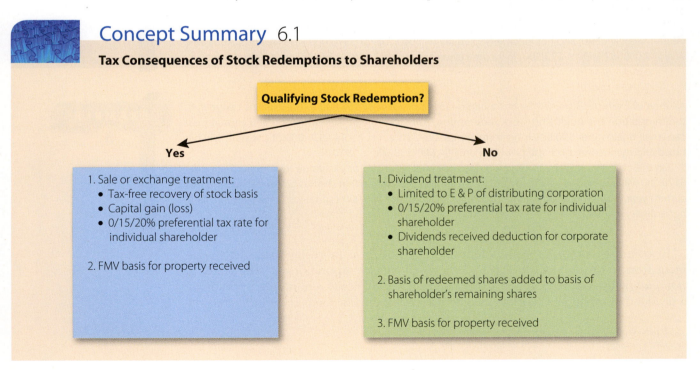

Qualifying Stock Redemption?

Yes

1. Sale or exchange treatment:
   - Tax-free recovery of stock basis
   - Capital gain (loss)
   - 0/15/20% preferential tax rate for individual shareholder

2. FMV basis for property received

No

1. Dividend treatment:
   - Limited to E & P of distributing corporation
   - 0/15/20% preferential tax rate for individual shareholder
   - Dividends received deduction for corporate shareholder

2. Basis of redeemed shares added to basis of shareholder's remaining shares

3. FMV basis for property received

The Code establishes the criteria for determining whether a transaction is a qualifying stock redemption for tax purposes. Section 302(b) provides four types of qualifying stock redemptions. In addition, § 303 allows certain distributions of property to an estate in exchange for a deceased shareholder's stock to be treated as a qualifying stock redemption. Each of these five types of qualifying redemptions is discussed later in this section.

6-2a Historical Background and Overview

Under prior law, the *dividend equivalency rule* was used to determine which stock redemptions qualified for sale or exchange treatment. Under that rule, if the facts and circumstances of a redemption indicated that it was essentially equivalent to a dividend, the redemption did not qualify for sale or exchange treatment. Instead, the entire amount received by the shareholder was taxed as dividend income to the extent of the corporation's E & P.

The uncertainty and subjectivity surrounding the dividend equivalency rule led Congress to enact several objective tests for determining the status of a redemption. Five types of stock redemptions qualify for sale or exchange treatment:

- Distributions not essentially equivalent to a dividend ("not essentially equivalent redemptions"; see text Section 6-2c).
- Distributions substantially disproportionate in terms of shareholder effect ("disproportionate redemptions"; see text Section 6-2d).
- Distributions in complete termination of a shareholder's interest ("complete termination redemptions"; see text Section 6-2e).
- Distributions to noncorporate shareholders in partial liquidation of a corporation ("partial liquidations"; see text Section 6-2f).
- Distributions to pay a shareholder's death taxes ("redemptions to pay death taxes"; see text Section 6-2g).

Concept Summary 6.2 later in this chapter summarizes the requirements for each of the qualifying stock redemptions.

6-2b Stock Attribution Rules

As explained earlier, to qualify for sale or exchange treatment, a stock redemption generally must result in a substantial reduction in the shareholder's ownership interest in the corporation. In determining whether a stock redemption has sufficiently reduced a shareholder's interest, the stock owned by certain related parties is attributed to the redeeming shareholder.[2]

Congress created stock **attribution** rules to serve this purpose. Under these rules, related parties are defined to include the following family members: spouses, children, grandchildren, and parents. Attribution also takes place *from* and *to* partnerships, estates, trusts, and corporations (50 percent or more ownership required in the case of regular corporations). Exhibit 6.1 summarizes the stock attribution rules.

The Big Picture

Return to the facts of *The Big Picture* on p. 6-1. Assume instead that Christina owns only 80% of the stock in Orange Corporation, with the other 20% being held by her two children. For purposes of the stock attribution rules, Christina is treated as owning 100% of the stock in Orange Corporation. She owns 80% directly and, because of the family attribution rules, 20% indirectly through her children.

EXAMPLE 6

---

[2]§ 318.

EXHIBIT 6.1 — Stock Attribution Rules

Deemed or Constructive Ownership

• Family	An individual is deemed to own the stock owned by his or her spouse, children, grandchildren, and parents (not siblings or grandparents).
• Partnership	A partner is deemed to own the stock owned by a partnership to the extent of the partner's proportionate interest in the partnership.
	Stock owned by a partner is deemed to be owned in full by a partnership.
• Estate or trust	A beneficiary or an heir is deemed to own the stock owned by an estate or a trust to the extent of the beneficiary's or heir's proportionate interest in the estate or trust.
	Stock owned by a beneficiary or an heir is deemed to be owned in full by an estate or a trust.
• Corporation	Stock owned by a regular corporation is deemed to be owned proportionately by any shareholder owning 50% or more of the corporation's stock.
	Stock owned by a shareholder who owns 50% or more of a regular corporation is deemed to be owned in full by the corporation.

EXAMPLE 7

Chris owns 40% of the stock in Gray Corporation. The other 60% is owned by a partnership in which Chris has a 20% interest. Chris is deemed to own 52% of Gray Corporation: 40% directly and, because of the partnership interest, 12% indirectly (20% × 60%).

As discussed later, the *family* attribution rules (refer to Example 6) can be waived in the case of some complete termination redemptions. In addition, the stock attribution rules do not apply to partial liquidations or redemptions to pay death taxes.

When a redemption *fails* to satisfy any of the qualifying stock redemption rules, the basis of the redeemed shares does not disappear. Typically, the basis will attach to the basis of the redeeming shareholder's remaining shares in the corporation. If, however, the redeeming shareholder has terminated his or her direct stock ownership and the redemption is nonqualified due to the attribution rules, the basis of the redeemed shares will attach to the basis of the constructively owned stock.[3] In this manner, a nonqualified stock redemption can result in stock basis being shifted from one taxpayer (the redeeming shareholder) to another taxpayer (the shareholder related under the attribution rules).

EXAMPLE 8

Floyd and Fran, husband and wife, each own 50 shares in Grouse Corporation, representing 100% of the corporation's stock. All of the stock was purchased for $50,000. Both Floyd and Fran serve as directors of the corporation. The corporation redeems Floyd's 50 shares, but he continues to serve as a director of the corporation. The redemption is treated as a dividend distribution (assuming adequate E & P) because Floyd constructively owns Fran's stock, or 100% of the Grouse stock outstanding. Floyd's $25,000 basis in the 50 shares redeemed attaches to Fran's stock; thus, Fran now has a basis of $50,000 in the 50 shares she owns in Grouse.

6-2c Not Essentially Equivalent Redemptions

Under § 302(b)(1), a redemption qualifies for sale or exchange treatment if it is "not essentially equivalent to a dividend." This is a continuation of the dividend equivalency rule. It was retained principally for redemptions of preferred stock because preferred shareholders often have no control over when corporations redeem preferred stock.[4]

---

[3]Reg. § 1.302–2(c).   [4]See S.Rept. No. 1622, 83d Cong., 2d Sess. 44 (1954).

Like its predecessor, the **not essentially equivalent redemption** is a subjective test. Each case must be resolved based on all the facts and circumstances.[5]

Based upon the Supreme Court's decision in *U.S. v. Davis*,[6] a redemption will qualify as a not essentially equivalent redemption only when the shareholder's interest in the redeeming corporation has been meaningfully reduced. In determining whether the **meaningful reduction test** has been met, the stock attribution rules apply. A decrease in the redeeming shareholder's voting control appears to be the most significant indicator of a meaningful reduction,[7] but reductions in the rights of the shareholders to share in corporate earnings or to receive corporate assets on liquidation also are considered.[8]

Meaningful Reduction Test

EXAMPLE 9

Pat owns 58% of the common stock of Falcon Corporation. As a result of a redemption of some of his stock, Pat's ownership interest in Falcon is reduced to 51%.

Because Pat continues to have voting control over Falcon after the redemption, the distribution is treated as essentially equivalent to a dividend. As a result, the entire amount of the distribution is treated as a dividend (assuming adequate E & P).

EXAMPLE 10

Maroon Corporation redeems 2% of its stock from Maria. Before the redemption, Maria owned 10% of Maroon Corporation. In this case, the redemption *may* qualify as a not essentially equivalent redemption. Maria experiences a reduction in her voting rights, her right to participate in current earnings and accumulated surplus, and her right to share in net assets upon liquidation.

6-2d Disproportionate Redemptions

A stock redemption qualifies for sale or exchange treatment under § 302(b)(2) as a **disproportionate redemption** if *both* of the following conditions are met:

- After the distribution, the shareholder owns *less than* 80 percent of the interest owned in the corporation before the redemption.
- After the distribution, the shareholder owns *less than* 50 percent of the total combined voting power of all classes of stock entitled to vote.

In determining a shareholder's ownership interest before and after a redemption, the attribution rules apply. Compare Examples 11 and 12.

Disproportionate Redemption Tests

EXAMPLE 11

Paulina, Carl, and Dan, unrelated individuals, own 30 shares, 30 shares, and 40 shares, respectively, in Wren Corporation. Wren has 100 shares outstanding and E & P of $200,000. The corporation redeems 20 shares of Dan's stock for $30,000. Dan paid $200 a share for the stock two years ago. Dan's ownership in Wren Corporation before and after the redemption is as follows:

	Total Shares	Dan's Ownership	Ownership Percentage	80% of Original Ownership
Before redemption	100	40	40% (40 ÷ 100)	32% (80% × 40%)
After redemption	80	20	25% (20 ÷ 80)*	

*Note that the denominator of the fraction is reduced after the redemption (from 100 to 80).

Dan's 25% ownership after the redemption meets both tests of § 302(b)(2). It is less than 80% of his original ownership and less than 50% of the total voting power. The distribution qualifies as a disproportionate redemption and receives sale or exchange treatment. As a result, Dan has a long-term capital gain of $26,000 [$30,000 − $4,000 (20 shares × $200)].

[5]Reg. § 1.302–2(b)(1).

[6]70–1 USTC ¶9289, 25 AFTR 2d 70–827, 90 S.Ct. 1041 (USSC, 1970).

[7]See, for example, *Jack Paparo*, 71 T.C. 692 (1979).

[8]See, for example, *Grabowski Trust*, 58 T.C. 650 (1972).

Disproportionate Redemption Tests

EXAMPLE 12

Assume in Example 11 that Carl and Dan are father and son. In this case, the redemption would *not* qualify for sale or exchange treatment because of the *attribution rules*. Dan is deemed to own Carl's stock before and after the redemption. Dan's ownership in Wren Corporation before and after the redemption is as follows:

	Total Shares	Dan's Direct Ownership	Carl's Ownership	Dan's Direct and Indirect Ownership	Ownership Percentage	80% of Original Ownership
Before redemption	100	40	30	70	70% (70 ÷ 100)	56% (80% × 70%)
After redemption	80	20	30	50	62.5% (50 ÷ 80)	

Dan's direct and indirect ownership of 62.5% fails to meet either of the tests of § 302(b)(2). After the redemption, Dan owns more than 80% of his original ownership and more than 50% of the voting stock. As a result, the redemption does not qualify for sale or exchange treatment and results in a dividend distribution of $30,000 to Dan. The basis in the 20 shares redeemed is added to Dan's basis in his remaining 20 shares.

A redemption that does not qualify as a disproportionate redemption may still qualify as a not essentially equivalent redemption if it meets the meaningful reduction test (see Example 10).

6-2e **Complete Termination Redemptions**

A redemption that terminates a shareholder's *entire* stock ownership in a corporation qualifies for sale or exchange treatment under § 302(b)(3). The attribution rules generally apply in determining whether the shareholder's stock ownership has been completely terminated. However, the *family* attribution rules do not apply to a ==complete termination redemption== if *both* of the following conditions are met:

- The former shareholder does not hold or acquire any interest, other than that of a creditor, in the corporation for at least 10 years after the redemption (including an interest as an officer, a director, or an employee). This is called a "prohibited interest."
- The former shareholder files a statement agreeing to notify the IRS within 30 days if a prohibited interest is acquired in the 10-year postredemption period, and retains all records related to the redemption during this time period.

The acquisition of stock in the corporation by bequest or inheritance is not a prohibited interest. The required statement must be signed by the former shareholder and attached to the tax return for the year in which the redemption occurs.[9]

Family Attribution Waiver

EXAMPLE 13

Kevin owns 50% of the stock in Green Corporation, and the remaining interests in Green are held as follows: 40% by Wilma (Kevin's wife) and 10% by Carmen (a key employee). Green redeems all of Kevin's stock for its fair market value. As a result, Wilma and Carmen are the only remaining shareholders, now owning 80% and 20%, respectively.

If the two requirements for the family attribution waiver are met, the transaction will qualify as a complete termination redemption and will result in sale or exchange treatment. If the waiver requirements are not satisfied, Kevin will be deemed to own Wilma's (his wife's) stock and the entire distribution will be taxed as a dividend (assuming adequate E & P).

---

[9]Reg. § 1.302–4(a).

Family Attribution Waiver

Assume in Example 13 that Kevin qualifies for the family attribution waiver for the redemption. In the year of the redemption, Kevin treats the transaction as a sale or exchange. However, if he purchases Carmen's stock seven years after the redemption, he has acquired a prohibited interest and the redemption distribution is reclassified as a dividend. Kevin must notify the IRS and will owe additional taxes due to this revised treatment.

EXAMPLE
14

6-2f **Partial Liquidations**

Under § 302(b)(4), a *noncorporate* shareholder receives sale or exchange treatment for a distribution that qualifies as a <mark>partial liquidation</mark>. A partial liquidation is a distribution that (1) is *not essentially equivalent to a dividend* and (2) is both pursuant to a plan and made within the plan year or within the succeeding taxable year. A stock redemption pursuant to a partial liquidation may be pro rata with respect to the shareholders. In the case of a pro rata distribution, an actual surrender of stock is not required to qualify the transaction as a partial liquidation.[10]

In determining whether a distribution is not essentially equivalent to a dividend, the effect of the distribution on the *corporation* is examined.[11] Consequently, to qualify as a partial liquidation, the distribution must result in a *genuine contraction* of the business of the corporation. Compare Examples 15 and 16.

Dove Corporation owned a building with seven floors. Part of the building was rented, and part was used directly in Dove's business. A fire destroyed the two top floors, and Dove received insurance proceeds in reimbursement for the damage sustained. For business reasons, Dove did not rebuild the two floors and, instead, chose to operate on a smaller scale than before the fire.

Pursuant to a plan adopted in the current year, Dove uses the insurance proceeds to redeem some stock from its noncorporate shareholders. Because a genuine contraction of the business occurs, the distribution is not essentially equivalent to a dividend and qualifies as a partial liquidation.[12]

EXAMPLE
15

Applying the genuine contraction of a corporate business concept has proved difficult due to the lack of objective tests. The IRS has ruled that neither the sale of investments nor the sale of excess inventory will satisfy the genuine contraction test.[13] Because the genuine contraction test is subjective, taxpayers should seek a favorable ruling from the IRS before proceeding.

The Big Picture

Return to the facts of *The Big Picture* on p. 6-1. Assume that Orange Corporation loses a major customer and that a severe drop in sales occurs. The corporation reduces its inventory investment and has $1,200,000 of excess cash on hand as a result. It distributes the excess cash to Christina in redemption of 10% of her stock.

Because Christina's ownership interest in Orange remains unchanged (100%), the redemption does not qualify as a not essentially equivalent redemption, a disproportionate redemption, or a complete termination redemption. Further, the reduction in inventory does not qualify as a genuine contraction of Orange Corporation's business; thus, the distribution is not a partial liquidation. Therefore, the $1,200,000 is dividend income to Christina. The $80,000 basis in the stock redeemed (10% × $800,000) attaches to the basis of Christina's remaining shares of Orange.

EXAMPLE
16

---

[10]See *Fowler Hosiery Co. v. Comm.*, 62–1 USTC ¶9407, 9 AFTR 2d 1252, 301 F.2d 394 (CA–7, 1962); and Rev.Rul. 90–13, 1990–1 C.B. 65.

[11]§ 302(e)(1)(A).

[12]See *Joseph W. Imler*, 11 T.C. 836 (1948), *acq.* 1949–1 C.B. 2; and Reg. § 1.346–1(a)(2).

[13]Rev.Rul. 60–322, 1960–2 C.B. 118.

A safe-harbor rule, the *termination of a business* test, will satisfy the "not essentially equivalent to a dividend" requirement. A distribution will qualify under the termination of a business test if all of the following conditions are met:

- The corporation has two or more qualified trades or businesses. A qualified trade or business is any trade or business that (1) has been actively conducted for the five-year period ending on the date of the distribution and (2) was not acquired in a taxable transaction during that five-year period.
- The distribution consists of the assets of a qualified trade or business or the proceeds from the sale of such assets.
- The corporation is actively engaged in the conduct of a qualified trade or business immediately after the distribution.

EXAMPLE 17

Swan Corporation, the owner and operator of a wholesale grocery business with a substantial amount of excess cash, purchased a freight-hauling concern. Six years later, Swan distributes the freight-hauling assets in kind on a pro rata basis to its shareholders.

The distribution satisfies the termination of a business test. Swan had conducted both businesses for at least five years and continues to conduct the wholesale grocery business.

As a result, for noncorporate shareholders, the distribution qualifies as a partial liquidation and is treated as a sale or exchange to Swan's noncorporate shareholders. For Swan's corporate shareholders, the distribution will be taxed as dividend income (assuming adequate E & P).

6-2g Redemptions to Pay Death Taxes

Section 303 provides sale or exchange treatment to a redemption of stock included in, and representing a substantial part of, a decedent's gross estate. This provision provides an estate with liquidity to pay death-related expenses when a significant portion of the estate consists of stock in a closely held corporation.

Because closely held corporation stock is not easily marketable, a stock redemption usually represents the only way to dispose of the stock. The redemption might not satisfy any of the other qualifying stock redemption provisions because of the attribution rules (e.g., attribution to estate from beneficiaries). A ==redemption to pay death taxes== provides sale or exchange treatment without regard to the attribution rules. However, this treatment is limited to the sum of the death taxes and funeral and administration expenses. A redemption in excess of these expenses may qualify for sale or exchange treatment under one of the § 302 provisions.

An estate's basis in property acquired from a decedent is generally the property's fair market value on the date of death.[14] Typically, there is little change in the fair market value of stock from the date of a decedent's death to the date of a redemption to pay death taxes. When the redemption price is the same as the estate's basis in the stock, the estate will recognize no gain (or loss) on the transaction.

Section 303 applies only to a distribution made with respect to stock of a corporation that is included in the gross estate of a decedent and whose value *exceeds* 35 percent of the value of the adjusted gross estate.[15] (For definitions of *gross estate* and *adjusted gross estate*, see the Glossary in Appendix C.)

EXAMPLE 18

Juan's adjusted gross estate is $15,000,000. The death taxes and funeral and administration expenses of the estate total $1,440,000. Included in the gross estate is stock of Yellow Corporation valued at $5,600,000. Juan had acquired the stock nine years ago at a cost of $600,000. Yellow redeems $1,440,000 of the stock from Juan's estate.

continued

---

[14]If available and elected, an alternate valuation date would apply. § 1014(a).

[15]§ 303(b)(2)(A). For purposes of this test, the stock of two or more corporations in which the decedent held a 20% or more interest (by value) is treated as the stock of one corporation [§ 303(b)(2)(B)].

Because the value of the Yellow stock in Juan's estate exceeds the 35% threshold ($5,600,000 ÷ $15,000,000 = 37.3%), the redemption qualifies under § 303 as a sale or exchange to Juan's estate. Assuming that the value of the stock has remained unchanged since the date of Juan's death, there is no recognized gain (or loss) on the redemption [$1,440,000 (amount realized) − $1,440,000 (estate's stock basis)].

Concept Summary 6.2

Summary of the Qualifying Stock Redemption Rules

Type of Redemption	Requirements to Qualify
Not essentially equivalent to a dividend [§ 302(b)(1)]	Meaningful reduction in the shareholder's voting interest. Reduction in the shareholder's right to share in earnings or in assets upon liquidation also is considered.
	Stock attribution rules apply.
Substantially disproportionate [§ 302(b)(2)]	Shareholder's interest in the corporation, after the redemption, must be less than 80% of interest before the redemption and less than 50% of the total combined voting power of all classes of stock entitled to vote.
	Stock attribution rules apply.
Complete termination [§ 302(b)(3)]	Entire stock ownership terminated.
	In general, stock attribution rules apply. However, *family* attribution rules are waived when the former shareholder has no interest, other than as a creditor, in the corporation for at least 10 years after the redemption and files an agreement to notify the IRS of any prohibited interest acquired during the 10-year period. Shareholder must retain all necessary records during the 10-year period.
Partial liquidation [§ 302(b)(4)]	Not essentially equivalent to a dividend.
	• Genuine contraction of corporation's business.
	• Termination of a business.
	➤ Corporation has two or more qualified trades or businesses.
	➤ Corporation terminates one qualified trade or business while continuing another qualified trade or business.
	Distribution may be in form of cash or property.
	Redemption may be pro rata.
	Stock attribution rules do not apply.
Redemption to pay death taxes [§ 303]	Value of the stock of one corporation in the gross estate exceeds 35% of the value of the adjusted gross estate.
	Redemption limited to the sum of death taxes and funeral and administration expenses.
	Generally tax-free because the estate's tax basis of stock is FMV on the date of the decedent's death and the value is unchanged at redemption.
	Stock attribution rules do not apply.

6-3 STOCK REDEMPTIONS—EFFECT ON THE CORPORATION

LO.2

Determine the tax impact of stock redemptions on the distributing corporation.

Thus far, the discussion has focused on the tax consequences of stock redemptions to the *shareholder*. There are also several tax issues surrounding the redeeming *corporation* that must be addressed:

- The recognition of gain or loss on property distributed pursuant to a redemption,
- The effect of a qualifying stock redemption on a corporation's E & P, and
- The deductibility of expenditures incurred in connection with a redemption.

These issues are discussed in the following paragraphs.

6-3a **Recognition of Gain or Loss**

Distributions in redemption of stock, qualifying or not, are nonliquidating distributions. Section 311 provides that corporations recognize *gain* on all nonliquidating distributions of appreciated property as if the property had been sold for its fair market value. When distributed property is subject to a corporate liability and that liability is greater than the property's fair market value, the liability amount is used to determine the recognized gain.

Losses are not recognized on nonliquidating distributions of property. Therefore, a corporation should avoid distributing loss property (fair market value less than basis) in a stock redemption. However, the corporation could sell the property in a taxable transaction, recognize a loss, and then distribute the proceeds.

To carry out a stock redemption, Blackbird Corporation distributes land (basis of $80,000, fair market value of $300,000) to a shareholder. Blackbird has a recognized gain of $220,000 ($300,000 − $80,000). If the land is subject to a liability of $330,000, Blackbird has a recognized gain of $250,000 ($330,000 − $80,000). If the value of the property distributed was less than its adjusted basis, the realized loss would not be recognized.

6-3b **Effect on Earnings and Profits**

In a qualifying stock redemption, the E & P of the distributing corporation is reduced by no more than the percentage of the corporation's stock redeemed.[16]

Navy Corporation has 100 shares of stock outstanding. In a qualifying stock redemption, Navy distributes $200,000 in exchange for 30 of its shares. At the time of the redemption, Navy has paid-in capital of $120,000 and E & P of $450,000. Navy's E & P is reduced by $135,000 (30% of the corporation's E & P). The remainder of the redemption price ($65,000) is a reduction of the Navy paid-in capital account.

If, instead, the 30 shares were redeemed for $80,000, E & P would be reduced by $80,000, the amount paid by the corporation to carry out the stock redemption.

6-3c **Redemption Expenditures**

In redeeming its shares, a corporation may incur certain expenses such as accounting, brokerage, legal, and loan fees. Section 162(k) specifically denies a deduction for expenditures incurred in connection with a stock redemption. The disallowance does not apply to amounts otherwise deductible as interest under § 163, such as interest from debt-financed redemptions.

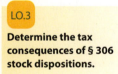

Determine the tax consequences of § 306 stock dispositions.

6-4 **STOCK REDEMPTIONS—PREFERRED STOCK BAILOUTS**

Stock redemptions that do not fall within any of the qualifying stock redemption provisions are treated as dividend distributions to the extent of the corporation's E & P. To obtain sale or exchange treatment, resourceful taxpayers devised ways to circumvent the redemption provisions. The **preferred stock bailout** was one type of transaction devised in an attempt to obtain the benefits of a qualifying stock redemption without the associated disadvantages.[17]

---

[16]§ 312(n)(7).

[17]See, for example, *Chamberlin v. Comm.*, 53–2 USTC ¶9576, 44 AFTR 494, 207 F.2d 462 (CA–6, 1953), *cert. den.* 74 S.Ct. 516 (USSC, 1954). Section 304, dealing with sales of stock to related corporations, was also enacted to close a loophole associated with a different form of stock redemption-like transaction.

6-4a Background

In a typical preferred stock bailout, a corporation issued a nontaxable (nonvoting) preferred stock dividend on common stock,[18] the shareholder assigned a portion of his or her basis in the common stock to the preferred stock,[19] and the preferred stock was sold to a third party. Because the disposition did not take the form of a stock redemption, the related limitations on sale or exchange treatment did not apply. As a result, the sale of the preferred stock was treated like any other capital asset disposition where the sales proceeds were offset by the stock's basis and the gain was taxed using the favorable capital gains rate. Unlike a sale of common shares, however, the sale of the preferred stock did not reduce the shareholder's ownership interest in the corporation.

6-4b Tax Consequences

The tax avoidance possibilities of the preferred stock bailout just described led to the enactment of § 306. In a sale of *§ 306 stock* to a third party, the shareholder generally has ordinary income on the sale equal to the fair market value of the preferred stock on the date of the stock dividend.[20] The ordinary income is *treated* as a dividend for purposes of the preferential tax rate on dividend income[21] but has no effect on the issuing corporation's E & P. No loss is recognized on the sale of the preferred stock;[22] instead, the unrecovered basis in the preferred stock sold is added to the basis of the shareholder's common stock.[23] If instead of a sale to a third party the issuing corporation redeems the preferred stock from the shareholder, the redemption proceeds constitute dividend income to the extent of the corporation's E & P.[24]

The Big Picture

EXAMPLE 21

Return to the facts of *The Big Picture* on p. 6-1. Assume that in early January of the current year, Orange Corporation (E & P of $4,000,000) declares and issues a nontaxable preferred stock dividend of 1,000 shares to Christina. After the stock dividend, the fair market value of one share of common is $1,080, and the fair market value of one share of preferred is $1,200. Two days later, Christina sells the 1,000 shares of preferred stock to Emily, an unrelated party, for $1,200,000. Section 306 produces the following results:

- After the distribution and before the sale, the preferred stock has a basis to Christina of $80,000 [($1,200,000 value of preferred ÷ $12,000,000 value of preferred and common) × $800,000 (original basis of common stock)]. At this time, the common stock has a new basis of $720,000.

- The sale of the preferred stock generates $1,200,000 of ordinary income to Christina. This is the amount of dividend income Christina would have recognized had cash been distributed instead of preferred stock (i.e., the § 306 taint). The preferential tax rate on dividend income is applicable to the $1,200,000.

- The $80,000 basis allocated to the preferred stock is added back to the basis of the common stock; thus, the common stock basis is increased back to $800,000.

- Orange Corporation's E & P is unaffected by either the stock dividend or its subsequent sale.

6-4c Section 306 Stock

Section 306 stock is stock other than common that (1) is received as a nontaxable stock dividend, (2) is received tax-free in a corporate reorganization or separation to the extent that either the effect of the transaction was substantially the same as the receipt of a stock dividend or the stock was received in exchange for § 306 stock, or (3) has a basis determined by reference to the basis of § 306 stock (e.g., a gift of § 306 stock).

---

[18]See § 305(a).

[19]See § 307(a).

[20]The ordinary income taint is limited to the stock's ratable share of the corporation's E & P at the date of the distribution. If the amount realized in the sale exceeds the ordinary income taint, the excess is applied against the basis of the preferred stock. § 306(a)(1).

[21]§ 306(a)(1)(D).

[22]§ 306(a)(1)(C).

[23]Reg. § 1.306–1(b)(2), Example (2).

[24]See § 306(a)(2).

(Corporate reorganizations are discussed in Chapter 7.) If a corporation has no E & P on the date of distribution of a nontaxable preferred stock dividend, the stock will not be § 306 stock.[25]

LO.4

Determine the tax consequences of complete liquidations for both the corporation and its shareholders.

6-5 LIQUIDATIONS—IN GENERAL

When a corporation makes a nonliquidating distribution (e.g., stock redemption), the entity continues as a going concern. With a complete liquidation, however, corporate existence terminates, as does each shareholder's ownership interest. A complete liquidation, like a qualifying stock redemption, produces sale or exchange treatment to the *shareholder*. However, the tax effects of a liquidation to the *corporation* vary somewhat from those of a redemption. Sale or exchange treatment is the general rule for the liquidating corporation, although some losses are disallowed.

6-5a The Liquidation Process

A corporate liquidation occurs when a corporation ceases to be a going concern. The corporation continues solely to wind up affairs, pay debts, and distribute any remaining assets to its shareholders. A legal dissolution under state law is not required. Further, a corporation can retain a nominal amount of assets to pay remaining debts and/or preserve its legal status and still liquidate for tax purposes.[26]

Shareholders may decide to liquidate a corporation for one or more reasons, including:

- The corporate business has been unsuccessful.
- The shareholders want to acquire the corporation's assets.
- Another person or entity wants to purchase the corporation's assets. The purchaser may buy the shareholders' stock and then liquidate the corporation to acquire the assets. Alternatively, the purchaser may buy the assets directly from the corporation. After the assets are sold, the corporation distributes the sales proceeds to its shareholders and liquidates.

As one might expect, the different means used to liquidate a corporation produce varying tax results.

6-5b Liquidating and Nonliquidating Distributions Compared

As noted previously, a *nonliquidating* distribution of noncash property produces gain (but not loss) recognition to the distributing corporation. For the shareholder, the receipt of cash or other property produces dividend income to the extent of the corporation's E & P or, in the case of a qualifying stock redemption, results in sale or exchange treatment.

Like a qualifying stock redemption, a *liquidation* produces sale or exchange treatment for the shareholders. E & P has no impact on the gain or loss recognized.[27] However, in a liquidation, a corporation generally recognizes gain *and* loss on any assets distributed.

EXAMPLE 22

Goose Corporation, with E & P of $40,000, makes a cash distribution of $50,000 to a shareholder. The shareholder's basis in the Goose stock is $20,000. If the distribution is not a qualifying stock redemption or in complete liquidation, the shareholder recognizes dividend income of $40,000 (the amount of Goose's E & P) and treats the remaining $10,000 of the distribution as a return of capital (i.e., stock basis is reduced to $10,000).

If the distribution is a qualifying stock redemption or is pursuant to a complete liquidation, the shareholder has a capital gain of $30,000 ($50,000 distribution − $20,000 stock basis). In the case of these distributions, Goose's E & P does not affect the shareholder's tax result.

---

[25]§ 306(c).

[26]Reg. § 1.332–2(c).

[27]§ 331.

In the event a corporate distribution results in a *loss* to the shareholder, another distinction exists between nonliquidating distributions and liquidations. Section 267 disallows recognition of losses between related parties in nonliquidating distributions but not in complete liquidations.

EXAMPLE 23

The stock of Tern Corporation is owned equally by three sisters, Pam, Meghann, and Natalie. When Natalie's basis in her stock is $40,000, the corporation distributes $30,000 to her in cancellation of all of her shares.

If the distribution is a qualifying stock redemption, the $10,000 realized loss is not recognized because Natalie and Tern Corporation are related parties. Under § 267, Natalie is deemed to own more than 50% in value of the corporation's outstanding stock. Natalie's direct ownership is 33⅓%, but through her sisters, she owns indirectly another 66⅔% for a total of 100%.

On the other hand, if the distribution is pursuant to a complete liquidation, Natalie's $10,000 realized loss is recognized.

The rules governing the basis of property received from a corporation are identical for both nonliquidating and liquidating distributions. Under § 301(d), the basis of property received in a *nonliquidating distribution* is its fair market value on the date of distribution, while § 334(a) provides the same treatment for property received in a *liquidating distribution*.

Text Section 6-6 discusses the tax consequences of a complete liquidation for the distributing corporation, and text Section 6-7 discusses the shareholder impacts. Because the tax rules differ when a subsidiary corporation is liquidated, these rules are discussed separately in text Section 6-8.

6-6 LIQUIDATIONS—EFFECT ON THE DISTRIBUTING CORPORATION

A corporation generally recognizes gain or loss on the distribution of property in a complete liquidation, but there are several exceptions to this rule.

6-6a The General Rule

Under § 336(a), a corporation recognizes *gain or loss* on the distribution of property in a complete liquidation as if the property were sold at its fair market value. This treatment is consistent with the notion of double taxation that is inherent in operating a business as a C corporation—once at the corporate level and again at the shareholder level.

As in the case of a nonliquidating distribution, if distributed property is subject to a corporate liability that is greater than the fair market value of the property, the liability amount is used to calculate gain or loss.

EXAMPLE 24

As part of a complete liquidation, Warbler Corporation distributes to its shareholders land held as an investment (basis of $200,000, fair market value of $300,000).

If no liability is involved, Warbler has a gain of $100,000 on the distribution ($300,000 − $200,000). The same result occurs (a gain of $100,000) if the land is subject to a liability of $250,000.

If, instead, the liability were $350,000, Warbler's gain on the distribution would be $150,000 ($350,000 − $200,000).

Liquidation expenses incurred by a corporation are deductible as trade or business expenses under § 162. Examples include accounting and legal costs of drafting and implementing a plan of liquidation and the cost of revoking the corporation's charter. However, expenses related to the sale of property (e.g., brokerage commissions and legal costs incurred in title transfers) reduce the amount realized on the sale.

There are four exceptions to the general rule of gain and loss recognition by a liquidating corporation:

- *Losses* are not recognized on certain liquidating distributions to related-party shareholders.

- *Losses* are not recognized on certain sales and liquidating distributions of property that was contributed to the corporation with a built-in loss shortly before the adoption of a plan of liquidation.

- A subsidiary corporation does not recognize *gains or losses* on liquidating distributions to its parent corporation.

- A subsidiary corporation does not recognize *losses* on liquidating distributions to its minority shareholders.

The first two exceptions, referred to as the "antistuffing rules," are discussed in detail in text Section 6-6b and are summarized in Concept Summary 6.3. The last two exceptions, dealing with the liquidation of a subsidiary corporation, are discussed in text Section 6-8.

6-6b **Antistuffing Rules**

When property is transferred to a corporation in a § 351 transaction or as a contribution to capital, carryover basis rules generally apply (see Chapter 4). Usually, the transferee corporation takes a basis in the property equal to that of the transferor-shareholder, and the shareholder takes an equal basis in the stock received in the exchange (or adds this amount to existing stock basis in the case of a capital contribution). Without special limitations, a transfer of loss property (fair market value less than basis) in a carryover basis transaction would present opportunities for the duplication of losses.

The Big Picture

EXAMPLE 25

Return to the facts of *The Big Picture* on p. 6-1. Assume that Christina transfers property (basis of $100,000, fair market value of $55,000) to Orange Corporation in exchange for additional stock. The exchange qualifies under § 351. Absent any exceptions to the contrary, the general rule of carryover basis would apply and Orange would take a carryover basis of $100,000 in the property while Christina would take a $100,000 basis in the additional stock.

A sale or liquidating distribution of the property by Orange Corporation would produce a $45,000 loss [$55,000 (fair market value of property) − $100,000 (property basis)]. Similarly, a sale by Christina of the stock acquired in the § 351 exchange would also generate a $45,000 loss [$55,000 (fair market value of stock) − $100,000 (stock basis)].

Congress addressed this loss duplication issue by enacting two loss limitation ("antistuffing") rules under § 336(d) that apply to corporations on liquidation—loss property distributed to related parties and certain loss property distributed or sold that had been contributed with a built-in loss. The effect of these rules is to disallow some or all of a loss realized by a corporation in liquidating distributions (and, in some cases, sales) of certain property. Each of these rules is discussed below.

These two antistuffing rules limited the duplication of losses realized on a corporation's liquidation, but loss duplication was still possible in other situations (e.g., if the corporation sold high-basis property in the normal course of business rather than in a liquidation).

As a result, Congress enacted § 362(e)(2), which requires a corporation to step down the basis of property acquired in a § 351 or contribution to capital transaction by the amount of any net built-in loss embodied in such property. The basis step-down is required when a shareholder transfers properties having an aggregate basis in excess of their aggregate fair market value ("net built-in loss"), and it is allocated proportionately among the properties having built-in losses. Alternatively, the transferor-shareholder can elect to reduce his or her stock basis by the amount of net built-in loss. (See Chapter 4 for a complete discussion of the basis step-down rules.)

Although the antistuffing rules of § 336(d) continue to apply in the case of liquidating distributions (and certain sales) of loss property, their bite has been lessened somewhat by the § 362(e)(2) basis step-down rules.

Related-Party Loss Limitation

Losses are disallowed on distributions to *related parties* in either of the following cases:

- The distribution is *not* pro rata, or
- The property distributed is disqualified property.[28]

A corporation and a shareholder are considered related if the shareholder owns (directly or indirectly) more than 50 percent in value of the corporation's outstanding stock.[29]

A *pro rata distribution* is a distribution where *each* shareholder receives his or her proportionate share of the corporate asset distributed. Examples 26 and 27 illustrate a non pro rata distribution. *Disqualified property* is property that is acquired by the liquidating corporation in a § 351 or contribution to capital transaction during the five-year period ending on the date of the distribution. The related-party loss limitation can apply even if the property was appreciated (fair market value greater than basis) when it was transferred to the corporation. See Examples 28 and 29.

Related-Party Loss Limitations

EXAMPLE 26

Bluebird Corporation stock is owned by Ana and Sanjay, who are unrelated. Ana owns 80% and Sanjay owns 20% of the stock in the corporation. Bluebird has the following assets (none of which were acquired in a § 351 or contribution to capital transaction); all are distributed in complete liquidation of the corporation.

	Adjusted Basis	Fair Market Value
Cash	$600,000	$600,000
Equipment	150,000	200,000
Building	400,000	200,000

Assume that Bluebird Corporation distributes the equipment to Sanjay and the cash and the building to Ana. Bluebird recognizes a gain of $50,000 on the distribution of the equipment. The loss of $200,000 on the building is disallowed because the property is distributed to a related party and the distribution is not pro rata (i.e., the building is not distributed 80% to Ana and 20% to Sanjay).

EXAMPLE 27

Assume in Example 26 that Bluebird Corporation distributes the cash and equipment to Ana and the building to Sanjay.

As in Example 26, Bluebird recognizes the $50,000 gain on the equipment. However, it now recognizes the $200,000 loss on the building because the property is not distributed to a related party (i.e., Sanjay does not own more than 50% of the stock in Bluebird Corporation).

EXAMPLE 28

Wren Corporation's stock is held equally by three brothers. Four years before Wren's liquidation, the shareholders transfer jointly owned property (basis of $150,000, fair market value of $200,000) to the corporation in return for stock in a § 351 transaction. When the property is worth $100,000, it is distributed pro rata to the brothers in a liquidating distribution.

Because disqualified property is involved and each brother owns directly and indirectly more than 50% of the stock (each owns 100% in this situation), none of the $50,000 realized loss [$100,000 (fair market value) − $150,000 (basis)] is recognized by Wren Corporation.

---

[28]§ 336(d)(1).

[29]Section 267 provides the definition of a related party for purposes of this provision. The rules are similar to the stock attribution rules discussed earlier in this chapter; one exception, however, is that stock owned by a sibling is treated as owned by the taxpayer under § 267.

EXAMPLE 29

Assume in Example 28 that the property's fair market value is $100,000 at the time of the § 351 transfer and $75,000 at the time of the liquidating distribution to the brothers. As a result of the § 362(e)(2) basis step-down rules, Wren Corporation's basis in the property is $100,000 [$150,000 (basis to brothers) − $50,000 (net built-in loss of property transferred)].

In a liquidating distribution of the property to the brothers, Wren would realize a loss of $25,000 [$75,000 (fair market value of property at distribution) − $100,000 (Wren's stepped-down basis in property)]. Because this is a distribution of disqualified property to related parties, none of the $25,000 loss is recognized by Wren.

Built-In Loss Limitation

A second loss limitation applies to sales, exchanges, or distributions of built-in loss property (fair market value less than basis) that is transferred to a corporation shortly before the corporation is liquidated. The *built-in loss limitation* applies when *both* of the following conditions are met:

- The property was acquired by the corporation in a § 351 (or contribution to capital) transaction.
- This acquisition was part of a plan whose principal purpose was to recognize a loss on that property by the liquidating corporation. A tax avoidance purpose is presumed in the case of transfers occurring *within two years* of a liquidation plan being adopted.

This disallowance rule applies only to the extent that a property's built-in loss at transfer is not eliminated by a § 362(e)(2) stepped-down basis. Some built-in losses on property transfers will avoid the basis step-down either because built-in gain properties were also transferred by the shareholder (see Example 30) or because the shareholder elected to step down the basis of his or her stock instead. Any loss related to a decline in a property's value *after* its transfer to the corporation is not subject to the built-in loss limitation.[30]

EXAMPLE 30

In the current year, Brown Corporation acquires two properties from a shareholder in a transaction that qualifies under § 351.

	Shareholder's Basis	Fair Market Value	Built-In Gain/(Loss)
Land	$100,000	$50,000	($50,000)
Securities	10,000	35,000	25,000
			($25,000)

The net built-in loss of $25,000 results in a stepped-down basis of $75,000 in the land for Brown Corporation [$100,000 (shareholder's basis) − $25,000 (step-down equal to net built-in loss)]. Later in the year, Brown adopts a plan of liquidation and distributes the land to an unrelated shareholder when the land is worth $30,000.

Of the $45,000 loss realized by Brown on the distribution [$30,000 (value of land on date of distribution) − $75,000 (basis in land)], $25,000 is disallowed by the built-in loss limitation [$50,000 (value of land when acquired by Brown) − $75,000 (stepped-down basis in land)] and $20,000 is recognized (equal to the decline in value occurring after acquisition by Brown).

The built-in loss limitation applies to a broader range of transactions than the related-party exception, which disallows losses only on certain *distributions* to related parties (i.e., more-than-50 percent shareholders). The built-in loss limitation can apply to distributions of property to any shareholder, including an unrelated party, and to a *sale or exchange* of property by a liquidating corporation. However, the limitation is narrower than the related-party exception in that it applies only to property that had a built-in loss upon its acquisition by the corporation (as adjusted by the basis step-down rules).

[30]§ 336(d)(2).

Assume in Example 30 that the land was worth $120,000 on the date Brown Corporation acquired the property. Since there is no net built-in loss on the transfer, Brown will have a basis of $100,000 in the land. If the distribution is to an unrelated shareholder, Brown Corporation will recognize the entire $70,000 loss [$30,000 (fair market value on date of distribution) − $100,000 (basis)].

However, if the distribution is to a related party, Brown cannot recognize any of the loss under the related-party loss limitation because the property is disqualified property. When the distribution is to a related party, the loss is disallowed even though the entire decline in value occurred during the period the corporation held the property.

EXAMPLE 31

Property held by the corporation for more than two years prior to the liquidation is usually not subject to the built-in loss limitation. Further, the presumption of a tax avoidance purpose for property transferred to a corporation in the "two years prior to liquidation" window can be contested if there is a clear and substantial business purpose for the transfer. When there is a business reason for the transfer, the built-in loss limitation will not apply. Compare Examples 32 and 33.

Presumption of Tax Avoidance Purpose

Cardinal Corporation's stock is held by two unrelated individuals: 60% by Manuel and 40% by Jack. One year before Cardinal's liquidation, Manuel transfers land (basis of $150,000, fair market value of $100,000) and equipment (basis of $10,000, fair market value of $70,000) to the corporation as a contribution to capital. Since there is no net built-in loss on the transfer, Cardinal will have a basis of $150,000 in the land. There is no business reason for the transfer.

In liquidation, Cardinal distributes the land (now worth $90,000) to Jack. Even though the distribution is to an unrelated party, the built-in loss of $50,000 is not recognized. However, Cardinal Corporation can recognize the loss of $10,000 ($90,000 − $100,000) that occurred while it held the land.

If, instead, the land is distributed to Manuel, a related party, the entire $60,000 loss is disallowed under the related-party loss limitation.

EXAMPLE 32

Concept Summary 6.3

Summary of Antistuffing Loss Disallowance Rules

Related-Party Loss Limitation

Distribution of loss property to a related party *and* distribution is not pro rata *or* property is disqualified property.

- Related party if shareholder owns directly or indirectly *more than* 50% in value of the stock.
  - Section 267 attribution rules apply. Similar to § 318 attribution rules but includes stock owned by siblings.
- Distribution is pro rata if each shareholder receives proportional interest in property.
- Disqualified property is property acquired by the corporation within five years of the distribution date in a § 351 or contribution to capital transaction.

Limitation can apply even if a corporation acquired property by purchase or in a carryover basis transaction with no built-in loss (i.e., fair market greater than basis).

Limitation does not apply to *sales* of loss property.

Built-In Loss Limitation

Distribution, sale, or exchange of certain built-in loss property (fair market value less than basis).

- Property was acquired in a § 351 or contribution to capital transaction.
- Acquisition was part of a plan whose principal purpose was to recognize a loss on the property by the corporation upon liquidation.
  - Presumption of tax avoidance purpose if property was acquired within two years of the date of the plan of liquidation.
  - Clear and substantial business purpose for a transfer of property to a corporation can rebut the presumption.
  - Transfers occurring more than two years before liquidation are rarely subject to the loss limitation.

Loss limitation applies only to amount of the built-in loss at the time of transfer to a corporation (excess of corporation's basis in property over fair market value of property).

- Basis step-down rules will eliminate many built-in losses. However, loss limitation remains applicable where built-in loss is not entirely eliminated by the basis step-down (i.e., built-in gain property transferred with built-in loss property) or where the shareholder elected to step down basis of stock.

Presumption of Tax Avoidance Purpose

EXAMPLE 33

Assume in Example 32 that the land and equipment are transferred to Cardinal Corporation because a bank required the additional capital investment as a condition to making a loan to the corporation.

Because there is a business purpose for the transfer, all of the $60,000 loss is recognized if the land is distributed to Jack in liquidation.

If, instead, the land is distributed to Manuel, a related party, the entire loss is still disallowed under the related-party loss limitation.

6-7 LIQUIDATIONS—EFFECT ON THE SHAREHOLDER

The tax consequences to the shareholders of a corporation in the process of liquidation are generally governed by § 331. The exception to this rule, § 332, applies in the liquidation of a subsidiary (discussed in text Section 6-8).

Section 331(a) requires sale or exchange treatment for the shareholders. As a result, the difference between the fair market value of the assets received from the corporation and the adjusted basis of the stock surrendered is the gain or loss recognized by the shareholder. The fair market value of property received subject to a corporate liability is reduced by the amount of the liability. Typically, the stock is a capital asset in the hands of the shareholder, and capital gain or loss results. The taxpayer must be able to document the adjusted basis of the stock. Without documentation, the stock is deemed to have a zero basis.[31] The basis of property received in a liquidation is the property's fair market value on the date of distribution.[32] If installment notes are distributed in liquidation, shareholders can use the installment method to defer to the point of collection the portion of their gain that is attributable to the notes.[33]

Any taxes paid by a corporation as a result of liquidation gains will reduce the proceeds available to be distributed to the shareholders. This will reduce the amount realized by the shareholders, which will then reduce their gain (or increase the loss) recognized.

EXAMPLE 34

Purple Corporation's assets are valued at $2,000,000 after payment of all corporate debts, except for $300,000 of taxes payable on net gains it recognized on the liquidation. Shawn, an individual and the sole shareholder of Purple, has a basis of $450,000 in his stock.

Shawn has a gain recognized of $1,250,000 [$1,700,000 amount realized ($2,000,000 − $300,000) − $450,000 basis] as a result of the liquidation.

ETHICS & EQUITY Transferee Liability for Tax Deficiency of Liquidated Corporation

In 2017, Loon Corporation distributed all of its remaining assets to two equal shareholders in a complete liquidation. The two shareholders, Gloria Martinez and Roger Stinson, each received a distribution of $250,000 for their stock in Loon.

In 2019, the IRS audited Loon Corporation and assessed additional income tax of $175,000 (plus penalties and interest) against the corporation. Since Loon was defunct and without assets, the IRS then assessed the entire deficiency against Gloria Martinez, based on transferee liability. The IRS did not attempt to collect any of the deficiency from Roger Stinson.

Is this an equitable solution to the collection of Loon's tax liability?

---

[31]See *John Calderazzo*, 34 TCM 1, T.C.Memo. 1975–1; and *Coloman v. Comm.*, 76–2 USTC ¶9581, 38 AFTR 2d 5523, 540 F.2d 427 (CA–9, 1976).

[32]§ 334(a).

[33]§ 453(h). Shareholders must allocate their stock basis between the notes and the other assets received in the liquidation. Upon distribution, the

corporation generally recognizes gain (or loss) equal to the difference between the fair market value of the notes and the corporation's basis in the notes. § 453B(a).

6-8 LIQUIDATIONS—PARENT-SUBSIDIARY SITUATIONS

LO.5

Determine the tax consequences of subsidiary liquidations for both the parent and the subsidiary corporations.

Section 332, an exception to the general rule of § 331, provides that a parent corporation does *not* recognize gain or loss on a liquidation of a subsidiary. In addition, the subsidiary corporation recognizes *neither gain nor loss* on liquidating distributions of property to its parent.[34]

There are three requirements for applying § 332:

- The parent must own at least 80 percent of the subsidiary's stock (both voting power and value).
- All of the subsidiary's property must be distributed in complete cancellation of all of its stock within the taxable year or within three years from the close of the tax year in which the first distribution occurred.
- The subsidiary must be solvent.[35]

If these requirements are met, nonrecognition of gains and losses is *mandatory*. However, if the subsidiary is insolvent, the parent corporation will have an ordinary loss deduction under § 165(g) equal to its basis in the subsidiary stock.

If the liquidation involves several distributions, the 80 percent test must be met on the date the plan of liquidation is adopted and maintained until the final liquidating distribution is received by the parent.[36] If the parent fails the 80 percent test at any time, the provisions for nonrecognition of gain or loss do not apply to any distribution.[37]

The parent-subsidiary rules are contrasted with other liquidation rules in Concept Summary 6.4 later in the chapter.

6-8a Minority Shareholder Interests

In a § 332 parent-subsidiary liquidation, up to 20 percent of the subsidiary's stock can be owned by minority shareholders. In such liquidations, a distribution of property to a minority shareholder is treated in the same manner as a *nonliquidating* distribution. That is, the subsidiary corporation recognizes gain (but not loss) on the property distributed to the minority shareholder.[38]

> The stock of Tan Corporation is held by Mustard Corporation (80%) and by Arethia, an individual (20%). Tan Corporation is liquidated pursuant to a plan adopted earlier in the year. At the time of its liquidation, Tan Corporation has assets with a basis of $100,000 and fair market value of $500,000. Tan Corporation distributes the property pro rata to Mustard Corporation and to Arethia.
>
> Tan must recognize a gain of $80,000 [($500,000 fair market value − $100,000 basis) × 20% minority interest]. Because the corporate tax due in this liquidation relates entirely to the minority shareholder distribution, that amount most likely will be deducted from the $100,000 distribution ($500,000 × 20%) going to Arethia. The remaining gain of $320,000 is not recognized because it relates to property being distributed to Mustard, the parent corporation.

EXAMPLE 35

A minority shareholder is subject to the general rule requiring the recognition of gain or loss in a liquidation. As a result, the difference between the fair market value of the assets received and the basis of the minority shareholder's stock is the amount of gain or loss recognized. The basis of property received by the minority shareholder is the property's fair market value on the date of distribution.[39]

---

[34]§ 337(a). This is an exception to the general rule of § 336.

[35]§ 332(b) and Reg. §§ 1.332–2(a) and (b).

[36]Establishing the date of the adoption of a plan of complete liquidation could be crucial in determining whether § 332 applies. See, for example, *George L. Riggs, Inc.*, 64 T.C. 474 (1975).

[37]§ 332(b)(3) and Reg. § 1.332–2(a).

[38]§§ 336(a) and (d)(3).

[39]§ 334(a).

GLOBAL TAX ISSUES   Basis Rules for Liquidations of Foreign Subsidiaries

The basis of property acquired by a parent corporation in the liquidation of a subsidiary corporation is generally equal to the basis the subsidiary had in such property. However, legislation a number of years ago modified the basis rules regarding property acquired by a U.S. parent in certain § 332 liquidations of foreign subsidiaries.

In general, if the aggregate basis in a foreign subsidiary's assets exceeds their aggregate fair market value, the U.S. parent will take a fair market value basis in the property acquired. The purpose of this amendment is to deny the importation of built-in losses (excess of basis over fair market value). [See §§ 334(b)(1)(B) and 362(e)(1)(B).]

6-8b Indebtedness of the Subsidiary to the Parent

If a subsidiary transfers appreciated property to its parent to satisfy a debt, it must recognize gain on the transaction unless the subsidiary is liquidating and the conditions of § 332 apply. When § 332 applies, the subsidiary does not recognize gain or loss upon the transfer of property to the parent in satisfaction of indebtedness.[40]

EXAMPLE 36

Eagle Corporation owes its parent, Finch Corporation, $20,000. It satisfies the obligation by transferring land (basis of $8,000, fair market value of $20,000) to Finch. Normally, Eagle would recognize a gain of $12,000 on the transaction. However, if the transfer relates to a liquidation under § 332, Eagle does not recognize a gain.

This nonrecognition provision does not apply to the parent corporation. The parent corporation recognizes gain or loss on the receipt of property in satisfaction of indebtedness even if the property is received during liquidation of the subsidiary.

EXAMPLE 37

Pelican Corporation owns bonds (basis of $95,000) of its subsidiary, Crow Corporation, that were acquired at a discount. Upon liquidation of Crow pursuant to § 332, Pelican receives a distribution of $100,000, the face amount of the bonds. The transaction has no tax effect on Crow. However, Pelican Corporation recognizes a gain of $5,000 [$100,000 (amount realized) − $95,000 (basis in bonds)].

6-8c Basis of Property Received by the Parent Corporation—The General Rule

Property received by the parent corporation in the complete liquidation of a subsidiary has the same basis it had in the hands of the subsidiary.[41] Unless the parent corporation makes a § 338 election (discussed in text Section 6-8d), this carryover basis in the assets generally will differ from the parent's basis in the stock of the subsidiary. Because the liquidation is a nontaxable exchange, the parent's gain or loss on the difference in basis is not recognized. Further, the parent's basis in the stock of the subsidiary disappears.

Basis Issues in Subsidiary Liquidations

EXAMPLE 38

Lark Corporation has a basis of $200,000 in the stock of Heron Corporation, a subsidiary in which it owns 85% of all classes of stock. Lark purchased the Heron stock 10 years ago. In the current year, Lark liquidates Heron and acquires assets that are worth $800,000 and have a tax basis to Heron of $500,000.

Lark Corporation takes a basis of $500,000 in the assets, with a potential gain on their sale of $300,000. Lark's $200,000 basis in Heron's stock disappears.

---

[40]§ 337(b)(1).

[41]§ 334(b)(1) and Reg. § 1.334–1(b). But see § 334(b)(1)(B) (exception for property acquired in some liquidations of foreign subsidiaries).

Basis Issues in Subsidiary Liquidations

Indigo Corporation has a basis of $600,000 in the stock of Kackie Corporation, a wholly owned subsidiary acquired 10 years ago. It liquidates Kackie Corporation and receives assets that are worth $400,000 and have a tax basis to Kackie of $300,000.

Indigo Corporation takes a basis of $300,000 in the assets it acquires from Kackie. If Indigo sells the assets, it has a gain of $100,000 even though its basis in the Kackie stock was $600,000. Indigo's loss on its stock investment in Kackie will never be recognized.

In addition to the parent corporation taking the subsidiary's basis in its assets, the parent's holding period for the assets includes that of the subsidiary.[42] Further, the carry-over rules of § 381 apply (see Chapter 7). As a result, the parent acquires other tax attributes of the subsidiary, including the subsidiary's net operating loss carryover, business credit carryover, capital loss carryover, and E & P.

6-8d Basis of Property Received by the Parent Corporation—§ 338 Election

As discussed above, the liquidation of a subsidiary generally is a nontaxable transaction resulting in the nonrecognition of gain or loss for both the parent and the subsidiary corporations and the carryover of the subsidiary's asset bases (and other tax attributes). This treatment reflects the fact that such a liquidation often is merely a change in corporate structure and not a change in substance. This is particularly the case when the parent has owned the stock of the subsidiary since the subsidiary's inception. In these cases, the carried-over bases are comparable to what the parent would have if it, and not the subsidiary, had originally acquired the assets.

The carryover basis rule for § 332 liquidations can result in some inequities when the subsidiary has been in existence for some time prior to the parent's acquisition of the subsidiary's stock. The parent's basis in the stock of the subsidiary will reflect the fair market value of the subsidiary's assets (and goodwill) at the time of the stock purchase. As a result, the parent's basis in the stock of the subsidiary will usually be greater than the subsidiary's basis in its assets. In this case, a subsidiary liquidation under § 332 would result in the parent taking a basis in the subsidiary's assets that is less than the parent's basis in the stock of the subsidiary. This is the case even if the parent acquired the subsidiary stock solely to obtain the subsidiary's assets.

If the parent could treat the purchase of the subsidiary stock as a purchase of its assets, the parent could take a basis in the assets equal to the acquisition cost of the stock. In most cases, this would mean a higher asset basis and, as a result, larger depreciation deductions and lower gains upon disposition for the parent. To obtain this stock-basis-for-asset-basis result, taxpayers successfully devised stock purchase/subsidiary liquidation transactions that fell outside § 332.[43] Congress codified this treatment by enacting § 338, which permits the purchase of a controlling interest of stock to be treated as a purchase of the subsidiary's assets.

Requirements for Application

A corporation (the "parent") may *elect* the provisions of § 338 if it acquires at least 80 percent of the stock (both voting power and value) of another corporation (the "subsidiary") within a 12-month period ("*qualified stock purchase*"). The stock must be acquired in a *taxable* transaction (i.e., a transaction where § 351 and other nonrecognition provisions do not apply). An acquisition of stock by any member of an affiliated group that includes the parent corporation is considered to be an acquisition by

---

[42]§ 1223(2).

[43]See, for example, *U.S. v. M.O.J. Corp.*, 60–1 USTC ¶9209, 5 AFTR 2d 535, 274 F.2d 713 (CA–5, 1960). See also *Kimbell-Diamond Milling Co.*, 14 T.C. 74

(1950), *aff'd* 51–1 USTC ¶9201, 40 AFTR 328, 187 F.2d 718 (CA–5, 1951), *cert. den.* 72 S.Ct. 50 (USSC, 1951) (IRS argued stock-for-asset basis).

Concept Summary 6.4

Summary of Liquidation Rules

Effect on the Shareholder	Basis of Property Received	Effect on the Corporation
§ 331—The general rule provides for gain or loss treatment on the difference between the FMV of property received and the basis of the stock in the corporation. Gain allocable to installment notes received can be deferred to the point of collection.	§ 334(a)—Basis of assets received by the shareholder will be the FMV on the date of distribution (except for installment obligations on which gain is deferred to the point of collection).	§ 336—Gain or loss is recognized for distributions in kind and for sales by the liquidating corporation. Losses are not recognized for distributions to related parties if the distribution is not pro rata or if disqualified property is distributed. Losses may be disallowed on sales and distributions of built-in loss property even if made to unrelated parties.
§ 332—In liquidation of a subsidiary, no gain or loss is recognized by the parent. Subsidiary must distribute all of its property within the taxable year or within three years from the close of the taxable year in which the first distribution occurs. Minority shareholders are taxed under the general rule of § 331.	§ 334(b)(1)—Property has the same basis that it had in the hands of the subsidiary. Parent's basis in the stock disappears. Carryover rules of § 381 apply. Minority shareholders get FMV basis under § 334(a).	§ 337—No gain or loss is recognized by the subsidiary on distributions to the parent. Gain (but not loss) is recognized on distributions to minority shareholders.
	§ 338—Subsidiary need not be liquidated. If subsidiary is liquidated, parent's basis in the assets is the new stepped-up (or -down) basis. Parent's basis in the stock disappears. Carryover rules of § 381 apply, but such amounts are likely to be nominal.	§ 338—Gain or loss is recognized by the subsidiary. Subsidiary is treated as a new corporation, and its basis in the assets is stepped up (or down) to reflect the parent's basis in the subsidiary stock plus subsidiary's liabilities. New basis is allocated among various asset classes.

the parent. The **§ 338 election** must be made by the fifteenth day of the ninth month beginning after the month in which a qualified stock purchase occurs. If made, the election is irrevocable.

Tax Consequences

If § 338 is elected, the subsidiary is treated as having sold its assets on the qualified stock purchase date for a value that is determined with reference to the parent's basis in the subsidiary stock plus any liabilities of the subsidiary ("aggregate deemed sale price").[44] The subsidiary is then treated as a new corporation that purchased those assets for a similarly computed amount ("adjusted grossed-up basis") on the day following the qualified stock purchase date.[45] The deemed sale results in gain (or loss) recognition by the subsidiary, and the deemed purchase results in a stepped-up (or -down) basis for the subsidiary's assets.[46] The subsidiary may, but need not, be liquidated. If the subsidiary is liquidated, the parent will obtain a carryover of the stepped-up (or -down) basis of the subsidiary's assets.

A Comparison of the General Rule and the § 338 Election

Under § 332, the liquidation of a subsidiary is tax-free to both the subsidiary (except for any minority interest) and the parent corporation. Under § 338, the subsidiary recognizes gain (or loss) on the deemed disposition of its assets, while the liquidation of the subsidiary remains tax-free to the parent. Although a carryover basis rule applies in both cases, the subsidiary's assets generally will have a stepped-up basis as a result

---

[44]See §§ 338(a)(1) and (b) and Reg. § 1.338–4.

[45]See §§ 338(a)(2) and (b) and Reg. § 1.338–5.

[46]For the rules governing the allocation of the purchase price to the assets, see § 338(b)(5) and Reg. § 1.338–6.

of the § 338 election and a liquidation of the subsidiary will result in a carryover of the stepped-up basis to the parent. Regardless of whether a § 338 election is made, a liquidation of the subsidiary results in a carryover of its other tax attributes (e.g., E & P) to the parent. However, when the election is made, the subsidiary is treated as a new corporation as of the day following the qualified stock purchase date; as a result, any tax attributes acquired by the parent are likely to be nominal (or zero) in amount.

The holding period of the subsidiary's assets is determined with reference to the substance of the transaction. When the subsidiary is liquidated and there is no § 338 election, the subsidiary's historical holding period in its assets carries over to the parent. This is the typical carryover rule found in other nonrecognition provisions. A § 338 election, however, assumes a sale and repurchase of the subsidiary's assets. As a result of these deemed transactions, the holding period starts anew. If there is a § 338 election and the subsidiary is liquidated, the holding period of the property received by the parent begins on the date of the qualified stock purchase. On the other hand, if there is a § 338 election and the subsidiary is not liquidated, the holding period of the assets begins on the day *after* the qualified stock acquisition date. Exhibit 6.2 illustrates the consequences of a § 338 election to both the parent and subsidiary corporations.

EXHIBIT 6.2	**Consequences of a Section 338 Election**

Assume the following:

- Parent acquires 100% of Subsidiary's stock for $750,000 on August 5, 2019.
- Subsidiary (E & P of $400,000) has only one asset, land (fair market value of $1,000,000, basis of $504,000), no liabilities, and no loss or tax credit carryovers.
- Parent files a timely § 338 election, and both aggregate deemed sale price (ADSP) and adjusted grossed-up basis (AGUB) are $815,392.

Subsidiary Is Liquidated

Consequences to Subsidiary:

Deemed to have sold the land for ADSP of $815,392, which results in a recognized gain of $311,392 [$815,392 (ADSP) − $504,000 (basis)], and tax of $65,392 ($311,392 × 21%). The land's new basis is $815,392 (AGUB). No gain or loss recognized on distribution of land to Parent.

Consequences to Parent:

No gain or loss recognized on receipt of land from Subsidiary. Basis in land is $815,392; holding period for the land begins on August 5, 2019; and basis in Subsidiary stock disappears. Acquires Subsidiary's E & P, but that amount is $0 as a result of the § 338 election.

Subsidiary Is *Not* Liquidated

Consequences to Subsidiary:

Deemed to have sold the land for ADSP of $815,392, which results in a recognized gain of $311,392 [$815,392 (ADSP) − $504,000 (basis)], and tax of $65,392 ($311,392 × 21%). Treated as a new corporation (e.g., E & P of $0) as of August 6, 2019: land's new basis is $815,392 (AGUB); and holding period for the land begins on August 6, 2019.

Consequences to Parent:

No tax consequences. Basis in Subsidiary stock remains unchanged at $750,000.

6-9 TAX PLANNING

LO.6
Identify planning opportunities available to minimize the tax impacts of stock redemptions and complete liquidations.

The qualifying stock redemption rules provide unique tax saving opportunities for shareholders of family owned and other closely held corporations. In addition, the tax consequences of corporate liquidations can be minimized with proper planning.

6-9a **Stock Redemptions**

Stock redemptions offer several possibilities for tax planning:

- Stock redemptions are particularly well suited for purchasing the interest of a retiring or deceased shareholder. Rather than the remaining shareholders buying the stock of the retiring or deceased shareholder, corporate funds are used to redeem these shares. A life insurance policy held by the corporation on a shareholder can be used to fund a redemption. Upon the shareholder's death, the corporation receives tax-free life insurance proceeds that are used to redeem the stock of the deceased shareholder. The ability to use the corporation's funds to buy out a shareholder's interest is also advantageous in property settlements between divorcing taxpayers.

- A third party who wants to purchase all of the stock of a corporation can utilize a stock redemption to finance some of the stock acquisition cost. This technique is referred to as a "bootstrap acquisition." The third party first purchases a small amount of stock from the shareholders. The corporation then redeems all of its outstanding stock except that of the third party. The third party becomes the sole shareholder of the corporation, but corporate funds finance most of the acquisition. Some leveraged buyouts (LBOs) are structured like a bootstrap acquisition.

- The timing and sequence of a redemption should be considered carefully, because a series of redemptions may have the effect of a dividend distribution. The following example illustrates this point.

EXAMPLE
40

Sparrow Corporation's stock is held by three unrelated shareholders: Alma (60 shares), Antonio (20 shares), and Ali (20 shares). The corporation redeems 24 of Alma's shares. Shortly thereafter, it redeems 5 of Antonio's shares. Does Alma's redemption qualify as a disproportionate redemption?

Taken in isolation, Alma's redemption satisfies the 80% and 50% tests. Yet, if the IRS takes into account the later redemption of Antonio's shares, Alma has not satisfied the 50% test; she still owns $36/71$ of the corporation after the two redemptions. A greater time lag between the redemptions places Alma in a better position to argue against collapsing the two redemptions as parts of one integrated plan.

- For a family corporation in which all of the shareholders are related to each other, the only hope of achieving sale or exchange treatment may lie in the use of a complete termination redemption. Here, strict compliance with the requirements for the family attribution waiver is critical (e.g., the withdrawing shareholder does not acquire a prohibited interest in the corporation within 10 years).

- In a redemption to pay death taxes, the amount sheltered from dividend treatment is limited to the sum of death taxes and funeral and administration expenses. The estate tax exemption amount was nearly doubled by the Tax Cuts and Jobs Act (TCJA) of 2017 (after adjustment for inflation). This change will result in far fewer taxpayers incurring any Federal estate tax, and further limiting the applicability of qualified redemption treatment under § 303. However, a redemption in excess of the limitation can qualify for sale or exchange treatment under one of the other qualifying stock redemption rules.

- A qualifying stock redemption financed by installment notes can provide tax benefits to both the corporation and the shareholder. For the corporation, the related interest expense is deductible (subject to the business interest expense limitation; see Chapter 3), while the shareholder can use the installment method to defer to the point of collection the gain that is attributable to the notes.

6-9b **Corporate Liquidations**

With the exception of parent-subsidiary liquidations, liquidating distributions are taxed at both the corporate level and the shareholder level. When a corporation liquidates, it can, as a general rule, claim losses on assets that have depreciated in value. These assets should not be distributed in the form of a property dividend or stock redemption because losses are not recognized on nonliquidating distributions.

Shareholders faced with large prospective gains in a liquidation may consider shifting part or all of that gain to other taxpayers. One approach is to donate stock to charity. A charitable contribution of the stock produces a deduction equal to the stock's fair market value (see Chapter 3). Alternatively, the stock may be given to family members in the 10 or 12 percent marginal tax bracket. Here, some or all of the gain on liquidation could be taxed at the 0 percent preferential rate on long-term capital gains. However, there is a risk that the donor may be deemed to have made an anticipatory assignment of income. If so, the gain is still taxed to the donor. In addition, any gift tax issues on the stock transfer must be considered (see Chapter 18). Advance planning of stock transfers, therefore, is crucial in arriving at the desired tax result.

The installment sale rules might also provide some relief. Rather than distributing assets to its shareholders, a sale of the liquidating corporation's assets in exchange for installment notes should be considered. Shareholders receiving the notes in a liquidation can then report their gain on the installment method as payments on the notes are collected. Gain deferred under the installment method is subject to the tax rates applicable in each year of collection. Taxpayers may be able to reduce the tax consequences of an installment sale by directing collections to a year in which a lower rate applies to the capital gain.

6-9c Parent-Subsidiary Liquidations

The nonrecognition provision applicable to the liquidation of a subsidiary, § 332, is not elective. Nevertheless, some flexibility may be available.

- Whether § 332 applies depends on the 80 percent stock ownership test. A parent corporation may be able to avoid § 332 by reducing its stock ownership in the subsidiary below this percentage to allow for recognition of a loss. On the other hand, the opposite approach may be desirable to avoid gain recognition. A corporate shareholder possessing less than the required 80 percent ownership may want to acquire additional stock to qualify for § 332 treatment.

- Once § 332 becomes effective, less latitude is allowed in determining the parent's basis in the subsidiary's assets. Generally, the subsidiary's existing basis in its assets carries over to the parent. If a timely § 338 election is made, the subsidiary's basis in its assets is stepped up to reflect, in part, the parent's basis in the subsidiary stock. If the subsidiary also is liquidated, the parent obtains assets with the stepped-up basis.

- An election to have the § 338 rules apply should be carefully weighed since the election can be detrimental. The income tax liability on the subsidiary's recognized gain that results from the deemed sale of its assets is the cost under § 338 for obtaining the stepped-up basis. As a result, a § 338 election may be a viable option only when the subsidiary possesses loss and/or credit carryovers that can be used to offset the associated tax.

6-9d Asset Purchase versus Stock Purchase

The acquisition of a corporation's assets generally takes one of two forms. In one form, the acquirer purchases the stock of the target corporation and then the target (subsidiary) is liquidated. In the other form, the acquirer purchases the assets of the target corporation and then the target distributes the proceeds to its shareholders in liquidation. Nontax considerations may affect the form of acquisition, with each form having both favorable and unfavorable aspects.

An asset purchase requires that title be transferred and that creditors be notified. Further, an asset purchase may not be feasible if valuable nontransferable trademarks, contracts, or licenses are involved. Alternatively, an asset purchase may be preferable to a stock purchase if the target's shareholders refuse to sell their stock. In addition, an asset purchase avoids the transfer of liabilities (including unknown liabilities) generally inherent in stock acquisitions. An asset purchase also has the advantage of allowing the purchaser to avoid the acquisition of unwanted assets, whereas a stock purchase would involve all of a target's assets.

REFOCUS ON THE BIG PICTURE

A FAMILY ATTRIBUTION WAIVER IS A VALUABLE TOOL IN SUCCESSION PLANNING

With proper planning, a complete termination redemption could be utilized to achieve Christina's objectives. In the years remaining before her retirement, Christina should ensure that her children are actively involved in the management and strategy decisions of Orange Corporation. Also, an ownership interest in Orange should be shifted to each of the children so that they are in minority shareholder positions by the time Christina retires. The children could purchase Orange shares from Christina or newly issued shares from Orange. Alternatively, Christina could make annual gifts of Orange stock to the children. In addition to eliminating the need for the children to raise capital for a stock purchase, this alternative would produce favorable estate tax consequences.

When Christina retires, Orange would redeem her remaining ownership interest, and the two children would be the sole shareholders of Orange Corporation. Assuming that Christina satisfies the requirements of the family attribution waiver, the transaction would qualify as a complete termination redemption. Orange Corporation could issue promissory notes to finance the stock redemption and deduct the related interest expense, and Christina could use the installment method to report her gain. (The notes should specify a reasonable rate of interest.)

What If?

What if Christina passes away before her retirement date? A redemption to pay death taxes could be utilized to redeem Orange stock from Christina's estate, since it appears that the requirements of § 303 would be satisfied. However, a redemption would qualify under § 303 only to the extent of the estate's death taxes and funeral and administration expenses. A redemption of an amount greater than the sum of these expenditures probably would not satisfy any of the § 302 qualifying stock redemption provisions, because the children would be the primary or sole beneficiaries of Christina's estate. After the redemption to pay death taxes, the estate's remaining shares of Orange would be distributed to the children, and they would control 100 percent of the outstanding shares of the corporation.

STOCK4B CREATIVE/STOCK4B-RF/GETTY IMAGES

Key Terms

Attribution, 6-5

Complete termination redemption, 6-8

Corporate liquidation, 6-14

Disproportionate redemption, 6-7

Meaningful reduction test, 6-7

Not essentially equivalent redemption, 6-7

Partial liquidation, 6-9

Preferred stock bailout, 6-12

Redemption to pay death taxes, 6-10

Section 338 election, 6-24

Stock redemption, 6-2

Discussion Questions

1. **LO.1** Why does the Code limit sale or exchange treatment on stock redemptions to qualifying stock redemptions?

Critical Thinking   2. **LO.1, 2, 6** Chao, Louis, and Mari, unrelated individuals, own all of the shares of Cerise Corporation. All three shareholders have been active in the management of Cerise since its inception. In the current year, Chao wants to retire and sell all of her shares in the corporation. What issues should be considered in determining whether Chao should sell her stock to one of the other shareholders, to Cerise Corporation, or to a third party?

3. **LO.1** Corporate shareholders typically prefer dividend treatment on a stock redemption. Why?

4. **LO.1** Do the stock attribution rules apply to all stock redemptions? Explain.

5. **LO.1** Briefly discuss the requirements for a redemption to qualify as a not essentially equivalent redemption.

6. **LO.1** If a redemption is treated as a dividend ("nonqualified stock redemption"), what happens to the basis of the stock redeemed?

7. **LO.1** Explain the requirements for a disproportionate redemption.

8. **LO.1, 2** Tammy and Barry formed Pheasant Corporation several years ago in a   Critical Thinking
transaction that qualified under § 351. Both shareholders serve as officers and on the board of directors of Pheasant. In the current year, Pheasant Corporation redeemed all of Barry's shares in the corporation with a property distribution. What are the tax issues for Barry and Pheasant?

9. **LO.1, 6** Lauren owns 600 shares in Viridian Corporation. The remaining 400 shares of Viridian are owned by Lauren's son, Brett. Currently, Lauren is both president and chair of the board of directors of Viridian Corporation. If Viridian redeems Lauren's 600 shares, can the redemption qualify for sale or exchange treatment? Explain.

10. **LO.1** To qualify as a partial liquidation, a distribution must not be essentially equivalent to a dividend. Discuss how this requirement is satisfied.

11. **LO.1, 2** Brown Corporation operates several trades and businesses. In the current   Critical Thinking
year, Brown discontinues the operation of one of its trades and businesses. Brown is considering distributing to its shareholders either the assets of the discontinued business or the proceeds from the sale of such assets. Considering both of these alternatives, what are the tax issues for Brown Corporation and its shareholders?

12. **LO.1, 2** Explain the requirements for a redemption to pay death taxes. What are the tax consequences of a redemption to pay death taxes for the shareholder and the corporation?

13. **LO.1, 2** Angie and her daughter, Ann, who are the only shareholders of Bluebird   Critical Thinking
Corporation, each paid $200,000 four years ago for their shares in Bluebird. Angie also owns 20% of the stock in Redbird Corporation. The Redbird stock is worth $1,000,000, and Angie's basis in the stock is $100,000. Angie dies in the current year leaving all of her property to her husband, Gary, but Ann wants to be the sole shareholder of Bluebird Corporation. Bluebird has assets worth $8,000,000 (basis of $1,400,000) and E & P of $2,000,000. Angie's estate is worth approximately $16,000,000. Angie has made gifts during her lifetime to Ann. What are the tax issues for Angie's estate, Ann, and Bluebird?

14. **LO.1, 2, 6** Donna and Steven own all the stock in Pink Corporation (E & P of   Critical Thinking
$2,000,000). Each owns 1,000 shares and has a basis of $75,000 in the shares. Donna and Steven are married and have two minor children. Pink Corporation has had considerable earnings in the past few years and has substantial cash flow. Pink pays Donna an annual salary of $250,000. Steven is currently unemployed. Donna and Steven own a house worth $600,000 with an adjusted basis of $450,000. The couple decides to divorce in the current year. They want to sell their residence and each purchase a new home. Donna wants to acquire Steven's stock in Pink Corporation but does not have adequate cash to buy his one-half interest. What are the tax issues for Donna, Steven, and Pink Corporation?

15. **LO.3** In general, what are the tax consequences surrounding the sale of § 306 stock?

16. **LO.4** Under what circumstances are losses disallowed to a corporation in liquidation?

17. **LO.4** For purposes of the related-party loss limitation within the context of a complete liquidation of a corporation, what is the definition of *disqualified property*?

18. **LO.4** For the built-in loss limitation to apply, the property must have been acquired by the corporation as part of a plan whose principal purpose was to recognize a loss on the property by the liquidating corporation. Explain.

19. **LO.4** Explain the tax consequences to a shareholder of a corporation in the process of liquidation under the general rule of § 331.

20. **LO.5** Discuss the tax consequences to the parent corporation in a § 332 liquidation of a subsidiary.

21. **LO.5** In terms of the rules applying to a § 332 parent-subsidiary liquidation, comment on each of the following:
    a.   The parent corporation's ownership interest in the subsidiary.
    b.   The period of time in which the subsidiary must liquidate.
    c.   The solvency of the subsidiary.

22. **LO.5** A subsidiary corporation is liquidated under § 332. Pursuant to its liquidation, the subsidiary distributed property to a minority shareholder. With respect to this distribution, what are the tax consequences to the subsidiary corporation and to the minority shareholder?

23. **LO.5** In general, what are the tax consequences of a § 338 election?

24. **LO.5** From the perspective of the parent corporation, contrast the tax consequences of a subsidiary liquidation under the general nonrecognition rules with a subsidiary liquidation that follows a § 338 election.

Computational Exercises

25. **LO.1** During the current year, Gnatcatcher, Inc., (E & P of $1,000,000) distributed $200,000 each to Brandi and Yuen in redemption of some of their Gnatcatcher stock. The two shareholders acquired their shares five years ago. Each shareholder is in the 32% tax bracket, and each had a $45,000 basis in her redeemed stock.
    a.   Assume that the distribution to Brandi is a qualifying stock redemption. Determine Brandi's tax liability on the distribution.
    b.   Assume that the distribution to Yuen is a nonqualified stock redemption. Determine Yuen's tax liability on the distribution.

26. **LO.1** Rosalie owns 50% of the outstanding stock of Salmon Corporation. In a qualifying stock redemption, Salmon distributes $80,000 to Rosalie in exchange for one-half of her shares, which have a basis of $100,000. Compute Rosalie's recognized loss, if any, on the redemption.

27. **LO.1** Derk owns 250 shares of stock in Rose Corporation. The remaining 750 shares of Rose are owned as follows: 150 by Derk's daughter, 200 by Derk's aunt, and 400 by a partnership in which Derk has an 80% interest. Determine the number of shares Derk owns (directly and indirectly) in Rose Corporation.

28. **LO.2** Indigo Corporation wants to transfer cash of $150,000 or property worth $150,000 to one of its shareholders, Linda, in a redemption transaction that will be treated as a qualifying stock redemption. If Indigo distributes property, the corporation will choose between two assets that are each worth $150,000 and are no longer needed in its business: Property A (basis of $75,000) and Property B (basis of $195,000).

    a. Compute Indigo's recognized gain or loss if it distributes Property A in redemption of Linda's shares.

    b. Compute Indigo's recognized gain or loss if it distributes Property B in redemption of Linda's shares.

    c. Compute Indigo's recognized gain or loss if it sells Property B to an unrelated party, then distributes the sale proceeds in redemption of Linda's shares.

29. **LO.2** Caramel Corporation has 5,000 shares of stock outstanding. In a qualifying stock redemption, Caramel distributes $145,000 in exchange for 1,000 of its shares. At the time of the redemption, Caramel has paid-in capital of $800,000 and E & P of $300,000. Calculate the reduction to Caramel's E & P as a result of the distribution.

30. **LO.1, 4** Sunset Corporation, with E & P of $400,000, makes a cash distribution of $120,000 to a shareholder. The shareholder's basis in the Sunset stock involved is $50,000.

    a. Determine the tax consequences to the shareholder if the distribution is a non-qualified stock redemption.

    b. Determine the tax consequences to the shareholder if the distribution is a qualifying stock redemption.

    c. Determine the tax consequences to the shareholder if the distribution is pursuant to a complete liquidation of Sunset.

31. **LO.4** Pursuant to a complete liquidation, Carrot Corporation distributes to its shareholders real estate held as an investment (basis of $650,000, fair market value of $880,000).

    a. Determine the gain or loss recognized by Carrot on the distribution if no liability is involved.

    b. Determine the gain or loss recognized by Carrot on the distribution if the real estate is subject to a liability of $690,000.

    c. Determine the gain or loss recognized by Carrot on the distribution if the real estate is subject to a liability of $885,000.

32. **LO.4** Osprey Corporation stock is owned by Pedro and Pittro, who are unrelated. Pedro and Pittro each own 50% of the stock in the corporation. Osprey has the following assets (none of which were acquired in a § 351 or contribution to capital transaction) that are distributed in complete liquidation of the corporation.

	Adjusted Basis	Fair Market Value
Cash	$300,000	$300,000
Land	200,000	440,000
Equipment	250,000	140,000

Assume that Osprey Corporation distributes the land to Pedro and the cash and equipment to Pittro.

    a. Determine Osprey's recognized gain or loss on the distribution of land.

    b. Determine Osprey's recognized gain or loss on the distribution of the equipment.

33. **LO.4** On January 4, 2019, Martin Corporation acquires two properties from a share-holder solely in exchange for stock in a transaction that qualifies under § 351. The shareholder's basis, the fair market value, and the built-in gain (loss) of each property are:

	Shareholder's Basis	Fair Market Value	Built-In Gain (Loss)
Property 1	$300,000	$375,000	$ 75,000
Property 2	525,000	400,000	(125,000)
Net built-in loss			($ 50,000)

Martin adopts a plan of liquidation later in the year and distributes Property 2 to a 30% shareholder when the property is worth $350,000.

a.   Compute Martin's basis in Property 1 and in Property 2 as of January 4, 2019.

b.   Compute Martin's realized and recognized loss on the liquidating distribution of Property 2.

34. **LO.4** Green Corporation's assets are valued at $920,000 after payment of all corporate debts, except for $134,000 of taxes payable on net gains it recognized on the liquidation. Bruno, an individual and the sole shareholder of Green, has a basis of $280,000 in his stock. Compute the gain or loss recognized by Bruno on the liquidation of Green Corporation.

35. **LO.5** The stock of Quail Corporation is held as follows: 85% by Pheasant Corporation and 15% by Gisela, an individual. Quail Corporation is liquidated in December of the current year pursuant to a plan adopted earlier in the year. At the time of its liquidation, Quail Corporation has assets with a basis of $730,000 and fair market value of $1,000,000. Quail Corporation distributes the property pro rata to Pheasant Corporation and to Gisela.

a.   Compute Quail's recognized gain or loss on the distribution of property to Pheasant.

b.   Compute Quail's recognized gain or loss on the distribution of property to Gisela.

36. **LO.5** Blush Corporation owns long-term bonds (basis of $1.3 million) of its subsidiary, Brass Corporation, that were acquired at a discount. Upon liquidation of Brass pursuant to § 332, Blush receives a distribution of $1.5 million, the face amount of the bonds. Determine Blush Corporation's recognized gain or loss on the distribution.

37. **LO.5** Goose Corporation has a basis of $2.4 million in the stock of Swift Corporation, a wholly owned subsidiary acquired 30 years ago. Goose liquidates Swift Corporation and receives assets that are worth $2 million and have a basis to Swift of $1.7 million.

a.   Determine Goose Corporation's recognized gain or loss on the liquidation.

b.   Determine Goose Corporation's basis in the assets received in liquidation.

Problems

Critical Thinking   38. **LO.1, 2, 6** Teal Corporation, with E & P of $2,000,000, distributes property with a basis of $150,000 and a fair market value of $400,000 to Grace. She owns 15% of the outstanding Teal shares.

a.   What are the tax consequences to Teal Corporation and to Grace if the distribution is a nonqualified stock redemption?

b. What are the tax consequences in part (a) if Grace is a corporation?

c. What are the tax consequences to Teal Corporation and to Grace if the distribution is a qualifying stock redemption? Assume that Grace's basis in the redeemed shares is $90,000.

d. What are the tax consequences in part (c) if Grace is a corporation?

e. If the parties involved could choose from among the preceding options, which would they choose? Why?

39. **LO.1** Julio Gonzales is in the 32% tax bracket. He acquired 2,000 shares of stock in Gray Corporation seven years ago at a cost of $50 per share. In the current year, Julio received a payment of $150,000 from Gray Corporation in exchange for 1,000 of his shares in Gray. Gray has E & P of $1,000,000. What income tax liability would Julio incur on the $150,000 payment in each of the following situations? Assume that Julio has no capital losses.

a. The stock redemption qualifies for sale or exchange treatment.

b. The stock redemption does not qualify for sale or exchange treatment.

c. For part (b), prepare Julio's Schedule B (Form 1040) to reflect the tax reporting required of the transaction. Julio's Social Security number is 123-45-6789. Assume that Julio did not have an interest in or signature authority over any financial account in a foreign country; in addition, he did not have any relationship with a foreign trust.

40. **LO.1** How would your answer to parts (a) and (b) of Problem 39 differ if Julio were a corporate shareholder rather than an individual shareholder and the stock ownership in Gray Corporation represented a 25% interest?

41. **LO.1** Assume in Problem 39 that Julio has a capital loss carryover of $50,000 in the current tax year. Julio has no other capital gain transactions during the year. What amount of the capital loss may Julio deduct in the current year in the following situations?   **Critical Thinking**

a. The $150,000 payment from Gray Corporation is a qualifying stock redemption for tax purposes.

b. The $150,000 payment from Gray Corporation is a nonqualified stock redemption for tax purposes.

c. If Julio had the flexibility to structure the transaction as described in either part (a) or part (b), which form would he choose? Why?

42. **LO.1** How would your answer to parts (a) and (b) of Problem 41 differ if Julio were a corporate shareholder rather than an individual shareholder and the stock ownership in Gray Corporation represented a 25% interest?

43. **LO.1** Silver Corporation has 2,000 shares of common stock outstanding. Howard owns 600 shares, Howard's grandfather owns 300 shares, Howard's mother owns 300 shares, and Howard's son owns 100 shares. In addition, Maroon Corporation owns 500 shares. Howard owns 70% of the stock in Maroon Corporation.

a. Applying the § 318 stock attribution rules, how many shares does Howard own in Silver Corporation?

b. Assume that Howard owns only 40% of the stock in Maroon Corporation. How many shares does Howard own, directly and indirectly, in Silver Corporation?

c. Assume the same facts as in part (a) above, but in addition, Howard owns a 25% interest in Yellow Partnership. Yellow owns 200 shares in Silver Corporation. How many shares does Howard own, directly and indirectly, in Silver Corporation?

44. **LO.1** Shonda owns 1,000 of the 1,500 shares outstanding in Rook Corporation (E & P of $1,000,000). Shonda paid $50 per share for the stock seven years ago.

The remaining stock in Rook is owned by unrelated individuals. What are the tax consequences to Shonda in the following independent situations?

    a.   Rook Corporation redeems 450 shares of Shonda's stock for $225,000.

    b.   Rook Corporation redeems 600 shares of Shonda's stock for $300,000.

Communications
Critical Thinking

45. **LO.1, 2** Stork Corporation (E & P of $850,000) has 1,000 shares of common stock outstanding. The shares are owned by the following individuals: Lana Johnson, 400 shares; Lori Jones (Lana's mother), 200 shares; and Leo Jones (Lana's brother), 400 shares. Lana paid $200 per share for the Stork stock eight years ago. Lana is interested in reducing her stock ownership in Stork via a stock redemption for $1,000 per share, the fair market value of the stock. Stork Corporation would distribute cash for the entire redemption transaction. In late October, Lana inquired as to the minimum number of shares she would have to redeem to obtain favorable long-term capital gain treatment and the overall tax consequences of such a redemption to both her and Stork Corporation.

    a.   Prepare a letter to Lana (1000 Main Street, St. Paul, MN 55166) and a memo for the file in which you explain your conclusions.

    b.   Using Microsoft Excel (or a similar software program), create a spreadsheet template that computes the minimum shares that must be redeemed to qualify for a disproportionate redemption. For Microsoft Excel, use the Solver Add-in in your template.

46. **LO.1** Cyan Corporation (E & P of $700,000) has 4,000 shares of common stock outstanding. The shares are owned as follows: Angelica, 2,000 shares; Dean (Angelica's son), 1,500 shares; and Walter (Angelica's uncle), 500 shares. In the current year, Cyan redeems all of Angelica's shares. Determine whether the redemption can qualify for sale or exchange treatment under the complete termination redemption rules in each of the following independent circumstances.

    a.   Angelica remains as a director of Cyan Corporation.

    b.   Three years after the redemption, Angelica loans $100,000 to Cyan Corporation and receives in return a two-year note receivable.

    c.   Dean replaces Angelica as president of Cyan Corporation.

    d.   Six years after the redemption, Angelica receives 250 shares in Cyan as a gift from Walter.

47. **LO.1, 2** Robert and Lori (Robert's sister) own all of the stock in Swan Corporation (E & P of $1,000,000). Each owns 500 shares and has a basis of $85,000 in the shares. Robert wants to sell his stock for $600,000, the fair market value, but he will continue to be employed as an officer of Swan Corporation after the sale. Lori would like to purchase Robert's shares, becoming the sole shareholder in Swan, but Lori is short of funds. What are the tax consequences to Robert, Lori, and Swan Corporation under the following circumstances?

    a.   Swan Corporation distributes cash of $600,000 to Lori, and she uses the cash to purchase Robert's shares.

    b.   Swan Corporation redeems all of Robert's shares for $600,000.

48. **LO.1, 2** For the last eleven years, Lime Corporation has owned and operated four different trades or businesses. Lime also owns stock in several corporations that it purchased for investment purposes. The stock in Lime Corporation is held equally by Sultan, an individual, and by Turquoise Corporation. Both Sultan and Turquoise own 1,000 shares in Lime that were purchased nine years ago at a cost of $200 per share. Determine whether the following independent transactions qualify as partial liquidations under § 302(b)(4). In each transaction, determine the tax consequences to Lime Corporation, to Turquoise Corporation, and to Sultan.

    a.   Lime Corporation sells one of its trades or businesses (basis of $500,000, fair market value of $700,000) and distributes the proceeds equally to Sultan and Turquoise Corporation in redemption of 250 shares from each shareholder. Lime Corporation has E & P of $2,100,000 as of the date of the distribution.

b. Lime Corporation distributes the stock (basis of $425,000, fair market value of $700,000) it holds in other corporations to Sultan and Turquoise Corporation equally in redemption of 250 shares from each shareholder. Lime Corporation has E & P of $2,100,000 as of the date of the distribution.

49. **LO.1** The gross estate of Raul, decedent, includes stock in Iris Corporation (E & P of $8,000,000) valued at $6,000,000. At the time of his death, Raul owned 60% of the Iris stock outstanding and he had a basis of $840,000 in the stock. The death taxes and funeral and administration expenses related to Raul's estate amount to $2,000,000, and the adjusted gross estate is $16,000,000. The remainder of the Iris stock is owned by Monica, Raul's daughter and sole heir of his estate. What are the tax consequences to Raul's estate if Iris Corporation distributes $6,000,000 to the estate in redemption of all of its stock in the corporation?

50. **LO.1, 2** Broadbill Corporation (E & P of $650,000) has 1,000 shares of common stock outstanding. The shares are owned by the following individuals: Tammy, 300 shares; Yvette, 400 shares; and Jeremy, 300 shares. Each of the shareholders paid $50 per share for the Broadbill stock four years ago. In the current year, Broadbill Corporation distributes $75,000 to Tammy in redemption of 150 of her shares. Determine the tax consequences of the redemption to Tammy and to Broadbill under the following independent circumstances.
    a. Tammy and Jeremy are grandmother and grandson.
    b. The three shareholders are siblings.

51. **LO.2** Crane Corporation has 2,000 shares of stock outstanding. It redeems 500 shares for $370,000 when it has paid-in capital of $300,000 and E & P of $1,200,000. The redemption qualifies for sale or exchange treatment for the shareholder. Crane incurred $13,000 of accounting and legal fees in connection with the redemption transaction and $18,500 of interest expense on debt incurred to finance the redemption. What is the effect of the distribution on Crane Corporation's E & P? Also, what is the proper tax treatment of the redemption expenditures? Prepare a letter to the president of Crane Corporation (506 Wall Street, Winona, MN 55987) and a memo for the file in which you explain your conclusions.   *Communications*

52. **LO.3** Ramon and Sophie are the sole shareholders of Gull Corporation. Ramon and Sophie each have a basis of $100,000 in their 2,000 shares of Gull common stock. When its E & P was $700,000, Gull Corporation issued a preferred stock dividend on the common shares of Ramon and Sophie, giving each 1,000 shares of preferred stock with a par value of $100 per share. At the time of the stock dividend, fair market value of one share of common stock was $150 and fair market value of one share of preferred stock was $75.
    a. What are the tax consequences of the distribution to Ramon and Sophie?
    b. What are the tax consequences to Ramon if he later sells his preferred stock to Anthony for $75,000? Anthony is not related to Ramon.
    c. What are the tax consequences if, instead of Ramon selling the preferred stock to Anthony, Gull Corporation redeems the stock from Ramon for $75,000? Assume that Gull's E & P at the time of the redemption is $650,000.

53. **LO.1, 2, 4** Dove Corporation (E & P of $800,000) has 1,000 shares of stock outstanding. The shares are owned as follows: Julia, 600 shares; Maxine (Julia's sister), 300 shares; and Janine (Julia's daughter), 100 shares. Dove Corporation owns land (basis of $300,000, fair market value of $260,000) that it purchased as an investment seven years ago. Dove distributes the land to Julia in exchange for all of her shares in the corporation. Julia had a basis of $275,000 in the shares. What are the tax consequences for both Dove Corporation and Julia if the distribution is:
    a. A qualifying stock redemption?
    b. A liquidating distribution?

54. **LO.4** Pursuant to a complete liquidation, Oriole Corporation distributes to its shareholders land held for three years as an investment (adjusted basis of $250,000, fair market value of $490,000). The land is subject to a liability of $520,000.

    a. What are the tax consequences to Oriole Corporation on the distribution of the land?

    b. If the land is, instead, subject to a liability of $400,000, what are the tax consequences to Oriole on the distribution?

55. **LO.4** The stock of Mulberry Corporation is owned by Archana (60%) and Anar (40%), who are mother and daughter. Pursuant to a plan of complete liquidation adopted earlier in the current year, Mulberry distributes land worth $575,000 to Anar (basis of $100,000 in Mulberry stock). The land was purchased by Mulberry Corporation three years ago for $650,000, and it is distributed subject to a liability of $425,000. What amount of gain or loss is recognized by Mulberry Corporation and by Anar with respect to the distribution of the land?

56. **LO.4** Last year Lory Corporation, a land development company, acquired land and construction equipment from its sole shareholder in a § 351 transaction. At the time, the land had a basis of $790,000 and a fair market value of $650,000 and the equipment had a basis of $130,000 and a fair market value of $300,000. The assets were transferred to Lory Corporation for the purpose of developing the land and constructing a residential home community. However, the residential housing market suffered a steep decline in the current year, and as a result of financial difficulties, Lory Corporation was forced to sell its assets and liquidate. Pursuant to a plan of liquidation adopted during the year, Lory sold the land to an unrelated party for its current fair market value of $500,000. What amount of loss, if any, is recognized by Lory Corporation on the sale of the land?

57. **LO.4** Last year a shareholder transferred land (basis of $650,000, fair market value of $575,000) to Roadrunner Corporation in a § 351 transaction. This was the only property transferred to Roadrunner at that time. During the current year, Roadrunner Corporation adopted a plan of liquidation and distributed the land to Rhonda, a 15% shareholder. On the date of the distribution, the land had a fair market value of $400,000. Roadrunner Corporation never used the land for business purposes during the time it owned the property. What amount of loss may Roadrunner recognize on the distribution of the land?

Decision Making   58. **LO.4** Last year Pink Corporation acquired land and securities in a § 351 tax-free exchange. On the date of the transfer, the land had a basis of $720,000 and a fair market value of $1,000,000 and the securities had a basis of $110,000 and a fair market value of $250,000. Pink Corporation has two shareholders, Maria and Paul, unrelated individuals. Maria owns 85% of the stock in Pink Corporation, and Paul owns 15%. The corporation adopts a plan of liquidation in the current year. On this date, the value of the land has decreased to $500,000. What is the effect of each of the following on Pink Corporation? Which option should be selected?

    a. Distribute all of the land to Maria.

    b. Distribute all of the land to Paul.

    c. Distribute 85% of the land to Maria and 15% to Paul.

    d. Distribute 50% of the land to Maria and 50% to Paul.

    e. Sell the land and distribute the proceeds of $500,000 proportionately to Maria and to Paul.

Decision Making   59. **LO.4** Assume in Problem 58 that the land had a fair market value of $630,000 on the date of its transfer to Pink Corporation. On the date of the liquidation, the land's fair market value has decreased to $500,000. How would your answer to Problem 58 change if:

    a. All of the land is distributed to Maria?

    b. All of the land is distributed to Paul?

c.   The land is distributed 85% to Maria and 15% to Paul?

d.   The land is distributed 50% to Maria and 50% to Paul?

e.   The land is sold and the proceeds of $500,000 are distributed proportionately to Maria and to Paul?

60. **LO.4** Pursuant to a complete liquidation in the current year, Scarlet Corporation distributes to Jake land (basis of $425,000, fair market value of $390,000) that was purchased three years ago and held as an investment. The land is subject to a liability of $250,000. Jake, who owned 35% of the Scarlet Corporation shares outstanding, had a basis of $60,000 in the stock. What are the tax consequences of the liquidating distribution to Scarlet Corporation and to Jake?

61. **LO.4, 5** The stock of Magenta Corporation is owned by Fuchsia Corporation (95%) and Marta (5%). Magenta is liquidated in the current year, pursuant to a plan of liquidation adopted earlier in the year. In the liquidation, Magenta distributes various assets worth $950,000 (basis of $620,000) to Fuchsia (basis of $700,000 in Magenta stock) and a parcel of land worth $50,000 (basis of $75,000) to Marta (basis of $30,000 in Magenta stock). Assuming that the § 338 election is not made, what are the tax consequences of the liquidation to Magenta, Fuchsia, and Marta?

62. **LO.4, 5** The stock in Ivory Corporation is owned by Gold Corporation (80%) and Imelda (20%). Gold Corporation purchased its shares in Ivory nine years ago at a cost of $650,000, and Imelda purchased her shares in Ivory four years ago at a cost of $175,000. Ivory Corporation has the following assets that are distributed in complete liquidation:

	Adjusted Basis	Fair Market Value
Cash	$600,000	$600,000
Inventory	80,000	200,000
Equipment	350,000	200,000

a.   Assume that Ivory Corporation distributes the cash and inventory to Gold Corporation and the equipment to Imelda. What are the tax consequences of the distributions to Ivory Corporation, to Gold Corporation, and to Imelda?

b.   Assume that Ivory Corporation distributes the cash and equipment to Gold Corporation and the inventory to Imelda. What are the tax consequences of the distributions to Ivory Corporation, to Gold Corporation, and to Imelda?

63. **LO.5** Orange Corporation purchased bonds (basis of $350,000) of its wholly owned subsidiary, Green Corporation, at a discount. Upon liquidation of Green pursuant to § 332, Orange receives payment in the form of land worth $400,000, the face amount of the bonds. Green Corporation had a basis of $320,000 in the land. What are the tax consequences of this land transfer to Green Corporation and to Orange Corporation?

64. **LO.5** On July 20, 2018, Lilac Corporation purchased 25% of the Coffee Corporation stock outstanding. Lilac Corporation purchased an additional 40% of the stock in Coffee on March 22, 2019, and an additional 20% on May 2, 2019. On September 25, 2019, Lilac Corporation purchased the remaining 15% of Coffee Corporation stock outstanding. For purposes of the § 338 election, on what date does a qualified stock purchase occur? What is the due date for making the § 338 election?

65. **LO.5** On April 23, 2019, Auk Corporation acquires 100% of the outstanding stock of Amazon Corporation (E & P of $750,000) for $1,200,000. Amazon Corporation has assets with a fair market value of $1,400,000 (basis of $800,000), no liabilities, and no loss or tax credit carryovers. Auk Corporation files a timely

§ 338 election. Assume that both the aggregate deemed sale price (ADSP) and adjusted grossed-up basis (AGUB) are $1,306,329.

    a.   What are the tax consequences of the § 338 election to Amazon Corporation and to Auk Corporation?

    b.   Assume that Amazon Corporation is liquidated immediately following the § 338 election. What are the tax consequences of the liquidation to Amazon Corporation and to Auk Corporation?

Research Problems

THOMSON REUTERS
CHECKPOINT™

Note: Solutions to the Research Problems can be prepared by using the Thomson Reuters Checkpoint™ online tax research database, which accompanies this textbook. Solutions can also be prepared by using research materials found in a typical tax library.

Communications

Critical Thinking

Research Problem 1. Your firm has a new individual client, Carla Navarro, who has been assigned to you for preparation of the current year's tax return. Upon review of Carla's tax returns from prior years, you notice that she reported a large capital gain from a stock redemption in 2018. Upon further investigation, you determine that stock in the corporation was owned by some of Carla's family members at the time of the redemption and that the only way the redemption would have qualified for sale or exchange treatment would have been if Carla had availed herself of the family attribution waiver for a complete termination redemption. You establish that the redemption terminated Carla's direct stock ownership in the corporation, that she had no interest in the corporation since the redemption, and that she retained all records pertaining to the redemption. However, you cannot find any evidence that the notification agreement required of a family attribution waiver was properly filed. When asked about the missing agreement, Carla indicated that she knew nothing about any required agreement and that if such an agreement was required, her previous CPA should have taken care of it. Your partner has asked you to research whether it is still possible to file an effective family attribution waiver agreement for Carla. In a memo for the tax file, summarize the results of your research.

Critical Thinking

Research Problem 2. Tammy Olsen has owned 100% of the common stock of Green Corporation (basis of $75,000) since the corporation's formation in 2009. In 2016, when Green had E & P of $320,000, the corporation distributed to Tammy a nontaxable dividend of 500 shares of preferred stock (value of $100,000 on date of distribution) on her common stock interest (value of $400,000 on date of distribution). In 2017, Tammy donated the 500 shares of preferred stock to her favorite charity, State University. Tammy deducted $100,000, the fair market value of the stock on the date of the gift, as a charitable contribution on her 2017 income tax return. Tammy's adjusted gross income for 2017 was $420,000. Six months after the contribution, Green Corporation redeemed the preferred stock from State University for $100,000. Upon audit of Tammy's 2017 return, the IRS disallowed the entire deduction for the gift to State University, asserting that the preferred stock was § 306 stock and that § 170(e)(1)(A) precluded a deduction for contributions of such stock. What is the proper tax treatment for Tammy's contribution of Green Corporation preferred stock?

Partial list of research aids:
Reg. § 1.170a–4(b)(1).
§ 306(b)(4).

Research Problem 3. Shelly Zumaya (2220 East Hennepin Avenue, Minneapolis, MN 55413) is the president and sole shareholder of Kiwi Corporation (stock basis of $400,000). Incorporated in 2008, Kiwi Corporation's sole business has consisted of the purchase and resale of used farming equipment. In December 2017, Kiwi transferred its entire inventory (basis of $1,200,000) to Shelly in a transaction described by the parties as a sale. According to Shelly and collaborated by the minutes of the board of directors, the inventory was sold to her for the sum of $2,000,000, the fair market value of the inventory. The terms of the sale provided that Shelly would pay Kiwi Corporation the $2,000,000 at some future date. This debt obligation was not evidenced by a promissory note, and to date, Shelly has made no payments (principal or interest) on the obligation. The inventory transfer was not reported on Kiwi's 2017 tax return as either a sale or a distribution. After the transfer of the inventory to Shelly, Kiwi Corporation had no remaining assets and ceased to conduct any business. Kiwi did not formally liquidate under state law. On an audit of Kiwi Corporation's 2017 tax return, the IRS asserted that the transfer of inventory constituted a liquidation of Kiwi; as a result, the corporation recognized a gain on the liquidating distribution in the amount of $800,000 [$2,000,000 (fair market value) − $1,200,000 (inventory basis)]. Further, because Kiwi Corporation is devoid of assets, the IRS assessed the entire tax liability against Shelly, based on transferee liability. Finally, the IRS assessed a tax due from Shelly for her gain recognized in the purported liquidating distribution. Shelly has contacted you regarding the IRS's determination. Prepare a letter to Shelly Zumaya and a memo for the file, documenting your research.

Communications

Critical Thinking

Use internet tax resources to address the following questions. Look for reliable web-sites and blogs of the IRS and other government agencies, media outlets, businesses, tax professionals, academics, think tanks, and political outlets.

Research Problem 4. Stock buy-back (redemption) programs are a frequent occurrence among publicly traded corporations. Using the internet as your sole research source, find at least six publicly traded corporations that announced stock buy-back programs in 2018. What are some of the reasons noted by these corporations for the buy-back programs? Summarize your findings in an e-mail and send it to your instructor.

Communications

Research Problem 5. The requirements for effectively liquidating a corporate entity under state law vary from state to state. Using the internet as your sole research source, prepare an outline discussing how an entity incorporated in your home state is liquidated, including any reporting requirements associated with such liquidation.

Communications

Research Problem 6. Although the requirements for a § 332 parent-subsidiary liquidation are fairly straightforward, some planning and reporting issues must be addressed to ensure the proper outcome. Using the internet as your sole research source, prepare an outline discussing the general requirements for a § 332 parent-subsidiary liquidation, including any associated planning and reporting considerations.

Communications

Research Problem 7. Browse the internet sites of several public accounting firms, and find discussions comparing stock purchases with asset purchases when acquiring a business. Based solely on your findings, prepare an outline of the advantages and disadvantages of each form of acquisition.

Communications

Becker CPA Review Questions

1. Krol Corp. distributed marketable securities in redemption of its stock in a complete liquidation. On the date of distribution, these securities had a basis of $100,000 and a fair market value of $150,000. What gain does Krol have as a result of the distribution?

   a. $0

   b. $50,000 capital gain

   c. $50,000 § 1231 gain

   d. $50,000 ordinary gain

2. A corporation was completely liquidated and dissolved during year 14. The filing fees, professional fees, and other expenditures incurred in connection with the liquidation and dissolution are:

   a. Deductible in full by the dissolved corporation.

   b. Deductible by the shareholders and *not* by the corporation.

   c. Treated as capital losses by the corporation.

   d. Not deductible either by the corporation or shareholders.

3. Generally, in a direct distribution of assets to the shareholders that results in a complete corporate liquidation:

   a. There is no taxable event.

   b. The corporation recognizes no gain or loss because it transfers the assets to the shareholders at the corporation's basis immediately before the distribution.

   c. The shareholders recognize dividend income in the amount of the fair market value of property received.

   d. The shareholders recognize gain or loss to the extent the fair market value of the distributed assets differs from the adjusted basis of the stock.

4. Olinto Corp., an accrual basis calendar year C corporation, had no corporate shareholders when it liquidated in year 12. In cancellation of all their Olinto Corp. stock, each Olinto Corp. shareholder received in year 12 a liquidating distribution of $12,000 cash and land with a corporate tax basis of $15,000 and a fair market value of $20,500. Before the distribution, each shareholder's tax basis in Olinto Corp. stock was $16,500. What amount of gain should each Olinto Corp. shareholder recognize on the liquidating distribution?

   a. $0

   b. $10,500

   c. $4,000

   d. $16,000

Corporations: Reorganizations

LEARNING OBJECTIVES: *After completing Chapter 7, you should be able to:*

LO.1 Identify the general requirements of corporate reorganizations.

LO.2 Determine the tax consequences of a corporate reorganization.

LO.3 Explain the statutory requirements for the different types of reorganizations.

LO.4 Delineate the judicial and administrative conditions for a nontaxable corporate reorganization.

LO.5 Apply the rules pertaining to the carryover of tax attributes in a corporate reorganization.

LO.6 Structure corporate reorganizations to obtain the desired tax consequences.

CHAPTER OUTLINE

Structuring Acquisitions

Rock & Water Corporation (R&W) specializes in industrial park landscaping featuring rock walls, holding ponds, water fountains, and indigenous vegetation. One of R&W's central missions is to cause as little negative impact on the environment as possible. Until recently, R&W applied this policy only to its own work, but the new CEO, Tony Turner, wants to extend its corporate responsibility to its suppliers.

R&W uses several types of chemicals and fertilizers in its business and is aware that three of its suppliers do not use environmentally sound practices. Realizing that simply changing suppliers will not eliminate these problematic practices, R&W is considering acquiring these three suppliers. Using this strategy, R&W would control the production practices of these corporations.

R&W is unsure about how to structure these potential acquisitions of its suppliers and seeks your advice. R&W gives you the following information about these potential acquisitions.

- BrineCo is a profitable corporation that has been owned predominantly by the Adams family since its incorporation in 1990. It has virtually no debt because most of its assets date from its incorporation.

- AcidCo, started in 1997, has been having legal troubles and has continually been fined since more stringent EPA standards came into existence. Besides chemicals used by R&W, AcidCo produces acids for the mining industry. R&W is only interested in acquiring the landscaping chemical business.

- ChemCo is a new fertilizer producer with the technology to produce environmentally safe products. Its management is inexperienced, however, and the result has been inefficiencies in production and unintended harm to its surroundings. ChemCo has yet to show a profit.

How will you advise R&W to approach each of these acquisitions?

Read the chapter and formulate your response.

One tenet of U.S. tax policy is to encourage business development. Accordingly, the tax laws allow entities to form without taxation, assuming that certain requirements are met. As an extension of this policy, corporate restructurings are also favored with tax-free treatment. Corporations may engage in a variety of acquisitions, combinations, consolidations, and divisions tax-free, as long as the "reorganization" requirements in the Code are met.

Because the dollar value of most reorganizations is substantial, the tax implications are significant; thus, the tax law often dictates the form of the restructuring. The taxable gain for shareholders is likely to be treated as either a dividend or a capital gain. For individual shareholders, both qualified dividends and long-term capital gains are subject to beneficial tax rates. Corporate shareholders are allowed the dividends received deduction if reorganization gains are categorized as dividends. However, because corporations receive no tax rate reduction for capital gains, corporations involved in restructurings would be taxed at the 21 percent marginal rate on any gains classified as capital.

Careful reorganization planning can reduce or totally eliminate the possible current taxes for both the corporations and their shareholders. Consequently, when feasible, parties contemplating a corporate reorganization should obtain a letter ruling from the IRS determining the income tax effect of the transactions. Assuming that the parties proceed with the transactions as proposed in the ruling request, a favorable ruling provides, in effect, an insurance policy as to the tax treatment of the restructuring.[1]

7-1 REORGANIZATIONS—IN GENERAL

LO.1

Identify the general requirements of corporate reorganizations.

Although the term **reorganization** is commonly associated with a corporation in financial difficulty, for tax purposes, the term refers to any corporate restructuring that may be tax-free under § 368. To qualify as a tax-free reorganization, a corporate restructuring must meet not only the specific requirements of the tax Code but also several general requirements. These requirements include the following.

1. There must be a *plan of reorganization*.
2. The reorganization must meet the *continuity of interest* and the *continuity of business enterprise* tests provided in the Regulations.
3. The judicial doctrine of having a *sound business purpose* must be met.
4. The court-imposed *step transaction* doctrine should not be applicable.

All of these concepts are discussed in this chapter. The initial and most important consideration, however, is whether the reorganization qualifies for nonrecognition status under § 368.

7-1a Summary of the Different Types of Reorganizations

The tax law specifies seven corporate restructurings or *reorganizations* that will qualify as nontaxable exchanges. If the transaction fails to qualify as a reorganization, it will not receive the special tax-favored treatment. Therefore, a corporation considering a business reorganization must determine in advance whether the proposed transaction specifically falls within one of these seven types.

The Code states, in § 368(a)(1), that the term *reorganization* applies to any of the following.

A. A statutory merger or consolidation
B. The acquisition by a corporation of another using solely stock of each corporation (voting-stock-for-stock exchange)
C. The acquisition by a corporation of substantially all of the property of another corporation in exchange for voting stock (voting-stock-for-asset exchange)

---

[1] To expedite the letter ruling process, the IRS attempts to issue rulings within 10 weeks from the date of request. Rev.Proc. 2005–68, 2005–2 C.B. 694.

D. The transfer of all or part of a corporation's assets to another corporation when the original corporation's shareholders are in control of the new corporation immediately after the transfer (divisive exchange: spin-off, split-off, or split-up)

E. A recapitalization

F. A mere change in identity, form, or place of organization

G. A transfer by a corporation of all or a part of its assets to another corporation in a bankruptcy or receivership proceeding

These seven types of tax-free reorganizations typically are designated by their identifying letters: "Type A," "Type B," "Type C," etc. Each will be described in more detail later in the chapter.

7-1b **Summary of Tax Consequences in a Tax-Free Reorganization**

LO.2

Determine the tax consequences of a corporate reorganization.

The tax treatment for the parties involved in a tax-free reorganization almost parallels the treatment under the like-kind exchange provisions of § 1031. Unfortunately, the like-kind exchange provisions only apply to real estate and not to the exchange of stock or securities.[2]

Therefore, the general rule is that when an investor exchanges stock in one corporation for stock in another, the exchange is a taxable transaction. If the transaction qualifies as a reorganization under § 368, the tax treatment, in substance, is similar to a nontaxable exchange of real estate like-kind property. The four-column template of Concept Summary 7.1 is useful in computing the gain or loss recognized and the basis in the new stock received in a corporate reorganization.

Concept Summary 7.1

Gain and Basis Rules for Nontaxable Exchanges

(1) Realized Gain/Loss	(2) Recognized Gain (Not Loss)	(3) Postponed Gain/Loss	(4) Basis of New Asset
Amount realized − Basis of asset(s) surrendered	Lesser of boot received or gain realized	Realized gain/loss (column 1) − Recognized gain (column 2)	FMV of asset (stock) received − Postponed gain (column 3) or + Postponed loss (column 3)
Realized gain/loss	Recognized gain	Postponed gain/loss	Basis in new asset (stock)

EXAMPLE 1

Castel holds 1,000 shares of Lotus stock that were purchased for $6,000 several years ago. In a merger of Lotus into Blossom, Inc., Castel exchanges these 1,000 Lotus shares for 500 Blossom shares. The Lotus stock and the Blossom stock both are valued at $10,000. Assuming that this exchange qualifies for tax-free treatment under § 368, Castel's recognized gain and basis in the Blossom stock are computed as follows.

Realized Gain	Recognized Gain	Postponed Gain	Basis in Blossom Stock
$10,000	$−0−	$4,000	$10,000
−6,000			−4,000
$ 4,000			$ 6,000

The exchange of Castel's stock has no tax consequences for Lotus or Blossom.

---

[2]§ 1031(a)(2).

Gain or Loss

Corporations meeting the § 368 requirements do not recognize gains or losses on restructurings. However, recognition, and therefore taxation, occurs when other property is transferred by the acquiring corporation in the reorganization. **Other property**, also called **boot**, is any asset other than stock or securities exchanged in the reorganization.[3] If boot is transferred, gain but not loss may be recognized.

EXAMPLE 2

In a qualifying reorganization, Acquiring exchanges $800,000 of stock and land valued at $200,000 ($150,000 basis) for all of Target's assets, which have a value of $1,000,000 and a $600,000 basis. Due to the boot (land) it used in the transfer, Acquiring recognizes a $50,000 gain ($200,000 − $150,000) on the reorganization. If Target distributes the land to its shareholders, it does not recognize gain. If Target retains the land, however, it recognizes a gain to the extent of the *boot* received, $200,000.

Generally, the shareholders of corporations involved in a tax-free reorganization do not recognize gain or loss when exchanging their stock unless they receive boot in addition to stock. As demonstrated in Concept Summary 7.1, the gain recognized by the stockholder is the lesser of the boot received or the realized gain. This is analogous to the treatment of boot in a real estate like-kind exchange. The only instance when shareholders may recognize (deduct) losses in reorganizations is when they receive solely boot and no stock.

EXAMPLE 3

Kalla, the sole shareholder of Target in Example 2, has a $700,000 basis in her stock. She exchanges her Target stock for the $800,000 of Acquiring stock plus the land ($200,000) transferred by Acquiring to Target. The recognized gain for Kalla is the lesser of boot received (land, $200,000) or realized gain ($300,000). Thus, Kalla incurs a $200,000 recognized gain on the reorganization.

Realized Gain	Recognized Gain	Postponed Gain	Basis in Acquiring Stock
$1,000,000*	$200,000	$ 300,000	$800,000
−700,000	Boot	−200,000	−100,000
$ 300,000		$ 100,000	$700,000

*$800,000 Acquiring stock + $200,000 land.

Once the gain is recognized, its tax character must be determined. The following are the possibilities for gain characterization.

- The gain is taxed as a dividend to the extent of the shareholder's proportionate share of earnings and profits (E & P). The remaining gain generally is capital gain.
- If the requirements of § 302(b) can be met, the transaction is treated similar to a stock redemption, receiving capital gain treatment (see text Section 6-2).

The Big Picture

EXAMPLE 4

Return to the facts of *The Big Picture* on p. 7-1. R&W proceeds with its acquisition of BrineCo. Sam Adams acquired his 5% interest in BrineCo 15 years ago for $55,000. He exchanges his BrineCo stock for $50,000 cash and 2% of R&W's outstanding stock worth $100,000. At the time of the reorganization, BrineCo's E & P is $60,000. Sam's recognized gain and basis in the R&W stock are computed as follows.

continued

---

[3]§§ 361(a) and (b).

Realized Gain	Recognized Gain	Postponed Gain	Basis in R&W Stock
$150,000*	$50,000	$95,000	$100,000
−55,000	Boot	−50,000	−45,000
$ 95,000		$45,000	$ 55,000

*$100,000 R&W stock + $50,000 cash.

The first $3,000 ($60,000 BrineCo E & P × 5% ownership) of the $50,000 gain recognized by Sam is taxed as a dividend, and the remaining $47,000 is treated as a long-term capital gain.

Debt security holders receive treatment similar to shareholders. They recognize gain only when the principal (face) amount of the securities received is greater than the principal (face) amount of the securities surrendered. If securities are received and none are relinquished, gain will be recognized.

The term **security** is not defined in the Code or the Regulations. Generally, however, debt instruments with terms longer than 10 years (e.g., bonds) are treated as securities, and those with terms of 5 years or less (e.g., notes) are not. An exception to this general rule occurs when the debt instrument issued by the acquiring corporation is exchanged for target securities having the same term and/or maturity date.[4]

EXAMPLE 5

Addison holds a debt instrument from Hibiscus with a principal value of $10,000 and a maturity date of December 31, 2022. In connection with the merger of Hibiscus and Tea, Addison exchanges Hibiscus debt for a $10,000 Tea note that also matures on December 31, 2022. Even though the Tea notes do not have a term remaining of more than five years, they qualify for tax-free reorganization treatment because they have the same term as the Hibiscus security.

Assume, instead, that in exchange for the $10,000 debt instrument, Addison receives a note from Tea with a $15,000 principal value. Addison recognizes a $5,000 capital gain on the exchange. The basis in the Tea bond is $15,000 ($10,000 original basis + $5,000 gain recognized).

Basis

The assets transferred from the target corporation to the acquiring corporation retain their basis (called carryover basis). The acquiring corporation's carryover basis is increased by any gain recognized by the target corporation on the reorganization, as shown in Concept Summary 7.2.

EXAMPLE 6

Target exchanges its assets with a value of $5,000,000 and a $3,000,000 basis for $4,500,000 of Acquiring stock and $500,000 of land. Target does not distribute the land to its shareholders. Target recognizes a $500,000 gain on the reorganization due to the boot (land) not being distributed. Acquiring's basis in the assets received from Target is $3,500,000 [$3,000,000 (Target's basis) + $500,000 (Target's gain recognized)].

Concept Summary 7.2

Basis to Acquiring Corporation of Property Received

Target's basis in property transferred	$xx,xxx
Plus: Gain recognized by Target on the transaction	x,xxx
Equals: Basis of property to Acquiring corporation	$xx,xxx

[4]Rev.Rul. 2004–78, 2004–2 C.B. 108.

In a tax-free reorganization, the shareholder/bondholder starts with a tax basis in the stock and securities received that is equal to the basis of the stock and securities surrendered (called substituted basis). This basis is decreased by the fair market value of boot received and increased by the gain and/or dividend income recognized on the transaction.

Basis also may be computed using the Concept Summary 7.1 template. Using the template, the fair market value of the stock and securities received is reduced by the gain (or increased by the loss) postponed. This basis computation ensures that the postponed gain or loss is recognized when the new stock or securities are disposed of in a future taxable transaction.

Basis Computations

EXAMPLE 7

All of Quinn's Target stock is exchanged for Acquiring stock plus $3,000 cash. The exchange is pursuant to a tax-free reorganization. Quinn paid $10,000 for the Target stock two years ago. The Acquiring stock received by Quinn has a $12,000 fair market value. Quinn has a $5,000 realized gain, which is recognized to the extent of the boot received, $3,000. The basis in the Acquiring stock is $10,000.

Realized Gain	Recognized Gain	Postponed Gain	Basis in Acquiring Stock
$15,000*	$3,000	$5,000	$12,000
−10,000	Boot	−3,000	−2,000
$ 5,000		$2,000	$10,000

*$12,000 Acquiring stock + $3,000 cash.

EXAMPLE 8

Assume the same facts as in Example 7, except that Quinn's Target stock basis was $16,000. Quinn realizes a $1,000 loss on the exchange, none of which is recognized. The basis in the Acquiring stock is computed as follows.

Realized Gain	Recognized Loss	Postponed Loss	Basis in Acquiring Stock
$15,000*	$−0−	($1,000)	$12,000
−16,000		− 0	+ 1,000
($ 1,000)		($1,000)	$13,000

*$12,000 Acquiring stock + $3,000 cash.

7-2 TYPES OF TAX-FREE REORGANIZATIONS

 LO.3

Explain the statutory requirements for the different types of reorganizations.

Each of the seven reorganizations authorized by the Code has specific requirements that must be met in order to qualify for the benefits of nontaxable treatment. The following sections provide these requirements.

7-2a Type A

The "Type A" reorganizations can be classified as either mergers or consolidations. A **merger** is the union of two or more corporations, with one of the corporations retaining its corporate existence and absorbing the others. The other corporations cease to exist. A **consolidation** occurs when a new corporation is created to take the place of two or more corporations. The "Type A" reorganizations are illustrated in Exhibit 7.1. To qualify as a "Type A" reorganization, mergers and consolidations must comply with the requirements of foreign, state, and Federal statutes.[5]

---

[5] For example, the U.S. states generally control the definition of property rights; therefore, state law should be consulted for issues related to who holds title to assets, etc.

EXHIBIT 7.1 | "Type A" Reorganization

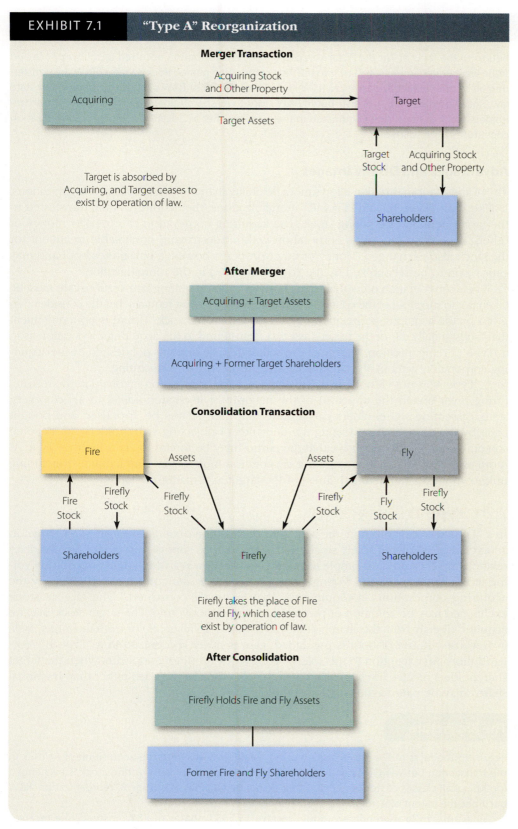

Merger Transaction

Acquiring Stock and Other Property

Target Assets

Target is absorbed by Acquiring, and Target ceases to exist by operation of law.

Target Stock

Acquiring Stock and Other Property

Shareholders

After Merger

Acquiring + Target Assets

Acquiring + Former Target Shareholders

Consolidation Transaction

Fire — Assets — Fly

Fire Stock | Firefly Stock | Firefly Stock | Firefly Stock | Fly Stock | Firefly Stock

Shareholders | Firefly | Shareholders

Firefly takes the place of Fire and Fly, which cease to exist by operation of law.

After Consolidation

Firefly Holds Fire and Fly Assets

Former Fire and Fly Shareholders

The Big Picture

EXAMPLE 9

Return to the facts of *The Big Picture* on p. 7-1. The R&W formation occurred as follows: Roca and Agua were united under state law into the new corporation named Rock & Water (R&W) by transferring all of their respective assets to R&W in exchange for all of R&W's stock. By operation of state law, Roca liquidated when it distributed R&W stock to its shareholders in exchange for the shareholders' stock in Roca. Agua liquidated in the same manner as Roca. This "Type A" reorganization constitutes a consolidation.

Advantages and Disadvantages

The "Type A" reorganization allows more flexibility than the other types of reorganizations. Unlike both "Type B" and "Type C" reorganizations, the acquiring stock transferred to the target need not be voting stock. The acquiring corporation can transfer money or other property to the target corporation without destroying nontaxable treatment for the stock also exchanged. Money or other property, however, constitutes boot and may cause gain to be recognized by the parties involved in the reorganization.

When consideration other than stock is given by the acquiring corporation, care must be taken not to run afoul of the continuity of interest test. This test requires that the consideration given by the acquiring corporation be at least 40 percent stock.[6] There is no requirement that "substantially all" of the target's assets be transferred to the acquiring corporation as in a "Type C" reorganization. The target can sell or dispose of assets not desired by the acquiring corporation without affecting the tax-free nature of the restructuring.

A "Type A" is not without its disadvantages. Each corporation involved in the restructuring must obtain the approval of the majority of its shareholders. In almost every state, dissenting shareholders can require that their shares be appraised and bought back by the corporation. Meeting the demands of objecting shareholders can become so cumbersome and expensive that the parties may be forced to abandon the "Type A" reorganization. Finally, the acquiring corporation must assume *all* liabilities (including unknown and contingent liabilities) of the target as a matter of state law.

7-2b Type B

In a "Type B" reorganization, the acquiring corporation obtains "control" of the target in an exchange involving solely stock. Both corporations survive, and a parent-subsidiary relationship is created. In simple terms, this transaction is an exchange of acquiring voting stock for target stock. Voting stock must be the *sole* consideration given by the acquiring corporation,[7] a requirement that is strictly construed.[8] The target's stock exchanged may be common or preferred, voting or nonvoting. The target stock may be acquired directly from the shareholders (as Exhibit 7.2 illustrates) or from the target itself.

Because the use of boot is precluded, gain is never recognized in a "Type B" reorganization. An exception to the solely voting stock requirement occurs when the target shareholders receive fractional shares of the acquiring stock. Cash rather than fractional shares may be paid to the target shareholders.[9]

The Big Picture

EXAMPLE 10

Return to the facts of *The Big Picture* on p. 7-1. R&W proceeds with the acquisition of AcidCo. In the transaction between R&W and AcidCo shareholders, 20% of R&W voting stock is exchanged for 90% of all classes of stock in AcidCo. The exchange qualifies as a "Type B" reorganization. R&W becomes the parent of AcidCo.

Gina, an AcidCo shareholder, should receive 15,555.5 shares of R&W. Instead, she receives 15,555 shares and $50. The receipt of the $50 does not disqualify the reorganization from receiving "Type B" treatment. Gina recognizes gain on the fractional share.

---

[6]Reg. 1.368–1(e)(2)(v), Ex.1.

[7]The exchange of the acquiring corporation's bonds for the target's bonds may be considered a separate and distinct transaction from a "Type B" reorganization. Rev.Rul. 98–10, 1998–1 C.B. 643. Consequently, this exchange will not affect an otherwise qualifying "Type B" reorganization.

[8]*A. S. Heverly v. Comm.*, 80–1 USTC ¶9322, 45 AFTR 2d 80–1122, 621 F.2d 1227 (CA–3, 1980), and *E. S. Chapman v. Comm.*, 80–1 USTC ¶9330, 45 AFTR 2d 80–1290, 618 F.2d 856 (CA–1, 1980).

[9]Rev.Rul. 66–365, 1966–2 C.B. 116.

EXHIBIT 7.2	"Type B" Reorganization

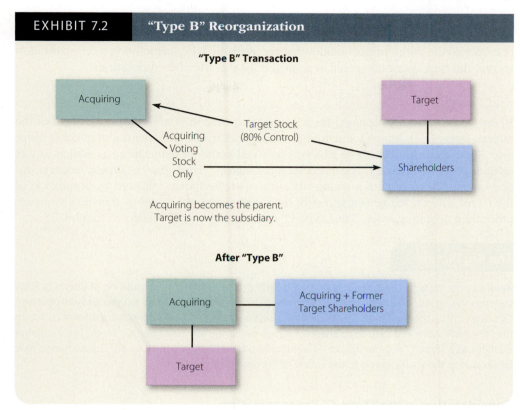

"Type B" Transaction

Acquiring becomes the parent.
Target is now the subsidiary.

After "Type B"

Control Requirements

In the "Type B" reorganization, the acquiring corporation must be in "control" of the target immediately after the reorganization. **Control** for this purpose requires owning at least 80 percent of all classes of the target's stock. The 80-percent-control-after-reorganization requirement does not mean that all 80 percent must be "acquired" in the restructuring transaction. Stock previously purchased in separate transactions can be counted in determining the 80 percent ownership.[10]

EXAMPLE

11

Acquiring purchased 30% of Target's stock for cash six years ago. It acquires another 55% in the current year by exchanging 10% of its voting stock with Target's shareholders. Thus, even though some of the Target shares were acquired with cash, the "Type B" requirements are satisfied through the current 55% exchange because Acquiring ends up with 85% of Target's stock.

What if Acquiring purchased 30% of Target's stock for cash three months ago? Now the acquisition of the additional 55% of Target's stock for voting stock seems to be part of a two-step transaction. The acquisition of the remaining stock for voting stock is probably not tax-free due to the step transaction doctrine.

Disadvantages and Advantages

The solely voting stock consideration requirement is a substantial disadvantage of the "Type B" reorganization. Another disadvantage is that if the acquiring corporation does not obtain 100 percent control of the target, problems may arise with the minority interest remaining in the target.

Nevertheless, the voting-stock-for-stock acquisition has the advantage of simplicity. Generally, the target shareholders act individually in transferring their stock to the acquiring corporation. Accordingly, the target itself and the acquiring corporation's shareholders are not directly involved.

---

[10]Reg. § 1.368–2(c).

Type A and Type B tax-free reorganizations often make sense and save corporations millions of dollars. However, they may not always be the best choice. It is important to consider all the different possibilities that are available when structuring a reorganization so that the best economic result is achieved for the affected corporations.

7-2c Type C

In the "Type C" reorganization, the acquiring corporation obtains substantially all of the target's assets in exchange for acquiring voting stock and a limited amount of other property. The target must distribute all assets received in the reorganization, as well as any of its own property retained. The target then liquidates.[11] Therefore, a "Type C" reorganization essentially consists of a voting-stock-for-assets exchange followed by liquidation of the target. The exchange is tax-free for the target shareholders unless they receive assets other than acquiring stock. The "Type C" reorganization is illustrated in Exhibit 7.3.

The Big Picture

EXAMPLE 12

Return to the facts of *The Big Picture* on p. 7-1. R&W proceeds with the acquisition of ChemCo. R&W transfers voting stock representing a 30% ownership interest to ChemCo for substantially all of Chem-Co's assets. After the exchange, ChemCo's only assets are cash and R&W voting stock. ChemCo distributes the R&W stock and cash to its shareholders in exchange for their ChemCo stock. The exchange qualifies as a "Type C" reorganization if ChemCo liquidates after the distribution. The exchange may be taxable to the shareholders to the extent of the cash they received.

Consideration in the "Type C" Reorganization

The acquiring corporation's consideration in a "Type C" reorganization normally consists of voting stock. However, there are exceptions. Cash and other property do not destroy a "Type C" reorganization if at least 80 percent of the fair market value of the target's gross property is obtained with voting stock.

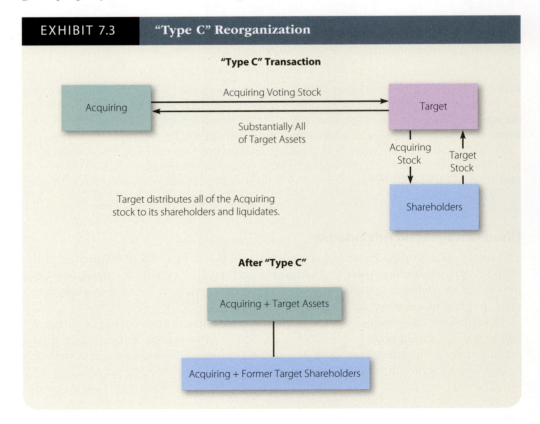

EXHIBIT 7.3   "Type C" Reorganization

---
[11]Distributions may be to creditors as well as to shareholders. § 368(a)(2)(G).

Although the acquiring corporation has more freedom in the consideration given in a "Type C" than in a "Type B," this freedom is not without a cost. When the acquiring corporation gives solely voting stock for target assets, the target's liabilities assumed by the acquiring corporation are not considered other property (i.e., not boot) in the exchange, and the 80-percent-of-property requirement is met.[12]

Target exchanges $850,000 of assets and a $250,000 liability for Acquiring stock worth $600,000. Target distributes the stock to its shareholders and liquidates. The transaction qualifies as a "Type C" reorganization. The liability is not treated as boot because Acquiring obtained 100% of Target's assets for voting stock.

Li bought all of the Target stock for $400,000 nine years ago. Li will not recognize a gain on the exchange because solely stock is received. Li's basis in the $600,000 of Acquiring stock will be a substituted basis of $400,000.

EXAMPLE 13

However, liabilities assumed by the acquiring corporation *are* treated as boot if the target receives any property other than acquiring's voting stock in the reorganization.[13] Target liabilities assumed by the acquiring corporation are likely to exceed 20 percent of the fair market value of the target assets acquired and, consequently, destroy the "Type C" reorganization.

Assume the same facts as in Example 13, except Target exchanged its $850,000 assets and a $250,000 liability for Acquiring stock worth $590,000 and $10,000 in cash. The liability now is considered boot because Target also received cash. The boot amounts to $260,000 ($250,000 liabilities + $10,000 cash), which exceeds 20% of the fair market value of Target's assets ($850,000 × 20% = $170,000). This transaction would not qualify as a "Type C" reorganization. Li recognizes a $200,000 gain on the exchange ($600,000 − $400,000).

EXAMPLE 14

As with a "Type B," the acquiring corporation's prior ownership of the target's stock will not prevent the transaction from qualifying as a "Type C" reorganization. If the acquiring corporation purchased stock in the target in an earlier unrelated transaction, the previously acquired stock will not be considered in determining whether 80 percent of the target's assets were obtained with the acquiring corporation's stock.[14]

Asset Transfers

The "Type C" reorganization requires that substantially all of the target corporation's assets be transferred to the acquiring. However, there is no statutory definition of "substantially all." To receive a favorable IRS ruling, the target must transfer to the acquiring corporation at least 90 percent of its net asset value and 70 percent of its gross asset value.[15]

"Type A" and "Type C" Reorganizations Compared

The outcome of a "Type C" reorganization and a "Type A" merger are similar, as can be seen by comparing the diagrams for these reorganizations (Exhibit 7.3 versus Exhibit 7.1). However, their requirements differ. A "Type C" has more restrictions regarding the consideration that may be used by the acquiring corporation.

Nevertheless, the "Type C" can be preferable to the "Type A": in the "Type C," the acquiring corporation assumes only the target liabilities for which it negotiates.

---

[12]§ 368(a)(1)(C).

[13]§ 368(a)(2)(B).

[14]Reg. § 1.368–2(d).

[15]Rev.Proc. 77–37, 1977–2 C.B. 568, amplified by Rev.Proc. 86–42, 1986–2 C.B. 722. Where 70% of the assets were transferred and 30% were retained

to discharge the target's liabilities prior to liquidation, the IRS found that substantially all of the assets were transferred. Rev.Rul. 57–518, 1957–2 C.B. 253.

Normally, the acquiring corporation in a "Type C" is not liable for unknown or contingent liabilities of the target.

7-2d Type D

The first three types of tax-free corporate reorganizations are designed for corporate combinations. The "Type D" reorganization is different; it is generally used to effect a corporate division, called a **divisive reorganization** . In contrast with other restructurings, the entity transferring assets in the "Type D" reorganization is considered the acquiring corporation, and the corporation receiving the property is the target.

A "Type D" reorganization also can be utilized to combine corporations. When combining, it is the larger corporation (acquiring) that is transferring its assets to the smaller corporation (target). This is sometimes called the "minnow swallowing the whale" because, after the restructuring, it is the smaller target that continues to exist and the larger acquiring that terminates. An acquisitive "Type D" reorganization is useful when the target corporation has a nontransferable license or right and therefore must be the entity that continues after the restructuring.

Divisive Type D Reorganization

Rather than combining, shareholders may divide the corporation by transferring its assets among two or more corporations. This might occur for many reasons, including antitrust problems, differing opinions among shareholders, product liability concerns, increasing shareholder value, and family tax planning. The more typical divisive "Type D" reorganization allows shareholders to accomplish their goals without incurring a current tax liability. In a divisive reorganization, one or more corporations (called New) are formed to receive part or all of the transferring (called Original) corporation's assets. In exchange for its assets, Original must receive New stock.

The remaining requirements for divisive "Type D" reorganizations are as follows.

- Stock received by Original must constitute control (80 percent) of New.
- Stock of New must be transferred to Original's shareholders.
- Both the assets transferred and the assets retained by Original must represent active businesses that were owned and conducted by Original for at least five years before the transfer.

Divisive "Type D" Reorganizations

EXAMPLE 15

Bell is a manufacturing corporation. It also owns investment securities. Bell transfers the investments to New Corporation and distributes the New stock to Bell's shareholders. The transaction does not qualify as a "Type D" reorganization; merely holding investments does not constitute a trade or business. The Bell shareholders are taxed on the stock they receive.

EXAMPLE 16

Jane and Ivan are the sole shareholders of WB. WB was organized 10 years ago and is actively engaged in manufacturing two products, widgets and bolts. Considerable friction has developed between Jane and Ivan, who now want to divide the business. Jane receives the assets used in manufacturing widgets, and Ivan continues manufacturing bolts. Dividing the business assets between the shareholders can be accomplished tax-free using one of the divisive "Type D" reorganizations.

Divisive "Type D" Reorganizations

EXAMPLE 17

Cube, Inc., has manufactured a single product at two plants for the past 10 years. It transfers one plant and related activities to a new corporation, Square, Inc. Cube then distributes the Square stock to its shareholders. Each plant's activities constitute a trade or business. The transaction qualifies as a "Type D" reorganization.

Spin-Offs, Split-Offs, and Split-Ups

The three types of divisive "Type D" reorganizations are spin-offs, split-offs, and split-ups.

- In a **spin-off**, New is formed to receive some of Original's assets in exchange for the New stock.[16] Original's shareholders receive the New stock without surrendering any of their Original stock. The shareholders' basis in their Original stock is allocated between the Original stock and the New stock, based on the relative fair market value of each.

- A **split-off** resembles a spin-off except that in a split-off, the shareholders surrender Original stock in exchange for the New stock. The stock basis is computed in the same manner as for a spin-off.

- In a **split-up**, two or more corporations are formed to receive substantially all of Original's assets. The stock of each New corporation is exchanged for Original stock and then Original liquidates. The shareholders' basis in the relinquished Original stock carries over as the basis of stock they receive in the New corporations.

The spin-off and split-off are illustrated in Exhibit 7.4, and the split-up is illustrated in Exhibit 7.5.

Spin-Offs, Split-Offs, and Split-Ups

EXAMPLE 18

Shawnee purchased 10% (500 shares) of OriginalCo eight years ago for $60,000. Before the **spin-off** reorganization, OriginalCo's stock value was $900,000, and Shawnee's shares were valued at $90,000, or $180 per share ($90,000 ÷ 500 shares). OriginalCo spins off 30% of its business assets into NewCo (fair value $270,000) and distributes 3,000 shares of NewCo stock to its shareholders. Shawnee's 300 NewCo shares are worth $27,000. After the spin-off, the value of OriginalCo is reduced to $630,000 ($900,000 × 70%); therefore, the value of Shawnee's stock in OriginalCo is $63,000 ($630,000 × 10%). Shawnee's $60,000 beginning basis in OriginalCo is allocated to the two companies' stock as follows: $18,000 to NewCo stock [$60,000 × ($27,000 / $90,000)] and $42,000 to OriginalCo stock [$60,000 × ($63,000 / $90,000)].

EXAMPLE 19

Assume the same facts as in Example 18, except that OriginalCo creates NewCo and FreshCo through a **split-up**. It transfers 30% of its assets to NewCo and the remaining assets to FreshCo for all of the stock in both corporations. Shawnee is required to surrender all of the OriginalCo stock (500 shares) to receive the 300 NewCo shares and 700 shares of FreshCo. Shawnee's NewCo stock is worth $27,000 ($90,000 × 30%), and the FreshCo stock is worth $63,000 ($90,000 × 70%). Shawnee's $60,000 beginning basis in OriginalCo is allocated to the two companies' stock as follows: $42,000 to the FreshCo stock [$60,000 × ($63,000 / $90,000)] and $18,000 to the NewCo shares [$60,000 × ($27,000 / $90,000)].

The Big Picture

EXAMPLE 20

Return to the facts of *The Big Picture* on p. 7-1. R&W proceeds with its acquisition of AcidCo. Gina and Gary are equal shareholders of AcidCo, which they organized six years ago with contributions of $300,000 each. To prepare for the restructuring transaction with R&W, AcidCo creates a new corporation, MineCo. Through a **split-off**, MineCo receives the mining business division, which is 40% of AcidCo's value. AcidCo retains all of the landscaping chemical business assets (60% of the corporate value). These are the assets that R&W wants.

continued

---

[16]Alternatively, an existing corporation can be the target in a divisive "Type D" reorganization.

The MineCo stock received in exchange for AcidCo's assets is transferred equally to Gary and Gina in exchange for 40% of their shares in AcidCo. Gina and Gary now are 100% owners of both AcidCo and MineCo. Gary and Gina have a basis in their AcidCo stock of $180,000 ($300,000 × 60%) and $120,000 in MineCo ($300,000 × 40%).

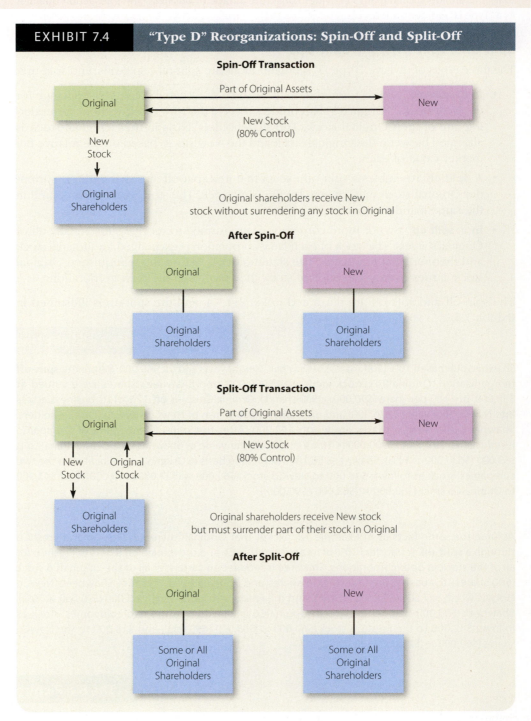

| EXHIBIT 7.4 | "Type D" Reorganizations: Spin-Off and Split-Off |

A summary of the advantages and disadvantages of the "Type A" through "Type D" reorganizations is found in Concept Summary 7.3.

7-2e Type E

The "Type E" reorganization is a **recapitalization**—a major change in the character and amount of outstanding capital stock, securities, or paid-in capital of a corporation. The

EXHIBIT 7.5	"Type D" Reorganization: Split-Up

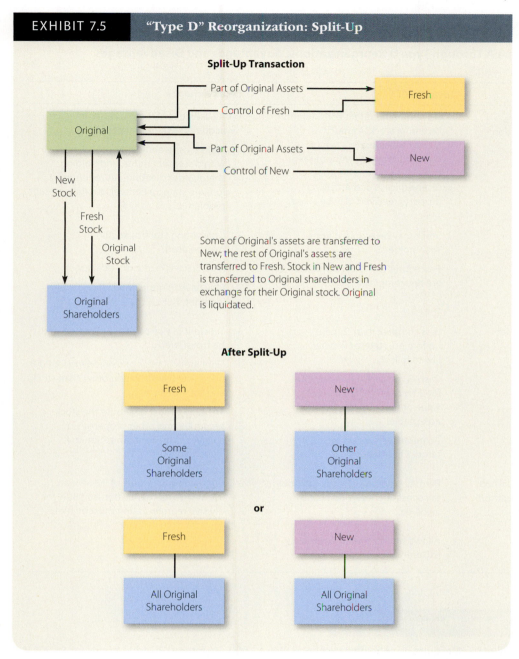

transaction is significant only for the stock- or bondholders who exchange their equity or securities. Because no property, stocks, or bonds are exchanged with another corporation, the "Type E" reorganization has no tax implications for the corporation involved. Further, transactions in a corporation's own stock or bonds are not taxable events to that corporation.[17]

The following types of exchanges qualify for nonrecognition treatment as "Type E" reorganizations: bonds for stock, stock for stock, and bonds for bonds. A corporation can exchange its common stock for preferred stock or its preferred stock for common stock tax-free. The exchange of bonds for other bonds is tax-free when the principal (face) amount of the debt received is not more than the surrendered debt's principal (face) amount.

[17]Reg. §§ 1.1032–1(a) and (c).

Concept Summary 7.3

Summary of Type A Through Type D Reorganizations: Advantages and Disadvantages

Reorganization	Type	Advantages	Disadvantages
A	Merger or consolidation	• No requirement that consideration be voting stock. As much as 60% of consideration can be cash and property without tax consequences for the stock received (cash and other property received may be taxed).	• All liabilities of target are assumed by acquiring as a matter of law. • Majority shareholder approval, dealing with dissenters' rights, and holding shareholder meetings, as required by foreign, state, or Federal law, may present problems.
B	Voting-stock-for-stock exchange	• Stock may be acquired from shareholders. • Procedures to effect reorganization are not complex.	• *Only* voting stock of acquiring may be used. • Must have 80% control of a target. • May have minority interest remaining in target.
C	Stock-for-assets exchange	• Less complex than "Type A"; no foreign, state, or Federal law to follow. • Cash or property consideration for 20% or less of fair market value of property transferred is acceptable. • Acquiring assumes only the target's liabilities that it chooses.	• *Substantially all* assets of the target must be transferred. • Liabilities count as *other property* for 20% rule if any consideration other than stock and liabilities is used. • The target must distribute the stock, securities, and other properties it receives in the reorganization to its shareholders.
D	Corporate division: spin-off, split-off, split-up	• Permits corporate division without tax consequences if no *boot* is involved.	• Control requirements of 50% for an acquisitive reorganization and 80% for a divisive reorganization must be met.
	Acquisitive	• Allows smaller target to retain its existence.	

"Type E" Reorganizations

EXAMPLE 21

All of the Mesquite bondholders exchange their $1,000, 3% interest-bearing bonds for $1,000, 4% interest-bearing bonds. This qualifies as a "Type E" reorganization because the surrendered bonds' face amount is equal to the face amount of the bonds received.

The Big Picture

EXAMPLE 22

Return to the facts of *The Big Picture* on p. 7-1. BrineCo's stock is owned by Gomez and Angel Adams (80%) and their two children Sam (5%) and Abigail (15%). The Adamses want to relinquish their corporate control to their children. The Adamses exchange their $2.4 million common voting stock for $2.4 million nonvoting preferred stock. The exchange qualifies as a "Type E" reorganization.

"Type E" Reorganizations

EXAMPLE 23

Cedar exchanges each of its $1,000 bonds for 10 shares of common stock worth $120 per share (10 × $120 = $1,200). This qualifies as a "Type E" reorganization, and no gain is recognized because the bonds are exchanged for stock. The bondholder's basis in the 10 shares of common stock is $1,000. The $200 built-in gain ($1,200 − $1,000) will be recognized when the stock is sold.

7-2f **Type F**

The "Type F" reorganization is "a mere change in identity, form, or place of organization . . . however effected."[18] Because "Type F" reorganizations involve only slight changes to a single operating corporation, the successor is the same corporation as its predecessor. Consequently, the tax characteristics of the predecessor carry over to the successor. A "Type F" reorganization neither jeopardizes the status of § 1244 stock nor terminates a valid S corporation election, unless such a termination is desired.

Conifer changes its name to Evergreen. This is a "Type F" reorganization. Evergreen is organized as an S corporation. Its shareholders want to revoke the S election. Changing from an S corporation to a C corporation also qualifies as a "Type F" reorganization.

7-2g **Type G**

Bankruptcy legislation introduced "Type G" reorganizations. In an acquisitive "Type G" restructuring, substantially all of the debtor corporation's assets are transferred to an acquiring corporation in exchange for its stock and securities. The stock and securities are distributed to the senior creditors in exchange for their claims against the debtor. To qualify for "Type G" treatment, the debtor must be insolvent before the reorganization and may be in Chapter 11 bankruptcy or a similar Federal or state court proceeding.

Like other reorganizations, the "Type G" must meet the judicial requirements explained in text Section 7-3. However, the continuity of interest test is more lenient here. When a corporation is insolvent, the creditors become the true owners of the corporate assets; thus, they should be the ones with the continuing interest in the insolvent corporation.[19] The former shareholders need not receive stock in the acquiring corporation for the restructuring to qualify as a "Type G" reorganization.[20]

It is likely in an insolvency that the debtor corporation will have most or all of its liabilities discharged. Ordinarily, discharge of indebtedness is income under § 61; however, § 108 precludes such treatment by allowing exclusion of such gain—with a price. First, the amount of the exclusion is limited to the degree to which the corporation is insolvent. Cancellation of debt (COD) in excess of the amount of insolvency is taxable. Then, the acquiring corporation must reduce certain tax attributes (generally credits or loss carryforwards) and depreciable property carried over from the bankrupt corporation to the extent of the excluded income.

The practical result of this reduction of attributes and basis in depreciable property is to provide more of a temporary deferral of COD income, rather than a permanent exclusion. The attributes must be reduced in the following order, unless the corporation elects to reduce its basis in any depreciable assets it receives from the bankrupt corporation first.[21]

- Net operating losses (NOLs).
- General business credits (GBCs).
- Minimum tax credits (MTCs).
- Capital loss carryovers.
- Basis in property.

Worthless files for Chapter 11 protection when its liabilities exceed its assets by $100,000. Worthless has a $60,000 NOL carryover and a $30,000 capital loss carryover at the time of its restructuring. Through a "Type G" reorganization, NewStart, Inc., becomes the successor to Worthless. NewStart must reduce the carryover attributes by $100,000. Consequently, NewStart has no NOL or capital loss carryovers from Worthless, and it must reduce the basis in the assets by $10,000 ($100,000 total COD relief − $60,000 NOL − $30,000 capital losses = $10,000 basis reduction).

---

[18]§ 368(a)(1)(F).

[19]*Helvering v. Alabama Asphaltic Limestone Co.*, 42–1 USTC ¶9245, 28 AFTR 567,62 S.Ct. 540 (USSC, 1942).

[20]PLR 8909007; Reg. § 1.368–1(e)(8), Example 10.

[21]Cancellation of debt (COD) income is the amount of debt forgiven by creditors that would constitute gross income if the corporation owing the debt were solvent. The COD income relief is the amount of debt forgiven that is not taxed due to the insolvency (i.e., to the extent that liabilities are greater than asset values) § 108(d)(3).

LO.4

Delineate the judicial and administrative conditions for a nontaxable corporate reorganization.

7-3 JUDICIAL DOCTRINES

Besides the statutory requirements for reorganizations, several judicially created doctrines have become basic requirements for tax-free treatment. In addition, a reorganization plan that is consistent with one of the Code reorganizations is required.

7-3a Sound Business Purpose

Even if the statutory reorganization requirements are literally followed, a transaction will not be tax-free unless it exhibits a **business purpose**.[22] The business purpose requirement restricts nonrecognition treatment to transactions that are motivated by valid corporate, rather than shareholder, purposes that go beyond tax avoidance.

In some cases, shareholder and corporate purposes may be so closely aligned that it may seem as though the reorganization is motivated by one or more shareholder purposes. In the event of such an alignment, the corporate purpose is deemed to be the motivation for the transaction.[23]

7-3b Continuity of Interest

The **continuity of interest** requirement prevents transactions that appear to be sales from qualifying as nontaxable reorganizations. Therefore, the continuity of interest test provides that if the shareholders have substantially the same investment after the restructuring as before, the transaction may qualify as a nontaxable event. To qualify for tax-favored status, the target corporation shareholders must receive an equity interest in the acquiring corporation.[24]

EXAMPLE 26

Okal owns 100% of Target. Target merges into Acquiring. Okal receives 1% of Acquiring's outstanding stock in exchange for all of his Target stock. The continuity of interest test is met; Okal received only stock for his interest in Target.

As indicated in the discussion for "Type A" reorganizations, the continuity of interest test is met when the target shareholders receive acquiring stock that is at least 40 percent of their prior target stock ownership. Not all target shareholders need to receive stock in the surviving corporation; the requirement is applied to the aggregate consideration given by the acquiring corporation.

EXAMPLE 27

Target merges into Acquiring pursuant to state statutes. Under the merger plan, Target's shareholders can elect to receive either cash or Acquiring stock. The shareholders holding 45% of Target's stock elect to receive cash; the remaining 55% receive Acquiring stock. This plan satisfies the continuity of interest test. The shareholders receiving cash are taxed on the transaction, and those receiving stock are not taxed.

7-3c Continuity of Business Enterprise

The **continuity of business enterprise** requirement ensures that tax-free reorganization treatment is limited to situations where there is a continuing interest in the target's business. Specifically, this test requires the acquiring corporation to either (1) continue the target's historic business (**historic business test**) or (2) use a significant portion of the target's assets in its business (**asset use test**). Continuing one of the target's significant

---

[22]Reg. §§ 1.368–1(c) and 1.355–2. See also *Gregory v. Helvering,* 35–1 USTC ¶9043, 14 AFTR 1191, 55 S.Ct. 266 (USSC, 1935).

[23]Reg. § 1.355–2(b) and *Comm. v. Marne S. Wilson,* 66–1 USTC ¶9103, 16 AFTR 2d 6030, 353 F.2d 184 (CA-9, 1966).

[24]*Pinellas Ice & Cold Storage v. Comm.,* 3 USTC ¶1023, 11 AFTR 1112, 53 S.Ct. 257 (USSC, 1933), *LeTulle v. Scofield,* 40–1 USTC ¶9150, 23 AFTR 789, 60 S.Ct. 313 (USSC, 1940), and Reg. §§ 1.368–1(b) and (c).

business lines satisfies the historic business test. Determining whether the acquiring corporation's use of the target's assets is "significant" is based on facts and circumstances.[25]

The continuity of interest and business doctrines apply to reorganizations that involve two or more corporations. When the reorganization involves only one corporation, the continuation of the interest or business is automatically met.

7-3d Step Transaction

The **step transaction** doctrine prevents taxpayers from engaging in a series of transactions for the purpose of obtaining tax benefits that are otherwise not allowed if the transaction was accomplished in a single step.

The step transaction doctrine is a problem for reorganizations such as a "Type C" and acquisitive "Type D," when the transferring corporation must transfer substantially all of its assets to the receiving corporation. If the transferring corporation attempts to dispose of its unwanted assets before a reorganization, the step transaction doctrine could ruin the reorganization's tax-favored status. The receiving corporation would have failed to obtain substantially all of the assets. Without direct evidence to the contrary, the IRS generally views any transactions occurring within one year of a reorganization as part of the restructuring.[26] The step transaction doctrine also may be an issue for "Type B" and "Type C" reorganizations when stock of the Target is purchased by the Acquiring in close proximity in time to a reorganization transaction.

---

[25]Reg. § 1.368–1(d).

[26]Reg. § 1.368–2(c), but in Rev.Rul. 69–48, 1969–1 C.B. 106, the IRS applied the step transaction doctrine to transactions that were 22 months apart.

> ### FINANCIAL DISCLOSURE INSIGHTS When an Acquisition Fails
>
> What happens when an acquisition is not as great of a deal as expected? Westinghouse Electric's Japanese nuclear business failure caused an approximately $6.4 billion goodwill write-down for its parent, Toshiba Co.
>
> When a corporation acquires another business, a value is determined for its net assets. If the price paid exceeds the value of the net assets, goodwill is recorded in the accounting records. The writing down of goodwill from the acquisition means that the expected value did not materialize; the acquirer overpaid for the target. In recent years, goodwill has been soaring due to the excess being paid in mergers and acquisitions. It accounts for more than 30 percent of net assets in S&P 500 companies.
>
> At least annually, firms are required to assess the value of their goodwill. If the existing book value cannot be supported, it must be written down through an impairment charge. Financial markets tend to discount the write-downs because they are a noncash charge. However, as with Toshiba, a huge write-down can indicate that management botched its valuation of the target and substantially overpaid for its acquisition. Over the last decade, the amount of goodwill has increased substantially, which may indicate that companies have been overpaying for acquisitions. This can lead to dramatic effects on the balance sheets and corporate earnings when the goodwill is considered impaired.

LO.5

Apply the rules pertaining to the carryover of tax attributes in a corporate reorganization.

7-4 TAX ATTRIBUTE CARRYOVERS

Some target corporation tax attributes (loss carryovers, tax credits, and E & P deficits) are welcomed by the successor corporation. Others may prove less desirable (positive E & P and assumption of liabilities). The mandatory carryover rules should be carefully considered in every corporate acquisition; they may, in fact, determine the form of the transaction.

7-4a Assumption of Liabilities

Because a reorganization must result in some continuation of the previous corporation's business activities, existing liabilities are rarely liquidated (a "Type G" reorganization is the exception). The acquiring corporation either assumes the target's liabilities or takes the target's assets subject to their liabilities. These liabilities generally are not considered boot when determining gain recognition for the corporations involved in the restructuring.

Liabilities are problematic only in the "Type C" reorganization, when the acquiring corporation transfers other property to the target as well as stock. In this situation, the liabilities are considered boot and, therefore, can cause a violation of the 80-percent-of-assets-for-voting-stock requirement.

7-4b Allowance of Carryovers

When a corporation acquires a target's property, it also acquires the target's tax attributes. Section 381 determines which of the target's tax benefits can be carried over to the successor. The "Type B," "Type E," and "Type F" reorganizations do not fall under the § 381 carryover rules because the original corporation remains intact and retains its own tax attributes.

A divisive "Type D" reorganization also is not subject to § 381. In a spin-off or split-off, the original entity retains its tax attributes, and the new corporation starts fresh with regard to its tax attributes (with the exception of E & P). In a split-up, on the other hand, the tax attributes of the original corporation disappear when it liquidates.

7-4c Net Operating Loss Carryovers

A target's NOL is one of the beneficial tax attributes (and sometimes its most valuable asset) that may be carried over to the acquiring corporation. Although the NOL cannot be carried back to a prior acquiring corporation tax year, it can be used prospectively. Thus, an NOL is valuable to the acquirer because it can offset future income of the combined successor corporation.

The Big Picture

Return to the facts of *The Big Picture* on p. 7-1. R&W proceeds with its acquisition of ChemCo. Prior to the merger, ChemCo accumulated a $3,000,000 NOL. After the reorganization, R&W generates $5,000,000 of taxable income. ChemCo's $3,000,000 NOL carries over to offset the $5,000,000 taxable income, reducing it to $2,000,000. R&W saves $750,000 in state and Federal income taxes by being able to utilize ChemCo's NOL carryover ($3,000,000 NOL carryover × 25% combined income tax rate). Accordingly, the $3,000,000 NOL is worth $750,000 to R&W.

EXAMPLE
28

Ownership Changes

To curtail the tax benefits received from NOL carryovers, § 382 limits the yearly NOL amount that may be utilized by the successor corporation. The **§ 382 limitation** applies when there is a more than 50-percentage-point **ownership change** (by value) for the target (loss) common shareholders. Whether an ownership change occurs is determined by examining the common stock ownership during the testing period, generally the three years prior to the date of the ownership change (change date).

Target, which holds a $100,000 NOL, merges into Acquiring under a plan where Target shareholders receive 40% of Acquiring's stock valued at $900,000. As a group, Target shareholders have experienced a more than 50-percentage-point ownership change. They went from owning 100% of Target to 40% of Acquiring (60-percentage-point change). The maximum annual use of Target's $100,000 NOL by Acquiring will be limited.

EXAMPLE
29

When an ownership change occurs, the yearly NOL amount usable by the successor corporation is restricted. The limit is based on the fair market value of the loss corporation's stock (both common and preferred) multiplied by the Federal **long-term tax-exempt rate**.[27] The stock received in a reorganization or the price paid for the loss corporation's stock generally indicates its fair market value.

The objective of the § 382 limitation is to restrict NOL use to a hypothetical future income stream based on what would be received if the stock was sold and the proceeds were invested in long-term tax-exempt securities. The formula for computing the § 382 limitation is:

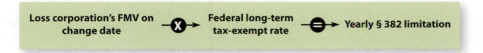

Loss corporation's FMV on change date **X** Federal long-term tax-exempt rate **=** Yearly § 382 limitation

Section 382 does not disallow an NOL; it merely limits the amount of NOL the successor corporation can use on an annual basis. In some cases, however, due to the § 382 limitation, the NOL may expire before it is utilized fully. Therefore, the effects of a § 382 limitation should be considered when determining the tax benefits the acquiring corporation receives from the target's NOL.

Because the NOL tax benefit may be the target's most valuable asset, a present value analysis is appropriate when determining the amount the acquiring corporation is willing to exchange for the NOL asset. Tax benefits received in future years are not worth as much as current tax benefits. The farther in the future the NOL deduction is taken, the less it is worth today. At some point, depending on the discount factor used, an NOL postponed to distant future years may be almost worthless today, in present value terms. Present value table excerpts are found in Appendix F of this text.

---

[27]Long-term tax-exempt rates are published quarterly in the Internal Revenue Bulletin (e.g., Rev.Rul. 2018–23, 2018–36 I.R.B. 405).

Value of an NOL

EXAMPLE 30

MakingIt acquires WashedUp in a transaction subjecting WashedUp's $600,000 NOL to a $40,000 per year § 382 limitation. After the acquisition, 15 years remain for deducting WashedUp's NOL. Given that MakingIt uses a discount factor of 6% for evaluating the benefit of possible transactions, the present value of a $40,000 deduction every year for the next 15 years, assuming a state and Federal corporate tax rate of 25%, is $97,122. Thus, MakingIt should not value the NOL for more than $97,122. Based on the time value of money, the NOL is worth much less than its face value!

$40,000 × 25% tax rate = $10,000 tax saving per year × 9.7122 (discount factor for present value of annuity for 15 years at a 6% discount rate) = $97,122 present value of NOL

EXAMPLE 31

Assume the same facts as Example 28, except that the § 382 yearly limitation is $120,000 rather than $40,000. Now the NOL can be fully deducted in 5 years rather than 15 years. Using the same discount factor (6%), the value of the NOL benefit to MakingIt increases significantly.

$120,000 × 25% tax rate = $30,000 tax savings per year × 4.2124 (discount factor for present value of annuity for 5 years at 6%) = $126,372

A further limitation on using NOL carryforwards arises in the year the ownership change occurs (change year). The NOL amount available to the successor in the change year is limited to the percentage of days remaining in the tax year after the change day. The § 382 yearly NOL limitation is multiplied by this percentage.

> **Yearly § 382 limitation**
> **× Number of days remaining in year/365 (366 in leap year)[28]**
> **= Initial year § 382 limitation**

Finally, the NOL carryover is disallowed for future taxable years if the successor fails to satisfy the continuity of the target's business enterprise requirement for at least two years following any ownership change.[29] This means that the target's historic business or asset use test must be met by the successor.

EXAMPLE 32

On December 1, Minus transfers all of its assets to Plus (a calendar year corporation) in exchange for 40% of Plus's stock. For the merger, Minus is valued at $900,000 and has an NOL carryover of $200,000. The long-term tax-exempt rate is 3%. Because a more than 50-percentage-point ownership change has occurred for Minus's shareholders, the amount of NOL available for use in the merger year is $2,219 [$900,000 × 3% = $27,000 × (30/365)]. The NOL available to reduce the successor corporation's taxable income in the next year is $27,000. If Plus fails to continue Minus's historic business or use a significant portion of its assets for a two-year period, Plus cannot use any of Minus's NOL.

7-4d **Earnings and Profits**

The E & P of an acquired corporation carries over to a successor corporation.[30] Thus, the positive E & P of the acquiring and target are added together and become the accumulated E & P for the successor. However, when the target has a negative E & P, the negative amount cannot be added to the acquirer's positive E & P.[31] Rather, the target deficit may be used only to offset E & P accumulated by the successor after the change date.[32]

---

[28]Reg. § 1.382–2T(f)(20).

[29]§ 382(c)(1).

[30]*Comm. v. Sansome*, 3 USTC ¶978, 11 AFTR 854, 60 F.2d 931 (CA–2, 1931), cert. den. 53 S.Ct. 291 (USSC, 1932).

[31]*Comm. v. Phipps*, 49–1 USTC ¶9204, 37 AFTR 827, 69 S.Ct. 616 (USSC, 1949).

[32]§ 381(c)(2) and Reg. § 1.381(c)(2)–1(a)(5).

The successor, therefore, must maintain two separate E & P accounts after the change date: one account contains the acquirer's positive accumulated E & P as of the change date, and the other contains the deficit transferred from the target plus the E & P accumulated since the change date. Dividends can be paid from the acquirer's positive pre-transfer E & P and from any post-transfer positive E & P balances.

In reality, many C corporations do not maintain up-to-date E & P accounts, and E & P is not tracked at the divisional level. An accurate calculation of E & P may require examination of all the tax returns of the acquirer or target from all prior periods to determine the correct accumulated E & P and account for any future distribution!

See Concept Summary 7.4 for a summary of E & P treatment in corporate reorganizations.

Concept Summary 7.4

Treatment of E & P Carried to Successor

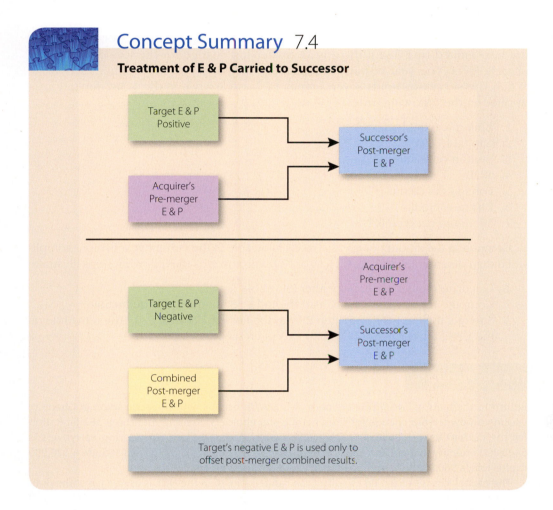

Target's negative E & P is used only to offset post-merger combined results.

Target is merged into Acquiring on December 31. On this date, the E & P balance for Target is a negative $75,000, and for Acquiring, it is a positive $400,000. In the next year, current E & P for the Succeeding Corporation is $50,000. Succeeding now has two E & P balances: pre-merger positive $400,000 and post-merger negative $25,000 ($50,000 − $75,000).

EXAMPLE 33

	Prior E & P Balance	Post E & P Balance
Current Year		
Acquiring	$400,000	
Target		($75,000)
Next Year		
Merged Succeeding		50,000
Ending Balances	$400,000	($25,000)

In corporate "Type D" divisions, the E & P of the original corporation is allocated among the newly created corporations and the original, based on the fair market values of each entity.[33]

Gaming distributes its computer gaming business to the newly created Compgame in a transaction qualifying as a "Type D" spin-off reorganization. Before the distribution, Gaming is worth $1,000,000 and its E & P balance is $300,000. After the spin-off, Gaming's value is $600,000, and Compgame's value is $400,000. Compgame starts with an E & P balance of $120,000 ($300,000 × $400,000/ $1,000,000), and Gaming retains an E & P balance of $180,000 ($300,000 − $120,000).

7-4e Other Carryovers

The capital losses and excess tax credits carried over to the successor corporation are also limited by § 382 if there is an ownership change for the loss corporation's shareholders. The year-of-transfer limitations also apply to these other carryovers. When the successor holds several types of loss carryovers, the § 382 limitation is applied in the following order.

1. Built-in capital losses
2. Capital losses
3. Built-in ordinary losses
4. NOLs
5. Foreign tax credits
6. Business credits
7. Minimum tax credits[34]

Computing the amount of excess credits allowable in the current year is more complicated than determining the capital loss or NOL carryover, as the following steps illustrate.

1. Calculate regular tax liability after allowable losses.
2. Compute regular tax liability as if the full § 382 limitation is deductible.
3. Subtract the tax liability in step 2 from the tax liability in step 1. The remainder is the § 382 limitation applicable to excess credits.

The Big Picture

EXAMPLE 35

Return to the facts of *The Big Picture* on p. 7-1. R&W proceeds with the acquisition of ChemCo, causing an ownership change for the ChemCo shareholders. Assume that the § 382 limitation for the current year is $150,000. The R&W taxable income before considering carryovers is $400,000 ordinary income and $100,000 capital gain. The ChemCo carryovers include a $20,000 capital loss, a $60,000 NOL, and $30,000 of excess business credits.

The capital loss is utilized first to offset the capital gain; then the NOL is used against the ordinary income. Taxable income becomes $420,000 [($100,000 − $20,000) + ($400,000 − $60,000)]. If the full § 382 limitation were utilized, taxable income for R&W becomes $350,000 [($400,000 + $100,000) − $150,000].

The benefit from all loss corporation carryovers taken in the current year cannot, in total, exceed the calculated yearly § 382 limitation. Nor can the loss carryovers exceed the year-of-transfer limitation.

A summary of the tax attribute carryover rules is provided in Concept Summary 7.5, and a comprehensive summary of corporate reorganizations is provided in Concept Summary 7.6.

[33]Reg. § 1.312–10.   [34]Reg. § 1.383–1(d).

Concept Summary 7.5

Summary of Carryover Rules

Tax attributes that carry over from a loss corporation to the successor corporation.

1. Loss carryovers—subject to the § 382 limitation.
   A. Annual limitations on carryover use are evoked when there is an ownership change—a more than 50-percentage-point change in ownership.
   B. Annual carryover usage cannot exceed the value of the old loss corporation on the change date (date of transfer) multiplied by the highest Federal long-term tax-exempt interest rate.
   C. Year of transfer. The loss claimed in the year of transfer is limited to the annual limitation multiplied by a percentage representing the remaining days in the year of transfer.
   D. Loss corporation carryovers are applied to the § 382 limitation in this order: built-in

capital losses, capital loss carryovers, built-in ordinary losses, NOL carryovers, foreign tax credits, business credit carryovers, and minimum tax credit carryovers.

2. Earnings and profits.
   A. Positive E & P of the target carries over to the acquirer.
   B. If either corporation has a deficit in E & P, the successor corporation will have two E & P accounts. One account contains the total positive accumulated E & P as of the date of the transfer. The other contains the total deficit as of the date of the transfer. Future positive E & P may offset the deficit E & P account.

3. Other tax attributes.
   A. Depreciation and cost recovery methods carry over.
   B. The installment method of reporting carries over.

Concept Summary 7.6

Comprehensive Summary of Corporate Reorganizations

Reorganization Type	Type of Consideration	Amount of Stock Ownership	Carryover of Tax Attributes	Treatment of E & P	Resulting Corporation(s)
"Type A" merger	Stock, cash, and property	At least 40% continuing interest by target shareholders	Yes	Combine if positive	Acquiring corporation continues, and target ceases to exist.
"Type A" consolidation	Stock, cash, and property	At least 40% continuing interest by contributing corporations' shareholders	Yes	Combine if positive	New corporation continues, and contributing corporations cease to exist.
"Type B"	Solely voting stock	At least 80% control of target	No, remain with target	Remains with target	Parent-subsidiary relationship
"Type C"	Voting stock and limited other cash and property	At least 80% of target assets acquired with voting stock	Yes	Combine if positive	Acquiring continues, and target corporation ceases to exist.
"Type D" divisive	Assets of distributing corporation	At least 80% control of targets	No, remain with original	Allocate among entities	Original and targets continue except for split-up; only targets continue.
"Type E"	Stock for stock Bonds for bonds Bonds for stock	N/A	Yes	N/A	Original continues.
"Type F"	N/A	N/A	Yes	Carries over	Old original continues as new corporation.
"Type G"	Stock	At least 40% continuing interest by creditors	Yes	N/A	Acquiring corporation continues, and debtor corporation ceases to exist.

LO.6

Structure corporate reorganizations to obtain the desired tax consequences.

7-5 **TAX PLANNING**

Reorganizations are valuable tools in corporate tax-free restructurings. However, it may not be possible to achieve the desired corporate structure by utilizing a single reorganization type. For this reason, reorganizations should not be seen as mutually exclusive transactions; they can be combined with other tax-favored transactions into a comprehensive plan.

7-5a **Assessing the Possible Benefits of Restructuring Options**

The tax law allows a series of tax-favored transactions to be recognized as legitimate separate steps when the statutory requirements for each are met. Thus, the step transaction doctrine can be used to facilitate the tax treatment desired by the taxpayer.

EXAMPLE 36

Black operates two businesses, both of which have been in existence for five years. One business is a manufacturing operation; the other is a wholesale distributorship. White wants to acquire only the manufacturing business and refuses to acquire all of Black's assets.

What course of action might be advisable to transfer the manufacturing operation from Black to White with the least, if any, tax costs? Compare the following three possibilities.

1. Black transfers the manufacturing operation to White in return for 51 percent of White's stock.
2. Black forms Orange and transfers the manufacturing business to it in return for all of Orange's stock. The Orange stock is then distributed to Black's shareholders. This portion of the arrangement is a nontaxable spin-off. Orange now transfers the manufacturing operation to White in exchange for 51 percent of White's stock.
3. Rather than transferring the manufacturing business as described in possibility 2, Black transfers the wholesale distributorship to Orange. White exchanges 51 percent of its voting stock for the Black stock. Black is now a subsidiary of White.

Possibility 1 probably will not fit within the definition of a "Type C" reorganization because Black does not transfer substantially all of its assets in return for White stock. The manufacturing operation is transferred, but the wholesale distributorship is not. As a result, Black continues to exist. It cannot qualify as a "Type A" reorganization either, because the target must liquidate after the reorganization.

Possibility 2 is a spin-off of the assets *desired* by White, followed by a "Type C" reorganization between Orange and White. This approach is acceptable to the IRS even though White does not acquire "substantially all" of Black's assets. The transaction is treated as successfully creating a separate corporation (Orange) through a "Type D" reorganization. The "Type C" is considered to be only between White and Orange. Black is not a party to the latter reorganization.[35]

Possibility 3 follows a different approach. It starts with the spin-off of the *unwanted* assets and concludes with White obtaining the *wanted* assets by exchanging 51 percent of its stock for the Black stock. Taken by itself, this last step satisfies the

---

[35]Rev.Rul. 2003–79, I.R.B. 2003–29.

voting-stock-for-stock requirement of a "Type B" reorganization. If, however, the step transaction doctrine is applied and the spin-off is disregarded, the Orange stock distributed to Black's shareholders might be considered as property *other than voting stock* in White. The IRS has not chosen to take this position and probably will recognize the nontaxability of a spin-off of *unwanted* assets followed by a "Type B" reorganization.[36]

Carryover Considerations

Careful consideration of the restructuring alternatives can help preserve desirable tax carryover attributes.

Acquiring wants to obtain the assets of Target. These assets have a $600,000 basis to Target and a $500,000 fair market value. Target has incurred losses in its operations during the past several years and possesses a $150,000 NOL, with 15 years of carryover remaining. Acquiring plans to continue the business conducted by Target, hoping to do so on a profitable basis.

EXAMPLE
37

To accomplish the planned acquisition of Target's assets, Acquiring could consider the following alternatives.

1. Using cash and/or other property, Acquiring purchases the assets directly from Target. Following the purchase, Target liquidates and distributes the cash and/or property to its shareholders.
2. Utilizing a "Type A" or "Type C" reorganization, Target merges into Acquiring. In exchange for their stock, Target shareholders receive stock in Acquiring.

A satisfactory solution must center around the preservation of Target's favorable tax attributes—the high basis in the assets and the NOL carryover. Alternative 1 is highly unsatisfactory. It will not retain Target's favorable tax attributes. The purchase price (probably $500,000) becomes the basis of the assets in the hands of Acquiring. Further, any unused NOLs disappear upon Target's liquidation. Target incurs a realized loss of $100,000 [$600,000 (basis in the assets) − $500,000 (sale proceeds)] from the sale of its assets. Yet the realized loss may generate little, if any, tax savings to Target. In view of Target's unabsorbed NOL carryover, it appears doubtful that the company will generate much taxable income in the year of sale.

Alternative 2, using a "Type A" or "Type C" reorganization, appears to be a better result. Presuming that Acquiring can establish a business purpose for the reorganization, the beneficial tax attributes of Target are preserved for Acquiring. The preservation of favorable tax attributes, such as the NOL carryover, should be considered when acquiring a small corporation.

How much should Acquiring offer for Target in Alternative 2? By preserving the NOL tax attribute, Acquiring is obtaining a value greater than the fair market value of the assets of $500,000. Assume the following facts.

- The Federal long-term interest rate is 3 percent.
- Acquiring earns a 6 percent after-tax rate of return.
- Acquiring's marginal state and Federal income tax rate is 25 percent for all years involved.

---

[36]Rev.Rul. 70–434, 1970–2 C.B. 83.

The § 382 limitation would allow Acquiring to utilize $15,000 of the NOL each year ($500,000 × 3%). Thus, it would take Acquiring 10 years to utilize the NOL ($150,000 ÷ $15,000).

$$\$15,000 \times 25\% = \$3,750 \text{ tax benefit} \times 7.3601 \text{ factor (10-year annuity at 6\%)}$$
$$= \$27,600 \text{ present value of NOL}$$

Therefore, Acquiring should not pay more than $27,600 for the NOL.

REFOCUS ON THE BIG PICTURE

STRUCTURING ACQUISITIONS

Rock & Water Corporation (R&W) wants to acquire three of its suppliers. The first is BrineCo, a profitable corporation owned by the Adams family since its incorporation, which has virtually no debt. Senior Adams family members are ready to retire, and the younger generation has no interest in the business. Consequently, all members would like some cash in the transaction. The "Type A" reorganization allows R&W to exchange cash and stock for those assets it wants to acquire. Acquiring BrineCo's few liabilities will not be an issue, nor will obtaining the approval of the BrineCo shareholders. All assets not transferred to R&W, plus the stock and cash received from R&W, are distributed to the Adams family in complete liquidation of BrineCo.

The next target, AcidCo, is struggling financially and legally. Because its lines of business are active and have existed for more than five years, AcidCo can, through a divisive "Type D" reorganization, spin off or split off its mining acid business and retain the landscaping chemical line for the transaction with R&W. The AcidCo shareholders exchange their stock for R&W voting stock in a "Type B" reorganization. This restructuring protects R&W's assets from AcidCo's legal liability issues.

Finally, ChemCo's inexperienced management team has yet to turn a profit. R&W uses a "Type C" reorganization to acquire substantially all of ChemCo's assets, and it selects which liabilities it assumes. To avoid having the liability assumption treated as boot, R&W uses solely voting stock for the exchange. ChemCo terminates after the reorganization. Given that ChemCo holds beneficial tax carryovers, R&W must meet the continuity of business enterprise requirement for at least two years.

The § 382 limitation applies because ChemCo shareholders experience a greater than 50-percentage-point ownership change. R&W performs a net present value analysis to determine what it is willing to pay for ChemCo's tax attributes. R&W now keeps two E & P accounts: one for its pre-merger E & P and another with ChemCo's negative E & P. Only the latter is offset by future profits of the combined company.

Key Terms

Asset use test, 7-18

Boot, 7-4

Business purpose, 7-18

Consolidation, 7-6

Continuity of business enterprise, 7-18

Continuity of interest, 7-18

Control, 7-9

Divisive reorganization, 7-12

Historic business test, 7-18

Long-term tax-exempt rate, 7-21

Merger, 7-6

Other property, 7-4

Ownership change, 7-21

Recapitalization, 7-14

Reorganization, 7-2

Section 382 limitation, 7-21

Security, 7-5

Spin-off, 7-13

Split-off, 7-13

Split-up, 7-13

Step transaction, 7-19

Discussion Questions

1. **LO.1** Explain why a private letter ruling from the IRS is like an insurance policy for a corporate reorganization.

2. **LO.2** How is the four-column template in Concept Summary 7.1 used to determine a shareholder's basis in the stock received in a corporate restructuring?

3. **LO.3** What is the difference between a "Type A" merger and a "Type A" consolidation?

4. **LO.3** Explain the stock and control requirements in a "Type B" reorganization. After a "Type B" reorganization, what is the relationship between the corporations participating in the restructuring?

5. **LO.3** What advantage does a "Type C" reorganization have over a "Type A" reorganization with regard to transferred liabilities? What disadvantage does a "Type C" reorganization have over a "Type A" reorganization with regard to transferred liabilities? — *Critical Thinking*

6. **LO.3** What is the difference between a split-up, a split-off, and a spin-off?

7. **LO.4** Briefly describe the judicial doctrines of sound business purpose, continuity of business enterprise, and the step transaction doctrine.

8. **LO.3** Explain what a corporation is trying to accomplish when using a "Type E" reorganization. When using a "Type F" reorganization. — *Critical Thinking*

9. **LO.5** Explain how the earnings and profits (E & P) of the acquired corporation are treated by the successor corporation when the E & P balance is positive. When the E & P balance is negative. How are earnings and profits treated in a divisive "Type D" reorganization?

10. **LO.5, 6** Why should the acquiring corporation perform present value calculations when it is planning to merge with a target holding business credit carryforwards?

11. **LO.5** AndyCo acquires DrewCo in a merger, becoming AndrewCo. AndyCo has $1,000,000 in positive accumulated E & P before the merger, and DrewCo has negative accumulated E & P of $400,000 before the merger.

    AndrewCo wants to make a distribution to its shareholders after the end of its first year. How much of the distribution is treated as a dividend if AndrewCo expects to have minimal negative current E & P at the end of its first year?

Computational Exercises

12. **LO.2** Rebecca holds 100 shares of Gotchas stock that she purchased for $1,000 several years ago. In a merger of Gotchas into Solis, Inc., Rebecca exchanges her 100 Gotchas shares for 1,000 Solis shares and $500. Gotchas is valued at $40.00 per share and Solis at $3.50 per share. Prepare your solution using spreadsheet software such as Microsoft Excel.

    a.   What is Rebecca's realized and recognized gain/loss from the reorganization?

    b.   What is Rebecca's basis in her Solis stock?

13. **LO.2** In a qualifying reorganization, Cato exchanges $1,200,000 worth of stock and property valued at $500,000 ($245,000 basis) for all of Firestar's assets, which have a value of $1,700,000 and a $500,000 basis. Firestar distributes the property received from Cato. The exchange meets the § 368 requirements.

    a.   What is Cato's recognized gain/loss from the reorganization?

    b.   What is Firestar's recognized gain/loss from the reorganization?

14. **LO.2** Townsend, the sole shareholder of Pruett Corporation, has a $480,000 basis in his stock. He exchanges his Pruett stock for $600,000 of Rogers voting common stock plus land with a fair market value of $100,000 and basis of $25,000 that is transferred by Rogers to Pruett. This exchange qualifies under § 368.

    a.   What is Townsend's recognized gain/loss from the reorganization? Prepare your solution using spreadsheet software such as Microsoft Excel.

    b.   What is the gain/loss recognized by Pruett Corporation and Rogers Corporation on the reorganization?

    c.   What is Townsend's basis in the Rogers stock and the land received?

15. **LO.2** Hosha exchanges all of her Leaf stock for Petal stock plus $5,000 cash. The exchange is pursuant to a tax-free reorganization. Hosha paid $25,000 for the Leaf stock five years ago. The Petal stock received by Hosha has an $18,000 fair market value.

    a.   What is Hosha's realized and recognized gain/loss from the reorganization? Prepare your solution using spreadsheet software such as Microsoft Excel.

    b.   What is Hosha's basis in the Petal stock she received?

16. **LO.5** Whitney Corporation acquires Jessamine Corporation. Prior to the merger, Jessamine accumulated a $12 million NOL. After the reorganization, Whitney generates $30 million of taxable income. Whitney is subject to a marginal state and Federal tax rate of 25%; the § 382 limitation does not apply.

    How much does Whitney Corporation save in Federal income taxes by being able to utilize Jessamine's NOL carryover?

17. **LO.5** Park Corporation distributes its shoe manufacturing line of business to the newly created ShoeBiz Corporation in a transaction qualifying as a "Type D" spin-off reorganization. Before the distribution, Park is worth $4,000,000 and its E & P balance is $630,000. After the spin-off, Park's value is $3,000,000 and ShoeBiz's value is $1,000,000.

    After the "Type D" reorganization, what is the E & P balance for ShoeBiz and for Park?

18. **LO.3** Determine whether the following transactions are taxable. If a transaction is not taxable, indicate what type of reorganization is effected, if any.

    a. Alpha Corporation owns assets valued at $400,000 and liabilities of $100,000. Beta Corporation transfers $160,000 of its voting stock and $40,000 in cash for 75% of Alpha's assets and all of its liabilities. Alpha distributes its remaining assets and the Beta stock to its shareholders. Alpha then liquidates. *[handwritten: 40,000 boot merger]*

    b. Beta Corporation owns assets valued at $1,500,000 with liabilities of $700,000, and Alpha holds assets valued at $350,000 with liabilities of $150,000. Beta transfers 200,000 shares of stock and $50,000 cash, and it accepts $100,000 of Alpha's liabilities, in exchange for all of the Alpha assets. Alpha distributes the Beta stock to its shareholders for their Alpha stock and then ceases to exist. *[handwritten: NOT type A]*

    c. Alpha Corporation obtained 200,000 shares of Beta Corporation's stock 10 years ago. In the current year, Alpha exchanges 40% of its stock for 500,000 of the remaining 600,000 shares of Beta stock. After the transaction, Alpha owns 700,000 of the 800,000 Beta shares outstanding. *[handwritten: Not type A]*

    d. Alpha Corporation has two divisions that have been in existence for seven years. The nail division has assets valued at $500,000 and liabilities of $120,000, whereas the hammer division has assets valued at $645,000 and liabilities of $25,000. Alpha would like the two divisions to be separate corporations. It creates Beta Corporation and transfers all of the hammer division assets and liabilities in exchange for 100% of Beta's stock. Alpha then distributes the Beta stock to its shareholders.

    e. Alpha Corporation owns assets valued at $750,000 with liabilities of $230,000, and Beta holds assets valued at $1,500,000 with liabilities of $500,000. Beta transfers 33% of its stock for $700,000 of Alpha's assets and $200,000 of its liabilities. Alpha distributes the Beta stock and its remaining assets and liabilities to its shareholders in exchange for their stock in Alpha. Alpha then terminates.

    f. Beta Corporation has not been able to pay its creditors in the last year. To avoid foreclosure, Beta transfers its assets valued at $650,000 and liabilities of $700,000 to a new corporation, Alpha, Inc., in accordance with a state court proceeding. The creditors receive shares of Alpha voting stock valued at $300,000 and cancel the outstanding debt. The former Beta shareholders receive the remaining shares in Alpha.

19. **LO.2** Cornell purchased a 15-year, $50,000 bond from Fulvous Corporation for $20,000 eight years ago. Interest of $2,300 has been amortized over the eight years and added to Cornell's bond basis. In the current year, Fulvous is acquired by Glaucous in a "Type A" reorganization. Cornell exchanges his Fulvous bond for a 7-year, $55,000 Glaucous bond. How does Cornell treat this exchange for Federal income tax purposes? Prepare your solution using spreadsheet software such as Microsoft Excel.

20. **LO.2** Citron enters into a "Type C" restructuring with Ecru. Ecru transfers $800,000 of its voting stock for Citron's $1,500,000 (basis $600,000) and $700,000 liabilities. Citron retains one asset, land, which it distributes to its sole individual shareholder, Electra. The land is valued at $150,000, and its basis is $80,000. Electra's basis in her Citron stock is $970,000.

    Determine the Federal income tax consequences for Citron, Ecru, and Electra, including Ecru's basis in the assets it receives from Citron. Determine Electra's basis in the Ecru stock she receives, using spreadsheet software such as Microsoft Excel.

21. **LO.2, 3** Spinone Corporation directs its sole shareholder, James, to exchange all of his common stock valued at $200,000 (basis of $50,000) for $100,000 of common stock, $70,000 of preferred stock, and $30,000 in cash. In addition, Spinone

directs its sole bondholder, Karen, to exchange her $150,000 of bonds paying 6.0% for $160,000 of bonds paying 5.6%. How are these transactions treated for income tax purposes by James, Karen, and Spinone? Determine James's basis in his common and preferred stock using spreadsheet software such as Microsoft Excel.

22. **LO.2** Quail Corporation was created six years ago through contributions from Kasha ($900,000) and Frank ($100,000). In a transaction qualifying as a reorganization, Quail exchanges all of its assets currently valued at $1,800,000 (basis of $1,200,000) for Covey Corporation stock valued at $1,700,000 plus $100,000 in Covey bonds. Quail distributes the Covey stock and bonds proportionately to Frank and Kasha in exchange for their stock in Quail. Quail's current and accumulated E & P before the reorganization amounts to $70,000.

   a.   How do Kasha and Frank treat this transaction for income tax purposes? What is Kasha's and Frank's basis in their Covey stock? Prepare your solution using spreadsheet software such as Microsoft Excel.

   b.   How do Quail and Covey treat this transaction for income tax purposes? What is Covey's basis in the assets it receives from Quail?

23. **LO.2** Jed acquired 25% of the stock of Alpha (basis of $100,000) 12 years ago, and the other 75% was purchased by Zia (basis of $400,000) three years ago.
   Alpha enters into a tax-free consolidation with Beta, in which Jed will receive an 8% interest in the new AlphaBeta (value $90,000) plus $36,000 cash, and Zia will receive a 28% interest (value $315,000) plus land worth $63,000. Alpha's basis in the land is $35,000.
   Before the reorganization or distributions to its shareholders, Alpha's value is $504,000, and Beta's value is $720,000.

   a.   What is Jed's and Zia's recognized gain or loss on the reorganization? What is each shareholder's basis in his or her AlphaBeta stock? Prepare your solution using spreadsheet software such as Microsoft Excel.

   b.   What is Alpha's and Beta's recognized gain or loss on the reorganization?

   c.   Diagram the consolidation of Alpha and Beta Corporation.

24. **LO.2, 3** Target Corporation holds assets with a fair market value of $4,000,000 (adjusted basis of $2,200,000) and liabilities of $1,500,000. It transfers assets worth $3,700,000 to Acquiring Corporation in a "Type C" reorganization, in exchange for Acquiring voting stock and the assumption of $1,400,000 of Target's liabilities.
   Target retained a building worth $300,000 (adjusted basis of $225,000). Target distributes the Acquiring voting stock and the building with its $100,000 mortgage to Wei, its sole shareholder, for all of her stock in Target. Wei's basis in her stock is $2,100,000.

   a.   Explain whether this transaction meets the requirements for a "Type C" reorganization.

   b.   What is the value of the stock transferred from Acquiring to Target?

   c.   What is the amount of gain (loss) recognized by Wei, Target, and Acquiring on the reorganization?

   d.   What is Wei's basis in the stock and building she received? Prepare your solution using spreadsheet software such as Microsoft Excel.

25. **LO.3** Determine whether the following transactions are taxable. If a transaction is not taxable, indicate what type of reorganization is effected, if any.

   a.   AlphaPsi Corporation owns two lines of business that it has conducted for the last eight years. For liability protection, AlphaPsi's shareholders decide that it would be best to separate into two corporations. The assets and liabilities of the garbage collection division are transferred to Alpha Corporation in exchange for all of its stock. The manufacturing division's assets and liabilities are exchanged for all of the stock of Psi Corporation. The Alpha and Psi stocks are distributed to the AlphaPsi shareholders in return for all of their AlphaPsi stock. Then AlphaPsi liquidates.

b. Alpha, Inc., owns assets valued at $1,000,000 and liabilities of $450,000. Beta Corporation transfers $500,000 of its voting stock and $50,000 in cash for all of Alpha's assets. Beta assumes Alpha's liabilities. Alpha distributes the Beta stock and cash to its shareholders and then liquidates.

c. Alpha Corporation moves its headquarters and state of legal incorporation from Salem, Oregon, to Dover, Delaware. It also changes its name to Beta, Inc.

d. Beta Company holds assets valued at $850,000 and liabilities of $50,000. Alpha, Inc., transfers $790,000 of its voting and $10,000 of nonvoting common stock for all of Beta's common and preferred stock. Beta becomes a subsidiary of Alpha.

e. Alpha, Inc., owns assets valued at $600,000 and liabilities of $150,000. Beta Corporation exchanges $270,000 of its voting stock and investments worth $180,000 for all of Alpha's assets and liabilities. Alpha distributes the Beta stock to its shareholders for 60% of their stock and retains the investments.

f. Beta Company holds assets valued at $3,000,000 and liabilities of $100,000. Nu Company transfers $2,850,000 of its voting stock for 95% of Beta's assets. Beta distributes the Nu stock, the remaining assets, and the liabilities to its shareholders; it then liquidates.

26. **LO.3, 6** Brown Corporation was organized seven years ago by Red Corporation (55%), Blue Corporation (35%), and Yellow Corporation (10%). Brown has been quite successful and now owns assets worth $12 million (basis of $4.4 million) with liabilities of $2 million. Red would like to obtain a controlling interest in Brown by using a "Type B" or "Type C" reorganization. Blue is willing to relinquish its interest in Brown, but Yellow is hesitant because it does not want to be a shareholder in Red.

    Critical Thinking

a. Explain whether Red can accomplish its acquisition of Brown by using either a "Type B" or a "Type C" reorganization.

b. Draw a diagram of the reorganization(s) that Red can use to accomplish its acquisition of Brown.

27. **LO.3, 6** Drab Corporation just obtained exclusive rights to a new revolutionary fertilizer that is sure to be an instant success in the gardening industry. Unfortunately, Drab does not control the capital to market the product adequately. Therefore, it is considering joining forces with Olive, a corporation with substantial liquid assets and experience in marketing new products. This union, Drab believes, would give both corporations a competitive edge due to this product and the positive reputation each corporation has. Name recognition is so important in gardening marketing that Drab hates to lose this if it merges.

    Communications

Drab's president, Lee Xanders, provides you with the following information and requests your guidance as to what type of reorganization Drab and Olive should consider.

Corporation	FMV of Assets	Adjusted Basis	Liabilities
Drab	$600,000	$480,000	$400,000
Olive	900,000	500,000	100,000

Write a letter to Ms. Xanders explaining the benefits of using a "Type A" consolidation or a "Type C" merger. Drab's address is Route 1, Box 2440, Mason, OH 45040.

28. **LO.3, 6** Big Corporation currently owns 25% of Small, Inc. Big acquired this stock two years ago by exchanging $375,000 of its preferred stock with Allie, one of the original owners of Small. Big had tried to acquire the assets of Small, but management was not in favor of the acquisition. In the current year, Big enters into a transaction with Small shareholders in which it acquires $712,500 of Small's voting stock and $200,000 of preferred stock. Big now owns 95% of the Small common stock and 100% of its preferred stock.

    Critical Thinking

a. Diagram the current-year corporate reorganization.

b. Identify the Federal income tax issues in the proposed transaction.

Critical Thinking
Communications

29. **LO.3, 6** Eta Corporation approaches Lily White, the CEO and sole shareholder of MuCo, regarding the acquisition of MuCo's cat toy division assets (worth $1,300,000). Because selling the assets would create a $600,000 gain, ($1,300,000 value − $700,000 basis), Lily declines the offer.

Eta counters and suggests a "Type C" reorganization as a method of acquiring all of MuCo by exchanging its voting stock for all assets (now worth $1,500,000) and all liabilities ($650,000) of MuCo. The other division of MuCo, Cat Publications, is small, with assets worth $200,000 and liabilities of $150,000. Lily agrees to the reorganization if MuCo receives the net value of the Cat Publication division ($50,000) in cash, because Lily would like money as well as stock.

Lily requests your advice on whether the transaction can be structured as a "Type C" reorganization as it is currently described. If it cannot meet the "Type C" requirements, suggest an alternative plan that will allow the transaction to qualify as a "Type C" reorganization. MuCo's address is 3443 E. Riverbank Road, Walla Walla, WA 99362. Include your analysis in a letter to Ms. White.

Critical Thinking

30. **LO.3, 6** Puce has two individual shareholders, Abram and Carmella. The shareholders purchased their stock in Puce four years ago at a cost of $500,000 each. For the past nine years, Puce has been engaged in two lines of business, manufacturing and wholesale distribution. Puce also owns substantial investments that it has held for at least six years.

For liability protection, Puce would like to segregate its businesses by placing wholesale distribution into one corporation and manufacturing into another corporation. Puce would distribute the stock of the new corporations to its shareholders, and Puce would retain only the investment assets.

a.   Discuss the immediate income tax consequences of the proposed transaction.

b.   As Puce's tax adviser, how would you structure the transaction?

c.   Draw a diagram of your proposed reorganization and its results.

31. **LO.3** TriStateCo, an Idaho corporation, has operated landfills in Washington (WA), Idaho (ID), and Oregon (OR) for the past 20 years. The states are changing their environmental laws governing landfills, and it is cumbersome for each landfill to meet the requirements of all three states. TriStateCo thinks it would be more efficient to have the landfills incorporated in the states in which they are located.

The net asset values of the landfills by state are as follows: ID, $600,000; OR, $800,000; and WA, $700,000.

a.   Suggest how TriStateCo can divide itself into three companies, named by their state location.

b.   Draw a diagram of your proposed reorganization and its results.

Decision Making

32. **LO.2, 3** The Rho Corporation was incorporated eight years ago by Tyee and Danette. Tyee received 5,000 shares of common stock for his $100,000 contribution, and Danette received 10,000 shares of common stock for her $200,000 contribution. Five years ago, both Tyee and Danette acquired $50,000 of Rho bonds paying 3% interest.

In the current year, Rho's common stock is valued at $900,000. SheenCo would like to acquire a 25% interest in Rho by purchasing common stock from Rho. Tyee and Danette see this as a good time to restructure Rho's capital. They would like to own bonds paying 5% interest, instead of 3%, and each would like to receive $120,000 of preferred stock (par of $100 per share) in exchange for some of his or her common stock. What Federal income tax advice would you give to Rho?

33. **LO.3** Beach Corporation, a seaside restaurant, is owned by 20 unrelated shareholders. This year Beach made the national news for polluting the surrounding beach and ocean with garbage; it was fined $200,000. Beach fired its chief executives and appointed a new board of directors. The new president, Sandy Shores, vowed to clean up Beach's pollution and become more socially responsible.

To put this damaging episode behind them, the board of directors wants to change Beach's name to Protected Bay. Further, it would like to change from a C corporation to an S corporation to make the owners feel more responsible for the business. Explain how these corporate changes can be accomplished and the Federal income tax implications for Beach.

34. **LO.3** Rufous Corporation just lost a $1,500,000 product liability lawsuit. Its assets currently are worth $2,000,000, and its outstanding liabilities amount to $800,000 without considering the lawsuit loss. As a result of the lawsuit, Rufous's future revenue stream appears to be substantially impaired. Rufous's president, Hunter Green, asks your advice regarding the possibilities of restructuring the corporation. Write a memo for the tax research file explaining Hunter's choices in restructuring Rufous.

Communications

35. **LO.3, 4** Aqua Corporation is a retail operation specializing in pool equipment and outdoor furniture. It is very interested in merging with Icterine Corporation, a lamp manufacturer; Aqua is very profitable, and Icterine has large business credits that it has not been able to utilize.

Critical Thinking

Aqua proposes to exchange about 40% of its stock and $200,000 for most of Icterine's assets. The assets not acquired by Aqua will be distributed to Icterine's shareholders. Aqua stock will be distributed to most of Icterine's shareholders, while dissenting Icterine shareholders will receive the cash.

Aqua is not interested in the lamp business except for the possibility of making pool lights. It therefore will sell off Icterine's assets except those that can be retooled to manufacture pool lights. What are the Federal income tax issues to be considered in these transactions?

36. **LO.4** Midori Corporation is a distiller of fine liqueurs. The market for this specialty product is thin but very lucrative. Midori wants to diversify its product line and is interested in acquiring Verdigris, which specializes in exotic teas and spices.

Critical Thinking

Because the spice products are of no interest to Midori, it suggests that Verdigris dispose of this line of business before the merger. Midori would then exchange 15% of its stock and $500,000 for the remaining assets of Verdigris. The Midori stock would be distributed to 30% of the Verdigris shareholders for their stock; the remaining Verdigris shareholders would receive cash.

What income tax problems can you identify with the proposed transactions?

37. **LO.5** Through a "Type B" reorganization, Golden Corporation acquired 90% of RetrieverCo stock by October 2 of the current tax year ending December 31. At the time the 90% was acquired, RetrieverCo was worth $800,000 and the Federal long-term tax-exempt rate was 3%. RetrieverCo holds capital loss carryovers of $50,000. If Golden reports taxable income of $300,000, which includes $30,000 capital gains, how much of the RetrieverCo capital loss carryover may Golden use in the current year to offset its income?

38. **LO.5** Through an acquisitive "Type D" reorganization, Border, Inc., is merged into Collie Corporation on September 2 of the current calendar tax year. The Federal long-term tax-exempt rate for September is 3%. Border shareholders receive 70% of the Collie stock in exchange for all of their Border shares. Border liquidates immediately after the exchange. At the time of the merger, Border was worth $1,000,000 and held a $500,000 NOL.

If Collie reports taxable income of $400,000 for the current year, how much of the Border NOL can be utilized in the current year? How much of the Border NOL may Collie utilize next year if its taxable income remains the same?

39. **LO.3, 5** Through a "Type C" reorganization, Springer Corporation was merged into Spaniel Corporation last year. Springer shareholders received 40% of the Spaniel stock in exchange for all of their Springer shares. Springer liquidated

Decision Making

immediately after the exchange. At the time of the merger, Springer was worth $2,000,000. The Springer shareholders are promised that Spaniel will purchase for $3,000,000 all of their stock five years after the reorganization. If the shareholders use a 5% discount rate, demonstrate whether this offer should be accepted. *Hint*: Use text Appendix F in your analysis.

Decision Making   40. **LO.5** Mila purchased a Zaffre Corporation $100,000 bond 10 years ago for its face value. The bond pays 5% interest annually. In a "Type E" reorganization, Zaffre exchanges Mila's bond with 10 years remaining for a 15-year bond also having a face value of $100,000 but paying 4.5% annual interest.

Mila earns a 3% after-tax rate of return, and she is in the 25% state and Federal income tax bracket for all years. Determine whether this is an equitable exchange for Mila. Prepare your solution using spreadsheet software such as Microsoft Excel. *Hint*: Use text Appendix F in your analysis.

41. **LO.5** Sinopia completed a corporate restructuring transaction with Cyan on May 31 of the current year. Cyan distributed 30% of Sinopia's stock to its shareholders in exchange for all of their stock in Cyan. At the completion of the reorganization, Cyan's assets were worth $900,000, its liabilities were $350,000, and it held an NOL carryover of $207,674. The applicable Federal long-term tax-exempt rate is 3%, and Sinopia is in the 25% state and Federal income tax bracket.

What is the amount of NOL that Sinopia may use in the current year? What is the net present value of the NOL carried forward to future years? Sinopia earns a 6% after-tax rate of return. Prepare your solution using spreadsheet software such as Microsoft Excel. *Hint*: Use text Appendix F in your analysis.

Decision Making   42. **LO.5** Zeta Corporation is interested in acquiring Tau Corporation through a "Type A" reorganization on January 2 of the current year. Zeta is valued at $50,000,000 and generates taxable income of $5,000,000 per year, whereas Tau is valued at $7,000,000 and holds a $1,470,000 NOL with nine years remaining in its carryover period. If Zeta earns a 7% after-tax rate of return and the Federal long-term tax-exempt rate is 3%, what value should Zeta place on Tau's NOL? Construct a spreadsheet to support your solution that includes a present value analysis. Prepare your solution using spreadsheet software such as Microsoft Excel. Use a marginal state and Federal income tax rate of 25%.

43. **LO.5** On December 31, 2017, Alpha Corporation, valued at $10,000,000, acquired BetaCo when BetaCo was valued at $5,000,000. BetaCo holds a capital loss carryforward of $220,000 and excess business credits of $435,000. At the end of 2018, Alpha reports taxable income before any carryovers of $750,000, consisting of $150,000 capital gains and $600,000 operating income. The applicable Federal long-term rate is 4%, and Alpha earns an 8% after-tax rate of return.

a.   How much of the BetaCo carryovers may Alpha utilize in 2018?

b.   Alpha expects to generate $600,000 of taxable operating income for 2019 and 2020. In 2021, it expects to record $700,000 taxable income, including $100,000 of capital gains. What is the value of the capital loss carryforward to Alpha after 2018? Prepare your solution using spreadsheet software such as Microsoft Excel. Use a marginal state and Federal income tax rate of 25%. *Hint*: Use text Appendix F in your analysis.

44. **LO.5** Through a "Type A" reorganization, VizslaCo acquires 100% of Puli Corporation by exchanging 30% of its stock for all of Puli's assets and liabilities. The VizslaCo stock was exchanged for all of the stock of the Puli shareholders. Then Puli liquidated. The net value of Puli's assets at the time of the restructuring was $500,000, and the Federal long-term tax-exempt rate was 3%. Puli held business tax credit carryovers of $37,500. If VizslaCo is always in the 25% state and Federal income tax bracket, what is the value of these credits to VizslaCo assuming that it uses a discount rate of 8%? Prepare your solution using spreadsheet software such as Microsoft Excel. *Hint*: Use text Appendix F in your analysis.

45. **LO.5** Shepherd Corporation is considering acquiring RentCo by exchanging its stock (value of $10 per share) for RentCo's only asset, a tract of land (adjusted basis of $150,000 and no liability). The yearly net rent that RentCo receives on the land is $50,000. Shepherd anticipates that it will receive the same net rent for the land over the next 20 years. At the end of that time, it would sell the land for $400,000.

    What is the maximum number of shares that RentCo shareholders can expect Shepherd to offer for 100% of their RentCo stock? Assume that Shepard uses a 10% discount rate and is in the 25% state and Federal income tax bracket for all years. What type of reorganization is this contemplated transaction? *Hint*: Use text Appendix F in your analysis.

46. **LO.3** Ten years ago, Xio and Xandra each invested $300,000 to create Xava Corporation. Xava develops and manufactures rock climbing and bungee jumping equipment. The business has become very profitable (it now is valued at $3,000,000), and Xandra would like to cash out the profits and sell the business. Xio, however, wants to reinvest the profits and expand the business into ice diving.

    Because they have different expectations, Xio and Xandra agree that the best solution is to divide up the company. Xandra will receive the bungee division; Xio, the rock climbing. After the reorganization, Xandra sells her stock in the bungee division for $1,500,000 at the beginning of the current year. Xio retains her ownership of the rock climbing division.

   a.   What type of reorganization would be used to divide Xava Corporation between Xio and Xandra?

   b.   Xio sells the rock climbing stock for $2,000,000 at the end of six years. Using a 7% discount factor, determine whether Xandra or Xio made a better decision. Assume a 20% tax rate on long-term capital gains. (*Hint:* Determine the present value of the after-tax cash flow for Xio and Xandra on the sale of the stock by constructing a Microsoft Excel spreadsheet.)

Decision Making

Research Problems

Note: Solutions to the Research Problems can be prepared by using the Thomson Reuters Checkpoint™ online tax research database, which accompanies this textbook. Solutions can also be prepared by using research materials found in a typical tax library.

THOMSON REUTERS
CHECKPOINT™

Research Problem 1. Nye Tools, incorporated in 2005, makes tools and devices for the automotive industry. The original shareholders were Andre (700 shares) and his brother Roscoe (300 shares). In 2010, Andre transferred 100 shares to his wife and Roscoe sold 50 shares to a business associate. In January 2016, Nye spun off the devices division, creating Nye Devices. In this transaction, Andre exchanged 500 shares of Tools for 500 shares of Devices. Roscoe did not receive any shares of Devices. Wanting to relinquish all ownership of Nye Tools, Andre and his wife sold their remaining 200 shares to Roscoe in 2017.

    From 2015 to 2017, Nye Tools accumulated substantial business credits, which it could not fully utilize. Finally, in 2018, Tools incurred sufficient tax liability to offset all of its business credit carryovers. The IRS audited Nye Tools's 2018 return and is questioning whether the business credit carryovers should be limited due to an ownership change. Roscoe believes there has been no ownership change because of stock attribution rules.

    Determine whether Roscoe should try to negotiate with the IRS or litigate over the business credit issue. Support your analysis with citations to primary tax sources.

Research Problem 2. Paloma purchased all of the outstanding Dove stock six years ago. Dove has prospered under Paloma's direction, and now Hawk Corporation is interested in acquiring Dove, but not directly. Hawk forms a new subsidiary, called Starling, whose purpose is to merge with Dove. Starling (the target) transfers its asset, Hawk stock, to Dove (acquiring) in exchange for all of the Dove stock.

Dove distributes the Hawk stock to Paloma in exchange for her Dove stock. Starling distributes the Dove stock to its shareholder, Hawk, and then ceases to exist. Dove is now a wholly owned subsidiary of Hawk, and Paloma is a Hawk shareholder.

Hawk immediately liquidates Dove to acquire all of Dove's assets and liabilities. Hawk continues Dove's previous line of business. The end result is that Hawk has all of Dove's assets and liabilities and that Paloma is a shareholder of Hawk.

Explain whether this reverse triangular restructuring qualifies as a reorganization under § 368, or whether the step transaction doctrine causes it to be disqualified.

Research Problem 3. Hawaii Corporation, which is owned equally by two brothers and their younger sister, has been in the business of growing coffee and onions for the last 10 years. Lately, the brothers have been disagreeing regarding the management, operations, and expansion of the business. A professional mediator concludes that the only way to resolve the issues is to divide the entity. The older brother will retain the coffee business and the Hawaii name. The younger brother and sister will receive stock in a newly formed entity, Maui Corporation, in exchange for their stock in Hawaii. Maui will continue growing onions, but it likely will expand into other products.

Hawaii is organized as an S corporation, and Maui will elect S status at the earliest possible date. The transaction will take place as follows: Hawaii will transfer the onion farming assets to Maui in exchange for all of its stock. Hawaii then will exchange all of the younger brother's and sister's stock in Hawaii for all of the stock in Maui. After the transaction, the older brother will own all of Hawaii, and the younger brother and sister will own all of Maui.

Will this division of Hawaii qualify as a "Type D" reorganization? Explain. Will this division terminate Hawaii's S election or prevent Maui from electing S status? Explain. See Chapter 12 for more detailed information about S corporations.

Use internet tax resources to address the following questions. Look for reliable websites and blogs of the IRS and other government agencies, media outlets, businesses, tax professionals, academics, think tanks, and political outlets.

Communications   **Research Problem 4.** While there are tax consequences to corporate reorganizations, there are non-tax issues that should be considered. Read "Reorganizations Without Tears" by Beauchamp, Heidarti-Robertson, and Heywood (**https://tinyurl.com/heidarti**). Send a one-page summary of the article to your instructor.

Communications   **Research Problem 5.** Find a recent merger or acquisition in the beverage industries (e.g., soft drinks, beer, wine). Prepare a written summary of the transaction, including a diagram of the deal and the names of the companies involved, and send your document to your instructor.

Consolidated Tax Returns

LEARNING OBJECTIVES: *After completing Chapter 8, you should be able to:*

LO.1 Apply the fundamental concepts of consolidated tax returns.

LO.2 Identify the sources of the rules for consolidated taxable income.

LO.3 List the major advantages and disadvantages of filing consolidated tax returns.

LO.4 Identify the corporations that are eligible to file on a consolidated basis.

LO.5 Explain the compliance aspects of consolidated returns.

LO.6 Compute a group's consolidated taxable income and a parent's investment basis in a subsidiary.

LO.7 Account for the intercompany transactions of a consolidated group.

LO.8 Identify limitations that restrict the use of losses and credits of group members derived in separate return years.

LO.9 Derive deductions and credits on a consolidated basis.

LO.10 Demonstrate tax planning opportunities available to consolidated groups.

CHAPTER OUTLINE

THE BIG PICTURE

A CORPORATION CONTEMPLATES A MERGER

Alexander Corporation has had a long-term association with one of its chip suppliers, Hamilton Corporation. In the past, Hamilton was a highly profitable operation and was even able to make loans to Alexander to cover short-term working capital needs. Recently, however, Hamilton has been consistently late in meeting current obligations. Alexander has had to grant extensions of up to nine months on Hamilton's payables. Several vendors have even ceased doing business with Hamilton. Nevertheless, Alexander feels confident that Hamilton's fortunes will improve. If this financial turnaround occurs, Alexander will continue dealing with Hamilton in the same manner as in the past.

But Alexander's tax advisers have suggested another alternative. They say that Alexander should consider acquiring Hamilton in a merger or other takeover that qualifies as a tax-favored reorganization (see Chapter 7) to avoid any immediate Federal income tax liability. Hamilton's downturn has left it with sizable net operating losses that would be attractive to Alexander for use on future joint tax returns. Because Hamilton's name, reputation, and location still have value in the marketplace, it could continue as a separate division or subsidiary of Alexander. Furthermore, the takeover would give other businesses greater assurance of Hamilton's financial viability. Finally, there could be tax advantages to Alexander, the new parent of a two-corporation group.

Evaluate this and other viable alternatives for Alexander, taking into account various possible outcomes (e.g., the success or failure of Hamilton's business).

Read the chapter and formulate your response.

o this point, our discussion has centered on the computation of the tax liability of stand-alone corporations. This is an appropriate approach to the study of corporate taxation; more than 90 percent of the roughly 7 million U.S. corporations are closely held (i.e., either by a small group of operators/investors or by members of the same family).

Although some of these family businesses operate in a multiple-corporation environment, the vast majority of the assets held by businesses nationwide are owned by no more than 60,000 large entities, both domestic and offshore. These corporations conduct the country's "big business," and they account for virtually all of the country's net assets, business receipts, and net Federal corporate taxable income. In addition, these corporate groups are subject to some special tax rules, which are the subject of this chapter.

8-1   THE CONSOLIDATED RETURN RULES

8-1a   Motivations to Consolidate

Corporate conglomerates are present in every aspect of life. The local dairy or bakery is likely to be owned by General Mills or General Foods. Oil and insurance companies own movie-making corporations. Professional sports teams are corporate cousins of the media outlets that carry their games. The same corporate group that produces night-lights for a child's nursery may manufacture control equipment for bombers and other elements of the Defense Department's arsenal.

What brings together these sometimes strange corporate bedfellows? For the most part, nontax motivations provide the strongest incentives for multiple-corporation acquisitions and holdings. Among the many commonly encountered motivations are the following.

- A desire to isolate assets of other group members from the liabilities of specific operating divisions (e.g., to gain limited liability for a tobacco or asbestos company within an operating conglomerate).

- A need to carry out specific estate planning objectives (e.g., by transferring growth or high-risk assets to younger-generation shareholders).

- A preference to isolate the group's exposure to losses and liabilities incurred in joint ventures with "outside" entities (especially when such venturers are not based in the United States).

- A desire to move an affiliate from control of its activities in a "business-unfriendly" state to that of its new parent entity, which is resident in a "business-friendly" jurisdiction.

- A perception that separate divisions/group members will be worth more on the market if they maintain unique identities or otherwise avoid a commingling of assets and liabilities with other group members (e.g., where a trade name or patent is especially valuable or carries excessive goodwill in the marketplace).

- Conversely, an attempt to shield the identities of a subsidiary's true owners from the public where negative goodwill exists (e.g., with respect to the consequences of a nuclear or industrial accident or the use of a long-held name of an oil or tobacco company).

Although nontax concerns may be the primary reason for the creation of many conglomerates, tax incentives also may play a role. To a large extent, these incentives can be found in the rules that control the filing of **consolidated returns**. In general terms, the tax law allows certain corporate groups to be treated as a single entity. This enables the group to use available tax provisions optimally among its members and to shelter the income of profitable members with the losses of other members. Thus, through the consolidated return rules, corporate taxpayers have an opportunity to manage the combined tax liability of the members of the group.

The consolidated return rules may be available to a taxpayer as a result of various business decisions.

- A consolidated return may result from a merger, an acquisition, or another corporate combination (discussed in Chapter 7).

When Dover Corporation acquires all of the stock of Edwards Corporation, a new corporate group, Dover and Edwards Corporation, is formed. The two group members can elect to file their tax return on a consolidated basis.

- A group of business taxpayers may be restructured to comply with changes in regulatory requirements, meet the demands of a competitive environment, or gain economies of scale and operate more efficiently in a larger arrangement. Consequently, an election to file a consolidated return becomes available.

External Corporation, a retailer, acquires Internal Corporation, a wholesaler, in an effort to control its flow of inventory in unstable economic times. The two group members can elect to file their tax returns on a consolidated basis.

- The taxpayers may be seeking to gain tax, financial reporting, and other financial advantages that are more readily available to corporate combinations.

Over the next three years, Mary Corporation will be selling a number of its business assets at a loss. If Norbert Corporation acquires all of Mary's stock and the group elects to file its tax returns on a consolidated basis, Norbert will be able to combine its gains from the sale of business property with Mary's losses in computing the group's consolidated § 1231 gain/loss for the year.

8-1b Source and Philosophy of Consolidated Return Rules

LO.2

Identify the sources of the rules for consolidated taxable income.

Some form of consolidated corporate tax return has been allowed for Federal purposes since World War I. Congress has delegated most of its legislative authority involving consolidated returns to the Treasury. As a result, the majority of the rules that affect consolidated groups are found in the Regulations. The Code provisions dealing with consolidated returns are strictly definitional in nature and broad in scope;[1] the related Regulations dictate the computational and compliance requirements of the group.[2]

As discussed in Chapter 1, "legislative" Regulations of this sort carry the full force and effect of law. Challenges to the content of these Regulations seldom are supported by the courts. Consequently, taxpayers generally participate actively in the hearings process in an effort to have their interpretations included in the final Regulations.

The length and detail of these Regulations make the consolidated return rules among the most complex in the Federal income tax law. For the most part, the underlying objective of the rules remains one of organizational neutrality; that is, a group of closely related corporations should have neither a tax advantage nor a disadvantage relative to taxpayers who file separate corporate returns.

---

[1]§§ 1501–1505.

[2]Reg. §§ 1.1501–1, 1.1502–0 through 1.1502–100, 1.1503–1 through 1.1503–2, and 1.1504–1.

ETHICS & EQUITY Delegating Authority to the Nonelected

In no other area of the tax law has Congress given the Treasury such leeway in crafting both major principles and details as in the area of consolidated returns. Because Treasury staff members are not elected officials, this delegation of authority might appear to be a shirking of congressional duty and a dangerous assignment of legislative power to an isolated group of individuals.

To what extent should Congress delegate its powers over the country's largest businesses (not only the largest players in the global economy but also the largest contributors to campaign and reelection funds)? Can the delegation of congressional powers to Washington-based civil servants, who are virtually immune to the checks and balances of the election process, be healthy for all taxpayers?

You are a member of the House Ways and Means Committee, and your chances of reelection are jeopardized when you must take a position on a consolidated tax return issue: taxes on old-line manufacturers would increase, whereas those on more environmentally friendly, high-tech industries would fall. Should you avoid the debate altogether by deferring the issue to the Regulations process?

LO.3

List the major advantages and disadvantages of filing consolidated tax returns.

8-2 ASSESSING CONSOLIDATED RETURN STATUS

Before making an election to file consolidated tax returns, eligible taxpayers must weigh the resulting tax advantages and disadvantages. (The eligibility requirements are explained in the next section.)

The potential advantages of filing consolidated returns are many.

- The operating and capital loss carryovers of one group member may be used to shelter the corresponding income of other group members.
- The taxation of all intercompany dividends may be eliminated.
- Recognition of income from certain intercompany transactions can be deferred, gaining an advantage as to the time value of money.
- Certain deductions and credits may be optimized by using consolidated amounts in computing pertinent limitations (e.g., the deductions for charitable contributions and dividends received).
- The tax basis of investments in the stock of subsidiaries is increased as the members contribute to consolidated taxable income.
- The shareholdings of all group members can be used in meeting other statutory requirements.[3]

Consolidated returns also have a number of potential disadvantages.

- The election is binding on all subsequent tax years of the group members unless either the makeup of the affiliated group changes or the IRS consents to a revocation of the election.
- Recognition of losses from certain intercompany transactions is deferred, a detriment as to the time value of money.

---

[3]For example, for purposes of the § 165(g)(3) ordinary deduction for losses from worthlessness of securities. For the 80% corporate control requirement of § 351, see the discussion in text Section 4-1d.

FINANCIAL DISCLOSURE INSIGHTS **GAAP and Tax Treatment of Consolidations**

Both U.S. financial accounting and tax rules use the term *consolidation*, but there is only a slight resemblance in the content of those rules. Here are some of the key similarities and differences between the book and tax treatment of conglomerates.

- GAAP consolidations for the most part are *mandatory* when specified ownership levels are met. Federal income tax consolidation is an *election* by the affiliates to join the parent's tax return.

- GAAP consolidations can include entities such as partnerships and non-U.S. entities. Federal income tax rules generally limit the consolidated return only to U.S. C corporations.

- Ownership levels required for a U.S. subsidiary to consolidate with a parent differ between the book and tax rules. For example, not only does GAAP set a lower maximum for consolidation (50 percent *versus* 80 percent) but consolidation may not be elective (see above). Furthermore, the categorization and treatment of minority interests may vary.

- Tax rules treat a merger or an acquisition of a target corporation by a parent as a like-kind exchange, assuming that the requirements of a § 368 reorganization are met (see Chapter 7). Under GAAP, the transaction usually is reported as a purchase of the target's identifiable assets and liabilities.

- After a takeover occurs, book cost amounts are "stepped up" or down to fair market value and any excess purchase price is deemed to be goodwill. For Federal income tax purposes, if reorganization treatment is available, the target's basis in its assets carries over to the parent's accounts.

- Goodwill is treated differently under book and tax rules. Financial accounting goodwill cannot be amortized, but impairments to its value are reported as operating losses. Book income results if that impairment of the goodwill is reversed, for example, because the value of the goodwill has increased. For Federal income tax purposes, purchased goodwill is amortized over 15 years.

- The tax basis of investments in the stock of subsidiaries is decreased when the members generate operating losses and when distributions are made from members' E & P.

- The requirement that all group members use the parent's tax year creates short tax years for the subsidiaries when they join the group. As a result, a subsidiary's income may be bunched together needlessly, tax return due dates can be accelerated, and one of the years of its charitable contribution and loss carryforward periods may be lost.

- Additional administrative costs are incurred in complying with the consolidated return Regulations.

Who Should Consolidate?

EXAMPLE 4

The following taxpayers should consider filing consolidated returns.

- Major Insurance Corporation generates billions of dollars of taxable income every year. Independent Movie Productions, Ltd., is concerned with artistic integrity, and its annual taxable loss totals $40 to $45 million per year. The accumulated losses are of no use to Independent in generating tax-related cash flow, but Major can use them to effect an immediate tax reduction at its marginal Federal income tax rate.

- Every year Parent contributes $1.2 million of its $10 million taxable income to charity. Thus, because of the 10% of taxable income limitation, Parent cannot deduct the full amount of the gift in computing taxable income. SubCo generates $3 million of taxable income every year, and it makes no charitable contributions. By filing a consolidated return with SubCo, Parent can deduct its full gift against consolidated taxable income.

EXAMPLE

5

Who Should Consolidate?

The following corporations might make unattractive consolidated return partners.

- Parent sells an asset to SubCo at a $500,000 realized loss. Under the intercompany transactions rules discussed later in the chapter, this loss cannot be recognized by the consolidated group until the asset subsequently is sold to Outsider.

- SubCo generates a steady level of taxable income every year operating outside the United States, generating intangible income in the pharmaceutical industry. This type of income is subject to an additional tax for SubCo's 100% U.S. owner, ParentCo, as discussed in text Section 9-5e. The consolidation results in an increase in the effective tax rate of ParentCo.

8-3 ELECTING CONSOLIDATED RETURN STATUS

A corporation can join in a consolidated tax return if it meets three requirements, as illustrated in Concept Summary 8.1.

- It is a member of an **affiliated group** .
- It is not ineligible to file on a consolidated basis.
- It meets the initial and ongoing compliance requirements specified in the Code and Regulations.

Concept Summary 8.1

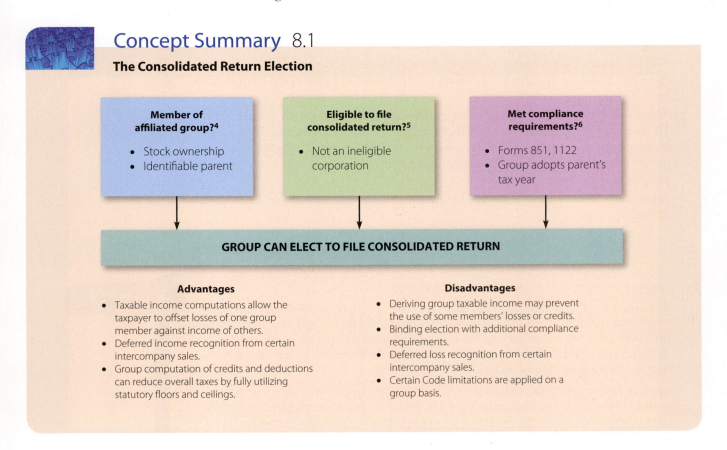

The Consolidated Return Election

Member of affiliated group?[4]	Eligible to file consolidated return?[5]	Met compliance requirements?[6]
• Stock ownership • Identifiable parent	• Not an ineligible corporation	• Forms 851, 1122 • Group adopts parent's tax year

GROUP CAN ELECT TO FILE CONSOLIDATED RETURN

Advantages

- Taxable income computations allow the taxpayer to offset losses of one group member against income of others.
- Deferred income recognition from certain intercompany sales.
- Group computation of credits and deductions can reduce overall taxes by fully utilizing statutory floors and ceilings.

Disadvantages

- Deriving group taxable income may prevent the use of some members' losses or credits.
- Binding election with additional compliance requirements.
- Deferred loss recognition from certain intercompany sales.
- Certain Code limitations are applied on a group basis.

---

[4] §§ 1504(a)(1) and (2).

[5] This is a negative definition, rooted in §§ 1504(b) through (f).

[6] See especially Reg. §§ 1.1502–75, –76, and –77.

8-3a **Affiliated Group**

An affiliated group exists when one corporation owns at least 80 percent of the voting power and stock value of another corporation.[7] Multiple tiers and chains of corporations are allowed as long as the group has an identifiable parent corporation (i.e., at least one corporation must own 80 percent of another group member).[8]

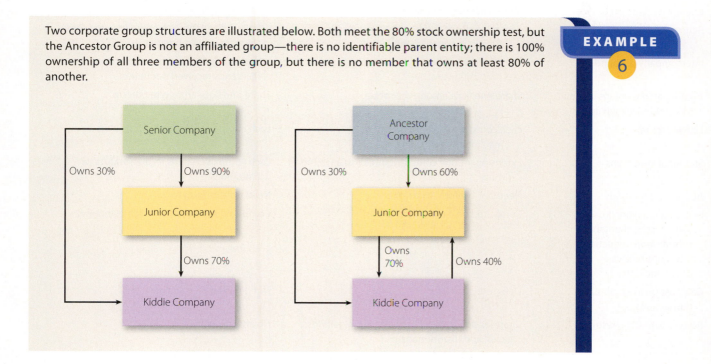

> Two corporate group structures are illustrated below. Both meet the 80% stock ownership test, but the Ancestor Group is not an affiliated group—there is no identifiable parent entity; there is 100% ownership of all three members of the group, but there is no member that owns at least 80% of another.

EXAMPLE 6

Members of an affiliated group can file tax returns in either of two ways.

- File a separate tax return for each member of the group, and claim a 100 percent dividends received deduction for payments passing among them.[9]
- Elect to file income tax returns on a consolidated basis for two or more of the affiliates. No 100 percent dividends received deduction is allowed for payments among group members.

Exhibit 8.1 provides additional details as to the tax effects of making a consolidated return election.

8-3b **Affiliated versus Controlled Group**

In a controlled group of corporations, the entities are related in some way, such as having common shareholders. Controlled groups include parent-subsidiary groups, brother-sister groups, combined groups, and certain insurance companies. Controlled groups are required to share certain elements of tax calculations, such as the $250,000 accumulated earnings credit (see text Section 3–2c),[10] or tax credits, such as the research tax credit.[11] An affiliated group is similar but not identical to a parent-subsidiary controlled group.

---

[7]§§ 1504(a)(2), 1504(a)(5)(C), (D).
[8]§ 1504(a)(1).
[9]§ 243(a)(3).

[10]§§ 535(c)(2) and 1561(a)(2).
[11]Reg § 1.41–6(b)(1).

EXHIBIT 8.1	Comparison of Tax Effects Available to Affiliated Group	

Attribute	Treatment If Consolidated Returns Are Filed	Treatment If Separate Returns Are Filed
Tax year	All companies use the parent's tax year.	Companies use various tax years.
Change to common tax year	Required, no IRS permission needed.	Requires IRS permission.
Returns of acquired companies	Separate returns through date of consolidation, then join in consolidated return.	Continue filing for each company's tax year. No extra returns needed.
Intercompany dividend	Eliminated, not taxed.	Include in taxable income, then claim dividends received deduction.
Accumulated earnings credit, $150,000/$250,000 floor	Share one floor among the group.	Share one floor among the group.
Liability for tax	Each company liable for the entire consolidated tax liability.	Each company liable only for its own tax.
Statute of limitations	Extension for one company applies to all in the group.	Each company retains its own statute of limitations.
Accounting methods	Need not conform to parent.	Need not conform to parent.
NOLs, capital gains/losses, § 1231 gains/losses, charitable contribution deductions, dividends received deductions, etc.	Computed on a consolidated basis.	Computed separately for each company.
Gain/loss on intercompany transactions	Deferred.	Not deferred.
Basis of parent's investment	Changes due to subsidiary operating gain/loss, taxes, and distributions.	No adjustments.

In addition, members of a controlled group must defer the recognition of any realized loss on intercompany sales until a sale is made at a gain to a nongroup member.[12] Similarly, any gain on the sale of depreciable property between members of a controlled group is recognized as ordinary income.[13]

A parent-subsidiary controlled group exists when one corporation owns at least 80 percent of the voting power or stock value of another corporation on the last day of the tax year.[14] Multiple tiers of subsidiaries and chains of ownership are allowed, as long as the group has an identifiable parent corporation. Thus, the Ancestor Group in Example 6 also is not a parent-subsidiary controlled group.

EXAMPLE 7

Aqua Corporation owns 80% of White Corporation. Aqua and White corporations are members of a parent-subsidiary controlled group. Aqua is the parent corporation, and White is the subsidiary.

---

[12]§§ 267(a)(1), (b)(3), and (f).

[13]§§ 1239(a) and (c).

[14]§ 1563(a)(1). For this purpose, stock attribution rules apply. In addition, all stock options are considered to be exercised by their holders. §§ 1563(d)(1) and (e)(1) through (3).

The parent-subsidiary relationship described in Example 7 is easy to recognize because Aqua Corporation is the direct owner of White Corporation. Real-world business organizations often are more complex, sometimes including numerous corporations with chains of ownership connecting them. In these complex corporate structures, determining whether the controlled group classification is appropriate becomes more difficult. The ownership requirements can be met through direct ownership (as in Example 7) or through indirect ownership.

Affiliated Groups

EXAMPLE 8

Red Corporation owns 80% of the voting stock of White Corporation, and White owns 80% of the voting stock of Blue Corporation. Red, White, and Blue constitute a controlled group in which Red is the common parent and White and Blue are subsidiaries. The same result would occur if Red, rather than White, owned the Blue stock.

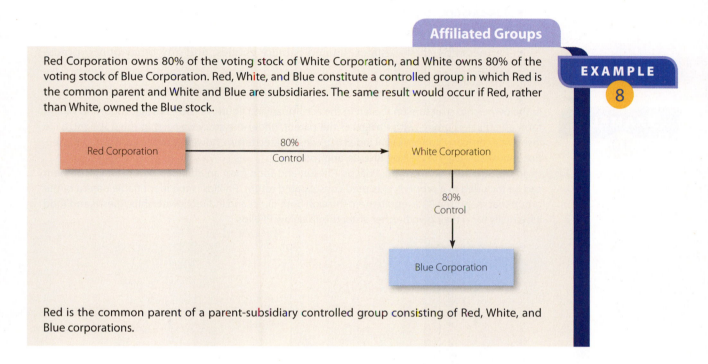

Red is the common parent of a parent-subsidiary controlled group consisting of Red, White, and Blue corporations.

EXAMPLE 9

Brown Corporation owns 80% of the stock of Green Corporation, which owns 30% of Blue Corporation. Brown also owns 80% of White Corporation, which owns 50% of Blue Corporation. Brown, Green, Blue, and White corporations constitute a parent-subsidiary controlled group in which Brown is the common parent and Green, Blue, and White are subsidiaries.

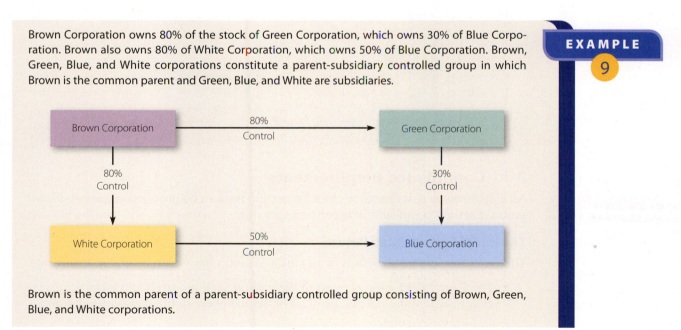

Brown is the common parent of a parent-subsidiary controlled group consisting of Brown, Green, Blue, and White corporations.

LO.4

Identify the corporations that are eligible to file on a consolidated basis.

8-3c **Eligibility for the Consolidation Election**

The Code lists a number of corporations that may *not* use a consolidated return to report their taxable income.[15] Thus, these corporations cannot be used to meet the stock ownership tests, and their taxable incomes cannot be included in a consolidated return. Some of the most frequently encountered entities that are ineligible for consolidated return status include the following.

- Corporations established outside the United States or in a U.S. possession.
- Tax-exempt corporations.[16]
- Insurance companies.
- Partnerships, trusts, estates, limited liability entities, and any other noncorporate entities.[17]

EXAMPLE

10

In the ownership structure on the left in the accompanying figure, Phillips, Rhesus, Todd, and Valiant form an affiliated group, with Phillips as the parent, under the stock ownership rules. Valiant, a life insurance company, cannot be included in a consolidated return, however, so the consolidation election is available only to Phillips, Rhesus, and Todd.

In the structure on the right, Phillips, Rhesus, and Todd form an affiliated group, and all of them can be included in a properly executed consolidated return. Phillips is the identifiable parent of the group that meets the 80% requirement through both direct and indirect ownership. Rhesus and Todd essentially form their own brother-sister group below Phillips.

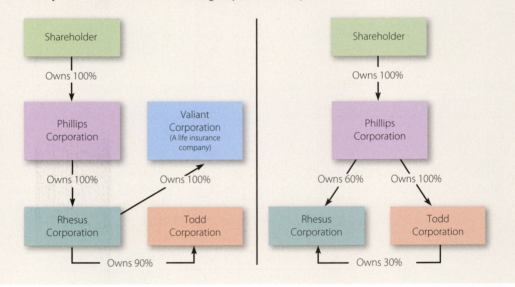

LO.5

Explain the compliance aspects of consolidated returns.

8-3d **Compliance Requirements**

An eligible entity that meets the stock ownership test can be included in a consolidated group if several compliance requirements are met.

The Initial Consolidated Return

The first consolidated tax return of an affiliated group must meet certain requirements.

- The Form 1120 for the tax year of the consolidated group should include the taxable results of the operations of all of the members of the consolidated group.[18]

---

[15]§ 1504(b).

[16]This includes any entity that is exempt from tax under § 501. See Chapter 15 for a discussion of the qualification of organizations for exempt status.

[17]Some less frequently encountered entities also are prohibited from filing on a consolidated basis. These include regulated investment companies (mutual funds) and real estate investment trusts. §§ 1504(b)(4) through (7).

[18]A consolidation election is inferred even when specific aspects of pertinent forms are completed incorrectly, as long as the members' combined operations are reported on the Form 1120. *American Pacific Whaling Co. v. Comm.*, 35–1 USTC ¶9065, 14 AFTR 887, 74 F.2d 613 (CA–9, 1935).

This return is filed in lieu of the separate returns of the group members.[19] The identified group then continues to file on a consolidated basis until an eligible group no longer exists or an election to "de-consolidate" is made.[20]

- A Form 1122 should be attached to the first consolidated tax return for each of the subsidiaries included in the group.[21] This form represents a consent by the affiliate to be included in the consolidated group.

The consolidation election must be made no later than the extended due date of the parent's return for the year. Only in the case of an inadvertent error can the election to consolidate be rescinded once this extended due date passes.

The Big Picture

EXAMPLE 11

Return to the facts of *The Big Picture* on p. 8-1. Assume that both Alexander and Hamilton use calendar tax years and that they want to file their Federal income tax returns on a consolidated basis starting with tax year 1. Alexander does not elect an extended due date for its year 1 return.

If the consolidation election is to be effective, Alexander must file a Form 1120 that includes the taxable income/loss for both corporations by April 15, year 2. Hamilton must execute a Form 1122 and attach it to the consolidated Form 1120.

If Alexander and Hamilton convert their separate tax returns to the consolidated format in this manner, the election to consolidate is in force for all future tax years, or until the IRS approves Alexander's application to revoke it.

An application to terminate the consolidation election must be filed at least 90 days prior to the extended due date of the consolidated return.[22] Generally, when a subsidiary leaves an ongoing consolidated group, it must wait five years before it can reenter the same parent's consolidated group.[23]

Subsequent Consolidated Returns

Every tax year, the consolidated tax return must include Form 851, Affiliations Schedule. This report identifies all of the corporations in the electing group, summarizes pertinent shareholdings and stock ownership changes that occurred during the tax year, and lists the estimated tax payments made by the group members for the year. Affiliates joining an existing consolidated group need not file a Form 1122 though.

Return Due Date

Generally, consolidated tax returns are due on the fifteenth day of the fourth month following the close of the group's tax year (this is April 15 for a calendar year taxpayer). A six-month extension to file the return can be obtained by executing Form 7004, but an estimated payment of the remaining tax liability for the group must accompany the extension application.[24]

Liability for Taxes

Liabilities and Payments An electing group's regular tax liability is computed applying the C corporation tax rate to consolidated taxable income for the tax year. Group members are jointly and severally liable for the entire consolidated income tax liability.[25]

---

[19]Reg. § 1.1502–75(a)(1).

[20]Reg. § 1.1502–75(c). The IRS permits such an election only rarely: on the parent's assertion of (1) a good-cause reason to disengage from consolidated status or (2) a substantial change in the tax law that adversely affects the consolidated tax liability.

[21]Reg. § 1.1502–75(b).

[22]Reg. § 1.1502–75(c)(1)(i).

[23]§ 1504(a)(3); Rev.Proc. 2002–32, 2002–1 C.B. 959; Rev.Proc. 2006–21, 2006–1 C.B. 1050.

[24]See text Section 3-3a for additional information on the corporate due dates.

[25]Reg. § 1.1502–6(a).

This rule applies to interest and penalties imposed as a result of audits as well as to tax liabilities. Furthermore, the IRS is not bound to follow internal agreements among group members in apportioning the liability.[26]

EXAMPLE 12

Parent Corporation, a calendar year taxpayer, acquired 100% of the stock of calendar year SubCo on December 20, 2017. The group filed on a consolidated basis from that date until December 31, 2019, when all of the SubCo stock was sold to Offshore Corporation.

An IRS audit determined that Parent owed an additional $10 million in Federal income taxes relating to a sale it made on December 30, 2017. By late 2020, however, Parent's cash-flow difficulties had brought it close to bankruptcy and forced it to cease activities.

Due to the consolidation election, the IRS can assess the delinquent taxes from SubCo (and Offshore). SubCo is liable for the full amount of any consolidated tax liability, even when it is not the source of the income that led to the tax.

Starting with the third consolidated return year, estimated tax payments must be made on a consolidated basis.[27] Prior to that year, estimates can be computed and paid on either a separate or consolidated basis.

Tax-Sharing Agreements Federal corporate income tax liabilities are apportioned equally among the group members unless all members consent to some other method through an annual election. The most commonly used tax-sharing agreements are the *relative taxable income* and *relative tax liability* methods.

Under the relative taxable income method,[28] the consolidated tax liability is allocated among the members based on their relative amounts of separate taxable income. When the relative tax liability method is used,[29] the consolidated tax liability is allocated based on the relative hypothetical separate tax liabilities of the members. IRS permission is required for the group to change from one allocation method to another, but such permission is granted automatically for these and other common tax-sharing methods.[30]

EXAMPLE 13

The Parent consolidated group reports the following results for the tax year.

	Parent	SubOne	SubTwo	SubThree	Consolidated
Ordinary income	$400	$100	$–0–	($20)	$480
Capital gain/loss	–0–	–0–	100	(25)	75
§ 1231 gain/loss	50	–0–	(50)	–0–	–0–
Separate taxable incomes	$450	$100	$ 50	($20)	
				with a $25 capital loss carryover	
Consolidated taxable income					$555
Consolidated tax liability (21% tax rate)					$117
Research credit, from SubOne					(19)
Net tax due					$ 98

continued

[26]Reg. § 1.1502–6(c).
[27]Reg. § 1.1502–5(a)(1).
[28]§ 1552(a)(1); Reg. § 1.1552–1(a)(1).
[29]§ 1552(a)(2); Reg. § 1.1552–1(a)(2).
[30]Rev.Proc. 90–39, 1990–2 C.B. 365; Rev.Proc. 2006–21, 2006–1 C.B. 1050.

If the group has consented to the relative taxable income method, the consolidated tax liability is allocated as follows.

	Separate Taxable Income	Allocation Ratio	Allocated Tax Due
Parent	$450	450/600	$74
SubOne	100	100/600	16
SubTwo	50	50/600	8
SubThree	–0–	–0–	–0–
Totals	$600		$98

The results are different if the relative tax liability method is in effect. Specifically, SubOne gets an immediate tax benefit for the tax credit it brings to the group. Under neither method, though, does SubThree get any tax benefit from the losses it brings to the consolidated group.

	Separate Taxable Income	Separate Tax Liability	Allocation Ratio	Allocated Tax Due
Parent	$450	$ 94.5	94.5/107	$87
SubOne	100	2.0*	2/107	2
SubTwo	50	10.5	10.5/107	9
SubThree	–0–	–0–	–0–	–0–
Totals	$600	$107.0		$98

*After applying research credit.

Tax Accounting Periods and Methods

All of the members of a consolidating group must use the parent's tax year.[31] As a result, the group may be required to file a short-year return for the first year a subsidiary is included in the consolidated return, so that the parent's year-end can be adopted.

When a mid-year acquisition occurs, both short years are used in tracking the carryforward period of unused losses and credits. Short-year income and deductions are apportioned between the pre- and postacquisition periods. At the election of the corporation being acquired, the apportionment may be done either on a daily basis or as the items are recorded for financial accounting purposes.[32]

EXAMPLE

14

All of the stock of calendar year SubCo is acquired by Parent Corporation on July 15, year 1 (not a leap year). The corporations elect to file a consolidated return immediately upon the acquisition.

SubCo had generated a long-term capital loss in a prior tax year. As of January 1, year 2, only one year remains in the five-year carryforward period for the capital loss.

According to SubCo's financial accounting records, $400,000 of its $1,000,000 accounting and taxable income for the year was generated in year 1 after the acquisition. At SubCo's election, either $400,000 (the "books" apportionment method) or $465,753 [(170 postacquisition days/365 days) × $1,000,000 income] (the "daily" method) can be included in the first consolidated return.

Generally, members of a consolidated group can continue to use the tax accounting methods that were in place prior to the consolidation election.[33] Thus, the members of a consolidated group may use different accounting methods. On the other hand, because the $25 million gross receipts test with respect to use of the cash method of accounting is applied on a consolidated basis,[34] some of the group members may need to switch from the cash to the accrual method of tax accounting.

---

[31]Reg. § 1.1502–76(a)(1).

[32]Reg. § 1.1502–76(b)(4).

[33]Reg. § 1.1502–17(a).

[34]§§ 448(a)(1) and (c)(1). The $25 million amount is indexed for inflation; it is $26 million for 2019. § 448(c)(4).

8-3e **State Tax Effects**

A Federal election to form a consolidated group may not be binding for state income tax purposes. Some states allow only separate return filing, and others may define the members of an electing group or tax their income differently than the Federal rules do. Many states limit the deductions for net operating losses, passive activity losses, and the like to only in-state operations. See text Section 16-3c for additional discussion of the multistate taxation of related corporations.

Concept Summary 8.2 enumerates the major features of the Federal election to file a consolidated income tax return.

Concept Summary 8.2

The Consolidated Tax Return

1. Groups of corporations form for a variety of tax and non-tax reasons. The election to file Federal income tax returns on a consolidated basis allows certain affiliated group members to use their positive tax attributes (e.g., loss or credit carryovers) to offset negative tax attributes (e.g., positive taxable income) of other members.

2. Consolidated tax returns are limited to eligible corporations that satisfy stock ownership tests and meet various compliance requirements. For instance, all group members must conform their tax years to that of the parent of the group. Group members may use different tax accounting methods, however.

3. Group members are jointly and severally liable for the overall income tax liability of the group. For the most part, computations of estimated tax liabilities must be made on a consolidated basis. Methods are adopted under which the members determine their proportionate payment of any Federal income tax liabilities.

4. A consolidated group shares a common tax year, but members can retain or adopt different tax accounting methods.

LO.6

Compute a group's consolidated taxable income and a parent's investment basis in a subsidiary.

8-4 **STOCK BASIS OF SUBSIDIARY**

Upon acquiring a subsidiary, the parent corporation records a stock basis on its tax balance sheet equal to the acquisition price. At the end of every consolidated return year, the parent records one or more adjustments to this stock basis, as in the financial accounting "equity" method. This treatment prevents double taxation of gain (or deduction of loss) upon the ultimate disposal of the subsidiary's shares.[35] The adjustments are recorded on the last day of the consolidated return year or on the (earlier) date of the disposal of the shares.[36]

In this regard, positive adjustments to stock basis include the following.

- An allocable share of consolidated taxable income for the year.

- An allocable share of the consolidated operating or capital loss of a subsidiary that could not utilize the loss through a carryback to a prior year.

Negative adjustments to stock basis include the following.

- An allocable share of a consolidated taxable loss for the year.

- An allocable share of any carryover operating or capital losses that are deducted on the consolidated return and have not previously reduced stock basis.

- Dividends paid by the subsidiary to the parent out of the subsidiary's E & P.

---

[35]This procedure parallels the accounting for tax basis in a partnership or an S corporation. See Chapters 10 and 12.

[36]Reg. § 1.1502–32(a). Basis adjustments also are allowed when necessary to determine a tax liability (e.g., when member stock is bought or sold).

The Big Picture

EXAMPLE 15

Return to the facts of *The Big Picture* on p. 8-1. Assume that Alexander acquired all of the outstanding Hamilton stock on January 1, year 1, for $1,000,000. The parties immediately elected to file consolidated Federal income tax returns. Hamilton reported a 2018 taxable loss of $100,000, but it generated $40,000 taxable income in year 2 and $65,000 in year 3. Hamilton paid a $10,000 dividend to Alexander in mid-year 3.

Alexander holds the following stock bases in Hamilton on the last day of each of the indicated tax years.

| **Year 1** | $900,000 | **Year 2** | $940,000 | **Year 3** | $995,000 |

When accumulated postacquisition negative adjustments to the stock basis of the subsidiary exceed the acquisition price plus prior positive adjustments, the stock basis becomes zero and an **excess loss account** is created.[37] This account (1) allows the consolidated return to recognize the losses of the subsidiary in the current year and (2) enables the group to avoid the need to reflect a negative stock basis on its tax-basis balance sheet. If the subsidiary stock is redeemed or sold to a nongroup member while an excess loss account exists, the seller recognizes the balance of the account as capital gain income.[38]

EXAMPLE 16

Parent Corporation acquired all of the stock of SubCo early in year 1, for $100,000. As a result of SubCo's operations, the group records the amounts listed.

Year	Operating Gain/(Loss)	Stock Basis	Excess Loss Account
1	($40,000)	$60,000	$ –0–
2	(80,000)	–0–	20,000
3	30,000	10,000	–0–

If Parent sells the SubCo stock for $50,000 at the end of year 2, Parent recognizes a $70,000 capital gain ($50,000 amount realized − $0 adjusted basis in stock + $20,000 recovery of excess loss account). If the sale takes place at the end of year 3, the capital gain is $40,000.[39]

In a chain of more than one tier of subsidiaries, the computation of the stock basis amounts starts with the lowest-level subsidiary, then proceeds up the ownership structure to the parent's holdings.[40]

There is no such concept as consolidated E & P in the Federal income tax law. Rather, each entity accounts for its own share of consolidated taxable income on an annual basis, immediately recognizing within E & P any gain or loss on intercompany transactions and reducing E & P by an allocable share of the consolidated tax liability.[41]

8-5 COMPUTING CONSOLIDATED TAXABLE INCOME

When an affiliated group computes its taxable income for the year, it does not simply add together the separate taxable income amounts of its members. Two groups of transactions are removed from the members' tax returns and receive special treatment. Then the special items are recombined with the remaining items of members' taxable incomes

[37]Reg. § 1.1502–19.

[38]Reg. §§ 1.1502–19(a)(1) and (2).

[39]The year 3 subsidiary income is used first to eliminate the excess loss account (i.e., before it creates a positive stock basis). Reg. § 1.1502–32(e)(3).

[40]Reg. § 1.1502–19(b)(3).

[41]Reg. § 1.1502–33(d). In the absence of an election to use some other allocation method, the consolidated tax liability is allocated to each group member according to the relative taxable income method.

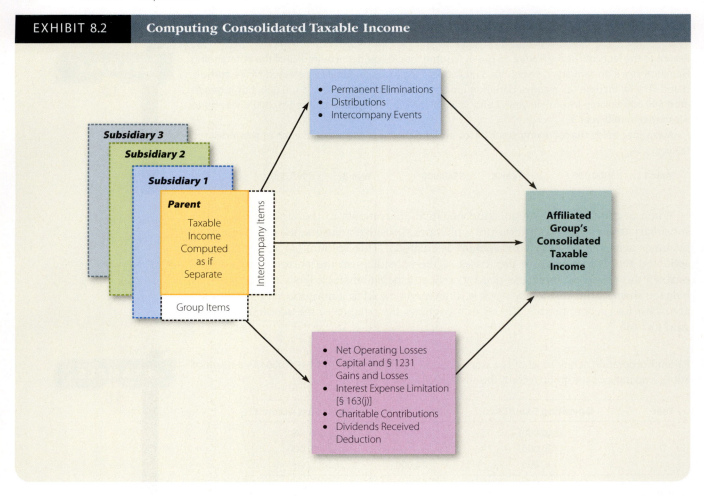

EXHIBIT 8.2   **Computing Consolidated Taxable Income**

to obtain the group's consolidated taxable income for the year. Exhibit 8.2 illustrates how consolidated taxable income is constructed using this sequential approach.

1. Taxable income is computed for each member on a separate basis.
2. "Group items" and "intercompany items" are isolated and receive special treatment.
3. The remaining separate incomes are combined with the group and intercompany items, resulting in consolidated taxable income.

The Code requires this computational procedure to accomplish several goals.

- Certain transactions are accounted for on a consolidated basis (e.g., charitable contributions and capital gains and losses). This requires that the transactions be isolated from the separate tax returns and computed on a groupwide basis.

- Gains and losses from certain intercompany transactions are deferred until a later tax year. Consequently, they are removed from the tax returns of the members that generated them.

- A few intercompany transactions (e.g., dividend payments) are removed from the taxable income calculation altogether, never to appear in a consolidated return.

8-5a Computational Procedure

The remainder of this chapter will follow the computational procedure suggested in Exhibit 8.2. Exhibit 8.3 presents a skeleton worksheet to be used for the procedure in the related examples. More information is added to the worksheet for every additional subsidiary. In each case, the starting point for this procedure is the separate taxable incomes of all of the group members. Adjustments then are made for group and intercompany items, as indicated in the footnotes to the worksheet.

EXHIBIT 8.3	Consolidated Taxable Income Worksheet

	Separate Taxable Income	Adjustments	Post-Adjustment Amounts
Parent information	_____	_____	_____
Subsidiary information	_____	_____	_____
Group-basis transactions	_____	_____	_____
Intercompany events	_____	_____	_____
Consolidated taxable income			_____

*Permanent eliminations.   **Group-basis transaction.   †Matching rule.

EXAMPLE 17

Parent Corporation owns 100% of the stock of SubCo. This year Parent's taxable income amounted to $100,000 and SubCo generated a $40,000 taxable loss. There were no transactions between the two corporations, and they incurred no capital or § 1231 gains/losses, charitable contributions, dividend income, or other items that are accounted for on a group basis. Accordingly, no adjustments are required, and consolidated taxable income is $60,000.

	Separate Taxable Income	Adjustments	Post-Adjustment Amounts
Parent information	$100,000	_____	$100,000
SubCo information	(40,000)	_____	(40,000)
Group-basis transactions	_____	_____	_____
Intercompany events	_____	_____	_____
Consolidated taxable income			$ 60,000

*Permanent eliminations.   **Group-basis transaction.   †Matching rule.

8-5b Typical Intercompany Transactions

LO.7
Account for the intercompany transactions of a consolidated group.

General Rules

When one member of a consolidated group engages in a transaction with another member of the group, an intercompany transaction occurs. In contrast to the financial accounting treatment of most such transactions, the most commonly encountered items *remain in* the members' separate taxable incomes and therefore cancel each other out on a consolidated basis. For instance, when one group member performs services for another member during the year, the purchaser of the services incurs a deductible expenditure; the service provider generates includible income. The net result is a zero addition to consolidated taxable income.[42]

This two-step procedure prevents the group from avoiding any related-party loss disallowances. Furthermore, when the members involved in the transaction are using different tax accounting methods, the payor's deduction for the expenditure is deferred until the year in which the recipient recognizes the related gross income.[43]

EXAMPLE 18

In the current year, Parent Corporation provided consulting services to its 100% owned subsidiary, SubCo, under a contract that requires no payments to Parent until next year. Both parties use the accrual method of tax accounting. The services that Parent rendered are valued at $100,000. In addition, Parent purchased $15,000 of supplies from SubCo.

continued

---

[42]Reg. §§ 1.1502–13(a)(1)(i) and (b)(1).   [43]§§ 267(a)(2) and (b)(3); Reg. § 1.1502–13(b)(2).

Including these transactions, Parent's taxable income for the year amounted to $500,000. SubCo reported $150,000 of separate taxable income. The group is not required to make any eliminating adjustments. The members' deductions incurred offset the income included by the other party to the intercompany transaction. The consolidated taxable income includes both Parent's $15,000 deduction for supplies and SubCo's $15,000 gross receipts from the sale, so the consolidated taxable income computation *de facto* results in an elimination similar to the kind made in financial accounting. No further adjustment is needed.

	Separate Taxable Income	Adjustments	Post-Adjustment Amounts
Parent information	$500,000	_____	$500,000
SubCo information	150,000	_____	150,000
Group-basis transactions	_____	_____	_____
Intercompany events	_____	_____	_____
Consolidated taxable income			$650,000
*Permanent eliminations.	**Group-basis transaction.		†Matching rule.

Assume instead that Parent is a cash basis taxpayer. Because Parent will not recognize the $100,000 of service income earned in the current year until the next tax period, SubCo's related deduction also is deferred until the following year. Thus, the intercompany item—SubCo's deduction—must be eliminated from consolidated taxable income. Additional record keeping is required to keep track of this intercompany transaction (and all others like it) so that the deduction is claimed in the appropriate year.

	Separate Taxable Income	Adjustments	Post-Adjustment Amounts
Parent information	$400,000	_____	$400,000
SubCo information	150,000	+ $100,000 due to use of different tax accounting methods	250,000
Group-basis transactions	_____	_____	_____
Intercompany events	_____	_____	_____
Consolidated taxable income			$650,000
*Permanent eliminations.	**Group-basis transaction.		†Matching rule.

Several other rules apply to intercompany transactions. Dividends received from other group members are eliminated from the recipients' separate taxable incomes, and no dividends received deduction is allowed.[44] When the distribution consists of noncash assets, the subsidiary payor realizes (but defers recognition of) any gain on the distributed property until the asset leaves the group; the (eliminated) dividend amount equals the fair market value of the asset.[45]

---

[44]Reg. § 1.1502–13(f)(2). If the distribution exceeds the payor's E & P, the stock basis of the payor is reduced. When the basis reaches zero, an excess loss account is created. Reg. § 1.1502–19(a). Cf. text Section 5-2d. Dividends received from nongroup members may result in a dividends received deduction; they constitute a group-basis item (discussed later in the chapter).

[45]§§ 301(b)(1) and (d); § 311(b)(1); Reg. §§ 1.1502–13(c)(7) and (f)(7).

Parent Corporation received a $50,000 cash dividend from 100%-owned SubCo in the current year. Including this item, Parent's separate taxable income amounted to $200,000, and SubCo reported $240,000 separate taxable income.

Parent cannot claim a dividends received deduction for this payment, but the dividend is eliminated in computing consolidated taxable income. No elimination is required for SubCo, as dividend payments are nondeductible.

	Separate Taxable Income	Adjustments	Post-Adjustment Amounts
Parent information	$200,000	−$50,000 dividend received from SubCo*	$150,000
SubCo information	240,000		240,000
Group-basis transactions			
Intercompany events			
Consolidated taxable income			$390,000

*Permanent eliminations. **Group-basis transaction. †Matching rule.

Members' Net Operating Losses

LO.8

Identify limitations that restrict the use of losses and credits of group members derived in separate return years.

Often the election to file consolidated returns is at least partly motivated by the parent corporation's desire to use the positive tax attributes of the subsidiary corporation, especially its NOLs. A number of provisions, however, discourage corporate acquisitions that are solely tax-motivated.[46]

The usual corporate NOL computations are available for the losses of the consolidated group. For tax years prior to 2018, such losses were carried back 2 years and then forward 20 years, although the parent could elect to forgo the carryback deductions for the group.[47] Losses arising after 2017 may not be carried back, only forward.[48] Such losses carry forward indefinitely until fully utilized. The losses may not reduce taxable income by more than 80 percent in the year the loss is applied.[49]

The consolidated NOL is derived after removing any consolidated charitable contribution deduction and capital gain or loss from consolidated taxable income. These items are treated separately because they have their own carryover periods and rules.

GLOBAL TAX ISSUES Consolidated Returns and NOLs

Very few countries outside the United States allow the use of consolidated returns. In the view of most countries, tax deductions for operating losses should be used only by those who generated them, not by some sister or other related corporation. This is as much a social principle (the sanctity of the corporate entity) as a revenue-raising provision (NOL deductions mean lower tax collections).

The way European business is conducted makes this result more understandable, because the tax laws of the various countries must ensure that operating losses generated in Tedesco, for instance, are not shifted to Cadenza and converted to deductions there.

---

[46]See text Section 7-4c and §§ 269, 381, 382, and 482.
[47]§ 172(b)(3).
[48]§ 172(b)(1)(A)(i).
[49]§ 172(a)(2).

Parent Corporation and SubCo have filed consolidated returns since both entities were incorporated in 2018. Neither group member incurred any capital gain or loss transactions during 2018–2021, nor did they make any charitable contributions. Taxable income computations for the members include the following.

Year	Parent's Taxable Income	SubCo's Taxable Income	Consolidated Taxable Income
2018	$100,000	$ 40,000	$140,000
2019	100,000	(40,000)	60,000
2020	100,000	(140,000)	?
2021	100,000	210,000	?

The 2020 consolidated loss of $40,000 is carried forward to reduce the 2021 consolidated taxable income.

Membership Changes Complications arise, however, when the corporations enter or depart from a consolidated group; members' operating losses are either incurred in a "separate return year" and deducted in a "consolidated return year" or vice versa. A variety of restrictions limit the availability of such deductions to discourage profitable corporations from acquiring unprofitable entities simply to file immediate refund claims based on loss and credit carryforwards. Exhibit 8.4 summarizes the applicable SRLY (separate return limitation year) limitations.

Where the members of a consolidated group change over time, the taxpayer apportions the consolidated NOL among the group members. When more than one group member generates a loss for the consolidated year, the following formula is used to apportion the loss among the electing group's members.

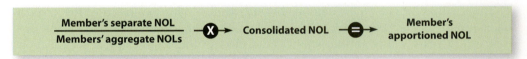

$$\frac{\text{Member's separate NOL}}{\text{Members' aggregate NOLs}} \quad \times \quad \text{Consolidated NOL} \quad = \quad \text{Member's apportioned NOL}$$

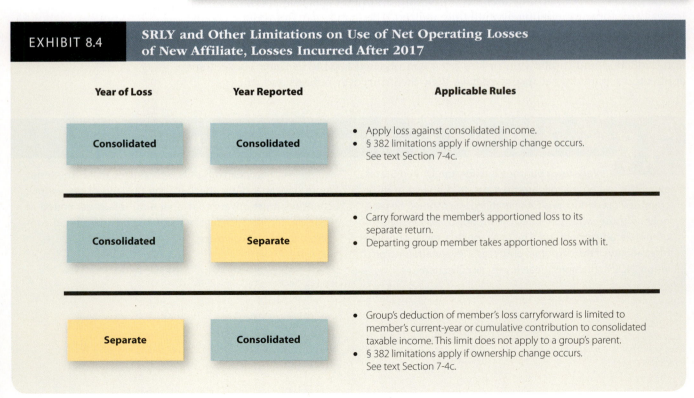

EXHIBIT 8.4	SRLY and Other Limitations on Use of Net Operating Losses of New Affiliate, Losses Incurred After 2017

Year of Loss	Year Reported	Applicable Rules
Consolidated	Consolidated	• Apply loss against consolidated income. • § 382 limitations apply if ownership change occurs. See text Section 7-4c.
Consolidated	Separate	• Carry forward the member's apportioned loss to its separate return. • Departing group member takes apportioned loss with it.
Separate	Consolidated	• Group's deduction of member's loss carryforward is limited to member's current-year or cumulative contribution to consolidated taxable income. This limit does not apply to a group's parent. • § 382 limitations apply if ownership change occurs. See text Section 7-4c.

Parent Corporation and SubCo have filed consolidated returns since year 2. Both entities were incorporated in year 1. Neither group member incurred any capital gain or loss transactions during years 1–4, nor did they make any charitable contributions. Taxable income computations for the members are listed below. All tax years occur after 2017.

EXAMPLE 21

Year	Parent's Taxable Income	SubCo's Taxable Income	Consolidated Taxable Income
1*	$100,000	$ 40,000	N/A
2**	100,000	(40,000)	$ 60,000
3**	100,000	(140,000)	(40,000)
4**	100,000	210,000	270,000

*Separate return year.
**Consolidated return year.

SubCo's losses are applied against consolidated income. The year 3 consolidated loss carries forward to year 4. SubCo did not bring any NOLs into the consolidated group as a carryforward.

When a corporation leaves a consolidated group, it takes with it any apportioned share of any unused loss carryforwards. The losses are used on its subsequent separate returns.

Parent Corporation, SubOne, and SubTwo have filed consolidated returns since year 1, the year in which all of the entities were incorporated. None of the group members incurred any capital gain or loss transactions during years 1–4, nor did they make any charitable contributions. Taxable income computations for the members are listed below. All tax years occur after 2017.

On the first day of year 4, a third-party investor purchases all of the stock of SubTwo. On its year 4 separate return, SubTwo can deduct its $53,333 share ($80,000 consolidated loss × $120,000 SubTwo's loss/$180,000 total losses in the group) of the year 3 $80,000 NOL carryforward.[50]

EXAMPLE 22

Year	Parent's Taxable Income	SubOne's Taxable Income	SubTwo's Taxable Income	Consolidated Taxable Income
1*	$100,000	$100,000	$ 40,000	$240,000
2*	100,000	100,000	(40,000)	160,000
3*	100,000	(60,000)	(120,000)	(80,000)
4**	100,000	100,000	210,000	N/A

*Consolidated return year.
**Separate return year.

SRLY Rules When an NOL is carried forward from a separate return year onto a consolidated return, another set of limitations, known as the **separate return limitation year (SRLY)** rules, applies.[51] The consolidated return can include an NOL carryforward from the member's SRLY period only to the extent of the lesser of its (1) current-year or (2) cumulative positive contribution to consolidated taxable income.[52] The SRLY rules apply to capital loss and credit carryforwards as well.

The SRLY limitations never apply to the electing group's identifiable parent.[53]

---

[50]SubTwo cannot take the entire $120,000 NOL that is attributable to it. Reg. §§ 1.1502–79(a)(1)(ii) and (b)(2)(ii). Losses are absorbed in the current consolidated return year before any loss apportionment occurs.

[51]Reg. § 1.1502–21(c).

[52]Reg. § 1.1502–21(c)(1)(i).

[53]Reg. § 1.1502–1(f)(2)(i), known as the "lonely parent" rule.

SRLY Limitations

EXAMPLE 23

Parent Corporation and SubCo have filed consolidated returns since year 2. Both entities were incorporated in year 1. Neither group member incurred any capital gain or loss transactions during years 1–4, nor did they make any charitable contributions. Taxable income computations for the members are listed below. All tax years occur after 2017.

Year	Parent's Taxable Income	SubCo's Taxable Income	Consolidated Taxable Income
1*	$100,000	($40,000)	N/A
2**	100,000	(10,000)	$90,000
3**	100,000	15,000	?
4**	100,000	70,000	?

  *Separate return year.
**Consolidated return year.

The thrust of the SRLY rules is to limit Parent's deduction of SubCo's losses from a separate return year against consolidated income. Accordingly, none of SubCo's separate return loss carried forward from year 1 can be deducted in computing year 2 consolidated taxable income; the deduction is limited to the lesser of SubCo's current-year (zero) or cumulative (zero) contribution to consolidated taxable income.

In computing year 3 consolidated taxable income, the SubCo SRLY loss deduction is limited to $5,000, the lesser of SubCo's current-year ($15,000) or cumulative ($5,000) contribution to consolidated taxable income. The remaining SRLY deduction reduces consolidated taxable income beginning in year 4.

EXAMPLE 24

Parent Corporation and SubCo have filed consolidated returns since year 2. Both entities were incorporated in year 1. Neither group member incurred any capital gain or loss transactions during years 1–4, nor did they make any charitable contributions. Taxable income computations for the members are listed below. All tax years occur after 2017.

Year	Parent's Taxable Income	SubCo's Taxable Income	Consolidated Taxable Income
1*	($ 40,000)	$100,000	N/A
2**	(100,000)	(10,000)	($110,000)
3**	20,000	165,000	?
4**	100,000	70,000	?

  *Separate return year.
**Consolidated return year.

The year 3 consolidated return can include a deduction for Parent's entire year 1 NOL of $40,000. The deduction is not limited to the lesser of Parent's current-year ($20,000) or cumulative (zero) contribution to consolidated taxable income. SRLY rules do not apply to the group's parent.

When both the SRLY rules and a § 382 limitation apply because an ownership change has occurred (see Chapter 7), the § 382 provisions override the SRLY limits.[54]

---

[54]Reg. §§ 1.1502–21(g) and –22(g).

The Parent consolidated group includes SubTwo, which was acquired as part of a § 382 ownership change. SubTwo brought with it to the group a $180,000 NOL carryforward, $125,000 of which is available this year under the SRLY rules due to SubTwo's positive contribution to the group's taxable income. The § 382 limitation with respect to SubTwo is $100,000. Accordingly, only $100,000 of the SubTwo NOL can be used to reduce consolidated taxable income this year.

If the § 382 limitation had been $200,000 instead, the full $180,000 NOL deduction would have been allowed. The § 382 rules prevail even with respect to SRLY losses that overlap with the same tax year.

8-5c Computation of Group Items

LO.9

Derive deductions and credits on a consolidated basis.

Several income and deduction items are derived on a consolidated-group basis. Therefore, statutory limitations and allowances are applied to the group as though it were a single corporation. This computational convention allows group members to match various types of gains and losses and to increase specific limitations, required by the Code, in a manner that optimizes the overall tax benefit.

Specifically, the following items are computed on a group basis with the usual C corporation tax effects applied to the combined group amounts.

- Net capital gain/loss.
- § 1231 gain/loss.
- § 163(j) interest expense limitation.
- Various tax credits and recapture amounts.

- Casualty/theft gain/loss.
- Charitable contributions.
- Dividends received deduction.
- Net operating loss.

Following the computational procedure of Exhibits 8.2 and 8.3, all of the group-basis items are removed from each member's separate taxable income. Then, using the consolidated taxable income figure to that point, statutory limitations are applied to determine group-basis gains, losses, income, and deductions.

Parent Corporation's current-year taxable income included $300,000 net income from operations and a $50,000 net long-term capital gain. Parent also made a $40,000 contribution to State University. Accordingly, its separate taxable income amounted to $315,000.

Income from operations	$ 300,000
Capital gain income	+ 50,000
Charitable contribution (maximum)	− 35,000
Separate taxable income	$ 315,000

SubCo generated $170,000 income from operations and incurred a $45,000 short-term capital loss. Thus, its separate taxable income was $170,000, and aggregate separate taxable income for the group amounted to $485,000.

Upon consolidation, a larger amount of Parent's charitable contribution is deductible, and its capital gain is almost fully sheltered from current-year tax.

continued

	Separate Taxable Income	Adjustments	Post- Adjustment Amounts
Parent information	$315,000	−$50,000 capital gain income**	$300,000
		+$35,000 charitable contribution deduction**	
SubCo information	170,000	$45,000 short-term capital loss**	170,000
Group-basis transactions		+$5,000 net long-term capital gain	−35,000
		−$40,000 charitable contribution deduction (maximum for group is $47,500)[55]	
Intercompany events			
Consolidated taxable income			$435,000

*Permanent eliminations.   **Group-basis transaction.   †Matching rule.

Computing these items on a group basis does not always result in a reduction of aggregate group taxable income.

EXAMPLE 27

Parent Corporation owns 15% of the stock of Outsider Corporation throughout the year. Outsider paid a $150,000 dividend to Parent during the year. Parent also generated $400,000 of taxable operating income and sold a § 1231 asset at a $10,000 gain. Parent's separate taxable income is computed below.

Operating income	$ 400,000
Dividend income	+ 150,000
§ 1231 gain	+ 10,000
Dividends received deduction (50%)	− 75,000
Separate taxable income	$ 485,000

A 10% owner of Outsider, SubCo received a $100,000 cash dividend from that entity. SubCo's operations produced a $20,000 net taxable loss for the year, and it sold a § 1231 asset at a $4,000 loss. Thus, SubCo's separate taxable income is computed as follows.

Operating income	($ 20,000)
Dividend income	+ 100,000
§ 1231 loss	− 4,000
Dividends received deduction[56]	− 38,000
Separate taxable income	$ 38,000

A consolidated return for Parent and SubCo increases the group's dividends received deduction,[57] but it wastes the opportunity to claim SubCo's § 1231 loss as an ordinary deduction.

continued

---

[55]§ 170(b)(2)(A).

[56]Limited to 50% of taxable income before the deduction. § 246(b)(1).

[57]The group cannot apply a 65% rate for the dividends received deduction, even though aggregate group ownership in Outsider now exceeds 20%. Reg. § 1.1502–26(a)(1)(i).

	Separate Taxable Income	Adjustments	Post-Adjustment Amounts
Parent information	$485,000	−$150,000 dividend received from Outsider**	$400,000
		−$10,000 § 1231 gain**	
		+$75,000 dividends received deduction**	
SubCo information	38,000	−$100,000 dividend received from Outsider**	−20,000
		+$4,000 § 1231 loss	
		+$38,000 dividends received deduction	
Group-basis transactions		+$250,000 dividend received from Outsider	+131,000
		−$125,000 dividends received deduction (50% × $250,000)	
		+$6,000 § 1231 gain	
Intercompany events			
Consolidated taxable income			$511,000

*Permanent eliminations.	**Group-basis transaction.	†Matching rule.

8-5d **The Matching Rule**

A special class of intercompany transactions receives deferral treatment.[58] The gain or loss realized on these transactions is removed from consolidated taxable income until the sold asset leaves the affiliated group. The purpose of this matching rule is to prevent group members from accelerating loss deductions that relate to sales of assets within the group. In effect, for purposes of these intercompany transactions, the group is treated as a single corporation with multiple operating divisions.

The matching rule applies to sales of assets or the performance of services among group members. The entire deferred gain or loss enters the consolidated taxable income computation when, for example, the asset is transferred outside the group through a subsequent sale. The matching rule also affects cost recovery computations when a group member purchases a business asset in an intercompany transaction.

Full gain or loss recognition also can be triggered under the acceleration rule when the transferor of the property leaves the group or the consolidation election is terminated.[59] The acceleration rule applies when it no longer is possible to produce a proper result under the matching rule.

Generally, the gain or loss on the sale outside the group is recognized in the same manner as it would have been on the initial transfer.

In most cases, the matching rule is attractive to the group when intercompany sales take place at a gain. When such sales generate losses, however, the mandatory nature of the rule may become burdensome.

Concept Summary 8.3 reviews some of the advanced features of the Federal election to file a consolidated income tax return.

---

[58]Reg. § 1.1502–13.

[59]Reg. § 1.1502–13(d)(1)(i).

EXAMPLE

28

Parent Corporation sold a plot of land to SubCo in the current year for $100,000. Parent had acquired the land 10 years ago for $40,000. The consolidated return also reflects the operating results of the parties: Parent generated $10,000 income, and SubCo produced a $100,000 gain.

This intercompany transaction triggers the matching rule: Parent's $60,000 realized gain is deferred through an elimination in the computation of consolidated taxable income. The $60,000 gain is recognized by the group when SubCo later sells the land to Outsider Corporation.

	Separate Taxable Income	Adjustments	Post-Adjustment Amounts
Parent information	$ 70,000	_____	$ 70,000
SubCo information	100,000	_____	100,000
Group-basis transactions			
Intercompany events		−$60,000 gain on intercompany sale to SubCo†	−60,000
Consolidated taxable income			$110,000

*Permanent eliminations.   **Group-basis transaction.   †Matching rule.

SubCo sold the land to Outsider for $110,000 in a year in which its operating income totaled $60,000 (exclusive of the sale of the land). Parent's operating income amounted to $170,000.

	Separate Taxable Income	Adjustments	Post-Adjustment Amounts
Parent information	$170,000	_____	$170,000
SubCo information	70,000	_____	70,000
Group-basis transactions			
Intercompany events		+$60,000 restored gain on Parent's sale to SubCo†	+60,000
Consolidated taxable income			$300,000

*Permanent eliminations.   **Group-basis transaction.   †Matching rule.

Concept Summary 8.3

The Consolidated Taxable Income

1. In computing consolidated taxable income, certain items are aggregated among the members; some intercompany gains and losses are deferred until later tax periods.
2. Group items, such as charitable contributions and § 1231 gains and losses, are treated in a different manner when computing consolidated taxable income. They are removed from the aggregate taxable income computations, and then various limitations are applied to the combined amounts from all of the affiliates.
3. Gain or loss recognition may be deferred for a transaction between affiliates under the matching rule.

8-6 TAX PLANNING

LO.10
Demonstrate tax planning opportunities available to consolidated groups.

8-6a Choosing Consolidated Return Partners

Taxpayers should optimize their overall tax benefits when choosing consolidated return partners. Within the limitations of the rules discussed earlier in the chapter, attributes of potential target corporations might include some of the following.

- Loss and credit carryovers.
- Passive activity income, loss, or credits.
- Gains that can be deferred through intercompany sales.
- Excess limitation amounts (e.g., with respect to charitable contributions).
- § 1231 gains, losses, and lookback profiles.

8-6b Consolidation versus 100 Percent Dividends Received Deduction

When adequate ownership is held, a 100 percent dividends received deduction is available for payments received from subsidiaries with whom a consolidated return is *not* filed. Thus, this tax benefit is still available when the taxpayer wants to affiliate with an insurance company, a foreign entity, or other ineligible corporation. The 100 percent deduction also is attractive if the parent cannot find potential group partners with the desired level of complementary tax attributes.

8-6c Protecting the Group Members' Liability for Tax Payments

Because all group members are responsible for consolidated tax liabilities, interest, and penalties, target subsidiaries and their (present and potential) shareholders should take measures to protect their separate interests.

A short tax year may be created when a member with a nonmatching tax year joins or leaves the group. When this occurs, the group should consider measures to limit the ensuing negative tax consequences. For instance, additional income can be accelerated into the short year of acquisition. This will reduce any loss carryforwards when the carryover period is effectively shortened due to the takeover.

In the context of a corporate takeover, the controlling intercompany documents should address the tax-sharing agreement. Members should allow for reimbursement between affiliates when a member cannot pay its allocated portion of the group's income tax liability. Another provision in the agreement should address the allocation of taxes caused by the takeover itself. For example, should some of the resulting tax liability be paid by affiliates, or should it be paid entirely by the target corporation?

Return to the facts of Example 12. Exposure by SubCo and its successive shareholders to tax (and all other) liabilities of Parent Corporation should be minimized by including appropriate clauses in purchase contracts and related documents. For instance, (1) Parent Corporation could alter its negotiating position so that it pays less to acquire the SubCo stock or (2) SubCo might attempt to recover any Parent taxes that it pays through courts other than the Tax Court.

EXAMPLE
29

SHOULD THE AFFILIATED GROUP FILE A CONSOLIDATED RETURN?

If Alexander and Hamilton are restructured as an affiliated group in a qualifying reorganization and both corporations continue to exist as separate entities, the parties should consider an election to file their Federal income tax returns on a consolidated basis. Assuming that Hamilton begins to generate positive taxable income in the near future as expected, the NOLs and other attractive tax attributes that Hamilton brings to the group will be of great benefit to both corporations.

The group also may benefit from other aspects of Hamilton's tax situation, including its accumulated capital and passive losses, and credits that have been carried forward due to a lack of tax liability. In all likelihood, Alexander and Hamilton are a "good match" as potential consolidated return partners.

What If?

But what if Alexander's expectations for a turnaround in Hamilton's business fortunes prove to be incorrect and the subsidiary continues to generate NOLs? The SRLY rules and § 382 limitations may prevent the deductions and credits acquired from Hamilton from being of immediate use to the affiliated group. A consolidation election is beneficial only if the Hamilton subsidiary generates positive postacquisition taxable income.

Key Terms

Acceleration rule, 8-25	Controlled group, 8-7	Separate return limitation year (SRLY), 8-21
Affiliated group, 8-6	Excess loss account, 8-15	
Consolidated returns, 8-2	Matching rule, 8-25	

Discussion Questions

Communications 1. **LO.1** You are making a presentation to the board of directors of HugeCo about the merits of acquiring Bitty, Ltd., an important supplier. One board member, knowing that you are a tax specialist, asks you to list some of the nontax reasons to make the acquisition. List at least four such motivations in a PowerPoint slide.

2. **LO.1** In working as the tax consultant for LargeCo, Megan discovers that for the first time, the corporation is eligible to form a consolidated group for filing its Federal corporate income tax returns. List two or more of the events that likely have occurred involving LargeCo that triggered the availability of the consolidation election. Include nontax events in making the list.

Critical Thinking 3. **LO.2** The tax rules governing the Federal consolidated tax return elections are largely in the form of Treasury Regulations and IRS rulings. Why? When is the split between the legislative and executive branches in tax-writing responsibilities:

    a.   Appropriate?

    b.   Inappropriate?

4. **LO.2, 3, 4** Financial accounting rules do not always match the tax treatment of transactions involving groups of U.S. corporations. List at least two areas where tax and accounting rules differ when groups of affiliated corporations are involved.

5. **LO.3** The local CPA Society is presenting its annual tax conference. Most of the attendees will be career tax professionals who work with smaller clients. You have been asked to submit an outline for your talk "When to Use a Consolidated Tax Return: Federal Tax Law Issues." Organize an outline that lists the advantages and disadvantages of a consolidation election. Include at least five points in each category. Keep your points at the introductory level, since most of the members of your audience know the rest of the tax law well but do not work regularly in this area.

   Communications

6. **LO.3, 4, 5** List the structural and compliance requirements under Federal income tax law that must be met before a parent and its affiliates are allowed to file on a consolidated basis. Consider only the requirements for the group to file its *first* consolidated return.

7. **LO.3, 10** Black, Brown, and Red corporations are considering a corporate restructuring that would allow them to file Federal income tax returns on a consolidated basis. Black holds significant NOL carryforwards from several years ago, all after 2017. Brown always has been profitable and is projected to remain so. Red has been successful, but its product cycles are mature and operating losses are likely to begin three years from now and last for a decade. What tax issues should the corporations consider before electing to file on a consolidated basis?

   Critical Thinking

8. **LO.3, 10** Continue with the facts presented in Question 7. In addition, assume that Brown Corporation has a history of making large, continuous charitable contributions that are important in its community. In the next three years, Brown's largest investment assets will be priced such that they will be attractive candidates for sale. Modify your list of tax issues to include these considerations.

   Critical Thinking

9. **LO.3, 5, 9, 10** Indicate whether each of the following would make good consolidated return partners in computing the affiliated group's Federal income tax. Explain why or why not.

   a. SubCo has a number of appreciated assets that it wants to sell to its parent, Huge Corporation.

   b. SubCo has a number of assets that it wants to sell to its parent, Huge. The assets have declined in market value since SubCo purchased them.

   c. ParentCo uses cost depletion in accounting for its natural resources, whereas SubCo wants to continue to claim percentage depletion.

   d. ParentCo uses a calendar tax year, whereas SubTwo has been using a September 30 tax year-end.

10. **LO.3, 5, 10** Indicate whether each of the following would make good consolidated return partners in computing the affiliated group's Federal income tax. Explain why or why not.

   a. ParentCo would like to file on a consolidated basis with SubOne because the subsidiary will be generating sizable operating losses in the next two tax years. Starting with the third tax year, though, SubOne will enter a highly profitable period.

   b. This year ParentCo generated $4 million in taxable income, and its wholly owned subsidiary, Small Corporation, reported a $3 million operating loss. Next year, though, Small is projected to start a four-year period with $20 million total taxable profits.

   c. ParentCo is highly profitable and makes a large annual gift in support of the local tax-exempt zoological gardens. SubCo reports sizable operating losses every year.

11. **LO.4** Provide the information required to complete the following chart.

Group of Entities	Eligible to Join a Consolidated Group?	Why or Why Not Eligible?
a. Lima City Choral Artists Co-op	_____	_____
b. Columbus United Health Insurance, Ltd.	_____	_____
c. Bethke Services, Inc.	_____	_____
d. Tequila Teléfono, organized in El Salvador	_____	_____
e. Vermont, South Carolina, and Utah Barbershops, Inc.	_____	_____
f. Capital Management Partnership	_____	_____
g. Henry Pontiac Trust	_____	_____

12. **LO.5** The Pelican Group cannot decide whether to start to file on a consolidated basis for Federal income tax purposes, effective for its tax year beginning January 1, 2020. Its computational study of the effects of consolidation is taking longer than expected. What is the latest date by which the group must make this critical decision? What tax forms must be filed by that date?

Decision Making   13. **LO.5** The consolidated tax liability for most affiliated groups is assigned among the parent and its subsidiaries—each entity is responsible for "its share" of the tax. The Regulations allow several methods to be used to compute these allocations. In this context, define the two most commonly encountered tax-sharing methods used by Federal consolidated tax return groups. When would a subsidiary corporation prefer one method over another?

   a.   The *relative taxable income* method.

   b.   The *relative tax liability* method.

Communications   14. **LO.6** Your firm has assigned you to work with Jeri Byers, the tax director of a small group of corporations. The group qualifies to file on a consolidated basis and plans to make its first election to file in that manner. In a memo for Jeri's tax file, describe some of the more important adjustments she will need to make to keep track of the parent corporation's basis in the stock of each of the subsidiaries.

Decision Making   15. **LO.6** Friar Corporation is the parent entity in a Federal consolidated group for corporate income tax purposes. It has a $3 million basis in the stock of its wholly owned subsidiary, Abbey, Ltd. This year Abbey reports a $4 million taxable loss.

   a.   What is Friar's basis in the Abbey stock after accounting for this operating loss?

   b.   Friar is considering a sale of the Abbey stock, since prospects for Abbey's future earnings are not encouraging. Comment on the tax consequences that would result if this sale occurs as they pertain to the stock basis computations.

16. **LO.6** Certain Corporation is the parent entity in a Federal consolidated group for corporate income tax purposes. When its wholly owned subsidiary, Likely, Inc., reports an operating profit, Certain's basis in the Likely stock increases, as does the balance in the consolidated E & P account for the group. Comment on this statement.

17. **LO.6** Outline the process by which a consolidated group computes its Federal taxable income. Your description should match the approach taken in Exhibit 8.2.

Critical Thinking   18. **LO.8** Mini Corporation brought a $7 million NOL carryforward into the Mucho Group of corporations that elected to file on a consolidated basis as of the beginning of this year. Combined results for the year generated $15 million taxable income, $2 million of which was attributable to Mini's activities for the year. Has Mini been a good consolidation partner? Explain.

19. **LO.8** The consolidated return Regulations employ the "SRLY" rules to limit the losses a parent can claim with respect to a newly acquired subsidiary. Explain the tax policy behind the SRLY rules. Describe how they affect the timing of loss deductions after an acquisition.

20. **LO.9** The computational method of Exhibit 8.2 indicates that consolidated taxable income includes a number of group items where limitations are applied on an aggregate basis. In no more than two slides, list as many group items as you can.   Communications

21. **LO.9, 10** Intercompany transactions of a consolidated group can be subject to a "matching rule" and an "acceleration rule."   Decision Making
    a. Define both terms.
    b. As a tax planner structuring an intercompany transaction, when would it be beneficial to use either rule?

22. **LO.9** Use a timeline to diagram the gain/loss recognition by this affiliated group.   Communications
    • Year 1: SubCo purchases a nondepreciable asset for $400.
    • Year 3: SubCo sells the asset to Parent for $575.
    • Year 4: Parent sells the asset to Stranger (not an affiliate) for $660.

23. **LO.9** Use a timeline to diagram the gain/loss recognition by this affiliated group.   Communications
    • Year 1: SubCo purchases an asset for $400.
    • Year 3: SubCo sells the asset to Parent for $300.
    • Year 4: Parent sells the asset to Stranger (not an affiliate) for $240.

Computational Exercises

24. **LO.5** The Parent consolidated group reports the following results for the tax year.

Entity	Income or Loss
Parent	$10,000
Sub1	(1,500)
Sub2	4,000
Sub3	2,000

    a. What is the group's consolidated taxable income and consolidated tax liability?
    b. If the Parent group has consented to the relative taxable income method, how will the consolidated tax liability be allocated among the Parent and Subsidiaries 1, 2, and 3?

25. **LO.6** Clifton Corporation acquired all of the outstanding Gillion stock on January 1, year 1, for $2,400,000. The parties immediately elected to file consolidated Federal income tax returns.

    Gillion reported a year 1 taxable loss of $250,000, but it generated $400,000 of taxable income in year 2 and $180,000 in year 3. Gillion paid a $100,000 dividend to Clifton in year 2 and $300,000 in year 3. Compute Clifton's stock basis in Gillion on the last day of each of the following tax years.
    a. Year 1.
    b. Year 2.
    c. Year 3.

26. **LO.8** Parent and Child corporations have filed on a consolidated basis since the mid-1970s. The group reports the following amounts for the current tax year.

What is the Parent group's net operating loss for the year that is available for carryforward?

Operating loss, including the following	$2,500,000
Charitable contributions	600,000
Net capital gain	1,100,000
Dividends received deduction	450,000

27. **LO.8** Put owned all of the stock of Call when the two corporations were formed a decade ago. The group immediately elected to file on a consolidated basis. Now Call's management team has purchased the company from the parent and intends to carry on and expand the business into new markets.

    When Call left the Put consolidated group, the group held a $5,000,000 2018 NOL carryforward, $2,000,000 of which was attributable to Call's operations under formulas approved by all of the parties. Call will generate $700,000 in taxable income on each of its first five years' worth of separate returns.

    Advise Call as to who "owns" the carryforwards after the corporate division.

28. **LO.9** Parent Corporation's current-year taxable income included $100,000 net income from operations and a $10,000 net long-term capital gain. Parent also made a $5,000 charitable contribution. SubCo generated $45,000 income from operations and incurred a $2,000 short-term capital loss.

    a.   How much is Parent's separate taxable income?

    b.   How much is SubCo's separate taxable income?

    c.   How much is consolidated taxable income?

Problems

29. **LO.3, 7** Your client, Big Corporation, and its wholly owned subsidiary, LittleCo, file a consolidated return for Federal income tax purposes. Indicate both the financial accounting and the tax treatment of the following transactions.

    a.   LittleCo pays a $1,000,000 dividend to Big.

    b.   LittleCo sells investment land to Big. LittleCo's basis in the land is $200,000. The sale price is $600,000.

    c.   Six months after purchasing the land from LittleCo, Big sells the investment land to Phillips, an unrelated party, for $750,000.

30. **LO.3, 5** Boulder Corporation owns all of the stock of PebbleCo, so they constitute a Federal affiliated group and a parent-subsidiary controlled group. By completing the following chart, delineate for Boulder's tax department some of the effects of an election to file Federal consolidated income tax returns.

Situation	If the Group Files a Consolidated Return	If Separate Income Tax Returns Continue to Be Filed
a. PebbleCo pays a $1,000,000 cash dividend to Boulder.	_____	_____
b. Boulder's tax liability is $95,000, and Pebble's liability totals $75,000.	_____	_____
c. Boulder uses the LIFO method for its inventories, but Pebble wants to use FIFO for its own inventories.	_____	_____

31. **LO.5** Grand Corporation owns all of the stock of Junior, Ltd., a corporation that has been declared bankrupt and holds no net assets. Junior still owes $1 million to Wholesale, Inc., one of its suppliers, and $2.5 million to the IRS for unpaid Federal income taxes. Grand and Junior always have filed Federal income tax returns on a consolidated basis. What is Grand's exposure concerning Junior's outstanding income tax liabilities?

32. **LO.5** The Chief consolidated group reports the following results for the tax year. Dollar amounts are listed in millions.

	Parent	SubOne	SubTwo	SubThree	Consolidated
Ordinary income	$600	$200	$140	($90)	$ 850
Capital gain/loss	–0–	–0–	60	(25)	35
§ 1231 gain/loss	250	–0–	(50)	–0–	200
Separate taxable incomes	$850	$200	$150	($90) with a $25 capital loss carryover	
Consolidated taxable income					$1,085
Consolidated tax liability					$ 228
Energy tax credit, from SubOne					(20)
Net tax due					$ 208

Determine each member's share of the consolidated tax liability. All of the members have consented to use the relative taxable income method.

33. **LO.5** Assume the same facts as in Problem 32, except that the group members have adopted the relative tax liability tax-sharing method.

34. **LO.6** Senior, Ltd., acquires all of the stock of JuniorCo for $30 million at the beginning of year 1. The group immediately elects to file income tax returns on a consolidated basis. Senior's operations generate a $50 million profit every year. In year 2, JuniorCo pays its parent a $9 million dividend. Operating results for JuniorCo are as follows. Compute Senior's basis in the JuniorCo stock as of the end of years 1, 2, and 3. All tax years occur after 2017.

Tax Year	Taxable Income
1	$ 4 million
2	12 million
3	15 million

35. **LO.6** Continue with the facts of Problem 34.
   a. Assume instead that JuniorCo's tax year 2 produced a $6 million NOL.
   b. Same as part (a), except that JuniorCo's tax year 2 produced a $40 million NOL.
   c. Continue with the facts of part (b). Express as a Microsoft Excel command the computation of Senior's excess loss account as of the end of each of the tax years discussed.

36. **LO.6** WhaleCo acquired all of the common stock of MinnowCo early in year 1 for $900,000, and MinnowCo immediately elected to join WhaleCo's consolidated Federal income tax return. As part of the takeover, WhaleCo also acquired $300,000 of MinnowCo bonds. The results of MinnowCo for the first few years of the group operations were reported as follows.

Tax Year	Operating Gain/Loss	Stock Basis
1	$ 100,000	_____
2	(800,000)	_____
3	(600,000)	_____

Determine WhaleCo's basis in its MinnowCo common stock as of the end of each tax year.

37. **LO.6** Continue with the facts of Problem 36. WhaleCo has determined that it will sell all of its MinnowCo stock at the end of year 3 for $250,000. Taking into account the rules regarding excess loss accounts, determine WhaleCo's gain/loss from its sale of the MinnowCo stock.

38. **LO.6** Compute consolidated taxable income for calendar years 1–4 for Blue Group, which elected consolidated status immediately upon creation of the two member corporations in January of year 1. All recognized income relates to the consulting services of the firms. No intercompany transactions were completed during the indicated years.

Tax Year	Blue Corporation	Orange Corporation
1	$250,000	($ 70,000)
2	250,000	(30,000)
3	250,000	(240,000)
4	250,000	85,000

39. **LO.6, 8** Determine consolidated taxable income for calendar years 1–4 for Yeti Group, which elected consolidated status immediately upon the creation of the two member corporations on January 1 of year 1. All recognized income is ordinary in nature, and no intercompany transactions were completed during the indicated years. All tax years occur after 2017.

Tax Year	Yeti Corporation	Snowman Corporation
1	$450,000	$ 70,000
2	450,000	(310,000)
3	450,000	(600,000)
4	450,000	75,000

40. **LO.8** Cougar, Jaguar, and Ocelot corporations have filed on a consolidated, calendar year basis for many years. At the beginning of the tax year, the group elects to de-consolidate. The group's $6 million NOL carryforward can be traced in the following manner: one-half to Cougar's operations and one-quarter each to Jaguar's and Ocelot's. How will Ocelot treat the NOL on its separate tax return?

41. **LO.8** The Giant consolidated group includes SubTwo, which was acquired as part of a § 382 ownership change. SubTwo brought with it to the group a large NOL carryforward, $3,000,000 of which is available this year under the SRLY rules due to SubTwo's positive contribution to the group's taxable income. The § 382 limitation with respect to SubTwo is $500,000.

    a.   How much of SubTwo's NOL can be used this year to reduce consolidated taxable income?

    b.   Express this computation as a Microsoft Excel command.

42. **LO.8** Child Corporation joined the Thrust consolidated group in year 1. At the time it joined the group, Child held a $2,000,000 NOL carryforward. On a consolidated basis, the members of Thrust generated significant profits for many years.

Child's operating results during the first few consolidated return years were as follows. The § 382 rules do not apply to the group. All tax years occur after 2017.

Tax Year	Taxable Income
1	($ 100,000)
2	1,600,000
3	1,800,000

a. How will Child's NOLs affect consolidated taxable income for each of these years?

b. Express your computations for years 2 and 3 as a Microsoft Excel formula.

43. **LO.7, 9** B.I.G. Corporation sold a plot of undeveloped land to SubCo this year for $100,000. B.I.G. had acquired the land several years ago for $40,000. The consolidated return also reflects the operating results of the parties: B.I.G. generated $130,000 income from operations, and SubCo produced a $20,000 operating loss.

    Critical Thinking

a. Use the computational worksheet of Exhibit 8.3 to derive the group members' separate taxable incomes and the group's consolidated taxable income.

b. Same as part (a), except that five years later SubCo sold the land to Outsider Corporation for $130,000, when its operating income totaled $20,000 (exclusive of the sale of the land), and Parent's operating income amounted to $90,000.

c. Using a 25% combined state and Federal income tax rate and the materials from text Appendix F, compute the benefit to the group of deferring the gain on the sale of the land. The B.I.G. group uses a 4% after-tax internal rate of return for purposes of this analysis.

Research Problems

Note: Solutions to the Research Problems can be prepared by using the Thomson Reuters Checkpoint™ online tax research database, which accompanies this textbook. Solutions can also be prepared by using research materials found in a typical tax library.

THOMSON REUTERS
CHECKPOINT™

Research Problem 1. The Cardinal Group had filed on a consolidated basis for several years with its wholly owned subsidiary, Swallow, Inc. The group used a calendar tax year.

On January 25, 2016, Heron acquired all of the stock of Cardinal, including its ownership in Swallow, an important supplier for Heron's manufacturing process. All parties in the new group intended to file on a consolidated basis immediately and, indeed, used consolidated amounts in filing the 2016 Heron Group return on September 10, 2017.

During the audit of Heron Group's 2016 tax return, the IRS disallowed the use of the consolidated method because no Forms 1122 had ever been filed for the affiliates in the new group. In a memo for the tax research file, summarize the possibilities for the Heron Group to be granted an extension to elect consolidated return status.

Research Problem 2. Graeter Corporation acquired all of the stock of Lesser Corporation in 2016, and the entities have filed a state and Federal consolidated income tax return ever since. Now an audit notice from the state unemployment tax administration makes it clear that Lesser underpaid its state and Federal payroll taxes by $2 million. Lesser's cash flow at this time is poor, and it has insufficient funds to pay the delinquent amount plus interest and penalties. Can the state revenue agency collect the outstanding payroll tax from Graeter under the Federal "joint and several liability" rule for tax obligations of consolidated return affiliates? Explain.

Use internet tax resources to address the following questions. Look for reliable websites and blogs of the IRS and other government agencies, media outlets, businesses, tax professionals, academics, think tanks, and political outlets.

Data Analytics

Communications

Critical Thinking

Research Problem 3. Using data from the IRS Stats website, assess the size of the businesses that file Federal consolidated returns, and their taxable activities. In a table that you send to your instructor, make a side-by-side comparison of (a) all C corporations using Forms 1120 to (b) the consolidated groups that file Forms 1120; in the table, compare each of the following, for the latest tax year with available data. Examine only domestic corporations. Then, from the list below, make three observations about your findings.

- Number of returns.
- Total (Schedule L) assets owned.
- Taxable income.
- Tax liability.
- Research credit claimed.
- Foreign tax credit claimed.

Communications

Research Problem 4. Find several journal articles and web postings addressing the consolidation election. Construct a list titled "Consolidated Returns: Compliance Tips and Traps." Submit this document to your instructor. Provide citations for your research.

Communications

Research Problem 5. Identify the key details of the evolution and development of the Federal consolidated tax return rules. When were consolidated returns elective? When were they first required? What political forces were at work when the major 1966 and 1995 changes to the pertinent Federal income tax Regulations were adopted? When were NOL deduction limitations tightened or relaxed? Why? Arrange your findings using a timeline and no more than three slides.

Data Analytics

Communications

Research Problem 6. Send your instructor a graph of the number of Federal consolidated income tax returns that the IRS has received over the last 25 years, using 5-year intervals for your data points. On the same graph, indicate the total assets reported by the tax filers on their consolidated Form 1120 balance sheets.

Becker CPA Review Question

1. Which of the following statements is *not* true?
    a. Affiliated corporations that file consolidated returns can take a 100% dividends received deduction.
    b. The dividends received deduction for a small investment in an unrelated corporation is 50%.
    c. The dividends received deduction for a large investment in a corporation is 65%.
    d. There is no income limitation on the dividends received deduction.

CHAPTER

9

Taxation of International Transactions

LEARNING OBJECTIVES: *After completing Chapter 9, you should be able to:*

LO.1 Explain the framework underlying the U.S. taxation of cross-border transactions.

LO.2 Describe the interaction between Internal Revenue Code provisions and tax treaties.

LO.3 Apply the rules for sourcing income and deductions into U.S. and foreign categories.

LO.4 Apply foreign currency exchange rules as they affect the tax consequences of international transactions.

LO.5 Work with the U.S. tax provisions affecting U.S. persons earning foreign-source income, including the rules relating to cross-border asset transfers, antideferral provisions, and the foreign tax credit.

LO.6 Apply the U.S. tax provisions concerning nonresident alien individuals and foreign corporations.

CHAPTER OUTLINE

MONKEY BUSINESS IMAGES/SHUTTERSTOCK.COM

GOING INTERNATIONAL

VoiceCo, a domestic corporation, designs, manufactures, and sells specialty microphones for use in theaters. All of its activities take place in Florida, although it ships products to customers all over the United States. When it receives inquiries about its products from potential non-U.S. customers, VoiceCo decides to test the overseas market and places ads in various trade journals that have an international focus. Soon it is taking orders from offshore customers.

VoiceCo is concerned about its potential worldwide income tax exposure. Although it has no assets or employees outside the United States, it now is involved in international commerce. Is VoiceCo subject to income taxes in any other countries? Must it pay U.S. income taxes on the profits from its overseas sales? What if VoiceCo pays taxes to other countries? Does it receive any benefit from these payments on its U.S. tax return?

Later, VoiceCo establishes a manufacturing plant in Ireland to meet the European demand for its products. VoiceCo incorporates the Irish operation as VoiceCo-Ireland, an Irish corporation. Ireland imposes only a 12.5 percent tax on VoiceCo-Ireland's profits. How does U.S. corporate income tax law affect these activities?

Read the chapter and formulate your response.

n today's global business environment, most large businesses are truly international in scope. Large U.S. corporations earn on average more than 20 percent of their profits overseas, with offshore sales by "all-American" companies Coca-Cola and Apple exceeding 60 percent of their totals for a typical year. "Offshore" companies like Honda and Toyota operate large manufacturing plants in the United States, with perhaps one-third of their total sales taking place in the United States.

Global trade is an integral part of the U.S. economy. In a recent year, U.S. exports and imports of goods and services totaled $2.3 trillion and $2.9 trillion, respectively. This international trade creates significant U.S. tax consequences for both U.S. and foreign entities. In the most recent year for which data are available, U.S. corporations reported $433 billion in foreign-source taxable income, paid $228 billion in income taxes to foreign governments, and claimed foreign tax credits of about $118 billion. U.S. corporations controlled by non-U.S. owners reported $172 billion in U.S. gross receipts.

Cross-border transactions create the need for special tax considerations for both the United States and its trading partners. Tax planning opportunities can arise as different countries raise revenue through income and other taxes, applying various tax bases and tax rates. Exhibit 9.1 includes data about the top statutory tax rates that various countries apply to corporate taxable income.

From a U.S. perspective, international tax laws should promote the global competitiveness of U.S. enterprises while protecting the tax revenue base of the United States. These two objectives sometimes conflict, however. The need to deal with both contributes to the complexity of the rules governing the U.S. taxation of cross-border transactions.

EXAMPLE 1

U.S. persons engage in activities outside the United States for many different reasons. Consider two U.S. corporations that have established sales subsidiaries in foreign countries. Dedalus, Inc., operates in Germany, a high-tax country, because customers demand local attention from sales agents. Mulligan, Inc., operates in the Cayman Islands, a low-tax country, simply to shift income outside the United States. U.S. tax law must fairly address both situations with the same law.

U.S. multinational taxpayers—and tax professionals—must understand the Federal tax rules related to international business, so that these can be incorporated into their overall tax plans. Generally, this involves reducing the exposure to double taxation of business profits, locating cash and other assets where they will be the most productive, and decreasing the present value of income tax liabilities (e.g., by accelerating losses and deductions, deferring taxable income recognition).

EXHIBIT 9.1	Top Statutory Corporate Income Tax Rates for Selected Countries, 2018
Bermuda	0.0%
Ireland	12.5%
United Kingdom	19.0%
Sweden	22.0%
United States	27.0%
Germany	30.0%
Mexico	30.0%
Japan	30.9%
France	33.0%

Note: Includes additional taxes on corporate taxable income levied by states, cities, provinces, cantons, and other smaller jurisdictions. Deductions, exemptions, and credits can reduce an entity's effective tax rate below the top statutory rate.

9-1 **OVERVIEW OF INTERNATIONAL TAXATION**

LO.1

Explain the framework underlying the U.S. taxation of cross-border transactions.

U.S. international tax provisions are concerned primarily with two types of potential tax-payers: U.S. persons earning foreign-source income and foreign (non-U.S.) persons earning U.S.-source income.[1] U.S. persons earning U.S.-source income are taxed using only the domestic provisions of the Internal Revenue Code. Non-U.S. persons earning foreign-source income are not within the taxing jurisdiction of the United States (unless this income is connected to a U.S. trade or business). Exhibit 9.2 illustrates this categorization.

Most countries in the developed world use a *territorial* taxing system, under which only the taxable income generated within the country's borders is subject to tax there, regardless of who the taxpayer is. By taxing all events for all taxpayers that occur within their borders and nothing else, most business income generated in those countries is subject to tax only at one time and in one place. For the most part, U.S. corporate income tax law applies a territorial system for transactions entered into by non-U.S. persons.

In addition, most countries have been cutting their business income tax rates over the last two decades. As a result, taxes have become a significant device by which countries compete for business, capital, and jobs.

Legacy U.S. business income tax provisions apply a *worldwide* system for U.S. persons. Under these rules, a U.S. person is subject to the U.S. income tax for all taxable income, regardless of where it is generated. This means that an item of taxable income for a U.S. entity could be subject to income tax in the United States and, simultaneously, in the non-U.S. country where it arises. Strict worldwide taxation systems are rare today throughout the developed world.

This potential for the *double taxation* of business income for a U.S. person under a worldwide system is addressed in the Code in several ways under legacy law, the most important of which is the **foreign tax credit (FTC)**. A credit was allowed against the U.S. income tax for income taxes paid on income generated in another country, up to the amount of U.S. income tax that would result from the same income.[2]

Tax reform provisions adopted by the United States in 2017 were designed to accomplish several goals, all of which are likely to increase the competitiveness of U.S. businesses that operate in multiple countries and encounter territorial taxing systems and other countries' relatively low income tax rates.[3]

The worldwide taxing system still undergirds the income taxation of cross-border transactions conducted by U.S. persons, but important provisions overlay the legacy rules, especially for large entities. These include the means by which to:

- Move toward a territorial system of taxation for U.S. businesses.
- Provide incentives for U.S. businesses to locate jobs in the United States and repatriate foreign profits back to the United States.
- Prevent U.S. entities from shifting taxable income outside the United States into low-tax-rate countries.

The U.S. taxation of cross-border transactions can be organized in terms of "outbound" and "inbound" taxation. **Outbound taxation** refers to the U.S. taxation of foreign-source income earned by U.S. taxpayers. **Inbound taxation** refers to the U.S. taxation of U.S.-source income earned by non-U.S. taxpayers.

---

[1]The term *person* includes an individual, corporation, partnership, trust, estate, or association; § 7701(a)(1). The terms *domestic* and *foreign* are defined in §§ 7701(a)(4) and (5).

[2]A carryback or carryforward of an FTC arose when the foreign tax paid exceeded the amount of the corresponding Federal income tax liability for the tax year.

[3]Largely, the provisions contained in the Tax Cuts and Jobs Act (TCJA) of 2017 are effective beginning with the 2018 tax year. In this chapter, we assume that all taxpayers use a calendar tax year.

| EXHIBIT 9.2 | U.S. Taxation of Cross-Border Transactions |

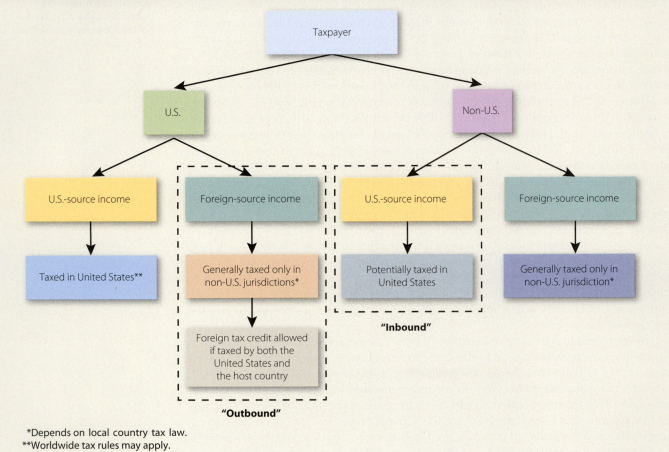

*Depends on local country tax law.
**Worldwide tax rules may apply.

GLOBAL TAX ISSUES   Tax Reform Can Make Strange Bedfellows

As governments around the world seek new revenues to balance budgets, pay down debts, and stabilize their economies, new levels of political cooperation can emerge. Age-old banking secrecy rules and tax laws that allow entities to shift taxable income into low-taxing jurisdictions all are under serious scrutiny. The Organization for Economic Cooperation and Development (OECD), a group of about 35 developed countries dedicated to expanding economic progress and world trade, has developed a plan to curtail income shifting (called "tax base erosion") that solely is meant to reduce taxes. The Group of 20, the largest economies in the world, has signed on to the principles of stopping base erosion as part of international tax reform. U.S. tax law now includes some anti-income-shifting rules.

Public pressure on such notable U.S. entities as Apple, Amazon, Google, and Starbucks has forced compromises in the U.S. companies' aggressive interpretation of tax law and treaties so that reported taxable income amounts might more closely correspond to where its customers reside (i.e., where its profit is earned, say in Germany, rather than where its holding company might exist, like in Luxembourg).

As these efforts to increase the tax liabilities of multinational entities expand, tax planners will need to find effective techniques to manage the tax costs of their operations.

The Big Picture

EXAMPLE 2

Return to the facts of *The Big Picture* on p. 9-1. Assume that VoiceCo operates an unincorporated manufacturing branch in Singapore to take advantage of local materials and low labor costs. This branch income is taxed in the United States as part of VoiceCo's worldwide income, but it also is taxed in Singapore. Without the availability of a foreign tax credit to mitigate this double taxation, VoiceCo would suffer an excessive tax burden and could not compete in a global environment. VoiceCo should arrange its affairs so that the territorial rules of U.S. tax law apply and double taxation on that income is avoided.

The Big Picture

EXAMPLE 3

Return to the facts of *The Big Picture* on p. 9-1. VoiceCo's major competitor is a Swiss-based foreign corporation with operations in the United States. Although not a U.S. person, the Swiss competitor is taxed in the United States on its U.S.-source business income. If the Swiss competitor could operate free of U.S. tax, VoiceCo would face a serious competitive disadvantage.

9-2 TAX TREATIES

LO.2

Describe the interaction between Internal Revenue Code provisions and tax treaties.

The U.S. tax rules governing cross-border transactions are based on both the Internal Revenue Code and **tax treaties**. U.S. tax treaties are bilateral agreements between countries that provide tax relief for those persons covered by the treaties. Tax treaty provisions must be harmonized with the treatment otherwise called for under the Internal Revenue Code or foreign tax statutes.[4] If there is a conflict, preference is given to whichever is newer, the treaty or the law; this is known as the "later in time" rule.

Almost 70 income tax treaties between the United States and other countries are in effect (see Exhibit 9.3). These treaties generally provide *taxing rights* related to the taxable income of residents of one treaty country who have income sourced in the other treaty country. For the most part, neither country is prohibited from taxing the income of its own residents. The treaties generally give one country primary taxing rights, and they require the other country to allow a credit for the taxes paid on the twice-taxed income.

EXAMPLE 4

ForCo, Ltd., a resident of a country with which the United States has an income tax treaty, earns income attributable to a permanent establishment (e.g., a place of business) in the United States.

Under the treaty, the United States has primary taxing rights related to this income. The other country can require that the income be included in gross income and can subject the income to its income tax, but it must allow a credit, an exemption, or some other offset for the taxes paid to the United States on the income.

Treaty language usually allows the country of the taxpayer's residence to levy a tax first. Alternatively, treaties allow a tax if there is a *permanent establishment* in a treaty country to which the income is attributable. Generally, a permanent establishment is a branch, an office, a factory, a workshop, a warehouse, or another fixed place of business.

Most U.S. income tax treaties reduce the withholding tax rate on certain items of investment income, such as interest and dividends. Exhibit 9.4 summarizes the treaty-based withholding rates for selected countries. Lacking a treaty provision, the withholding rate likely would be 30 percent.

The United States has developed a Model Income Tax Convention as the starting point for negotiating income tax treaties with other countries.[5]

---

[4] § 7852(d)(1).

[5] Treasury Department Model Income Tax Convention (November 17, 2016). See **tinyurl.com/16model**.

EXHIBIT 9.3	U.S. Income Tax Treaties in Force as of 2018		
Armenia	France	Lithuania	South Africa
Australia	Georgia	Luxembourg	Spain
Austria	Germany	Malta	Sri Lanka
Azerbaijan	Greece	Mexico	Sweden
Bangladesh	Hungary	Moldova	Switzerland
Barbados	Iceland	Morocco	Tajikistan
Belarus	India	Netherlands	Thailand
Belgium	Indonesia	New Zealand	Trinidad
Bulgaria	Ireland	Norway	Tunisia
Canada	Israel	Pakistan	Turkey
China	Italy	Philippines	Turkmenistan
Cyprus	Jamaica	Poland	Ukraine
Czech Republic	Japan	Portugal	United Kingdom
Denmark	Kazakhstan	Romania	Uzbekistan
Egypt	Korea	Russia	Venezuela
Estonia	Kyrgyzstan	Slovak Republic	
Finland	Latvia	Slovenia	

EXHIBIT 9.4	Selected Tax Treaty Withholding Rates, Income Paid by U.S. Entity		
	Interest	Dividends (in General)	Dividends Paid by U.S. Subsidiary to a Foreign Parent Corporation
Australia	10%	15%	5%
Canada	0%	15%	5%
Ireland	0%	15%	5%
Japan	10%	10%	5%
Mexico	15%	10%	5%
Philippines	15%	25%	20%
Non-treaty countries	30%	30%	30%

9-3 SOURCING OF INCOME AND DEDUCTIONS

LO.3

Apply the rules for sourcing income and deductions into U.S. and foreign categories.

The *sourcing* of income and deductions inside and outside the United States has a direct bearing on a number of tax provisions affecting both U.S. and offshore taxpayers. For example, non-U.S. taxpayers generally are taxed only on U.S.-source income, and U.S. taxpayers apply the sourcing rules in making several income, credit, and deduction computations. As a result, an examination of the sourcing rules often is the starting point in addressing international tax computational issues.

9-3a U.S.-Source Income

The determination of the source of income depends on the type of income realized (e.g., income from the sale of property versus income for the use of property).[6]

---

[6]Rules pertaining to the sourcing of income are found in §§ 861 through 865.

Interest

Interest income received from the U.S. government, from the District of Columbia, and from noncorporate U.S. residents or domestic corporations is U.S.-source income.

There are a few exceptions to this rule. Certain interest received from a U.S. corporation that earned 80 percent or more of its active business income from offshore sources over the prior three-year period is treated as foreign-source income. Interest received on amounts deposited with an overseas branch of a U.S. corporation also is treated as foreign-source income if the branch is engaged in the commercial banking business.

John holds a bond issued by Alpha, a domestic corporation. For the immediately preceding three tax years, 82% of Alpha's gross income has been active foreign business income. The interest income that John receives for the current tax year from Alpha is foreign-source income.

EXAMPLE 5

Dividends

Dividends received from domestic corporations typically are U.S.-source income. Typically, dividends paid by a non-U.S. corporation constitute foreign-source income. However, if an offshore corporation earned 25 percent or more of its gross income from income effectively connected with a U.S. trade or business during the three-year period immediately preceding the year of the dividend payment, that percentage of the dividend is treated as U.S.-source income.

Ann receives dividend income from the following corporations during the current tax year.

EXAMPLE 6

Amount	Corporation	Effectively Connected U.S. Income for Past Three Years	U.S.-Source Income
$500	Green, domestic	85%	$500
600	Brown, domestic	13%	600
300	Orange, foreign	92%	276

Because Green Corporation and Brown Corporation are domestic corporations, the dividends they pay are U.S.-source income. Orange Corporation is a non-U.S. corporation that earned 92% of its business income over the prior three years from income effectively connected with a U.S. trade or business. Because Orange meets the 25% threshold, 92% of its dividend is U.S. source.

Personal Services Income

The source of income from personal services is determined by the location in which the services are performed (inside or outside the United States). A limited *commercial traveler* exception is available. Under this exception, personal services income must meet *all* of the following requirements to avoid being classified as U.S.-source income.

- The services must be performed by a nonresident alien who is in the United States for 90 days or less during the taxable year.
- The compensation may not exceed $3,000 in total for the services performed in the United States.
- The services must be performed on behalf of:
  - A nonresident alien, non-U.S. partnership, or non-U.S. corporation that is not engaged in a U.S. trade or business, or
  - An office or place of business maintained in a country outside the United States by an individual who is a citizen or resident of the United States, a domestic partnership, or a domestic corporation.

EXAMPLE 7

Mark, a nonresident alien, is an engineer employed by a foreign oil company. He spent four weeks in the United States arranging the purchase of field equipment for his company. His salary for the four weeks was $3,500.

Even though the oil company is not engaged in a U.S. trade or business and Mark was in the United States for less than 90 days during the taxable year, the income is U.S.-source income because it exceeds $3,000.

Rents and Royalties

Income received for the use of tangible property is sourced to the country in which the property is located. The source of income received for the use of intangible property (e.g., patents, copyrights, processes, and formulas) is the country where the property is used.

Sale or Exchange of Property

Generally, the location of *real property* determines the source of any income derived from the property. Income from the disposition of U.S. real property interests is U.S.-source income.

The source of income from the sale of *personal property* (assets other than real property) depends on several factors, including the following.

- Whether the property was produced by the seller.
- What type of property was sold (e.g., inventory or a capital asset).
- Where the residence of the seller was.

Generally, income, gain, or profit from the sale of personal property is sourced according to the residence of the seller. Income from the sale of *purchased* inventory, however, is sourced in the country where the sale takes place.[7]

When the seller has *produced* the inventory, the income is sourced to the country where the assets were produced.

Income from the sale of personal property other than inventory is sourced at the residence of the seller unless one of the following exceptions applies.

- Gain on the sale of depreciable personal property is sourced according to prior depreciation deductions to the extent of the deductions. Any excess gain is sourced the same as the sale of inventory.
- Gain on the sale of intangibles is sourced according to prior amortization deductions to the extent of the deductions. Contingent payments, however, are sourced as royalty income.
- Gain attributable to an office or a fixed place of business maintained outside the United States by a U.S. resident is foreign-source income.
- Income or gain attributable to an office or a fixed place of business maintained in the United States by a nonresident is U.S.-source income.

Losses are sourced depending on the nature of the property. Different rules exist for the disposition of stock versus other personal property.[8]

Transportation and Communication Income

Income from transportation beginning *and* ending in the United States is U.S.-source income. Fifty percent of the income from transportation beginning *or* ending in the United States is U.S.-source income, unless the U.S. point is only an intermediate stop.

---

[7] §§ 861(a)(6) and 865. The sale is deemed to take place where title passes. See Reg. § 1.861–7(c) regarding title passage. There has been considerable conflict in this area of tax law. See, for example, *Liggett Group, Inc.*, 58 TCM 1167, T.C.Memo. 1990–18.

[8] See Reg. § 1.861–8(e)(7) and Reg. § 1.865–1(a)(1). See Reg. §§ 1.865–2(a)(1) and (2) regarding the source of losses on the disposition of stock.

Income from space and ocean activities conducted outside the jurisdiction of any country is sourced according to the residence of the person conducting the activity.

International communication income derived by a U.S. person is one-half U.S.-source when transmission is between the United States and another country. International communication income derived by non-U.S. persons is foreign-source income unless it is attributable to an office or another fixed place of business in the United States. In that case, it is U.S.-source income.

Software Income

Income from the sale or license of software is sourced depending on how the income is classified. A transfer of software is classified as either the transfer of a copyright (e.g., the right to the computer program itself) or the transfer of a copyrighted article (the right to use a copy of the computer program).[9] If the transfer is considered a transfer of a copyright, the income is sourced using the royalty income rules. If the transfer is considered a transfer of a copyrighted article, the income is treated as resulting from a sale of the article and is sourced based on the personal property sales rules.

9-3b Foreign-Source Income

Income items are determined to be foreign-source using a simple rule. Any income that is not U.S.-source income constitutes foreign-source income.[10]

9-3c Allocation and Apportionment of Deductions

The United States levies a tax on *taxable income* (gross income minus deductions). Deductions and losses, therefore, also must be *allocated* and *apportioned* between U.S.- and foreign-source gross income to determine U.S.- and foreign-source taxable income. Deductions directly related to an activity or property are *allocated* to classes of income. Then these deductions are *apportioned* between U.S.- and foreign-source on a reasonable basis.[11]

EXAMPLE 8

Ace, Inc., a domestic corporation, reports $2,000,000 of gross income and a $50,000 expense that is related to real estate sales and rental activities. The expense is *allocated* and *apportioned* using gross income as a basis in the following way.

	Gross Income		Expense Allocation	Expense Apportionment	
	Foreign	U.S.		Foreign	U.S.
Sales	$1,000,000	$500,000	$37,500*	$25,000	$12,500**
Rentals	400,000	100,000	12,500	10,000	2,500***
Totals			$50,000	$35,000	$15,000

*$50,000 × ($1,500,000/$2,000,000).   ***$12,500 × ($100,000/$500,000).
**$37,500 × ($500,000/$1,500,000).

If, instead, Ace could show that $45,000 of the expense was directly related to sales income, the $45,000 would be allocated specifically to that class of gross income, with the remainder allocated and apportioned ratably based on gross income.

Interest expense is allocated and apportioned based on the theory that borrowed money can be raised and spent in any country without being earmarked to any specific location or use (i.e., it is *fungible*). With limited exceptions, interest expense is attributable to all of the activities and property of the taxpayer, regardless of the specific

---

[9]Reg. § 1.861–18.
[10]§ 862.

[11]Reg. § 1.861–8.

purpose for incurring the debt on which interest is paid. Taxpayers allocate and apportion interest expense on the basis of the tax book value of the leveraged assets.[12]

The Big Picture

EXAMPLE 9

Return to the facts of *The Big Picture* on p. 9-1. Assume that VoiceCo generates U.S.-source and foreign-source gross income for the current year. VoiceCo's assets (measured at tax book value) are as follows.

Assets generating U.S.-source income	$18,000,000
Assets generating foreign-source income	5,000,000
	$23,000,000

VoiceCo incurs interest expense of $800,000 for the current year. Interest expense is apportioned to foreign-source income as follows.

$$\frac{\$5,000,000 \text{ (foreign assets)}}{\$23,000,000 \text{ (total assets)}} \times \$800,000 = \$173,913$$

Different rules apply to research and development (R&D) expenditures, certain costs of day-to-day management, legal and accounting fees and expenses, income taxes, and losses. Although U.S. companies incur about 90 percent of their R&D expenditures at U.S. facilities, several billion dollars are spent on offshore R&D each year. If the R&D relates to offshore product sales, a portion of a U.S. company's R&D expense is treated as foreign source.

Concept Summary 9.1

The Sourcing Rules

The Code and Regulations include rules that designate income and deduction items as U.S.-source or foreign-source. These rules are important for several purposes.

- A U.S. taxpayer uses U.S.- and foreign-source amounts in computing various income, credits, and deductions.

- A non-U.S. taxpayer is subject to U.S. Federal income taxes only on U.S.-source taxable income.

- An expatriate from the United States (e.g., an employee of a U.S. business entity who temporarily is stationed overseas) can claim a foreign earned income exclusion only on foreign-source income (§ 911; not otherwise discussed in this chapter).

9-3d **Transfer Pricing**

Income Shifting

Taxpayers may be tempted to minimize taxation by manipulating the source of income and the allocation of deductions arbitrarily through **transfer pricing**. This manipulation is more easily accomplished between or among related persons. A transfer pricing arrangement sets the internal prices at which goods and services are sold between, for instance, a parent corporation and its subsidiary. *Transfer pricing* also can refer to the use of charges, such as fees for management services and database access, that are assessed on one related party by another. In this way, net profits can be shifted from

---

[12]Reg. § 1.861–9T. Reg. § 1.861–10T(b) describes circumstances in which interest expense can be directly allocated to specific debt. This exception to the fungibility concept is limited to cases in which specific property is purchased or improved with nonrecourse debt.

one entity to a different entity, thereby achieving a tax advantage. For instance, an entity in a high-tax country might pay a management fee to its parent in a low-tax country. Doing so creates a valuable deduction in a high-tax jurisdiction, with the related income (the management fee received) subject to a lower tax rate.

The IRS uses § 482 to counter such actions. This provision gives the IRS the power to reallocate gross income, deductions, credits, or allowances between or among organizations, trades, or businesses owned or controlled directly or indirectly by the same interests. This can be done whenever the IRS determines that reallocation is necessary to prevent the evasion of taxes or to reflect income more clearly.

Section 482 is a "one-edged sword" available only to the IRS. A taxpayer generally cannot invoke § 482 to reallocate income and expenses.[13]

ETHICS & EQUITY The Costs of Good Tax Planning

High Tech Tops (HTT), a C corporation based in California, manufactures resilient cases and covers for laptops, smartphones, and tablets. Its sales and profits have more than doubled in each of the last five years (i.e., the company is growth-oriented and recession-proof). Its employees and contractors make above-average wages, so they make important contributions to the local individual income, sales, and property tax collections.

But the Federal and state corporate income tax is another story. Using legal and effective transfer pricing techniques, HTT shifts most of its operating profits to low-tax subsidiaries in Ireland and Singapore. Most of the firm's executives, engineers, and designers are based in the United States, but almost all of the sales operations are run from overseas. HTT's customers live around the world, but its tax liabilities are concentrated in the low-tax jurisdictions.

You are the president of State University, across town from HTT's headquarters. The company sends hundreds of its employees to take graduate and professional courses on your campus, and several of the corporate leaders are frequent guest speakers and adjunct lecturers in classes.

Still, the state income tax the company avoids through its transfer pricing plans would fund millions of dollars of campus growth and improvements for State University.

Should you become involved in the politics of the matter and lobby at your statehouse for tighter rules on transfer pricing? Such an action might result in tax increases that would improve your university's situation, but it also might force HTT to consider moving its headquarters to another location.

EXAMPLE 10

Consider the transaction depicted in Exhibit 9.5. A U.S. corporation manufactures and sells inventory to an unrelated foreign customer. The sales price for the inventory is $1,000, and the related cost of goods sold (COGS) is $600. All of the resulting profit of $400 is taxed to the U.S. corporation, resulting in an $84 U.S. income tax liability ($400 × 21%). If the U.S. corporation has no business presence in the foreign jurisdiction and is merely selling to a customer located there, the foreign government is unlikely to impose any local income tax on the U.S. corporation. Consequently, the total tax burden imposed on the inventory sale is $84.

Suppose instead that the U.S. corporation attempts to reduce its total tax expense by channeling the inventory sale through a subsidiary in the same country as the foreign customer. In this case, because the U.S. corporation controls the foreign subsidiary, it chooses an intercompany sales price (the transfer price) that effectively moves a portion of the profits from the United States to the non-U.S. country.

By selling the inventory it manufactured to its 100%-owned foreign subsidiary for $700, the U.S. corporation reports only $100 of profits and an associated U.S. tax liability of $21. The subsidiary then sells the inventory to the ultimate customer for $1,000 and, with a $700 COGS, earns a $300 profit. In this example, the non-U.S. country imposes only a 10% tax on corporate profits, resulting in an income tax there of $30 ($300 × 10%). By using a related offshore entity in a lower-tax jurisdiction, the U.S. corporation has lowered its overall tax liability on the sale from $84 (all U.S.) to $51 ($21 U.S. and $30 foreign).

continued

---

[13]Reg. § 1.482–1(a)(3).

Will the IRS agree to $700 as the appropriate transfer price in considering whether to apply § 482? The IRS may question why the subsidiary deserved to earn $300 of the total $400 profit related to the manufacture and sale of the inventory. In general, the U.S. corporation must document the functions performed by its subsidiary, the assets it owns that assist in producing the income, or the risks it takes (e.g., credit risk), to justify its profit assignment.

If the IRS does not consider the $300 profit earned by the subsidiary to be appropriate, it will use § 482 to adjust the transfer price upward. If the IRS determines that the transfer price should have been, for example, $990, then the U.S. corporation reports a $390 profit (with $82 of U.S. income tax) and the non-U.S. corporation earns a $10 profit (with $1 of the other country's income tax). With this change in transfer price, the U.S. corporation reduces its tax liability, but only by $1 [$84 − ($82 + $1)].

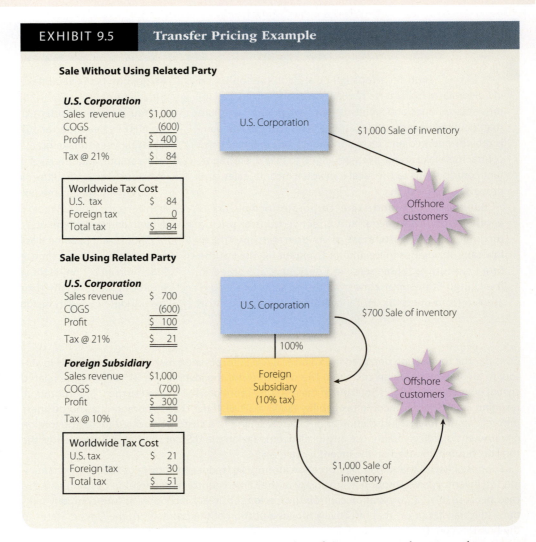

EXHIBIT 9.5   **Transfer Pricing Example**

The IRS imposes an accuracy-related penalty of 20 percent when it makes a net transfer price adjustment in a taxable year that exceeds the lesser of $5 million or 10 percent of the taxpayer's gross receipts, or when the transfer price is overstated by 200 percent or more.[14] The penalty is doubled for "gross misstatements" of taxable income due to transfer pricing arrangements.

Preemptive Transfer Pricing Arrangements

As an aid to reducing pricing disputes, the IRS initiated the Advance Pricing Agreement (APA) program, where the taxpayer can propose a transfer pricing method for certain future cross-border transactions.[15] The taxpayer provides relevant data, which then are

---

[14]§ 6662(e)(1)(B).

[15]Rev.Proc. 2015–41, 2015–35 I.R.B. 263. The IRS offers an application template based on this document.

evaluated by the IRS. If accepted, the APA provides a safe-harbor transfer pricing result for the taxpayer, preempting most later IRS adjustments.

APAs can be complex in their application, and they may take three or four years to negotiate fully. About 275 APAs have been executed over the past three years, and another 400 are pending. About 75 percent of the APAs affect transfer pricing between the United States and Japan, Canada, and India. About half of the APAs involve taxpayers in the manufacturing industries. Most APAs are effective for five years.

Additional Tax for Base Erosion

The Code provides another sanction for large C corporations that appear to shift "too much" taxable income to other countries where a lower income tax rate may be available. The *base erosion anti-abuse* provision applies to U.S. and non-U.S. corporations with average annual gross receipts of at least $500 million for the prior three tax years.

An alternative tax computation applies to the entity when "excessive" deductible royalties, management fees, and similar payments are made to a related (25 percent ownership) non-U.S. person. If these base erosion items total at least 3 percent of total deductible payments for the year, the entity pays a Federal corporate income tax equal to the *greater of* the corporation's regular tax liability, or:

10% ✕ Taxable income (after adding back the base erosion items)[16]

The base erosion anti-abuse tax (BEAT) is similar in nature to provisions adopted in the last decade by other developed countries that want to keep the income tax base indicative of where multinational profits are earned. The BEAT provisions effectively act as a minimum tax to keep a taxpayer from unduly reducing its U.S. taxable income to zero (or close to it), by using income-shifting deductions and other devices with a related party.

Base erosion items do not include those related to cost of goods sold and other active trade or business expenses, like salaries, or those where a withholding tax already applies.

EXAMPLE 11

ReichCo, a non-U.S. conglomerate, generates $3 billion in gross receipts annually. Its U.S. subsidiary, GiantCo, accounts for $750 million of the annual gross receipts (and its average annual gross receipts for the last three years is $685 million).

GiantCo generates U.S. taxable income of $120 million ($750 million gross receipts − $630 million total deductions). Included in the total deductions is a $250 million management fee that it pays to ReichCo. GiantCo reports no U.S. tax credits. The corporate income tax rate in ReichCo's country is 15%. GiantCo is subject to the base erosion tax.

- Its average annual gross receipts for the last three years are at least $500 million.

- Base erosion items are at least 3% of deductible items for the year ($250 million base erosion items ÷ $630 million total deductions = 40%).

Now determine whether a base erosion tax is due. GiantCo pays the *greater of*:

- Regular U.S. income tax: $25.2 million = 21% × $120 million taxable income, or

- The base erosion tax: $37 million = 10% × $370 million modified taxable income
  ($120 million taxable income + $250 million base erosion items).

Apparently tempted by the low tax rate of its parent ReichCo, GiantCo has shifted "too much" income to the non-U.S. country with its deductible management fee. It incurs the base erosion anti-abuse tax for the tax year. GiantCo pays its regular U.S. corporate income tax of $25.2 million, plus the anti-abuse tax equal to the excess amount of $11.8 million, for a total of $37 million. GiantCo's U.S. income tax liability has increased by about one-half due to the anti-abuse tax.

---

[16]§ 59A. The 10% tax rate is 5% for the 2018 tax year and 12.5% after 2025. The BEAT rate is not used for book purposes in deriving the deferred tax accounts.

LO.4

Apply foreign currency exchange rules as they affect the tax consequences of international transactions.

9-4 FOREIGN CURRENCY GAIN/LOSS

An exchange rate provides the relative value of a foreign currency to the U.S. dollar. Changes in this rate affect the dollar value of overseas property held by the taxpayer, the dollar value of non-U.S. debts, and the dollar amount of gain or loss on a transaction denominated in a foreign currency.[17] Almost every international tax issue requires consideration of currency exchange implications.

EXAMPLE 12

Dress, Inc., a domestic corporation, purchases merchandise for resale from Fiesta, Inc., a non-U.S. corporation, for 50,000K (a foreign currency). On the date of purchase, 1K is equal to $1 U.S. (1K:$1). At this time, the account payable is $50,000.

On the date of payment by Dress (the foreign exchange date), the exchange rate is 1.25K:$1. In other words, the foreign currency has been devalued in relation to the U.S. dollar, and Dress will pay Fiesta 50,000K, which will cost Dress only $40,000. Dress must record the purchase of the merchandise at $50,000 and recognize a foreign currency gain of $10,000 ($50,000 − $40,000).

The foreign currency exchange rates, however, have no effect on the transactions of a U.S. person who arranges all international transactions in U.S. dollars.

EXAMPLE 13

Sellers, Inc., a domestic corporation, purchases goods from Rose, Ltd., a foreign corporation, and pays for these goods in U.S. dollars. Rose then exchanges the U.S. dollars for the currency of the country in which it operates. Sellers has no foreign exchange considerations with which to contend.

If, instead, Rose required Sellers to pay for the goods in a foreign currency, Sellers would have to exchange U.S. dollars to obtain the foreign currency to make payment. If the exchange rate changed from the date of purchase to the date of payment, Sellers would have a foreign currency gain or loss on the currency exchange.

In recent years, U.S. currency abroad has amounted to more than 50 percent of the U.S. currency in circulation. Taxpayers may find it necessary to translate amounts denominated in foreign currency into U.S. dollars for any of the following purposes.

- Purchase of goods, services, and property.
- Sale of goods, services, and property.
- Collection of foreign receivables.
- Payment of foreign payables.
- Foreign tax credit calculations.

The IRS maintains that transactions involving virtual currencies and cryptocurrencies do not create foreign currency gain or loss.[18]

The Code generally adopts the **functional currency** approach. For book and tax purposes, the currency of the economic environment in which the non-U.S. entity operates generally is used as the monetary unit to measure gains and losses.

All income tax determinations are made in the taxpayer's functional currency.[19] A taxpayer's default functional currency is the U.S. dollar. In most cases, a **qualified business unit (QBU)** operating in another country uses that country's currency as its functional currency. A QBU is a separate and clearly identified unit of a taxpayer's trade or business (e.g., a foreign branch).[20]

---

[17]§ 988(b).

[18]Notice 2014–21, 2014–16 I.R.B. 938.

[19]§ 985. These rules are similar to those of ASC 830.

[20]Reg. § 1.989(a)–1(b). An individual is not a QBU; however, a trade or business conducted by an individual may be a QBU.

9-5 **U.S. PERSONS WITH OFFSHORE INCOME**

LO.5

Work with the U.S. tax provisions affecting U.S. persons earning foreign-source income, including the rules relating to cross-border asset transfers, antideferral provisions, and the foreign tax credit.

U.S. taxpayers often "internationalize" gradually over time. A U.S. business may operate on a strictly domestic basis for several years, then explore offshore markets by exporting its products abroad, and later license its products to an overseas manufacturer or enter into a joint venture with a non-U.S. partner. If its forays into these markets are successful, the U.S. business may create a foreign branch and then a subsidiary, moving a portion of its operations abroad by establishing a sales or manufacturing facility.

Exhibit 9.6 shows a typical timeline for "going global." Both U.S. and offshore entities generally move into international markets in this manner. Each step in this process generates increasingly significant international income tax consequences.

The Big Picture

EXAMPLE

14

Return to the facts of *The Big Picture* on p. 9-1. It appears that VoiceCo has moved along the Exhibit 9.6 Global Activities Timeline, in that it is making export sales, and it has a manufacturing plant in Ireland.

9-5a **Export Property, Licenses, Foreign Branches**

The easiest way for a U.S. business to engage in global commerce is simply to sell U.S.-produced goods and services abroad. These sales can be conducted with little or no foreign presence and allow the business to explore offshore markets without making costly financial commitments to overseas operations. Under the worldwide provisions of the U.S. tax law, a U.S. person immediately includes gross income from export sales.

Whether foreign taxes must be paid on this export income depends on the laws of the non-U.S. jurisdiction and whether the U.S. taxpayer is deemed to have a business presence there (i.e., a "permanent establishment"). In many cases, this export income is not taxed by the receiving country.

Fees from licensing arrangements generally are recognized by the U.S. taxpayer when earned or collected; these usually entail royalties and profit sharing payments.

Profits and losses from branch operations are recognized immediately (i.e., the operating results flow through to the U.S. parent's tax return in the same tax year). Branch operating losses generally produce an immediate deduction, and branch profits are taxed in the year earned. This often means that entities that generate current operating losses should remain branches of the U.S. parent. On the other hand, a profitable foreign branch can create a cash-flow problem if the U.S. tax liability is due before the cash related to those profits is repatriated to the U.S. parent.

Foreign Tax Credit

Income and loss from the export, licensing, and branch operations of a U.S. person are taxed under the worldwide system of business taxation. If the non-U.S country also imposes an income tax on such income, the possibility of double taxation arises. Problems associated with double taxation include the stacking of tax rates for the various countries upon each other, resulting in high effective tax rates on the dual-taxed income, and the harmonization of the tax rules of the various countries to the taxpayer's detriment.

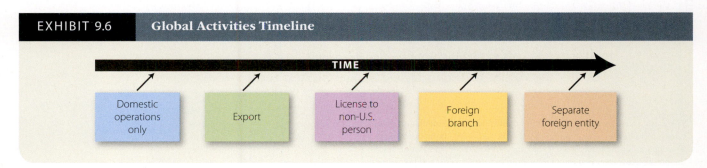

EXHIBIT 9.6 **Global Activities Timeline**

Concerns involving double taxation most often are addressed through language in applicable tax treaties, ideally assigning taxable income to only one of the countries involved, and through tax credits and exemptions in the taxpayer's home country. The United States long has allowed a foreign tax credit (FTC) for this purpose, typically for use when the dual-taxed transaction occurs in a non-treaty country.[21] The FTC is an annual taxpayer election; lacking an FTC election, the tax payments are claimed as deductions against gross income.

The FTC is allowed against the taxpayer's regular tax liability, such that only the non-U.S. tax obligation is paid on the dual-taxed income. The FTC is limited, though, to the U.S. tax that would be incurred on the income amount. As a result, the credit equals the *lesser of* (1) the foreign tax actually paid or (2) the corresponding U.S. income tax amount,[22] using the sourcing rules discussed in text Section 9-3, with the following formula.

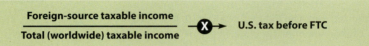

$$\frac{\text{Foreign-source taxable income}}{\text{Total (worldwide) taxable income}} \quad \text{X} \longrightarrow \quad \text{U.S. tax before FTC}$$

Where a foreign tax payment is not allowed as a current-year credit under the *lesser of* rule, the disallowed amount is allowed in another tax year as a carryover. FTCs are carried back 1 year and forward 10 years. FTC carryovers tend to occur when the effective tax rate that applies to the dual-taxed income is lower in the United States than it is in the other country.

EXAMPLE

15

BlueCo, a U.S. corporation, manufactures and sells most of its products in the United States. It also conducts some business in the European Union through various branches. During the current year, BlueCo reports taxable income of $700,000, of which $500,000 is U.S.-source and $200,000 is foreign-source. Foreign income taxes paid amounted to $45,000. BlueCo's U.S. income tax liability is $147,000. What is its allowable foreign tax credit?

(1) Foreign taxes paid	$45,000
(2) U.S. tax associated with dual-taxed income	
$\dfrac{\$200,000 \text{ (Foreign-source TI)}}{\$700,000 \text{ (Total TI)}} \times \$147,000 \text{ (U.S. tax)}$	$42,000
(3) FTC allowed [lesser of (1) or (2)]	$42,000
(4) FTC carryforward [(1) − (2), but not below $0]	$ 3,000

A separate FTC is computed for each of four types of taxable income. These FTC "baskets" were devised so that a taxpayer could not claim credits against a high-taxed type of income (like business profits) from foreign taxes paid concerning a low-taxed type of income (like portfolio interest, perhaps under treaty language). The taxpayer's FTC for the year is the sum of the separately computed amounts; there might be a carryforward in one basket and none in another, but the FTCs cannot be combined among baskets. The FTC baskets separately treat the following types of income.

- Active, business income.
- Portfolio income, like dividends and capital gains.
- Income from foreign branches.
- Certain intangible income (see text Section 9-5e).

---

[21]The credit is allowed via § 27, but the qualifications and calculation procedure for the FTC are contained in §§ 901–908. Although taxpayers can claim a deduction for the foreign taxes paid, instead of a credit, in most instances, the credit is advantageous since it is a direct offset against the tax liability.

[22]§ 904.

FINANCIAL DISCLOSURE INSIGHTS **Overseas Operations and Book-Tax Differences**

Non-U.S. operations account for a large portion of the permanent book-tax differences of U.S. business entities. These differences may relate to different tax bases, different tax rate structures, or special provisions concerning tax-based financing with the other country. For instance, lower tax rates applied by Ireland, Bermuda, and the Netherlands recently reduced Apple's current-year tax rate by about 25 percent.

Tax planning strategies using non-U.S. operations also are found in the deferred tax asset and liability accounts. Tax deferrals allowed under current U.S. tax rules and carryforwards of the foreign tax credit can be substantial for some businesses. For example, IBM recently reported a deferred tax asset relating to delays in using its FTCs amounting to about $800 million. For the operating arm of General Electric, that amount was about $1.5 billion.

To qualify for the FTC, the foreign levy must resemble a tax on net income, like the Federal income tax. For instance, it cannot be a tax on gross receipts, on the right to extract minerals, or on property values.[23] Such tax payments can be deducted by the taxpayer, though. A tax is available for the FTC when it is paid or accrued, according to the taxpayer's method of tax accounting. Concept Summary 9.2 summarizes the FTC rules.

Concept Summary 9.2

The Foreign Tax Credit

The foreign tax credit (FTC) is related to the worldwide system of income taxation that applies under U.S. income tax law to many cross-border transactions. The credit works to eliminate the exposure of a taxpayer to the double taxation of income that is generated in another country. In effect, foreign income taxes are used to reduce the Federal income tax liability, in a form of "revenue sharing" by the governments involved.

- The FTC is available to C corporations and individuals.

- The FTC is an annual taxpayer election. If the FTC is not used for foreign taxes, a deduction may be claimed.

- The FTC is allowed for taxes paid by the taxpayer directly or through a foreign withholding procedure.

- An FTC is allowed only for income taxes on net taxable income that are levied by the host country. Other forms of fees or non-income taxes can be claimed by the taxpayer as a deduction.

- The taxpayer's taxable income and foreign tax payments are split among four income "baskets" (i.e., among business, investment, foreign branch, and certain intangible income).

- The FTC then is allowed in each income basket.
  - The FTC for the year in each basket equals the lesser of (1) the foreign taxes paid or accrued or (2) the share of the U.S. tax liability that corresponds to the foreign-source income of the taxpayer as a percentage of worldwide taxable income.
  - In this way, if the taxpayer is operating in a jurisdiction that applies an income tax rate that is higher than that of the United States, the credit cannot be used to offset income tax that relates to other types of income.

- If foreign taxes were paid but are not allowed for the current tax year because of this "lesser of" limitation, the credit is carried back 1 year and then forward 10 years.

Special Tax Rate for Intangible Income

The U.S. tax law provides an incentive for domestic C corporations to generate taxable income overseas in the form of intangible income, with most personnel and activities still in the United States.[24] A lower tax rate (effectively 13.125 percent) applies to income from intangible assets that the U.S. entity employs overseas. The lower tax rate is meant to encourage U.S. C corporations to conduct international business that leverages U.S. expertise (especially in technological fields) in operations around the world. The lower tax rate is meant to affect how domestic C corporations position their assets and personnel in various countries.

---

[23]§ 904(c).

[24]§ 250. The provision creates the computational amount known as foreign-derived intangible income (FDII).

The special tax rate is derived after allowing deductions against foreign-source income in excess of a normalized return on the entity's tangible assets. The details of those computations are not discussed here.[25] The special tax rate does not apply to the sale of goods or services, or to income that otherwise is taxed under Subpart F of the Code (see text Section 9-5d). The base for the lower tax rate is limited to the entity's foreign-source taxable income for the year.

9-5b Creating a Cross-Border Business Entity

As part of "going international," a U.S. taxpayer may decide to transfer assets outside the United States so that all related business will be conducted overseas. This may take the form of a cash investment or a transfer of assets of a U.S. entity. After the transfer, the U.S. investor has created the equivalent of a new corporation.

In situations where potential taxable income is transferred to a corporation outside the U.S. taxing jurisdiction, the exchange may trigger an income tax. The tax result of transferring property to a non-U.S. corporation depends on the nature of the exchange, the assets involved, the income potential of the property, and the character of the property in the hands of the transferor or transferee. Exhibit 9.7 summarizes the taxation of cross-border asset transfers.

As discussed in Chapters 6 and 7, when assets are exchanged for corporate stock in a domestic transaction, realized gain or loss may be deferred rather than recognized. Similarly, deferral treatment may be available when the following "outbound" capital changes occur (i.e., moving corporate business across country borders and outside the United States).

- A U.S. corporation starts up a new corporation outside the United States (§ 351).
- A U.S. corporation liquidates a U.S. subsidiary into an existing foreign subsidiary (§ 332).
- A U.S. corporation incorporates a non-U.S. branch of a U.S. corporation, forming a new foreign corporation (§ 351).
- A foreign corporation uses a stock swap to acquire a U.S. corporation ("Type B" reorganization).
- A foreign corporation acquires substantially all of a U.S. corporation's net assets ("Type C" reorganization).

EXHIBIT 9.7   Taxation of Cross-Border Asset Transfers

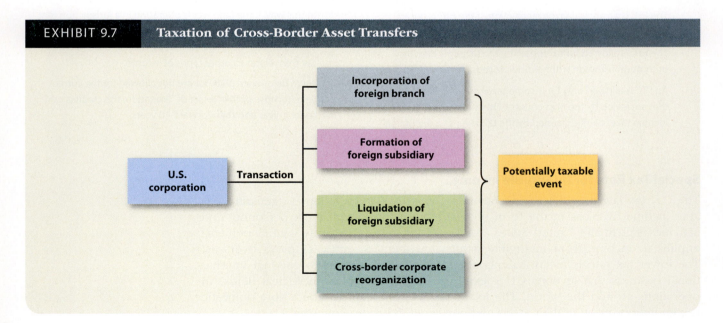

However, when non-U.S. corporations are involved, gain deferral is not allowed when assets leave the U.S. taxing jurisdiction.[26] Consequently, the United States recognizes this gain when these assets are transferred outside the United States.

> **EXAMPLE 16**
>
> Amelia, Inc., a domestic corporation, incorporates its profitable Irish manufacturing branch and creates a new wholly owned foreign corporation, St. George, Ltd., to engage in manufacturing activities in Ireland. The transfer qualifies for tax deferral under § 351. The branch assets always have been used in Ireland. Amelia transfers the following branch assets to St. George upon its creation.
>
> | Asset | Tax Basis | Market Value | Built-In Gain/Loss |
> |---|---|---|---|
> | Raw materials inventory | $100 | $ 400 | $ 300 |
> | Accounts receivable | 200 | 250 | 50 |
> | Land | 450 | 925 | 475 |
> | Equipment, furniture, and fixtures | 150 | 50 | (100) |
> | Total | $900 | $1,625 | $ 725 |
>
> Although the $725 in realized gain would be deferred under § 351 in a purely domestic event, Amelia's gain potentially is taxable because the assets are leaving the U.S. taxing jurisdiction. All of the realized gain is recognized by Amelia when the transfer occurs. Gain is recognized on an asset-by-asset basis with no offset for losses on other assets.

The transfer of intangible assets is treated separately as a transfer pursuant to a sale for contingent payments.[27] These amounts are treated as received by the transferor over the life of the intangible; they then constitute ordinary income. For this purpose, intangible assets include goodwill and the value of the entity's workforce in place.

9-5c Tax Havens

Many outbound transfers of assets to foreign corporations are to countries with tax rates higher than or equal to the U.S. rate; tax avoidance is not the motive for these transfers. Some U.S. corporations, however, make their offshore investment in (or through) a tax haven. A **tax haven** is a country where either locally sourced income or residents are subject to zero or low levels of local income taxation. The Bahamas, Ireland, the Netherlands, the Cayman Islands, and Bermuda, among other countries, are seen as tax havens. U.S. corporations shift sizable amounts of taxable income annually to these countries.

A tax haven usually has adopted rules that allow taxpayers to establish residency with a minimal presence. Tax haven countries also may have in effect provisions limiting the exchange of financial and commercial information.[28]

Exhibit 9.8 illustrates this use of a tax haven by a U.S. corporation. The U.S. corporation uses a foreign subsidiary in a low- or no-tax country to earn either investment income or a portion of income from business activities (as illustrated previously in the transfer pricing discussion). Because the foreign subsidiary cannot be consolidated with the domestic parent under U.S. tax law and is not itself engaged in any U.S. trade or business, the subsidiary is not subject to U.S. taxation. Without the application of the transfer pricing rules, the base-erosion tax, or the Subpart F rules (discussed in text Section 9-5d), the subsidiary's income escapes U.S. taxation.

A tax haven also can, in effect, be created by an income tax treaty. For example, under an income tax treaty between Country A and Country B, residents of Country A are subject to a withholding tax of only 5 percent on dividend and interest income sourced in Country B. The United States and Country A have a similar treaty. The United States does not have a treaty with Country B, and the withholding tax is 30 percent. A U.S. corporation can create a foreign subsidiary in Country A and use that subsidiary to make investments in Country B.

---

[26]§ 367.

[27]§§ 367(d) and 936(h)(3)(B).

[28]§ 894(c) contains additional limitations on the use of treaty benefits.

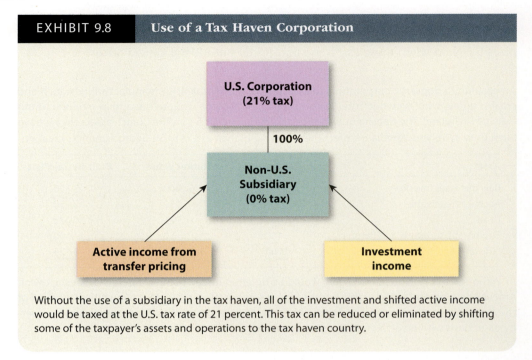

EXHIBIT 9.8   Use of a Tax Haven Corporation

U.S. Corporation (21% tax)

100%

Non-U.S. Subsidiary (0% tax)

Active income from transfer pricing

Investment income

Without the use of a subsidiary in the tax haven, all of the investment and shifted active income would be taxed at the U.S. tax rate of 21 percent. This tax can be reduced or eliminated by shifting some of the taxpayer's assets and operations to the tax haven country.

This practice often is referred to as treaty shopping . If the Country B investment income had been earned directly by the U.S. corporation, it would have been subject to a 30 percent withholding tax. As a result of investing through the foreign subsidiary created in Country A, the U.S. parent corporation pays only 10 percent in foreign taxes on the income earned (i.e., 5 percent to Country B and 5 percent to Country A).

9-5d Offshore (Foreign) Corporations Controlled by U.S. Persons

To minimize current tax liability, taxpayers often shift an income-generating activity to an entity that is not within the U.S. taxing jurisdiction. When a foreign corporation is used in this manner, offshore taxable income may be subject to lower income tax rates, and they may attract certain treaty benefits. U.S. tax law extends a worldwide approach to some of this income, treating such items on a pass-through basis that triggers immediate U.S. income taxation, even though a separate foreign corporation, and not just a branch, is used.

Controlled Foreign Corporations

An elaborate anti-deferral system is in place that attempts to keep U.S. taxpayers from sheltering current taxable income by using foreign subsidiaries. Subpart F of the Code provides that certain types of income generated by controlled foreign corporations (CFCs) are included in current-year gross income by the U.S. shareholders, without regard to actual distributions.[29] Subpart F and CFC rules thus create an immediate "flow-through" of taxable income from the foreign subsidiary to its U.S. shareholders.

About 100,000 CFCs exist, largely in the United Kingdom, Canada, China, Mexico, Germany, and the Netherlands.

A controlled foreign corporation (CFC) is any non-U.S. corporation in which more than 50 percent of (1) the total combined voting power of all classes of stock entitled to vote or (2) the total value of the stock of the corporation is owned by U.S. shareholders on any day during the taxable year of the foreign corporation. The offshore subsidiaries of most multinational U.S. parent corporations are CFCs.

---

[29] §§ 951 through 964.

For this purpose, a U.S. shareholder is defined as a U.S. person who owns, or is considered to own, 10 percent or more of the total combined voting power of all classes of voting stock of the non-U.S. corporation. Stock owned directly, indirectly, and constructively is counted.

When Subpart F applies, U.S. shareholders include in gross income their pro rata share of Subpart F income and the increase of the CFC's investment in U.S. property for the tax year. The taxpayer includes a proportionate share of gross income in the year in which the CFC's taxable year ends.

Subpart F Constructive Dividends

Gray, Inc., a calendar year corporation, is a CFC for the entire tax year. Chance Company, a U.S. corporation, owns 60% of Gray's one class of stock for the entire year. Subpart F income is $100,000, and no distributions have been made during the year.

Chance, a calendar year taxpayer, includes $60,000 in gross income as a constructive dividend from Gray for the tax year.

EXAMPLE 17

Groth, Inc., is a CFC until July 1 of the calendar tax year (not a leap year) and earns $100,000 of Subpart F income. Terry, a U.S. citizen, owns 30% of its one class of stock for the entire year.

Terry includes $14,877 [$100,000 × 30% × (181 days/365 days)] in gross income as a constructive dividend from Groth for the tax year.

EXAMPLE 18

Subpart F Income Only certain income earned by the CFC triggers immediate U.S. taxation as a constructive dividend. This Subpart F income can be characterized as income with little or no economic connection with the CFC's country of incorporation. Subpart F income typically includes foreign base company income (FBCI), such as:

- Foreign personal holding company income.
- Foreign base company sales income.
- Foreign base company services income.

Foreign personal holding company (FPHC) income commonly includes:

- Dividends, interest, royalties, rents, and annuities.
- Excess gains over losses from the sale or exchange of property that gives rise to FPHC income.
- Excess of foreign currency gains over foreign currency losses (other than amounts directly related to the business needs of the CFC).

Foreign base company (FBC) sales income is income derived by a CFC where the CFC has very little connection with the process that generates the income and a related party is involved. If the CFC earns income from the sale of property to customers outside the CFC's country of incorporation and either the supplier or the customer is related to the CFC, this typically constitutes FBC sales income. FBC sales income usually involves three different countries in the arrangement, as illustrated in Concept Summary 9.3.

Ulysses, Ltd., is a CFC organized in the United Kingdom and owned 100% by Joyce, Inc., a U.S. corporation. Ulysses purchases finished inventory from Joyce and sells the inventory to customers in Hong Kong. This sales income constitutes FBC sales income.

EXAMPLE 19

Concept Summary 9.3

Subpart F Income and a CFC

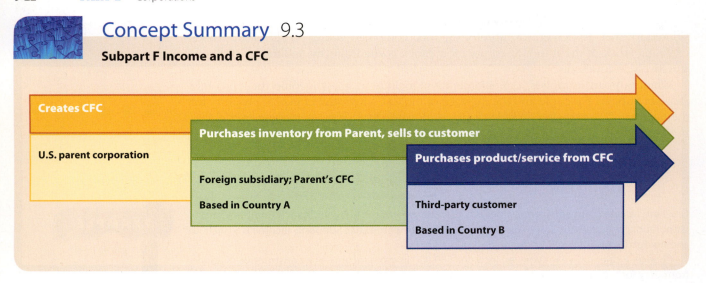

An exception applies to property that is manufactured, produced, grown, or extracted in the country in which the CFC was organized or created and to property sold for use, consumption, or disposition within that country. In both of these situations, fewer than three countries are involved, and the CFC has participated in the economic process that generates the income. No Subpart F income is created.

EXAMPLE 20

If Ulysses, from Example 19, purchases raw materials from Joyce and performs substantial manufacturing activity in the United Kingdom before selling the inventory to customers in Hong Kong, the income is not FBC sales income.

Even without the manufacturing activity, sales to customers within the United Kingdom would not produce FBC sales income.

FBC services income is income derived from the performance of services for or on behalf of a related person and performed outside the country in which the CFC was created or organized. Income from services performed in connection with the sale of property by a CFC that has manufactured, produced, grown, or extracted such property is *not* FBC services income.

Potentially large amounts of offshore profits (e.g., active trade or business income not involving related persons) escape the definition of Subpart F income, resulting in no immediate U.S. income taxation.

Subpart F Income Exceptions Several exceptions apply to the Subpart F rules discussed above.

- A *de minimis* rule provides that if the total amount of a foreign corporation's FBCI for the taxable year is less than the smaller of 5 percent of the CFC's gross income or $1 million, *none* of its gross income is treated as FBCI for the tax year.

- A *full inclusion* rule applies if a foreign corporation's FBCI exceeds 70 percent of total gross income. In this case, *all* of the corporation's gross income for the tax year is treated as Subpart F income.

- FBCI subject to high foreign taxes is not included under Subpart F. The taxpayer must establish that the income was taxed by the other country at an effective rate of more than 90 percent of the Federal corporate income tax rate. For example, the other country's effective income tax rate must be greater than 18.9 percent (90% × 21%, where 21 percent is the current U.S. corporate rate).

Subpart F Income

USP, Inc., is the sole U.S. shareholder of Gaelic, Inc., a CFC. During the taxable year, Gaelic reports gross income of $12,000,000 and FBCI of $521,000.

Since Gaelic's FBCI is less than the smaller of (1) 5% of gross income ($600,000; $12,000,000 × 5%) or (2) $1,000,000, the *de minimis* rule applies and *none* of Gaelic's gross income is treated as FBCI for the year.

EXAMPLE 21

Assume the same facts as in the previous example, except that Gaelic's FBCI is $8,500,000. Here, FBCI is 70.8% of gross income ($8,500,000 ÷ $12,000,000).

Under the *full inclusion* rule, *all* of Gaelic's gross income is treated as Subpart F income.

EXAMPLE 22

Investment in U.S. Property In addition to Subpart F income, U.S. shareholders include in gross income their pro rata share of the CFC's increase in investment in U.S. property for the taxable year.[30] U.S. property generally includes U.S. real property, debt obligations of U.S. persons, cash held in U.S. banks, and stock in certain related domestic corporations. Here, the U.S. shareholders pay current Federal income tax because the CFC has "repatriated" *assets* to the United States, and immediate taxation occurs. The CFC must have sufficient E & P to support such a deemed dividend.

Fleming, Ltd., a CFC, earned no Subpart F income for the taxable year. If Fleming lends $100,000 to Lynn, its sole U.S. shareholder, this debt is considered an investment in U.S. property by Fleming because it now owns a U.S. note receivable. Holding the note triggers a constructive dividend of $100,000 to Lynn, assuming that Fleming has sufficient E & P.

EXAMPLE 23

Other Tax Consequences of Being a CFC The Subpart F and CFC rules create an immediate flow-through of taxable income, regardless of distributions received by the taxpayer. This works in a manner similar to that of the income taxation of partnerships, S corporations, and similar entities (see Chapters 10 through 13). A foreign tax credit is allowed with respect to a Subpart F income inclusion.[31]

A U.S. shareholder's basis in CFC stock is increased by constructive dividends and decreased by subsequent distributions of previously taxed income. The various constructive dividend possibilities for CFC income appear in Concept Summary 9.4.

Singh, a U.S. shareholder in the CFC Bombay United, records a $100,000 constructive dividend from the entity as foreign base company services income under Subpart F rules. Singh's basis in the Bombay United stock increases correspondingly by $100,000.

EXAMPLE 24

9-5e **Movement Toward a Territorial System**

U.S. income tax law generally applies a worldwide system with respect to the cross-border activities of U.S. persons, but most of the rest of the developed world uses a territorial approach. Congress believes that moving toward a territorial system will increase the competitiveness of U.S. businesses in the global marketplace, and it has taken steps to adopt some territorial aspects within current law, although the worldwide system still undergirds the taxation of outbound transactions.

Legacy law promoted a "defer until repatriation" strategy by U.S. taxpayers: unless Subpart F or some other rule applied, gross income from overseas operations was not recognized by a U.S. entity until the profits were paid back into the United States in the form of dividend payments from a CFC to its domestic parent. Over time, about $3 trillion in unrepatriated profits had been accumulated offshore by U.S. taxpayers, especially in the tech and pharma industries; this unrepatriated cash represented

---

[30]§ 956.   [31]§ 960.

Concept Summary 9.4

Income of a CFC That Is Included in Gross Income of a U.S. Shareholder, Selected

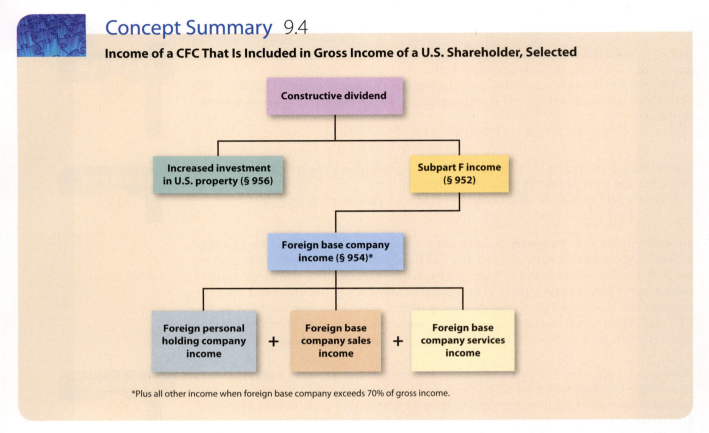

*Plus all other income when foreign base company exceeds 70% of gross income.

about $1 trillion in deferred U.S. income tax collections. Congress used parts of the TCJA of 2017 to encourage the repatriation of these funds.

Effective in 2018, C corporations are allowed a limited version of territorial taxation, while also being encouraged to repatriate any profits accumulated from past tax years. A dividends received deduction (DRD) of 100 percent is allowed for amounts paid to a U.S.-parent C corporation from the earnings and profits (E & P) of a non-U.S., "10%-owned" subsidiary.[32] This rule fully exempts from U.S. taxation the foreign-source profits that underlie the dividend payment (thereby resembling a territorial taxing system), and it encourages the return of cash accumulations to the U.S. economy (perhaps in large amounts).

EXAMPLE

25

OffCo, a 100%-owned Nigerian subsidiary of the U.S. C corporation BossCo, earned a current-year profit of $10 million, and it immediately paid all of this amount to its parent in the form of a dividend. The income did not represent Subpart F income for BossCo.

BossCo reports zero gross income for OffCo's current activities; its income from the dividend received is fully offset by the 100% DRD.

The DRD is allowed even if the foreign affiliate is not a CFC of the U.S. parent. Subpart F pass-through constructive dividends do not qualify for the DRD. To qualify for the DRD, the U.S. parent must have owned the stock of the offshore affiliate for at least one year; this requirement may present problems when the entities were involved in recent merger or takeover activity.

In addition, any recognized gain on the sale or other disposition of stock of a 10%-owned CFC by a U.S. shareholder is treated as dividend income and triggers the DRD, to the extent of the transferor's share of unrepatriated, untaxed E & P of the corporation.[33] No foreign tax credit is allowed relative to dividends taxed under this provision.

One-Time 2017 Transition Tax The adoption of the U.S. version of territorial taxation, allowing significant amounts of offshore profits to fully escape Federal income taxation,

---

[32]§ 245A; "10%-owned" means owning 10% or more of the voting stock of the foreign corporation.

[33]§ 1248.

came at a potentially steep price for some entities. Included in the 2017 Subpart F income of C corporations with unrepatriated E & P was the U.S. parent's share of the untaxed, unrepatriated post-1986 E & P of its 10%-owned foreign subsidiaries, measured typically as of the end of 2017.[34] This E & P triggered significant tax obligations for many U.S. entities, affecting both book and taxable income amounts.

This E & P was subjected to a tax rate of 15.5 percent (8 percent if the E & P was distributed in a form other than cash).[35] The tax was payable immediately, or by election the payment could be spread out over eight years.[36] No foreign tax credit was allowed against the one-time tax liability.[37] The one-time transition tax applied whether or not the foreign affiliate made an actual distribution of its E & P to its shareholders, although many C corporations that were liable for the tax constructed plans to commence distributions, often over a period of years.

> **EXAMPLE 26**
>
> HomeCo, a U.S. C corporation, ran its overseas operations through AwayCo, a 100%-owned subsidiary based in a low-tax country with which the United States does not hold a tax treaty. E & P accumulated within AwayCo amounted to $50 million in cash, which remained unrepatriated, deferring the U.S. income taxation on those profits.
>
> HomeCo's 2017 Subpart F income included this $50 million, and HomeCo incurred a one-time transition tax of $7.75 million ($50 million × 15.5% tax rate). HomeCo properly elected to pay this obligation over eight years.

The tax was payable by the U.S. parent, or by individual investors and partners/members of pass-through entities if the shares were held in that manner. An S corporation with E & P was allowed to defer the income recognition and tax liability until its S election was terminated or lost, or until it ceased doing business.[38]

Additional Tax on Intangible Income In the context of the adoption of a form of territorial taxation, Congress feared that U.S. CFCs would transfer portable types of income overseas, to avoid Federal income taxation permanently and in full. To counter these possibilities, a tax applies at an effective rate of 10.5 percent on the shareholders of a CFC, where the entity generates intangible income that is foreign-sourced (called global intangible low-taxed income, or GILTI).[39]

Income taxed under this provision is not classified as Subpart F income, although it is taxed in a similar manner (i.e., in the immediate recognition year).[40] The tax does not apply to income that is effectively connected to a U.S. business, nor to items already taxed under Subpart F. The base for the 10.5 percent tax is computed to allow for a normal return on the CFC's tangible assets; those calculations are not discussed here.[41]

The foreign tax credit is allowed against this tax, but only to the extent of 80 percent of the foreign taxes paid, and without any carryover allowed to another tax year.

> **EXAMPLE 27**
>
> HornCo, a U.S. C corporation, conducts its overseas operations through its Algerian CFC, OtterCo. OtterCo's intangible income for the tax year totaled $5,000,000, on which it paid $200,000 Algeria income tax. These items did not constitute Subpart F income, and they were not effectively connected to HornCo's U.S. businesses.
>
> HornCo includes the $5,000,000 intangible income in its own gross income for the year, and its shareholders are liable for a tax of $525,000 ($5,000,000 × 10.5%). Against this amount, HornCo shareholders can claim an aggregate foreign tax credit of $160,000 ($200,000 foreign tax paid × 80% maximum credit), with no carryover of the remaining $40,000 foreign tax paid.

When GILTI is generated by a CFC that is owned by a partnership, S corporation, or other flow-through entity, this income is subject to tax in full at the owners' applicable income tax rates.

---

[34]§ 965(a).

[35]§ 965(c).

[36]§ 965(h).

[37]§ 965(g).

[38]§ 965(i).

[39]§ 951A.

[40]§ 951A(f).

[41]§§ 951A(b)–(d).

9-6 U.S. TAXATION OF NONRESIDENT ALIENS AND FOREIGN CORPORATIONS

Generally, only the U.S.-source income of nonresident alien individuals and foreign corporations is subject to U.S. taxation. This reflects the reach of the U.S. tax jurisdiction. The constraint, however, does not prevent the United States from also taxing the foreign-source income of nonresident alien individuals and non-U.S. corporations when that income is effectively connected with the conduct of a U.S. trade or business, in the manner of territorial taxation.[42]

9-6a Nonresident Alien Individuals

A nonresident alien (NRA) individual is not a citizen or resident of the United States. For example, Prince William is an NRA because he is not a citizen or resident of the United States. Citizenship is determined under the immigration and naturalization laws of the United States.[43] Usually, citizenship statutes are broken down into two categories: nationality at birth or through naturalization.

Residency

An individual is a resident of the United States for income tax purposes if he or she meets either the green card test or the substantial presence test.[44] If either of these tests is met for the calendar year, the individual is deemed a U.S. resident for the year.

A non-U.S. person issued a green card is considered a U.S. resident on the first day he or she is physically present in the United States after issuance. The green card is Immigration Form I–551. Newly issued cards no longer are green, but the form still is referred to as the "green card." Status as a U.S. resident remains in effect until the green card has been revoked or the individual has abandoned lawful permanent resident status.

The *substantial presence* test is applied to an alien without a green card. It is a mathematical test involving physical presence in the United States. An individual who is physically present in the United States for at least 183 days during the calendar year is a U.S. resident for income tax purposes.

This 183-day requirement also can be met over a three-year period that includes the two immediately preceding years and the current year, as long as the individual is present in the United States at least 31 days during the current year.[45] For this purpose, each day of the current calendar year is counted as a full day, each day of the first preceding year as one-third day, and each day of the second preceding year as one-sixth day. A nominal presence of 10 days or less can be ignored in determining whether the substantial presence test is met.

EXAMPLE 28

Li, who is not a U.S. citizen, was present in the United States for 90 days in 2017, 180 days in 2018, and 110 days in 2019. For Federal income tax purposes, Li is a U.S. resident for 2019, because she was physically present for 185 days [(90 days × $\frac{1}{6}$) + (180 days × $\frac{1}{3}$) + (110 days × 1)] during the three-year period.

When counting days of physical presence in the United States, there are several exceptions. Commuters from Mexico and Canada who are employed in the United States but return home each day do not count those work days as days of physical presence. The same is true for individuals who are prevented from leaving the United States by medical conditions that arose while the individuals were in the United States. Some individuals are exempt altogether from the substantial presence test, including

---

[42]§§ 871, 881, and 882.
[43]Title 8, Aliens and Nationality, *United States Code.*

[44]§ 7701(b).
[45]§ 7701(b)(3)(A).

foreign government-related individuals (e.g., diplomats), qualified teachers, trainees and students, and certain professional athletes.

Nonresident Aliens Not Engaged in a U.S. Trade or Business

Certain U.S.-source income that is *not* effectively connected with the conduct of a U.S. trade or business is subject to a flat 30 percent tax. This income includes dividends, certain interest, rents, royalties, certain compensation, premiums, annuities, and other similar income. This tax generally requires the payors of the income to withhold 30 percent of gross amounts.[46] The withholding procedures work to eliminate the problems of ensuring payment by nonresidents and determining allowable deductions as well as, in most instances, the filing of tax returns by nonresidents.

Interest received from certain portfolio debt investments, even though U.S. sourced, is exempt from taxation when earned by non-U.S. persons. Interest earned on bank deposits also is exempt as long as it is not effectively connected with the conduct of a U.S. trade or business. These rules encourage offshore investors to purchase U.S. Treasury bonds and notes and to deposit U.S. currency in domestic bank accounts.

Capital gains *not* effectively connected with the conduct of a U.S. trade or business are exempt from this tax, as long as the NRA was not present in the United States for 183 days or more during the taxable year. If an NRA has not established a taxable year, the calendar year is used. NRAs are not permitted to carry forward capital losses.[47]

Nonresident Aliens Engaged in a U.S. Trade or Business

Two important definitions determine the U.S. tax consequences to NRAs with U.S.-source income: "the conduct of a **U.S. trade or business**" and "**effectively connected income**." Specifically, for an NRA's noninvestment income to be subject to U.S. taxation, the NRA must be considered engaged in a U.S. trade or business and must earn income effectively connected with that business.

General criteria for determining whether a U.S. trade or business exists include the location of production activities, management, distribution activities, and other business functions. Trading in commodities and securities ordinarily does not constitute a trade or business. Dealers, however, need to avoid maintaining a U.S. trading office and trading for their own accounts.

The Code does not explicitly define a U.S. trade or business, but case law looks for activities carried on in the United States that are regular, substantial, and continuous.[48] Once an NRA is considered engaged in a U.S. trade or business, all U.S.-source income other than investment and capital gain income is considered effectively connected to that trade or business and is therefore subject to U.S. taxation.

EXAMPLE 29

Vito, an NRA, produces wine for export. During the current year, Vito earns $500,000 from exporting wine to unrelated wholesalers in the United States. The title to the wine passes to the U.S. wholesalers in New York. Vito has no offices or employees in the United States. The income from wine sales is U.S.-source income, but because Vito is not engaged in a U.S. trade or business, the income is not subject to taxation in the United States.

Vito begins operating a hot dog cart in New York City. This activity constitutes a U.S. trade or business. Consequently, all U.S.-source income other than investment or capital gain income is taxed in the United States as income effectively connected with a U.S. trade or business. As a result, both the hot dog cart profits and the $500,000 in wine income are subject to U.S. income tax.

---

[46]§§ 871 and 1441. Tax treaty provisions can change these rates.

[47]§ 871(a)(2).

[48]See, for example, *Higgins v. Comm.*, 41–1 USTC ¶9233, 25 AFTR 1160, 61 S.Ct. 475 (1941) and *Continental Trading, Inc. v. Comm.*, 59–1 USTC ¶9316, 3 AFTR 2d 923, 265 F.2d 40 (CA–9, 1959).

Effectively connected income is taxed at the same rates that apply to U.S. citizens and residents, and deductions for expenses attributable to that income are allowed. NRAs with income effectively connected with the conduct of a U.S. trade or business also are subject to the alternative minimum tax.

9-6b Foreign Corporations

A corporation created or organized in the United States is a domestic corporation. A foreign corporation is one that is not domestic. Although McDonald's is a global corporation, it is considered a domestic corporation for U.S. tax purposes, solely because it was organized in the United States.

Foreign corporations are taxed very much like NRAs. Capital gain income is exempt from tax, and a flat 30 percent tax rate is applied to U.S.-source investment income items if they are not effectively connected with a U.S. trade or business. Foreign corporations conducting a trade or business in the United States are subject to Federal income taxation on any U.S.-source income effectively connected with the trade or business.

9-6c Foreign Investment in Real Property Tax Act

At one time, NRAs and foreign corporations could avoid U.S. taxation on gains from the sale of U.S. real estate if the gains were treated as capital gains and were not effectively connected with the conduct of a U.S. trade or business. In the mid-1970s, midwestern farmers pressured Congress to eliminate what they saw as a tax advantage that would allow nonresidents to bid up the price of farmland. This and other concerns about foreign ownership of U.S. real estate led to the enactment of the **Foreign Investment in Real Property Tax Act (FIRPTA)**.

Under FIRPTA, gains and losses realized by NRAs and foreign corporations from the sale or other disposition of U.S. real property interests (USRPIs) are treated as effectively connected with the conduct of a U.S. trade or business, even when those individuals or corporations are not actually so engaged. Any direct interest in real property situated in the United States and any interest in a domestic corporation (other than solely as a creditor) are U.S. real property interests.

NRA individuals must pay a tax equal to the *lesser of*:

- The applicable tax on their alternative minimum taxable income, or
- Regular U.S. rates on the net U.S. real property gain for the taxable year.[49]

Any purchaser acquiring a USRPI from a foreign person must withhold 10 percent of the amount realized on the disposition.[50]

9-6d Expatriation to Avoid U.S. Taxation

U.S. taxation of U.S.-source income is required of individuals who relinquished their U.S. citizenship within 10 years of deriving that income if they gave up their citizenship to avoid U.S. taxation. Furthermore, NRAs who lost U.S. citizenship within a 10-year period immediately preceding the close of the tax year must pay taxes on their U.S.-source income as though they were still U.S. citizens. This provision applies only if the expatriation had as one of its principal purposes the avoidance of U.S. taxes. Individuals are presumed to have a tax avoidance purpose if they meet either of the following criteria.[51]

- Average annual net income tax for the five taxable years ending before the date of loss of U.S. citizenship is more than $168,000 for 2019.
- Net worth as of that date is at least $2 million.

These provisions also apply to "long-term lawful permanent residents" who cease to be taxed as U.S. residents. A long-term permanent resident is an individual (other than

---

[49]§ 897.
[50]§ 1445.

[51]§ 877(a)(2). The dollar amounts are adjusted for inflation each year.

a citizen of the United States) who is a lawful permanent resident of the United States in at least 8 taxable years during the previous 15-year period. An exception applies to certain individuals with dual citizenship.

The United States continues to treat individuals as U.S. citizens or residents until the taxpayers provide required information and an expatriation notice. Expatriates who are subject to the 10-year rule outlined previously must file an information disclosure statement annually. If an expatriate is physically present in the United States for more than 30 days during a calendar year during the 10-year period, the individual is taxed as a U.S. citizen or resident.[52] These expatriation rules, taken as a whole, make it difficult to give up U.S. citizenship or residency simply to avoid U.S. taxation.

9-7 REPORTING REQUIREMENTS

The U.S. tax provisions involving cross-border transactions include numerous reporting requirements. In addition, civil and criminal penalties for noncompliance can apply.

A domestic C corporation reports non-U.S. results on its Form 1120. A non-U.S. corporation with a U.S. income tax liability files Form 1120–F.

A domestic corporation that is 25 percent or more foreign-owned must file an information return and maintain certain records for review by the IRS.[53] In addition, any foreign corporation carrying on a trade or business in the United States must file an information return and maintain records in a similar manner.[54]

U.S. shareholders of a CFC must file a Form 5471. Asset transfers to foreign corporations or partnerships under certain tax-deferred transactions require information returns at the time of the transfer.[55] U.S. taxpayers that control foreign corporations or partnerships also must file annual information returns related to these entities.[56]

9-8 TAX PLANNING

Return to the timeline of Exhibit 9.6, and consider the decision to operate a multi-national business entity as a branch and when to convert the structure of the business to an overseas subsidiary. Exhibit 9.9 identifies the major advantages and disadvantages for each of these decisions from a Federal income tax standpoint.

Additional tax planning opportunities and considerations are discussed below.

9-8a The Foreign Tax Credit Limitation and Sourcing Provisions

The FTC limitation is partially based on the amount of foreign-source taxable income in the numerator of the limitation formula. Consequently, the sourcing of income is extremely important. Generally, in this regard, the U.S. taxpayer benefits when the sourcing rules work to:

- Generate *income* items that are *foreign-source*, to maximize net foreign-source income (the numerator of the FTC fraction). Alternatively, a branch or flow-through entity might want overseas income to be U.S.-source, to increase its 20 percent deduction for qualified business income.[57]

- Realize *deduction* items as *U.S.-source*, to minimize any reduction in net foreign-source income (the numerator of the FTC fraction).

---

[52] § 877(g)(1).

[53] § 6038A.

[54] § 6038C.

[55] § 6038B.

[56] § 6038.

[57] § 199A. See text Section 2-3k.

EXHIBIT 9.9	Foreign Branch vs. Separate Overseas Entity: Tax Considerations

U.S. Income Tax Considerations	Operate as a Branch of the U.S. Corporation	Operate Through a Separate Overseas Entity (e.g., Subsidiary)
Advantages	• Current U.S. deduction for foreign losses (i.e., flow-through treatment) • If permanent establishment tests are met, treaty benefits are available • Income taxes paid to other jurisdictions may qualify for foreign tax credit, thereby reducing exposure to double taxation • Lower tax rate on certain intangible income	• Exemption for U.S. income taxation on profits repatriated as dividends (except for Subpart F income) • Availability of income shifting by transfer pricing strategies (e.g., by paying management fees or setting internal pricing levels) • Liability protection for U.S. net assets from overseas operations
Disadvantages	• Current profits are subject to immediate U.S. taxation (i.e., flow-through treatment, even without cash repatriations) • Local tax and financial incentives may not be available (i.e., to an "outside" entity)	• Exposure to taxes on intangible income • Subpart F rules might accelerate recognition of gross income from offshore profits • IRS might use § 482 powers to reallocate income/deductions to the United States

Income that is taxed by an overseas tax jurisdiction benefits from the FTC only to the extent that it is classified as foreign-source income under U.S. tax law. As a result, elements that affect the sourcing of income, such as the place of title passage, should be considered carefully before a transaction is undertaken.

It further may be possible for a U.S. corporation to alleviate the problem of excess foreign taxes by using the following techniques.

- Generate "same basket" foreign-source income that is subject to a tax rate lower than the U.S. tax rate.

- Reduce, by relocating operations, highly taxed foreign-source income in favor of foreign-source income that is taxed at a lower rate.

- Deduct foreign taxes for years when the deduction benefit would exceed the FTC benefit.

EXAMPLE 30

Donohoe, Inc., a U.S. corporation, reports total U.S. taxable income of $100,000, classified as follows.

	Total	U.S.-Source Income	Foreign-Source Income—Active Basket
Gross income	$150,000	$100,000	$ 50,000
Deductions	(50,000)	(40,000)	(10,000)
Taxable income	$100,000	$ 60,000	$ 40,000

U.S. income tax before the FTC is $21,000, and Donohoe's FTC limitation is $8,400 [($40,000 ÷ $100,000) × $21,000]. If, through planning and analysis, Donohoe is able to convert $5,000 of the deductions related to foreign-source income to U.S. source, the total taxable income would remain the same, but the FTC limitation would increase to $9,450 [($45,000 ÷ $100,000) × $21,000].

9-8b **Transfer Pricing**

U.S. multinational companies earn income across many different jurisdictions and operate through several different types of entities (e.g., subsidiary corporations, joint ventures, and partnerships). With proper planning and documentation, a U.S. corporation can organize its intercompany payments for goods and services, interest on debt, and royalties for use of intangible property in such a way as to minimize its worldwide tax burden. For example, a U.S. multinational may choose to borrow in high-tax jurisdictions (where the interest deduction will be more valuable) and earn royalty income in low-tax jurisdictions (where the income escapes heavy taxation). The anti-base-erosion tax might restrict these arrangements.

REFOCUS ON THE BIG PICTURE

GOING INTERNATIONAL

Now you can address the questions about VoiceCo's activities that were posed at the beginning of the chapter. Simply selling assets overseas may not trigger any host country income tax consequences, but such income is taxed currently to VoiceCo in the United States. When VoiceCo sets up an Irish corporation as a manufacturer, it can avoid deemed dividends under Subpart F.

VoiceCo must file Form 5471 to report the activities of its foreign subsidiary. If VoiceCo receives dividends from such a subsidiary, it can claim exemption from U.S. taxation.

What If?

Suppose that although VoiceCo's European sales become a substantial part of its total revenues, it decides not to create a foreign subsidiary. Instead, because shipping costs are high and customers demand quick turnaround on product orders, VoiceCo decides to license its design and manufacturing process to a local European musical instruments company for sales in Europe. The European company pays VoiceCo a royalty equal to 25 percent of the sales price on all of its sales of microphones based on VoiceCo's design. The royalty income is foreign-source, because the underlying intangible property is exploited outside the United States.

The European country imposes a 5 percent withholding tax on all royalty payments to VoiceCo. The royalties are part of its worldwide income and so are currently taxed to VoiceCo in the United States. Will VoiceCo receive a foreign tax credit for the withholding tax?

MONKEY BUSINESS IMAGES/SHUTTERSTOCK.COM

Key Terms

Controlled foreign corporation (CFC), 9-20

Effectively connected income, 9-27

Foreign Investment in Real Property Tax Act (FIRPTA), 9-28

Foreign tax credit (FTC), 9-3

Functional currency, 9-14

Inbound taxation, 9-3

Nonresident alien (NRA), 9-26

Outbound taxation, 9-3

Qualified business unit (QBU), 9-14

Subpart F income, 9-21

Tax haven, 9-19

Tax treaties, 9-5

Transfer pricing, 9-10

Treaty shopping, 9-20

U.S. shareholder, 9-21

U.S. trade or business, 9-27

Discussion Questions

1. **LO.1** "U.S. persons are taxed on their worldwide income." Explain.

2. **LO.1, 5** Liang, a U.S. citizen, owns 100% of ForCo, a non-U.S. corporation not engaged in a U.S. trade or business. Is Liang subject to any U.S. income tax on her dealings with ForCo? Explain.

Critical Thinking   3.   **LO.5** Randall operates his distribution business in several countries. He wants to move some equipment to a new office in South Africa. This equipment includes assets with a large acquisition price and accumulated MACRS depreciation. The assets to be transferred would generate a $1 million realized gain if sold. Advise Randall on the tax effects of his proposed asset transfer.

Communications   4.   **LO.5** Joy Marcus owns several income-producing assets, including a stock portfolio and a small services proprietorship. She wants to start up a new corporation in the country Molto, where the income tax rates are about one-third of those in the United States, and transfer all of her assets and operations there.

How tax-effective is Joy's plan in shifting the income from her activities when they are placed in the Molto corporation? Write a memo for the tax research file highlighting the Federal income tax rules that apply.

5.   **LO.5** Five unrelated U.S. individuals own all of the shares of Popping, a corporation organized in the United States but operating fully in the country Vivace. Mariam, one of the shareholders, asks you whether the income from Popping will be taxed to her immediately as earned; she believes the entity is classified as "a controlled foreign corporation (CFC)." Explain how the Federal income tax law applies to the profits earned by Popping. Use the correct Federal income tax terminology in your comments.

6.   **LO.5** QuinnCo could not claim all of the income taxes it paid to Japan as a foreign tax credit (FTC) this year. What computational limit probably kept QuinnCo from taking its full FTC? Explain.

7.   **LO.5** FoldIt, a U.S. business, paid income taxes to Mexico relative to profitable sales of shipping boxes it made in that country. Can it claim a deduction for these taxes in computing U.S. taxable income? A tax credit? Both? Explain.

Critical Thinking   8.   **LO.5** Molly, Inc., a domestic corporation, generates income from the receipt of royalty income from patents that it owns. Molly wants to avoid U.S. income tax on these royalties, so it has its 100%-owned subsidiary, based in Nigeria, hold the patents and collect the royalties.

What U.S. income tax issues must be considered in assessing this arrangement by Molly, Inc.?

9.   **LO.5** HiramCo, a U.S. entity, operates a manufacturing business in both Mexico and Costa Rica, and it holds its investment portfolio in Sweden. How many foreign tax credit computations must HiramCo make? Be specific, and use the term *basket* in your answer.

Communications   10.   **LO.1, 6** Write a memo for the tax research file on the difference between "inbound" and "outbound" activities in the context of U.S. taxation of international income.

Communications   11.   **LO.1, 3, 5** Draft a short speech that you will give to your university's Business Club. The title of your talk is "What Is Worldwide Taxation and How Can I Avoid It?" Be certain to include the term *territorial taxing system* in your presentation.

Computational Exercises

12.   **LO.3** Shonda receives dividend income from the following foreign and domestic corporations in the current tax year.

Corporation	Dividends Received	Percentage of U.S. Income for Past 3 Years
Silver (foreign)	$1,500	35%
Bronze (domestic)	1,000	20%
Copper (domestic)	2,000	80%

Determine the amount of U.S.-source income for each corporation.

13. **LO.5** Cordeio, Inc., is a CFC for the entire tax year (not a leap year). Yancy Company, a U.S. corporation, owns 75% of Cordeio's one class of stock for the entire year. Subpart F income is $450,000, and no distributions have been made during the year. Both entities use the calendar tax year.
    a. What amount does Yancy include in gross income as a constructive dividend for the tax year?
    b. Assume that Cordeio is a CFC until March 1 of the calendar tax year. What amount does Yancy include in gross income as a constructive dividend for the tax year?

14. **LO.5** Enders, Inc., a domestic corporation that invests in foreign securities, reports total taxable income for the tax year of $290,000, consisting of $208,800 in U.S.-source business profits and $81,200 of Subpart F income from foreign sources. Income taxes of $24,000 were withheld by foreign tax authorities. Enders's U.S. tax before the FTC is $60,900.
    a. Compute Enders's FTC for the tax year.
    b. Express your answer as a Microsoft Excel formula.

15. **LO.5** By the end of 2017, Klein, a domestic corporation, had accumulated $10 million in cash from the overseas operations of its Liberia subsidiary. Klein made no distributions of these accumulated profits during 2017. Compute the one-time transition tax liability that was incurred by Klein.

16. **LO.6** Velocity, Inc., a foreign corporation, earned $500,000 U.S.-source income from royalties that it collected and $400,000 interest from its investment in U.S. Treasury bonds. Compute Velocity's U.S. income tax on these amounts.

Problems

17. **LO.3, 5** BlueCo, a domestic corporation, incorporates GreenCo, a new wholly owned entity in Germany. Under both German and U.S. legal principles, this entity is a corporation. BlueCo faces a 21% U.S. tax rate.

    GreenCo earns $1.5 million in net profits from its German manufacturing activities and makes no dividend distributions to BlueCo. How much U.S. income tax will BlueCo pay for the current year as a result of GreenCo's earnings, assuming that it incurs no deemed dividend under Subpart F?

18. **LO.3** Emma, a U.S. resident, received the following income items for the current tax year. Identify the sourcing of each item as either U.S. or foreign.
    a. $600 interest from a savings account at a Florida bank.
    b. $5,000 dividend from U.S. Flower Company, a U.S. corporation that operates solely in the eastern United States.
    c. $7,000 dividend from Stern Corporation, a U.S. corporation that generated total gross income of $4,000,000 from the active conduct of a foreign trade or business for the immediately preceding three tax years. Stern's total gross income for the same period was $5,000,000.
    d. $10,000 dividend from International Consolidated, Inc., a foreign corporation that reported gross income of $4,000,000 effectively connected with the conduct of a U.S. trade or business for the immediately preceding three tax years. International's total gross income for the same period was $12,000,000.
    e. $5,000 interest on Warren Corporation bonds. Warren is a U.S. corporation that derived $6,000,000 of its gross income for the immediately preceding three tax years from operation of an active foreign business. Warren's total gross income for this same period was $7,200,000.

Communications

19. **LO.3** Gloria Martinez, an NRA, is a professional golfer. She played in seven tournaments in the United States in the current year and earned $250,000 in prizes from these tournaments. She deposited the winnings in a bank account she opened in Mexico City after her first tournament win.

    Gloria played a total of 30 tournaments for the year and earned $800,000 in total prize money. She spent 40 days in the United States, 60 days in England, 20 days in Scotland, and the rest of the time in South America. Write a letter to Gloria explaining how much U.S.-source income she will generate, if any, from her participation in these tournaments and whether any of her winnings are subject to U.S. taxation. Gloria's address is AV Rio Branco, 149-4#, Rio de Janeiro, RJ 20180, Brazil.

20. **LO.3** Determine whether the sourcing of income for the following sales is U.S. or foreign.
    a. Suarez, an NRA, sells stock in Home Depot, a U.S. corporation, through a broker in San Antonio.
    b. Chris sells stock in IBM, a U.S. corporation, to her brother, Rich. Both Chris and Rich are NRAs, and the sale takes place outside the United States.
    c. Crows, Inc., sells inventory produced in the United States to customers in Europe. Title passes in the international waters of the Atlantic Ocean.
    d. Doubles, Inc., a U.S. corporation, manufactures equipment in Malaysia and sells the equipment to customers in the United States.

21. **LO.3, 6** Determine whether the sourcing of income in each of the following situations is U.S. or foreign.
    a. USCo sells depreciable personal property (produced in the United States) that it has been using in its foreign branch operations. The property sells for $180,000, has a tax basis of $75,000, and has been depreciated for tax purposes to the extent of $90,000. The property is located in a foreign country but is sold to another domestic corporation. The sales transaction takes place in the United States.
    b. Jacques, an NRA, sells an apartment building to Julie, a U.S. resident, at a $200,000 gain. The building is located in Denver. The closing takes place in Jacques's country of residence.
    c. Carla, an NRA, is an employee of a non-U.S. corporation. During the tax year, she spends 80 days in the United States purchasing cloth for her employer, a clothing manufacturer. Her yearly salary is $150,000 (translated into U.S. dollars). Carla spends a total of 200 days working during the year. Her employer has no other business contacts with the United States.
    d. Development, Inc., a U.S. corporation, earns $1,100,000 in royalty income from Far East, Ltd., a foreign corporation, for the use of several patented processes in Far East's manufacturing business located in Singapore.

22. **LO.3** Chock, a U.S. corporation, purchases inventory for resale from distributors within the United States and resells this inventory at a $1 million profit to customers outside the United States. Title to the goods passes outside the United States. What is the sourcing of Chock's inventory sales income?

23. **LO.3** Willa, a U.S. corporation, owns the rights to a patent related to a medical device. Willa licenses the rights to use the patent to IrishCo, which uses the patent in its manufacturing facility located in Ireland. What is the sourcing of the $1 million royalty income received by Willa from IrishCo for the use of the patent?

24. **LO.3** USCo incurred $100,000 in interest expense for the current year. The tax book value of USCo's assets generating foreign-source income is $5,000,000. The tax book value of USCo's assets generating U.S.-source income is $45,000,000. Corresponding fair market values for the assets are $3,000,000 and $33,000,000, respectively. How much of the interest expense is allocated and apportioned to foreign-source income?

25. **LO.3** LearCo, a non-U.S. conglomerate, generates $4 billion in gross receipts annu- **Critical Thinking** ally. Its U.S. subsidiary, KingCo, accounts for $750 million of the annual gross receipts; KingCo's average annual gross receipts for the last three years is $820 million. KingCo generates U.S. taxable income income of $180 million, after deducting a $350 million management fee that it pays to LearCo. KingCo reports no U.S. tax credits. The corporate income tax rate in LearCo's country is 14%. What are the tax implications (if any) of this arrangement?

26. **LO.4** Honk, Inc., a U.S. corporation, purchases weight-lifting equipment for resale from HiDisu, a Japanese corporation, for 60 million yen. On the date of purchase, 110 yen is equal to $1 U.S. (¥110:$1). The purchase is made on December 15, 2018, with payment due in 90 days. Honk is a calendar year taxpayer. On December 31, 2018, the foreign exchange rate is ¥112:$1.

    On February 2, 2019, the invoice is paid when the exchange rate is ¥115:$1. What amount of foreign currency gain or loss, if any, must Honk recognize for 2018 as a result of this transaction? For 2019?

27. **LO.5** Locket, a U.S. C corporation, makes a sale to a customer in Sustainia, a coun- try that applies a 25% income tax to business profits. The customer found out about Locket through an internet search. Locket has no facilities or employees outside the United States. Locket's profit on the sale totals $25,000. Where is the tax levied on this profit?

28. **LO.5** USCo incorporated its foreign branch operations in Italy by transferring the branch's assets to a foreign corporation in return solely for stock in the new corporation. All of the branch's assets are located outside the United States and are used in the active conduct of a foreign trade or business. Is this transaction eligible for tax deferral under § 351? Explain.

29. **LO.5** Brutus Corporation transferred inventory (basis of $10, fair market value of $30) and machinery used in a U.S. factory (adjusted basis of $50, fair market value of $75) to MapleLeaf, a newly formed corporation in Canada, in exchange for all of MapleLeaf's stock. Brutus previously deducted $30 of depreciation related to the machinery on its U.S. tax return.

    How much gain, if any, must Brutus recognize on the transfers of the property to MapleLeaf?

30. **LO.5** Packard, Inc., a domestic corporation, operates a branch in Mexico. Over **Critical Thinking** the last 10 years, this branch has generated $30 million in losses. For the last **Communications** 3 years, however, the branch has been profitable and has earned enough income to offset the prior losses in full. Most of the assets are fully depreciated, and a net gain would be recognized if the assets were sold.

    Packard's CFO believes that Packard should incorporate the branch now, so that this potential gain can be transferred to a foreign corporation, deferring the real- ized gain on the transfer under § 351. Draft a memo to Akiko Henderson, the CFO, addressing the tax issues involved in the proposed transaction.

31. **LO.5** USCo owns 65% of the voting stock of LandCo, a Country X corporation. Terra, an unrelated Country Y corporation, owns the other 35% of LandCo. LandCo owns 100% of the voting stock of OceanCo, a Country Z corporation. Assuming that USCo is a U.S. shareholder, do LandCo and OceanCo meet the definition of a CFC? Explain.

32. **LO.5** Hart Enterprises, a U.S. corporation, owns 100% of OK, Ltd., an Irish corporation. OK's gross income for the year is $10,000,000. Determine OK's Subpart F income (before any expenses) from the transactions that it reported this year.

    a. OK received $600,000 from sales of products purchased from Hart and sold to customers outside Ireland.

b. OK received $1,000,000 from sales of products purchased from Hart and sold to customers in Ireland.

c. OK received $400,000 from sales of products purchased from unrelated suppliers and sold to customers in Germany.

d. OK purchased raw materials from Hart, used these materials to manufacture finished goods, and sold these goods to customers in Italy. OK earned $300,000 from these sales.

e. OK received $100,000 for the performance of warranty services on behalf of Hart. These services were performed in Japan for customers located in Japan.

f. OK received $50,000 in dividend income from investments in Canada and Mexico.

33. **LO.5** Brandy, a U.S. corporation, operates a manufacturing branch in Chad, which does not have an income tax treaty with the United States. Brandy's worldwide Federal taxable income is $30,000,000; it is subject to a 21% marginal tax rate. Profits and taxes in Chad for the current year are summarized as follows. Compute Brandy's foreign tax credit associated with its operations in Chad.

Income Item	Chad Income This Year	Chad Tax Rate	Chad Tax Paid
Manufacturing profits	$2,500,000	20%	$500,000
Dividend	300,000	5%	15,000

34. **LO.5** Weather, Inc., a domestic corporation, operates in both Fredonia and the United States. This year, the business generated taxable income of $600,000 from foreign sources and $900,000 from U.S. sources. All of Weather's foreign-source income is in the general limitation basket. Weather's total taxable income is $1,500,000. Weather pays Fredonia taxes of $228,000. What is Weather's FTC for the tax year? Assume a 21% U.S. income tax rate.

35. **LO.5** Blunt, Inc., a U.S. corporation, earned $600,000 in total taxable income, including $80,000 in foreign-source taxable income from its German branch's manufacturing operations and $30,000 in foreign-source taxable income from its Swiss branch's engineering services operations. Blunt paid $20,000 in German income taxes and $1,800 in Swiss income taxes. Compute Blunt's U.S. tax liability after any available FTCs. Blunt's Federal income tax rate is 21%.

36. **LO.5** Dunne, Inc., a U.S. corporation, earned $500,000 in total taxable income, including $50,000 in foreign-source taxable income from its branch manufacturing operations in Brazil and $20,000 in foreign-source income from interest earned on bonds issued by Dutch corporations. Dunne paid $25,000 in Brazilian income taxes and $3,000 in Dutch income taxes. Compute Dunne's U.S. tax liability after any available FTCs. Dunne's U.S. tax rate is 21%.

37. **LO.5** ABC, Inc., a domestic corporation, reports $50 million of taxable income, including $15 million of foreign-source taxable income from services rendered, on which ABC paid $2.5 million in foreign income taxes. The U.S. tax rate is 21%. What is ABC's foreign tax credit?

Critical Thinking 38. **LO.1, 5** Indeco, a U.S. C corporation, operates Grange, a sales branch in Staccato. Indeco's U.S. corporate marginal tax rate is 21%; it is 15% for Staccato. Grange's pretax profit for the year is $1 million. There is no income tax treaty between the United States and Staccato. Staccato's currency is the U.S. dollar.

Compute Indeco's combined U.S. and foreign income tax on the Grange profits under each of the following assumptions.

	U.S. Income Tax	Staccato Income Tax	Combined Tax Liability
a. U.S. income tax law allows no deduction or credit for foreign income taxes paid.	_____	_____	_____
b. U.S. income tax law allows only a deduction for foreign income taxes paid.	_____	_____	_____
c. U.S. income tax law allows only an exclusion of foreign branch profits.	_____	_____	_____
d. U.S. income tax law allows only a credit for the full amount of foreign income taxes paid.	_____	_____	_____
e. U.S. income tax law allows only a credit for the full amount of foreign income taxes paid. The applicable Staccato tax rate is now 30%.	_____	_____	_____
f. U.S. income tax law allows only a credit for the full amount of foreign income taxes paid, but limited currently to the corresponding tax on this income at U.S. rates. The applicable Staccato tax rate is now 30%.	_____	_____	_____

39. **LO.5** Night, Inc., a domestic corporation, earned $300,000 from foreign manufacturing activities on which it paid $36,000 of foreign income taxes. Night's foreign sales income is taxed at a 50% foreign tax rate. What amount of foreign sales income can Night earn without generating any excess FTCs for the current year? Assume a 21% U.S. tax rate.   *Critical Thinking*

40. **LO.3, 4, 5** You are the head tax accountant for Venture Company, a U.S. corporation. The board of directors is considering expansion overseas and asks you to present a summary of the U.S. tax consequences of investing overseas through an offshore foreign subsidiary. Prepare a detailed outline of the presentation you will make to the board.   *Communications*

41. **LO.2, 6** IrishCo, a manufacturing corporation resident in Ireland, distributes products through a U.S. office. Current-year taxable income from such sales in the United States is $12,000,000. IrishCo's U.S. office deposits working capital funds in short-term certificates of deposit with U.S. banks. Current-year interest income from these deposits is $150,000.

    IrishCo also invests in U.S. securities traded on the New York Stock Exchange. This investing is done by the home office. For the current year, IrishCo records realized capital gains of $300,000 and dividend income of $50,000 from these stock investments.
    a. Compute IrishCo's U.S. tax liability, assuming that the U.S.-Ireland income tax treaty reduces withholding on dividends to 15% and on interest to 5%.
    b. Express your solution as a Microsoft Excel command.

42. **LO.6** Calabra, S.A., a Peruvian corporation, manufactures inventory in Peru. The inventory is sold to independent distributors in the United States; title passes to the purchaser in the United States. Calabra has no employees or operations within the United States. All sales activities are conducted via telephone and internet communication between Calabra's home office and its U.S. customers. Explain whether Calabra incurs any income effectively connected with a U.S. trade or business.

43. **LO.6** Clario, S.A., a Peruvian corporation, manufactures furniture in Peru. It sells the furniture to independent distributors in the United States. Because title to the furniture passes to the purchasers in the United States, Clario reports $2,000,000 in U.S.-source income. Clario has no employees or operations in the United States related to its furniture business.

     As a separate line of business, Clario buys and sells antique toys. Clario has a single employee operating a booth on weekends at a flea market in Waldo, Florida. The antique toy business generated $85,000 in net profits from U.S. sources during the current year.

     What is Clario's effectively connected income for the current year?

44. **LO.3, 6** Carter, Ltd., a Bohemia corporation, operates a sales branch in the United States that constitutes a U.S. trade or business. Rather than return the profits from the sales branch to the Bohemia home office, Carter invests the profits in certificates of deposit at U.S. banks. Explain whether the interest earned on these CDs is considered effectively connected with Carter's U.S. trade or business.

45. **LO.6** Martinho is a citizen of Brazil and lives there year-round. He has invested in a plot of Illinois farmland with a tax basis to him of $1 million. Martinho has no other business or investment activities in the United States. He is not subject to the alternative minimum tax.

     a. Upon sale of the land for $1.5 million to Emma, an Illinois individual, what are the Federal income tax consequences to Martinho?

     b. What are the Federal income tax withholding requirements with respect to Martinho's sale? Who pays the withheld amount to the U.S. Treasury?

Critical Thinking

Communications

46. **LO.6** Sarah Liu is single, an attorney, and a U.S. citizen. Liu recently attended a seminar where she heard that she could give up her U.S. citizenship, move to Bermuda (where she would pay no income tax), and operate a law practice long distance via the internet with no U.S. tax consequences. Write a letter informing Liu of the tax consequences of the proposed actions. Liu's address is 1005 NE Farwell Street, Gainesville, GA 32612.

47. **LO.6** ForCo, a foreign corporation not engaged in a U.S. trade or business, received a $600,000 dividend from USCo, a domestic corporation. ForCo incurred $45,000 in expenses related to earning the dividend. All of USCo's income is from U.S. sources. ForCo is not eligible for any treaty benefits. What is the withholding tax on the dividend paid to ForCo?

48. **LO.6** ForCo, a foreign corporation not engaged in a U.S. trade or business, received a $250,000 dividend from USCo, a domestic corporation. ForCo incurred $40,000 in expenses related to earning the dividend. All of USCo's income is from U.S. sources. ForCo is not eligible for any treaty benefits. What is the withholding tax on the dividend paid to ForCo?

49. **LO.6** ForCo, a foreign corporation not engaged in a U.S. trade or business, received an $800,000 dividend from USCo, a domestic corporation. ForCo incurred $75,000 in expenses related to earning the dividend. All of USCo's income is from U.S. sources. ForCo is eligible for an income tax treaty that limits withholding on dividends to 10%. What is the withholding tax on the dividend paid to ForCo?

Note: Solutions to the Research Problems can be prepared by using the Thomson Reuters Checkpoint™ online tax research database, which accompanies this textbook. Solutions can also be prepared by using research materials found in a typical tax library.

THOMSON REUTERS
CHECKPOINT™

Research Problem 1. Jerry Jeff Keen, the CFO of Boots Unlimited, a Texas corporation, has come to you regarding a potential restructuring of business operations. Boots has long manufactured its western boots in plants in Texas and Oklahoma. Recently, Boots has explored the possibility of setting up a manufacturing subsidiary in Ireland, where manufacturing profits are taxed at 10%. Jerry Jeff sees this as a great idea, given that the alternative is to continue all manufacturing in the United States, where profits are taxed at 21%.

Communications

Critical Thinking

Boots plans to continue all of the cutting, sizing, and hand tooling of leather in its U.S. plants. This material will be shipped to Ireland for final assembly, with the finished product shipped to retail outlets all over Europe and Asia.

Your initial concern is whether the income generated by the Irish subsidiary will be considered foreign base company income. Address this issue in a research memo, along with any planning suggestions.

Partial list of research aids:
§ 954(d).
Reg. § 1.954–3(a).
Bausch & Lomb, 71 TCM 2031, T.C.Memo. 1996–57.

Research Problem 2. Polly Ling is a successful professional golfer. She is a resident of a country that does not have a tax treaty with the United States. Ling plays matches around the world, about one-half of which are in the United States. Ling's reputation is without blemish; in fact, she is known as being exceedingly honest and upright, and many articles discuss how she is a role model for young golfers due to her tenacious and successful playing style and her favorable character traits. Every year, she reports the most penalty strokes on herself among the participants in women's matches, and this is seen as reinforcing her image as an honest and respectful competitor.

This combination of quality play and laudable reputation has brought many riches to Ling. She comes to you with several Federal income tax questions. She knows that as a non-U.S. resident, any of her winnings from tournament play that occur in the United States are subject to U.S. income taxation. But what about each of the following items? How does U.S. tax law affect Ling? Apply the sourcing rules in this regard, and determine whether the graduated U.S. Federal income Tax Rate Schedules apply.

- Endorsement income from YourGolf for wearing clothing during matches with its logo prominently displayed. Ling must play in at least 10 tournaments per year that are televised around the world. She also must participate in photo sessions and in blogs and tweets associated with the tournaments. Payment to Ling is structured as a flat fee, with bonuses paid if she finishes in the top five competitors for each match. This is known as an *on-court endorsement*.

- Endorsement income from GolfZone for letting the company use her likeness in a video game that simulates golf tournaments among known golfers and other players that the (usually middle-aged men and women) gamers identify. In this way, the gamer seems to be playing against Ling on famous golf courses. Two-thirds of all dollar sales of the game licenses are to U.S. customers.

- Endorsement income from Eliteness for appearing in print and internet ads that feature Ling wearing the company's high-end watches. One-fifth of all dollar sales of the watches are to U.S. customers. The latter two items are known as *off-court endorsements*.

Use internet tax resources to address the following questions. Look for reliable websites and blogs of the IRS and other government agencies, media outlets, businesses, tax professionals, academics, think tanks, and political outlets.

Data Analytics

Communications

Research Problem 3. Locate data on the size of the international economy, including data on international trade, foreign direct investment by U.S. firms, and investment in the United States by foreign firms. Useful web locations include **census.gov** and **bea.gov**. Prepare an analysis of the data for a three-year period using spreadsheet and graphing software, and e-mail the results to your instructor.

Communications

Research Problem 4. For your analysis, choose 10 countries, one of which is the United States. Create a table showing whether each country applies a worldwide or territorial approach to international income taxation. Then list the country's top income tax rate on business profits. Send a copy of this table to your instructor.

Communications

Research Problem 5. Find the text of various tax treaties currently in force in the United States. In an e-mail to your instructor, address the following items.
   a.   How does the U.S. income tax treaty with Germany define "business profits" for multinational businesses?
   b.   How does the U.S. income tax treaty with Japan treat the FIRPTA provisions?
   c.   List five countries with which the United States has entered into an estate tax treaty.
   d.   What is the effective date of the latest income tax treaty with the United Kingdom?
   e.   List five countries with which the United States does not have in force a bilateral income tax treaty.

Communications

Research Problem 6. At **crsreports.congress.gov**, find a 2018 report that analyzes the 2017 tax law changes concerning international corporate taxation. In no more than one page each, summarize an important tax issue that:
   a.   Existed under legacy income tax law.
   b.   Arose after the 2017 tax reform provisions were adopted.

PART 3

FLOW-THROUGH ENTITIES

CHAPTER **10**
Partnerships: Formation, Operation, and Basis

CHAPTER **11**
Partnerships: Distributions, Transfer of Interests, and Terminations

CHAPTER **12**
S Corporations

Unlike C corporations, some business entities are taxed under the conduit principle. Generally, this means the tax attributes of various transactions are retained as they flow through the entity directly to the owners. Usually, no Federal income tax is imposed at the entity level. Part 3 of this text discusses two types of flow-through entities—partnerships and corporations that make an S election. Similarities and differences in the taxing systems for the two types of entities are highlighted.

CHAPTER

10

Partnerships: Formation, Operation, and Basis

LEARNING OBJECTIVES: *After completing Chapter 10, you should be able to:*

LO.1 Distinguish among the various types of entities treated as partnerships for tax purposes.

LO.2 Describe the conceptual basis for partnership taxation and how partnership income is reported and taxed.

LO.3 Determine the tax effects of forming a partnership with cash and property contributions.

LO.4 Identify elections available to a partnership and specify the tax treatment of expenditures of a newly formed partnership.

LO.5 Specify the accounting methods available to a partnership.

LO.6 List and explain the methods of determining a partnership's tax year.

LO.7 Calculate a partnership's taxable income and separately stated items and describe how the partnership's income is reported.

LO.8 Outline and discuss the requirements for allocating income, gains, losses, deductions, and credits among the partners and describe how that income is reported.

LO.9 Determine a partner's basis in the partnership interest.

LO.10 Explain how liabilities affect a partner's basis.

LO.11 Illustrate a partner's capital account rollforward and explain why the year-end balance might differ from the partner's year-end basis in the partnership interest.

LO.12 List and review the limitations on deducting partnership losses.

LO.13 Identify other issues related to partners and partnerships.

LO.14 Provide insights regarding advantageous use of a partnership.

CHAPTER OUTLINE

WHY USE A PARTNERSHIP, ANYWAY?

For 15 years, Maria has owned and operated a seaside bakery and café called The Beachsider. Each morning, customers line up on the boardwalk in front of the building and enjoy fresh coffee and croissants while waiting for a table. "The building is too small," Maria commented to her landlord, Kyle. "Is there any way we can expand?" The Beachsider occupies one of several buildings on 3 acres of a 10-acre parcel that Kyle inherited several years ago. The remaining 7 acres are undeveloped.

Kyle and Maria talked to Josh, a real estate developer, and he proposed an expansion to The Beachsider and upgrades to the other buildings. The improvements would preserve the character of the original retail center, and the remaining acreage would be available for future expansion.

They liked his ideas, so Kyle, Maria, and Josh agreed to form a partnership to own and operate The Beachsider and to improve and lease the other buildings. Josh summarized the plan as follows: "Kyle and Maria will each contribute one-half of the capital we need. Kyle's real estate is valued at about $2,000,000. Maria's bakery equipment and the café furnishings are valued at about $500,000. The improvements will cost about $1,500,000 of cash, which Maria has agreed to contribute to the partnership."

Josh continued, "You have agreed that I do not need to contribute any capital to the partnership. I will oversee the construction, and when it is complete, I will vest in a 5 percent interest in the partnership's capital. On an ongoing basis, I will oversee the partnership's operations in exchange for a fixed salary and 20 percent of the partnership's ongoing profits. The construction should be completed in June of this year, and my capital interest is estimated to be valued at $200,000 at that time."

What are the tax consequences if the trio forms Beachside Properties as a partnership to own and operate the retail center? What issues might arise later in the life of the entity?

Read the chapter and formulate your response.

We'll talk about partnerships and S corporations in this chapter and the next two chapters. These entities are called *flow-through* or *pass-through* entities, because the entity's income, gains, losses, deductions, credits, and general tax information flow through and are taxed or attributed to the owners. As we'll discuss, the flexibility of the pass-through entity and its single level of taxation offer the potential for significant tax and business advantages over a C corporation.

This chapter addresses partnership formation and operations. Chapter 11 focuses on partnership distributions, dispositions of partnership interests, and optional basis adjustments. Chapter 12 discusses the taxation of S corporations.

10-1 OVERVIEW OF PARTNERSHIP TAXATION

Let's look at some of the general concepts that apply to all partnerships.

10-1a What Is a Partnership?

LO.1

Distinguish among the various types of entities treated as partnerships for tax purposes.

Partnerships are governed by Subchapter K of the Internal Revenue Code. A partnership is defined as an association formed by two or more persons to carry on a trade or business, with each contributing money, property, labor, or skill, and with all expecting to share in profits and losses. A "person" can be an individual, trust, estate, corporation, association, or another partnership.[1] The entity must be unincorporated and cannot be otherwise classified as a corporation, trust, or estate.

Types of Partnerships

You'll encounter several types of partnerships, each suited for different situations. Partnership entities are defined and formed under state law. They are typically distinguished based on the classification of the partners as **general partners** or **limited partners** and the types of business permitted to be conducted.

- General partners can participate in managing the entity. If entity debt is recourse to the partnership (i.e., secured by all partnership assets rather than specific partnership properties), a general partner legally can be called upon for repayment.

- Limited partners are typically not permitted to participate in entity management. They are only liable for partnership debts to the extent of any unpaid contributions they have contractually agreed to make to the partnership.

Some of the more common types of entities treated as partnerships include the following.

- A **general partnership (GP)** consists of two or more general partners who may participate in management; there are no limited partners. General partnerships often are used for operating activities (e.g., product manufacturing or sales) and corporate joint ventures.

- A **limited partnership (LP)** is a partnership with at least one general partner and one or more limited partners.[2] These partnerships often have numerous limited partners and are used to raise capital for real estate development, oil and gas exploration, research and development, and various financial product investment

---

[1] §§ 7701(a)(1) and (2).

[2] A limited liability limited partnership (LLLP) is an extension of the limited partnership form in which all partners, whether general or limited, are accorded limited liability. At this writing, about half of U.S. states permit formation of LLLPs or recognize LLLPs formed in another state. LLLPs are not discussed further in this chapter.

vehicles. To reduce exposure to the entity's liabilities, the general partners are often entities that, themselves, have limited liability, such as a C corporation (or a limited liability company, discussed next).

- In a **limited liability company (LLC)**, the owners (termed "members") are a hybrid type of partner. With respect to the LLC's debts, members are treated as limited partners. However, LLC members generally participate in management of the LLC. Therefore, an LLC combines the corporate benefit of limited liability for the owners with the benefits of partnership taxation, including the single level of tax. A properly structured multiowner[3] LLC is generally treated as a partnership for all Federal tax purposes.[4]

- In most states, a **limited liability partnership (LLP)** is treated similarly to a general partnership; however, an LLP partner is not personally liable for any malpractice committed by other partners. The LLP is currently the organizational form of choice for the large accounting firms.

A **partnership agreement** is signed by each partner. This document outlines the rights and obligations of the partners; the allocation of income, deductions, and cash flows; initial and future capital contribution requirements; conditions for terminating the partnership; and other matters. The governing agreement of an LLC is known as an **operating agreement**.

Concept Summary 10.1 summarizes characteristics of the various entities treated as partnerships.

The Big Picture

EXAMPLE 1

Return to the facts of *The Big Picture* on p. 10-1. When Beachside Properties is formed, Kyle, Maria, and Josh must first decide which type of entity to form. They've narrowed the decision to a C corporation or a partnership. Assume that all three owners are single individuals in the highest tax brackets before considering Beachside's income.

If they form a C corporation, the entity will pay them modest salaries and distribute all of Beachside's remaining cash flows currently as dividends. The amounts paid as wages would be subject to a 37% tax (plus employment taxes, discussed near the end of the chapter). The C corporation's taxable income (after deducting wages) would be taxed at 21%. The remaining 79% of income can be distributed and would be taxed at 23.8% (20% tax rate on qualified dividends plus 3.8% net investment income tax) for a combined effective tax rate of about 39.8%.

If they form a partnership, the income will be subject to one 37% tax (again, plus employment taxes, discussed later). This single level of tax is less than the 39.8% combined effective rate that would apply to a C corporation's taxable income. In addition, to the extent the income is qualified business income (as described later in this chapter), the partners can deduct 20% of their shares of income, effectively lowering the tax rate to 29.6%.

As a result of the potential tax savings, Kyle, Maria, and Josh decided to form a partnership. They must next decide which type of partnership to utilize.

With a GP, Kyle, Maria, and Josh would each be jointly and severally liable for all entity debts. With an LP, one of the partners would be designated as a general partner and would be liable for all entity debts. Neither of these is ideal if there's a way all three owners can have limited liability.

An LLP is not considered because LLPs are typically reserved for service-providing entities.

With an LLC, each partner's losses will be limited to the partner's contributed capital. Therefore, Kyle, Maria, and Josh decide to form Beachside Properties as an LLC.

---

[3]Note that an LLC might have only one owner. Single-member LLCs (SMLLCs) are treated as sole proprietorships or disregarded entities rather than partnerships. SMLLCs are not discussed further in this chapter.

[4]In most of the examples in Chapters 10 and 11, the entities are structured as LLCs for state law purposes. Unless otherwise indicated, assume that these entities are treated as partnerships for Federal income tax purposes.

Concept Summary 10.1

Comparison of Partnership Types

The following table summarizes information about the types of partnerships and limited liability entities discussed in this chapter.

Type of entity	Types of owners	Are owners liable for entity debts?	May owners participate in entity management?	Types of businesses operated by entity*
General partnership (GP)	General partners only	Yes, recourse to GP No, debt secured only by property	Yes	Operating businesses, and joint ventures formed by other operating businesses
Limited partnership (LP)	Limited partners plus at least one general partner**	Yes, for general partners No, for limited partners	Yes, for general partners No, for limited partners	Entities raising capital from investors
Limited liability company (LLC)	"Members" have some general and some limited characteristics	No	Yes, generally	Generally, operating businesses and non-professional service businesses
Limited liability partnership (LLP)	General partners with limited liability for malpractice committed by other partners	Yes, for general liabilities and partner's own malpractice	Yes	Professional service entities such as accounting and law firms

*In general; permitted business operations depend on state law.

**The general partner is often a C corporation or LLC, to minimize exposure to entity liabilities.

Describe the conceptual basis for partnership taxation and how partnership income is reported and taxed.

10-1b Key Concepts in Taxation of Partnership Income

A partnership is not a taxable entity.[5] Rather, the taxable income or loss of the partnership flows through to the partners at the end of the partnership's tax year.[6] The partnership itself pays no Federal income tax.[7] Instead, the partners report their allocable share of the partnership's income or loss on their tax returns and pay any tax due. As discussed in Chapter 11, a partner's withdrawals are not generally taxable (unless they exceed the partner's basis in the partnership interest).

EXAMPLE 2

Adam contributes land with a basis and value of $60,000 in exchange for a 40% share of the profits and losses of the calendar year ABC LLC. In 2019, ABC generates $200,000 of ordinary taxable income and distributes cash of $5,000 to Adam. Adam is taxed on his $80,000 allocable share of income. He is not separately taxed on the $5,000 distribution.

The same result would arise if ABC reported a loss: 40% of the loss would be allocated to Adam, and he would deduct the loss, subject to the loss limitation rules discussed later.

Conceptual Framework for Partnership Taxation

The unique tax treatment of partners and partnerships can be traced to two legal concepts: the **aggregate** (or **conduit**) **concept** and the **entity concept**.

---

[5]§ 701.

[6]§ 702.

[7]However, as discussed in text Section 10-3, the partnership may be required to pay employment taxes for its employees (not partners) or certain U.S. state franchise taxes or fees.

Aggregate (or Conduit) Concept The aggregate concept treats the partnership as a channel through which income, credits, deductions, and other items flow to the partners. The partnership is regarded as a collection of taxpayers joined in an agency relationship. For example, the income tax is imposed on the partners rather than the partnership.

Entity Concept The entity concept treats partners and partnerships as separate units and gives the partnership its own tax "personality." For example, the partnership must file an information return that summarizes its activities for the tax year.

Combined Concepts The "aggregate" concept governs most of the "general rules" for partnerships; the "entity" concept governs many of the exceptions to those general rules. Some rules are governed by both aggregate and entity concepts.

Inside and Outside Basis

The partnership basis rules are the key reason single taxation of partnership income is possible. A partnership has an **inside basis** for each asset it owns, and each partner has an **outside basis** in the partnership interest. In general, the partnership basis rules—an aggregate concept—ensure that the partnership's total inside basis in all assets equals the sum of the outside basis of all partners' partnership interests. In Chapter 10, you can assume that inside basis equals outside basis. In Chapter 11, we'll discuss situations that can result in inside/outside basis differences.

When income or gain flows through to a partner from the partnership, the partner's outside basis in the partnership interest is increased. When a deduction or loss flows through to a partner, the outside basis is reduced. These adjustments ensure that partnership items are taxed only once.

EXAMPLE 3

In Example 2, Adam's outside basis in the LLC interest is $60,000 after his contribution of land in exchange for the LLC interest. The LLC's inside basis in the land is also $60,000. When Adam reports his $80,000 share of the LLC's income, his outside basis is increased to $140,000.

If Adam sold his interest at the beginning of 2020 for $140,000, he would have no gain or loss. If, instead, there were no adjustments to basis, Adam's outside basis would be only $60,000, and he would be taxed on an $80,000 gain in addition to paying tax on his $80,000 share of ABC's income. Without the basis adjustment, the LLC's income would be subject to double taxation.

Separately Stated Items

Typically, a partnership combines income and expenses related to the partnership's trade or business activities into a single income or loss amount that is passed through to the partners. As shown in Example 20, later in the chapter, most other partnership items, such as investment income, gains, and losses, are **separately stated items**.

In keeping with the aggregate theory, these items flow through separately because the items *might* affect any two partners' tax liabilities in different ways.[8] For example, charitable contributions are separately stated because partners need to compute their own deductions for charitable contributions.

Partners' Ownership and Allocation of Partnership Items

Another "aggregate" concept is that each partner typically owns both a **capital interest** and a **profits (loss) interest** in the partnership. A capital interest is measured by a partner's **capital sharing ratio**, which is the partner's percentage ownership of the capital of

---

[8]§ 703(a)(1).

the partnership. Generally, this is the share of capital the partner would receive if the entity was liquidated.

A profits (loss) interest is simply the partner's share of the partnership's current operating results. **Profit and loss sharing ratios** are usually specified in the partnership agreement and are used to determine each partner's allocation of the partnership's ordinary taxable income (loss) and separately stated items.[9]

A key advantage of partnerships is that these ratios and allocations can differ for a given partner, provided the **capital account maintenance** rules discussed later in the chapter are followed. These rules generally work to ensure that everything evens out over time—at the latest, by the time the partnership liquidates.

The partnership agreement may provide for a **special allocation** of various items to specified partners. It may also allocate items in a different proportion from the general profit and loss sharing ratios. As discussed later in the chapter, for a special allocation to be recognized for tax purposes, it must produce nontax economic consequences to the partners receiving the allocation.[10]

EXAMPLE

4

In Example 2, Adam contributed $60,000 of cash in exchange for a 40% share of ABC LLC's profits. Assume that the other LLC members, Beth and Carl, only contributed capital of $20,000 each for their 30% share of profits, for a total of $100,000 of contributed capital. When the partnership is formed, Adam's capital sharing ratio is 60%, because he would be entitled to 60% of the partnership's $100,000 of capital if the partnership was liquidated immediately.

Adam's profit sharing ratio is 40%, per Example 2. In addition, the LLC's operating agreement could easily allocate 30% of losses to Adam and provide a special allocation of 100% of depreciation deductions to him.

Because of the capital account maintenance rules, by the time the partnership liquidates, Adam will receive the capital he deserves. Each year, his capital sharing ratio will be adjusted to reflect his percentage ownership.

Partnership Reporting

In keeping with the entity concept, a partnership must file an information return, Form 1065. This return accumulates information related to the partnership's operations and separately stated items. The partnership makes most elections regarding the treatment of partnership items, but no tax is calculated. This return is due by the fifteenth day of the third month following the end of the tax year. For a calendar year partnership, this deadline is March 15. The partnership may request (by the original due date) an automatic six-month extension of time for filing (to September 15 for a calendar year partnership). Note that these due dates are one month earlier than the due date and extended deadline for individual taxpayers.

In addition to Form 1065, the partnership return includes a **Schedule K–1** for each partner that shows that partner's share of partnership items. Each partner receives a copy of Schedule K–1 for use in preparing the respective partner's tax return.

LO.3

Determine the tax effects of forming a partnership with cash and property contributions.

10-2 FORMATION OF A PARTNERSHIP: TAX EFFECTS

When a partnership is formed, the partners contribute cash and other property in exchange for the partnership interest. This transaction has implications for both the partners and the partnership. Are any gains or losses recognized? What is the basis for each property and the basis of each partnership interest? How does the partnership recover (depreciate, deduct, amortize) the basis of contributed property? What issues must the partnership address in its initial year?

---

[9]§ 704(a).   [10]§ 704(b).

10-2a **Contributions to the Partnership**

Congress intended the partnership formation transaction to be tax-neutral, so partnerships can be formed without (generally) prohibitive tax consequences.

Gain or Loss Recognition

As a general rule, neither the partner nor the partnership recognizes any realized gain or loss arising on contribution of property to a partnership. This applies upon formation of the entity or if the contribution occurs at some later date. The realized gain or loss is deferred, rather than forgiven.[11]

Alicia transfers assets to the Wren LLC on the day the entity is created, in exchange for a 60% profit and loss interest worth $60,000. She contributes cash of $40,000 and retail display fixtures (basis to her as a sole proprietor, $8,000; fair market value, $20,000). Alicia *realizes* a $12,000 gain [$60,000 fair market value of LLC interest less $48,000 basis ($40,000 cash plus $8,000 basis in fixtures)].

Alicia *does not recognize* the $12,000 realized gain in the year of contribution. She received only a nonliquid LLC interest; she received no cash with which to pay any resulting tax liability.

Similarly, if Alicia's basis had been $25,000 in the contributed assets, § 721 would have disallowed the $5,000 realized loss [$60,000 − ($40,000 + $25,000)].

Basis Issues

When a partner makes a tax-deferred contribution of an asset to the capital of a partnership, any potential gain or loss recognition is merely postponed, instead of being permanently excluded.[12]

Partnership's Basis in Assets The partnership takes a *carryover basis* in the contributed assets it receives. This means that the partner's basis in the asset carries over to become the partnership's inside basis in the asset.

Partner's Basis in the Partnership Interest The partner takes a *substituted basis* in the partnership interest. This means that the partner's basis in the contributed assets transfers over to become the partner's outside basis in the partnership interest.

Holding Period

Partnership's Holding Period in Assets The partnership's holding period for the contributed assets includes the period during which the partner owned the asset.

Partner's Holding Period in the Partnership Interest The partner's holding period in the partnership interest depends on the type of contributed assets. To the extent a partner contributes capital and § 1231 assets, the partner's holding period in the partnership interest is the same as that partner's holding period for these assets. To the extent the partner contributes cash or noncapital/§ 1231 assets, the holding period in the partnership interest begins on the date the partnership interest is acquired.

---

[11]§ 721.

[12]§ 723.

Luis transfers a capital asset in exchange for a one-third interest in JKL LLC. The asset has an adjusted basis to Luis of $10,000 and a fair market value of $30,000. Luis has a $20,000 realized gain on the exchange ($30,000 − $10,000), but under § 721, he does not recognize any of the gain.

Luis's outside basis for his LLC interest is a substituted basis of $10,000. This rule ensures that Luis's $20,000 deferred gain would be recognized on a subsequent sale at its $30,000 fair market value. Because Luis contributed a capital asset, his holding period "tacks" and becomes his holding period for the partnership interest.

The LLC's inside basis for the contributed property is a carryover basis of $10,000. This basis ensures that Luis's $20,000 deferred gain would be recognized if the LLC sold the property for its $30,000 fair market value. Luis's holding period for the capital asset becomes the partnership's holding period for the asset.

Note that if Luis had contributed cash for the interest, both his and the partnership's holding periods would begin on the date the cash was contributed.

10-2b Exceptions to the General Rule of § 721

In certain situations, the nonrecognition provisions do not apply. The most widely applicable situations are when:

- Appreciated stocks are contributed to an investment partnership,
- The transaction is essentially a disguised sale or exchange of properties, or
- The partnership interest is received in exchange for services rendered to the partnership by the partner.

Investment Partnership

If the transfer consists of appreciated stocks and securities and the partnership is an investment partnership, it is possible that the contributing partner will recognize the inherent realized gain at the time of the contribution.[13] This rule prevents investors from using the partnership form to diversify their investment portfolios on a tax-free basis.

Disguised Sale or Exchange

If a transaction appears to be a sale or exchange of property rather than a contribution, it is deemed a **disguised sale** and § 721 cannot be used to defer a gain or loss. For example, if a partner contributes appreciated property to a partnership and soon thereafter receives a distribution from the partnership, the distribution could be viewed as a payment to purchase the property.[14]

Kim's basis in her KLM partnership interest was $50,000. She transfers to the partnership a property with an adjusted basis of $10,000 (and a fair market value of $30,000), resulting in a basis of $60,000 in her partnership interest. Two weeks later, the partnership distributes $30,000 cash to Kim. Under the general rule, the distribution would not be taxable to Kim but instead reduces her basis in the partnership interest to $30,000 ($60,000 basis − $30,000 cash distribution). However, the transaction appears to be a disguised purchase-sale transaction. Therefore, Kim must recognize gain of $20,000 on transfer of the property, and the partnership is deemed to have purchased the property for $30,000.

A similar rule applies when a contribution of property is followed by a distribution of other property.[15] For example, a contribution of land followed by a distribution to that partner of stock recently contributed by another partner likely will be treated as a taxable exchange of properties.

---

[13]§ 721(b).

[14]§ 707(a)(2)(B) and related Regulations.

[15]Reg. § 1.731–1(c)(3).

Extensive Regulations outline situations in which the IRS may presume that a disguised sale has occurred. For example, a disguised sale is presumed to exist if both of the following occur.

- A contractual agreement requires a contribution by one partner to be followed within two years by a specified distribution from the partnership.
- The distribution is to be made without regard to partnership profits. In other words, the forthcoming distribution is not subject to significant "entrepreneurial risk."

If the distribution occurs more than two years after the property contribution, or if it is deemed "reasonable" in relation to the partner's invested capital, the distribution is *not* presumed to be a disguised sale.

Services

A partner may receive an interest in partnership capital or profits in exchange for services rendered to the partnership. In certain circumstances, special rules will apply.

Capital Interest Received in Exchange for Services When a partner receives a fully vested interest in partnership capital (i.e., unrestricted liquidation rights) in exchange for services, the value of the interest is generally taxable to the partner as ordinary compensation income. Services are not treated as "property" that can be transferred to a partnership on a tax-free basis. Generally, the partner's ordinary income equals the amount the partner would receive if the partnership was liquidated immediately following the contribution of services, less any amount the partner paid for the interest.[16]

The partnership may deduct any amount included in the service partner's income if the services are of a deductible nature.[17] Otherwise, they must be capitalized. Any deduction related to the service partners' interest is generally allocated to the other partners in the partnership.

Profits Interest Received in Exchange for Services Transfer of a partnership *profits* interest in exchange for services is generally taxed to the recipient partner as the profits are earned. The amount of the partnership's future profits cannot typically be determined, so there is no current value to the interest.[18]

If the future profits interest is classified as a **carried interest**, special rules apply. The effect of these rules is that, for certain types of interests received in exchange for services, future capital gain allocations can be recharacterized as ordinary income to the partner. The details of carried interests are beyond the scope of this chapter, but you should note that a carried interest does *not* arise to the extent the partner "pays" a fair value for a *capital* interest, either with contributed cash or other assets or through income recognition under § 83.

EXAMPLE 8

Dave receives his one-third capital and profits interest in BCD LLC (valued at $20,000) as compensation for tax planning services he provided before the LLC was formed.

Dave recognizes $20,000 of compensation income, and he takes a $20,000 basis in his LLC interest. The interest is not a carried interest because Dave "pays" for the capital interest by recognizing the value as compensation income.

The same result would occur if the LLC had paid Dave $20,000 for his services and he immediately contributed that amount to the entity for a one-third ownership interest. The LLC will probably treat the $20,000 as an amortizable startup expense.

---

[16]§ 83(a); for treatment when there is a "substantial risk of forfeiture," also see Reg. § 1.83–3, Prop.Reg. § 1.83–3(l), and Notice 2005–43, 2005–1 C.B. 1221 (5/20/2005).

[17]§ 83(h).

[18]For situations in which the future interest might be taxable, see Rev.Proc. 93–27, 1993–2 C.B. 343, as clarified by Rev.Proc. 2001–43, 2001–2 C.B. 191.

10-2c Other Issues Related to Contributed Property

When property is contributed to a partnership, other issues arise, including cost recovery, allocations related to the property, and subsequent dispositions of the property.

Depreciation Method and Period

If a partner contributes depreciable property, the partnership generally "steps into the shoes" of the contributing parter and continues to use the depreciation schedule and calculations the partner used. The partnership may not claim a § 179 deduction with respect to contributed property.

Amortization of Intangible Assets

Similarly, if a partner contributes an existing intangible asset to the partnership, the partnership generally will "step into the shoes" of the partner in determining future amortization deductions. Section 197 intangible assets are amortized over 15 years and include purchased goodwill, going-concern value, information systems, customer- or supplier-related intangible assets, patents, licenses obtained from a governmental unit, franchises, trademarks, covenants not to compete, and other items. Other intangible assets (i.e., not addressed in § 197) are amortized over their useful life, if any.[19]

**EXAMPLE
9**

On September 1, 2017, at a cost of $120,000, James obtained a license to operate a television station from the Federal Communications Commission. The license is effective for 20 years. On January 1, 2019, he contributes the license to the JS LLC in exchange for a 60% interest. The value of the license is still $120,000 at that time.

The license is a § 197 intangible asset because it is a covered property with a term greater than 15 years. The cost is amortized over 15 years. James claims amortization for 4 months in 2017 and 12 months in 2018. Thereafter, the LLC steps into James's shoes in claiming amortization deductions over the remaining 13 years and 8 months.

Character of Gain or Loss on Disposition of Receivables, Inventory, and Built-In Loss Properties

When a partner contributes certain types of property to a partnership, the aggregate theory comes into play if the partnership later sells it. In three situations, the character of the partnership's gain or loss is not necessarily what you would expect.[20]

Ordinary Income Property If the partner contributes either of the following types of property, the partnership's later sale of the property results in ordinary income for:

- Accounts receivable where the contributing partner has not yet recognized the related income (e.g., cash basis accounts receivable).

- Inventory (in the contributing partner's hands) that would have resulted in ordinary income if the partner had sold it, *if* the partnership sells the inventory *within five years of the contribution date.*

Capital Loss Property Similarly, if the partner contributes property with a "built-in" capital loss at the contribution date, the partnership's later sale of that property *within five years of the contribution date* results in a capital loss. The capital loss is limited to the "built-in" loss at the contribution date.

---

[19]Reg. § 1.167(a)–3.   [20]§ 724.

Deon contributed accounts receivable, inventory, and land to DR LLC as follows.

	Adjusted Basis	Fair Market Value
Receivables	$ –0–	$20,000
Inventory	25,000	50,000
Land (investment property to Deon)	12,000	9,000

Soon after formation, DR collects $20,000 cash for the receivables and sells the inventory for $50,000 cash. The LLC recognizes ordinary income of $20,000 for the receivables and $30,000 for the inventory, even if the property is not an ordinary trade receivable or inventory in the LLC's hands.

DR uses the land as a parking lot for a year (§ 1231 property) and then sells it for $7,000. The LLC's loss on the land is $5,000 ($12,000 adjusted basis − $7,000 selling price). DR classifies the $3,000 precontribution loss ($12,000 − $9,000) as a capital loss because it would have been a capital loss to Deon. The remaining $2,000 loss ($9,000 − $7,000) is a § 1231 loss based on DR's use of the land.

Allocations Related to Contributed Property

As discussed later in the chapter, special allocations must be made relative to contributed property that is appreciated or depreciated. The partnership's income and losses must be allocated to ensure that the inherent gain or loss is not shifted away from the contributing partner. So in Example 10, the precontribution portion of the income, gains, and losses would be allocated to Deon.

The Big Picture

Return to the facts of *The Big Picture* on p. 10-1. Assume that Kyle's $2,000,000 of contributed real estate consists of land with a $600,000 basis and a fully depreciated building and fixtures ($0 basis). Maria has fully depreciated the $500,000 of bakery equipment and café furnishings that she contributed and so has a $0 basis in those assets.

When Beachside Properties LLC is formed, no tax arises for the LLC or for Kyle or Maria. Kyle does not recognize his $1,400,000 realized gain, nor does Maria recognize her $500,000 realized gain.

Kyle takes a substituted basis of $600,000 for his interest, and Maria takes a substituted basis of $1,500,000 ($1,500,000 of contributed cash + $0 basis in contributed property). Beachside Properties assumes a carryover basis of $600,000 for the real estate contributed by Kyle and $0 for the property contributed by Maria. If there had been a remaining depreciable basis for any of the contributed property, the LLC would have "stepped into the member's shoes" in calculating depreciation deductions. Any future income related to the precontribution gains will be allocated to the contributing partner.

When Josh vests in his 5% *capital interest* in the LLC, the $200,000 value of the interest is taxable to him because he received it in exchange for services. Beachside Properties will capitalize this amount and allocate it to the building expansion and new fixtures. Josh's 20% interest in the *future profits* of the LLC will be taxed to him as profits are earned by the LLC.[21]

Concept Summary 10.2 reviews the rules that apply to partnership asset contribution and basis adjustments.

---

[21]While beyond the scope of the text, note that the 15% difference between the "paid for" capital interest and the future services interest *might* be considered a "carried interest." As such, a portion of future capital gains allocated to Josh from the LLC *might* be recharacterized as ordinary income under the rules of § 1061.

Concept Summary 10.2

Partnership Formation and Initial Basis Computation

1. Under the general rule of § 721, partners or partnerships do not recognize gain or loss when property is contributed in exchange for capital interests.

2. Partners take a substituted basis in their partnership interest *(outside basis)* equal to the basis of the property contributed to the partnership.

3. The partnership takes a carryover basis in assets received *(inside basis)* equal to the partner's basis in those assets.

4. The partner's holding period in the partnership interest begins when the interest is acquired (for cash or "other" property contributions) and/or on the date the contributed property was acquired (for contributions of capital or § 1231 property).

5. The partnership's holding period for contributed property includes the contributing partner's holding period.

6. The partnership "steps into the partner's shoes" in calculating depreciation and amortization of contributed property.

7. Rules prevent the recharacterization of ordinary income as capital gains for inventory and accounts receivable and prevent conversion of capital losses to ordinary losses.

8. The general rule of § 721 does not apply to partnership interests received upon formation of certain investment partnerships, as a disguised sale or exchange, or as a fully vested capital interest received in exchange for services.

LO.4

Identify elections available to a partnership and specify the tax treatment of expenditures of a newly formed partnership.

10-2d Tax Accounting Elections

A newly formed partnership must make numerous tax accounting elections stating how certain transactions or tax attributes should be handled. In general, these elections must be made by the partnership rather than by the partners individually.[22] For example, as discussed later in the chapter, the partnership selects its taxable year and accounting method and elects the treatment of organizational and startup expenditures. As discussed in text Section 11-5, the partnership also makes any optional basis adjustment election and calculations under § 754 (available only to partnerships).

The partnership, rather than the partners, makes other elections and calculations under general tax accounting rules, including the following.

- Cost recovery methods and assumptions.
- § 179 deductions for certain tangible personal property.
- Inventory method.
- Calculation of the partnership's allowable business interest expense deduction.
- Calculation of all partnership tax credits except foreign tax credit.
- Cost or percentage depletion method, excluding oil and gas wells.
- Amounts and treatment of research and experimental expenditures.

Each partner is bound by the decisions made by the partnership relative to these items. If the partnership fails to make an election, a partner cannot make the election individually.

There are three rather narrow exceptions to this general rule. Each *partner* is required to make a specific election for the following tax issues.

- Whether to reduce the basis of depreciable property first when excluding income from discharge of indebtedness.
- Whether to claim cost or percentage depletion for oil and gas wells.
- Whether to take a deduction or credit for taxes paid to non-U.S. jurisdictions.

10-2e Initial Costs of a Partnership

In its initial stages, a partnership incurs expenses related to some or all of the following activities: forming the partnership (organizational costs), starting business operations (startup costs), admitting partners to the partnership, marketing and selling partnership units to prospective partners (syndication costs), and acquiring assets.

---

[22]§ 703(b).

Organizational and Startup Costs

Organizational costs include expenditures that are (1) incident to the creation of the partnership; (2) chargeable to a capital account; and (3) of a character that, if incident to the creation of a partnership with an ascertainable life, would be amortized over that life. The types of expenditures treated as organizational costs for a partnership parallel those outlined in text Section 3-1k for corporations.

Startup costs include operating costs that are incurred after the entity is formed but before it begins business.

For tax purposes, organizational costs and startup costs follow the rules illustrated in text Section 3-1k, Examples 24 to 26. Each type of cost is considered separately, so for each category, the partnership can deduct up to $5,000 immediately (subject to phaseout) with the excess amortized over 180 months, beginning with the month in which the partnership begins business.[23]

This treatment is elected simply by deducting the proper amounts on the tax return.[24]

EXAMPLE

12

Bluejay LLC was formed on June 1, 2019, and started business on July 1. Bluejay adopts a calendar year. During 2019, Bluejay incurred $4,000 in legal fees for drafting the LLC's operating agreement and $2,200 in accounting fees for tax advice of an organizational nature, for a total of $6,200 of organizational costs.

That same month, Bluejay also incurred $20,000 of preopening advertising expenses and $34,000 of salaries and training costs for new employees, for a total of $54,000 of startup costs.

Using the calculations shown in text Section 3-1k, Bluejay can deduct $5,040 of organizational costs {[$5,000 current deduction] + [$40 amortization ($1,200 × 6/180)]} and $2,767 of startup costs {[$5,000 − ($54,000 − $50,000) current deduction] + [$1,767 amortization ($53,000 × 6/180)]} on its 2018 tax return.

Syndication Costs

Syndication costs are capitalized, but no amortization election is available.[25] Syndication costs include expenditures incurred for promoting and marketing partnership interests such as brokerage fees, registration fees, certain legal fees, accounting fees related to the offering materials, and printing costs of the prospectus and other selling materials. Recall that this parallels the corporate tax treatment of stock marketing, issuance, and brokerage costs.

Acquisition Costs of Depreciable Assets

As mentioned earlier, the partnership typically determines its depreciation deductions by "stepping into the shoes" of the contributing partner. If additional costs are incurred, though, the additional basis is treated as a new MACRS asset, placed in service on the date the partnership places the asset in service. For example, legal fees and transfer taxes incurred in transferring assets to a partnership must be capitalized. Cost recovery for these amounts commences when the underlying property is placed in service.

10-2f Method of Accounting

A newly formed partnership may adopt either the cash or accrual method of accounting or a hybrid of these two methods.

If a partnership uses the accrual method of accounting, its income must be reported no later than the date that income would be reported on the partnership's "applicable financial statement" (e.g., an audited financial statement) or other similar financial statement.[26]

LO.5

Specify the accounting methods available to a partnership.

---

[23]§ 709(b) and § 195(b)(1).
[24]Reg. § 1.709–1 and Reg. § 1.195–1.

[25]§ 709(a).
[26]§§ 451(a) and (b).

This rule is designed to ensure that any advance payments (i.e., cash receipts) received by the taxpayer are reported in taxable income at least as quickly as they are reported in book income.

Two exceptions limit use of the cash method of accounting by partnerships.[27] The cash method may *not* be adopted by a partnership that:

- Has one or more C corporation partners, or
- Is a tax shelter.

As an "exception to the exception," a nontax shelter partnership with a C corporation partner may still elect to use the cash method if:

- The partnership meets the $26 million gross receipts test described below;
- The C corporation partner(s) is a qualified personal service corporation, such as an incorporated attorney; or
- The partnership is engaged in the business of farming.

A partnership meets the $26 million gross receipts test if it has not received average annual gross receipts of more than $26 million for 2019. "Average annual gross receipts" is the average of gross receipts for the three tax years ending with the tax period *prior to* the tax year in question. If the gross receipts test is not met, the partnership must change to the accrual method the next tax year.

A tax shelter is a partnership whose interests have been sold in a registered offering, a partnership in which 35 percent of the losses are allocated to limited partners, or a partnership with a significant purpose to avoid or evade Federal income tax..

EXAMPLE 13

Jason and Julia are both attorneys. In 2016, each of them formed a professional personal service corporation to operate their separate law practices. In 2019, the two attorneys decide to form the JJ Partnership, which consists of the two professional corporations. In 2019, JJ's gross receipts are $26 million.

Because JJ's two corporate partners are both personal service corporations, JJ may adopt the cash method in 2019. It may continue to use the cash method in 2020, even though its average annual gross receipts are greater than $26 million. [In this case, average annual gross receipts would be calculated considering only JJ's one year (2019) prior history.] Alternatively, JJ may adopt the accrual method of accounting or a hybrid of the cash and accrual methods.

LO.6

List and explain the methods of determining a partnership's tax year.

10-2g **Taxable Year of the Partnership**

A partnership must use either the <mark>required taxable year</mark> or one of three alternate taxable years. Partnership taxable income (and any separately stated items) flows through to each partner at the end of the *partnership's* taxable year. A *partner's* taxable income, then, includes the distributive share of partnership income for any *partnership* taxable year that ends during the partner's tax year.

Deferral of Partnership Income

The required taxable year rules prevent excessive deferral of taxation of partnership income. How might deferral arise? In the hypothetical example of Exhibit 10.1, the partners have a calendar tax year. If the partnership's adopted year ended on January 31, the reporting of income from the partnership and payment of related taxes would be deferred for up to 11 months. For instance, income earned by the partnership in

---

[27]§ 448. For tax years beginning before 2018, a $5 million average annual gross receipts test applied to *all* three-year tax periods before the test year. Consequently, a partnership might have been required to use the accrual method in prior years before being permitted to change to the cash method in 2018. The $26 million threshold is indexed for inflation; it was $25 million for 2018.

EXHIBIT 10.1	**Deferral Benefit If Partnership Could Use a Fiscal Year and All Partners (Individual Taxpayers) Used the Calendar Year**

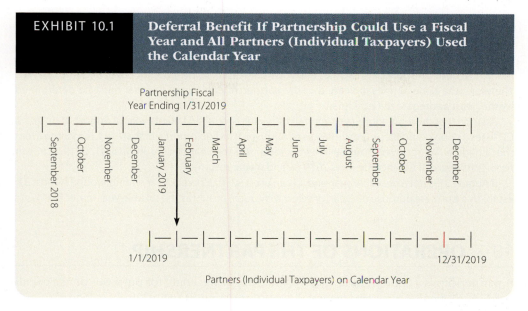

February 2018 would not be taxable to the partners until the partnership's tax year closes on January 31, 2019. It would be reported in the partners' tax returns for the year ended December 31, 2019, which is not due until April 15, 2020. Even though each partner would be required to make quarterly estimated tax payments, some deferral might still be possible.

Required Taxable Year

The partnership's required taxable year is determined under the first of three rules that applies.[28] The rules are evaluated in order. First, the partnership uses the tax year of the "majority partners" if partners owning more than 50 percent of partnership capital and profits have the same tax year.

If there are no "majority partners" (e.g., if there are two 50 percent partners with different tax years), we go to the second rule. Under this rule, the partnership uses the tax year of the "principal partners" if all partners who own 5 percent or more of capital or profits have the same tax year. If any 5 percent partner has a different year from the other 5 percent partners (or if there is no partner who owns a 5 percent capital or profits interest), we keep testing.

Here's the third rule: if no year-end can be determined under the first two rules, the partnership determines a year under the **least aggregate deferral rule** as outlined in the Regulations for § 706.

Alternative Tax Years

If the required tax year is undesirable to the entity, three alternative tax years may be available.

- Establish to the IRS's satisfaction that a *business purpose* exists for a different tax year. This will typically be a "natural business year" (as defined)[29] that ends following a peak season or shortly thereafter.

- Elect a tax year so that taxes on partnership income are deferred for not more than *three months* from the *required* tax year.[30] This election is highly restrictive, can be expensive, and is not often made.

- Elect a 52- to 53-week taxable year that ends the same week as the required taxable year (or the taxable year elected under the three-month deferral rule) would end.

---

[28]§ 706(b).

[29]Rev.Proc. 2006–46, 2006–2 C.B. 859, § 5.07.

[30]§ 444.

EXAMPLE 14

Crimson, Inc., and Indigo, Inc., (both subchapter C corporations) are equal partners in the CI Partnership. Crimson uses the calendar year, and Indigo uses a fiscal year ending August 31. Neither Crimson nor Indigo is a majority partner as neither owns more than 50%. Although Crimson and Indigo are both principal partners (i.e., each owns at least 5%), they do not have the same tax year. Therefore, the general rules indicate that the partnership's required tax year must be determined by the "least aggregate deferral rule."

Assume that the least aggregate deferral rule yields a required taxable year of August 31. In 2019, CI closes its books and files a Form 1065 as of August 31. Indigo reports its share of CI's income (from the Schedule K–1 received from CI) in its tax return for the year ending August 31, 2019. Crimson reports its share of CI's income in its 2019 calendar year return.

If August 31 is not a desirable year-end, CI can use a 52- to 53-week year ending around August 31; establish a business purpose tax year; or select May, June, or July as the taxable year under § 444.

LO.7

Calculate a partnership's taxable income and separately stated items and describe how the partnership's income is reported.

10-3 OPERATIONS OF THE PARTNERSHIP

A partnership is a tax-reporting, rather than a taxpaying, entity for purposes of its Federal (and state) income tax computations. Almost any type of entity can be a partner: individuals, corporations, trusts, estates, or another partnership, for example. Consequently, the partnership's income, deductions, credits, and alternative minimum tax (AMT) preferences and adjustments can ultimately be reported and taxed on any of a number of income tax returns [e.g., Forms 1040 (individuals), 1041 (fiduciaries, see Chapter 20), 1120 (C corporations), and 1120S (S corporations)].

A partnership is subject to all other taxes in the same manner as any other business. Thus, the partnership files returns and pays appropriate sales taxes and property taxes. For employees (not partners), the partnership files returns and pays Social Security, unemployment, and other payroll taxes. In some states, franchise taxes are assessed based on partnership net income or gross receipts, or capital or asset values.

10-3a Measuring and Reporting Partnership Income

The partnership's Form 1065 organizes and reports the transactions of the entity for the tax year.

Income Measurement

A partnership measures and reports two kinds of income: ordinary business income (Form 1065, page 1, shown on p. 10-21) and separately stated items (Form 1065, Schedule K, shown on p. 10-22). The partnership's ordinary business income from Form 1065, page 1, also is reported on Schedule K, line 1. To get a full picture of a partnership's activities, review its Schedule K. Information from Schedule K is allocated to the partners on their Schedules K–1.

Ordinary Business Income A partnership's ordinary business income consists of any income or expenses that are not required to be separately stated. For example, the partnership's sales revenues, utilities, rent expense, and depreciation expense related to business assets are reported on Form 1065, page 1. As mentioned earlier, the partnership makes elections related to inventory, depreciation, research and experimentation expenses, and similar business-related amounts, so it makes sense that the partners don't need separate information about these calculations. The partnership also calculates and claims the allowable business interest expense deduction, but any disallowed interest expense is treated as a separately stated item, as discussed later.

Separately Stated Items A separately stated item is any item with tax attributes that could affect partners differently. Among the many income and deduction items passed through separately are the following.

- Net short-term and net long-term capital gains or losses.
- § 1231 gains and losses.
- Charitable contributions.

- Portfolio income items (qualified and ordinary dividends, interest, and royalties).
- Expenses related to portfolio income.
- Disallowed business interest expense and related information.
- Immediately expensed tangible personal property (§ 179).
- Guaranteed payments, discussed later in this section.
- Passive activity items such as rental real estate income or loss.
- Intangible drilling and development costs.
- General business tax credits (the partnership calculates the credit and allocates the credit to the partners so they can apply their limitations).
- Taxes paid to non-U.S. countries and to U.S. possessions (the partners calculate this credit and determine any limitations).[31]

The reason for separately reporting the preceding items is rooted in the aggregate or conduit concept. These items affect various exclusions, deductions, and credits at the partner level and must pass through without loss of identity so that the proper tax for each partner may be determined.[32]

A partnership is not allowed to claim the following deductions.

- Net operating losses (NOLs).
- Depletion of oil and gas interests.
- Dividends received deduction.

Deductions taken by individuals, such as standard deductions, are not available to the partnership. If a partnership makes a payment on behalf of a partner, such as for alimony, medical expenses, or items that might constitute deductions to individuals, the partnership treats the payment as a distribution or guaranteed payment to the partner, and the partner determines whether any deduction is permitted.

The Big Picture

EXAMPLE 15

Return to the facts of *The Big Picture* on p. 10-1. In its second year of operations, Beachside Properties LLC reports income and expenses from operating the café as well as rent income and expenses from leasing the other buildings, as follows.

Sales revenue	$2,000,000
Cost of sales	800,000
W–2 wages paid to employees	500,000
Cost recovery deductions (related to the Beachsider café business only)	91,984
Utilities, supplies, and other ordinary business expenses	128,016
Taxes and licenses (including payroll taxes)	60,000
Guaranteed payments to LLC members	240,000
Charitable contributions	6,000
Short-term capital gain	12,000
Net income from rental real estate (net of all expenses, including $26,153 depreciation on rental property)	300,000
Qualified dividends received	4,000
Exempt income (bond interest)	2,100
Alternative minimum tax (AMT) adjustment (cost recovery)	18,224
Payment of medical expenses on behalf of Kyle	4,000
Distribution of cash to Maria	30,000

Beachside will determine its ordinary income or loss for the year, along with its separately stated items. As discussed next, the guaranteed payments are either deducted or capitalized by the LLC; they are reported as ordinary income by the member who receives them. Beachside also reports any additional information the partners might need to prepare their individual income tax returns.

continued

---

[31]§ 702(a).　　　　　[32]§ 702(b).

The LLC cannot deduct the payment for Kyle's medical expenses. This payment is probably handled as a distribution to Kyle, who may report it as a medical expense on his Schedule A in determining his itemized deductions. Similarly, the LLC cannot deduct the distribution to Maria (distributions are discussed in Chapter 11). The AMT adjustment is not a separate component of the LLC's income. However, it must be reported to Beachside's members so that they can properly calculate any AMT liability. Other information will also be passed through, including information for business interest deduction carryovers, qualified business income (the § 199A deduction), and self-employment and other taxes. These topics are discussed later.

Last year (the first year of operations), the LLC reported a $250,000 net loss from operations. Beachside could not deduct that loss; instead, it was passed through to the LLC members. Loss deduction limitations might have applied at the member level. These limitations are discussed later in the chapter.

Guaranteed Payments Paid by the Partnership

A **guaranteed payment** is a payment to a partner for services performed by the partner or for the use of the partner's capital. These payments resemble the salary or interest payments of other businesses.[33] The partnership either deducts or capitalizes the payment, depending on its nature. As discussed later, regardless of the partnership's treatment, the partner reports the payment as ordinary income.

Guaranteed payments are usually expressed as a fixed-dollar amount or as a percentage of capital the partner has invested in the partnership. By definition, a guaranteed payment cannot be calculated based on partnership income (e.g., as a percentage of annual income).

The Big Picture

EXAMPLE 16

Return to the facts of *The Big Picture* as updated in Example 15. Assume that Josh was elected as managing member of Beachside Properties LLC; he has the sole authority to contract for the LLC and works 1,000 hours per year in the business. Maria works 1,000 hours per year in the café. After transferring his land to Beachside, Kyle has generally not been involved in the LLC's operations. In addition, recall that the LLC uses capital contributed by Maria and Kyle of $2,000,000 each.

Josh and Maria both receive guaranteed payments of $5,000 per month for services to the LLC. In addition, Maria and Kyle both receive guaranteed payments of $5,000 per month for the LLC's use of their capital. The guaranteed payments total $240,000 for the year (12 months × $5,000 × 4 payments). Beachside may deduct these payments.

Deductible guaranteed payments, like any other deductible expenses of a partnership, can create an ordinary loss for the entity.[34]

Partnership Reporting

Form 1065 Ordinary Income and Separately Stated Items The partnership's income is reported on Form 1065, which contains five pages. Pages 1, 4, and 5 of the Beachside Form 1065 for its second tax year are constructed on pages that follow. The entire Form 1065 can be found in Appendix B; all U.S. Federal tax forms can be downloaded at **irs.gov**.

---

[33]§ 707(c).

[34]Per Rev.Rul. 2007–40, 2007–1 C.B. 1426, if the partnership distributes appreciated property to pay a guaranteed payment, the partnership recognizes any gain on the transfer.

Form 1065 is organized as follows.

- Page 1 summarizes the partnership's ordinary income and loss from trade or business activities. Cost of goods sold (line 2) is calculated on Form 1125–A (not shown) and carried to this page.[35]

- Pages 2 and 3 provide information about the partnership's activities and general information about the partners.

- Page 4 (Schedule K) summarizes the partnership's ordinary income or loss, separately stated items, and other information the partners need to prepare their returns. Schedule K, line 1, shows the ordinary income/loss from page 1.

- Page 5 provides several schedules, including a balance sheet (Schedule L), a reconciliation of book and "taxable" income [Schedules M–1 and the Analysis of Net Income (Loss)], and a reconciliation of partners' beginning and ending capital (Schedule M–2).

The Big Picture

EXAMPLE 17

Continue with the facts of Examples 15 and 16, and refer to pages 1, 4, and 5 of Beachside's Form 1065 following in this chapter. Beachside's ordinary income on Form 1065, page 1, is $180,000 after considering the sales revenue, cost of sales, guaranteed payments, and other operating expenses.

On Schedule K (Form 1065, page 4), Beachside's separately stated income and deduction items (lines 1 to 13a) include net income from rental real estate, guaranteed payments (reported as income by the members), qualified dividends received, short-term capital gain, and charitable contributions.

Beachside's real estate rental operations are reported separately from the bakery's income on a Form 8825 (not shown) and included with Beachside's tax return. Beachside's *deduction* for guaranteed payments is shown on Form 1065, page 1, and the amount the LLC members must report as *income* is shown on Schedule K, line 4.

Other Items Reported on Schedule K Starting on Schedule K, line 13d, the partnership must also report any additional information the partners need to prepare a complete and accurate income tax return. This information includes the following.

- The partner's share of tax credits calculated at the partnership level.

- Information the partner uses to make various tax or credit calculations (e.g., foreign tax credit or deduction, self-employment tax, net investment income tax, alternative minimum tax).

- Information the partner needs for other calculations and limitations (e.g., information for the qualified business income deduction or interest expense deductions discussed later in the chapter).

- Information the partner needs to calculate the basis in the partnership interest (e.g., cash and property distributions received, tax-exempt/nondeductible items).

- Any additional information (e.g., summary schedules for each partnership activity) the partners might need in preparing their tax returns.

Partnership Interest Expense If a partnership pays interest expense, it must be allocated among the partnership's various activities, generally based on how and why the underlying debt arose. For example, some interest expense might relate to funds borrowed for investment purposes. In that case, it is classified as investment interest expense and must be separately stated on Schedule K, line 13b.

---

[35]A "Tax and Payment" section is completed in unusual situations where the partnership must pay interest related to certain permitted tax deferral situations (e.g., as to long-term contracts).

Special rules apply to business interest expense, as discussed in text Section 3-1f. For a partnership or an S corporation, in the year the interest expense arises, the entity determines the amount that can be deducted.[36] If the partnership (or S corporation) meets the $26 million gross receipts test (discussed in connection with the cash method of accounting in text Section 10-2f), or if the underlying debt relates to certain types of businesses (e.g., real estate or farming, if elected), the business interest expense limitation does not apply. For other businesses, the entity's business interest expense is limited to 30 percent of "adjusted taxable income" (taxable income before deduction for interest, taxes, depreciation, and amortization), plus business interest income. The entity deduction is a nonseparately stated item, so it would be deducted on page 1 of the partnership or S corporation return.

Any disallowed business interest expense is passed through to the partners (reducing their basis in the partnership interest) and can be used to offset the partnership's "excess taxable income" in future years.

The Big Picture

EXAMPLE 18

Continue with the information in Examples 15 to 17. In addition to the business income and separately stated items described in Example 17, the LLC also reports the following information that the LLC members will use in preparing their tax returns.

Additional Information (Schedule K)	
Net earnings (loss) from self-employment (line 14a)	$150,000
AMT adjustment—cost recovery (line 17a)	18,224
Tax-exempt income—bond interest (line 18a)	2,100
Distributions (line 19a)	34,000
Investment income (line 20a)	12,000
Other information for LLC member-level calculations	

Investment income on line 20a (used to calculate any allowable investment interest expense deduction) includes Beachside's short-term capital gains but does not include favorably taxed qualified dividends.

Other information for LLC member-level calculations is reported on supporting schedules and includes net investment income (for calculating the net investment income tax), excess taxable income (for calculating business interest expense carryover deductions), and information the members need for qualified business income calculations.

Reconciling Taxable Income The partnership reconciles "book" income with income reported on the return. Refer to pages 4 and 5 of Beachsider's Form 1065 on the following pages.

The partnership calculates "taxable income"—the net of the partnership's ordinary and separately stated income and expense amounts on Schedule K (generally, lines 1 to 13 less any foreign tax payments shown on line 16p). It reports that amount on line 1 of the Analysis of Net Income (Loss) (page 5 of Form 1065). Note that, because guaranteed payments are shown separately on Schedule K, line 4, the partnership's "taxable income" is calculated *before* the deduction for guaranteed payments.

Book income is reconciled to this "taxable income" on either Schedule M–1 or Schedule M–3. Schedule M–1 is found on page 5 of Form 1065. Schedule M–3 is a separate three-page form and is often required (in lieu of Schedule M–1) for larger partnerships. The Schedule M–1 or Schedule M–3 is completed similarly to the forms shown for a C corporation; see text Sections 3-3c and 3-3e.

---

[36]§ 163(j)(4).

Form **1065**		**U.S. Return of Partnership Income**		OMB No. 1545-0123

Department of the Treasury
Internal Revenue Service

For calendar year 2018, or tax year beginning _____, 2018, ending _____, 20_____ .
▶ Go to *www.irs.gov/Form1065* for instructions and the latest information.

2018

A Principal business activity *Restaurant/Commercial Rental*	**Type or Print**	Name of partnership *Beachside Properties LLC*	**D** Employer identification number *11-1111111*
B Principal product or service *Food service*		Number, street, and room or suite no. If a P.O. box, see instructions. *1600 Ocean Vista Way*	**E** Date business started *1/1/2016*
C Business code number *722110*		City or town, state or province, country, and ZIP or foreign postal code *Surfside*	**F** Total assets (see instructions) $ *3,218,100*

G Check applicable boxes: **(1)** ☐ Initial return **(2)** ☐ Final return **(3)** ☐ Name change **(4)** ☐ Address change **(5)** ☐ Amended return

H Check accounting method: **(1)** ☐ Cash **(2)** ☒ Accrual **(3)** ☐ Other (specify) ▶ _____

I Number of Schedules K-1. Attach one for each person who was a partner at any time during the tax year. ▶ _____ *3*

J Check if Schedules C and M-3 are attached . . . . ▶ ☐

Caution: Include **only** trade or business income and expenses on lines 1a through 22 below. See instructions for more information.

Income

1a	Gross receipts or sales	**1a**	2,000,000	
b	Returns and allowances	**1b**		
c	Balance. Subtract line 1b from line 1a	**1c**		2,000,000
2	Cost of goods sold (attach Form 1125-A)	**2**		800,000
3	Gross profit. Subtract line 2 from line 1c	**3**		1,200,000
4	Ordinary income (loss) from other partnerships, estates, and trusts (attach statement) . .	**4**		
5	Net farm profit (loss) (attach Schedule F (Form 1040))	**5**		
6	Net gain (loss) from Form 4797, Part II, line 17 (attach Form 4797)	**6**		
7	Other income (loss) (attach statement)	**7**		
8	**Total income (loss).** Combine lines 3 through 7	**8**		1,200,000

Deductions (see instructions for limitations)

9	Salaries and wages (other than to partners) (less employment credits) . . .	**9**		500,000
10	Guaranteed payments to partners	**10**		240,000
11	Repairs and maintenance	**11**		
12	Bad debts	**12**		
13	Rent	**13**		
14	Taxes and licenses	**14**		60,000
15	Interest (see instructions)	**15**		
16a	Depreciation (if required, attach Form 4562)	**16a**	91,984	
b	Less depreciation reported on Form 1125-A and elsewhere on return	**16b**		
		16c		91,984
17	Depletion (**Do not deduct oil and gas depletion.**)	**17**		
18	Retirement plans, etc.	**18**		
19	Employee benefit programs	**19**		
20	Other deductions (attach statement)	**20**		128,016
21	**Total deductions.** Add the amounts shown in the far right column for lines 9 through 20 .	**21**		1,020,000
22	**Ordinary business income (loss).** Subtract line 21 from line 8	**22**		180,000

Tax and Payment

23	Interest due under the look-back method—completed long-term contracts (attach Form 8697)	**23**		
24	Interest due under the look-back method—income forecast method (attach Form 8866) .	**24**		
25	BBA AAR imputed underpayment (see instructions)	**25**		
26	Other taxes (see instructions)	**26**		
27	**Total balance due.** Add lines 23 through 27	**27**		
28	Payment (see instructions)	**28**		
29	**Amount owed.** If line 28 is smaller than line 27, enter amount owed	**29**		
30	**Overpayment.** If line 28 is larger than line 27, enter overpayment	**30**		

Sign Here

Under penalties of perjury, I declare that I have examined this return, including accompanying schedules and statements, and to the best of my knowledge and belief, it is true, correct, and complete. Declaration of preparer (other than partner or limited liability company member) is based on all information of which preparer has any knowledge.

▶ _____
Signature of partner or limited liability company member

▶ _____
Date

May the IRS discuss this return with the preparer shown below? See instructions. ☐ **Yes** ☐ **No**

Paid Preparer Use Only

Print/Type preparer's name	Preparer's signature	Date	Check ☐ if self-employed	PTIN
Firm's name ▶			Firm's EIN ▶	
Firm's address ▶			Phone no.	

For Paperwork Reduction Act Notice, see separate instructions.   Cat. No. 11390Z   Form **1065** (2018)

Form 1065 (2018) *Beachside Properties LLC*   *11-1111111*   Page **4**

Schedule K		Partners' Distributive Share Items				Total amount	

Income (Loss)

1	Ordinary business income (loss) (page 1, line 22)				**1**	180,000	
2	Net rental real estate income (loss) (attach Form 8825)				**2**	300,000	
3a	Other gross rental income (loss)		**3a**				
b	Expenses from other rental activities (attach statement)		**3b**				
c	Other net rental income (loss). Subtract line 3b from line 3a				**3c**	0	
4	Guaranteed payments				**4**	240,000	
5	Interest income				**5**		
6	Dividends and dividend equivalents: **a** Ordinary dividends				**6a**	4,000	
	b Qualified dividends		**6b**	4,000			
	c Dividend equivalents		**6c**				
7	Royalties				**7**		
8	Net short-term capital gain (loss) (attach Schedule D (Form 1065))				**8**	12,000	
9a	Net long-term capital gain (loss) (attach Schedule D (Form 1065))				**9a**		
b	Collectibles (28%) gain (loss)		**9b**				
c	Unrecaptured section 1250 gain (attach statement)		**9c**				
10	Net section 1231 gain (loss) (attach Form 4797)				**10**		
11	Other income (loss) (see instructions) Type ▶				**11**		

Deductions

12	Section 179 deduction (attach Form 4562)				**12**		
13a	Contributions				**13a**	6,000	
b	Investment interest expense				**13b**		
c	Section 59(e)(2) expenditures: **(1)** Type ▶ _____ **(2)** Amount ▶				13c(2)		
d	Other deductions (see instructions) Type ▶				**13d**		

Self-Employment

14a	Net earnings (loss) from self-employment				**14a**	150,000	
b	Gross farming or fishing income				**14b**		
c	Gross nonfarm income				**14c**	720,000	

Credits

15a	Low-income housing credit (section 42(j)(5))				**15a**		
b	Low-income housing credit (other)				**15b**		
c	Qualified rehabilitation expenditures (rental real estate) (attach Form 3468, if applicable)				**15c**		
d	Other rental real estate credits (see instructions) Type ▶				**15d**		
e	Other rental credits (see instructions) Type ▶				**15e**		
f	Other credits (see instructions) Type ▶				**15f**		

Foreign Transactions

16a	Name of country or U.S. possession ▶						
b	Gross income from all sources				**16b**		
c	Gross income sourced at partner level				**16c**		
	Foreign gross income sourced at partnership level						
d	Section 951A category ▶ _____ **e** Foreign branch category ▶				**16e**		
f	Passive category ▶ _____ **g** General category ▶ _____ **h** Other (attach statement)				**16h**		
	Deductions allocated and apportioned at partner level						
i	Interest expense ▶ _____ **j** Other				**16j**		
	Deductions allocated and apportioned at partnership level to foreign source income						
k	Section 951A category ▶ _____ **l** Foreign branch category ▶				**16l**		
m	Passive category ▶ _____ **n** General category ▶ _____ **o** Other (attach statement)				**16o**		
p	Total foreign taxes (check one): ▶ Paid ☐ Accrued ☐				**16p**		
q	Reduction in taxes available for credit (attach statement)				**16q**		
r	Other foreign tax information (attach statement)						

Alternative Minimum Tax (AMT) Items

17a	Post-1986 depreciation adjustment				**17a**	18,224	
b	Adjusted gain or loss				**17b**		
c	Depletion (other than oil and gas)				**17c**		
d	Oil, gas, and geothermal properties—gross income				**17d**		
e	Oil, gas, and geothermal properties—deductions				**17e**		
f	Other AMT items (attach statement)				**17f**		

Other Information

18a	Tax-exempt interest income				**18a**	2,100	
b	Other tax-exempt income				**18b**		
c	Nondeductible expenses				**18c**		
19a	Distributions of cash and marketable securities				**19a**	34,000	
b	Distributions of other property				**19b**		
20a	Investment income				**20a**	12,000	
b	Investment expenses				**20b**		
c	Other items and amounts (attach statement)					*	

* As shown in Example 25 later in the chapter, a supporting schedule will show the partnership's totals for additional information related to the partners' qualified business income deduction.

Form **1065** (2018)

Form 1065 (2018)   *Beachside Properties LLC*   *11-1111111*   Page **5**

Analysis of Net Income (Loss)

1	Net income (loss). Combine Schedule K, lines 1 through 11. From the result, subtract the sum of Schedule K, lines 12 through 13d, and 16p					**1**	*730,000*

2	Analysis by partner type:	**(i)** Corporate	**(ii)** Individual (active)	**(iii)** Individual (passive)	**(iv)** Partnership	**(v)** Exempt Organization	**(vi)** Nominee/Other
a	General partners						
b	Limited partners		*486,000*	*244,000*			

Schedule L — Balance Sheets per Books

	Assets	Beginning of tax year (a)	(b)	End of tax year (c)	(d)
1	Cash		*97,503*		*123,740*
2a	Trade notes and accounts receivable . . .				
b	Less allowance for bad debts		*0*		*0*
3	Inventories		*60,000*		*80,000*
4	U.S. government obligations				
5	Tax-exempt securities		*40,000*		*40,000*
6	Other current assets (attach statement) . .				
7a	Loans to partners (or persons related to partners)				
b	Mortgage and real estate loans				
8	Other investments (attach statement) . . .		*120,000*		*860,000*
9a	Buildings and other depreciable assets . .	*3,400,000*		*3,400,000*	
b	Less accumulated depreciation	*1,767,503*	*1,632,497*	*1,885,640*	*1,514,360*
10a	Depletable assets				
b	Less accumulated depletion		*0*		*0*
11	Land (net of any amortization)		*600,000*		*600,000*
12a	Intangible assets (amortizable only) . . .	*10,000*		*10,000*	
b	Less accumulated amortization	*10,000*	*0*	*10,000*	*0*
13	Other assets (attach statement)				
14	Total assets		*2,550,000*		*3,218,100*
	Liabilities and Capital				
15	Accounts payable				
16	Mortgages, notes, bonds payable in less than 1 year				
17	Other current liabilities (attach statement) .				
18	All nonrecourse loans		*500,000*		*600,000*
19a	Loans from partners (or persons related to partners)				
b	Mortgages, notes, bonds payable in 1 year or more				
20	Other liabilities (attach statement)				
21	Partners' capital accounts		*2,050,000*		*2,618,100*
22	Total liabilities and capital		*2,550,000*		*3,218,100*

Schedule M-1 — Reconciliation of Income (Loss) per Books With Income (Loss) per Return

Note: The partnership may be required to file Schedule M-3. See instructions.

1	Net income (loss) per books	*492,100*	**6**	Income recorded on books this year not included on Schedule K, lines 1 through 11 (itemize):		
2	Income included on Schedule K, lines 1, 2, 3c, 5, 6a, 7, 8, 9a, 10, and 11, not recorded on books this year (itemize): _____	*0*	**a**	Tax-exempt interest $ *2,100* _____		*2,100*
3	Guaranteed payments (other than health insurance)	*240,000*	**7**	Deductions included on Schedule K, lines 1 through 13d, and 16p, not charged against book income this year (itemize):		
4	Expenses recorded on books this year not included on Schedule K, lines 1 through 13d, and 16p (itemize):		**a**	Depreciation $ _____		*0*
a	Depreciation $ _____		**8**	Add lines 6 and 7		*2,100*
b	Travel and entertainment $ _____	*0*	**9**	Income (loss) (Analysis of Net Income (Loss), line 1). Subtract line 8 from line 5 .		*730,000*
5	Add lines 1 through 4	*732,100*				

Schedule M-2 — Analysis of Partners' Capital Accounts

1	Balance at beginning of year . . .	*2,050,000*	**6**	Distributions: **a** Cash		*34,000*
2	Capital contributed: **a** Cash . . .	*110,000*		**b** Property		
	b Property . .		**7**	Other decreases (itemize): _____		
3	Net income (loss) per books	*492,100*		_____		
4	Other increases (itemize): _____	*0*	**8**	Add lines 6 and 7		*34,000*
5	Add lines 1 through 4	*2,652,100*	**9**	Balance at end of year. Subtract line 8 from line 5		*2,618,100*

GLOBAL TAX ISSUES   Withholding Requirements for non-U.S. Partners

A U.S. partnership may have non-U.S. partners subject to U.S. tax on their partnership income. The Code provides tax withholding rules to counter the challenge of collecting tax from parties not physically present in the United States. The rules differ depending on whether the income is "effectively connected with a U.S. trade or business," derived from investment property, or related to real estate transactions.

If the partnership purchases real property from a non-U.S. seller, for example, the partnership generally must withhold 10 percent of the purchase price. If a partnership sells a U.S. real property interest, it typically withholds tax at the partner's highest tax rate applied to the gain allocated to a foreign partner. Further, if the partnership receives dividends, interest, rents, or other income described in

§ 1441(b), it typically withholds 30 percent of the non-U.S. partner's distributive share of such income.

Finally, if the partnership generates U.S. business income, it must withhold and pay an amount equal to the highest U.S. tax rate applicable to the non-U.S. taxpayer's allocable share of partnership income.

Many of these withholding requirements can be reduced or eliminated through various alternative procedures available in the Regulations (designed to ensure that the withholding does not exceed the actual tax that might be due, while still protecting the U.S. revenue) or through tax treaties between the United States and the overseas jurisdiction.

Source: See IRC §§ 1441(b), 1445(a) and (e), and 1446(a) and related Regulations.

The Big Picture

EXAMPLE 19

Continue with the facts in Examples 15 to 18, and follow along on Beachside's Form 1065, page 5. To calculate Beachside's "taxable income" on the Analysis of Net Income (Loss) schedule, we combine the ordinary income of $180,000, guaranteed payments of $240,000, and the four separately stated income and deduction amounts [lines 2, 6a, 8, and 13a (negative)] from Beachside's Schedule K. This net amount is $730,000 and is the amount to which the $492,100 (assumed) of book income is reconciled on Schedule M–1, line 9.

Reconciling Partners' Capital Schedule M–2 reconciles partners' beginning and ending capital accounts, considering contributions to and distributions from the partnership as well as the partnership's income, gains, losses, and deductions. Schedule M–2 can be prepared using any of several methods, including the tax basis, generally accepted accounting principles (GAAP), or the "§ 704(b) book" method. The method used on Schedule M–2 should also be used in preparing the capital account reconciliation on the partners' Schedules K–1.

Schedule L (on page 5 of Form 1065) generally shows an accounting-basis balance sheet. If the capital reconciliation method used in Schedule M–2 differs from the method used for Schedule L, a reconciling schedule should be provided.

The Big Picture

EXAMPLE 20

Continue with Examples 15 to 19 and the Beachside Properties Form 1065 excerpts. Beachside prepares its Schedule L and Schedule M–2 using the same method, so Beachside's beginning and ending capital accounts have the same balances on both Schedule L and Schedule M–2.

In addition to Beachside's book income, Schedule M–2 also reflects the $30,000 cash distribution to Maria, payment of medical expenses of $4,000 to Kyle, and (as discussed later) a $110,000 cash contribution from Maria.

LO.8

Outline and discuss the requirements for allocating income, gains, losses, deductions, and credits among the partners and describe how that income is reported.

10-3b Partner Allocations and Reporting

Partnership items—ordinary income, separately stated items, and other related information—must be allocated among the partners. These allocations must have economic effect and substantiality, and they must take into account any precontribution gains and losses.

Economic Effect

Partnership allocations are made in accordance with the partnership agreement or an LLC's operating agreement. These allocations can be flexible. Profits, losses, and cash flows are not required to be allocated in accordance with capital ownership, as is the case under state law for most corporate entities. Partnership allocations have, at times, been used to manipulate the allocation of tax benefits among partners. Extensive Regulations[37] are designed to ensure that allocations do not result in undue tax revenue losses to the Treasury. The rules are complex, but the primary general rule—the economic effect test —can be easily understood.

The economic effect test has three general requirements.

- Section 704(b) book capital accounts must be maintained as described in the Regulations. These capital accounts reflect contributions and distributions at their fair market values. An allocation of income or gain to a partner must increase the partner's capital account, and an allocation of deduction or loss must decrease the partner's capital account.

- When the partnership interest is liquidated, if a partner has a *positive* balance in the capital account, the partner must receive net assets with a fair market value equal to that positive balance.

- When the partnership interest is liquidated, if a partner has a *negative* balance in the capital account, the partner must "restore" that account, generally by contributing cash. Alternative tests (beyond the scope of this text) may also be used to meet this requirement.

These capital account maintenance requirements are designed to ensure that a partner bears the economic burden of a loss or deduction allocation and receives the economic benefit of an income or gain allocation.

The Big Picture

EXAMPLE 21

Continue with Examples 15 to 17 and the Beachside Properties Form 1065 excerpts. Maria arrives at the bakery at 4 A.M. (or earlier) six days a week to make sure her cinnamon rolls and croissants are ready when the café opens at 7. Consequently, the other LLC members have agreed with Maria that she should be allocated the first $30,000 of gross revenues (and cash flows) from bakery operations each year, starting in year 2. All other revenues and expenses (including W–2 wages and depreciation expense) are allocated in the expected 40%/40%/20% ratios to Kyle, Maria, and Josh, respectively.

Beachside's Form 1065, page 1, for the LLC's second year of operations includes only the bakery's retail operations. To simplify the illustration, assume that the § 704(b) book income and taxable income are the same amount. Maria is entitled to the first $30,000 shown on that page. The remaining $150,000 of ordinary income and all other items of partnership income, gain, loss, or deduction are allocated based on the members' profit sharing percentages.

Assume *for this example only* that the bakery operations are the only item impacting the § 704(b) book capital accounts this year and that the initial § 704(b) book capital amounts are as follows.

	Maria	Kyle	Josh
Beginning § 704(b) book capital	$1,900,000	$1,900,000	$150,000
Special allocation of gross income	30,000	—0—	—0—
Allocation of remaining net income	60,000	60,000	30,000
Ending § 704(b) book capital	$1,990,000	$1,960,000	$180,000

This allocation will be respected as long as the members eventually (i.e., any time on or before liquidation) receive cash and property that reflects these ending capital account values.

---

[37]Reg. § 1.704–1(b).

Substantiality

Partnership allocations must also have "substantial" effect. In general, an allocation does not meet the "substantial" test unless it has economic consequences in addition to tax consequences that might benefit a subset of the partners. Allocations are not generally permitted if they are for tax reasons only or if an allocation in one tax year is required to be offset by an equal allocation in a future tax year.

The Big Picture

EXAMPLE 22

In Example 21, assume instead (for this example only) that the $30,000 special allocation of net income was awarded to Maria in year 2 simply to allow Maria to utilize her personal expiring net operating loss carryover and that an offsetting $30,000 special allocation of deductions would be made to Maria the following tax year.

Even though the LLC's allocations meet the "economic effect" tests, they would not be permitted because there is no substantial nontax economic reason for the allocations. The allocations over the two-year period are intended only to reduce the LLC members' combined income tax liability.

Precontribution Gain or Loss

If property is contributed to a partnership, the difference between the property's fair market value and its basis at the contribution date is a **precontribution gain or loss**. The partnership keeps track of these built-in gains and losses in its § 704(b) book accounting records. Any income, gain, loss, or deduction related to such property must be allocated among the partners to take the precontribution amount into account.[38]

An easy example occurs when a gain or loss is recognized when a nondepreciable contributed property is later sold by the partnership. The precontribution portion of the gain or loss is allocated to the contributing partner.

As you can imagine, allocations are more challenging when depreciable property is involved. Regulations (beyond the scope of this chapter) describe several permitted depreciation allocation methods.[39]

The Big Picture

EXAMPLE 23

Return to the facts of *The Big Picture* on p. 10-1. When Beachside Properties LLC was formed, Kyle contributed land (value of $800,000 and basis of $600,000) and buildings (value of $1,200,000 and basis of $0). Maria contributed $1,500,000 of cash, plus equipment and furnishings (value of $500,000 and basis of $0). For § 704(b) book capital account purposes, Beachside records the land and other properties at their fair market values. For tax purposes, the LLC takes carryover bases in the properties. The LLC must keep track of the differences between the basis in each property and the value at the contribution date. If any of this property is sold, the gain must be allocated to the contributing partner to the extent of any previously unrecognized built-in gain.

For example, if Beachside sells the land contributed by Kyle for $1,100,000, the gain would be calculated and allocated as follows.

	§ 704(b) Book	Tax
Amount realized	$1,100,000	$1,100,000
Less: Adjusted basis	800,000	600,000
Gain realized	$ 300,000	$ 500,000
Built-in gain to Kyle	—0—	200,000
Remaining gain (allocated proportionately)	$ 300,000	$ 300,000

For tax purposes, Kyle would recognize $320,000 of the gain [($300,000 × 40%) + $200,000 built-in gain], Maria would recognize $120,000 ($300,000 × 40%), and Josh would recognize $60,000 ($300,000 × 20%).

---

[38]§§ 704(c)(1)(A) and (C).   [39]Reg. § 1.704–3.

Schedule K–1

Once the partnership's items are calculated on Schedule K, they are allocated among the partners on their Schedules K–1. Schedule K summarizes the tax-related items for the entire partnership. Schedule K–1 summarizes the tax-related items for each partner after considering the allocation conventions outlined in the partnership agreement or required under the Code and Regulations. For each partnership item, the sum of the amounts allocated to all of the partners on Schedules K–1 should equal the partnership's total amount per Schedule K.

Refer to Maria's Schedule K–1 from Beachside Properties on the next page. Part I includes information about the partnership. Part II includes information about the partner, including the partner's profit, loss, and capital sharing percentages; share of partnership liabilities at the beginning and end of the year; and changes in the partner's capital account during the year.

Part III includes the information the partners use in completing their tax return. As a parallel to Schedule K, you'll find that Schedule K–1, lines 1 to 13 reflect the partner's distributive share of the partnership's income and deductions, including any amounts specially allocated to that partner; lines 14 to 17 include information the partner needs to calculate other amounts (e.g., self-employment tax, alternative minimum tax); lines 18 and 19 help the partner calculate the outside basis in the partnership interest; and line 20 provides additional information the partner might need (e.g., information for the "qualified business income" deduction, discussed later in this section).

The Big Picture

EXAMPLE
24

Continue with the Beachside Properties examples and the Form 1065 excerpts. Also refer to Maria's Schedule K–1. Maria, a 40% owner, will receive a Schedule K–1 from Beachside Properties. Part III, line 1, of Maria's Schedule K–1 reflects her $30,000 special allocation of ordinary income, plus her normal allocation of 40% of the remaining ordinary income, for a total of $90,000 (calculated in Example 21). She is also allocated 40% of all separately stated items.

On her Form 1040, Maria includes $90,000 of ordinary income, a $2,400 charitable contribution, a $4,800 short-term capital gain, $120,000 of passive rental income, and $1,600 of qualified dividend income. On the first page of Form 1040, Maria lists her $840 share of tax-exempt interest. She must also report as ordinary income the $120,000 guaranteed payment she received. (Similarly, Kyle and Josh will each report his respective guaranteed payment of $60,000.) In determining her AMT liability (if any), Maria takes into account a $7,290 positive adjustment.

Note that the specially allocated income simply increases Maria's amount on line 1 and decreases the amounts allocated to the other members. Kyle's and Josh's allocations on line 1 will be $60,000 and $30,000, respectively.

In her personal tax return, Maria combines the partnership's amounts with similar items from sources other than Beachside. For example, if Maria has a $3,000 long-term capital loss from a stock transaction, the overall net short-term capital gain calculated on Schedule D of her Form 1040 is $1,800.

For each LLC item, the sum of the allocated amounts on Josh's, Kyle's, and Maria's K–1s will equal the totals on Beachside Properties' Schedule K. Thus, the three amounts on Schedule K–1, line 1, after the special allocation ($90,000 + $60,000 + $30,000), equal the total $180,000 of ordinary income shown on Beachside's Form 1065, Schedule K, line 1.

Guaranteed Payments Received by Partners

A partner who receives guaranteed payments during a partnership year must include the payments in income as if they were received on the last day of the partnership year. Guaranteed payments are always taxable as ordinary income to the recipient partner.

The amount the partner receives is reported on Schedule K–1, line 4. The partner uses this information (in lieu of a Form W–2 or 1099) to report the income on the partner's tax return. A guaranteed payment often is subject to self-employment tax and, potentially, other additional taxes, as discussed later in the chapter.

Schedule K-1
(Form 1065)
Department of the Treasury
Internal Revenue Service

2018

For calendar year 2018, or tax year

beginning / / 2018 ending / /

Partner's Share of Income, Deductions, Credits, etc.
► See back of form and separate instructions.

651118

OMB No. 1545-0123

☐ Final K-1   ☐ Amended K-1

Part I	**Information About the Partnership**

A Partnership's employer identification number
11-1111111

B Partnership's name, address, city, state, and ZIP code

Beachside Properties LLC
1600 Ocean Vista Way
Surfside

C IRS Center where partnership filed return
P.O. Box 409101, Ogden, UT 84409

D ☐ Check if this is a publicly traded partnership (PTP)

Part II	**Information About the Partner**

E Partner's identifying number
111-11-1111

F Partner's name, address, city, state, and ZIP code

Maria LeClerc
1600 Ocean Vista Way
Surfside

G ☐ General partner or LLC member-manager   ☒ Limited partner or other LLC member

H ☒ Domestic partner   ☐ Foreign partner

I1 What type of entity is this partner? *Active Individual*

I2 If this partner is a retirement plan (IRA/SEP/Keogh/etc.), check here ☐

J Partner's share of profit, loss, and capital (see instructions):

	Beginning	Ending
Profit	40.000000 %	40.000000 %
Loss	40.000000 %	40.000000 %
Capital	47.500000 %	47.500000 %

K Partner's share of liabilities:

	Beginning	Ending
Nonrecourse	$ 200,000	$ 240,000
Qualified nonrecourse financing	$	$
Recourse	$	$

L Partner's capital account analysis:

Beginning capital account	$ 1,400,000
Capital contributed during the year	$ 110,000
Current year increase (decrease)	$ 214,840
Withdrawals & distributions	$ 30,000
Ending capital account	$ 1,694,840

☒ Tax basis   ☐ GAAP   ☐ Section 704(b) book
☐ Other (explain)

M Did the partner contribute property with a built-in gain or loss?
☒ Yes   ☐ No
If "Yes," attach statement (see instructions)

Part III	**Partner's Share of Current Year Income, Deductions, Credits, and Other Items**		
1	Ordinary business income (loss) 90,000	15	Credits
2	Net rental real estate income (loss) 120,000		
3	Other net rental income (loss)	16	Foreign transactions
4	Guaranteed payments 120,000		
5	Interest income		
6a	Ordinary dividends 1,600		
6b	Qualified dividends 1,600		
6c	Dividend equivalents		
7	Royalties		
8	Net short-term capital gain (loss) 4,800	17 A	Alternative minimum tax (AMT) items 7,290
9a	Net long-term capital gain (loss)		
9b	Collectibles (28%) gain (loss)		
9c	Unrecaptured section 1250 gain	18	Tax-exempt income and nondeductible expenses
10	Net section 1231 gain (loss)	A	840
11	Other income (loss)		
		19 A	Distributions 30,000
12	Section 179 deduction		
13 A	Other deductions 2,400	20 A	Other information 4,800
		Y	60,000
		Z	210,000
		AA	200,000
14 A	Self-employment earnings (loss) 60,000	AB	600,000
C	480,000		

*See attached statement for additional information.

For IRS Use Only

For Paperwork Reduction Act Notice, see Instructions for Form 1065.   www.irs.gov/Form1065   Cat. No. 11394R   **Schedule K-1 (Form 1065) 2018**

Qualified Business Income

Under § 199A, a noncorporate taxpayer can deduct up to 20 percent of "the combined qualified business income amount"; this produces the "QBI deduction." The deduction typically equals 20 percent of "qualified business income" (QBI), which is net of related deductions, including the self-employment tax deduction on QBI. Other limits relate to the taxpayer's modified taxable income and the entity's wages/capital investment. Further, the deduction might be limited if the business is a "specified service trade or business" ("SSTB") (e.g., certain service-oriented businesses). There is no cash outflow related to this deduction; it just works to lower the noncorporate party's effective tax rate on this income. For more information on the QBI deduction, the wages/capital investment limitations, SSTBs, and specific calculations, see text Section 2-3.

For a partner, QBI does not include guaranteed payments received for *services* provided to the partnership or payments from the partnership under § 707(a) for *services* unrelated to the partnership's business (e.g., payments by a restaurant LLC to a member for providing accounting services). In addition, the regulations provide that guaranteed payments for use of the partner's *capital* do not constitute QBI.[40]

The deduction is calculated at the partner level. The partnership is charged with calculating the partnership's QBI and reporting, on Schedules K–1, any information the partners need to complete their tax returns.[41] The partner's QBI generally equals the partner's share of business income on Schedule K–1 Part III, lines 1, 2, and 3 (trade or business income and/or rental income), reduced by business expenses on lines 12 and 13. The net amount is shown on Schedule K–1, line 20, code Z.

The additional information needed to calculate various limitations [e.g., W–2 wages and the "unadjusted basis immediately after acquisition of qualified property" (termed UBIA in the regulations)] is reported on Schedule K–1, line 20, codes AA to AD. These amounts are allocated in the same manner in which the related wage and depreciation deductions are allocated to the partners or shareholders. If the entity has multiple trades or businesses and/or income from SSTBs, additional schedules should be provided with allocated amounts for each business.[42]

The Big Picture

EXAMPLE

25

Continue with the Beachside Properties examples and the Form 1065 excerpts. Beachside has income from real estate and from a restaurant, both of which are qualified trades or businesses and produce QBI; neither is an SSTB. On Maria's Schedule K–1, Beachside reports ordinary business income of $90,000 (line 1, per Example 24), net rental real estate income of $120,000 (line 2), and qualified business income of $210,000 (line 20, code Z). It also provides supporting schedules for the two businesses. The other separately stated income and deduction amounts (including guaranteed payments received for performance of services and use of the partners' capital, and the charitable contribution on line 13) are nonbusiness income or deductions and do not affect the QBI calculation.

Per Example 15, the LLC pays W–2 wages of $500,000. Per Example 11, the property contributed by Kyle and Maria is either land (ineligible) or fully depreciated property. Immediately after formation, the LLC spent $1,500,000 on improvements, so this is the LLC's UBIA. The LLC computes these amounts for Kyle, Maria, and Josh in the 40%/40%/20% proportions, respectively, in which the related wage expense and depreciation deductions are allocated. Maria's allocated amounts are shown on her Schedule K–1, line 20, codes AA (W–2 wages) and AB (UBIA).

---

[40]Reg. § 1.199A–3(b)(1)(ii).
[41]§ 199A(f)(1).

[42]See Reg. § 1.199A–6 for complete information related to computational and reporting rules.

Concept Summary 10.3 reviews the tax-reporting rules for partnership items at both the partnership and partner levels.

Concept Summary 10.3

Tax Reporting of Partnership Items

Item	Partnership reports on Form 1065	Partner's share reported on Schedule K–1, Part III
1. Partnership ordinary income or loss.	Page 1, line 22. Schedule K, line 1.	Line 1. Special allocations, basis adjustments, and loss limitations may apply.
2. Guaranteed payments to partners for capital or services.	Page 1, line 10, if deductible; otherwise capitalized. All amounts on Schedule K, line 4, for partner reporting.	Line 4. Partner reports as ordinary income; no basis adjustment.
3. Separately stated income and deduction items such as portfolio income, capital gain and loss, and § 179 deductions.	Schedule K, lines 2, 3, and 5 to 13.	Lines 2, 3, and 5 to 13. Special allocations, basis adjustments, and loss limitations may apply.
4. Net earnings from self-employment.	Schedule K, line 14a.	Line 14, Code A.
5. Additional information so that the partner can make various calculations (e.g., AMT, foreign tax credits, net investment income tax, and the partner's outside basis).	Schedule K, lines 15 to 20.	Lines 15 to 20. Each partner's share of each item is passed through and considered in various calculations.
6. Qualified business income.	Schedule K, line 20 supporting schedule.	Line 20, Code Z and Codes AA to AD.

ETHICS & EQUITY   Built-In Appreciation on Contributed Property

In the "old days," one partner could contribute cash and another partner could contribute an equal value of appreciated property with no subsequent record-keeping requirements. Future depreciation deductions and gains on sale of the property could be allocated to both partners equally, thereby shifting income from one taxpayer to another. A partner in a lower tax bracket (or with expiring net operating losses and the like) could report the share of the gain on sale of the asset with a relatively low corresponding tax burden.

Section 704(c)(1)(A) was added to the Code to ensure that the partner contributing the property pays tax on any built-in gain. This prevents income shifting among taxpayers and loss of revenue to the U.S. Treasury.

There is no corresponding provision for S corporations—gains and losses and depreciation expense are allocated among the shareholders without regard to any built-in appreciation on contributed property.

Assume that a new partner or shareholder owns land valued at $100,000 in which the tax basis is $60,000. How would the "incidence of taxation" differ for the entities and owners if (1) the owner (partner or shareholder) sold the property and contributed the $100,000 proceeds versus (2) the owner (partner or shareholder) contributed that same property with the entity selling it for $100,000? What theory of partnership taxation supports this difference in treatment?

LO.9

Determine a partner's basis in the partnership interest.

10-3c **Partner's Basis**

Each partner has an outside basis in the partnership interest. That basis is increased/(decreased) over time for the partner's share of income/(deductions), contributions/(distributions), and increases/(decreases) in the partner's share of partnership liabilities.

The partner's basis is important for determining the treatment of distributions from the partnership to the partner and establishing the deductibility of partnership losses. When a partnership interest is sold (or liquidated by the partnership), the partner's gain or loss is determined by reference to the adjusted basis of the partnership interest (see Chapter 11).

Generally, the total of the partners' outside bases equals the partnership's inside basis in its assets. However, as noted in Chapter 11, certain transactions can throw this parity out of balance.

A partner's basis is not reflected anywhere on the Schedule K–1. Instead, each partner should maintain a personal record of the basis in the partnership interest.

Basis—Effect of Partnership Operations

As discussed earlier, the partner's initial outside basis generally equals the partner's basis in contributed assets. This could be a cost basis (plus any amount recognized as income on contribution of services) or a basis determined under the gift or inheritance rules. After the partner is admitted to the partnership, the partner's basis is adjusted for numerous items. The following items *increase* a partner's adjusted basis.

- The partner's proportionate share of partnership income (including capital gains and tax-exempt income).

- The partner's proportionate share of any increase in partnership liabilities (as discussed in the next section).

- Contributions of cash or property from the partner to the partnership after the partnership is formed.

The following items *decrease* the partner's adjusted basis in the partnership.

- The partner's proportionate share of partnership deductions and losses [including capital losses, foreign taxes, charitable contributions (including the allocable basis of donated property), and suspended business interest expense that will be available for future tax years].

- The partner's proportionate share of nondeductible expenses.

- The partner's proportionate share of any reduction in partnership liabilities.[43]

- Distributions of cash or property from the partnership to the partner after the partnership is formed.

Under no circumstances can the partner's adjusted basis for the partnership interest be reduced below zero.

As shown in Example 3 earlier in the chapter, increasing the adjusted basis for the partner's share of partnership taxable income is logical because the partner has already been taxed on the income. By increasing the partner's basis, the partner is not taxed again on the income when he or she sells the interest or receives a distribution from the partnership.

Using the same logic, tax-exempt income (or noncapitalizable, nondeductible expenditures) should increase (decrease) the partner's basis. If the income is exempt in the current period, it should not contribute to the recognition of gain when the partner either sells the interest or receives a distribution from the partnership.

Basis—Effect of Partnership Liabilities

LO.10

Explain how liabilities affect a partner's basis.

All partnership debt is allocated among the partners and included in the partners' bases.[44] [In contrast, the liabilities of an S corporation are generally *not* included in the shareholder's bases (see text Section 12-3f).] Partnership debt includes any partnership obligation that creates an asset; results in an expense to the partnership; or results in a nondeductible, noncapitalizable item at the partnership level. This definition includes certain contingent liabilities.[45] The definition also includes most debt that is considered a liability under financial accounting rules. However, partnership debt does *not* include accounts payable of a cash basis partnership.

---

[43]§§ 705 and 752.

[44]§ 752.

[45]Reg. § 1.752–1(a)(4)(ii).

An increase in a partner's share of partnership debt is treated as a cash contribution by the partner to the partnership and increases the partner's basis. A decrease in a partner's share of partnership debt is treated as a cash distribution from the partnership to the partner and decreases the partner's basis.

EXAMPLE 26

Jim and Becky contribute property to form the JB Partnership. Jim contributes cash of $30,000. Becky contributes land with an adjusted basis and fair market value of $45,000, subject to a liability of $15,000; the partnership assumes the debt (treated as a distribution to Becky). The partnership borrows $50,000 to finance construction of a building on the contributed land.

At the end of the first year, the accrual basis partnership owes $3,500 in trade accounts payable to various vendors. Disregard any operating activities and deductions related to these debts. If Jim and Becky share equally in liabilities, the partners' bases in their partnership interests are determined as follows.

Jim's Basis		Becky's Basis	
Contributed cash	$30,000	Basis in contributed land	$ 45,000
		Less: Debt assumed by partnership	(15,000)
Share of debt on land	7,500	Share of debt on land	7,500
Initial basis	$37,500	Initial basis	$ 37,500
Share of construction loan	25,000	Share of construction loan	25,000
Share of trade accounts payable (accrual basis)	1,750	Share of trade accounts payable (accrual basis)	1,750
Basis, end of first year	$64,250	Basis, end of first year	$ 64,250

Assume in the following year that the partnership pays off its accounts payable, debt on land, and construction loan. The partner's bases would be correspondingly decreased and (disregarding any other operating activities) would become $30,000 each at the end of that second year.

Allocation of Liabilities—In General In the above example, liabilities were allocated equally between the two partners. However, it's not generally that simple. Look at Maria's Schedule K–1 on p. 10-28. In Part II, item K, you can see that partnership debt, at the beginning and end of the partnership's tax year, is allocated based on whether it is recourse, nonrecourse, or qualified nonrecourse financing. **Recourse debt** is partnership debt for which the partnership or at least one of the partners is personally liable. This personal liability can exist, for example, through the operation of state law or through personal guarantees that a partner makes to the creditor. **Nonrecourse debt** is debt for which no partner is personally liable. Lenders of nonrecourse debt generally require that collateral be pledged against the loan. Upon default, the lender can claim only the collateral, not the partners' personal assets. **Qualified nonrecourse financing** is a subset of nonrecourse debt that applies for purposes of the at-risk limitation discussed later in the chapter. Qualified nonrecourse financing is generally bank debt (or similar third-party debt) on real estate.

In general (disregarding any personal guarantees of any partnership debt), recourse debt is allocated among *general partners only*, and nonrecourse debt is allocated among *all partners*. If any partner or LLC member personally guarantees a debt, it is treated as a recourse debt with respect to that partner. For an LLC, most debt will, by default, be treated as nonrecourse debt because the LLC members, by definition, have no liability for entity debts.

Recourse Debt Rules Recourse debt is allocated based on each partner's "economic risk of loss." For a partnership in which all contributions and allocations have been proportionate to the capital contributions, recourse debt is allocated among the general partners in proportion to their *loss sharing* ratios. In more complex situations, the partner's economic risk of loss is determined under a <mark>constructive liquidation scenario</mark> outlined in the Regulations.[46]

Hill, Inc., and Dart, Inc., own the newly created HD Partnership, where both entities are treated as general partners. Assume that all contributions and allocations are equal (50%/50%). At the end of the year, HD has $40,000 of recourse accounts payable and a $100,000 personal property loan that is guaranteed by Dart.

Because recourse debt is allocated according to *loss* sharing ratios, each partner is allocated 50% of the accounts payable, and Dart is allocated 100% of the guaranteed debt. Hill's share of recourse debt is $20,000, and Dart's share is $120,000.

EXAMPLE 27

Nonrecourse Debt Rules Nonrecourse debt (including qualified nonrecourse financing) is allocated among all the partners. For our purposes, it is allocated to the partners in accordance with their *profit sharing* ratios.[47]

In Example 27, assume instead that HD is an LLC instead of a general partnership. Also assume that 40% of profits are allocated to Hill and 60% are allocated to Dart. (Losses are still allocated equally.)

In an LLC, accounts payable are treated as *nonrecourse* debt and are allocated according to *profit* sharing ratios. Therefore, the $40,000 of accounts payable are allocated $16,000 (40%) to Hill and $24,000 (60%) to Dart. The debt guaranteed by Dart remains a recourse debt allocated 100% to Dart. Therefore, Hill's Schedule K–1 will show $16,000 of nonrecourse debt, and Dart's will show $24,000 of nonrecourse debt and $100,000 of recourse debt.

EXAMPLE 28

Exhibit 10.2 summarizes the rules for computing a partner's basis in a partnership interest and the order in which the rules are applied.

The Big Picture

Return to the facts of *The Big Picture* on p. 10-1. Example 24 described how the income and deduction items of Beachside Properties LLC are allocated to Maria on her Schedule K–1. But how is Maria's basis affected by those items?

Assume that at the beginning of that tax year (Beachside's second year of operations), Maria's basis in her LLC interest was $1,600,000, including a $200,000 share of the LLC's $500,000 of nonrecourse debt. At the end of the year, Beachside had $600,000 of debt, which was again treated as nonrecourse to all of the LLC members.

During the year, Maria contributes to the LLC cash of $110,000 and additional property (basis of $0 and fair market value of $50,000). Maria also received a cash distribution equal to her $30,000 special allocation of the LLC's gross income. Maria's share of Beachside's income, gain, and deductions is as described in Example 24 and on her Schedule K–1.

EXAMPLE 29

continued

---

[46]See Reg. § 1.752–2 and related Regulations and Proposed Regulations. Under the constructive liquidation scenario, debts are allocated based on which partner would be required to pay the debt in the event of a hypothetical catastrophic event that left all of the partnership's assets worthless. The assumed losses are allocated among the partners, and the debt is allocated in proportion to the partners' negative capital accounts after this deemed allocation.

[47]Reg. § 1.752–3. This Regulation outlines a first stage allocation of minimum gain and a second stage allocation where liabilities on contributed property exceed the tax basis of the contributed property. These first two stages are beyond the scope of this text.

Maria's basis can be calculated using the ordering rules shown in Exhibit 10.2. At the end of the year, Maria's basis is as follows.

Beginning basis (including beginning liability share)	$1,600,000
Contributions, including increase in share of liabilities	
Share of net increase in LLC liabilities [40% × ($600,000 − $500,000)]	40,000
Cash contribution to LLC capital	110,000
Maria's basis in noncash capital contribution	–0–
Share of LLC income items	
Ordinary LLC income	90,000
LLC's net passive activity income from rental real estate	120,000
Tax-exempt income	840
Short-term capital gain	4,800
Qualified dividend income	1,600
Distributions and withdrawals	
Capital withdrawal (distribution related to special allocation of income)	(30,000)
Share of LLC deduction items	
Charitable contribution	(2,400)
Ending basis (including ending liability share)	$1,934,840

EXHIBIT 10.2	Partner's Basis in Partnership Interest

Basis is generally adjusted in the following order every tax year.

Initial basis or beginning basis for the taxable year.

+ Partner's contributions, including increases in the partner's share of partnership debt

+ Partner's share of the partnership's

- Taxable income items

- Exempt income items

- Excess of depletion deductions over adjusted basis of property subject to depletion

− Partner's distributions and withdrawals, including decreases in the partner's share of partnership debt

− Partner's share of the partnership's

- Separately stated foreign taxes, charitable contributions (limited to the basis of contributed property), and other deductions

- Nondeductible items not chargeable to a capital account

- Special depletion deduction for oil and gas wells

- Other loss items

The basis of a partner's interest can never be negative.

LO.11

Illustrate a partner's capital account rollforward and explain why the year-end balance might differ from the partner's year-end basis in the partnership interest.

10-3d Partner's Capital Account

As mentioned earlier in the chapter, the partner's basis is not the same as the partner's capital account. Think of the capital account as an accounting calculation of the partner's ownership in the entity.

The capital account analysis (sometimes called a "rollforward" or "reconciliation") is shown on the partner's Schedule K–1 (see text Section 10-3b). This calculation shows the change in the partner's capital account from the beginning to the end of the tax year.

This capital account analysis can be prepared using any of several methods, including the tax basis, GAAP, or the § 704(b) book method. The method selected is indicated on the Schedule K–1 and should be the same method that was used in preparing the partnership's Schedule M–2 (Analysis of Partners' Capital Accounts). The partnership might need to keep track of partners' capital using more than one method—for example, using both GAAP and the § 704(b) book method.

The total of the partners' beginning and ending capital accounts on all Schedules K–1 should equal the beginning and ending balances shown on the partnership's Schedule M–2. These amounts should also generally equal the balances shown on the partnership's balance sheet (Schedule L) (or an explanation of the differences should be attached).

The partner's ending capital account balance is rarely the same amount as the partner's tax basis. For example, a partner's tax basis includes the partner's share of partnership liabilities; these liabilities are not included in partner's capital. The partner's share of partnership liabilities is shown separately in Part II of Schedule K–1.

Sometimes the partner's ending basis in the partnership interest can be estimated by adding the partner's ending capital and the partner's share of liabilities. This would be accurate, for example, when the partner has been in the partnership since its inception and the capital account analysis is prepared on a tax basis.

> **The Big Picture**
>
> **EXAMPLE 30**
>
> Maria's Schedule K–1 shows her capital account rollforward from the prior year to the current year. Her capital account was calculated on a tax basis, and the beginning capital account balance was $1,400,000. The reconciliation shows the $110,000 of cash Maria contributed, the $0 basis of other contributed property, and the $30,000 distribution related to the special allocation of cash to Maria.
>
> The current-year increase (decrease) of $214,840 is the combination (additions and subtractions) of Maria's amounts shown on Schedule K–1, Part III, lines 1 to 13, plus the tax-exempt income shown on line 18. (Note that the ordinary/qualified dividends are only included one time.)
>
> Maria's ending tax-basis capital account on Schedule K–1 is $1,694,840. Her Schedule K–1 shows a $240,000 share of nonrecourse liabilities. While this will not always be the case, the sum of these amounts equals her ending tax basis of $1,934,840 as calculated in Example 29.

10-3e Loss Limitations

LO.12

List and review the limitations on deducting partnership losses.

Partnership losses flow through to the partners to be reported on their tax returns. However, the loss deduction might be limited at the partner level. When limitations apply, all or a portion of the losses are suspended until a triggering event occurs. No time limit is imposed on such loss carryforwards.

The following different limitations might apply.

1. **Basis limitation [§ 704(d)].** This limitation allows a loss deduction only to the extent of the partner's adjusted outside basis.
2. **At-risk limitation (§ 465).** Losses that are deductible under the basis limitation are deductible only to the extent the partner is at risk for the partnership interest.
3. **Passive activity loss limitation (§ 469).** Any losses that survive this second limitation may be subject to the passive activity loss rules.
4. **Excess business losses [§ 461(l)].** If a loss passes the above three limitations, a noncorporate taxpayer must consider whether the excess business loss limitation applies.

The partner can only deduct losses that make it through all of the hurdles. Special rules apply to losses from real estate activities.

> **EXAMPLE 31**
>
> Megan is a 50% partner in Green LLC, which does not invest in real estate. On January 1, 2019, Megan's adjusted basis for her LLC interest is $50,000, and her at-risk amount is $35,000. Her share of losses from Green for 2019 is $60,000, all of which is passive. She has another investment that produced $25,000 of passive activity income. She has no other passive or active losses. Megan can deduct $25,000 of Green's losses on her Form 1040 for 2019, calculated as follows.
>
> *continued*

Applicable Provision	Deductible Loss	Suspended Loss
§ 704(d) basis limitation	$50,000	$10,000
At-risk limitation	35,000	15,000
Passive activity loss limitation	25,000	10,000
Excess business loss limitation	25,000	–0–

Megan can deduct only $50,000 under the basis limitation. Of this $50,000, only $35,000 is deductible under the at-risk limitation. Under the passive activity loss limitation, passive losses can be deducted only against passive income. The net passive income/loss from the two investments is $0, so the excess business loss limitation does not apply. Thus, Megan can deduct $25,000. This amount, plus the three suspended loss amounts, equals the original $60,000 loss.

Basis Limitation

For the first limitation, basis is determined at the end of the partnership's taxable year. It is adjusted for any partnership income and gain items and contributions and distributions made during the year, but it is determined *before considering any loss or deduction items for the year*. (In Exhibit 10.2, basis would be calculated through "partner's distributions and withdrawals.")

Losses that cannot be deducted because of this rule are suspended and carried forward (never back) for use against future increases in the partner's adjusted basis. Such increases might result from additional capital contributions, from sharing in additional partnership debts, or from future partnership income.

At-Risk Limitation

Under the at-risk rules, certain loss deductions are limited to amounts that are economically invested in the partnership. Limited losses are those from business and income-producing activities allocated to individual partners and closely held C corporation partners. Suspended losses are carried forward until a partner has a sufficient amount at risk in the activity to absorb them.[48]

Invested amounts include cash, the adjusted basis of property contributed by the partner, and the partner's share of partnership earnings that have not been withdrawn.[49]

Recourse debt generally is included in the amount at risk, but nonrecourse debt is not. As an exception, qualified recourse financing is deemed to be at risk.[50] In general terms, qualified nonrecourse financing is nonrecourse financing provided by a bank, retirement plan, or similar party or by a Federal, state, or local government for the purchase of real estate.

EXAMPLE 32

In Example 31, Megan's amount at risk was $35,000, and $15,000 was suspended under the at-risk limitation. Assume that this limitation applied because Megan's basis in her partnership interest included a $15,000 nonrecourse debt that could not be included in her amount at risk.

If, instead, the activity was a real estate activity and the debt was qualified nonrecourse financing, Megan's basis and at-risk amounts would have been the same ($50,000) and no additional loss deduction would have been suspended under the at-risk rules.

Passive Activity Loss Limitation

The third loss limitation is that passive activity losses can generally only be deducted to the extent they offset passive activity income.[51] These rules apply to partners who are individuals, estates, trusts, closely held C corporations, or personal service corporations.

---

[48]§ 465(a)(2).
[49]§ 465(a).
[50]§ 465(b)(6).
[51]§ 469(a)(1).

Passive activity income is income from a trade or business activity in which the partner does not materially participate on a regular, continuous, and substantial basis,[52] or income from many rental activities.

Material participation means that the partner should have substantial involvement in daily operations of the activity. By definition, a partner treated as a limited partner is typically considered *not* to materially participate in partnership activities.[53]

Rent income from real or personal property generally is passive activity income, regardless of the partner's level of participation. The primary exception is that rental real estate is not treated as a passive activity for a person who qualifies as a real estate professional.

As a special allowance, individuals can offset up to $25,000 of passive activity losses from rental real estate against active and portfolio income.[54] (This amount is phased out at a rate of $0.50 for every excess dollar, starting at $100,000 of modified adjusted gross income.) This deduction is available to those who actively (rather than materially) participate in rental real estate activities.

For additional information regarding loss limitations, the passive activity loss rules, and the rental real estate exception, refer to *Individual Income Taxes* (South-Western Federal Taxation), Chapter 11.

Excess Business Losses of Noncorporate Taxpayers

If a noncorporate taxpayer has net trade or business losses that (1) pass the above three tests and (2) exceed a threshold amount, the excess loss is carried forward as part of the taxpayer's net operating loss carryover.[55] The threshold is $255,000 (2019) for single taxpayers and $510,000 (2019) for married taxpayers filing a joint tax return. These amounts are adjusted for inflation each year.

The limitation is applied at the partnership or S corporation shareholder level. As examples, losses from farming, active business losses, or losses of a real estate professional might be subject to this rule.

10-4 OTHER ISSUES

LO.13

Identify other issues related to partners and partnerships.

Individual partners are subject to additional taxes on their partnership income. Certain transactions between a partner and a partnership are subject to special rules. These issues are the focus of this section.

10-4a Self-Employment and Net Investment Income Tax

A partner is not treated as an employee for tax purposes. Thus, certain types of partnership income allocated to an individual taxpayer may be considered "net earnings from self-employment" [subject to self-employment (SE) tax] or "net investment income" [subject to the tax on net investment income (NII)].

Self-Employment Tax

Self-employed individuals may be liable for an SE tax, consisting of a 12.4 percent tax for old-age, survivors, and disability insurance (on up to $132,900 of SE income in 2019, less any wages on which the tax is withheld) and a 2.9 percent tax for hospital insurance (on all SE income). An additional Medicare tax of 0.9 percent applies to SE income in excess of $250,000 for married taxpayers filing joint tax returns (or half that amount if a separate return is filed, or $200,000 for other taxpayers). The taxpayer calculates the SE tax on Schedule SE and the additional Medicare tax on Form 8959.

SE Treatment of Distributive Shares SE income includes a general partner's distributive share of income from a partnership's trade or business, whether or not that income is distributed (e.g., income reported on line 1 of Schedule K–1). It also includes the distributive share allocated to a "limited partner" that is in the nature of compensation for services

---

[52]§§ 469(c)(1) and (2).

[53]§ 469(h)(2).

[54]§ 469(i).

[55]§§ 461(l)(1) and (4).

performed for or on behalf of the partnership.[56] However, SE income does not include the distributive share allocated to a limited partner who merely is an investor in the entity.

SE Treatment of Guaranteed Payments For both general and limited partners, any guaranteed payments for *services* are subject to the SE tax. Guaranteed payments for use of the partner's *capital* are not subject to the SE tax.

Treatment as a General versus a Limited Partner For SE tax purposes, a taxpayer could save up to 15.3 percent of any distributive share by being treated as a *limited* partner. As a result, this has been a contentious area for the IRS. According to Proposed Regulations dating from 1997, a partner or an LLC member will be treated as a *general* partner if:

- The partner has personal liability for partnership debts by virtue of status as a partner,
- The partner can enter into contractual relationships on behalf of the partnership, or
- The partner works more than 500 hours in the partnership's trade or business during the tax year.

The Big Picture

EXAMPLE 33

Return to the facts of *The Big Picture* in Examples 16 and 24. Beachside's Schedule K and Schedules K–1 were prepared in accordance with these Proposed Regulations, with the members' distributive shares and guaranteed payments being treated as follows.

	Distributive Share (Proposed Regulations)	Guaranteed Payments [§ 1402(a)(13)]
Kyle	$60,000—not SE income	$60,000—not SE income (capital)
Maria	$90,000—not SE income*	$60,000—SE income (services) and $60,000—not SE income (capital)
Josh	$30,000—SE income	$60,000—SE income (services)

*See Prop.Reg. § 1.1402(a)–2(i), Example (iii).

Net Investment Income Tax

An individual taxpayer's "net investment income" (NII) is subject to an additional tax of 3.8 percent to the extent the taxpayer's modified adjusted gross income (MAGI) exceeds $250,000 for married taxpayers filing joint returns (or half that amount if a separate return is filed) or $200,000 for other taxpayers.[57] MAGI equals the taxpayer's adjusted gross income increased by any foreign earned income exclusion.[58] This tax is calculated on Form 8960.

Certain types of income allocated from a partnership are treated as net investment income (NII), including dividends, interest, passive activity income, and gains from property not used in a trade or business. In addition, the partner's distributive share is considered NII if the partner is a "passive" investor, as defined under the passive activity loss rules. The tax also applies to "income on investment of working capital," which includes guaranteed payments for use of a partner's capital. Tax-exempt income is not subject to this tax.

---

[56]§§ 1402(a) and (a)(13). See also Prop.Reg. § 1.1402(a)–2(h).

[57]§ 1411.

[58]§ 911.

The Big Picture

Refer to Maria's Schedule K–1 on p. 10-28. Maria's NII includes the $60,000 guaranteed payment she received in exchange for capital plus her distributive share of the partnership's qualified dividends ($1,600) and net short-term capital gains ($4,800). It does not include the $840 of tax-exempt interest reported to her on line 18.

Maria will prepare Form 8960 to calculate her net investment income tax. Assuming that Maria has no net investment income from other sources and files as a single taxpayer, she will pay a tax of 3.8% on the lesser of $66,400 ($60,000 + $1,600 + $4,800) or the excess of her modified AGI over $200,000.

EXAMPLE
34

10-4b Transactions between a Partner and a Partnership

Certain transactions between a partner and the partnership are treated as if the partner were an outsider, dealing with the partnership at arm's length.[59] This includes loan transactions, rental payments, sales of property between the partner and the partnership, and payments for services when the services are short-term technical services the partner also provides for parties other than the partnership.

On the other hand, for some transactions, the partner and partnership are treated as related parties, and the tax treatment is adjusted accordingly.

Sales of Property

Certain sales of property are subject to special rules. No loss is recognized on a sale of property between a person and a partnership when the person owns, directly or indirectly, more than 50 percent of partnership capital or profits.[60] The disallowed loss might not vanish entirely, however. If the transferee eventually sells the property at a gain, the disallowed loss reduces the gain the transferee would otherwise recognize.

Blake sells land (basis to him, $30,000; fair market value, $45,000) to a partnership in which he controls a 60% capital interest. The partnership pays him only $20,000 for the land. Blake cannot deduct his $10,000 realized loss.

Assume that the partnership sells the land to an outsider at a later date and receives a sales price of $44,000. The partnership can reduce its $24,000 realized gain on the subsequent sale ($44,000 sales proceeds less $20,000 basis) by the amount of Blake's $10,000 prior disallowed loss ($30,000 − $20,000). Thus, the partnership recognizes only a $14,000 gain on its sale of the land.

EXAMPLE
35

Using a similar rationale, any gain that is realized on a sale or exchange between a partner and a partnership in which the partner controls a capital or profits interest of more than 50 percent must be recognized as ordinary income, unless the asset is a capital asset to both the seller and the purchaser.[61] Note that this provision recharacterizes the gain from capital gain to ordinary income, whereas the above provision disallows a realized loss.

---

[59]§ 707(a).
[60]§ 707(b).

[61]§ 707(b)(2).

10-5 **TAX PLANNING**

Proper Federal tax planning should be used at all stages of entity formation and operations to ensure that the results match the partners' expectations.

10-5a **Choosing Partnership Taxation**

LO.14

Provide insights regarding advantageous use of a partnership.

A partnership often provides tax advantages over a C or S corporation. Partnership income is subject to only a single level of taxation; for partners who are individual taxpayers, the rate can be as high as 37 percent (or 40.8 percent for pass-through income subject to the net investment income tax). Individual partners can deduct up to 20 percent of QBI passed through from a partnership; the maximum effective tax rate on this income is 29.6 percent. Corporate income, however, is taxed at the entity level (at 21 percent) and upon distribution to shareholders as dividends (at up to 23.8 percent for qualified dividends paid to individual shareholders). Partnership income may be subject to high tax rates at the partner level, but (especially for QBI) this tax will generally be lower than the combined layers of tax on corporate income.

Income tax rates, however, don't tell the full story. Self-employment tax or the net investment income tax might also apply. An active "general" partner might be subject to self-employment tax (up to 15.3 percent of income, plus additional Medicare tax of up to 0.9 percent) on the entire distributive share from the partnership, as well as on any guaranteed payments for services. A C or S corporation shareholder, however, will only be subject to employment taxes to the extent the shareholder receives wages from the entity. Distributions from a C corporation (dividends) might be subject to net investment income tax, but for partners or S corporation shareholders, this tax only applies to distributive shares of the entity's actual investment income.

When selecting a legal form in which to conduct business, a complete analysis, then, must consider the expected types and amounts of income for both the entity and the owners, plans to distribute cash flows (i.e., present value considerations), differences between actual salaries or wages that might be paid versus the amounts a partner would be required to report as self-employment income, and whether additional taxes might apply.

The chief disadvantage of partnerships is that the owners might be liable for entity debts (which only occurs with C or S corporations if the debt is guaranteed). However, most partnership entity forms limit the partners' personal liability for entity debts.

For both C and S corporations, income or loss allocations or distributions are required to be proportionate to ownership interests. A partnership, though, may adjust its allocations of income and cash flow among the partners each year according to their needs, as long as the allocation meets the substantial economic effect and capital account maintenance rules discussed in the chapter.

For smaller business operations, a partnership enables several owners to combine their resources at low cost. It offers simple filing requirements, the taxation of income only once, and the ability to discontinue operations relatively inexpensively.

For larger businesses, a partnership offers a unique ability to raise capital with low filing and reporting costs compared to corporate stock or bond issuances.

Concept Summary 10.4 outlines considerations in choosing to use a C corporation, an S corporation, or a partnership as a means of doing business.

Concept Summary 10.4

Major Advantages and Disadvantages of the Partnership Form

The partnership form may be attractive when one or more of the following factors is present.

- The entity will generate net taxable losses and/or valuable tax credits, which will be of use to the owners (subject to loss limitation rules).

- The entity will have individual partners and will generate qualified business income, of which up to 20% can be deducted.

- The partners' distributive shares of income will be taxed at lower individual tax rates (e.g., 10%, 12%, 22%, 24%, 32%, or 35%).

- Any individual partners will be passive or will have sufficient wages from other sources, so self-employment taxes will not apply.

- The owners want to avoid complex corporate administrative and filing requirements.

- The owners want to make special allocations of certain income or deduction items.

- Other means of reducing the effects of corporate double taxation (e.g., compensation to owners, interest, and rental payments) have been exhausted. {Corporate double taxation can result in total Federal tax at rates up to 39.8% [21% corporate rate + tax on the remaining 79% of income at 20% capital gains rates + (potentially) 3.8% net investment income tax].}

- The owners anticipate liquidating the entity within a short period of time. Liquidation of a C or S corporation would generate entity-level recognized gains on appreciated property distributed.

The partnership form may be less attractive when one or more of the following factors is present.

- The tax paid by the individual owners of a partnership is greater than the tax the entity would pay if it were a C corporation. [An individual partner in a partnership could pay Federal tax at up to 40.8% if the income is not QBI (37% top rate plus a potential 3.8% net investment income tax) plus potential self-employment taxes.]

- The entity is generating net taxable income without distributing any cash to the owners. The owners may not have sufficient cash with which to pay the tax on the entity's earnings. (Federal tax on corporate income is only 21% until that income is distributed to the shareholders.)

- The entity is in a high-exposure business, and the owners want protection from personal liability. An LLC or LLP, however, would limit personal liability.

- The entity has already been formed as a corporation, and conversion to partnership status could result in significant liquidation taxes.

10-5b Formation and Operation of a Partnership

Potential partners should ensure that they will not be taxed on gains realized when transferring assets to create the entity. A partner can make a tax-deferred contribution of assets to the entity either at the inception of the partnership or later. This possibility is not available to less-than-controlling shareholders in a corporation.

Partnership allocation rules should be used to the partners' best advantage. Special allocations of income, expense, or credit items must satisfy certain requirements to be acceptable to the IRS.

10-5c Basis Considerations and Loss Deduction Limitations

If a partnership incurs a loss for the taxable year, careful planning will help ensure that the partners can claim the deduction.

A partner can contribute capital to the partnership before the end of the tax year to ensure that there is adequate basis to absorb the loss. If economic conditions warrant, the partnership could incur additional debt. The partner's cash contribution or share of debt increases the partner's basis in the partnership interest. If the loss also meets the "at-risk," "passive," and "excess business loss" hurdles, the loss can be deducted.

In the following year, if the partnership is expected to report taxable income, the partner could withdraw cash or pay off debt equal to the income.

10-5d **Partnership Reporting Requirements**

The partnership return is generally due by the fifteenth day of the third month following the tax year-end (March 15 for a calendar year partnership).

The partners cannot file an accurate return until they receive the Schedule K–1 from the partnership. If a partnership return is filed (and Schedules K–1 provided to the partners) near this filing deadline, individual partners will have only limited time in which to complete their tax returns, and corporate partners will need to file an extension.

If a partner needs to file a return before the partnership prepares the partner's Schedule K–1, the partner can estimate income from the partnership and then file an amended return when the Schedule K–1 is received.

10-5e **Transactions between Partners and Partnerships**

A partner who owns a majority of the partnership generally should not sell property at a loss to the partnership, because the loss deduction is disallowed. Similarly, a majority partner should not sell a capital asset to the partnership at a gain if the asset is to be used by the partnership as a noncapital asset. The gain on this transaction is taxed as ordinary income to the selling partner rather than as capital gain.

The partner should consider leasing, rather than selling, property to a partnership. The partner recognizes rent income (which might be qualified business income, eligible for up to a 20 percent deduction), and the partnership has a rent expense. Alternatively, the partner can sell the property to an outside third party; then the third party can lease the property to the partnership for a fair rental.

10-5f **Drafting the Partnership Agreement**

A partner's distributive share of income, gain, loss, deduction, or credit is determined in accordance with the partnership agreement. In addition, the partner's status as a limited or general partner is often determined by reference to the rights the partner has in managing the entity. While a formal agreement is not always required, an agreement that sets forth the obligations, rights, and powers of the partners would provide some certainty as to the tax consequences of the partners' actions.

REFOCUS ON THE BIG PICTURE

WHY USE A PARTNERSHIP, ANYWAY?

RODERICK PAUL WALKER/ALAMY STOCK PHOTO

After considering the various types of partnerships, Kyle, Maria, and Josh decided to form Beachside Properties as an LLC (see Example 1). On formation of the entity, there was no tax to the LLC or to any of its members (see Example 11). Beachside Properties computes its income as shown in Examples 15 and 17. Beachside determines additional information the members will need (Example 18) and reconciles book and tax income and members' capital (Examples 19 and 20). Payments to the members for services or for the use of their capital are treated as guaranteed payments; the amounts are deducted by the LLC and reported as income by the LLC members (see Examples 16 and 24). The LLC members can claim a qualified business income deduction related to Beachside's operating income, rental income, and Kyle's and Maria's guaranteed payments for capital; the LLC will report additional information the members need to calculate their deduction limitations (see Example 25).

A portion of ordinary income was specially allocated to Maria under the substantial economic effect rules; precontribution gains will eventually be specially allocated under § 704(c); the remaining income is allocated according to profit sharing ratios (Examples 21 to 24). The LLC's income affects the members' bases and capital accounts as shown in Examples 29 and 30.

continued

An important consideration for the LLC members is whether their distributive shares and guaranteed payments will be treated as self-employment income or subject to net investment income tax (Examples 33 and 34).

What If?

What happens in the future when the LLC members decide to expand or renovate Beachside's facilities? At that time, the existing members can contribute additional funds, the LLC can obtain new members, or the entity can solicit third-party financing. An LLC is not subject to the 80 percent control requirement applicable to the formation of and subsequent transfers to a corporation. Therefore, new investors can contribute cash or other property in exchange for interests in the LLC—and the transaction will qualify for tax-deferred treatment.

Key Terms

Aggregate concept, 10-4

Capital account maintenance, 10-6

Capital interest, 10-5

Capital sharing ratio, 10-5

Carried interest, 10-9

Conduit concept, 10-4

Constructive liquidation scenario, 10-33

Disguised sale, 10-8

Economic effect test, 10-25

Entity concept, 10-4

General partners, 10-2

General partnership (GP), 10-2

Guaranteed payment, 10-18

Inside basis, 10-5

Least aggregate deferral rule, 10-15

Limited liability company (LLC), 10-3

Limited liability partnership (LLP), 10-3

Limited partners, 10-2

Limited partnership (LP), 10-2

Nonrecourse debt, 10-32

Operating agreement, 10-3

Outside basis, 10-5

Partnership agreement, 10-3

Precontribution gain or loss, 10-26

Profit and loss sharing ratios, 10-6

Profits (loss) interest, 10-5

Qualified nonrecourse financing, 10-32

Recourse debt, 10-32

Required taxable year, 10-14

Schedule K–1, 10-6

Section 704(b) book capital accounts, 10-25

Separately stated items, 10-5

Special allocation, 10-6

Syndication costs, 10-13

Discussion Questions

1. **LO.1** What is a partnership agreement? What types of provisions does it include?

2. **LO.1** What is the difference between a general partnership and a limited liability company? When might each type of entity be used? Why?

3. **LO.2, 4, 7, 8** Describe how a partnership reports its income for tax purposes. Who makes most elections related to partnership income and deductions? What two theories underlie most partnership tax rules? As an example, contrast the theories underlying the treatments of (1) the business interest expense limitation and (2) the qualified business income deduction.

4. **LO.3** Compare the provision for the nonrecognition of gain or loss on contributions to a partnership (i.e., § 721) with the similar provision related to corporate formation (i.e., § 351). What are the major differences and similarities?

5. **LO.3, 4** How does a partnership calculate depreciation on property that is contributed by a partner? If the partnership incurs additional costs that must be capitalized (i.e., transfer taxes related to changing the title), how are those costs treated?

6. **LO.4** What types of expenditures might a new partnership incur? How are those   Communications costs treated for Federal tax purposes? Create a chart describing the expenditure, the treatment, and the Code section requiring this treatment.

7.   **LO.5** When can a partnership use the cash method of accounting?

8.   **LO.7, 8** What is a guaranteed payment? How is it reported on Form 1065 and its various schedules? How is it reported to and by the partner? Describe ways in which a guaranteed payment for services differs from guaranteed payments for use of the partner's capital.

9.   **LO.7, 8** What is the purpose of the qualified business income deduction under § 199A? How is the deduction calculated? What information does the partnership report?

10.   **LO.8** What is the purpose of the three rules that implement the economic effect test?

11.   **LO.9, 10** Discuss the adjustments that must be made to a partner's basis in the partnership interest. When are such adjustments made? Why?

12.   **LO.11** What is a partner's capital account? Describe how a partner's ending capital account balance is determined.

13.   **LO.12** Describe the limitations that apply to the deductibility of a loss from a partnership. In what order are these limitations applied? Why do these rules exist?

14.   **LO.13** When is partnership income subject to self-employment tax or the net investment income tax by an individual partner?

Communications
Critical Thinking

15.   **LO.10, 12, 14** Write an e-mail to a client describing situations in which the partnership entity form might be more advantageous (or disadvantageous) than operating as a C corporation. Use subheadings and bullet points to highlight your major thoughts.

Computational Exercises

16.   **LO.2** Enercio contributes $100,000 in exchange for a 40% interest in the calendar year ABC LLC, which is taxed as a partnership. This year, the LLC generates $80,000 of ordinary taxable income and has no separately stated income or expenses. Enercio withdrew $10,000 from the partnership during the year.
     Enercio is taxed on what amount of ABC's income? On how much of the $10,000 distribution will Enercio be taxed?

17.   **LO.3** Henrietta transfers cash of $75,000 and equipment with a fair market value of $25,000 (basis to her as a sole proprietor, $10,000) in exchange for a 40% profit and loss interest worth $100,000.
     a.   How much are Henrietta's realized and recognized gains?
     b.   What is the amount of Henrietta's basis in her partnership interest?
     c.   What is the partnership's basis in the contributed equipment?

18.   **LO.3** Wozniacki and Wilcox form Jewel LLC, with each receiving a one-half interest in the capital and profits of the LLC. Wozniacki receives his one-half interest as compensation for tax planning services he rendered prior to the formation of the LLC. Wilcox contributes $50,000 cash. The value of a one-half capital interest in the LLC (for each of the parties) is $50,000.
     a.   How much income does Wozniacki recognize as a result of this transaction, and what is its character?
     b.   How much is Wozniacki's basis in the LLC interest? How will Jewel LLC treat this amount?

19. **LO.3** On January 2 of the current year, Fenton and Myers form the FM LLC. Their contributions to the LLC are as follows.

	Adjusted Basis	Fair Market Value
From Fenton:		
Cash	$ 50,000	$ 50,000
Accounts receivable	–0–	90,000
Inventory	25,000	60,000
From Myers:		
Cash	200,000	200,000

Within 30 days of formation, FM collects the receivables and sells the inventory for $60,000 cash. How much income does FM recognize from these transactions, and what is its character? Why does this result apply?

20. **LO.4** Candlewood LLC started business on September 1, and it adopted a calendar tax year. During the year, Candlewood incurred $6,500 in legal fees for drafting the LLC's operating agreement and $3,000 in accounting fees for tax advice of an organizational nature, for a total of $9,500 of organizational costs. Candlewood also incurred $30,000 of preopening advertising expenses and $24,500 of salaries and training costs for new employees before opening for business, for a total of $54,500 of startup costs. The LLC wants to take the largest deduction available for these costs.

How much can Candlewood deduct as organizational expenses? As startup expenses?

21. **LO.7** Penguin LLC operates a large apparel store with several employees and substantial debt. Each LLC member is active in the business and receives compensation from the LLC. The LLC invests its excess cash in government and corporate bonds, blue chip stocks, and a global mutual fund. It owns property that is subject to accelerated depreciation. What types of information must Penguin accumulate and report on its Schedule K?

22. **LO.7** This year, the Tastee Partnership reported income before guaranteed payments of $92,000. Stella owns a 90% profits interest and works 1,600 hours per year in the business. Euclid owns a 10% profits interest (with a basis of $30,000 at the beginning of the tax year) and performs no services for the partnership during the year. For services performed during the year, Stella receives a "salary" of $6,000 per month. Euclid withdrew $10,000 from the partnership during the year as a normal distribution of cash from Tastee (i.e., not for services).

   a.   What is the amount of guaranteed payments made by the partnership this year?

   b.   How much is the partnership's ordinary income after any permitted deduction for guaranteed payments?

   c.   How much income will Stella report?

   d.   How much income will Euclid report?

23. **LO.8** When Padgett Properties LLC was formed, Nova contributed land (value of $200,000 and basis of $50,000) and $100,000 cash, and Oscar contributed cash of $300,000. Both partners received a 50% interest in partnership profits and capital.

   a.   How is the land recorded for § 704(b) book capital account purposes?

   b.   What is Padgett's tax basis in the land?

   c.   If Padgett sells the land several years later for $300,000, how much tax gain will Nova and Oscar report?

24. **LO.9** At the beginning of the tax year, Barnaby's basis in the BBB Partnership was $50,000, including his $5,000 share of partnership debt. At the end of the tax year, his share of debt was $8,000. His share of the partnership's income for the year was $20,000, and he received cash distributions totaling $12,000. In addition, his

share of the partnership's nontaxable income was $1,000. How much is Barnaby's basis at the end of the tax year? Show your calculations.

25. **LO.10** On June 1 of the current tax year, Elisha and Ezra (who are equal partners) contribute property to form the Double E Partnership. Elisha contributes cash of $200,000. Ezra contributes a building and land with an adjusted basis and fair market value of $340,000, subject to a liability of $140,000. The partnership borrows $20,000 to finance construction of a parking lot in front of the building. At the end of the first year (December 31), the accrual basis partnership owes $8,200 in trade accounts payable to various creditors. The partnership reported net income of $30,000 for the year that they share equally.

Assume that Elisha and Ezra share equally in partnership liabilities. How much is Elisha's basis in the partnership interest on December 31? Ezra's?

26. **LO.10** Jokan contributes a nondepreciable asset to the Mahali LLC in exchange for a one-fourth (25%) interest in the LLC's capital and profits and a 30% interest in the LLC's losses. The asset has an adjusted tax basis to Jokan and the LLC of $60,000 and a fair market value and § 704(b) "book" basis on the contribution date of $150,000. The asset is encumbered by a nonrecourse note of $40,000 that has not been guaranteed by any of the LLC members.

How much of the nonrecourse debt is allocated to Jokan, and what is the amount of Jokan's basis in the LLC interest following the contribution?

27. **LO.12** Tobias is a 50% partner in Solomon LLC, which does not invest in real estate. On January 1, Tobias's adjusted basis for his LLC interest is $130,000, and his at-risk amount is $105,000. His share of losses from Solomon for the current year is $150,000, all of which is passive. Tobias owns another investment that produced $90,000 of passive activity income during the year. (Assume that Tobias is a single taxpayer, there were no distributions or changes in liabilities during the year, and that the Solomon loss is Tobias's only loss for the year from any activity.)

How much of Solomon's losses may Tobias deduct on his Form 1040? How much of the loss is suspended, and what Code provisions cause the suspensions?

28. **LO.13** Heather sells land (adjusted basis, $75,000; fair market value, $95,000) to a partnership in which she controls an 80% capital interest. The partnership pays her only $50,000 for the land.

a. How much loss does Heather realize and recognize?

b. If the partnership later sells the land to a third party for $80,000, how much gain does that partnership realize and recognize?

Problems

29. **LO.3, 8, 9** Emma and Laine form the equal EL Partnership. Emma contributes cash of $100,000. Laine contributes property with an adjusted basis of $40,000 and a fair market value of $100,000.

a. How much gain, if any, must Emma recognize on the transfer? Must Laine recognize any gain? If so, how much?

b. What is Emma's tax basis in her partnership interest? Her § 704(b) book basis?

c. What is Laine's tax basis in her partnership interest? Her § 704(b) book basis?

d. What tax basis does the partnership take in the property transferred by Laine?

e. How will the partnership account for the difference between the basis and value of the property transferred by Laine?

Critical Thinking 30. **LO.3, 9, 14** Kenisha and Shawna form the equal KS LLC with a cash contribution of $360,000 from Kenisha and a property contribution (adjusted basis of $380,000, fair market value of $360,000) from Shawna.

a. How much gain or loss, if any, does Shawna realize on the transfer? Does Shawna recognize any gain or loss? If so, how much?

b. What is Kenisha's tax basis in her LLC interest?

c. What is Shawna's tax basis in her LLC interest?

d. What tax basis does the LLC take in the property transferred by Shawna?

e. Are there more effective ways to structure the formation? Explain.

31. **LO.3, 8, 9** Liz and John formed the equal LJ Partnership on January 1 of the current year. Liz contributed $80,000 of cash and land with a fair market value of $90,000 and an adjusted basis of $75,000. John contributed equipment with a fair market value of $170,000 and an adjusted basis of $20,000. John had used the equipment in his sole proprietorship.   **Critical Thinking**

a. How much gain or loss will Liz, John, and the partnership realize?

b. How much gain or loss will Liz, John, and the partnership recognize?

c. What bases will Liz and John take in their partnership interests?

d. What bases will LJ take in the assets it receives?

e. Are there any differences between inside basis and outside basis? Explain.

f. How will the partnership depreciate any assets it receives from the partners?

g. Do additional considerations arise because of the difference between the basis and fair market values of the property John contributed? Explain.

32. **LO.3, 9, 14** Mike and Melissa want to form the equal MM Partnership. Melissa will contribute cash of $140,000. Mike has cash of $40,000 and land (fair market value of $100,000, adjusted basis of $136,000). Mike purchased the land several years ago as an investment (capital) asset. Mike and MM LLC are trying to decide between two alternatives for Mike's contribution.   **Critical Thinking**

Decision Making

- In Alternative 1, Mike will contribute the land to the LLC. MM will use the property as a § 1231 asset (a parking lot) and then sell it in six years at an estimated $100,000 price. (Disregard any potential improvements to the land.)

- In Alternative 2, Mike will sell the land immediately to a third party and contribute to MM the $100,000 cash proceeds from the sale. MM will use that cash to purchase similar land for $100,000 (also to be used as a parking lot).

Use the following additional assumptions: (1) neither Mike nor MM will realize other capital or § 1231 gains or losses now or in the future, (2) Mike's marginal tax rate is 35%, (3) a reasonable annual discount rate is 3%, and (4) the tax treatment of capital and § 1231 gains and losses does not change in the foreseeable future.

a. For each alternative, when would the $36,000 loss be recognized, to whom would the loss be allocated, what is the character of the loss, and over what time period can the loss be deducted?

b. In these two alternatives, calculate Mike's tax savings each year from deducting his share of any loss allocated to him that year. Use the tables in Appendix F (or Microsoft Excel) to calculate the present value of these savings. Considering only tax savings, as Mike's tax adviser, would you recommend Alternative 1 or Alternative 2? Why? What other issues should Mike consider?

c. How would the results in parts (a) and (b) change if MM were to sell the property in Alternative 1 after only four years? Answer conceptually; do not make calculations.

33. **LO.3, 9, 14** Sam and Drew are equal partners in SD LLC formed on June 1 of the current year. Sam contributed land that he inherited from his uncle in 2013. Sam's uncle purchased the land in 1986 for $30,000. The land was worth $100,000 when Sam's uncle died. The fair market value of the land was $200,000 at the date it was contributed to the partnership.   **Critical Thinking**

Drew has significant experience developing real estate. After the LLC is formed, he will prepare a plan for developing the property and secure zoning approvals for the LLC. Drew would normally bill a third party $50,000 for these efforts. Drew also will contribute $150,000 cash in exchange for his 50% interest in the LLC. The value of his 50% interest is $200,000.

a. How much gain or income will Sam recognize on his contribution of the land to the LLC? What is the character of any gain or income recognized?

b. What basis will Sam take in his LLC interest?

c. How much gain or income will Drew recognize on the formation of the LLC? What is the character of any gain or income recognized? Does Drew have a "carried interest"?

d. What basis will Drew take in his LLC interest?

e. Use Microsoft Excel to construct a balance sheet for SD LLC assuming that Drew's services are completed immediately after forming SD. The balance sheet should show two numeric columns, including the LLC's basis in assets and the fair market value of these assets.

f. Outline any planning opportunities that may minimize current taxation to any of the parties.

Decision Making   34. **LO.3, 14** During the current tax year, Dave and Stu formed the DS LLC with Dave contributing land with a basis of $360,000 and a fair market value of $600,000 at the contribution date. At the end of the year, the LLC distributes $300,000 of cash to Dave. The LLC made no distributions to Stu. Assume that there were no other income or loss transactions for the year that would affect Dave's basis in his LLC interest.

a. Under general tax rules, how would the payment to Dave be treated?

b. Under general tax rules, how much income or gain would Dave recognize as a result of the contribution and distribution?

c. Under general tax rules, what basis would the LLC take in the land Dave contributed?

d. What alternative treatment might the IRS try to impose?

e. Under the alternative treatment, how much income or gain would Dave recognize?

f. Under the alternative treatment, what basis would the LLC take in the land contributed by Dave?

g. How can the transaction be restructured to minimize risk of IRS recharacterization?

35. **LO.3, 9** The JM Partnership was formed to acquire land and subdivide it as residential housing lots. On March 1, 2019, Jessica contributed land valued at $600,000 to the partnership in exchange for a 50% interest. She had purchased the land in 2011 for $420,000 and held it for investment purposes (capital asset). The partnership holds the land as inventory.

On the same date, Matt contributed land valued at $600,000 that he had purchased in 2009 for $720,000. He also became a 50% owner. Matt is a real estate developer, but he held this land personally for investment purposes. The partnership holds this land as inventory.

In 2020, the partnership sells the land contributed by Jessica for $620,000. In 2021, the partnership sells the real estate contributed by Matt for $580,000.

a. What is each partner's initial basis in his or her partnership interest?

b. What is the amount of gain or loss recognized on the sale of the land contributed by Jessica? What is the character of this gain or loss?

c. What is the amount of gain or loss recognized on the sale of the land contributed by Matt? What is the character of this gain or loss?

d. How would your answer in part (c) change if the property was sold in 2026?

36. **LO.4** Tom and Missy form TM Partnership, Ltd. (a limited partnership), to own and   Critical Thinking
    operate certain real estate. Tom contributed land, and Missy contributed cash
    to be used for setting up the entity and creating a plan for developing the property.
    Once a development plan was in place, the partnership sold interests in the partner-
    ship to investors to raise funds for constructing a shopping center.

    The partnership incurred expenses of $30,000 for forming the entity and $60,000
    for starting the business (e.g., setting up the accounting systems, locating tenants,
    and negotiating leases). It also paid $5,000 in transfer taxes for changing the own-
    ership of the property to the partnership's name. The brokerage firm that sold the
    interests to the limited partners charged a 6% commission, which totaled $600,000.

    The calendar year partnership started business in November this year. How are
    these initial expenses treated by the partnership? How much is currently deductible,
    and how is the remainder treated for tax purposes? Show your calculations.

37. **LO.5** Browne and Red, both C corporations, formed the BR Partnership on   Critical Thinking
    January 1, 2019. Neither Browne nor Red is a personal service corpora-
    tion, and BR is not a tax shelter. BR's gross receipts were $22 million, $28 million,
    $31 million, and $32 million, respectively, for the next four tax years. Describe the
    methods of accounting available to BR in each tax year.

38. **LO.4** The Pelican Partnership was formed on August 1 of the current year and   Critical Thinking
    admitted Morlan and Merriman as equal partners on that date. The partners
    both contributed $300,000 of cash to establish a children's clothing store in a local
    shopping mall. The partners spent August and September buying inventory, equip-
    ment, supplies, and advertising for their "Grand Opening" on October 1. Following
    are some of the costs the partnership incurred during its first year of operations.

Legal fees to form partnership	$ 8,000
Advertising for "Grand Opening"	18,000
Advertising after opening	30,000
Consulting fees for establishing accounting system	20,000
Rent, five months at $2,000/month	10,000
Utilities at $1,000 per month	5,000
Salaries to salesclerks (beginning in October)	50,000
Payments to Morlan and Merriman for services	
($6,000/month each for three months, beginning in October)	36,000
Tax return preparation expense	12,000

    In addition, on October 1, the partnership purchased all of the assets of Granny
    Newcombs, Inc. Of the total purchase price for these assets, $200,000 was allocated
    to the trade name and logo.

    Determine how each of these costs is treated by the partnership, and identify the
    period over which the costs can be deducted, if any.

39. **LO.6** Cerulean, Inc., Coral, Inc., and Crimson, Inc., form the Three Cs Partnership
    on January 1 of the current year. Cerulean is a 50% partner, and Crimson and
    Coral are 25% partners. For reporting purposes, Crimson uses a fiscal year with an
    October 31 year-end, Coral uses the calendar year, and Cerulean uses a fiscal year
    with a February 28/29 year-end. In general terms, how is the required taxable year
    determined (no calculations required)? Explain. If the *required* taxable year is, for
    example, October 31, what alternative tax years could the new partnership consider?

40. **LO.7** CL LLC is a manufacturing business and reported taxable income of
    $40,000,000 before interest expense, taxes, depreciation, and amortization
    ("tax EBITDA"), plus $1,500,000 of separately stated investment income. CL incurred
    interest expense of $1,000,000 in connection with this investment income and
    $14,000,000 in connection with its trade or business.
    a. How much interest expense can CL deduct?
    b. How is the interest expense reported on CL's Schedule K?

    c.   What action, if any, is needed by the LLC members?

    d.   How would your answers to parts (a) through (c) change if CL's tax EBITDA was $4,000,000 (plus $150,000 of investment income), its average annual gross receipts for all prior tax years was $10,000,000 or less, and the interest expense amounts were $100,000 (investment) and $1,400,000 (business)?

41. **LO.3, 7, 8, 9** Phoebe and Parker are equal members of Phoenix Investors LLC. They are real estate investors who formed the LLC several years ago with equal cash contributions. Phoenix then purchased a parcel of land.

On January 1 of the current year, to acquire a one-third interest in the entity, Reece contributed to the LLC some land she had held for investment. Reece purchased the land five years ago for $75,000; its fair market value at the contribution date was $90,000. No special allocation agreements were in effect before or after Reece was admitted to the LLC. Phoenix holds all land for investment.

Immediately before Reece's property contribution, the balance sheet of Phoenix Investors LLC was as follows.

	Basis	FMV		Basis	FMV
Land	$30,000	$180,000	Phoebe, capital	$15,000	$ 90,000
			Parker, capital	15,000	90,000
	$30,000	$180,000		$30,000	$180,000

    a.   At the contribution date, what is Reece's basis in her interest in the LLC?

    b.   When does the LLC's holding period begin for the contributed land?

    c.   On June 30 of the current year, the LLC sold the land contributed by Reece for $90,000. How much is the recognized gain or loss? How is it allocated among the LLC members?

    d.   Use Microsoft Excel to prepare a balance sheet reflecting basis and fair market value for the LLC immediately after the land sale described in part (c). No other transactions occurred during the tax year.

42. **LO.3, 7, 8, 11** Marcus and Madison are equal members of an LLC. On January 1 of the current year, to acquire a one-third interest in the entity, Nora contributed a parcel of land she had held for investment. (At this time, the entity will be renamed MMN, LLC.) Nora had purchased the land for $120,000; its fair market value was $90,000 at the contribution date.

A few years later, the LLC sells Nora's land for $84,000. At the beginning of that year, Nora's tax basis capital account was $200,000 and Marcus and Madison's tax basis capital accounts were $170,000.

    a.   How much is the recognized gain or loss? How is it allocated among the LLC members?

    b.   Use Microsoft Excel to prepare schedules that roll the partners' tax basis capital accounts forward from before to immediately after the sale.

43. **LO.7, 8, 9, 10, 11** Amy and Mitchell share equally in the profits, losses, and capital of the accrual basis AM Products LLC. Amy is a managing member of the LLC (treated as a general partner) and is a U.S. person. At the beginning of the current tax year, Amy's capital account has a balance of $300,000, and the LLC has debts of $200,000 payable to unrelated parties. The debts are recourse to the LLC, but neither of the LLC members has personally guaranteed them. Assume that all LLC debt is shared equally between the partners. The following information about AM's operations for the current year is obtained from the LLC's records.

Ordinary income	$ 900,000
W–2 wages to employees	200,000
Depreciation expense	300,000
Interest income	4,000
Short-term capital loss	6,000
Long-term capital gain	12,000
Charitable contribution (cash)	4,000
Cash distribution to Amy	20,000
Unadjusted basis of partnership depreciable property	1,600,000

Year-end LLC debt payable to unrelated parties is $140,000. Assume that all transactions are reflected in Amy's beginning capital and basis in the same manner. Also assume that all AM Products' activities are eligible for the qualified business income deduction, and that the unadjusted basis of assets immediately after acquisition was $800,000.

a. Use Microsoft Excel to calculate Amy's basis in her LLC interest at the beginning and end of the tax year.

b. What income, gains, losses, and deductions does Amy report on her income tax return?

c. Based on the information provided, what other calculations is Amy required to make?

d. Use Microsoft Excel to prepare Amy's tax-basis capital account rollforward from the beginning to the end of the tax year. How does her ending capital account differ from her ending basis as calculated in part (a)?

e. Using the information from parts (a) to (d), prepare Amy's Schedule K–1 as if you were the preparer of AM Products LLC's tax return. Provide all information that Amy needs to the extent you can. For Parts I and II (items A to F), omit any missing information (e.g., last names, addresses, EINs).

44. **LO.7, 8, 9, 11** Barney is a managing LLC member (treated as a general partner) of BG LLC and is allocated qualified business income (QBI) from BG of $800,000. (BG is not a "specified service trade or business.") Barney's Schedule K–1 reflects a $300,000 share of BG's W–2 wages and a $1,200,000 share of BG's UBIA (unadjusted basis immediately after acquisition). Barney's taxable income excluding capital gains is $600,000, and Barney has no income from REITs, publicly traded partnerships, or other qualified businesses. Refer to the QBI discussion in this chapter, the discussion in text Section 2-3, and the flowchart in Concept Summary 2.2.

a. Calculate Barney's deduction under § 199A for qualified business income. Show your work, and show how any limitations are calculated.

b. How does Barney's § 199A deduction affect his (1) cash flow, (2) basis in the LLC interest, and (3) capital account?

45. **LO.7, 8, 9, 12** The KL Partnership is owned equally by Kayla and Lisa. At the beginning of the year, Kayla's basis is $20,000 and Lisa's basis is $16,000. Partnership debt did not change from the beginning to the end of the tax year. KL reported the following income and expenses for the current tax year.

Decision Making

Sales revenue	$150,000
Cost of sales	80,000
Distribution to Lisa	15,000
Depreciation expense	20,000
Utilities	14,000
Rent expense	18,000
Long-term capital gain	6,000
Payment to Mercy Hospital for Kayla's medical expenses	12,000

a. Prepare a Microsoft Excel spreadsheet that could be used in a CPA firm to accumulate KL's information that would be reported on Form 1065, page 1 [Ordinary business income (loss)] and page 4 (Schedule K). Include calculations and subtotals to ensure that the spreadsheet will automatically update if the information changes.

How much is the partnership's ordinary income on page 1? What information is shown on Schedule K?

b. Use the information in part (a) to prepare Form 1065, pages 1 and 4 (Schedule K) for the KL Partnership. On page 1, omit items A to J at the top if the facts do not provide that information. For Schedule K, line 14, assume that both partners are active in the partnership.

c. Add columns to your spreadsheet to allocate amounts to Kayla and Lisa. (For this requirement, disregard the income from self-employment and information related to the qualified business income deduction.) Show the partners' allocation percentages at the top of their columns, and use those percentages in formulas to allocate any separately stated items that should be allocated. (Note that some items are directly assigned to a partner.)

What information will be shown on Kayla's and Lisa's Schedules K–1, Part III? What items will Kayla and Lisa report on their Federal income tax returns?

d. Expand your spreadsheet. Add rows for beginning basis and ending basis below Kayla's and Lisa's columns, and calculate each partner's ending basis in the partnership interest. How do you make this calculation? What is each partner's basis in her partnership interest at the end of the tax year?

e. Consider the results if the partnership's revenues were $100,000 instead of $150,000. What happens if you update the revenues line on your spreadsheet? Are your new amounts correct for the Form 1065/Schedule K information, Schedule K–1 information, and partners' bases? Why or why not? What conclusions can you draw?

46. **LO.8, 9, 12** The RB LLC is owned equally by Romer and Brad. At the beginning of the year, Romer's basis is $40,000 and Brad's is $32,000. RB reported the following income and expenses for the current tax year.

Net ordinary business income (loss) (Form 1065, page 1, line 28)	($64,000)
Long-term capital gains	12,000
Distribution to Brad	(30,000)
Payment to Great Health Hospital for Romer's medical expenses	(24,000)

a. Use the ordering rules of Exhibit 10.2 (and the loss limitation rules), and calculate Romer's basis in his partnership interest at the end of the year. Based on this calculation, what does Romer report on his tax return?

b. Make the same calculation for Brad. What will Brad report on his tax return?

Critical Thinking 47. **LO.3, 7, 9, 10, 11** Suzy contributed assets valued at $360,000 (basis of $200,000) in exchange for her 40% interest in Suz-Anna GP (a general partnership in which both partners are active owners). Anna contributed land and a building valued at $640,000 (basis of $380,000) in exchange for the remaining 60% interest. Anna's property was encumbered by qualified nonrecourse financing of $100,000, which was assumed by the partnership.

The partnership reports the following income and expenses for the current tax year.

Sales	$560,000
Utilities, salaries, depreciation, and other operating expenses	360,000
Short-term capital gain	10,000
Tax-exempt interest income	4,000
Charitable contributions (cash)	8,000
Distribution to Suzy	10,000
Distribution to Anna	20,000

During the current tax year, Suz-Anna refinanced the land and building (i.e., the original $100,000 debt was repaid and replaced with new debt). At the end of the year, Suz-Anna held recourse debt of $100,000 for partnership accounts payable (recourse to the partnership but not personally guaranteed by either of the partners) and qualified nonrecourse financing of $200,000.

a. What is Suzy's basis in Suz-Anna after formation of the partnership? Anna's basis?

b. What income and separately stated items does the partnership report on Suzy's Schedule K–1? What income, deduction, and taxes does Suzy report on her tax return? What additional information is needed?

c. Assume that all partnership debts are shared proportionately. At the end of the tax year, what are Suzy's basis and amount at risk in her partnership interest?

d. Assume that Suz-Anna prepares the capital account rollforward on the partners' Schedules K–1 on a tax basis. What are Suzy's capital account balances at the beginning and end of the tax year? What accounts for the difference between Suzy's ending capital account and her ending tax basis in the partnership interest?

e. Now think about what would happen if Suz-Anna was formed as an LLC instead of a general partnership. How would Suz-Anna's ending liabilities be treated? How would Suzy's basis and amount at risk be different?

48. **LO.7** Burgundy, Inc., and Violet are equal partners in the calendar year BV LLC. Burgundy uses a fiscal year ending April 30, and Violet uses a calendar year. Burgundy receives an annual guaranteed payment of $100,000 for use of capital contributed by Burgundy. BV's taxable income (after deducting the payment to Burgundy, Inc.) is $80,000 for 2019 and $90,000 for 2020.

a. What is the amount of income from the LLC that Burgundy must report for its tax year ending April 30, 2020?

b. What is the amount of income from the LLC that Violet must report for her tax year ending December 31, 2020?

c. Now assume that Burgundy, Inc.'s annual guaranteed payment is increased to $120,000 starting on January 1, 2020, and the LLC's taxable income for 2019 and 2020 (after deducting Burgundy's guaranteed payment) is the same (i.e., $80,000 and $90,000, respectively). What is the amount of income from the LLC that Burgundy, Inc., must report for its tax year ending April 30, 2020?

49. **LO.3, 7, 9, 12** Bryan and Cody each contributed $120,000 to the newly formed BC   Critical Thinking
Partnership in exchange for a 50% interest. The partnership used the available funds to acquire equipment costing $200,000 and to fund current operating expenses. The partnership agreement provides that depreciation will be allocated 80% to Bryan and 20% to Cody. All other items of income and loss will be allocated equally between the partners.

Upon liquidation of the partnership, property will be distributed to the partners in accordance with their capital account balances. Any partner with a negative capital account must contribute cash in the amount of the negative balance to restore the capital account to $0.

In its first year, the partnership reported an ordinary loss (before depreciation) of $80,000 and depreciation expense of $36,000. In its second year, the partnership reported $40,000 of income from operations (before depreciation), and it reported depreciation expense of $57,600.

a. Use Microsoft Excel to calculate the partners' bases in their partnership interests at the end of the first and second tax years. Are any losses suspended? Explain.

b. Does the allocation provided in the partnership agreement have economic effect? Explain.

c. Now assume that on the first day of the third tax year, the partnership sells the equipment for $150,000. The gain on the sale is allocated equally to the partners. The partnership distributes all cash in accordance with the partners' capital account balances, and the partnership liquidates. How will partnership cash balances be distributed to the partners upon liquidation? (*Hint:* First, use Microsoft Excel to calculate the partners' bases in their partnership interests after reflecting any gain or loss on disposal of the equipment. Disregard any depreciation in year 3.) What observations can you make regarding the value of a deduction to each partner?

50. **LO. 9, 10** This year, Callie and Neil formed CN LLC. Callie contributed $300,000 of cash, and Neil contributed real estate valued at $450,000 (basis of $200,000). The property was subject to a recourse liability of $150,000 that was assumed by the LLC but is not guaranteed by either LLC member. Callie and Neil's profit sharing ratios are 40%/60%, respectively, but the loss sharing ratios are 50%/50%. Is the debt treated as a recourse debt or a nonrecourse debt to the LLC members? How is the debt allocated between Callie and Neil? What are Neil's and Callie's bases in the LLC interest immediately after the LLC was formed? Show your calculations.

Communications
Decision Making

51. **LO.3, 9, 10** Paul and Anna plan to form the PA LLC by the end of the current year to produce and sell specialty athletic apparel. Paul and Anna will both serve as member-managers of the LLC and will be active in its operations. The members will each contribute $80,000 cash, and in addition, the LLC will borrow $440,000 from First State Bank. The $600,000 will be used to buy equipment and to lease a property they can use as a small manufacturing facility and a storefront.

The bank has stated that the debt must be guaranteed, and Anna has agreed to guarantee the entire amount. At the end of the year, the LLC also expects to have accounts payable of $40,000 for inventory and supplies.

The LLC's operating agreement provides that all LLC items will be allocated equally. The agreement also provides that capital accounts will be properly maintained and that each member must restore any deficit in the capital account upon the LLC's liquidation.

If the LLC claims 100% bonus depreciation, it will report a loss of about $580,000 in its first year, which the LLC members would like to deduct.

Paul and Anna would like to know how the debt ($440,000 loan and $40,000 of accounts payable) will be allocated between them, and how that allocation affects their ability to deduct the losses. Paul and Anna are single individual taxpayers. If limitations arise, can any adjustments be made to ensure that the losses can be deducted? Consider all potential loss limitations and assume that neither Paul nor Anna will have business income or losses from other sources. Using the format (1) facts, (2) issues, (3) conclusion and recommendations, and (4) law and analysis, draft a memo to the PA LLC tax planning file for your manager's review that describes how the debt will be shared between Paul and Anna for purposes of computing the adjusted basis of each LLC interest. Include any planning ideas that could be addressed to improve the results.

Critical Thinking

52. **LO.9, 10, 12, 14** The BCD Partnership plans to distribute cash of $20,000 to partner Brad at the end of the tax year. The partnership reported a loss for the year, and Brad's share of the loss is $10,000. At the beginning of the tax year, Brad's basis in his partnership interest, including his share of partnership liabilities, was $15,000. The partnership expects to report substantial income in future years.

a. What ordering rules are used to calculate Brad's ending basis in his partnership interest?

b. How much gain or loss will Brad report for the tax year?

c. Will the deduction for the $10,000 loss be suspended? Why or why not?

d. Could any planning opportunities be used to minimize any negative tax ramifications of the distribution? Explain.

53. **LO.10, 12** Jasmine Gregory is a 20% member in Sparrow Properties LLC, which   Communications
is a lessor of residential rental property. Her share of the LLC's losses
for the current year is $100,000. Immediately before considering the deductibility
of this loss, Jasmine's capital account (which, in this case, corresponds to her basis
excluding liabilities) reflected a balance of $50,000. Jasmine has personally guaran-
teed a $10,000 debt of the LLC that is allocated to her as a recourse debt. Her share
of the LLC's nonrecourse debt is $30,000. This debt cannot be treated as qualified
nonrecourse financing. Jasmine spends several hundred hours a year working for
Sparrow Properties.

Jasmine is also a managing member of Starling Rentals LLC, which is engaged
in long-term (more than 30 days) equipment rental activities. (This is considered a
passive activity.) Jasmine's share of Starling's income is $36,000.

Jasmine is a single taxpayer. Her modified adjusted gross income before considering the LLCs' activities is $300,000, and she has no other business losses. The "active
participation" rental real estate deduction is not available to Jasmine. Determine
how much of Sparrow's $100,000 loss Jasmine can deduct on her current calendar
year return. Using the format (1) facts, (2) issues, (3) conclusion, and (4) law and
analysis, draft a memo for the client's tax file describing the loss limitations. Identify
the Code sections, if any, under which losses are suspended.

54. **LO.13** Four GRRLs Partnership is owned by four girlfriends. Lacy holds a 40%
interest; each of the others owns 20%. Lacy sells investment property to the
partnership for its fair market value of $200,000 (Lacy's basis is $250,000).

a. How much loss, if any, may Lacy recognize?

b. If the partnership later sells the property for $260,000, how much gain must it
recognize?

c. How would your answers in parts (a) and (b) change if Lacy owned a 60%
interest in the partnership?

d. If Lacy owned a 60% interest and her basis in the investment property was
$120,000 (instead of $250,000), how much, if any, gain would she recognize
on the sale? How would the gain be characterized?

Tax Return Problem

1. Ryan Ross (111-11-1112), Oscar Omega (222-22-2223), Clark Carey (333-33-3334),
and Kim Kardigan (444-44-4445) are equal active members in ROCK the Ages LLC.
ROCK serves as agent and manager for prominent musicians in the Los Angeles area.
The LLC's Federal ID number is 55-5555555. It uses the cash basis and the calendar
year and began operations on January 1, 2006. Its current address is 6102 Wilshire
Boulevard, Suite 2100, Los Angeles, CA 90036. ROCK was the force behind such
music icons as Rhiannon, Burgundy Six, Elena Gomez, Tyler Quick, Queen Bey,
and Bruno Mercury and has had a very profitable year. The following information
was taken from the LLC's income statement for the current year.

Revenues

Fees and commissions	$4,800,000
Taxable interest income from bank deposits	1,600
Tax-exempt interest	3,200
Net gain on stock sales	4,000
Total revenues	$4,808,800

Expenses

Advertising and public relations	$ 380,000
Charitable contributions	28,000
Section 179 expense	20,000
Employee W–2 wages	1,000,000
Guaranteed payment (services), Ryan Ross, office manager	800,000
Guaranteed payment (services), other members	600,000
Business meals subject to 50% disallowance	200,000
Travel	320,000
Legal and accounting fees	132,000
Office rentals paid	80,000
Interest expense on operating line of credit	10,000
Insurance premiums	52,000
Office expense	200,000
Payroll taxes	92,000
Utilities	54,800
Total expenses	$3,968,800

During the past couple of years, ROCK has taken advantage of bonus depreciation and § 179 deductions and fully remodeled the premises and upgraded its leasehold improvements. This year, ROCK wrapped up its remodel with the purchase of $20,000 of office furniture for which it will claim a § 179 deduction. (For simplicity, assume that ROCK uses the same cost recovery methods for both tax and financial purposes.) There is no depreciation adjustment for alternative minimum tax purposes. While the property is fully depreciated, it is not beyond the end of its depreciable life for purposes of the qualified business income deduction.

ROCK invests much of its excess cash in non-dividend-paying growth stocks and tax-exempt securities. During the year, the LLC sold two securities. On June 15, ROCK purchased 1,000 shares of Tech, Inc. stock for $100,000; it sold those shares on December 15 for $80,000. On March 15 of last year, ROCK purchased 2,000 shares of BioLabs, Inc. stock for $136,000; it sold those shares for $160,000 on December 15 of the current year. These transactions were reported to the IRS on Forms 1099–B; ROCK's basis in these shares *was* reported.

Net income per books is $840,000. On January 1, the members' capital accounts equaled $200,000 each. No additional capital contributions were made this year. In addition to their guaranteed payments, each member withdrew $250,000 cash during the year. The LLC's balance sheet as of December 31 of this year is as follows.

	Beginning	Ending
Cash	$ 444,000	$??
Tax-exempt securities	120,000	120,000
Marketable securities	436,000	300,000
Leasehold improvements, furniture, and equipment	960,000	980,000
Accumulated depreciation	(960,000)	(980,000)
Total assets	$1,000,000	$??

	Beginning	Ending
Operating line of credit	$ 200,000	$ 160,000
Capital, Ross	200,000	??
Capital, Omega	200,000	??
Capital, Carey	200,000	??
Capital, Kardigan	200,000	??
Total liabilities and capital	$1,000,000	$??

All debt is shared equally by the members. Each member has personally guaranteed the debt of the LLC. All members are active in LLC operations.

For purposes of QBI calculations, the LLC is not considered an SSTB, and ROCK's operations constitute an active trade or business. (Note that the § 179 deduction is a business-related expense.) The LLC's UBIA (unadjusted basis immediately after acquisition) equals the total original cost of all leasehold improvements, or $980,000.

The appropriate business code for the entity is 711410. For the Form 1065, page 5, Analysis of Net Income, put all amounts in cell 2(b)(ii). The LLC's Form 1065 was prepared by Ryan Ross and sent to the Ogden, UT IRS Service Center.

a. Prepare a Form 1065, pages 1, 4, and 5, for ROCK the Ages LLC using tax-basis information for Schedules L and M–2. Provide any special information the LLC members might need, including net income from self-employment and information for the § 199A calculation. Attach additional statements if needed.

b. If you are using tax return preparation software, prepare Forms 4562, 8949, and Schedule D.

c. Prepare Schedule K–1 for Ryan Ross, 15520 W. Earlson Street, Pacific Palisades, CA 90272.

Research Problems

Note: Solutions to the Research Problems can be prepared by using the Thomson Reuters Checkpoint™ online tax research database, which accompanies this textbook. Solutions can also be prepared by using research materials found in a typical tax library.

THOMSON REUTERS
CHECKPOINT™

Research Problem 1. Barney, an individual, and Aldrin, Inc., a domestic C corporation, have decided to form BA LLC. The new LLC will produce a product that Barney recently developed and patented. Barney and Aldrin, Inc., will each own a 50% capital and profits interest in the LLC. Barney is a calendar year U.S. taxpayer, while Aldrin, Inc., uses a July 1–June 30 fiscal year. The LLC does not have a "natural business year" and elects to be taxed as a partnership.

a. Determine the taxable year of the LLC under the Code and Regulations.

b. Two years after formation of the LLC, Barney sells half of his interest (25%) to Aldrin, Inc. Can the LLC retain the taxable year determined in part (a)? Why or why not?

Research Problem 2. Your clients, Grayson Investments, Inc. (Ana Marks, President), and Blake Caldwell, each contributed $200,000 of cash to form the Realty Management Partnership, a limited partnership. Grayson is the general partner, and Blake is the limited partner. The partnership used the $400,000 cash to make a down payment on a building. The rest of the building's $4,000,000 purchase price was financed with an interest-only nonrecourse loan of $3,600,000, which was obtained from an independent third-party bank.

Critical Thinking
Communications

The partnership allocates all partnership items equally between the partners except for the MACRS deductions and building maintenance, which are allocated 70% to Blake and 30% to Grayson. The partnership wants to satisfy the "economic effect" requirements of Reg. §§ 1.704–1 and 1.704–2 and will reallocate MACRS, if necessary, to satisfy the requirements of the Regulations.

Under the partnership agreement, liquidation distributions will be paid in proportion to the partners' positive capital account balances. Capital accounts are maintained as required in the Regulations. Grayson Investments has an unlimited obligation to restore its capital account, while Blake is subject to a qualified income offset provision.

Assume that all partnership items, except for MACRS, will net to zero throughout the first three years of the partnership operations. Also assume that each year's MACRS deduction will be $200,000 (to simplify the calculations).

Draft a letter to the partnership evaluating the allocation of MACRS in each of the three years under Reg. §§ 1.704–1 and –2. The partnership's address is 53 East Marsh Ave., Smyrna, GA 30082. Do not address the "substantial" test.

Research Problem 3. Andy has operated his moving company, MoveOn, as a sole proprietorship for several years. In the current tax year, MoveOn placed into service $700,000 of real property improvements eligible for immediate expensing under § 179 (but not eligible for bonus depreciation). Andy also joined with another local mover to form and operate a storage partnership, The Attic LLC. Andy holds a 90% capital and profits interest in The Attic.

This year, The Attic purchased and placed into service $2,900,000 of property eligible for expensing under § 179 (and not eligible for bonus depreciation). Andy has $800,000 of taxable income from MoveOn and a $750,000 share of ordinary income from his 90% ownership of The Attic, both before considering any § 179 expense. Assuming that Andy wants to maximize his current deductions (without sacrificing future deductions), how much can he elect to deduct under § 179? How are any remaining expenditures treated? **NOTE:** For simplification, disregard inflation adjustments that may be in effect, and simply use the information shown in the Code.

Use internet tax resources to address the following questions. Look for reliable websites and blogs of the IRS and other government agencies, media outlets, businesses, tax professionals, academics, think tanks, and political outlets.

Communications

Research Problem 4. Send your instructor a one-page summary of an article posted by a law firm that comments on pitfalls to avoid in drafting partnership agreements. Ideally, use the home page of a firm that has offices in your state.

Research Problem 5. Search for news or current reports related to partnerships, LLCs, or limited partnerships. What entities did you find that are taking advantage of the partnership entity form? In what industries do they operate? What are their gross receipts and asset holdings?

Data Analytics

Communications

Research Problem 6. The IRS Statistics on Income division accumulates information each year on the various types of businesses operating as partnerships. Go to **irs.gov/taxstats**, click "Partnerships," and then click "By Sector or Industry." Open the Microsoft Excel file for the most recent tax year available. For that year, sort and evaluate the data various ways to "dig deeper" into the various types of industries in which partnerships are used.

Write a memo to your instructor that describes some of the things you learned. For example, in which industries do you find the largest numbers of partnerships, the largest numbers of partners, and/or the largest concentration of gross and net assets? What conclusions can you draw? Support your findings with at least one graphic or chart prepared in Microsoft Excel.

Becker CPA Review Questions

1. Gray is a 50% partner in Fabco Partnership. Gray's tax basis in Fabco on January 1, year 4, was $5,000. Fabco made no distributions to the partners during year 4 and recorded the following:

Ordinary income	$20,000
Tax-exempt income	8,000
Portfolio income	4,000

What is Gray's tax basis in Fabco on December 31, year 4?

a. $21,000

b. $16,000

c. $12,000

d. $10,000

2. Nick, Chris, Stacey, and Mike are each 25% partners in Liberty Partnership, a general partnership. During the current year, the partnership had revenues of $300,000 and nonseparately allocated business expenses of $100,000, including a guaranteed payment of $30,000 to Nick for services rendered. Also, during the current year, the partnership had interest income of $10,000 and charitable contributions of $16,000. With regard to activity in the partnership, what should Stacey report on her income tax return for the current year?

	Ordinary Income	**Interest Income**	**Charitable Contributions**
a.	$200,000	$10,000	$16,000
b.	80,000	2,500	4,000
c.	57,500	2,500	4,000
d.	50,000	2,500	4,000

3. Duffy Associates is a partnership engaged in real estate development. Olinto, a civil engineer, billed Duffy $40,000 in the current year for consulting services rendered. In full settlement of this invoice, Olinto accepted $15,000 cash payment plus the following:

	Fair Market Value	**Carrying Amount on Duffy's Books**
10% partnership interest in Duffy	$10,000	N/A
Automobile	7,000	$3,000

What amount should Olinto, a cash basis taxpayer, report in his current-year return as income for the services rendered to Duffy?

a. $15,000   c. $32,000
b. $28,000   d. $40,000

4. On January 2 of the current year, Black acquired a 50% interest in New Partnership by contributing property with an adjusted basis of $7,000 and a fair market value of $9,000, subject to a mortgage of $3,000. What was Black's basis in New at January 2 of the current year?

a. $3,500   c. $5,500
b. $4,000   d. $7,500

5. At partnership inception, Black acquires a 50% interest in Decorators Partnership by contributing property with an adjusted basis of $250,000. Black recognizes a gain if:

I. The fair market value of the contributed property exceeds its adjusted basis.
II. The property is encumbered by a mortgage with a balance of $100,000.

a. I only   c. Both I and II
b. II only   d. Neither I nor II

6. When a partner's share of partnership liabilities increases, that partner's basis in the partnership interest:
   a. Increases by the partner's share of the liabilities.
   b. Decreases by the partner's share of the liabilities.
   c. Decreases, but not to less than zero.
   d. Is not affected.

7. A reduction of a partner's share of partnership liabilities will have what effect on the partner's basis in the partnership interest?

    a. There is no effect on partnership basis.

    b. The same result (basis reduction and/or gain recognition) as if the partner received a distribution of that same amount of cash.

    c. A reduction of the partner's basis by the amount of the partner's share of liability reduction, without regard to the amount of the partner's basis before the liability share reduction.

    d. An increase in the partner's basis by the amount of the partner's share of liability reduction, without regard to the amount of the partner's basis before the liability share reduction.

8. Peter, a 25% partner in Gold & Stein Partnership, received a $20,000 guaranteed payment in the current year for deductible services rendered to the partnership. Guaranteed payments were not made to any other partner. Gold & Stein's current-year partnership income consisted of:

Net business income before guaranteed payments	$80,000
Net long-term capital gains	10,000

    What amount of income should Peter report from Gold & Stein Partnership on his current-year tax return?

    a. $37,500   c. $22,500

    b. $27,500   d. $20,000

CHAPTER

11

Partnerships: Distributions, Transfer of Interests, and Terminations

LEARNING OBJECTIVES: *After completing Chapter 11, you should be able to:*

LO.1 Define terms related to distributions from a partnership.

LO.2 Determine the tax treatment of proportionate current distributions from a partnership to a partner.

LO.3 Determine the tax treatment of proportionate distributions that liquidate a partnership.

LO.4 Describe the rules that apply to property distributions with special tax treatment.

LO.5 Explain the general concepts governing tax treatment of disproportionate distributions.

LO.6 Determine the tax treatment under § 736 of payments from a partnership to a retiring or deceased partner.

LO.7 Calculate the selling partner's amount and character of gain or loss on the sale or exchange of a partnership interest.

LO.8 Describe tax issues related to other dispositions of partnership interests.

LO.9 Calculate the optional adjustments to basis under § 754.

LO.10 Outline the events that could terminate a partnership.

LO.11 Identify the special considerations of a family partnership.

LO.12 Describe the application of partnership provisions to limited liability companies (LLCs) and limited liability partnerships (LLPs).

LO.13 List and evaluate various tax planning considerations related to partnership distributions and sales of partnership interests.

CHAPTER OUTLINE

THE LIFE CYCLE OF A PARTNERSHIP

In the previous chapter, Josh, Kyle, and Maria created Beachside Properties LLC to own and operate the Beachsider Café and to own, manage, and lease the remaining properties in the Shorefront Center. The 10-acre center includes 3 developed acres (including the Beachsider Café) and 7 acres being held for expansion. Josh, Kyle, and Maria own, respectively, 20 percent, 40 percent, and 40 percent shares in the LLC's profits and losses and 5 percent, 47.5 percent, and 47.5 percent interests in its capital. The entity was formed as an LLC to limit the members' liability for claims against the LLC (see Chapter 10).

In the years since the LLC was formed, it's been business as usual: income each year and regular cash and property distributions to the LLC members. Meanwhile, property values have skyrocketed. The LLC interests and the net underlying assets are currently valued at approximately $10 million (including $1 million of goodwill for the Beachsider Café).

Josh wants to develop the remaining 7 acres at an estimated cost of $15 million. However, Kyle and Maria are ready to retire. Their interests are valued at $9.5 million, or 95 percent of the current $10 million net LLC value. Josh has found a group of developers who are willing to invest the $24.5 million necessary for improvements and to purchase Kyle's and Maria's interests.

There are two ways to accomplish the transition and make everyone happy. First, the LLC could admit the new members for $24.5 million of cash and use $9.5 million to redeem Kyle's and Maria's interests (with the remaining $15 million of cash being used for property improvements). Alternatively, Kyle and Maria could sell their LLC interests directly to the new members for $9.5 million; the new members then would contribute $15 million of cash to the LLC for the expansion. Although the two alternatives have identical economic effects, the tax results could differ substantially.

We'll look at several issues related to ongoing operations as well as the buyout. First, on an annual basis, how are the cash and property distributions treated by the LLC? For future planning, what are the tax consequences of admitting the new members to the LLC and *redeeming* Kyle's and Maria's interests? What are the results if the new members *buy* Kyle's and Maria's interests directly and contribute additional cash for development? Which alternative is best for Josh, the new owners, and the LLC? Which alternative is best for Kyle and Maria?

Read the chapter and formulate your response.

n the last chapter, we looked at forming and operating a partnership. In this chapter, we look at "life cycle" issues, such as:

- Routine ("current") distributions of cash or property.
- Distributions that liquidate the partnership or buy out a partner's interest.
- Sale of a partnership interest.

We also discuss the § 754 election (a special election a partnership can make to help keep inside basis and outside basis in balance), as well as partnership terminations, and we introduce family partnerships. At the end of the chapter, we take a deeper look at limited liability companies (LLCs) and limited liability partnerships (LLPs).

11-1 DISTRIBUTIONS FROM A PARTNERSHIP

Distributions don't typically cause the partner to recognize income or gain. Instead, the partner's outside basis is reduced by the amount of cash received. The partnership's inside basis in assets is also reduced. This reflects the aggregate theory, which holds that the partner essentially owns a share of the partnership's underlying assets.

The Big Picture

EXAMPLE 1

Return to the facts of *The Big Picture* on p. 11-1. Assume that Josh's outside basis in his Beachside Properties LLC interest is $300,000. The LLC distributes $50,000 cash to Josh. Josh does not recognize any current gain, but, instead, he reduces his basis in the entity to $250,000 ($300,000 original basis − $50,000 distribution).

This result applies whether or not Kyle and Maria, Beachside's other members, receive a similar distribution.

Each partner eventually receives a "fair share" from the partnership: the capital account maintenance requirements (discussed in text Section 10-3b) ensure that. At the end of the day (i.e., when the partnership liquidates, at the latest), distributions are in accordance with the partners' ending § 704(b) book capital accounts.

LO.1

Define terms related to distributions from a partnership.

11-1a Distributions in General

First, consider a few definitions. A *distribution* is a payment from a partnership to a partner with respect to the partner's ownership interest in the partnership.

Not all payments from a partnership to a partner are treated as distributions. For example, as discussed in text Section 10-4b, a partnership may pay rent to a partner for use of the partner's property, make a guaranteed payment to a partner for services or for use of the partner's capital, or purchase property from a partner.

Current versus Liquidating Distributions

If a payment *is* treated as a distribution from the partnership to the partner, it falls into one of two categories.

- Current (or nonliquidating) distributions.
- Liquidating distributions.

These distributions may consist of cash or partnership property. Whether a distribution is a **current distribution** or a **liquidating distribution** depends solely on whether the partner remains a partner in the partnership after the distribution is made.

Liquidating Distributions A *liquidating* distribution occurs either (1) when a partnership itself liquidates and distributes all of its property to its partners or (2) when an ongoing partnership redeems the interest of one of its partners (see text Section 11-2).

Current Distributions A *current* distribution (sometimes called a "nonliquidating distribution") is any other distribution from a continuing partnership to a continuing partner—that is, any distribution that is not a liquidating distribution.

Kate buys a 25% interest in the KLM LLC by contributing $40,000 cash. Her distributive share of the LLC's income that year is $25,000. Assume that the LLC distributes $65,000 ($25,000 share of profits + $40,000 initial capital contribution) to Kate on the last day of the LLC's tax year. Even though Kate's capital account and basis are reduced to $0, the distribution is a current distribution if Kate continues to be a member of the LLC. If the LLC liquidates or if Kate's interest is liquidated, it is a liquidating distribution.

EXAMPLE 2

Proportionate versus Disproportionate Distributions

Each distribution is also classified based on whether it is proportionate or disproportionate. In a proportionate distribution, a partner receives the appropriate share of certain ordinary income-producing assets of the partnership. A disproportionate distribution occurs when the distribution increases or decreases the distributee partner's interest in these assets. The tax treatment of disproportionate distributions illustrates yet another effect of the aggregate theory: the partner is deemed to own a share of each of the partnership's underlying ordinary-income-producing assets. These rules can be complex.

We'll start by discussing *proportionate* current and liquidating distributions. Then we'll give a brief overview of special rules and disproportionate distributions.

11-1b **Proportionate Current Distributions**

In general, neither the partner nor the partnership recognizes gain or loss when a proportionate current distribution occurs.[1] The partner usually takes a carryover basis for the assets distributed.[2] The distributee partner's outside basis is reduced (but not below zero) by the amount of cash and the adjusted basis of property distributed to the partner by the partnership.[3] As the following examples illustrate, a distribution does not change a partner's overall economic position.

LO.2

Determine the tax treatment of proportionate current distributions from a partnership to a partner.

Payton owns a 25% interest in the SP LLC. On the last day of the current tax year, Payton's basis in the LLC interest is $40,000 and its fair market value is $70,000. On that date, the LLC distributes $25,000 of cash plus a parcel of land (adjusted basis to the LLC is $13,000; fair market value is $30,000). The distribution is not taxable to Payton or the LLC. Payton's $40,000 basis is reduced by the $25,000 cash and the LLC's $13,000 basis in the land. After the distribution, Payton's basis in the LLC interest is $2,000, the basis in the land is a carryover basis of $13,000, and Payton has $25,000 of cash—for a before and after total basis of $40,000. Similarly, the fair market value of Payton's remaining interest in the LLC interest is (arguably) reduced to $15,000 [$70,000 − ($25,000 cash + $30,000 value of land)].

If Payton sells the land and remaining LLC interest on the first day of the next year (the day after the distribution), Payton realizes and recognizes gains of $17,000 ($30,000 − $13,000) on the land and $13,000 ($15,000 − $2,000) on the LLC interest. These gains total $30,000, which is the amount of the original deferred gain.

EXAMPLE 3

---

[1] §§ 731(a) and (b).
[2] § 732(a)(1).

[3] § 733.

Partnership distributions are governed by the aggregate theory; C corporation distributions are governed by the entity theory. In a C corporation, a distribution from current or accumulated income (earnings and profits) is taxable as a dividend to the shareholder, and the corporation does not receive a deduction for the amount distributed. This results in corporate income being subject to double taxation. In a partnership, a partner pays tax when the share of income is earned by the partnership; this income is not taxed again when distributed, so only a single level of taxation occurs.

Cash Distributions

Gain Recognition A proportionate current distribution of cash is taxable to the partner to the extent the distributed cash exceeds the partner's outside basis.[4]

Samantha's basis in her partnership interest is $50,000 on December 31, after accounting for the calendar year LLC's current-year operations. On that date, the LLC distributes $60,000 of cash to Samantha. She recognizes a $10,000 gain from this distribution ($60,000 cash received − $50,000 basis in her LLC interest). Most likely, this gain is taxed as a capital gain.[5]

Liability Reduction Treated as Cash Distribution Recall from Chapter 10 that the reduction of a partner's share of partnership debt is treated as a distribution of cash from the partnership to the partner. A reduction of a partner's share of partnership debt, then, first reduces the partner's basis in the partnership. Any reduction of a share of debt in excess of a partner's basis in the partnership is taxable to the partner as a gain.

Return to the facts of Example 4, except that, rather than cash being distributed, assume that Samantha's $50,000 basis in her LLC interest included a $60,000 share of the LLC's liabilities. If the LLC repays all of its liabilities, Samantha is treated as receiving a $60,000 cash distribution. The first $50,000 reduces her basis to $0. The last $10,000 creates a taxable gain to Samantha of $10,000.

Marketable Security Distributions Treated as Cash A distribution of marketable securities can also be treated as a distribution of cash. The rationale for this rule is discussed later in text Section 11-1d.

Loss Recognition Disallowed The distributee partner cannot recognize a loss on a proportionate current distribution of cash or property. This loss is deferred because tax law typically does not permit losses to be recognized until the loss is certain to occur and the amount is known—which does not happen until the final liquidating distribution is received.

Henry has a $50,000 basis in his partnership interest. On December 31, he receives a $10,000 cash distribution, and his partnership interest basis is reduced to $40,000.

The partnership has fallen on hard times, and Henry knows that future distributions will be minimal. However, he cannot recognize a current loss, even though a loss in the value of the partnership probably exists. The amount of the loss is not fixed and determinable because he still owns the partnership interest.

---

[4]§ 731(a)(1).

[5]§ 731(a). If the partnership holds any "hot assets," however, Samantha will probably recognize some ordinary income. See § 751(b) and the related discussion of ordinary income ("hot") assets and disproportionate distributions later in this chapter.

Property Distributions

In general, a distributee partner does not recognize gain from a property distribution, whether the distribution is current or liquidating. If the partnership's basis in the property is greater than the partner's basis in the partnership interest, the distributed asset takes the lower substituted basis. This ensures that the partner does not receive asset basis that is not "paid for."

EXAMPLE
7

Amanda holds a $50,000 basis in her LLC interest. The LLC distributes land that had a partnership basis of $60,000 and a fair market value of $100,000. Amanda does not recognize any gain on this distribution because it is a distribution of property, not cash. Amanda takes a substituted basis of $50,000 in the land. Her basis in her LLC interest is reduced by the basis she takes in the asset received, or $50,000. Therefore, Amanda has a $50,000 basis in the land and a $0 basis in her LLC interest, and she recognizes no gain on this distribution.

If she later sells the land for its $100,000 value, she will recognize a $50,000 gain, which includes the partnership's $40,000 inherent gain at the distribution date, plus the $10,000 excess value of the land over Amanda's basis in the partnership interest.

There are several exceptions to the general "no gain or loss" rules for property distributions. This discussion is deferred until text Section 11-1d.

Ordering Rules

When multiple properties are distributed, the assets are deemed distributed in the following order.

- Step 1. Cash is distributed first.
- Step 2. Unrealized receivables and inventory are distributed second.
- Step 3. All other assets are distributed last.

Unrealized Receivables and Inventory, Defined **Unrealized receivables** are generally cash basis receivables that will result in ordinary income when collected. In addition, for purposes of the distribution rules, unrealized receivables also include depreciation recapture income that would arise if the partnership sold its depreciable assets (regardless of whether the taxpayer uses the cash or accrual method).

Inventory, for purposes of these ordering rules, includes any partnership assets except cash, capital, or § 1231 assets. The definition is so broad that all accounts receivable are considered to be inventory, although only cash basis receivables are "unrealized receivables."

One often hears unrealized receivables and inventory referred to as **hot assets**. In general, the partnership rules work to ensure that each partner is accountable for his/her/its share of hot assets and the related built-in ordinary income.[6] The basis of the distributed hot assets cannot be increased, and the partner must recognize his/her/its share of ordinary income when the distributed assets are sold.

Basis in Distributed Property and Partnership Interest In a current distribution, the partner cannot **step up** (increase) the basis in distributed property beyond the partnership's basis. However, a current distribution can result in a **step down** (reduction to the property's basis). These potential decreases to basis are determined at each step of the asset distribution. For example, after a cash distribution (step 1), the partner's basis in the interest is recomputed. Then we can determine the effect of a distribution of unrealized receivables or inventory (step 2). If the remaining outside basis at the end of any step is insufficient to cover the entire inside basis of the assets in the next step, the basis in the remaining assets (step 3) is stepped down to equal the partner's remaining basis in the partnership interest.[7]

---

[6]§ 751.   [7]§ 732.

Effect of Ordering Rules

EXAMPLE 8

Lindsey holds a $48,000 basis in her partnership interest. On October 10, Lindsey receives a distribution from the partnership of (1) cash of $12,000, (2) cash basis receivables (inside basis $0; fair market value $10,000), and (3) land (inside basis and fair market value $60,000). Lindsey has a realized gain of $34,000 [$12,000 + $10,000 + $60,000 (values) − $48,000 (basis)].

However, none of that gain is recognized yet. The cash distribution (step 1) is considered first. No gain arises, because the cash does not exceed Lindsey's basis in the partnership interest before the distribution ($12,000 cash < $48,000 basis in interest). It reduces her basis in the partnership interest to $36,000 ($48,000 − $12,000). The receivables (step 2) are distributed next, taking a $0 carryover basis to Lindsey. Her partnership basis remains $36,000. The land is distributed last, (step 3). Lindsey's remaining $36,000 basis in the partnership interest is less than the partnership's basis in the land ($60,000), so Lindsey takes a substituted basis of $36,000 in the land and reduces the basis for her partnership interest to $0.

EXAMPLE 9

Assume the same facts as in Example 8 and that Lindsey sells the parcel of land early the following year for its fair market value of $60,000. She also collects $10,000 from the cash basis receivables. Now she recognizes all of the previously deferred $34,000 gain ($70,000 amount realized and collected − $36,000 basis for the land − $0 basis for the receivables).

In Examples 8 and 9, although Lindsey does not recognize any of the gain she realizes from the distribution, she has a zero outside basis for her partnership interest. If the partnership generates net losses in the following year, she will not be able to deduct them.

When more than one asset in a particular class is distributed, special rules apply, as discussed later under Proportionate Liquidating Distributions.

Concept Summary 11.1 reviews the general rules that apply to proportionate current partnership distributions.

ETHICS & EQUITY   Arranging Tax-Advantaged Distributions

The Sparrow Partnership plans to distribute $200,000 cash to its partners at the end of the year. Marjorie is a 40 percent partner and would receive $80,000. Her basis in the partnership is only $10,000, however, so she would be required to recognize a $70,000 gain if she receives a cash distribution. She has asked the partnership instead to purchase a parcel of land that she has found, on which she will build her retirement residence. The partnership then will distribute that land to her. Under the partnership distribution rules, Marjorie would take a $10,000 basis in land worth $80,000. Her basis in the partnership would be reduced to $0, and the $70,000 gain is deferred. Discuss whether this is an appropriate result.

LO.3

Determine the tax treatment of proportionate distributions that liquidate a partnership.

11-1c **Proportionate Liquidating Distributions**

Proportionate liquidating distributions consist of a single distribution or a series of distributions that result in the termination of the partner's entire interest in the partnership. This section examines the rules for liquidating distributions that arise when the partnership itself is liquidating. If the partnership continues in existence, the rules of § 736 (discussed in text Section 11-2) apply.

No Partnership Level Gain or Loss

In a proportionate liquidating distribution where the partnership liquidates, the partnership does not recognize either gain or loss. In contrast, if a corporation distributes property in a complete liquidation, the corporation recognizes gain or loss as if it sold all of its property at fair market value. This is another example of how the aggregate theory applies to partnerships and the entity theory applies to corporations.

Concept Summary 11.1

Proportionate Current Distributions (General Rules)

Gains and Losses

- Generally, neither the distributee partner nor the partnership recognizes any gain or loss on a proportionate current distribution of cash or property.

- Exception: Gain is recognized if *cash* (and deemed cash) distributions exceed the distributee partner's basis.

Basis in Partnership Interest and Property Received

- The partner's basis in the partnership interest is reduced by the partner's basis in distributed property received.

- General rule: Partner's basis in distributed property equals partnership's basis before distribution (carryover basis).

- Exception: Where the partner's *outside* basis is less than the partnership's *inside* (property) basis, partner's *outside* basis is assigned to distributed property (substituted basis).

Other Issues

- If the partner recognizes gain on a *proportionate* current distribution, the gain is a capital gain.

- Neither the partner nor the partnership recognizes loss on a *proportionate* current distribution of cash or property.

Proportionate Current Distribution Inputs and Calculations

Input the following information and complete the Calculations chart to determine the partner's (1) gain or loss and (2) basis in distributed property on a proportionate current distribution.

Inputs

Line 1 below	Partner's outside basis before distribution	_____
Line 2 below	*Step 1.* Cash and deemed cash distributed	_____
Line 5 below	*Step 2.* Partnership's basis in distributed hot assets	_____
Line 8 below	*Step 3.* Partnership's basis in other distributed property	_____

Calculations

1. Partner's outside basis (input above).	_____
2. Step 1. Cash and deemed cash distributed (input above).	_____
3. **Gain recognized by partner (excess of line 2 over line 1, if any).**	_____
4. Partner's remaining outside basis (line 1 − line 2). If less than $0, enter $0.	_____
5. Step 2. Partnership's basis in distributed hot assets (input above).	_____
6. **Partner's basis in distributed hot assets (lesser of line 4 or line 5).**	_____
7. Partner's remaining outside basis (line 4 − line 6). Cannot be < $0.	_____
8. Step 3. Partnership's basis in other distributed property (input above).	_____
9. **Partner's basis in other distributed property (lesser of line 7 or line 8).**	_____
10. Partner's remaining outside basis (line 7 − line 9). Cannot be < $0.	_____

Gain Recognition and Ordering Rules

When a partnership liquidates, the liquidating distributions to a partner usually consist of an interest in several or all of the partnership's assets. The ordering rules parallel those for current distributions, except that the partner's *entire* basis in the partnership interest is allocated to the assets received in the liquidating distribution, *unless* the partner is required to recognize a loss (see the discussion that follows).

The general ordering and gain recognition rules for a proportionate liquidating distribution are summarized as follows. You should recognize the first two steps from the previous discussion of current distributions.

- Step 1. Cash is distributed first. As with a proportionate current distribution, the cash distribution results in a capital gain if the amount distributed exceeds the partner's basis in the partnership interest. The cash distributed (including "deemed cash," such as relief of the partner's share of partnership debt) reduces the liquidated partner's outside basis dollar for dollar, except that the partner's basis cannot be reduced below zero.

- Step 2. Unrealized receivables and inventory are distributed second. As with proportionate nonliquidating distributions, these assets take a basis equal to the lesser of the *partnership's* inside basis in those assets or the *partner's* remaining outside basis. The partner's outside basis is reduced by the amount of basis assigned to these ordinary income-producing assets.

- Step 3. Here's where proportionate liquidating and nonliquidating distributions differ: for a liquidating distribution, if the liquidating partner has any remaining outside basis, that basis is allocated to all the assets received in step 3.[8]

EXAMPLE 10

When Tara's basis in her LLC interest is $70,000, she receives cash of $15,000 (step 1), a proportionate share of inventory (basis to LLC $20,000; fair market value $30,000) (step 2), and land (basis to LLC $8,000; fair market value $12,000) (step 3). The distribution liquidates both the LLC and Tara's entire LLC interest. The partnership has no hot assets other than the inventory, so this is a proportionate distribution.

Tara recognizes no gain or loss. Tara's $70,000 basis is reduced to $55,000 by the $15,000 cash received (step 1). The inventory (step 2) takes a basis to Tara of $20,000 and reduces her basis in the LLC interest to $35,000. The land (step 3) absorbs Tara's remaining LLC basis of $35,000.

Multiple Properties

When more than one asset in a particular class is distributed in either a proportionate current distribution or a proportionate liquidating distribution, special rules may apply. If a step-*down* is needed (i.e., the partner's remaining basis for the partnership interest is *less than* the partnership's basis for the distributed assets in the particular class), the partner's basis for each distributed asset is proportionately reduced, so as to reduce the differences between each asset's basis and its fair market value.

If, however, in a liquidating distribution, a step-*up* is needed (i.e., the partner's remaining basis for the partnership interest is *greater than* the partnership's basis for the distributed assets in the "other assets" class), the partner's basis for the assets in the class is determined such that the basis amounts ultimately are in proportion to the fair market values of the distributed assets in that class.

EXAMPLE 11

Assume the same facts as in Example 10, except that Tara receives two parcels of land instead of one. The LLC's basis for the parcels is $2,000 for Parcel 1 and $6,000 for Parcel 2. Each parcel has a fair market value of $6,000.

Tara again takes a $15,000 basis for the cash and a $20,000 carryover basis for the inventory. Now Tara has a $35,000 remaining basis that must be allocated to the two parcels of land (step 3). The partnership's inside basis for the land of $8,000 is stepped up by $27,000.

Without going through the detailed rules, the remaining $35,000 basis is allocated $17,500 to each parcel of land. The step-up allocation and ending basis follows the intuitive result because the properties' fair market values are equal.

Loss Recognition

The distributee partner recognizes a *loss* on a liquidating distribution only if both of the following are true.

1. The partner receives *only* cash, unrealized receivables, or inventory. The word *only* is important. A distribution of any other property precludes recognition of the loss.
2. The partner's outside basis exceeds the partnership's inside basis for the hot assets.

The basis of hot assets cannot be increased. Therefore, the step 2 assets take a carryover basis, and the partner claims a loss for any remaining basis in the partnership interest.[9]

---

[8]§§ 731 and 732.

[9]§ 731(a)(2).

Liquidating Distributions with Potential Losses

EXAMPLE 12

When Ramon's outside basis is $40,000, he receives a liquidating distribution of $7,000 cash and a proportionate share of inventory having a partnership basis of $3,000 and a fair market value of $10,000. Ramon is not allowed to "step up" the basis in the inventory, so it is allocated a $3,000 carryover basis. Ramon's unutilized outside basis is $30,000 ($40,000 − $7,000 − $3,000). Because he received a liquidating distribution of *only* cash and inventory, he recognizes a capital loss of $30,000 on the liquidation.

EXAMPLE 13

Assume the same facts as in Example 12, except that in addition to the cash and inventory, Ramon receives an antique desk he used while working at the partnership. The desk originally was purchased at a flea market for $100. Later, it was discovered that the desk was valued at $2,000, but because the desk was held as a § 1231 asset rather than an investment, it was depreciable. By the time the partnership liquidated, the desk was fully depreciated, with a basis of $0 and potential depreciation recapture (a "hot asset" for distribution purposes) of $100.

The $100 of potential depreciation recapture (with a $0 basis) is added to the hot assets in step 2. Therefore, Ramon's step 2 assets include inventory (basis $3,000, value $10,000) and depreciation recapture (basis $0, value $100).

As with the previous example, Ramon's basis is $30,000 after the step 2 allocation. Because the desk is not cash, an unrealized receivable, or inventory, he cannot recognize a loss. Therefore, Ramon's remaining basis of $30,000 in his partnership interest is allocated to the desk.

What can Ramon do with a $30,000 antique desk (valued at $2,000)? If he continues to use it in a trade or business, he can depreciate it. Once he has established his business use of the desk, he could sell it and recognize a large § 1231 loss, which would be treated as an ordinary loss if it is the only § 1231 loss of Ramon's tax year. (Because depreciation recapture is not recognized on a loss, the $100 of potential ordinary income from prior depreciation deductions simply disappears.)

If the antique desk, however, is held as an investment asset, it will generate a $28,000 *capital* loss if it is sold at its $2,000 value. With proper planning, no liquidated partner should be forced to recognize a capital loss instead of an ordinary loss.

If the withdrawing partner later sells distributed inventory, gain on the sale is ordinary income unless the sale occurs more than five years after the distribution.[10] The withdrawing partner's holding period for all other property received in a liquidating distribution includes the partnership's related holding period.

Concept Summary 11.2 outlines the general rules that apply to proportionate liquidating partnership distributions.

11-1d **Property Distributions with Special Tax Treatment**

This section discusses exceptions in which a *proportionate* distribution, either liquidating or nonliquidating, may result in gain to the partner.

LO.4

Describe the rules that apply to property distributions with special tax treatment.

Disguised Sales

As discussed in Chapter 10, a disguised sale is a transaction in which a partner contributes appreciated property to a partnership and soon thereafter receives a distribution of cash or property from the partnership. If the IRS determines that the payment is part of a "purchase" of the property, the partner must report a gain on the deemed sale, and the partnership takes a cost basis in the "purchased" property. See Chapter 10 for additional discussion.

Marketable Securities

A portion of a marketable security distribution might be treated as a cash distribution, resulting in a gain to the distributee partner if the partnership's basis in the security is greater than the partner's basis in the partnership interest.[11]

---

[10] § 735(a)(2).

[11] § 731(c).

Concept Summary 11.2

Proportionate Liquidating Distributions When the Partnership Also Liquidates (General Rules)

Gains and Losses

- Generally, neither the partner nor the partnership recognizes gain or loss when a partnership liquidates with a proportionate distribution of hot assets. This general rule applies to both cash and property distributions.

- Exception: Gain is recognized if cash (and deemed cash) distributions exceed the distributee partner's basis.

- Exception: A partner recognizes loss when (a) the partner receives only cash, unrealized receivables, or inventory and (b) the partner's outside basis is greater than the partnership's inside basis of the assets distributed.

Basis in Property Received

- A partner's basis in distributed assets must be determined in a certain order. Cash is distributed first, inventory and unrealized receivables second, and all other assets last.

- Assets in step 3 take a substituted basis equal to the distributee partner's remaining outside basis.

Other Issues

- For a *proportionate* liquidating distribution, any gain or loss recognized by the partner is usually capital in nature.

Proportionate Liquidating Distribution Inputs and Calculations

Input the following information and complete the Calculations chart to determine the partner's (1) gain or loss and (2) basis in distributed property on a proportionate liquidating distribution.

Inputs

Line 1 below	Partner's outside basis before distribution	_____
Line 2 below	Step 1. Cash and deemed cash distributed	_____
Line 5 below	Step 2. Partnership's basis in distributed hot assets	_____
Line 8 below	Step 3. Partnership's basis in other distributed property (N/A if no step 3 property was distributed)	_____

Calculations

1. Partner's outside basis (input above).	_____
2. Step 1. Cash and deemed cash distributed (input above).	_____
3. **Gain recognized by partner (excess of line 2 over line 1, if any).**	_____
4. Partner's remaining outside basis (line 1 − line 2). If less than $0, enter $0.	_____
5. Step 2. Partnership's basis in distributed hot assets (input above).	_____
6. **Partner's basis in distributed hot assets (lesser of line 4 or line 5).**	_____
7. Partner's remaining outside basis (line 4 − line 6). Cannot be < $0.	_____
8. Step 3. Partnership's basis in other distributed property (input above).	_____
9. **Partner's basis in other distributed property (If line 8 is $0 or positive, enter the amount from line 7; if line 8 is "N/A," enter $0).**	_____
10. **Loss recognized by partner (If line 8 is "N/A," enter amount from line 7; otherwise, enter $0).**	_____
11. Partner's remaining outside basis. Check: line 7 − line 9 − line 10 = $0.	$0

The primary purpose of this rule is to stop the tax avoidance that otherwise would occur if a partnership purchased marketable securities with the intent of immediately distributing them to the partner. As the "Ethics & Equity" feature earlier in this chapter indicated, a partnership can purchase property desired by a partner, distribute that property to the partner, and allow the partner to defer tax on any appreciation inherent in the partnership interest. Because of this rule, the partner and partnership cannot arrange such a transaction with marketable securities.

However, if the securities are *appreciated*, they probably have been held by the partnership for some time and, therefore, were not acquired in anticipation of being distributed to a partner. Therefore, under a complex set of rules, a portion of the marketable security value is reclassified as a property distribution (no gain) rather than a cash distribution (potential gain).

Unless otherwise indicated, the remaining examples in this chapter assume that the partnership is not distributing marketable securities.

Precontribution Gain

Taxable gains may arise on a distribution of property to a partner where precontribution (built-in) gains exist. Specifically, if a partner contributes appreciated property to a partnership, the contributing partner recognizes gain in two situations.

1. The contributed appreciated property is distributed to another partner within seven years of the contribution date.[12]
2. The partnership distributes *any* property other than cash to a contributing partner within seven years after that partner contributed appreciated property to the partnership.[13]

These situations result in gain recognition to the contributing partner, as well as adjustments to that partner's basis in the partnership interest and/or the basis in the precontribution gain property.

EXAMPLE 14

In 2019, Rick contributes nondepreciable property with an adjusted basis of $10,000 and a fair market value of $40,000 to the RTCO Partnership in exchange for a one-fourth interest in profits and capital. In 2020, when the property's fair market value is $50,000, the partnership distributes the property to Tom, another one-fourth partner. This is situation 1 above.

Because the precontribution gain property [$30,000 potential gain ($40,000 value at contribution date − $10,000 basis)] was contributed to the partnership less than seven years before it was distributed to another partner, the built-in gain on the property is taxable to Rick. Therefore, in 2020, when the property is distributed to Tom, *Rick* must pay tax on the $30,000 built-in gain. Rick increases his basis in his partnership interest by the $30,000 gain recognized, and Tom increases his basis in the property received by $30,000.

Note that if the partnership were to sell the property to an unrelated third party for $40,000 in 2020, the result would be the same for Rick. Recognized built-in gains are allocated to the partner who contributed the property, and the partner's outside basis is increased accordingly. See text Section 10-3b.

Situation 2 would arise if a different property were distributed to Rick within seven years. The tax calculations are slightly different in this case. Rick's gain is the lesser of (1) his (remaining) precontribution gain ($30,000) or (2) the excess of the property's fair market value over Rick's basis in the partnership. Exact calculations of Rick's basis in the property and the remaining basis in the partnership interest are beyond the scope of this text.

11-1e **Disproportionate Distributions**

LO.5

Explain the general concepts governing tax treatment of disproportionate distributions.

Disproportionate distributions are another exception to the general nonrecognition rules for partnership distributions. A disproportionate distribution occurs when a partnership distributes cash or property to a partner and that distribution increases or decreases the distributee partner's proportionate interest in hot assets. (Note that the partnership *can* distribute cash and *non-hot* assets in a different percentage than the partners' ownership interests. As long as the partners' interests in hot assets does not change, this would not be classified as a disproportionate distribution. For example, in a two-person partnership, Partner A could receive $10,000 cash and Partner B could receive $10,000 of investment property in a proportionate distribution.)

For the disproportionate distribution rules, hot assets include unrealized receivables (as described earlier) and substantially **appreciated inventory**. Substantially appreciated inventory is inventory that has a fair market value in excess of 120 percent of the partnership's adjusted basis for the inventory.[14]

The taxation of disproportionate distributions is based on the aggregate theory of taxation. Each partner is deemed to own a proportionate share of the underlying assets of the partnership, and each partner is responsible for recognizing and reporting the proportionate share of ordinary income related to substantially appreciated inventory and cash basis receivables.

---

[12]§ 704(c)(1)(B).

[13]§ 737.

[14]§ 751(b)(3)

Section 751(b) maintains each partner's proportionate share of ordinary income by recasting any transaction in which a disproportionate distribution of hot assets is made. If the distributee partner receives less than a proportionate share of hot assets, the transaction is treated as if two separate events occurred: (1) the partnership made a distribution of some of the hot assets to the distributee partner and (2) that partner immediately sold these hot assets back to the partnership. The partner recognizes ordinary income on the sale of the hot assets, and the partnership takes a cost basis for the hot assets purchased.

EXAMPLE

15

The balance sheet of the AB LLP is as follows on December 31 of the current tax year.

	Basis	**FMV**		**Basis**	**FMV**
Cash	$26,000	$26,000	Abby, capital	$13,000	$26,000
Unrealized receivables	–0–	26,000	Bob, capital	13,000	26,000
Total	$26,000	$52,000	Total	$26,000	$52,000

Abby and Bob are equal partners in the partnership. The partnership makes a liquidating distribution of the unrealized receivables to Abby and the cash to Bob. Because the unrealized receivables are a hot asset, Abby has received more than her proportionate share of the hot asset and Bob has received less than his proportionate share. Section 751 recasts the transaction into two separate events. First, Bob is deemed to receive a current distribution of his 50% share of hot assets (basis $0; fair market value $13,000), which he then immediately sells back to the partnership for $13,000 of the cash. Bob recognizes $13,000 ordinary income on the sale, and the partnership takes a $13,000 basis in the receivables purchased. The remaining $13,000 cash received by Bob reduces his adjusted basis for his partnership interest to $0 ($13,000 cash distributed − $13,000 adjusted basis).

Abby receives both the $13,000 receivables the partnership purchased from Bob and her share of the remaining $13,000 unrealized receivables. She takes a substituted basis of $13,000 in the receivables and reduces her adjusted basis for her partnership interest to $0. When she collects all $26,000 of the receivables, she will recognize $13,000 of ordinary income ($26,000 cash collected − $13,000 basis for receivables).

Although the mechanical rules of § 751(b) are complicated, the application of the rules in this example has ensured that each partner eventually recognizes his or her $13,000 share of ordinary income. Bob holds the cash and recognizes his share of the gain at the time the partnership is liquidated. Abby recognizes her share of the gain when she collects the unrealized receivables.

Although most of the problems and examples in this text involve proportionate distributions, be aware that disproportionate distributions occur frequently in practice. The calculation of ordinary income in disproportionate distributions can become extremely complex. These more difficult calculations are not discussed in this text.

LO.6

Determine the tax treatment under § 736 of payments from a partnership to a retiring or deceased partner.

11-2 SECTION 736—LIQUIDATING DISTRIBUTIONS TO RETIRING OR DECEASED PARTNERS

In text Sections 11-2, 11-3, and 11-4, we'll discuss special situations in which a partner leaves the partnership and the partnership (or a successor entity) continues in existence. Section 11-2 covers the situation where a partnership "redeems" the partner's interest. Section 11-3 covers the sale of a partnership interest between a partner and a third party. Section 11-4 covers special situations.

Section 736 applies when a partner's interest is liquidated by an ongoing partnership. For example, in *The Big Picture* at the beginning of the chapter, one alternative is for Beachside LLC to buy out Kyle's and Maria's LLC interests. Section 736 also applies when the partnership must buy out the interest of a successor who inherited an interest from a deceased partner.[15]

For both situations, the buy-out by the partnership is similar in concept to the redemption of a corporate shareholder's stock by the corporation. See text Section 6-1.

---

[15]A successor typically is the estate of the deceased or the party who inherits the decedent's interest.

11-2a General Partners in Service-Providing Partnerships

Section 736 generally is most relevant when the retiring or deceased partner was treated as a *general* partner in a *service-providing* partnership. The rules discussed in this section apply when:

- The deceased or retiring partner was a *general* partner or a partner *treated* as a general partner. For example, a member of an LLP might have been treated as a general partner if that partner had the right, under the partnership agreement, to enter contractual relationships on behalf of the LLP.

- The partnership must be "service providing," which happens if "capital is *not* a material income-producing factor for the partnership."[16] For our purposes, we'll label partnerships as either "service providing" or "capital intensive." (Note that an LLP would likely be "service providing" and an LLC more likely is "capital intensive.")

- The deceased or retiring partner *for purposes of text Section 11-2a* will generally be a person—an individual taxpayer—rather than a corporation, trust, or other entity.[17]

From a practical standpoint, if the service-providing partnership redeems the individual general partner's or successor's interest, the two parties (partner and partnership) negotiate a buyout package. The payments under the buyout package are classified as either § 736(a) *income* payments or § 736(b) *property* payments. It is critical to note that § 736 only *classifies* the payments between these two categories. Other rules determine the *tax effects* of that classification.

For our purposes *assume that all payments from the partnership are in **cash***. However, you should realize that the payments could be in the form of cash and/or other property, in which case the analysis can become sticky.

Income Payments

"Income" payments under § 736(a) typically represent compensation for the partner's share of the partnership's going-concern value. Payments by a service-providing partnership to a general partner are § 736(a) income payments if they fall into the following categories.

- Payments for the partner's pro rata share of unrealized receivables. For purposes of this rule, unrealized receivables are as defined previously for other distributions, except that they do *not* include potential depreciation recapture.

- Payments for the partner's pro rata share of partnership goodwill *if* the payment is "unstated" (not provided in the partnership agreement). If the payment is "stated" (outlined in the partnership agreement), it is a § 736(b) payment.

- Certain annuities and lump-sum payments to the partner. (Not discussed further.)

Property Payments

Any payments that are not § 736(a) payments are treated as § 736(b) property payments. These payments are just what they sound like: the partnership pays the retiring partner for the value of the partnership's underlying assets. Section 736(b) payments, therefore, include payments to the partner for the service-providing partnership's:

- Fixed assets and equipment.
- Inventory, whether or not it is classified as a hot asset.
- Accrual basis accounts receivable.
- Goodwill, if it is stated in the partnership agreement.

---

[16]Capital is a material income-producing factor if a partnership derives a substantial portion of its gross income from the use of capital, such as inventories or investments in plant, machinery, or equipment. Ordinarily, capital is not a material income-producing factor if the partnership's income consists principally of fees, commissions, or other compensation for personal services performed by partners or employees.

[17]Although not specifically required in the Code or Regulations, this convention makes sense given that § 736(a) payments (discussed next) must be made to a service-providing general partner.

11-2b Limited Partners or Capital-Intensive Partnerships

In contrast, if the payment is from a *capital-intensive* partnership to *any* partner *or* from a *service-providing* partnership to a partner treated as a *limited partner*, the entire payment is treated as a § 736(b) property payment.

Similarly, if the redeemed partner is any entity other than an individual taxpayer, the entire payment will generally be a § 736(b) payment. For example, if a joint venture with three corporate partners redeems the interest of one of the partners, the entire liquidation payment will probably be a § 736(b) property payment because the partnership is not likely to be considered a service-providing entity. (Tiered partnership arrangements could have a different result but are beyond the scope of this discussion.)

EXAMPLE 16

The ABC LLP reports the following balance sheet at the end of the current tax year.

	Basis	FMV		Basis	FMV
Cash	$36,000	$36,000	Anne, capital	$15,000	$27,000
Unrealized receivables	–0–	18,000	Bonnie, capital	15,000	27,000
Land	9,000	27,000	Cindy, capital	15,000	27,000
Total	$45,000	$81,000	Total	$45,000	$81,000

General partner in a service-providing partnership. Assume that Anne is an active (i.e., "general") partner retiring from the service-providing partnership. She receives $36,000 cash, none of which is stated in the partnership agreement to be for goodwill. Because the fair market value of Anne's share of the three recorded assets is only $27,000 ($\frac{1}{3}$ × $81,000), the $9,000 excess payment ($36,000 − $27,000) is for unstated goodwill.

The payment Anne receives for her interest in the cash and land is a § 736(b) property payment. This payment is $21,000, consisting of $12,000 paid for the cash ($\frac{1}{3}$ × $36,000 FMV) and $9,000 paid for Anne's share of the fair market value of the land ($\frac{1}{3}$ × $27,000 FMV).

The remaining $15,000 distribution [$36,000 total − $21,000 § 736(b) payment] is a § 736(a) payment, consisting of the $6,000 Anne receives for her share of the LLP's unrealized receivables, and the $9,000 payment for unstated goodwill.

Limited partner in any partnership or any partner in a capital-intensive partnership. If, instead, Anne was a limited partner in (service-providing) ABC LLP, the entire cash payment of $36,000 would be treated as a § 736(b) property payment.

11-2c Tax Treatment of § 736 Payments

As mentioned, § 736 only *classifies* the liquidation payment from the partnership; other provisions govern the *tax treatment*.

Tax Treatment of § 736(b) Property Payments

Section 736(b) property payments (including "stated" goodwill) may *not* be deducted by the *partnership*. Section 736(b) payments to the partner for "nonhot" assets are treated first as a return of the partner's outside basis in the partnership.[18] Once the entire basis is returned, any additional amounts are taxed to the partner as capital gain. If the cash distributions are not sufficient to return the partner's entire outside basis, the shortfall is treated by the partner as a capital loss.[19]

EXAMPLE 17

In Example 16, if Anne is a general partner in a service-providing partnership , the property payment of $21,000 cash includes amounts for Anne's share of land and cash only, neither of which is a hot asset.

- If Anne's outside basis is $15,000, she recognizes capital gain of $6,000 [($12,000 + $9,000) − $15,000] on the distribution.

- If Anne's outside basis is $25,000, she recognizes a $4,000 capital loss on the distribution [($12,000 + $9,000) − $25,000].

- The partnership cannot deduct any part of the $21,000 property payment.

---

[18] §§ 736(b) and 731(a)(1).   [19] § 731(a)(2).

As a corollary (and an easy-to-follow rule of thumb), if the partnership has *no* "hot assets" and if the liquidation payment is in cash (as assumed for our purposes), the partner's treatment of § 736(b) payments follows the proportionate liquidating distribution rules discussed in text Section 11-1c: the distribution results in a capital gain to the partner to the extent it exceeds the partner's basis and a capital loss to the extent it is less than the partner's basis.

If the partnership *does* have hot assets, and because we are assuming that all § 736 payments are made in cash, any portion of the payment related to hot assets is treated as discussed earlier under Disproportionate Distributions. For example, if Anne was a limited partner, the entire payment would be a § 736(b) property payment, and the cash payment in exchange for her $6,000 share of unrealized receivables would be a disproportionate distribution, as shown in Example 15.

Tax Treatment of § 736(a) Income Payments

All payments that are not § 736(b) payments are § 736(a) payments. Section 736(a) income payments are treated either as (1) a partner's distributive share of partnership income or (2) a guaranteed payment to the retiring partner.

Section 736(a) income payments are treated as a distributive share of partnership income (i.e., an allocation of the partnership's income for the year) if the partnership agreement or buy-out agreement states that they are determined by reference to the total amount of partnership income. For example, if the § 736(a) payment must equal 10 percent of ordinary income (or capital gain), then 10 percent of the partnership's total ordinary income (or capital gain) is allocated to the retiring partner and the remaining 90 percent is allocated to the partners remaining in the partnership. These amounts are taxed to the retiring partner according to their character to the partnership (as shown on the partner's Schedule K–1).[20] These payments simply reduce the amount of income/gain of a specific character that is allocated to the remaining partners.[21]

The payments treated as guaranteed payments are fully taxable as ordinary income to the distributee partner and are fully deductible by the continuing partnership. See text Sections 10-3a and 10-3b. [Note that the partner's income *character* might change depending on whether the payments are treated as guaranteed payments or distributive share/special allocations, but the total *amount* of the § 736(a) payment would not change.] The examples in this chapter are structured such that all § 736(a) payments are treated as guaranteed payments and result in an ordinary deduction to the partnership and ordinary income to the retiring partner.

EXAMPLE 18

Continue with the same facts as in Example 16 where the LLP is service-oriented and Anne is an active partner. Anne's § 736(a) payment is $15,000, consisting of a $6,000 cash payment ($18,000 × ⅓) for Anne's pro rata share of the unrealized receivables and the $9,000 payment for unstated goodwill.

Because the $15,000 § 736(a) income payment is not determined by reference to partnership income, the payment is classified as a guaranteed payment. It is included as ordinary income on Anne's tax return and is deductible by the partnership.

Exhibit 11.1 summarizes the taxation results of Examples 16 through 18 for situations where capital is or is not a material income-producing factor (or where the partner is a limited partner). In both cases, assume that Anne's basis in her partnership interest was $15,000 before the distribution.

Conceptually, you should recognize that the characterization under § 736 does not change the partner's overall gain: whether Anne was a general or limited partner (or whether the partnership was service-oriented or capital-intensive), Anne would recognize a total gain of $21,000. This is appropriate because she receives $36,000 cash against a basis of $15,000. However, the character of Anne's income (ordinary income or capital gain/loss) could differ as a result of the characterization of goodwill.

From the partnership's perspective, the classification will determine whether it can deduct any portion of the payment to the retiring partner. The partnership can

---

[20]§ 702(b).   [21]Reg. § 1.736–1(a)(4).

EXHIBIT 11.1	Summary of Tax Results—Examples 16 to 18	

	Tax Character to Anne	Deduction to ABC
General partner in service-oriented partnership.		
§ 736(b) (Example 17)	$ 6,000 capital gain	None
§ 736(a) (Example 18)	15,000 ordinary income	$15,000 deduction
Total gain	$21,000	

Limited partner OR capital-intensive partnership. Entire payment is a § 736(b) payment. The partnership cannot deduct the payment. If there are no hot assets, the partner's capital gain or loss equals the difference between the distribution and the partner's basis before the distribution. If the partnership has hot assets, the disproportionate distribution rules apply.

deduct § 736(a) payments for unstated goodwill or hot assets if the partnership is service-oriented and the payment is to a general partner. It cannot deduct those payments if the goodwill payment is stated in the partnership agreement, *or* if the partner is limited *or* the partnership is capital-intensive.

The Big Picture

EXAMPLE 19

Return to the facts of *The Big Picture* on p. 11-1. Assume that the members of Beachside Properties LLC decide to admit new partners for $24,500,000 and use $9,500,000 of the cash to redeem the interests of Kyle and Maria.

Because the LLC itself is not liquidating, the distribution to Kyle and Maria is classified under § 736. The current balance sheet for Beachside Properties LLC is as follows.

	Basis	Fair Market Value
Cash	$1,000,000	$ 1,000,000
Accounts receivable and inventory	500,000	1,000,000
Land	500,000	6,000,000
Buildings and other § 1231 property	2,000,000	3,000,000
Goodwill	–0–	1,000,000
Total assets	$4,000,000	$12,000,000
Debt	$2,000,000	$ 2,000,000
Capital, Josh	300,000*	500,000
Capital, Kyle	400,000*	4,750,000
Capital, Maria	1,300,000*	4,750,000
Net assets	$4,000,000	$12,000,000

*The LLC members' tax basis capital accounts correspond to their bases, excluding their shares of the LLC's liabilities. The members' bases are not proportionate because the bases of the contributed properties were not proportionate. Also, over time, some LLC income was retained to provide operating cash flows, and some of the members have withdrawn more cash than others.

Capital is a "material income-producing factor" for Beachside Properties LLC. Therefore, in this redemption scenario, the entire $9,500,000 distribution from the LLC to Kyle and Maria is a § 736(b) payment for their interests in the partnership's property regardless of whether Kyle and Maria are "active" members of the LLC and whether the LLC's operating agreement provides for partnership goodwill payments. Kyle and Maria recognize a gain to the extent that this cash distribution (including forgiveness of their shares of the LLC's debt) exceeds their bases in the LLC interests.

Because Kyle and Maria receive cash in lieu of their shares of the LLC's unrealized receivables (including potential depreciation recapture) and inventory, this is a disproportionate distribution. They recognize ordinary income to the extent that their gain relates to these receivables and inventory. The remaining gain is a capital gain.

Because there are no § 736(a) payments, the LLC cannot claim any deductions. Absent a § 754 election (discussed later), the basis of the LLC's property is not affected.

Concept Summary 11.3 reviews the rules for liquidating distributions under § 736.

Concept Summary 11.3

Liquidating Distributions of Cash When the Partnership Continues

1. Payments made by an ongoing partnership to a liquidating partner are classified as § 736(a) income payments or as § 736(b) property payments.

2. Section 736(b) property payments are payments for the liquidated partner's share of partnership assets.

3. Section 736(a) classification is required for certain payments if the partnership is a service provider and the partner is a general partner. These payments include amounts paid for the liquidated partner's share of certain unrealized receivables, certain goodwill that is not stated in the partnership agreement, and certain annuity payments.

4. Section 736(a) income payments are the payments mentioned in item 3 above and any other payments that are not classified as § 736(b) property payments [e.g., a payment that is negotiated to be a §736(a) payment].

5. To the extent that the § 736(b) property payment is for the partner's share of partnership hot assets, the disproportionate distribution rules apply. The partner is deemed to have received and sold his or her share of such assets to the partnership.

6. Section 736(b) payments that are for the partner's share of "nonhot" assets are taxed as a return of the partner's outside basis. Any excess cash received over the partner's outside basis is taxed as capital gain; any shortfall results in a capital loss.

7. Section 736(a) income payments are further classified as either guaranteed payments or distributive shares. In this chapter, the examples reflect guaranteed payment treatment (ordinary income to the partner; ordinary deduction to the partnership).

8. The partnership cannot deduct § 736(b) payments.

11-3 SALE OF A PARTNERSHIP INTEREST

LO.7

Calculate the selling partner's amount and character of gain or loss on the sale or exchange of a partnership interest.

A partner can sell or exchange all or part of a partnership interest. For example, in *The Big Picture* at the beginning of the chapter, one alternative is for Kyle and Maria to sell their LLC interests directly to the new developer. A sale of a partnership interest to a third party is similar in concept to a sale of corporate stock. However, because both the entity and aggregate theories are at work, the partner might be required to split the gain or loss on disposition of the partnership interest into ordinary and capital gains or losses.

11-3a General Rules

Generally, the sale or exchange of a partnership interest results in gain or loss, measured by the difference between the amount realized and the selling partner's basis in the partnership interest.[22]

Liabilities

In computing the amount realized and the basis of the interest sold, the selling partner's share of partnership liabilities must be considered, as discussed in text Section 10-3c. The purchasing partner includes any assumed indebtedness as a part of the consideration paid for the partnership interest, just as the selling partner includes the share of liabilities in the basis in the partnership interest. The concern is that the liabilities will be incorrectly excluded from either the selling price or basis when they should be included in both amounts.[23]

EXAMPLE 20

Cole originally contributed $50,000 in cash for a one-third interest in the CDE LLC. During the time Cole was a member of the LLC, his share of the LLC's income was $90,000 and he withdrew $60,000 cash. Cole's capital account balance is now $80,000, and the LLC's liabilities are $45,000, of which Cole's share is $15,000. Cole's outside basis is $95,000 ($80,000 capital account + $15,000 share of the LLC's debts).

Cole sells his LLC interest to Stephanie for $110,000 cash, with Stephanie also assuming Cole's share of the LLC's liabilities. The total amount realized by Cole is $125,000 ($110,000 cash received + $15,000 of the LLC's debts transferred to Stephanie). Cole's gain on the sale is $30,000 ($125,000 amount realized − $95,000 outside basis).

Stephanie's adjusted basis for her LLC interest is the purchase price of $125,000 ($110,000 cash paid + $15,000 assumed LLC debt).

---

[22]§ 741.   [23]§ 742.

Income Allocation

When a partner sells an entire interest in the partnership:

- Income for the partnership interest for the tax year is allocated between the buying partner and the selling partner (discussed next), and
- The partnership's tax year "closes" with respect to the selling partner.

The closing of the tax year causes the selling partner to report the share of income on the sale date rather than at the end of the partnership's tax year.

The selling partner's basis is adjusted for the allocated income or loss before the partner calculates the gain or loss on the sale of the interest.

EXAMPLE 21

On September 30, 2019, Erica sells her 20% interest in Evergreen LLC to Jason for $25,000. Erica is a calendar year taxpayer. Evergreen owns no hot assets, and its tax year ends on June 30.

On January 1, 2019, Erica's basis in Evergreen is $5,000. Here's what happens to Erica in calendar year 2019. First, on June 30, 2019, Evergreen's fiscal tax year closes, and Erica is allocated $3,000 of the LLC's income for that year.

On July 1, 2019, Erica's basis in the LLC interest is $8,000 ($5,000 beginning basis + $3,000 fiscal year 2018–2019 allocation). Evergreen determines that Erica's share of LLC income is $10,000 for the additional period she owned the LLC interest (July 1 to September 30, 2019). Because the LLC's tax year closes with respect to Erica, she must also report that $10,000 of income on her 2019 tax return. Her basis in the LLC interest is increased to $18,000, and she recognizes a $7,000 capital gain on the sale.

In her calendar year 2019 tax return, Erica reports income from two Schedules K–1 ($3,000 and $10,000), plus her gain on the sale ($7,000). This $20,000 of reported income accounts for the difference between her $5,000 basis at the beginning of the year and the $25,000 she received from Jason.

In general, the partnership may use the interim closing method or the proration method to allocate income among the partners when ownership interests vary during the year.[24] Under the proration method, the variation in the partnership interest is deemed to occur on a given day and partnership income is prorated and allocated on a daily basis to the time before and after the change. Under the interim closing method, the partnership's books are actually closed, and income is attributed to the before and after time periods. Under the interim closing method, the change in ownership occurs on the actual transfer date or under simplifying transfer dates permitted by the Regulations (e.g., at mid-month). Under either method, income for each period is allocated among the partners who owned interests during that period. If partnership earnings are seasonal, the two methods can produce vastly different results.

EXAMPLE 22

Cardinal, Inc., sold its 40% interest in the Owl Partnership to Sparrow, Inc., exactly halfway through the current tax year. Under the interim closing method, the partnership's income was $60,000 for the first half of the year, and its income for the last half of the year was $2,000. Cardinal is allocated 40% of $60,000, or $24,000, and Sparrow is allocated 40% of $2,000, or $800 of partnership income.

Under the proration method, the partnership's income for the year is $62,000, of which 40%, or $24,800, is allocated to the 40% interest. Based on the number of days each was a partner, both Cardinal and Sparrow report income of $12,400 for the current year.

If the partnership uses the cash method for certain items such as interest, taxes, rent, or other amounts that accrue over time, it must allocate these items to each day in the tax year over which they economically accrue and use the interim closing method for these items in determining the amount allocated to a selling partner.[25] Similarly, extraordinary items, as defined, are allocated to the exact time at which they occurred.

---

[24]§ 706(d)(1) and Regulations and 2015 Proposed Regulations thereunder.   [25]§ 706(d)(2).

Tax Reporting

The partnership is not required to issue a Schedule K–1 to the selling partner until the normal filing of its tax return. The partner, though, is required to include the share of partnership income as of the sale date. Consequently, the partner may have to obtain an extension for filing his or her personal return until the partnership provides a Schedule K–1. As you saw in Example 21, the partner may be required to report income from two partnership years in one tax return. The partners are required to report the sale to the partnership, and the partnership may be required to file an information statement with the IRS.

11-3b Hot Assets and Carried Interests

Special rules apply if the partnership owns hot assets or if the partnership interest is a "carried interest" (as defined in text Section 10-2b). If the partnership holds hot assets, the selling partner will incur both ordinary income (loss) and capital gain (loss) on the sale of the interest. Recall that *hot assets* are *unrealized receivables* and *inventory*, which, when collected or disposed of by the partnership, would cause it to recognize ordinary income or loss. When a partner sells the interest in a partnership, it is as if the partner sold the underlying share of the partnership's ordinary income (loss) assets. The primary purpose of this rule is to prevent a partner from converting ordinary income into capital gain through the sale of a partnership interest.[26]

Unrealized Receivables

The term *unrealized receivables* generally has the same meaning as in the earlier discussion of disproportionate distributions. As previously noted, unrealized receivables include the accounts receivable of a cash basis partnership and, for sale or exchange purposes, depreciation recapture potential.[27]

> The cash basis Canary LLP owns only a $10,000 receivable for rendering health care advice. Its basis in the receivable is zero because no income has been recognized. This item is a hot asset because ordinary income is not generated until Canary collects on the account.
>
> Jacob, a 50% partner, sells his interest to Mark for $5,000. If Jacob's basis in his partnership interest is $0, his total gain is $5,000. The entire gain is attributable to Jacob's 50% share of the unrealized receivable, so his gain is taxed as ordinary income.
>
> The result would be the same if the partnership's only asset was fully depreciated equipment with $10,000 of depreciation recapture potential.

EXAMPLE 23

Depreciation recapture represents ordinary income the partnership would recognize if it sold depreciable property. Under the aggregate theory, the selling partner's share of depreciation recapture potential is treated as an unrealized receivable and is taxed to the selling partner as ordinary income, rather than capital gain. (Recall that depreciation recapture is *not* treated as an unrealized receivable for § 736 purposes, discussed previously.)

> Andrew sells his 40% interest in the accrual basis Wren Partnership. The partnership's only asset is a depreciable business asset that it originally purchased for $25,000. The asset now has an adjusted basis of $15,000 and a market value of $30,000. Depreciation recapture potential is $10,000 ($25,000 − $15,000). If Wren sold the asset for $30,000, it would recognize $10,000 of ordinary income and $5,000 of § 1231 gain. Therefore, Andrew recognizes $4,000 ($10,000 × 40%) of ordinary income when he sells his partnership interest.

EXAMPLE 24

The effect of the hot asset rule is that a partner selling an interest in a partnership with hot assets must usually recognize both ordinary income (loss) and capital gain (loss).

---

[26]§ 751(a).

[27]§ 751(a)(1).

Sale of Partnership Interest with Hot Assets

EXAMPLE 25

Ahmad sells his one-third interest in the equal ABC LLP to Dave for $17,000 cash. On the sale date, the partnership's cash basis balance sheet reflects the following.

	Basis	FMV		Basis	FMV
Cash	$10,000	$10,000	Liabilities	$ 9,000	$ 9,000
Accounts receivables (for services)	–0–	30,000	Capital accounts		
Nonhot assets	14,000	20,000	Ahmad	5,000	17,000
			Beth	5,000	17,000
			Chris	5,000	17,000
Total	$24,000	$60,000	Total	$24,000	$60,000

The total amount realized by Ahmad is $20,000 ($17,000 cash price + $3,000 of debt assumed by Dave). If we assume that Ahmad's basis for his partnership interest is $8,000 ($5,000 capital account + $3,000 debt share), then the total gain recognized on the sale is $12,000 ($20,000 − $8,000).

Because the partnership has an unrealized receivable, the hot asset rule applies. If ABC sold the accounts receivable for $30,000, Ahmad's proportionate share of the ordinary income recognized on this sale would be $10,000 ($30,000 × ⅓). Consequently, $10,000 of the $12,000 recognized gain on the sale relates to Ahmad's interest in the unrealized receivables and is taxed to him as ordinary income. The remaining gain of $2,000 is taxed to him as a capital gain.

Note that Ahmad still reports a total of $12,000 of income or gain; the hot asset rule merely reclassifies part of the gain as ordinary income. The effect of the rule is that the partnership's inherent ordinary income is allocated to the partner who earned it.

EXAMPLE 26

Assume the same facts as in Example 25, except that Ahmad's basis in his partnership interest is $10,000. Under these circumstances, Ahmad still has $10,000 of ordinary income because of the unrealized receivables, but his capital gain or loss is zero ($20,000 − $10,000 basis − $10,000 ordinary income). The partner's share of ordinary income potential must always be recognized.

Inventory

For a sale or exchange of a partnership interest, the term *inventory* includes all partnership property except money, capital assets, and § 1231 assets. Receivables of an accrual basis partnership are included in the definition of inventory, because they are not cash, capital assets, or § 1231 assets.[28] This definition also is broad enough to include all items considered to be unrealized receivables. [This is the same "inventory" definition that applies for distribution purposes (other than § 736 distributions).]

EXAMPLE 27

Jan sells her one-third interest in the JKL LLC to Matt for $20,000 cash. On the sale date, the LLC's balance sheet reflects the following.

	Basis	FMV		Basis	FMV
Cash	$10,000	$10,000	Jan, capital	$15,000	$20,000
Inventory	21,000	30,000	Kelly, capital	15,000	20,000
Capital assets	14,000	20,000	Luis, capital	15,000	20,000
Total	$45,000	$60,000	Total	$45,000	$60,000

The overall gain on the sale is $5,000 ($20,000 − $15,000). Jan's share of the appreciation in the inventory is $3,000 [($30,000 − $21,000) × ⅓]. Therefore, she recognizes $3,000 of ordinary income because of the inventory and $2,000 of capital gain from the rest of the sale.

Sale of Carried Interests

As a further exception, if the partnership interest being sold is classified as a "carried interest," any gain on the sale of that interest is treated as a short-term capital gain, unless the interest has been held for more than three years.[29] Carried interests were introduced in text Section 10-2b. Most carried interests are held by investors for more than three years, so this provision likely will be encountered only rarely.

Concept Summary 11.4 outlines the rules that apply to sales of partnership interests.

Concept Summary 11.4

Sale of a Partnership Interest

1. A partnership interest is a capital asset and generally results in capital gain or loss when it is sold.

2. The outside bases of the selling and buying partners, as well as the pertinent selling price and purchase price, include an appropriate share of partnership debt. (The debt amount is the same on both sides of the transaction: buying and selling.)

3. Partnership income or loss for the year of the sale is allocated between the selling and buying partners. The selling partner's basis is adjusted before the gain or loss on the sale is calculated.

4. The partnership's tax year closes with respect to the selling partner on the sale date; the seller reports partnership income at that time, and income "bunching" may occur.

5. When the partnership owns hot assets, the selling partner's overall gain or loss is reclassified into ordinary income or loss and a capital gain or loss. The ordinary portion equals the partner's share of the partnership's potential ordinary income.

6. If the interest is a carried interest, gain on the sale is treated as a short-term capital gain (ordinary income) to the extent the holding period is three years or less.

The Big Picture

EXAMPLE 28

Return to the facts of *The Big Picture* on p. 11-1. Recall that the second restructuring option for Beachside Properties LLC is for Kyle and Maria to sell their interests directly to the new members of the LLC. The new members will pay $4,750,000 each to Kyle and Maria in exchange for their interests in the LLC. The new members will then contribute an additional $15,000,000 of cash to Beachside Properties for the expansion.

Refer to the balance sheet in Example 19. Kyle and Maria receive cash of $9,500,000 (total) plus relief of their shares of the LLC's debt. Their bases in the LLC interests equal their capital account balances plus their shares of the LLC's liabilities. The difference must be recognized as a gain.

The gain is ordinary income to the extent that it relates to Kyle's and Maria's 95% total share of the LLC's $500,000 potential gain on receivables and inventory, plus 95% of potential depreciation recapture. The remaining gain is a capital gain. Absent a § 754 election (discussed later), the basis of the LLC's property is not affected.

11-4 OTHER DISPOSITIONS OF PARTNERSHIP INTERESTS

LO.8

Describe tax issues related to other dispositions of partnership interests.

There are various other ways to terminate a partnership interest, including:

- Transferring the interest to a corporation.
- Like-kind exchanges.
- Death of a partner.
- Gifts.

11-4a Transfers to a Corporation

A partnership might incorporate to secure some of the advantages of a C corporation, to raise capital, to more easily retain capital for expansion, or when one or all partners are ready to retire from the business.

---

[29] § 1061(a).

Recall the controlled corporation rules of § 351 from text Section 4-1. These rules provide that gain or loss is not recognized on the transfer of property to a corporation solely in exchange for stock in that corporation if, immediately after the exchange, the stockholders are in control of the corporation.

Incorporation of a partnership can be structured in various ways, depending on the manner in which partnership assets are deemed to be transferred and whether the corporate stock is deemed to be issued in exchange for partnership assets or partnership interests. Specifics are beyond the scope of this text, but you should recognize that different incorporation methods could have different tax results. In most situations in which an existing partnership is incorporated and continues to operate, § 351 conditions are met, and the incorporation is a nontaxable exchange. If § 351 conditions are not met, the partners recognize gain or loss on the transfer according to standard rules for sales or exchanges.

11-4b Like-Kind Exchanges

An exchange of one partnership interest for an interest in another partnership cannot be treated as a like-kind exchange.[30] These exchanges are fully taxable under the sale or exchange rules discussed previously. However, an exchange of interests in the same partnership is generally a nontaxable event.[31]

11-4c Death of a Partner

If a partner in a partnership dies, several issues must be addressed.

- **Allocation of income.** The partnership's income is allocated between the decedent and the successor in interest just as with a sale or exchange.

- **Successor's basis.** The successor takes a basis in the partnership interest as determined under estate tax rules (generally a fair market value basis). That basis will likely differ from the underlying basis of the partner's share of partnership assets.

- **Automatic liquidation or sale.** The partnership might have a buy-sell agreement in effect that triggers liquidation or sale of the interest on death of the partner. That agreement will govern the tax treatment: if the transfer is structured as a liquidation, § 736 (discussed in text Section 11-2) will apply, and if the transfer is structured as a sale between the partners, § 741 (discussed in text Section 11-3) will apply.

- **Section 754 election.** As discussed in the next section, a § 754 election can remove the disparity that might arise between the successor's basis in the partnership interest and the successor's share of the partnership's basis in its assets.

11-4d Gifts

Generally, the donor of a partnership interest recognizes neither gain nor loss. If the donor's entire interest is transferred, all items of partnership income, loss, deduction, or credit attributable to the interest are prorated between the donor and donee.

The taxable year of the partnership does not close with respect to the donor, however, so the donor reports his or her share of partnership income or loss at the end of the partnership's tax year.

---

[30]§ 1031(a)(2)(D).

[31]Rev.Rul. 84–52, 1984–1 C.B. 157.

11-5 SECTION 754—OPTIONAL ADJUSTMENTS TO PROPERTY BASIS

LO.9

Calculate the optional adjustments to basis under § 754.

A potential § 754 adjustment arises any time a transaction could change the balance between the (total) partners' outside bases in their partnership interests and the partnership's inside basis in its assets. The transactions that could trigger an out-of-balance situation fall into two general categories: (1) sale or transfer of a partnership interest or (2) certain distributions of partnership property.

When one of these situations arises, the partnership can make an **optional adjustment election**, or **§ 754 election**. If this election is made, the inside basis of the partnership's property is adjusted to bring inside basis and outside basis back into balance.

For example, when a partner purchases an existing partnership interest (as in text Section 11-3), the purchase price reflects what the acquiring partner believes the interest in the partnership—and the partnership's underlying assets—is worth. Because the value of the assets probably differs from their inside bases, a discrepancy exists between the purchasing partner's outside basis and that partner's share of the inside basis of partnership assets. (As a comparison, think of the difference between the price a purchaser pays for corporate stock versus the inside basis of the corporation's assets.)

If the § 754 election is made, the partnership's basis in its assets can be adjusted to reflect the purchase price paid by the new partner. If the election is not made, the statute produces some inequitable results.

> **EXAMPLE 29**
>
> A partnership's sole asset is a building with an adjusted basis of $450,000 and a fair market value of $900,000. George buys a one-third interest in the partnership for $300,000 (one-third of the value of the building). The partnership does not make an election under § 754. Although the price George paid for the interest was based on fair market value, the building's depreciation continues to be determined on the partnership's adjusted basis of $450,000, of which George's share is only $150,000 rather than the $300,000 paid for the interest.

A result similar to that in Example 29 can take place when a partnership distributes cash to a partner (as in text Section 11-1) or redeems a retiring partner's interest with a cash payment (as in text Section 11-2) if the cash payments exceed the distributee/retiring partner's outside basis. Without a § 754 election, the partnership cannot increase the adjusted basis of its assets for the excess cash paid to the retiring partner.[32]

The partnership (not the partner) makes the § 754 election. The election is made by attaching a statement to a timely filed partnership return (including extensions).[33] The election applies to basis increases as well as basis decreases. An election is binding in the year for which it is made and for all subsequent years, unless the IRS consents to its revocation. Permission to revoke is granted for business reasons, such as a substantial change in the nature of the business or a significant increase in the frequency of interest transfers. Permission is not granted if it appears the primary purpose is to avoid downward adjustments to basis otherwise required under the election.

A basis adjustment is generally *required* if a sale or distribution occurs and the partnership has a **substantial built-in loss** or a **substantial basis reduction**—even if the partnership does not make (or have) a § 754 election. A substantial built-in loss exists relative to a sale of a partnership interest when the partnership's adjusted basis for all partnership property exceeds the fair market value of the property by more than $250,000, or if the partner would be allocated more than a $250,000 loss if all partnership assets were sold. A substantial basis reduction exists relative to a distribution when the distributee partner recognizes a loss (or basis reduction) of at least $250,000.[34]

---

[32]§§ 743(a) and 734(a), respectively.

[33]§ 754.

[34]§§ 743(d) and 734(d), respectively.

EXAMPLE 30

Refer to Example 29, but assume, instead, that the building had an adjusted basis of $300,000 and a fair market value of $150,000. Assume also that George purchased the one-third interest for $50,000 (an amount equal to one-third of the value of the building). Although the purchase price was based on fair market value, George obtains the benefit of *double* depreciation deductions because these deductions are calculated on the adjusted basis of the depreciable property ($300,000), which is twice the property's market value.

If the partnership has a § 754 election in effect, the downward basis adjustment is required. If there is no § 754 election in effect, it is unlikely the partnership would make one, because the result is disadvantageous. There is no substantial built-in loss, so the mandatory adjustment does not apply: the overall depreciation in the partnership's property is only $150,000 ($300,000 adjusted basis − $150,000 fair market value).

11-5a Adjustment: Sale or Exchange of an Interest

If the § 754 optional adjustment-to-basis election is in effect and a partner's interest is sold, exchanged, or inherited, the partnership adjusts the basis of its assets as follows.[35] The step-up or step-down is allocated among all the partnership's assets (except cash).

Purchaser's (transferee's) outside basis in the partnership	$ xxx
Less: Purchaser's (transferee's) share of the inside basis of all partnership property	(xxx)
Adjustment	$ xxx

The adjustment affects the basis of partnership property with respect to the transferee partner only, and all subsequent income, deductions, gains, and losses related to the step-up or step-down are allocated to the transferee. Any portion of the step-up that relates to depreciable property is depreciated as if it were a newly acquired asset. The transferee partner, therefore, shares in the depreciation taken by the partnership on the original asset and, in addition, reports *all* of the depreciation taken on the step-up basis created by the optional adjustment.

EXAMPLE 31

Keith is a member of the KLM LLC, and all members have equal interests in capital and profits. The LLC has made an optional adjustment-to-basis election. Keith sells his interest to Sean for $76,000. The balance sheet of the LLC immediately before the sale shows the following.

	Basis	FMV		Basis	FMV
Cash	$ 15,000	$ 15,000	Capital accounts		
Depreciable assets	150,000	213,000	Keith	$ 55,000	$ 76,000
			Leah	55,000	76,000
			Morgan	55,000	76,000
Total	$165,000	$228,000	Total	$165,000	$228,000

The adjustment is the difference between the basis of Sean's interest in the LLC (the $76,000 paid) and his share of the adjusted basis of the LLC's property ($55,000, or $165,000 × ⅓). Therefore, the optional adjustment that is added to the basis of the LLC's property is $21,000.

The $21,000 basis increase is allocated to the LLC's assets (except cash). In this case, KLM owns only fixed assets, so the step-up is treated as a new depreciable asset. Depreciation on the step-up is allocated to Sean.

If the LLC were to immediately sell the depreciable property for $213,000, the gain allocated to Leah and Morgan would be $21,000 ($71,000 share of sales price less $50,000 basis), but the gain allocated to Sean would be $0 [$71,000 share of sales price less $71,000 basis ($50,000 original basis + $21,000 step-up)].

---

[35]§§ 743(b), 755.

11-5b Adjustment: Partnership Distributions

Optional adjustments to basis are also available to the partnership when property is distributed to a partner. If a § 754 optional adjustment-to-basis election is in effect, the basis of partnership property is *increased* by:[36]

- Any gain recognized by a distributee partner (e.g., when a cash distribution exceeds the partner's basis).
- Any *step-down* in the basis of property received by the distributee partner (i.e., the excess of the partnership's adjusted basis for any distributed property over the adjusted basis of that property in the hands of the distributee partner).

Conversely, the basis of partnership property is *decreased* by:

- Any loss recognized by a distributee partner in a liquidating distribution (e.g., under § 736).
- Any *step-up* in the basis of property received by the distributee partner (i.e., the excess of the distributee partner's adjusted basis of any nonhot assets received in a distribution over the basis of that property to the partnership).

The basis adjustments created by distributions affect the bases of all remaining partnership properties. Therefore, any depreciation deductions taken on such basis adjustments are allocated to all partners remaining in the partnership after the distribution. The *partnership* also takes these basis adjustments into account in determining any gains or losses on subsequent sales of partnership properties.

Basis Adjustments Related to Partnership Distributions

Ryan has a basis of $50,000 in his partnership interest and receives a building with an adjusted basis to the partnership of $120,000 in termination of his interest. (Assume that the partnership has no hot assets.) The building's basis in Ryan's hands is a substituted basis of $50,000 under the proportionate liquidating distribution rules. If an optional adjustment-to-basis election is in effect, the partnership increases the basis of its remaining property by $70,000 and the depreciation expense related to this step-up is allocated to all remaining partners in the partnership.

Partnership's adjusted basis in distributed property	$120,000
Less: Distributee's basis in distributed property	(50,000)
Increase	$ 70,000

EXAMPLE 32

Assume the same facts as in Example 32, except that the partnership's basis in the building was $40,000. Ryan's basis in the building is still $50,000, and the partnership reduces the basis of its remaining property by $10,000.

Distributee's basis in distributed property	$ 50,000
Less: Partnership's adjusted basis in distributed property	(40,000)
Decrease	$ 10,000

EXAMPLE 33

Although these rules may seem confusing at first reading, understanding the theory on which they are based helps to clarify the situation. Section 734(b) assumes that the inside basis for all partnership assets equals the outside basis for all of the partners' interests immediately before the distribution. When this equality exists both before and after a distribution, no adjustment to the basis of partnership property

---

[36]§ 734(b).

is necessary. However, when the equality does not exist after the distribution, an adjustment can bring the inside and outside bases back into equality. This is the adjustment that is made by the two increases and the two decreases described in the bulleted lists above.

Assume that the Mockingbird LLC has an inside basis of $12,000 for its assets, which have a fair market value of $15,000. Aaron, Bill, and Chelsea each have outside bases of $4,000 for their LLC interests. If the LLC liquidates Aaron's interest with a $5,000 cash distribution, the resulting balance sheet is unbalanced.

	Inside (Assets)		Outside (Capital)
Before	$12,000	=	$12,000
Distribution	(5,000)	≠	(4,000)
After	$ 7,000	≠	$ 8,000

This unbalanced situation can be eliminated by adding $1,000 to the inside basis. Note that this is the same amount as the gain that Aaron recognizes on the distribution ($5,000 cash − $4,000 outside basis = $1,000 gain). Therefore, by adding the amount of Aaron's gain to the inside basis of the LLC's assets, the inside basis = outside basis formula is back in balance for the remaining LLC members.

Inside (Assets)		Outside (Capital)
$7,000	≠	$8,000
+1,000		
$8,000	=	$8,000

If the LLC liquidates Aaron's interest with a distribution of land having a $5,000 inside basis, the same unbalanced situation occurs. Although this transaction does not create any recognized gain for Aaron, the $1,000 optional adjustment is the excess of the $5,000 inside basis of the distributed property over the $4,000 substituted basis of that property to Aaron.

The Big Picture

Return to the facts of *The Big Picture* on p. 11-1 and Beachside's balance sheet in Example 19. Recall that the members of Beachside Properties LLC are considering two restructuring options. For either option, Beachside Properties could make a § 754 election and record an adjustment to the basis of the LLC's property.

- *Step-up related to sale of interests.* On a sale of the interests to the new LLC members, the step-up would equal the difference between the $9,500,000 purchase price and Kyle's and Maria's share of the inside basis of the LLC's property. This step-up of approximately $7,600,000 [$9,500,000 − (95% × $2,000,000 net assets)] would be allocated to the various LLC properties under the rules of § 755 (not discussed in this chapter). Deductions related to the step-up, such as depreciation, would be allocated to the new developer group.

- *Step-up related to distribution in liquidation of the LLC members' interests.* If the LLC redeems the interests of Kyle and Maria, the LLC can step up the bases of its remaining assets by the amount of gain recognized by Kyle and Maria. This step-up is approximately $7,800,000 [$9,500,000 distribution − $1,700,000 total basis in LLC interests (Kyle's basis of $400,000 + Maria's basis of $1,300,000)] and benefits all of the remaining members of the LLC (Josh and the new developer group).

continued

Note that the step-up and treatment differ depending on whether there is a sale or redemption, because Kyle's and Maria's share of the basis of the assets differs from their basis in the LLC interests and because of the difference in makeup of the member group to whom the resulting adjustments are allocated.

Concept Summary 11.5 outlines the rules related to basis adjustments under § 754.

Concept Summary 11.5

Basis Adjustments under § 754

1. A partnership can make a § 754 election if a transaction would cause the partnership's inside basis in assets to differ from the sum of the partners' outside bases in their partnership interests.

2. This situation could arise upon the sale of a partnership interest, the death of a partner, or a distribution of cash or property to a partner.

3. The § 754 election adjusts the partnership's basis in its assets to rebalance inside basis and outside basis.

4. A step-up in the partnership's asset basis arises when a purchasing partner pays more for an interest than the selling partner's share of the partnership's basis in its assets, when a distributee partner recognizes gain, or when a distributee partner takes a lower basis than the partnership had in distributed property.

5. A step-down in the partnership's asset basis arises when a purchasing partner pays less for the interest than the selling partner's share of the partnership's basis in its assets, when a distributee partner recognizes loss, or when a distributee partner takes a higher basis than the partnership had in distributed property.

6. An adjustment might be *required* (whether or not a § 754 election is in effect):
   - Upon sale of a partnership interest if the partnership has a "substantial built-in loss" (e.g., the partnership's basis in its assets exceeds their value by more than $250,000 or the partner would be allocated a loss of more than $250,000), or
   - Upon distribution of property, if there is a "substantial basis reduction" (i.e., a distributee partner recognizes more than a $250,000 loss or a distribution results in the partner having more than a $250,000 increase in the basis of distributed assets).

7. For a § 754 adjustment arising from sale of an interest, the resulting step-up or step-down is allocated to the acquiring partner.

8. For a § 754 election arising from a distribution of property, the resulting step-up or step-down is allocated to all remaining partners.

9. The partnership (not the partner) makes the election. It is binding for that year and all future years for which such transactions arise, unless the IRS consents to a revocation.

11-6 TERMINATION OF A PARTNERSHIP

Outline the events that could terminate a partnership.

When does a partnership's final tax year end? Technically, it ends when no part of the business continues to be carried on by any of the partners in a partnership.

The partnership terminates and its tax year closes when the partnership incorporates or when one partner in a two-party partnership buys out the other partner, thereby creating a sole proprietorship. A termination also occurs when the partnership ceases operations and liquidates.

The partnership taxable year usually does not close upon the death of a partner or upon the liquidation of a partner's interest, unless there is only one partner remaining.[37]

The partnership year does not close upon the entry of a new partner to the partnership. It also does not close upon the sale or exchange of an existing partnership interest.

When the partnership terminates, it distributes its assets as described in text Section 11-1c (Proportionate Liquidating Distributions) or 11-1e (Disproportionate Distributions).

---

[37]§ 706(c)(1).

Return to the facts of *The Big Picture* on p. 11-1. Before the sale or redemption, Kyle's and Maria's combined interests equal 95% of the LLC's capital and 80% of the LLC's profits interests. Whether the interests are sold to the new developer group or Beachside redeems the interests under § 736, the partnership continues in existence after the transaction.

LO.11

Identify the special considerations of a family partnership.

11-7 OTHER ISSUES

Partnership rules also generally apply to family partnerships, limited liability companies, and limited liability partnerships. This section examines the special considerations applicable to these entities.[38]

11-7a Family Partnerships

Family partnerships are owned and controlled primarily by members of the same family. For this purpose, "family" includes the individual's spouse, ancestors, lineal descendants, and trusts established for the benefit of any of those parties; it does not include siblings. Often, one primary reason for establishing a family partnership is the desire to save taxes. If the parents are in higher marginal tax brackets than the children, it would be nice if family tax dollars could be saved by allocating some of the partnership income to the children. However, rules are in place to minimize opportunities for tax avoidance.

Capital versus Services

A family member is recognized as a partner only in the following cases.

- Capital is a material income-producing factor in the partnership,[39] and the family member's capital interest is acquired in a bona fide transaction (even if by gift or purchase from another family member) in which both ownership and control over the interest are received.

- Capital is not a material income-producing factor, but the family member contributes substantial or vital services.

Gift of Capital Interest

If a family member receives a gift of a capital interest in a family partnership in which capital is a material income-producing factor, only part of the income may be allocated to this interest. First, the donor of the interest is allocated an amount of partnership income that represents reasonable compensation for services to the partnership. Then the remaining income is divided among the partners in accordance with their capital interests in the partnership. An interest purchased by one family member from another is considered to be created by gift for this purpose.[40]

Note that allocations to minor children might be subject to the "kiddie tax rules," which could require the income to be taxed at the tax rates applicable to estates and trusts, except to the extent the child performs services for the partnership. These rules are beyond the scope of this chapter.

---

[38]See § 704(e) for rules related to family partnerships.

[39]See footnote 16 for the definition of capital as a material income-producing factor.

[40]§ 704(e)(3).

GLOBAL TAX ISSUES Sale of Global Partnership Interests

In the past, the IRS and the Tax Court differed on whether partnership property sited in the United States but owned by a foreign partnership was "effectively connected with a U.S. trade or business." The issue is whether taxation is determined at the entity level (based on the domicile of the partnership) or at the property level (based on the underlying assets owned by the partnership). If the property (either the partnership interest or underlying property) is "effectively connected," then income from the sale of the property is subject to U.S. taxation and U.S. withholding.

A new provision in the tax law solves the issue by adopting a property-level analysis. It requires that, if a partnership interest owned by a foreign partner is sold, a portion of the gain or loss on the sale is treated as "effectively connected" income. The partnership determines the selling partner's distributive share of the gain or loss that would arise if all partnership assets were sold at fair market value. The portion of the gain or loss arising from U.S. assets is effectively connected with a U.S. trade or business.

The buyer of a partnership interest must either ascertain that the seller is a U.S. taxpayer or must withhold 10 percent of the selling price as prepayment of the non-U.S. seller's estimated tax on the sale.

Sources: IRC §§ 864(c)(8), effective for sales and exchanges on or after November 27, 2017, and 1446(f), effective for sales, exch66d dispositions of property after 2017.

> A partnership in which a parent transferred a 50% interest by gift to a child generated a profit of $90,000. Capital is a material income-producing factor. The parent performed services valued at $20,000. The child performed no services. Under these circumstances, $20,000 is allocated to the parent as compensation. Of the remaining $70,000 of income attributable to capital, at least 50%, or $35,000, is allocated to the parent. Depending on the child's age, income allocated to the child (e.g., $35,000) might be taxed at estate and gift tax rates because the child performed no services.

EXAMPLE 37

11-7b Limited Liability Companies

The limited liability company combines partnership taxation with limited personal liability for all owners of the entity.

LO.12

Describe the application of partnership provisions to limited liability companies (LLCs) and limited liability partnerships (LLPs).

Taxation of LLCs

A properly structured LLC with two or more owners is generally taxed as a partnership. Because none of the LLC members are personally liable for any debts of the entity, the LLC is effectively treated as a limited partnership with no general partners. As described in Chapter 10, this results in unusual application of partnership taxation rules in areas such as allocation of liabilities to the LLC members, inclusion or exclusion of debt for at-risk purposes, passive or active status of a member for passive activity loss purposes, and determination of a member's liability for self-employment tax.

Converting to an LLC

A partnership can convert to an LLC with few, if any, tax ramifications: the old elections of the partnership continue, and the partners retain their bases and ownership interests in the new entity. However, a C or S corporation that reorganizes as an LLC is treated as having liquidated prior to forming the new entity. The transaction is taxable to both the corporation and the shareholders.

Advantages of an LLC

An LLC offers certain advantages over a limited partnership, including the following.

- Generally, none of the owners of an LLC are personally liable for the entity's debts. General partners in a limited partnership have personal liability for partnership recourse debts.

- Limited partners cannot participate in the management of the partnership. All owners of an LLC have the legal right to participate in the entity's management.

Disadvantages of an LLC

The disadvantages of an LLC stem primarily from the lack of final Regulations in certain areas. There is only a limited body of case law interpreting the various state statutes, so the application of some provisions is uncertain. An additional uncertainty for LLCs that operate in more than one jurisdiction is which state's law will prevail and how it will be applied.

11-7c Limited Liability Partnerships

A limited liability partnership (LLP) is similar to a general partnership. The differences between the two entities are small but very significant. Recall that general partners are jointly and severally liable for all partnership debts. In some states, partners in a registered LLP are jointly and severally liable for contractual liabilities (i.e., they are treated as general partners for commercial debt). They are also always personally liable for their own malpractice or other torts. They are not, however, personally liable for the malpractice and torts of their partners. As a result, the exposure of their personal assets to lawsuits filed against other partners and the partnership is considerably reduced.

LLPs are treated as partnerships under Federal income tax statutes. They are most similar to general partnerships. An LLP must have formal documents of organization and register with the state. Because the LLP is a general partnership in other respects, it does not have to pay any state franchise taxes on its operations—an important difference between LLPs and LLCs in states that impose franchise taxes on LLCs.

When a general partnership converts to an LLP, it generally is treated as a continuation of the old partnership for tax purposes. This means that all of the old partnership's elections continue in the LLP, including accounting methods, the taxable year-end, and the § 754 election.

11-7d Partnership Administration and Anti-Abuse

Most larger partners will designate a "tax matters partner" who oversees the partnership's relationship with the IRS.

A partner's share of each partnership item should be reported on the partner's tax return in the same manner as presented on the partner's Schedule K–1. If a partner treats an item differently, the IRS should be notified of the inconsistent treatment.[41] If a partner fails to notify the IRS, a penalty may be added to the tax due.

Partnership taxation allows flexibility, which leaves the doors open for potential abuse. Regulations allow the IRS to disregard the form of a partnership transaction when it believes that the transaction (or series of transactions) is abusive.[42]

11-8 TAX PLANNING

LO.13

List and evaluate various tax planning considerations related to partnership distributions and sales of partnership interests.

11-8a Planning Partnership Distributions

In planning for any partnership distributions, be alert to the following possibilities.

- When gain recognition is undesirable, make sure that cash distributions from a partnership, including any debt assumptions or repayments, do not exceed the basis of the receiving partner's interest.

- When a partner is to receive a liquidating distribution and the full basis of the interest will not be recovered, the partner's capital loss can be ensured by providing that the only assets received by the partner are cash, unrealized receivables, and inventory. If a capital loss is undesirable, however, the partnership should also distribute a capital or § 1231 asset that will take the partner's remaining basis in the interest. A capital asset would defer the loss, and a § 1231 asset could yield a more favorable ordinary deduction or loss in the future.

---

[41]See § 6222.   [42]Reg. § 1.701–2.

- Current and liquidating distributions may result in ordinary income recognition for either the receiving partner or the partnership if hot assets are present. When such income is undesirable, consider making a proportionate distribution.

- If precontribution gain property is contributed to a partnership, gain to the contributing partner can be further deferred if the partnership waits seven years before (1) distributing the precontribution gain property to another partner or (2) distributing other partnership property to the precontribution gain partner if the value of the other property exceeds the partner's basis in the partnership.

- When the partnership agreement initially is drafted, consider including provisions that govern liquidating distributions of partnership income and property for purposes of § 736. The specifics of the agreement generally will be followed by the IRS if these and other relevant points are addressed early in the life of the entity.

11-8b Sales and Exchanges of Partnership Interests

Delaying Income for the Seller

A partner planning to dispose of a partnership interest in a taxable transaction might consider receiving a pro rata distribution of hot assets, followed by a sale of the remaining interest in the partnership. Although the partner will have ordinary income when these hot assets are collected or sold, the partner can spread the income over more than one tax year by controlling the collection or disposal dates.

Providing Basis for the Buyer

If a partnership interest is acquired by purchase, the purchaser may want to condition the acquisition on the partnership's promise to make an election to adjust the basis of partnership assets. Making the election under § 754 results in the basis in the partner's ratable share of partnership assets being adjusted to reflect the purchase price. Failure to do so could result in the loss of future depreciation deductions or could convert ordinary losses into capital losses.

11-8c Comparing Sales to Liquidations

When a partner disposes of an entire interest in a partnership for a certain sum, the *before-tax* result of a sale of that interest to another partner or partners is the same as the liquidation of the interest under § 736. In other words, if both transactions result in the partner receiving the same amount of pretax dollars, the partner should be ambivalent about which form the transaction takes unless one form offers tax savings that the other does not. The *after-tax* result of a sale of a partnership interest and a liquidation of a partner's interest by an ongoing partnership may differ considerably.

Payments over Time

One difference occurs when the payment for that interest is extended over several years. When a partner sells the partnership interest to another partner, the selling partner can postpone the recognition of income under the installment sale rules. These rules are very restrictive and require that gain and income be recognized at least as quickly as the proportionate share of the receivable is collected. However, in a liquidation, more flexibility may be available. Under § 736, the § 736(b) payments for partnership property can be made before the income payments under § 736(a). Furthermore, the § 736(b) payments can be treated as a return of basis first, with gain recognized only after the distributee partner has received amounts equal to the basis. This treatment results in a deferral of gain and income recognition under § 736 that is not available under the installment sale provisions.

Payments for Goodwill

Sale The partner who purchases a partnership interest often pays an amount that can be attributed, in part, to partnership goodwill. Purchased goodwill is included in a purchasing partner's outside basis for the partnership interest. The partner cannot amortize the goodwill unless the asset qualifies as a § 197 intangible, amortizable over 15 years, *and* the partnership makes an election under § 754 to adjust the basis of partnership assets to reflect the purchase price paid. Absent these conditions, the purchasing partner will not obtain a tax benefit from the goodwill until the partnership interest is sold, exchanged, or liquidated.

Liquidation Amounts paid by a service partnership in liquidation of a general partner's share of partnership goodwill can be treated as a § 736(a) payment, provided it is *not* required by the partnership agreement ("unstated goodwill"). If this constitutes a guaranteed payment, it is deductible by the partnership. If (1) capital is a material income-producing factor of the partnership or (2) the distributee partner was a limited partner, payments for goodwill constitute § 736(b) property payments. These payments are not deductible by the partnership and result in increased capital gain (or decreased capital loss) to the retiring partner.

Valuation Problems

Both the IRS and the courts usually consider the value of a partner's interest or any partnership assets agreed upon by all partners to be correct. Thus, when planning the sale or liquidation of a partnership interest, the results of the bargaining process should be documented. To avoid valuation problems on liquidation, include a formula or agreed-upon valuation procedure in the partnership agreement or in a related buy-sell agreement. Be alert to whether or not the parties want § 736(a) or (b) treatment for partnership goodwill, and provide appropriate documentation to achieve that goal.

11-8d Other Partnership Issues

Liquidating the Entity

The partnership liquidation rules demonstrate the tax advantages of the partnership form over the C corporation in the final stage of the business's life.

- A service partnership can effectively claim deductions for its payment to a retiring general partner for goodwill.

- The partnership liquidation itself is not a taxable event. Under corporate rules, however, liquidating distributions and sales in preparation for a distribution are fully taxable.

- Tax liability relative to the liquidation is generated at the partner level, but only upon a recognition event (such as receipt of cash in excess of basis or sale of an asset received in a distribution). The timing of this event is usually under the control of the (ex-)partner. In this manner, the tax obligations can be placed in the most beneficial tax year and rate bracket.

Family Partnerships

If possible, make certain that very young and elderly members of a family partnership contribute services to the entity, so that you can justify making income allocations to them.

Because there is no equivalent of the kiddie tax for elderly taxpayers, retention of the founding members of the partnership past the usual retirement age can facilitate the income-shifting goals of a family where the founding members are not independently wealthy.

REFOCUS ON THE BIG PICTURE

THE LIFE CYCLE OF A PARTNERSHIP

Two things are happening when the new developers become members of Beachside Properties LLC. The developers are buying out the interests of two existing LLC members, and they are providing cash with which to expand the LLC's operations.

The expansion itself raises no specific tax problems. An LLC can admit new members with no immediate tax consequences. In addition to the issues addressed earlier in the chapter, the LLC's operating agreement should be modified to ensure that there is no shift in ownership rights between Josh and the new LLC members.

What If?

Changing the facts, assume that the developers have only $5 million in cash, with good prospects for receiving an additional $10 million over the next two years and the remaining $9.5 million in the third year. The LLC has found a bridge loan and temporary financing of $12 million to cover costs during this interim period. This loan, though, is not large enough to fund the new development and to completely buy out Kyle's and Maria's interests. Thus, Kyle and Maria have agreed to accept installment payments for the sale or redemption of their interests.

Now the buyout of Kyle and Maria can be treated either as an installment sale or as a redemption under § 736 requiring a series of payments. Although the specific results of these arrangements are beyond the scope of this chapter, different tax consequences might arise as to the timing and character of Kyle's and Maria's gain recognition.

Key Terms

Appreciated inventory, 11-11	Liquidating distribution, 11-2	Step up, 11-5
Current distribution, 11-2	Optional adjustment election, 11-23	Substantial basis reduction, 11-23
Disproportionate distribution, 11-3	Proportionate distribution, 11-3	Substantial built-in loss, 11-23
Hot assets, 11-5	Section 754 election, 11-23	Unrealized receivables, 11-5
Inventory, 11-5	Step down, 11-5	

Discussion Questions

1. **LO.1, 2, 3, 5** What is the difference between the definition of a proportionate current distribution and a proportionate liquidating distribution? What is the significance of the word *proportionate*?

2. **LO.1, 2** How does a proportionate current distribution of cash from a partnership to a partner compare with one from a Subchapter C corporation to a shareholder?

3. **LO.4** What issues arise if a partner contributes appreciated property to a partnership and other property is later distributed to that partner?   Critical Thinking

4. **LO.6** Distinguish between the treatment of § 736 income and property payments. What are the tax consequences of such payments to the retiring partner, the remaining partners, and the partnership?

5.   **LO.7** When a partnership interest is sold during the partnership's taxable year, how is the income allocated between the buying partner and selling partner? When is the income reported?

6.   **LO.8** What tax consequences result from the death of a partner? What collateral issues might arise?

7.   **LO.9** Who makes the optional adjustment-to-basis election? How is the election made? What is its effect on future years? Are there situations in which the partnership would *not* make the election?

8.   **LO.10** Describe the various types of events that can cause a partnership termination.

Critical Thinking   9.   **LO.12, 13** To what extent are the personal assets of a general partner, limited partner, or member of an LLC subject to (a) contractual liability claims such as trade accounts payable and (b) malpractice claims against the entity? Answer the question for partners or members in a general partnership, an LLP, a nonprofessional LLC, and a limited partnership.

Computational Exercises

10.   **LO.2** Franco owns a 60% interest in the Dulera LLC. On December 31 of the current tax year, his basis in the LLC interest is $128,000. The fair market value of the interest is $140,000. In a proportionate current distribution, the LLC distributes $30,000 cash and equipment with an adjusted basis of $5,000 and a fair market value of $8,000 to him on that date.

     How much is Franco's adjusted basis in the LLC interest after the distribution, and what is the amount of his basis in the equipment received?

11.   **LO.2** Lola owns a one-half interest in the Lenax LLC. Her basis in this ownership interest is $22,000 at the end of the year, after accounting for the calendar year LLC's current operations. On that date, the LLC distributes $25,000 cash to Lola in a proportionate current distribution.

     What is the amount of any gain or loss Lola recognizes as a result of this distribution? What is her basis in the LLC interest?

12.   **LO.2** Pablo has a $63,000 basis in his partnership interest. On May 9 of the current tax year, the partnership distributes to him, in a proportionate current distribution, cash of $25,000, cash basis receivables with an inside basis of $0 and a fair market value of $16,000, and land with a basis and fair market value to the partnership of $80,000.

     a.   How much is Pablo's realized and recognized gain on the distribution?

     b.   What is Pablo's basis in the receivables, land, and partnership interest following the distribution?

13.   **LO.3** When Bruno's basis in his LLC interest is $150,000, he receives cash of $55,000, a proportionate share of inventory, and land in a distribution that liquidates both the LLC and his entire LLC interest. The inventory has a basis to the LLC of $45,000 and a fair market value of $48,000. The land's basis is $70,000, and the fair market value is $60,000.

     How much gain or loss does Bruno recognize, and what is his basis in the inventory and land received in the distribution?

14.   **LO.3** When Magdalena's outside basis is $58,000, she receives a liquidating distribution of $15,000 cash and a proportionate share of inventory having a partnership basis of $20,000 and a fair market value of $24,000. The distribution results in a liquidation of both the partnership and her interest.

     a.   How much is Magdalena's basis in the inventory received?

     b.   What is the amount of any gain or loss recognized on the liquidation?

15. **LO.4** Ryce contributes nondepreciable property with an adjusted basis of $60,000 and a fair market value of $95,000 to the Montgomery Partnership in exchange for a one-half interest in profits and capital. In the next tax year, when the property's fair market value is $100,000, the partnership distributes the property to Jarvis, the other one-half partner. Jarvis's basis in the partnership interest was $100,000 immediately before the distribution.

Which partner must recognize a gain, what is the amount recognized, and what is the effect on that partner's basis in the partnership interest? What is the effect on Jarvis's basis in the nondepreciable property received?

16. **LO.4** Ten years ago, Dudley contributed land to the Prosperity LLC. His basis in the land was $100,000. The fair market value at the contribution date was $115,000. This year, when the property's value was $200,000, the LLC distributed that property to partner Nicki. At that time, Dudley's basis in his LLC interest was $50,000 and Nicki's basis was $60,000. Assume that the partnership continues in existence and has no hot assets.

What gain or loss is recognized as a result of this distribution of precontribution gain property? What is Dudley's basis in his partnership interest following the distribution? What is Nicki's basis in the property received and her partnership interest following the distribution?

17. **LO.6** Wylie is a general partner in a service-providing partnership and receives cash of $145,000 in liquidation of his partnership interest, in which he has a basis of $110,000. The partnership owns no hot assets and continues in existence. After following all of the classification requirements of § 736, $100,000 of this amount is classified as a property payment [§ 736(b)] and $45,000 is classified as a guaranteed payment [§ 736(a)] (assume that this payment is for unstated partnership goodwill).

As a result of the liquidation proceeds, how much will Wylie recognize as a capital gain or loss, and how much will be ordinary income?

18. **LO.6** The Whitewater LLP is equally owned by three partners and shows the following balance sheet at the end of the current tax year.

	Basis	FMV
Cash	$60,000	$ 60,000
Unrealized receivables	–0–	15,000
Land	15,000	45,000
	$75,000	$120,000
Petula, capital	$25,000	$ 40,000
Prudence, capital	25,000	40,000
Primrose, capital	25,000	40,000
	$75,000	$120,000

Partner Petula is an active (i.e., "general") partner retiring from the service-oriented partnership. She receives $60,000 cash, none of which is stated to be for goodwill.

a.   How much of the payment is for "unstated goodwill"?

b.   How is the $60,000 allocated between a § 736(a) income payment and a § 736(b) property payment?

19. **LO.7** Sweeney originally contributed $175,000 in cash for a one-fourth interest in the Gilbert LLC. During the several years that Sweeney was a member of the LLC, his share of the LLC's income was $90,000 and he withdrew $75,000 cash. The LLC's liabilities are $80,000, of which Sweeney's share is $20,000. The LLC has $40,000 of hot assets, of which Sweeney's share is $10,000.

Sweeney sells his LLC interest to Jana for $225,000 cash, with Jana also assuming Sweeney's share of the LLC's liabilities.

How much is Sweeney's gain on the sale, and what is its character? How much is Jana's adjusted basis for her LLC interest?

20. **LO.7** On December 31, Yong sells his 10% interest in Catawissa LLC to Mei for $17,500. Yong is a calendar year taxpayer. Catawissa owns no hot assets, and its tax year ends on September 30. On October 1, Yong's basis in the LLC interest was $11,000. His share of current LLC income is $4,000 for the period in which he owned the LLC interest (October 1 to December 31).

    How much capital gain does Yong recognize on the sale?

21. **LO.7** The Lexington Partnership has a depreciable business asset (personal property) that it originally purchased for $60,000. The asset now has an adjusted basis of $36,000 and a market value of $70,000. The partnership has no other potential hot assets. Ambroz sells his 25% interest in the partnership.

    a. How much is Lexington's depreciation recapture potential?

    b. How much ordinary income does Ambroz recognize when he sells this partnership interest?

22. **LO.9** Dusan is a member of the Tonda LLC, and all members have equal interests in capital and profits. The LLC has made an optional adjustment-to-basis election. Dusan's interest is sold to Adele for $35,000. The balance sheet of the LLC immediately before the sale shows the following.

	Basis	FMV
Cash	$ 40,000	$ 40,000
Depreciable assets	80,000	100,000
	$120,000	$140,000
Dusan, capital	$ 30,000	$ 35,000
Randal, capital	30,000	35,000
Thom, capital	30,000	35,000
Erim, capital	30,000	35,000
	$120,000	$140,000

    a. How much is the § 754 adjustment?

    b. What is the amount of Adele's basis in the acquired interest?

    c. Which partners receive deductions related to the step-up?

23. **LO.9** Berdine has a basis of $32,000 in her partnership interest and receives land with an adjusted basis to the partnership of $78,000 in termination of her interest. (The partnership holds no hot assets.)

    a. Under the proportionate liquidating distribution rules, what is Berdine's basis in the distributed land?

    b. If an optional § 754 adjustment-to-basis election is in effect, by what amount does the partnership adjust the basis of its remaining property? If that adjustment is allocated to depreciable property, to whom does the partnership allocate the resulting depreciation deductions?

24. **LO.11** A partnership in which a parent transferred a 40% interest by gift to a child generated a profit of $130,000. Capital is a material income-producing factor. The parent performed services valued at $44,000; the child performed no services.

    How much income is allocated to the parent for services and for use of capital?

Problems

25. **LO.2** Gil's outside basis in his interest in the GO Partnership is $100,000. In a proportionate current distribution, the partnership distributes to him cash of $30,000, inventory (fair market value of $40,000, basis to the partnership of $20,000), and land (fair market value of $90,000, basis to the partnership of $40,000). The partnership continues in existence.

a.   Does the partnership recognize any gain or loss as a result of this distribution? Explain.

b.   Does Gil recognize any gain or loss as a result of this distribution? Explain.

c.   Calculate Gil's basis in the land, in the inventory, and in his partnership interest immediately following the distribution.

26. **LO.2** When Teri's outside basis in the TMF Partnership is $80,000, the partnership distributes to her $30,000 cash, an account receivable (fair market value of $60,000, inside basis to the partnership of $0), and a parcel of land (fair market value of $60,000, inside basis to the partnership of $80,000). Teri remains a partner in the partnership, and the distribution is proportionate to the partners.

a.   Use the format of Concept Summary 11.1 to create a spreadsheet to calculate the effects of the distribution. Set up an Input area for the amounts on lines 1, 2, 5, and 8. Code the formulas shown in the Calculations section of the concept summary to calculate the amounts in the remaining lines. You will use "sum," "min," and "max" formulas. Enter Teri's relevant facts in the input section of your spreadsheet.

b.   Based on the information in your spreadsheet, how much gain or loss will Teri recognize as a result of the distribution? Explain your answer.

c.   How much is Teri's basis in the land, account receivable, and TMF Partnership after the distribution? What can you conclude regarding Teri's basis in the assets and the fair market value she received?

d.   How would your answer to part (c) change if, instead, the partnership's basis in the land was $10,000 and its fair market value was $30,000 (and the cash and unrealized receivable distributions do not change)? Adjust the input section of your spreadsheet, and explain your findings.

27. **LO.2, 9** Consider each of the following independent situations, and answer the following questions.   **Decision Making**

a.   For each fact pattern, indicate:

- Whether the partner recognizes gain or loss.
- Whether the partnership recognizes gain or loss.
- The partner's adjusted basis for the property distributed.
- The partner's outside basis in the partnership after the distribution.

In each case, assume that the partnership owns no hot assets. Show your calculations in Microsoft Excel using a template similar to the format shown in Concept Summary 11.1. You will use "sum," "min," and "max" formulas.

(1) Kim receives $20,000 cash in partial liquidation of her interest in the partnership. Kim's outside basis for her partnership interest immediately before the distribution is $3,000.

(2) Kourtni receives $40,000 cash and land with an inside basis to the partnership of $30,000 (value of $50,000) in partial liquidation of her interest. Kourtni's outside basis for her partnership interest immediately before the distribution is $80,000.

(3) Assume the same facts as in part (2), except that Kourtni's outside basis for her partnership interest immediately before the distribution is $60,000.

(4) Klois receives $50,000 cash and inventory with a basis of $30,000 and a fair market value of $50,000 in partial liquidation of her partnership interest. Her basis was $90,000 before the distribution. All partners received proportionate distributions.

b.   For fact patterns (1) to (4) in part (a) above, are additional planning opportunities available to the partnership to maximize its inside basis in its assets? If so, by how much can the basis be increased? What is the effect of any basis increase to the distributee partner or the other partners?

Communications   28.   **LO.2** Cari Hawkins is a 50% partner in the calendar year Hawkins-Henry Partnership. On January 1, 2019, her basis in her partnership interest is $160,000. The partnership has no taxable income or loss for the current year. In a current distribution on December 15, the partnership distributes $120,000 cash to Cari and inventory proportionately to all partners. Cari's share of the inventory has an inside basis of $50,000 (fair market value of $60,000).

     In January 2020, Cari asks your advice regarding treatment of 2019 operations and distributions. Using the format (1) facts, (2) issues, and (3) conclusion and analysis, draft a letter to Cari at the Hawkins-Henry Partnership (1622 E. Henry Street, St. Paul, MN 55118). Without including specific citations, your letter should address the following points and provide enough information for the client to understand the applicable tax provisions.

     a.   How much gain or loss does the partnership recognize as a result of 2019 activities?

     b.   How much gain or loss must Cari recognize in 2019?

     c.   What is Cari's basis in inventory received?

     d.   What is Cari's basis in her partnership interest at the end of 2019?

     e.   Are there other considerations Cari and/or the partnership should address? Explain.

29.   **LO.2, 3** At the beginning of the tax year, Melodie's basis in the MIP LLC was $60,000, including her $40,000 share of the LLC's liabilities. At the end of the year, MIP distributed to Melodie cash of $10,000 and inventory (basis of $6,000, fair market value of $10,000). In addition, MIP repaid all of its liabilities by the end of the year.

     a.   If this is a proportionate current distribution, what is the tax effect of the distribution to Melodie and MIP? After the distribution, what is Melodie's basis in the inventory and in her MIP interest?

     b.   Would your answers to part (a) change if this had been a proportionate liquidating distribution? Explain.

Critical Thinking   30.   **LO.2, 3, 4, 5, 13** Vincent is a 50% partner in the TAV Partnership. He became a partner three years ago when he contributed land with a value of $60,000 and a basis of $30,000 (current value is $100,000). Tyler and Anita each contributed $30,000 cash for a 25% interest. Vincent's basis in his partnership interest is currently $150,000; the other partners' bases are each $75,000. The partnership holds the following assets.

	Basis	FMV
Cash	$200,000	$200,000
Accounts receivable	–0–	200,000
Marketable securities	70,000	100,000
Land	30,000	100,000
Total	$300,000	$600,000

     a.   In general terms (i.e., no calculations are required), describe the tax results to the partners and the partnership in each of the following independent scenarios where the partnership distributes the assets indicated in a current nonliquidating distribution at the end of its tax year. *Hint:* You should first determine whether the distributions are proportionate.

       (1)   TAV distributes a $50,000 (FMV) plot of land each to Tyler and Anita and $100,000 of accounts receivable to Vincent.

       (2)   TAV distributes $100,000 of cash to Vincent, $50,000 (FMV) of marketable securities to Tyler, and $50,000 (FMV) of accounts receivable to Anita.

       (3)   TAV distributes a $50,000 (FMV) interest in the land and $50,000 (FMV) of accounts receivable to Vincent and $25,000 of cash and $25,000 (FMV) of accounts receivable each to Anita and Tyler.

     b.   Now consider what would happen if the partnership distributed all of its assets in a liquidating distribution. In deciding the allocation of assets, what issues should the partnership consider to minimize each partner's taxable gains?

31. **LO.3** In each of the following independent liquidating distributions in which the partnership also liquidates, prepare a Microsoft Excel spreadsheet to determine the amount and character of any gain or loss to be recognized by each partner and the basis of each asset (other than cash) received. In each case, assume that distributions of hot assets are proportionate to the partners. You can use the format in Concept Summary 11.2, or you can create your own. In either case, be sure you can explain your rationale.

    a. Landon has a partnership basis of $40,000 and receives a distribution of $50,000 in cash.

    b. Mark has a partnership basis of $50,000 and receives $20,000 cash and a capital asset with a basis to the partnership of $25,000 and a fair market value of $40,000.

    c. Neil has a partnership basis of $100,000 and receives $40,000 cash, inventory with a basis to the partnership of $30,000, and a capital asset with a partnership basis of $20,000. The inventory and capital asset have fair market values of $20,000 and $30,000, respectively.

    d. Oscar has a partnership basis of $40,000 and receives a distribution of $10,000 cash and an account receivable with a basis of $0 to the partnership (value is $15,000).

32. **LO.3, 13** Jerome's basis in his partnership interest is $50,000. Jerome receives a pro rata liquidating distribution consisting of $10,000 cash, land with a basis of $40,000 and a fair market value of $60,000, and his proportionate share of inventory with a basis of $30,000 to the partnership and a fair market value of $50,000. Assume that the partnership also liquidates. *Decision Making* *Critical Thinking*

    a. How much gain or loss, if any, must Jerome recognize as a result of the distribution?

    b. What basis will Jerome take in the inventory and land?

    c. If Jerome sells the land two years later for $50,000, what are the tax consequences to him?

    d. What are the tax consequences to the partnership as a result of the liquidating distribution?

    e. Is any planning technique available to the partnership to avoid any "lost basis" results? Explain.

    f. Would your answers to parts (b) and (e) change if this had been a current distribution? Explain.

33. **LO.3** Parker's basis in his PQ Partnership interest is $180,000. Parker receives a pro rata liquidating distribution consisting of $20,000 cash, land with a basis of $80,000 and a fair market value of $100,000, and his proportionate share of inventory with a basis of $60,000 to PQ and a fair market value of $75,000. Assume that PQ also liquidates.

    a. How much gain or loss, if any, must Parker recognize on the distribution?

    b. What basis will Parker take in the inventory and land?

    c. What are the tax consequences to the partnership?

    d. Would your answer to part (a) or (b) change if this had been a current distribution? Explain.

34. **LO.3, 13** Paula's basis in her partnership interest is $60,000. In liquidation of her interest, the partnership makes a proportionate distribution to Paula of $20,000 of cash and inventory (basis of $5,000 and value of $7,000). No "other property" was distributed. (Assume that the partnership then liquidates.) *Decision Making*

    a. Use the format of Concept Summary 11.2 to create a spreadsheet to calculate the effects of the distribution. Set up an Input area for the amounts on lines 1, 2, 5, and 8. Code the formulas shown in the Calculations section of the concept summary to calculate the amounts in the remaining lines. You will use "sum," "min," "max," and "if/then/else" formulas. Enter Paula's relevant facts in the input section of your spreadsheet.

b.   Based on the information in your spreadsheet, how much gain or loss, if any, will Paula recognize on the distribution?

c.   What basis will Paula take in the inventory?

d.   What happens if the partnership also distributes artwork to Paula with a basis of $1,000 and a fair market value of $30,000? Adjust the input section of your spreadsheet, and explain your findings.

e.   Return to the original facts. Conceptually, how would your answer to part (b) or (c) change if this had been a current distribution? (You do not need to create a spreadsheet for the current distribution rules.) Explain.

35.   **LO.3** Jamie's basis in her partnership interest is $52,000. In a proportionate distribution in liquidation of the partnership, Jamie receives $2,000 cash and two parcels of land with bases of $10,000 and $18,000, respectively, to the partnership. The partnership holds both parcels of land for investment, and the parcels have fair market values of $20,000 each.

a.   How much gain or loss, if any, must Jamie recognize on the distribution?

b.   What basis will Jamie take in each parcel?

c.   If the land had been held as inventory by the partnership, what effect, if any, would it have on your responses to parts (a) and (b)?

Decision Making   36.   **LO.3, 13** Michelle has a basis in her partnership interest of $85,000. In a proportionate liquidating distribution of the partnership, Michelle receives $5,000 cash and a car (a § 1231 asset to the partnership) having a basis of $20,000 to the partnership and a fair market value of $30,000. For our purposes, disregard any potential depreciation recapture on the car.

a.   How much loss, if any, may Michelle recognize on the distribution?

b.   What basis will Michelle take in the car?

c.   Suppose Michelle's 18-year-old son uses the car for his personal use for one year before Michelle sells it for $28,000. How much loss may Michelle recognize on the sale of the car? What tax planning procedures should be considered?

37.   **LO.4** In 2016, Adrianna contributed land with a basis of $16,000 and a fair market value of $25,000 to the A&I Partnership in exchange for a 25% interest in capital and profits. In 2019, the partnership distributes this property to Isabel, also a 25% partner, in a current distribution. The fair market value had increased to $30,000 at the time the property was distributed. Isabel's and Adrianna's bases in their partnership interests were each $40,000 at the time of the distribution.

a.   How much gain or loss, if any, does Adrianna recognize on the distribution to Isabel? What is Adrianna's basis in her partnership interest following the distribution?

b.   What is Isabel's basis in the land she received in the distribution?

c.   How much gain or loss, if any, does Isabel recognize on the distribution? What is Isabel's basis in her partnership interest following the distribution?

d.   How much gain or loss would Isabel recognize if she later sells the land for its $30,000 fair market value? Is this result equitable?

e.   Would your answers to parts (a) and (b) change if Adrianna originally contributed the property to the partnership in 2007? Explain.

Decision Making   38.   **LO.6, 13** Damon owns a 20% interest as a general partner in the Vermillion Partnership, which provides consulting services. The partnership distributes $60,000 cash to Damon in complete liquidation of his partnership interest. Damon's share of partnership unrealized receivables immediately before the distribution is $20,000. The partnership has no other hot assets. Assume that none of the cash payment is for goodwill. Damon's basis for his partnership interest immediately before the distribution is $30,000.

a.   How is the cash payment treated under § 736?

b.   How much gain or loss must Damon recognize on the distribution? What is the character of these amounts?

c. How does the partnership treat the distribution to Damon?

d. What planning opportunities might the partnership want to consider?

e. How would your answers to parts (a), (b), and (c) change if Damon had been a limited partner?

39. **LO.6, 7, 9** The December 31 balance sheet of the GAB LLP reads as follows.

	Adjusted Basis	FMV
Cash	$300,000	$300,000
Receivables	–0–	100,000
Capital assets	60,000	80,000
Total	$360,000	$480,000
Gina, capital	$ 90,000	$120,000
Adelle, capital	180,000	240,000
Britney, capital	90,000	120,000
Total	$360,000	$480,000

Capital is not a material income-producing factor for the LLP. Gina is an active (general) partner and owner of a 25% interest in the LLP's profits and capital.

a. On December 31, Gina receives a distribution of $140,000 cash in liquidation of her partnership interest. Nothing is stated in the partnership agreement about goodwill. Gina's outside basis for the partnership interest immediately before the distribution is $90,000.

(1) How much is Gina's recognized gain from the distribution? What is the character of the gain?

(2) How much can GAB claim as a deduction?

(3) What action might the partnership want to take?

b. Now assume instead that Gina sells her partnership interest to Jess for $140,000 of cash.

(1) What is the amount and character of Gina's gain?

(2) What deductions can be claimed by the LLP?

(3) What action might Jess request of the partnership?

40. **LO.6, 7** Skylar is ready to retire and wants your professional opinion on the most advantageous way to dispose of a 40% limited ownership interest in the three-member STU LLC.

Decision Making

Critical Thinking

Communications

Option #1. Skylar will immediately sell the LLC interest to Partner Tameeka for $300,000 cash. Skylar will then invest the after-tax proceeds in a tax-exempt (Federal and state) municipal bond paying 4% interest per year, compounded at the end of each year. (Assume that there are no Federal or state income taxes on the interest earned on the bond.)

Option #2. STU will distribute a parcel of land (investment property) to Skylar in complete redemption of the 40% interest. STU's land was recently appraised for $260,000. The appraiser estimated that Skylar could sell the land for $400,000 (before taxes) at the end of eight years. For simplicity, determine the tax results of the land distribution under the proportionate liquidating distribution rules. [In this case, this result also arises if the distribution is a § 736(b) distribution.]

Other information. In either scenario, at the end of the eighth year, Skylar will convert the asset (bond or land) to cash to help cover living expenses. If needed, use the Present and Future Value Tables in Appendix F.

Assumptions:

- STU owns no hot assets and has no stated or unstated goodwill.
- Skylar's basis in the LLC interest is $100,000.
- The LLC's basis in the land is $80,000.
- Skylar's tax rate is 20% on capital gains.

Draft a memo to Skylar describing how each option would be treated for tax purposes, and the after-tax amount of cash Skylar would have on hand after cashing the bond or selling the land at the end of year 8. Based solely on this analysis, recommend one of these options to Skylar.

Communications   41. **LO.7** BDD Partnership is a service-oriented partnership that has three equal general partners. One of them, Barry Evans, sells his interest to another partner, Dale Allen, on December 31 (the last day of the current tax year) for $90,000 cash and the assumption of Barry's share of partnership liabilities. (Liabilities are shared equally by the partners.) Immediately before the sale (after reflecting operations for the year), the partnership's cash basis balance sheet was presented as shown below. Assume that the capital accounts *before* the sale reflect the partners' bases in their partnership interests, excluding liabilities. The payment exceeds the stated fair market value of the assets because of goodwill that is not recorded on the books.

	Basis	FMV		Basis	FMV
Cash	$120,000	$120,000	Note payable	$ 30,000	$ 30,000
Accounts receivable	–0–	90,000	Capital accounts		
Capital assets	30,000	75,000	Barry	40,000	85,000
			David	40,000	85,000
			Dale	40,000	85,000
Total	$150,000	$285,000	Total	$150,000	$285,000

a. What is the total amount realized by Barry on the sale?

b. How much, if any, ordinary income must Barry recognize on the sale?

c. How much capital gain must Barry report?

d. What is Dale's basis in the partnership interest acquired?

e. Refer to Reg. § 1.751–1(a)(3). What information is the seller required to provide? Draft a statement that meets these requirements.

f. How would Barry's tax result differ if, instead, BDD distributed $90,000 of its cash in liquidation of Barry's interest (with the remaining partners assuming Barry's share of partnership debt)? Why does this happen? The LLC's operating agreement does not address payment of goodwill to the partner.

42. **LO.7, 9** Diana, a partner in the cash basis HDA Partnership, has a one-third interest in partnership profits and losses. The partnership's balance sheet at the end of the current year is as follows.

	Basis	FMV		Basis	FMV
Cash	$120,000	$120,000	Hannah, capital	$ 90,000	$250,000
Receivables	–0–	240,000	Diana, capital	90,000	250,000
Land	150,000	390,000	Alexis, capital	90,000	250,000
Total	$270,000	$750,000	Total	$270,000	$750,000

Diana sells her interest in the HDA Partnership to Kenneth at the end of the current year for cash of $250,000.

a. How much income must Diana report on her tax return for the current year from the sale? What is its nature?

b. If the partnership does not make an optional adjustment-to-basis election, what are the type and amount of income that Kenneth must report in the next year when the receivables are collected?

c. Refer to Example 34. Describe how an out-of-balance situation arises and is resolved for Diana's *sale* of a partnership interest. (Note that Example 34 relates to a *distribution* that causes an out-of-balance situation.) Prepare a Microsoft Excel worksheet that illustrates the out-of-balance situation and how a § 754 adjustment can restore balance. Use the intuitive approach to allocate any step-up to partnership assets. *Hint:* You'll need to significantly modify the format for this situation.

d.   If the partnership did make an optional adjustment-to-basis election, what are the type and amount of income that Kenneth would report in the next year when the receivables are collected? If the land (which is used in the HDA Partnership's business) was sold for $420,000? Assume that no other transactions occurred that year.

43. **LO.7, 8, 10** At the end of last year, June, a 30% partner in the four-person BJJM Partnership, had an outside basis of $75,000 in the partnership, including a $60,000 share of partnership debt. June's share of the partnership's § 1245 recapture potential was $40,000. All parties use the calendar year. Describe the income tax consequences to June in both of the following independent situations that take place in the current year.

a.   On the first day of the tax year, June sells her partnership interest to Marilyn for $120,000 cash and the assumption by Marilyn of the appropriate share of partnership liabilities.

b.   June dies after a lengthy illness on April 1 of the current year. June's brother immediately takes June's place in the partnership.

44. **LO.11** Mona and Denise, mother and daughter, operate a local restaurant as an LLC. The MD LLC earned a profit of $200,000 in the current year. Denise's equal partnership interest was acquired by gift from Mona. Assume that capital is a material income-producing factor and that Mona manages the day-to-day operations of the restaurant without any help from Denise. Reasonable compensation for Mona's services is $50,000.

a.   How much of the LLC's income is allocated to Mona?

b.   What is the maximum amount of the LLC's income that can be allocated to Denise?

c.   Assuming that Denise is 15 years old, has no other income, and is claimed as a dependent by Mona, how is Denise's income from the LLC taxed?

Research Problems

Note: Solutions to the Research Problems can be prepared by using the Thomson Reuters Checkpoint™ online tax research database, which accompanies this textbook. Solutions can also be prepared by using research materials found in a typical tax library.

Research Problem 1. Your client, Paul, owns a one-third interest as a managing (general) partner in the service-oriented PRE LLP. He would like to retire from the limited liability partnership at the end of 2020 and asks your help in structuring the buyout transaction. He expects that his basis in the LLP interest will be about $60,000 at that time.

Decision Making

Based on interim financial data and revenue projections, the LLP's balance sheet is expected to approximate the following at the end of the year.

	Basis	FMV		Basis	FMV
Cash	$ 60,000	$ 60,000	Paul, capital	$ 60,000	$150,000
Accounts receivable	–0–	180,000	Rachel, capital	60,000	150,000
Land (capital asset)	120,000	210,000	Erik, capital	60,000	150,000
Total assets	$180,000	$450,000	Total capital	$180,000	$450,000

Although the LLP has some cash, the amount is not adequate to purchase Paul's entire interest in the current year. The LLP has proposed to pay Paul, in liquidation of his interest, according to the following schedule.

December 31, 2020	$50,000
December 31, 2021	$50,000
December 31, 2022	$50,000

Paul has agreed to this payment schedule, but the parties are not sure of the tax consequences of the buyout and have temporarily halted negotiations to consult with their tax advisers. Paul has retained you to determine the income tax ramifications of the buyout and to make sure he secures the most advantageous result available. Using the IRS Regulations governing partnerships, answer the following questions.

a. If the buyout agreement between Paul and PRE is silent as to the treatment of each payment, how will each payment be treated by Paul and the partnership?

b. As Paul's adviser, what payment schedule should Paul negotiate to minimize his current tax liability?

c. Regarding the LLP, what payment schedule would ensure that the remaining partners receive the earliest possible deductions?

d. Under the three alternatives in parts (a) to (c), what is the present value of Paul's after-tax cash received from the buyout? Which alternative do you recommend to your client, Paul? Does this change your recommendations in parts (a) through (c)? Paul's Federal and state tax rate for capital gains is 25%, and his marginal combined state and Federal rate for ordinary income is 40%. Paul typically earns 6% on his investments (after-tax discount rate); the first payment will be received one year from now (with the other payments one year apart). Use the present value tables in Appendix F. Each year's after-tax cash flow differs, so the after-tax payment does not constitute an annuity.

   Create a spreadsheet that summarizes the after-tax cash flows and present values of the three alternatives. You might use the format below for part (a), where the partnership agreement is silent, and then copy and modify the format for parts (b) and (c).

e. What additional planning opportunities might be available to the partnership?

Partnership Agreement Silent

		Basis Recovery	Taxable Gain	Tax on Ordinary Income	Tax on Taxable Gain	Total Tax on Distribution	Net After-Tax Proceeds	Discount Factor for Year	Discounted Proceeds
§ 736(a)	§ 736(b)								
2020									
2021									
2022		___	___	___	___	___	___	___	___

Communications **Research Problem 2.** The accrual basis Four Winds Partnership owned and operated three storage facilities in Milwaukee, Wisconsin. The partnership did not have a § 754 election in effect on March 1, 2019, when partner Taylor Barnes sold her 25% interest to Patrick Knight for $250,000. The partnership has no debt. There are no § 197 assets, and assume that there is no depreciation recapture potential on the storage facility buildings.

At the time of the transfer, the partnership's asset bases and fair market values were as follows.

	Basis	Fair Market Value
Cash	$ 50,000	$ 50,000
Accounts receivable	150,000	150,000
Storage facility 1	500,000	200,000
Storage facility 2	400,000	500,000
Storage facility 3	300,000	100,000
Total assets	$1,400,000	$1,000,000

The value of two of the properties is less than the partnership's basis because of downturns in the real estate market in the area.

Patrick's share of the inside basis of partnership assets is $350,000, and his share of the fair market value of partnership assets is $250,000.

a. What adjustment is required regarding Patrick's purchase of the partnership interest? Must a § 754 election be made? Why or why not?

b. Using the basis allocation rules of § 755 and the Regulations thereunder, calculate the amount of the total adjustment to be allocated to each of the partnership's assets. Present the information in the form of the statement that would be attached to the partnership's tax return as indicated by Reg. § 1.743–1(k)(1).

c. Would an adjustment be required if the partnership was a venture capital firm and, instead of storage facilities, its three primary assets were equity interests owned in target firms? What requirements would have to be satisfied to avoid making a basis adjustment?

Research Problem 3. ABC Partnership is engaged exclusively in providing consulting services, and capital is not a material income-producing factor. The ABC General Partnership agreement, which was drafted in 2014, did not explain how a retiring partner would be paid for his or her share of partnership goodwill. In 2018, the partnership executed an "Amendment of General Partnership Agreement," which provided that Partner Adam was to receive $100,000 cash from the partnership on July 1, 2019. The payment was designed to retire Adam's interest in the partnership. Of that amount, $30,000 was in return for Adam's one-third interest in the fair market value of the net assets of the partnership. The other $70,000 was referred to as "a guaranteed payment, or a payment for goodwill."

Saying that the "Amendment of General Partnership Agreement" is not clear, the IRS wants to treat the payment for goodwill as ordinary income to Adam and deductible by the partnership. (Assume that this approach maximizes the tax revenue for the government). Presuming that the taxpayers would prefer a return of basis and capital gain, what case law authority is available to support this position?

Use internet tax resources to address the following questions. Look for reliable websites and blogs of the IRS and other government agencies, media outlets, businesses, tax professionals, academics, think tanks, and political outlets.

Research Problem 4. On what form or attachment does a partnership report that it has made a § 754 election? Prepare such a form using the facts of Example 29 in the text.

Research Problem 5. For the most recent year available, what types of partnerships are most commonly used in various industries? Consider general and limited partnerships and LLCs; disregard LLPs and foreign partnerships. Which types of industries/partnerships account for the largest numbers of partners? Profits (or losses)? Why do you think these results might arise?

Data Analytics

Communications

Use the partnership information "by entity type" at **irs.gov/taxstats** to help you discover this data. For each situation, evaluate the industry total compared to "All Industries." Consider only "main categories." For example, consider "Finance and insurance" and "Real estate and rental and leasing" rather than subcategories such as "Securities and commodity contracts" or "Lessors of residential buildings and dwellings." *Hint:* Your total (for a given category) for separate industries should equal the total for "all industries."

In an e-mail to your instructor, describe your results. Support your findings with pie charts, line charts, and/or "stacked" area charts.

Becker CPA Review Questions

1. Hart's adjusted basis of his interest in a partnership was $30,000. He received a proportionate nonliquidating distribution of $24,000 cash plus a parcel of land with a fair market value and partnership basis of $9,000. Hart's basis for the land is:

   a. $9,000

   b. $6,000

   c. $3,000

   d. $0

2. Gearty's adjusted basis in Worthington Company, a partnership, was $18,000 at the time Gearty received the following proportionate nonliquidating distributions of partnership property.

Cash	$ 6,000
Land	
Adjusted basis	14,000
Fair market value	12,000
Inventory	
Adjusted basis	7,000
Fair market value	10,000

   What is Gearty's tax basis in the land received from the partnership?

   a. $0

   b. $5,000

   c. $12,000

   d. $14,000

3. Desi's adjusted basis of her partnership interest was $40,000 immediately before she received a distribution in full liquidation of her Makris partnership interest. (The partnership had no hot assets and also liquidated.) The distribution consisted of $25,000 in cash and land with a fair market value of $30,000. Makris's basis in the land was $10,000 immediately prior to the distribution. During the year, Desi sold the land for $50,000. How will Desi report the liquidating distribution and the sale on her income tax return?

	Liquidating Distribution	Sale of the Land
a.	No gain or loss	$35,000 capital gain
b.	No gain or loss	$40,000 capital gain
c.	$15,000 gain	$20,000 capital gain
d.	$5,000 loss	$40,000 capital gain

4. On December 31 of the current year, after receipt of his share of partnership income, Fox sold his interest in a limited partnership for $50,000 cash plus relief of all liabilities. On that date, the adjusted basis of Fox's partnership interest was $60,000, consisting of his capital account of $35,000 and his share of the partnership liabilities of $25,000. The partnership has no unrealized receivables or substantially appreciated inventory. What is Fox's gain or loss on the sale of his partnership interest?

   a. Ordinary loss of $10,000

   b. Ordinary gain of $15,000

   c. Capital loss of $10,000

   d. Capital gain of $15,000

CHAPTER

12

S Corporations

LEARNING OBJECTIVES: *After completing Chapter 12, you should be able to:*

LO.1 Explain the tax effects that S corporation status has on shareholders.

LO.2 Identify corporations that qualify for the S election.

LO.3 Explain how to make an S election.

LO.4 Explain how an S election can be terminated.

LO.5 Compute nonseparately stated income and identify separately stated items.

LO.6 Allocate income, deductions, and credits to shareholders.

LO.7 Determine how distributions to S corporation shareholders are taxed.

LO.8 Calculate a shareholder's basis in S corporation stock.

LO.9 Explain the tax effects that losses have on shareholders.

LO.10 Compute the built-in gains and passive investment income penalty taxes.

LO.11 Engage in tax planning for S corporations.

CHAPTER OUTLINE

LISA S./SHUTTERSTOCK.COM

DEDUCTIBILITY OF LOSSES AND THE CHOICE OF BUSINESS ENTITY

Cane, Inc., has been a C corporation for a number of years, earning taxable income of less than $100,000 per year. Thus, the business has been subject to the lower C corporation tax rates, but due to cheap imports from China, Cane's two owners, Smith and Jones, expect operating losses for the next two or three years. They hope to outsource some of the manufacturing to Vietnam and turn the company around. How can they deduct these anticipated future losses?

The corporation receives some tax-exempt income, generates a small amount of passive investment income, and holds some C corporation earnings and profits. Each owner draws a salary of $92,000. Cane has issued two classes of stock, voting and nonvoting common. Cane is located in Texarkana, Texas. Smith lives in Texas, and Jones lives in Arkansas. Both are married to nonresident aliens.

Should Smith and Jones elect to have Cane treated as an S corporation?

Read the chapter and formulate your response.

An individual establishing a business has a number of choices as to the form of business entity under which to operate. Chapters 2 through 7 outline many of the rules, advantages, and disadvantages of operating as a regular C corporation. Chapters 10 and 11 discuss the partnership entity, and Chapter 11 covers the limited liability company (LLC) and limited liability partnership (LLP) forms.

Another alternative, the **S corporation**, provides many of the benefits of partnership taxation and at the same time gives the owners limited liability protection from creditors. The S corporation rules, which are contained in **Subchapter S** of the Internal Revenue Code (§§ 1361–1379), were enacted to allow flexibility in the entity choice that businesspeople face. Thus, S status combines the legal environment of C corporations with taxation similar to that applying to partnerships. S corporation status is obtained through an election by a *qualifying* corporation with the consent of its shareholders.

<table>
<tr><td>

LO.1

Explain the tax effects that S corporation status has on shareholders.

</td></tr>
</table>

12-1 CHOICE OF BUSINESS ENTITY

S corporations (like C corporations) are organized under state law. Other than for income tax purposes, they are recognized as separate legal entities and generally provide shareholders with the same liability protection available to C corporations. For Federal income tax purposes, however, taxation of S corporations resembles that of partnerships. As with partnerships, the income, deductions, and tax credits of an S corporation flow through to shareholders annually, regardless of whether distributions of wealth (like cash) are made to the shareholders. Thus, income is taxed at the shareholder level and not at the corporate level. Payments to S shareholders by the corporation are distributed tax-free to the extent the distributed earnings were previously taxed.

Although the Federal tax treatment of S corporations and partnerships is similar, the two sets of computations are not identical. For instance, liabilities of the entity affect an owner's basis differently, and S corporations may incur a tax liability at the corporate level. Furthermore, an S corporation may not make a special allocation of tax items like a partnership can, and distributions of appreciated property are taxable in an S corporation situation (see Concept Summary 12.3 later in this chapter). In addition, a variety of C corporation provisions apply to S corporations. For example, the liquidation of C and S corporations is taxed in the same way. As a general rule, where the S corporation provisions are silent, C corporation rules apply.

A newly forming closely held business often makes a tax and legal entity choice between an S corporation and an LLC; both are flow-through entities for Federal income tax purposes and provide limited liability for the owners under nontax state law. In the typical year, over 4.8 million S corporations file Federal income tax returns, and filings are received from over 2 million LLCs and 4 million partnership returns. Concept Summary 12.1 lists several major factors to be considered when making this entity choice. See also Chapter 13 for comparisons of tax effects among business entities.

Concept Summary 12.1

Making an S Election

A number of considerations will affect a decision to make an S election.

- Avoid the S election if shareholders have high marginal income tax rates relative to the C corporation rate.

- If corporate losses are anticipated and there is unlikely to be corporate taxable income soon, S corporation status is advisable.

- If a C corporation holds an NOL carryover from prior years, the losses cannot be used in an S corporation year (except with respect to built-in gains).

- There may be tax advantages to the S shareholder who receives a flow-through of passive activity income.

- Tax-exempt income at the S level does not lose its special tax treatment for shareholders.

12-1a **An Overview of S Corporations**

As the following examples illustrate, S corporations can be advantageous even when the individual tax rate exceeds the corporate tax rate.

S Corporation Advantages

EXAMPLE 1

An S corporation earns $300,000 for the tax year. The marginal individual tax rate applicable to the entity's shareholders is 37% on ordinary income and 20% on dividends (ignoring the 3.8% investment income tax). The corporate tax rate is 21%, and the S corporation shareholders receive the full 20% qualified business income deduction (see text Section 12-3b). All after-tax income is distributed currently.

	C Corporation	S Corporation
Earnings	$300,000	$300,000
Less: Corporate tax	(63,000)	(–0–)
Available for distribution	$237,000	$300,000
Less: Tax at owner level	(47,400)	(88,800)
Available after-tax earnings	$189,600	$211,200

The S corporation generates an extra $21,600 of after-tax earnings ($211,200 − $189,600) when compared with a similar C corporation. The C corporation might be able to reduce this disadvantage by paying out its earnings as deductible compensation, rents, or interest expense. Tax at the owner level also can be deferred or avoided by not distributing after-tax earnings.

EXAMPLE 2

A new corporation elects S status and incurs a net operating loss (NOL) of $300,000. The shareholders may use their proportionate shares of the NOL to offset other taxable income in the current year, providing an immediate tax savings. In contrast, a newly formed C corporation is required to carry the NOL forward and does not receive any tax benefit in the current year. Hence, an S corporation can accelerate NOL deductions and thereby provide a greater present value for tax savings generated by the loss.

12-2 **QUALIFYING FOR S CORPORATION STATUS**

LO.2

Identify corporations that qualify for the S election.

There are certain conditions that a corporation must meet before S corporation status is available.

12-2a Definition of a Small Business Corporation

To achieve S corporation status, a corporation *first* must qualify as a  small business corporation . If each of the following requirements is met, then the entity can elect S corporation status.

- Is a domestic corporation (incorporated and organized in the United States).
- Is an eligible corporation (see the following section for ineligible types).
- Issues only one class of stock.
- Is limited to a theoretical maximum of 100 shareholders.
- Has only individuals, estates, and certain trusts and exempt organizations as shareholders.
- Has no nonresident alien shareholders.

No maximum or minimum dollar sales or capitalization restrictions apply to small business corporations.

Ineligible Corporations

Small business corporation status is not permitted for non-U.S. corporations, nor for certain banks and insurance companies.

Any domestic corporation that is not an ineligible corporation can be a qualified Subchapter S corporation subsidiary (QSSS) if another S corporation holds 100 percent of its stock and elects to treat the subsidiary as a QSSS.[1] QSSSs are separate entities for legal purposes, but they are treated merely as a division of the parent for Federal income tax purposes.

One Class of Stock

A small business corporation may have only one class of stock issued and outstanding.[2] This restriction permits differences in voting rights, but not differences in distribution or liquidation rights.[3] Thus, two classes of common stock that are identical, except that one class is voting and the other is nonvoting, are treated as a single class of stock for S corporation purposes. In contrast, voting common stock and voting preferred stock (with a preference on dividends) are treated as two classes of stock. Authorized and unissued stock or treasury stock of another class do not count as a second class of stock. Likewise, unexercised stock options, phantom stock, stock appreciation rights, warrants, and convertible debentures usually do not constitute a second class of stock.[4]

The Big Picture

EXAMPLE 3

Return to the facts of *The Big Picture* on p. 12-1. Cane, Inc., could elect S status as long as the two classes of common stock are identical except for differences in voting rights. In this situation, one class of common stock is voting and the other class is nonvoting. This situation does not violate the one-class-of-stock rule.

You learn that both shareholders have binding employment contracts with Cane, Inc. The amount of compensation paid by the corporation to Jones under her contract is reasonable, but the amount paid to Smith under his contract is excessive, resulting in a constructive dividend. Smith's employment contract was not designed to circumvent the one-class-of-stock requirement.

Because employment contracts are not considered governing provisions, Cane still is treated as though it has only one class of stock if an S election is made.

Although the one-class-of-stock requirement seems straightforward, debt still can be reclassified as stock, resulting in an unexpected loss of S corporation status.[5] To mitigate concern over possible reclassification of debt as a second class of stock, the law provides a set of *safe harbor provisions*.

First, straight debt *issued in an S corporation year* is not treated as a second class of stock and does not disqualify the S election.[6] The characteristics of straight debt include the following.

- The debtor is subject to a written, unconditional promise to pay on demand or on a specified date a sum certain in money.
- The interest rate and payment date are not contingent on corporate profits, management discretion, or similar factors.
- The debt is not convertible to stock.

In addition to straight debt under the safe harbor rules, short-term unwritten debt that is held by stockholders in the same proportion as their stock is not treated as a second class of stock, even if it otherwise would be reclassified as equity.[7]

Number of Shareholders

A small business corporation theoretically is limited to 100 shareholders. Several exceptions, though, allow the number of shareholders to exceed 100. For instance, if shares of stock are owned jointly by two individuals, they generally are treated as separate shareholders.

---

[1] § 1361(b)(3)(B).
[2] § 1361(b)(1)(D).
[3] § 1361(c)(4).
[4] Reg. § 1.1361–1(l)(1).

[5] Refer to the discussion of debt-versus-equity classification in text Section 4-2b.
[6] § 1361(c)(5)(A).
[7] Reg. § 1.1361–1(l)(1).

A group of family members may be treated as one shareholder for purposes of determining the number of shareholders. The term *members of the family* includes a "common ancestor, the lineal descendants of the common ancestor, and the spouses (or former spouses) of the lineal descendants or common ancestor."[8]

Fred and Wilma (husband and wife) jointly own 10 shares in Marlins, Inc., an S corporation, with the remaining 290 shares outstanding owned by 99 other unrelated shareholders. Fred and Wilma are divorced; pursuant to the property settlement approved by the court, the 10 shares held by Fred and Wilma are divided between them—5 to each.

Before the divorce settlement, Marlins had 100 shareholders under the small business corporation rules. After the settlement, it still has 100 shareholders and continues to qualify as a small business corporation. A former spouse is treated as being in the same family as the individual to whom he or she was married.

EXAMPLE 4

Type of Shareholder Limitation

Small business corporation shareholders may be resident individuals, estates, certain trusts, and certain tax-exempt organizations.[9] Charitable organizations, employee benefit trusts exempt from taxation, and a one-person LLC also can qualify as shareholders of an S corporation. This limitation prevents partnerships, corporations, limited liability partnerships, most LLCs, and most IRAs and Roth IRAs from owning S corporation stock. Partnerships and corporate shareholders could circumvent the 100-shareholder limitation as illustrated in the following example.

Saul and 105 of his friends want to form an S corporation. Saul reasons that if he and his friends form a partnership, the partnership can then form an S corporation and act as a single shareholder, thereby avoiding the 100-shareholder rule. Saul's plan will not work because partnerships cannot own stock in a small business corporation.

EXAMPLE 5

Although partnerships and corporations cannot own S corporation stock, small business corporations can be partners in a partnership or shareholders in a corporation. This approach allows the 100-shareholder requirement to be bypassed in a limited sense. For example, if two small business corporations, both with 80 shareholders, form a partnership, then the shareholders of both corporations can enjoy the limited liability conferred by S corporation status and a single level of tax on partnership profits.

Nonresident Aliens

Nonresident aliens cannot own stock in a small business corporation.[10] That is, individuals who are not U.S. citizens *must live in the United States* to own S corporation stock. Therefore, shareholders with nonresident alien spouses in community property states[11] cannot own S corporation stock because the nonresident alien spouse would be treated as owning half of the community property.[12] Similarly, if a resident alien shareholder moves outside the United States, the S election is terminated.

---

[8]§§ 1361(c)(1)(A)(ii) and (B)(i).

[9]§ 1361(b)(1)(B). Foreign trusts, charitable remainder trusts, and charitable lead trusts cannot be shareholders.

[10]§ 1362(b)(1)(C).

[11]Assets acquired by a married couple are generally considered community property in these states: Arizona, California, Idaho, Louisiana, Nevada, New Mexico, Texas, Washington, Wisconsin, and (if elected) Alaska.

[12]See *Ward v. U.S.*, 81–2 USTC ¶9674, 48 AFTR 2d 81–5942, 661 F.2d 226 (Ct.Cl., 1981), where the court found that the stock was owned as community property. Because the taxpayer-shareholder (a U.S. citizen) was married to a citizen and resident of Mexico, the nonresident alien prohibition was violated. If the taxpayer-shareholder had held the stock as separate property, the S election would have been valid.

The Big Picture

EXAMPLE 6

Return to the facts of *The Big Picture* on p. 12-1. Because Jones lives in Arkansas, a common law property state, the fact that she is married to a nonresident alien spouse would not affect an S election. However, because Smith lives in Texas, a community property state, his nonresident alien spouse would be treated as owning half of his community property stock, and an S election would not be allowed. To qualify for S status, Smith could move to Arkansas or his wife could move to Texas (becoming a resident alien).

LO.3

Explain how to make an S election.

12-2b **Making the Election**

To become an S corporation, the entity must file a valid election with the IRS. The election is made on Form 2553. For the election to be valid, it should be filed on a timely basis and all shareholders must consent.

For S corporation status to apply in the current tax year, the election must be filed either in the previous year or on or before the fifteenth day of the third month of the current year.

The Big Picture

EXAMPLE 7

Return to the facts of *The Big Picture* on p. 12-1. Suppose that in 2019, shareholders Smith and Jones decide to become an S corporation beginning January 1, 2020. Because the C corporation uses a calendar tax year, the S election can be made at any time in 2019 or by March 15, 2020. An election after March 15, 2020, is not effective until the 2021 calendar tax year.

Even if the 2½-month deadline is met, an S election is not valid unless the corporation qualifies as a small business corporation for the *entire* tax year. Otherwise, the election is not effective until the following tax year.

A corporation that does not yet exist cannot make an S corporation election.[13] Thus, for new corporations, a premature election may not be effective. A new corporation's 2½-month election period begins at the earliest occurrence of any of the following events.

- When the corporation has shareholders.
- When it acquires assets.
- When it begins doing business.[14]

EXAMPLE 8

Several individuals acquire assets on behalf of Rock Corporation on June 29, 2019, and they begin doing business on July 3, 2019. They subscribe to shares of stock, file articles of incorporation for Rock, and become shareholders on July 6, 2019. The S election must be filed no later than 2½ months after June 29, 2019 (i.e., on or before September 12), to be effective for 2019.

12-2c **Shareholder Consent**

A qualifying election requires the consent of all of the corporation's shareholders.[15] Consent must be in writing, and it generally must be filed by the election deadline. A consent extension is available only if Form 2553 is filed on a timely basis, reasonable cause is given, and the interests of the government are not jeopardized.[16]

---

[13]See, for example, *T.H. Campbell & Bros., Inc.*, 34 TCM 695, T.C.Memo. 1975–149; Ltr.Rul. 8807070.

[14]Reg. § 1.1372–2(b)(1). Also see, for example, *Nick A. Artukovich*, 61 T.C. 100 (1973).

[15]§ 1362(a)(2).

[16]Rev.Rul. 60–183, 1960–1 C.B. 625; *William Pestcoe*, 40 T.C. 195 (1963); Reg. § 1.1362–6(b)(3)(iii).

Vern and Yvonne decide to convert their C corporation into a calendar year S corporation for 2019. At the end of February 2019 (before the election is filed), Yvonne travels to Ukraine and forgets to sign a consent to the election. Yvonne will not return to the United States until June, and she cannot be reached by fax or e-mail.

Vern files the S election on Form 2553 and requests an extension of time to file Yvonne's consent to the election. Vern indicates that there is a reasonable cause for the extension: a shareholder is out of the country. Because the government's interest is not jeopardized, the IRS probably will grant Yvonne an extension of time to file the consent. Vern must file the election on Form 2553 on or before March 15, 2019, for the election to be effective for the 2019 calendar year.

Both husband and wife must consent if they own their stock jointly (as joint tenants, tenants in common, tenants by the entirety, or community property), even though they count as one shareholder.

Three shareholders, Amy, Monty, and Dianne, incorporate in January and file Form 2553. Amy is married and lives in California. Monty is single, and Dianne is married; both live in South Carolina. Because Amy is married and lives in a community property state, her husband also must consent to the S election. South Carolina is not a community property state, so Dianne's husband need not consent.

For current-year S elections, persons who were shareholders during any part of the taxable year before the election date but were not shareholders when the election was made also must consent to the election.[17]

On January 15, 2019, the stock of Columbus Corporation (a calendar year C corporation) was held equally by three individual shareholders: Jim, Sally, and LuEllen. On that date, LuEllen sells her interest to Jim and Sally. On March 14, 2019, Columbus Corporation files Form 2553. Jim and Sally indicate their consent by signing the form. Columbus cannot become an S corporation until 2020 because LuEllen did not indicate consent. Had all three shareholders consented by signing Form 2553, S status would have taken effect as of January 1, 2019.

12-2d **Loss of the Election**

An S election remains in force until it is revoked or lost. Election or consent forms are not required for future years. However, an S election can terminate if any of the following occurs.

- Shareholders owning a majority of shares (voting and nonvoting) voluntarily revoke the election.
- A new shareholder owning more than one-half of the stock affirmatively refuses to consent to the election.
- The corporation no longer qualifies as a small business corporation.
- The corporation does not meet the passive investment income limitation.

Voluntary Revocation

A **voluntary revocation** of the S election requires the consent of shareholders owning a majority of shares on the day the revocation is to be made.[18] A revocation filed up to and including the fifteenth day of the third month of the tax year is effective for the entire tax year, unless a later date is specified. Similarly, unless an effective date is specified, revocation made after the first 2½ months of the current tax year is effective for the following tax year.

LO.4

Explain how an S election can be terminated.

---

[17]§ 1362(b)(2)(B)(ii).   [18]§ 1362(d)(1).

EXAMPLE 12

The shareholders of Petunia Corporation, a calendar year S corporation, voluntarily revoke the S election on January 5 of the current year (not a leap year). They do not specify a future effective date in the revocation. If the revocation is properly executed and timely filed, Petunia will be a C corporation for the entire current tax year. If the election is not made until June, though, Petunia remains an S corporation for this year; it becomes a C corporation at the beginning of the next year.

A corporation can revoke its S status *prospectively* by specifying a future date when the revocation is to be effective. A revocation that designates a future effective date splits the corporation's tax year into a short S corporation year and a short C corporation year. The day on which the revocation occurs is treated as the first day of the C corporation year. The corporation allocates income or loss for the entire year on a pro rata basis, using the number of days in each short year.

EXAMPLE 13

Assume the same facts as in the preceding example, except that Petunia designates July 1 as the revocation date. Accordingly, June 30 is the last day of the S corporation's tax year. The C corporation's tax year runs from July 1 to December 31 of the current year. Income or loss for the 12-month period is allocated between the two short years (i.e., 184/365 to the C corporation year).

Rather than allocating on a pro rata basis, the corporation can elect to compute actual income or loss attributable to the two short years. This election requires the consent of everyone who was a shareholder at any time during the S corporation's short year and everyone who owns stock on the first day of the C corporation's year.[19]

EXAMPLE 14

Assume the same facts as in the preceding example, except that all of Petunia's shareholders consent to allocate the income or loss to the two short tax years based on its actual realization. Assume further that Petunia experiences a total loss of $102,000, of which $72,000 is incurred in the first half of the year. Because $72,000 of the loss occurs before July 1, this amount is allocated to the S corporation short year, and only $30,000 of the loss is allocated to the C corporation year.

Loss of Small Business Corporation Status

If an S corporation fails to qualify as a small business corporation at any time after the election has become effective, its status as an S corporation ends. The termination occurs on the day the corporation ceases to be a small business corporation.[20] Thus, if the corporation ever has more than 100 qualified shareholders, a second class of stock, a nonqualifying shareholder, or otherwise fails to meet the definition of a small business corporation, the S election is immediately terminated.

EXAMPLE 15

Peony Corporation has been a calendar year S corporation for three years. On August 13, one of its 100 shareholders sells *some* of her stock to an outsider. Peony now has 101 shareholders, and it ceases to be a small business corporation. For the tax year, Peony is an S corporation through August 12 and a C corporation from August 13 to December 31.

Passive Investment Income Limitation

The Code provides a <mark>passive investment income (PII)</mark> limitation for S corporations that were previously C corporations or for S corporations that have merged with C corporations. If an S corporation holds C corporation E & P and it generates passive investment income in excess of 25 percent of its gross receipts for three consecutive tax years, the S election is terminated as of the beginning of the fourth year.[21]

---

[19] § 1362(e)(3).
[20] § 1362(d)(2)(B).
[21] § 1362(d)(3)(A)(ii).

For 2017, 2018, and 2019, Diapason Corporation, a calendar year S corporation, received passive investment income in excess of 25% of its gross receipts. If Diapason holds accumulated E & P from years in which it was a C corporation, its S election is terminated as of January 1, 2020.

EXAMPLE 16

PII includes dividends, interest, rents, gains and losses from sales of capital assets, and royalties net of investment deductions. Rents are not considered PII if the corporation renders significant personal services to the occupant.

Violet Corporation owns and operates an apartment building. The corporation provides utilities for the building, maintains the lobby, and furnishes trash collection for tenants. These activities are not considered significant personal services, so any rent income earned by the corporation will be considered PII.

Alternatively, if Violet also furnishes maid services to its tenants (personal services beyond what normally would be expected from a landlord in an apartment building), the rent income would no longer be PII.

EXAMPLE 17

Reelection after Termination

After an S election has been terminated, the corporation must wait five years before reelecting S corporation status. The five-year waiting period is waived if:

- There is a more-than-50-percent change in ownership of the corporation after the first year for which the termination is applicable, or
- The event causing the termination was not reasonably within the control of the S corporation or its majority shareholders.

Conditions that a corporation must meet before S corporation status is available are illustrated in Exhibit 12.1.

12-3 OPERATIONAL RULES

S corporations are treated much like partnerships for tax purposes. With a few exceptions,[22] S corporations generally make tax accounting and other elections at the corporate level. Each year, the S corporation determines nonseparately stated income or loss and separately stated income, deductions, and credits. These items are taxed only once, at the shareholder level. All items are allocated to each shareholder based on average ownership of stock throughout the year. The *flow-through* of each item of income, deduction, and credit from the corporation to the shareholder is illustrated in Exhibit 12.2.

12-3a **Computation of Taxable Income**

An S corporation's taxable income or loss is determined in a manner similar to the tax rules that apply to partnerships, except that S corporations amortize organizational expenditures under the C corporation rules[23] and must recognize gains, *but not losses*, on distributions of appreciated property to shareholders.[24] Other provisions affecting only the computation of C corporation income, such as the dividends received deduction, do not extend to S corporations.[25] Finally, as with partnerships, certain deductions of individuals are not permitted, including alimony payments and the standard deduction.

In general, S corporation items are divided into (1) nonseparately stated income or loss and (2) separately stated income, losses, deductions, and credits that could affect

LO.5

Compute nonseparately stated income and identify separately stated items.

---

[22]A few elections can be made at the shareholder level (e.g., the choice between a foreign tax deduction or credit). But shareholders cannot make these accounting method elections; only the entity can do so. *Caselli*, 115 TCM 1448, T.C. Memo. 2018–81.

[23]§§ 248 and 1363(b).

[24]§ 1363(b).

[25]§ 703(a)(2).

EXHIBIT 12.1	Conditions Required to Elect S Corporation Status

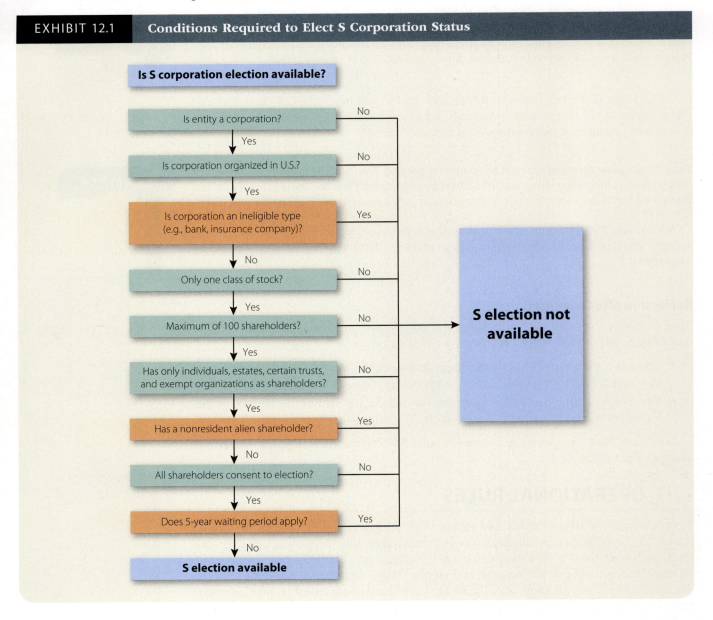

the tax liability of any shareholder in a different manner, depending on other factors in the shareholder's tax situation.

Nonseparate items are aggregated into an undifferentiated amount that constitutes S corporation ordinary income or loss. An S corporation's separately stated items are identical to those separately stated by partnerships. These items retain their tax attributes on the shareholder's return. Separately stated items are listed on Schedule K of the 1120S. They include the following.

- Tax-exempt income.
- Long-term and short-term capital gains and losses.
- § 1231 gains and losses.
- Charitable contributions (no grace period).
- Passive activity gains, losses, and credits.
- Certain portfolio income.
- § 179 deduction.

- Tax preferences and adjustments for the shareholders' potential alternative minimum tax.
- Depletion.
- Foreign income or loss.
- Recoveries of tax benefit items.
- Intangible drilling costs.
- Investment interest, income, and expenses.

EXHIBIT 12.2 **Flow-Through of Separate Items of Income and Loss to S Corporation Shareholders**

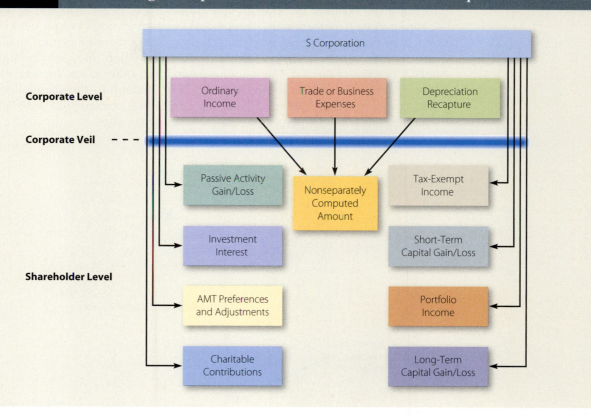

The following is the income statement for Jersey, Inc., an S corporation.

EXAMPLE 18

Sales		$ 40,000
Less cost of sales		(23,000)
Gross profit on sales		$ 17,000
Less: Interest expense	$1,200	
Charitable contributions	400	
Advertising expenses	1,500	
Other operating expenses	2,000	(5,100)
Book income from operations		$ 11,900
Add: Tax-exempt interest	$ 300	
Dividend income	200	
Long-term capital gain	500	1,000
Less: Short-term capital loss		(150)
Net income per books		$ 12,750

Jersey's ordinary income is calculated as follows, using net income for book purposes as the starting point.

Net income per books		$ 12,750
Separately stated items		
Deduct: Tax-exempt interest	$ 300	
Dividend income	200	
Long-term capital gain	500	(1,000)
Add: Charitable contributions	$ 400	
Short-term capital loss	150	550
Ordinary income		$ 12,300

The $12,300 of Jersey's ordinary income, as well as each of the five separately stated items, are divided among the shareholders based upon their stock ownership.

12-3b **Qualified Business Income Deduction**

To bring the taxation of flow-through entities such as S corporations closer to the C corporation 21 percent rate, shareholders of certain S corporations (and other qualified flow-through entities) may deduct up to 20 percent of certain qualified business income (QBI). With the full 20 percent deduction, the pass-through top rate is 29.6 percent (0.80 × 0.37), ignoring payroll and other taxes. Income earned by a C corporation that is distributed after-tax as a dividend to the shareholders may be subject to a maximum Federal income tax rate of 39.8 percent [0.21 + (0.79 × 0.238)], which includes the 3.8 percent investment income tax rate.

The <mark>qualified business income deduction (QBID)</mark> is:

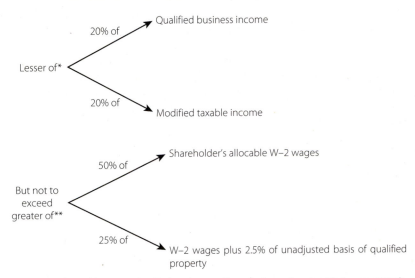

*Deduction limited for certain specified service-type S corporations where taxable income exceeds $160,700 (single; phased out at $210,700) and $321,400 (joint; phased out at $421,400). The phaseout percentage is the ratio of the excess over the threshold amount to $50,000 for individual taxpayers or $100,000 if married filing jointly.

**Does not apply if taxable income is equal to or less than $160,700 (single; phased out at $210,700) or $321,400 (joint; phased out at $421,400).

There are some important limitations on the QBID. The deduction is the smaller of 20 percent of (a) qualified business income or (b) taxable income reduced by net capital gains, and without considering the QBID (modified taxable income).[26] QBI does not include any service-related income paid by the S corporation, including reasonable compensation paid to the S corporation shareholder.[27]

QBI is the net amount of domestic qualified items of income, gains, deductions, and losses in the determination of taxable income with respect to the S shareholders qualified businesses. For a more detailed discussion of QBI, see text Section 2-3c.

In case of a qualified business loss in one year, the loss can be carried over to the next year to reduce QBI (but not below zero). Further, QBI does not include certain investment-type gains, deductions, or losses.

The W–2 wages limitation is the greater of (1) 50 percent of wages paid by the S corporation or (2) the sum of 25 percent of the W–2 wages plus 2.5 percent of the unadjusted basis (determined immediately after purchase) of all depreciable property.[28] An S corporation's W–2 wages are the sum of wages paid subject to withholding, elective deferrals, and deferred compensation (including wages paid to S corporation owners). See text Section 2-3f.

---

[26]§ 199A(a).

[27]§ 199A(e)(5)(A).

[28]§ 199A(b)(2)(B)(ii). For more detail, see D.L. Crumbley and J.R. Hasselback, "Attractiveness of S Corporations After 2017," *Tax Notes*, February 26, 2018.

EXAMPLE 19

Morris is the sole owner of an S corporation that manufactures shovels. This business has no employees, but the company purchases and places into service a shovel-making machine for $200,000 in 2020. Morris's limit on the qualified business income deduction is $5,000, calculated as follows: greater of 50% of W–2 wages ($0) or the sum of 25% of W–2 wages ($0) + 2.5% of the basis of the shovel-making machine (2.5% × $200,000 = $5,000).

This deduction has no effect on AAA or the shareholder's stock basis. If the S corporation is a specified service trade or business and the owner is over the threshold amount, the QBID is zero. See text Section 2-3g.

12-3c **Allocation of Income and Loss**

LO.6

Allocate income, deductions, and credits to shareholders.

Each shareholder is allocated a pro rata portion of nonseparately stated income or loss and all separately stated items. The pro rata allocation method assigns an equal amount of each of the S items to each day of the year. If a shareholder's stock holding changes during the year, this allocation assigns the shareholder a pro rata share of each item for *each* day the stock is owned. On the date of transfer, the transferor (and not the transferee) is considered to own the stock.[29]

The per-day allocation must be used, unless the shareholder disposes of his or her entire interest in the entity.[30]

EXAMPLE 20

Assume in the previous example that Pat, a shareholder, owned 10% of Jersey's stock for 100 days and 12% for the remaining 265 days of the tax year (not a leap year). Using the required per-day allocation method, Pat's share of the S corporation items is determined as follows.

	Schedule K Totals	Pat's Share 10%	Pat's Share 12%	Pat's Schedule K–1 Totals
Ordinary income	$12,300	$337	$1,072	$1,409
Tax-exempt interest	300	8	26	34
Dividend income	200	5	17	22
Long-term capital gain	500	14	44	58
Charitable contributions	400	11	35	46
Short-term capital loss	150	4	13	17

Pat's share of the Subchapter S ordinary income is the total of $12,300 × [0.10 × (100/365)] plus $12,300 × [0.12 × (265/365)], or $1,409. Each of the Schedule K–1 totals from the right column flows through to the appropriate lines on Pat's individual income tax return (Form 1040).

The Short-Year Election

If a shareholder's interest is completely terminated by a sale or by a disposition following death during the tax year, all shareholders holding stock during the year and the corporation may elect to treat the S taxable year as two taxable years. The first year ends on the date of the termination. Under this election, an interim closing of the books is undertaken, and the shareholders report their shares of the S corporation items as they occurred during the short tax year.[31]

---

[29]Reg. § 1.1377–1(a)(2)(ii).
[30]§§ 1366(a)(1) and 1377(a)(1).

[31]§ 1377(a)(2).

The short-year election provides an opportunity to shift income, losses, and credits among shareholders. The election is desirable in circumstances where more loss can be allocated to taxpayers with higher marginal rates.

EXAMPLE 21

Alicia, the owner of all of the shares of an S corporation, transfers her stock to Cindy halfway through the tax year. There is a $100,000 NOL for the entire tax year, but $30,000 of the loss occurs during the first half of the year. Without a short-year election, $50,000 of the loss is allocated to Alicia, and $50,000 is allocated to Cindy. If the corporation makes the short-year election, Cindy is allocated $70,000 of the loss. Of course, the sales price of the stock would probably be increased to recognize the tax benefits being transferred from Alicia to Cindy.

12-3d Tax Treatment of Distributions to Shareholders

The amount of any actual distribution of wealth (like cash) to an S corporation shareholder is equal to the cash plus the fair market value of any other property distributed. How the distribution is taxed depends upon whether the S corporation has C corporation **accumulated earnings and profits (AEP)** (described in text Section 5-2).

No C Corporation AEP

If the S corporation never has been a C corporation or if it holds no C corporation AEP, the distribution is a tax-free recovery of capital to the extent that it does not exceed the shareholder's basis in the stock of the S corporation. When the amount of the distribution exceeds the basis of the stock, the excess is treated as a gain from the sale or exchange of property (capital gain in most cases). The vast majority of S corporations fall into this easy-to-apply category.

EXAMPLE 22

Twirl, Inc., a calendar year S corporation, has no AEP. During the year, Juan, an individual shareholder of the corporation, receives a cash distribution of $12,200 from Twirl. Juan's basis in his stock is $9,700. Juan recognizes a capital gain of $2,500, the excess of the distribution over the stock basis ($12,200 − $9,700). The remaining $9,700 is tax-free, but it reduces Juan's basis in his stock to zero.

C Corporation AEP Exists

S corporations that hold C corporation AEP treat distributions of pre-election (C corporation) and post-election (S corporation) earnings differently. Distributions of AEP are taxed as dividends, while distributions of previously taxed S corporation earnings are tax-free to the extent of the shareholder's basis in the stock.

Concept Summary 12.2 outlines the taxation of distributions when this condition applies. These rules are intended to prevent two problems that result when a profitable C corporation (one holding C corporation accumulated E & P) has been converted to an S corporation.

- Manipulation in the shareholders' favor could result because the AEP would not be taxed when an S distribution is made; S corporation shareholders are taxed on income, not on distributions.

- On the other hand, double taxation could occur if the rules acted to tax as dividend income any AEP that exists when a distribution is made to the S shareholders; S distributions usually are free of income tax.

The Accumulated Adjustments Account A special account is required to track undistributed earnings of an S corporation that have been taxed to shareholders previously. Distributions from this account, known as the **accumulated adjustments account (AAA)**, are tax-free. The AAA begins with a zero balance on the first day of an S corporation's

Concept Summary 12.2

Classification Procedures for Distributions from an S Corporation

Where No Earnings and Profits Exist	Where Earnings and Profits Exist
	1. Distributions are tax-free to the extent of the AAA.*
	2. Distributions from AEP constitute dividend income.†
	3. Distributions are tax-free to the extent of the other adjustments account (OAA).*
1. Distributions are nontaxable to the extent of shareholder's basis of stock.*	4. Any residual distribution amount is nontaxable to the extent of shareholder's basis of stock.*
2. Excess is treated as gain from a sale or exchange of stock (capital gain in virtually all cases).	5. Excess is treated as gain from a sale or exchange of stock (capital gain in virtually all cases).

*The distribution reduces the stock basis. Once stock basis reaches zero, any distribution from the AAA is treated as a gain from the sale or exchange of stock. Thus, the shareholder's stock basis is an upper limit on what a shareholder may receive tax-free.

†The AAA bypass election is available to pay out AEP before reducing the AAA [§ 1368(e)(3)].

first tax year. Essentially, the AAA is the cumulative total of undistributed nonseparately and separately stated items for S corporation tax years. Calculation of the AAA should be made by all S corporations, but the AAA is most important to those that have been C corporations. The AAA provides a mechanism to ensure that the earnings of an S corporation are taxed to shareholders only once.

The AAA is computed by making adjustments in the order specified in Exhibit 12.3. Its balance typically is determined at the end of each year, rather than at the time distributions are made. When more than one distribution occurs in the same year, a pro rata portion of each distribution is treated as having been made out of the AAA.

In calculating the amount in the AAA for purposes of determining the tax treatment of current-year distributions, the net negative adjustments (e.g., the excess of losses and deductions over income) for that tax year are ignored. Tax-exempt income and related expenses (e.g., insurance proceeds and premiums paid for life insurance) do not affect the AAA.

A shareholder has a proportionate interest in the AAA, regardless of the size of his or her stock basis.[32] However, because the AAA is a corporate account, no connection exists between the prior accumulated S corporation income and any specific shareholder.[33]

EXHIBIT 12.3	Adjustments to the Corporate AAA

Increase by:

1. Schedule K income items other than tax-exempt income.
2. Nonseparately computed income.
3. Depletion in excess of basis in the property.

Decrease by:

4. Negative Schedule K adjustments other than distributions (e.g., losses and deductions).
5. Any portion of a distribution that is considered to be tax-free from the AAA (but not below zero).

Note: When the combination of items 1 through 4 results in a negative number, the AAA is adjusted first for the distribution and then for the adjustments in items 1 through 4.

---

[32]§ 1368(c).

[33]§ 1368(e)(1)(A).

Thus, the benefits of the AAA can be shifted from one shareholder to another shareholder. For example, when one S shareholder transfers stock to another shareholder, any AAA balance on the purchase date may be distributed tax-free to the purchaser. Similarly, issuing additional stock to a new shareholder in an S corporation with a positive balance in the AAA dilutes the account relative to the existing shareholders.

The AAA can have a negative balance. All losses decrease the AAA balance, even those in excess of the shareholder's stock basis. However, *distributions* may not make the AAA negative or increase a negative balance.

Distribution Ordering Rules A cash distribution from an S corporation with AEP comes first from the AAA.[34] Distributions from the AAA are tax-free. The remaining distribution is taxed as a dividend to the extent of AEP. After AEP is fully distributed, any residual amount is applied against the other adjustments account (OAA, discussed in the next section) and then the shareholder's remaining stock basis. The reduction in the shareholder's stock basis is a tax-free recovery of capital.[35] Any distributions once the stock basis reaches zero typically are taxed as capital gains.

Ordering Rules for Distributions

Short, a calendar year S corporation, distributes $1,300 cash to its only shareholder, Otis, on December 31. Otis's basis in his stock is $1,400, Short's AAA balance is $500, and Short holds $750 AEP before the distribution.

According to the distribution ordering rules, the first $500 is a tax-free recovery of basis from the AAA. The next $750 is a taxable dividend distribution from AEP. The remaining $50 of cash is a tax-free recovery of basis. Immediately after the distribution, Short holds a zero balance in its AAA and AEP. Otis's stock basis now is $850.

	Corporate AAA	Corporate AEP	Otis's Stock Basis*
Balance before the distribution	$ 500	$ 750	$1,400
Distribution ($1,300)			
From AAA	(500)		(500)
From AEP		(750)	
From stock basis			(50)
Balance after the distribution	$ –0–	$ –0–	$ 850

*Details of basis adjustments are discussed later in the chapter.

Assume the same facts as in the preceding example. During the following year, Short reports zero ordinary income and distributes $1,000 to Otis. Of the distribution, $850 is a tax-free recovery of basis, and $150 is taxed to Otis as a capital gain.

With the consent of all of its shareholders, an S corporation can elect to have a distribution treated as if it were made from AEP rather than from the AAA. This mechanism is known as an AAA **bypass election** . This election may be desirable as a simple means by which to eliminate a small AEP balance. See Exhibit 12.4.

EXAMPLE 25

Collett, a calendar year S corporation, has AEP of $12,000 and a balance of $20,000 in the AAA. Collett Corporation may elect to distribute the AEP first, creating a $12,000 dividend for its shareholders, before using the AAA.

---

[34]§§ 1368(c)(1) and (e)(1). Before 1983, different distribution rules applied, and an account similar to the AAA was in place, namely, **previously taxed income (PTI)** . An S corporation in existence before 1983 might still hold some PTI.

[35]§ 1368(c).

EXHIBIT 12.4	**Special Complications of Conversion of C Corporation to S Corporation**

- Positive accumulated earnings and profits (AEP) may cause distributions to be taxed as dividends.
- Positive AEP may trigger one or more corporate level taxes.
- Positive AEP with passive investment income exceeding 25 percent of gross income for three consecutive years causes loss of S status.
- Net operating loss from C years can only be used to reduce built-in gains.
- C corporation operating loss carryover period continues to run.
- S corporation may make a bypass election to distribute AEP before AAA.

Other Aspects of the AAA

Schedule M–2. S corporations report changes in the AAA on Schedule M–2 of Form 1120S. Schedule M–2 contains a column labeled **other adjustments account (OAA)**. This account includes items that affect basis but not the AAA, such as tax-exempt income and any related nondeductible expenses. For example, life insurance proceeds received and insurance premiums paid are traced through the OAA. Distributions are made from the OAA after AEP and the AAA are depleted to zero. Distributions from the OAA generally are tax-free.

EXAMPLE 26

Sparrow, an S corporation, records the following items.

AAA, beginning of the year	$ 8,500
Ordinary income	25,000
Tax-exempt interest	4,000
Key employee life insurance proceeds received	5,000
Payroll penalty expense	2,000
Charitable contributions	3,000
Unreasonable compensation	5,000
Premiums on key employee life insurance	2,100
Distributions to shareholders	16,000

Sparrow's Schedule M–2 for the current year appears as follows.

Schedule M-2	Analysis of Accumulated Adjustments Account, Shareholders' Undistributed Taxable Income Previously Taxed, Accumulated Earnings and Profits, and Other Adjustments Account (see instructions)			
		(a) Accumulated adjustments account	**(b)** Shareholders' undistributed taxable income previously taxed	**(c)** Accumulated earnings and profits	**(d)** Other adjustments account
1	Balance at beginning of tax year	8,500			
2	Ordinary income from page 1, line 21	25,000			
3	Other additions				9,000**
4	Loss from page 1, line 21	( )			
5	Other reductions	(10,000*)			(2,100)
6	Combine lines 1 through 5	23,500			6,900
7	Distributions	16,000			
8	Balance at end of tax year. Subtract line 7 from line 6	7,500			6,900

*$2,000 (payroll penalty) + $3,000 (charitable contributions) + $5,000 (unreasonable compensation).
**$4,000 (tax-exempt interest) + $5,000 (life insurance proceeds).

Schedule M–3: Net Income or Loss Reconciliation. S corporations that have total assets on Schedule L at the end of the tax year that equal or exceed $10 million must file Schedule M–3 in lieu of Schedule M–1. Only a few large S corporations must file a Schedule M–3. The schedule provides detailed information about the entity's book-tax differences, and it can be used by the IRS to target specific items that will be subjected to an audit.

Effect of Terminating the S Election. As a result of the reduced C corporation tax rate after 2017, there is the expectation that some S corporations will terminate the S election and convert to C corporation status. Normally, distributions to shareholders from a

C corporation are taxed as dividends to the extent of E & P. However, any distribution of *cash* by a corporation to shareholders during a one-year period[36] following S election termination receives special treatment. Such a distribution is treated as a tax-free recovery of stock basis to the extent that it does not exceed the AAA.[37] To take advantage of post-termination benefits, an S corporation must know the amount of both the AAA and the OAA as of the date the election terminates.

EXAMPLE 27

Quinn, the sole shareholder of Roman, Inc., a calendar year S corporation, elects during 2019 to terminate the S election, effective January 1, 2020. As of the end of 2019, Roman holds an AAA of $1,300. Quinn can receive a nontaxable distribution of cash during a post-termination period of approximately one year to the extent of Roman's AAA. Although a cash distribution of $1,300 during 2020 would be nontaxable to Quinn, it would reduce the basis of his stock.

LO.7

Determine how distributions to S corporation shareholders are taxed.

12-3e Tax Treatment of Noncash Property Distributions by the Corporation

An S corporation recognizes a gain on any distribution of appreciated property in the same manner as if the asset were sold to the shareholder at its fair market value.[38] The corporate gain is passed through to the shareholders. The character of the gain—capital gain or ordinary income—depends upon the type of asset being distributed. There is an important reason for this gain recognition rule. Without it, property might be distributed tax-free (other than for certain recapture items) and later sold without income recognition to the shareholder because the shareholder's basis in the property equals its fair market value.

The S corporation does not recognize a loss when distributing assets that are worth less than their basis. As with gain property, the shareholder's basis is equal to the asset's fair market value. Thus, the potential loss is postponed until the shareholder sells the stock of the S corporation. Because loss property receives a step-down in basis without any loss recognition by the S corporation, distributions of loss property should be avoided. See Concept Summary 12.3.

Concept Summary 12.3

Consequences of Noncash Distributions

	Appreciated Property	**Depreciated Property**
S corporation	Realized gain is recognized by the corporation, which passes it through to the shareholders. Such gain increases a shareholder's stock basis, generating a basis in the property equal to FMV. On the distribution, the shareholder's stock basis is reduced by the FMV of the property (but not below zero).	Realized loss is not recognized. The shareholder takes an FMV basis in the property.
C corporation	Realized gain is recognized under § 311(b) and increases E & P (net of tax). The shareholder reports a taxable dividend to the extent of corporate E & P equal to the property's FMV. The shareholder takes an asset basis equal to its FMV.	Realized loss is not recognized. The shareholder takes an FMV basis in the property.
Partnership	No gain to the partnership or partner. The partner takes a carryover basis in the asset, but the asset basis is limited to the partner's basis in the partnership.	Realized loss is not recognized. The partner takes a carryover basis in the asset, but the asset basis is limited to the partner's basis in the partnership.

---

[36]The period is approximately one year in length. The post-termination transition period is discussed later in the chapter.

[37]§§ 1371(e) and 1377(b).

[38]§ 311(b).

Noncash Distributions

EXAMPLE 28

Turnip, Inc., an S corporation for 10 years, distributes a tract of land held as an investment to Chang, its majority shareholder. The land was purchased for $22,000 many years ago and currently is worth $82,000. Turnip recognizes a capital gain of $60,000, which increases the AAA by $60,000. The gain appears on Turnip's Schedule K, and a proportionate share of it passes through to the shareholders' tax returns. Then the property distribution reduces the AAA by $82,000 (the fair market value). The tax consequences are the same for appreciated property, whether it is distributed to the shareholders and they dispose of it or the corporation sells the property and distributes the proceeds to the shareholders.

If the land had been purchased for $82,000 and was currently worth $22,000, Chang would take a $22,000 basis in the land. The $60,000 realized loss is not recognized at the corporate level. The loss does reduce Turnip's AAA, though not an attractive result for Turnip shareholders.

EXAMPLE 29

Assume the same facts as in the previous example, except that Turnip is a C corporation ($1,000,000 E & P balance) or a partnership. The partner's basis in the partnership interest is $100,000.

	Appreciated Property		
	S Corporation	**C Corporation**	**Partnership**
Entity gain/loss	$60,000	$60,000	$ –0–
Owner's gain/loss/dividend	60,000	82,000	–0–
Owner's basis in land	82,000	82,000	22,000
	Property That Has Declined in Value		
	S Corporation	**C Corporation**	**Partnership**
Entity gain/loss	$ –0–	$ –0–	$ –0–
Owner's gain/loss/dividend	–0–	22,000	–0–
Owner's basis in land	22,000	22,000	82,000

12-3f Shareholder's Basis in S Stock

LO.8

Calculate a shareholder's basis in S corporation stock.

The calculation of the initial tax basis of stock in an S corporation is similar to that for the basis of stock in a C corporation and depends upon the manner in which the shares are acquired (e.g., gift, inheritance, purchase, or exchange under § 351). Once the initial tax basis is determined, various transactions during the life of the corporation affect the shareholder's basis in the stock. Although each shareholder is required to compute his or her own basis in the S shares, neither Form 1120S nor Schedule K–1 provides a place for deriving this amount.

A shareholder's basis is increased by stock purchases and capital contributions. Operations during the year cause the following upward adjustments to basis.

- Nonseparately computed income.
- Separately stated income items (e.g., nontaxable income).
- Depletion in excess of basis in the property.

Basis then is reduced by distributions not reported as income by the shareholder (e.g., an AAA distribution). Next, the following items reduce basis (*but not below zero*).

- Nondeductible expenses of the corporation (e.g., fines, penalties, and illegal kickbacks).
- Nonseparately computed loss.
- Separately stated loss and deduction items.

As under the partnership rule, basis first is increased by income items; then it is decreased by distributions and finally by losses. In most cases, this *losses last* rule is advantageous to the S shareholder.

EXAMPLE 30

In its first year of operation, Iris, Inc., a calendar year S corporation in Clemson, South Carolina, earns income of $2,000. On February 2 in its second year of operation, Iris distributes $2,000 to Marty, its sole shareholder. During the remainder of the second year, the corporation incurs a $2,000 loss.

Before accounting for the entity's operating results, Marty's stock basis is zero. Under the S corporation ordering rules, the $2,000 distribution is tax-free AAA to Marty, and the $2,000 loss is suspended until Marty generates additional stock basis (e.g., from capital contributions or future entity profits).

A shareholder's basis in S stock never can be reduced below zero. Once stock basis reaches zero, any additional basis reductions from losses or deductions, but *not* distributions, decrease (but not below zero) the shareholder's basis in loans made to the S corporation. Any excess of losses or deductions over both bases is *suspended* until there are subsequent bases.

Once the basis of any debt is reduced, it later is increased (up to the original amount) by the subsequent *net* increase resulting from *all* positive and negative basis adjustments. The debt basis is adjusted back to the original amount by any "net increase" before any increase is made in the stock basis.[39] "Net increase" for a year is computed after taking distributions (other than those from AEP) into consideration.

A distribution in excess of stock basis does not reduce any debt basis. If a loss and a distribution occur in the same year, the loss reduces the stock basis last, *after* the distribution.

EXAMPLE 31

Stacey, a sole shareholder, has a $7,000 stock basis and a $2,000 basis in a loan that she made to Romulus, a calendar year S corporation with no AEP. At the beginning of the tax year, the corporation's AAA and OAA balances are zero. Ordinary income for the year is $8,200, during which Romulus received $2,000 of tax-exempt interest income.

Cash of $17,300 is distributed to Stacey on November 15. Stacey recognizes only a $100 capital gain.

	Corporate AAA	Corporate OAA	Stacey's Stock Basis	Stacey's Loan Basis
Beginning balance	$ –0–	$ –0–	$ 7,000	$2,000
Ordinary income	8,200		8,200	
Tax-exempt income		2,000	2,000	
Subtotal	$ 8,200	$ 2,000	$17,200	$2,000
Distribution ($17,300)				
From AAA	(8,200)		(8,200)	
From OAA		(2,000)	(2,000)	
From stock basis			(7,000)	
Ending balance	$ –0–	$ –0–	$ –0–	$2,000
Distribution in excess of basis = Capital gain			$ 100	

Pass-through losses can reduce loan basis, but distributions do not. Stock basis cannot be reduced below zero, so the $100 excess distribution does not reduce Stacey's loan basis.

The basis rules for an S corporation are similar to the rules for determining a partner's interest basis in a partnership. However, a partner's basis in the partnership interest includes the partner's direct investment plus a *ratable share* of any partnership liabilities.[40] If a partnership borrows from a partner, the partner receives a basis increase as if the partnership had borrowed from an unrelated third party.[41] In contrast, except for loans from the shareholder to the corporation, corporate borrowing has no effect on S corporation shareholder basis.

---

[39]§ 1367(b)(2); Reg. § 1.1367–2(e).

[40]§ 752(a).

[41]Reg. § 1.752–1(e).

The fact that a shareholder has guaranteed a loan made to the corporation by a third party has no effect on the shareholder's loan basis, unless payments actually have been made as a result of that guarantee.[42]

If a loan's basis has been reduced and is not restored, income is recognized when the S corporation repays the shareholder. If the corporation issued a note as evidence of the debt, repayment constitutes an amount received in exchange for a capital asset and the amount that exceeds the shareholder's basis is entitled to capital gain treatment.[43] However, if the loan is made on open account, the repayment constitutes ordinary income to the extent that it exceeds the shareholder's basis in the loan.[44] Each repayment is prorated between the gain portion and the repayment of the debt.[45] Thus, a written note should be given to ensure capital gain treatment for the income that results from a loan's repayment.

Effects of Debt

Sammy is a 57% owner of Falcon, an S corporation in Brooklyn, New York. At the beginning of the year, his stock basis is zero. Sammy's basis in a $12,000 loan made to Falcon and evidenced by Falcon's note has been reduced to $0 by prior losses. At the end of the year, he receives a $13,000 distribution. During the year, his net share of corporate taxable income is $11,000. Because there is no "net increase" (i.e., his share of income is less than the amount of the distribution), Sammy's debt basis is not restored. Instead, his share of income increases his stock basis to $11,000. Therefore, on receipt of the $13,000 distribution, $11,000 is a tax-free recovery of his stock basis, and $2,000 is a capital gain.[46]

EXAMPLE 32

Assume in the previous example that the distribution that Sammy receives is only $8,000. Because the "net increase" is $3,000 ($11,000 income share in excess of $8,000 distribution), the debt basis is restored by $3,000. Accordingly, the remaining income share not used to increase debt basis ($8,000) is used to increase Sammy's stock basis to $8,000. Therefore, on receipt of the $8,000 distribution, all $8,000 is tax-free, reducing the stock basis back to zero.

EXAMPLE 33

12-3g **Treatment of Losses**

Net Operating Loss

One major advantage of an S election is the ability to pass through any net operating loss of the corporation directly to the shareholders. A shareholder can deduct an NOL for the year in which the S corporation's tax year ends. The corporation does not deduct the NOL. A shareholder's basis in the stock is reduced to the extent of any pass-through of the NOL, and the entity's AAA is reduced by the same deductible amount.[47]

LO.9

Explain the tax effects that losses have on shareholders.

The Big Picture

Return to the facts of *The Big Picture* on p. 12-1. If Smith and Jones make the S election for Cane, Inc., they each can pass through any NOLs to the extent of the current stock basis. If the new S corporation incurs an NOL of $84,000 for the tax year, both shareholders are entitled to deduct $42,000 against other income for the tax year in which Cane's tax year ends. Any NOL incurred before the S election is in effect does not flow through to the two shareholders as long as the S election is maintained.

EXAMPLE 34

[42]See, for example, *Estate of Leavitt*, 90 T.C. 206 (1988), *aff'd* 89–1 USTC ¶9332, 63 AFTR 2d 89–1437, 875 F.2d 420 (CA–4, 1989); *Selfe v. U.S.*, 86–1 USTC ¶9115, 57 AFTR 2d 86–464, 778 F.2d 769 (CA–11, 1985); *James K. Calcutt*, 91 T.C. 14 (1988).

[43]*Joe M. Smith*, 48 T.C. 872 (1967), *aff'd* and *rev'd* in 70–1 USTC ¶9327, 25 AFTR 2d 70–936, 424 F.2d 219 (CA–9, 1970); Rev.Rul. 64–162, 1964–1 C.B. 304.

[44]Reg. § 1.1367–2. Open account debt is treated as if it were evidenced by a note if the shareholder's principal balance exceeds $25,000 at the end of the tax year.

[45]Rev.Rul. 68–537, 1968–2 C.B. 372.

[46]§ 1367(b)(2)(B); Reg. § 1.1367–2(e).

[47]§§ 1368(a)(1)(A) and (e)(1)(A).

Deductions for an S corporation's loss pass-throughs (e.g., NOL, capital loss, and charitable contributions) cannot exceed a shareholder's adjusted basis in the stock *plus* the basis of any loans made by the shareholder to the corporation. If a taxpayer is unable to prove the tax basis, the loss pass-through can be denied.

Distributions made by an S corporation are taken into account *before* applying the loss limitations for the year.

EXAMPLE 35

Pylon, Inc., a calendar year S corporation, is partly owned by Doris, who has a beginning stock basis of $10,000. During the year, Doris's share of a long-term capital gain (LTCG) is $2,000, and her share of an ordinary loss is $9,000. If Doris receives a $6,000 distribution, her deductible loss is calculated as follows.

Beginning stock basis	$10,000
Add: LTCG	2,000
Subtotal	$12,000
Less: Distribution	(6,000)
Basis for loss limitation purposes	$ 6,000
Deductible loss	($ 6,000)
Suspended loss	($ 3,000)

Doris's stock now has a basis of zero.

A shareholder's share of an NOL may be greater than both stock basis and loan basis. A shareholder is entitled to carry forward a loss to the extent that the loss for the year exceeds basis. Any loss carried forward may be deducted *only* by the *same* shareholder if and when the basis in the stock or loans to the corporation is restored.[48]

EXAMPLE 36

Dana has a stock basis of $4,000 in an S corporation. He has loaned $2,000 to the corporation and has guaranteed another $4,000 loan made to the corporation by a local bank. Although his share of the S corporation's NOL for the current year is $9,500, Dana may deduct only $6,000 of the NOL on his individual tax return; the loan guarantee had no effect on Dana's stock or loan basis.

Dana may carry forward $3,500 of the NOL, to be deducted when the basis in his stock or loan to the corporation is restored. Dana has a zero basis in both the stock and the loan after the flow-through of the $6,000 NOL.

Any loss carryover due to insufficient basis remaining at the end of an approximately one-year post-termination transition period is *lost forever*. The post-termination period includes the 120-day period beginning on the date of any determination pursuant to an audit of a taxpayer that follows the termination of the S corporation's election and that adjusts a Subchapter S item.[49] Thus, if a shareholder has a loss carryover, he or she should increase the stock or loan basis and flow through the loss before disposing of the stock.

Net operating losses from C corporation years cannot be utilized at the corporate level (except with respect to built-in gains, discussed in text Section 12-3h), nor can they be passed through to the shareholders. When a corporation is expecting losses in the future, an S election should be made *before* the loss years.

At-Risk Rules

S corporation shareholders, like partners, are limited in the amount of loss they may deduct by their "at-risk" amounts; see text Section 10-3e. These rules apply to the shareholders, but not to the corporation. An amount at risk is determined separately for each shareholder.

---

[48]§ 1366(d).   [49]§ 1377(b)(1).

Shareholder Ricketts has a basis of $35,000 in his S corporation stock. His share of this year's S corporation loss is $40,000.

Ricketts takes a $15,000 nonrecourse loan from a local bank and lends the proceeds to the S corporation. Ricketts now has a stock basis of $35,000 and a loan basis of $15,000. However, due to the at-risk rules, he can deduct only $35,000 of S corporation losses, reducing his stock basis to $0.

Passive Activity Losses and Credits

S corporations are not directly subject to the passive activity limits, but corporate rental activities are inherently passive, and other activities of an S corporation may be passive unless the shareholder(s) materially participate(s) in operating the business. If the corporate activity involves rentals or the shareholders do not materially participate, any loss or credit that flows through is passive. The shareholders can apply such losses or credits only against income from other passive activities.

12-3h Tax on Pre-Election Built-In Gain

LO.10

Compute the built-in gains and passive investment income penalty taxes.

In almost all cases, an S corporation does *not* pay an income tax, because all items flow through to the shareholders. But an S corporation that previously was a C corporation may be required to pay a built-in gains tax, LIFO recapture tax, general business credit recapture, or passive investment income tax.

Without the **built-in gains tax** (§ 1374), it would be possible to avoid the corporate double tax on a disposition of appreciated property by electing S corporation status.

The built-in gains tax generally applies to C corporations converting to S status. It is a *corporate-level* tax on any built-in gain recognized when the S corporation disposes of an asset in a taxable disposition within five calendar years after the date on which the S election took effect.[50] The holding period begins on the date of the S election.

General Rules

The base for the built-in gains tax includes any unrealized gain on appreciated assets (e.g., real estate, cash basis receivables, and goodwill) held by a corporation on the day it elects S status. The highest corporate tax rate (currently 21 percent) is applied to the unrealized gain when any of the assets are sold. Furthermore, the gain on the sale (net of the tax itself)[51] passes through as a taxable gain to shareholders.

Zinnia, Inc., a C corporation, owns a single asset with a basis of $100,000 and a fair market value of $500,000. Zinnia elects S corporation status. A corporate-level tax must be paid by Zinnia if it sells the asset after electing S status. Upon sale of the asset, the corporation owes a tax of $84,000 ($400,000 × 21%). The shareholders report a $316,000 taxable gain ($400,000 − $84,000). In this manner, the built-in gains tax effectively imposes a double tax on Zinnia and its shareholders.

The gain that is subject to the tax is limited to the *aggregate net* built-in gain of the corporation at the time it converted to S status. Thus, at the time of the S election, unrealized gains of the corporation are reduced by unrealized losses from the contributed assets. This net amount sets an upper limit on the tax base for the built-in gains tax.

Recognized built-in losses and built-in gains are netted each year to determine the built-in gains tax base. The tax base then is limited to the entity's taxable income for the year.[52]

An S corporation can offset built-in gains with NOLs or unexpired capital losses from C corporation years.

---

[50]§ 1374(d)(7)(B).
[51]§ 1366(f)(2).

[52]§§ 1374(c)(2), (d)(1), and (d)(2)(A).

The Big Picture

EXAMPLE 39

Return to the facts of *The Big Picture* on p. 12-1. If Cane, Inc., becomes an S corporation, a built-in gain may be recognized. Assuming that Cane reports a $50,000 built-in gain on conversion and that it holds a $20,000 NOL carryforward for C corporation years before the S election, the NOL carryforward is applied against the built-in gain. Cane's built-in gains tax applies only to $30,000.

LIFO Recapture Tax

To preclude deferral of gain recognition by a C corporation that is electing S status, any LIFO recapture amount at the time of the S election is subject to a corporate-level tax.

The taxable LIFO recapture amount equals the excess of the inventory's value under FIFO over the LIFO value. No negative adjustment is allowed if the LIFO value is higher than the FIFO value.

The resulting tax is payable in four equal installments, with the first payment due on or before the due date for the corporate return for the last C corporation year (without regard to any extensions). The remaining three installments are paid on or before the due dates of the succeeding corporate returns.

No interest is due if payments are made by the due dates, and no estimated taxes are due on the four tax installments. The basis of the LIFO inventory is adjusted to account for this LIFO recapture amount, but the AAA is not decreased by payment of the tax.

12-3i Passive Investment Income Penalty Tax

A tax is imposed on the excess passive income of S corporations that possess AEP from C corporation years. The tax rate is the highest corporate rate for the year (21 percent currently). The rate is applied to excess net passive income (ENPI), which is determined using the following formula, and illustrated in Example 40.

Passive investment income (PII) includes gross receipts derived from royalties, passive rents, dividends, interest, and annuities. Only the net gain from the disposition of capital assets is taken into account in computing PII gross receipts.[53] Net passive income is PII reduced by any deductions directly connected with the production of that income. Any PII tax reduces the gross income that flows through to the shareholders.

The excess net passive income cannot exceed the S corporation's taxable income for the year, calculated as if it were a C corporation.[54]

EXAMPLE 40

Barnhardt Corporation, an S corporation, generates gross receipts for the year totaling $264,000 (of which $110,000 is PII). Expenditures directly connected to the production of the PII total $30,000. Therefore, Barnhardt reports net PII of $80,000 ($110,000 − $30,000), and its PII for the tax year exceeds 25% of its gross receipts by $44,000 [$110,000 PII − (25% × $264,000)]. Excess net passive income (ENPI) is $32,000, calculated as follows.

$$\text{ENPI} = \frac{\$44,000}{\$110,000} \times \$80,000 = \$32,000$$

Barnhardt's PII tax is $6,720 ($32,000 × 21%).

---

[53]§§ 1362(d)(3)(B), (C).   [54]§ 1375(b)(1)(B).

12-3j **Other Operational Rules**

Several other points may be made about the possible effects of various Code provisions on S corporations.

- An S corporation is required to make estimated tax payments with respect to tax exposure because of any recognized built-in gain and excess passive investment income.

- An S corporation is *not* subject to the 10 percent of taxable income limitation applicable to charitable contributions made by a C corporation.

- Any family member who renders services or furnishes capital to an S corporation must be paid reasonable compensation. Otherwise, the IRS can make adjustments to reflect the value of the services or capital.[55] This rule may make it more difficult for related parties to shift Subchapter S taxable income to children or other family members.

- The flow-through of S items does not create self-employment income to the shareholder, nor is it subject to the additional Medicare tax on upper-income taxpayers.[56] This treatment is attractive compared to the treatment of a proprietorship or a partnership whose income is taxed as self-employment income to the owners. Compensation for services rendered to an S corporation is, however, subject to FICA taxes for the employee-shareholder, but it is not considered wages for the 20 percent QBID test.

S Corporations and SE Income

EXAMPLE 41

Mickey and Dana each own one-third of a fast-food restaurant, and their 14-year-old son owns the other shares. Both parents work full-time in the restaurant operations, but the son works infrequently. Neither parent receives a salary this year, when the taxable income of the S corporation is $160,000. The IRS can require that reasonable compensation be paid to the parents to prevent the full one-third of the $160,000 from being taxed to the son. Otherwise, this would be an effective technique to shift earned income to a family member to reduce the total family tax burden. Furthermore, low or zero salaries can reduce FICA taxes due to the Federal government and increase QBI for purposes of the QBID.

EXAMPLE 42

Dave is a professor at a southeastern university, earning a salary of $150,000. He also generates consulting income of $80,000. If the consulting business is organized as an S corporation, Dave should withdraw a reasonable salary from the S corporation for his services. The S corporation pays payroll and withholding tax on the salary. Dave receives a tax credit for any overpayment of the employee share of the FICA tax, but the S corporation does not receive a similar credit.

If the business is operated as a proprietorship, Dave is exempt from the Social Security portion of the self-employment tax because his university salary exceeds the annual FICA ceiling. Here, operating as a proprietorship offers a tax advantage over an S corporation.

- Some or all of the entity's income may be subject to a state-level income tax (e.g., a gross receipts tax or a "sting tax" on large S corporations in Massachusetts).

- An S corporation may issue § 1244 stock to its shareholders to obtain ordinary loss treatment. Review text Section 4-3c for the Federal income tax effects of such stock.

- The exclusion of gain on disposition of small business stock is *not* available for S stock.[57]

- Losses may be disallowed due to a lack of a profit motive. If the activities at the corporate level are not profit-motivated, the losses may be disallowed under the hobby loss rules.[58]

---

[55]§ 1366(e). In addition, beware of an IRS search for the "real owner" of the stock under Reg. § 1.1373–1(a)(2).

[56]Rev.Rul. 59–221, 1959–1 C.B. 225.

[57]§ 1202.

[58]§ 183; *Michael J. Houston*, 69 TCM 2360, T.C.Memo. 1995–159; *Mario G. De Mendoza, III*, 68 TCM 42, T.C.Memo. 1994–314.

- A penalty is imposed for failure to file (including extensions) timely S corporation returns. The penalty for returns filed in 2020 is $205 per month times the number of S corporation shareholders. The penalty is assessed against the corporation for a maximum of 12 months.[59]

- Partnership treatment applies for certain fringe benefits to more-than-2-percent shareholder-employees of S corporations. Thus, these shareholders are not entitled to exclude certain fringe benefits from gross income. A more-than-2-percent shareholder-employee is allowed an above-the-line (*for* AGI) deduction on Form 1040 for accident and health insurance premiums.[60]

LO.11

Engage in tax planning for S corporations.

12-4 TAX PLANNING

12-4a **When the Election Is Advisable**

Effective tax planning with S corporations begins with the determination of whether the election is appropriate. In this context, one should consider the following factors.

- Are losses from the business anticipated? If so, the S election may be highly attractive because these losses pass through to the shareholders.

- What are the tax brackets of the shareholders? If the shareholders are in high individual income tax brackets, it may be desirable to avoid S corporation status and have profits taxed to the entity at the lower C corporation rate (21 percent). However, the income still is not in the owners' hands.

- When the shareholders are in low individual income tax brackets, the pass-through of corporate profits is attractive, and reducing the combined income tax becomes the paramount consideration. Under these circumstances, the S election could be an effective tax planning tool.

- Does a C corporation hold an NOL carryforward? Such a loss cannot be used in an S year (except for purposes of the built-in gains tax).

- S corporations and partnerships have limited flexibility in the choice of a tax accounting period.[61]

12-4b **Making a Proper Election**

Once the parties have decided the election is appropriate, it becomes essential to ensure that the election is made properly.

- Make sure that all shareholders timely file a proper consent. If any doubt exists concerning the shareholder status of an individual, it would be wise to have that party issue a consent anyway.[62] Too few consents are fatal to the election; the same cannot be said for too many consents.

- Make sure the election is timely and properly filed. Either hand-carry the election to an IRS office or send it by certified or registered mail or use a commercial delivery service. The date used to determine timeliness is the postmark date, not the date the IRS receives the election. A copy of the election should become part of the corporation's permanent files.

---

[59]§ 6699.

[60]§ 1372(a); Notice 2008–1, 2008–2 I.R.B. 251.

[61]Entity tax-year constraints parallel those pertaining to partnerships, as discussed in text Section 10-2g. But the least aggregate deferral method is not used by S corporations.

[62]See *William B. Wilson*, 34 TCM 463, T.C.Memo. 1975–92.

- Ascertain when the timely election period begins to run for a newly formed corporation. An election made too soon (before the corporation is in existence) is worse than one made too late.

12-4c **Preserving the Election**

Recall that an election can be lost intentionally or unintentionally in several ways, and that a five-year waiting period generally is imposed before another S election is available. To preserve an S election, the following practices should be followed.

- As a starting point, all parties concerned should be made aware of the various transactions that lead to the loss of an election.
- Watch for possible disqualification of the eligibility rules for the S corporation and its shareholders. For example, the death of a shareholder could result in a nonqualifying trust becoming a shareholder.

12-4d **Planning for the Operation of the Corporation**

Accumulated Adjustments Account

Although the corporate-level accumulated adjustments account (AAA) is used primarily by an S corporation with accumulated earnings and profits (AEP) from a Subchapter C year, all S corporations should maintain an accurate record of the AAA. Because there is a grace period for distributing the AAA after termination of the S election, the parties must be in a position to determine the balance of the account.

The AAA bypass election may be used to eliminate a small E & P balance and pay a small current tax, but then to avoid future exposure to dividend distributions and the entity-level taxes of the S corporation.

Salary Structure

The amount of salary paid to a shareholder-employee of an S corporation can have varying tax consequences and should be considered carefully. Larger amounts might be advantageous if the maximum contribution allowed for the shareholder-employee under the corporation's retirement plan has not been reached. Smaller amounts may be beneficial if the parties are trying to shift taxable income to lower-bracket shareholders, reduce payroll taxes, curtail a reduction of Social Security benefits, or restrict losses that do not pass through because of the basis limitation.[63]

A strategy of decreasing compensation and correspondingly increasing distributions to shareholder-employees often results in substantial savings in employment taxes. This technique also increases the QBID for shareholders.

The Big Picture

Return to the facts of *The Big Picture* on p. 12-1. The two shareholders should consider reducing their $92,000 salary and instead receiving a larger undistributed share of the S corporation income. A shareholder's share of pass-through S corporation income is not treated as self-employment income, whereas traditional compensation is subject to the Social Security and Medicare taxes for the corporation and both employees.

EXAMPLE 43

---

[63]Rev.Rul. 74–44, 1974–1 C.B. 287; *Spicer Accounting, Inc. v. U.S.*, 91–1 USTC ¶50,103, 66 AFTR 2d 90–5806, 918 F.2d 90 (CA–9, 1990); *Radtke v. U.S.*, 90–1 USTC ¶50,113, 65 AFTR 2d 90–1155, 895 F.2d 1196 (CA–7, 1990); *Joseph M. Grey Public Accountant, P.C.*, 119 T.C. 121 (2002); *David E.* *Watson, PC, v. U.S.*, 2010–1 USTC ¶50,444, 105 AFTR 2d 2010–2624, 714 F.Supp.2d 954 (S.D. Iowa). The IRS uses salary surveys and other statistical methods to determine the appropriate compensation level. *McAlary Ltd.*, T.C. Summary Opinion 2013–62.

The IRS can require that reasonable compensation be paid to family members who render services or provide capital to the S corporation. The IRS also can adjust the items taken into account by family-member shareholders to reflect the value of services or capital they provided (refer to Example 41).

Deductions for various tax-free fringe benefits are denied to a more-than-2-percent shareholder-employee of an S corporation. Such benefits include group term life insurance, medical insurance, and meals and lodging furnished for the convenience of the employer. These items are treated as wages and are subject to most payroll taxes. The employee can deduct medical insurance premiums on his or her tax return.

The choice between a salary and pass-through income is not clear-cut.

- Although a salary is subject to payroll tax and pass-through income is not, pass-through income does not accrue Social Security benefits for its recipient.
- S corporation income distributions do not count as compensation for computing an employee's contribution formula for a qualified retirement plan.
- The IRS and the courts require an S shareholder to take a reasonable salary (see footnote 63).
- If a partner or proprietor reports salary income from other sources and the aggregate salaries exceed the annual FICA ceiling, a partnership or proprietorship entity may provide tax savings over an S corporation.

Loss Considerations

A net loss in excess of tax basis may be carried forward and deducted only by the same shareholder in succeeding years. Thus, before disposing of the stock, a shareholder should increase the basis of such stock/loan to flow through the loss. The next shareholder does not obtain the loss carryover.

Any unused loss carryover in existence upon the termination of the S election may be deducted only in the next tax year and is limited to the individual's *stock* basis (not loan basis) in the post-termination year.[64] The shareholder may want to purchase more stock to increase the tax basis to absorb the loss.

Avoiding the Passive Investment Income Tax

Too much passive investment income (PII) may cause an S corporation to incur a penalty tax on excessive passive investment income and/or terminate the S election. Several planning techniques can be used to avoid both of these unfavorable events. The corporation might reduce taxable income below the excess net passive income; similarly, PII might be accelerated into years in which there is an offsetting NOL.

The tax also can be avoided if the corporation generates needed gross receipts. By increasing gross receipts without increasing PII, the amount of PII in excess of 25 percent of gross receipts is reduced.

EXAMPLE 44

An S corporation has paid a passive investment income penalty tax for two consecutive years. In the next year, the corporation has a large amount of AAA. One planning technique to address this situation is to manufacture a large amount of gross receipts without increasing PII through an action such as a merger with a grocery store. If the gross receipts from the grocery store are substantial, the amount of the PII in excess of 25% of gross receipts is reduced.

---

[64]§ 1366(d)(3).

USING A PASS-THROUGH ENTITY TO ACHIEVE DEDUCTIBILITY OF LOSSES

As long as Smith and Jones, the owners of Cane, Inc., maintain C corporation status, they cannot deduct on their individual tax returns any NOLs the business incurs. For the owners to deduct any future NOLs on their Forms 1040, Cane needs to be operated as a flow-through entity. The most logical alternative is to make an S election or to become a limited liability company.

An S election may be appropriate for Cane. Cane should make a timely election on Form 2553, and both shareholders must consent to the election. The owners should make the election on or before the fifteenth day of the third month of the current year to claim losses for the current year. Otherwise, the S election becomes effective only at the beginning of the next tax year.

Normally, an S corporation does not pay any income tax because all items (including NOLs) flow through to the shareholders. A C corporation making an S election may be required to pay a corporate-level built-in gains tax or a LIFO recapture tax.

An S corporation can issue both voting and nonvoting common stock, provided that all shares have the same economic rights to corporate income or loss.

Cane might sell off the bonds that generate its tax-exempt income, which will not be reflected in the AAA. Although it is reflected in stock basis, tax-exempt income (as part of the OAA) is distributed to the shareholders only after the S corporation has distributed all of its C corporation earnings and profits.

What If?

Nonresident aliens cannot own S stock, so if joint ownership of the shares is desired among all of the spouses, a change in the spouses' residency must occur. When Cane begins to turn a profit, the S election will be less attractive, and termination of the S election should be considered by the parties.

Key Terms

Accumulated adjustments account (AAA), 12-14

Accumulated earnings and profits (AEP), 12-14

Built-in gains tax, 12-23

Bypass election, 12-16

Other adjustments account (OAA), 12-17

Passive investment income (PII), 12-8

Previously taxed income (PTI), 12-16

Qualified business income deduction (QBID), 12-12

S corporation, 12-2

Small business corporation, 12-3

Subchapter S, 12-2

Voluntary revocation, 12-7

Discussion Questions

1. **LO.1** Which of these taxes may be incurred by an S corporation?
   a. Corporate income tax.
   b. Tax on certain built-in gains.
   c. Property tax assessed by the county.

2. **LO.2** Which of the following are requirements to be an S corporation?
   a. Limited to an absolute maximum of 100 shareholders.
   b. Has no resident alien shareholders.
   c. Has only one class of stock.
   d. May have no straight debt.
   e. Cannot have any earnings and profits (E & P).

3. **LO.2** One shareholder of an S corporation takes a short-term unwritten cash advance of $9,100 during the tax year. Would this arrangement create a second class of stock? Explain.

4. **LO.2** Which of the following can be shareholders of an S corporation?

    a. Partnership.
    b. Limited liability partnership.
    c. Corporation.
    d. One-member limited liability company.

5. **LO.2** Joey lives in North Carolina, a common law state. He is a shareholder in an S corporation. If he marries a nonresident alien, will the S election terminate? Would your answer change if he lived in Louisiana? Explain.

Critical Thinking   6. **LO.2** Bob Roman, the major owner of an S corporation, approaches you for some tax planning help. He would like to exchange some real estate in a like-kind
Communications   transaction under § 1031 for real estate that may have some environmental liabilities. Prepare a letter to Bob outlining your suggestion. Bob's address is 8411 Huron Boulevard, West Chester, PA 19382.

Critical Thinking   7. **LO.2, 3** On March 5, 2019, the two 50% shareholders of a calendar year corporation decide to elect S status. One of the shareholders, Terry, purchased her stock from a previous shareholder (a nonresident alien) on January 18, 2019. Identify any potential problems for Terry and the corporation.

Communications   8. **LO.4** Caleb Samford calls you and says that his two-person S corporation was involuntarily terminated in February 2018. He asks you if they can make a new S election now, in November 2019. Draft a memo for your firm's tax research file, outlining what you told Caleb.

9. **LO.6** Using the categories in the following legend, classify each transaction as a plus (+) or minus (−) on Schedule M–2 of Form 1120S. An answer might look like one of these: +AAA or −OAA.

Legend
AAA = Accumulated adjustments account
OAA = Other adjustments account
NA = No direct effect on Schedule M–2

    a. Receipt of tax-exempt interest income.
    b. Administrative expenses.
    c. Depreciation recapture income.
    d. Nontaxable life insurance proceeds.
    e. Expenses related to tax-exempt securities.
    f. Charitable contributions.
    g. Business gifts in excess of $25.
    h. Nondeductible fines and penalties.

Critical Thinking   10. **LO.6, 11** Collette's S corporation holds a small amount of accumulated earnings and profits (AEP), thereby requiring the use of a more complex set of distribution rules. Collette's accountant tells her that this AEP forces the maintenance of the AAA figure each year. Discuss the issues that arise with respect to distributions when an S corporation holds AEP.

Communications   11. **LO.6, 8** Scott Tierney owns 21% of an S corporation. He is confused with respect to the amounts of the corporate AAA and his stock basis. Write a memo to Scott identifying the key differences between AAA and an S shareholder's stock basis.

12. **LO.8** For each of the following independent statements, indicate whether the transaction will increase (+), decrease (−), or have no effect (*NE*) on the basis of a shareholder's stock in an S corporation.

   a.   Expenses related to tax-exempt income.

   b.   Short-term capital gain.

   c.   Nonseparately computed loss.

   d.   Section 1231 gain.

   e.   Depletion *not* in excess of basis.

   f.   Separately computed income.

   g.   Nontaxable return-of-capital distribution by the corporation.

   h.   Advertising expenses.

   i.   Business gifts in excess of $25.

   j.   Depreciation recapture income.

   k.   Dividend income received by the S corporation.

   l.   LIFO recapture tax paid.

   m.   Collection of a bad debt previously deducted.

   n.   Long-term capital loss.

   o.   Cash distribution to shareholder out of AAA.

13. **LO.9** Sheila Jackson is a 50% shareholder in Washington, Inc., an S corporation.   Critical Thinking
   This year, Jackson's share of the Washington loss is $100,000. Jackson reports income from several other sources. Identify at least four tax issues related to the effects of the S corporation loss on Jackson's tax return.

14. **LO.1, 11** One of your clients is considering electing S status. Texas, Inc., is a   Decision Making
   six-year-old manufacturing company with two equal shareholders, both of whom paid $30,000 for their stock. Going into 2019, Texas holds a $110,000 NOL carryforward. Estimated income is $40,000 for 2019 and $25,000 for each of the next three years. Should Texas make an S election for 2019? Why or why not?

Computational Exercises

15. **LO.10** Matulis, Inc., a calendar year C corporation, owns a single asset with a basis of $325,000 and a fair market value of $800,000. Matulis holds a positive E & P balance. The entity elects S corporation status for 2020 and then sells the asset. Compute the corporate-level built-in gains tax that must be paid by Matulis.

16. **LO.10** TyroneCo, an S corporation with a positive E & P balance, reports gross receipts for the year totaling $400,000 (of which $200,000 is PII). Expenditures directly connected to the production of the PII total $80,000. Compute Tyrone's PII tax.

17. **LO.6** Dion, an S shareholder, owned 20% of MeadowBrook's stock for 292 days and 25% for the remaining 73 days in the year. Using the per-day allocation method, compute Dion's share of the following S corporation items.

	Schedule K Totals	Dion's Schedule K–1 Totals
Ordinary income	$60,000	
Tax-exempt interest	1,000	
Charitable contributions	3,400	

18. **LO.6** Noelle, the owner of all of the shares of ClockCo, an S corporation, transfers her stock to Grayson on April 1. ClockCo reports a $70,000 NOL for the entire tax year, but only $10,000 of the loss occurs during January–March. Without a short-year election, how much of the loss is allocated to Noelle and how much is allocated to Grayson? If the corporation makes the short-year election, how much of the loss is allocated to Grayson? The tax year is not a leap year.

19. **LO.6** Greiner, Inc., a calendar year S corporation, holds no AEP. During the year, Chad, an individual Greiner shareholder, receives a cash distribution of $30,000 from the entity. Chad's basis in his stock is $25,000. Compute Chad's ordinary income and capital gain from the distribution. What is his stock basis after accounting for the payment?

20. **LO.6** Holbrook, a calendar year S corporation, distributes $15,000 cash to its only shareholder, Cody, on December 31. Cody's basis in his stock is $20,000, Holbrook's AAA balance is $8,000, and Holbrook holds $2,500 AEP before the distribution. Complete the chart below using spreadsheet software such as Microsoft Excel.

	Distribution from Account	Effect on Stock Basis	Balance after Distribution
From AAA account			
From AEP account			
From Cody's stock basis			

21. **LO.7** Vogel, Inc., an S corporation for five years, distributes a tract of land held as an investment to Jamari, its majority shareholder. The land was purchased for $45,000 ten years ago and is currently worth $120,000.

    a. As a result of the distribution, what is Vogel's recognized capital gain? How much is reported as a distribution to shareholders?

    b. What is the net effect of the distribution on Vogel's AAA?

    c. Assume instead that the land had been purchased for $120,000 and was currently worth $45,000. How much would Vogel recognize as a loss? What would be the net effect on Vogel's AAA? What would be Jamari's basis in the land?

22. **LO.8** Jonas is a 60% owner of Ard, an S corporation. At the beginning of the year, his stock basis is zero. Jonas's basis in a $20,000 loan made to Ard and evidenced by Ard's note has been reduced to $0 by prior losses.

    During the year, Jonas's net share of Ard's taxable income is $10,000. At the end of the year, Ard makes a $15,000 cash distribution to Jonas. After these transactions, what is Jonas's basis in his stock, and what is his basis in the debt? What is Jonas's recognized capital gain?

23. **LO.9** Kaiwan, Inc., a calendar year S corporation, is partly owned by Sharrod, whose beginning stock basis is $32,000. During the year, Sharrod's share of a Kaiwan long-term capital gain (LTCG) is $5,000, and his share of an ordinary loss is $18,000. Sharrod then receives a $20,000 cash distribution. Compute the following.

    a. Sharrod's deductible loss.

    b. Sharrod's suspended loss.

    c. Sharrod's new basis in the Kaiwan stock.

Problems

24. **LO.5, 6** The profit and loss statement of Kitsch Ltd., an S corporation, shows $100,000 book income. Kitsch is owned equally by four shareholders. From supplemental data, you obtain the following information about items that are included in book income.

Selling expenses	($21,200)
Tax-exempt interest income	3,000
Dividends received	9,000
§ 1231 gain	7,000
Depreciation recapture income	11,000
Net income from passive real estate rentals	5,000
Long-term capital loss	(6,000)
Salary paid to owners (each)	(12,000)
Cost of goods sold	(91,000)

a. Compute Kitsch's nonseparately stated income or loss for the tax year.

b. What would be the share of this year's nonseparately stated income or loss items for James Billings, one of the Kitsch shareholders?

c. What is James Billings's share of tax-exempt interest income, if any? Is the income taxable to him this year?

25. **LO.5, 6** Maul, Inc., a calendar year S corporation, incurred the following items.

Tax-exempt interest income	$ 7,000
Sales	140,000
Depreciation recapture income	12,000
Long-term capital gain	20,000
§ 1231 gain	7,000
Cost of goods sold	(42,000)
Administrative expenses	(15,000)
Depreciation expense (MACRS)	(17,000)
Charitable contributions	(7,000)

a. Calculate Maul's nonseparately computed income or loss.

b. If Carl is a 40% owner of Maul, Inc., what is his share of the long-term capital gain?

26. **LO.5, 6** Zebra, Inc., a calendar year S corporation, incurred the following items this year. Sammy is a 40% Zebra shareholder throughout the year.

Operating income	$100,000
Cost of goods sold	(40,000)
Depreciation expense (MACRS)	(10,000)
Administrative expenses	(5,000)
§ 1231 gain	21,000
Depreciation recapture income	25,000
Short-term capital loss from stock sale	(6,000)
Long-term capital loss from stock sale	(4,000)
Long-term capital gain from stock sale	15,000
Charitable contributions	(4,500)

a. Calculate Sammy's share of Zebra's nonseparately computed income or loss.

b. Calculate Sammy's share of any Zebra long-term capital gain, if any.

c. Calculate Sammy's share of charitable contributions, if any.

27. **LO.6, 8, 9** Mary is a shareholder in CarrollCo, a calendar year S corporation. At the beginning of the year, her stock basis is $10,000, her share of the AAA is $2,000, and her share of corporate AEP is $6,000.

   At the end of the year, Mary receives from CarrollCo a $6,000 cash distribution. Mary's share of S corporation items includes a $2,000 long-term capital gain and a $10,000 ordinary loss. Determine the effects of these events on Mary's share of the entity's AAA, her stock basis, and CarrollCo's AEP using spreadsheet software such as Microsoft Excel.

28. **LO.6, 7** On January 1, Kinney, Inc., an S corporation, reports $4,000 of accumulated E & P and a balance of $10,000 in AAA. Kinney has two shareholders, Erin

and Frank, each of whom owns 500 shares of Kinney's stock. Kinney's nonseparately stated ordinary income for the year is $5,000.

Kinney distributes $6,000 to each shareholder on July 1, and it distributes another $3,000 to each shareholder on December 21. How are the shareholders taxed on the distributions? Ignore the 20% QBI deduction.

Critical Thinking   29. **LO.5, 6, 7** McLin, Inc., is a calendar year S corporation. Its AAA balance is zero.

    a.   McLin holds $90,000 of AEP. Tobias, the sole shareholder, has an adjusted basis of $80,000 in his stock. Determine the tax aspects if a $90,000 salary is paid to Tobias. Ignore the 20% QBI deduction.

    b.   Same as part (a), except that McLin pays Tobias a $90,000 cash distribution from AEP.

30. **LO.6, 7, 8** Tiger, Inc., a calendar year S corporation, is owned equally by four shareholders: Ann, Becky, Chris, and David. Tiger owns investment land that was purchased for $160,000 four years ago. On September 14, when the land is worth $240,000, it is distributed to David. Assuming that David's basis in his S corporation stock is $270,000 on the distribution date, discuss any Federal income tax ramifications. Ignore the 20% QBI deduction.

31. **LO.5** Jack and Mary, a married couple, report taxable income of $280,000, which includes $200,000 from Jack's solely owned S corporation. The S corporation paid wages of $100,000 to employees (which does not include his salary). Calculate the couple's QBI deduction, if any. No acquisitions of depreciable property were made during the year.

Communications   32. **LO.6, 8, 9, 11** Spence, Inc., a calendar year S corporation, generates an ordinary loss of $110,000 and makes a distribution of $140,000 to its sole shareholder, Storm Nelson. Nelson's stock basis and AAA at the beginning of the year are $200,000. Write a memo to your senior manager, Aaron McMullin, discussing the tax treatment of Spence's activities.

33. **LO.6** Lonergan, Inc., a calendar year S corporation in Athens, Georgia, had a balance in AAA of $200,000 and AEP of $110,000 on December 31, 2019. During 2020, Lonergan, Inc., distributes $140,000 to its shareholders, while sustaining an ordinary loss of $120,000. Calculate the balance in Lonergan's AAA and AEP accounts at the end of 2020.

34. **LO.6** If the beginning balance in Swan, Inc.'s OAA is $6,700 and the following transactions occur, what is Swan's ending OAA balance?

Depreciation recapture income	$ 21,600
Payroll tax penalty	(4,200)
Tax-exempt interest income	4,012
Nontaxable life insurance proceeds	100,000
Life insurance premiums paid (nondeductible)	(3,007)

35. **LO.6, 8** Cougar, Inc., is a calendar year S corporation. Cougar's Form 1120S shows nonseparately stated ordinary income of $80,000 for the year. Johnny owns 40% of the Cougar stock throughout the year. The following information is obtained from the corporate records.

Tax-exempt interest income	$ 3,000
Salary paid to Johnny	(52,000)
Charitable contributions	(6,000)
Dividends received from a non-U.S. corporation	5,000
Short-term capital loss	(6,000)
Depreciation recapture income	11,000
Refund of prior state income taxes	5,000

Cost of goods sold	($72,000)
Long-term capital loss	(7,000)
Administrative expenses	(18,000)
Long-term capital gain	14,000
Selling expenses	(11,000)
Johnny's beginning stock basis	32,000
Johnny's additional stock purchases	9,000
Beginning AAA	31,000
Johnny's loan to corporation	20,000

   a.   Compute Cougar's book income or loss.

   b.   Compute Johnny's ending stock basis.

   c.   Calculate Cougar's ending AAA balance.

36. **LO.6, 7, 8** Money, Inc., a calendar year S corporation in Denton, Texas, has two unrelated shareholders, each owning 50% of the stock. Both shareholders record a $400,000 stock basis as of January 1. At the beginning of the tax year, Money reports balances in AAA of $300,000 and AEP of $600,000. During the year, Money generates operating income of $100,000. At the end of the year, Money distributes securities worth $1,000,000, with an adjusted basis of $800,000. Determine the Federal income tax effects of these transactions.

37. **LO.6, 7, 8** Assume the same facts as in Problem 36, except that the two shareholders consent to an AAA bypass election.

38. **LO.7, 8, 9** At the beginning of the tax year, Lizzie holds a $10,000 stock basis as the sole shareholder of Spike, Inc., an S corporation. During the year, Spike reports the following. Determine Lizzie's stock basis at the end of the year and the treatment of her cash distribution.

Net taxable income from sales	$ 25,000
Net short-term capital loss	(18,000)
Cash distribution to Lizzie, 12/31	15,000

39. **LO.7, 8, 9** Assume the same facts as in Problem 38, except that the cash distribution to Lizzie amounts to $40,000. Determine Lizzie's stock basis at the end of the year and the treatment of her cash distribution.

40. **LO.7, 8** Jeff, a 52% owner of an S corporation, has a stock basis of zero at the beginning of the year. Jeff's basis in a $10,000 loan made to the corporation and evidenced by a corporate note has been reduced to zero by pass-through losses. During the year, his net share of the corporate taxable income is $11,000. At the end of the year, Jeff receives a $15,000 cash distribution. Discuss the tax effects of the distribution.

41. **LO.7, 8** Assume the same facts as in Problem 40, except that there is no cash distribution, but the corporation repays the loan principal to Jeff. Discuss the tax effects.

42. **LO.7, 8** Assume the same facts as in Problem 40, except that Jeff's share of corporate taxable income is only $8,000 and there is no cash distribution. However, the corporation repays the $10,000 loan principal to Jeff. Discuss the related Federal income tax effects. Assume that there was no corporate note (i.e., only an account payable). Does this change your answer? Explain.

43. **LO.9** Maple, Inc., is an S corporation with a single shareholder, Bob Maple. Bob believes that his stock basis in the entity is $50,000, but he has lost some of the records to substantiate this amount. Maple reports an ordinary loss for the year of $80,000. What are the Federal income tax aspects to consider?   Critical Thinking

44. **LO.6, 9** At the beginning of the year, Ann and Becky own equally all of the stock of Whitman, Inc., an S corporation. Whitman generates a $120,000 loss for

the year (not a leap year). On the 189th day of the year, Ann sells her half of the Whitman stock to her son, Scott. How much of the $120,000 loss, if any, belongs to Scott?

45. **LO.6, 9** In Problem 44, how much of the Whitman loss belongs to Ann and Becky? Becky's stock basis is $41,300.

Communications   46. **LO.5, 6, 8, 9**   A calendar year S corporation reports an ordinary loss of $80,000 and a capital loss of $20,000. Mei Freiberg owns 30% of the corporate stock and has a $24,000 basis in her stock. Determine the amounts of the ordinary loss and capital loss, if any, that flow through to Freiberg. Prepare a tax memo for the files, explaining your computations.

47. **LO.10** Whindy Corporation, an S corporation, reports a recognized built-in gain of $80,000 and a recognized built-in loss of $10,000 this year. Whindy holds an $8,000 unexpired NOL carryforward from a C corporation year. Whindy's ordinary income for the year is $65,000. Calculate any built-in gains tax.

48. **LO.10** Flint, an S corporation with substantial AEP, reports operating revenues of $410,000, taxable interest income of $390,000, operating expenses of $260,000, and deductions attributable to the interest of $150,000. Calculate any passive investment income penalty tax payable.

Critical Thinking   49. **LO.5, 6, 11** Bonnie and Clyde each own one-third of a fast-food restaurant, and their 13-year-old daughter owns all of the other shares. Both parents work full-time in the restaurant, but the daughter works infrequently. Neither Bonnie nor Clyde receives a salary during the year, when the ordinary income of the S corporation is $180,000.

An IRS agent estimates that reasonable salaries for Bonnie, Clyde, and the daughter are $30,000, $35,000, and $10,000, respectively. What adjustments would you expect the IRS to impose upon these taxpayers?

50. **LO.5** Bertha, a single individual, reports taxable income of $177,500, of which $130,000 is attributable to an S corporation that provides consulting services, after paying wages of $72,000 to employees (but not to Bertha). The entity made no acquisitions of depreciable property during the year. Calculate any 20% qualified business income deduction.

Critical Thinking   51. **LO.6, 10** Samuel Reese sold 1,000 shares of his stock in Maroon, Inc., an S corporation. He sold the stock for $15,700 after he had owned it for six years. Samuel had paid $141,250 for the stock, which was issued under § 1244. Samuel is married and is the owner of the 1,000 shares. Determine the appropriate treatment of any gain or loss on the stock sale.

Critical Thinking   52. **LO.7, 11** Blue is the owner of all of the shares of an S corporation, and Blue is considering receiving a salary of $110,000 from the business. She will pay the 7.65% FICA taxes on the salary, and the S corporation will pay the same amount of FICA tax. If Blue reduces her salary to $50,000 and takes an additional $60,000 as a cash distribution, how would her Federal income tax liabilities change?

Critical Thinking   53. **LO.1, 6, 8, 9, 11** Orange, Inc., a calendar year corporation in Clemson, South Carolina, elects S corporation status for 2019. The company generated a $74,000 NOL in 2018 and another NOL of $43,000 in 2019. Orange recorded no other transactions for the year.

At all times in 2018 and 2019, the stock of the corporation is owned by the same four shareholders, each owning 25% of the stock. Pete, one of the shareholders, holds a $6,020 basis in the Orange stock at the beginning of 2019. Identify the Federal income tax issues that Pete faces.

54. **LO.6** Based upon the following facts about Aqua, Inc., a calendar year S corporation, prepare the entity's Schedule M-2.

AAA, beginning of the year	$ 9,400
Ordinary income	24,600
Tax-exempt income	3,000
Key employee life insurance proceeds received	4,900
Payroll penalty expense	2,200
Charitable contributions	3,000
Unreasonable compensation	4,000
Premiums on key employee life insurance	2,300
Distribution to shareholders	17,000

Tax Return Problem

1. John Parsons (123-45-6781) and George Smith (123-45-6782) are 70% and 30% owners, respectively, of Premium, Inc. (11-1111111), a candy company located at 1005
16th Street, Cut and Shoot, TX 77303. Premium's S election was made on January 15,
2011, its date of incorporation. The following information was taken from the company's 2018 income statement.

Interest income	$ 100,000
Gross sales receipts	2,410,000
Beginning inventory	9,607
Direct labor	(203,102)
Direct materials purchased	(278,143)
Direct other costs	(249,356)
Ending inventory	3,467
Salaries and wages	(442,103)
Officers' salaries ($75,000 each to Parsons and Smith)	(150,000)
Repairs	(206,106)
Depreciation expense, tax and book	(15,254)
Interest expense	(35,222)
Rent expense (operating)	(40,000)
Taxes	(65,101)
Charitable contributions (cash)	(20,000)
Advertising expenses	(20,000)
Payroll penalties	(15,000)
Other deductions	(59,899)
Book income	704,574

A comparative balance sheet appears below.

	January 1, 2018	December 31, 2018
Cash	$ 47,840	$?
Accounts receivable	93,100	123,104
Inventories	9,607	3,467
Prepaid expenses	8,333	17,582
Building and equipment	138,203	185,348
Accumulated depreciation	(84,235)	(?)
Land	2,000	2,000
Total assets	$214,848	$844,422
Accounts payable	$ 42,500	$ 72,300
Notes payable (less than 1 year)	4,500	2,100
Notes payable (more than 1 year)	26,700	24,300
Capital stock	30,000	30,000
Retained earnings	111,148	?
Total liabilities and capital	$214,848	$844,422

Premium's accounting firm provides the following additional information.

Distributions to shareholders	$100,000
Beginning balance, Accumulated adjustments account	111,148

Using the preceding information, prepare a Form 1120S and Schedule K–1s for John Parsons and George Smith, 5607 20th Street, Cut and Shoot, TX 77303. Do not complete the Forms 1125–A, 1125–E, and 4562. If any information is missing, make realistic assumptions. Suggested software: ProConnect Tax Online.

Research Problems

THOMSON REUTERS
CHECKPOINT™

Note: Solutions to the Research Problems can be prepared by using the Thomson Reuters Checkpoint™ online tax research database, which accompanies this textbook. Solutions can also be prepared by using research materials found in a typical tax library.

Research Problem 1. Glow and Bro organized an S corporation and intended to have only one class of stock. They agreed that all distributions should be proportional to their stock ownership. During 2019, Bro withdrew large sums of money from the S corporation without Glow's knowledge. Glow's share of pass-through income was $500,000 on the Schedule K–1, but he only received $30,000 of cash distributions. The S corporation became bankrupt. The IRS determined that the two owners did not receive distributions that were proportionate to their ownership, but it taxed Glow (who is in the 37% tax bracket) on the $500,000.

Glow argued that a second class of stock was created: these substantially disproportionate distributions appear to create a preference in distribution, creating a second class of stock. Thus, the election was terminated, the entity was a C corporation, and Glow should be taxed only on the $30,000 distribution, taxed as a dividend because the entity was a C corporation. Glow also argued that the S corporation should take a theft loss deduction for Bro's withdrawals.

You are the U.S. Tax Court judge hearing the dispute. What are the proper Federal income tax results? Elaborate.

Research Problem 2. Sean Moon is president, secretary, treasurer, sole director, and sole shareholder of Streetz, an S corporation real estate company. He manages all aspects of the company's operations, and he is the only person working at the company that holds a real estate broker's license. Sean works 12-hour days and takes few days off. Streetz's gross receipts and net income figures were reported as follows.

Year	Gross Receipts	Net Income
1	$376,453	$122,605
2	405,244	161,660
3	518,189	231,454

Sean and his wife, Kim, filed joint Federal income tax returns, but they did not report any wages or salaries on line 7 of their Forms 1040. During year 3, Moon transferred $240,000 from the S corporation to his personal account.

You are an expert witness for the IRS. Identify the items you would present to the U.S. Tax Court with respect to the amount of Moon's compensation that is subject to employment taxes and any other taxes due for year 3 (especially the Medicare net investment income tax). *Hint:* This is a reasonable compensation issue.

Use internet tax resources to address the following questions. Look for reliable websites and blogs of the IRS and other government agencies, media outlets, businesses, tax professionals, academics, think tanks, and political outlets.

Research Problem 3. Prepare a graph of the growth in the number of S elections since 1980, using increments of no more than five years. On the same graph, show the maximum Federal income tax rates for those years as they applied to individuals and to C corporations. Send your graph and other observations in an e-mail to your instructor with some explanatory comments as to what you found. You might use the IRS Data Book and other items at **irs.gov** Tax Stats.

Data Analytics

Communications

Research Problem 4. Summarize the corrective actions required for a corporation to obtain a letter ruling under the inadvertent defective election provision since 1997. There have been almost 100 such letter rulings, and they have been limited to curing the defects that existed at the time the corporation filed its original Form 2553. Send your findings as a research memo in an e-mail to your instructor.

Communications

Becker CPA Review Questions

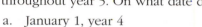

1. Village Corp., a calendar year corporation, began business in year 1. Village made a valid S corporation election on December 5, year 4, with the unanimous consent of its shareholders. The eligibility requirements for S status continued to be met throughout year 5. On what date did Village's S status become effective?

   a. January 1, year 4
   b. January 1, year 5
   c. December 5, year 4
   d. December 5, year 5

2. Fox Corp., an S corporation, had an ordinary loss of $36,500 for the year ended December 31, year 2. At January 1, year 2, Duffy owned 50% of Fox's stock. Duffy held the stock for 40 days in year 2 before selling the entire 50% interest to an unrelated third party. Duffy's basis for the stock was $10,000. Duffy was a full-time employee of Fox until the stock was sold. Duffy's share of Fox's loss was:

   a. $0
   b. $2,000
   c. $10,000
   d. $18,250

3. An S corporation has 30,000 shares of voting common stock and 20,000 shares of nonvoting common stock issued and outstanding. The S election can be revoked voluntarily with the consent of the shareholders holding, on the day of the revocation, the following number of outstanding shares.

	Shares of Voting Stock	Shares of Nonvoting Stock
a.	0	20,000
b.	7,500	5,000
c.	10,000	16,000
d.	20,000	0

4. The Haas Corp., a calendar year S corporation, has two equal shareholders. For the year ended December 31, year 6, Haas had net income of $60,000, which included $50,000 from operations and $10,000 from investment interest income. There were no other transactions that year. Each shareholder's basis in the stock of Haas will increase by:

   a. $50,000
   b. $30,000
   c. $25,000
   d. $0

5. Zinco Corp. was a calendar year S corporation. Zinco's S status terminated on April 1, year 6, when Case Corp. became a shareholder. During year 6 (365-day calendar year), Zinco had nonseparately computed income of $310,250. If no election was made by Zinco, what amount of the income, if any, was allocated to the S short year for year 6?

   a. $233,750   c. $76,500
   b. $155,125   d. $0

6. The Matthew Corporation, an S corporation, is equally owned by three shareholders—Emily, Alejandra, and Kristina. The corporation is on the calendar year basis for tax and financial purposes. On April 1 of the current year, Emily sold her one-third interest in the Matthew Corporation equally to the other two shareholders. For the current year, the corporation had nonseparately stated ordinary income of $900,000. For the current year, how much ordinary income should be allocated to Kristina on her Schedule K–1?

   a. $25,000   c. $337,500
   b. $75,000   d. $412,500

7. After a corporation's status as an S corporation is revoked or terminated, how many years is the corporation required to wait before making a new S election, in the absence of IRS consent to an earlier election?

   a. 1   c. 5
   b. 3   d. 10

8. As of January 1, year 6, Kane owned all the 100 issued shares of Manning Corp., a calendar year S corporation. On the 41st day of year 6, Kane sold 25 of the Manning shares to Rodgers. For the year ended December 31, year 6 (a 365-day calendar year), Manning had $73,000 in nonseparately stated income and made no distributions to its shareholders. What amount of nonseparately stated income from Manning should be reported on Kane's year 6 tax return?

   a. $56,750   c. $16,250
   b. $54,750   d. $0

9. An S corporation may deduct:

   a. Charitable contributions within the percentage of income limitation applicable to corporations.
   b. Net operating loss carryovers.
   c. Foreign income taxes.
   d. Compensation of officers.

PART 4

ADVANCED TAX PRACTICE CONSIDERATIONS

In this part of the text, we discuss some of the more complex issues that regularly are addressed by the tax professional.

By comparing the tax attributes of C corporations (Part 2) with those of flow-through entities (Part 3), a choice can be made as to the most appropriate tax and legal entity to use for conducting a business. A tax professional must understand how taxes are treated under GAAP in the reconciliation and reporting of tax and accounting information. When the taxpayer is exempt from Federal income taxation, disclosure and operating requirements often differ from those applicable to corporations. Many businesses operate in more than one U.S. state and must account for the taxable activities in each. Finally, the conduct of a tax professional's practice is bound by ethical and operational constraints, exposing both the taxpayer and the tax professional to penalties, interest, and other sanctions.

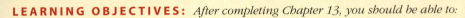

CHAPTER

13

Comparative Forms of Doing Business

LEARNING OBJECTIVES: *After completing Chapter 13, you should be able to:*

LO.1 Identify the principal legal and tax forms for conducting a business.

LO.2 Explain the relative importance of nontax factors in making business entity decisions.

LO.3 Distinguish between the forms for conducting a business according to whether they are subject to single taxation or double taxation.

LO.4 Identify techniques for avoiding double taxation and for controlling the entity tax.

LO.5 Review and illustrate the applicability and the effect of the conduit and entity concepts on an entity's operations.

LO.6 Analyze the effect of the disposition of a business on the owners and the entity for each of the forms for conducting a business.

LO.7 Compare the key tax rules for the various forms of doing business.

CHAPTER OUTLINE

SELECTION OF A TAX ENTITY FORM

Madison and Doug are going to start a dot-com business in which they both will participate on an active basis. They have an adequate amount in savings to finance the business. Limited liability is a significant factor for the owners, but equally important is the minimization of income taxes. Madison and Doug have narrowed the choice of business forms to a C corporation or a general partnership. Annual earnings of the business before taxes are expected to be $200,000, and any after-tax profit will be distributed to Madison and Doug. Assume that both Madison and Doug are single and have a marginal Federal income tax rate of 22 percent. Advise Madison and Doug on the choice of business form.

Read the chapter and formulate your response.

V arious tax and nontax factors affect the choice of the tax and legal form of business entity. The form that is appropriate at one point in the life of an entity and its owners may not be appropriate at a different time.

This chapter provides the basis for comparatively analyzing the tax consequences of business decisions for five types of tax entities (sole proprietorship, partnership, C corporation, S corporation, and limited liability company). Understanding the comparative tax consequences for the different types of entities and being able to apply them effectively to specific fact patterns can lead to effective tax planning.

13-1 **FORMS OF DOING BUSINESS**

LO.1

Identify the principal legal and tax forms for conducting a business.

The principal *legal* forms for conducting a business entity are a sole proprietorship, partnership, limited liability company, and corporation.[1] From a *Federal income tax* perspective, these same forms are available, with the corporate form divided into two types (S corporation and C or regular corporation). In most instances, the legal form and the tax form are the same. In some cases, however, the IRS may attempt to tax a business entity as a form different from its legal form. For example, a partnership, consisting of a parent and one or more children who do little work in the partnership business, might be treated as a sole proprietorship if the IRS determines there is no true partnership and the parent is merely trying to shift income to children in lower tax brackets.

The taxpayer generally is bound for tax purposes by the legal form that is selected. A major statutory exception to this is the ability of an S corporation to receive tax treatment similar to that of a partnership.[2] In addition, taxpayers sometimes can control which set of tax rules will apply to their business operations. The "check-the-box" Regulations provide an elective procedure that enables certain entities to be classified as partnerships for Federal income tax purposes even though they have corporate characteristics.[3] These Regulations have greatly simplified the determination of entity classification, and they commonly are used by multinational taxpayers.

A **limited liability company (LLC)** is a hybrid business form that combines the corporate characteristic of limited liability for the owners with the tax characteristics of a partnership.[4] All of the states now permit this legal form for conducting a business.

The most frequently cited benefit of an LLC is the limited liability of the owners. Compared to the other forms of ownership, LLCs offer additional benefits but also certain disadvantages. Refer to the coverage of the advantages and disadvantages of an LLC in text Sections 11-7b and 11-7c.

An individual conducting a sole proprietorship files Schedule C of Form 1040. If more than one trade or business is conducted, a separate Schedule C is filed for each trade or business. A partnership files Form 1065. An LLC that has elected to be taxed as a partnership also files Form 1065. A corporation files Form 1120, and an S corporation files Form 1120S. Exhibit 13.1 shows the number of business entities and the distribution among entity forms.

---

[1]A business entity can also be conducted in the form of a trust or an estate. These two forms are not discussed in this chapter. See Chapter 20.

[2]§§ 1361 and 1362.

[3]Reg. §§ 301.7701–1 through –4, and –6. If the business has only one owner, the elective procedure enables the entity to be classified as a sole proprietorship.

[4]Depending on state law, an LLC may be organized as a limited liability corporation or a limited liability partnership.

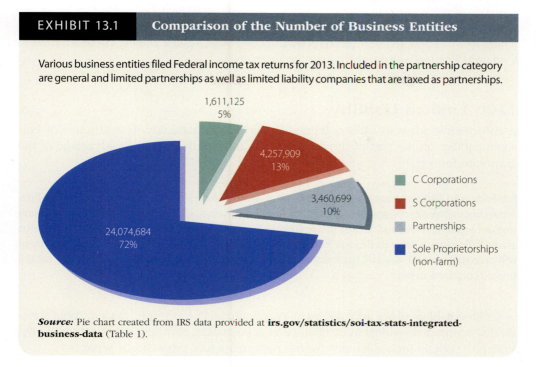

EXHIBIT 13.1	Comparison of the Number of Business Entities

Various business entities filed Federal income tax returns for 2013. Included in the partnership category are general and limited partnerships as well as limited liability companies that are taxed as partnerships.

1,611,125
5%

4,257,909
13%

3,460,699
10%

24,074,684
72%

- C Corporations
- S Corporations
- Partnerships
- Sole Proprietorships (non-farm)

Source: Pie chart created from IRS data provided at **irs.gov/statistics/soi-tax-stats-integrated-business-data** (Table 1).

13-2 NONTAX FACTORS

Taxes are only one of many factors to consider in making any business decision. Business decisions should also make economic and legal sense.

13-2a Capital Formation

The ability of an entity to raise capital is a factor that must be considered. A sole proprietorship is limited to the proprietor's capital. Compared to the sole proprietorship, the partnership has a greater opportunity to raise funds through the pooling of owner resources.

> Adam and Beth decide to form a partnership, AB. Adam contributes cash of $200,000, and Beth contributes land with an adjusted basis of $60,000 and a fair market value of $200,000. The partnership is going to construct an apartment building at a cost of $800,000. AB pledges the land and the building to secure a loan of $700,000.

EXAMPLE
1

The limited partnership offers greater potential than the general partnership form because a limited partnership can secure funds from investors (limited partners).

> Carol and Dave form a limited partnership, CD. Carol contributes cash of $200,000, and Dave contributes land with an adjusted basis of $60,000 and a fair market value of $200,000. The partnership is going to construct a shopping center at a cost of $5,000,000. Included in this cost is the purchase price of $800,000 for land adjacent to that contributed by Dave. Thirty limited partnership interests are sold for $100,000 each to raise $3,000,000. CD also pledges the shopping center (including the land) and obtains nonrecourse creditor financing of $2,000,000.

EXAMPLE
2

Both the at-risk and the passive activity loss provisions restrict the tax attractiveness of investments in real estate, particularly in the limited partnership form. In most cases, the tax consequences have a critical effect on the economic results.[5]

Of the different forms of business entities, the corporate form offers the greatest ease and potential for obtaining financing, because it can issue additional shares of stock. The ultimate examples of this form are the large public companies listed on the stock exchanges.

LO.2

Explain the relative importance of nontax factors in making business entity decisions.

---

[5]See the related discussion in text Sections 10-3e, 13-5e, and 13-5f.

Marble, Inc., a publicly traded corporation can raise additional capital by issuing new shares of stock. It must follow Federal and state securities laws, but otherwise, a public offering can be attractive to third-party investors with no other connection to the entity.

13-2b Limited Liability

A corporation offers its owners limited liability under state law. This absence of personal liability on the part of the owners is the most frequently cited advantage of the corporate form.

Ed, Fran, and Gabriella each invest $25,000 for all the shares of stock of Brown Corporation. Brown obtains creditor financing of $100,000. Brown is the defendant in a personal injury suit resulting from an accident involving one of its delivery trucks. The court awards a judgment of $2,500,000 to the plaintiff. The award exceeds Brown's insurance coverage by $1,500,000. Even though the judgment will probably result in Brown's bankruptcy, the shareholders will have no personal liability for the unpaid corporate debts.

Limited liability is not available to all corporations. For example, laws in some states do not permit professional individuals (e.g., accountants, attorneys, architects, and physicians) to obtain limited liability for the performance of professional services.

Even if state law provides for limited liability, the shareholders of small corporations may have to forgo this benefit. Often, such a corporation may be unable to obtain external financing (e.g., a bank loan) unless the shareholders guarantee the loan.

Owners also may achieve limited liability with LLCs and LLPs if allowed under state law.[6] As with a corporation though, external funding may involve owner guarantees, which will expose the owners to liability.

Sarah and Juan want to form a bike rental business. Entity forms available to them include corporation, partnership, and LLC. Regardless of which form they choose, when they go to the bank for a loan to help get their business started, the bank will likely require them to guarantee the loan. That means that if the business cannot repay the loan, Sarah and Juan must repay it out of their personal funds.

13-2c Other Factors

Other nontax factors may be significant in selecting an organization form, including the following.

- Estimated life of the business.
- Number of owners and their roles in the management of the business.
- Freedom to choose the methods of transferring ownership interests.
- Organizational formality, including the related cost and extent of government regulation.
- Ease of increasing equity by admitting new owners.

13-3 SINGLE VERSUS DOUBLE TAXATION

LO.3

Distinguish between the forms for conducting a business according to whether they are subject to single taxation or double taxation.

One area of difference among business entity types is that one is subject to double taxation and others are pass-throughs. In addition, state tax treatment can vary among entities.

13-3a Overall Effect on Entity and Owners

The sole proprietorship, partnership, and LLC are subject to a *single* level of taxation. This result occurs because the owner(s) and the entity generally are not considered as separate persons for income tax purposes. Thus, income tax liability is levied at the owner level rather than at the entity level.

---

[6]See text Section 10-1a for a review of types of partnerships.

On the other hand, the corporate form can be subject to *double* taxation. This frequently is cited as the major tax disadvantage of the corporate form. Under double taxation, the entity is taxed on the earnings of the corporation, and the owners later are taxed on distributions to the extent they are made from corporate earnings.

The S corporation provides a way to avoid double taxation and perhaps to subject the earnings to a lower income tax rate (the individual shareholder's tax rate may be lower than the flat 21 percent corporate tax rate). However, the ownership structure of an S corporation is restricted in both the number and type of shareholders. In addition, statutory exceptions subject the entity to taxation in rare circumstances. To the extent these exceptions apply, double taxation may result. Finally, the distribution policy of the S corporation may create difficulties with the *wherewithal to pay* concept.

EXAMPLE 6

Hawk Corporation has been operating as an S corporation since it began its business two years ago. For both of the prior years, Hawk incurred a tax loss. Hawk reports taxable income of $75,000 this year and expects that its earnings will increase in the foreseeable future. Part of this earnings increase will result from Hawk's expansion into other communities in the state. Because most of this expansion will be financed internally, no dividend distributions will be made to the shareholders.

Assuming that all of Hawk's shareholders are in the 24% tax bracket, their combined tax liability for this year will be $18,000 ($75,000 × 24%). Although the S corporation election will avoid double taxation, the shareholders may have a wherewithal to pay problem (i.e., they owe tax on their share of Hawk's income even though they did not receive any cash distribution from Hawk).

In addition, the actual tax liability for this year would have been less if Hawk had not been an S corporation ($75,000 × 21% = $15,750).

The information in Example 6 illustrates two additional tax concepts. First, the wherewithal to pay problem could be resolved by terminating the S corporation election. A tax liability would then be imposed at the corporate level. Because the corporation did not intend to make any dividend distributions, current double taxation of entity income would be avoided. Terminating the election also reduces the overall shareholder-corporation tax liability by $2,250 ($18,000 − $15,750).

Second, tax decisions on the form of business organization should consider more than the current taxable year. If the S election is terminated, another election will not be available for five years. If the earnings exceed the expansion needs, Hawk could encounter an accumulated earnings tax problem (at a 20 percent tax rate) if it is a C corporation.[7] Thus, the decision to revoke the election should have at least a five-year time frame. Perhaps a better solution would be to retain the election and distribute enough dividends to the S corporation shareholders to enable them to pay the shareholder tax liability.

Two other variables that relate to the adverse effect of double taxation are the timing and form of corporate distributions. If no distributions are made in the short run, then only single taxation occurs.[8] To the extent a second round of taxation does occur in the future, the cash-flow effect should be discounted to its present value. Furthermore, when the distribution is made, is it in the form of a dividend or a return of capital (a stock redemption or a complete liquidation)?[9]

Type of Distribution and Tax Effect

EXAMPLE 7

Gray Corporation reports taxable income of $100,000 for 2019. Gray's tax liability is $21,000. All of Gray's shareholders are in the 24% bracket. If dividends of $79,000 are distributed during the year, the shareholders incur a tax liability of $11,850 ($79,000 × 15%), assuming that the distributions are qualified dividends. The combined corporation-shareholder tax liability is $32,850 ($21,000 + $11,850), for a combined effective tax rate of 32.9%.

---

[7]The absence of distributions to shareholders could create an accumulated earnings tax problem under § 531. However, as long as earnings are used to finance expansion, the "reasonable needs" provision will be satisfied and the corporation will avoid the accumulated earnings tax.

[8]This assumes that there is no accumulated earnings tax exposure. See the subsequent discussion of distributions in text Section 13-4b.

[9]See the coverage of dividends in Chapter 5 and of stock redemptions and complete liquidations in Chapter 6.

EXAMPLE
8

Assume the same facts as in Example 7, except that the form of the distribution is a stock redemption and the basis for the redeemed shares is $59,000. The shareholders record a recognized gain of $20,000 and a tax liability of $3,000 ($20,000 × 15% beneficial capital gains rate). The combined corporation-shareholder tax liability is $24,000 ($21,000 + $3,000), for a total effective tax rate of 24%.

The differences in the tax consequences in Examples 7 and 8 are more obvious when illustrated in graphic form (see Exhibit 13.2). Recall from the Chapters 5 and 6 discussion of dividend distributions and redemptions that the corporation's E & P affects whether a distribution is treated as a dividend versus a return of capital versus a capital gain. For Example 7, if distributions are made in years where the E & P is less than the distribution, the tax effect to the shareholder is reduced (the excess would be a return of capital and perhaps even a capital gain). See text Section 5-1.

13-3b Alternative Minimum Tax

Individuals are subject to the alternative minimum tax (AMT), but C corporations are not.[10] For the sole proprietorship, the effect is direct (the AMT liability calculation is included with the tax form that reports the entity's taxable income—Form 1040). For the partnership, LLC, and S corporation, the effect is indirect (the tax preferences and adjustments are passed through from the entity to the entity's owners, and the AMT liability calculation is not attached to the tax form that reports the entity's taxable income—Form 1065 or Form 1120S).

The 2017 tax law changes greatly reduced the number of individuals subject to the AMT. Partnerships and S corporations still need to report certain information on their returns to enable the individual owners to determine whether they are subject to the AMT.

13-3c State Taxation

In selecting a form for doing business, the determination of the tax consequences should not be limited to Federal income taxes. Consideration also should be given to state income taxes and, if applicable, local income, gross receipts, and other transaction taxes.[11]

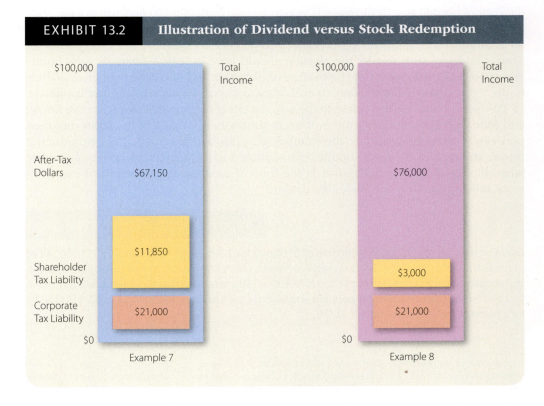

EXHIBIT 13.2   **Illustration of Dividend versus Stock Redemption**

---

[11]See the discussion of multistate corporate taxation in Chapter 16.

GLOBAL TAX ISSUES   Tax Rates and Economic Activity

Tax rates affect economic activity. The maximum corporate income tax rates for selected countries for 2018 are shown in the table.

Most of these countries, including for the United States, have reduced their corporate tax rates in recent years. The primary motivation for doing so was to increase the country's attractiveness as a location for foreign investment.

Country	Tax Rate
Australia	30.0%
Canada	15.0%
Denmark	22.0%
France	34.43%
Ireland	12.5%
Japan	23.2%
Mexico	30.0%
United Kingdom	19.0%
United States (prior to 2018)	35.0%
United States (after 2017)	21.0%

Source: OECD Tax Database; available at **https://stats.oecd.org/index. aspx?DataSetCode=Table_II1**.

The S corporation provides a good illustration of this point. Suppose the forms of business being considered are a limited partnership and a corporation. An operating loss is projected for the next several years. The owners decide to operate the business in the corporate form. The principal nontax criterion for the decision is the limited liability offered by the corporation. The owners consent to an S election so that the corporate losses can be passed through to the shareholders to deduct on their individual tax returns.

However, assume that state law does not permit the S election to be effective at the state level. Thus, the owners will not receive the tax benefits of the loss deductions that would have been available on their state income tax returns if they had chosen the limited partnership form. As a result of providing limited liability to the owner who would have been the general partner for the limited partnership, the loss deduction at the state level is forgone.

13-4 CONTROLLING THE ENTITY TAX

LO.4

Identify techniques for avoiding double taxation and for controlling the entity tax.

Of the five forms of business entities, it appears at first glance that only the C corporation needs to be concerned with controlling the entity tax. However, from the broader perspective of controlling the tax liability related to the business entity's profits, whether that tax is imposed at the entity or owner level, tax planning is relevant for all five business forms.

Techniques that can be used to minimize the current-period tax liability include the following.

1. Distribution policy.
2. Recognition of the interaction between the regular tax liability and the AMT liability.
3. Utilization of special allocations.
4. Favorable treatment of certain fringe benefits.
5. Minimization of double taxation.
6. Consideration of the qualified business income deduction.

Some of these techniques apply to all five forms of business entities. Others apply to only a subset of the five forms. Even those that apply to all do not minimize taxes equally for all forms. Because the first three techniques are discussed elsewhere in this text, only the last three are discussed here.

13-4a **Favorable Treatment of Certain Fringe Benefits**

Ideally, a fringe benefit produces the following tax consequences.

- Deductible by the entity (employer) that provides the fringe benefit.
- Excludible from the gross income of the taxpayer (employee) who receives the fringe benefit.

From the perspective of the owner or owners of an entity, when the entity provides such favorably taxed fringe benefits to an owner, the benefits are paid for with *before-tax* dollars.

EXAMPLE 9

Rocky, the owner and employee of Rocky's Ranch, a C corporation, is provided with meals and lodging that qualify for exclusion treatment (i.e., provided for the convenience of the employer). The annual cost of the meals and lodging to Rocky's Ranch is $3,000 and $7,000, respectively. Because 50% of the cost of the meals and 100% of the lodging costs are deductible in calculating the taxable income of Rocky's Ranch on Form 1120, the after-tax cost to the corporation is only $8,215 [$10,000 − (21% × $8,500)].

Because the $10,000 is excluded in calculating Rocky's gross income, there is no additional tax cost at the owner level. If Rocky had paid for the meals and lodging himself, no deduction would have been permitted because these expenditures are nondeductible personal expenditures. Thus, from Rocky's perspective, the receipt of excludible meals and lodging of $10,000 is equivalent to receiving a dividend distribution from the corporation of $11,765 [$10,000/(100% − 15%)], assuming that he is in the 15% capital gain tax bracket.

Example 9 illustrates how certain fringe benefits can be used to benefit the owner of an entity and at the same time have a beneficial effect on the combined tax liability of the entity and the owner. Because this structure is generous to taxpayers, Congress has enacted various nondiscrimination provisions that generally negate favorable tax treatment if the fringe benefit program is discriminatory. In addition, the Code includes several statutory provisions that make the favorably taxed fringe benefit treatment available only to *employees* (e.g., group term life insurance and meal and lodging exclusion).[12]

The IRS defines the term *employee* restrictively. For the owner of a business entity to be treated as an employee, the entity must be a corporation.[13] For fringe benefit purposes, an S corporation is treated as a partnership, and a greater-than-2-percent shareholder is treated as a partner.[14]

Classification of an owner as a nonemployee produces two negative results. First, the deduction for the cost of the fringe benefit to the entity is disallowed at the entity level. Second, the owner whose fringe benefit has been paid for by the entity must include the cost of the fringe benefit in gross income.

Not all favorably taxed fringe benefits receive exclusion treatment. Although not as attractive to the recipient, another approach provided in the Code is deferral treatment (e.g., pension plans and profit sharing plans).

13-4b **Minimizing Double Taxation**

Only the corporate form is potentially subject to double taxation. Several techniques are available for eliminating or at least reducing the second layer of taxation.

- Transferring funds to the shareholders in a manner that is deductible to the corporation.
- Not making distributions to the shareholders.
- Making distributions that qualify for return of capital treatment at the shareholder level.
- Making the S election.

Moreover, the lower tax rate for qualified dividends reduces the negative impact of double taxation (see text Section 5-3b).

---

[12]§§ 79 and 119.

[13]Reg. § 1.79–0(b). The IRS has not been completely successful in litigating a defense of this position.

[14]§ 1372(a).

Transferring Funds That Are Deductible

Typical forms of transfer that will result in a deduction to the corporation are (1) salary payments to shareholder-employees, (2) lease payments to shareholder-lessors, and (3) interest payments to shareholder-creditors.

Recognizing the tax benefit of this technique and the relationship between a corporation and its shareholders, the IRS scrutinizes these types of transactions carefully. All three types are evaluated in terms of *reasonableness*.[15] In addition, the interest payments may result in the IRS raising the <mark>thin capitalization</mark> issue and reclassifying some or all of the debt as equity.[16] IRS success with either approach raises the specter of double taxation.

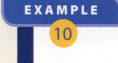

Transfers to Shareholders

EXAMPLE 10

Donna owns all of the stock of Green and is the chief executive officer. Green's taxable income before salary payments to Donna is as follows.

Year 1	$ 80,000
Year 2	50,000
Year 3	250,000

Each year, Donna receives a monthly salary of $3,000. In December of each year, she reviews the operations for the year and determines the year-end bonus to be paid to the key officers (only Donna for bonus purposes). Donna's yearly bonuses are recorded as follows.

Year 1	$ 44,000
Year 2	14,000
Year 3	214,000

The obvious purpose of Green's bonus program is to reduce the corporate taxable income to zero and thereby avoid double taxation. An examination of Green's tax return by the IRS would likely result in a deduction disallowance for unreasonable compensation. If that happens, the excess will be treated as a distribution to Donna taxed as a dividend to the extent Green has E & P.

Donna, Green, and the tax preparer(s) for these taxpayers must address reasonable compensation and dividend distributions before filing the corporate and individual tax returns; they cannot ignore the matter and hope the IRS does not audit Green or Donna.

EXAMPLE 11

Tom and Vicki each contribute $20,000 to TV Corporation for all of the stock of TV. In addition, they each lend $80,000 to TV. The loan is documented by formal notes, the interest rate is 7%, and the maturity date is 10 years from the date of the loan.

The notes provide the opportunity for the corporation to make payments of $5,600 each year to both Tom and Vicki and for the payments not to be subject to double taxation. That is, the interest payments are includible in the gross income of Tom and Vicki, but are deductible by TV in calculating its taxable income. At the time of repayment in 10 years, neither Tom nor Vicki will record any gross income from the repayment, because the $80,000 amount realized is equal to the basis for the note of $80,000 (return of capital concept).

It is important that the loans be valid transactions; there must be a loan document with required interest payments and a maturity date. The loan terms and interest rate should be similar to what a third-party lender would require. Otherwise, the loans can be reclassified as equity. If the notes are reclassified as equity, Tom and Vicki's includible gross income of $5,600 each would remain the same (interest income would be reclassified as dividend income that may be taxed at the rate of 15% or 20%, depending on the shareholder's taxable income). However, because the dividend payments are not deductible by TV, the corporation's taxable income would increase by $11,200 ($5,600 × 2). The "repayment" of the notes in 10 years likely would result in dividend income treatment for Tom and Vicki.

Not Making Distributions

Double taxation will not occur unless the corporation makes (actual or deemed) distributions to the shareholders. Dividend payments are not mandatory, like interest; they are discretionary to the entity's board of directors. By choosing not to make current distributions, a C corporation's exposure to double taxation can be eliminated.

---

[15]§ 162(a)(1). *Mayson Manufacturing Co. v. Comm.*, 49–2 USTC ¶9467, 38 AFTR 1028, 178 F.2d 115 (CA–6, 1949); *Harolds Club v. Comm.*, 65–1 USTC ¶9198, 15 AFTR 2d 241, 340 F.2d 861 (CA–9, 1965).

[16]§ 385; Rev.Rul. 83–98, 1983–2 C.B. 40; *Bauer v. Comm.*, 84–2 USTC ¶9996, 55 AFTR 2d 85–433, 748 F.2d 1365 (CA–9, 1984).

A policy of no distributions to shareholders can avoid the second layer of taxation forever. This will occur if the shares of stock are bequeathed to the taxpayer's beneficiaries. As a result of the step-up in basis rules for inherited property, the basis of the stock for the beneficiaries becomes the fair market value at the date of the decedent's death rather than the decedent's basis.

A closely held C corporation that does not make distributions eventually may encounter an accumulated earnings tax problem unless the reasonable needs requirement is satisfied. The accumulated earnings tax rate of 20 percent is higher than the 15 percent rate for qualified dividends that most individual taxpayers are subject to.[17]

For certain high-income taxpayers, the tax rate for qualified dividends is 20 percent. In addition, high-income individuals may also owe the net investment income tax (NIIT) of 3.8 percent on their dividend income.

Dolphin Corporation, a C corporation, manufactures exercise machines. Business has been very good, and profits exceed $500,000 for each of the past few years after paying employee salaries, bonuses, and all expenses. Dolphin has no plans for expanding its business or adding any new product lines. It has invested its extra cash in technology and oil and gas stocks. If Dolphin has not paid dividends, it could be at risk of the accumulated earnings tax.

Return of Capital Distributions

Another approach to controlling the entity tax is through a stock redemption or liquidation. The magnitude of the effect of double taxation can be reduced if the corporate distributions to the shareholders can qualify for return of capital rather than dividend treatment. For an ongoing corporation, the stock redemption provisions offer an opportunity to reduce the includible gross income at the shareholder level (see Examples 7 and 8). The corporate liquidation provisions can be used if the business entity will cease to operate in corporate form. Under redemption and liquidation rules, the distribution may be treated as a sale of some or all of the shareholder's stock resulting in a tax-free recovery of basis and capital gain.

Copper Corporation makes a distribution of $60,000 to its shareholders. Mark and Min, two of the shareholders, receive $25,000 and $10,000, respectively. The form of the distribution permits the shareholders to surrender a certain number of shares of stock. The potential exists that the distribution can qualify for stock redemption treatment at the shareholder level. Mark satisfies the requirements for a substantially disproportionate distribution (see text Section 6-2d). Min does not qualify for capital gain treatment, because she is in control of the corporation after the distribution (she owns 60% of the stock). Assuming that Mark's basis for the shares redeemed is $20,000, he reports a capital gain of $5,000 ($25,000 − $20,000). Min incurs dividend income of $10,000. She must allocate her stock basis among her remaining shares.

Electing S Corporation Status

Making an S election generally eliminates double taxation by making the corporation a tax reporter rather than a taxpayer. Therefore, the only tax levy is at the shareholder level. Factors to consider in making this election include the following.

- Are all of the shareholders willing to consent to the election?
- Can the qualification requirements for S status be satisfied at the time of the election?
- Because the S qualification requirements become maintenance requirements, can these requirements continue to be satisfied?
- For what period will the conditions that make the S election beneficial continue to prevail?
- Will the corporate distribution policy create wherewithal to pay problems at the shareholder level?

---

[17]§ 531. See the discussion of the accumulated earnings tax in text Section 3-2c.

13-4c Considering the Qualified Business Income Deduction

Another technique to minimize the tax liability of the business entity is to operate as a sole proprietorship, partnership (including an LLC taxed as a partnership), or S corporation. A deduction is available for individuals (and estates and trusts) that own these forms of business. The purpose of the <mark>qualified business income deduction</mark> is to, in effect, lower the tax rate applicable to the owner to compensate for how tax reform lowered the rate for C corporations from a maximum of 35 percent to a flat 21 percent.

Section 199A identifies the qualified business income (QBI) deduction. The QBI deduction generally reduces the individual business owner's taxable income by 20 percent of the QBI (see Chapter 2).

EXAMPLE 14

Sarah, a single taxpayer, owns a car wash business. The car wash generates net income of $100,000 before considering any salary for Sarah. Assume that Sarah reports non-capital gain income equal to the standard deduction amount. If this business operates in a sole proprietorship form, Sarah claims a § 199A deduction of $20,000. Her income tax liability on the $80,000 of remaining income is $13,459 (using the 2019 Tax Rate Schedule for unmarried individuals).

If this business is instead operated as a C corporation, that entity's income tax liability for $100,000 of income would be $21,000. Sarah must also consider that the C corporation would pay her a salary for her work performed and possibly also a dividend in her role as investor. The salary would lower the taxable income of the C corporation and be taxable to Sarah. A dividend would not be deductible by the C corporation and would be taxable to Sarah at her capital gain rate.

Although this example indicates lower taxes for the sole proprietorship form, if increased income levels placed Sarah above the 22% bracket, the C corporation form might be a better option.

13-5 CONDUIT VERSUS ENTITY TREATMENT

LO.5

Review and illustrate the applicability and the effect of the conduit and entity concepts on an entity's operations.

Under the <mark>conduit concept</mark>, the entity is viewed as merely an extension of the owners. Under the <mark>entity concept</mark>, the entity is regarded as being separate and distinct from its owners. The tax effects of these different legal theories are examined in this section of the chapter.

The sole proprietorship is not analyzed separately because the owner and the business are in essence the same taxpayer. Recognition of a realized gain or loss does not occur when an owner contributes an asset to a sole proprietorship. Instead, the basis generally is a carryover basis. If an asset, such as a car, is converted from personal use to business use, its basis in the business is the lower of the owner's basis at the date of conversion or its fair market value.

13-5a Effect on Recognition at Time of Contribution to the Entity

The conduit approach applies for the partnership and LLC, and § 721 provides for no recognition of gain or loss on the contribution of property to the partnership or LLC in exchange for an ownership interest. Such deferral applies to both a contribution associated with the formation of the partnership or LLC and later contributions. The partnership or LLC takes a carryover basis for the contributed property, and the owners take a carryover basis for their ownership interests.[18]

Because the entity approach applies for the corporation, the transfer of property to a corporation in exchange for its stock is a taxable event. However, if the § 351 control requirement (80 percent) is satisfied, no gain or loss is recognized. In this case, both the corporate property and the shareholders' stock take a carryover basis.[19] This control requirement makes it more likely that shareholders who contribute appreciated property to the corporation *after* the formation of the corporation will recognize gain.

---

[18]See the pertinent discussion in text Section 10-2a.   [19]See the pertinent discussion in text Section 4-1a.

To the extent the fair market value of property contributed to the entity at the time of formation is not equal to the property's adjusted basis, it may be desirable to make a special allocation associated with the subsequent sale of the contributed property by the entity. With a special allocation, the owner contributing the property receives the tax benefit or detriment for any recognized gain or loss that subsequently results because of the initial difference between the adjusted basis and the fair market value.

For the partnership or LLC, this special allocation treatment is mandatory. No such allocation is available for the C corporation, because the gain or loss is recognized at the corporation level rather than at the shareholder level. For the S corporation, no special allocation is available. The recognized gain or loss will be reported on the shareholders' tax returns based on their stock ownership.

Asset Contributions: Special Allocations

EXAMPLE 15

Khalid contributes land with an adjusted basis of $10,000 and a fair market value of $50,000 for a 50% ownership interest in Maple Company. At the same time, Tracy contributes cash of $50,000 for the remaining 50% ownership interest. Because the entity is unable to obtain the desired zoning, it subsequently sells the land for $50,000.

If Maple is a C corporation, Khalid has a realized gain of $40,000 ($50,000 − $10,000) and a recognized gain of $0 resulting from the contribution. His basis for the Maple stock is $10,000, and the corporation has a basis for the land of $10,000. The corporation records a realized and recognized gain of $40,000 ($50,000 − $10,000) when it sells the land. Thus, what should have been Khalid's recognized gain becomes the corporation's taxable gain.

There is no way the corporation can directly allocate the recognized gain to Khalid. The corporation could distribute the land to Khalid and let him sell the land, but the distribution may be taxable to Khalid as a dividend, and gain may be recognized at the corporate level on the distribution.

EXAMPLE 16

Assume the same facts as in Example 15, except that Maple Company is a partnership or an LLC. The tax consequences are the same as in the C corporation illustration except for the $40,000 recognized gain on the sale of the land. Maple records a realized and recognized gain of $40,000 ($50,000 − $10,000). However, even though Khalid's share of profits and losses is only 50%, all of the $40,000 recognized gain is allocated to him. If Maple is an S corporation, the tax consequences are the same as in Example 15, except that Khalid and Tracy each report $20,000 of the recognized gain on their tax returns.

13-5b Effect on Basis of Ownership Interest

In the case of a partnership or an LLC, the contribution of property to the entity in exchange for an ownership interest is not a taxable event under § 721. Therefore, the owner's basis for the ownership interest is a carryover basis. For C and S corporations, the nontaxable and related carryover basis results are appropriate only if the 80 percent control requirement of § 351 is satisfied. If the control requirement is not satisfied, any realized gain or loss on the transaction is recognized, and the stock basis is equal to the fair market value of the contributed property.

In a partnership or an LLC, profits and losses of the entity affect the owner's basis in the entity interest. Likewise, the owner's basis is increased by the share of entity liability increases and is decreased by the share of entity liability decreases. Accordingly, the owner's basis can change frequently.[20]

For the C corporation, the shareholder's basis for the stock is not affected by corporate profits and losses or corporate liability increases or decreases.

---

[20]§§ 705 and 752.

The treatment of an S shareholder falls between that of the owner of a partnership or LLC interest and the C corporation shareholder. The S shareholder's stock basis is increased by the share of profits and decreased by the share of losses, but it is not affected by corporate liability increases or decreases.

The Big Picture

EXAMPLE 17

Return to the facts of *The Big Picture* on p. 13-1. In the first year of operations, the entity chosen by Madison and Doug (either a partnership or a C corporation) needs additional working capital. The owners decide to have the entity obtain a loan of $30,000. The profits for the year are $10,000. Madison and Doug are equal owners of the entity, each having contributed $40,000 of cash to the entity.

If the entity is a partnership or an LLC, each owner's basis at the end of the period is $60,000 ($40,000 investment + $15,000 share of liability + $5,000 share of profits). If the entity is instead a C corporation, each owner's basis is $40,000 (the original investment). If the entity is an S corporation, each owner's basis is $45,000 ($40,000 investment + $5,000 share of profits).

ETHICS & EQUITY Income Tax Basis That Does Not Change?

Howard purchased stock in Green, a C corporation, for $100,000. In a later year, Green made a valid S election. This year, Howard sells his stock in Green for $120,000.

Because he paid $100,000 for the stock, Howard plans to recognize a long-term capital gain of $20,000 from the sale. Do you agree with Howard's proposed reporting? Explain.

13-5c Effect on Results of Operations

The entity concept is the source of double taxation for the C corporation form (the corporation is taxed on its earnings, and the shareholders are taxed on the distribution of earnings). Thus, from the perspective of taxing the results of operations, the entity concept appears to produce a disadvantage for the corporation. However, whether the entity concept actually generates disadvantageous results depends on the relative tax rates of the entity and its owners, and on the nature of the income/loss that the entity generates.

As discussed in text Section 13-4b, techniques exist for getting cash out of the corporation to the shareholders without incurring double taxation (e.g., compensation payments to shareholder-employees, lease rental payments to shareholder-lessors, and interest payments to shareholder-creditors). Because these payments are deductible to the corporation, they reduce corporate taxable income. If the payments can be used to reduce corporate taxable income to zero, the corporation incurs a zero current tax liability.

Individual tax rates (plus any additional Medicare tax) often exceed the corporate tax rate (21 percent). In such cases, the use of a flow-through entity may be unattractive.[21]

Application of the entity concept results in the earnings components losing their identity when they are passed through to shareholders in the form of dividends. This may produce a negative result for capital gains. Because capital gains lose their identity when passed through in the form of dividends, they cannot be used to offset capital losses at the shareholder level.

An even more negative result is produced when dividends are paid out of tax-exempt income. Tax-exempt income is excluded in calculating corporate taxable income, but it is included in calculating current earnings and profits. Thus, what should not be subject to taxation (an exclusion) is taxed because of the entity concept.

The partnership, the LLC, and the S corporation use the conduit concept in reporting the results of operations. Any item that is subject to special treatment on the taxpayer owners' tax return is reported separately to the owners. Other items are reported as ordinary income.[22]

---

[21]Long-term capital gains are taxed at ordinary income rates for C corporations. See text Section 3-1d.

[22]§§ 701, 702, 1363, and 1366.

EXAMPLE 18

Birch Company earned $10,000 of interest on municipal (tax-exempt) bonds this year. Birch also donated $50,000 to the United Way. Regardless of entity type, the interest income is not taxable. However, if Birch is a C corporation, this income increases E & P. If Birch distributes the earnings to shareholders, the dividends are taxable. If Birch were instead a partnership or an S corporation, the $10,000 of interest income would be separately reported on Schedule K–1 to be given to each owner.

For the charitable contribution, if Birch is a C corporation, the entity reports the deduction and applies any limitation at the entity level. In contrast, if Birch is a partnership or an S corporation, the contribution is reported on Schedule K–1 and each owner must individually determine how to report their share of the donation.

Many of the problems the entity concept may produce for the C corporation form are not present for the partnership, LLC, or S corporation. Included in this category are double taxation, problems with the reasonableness requirement, and loss of identity of the income or expense item at the owner level.

Only the partnership and LLC completely apply the conduit concept in reporting the results of operations. In several circumstances, the S corporation is subject to taxation at the corporate level, including the tax on built-in gains and the tax on certain passive investment income.[23] This limited application of the entity concept necessitates additional planning to attempt to avoid taxation at the corporate level.

13-5d Effect on Recognition at Time of Distribution

The application of the conduit concept results in distributions not being taxed to the owners. The application of the entity concept produces the opposite result. Therefore, distributions can be made to partners, to LLC owners, or to S shareholders tax-free, whereas the same distribution would produce dividend income treatment for C corporation shareholders.

In this regard, a distinction must be made between distributions of earnings and other distributions for the S corporation. The S corporation generally is treated as a conduit with respect to its operations, except when an entity-level tax applies. Earnings distributions are subject to conduit treatment and generally are tax-free; a few S corporations have C corporation earnings and profits and trace their distributions through the accumulated adjustments account (AAA), perhaps creating dividend income.[24] Distributions in excess of earnings qualify for return of capital treatment.

A combination entity/conduit concept applies to property distributions to S shareholders. As discussed, the conduit concept applies with respect to the shareholder. However, if the property distributed has appreciated in value, the realized gain is recognized at the corporate level (same treatment as a C corporation). Then the conduit concept is applied as a pass-through of the gain to the shareholders.

The Big Picture

EXAMPLE 19

Return to the facts of *The Big Picture* on p. 13-1. Madison and Doug decide to name their business MD Corporation. MD is an S corporation that is owned as follows: Madison 60% and Doug 40%. MD distributes two parcels of land to each owner. MD holds a basis of $10,000 for each parcel. The fair market value of each of the parcels is as follows.

Madison	$22,000
Doug	18,000

The distribution results in a $20,000 ($40,000 − $20,000) recognized gain for MD. Madison reports $12,000 of the gain and Doug reports $8,000 of the gain on their individual income tax returns.

---

[23]§§ 1374 and 1375. [24]§ 1368.

13-5e **Effect on Passive Activity Losses**

The passive activity loss rules are effective for the partnership, LLC, and S corporation, but they apply to the C corporation only for personal service corporations and closely held corporations. A *closely held corporation* is a corporation where more than 50 percent of the value of the outstanding stock at any time during the last half of the taxable year is owned by or for not more than five individuals.

For this purpose, a C corporation is a personal service corporation if all of the following apply.

- The principal activity of the corporation is the performance of personal services.
- The services are substantially performed by owner-employees.
- Owner-employees own more than 10 percent in value of the stock of the corporation.

For the closely held corporation, passive activity losses cannot be offset against portfolio income, but they can be offset against active income.

Because the conduit concept applies, any passive activity results are separately stated at the partnership, LLC, or S corporation level and are passed through to the owners so that they can properly report the passive activity information to their owners for use in preparing their own tax returns.

13-5f **Effect of At-Risk Rules**

The at-risk rules apply to the partnership, LLC, and S corporation and to closely held C corporations (defined the same as under the passive loss rules).

The application of the at-risk rules can produce a harsher result for the partnership and the LLC than for the S corporation.

Entity Type and the At-Risk Rules

EXAMPLE 20

Walt is the general partner and Scott and Luan are the limited partners in the WSL limited partnership. Walt contributes land with an adjusted basis of $40,000 and a fair market value of $50,000 for his partnership interest, and Scott and Luan each contribute cash of $100,000 for their partnership interests. They agree to share profits and losses equally.

To finance construction of an apartment building, the partnership obtains $600,000 of nonrecourse financing (not qualified nonrecourse financing) using the land and the building as the pledged assets. Each partner's basis for the partnership interest is computed as follows.

	Walt	Scott	Luan
Contribution	$ 40,000	$100,000	$100,000
Share of nonrecourse debt	200,000	200,000	200,000
Basis	$240,000	$300,000	$300,000

Without the at-risk rules, Scott and Luan could pass through losses up to $300,000 each, even though they invested only $100,000 and have no personal liability for the nonrecourse debt. However, the at-risk rules limit the loss pass-through to the at-risk basis, which is $100,000 for Scott and $100,000 for Luan.

Because Walt is not at risk for the nonrecourse debt, his at-risk basis is $40,000. If the mortgage were recourse debt, his at-risk basis would be $640,000 ($40,000 + $600,000).

Entity Type and the At-Risk Rules

EXAMPLE

21

Assume the same facts as in Example 20, except that the entity is an S corporation and Walt receives 20% of the stock and Scott and Luan each receive 40%. The basis for their stock now is:

Walt	$ 40,000
Scott	100,000
Luan	100,000

The nonrecourse debt does not affect the calculation of stock basis. The stock basis for each shareholder would remain the same even if the debt were recourse debt. Only direct loans by the shareholders increase the ceiling on loss pass-through (basis for stock plus basis for loans by shareholders).

13-5g **Effect of Special Allocations**

An advantage of the conduit concept over the entity concept is the ability to make special allocations. Special allocations are not permitted for the C corporation. Indirectly, however, the corporate form may be able to achieve results similar to those produced by special allocations through payments to owners (e.g., salary payments, lease rental payments, and interest payments) and through different classes of stock (e.g., preferred and common). However, even in these cases, the breadth of the treatment and the related flexibility are less than that achievable under the conduit concept.

Although the S corporation is a conduit, it is treated more like a C corporation than a partnership or an LLC with respect to special allocations. This treatment results from the application of the per-share and per-day rule (see text Section 12-3c). Although the S corporation is limited to one class of stock, it still can make deductible payments to its shareholders. However, the IRS can reallocate income among members of a family if fair returns are not provided for services rendered or capital invested.[25]

EXAMPLE

22

The stock of an S corporation is owned by Debra (50%), Helen (25%), and Joyce (25%). Helen and Joyce are Debra's adult children. Debra is in the 32% Federal income tax bracket, and Helen and Joyce are in the 12% bracket. Only Debra is an employee of the corporation. She is paid an annual salary of $20,000, whereas employees with similar responsibilities in other corporations earn $100,000. The corporation generates earnings of approximately $200,000 each year.

It appears that the reason Debra is paid a low salary is to enable more of the earnings of the S corporation to be taxed to Helen and Joyce, who are in lower tax brackets. Thus, the IRS could reallocate a larger salary to Debra.

The partnership and LLC have many opportunities to use special allocations, including the following.

- The ability to share profits and losses differently from the share in capital.
- The ability to share profits and losses differently.
- The special allocation required for the difference between the adjusted basis and The fair market value of contributed property.
- The special allocation of any item permitted if the substantial economic effect rule is satisfied.
- The optional adjustment to basis that results from distributions.
- The optional adjustment to basis that results from an acquisition by purchase, taxable exchange, or inheritance.

---

[25]§ 1366(e).

13-6 **FICA, SELF-EMPLOYMENT TAXES, AND NIIT**

Payroll (employment) taxes can be a significant cost for a business and its owners, with a combined tax rate of 15.3 percent. Such costs can be classified into two categories.

- FICA taxes (Social Security and Medicare).
- Self-employment tax.

13-6a **FICA**

FICA (Federal Insurance Contribution Act) taxes are imposed on the wages of employees using the following rates.[26]

Social Security	6.2%
Medicare	1.45%

A 0.9 percent additional Medicare tax is imposed on all wages in excess of $200,000 ($250,000 for joint returns, $125,000 for married filing separate returns).

All of the wages of an employee are subject to Medicare taxes. However, FICA withholding for the Social Security taxes is applied to only the first $132,900 (in 2019) of an employee's earned wages. In addition, the employer must pay to the IRS an amount equal to the FICA tax normally withheld from employee wages (i.e., a matching 6.2% + 1.45%).[27]

13-6b **Self-Employment Tax**

The purpose of the self-employment tax is to provide Social Security and Medicare benefits for self-employed individuals. This requires the self-employed taxpayer to pay both the employee and employer shares of the Social Security and Medicare tax. For 2019, the self-employment tax is 15.3 percent [(6.2 + 1.45) × 2] of self-employment income up to $132,900 and 2.9 percent (1.45 × 2) of self-employment income in excess of $132,900.[28]

As in the case of employees, an additional Medicare tax of 0.9 percent is imposed on self-employment income in excess of $200,000 ($250,000 for joint returns, $125,000 for married filing separate returns). This additional Medicare tax is imposed if combined wages and self-employment income exceed the taxpayer's threshold amount. If self-employment income is negative (a loss), it is treated as zero in computing the additional Medicare tax.

EXAMPLE 23

Brian, a single individual, works as an employee of ABC Company. Brian also runs a consulting practice as a sole proprietor. Brian reported:

Wages from ABC (Box 5 of Form W–2)	$170,000
Net income from consulting business	45,000

As a single individual, Brian's threshold for the additional Medicare tax is $200,000. Because his combined wages and self-employment income exceeds this threshold by $15,000 ($170,000 + $45,000 − $200,000), Brian is liable for the additional Medicare tax. The amount owed is $135 ($15,000 × 0.9%).

Individuals may deduct one-half of the self-employment tax paid. This is a deduction for AGI ("above-the-line"). No portion of the additional Medicare tax (the 0.9 percent) is deductible.[29]

---

[26]§ 3101.
[27]§ 3111.

[28]§ 1401.
[29]§ 164(f).

13-6c **Net Investment Income Tax (NIIT)**

Another additional Medicare tax applies on the unearned income of high-bracket individuals, trusts, and estates. Although this is not a payroll tax (because it is imposed on unearned income), its rate of 3.8 percent is tied to payroll tax rates. The 3.8 percent rate is based on the combined employer and employee Medicare tax rate of 1.45 percent for each, plus the additional Medicare tax of 0.9 percent (2.9% plus 0.9%).

The NIIT applies to net investment income (NII). For individuals, high income is defined as more than $200,000 ($250,000 if married filing jointly). For this purpose, income for most individuals equals AGI plus any foreign income exclusion, or modified AGI (MAGI). The tax rate of 3.8 percent applies to the lesser of NII or MAGI in excess of the threshold amount. The tax is reported on Form 8960.

NII includes traditional forms of investment income (interest and dividends, for example), as well as rents and income from passive activities. For planning purposes, taxpayers subject to the NIIT must consider the effect of transactions on NII and MAGI. For example, a year-end bonus an employee receives may cause his or her MAGI to cross the threshold amount for the NIIT. High-income taxpayers may want to consider investments in tax-exempt bonds and use other planning strategies to reduce exposure to the NIIT.

EXAMPLE 24

Jane, a single individual, reports the following income and expenses.

Interest income	$ 11,000
Dividend income	9,000
Net capital gain	34,000
Expenses allocable to her investment income (such as state income taxes related to her NII)	3,200
Wage income	190,000

Jane's MAGI is $244,000 ($190,000 + $11,000 + $9,000 + $34,000). Her NII is $50,800 ($11,000 + $9,000 + $34,000 − $3,200). Jane compares these amounts.

(a) NII	$ 50,800
(b) MAGI − $200,000	44,000

She multiplies the lesser amount by 3.8% to compute NIIT of $1,672 ($44,000 × 3.8%). Jane reports this tax on her Form 1040.

Although the NIIT does not apply to partnerships and S corporations, it can apply to their owners. These pass-through entities need to report certain information to the owners so that they can apply the NIIT correctly.

For more information on tax rules included in the ACA, see this text's online appendix, Affordable Care Act Provisions.

13-6d **Effect on the Entity and Its Owners**

Depending on the type of tax entity, FICA taxes and self-employment taxes have different effects on the entity and its owners as follows.

- *Sole proprietorship.* The wages of employees of the sole proprietorship are subject to FICA taxes, which must be matched by the sole proprietorship. The Schedule C income of the sole proprietorship is subject to the self-employment tax.

- *Partnership.* The wages of employees of the partnership are subject to FICA taxes, which must be matched by the partnership. A partner is not considered to be an employee. However, guaranteed payments (i.e., compensation for services rendered) made by the partnership to a partner are treated as self-employment income subject to the self-employment tax.[30] The partner's distributive share of the net earnings of the partnership is subject to self-employment tax.

- *Limited partnership.* The wages of employees of the limited partnership are subject to FICA taxes, which must be matched by the limited partnership. A limited partner is not considered to be an employee. However, guaranteed payments (i.e., compensation for services rendered) made by the limited partnership to a partner are treated as self-employment income subject to the self-employment tax.[31] A limited partner's distributive share of the net earnings of the limited partnership is not subject to self-employment tax.

- *C corporation.* The wages of employees of the corporation are subject to FICA taxes, which must be matched by the corporation. A shareholder who works for the corporation is an employee of the corporation and is subject to FICA taxes as an employee. The net earnings of the corporation have no effect on such a shareholder's self-employment income.

- *S corporation.* The wages of employees of the corporation are subject to FICA taxes, which must be matched by the corporation. A shareholder who works for the corporation is an employee of the corporation and is subject to FICA taxes as an employee. A shareholder's share of the net earnings of the corporation is not self-employment income, although the shareholder is subject to income tax on such earnings. In this respect, the shareholder of an S corporation receives more beneficial treatment than a sole proprietor or a partner whose share of the entity's net earnings is subject to self-employment tax.

- *LLC.* The wages of employees of an LLC are subject to FICA taxes, which must be matched by the LLC. If an LLC owner is treated as a limited partner, the LLC owner's distributive share of the net earnings of the LLC is not subject to the self-employment tax. Conversely, if an LLC owner is not treated as a limited partner, the LLC owner's distributive share of the net earnings of the LLC is subject to the self-employment tax.

13-7 DISPOSITION OF A BUSINESS OR AN OWNERSHIP INTEREST

LO.6

Analyze the effect of the disposition of a business on the owners and the entity for each of the forms for conducting a business.

A key factor in evaluating the tax consequences of disposing of a business is whether the disposition is viewed as the sale of an ownership interest or as a sale of assets. Generally, the tax consequences are more favorable if the transaction is treated as a sale of the ownership interest.

13-7a Sole Proprietorship

Regardless of the form of the transaction, the sale of a sole proprietorship is treated as the sale of individual assets. Thus, gains and losses must be calculated separately for each asset sold. Classification as capital gain or ordinary income depends on the nature and holding period of each individual asset. Ordinary income property such as inventory will result in ordinary gains and losses. Section 1231 property such as land, buildings, and machinery used in the business will produce § 1231 gains and losses (subject to depreciation recapture under §§ 1245 and 1250). Capital assets such as investment land and stocks qualify for capital gain or loss treatment.

If the amount realized exceeds the fair market value of the identifiable assets, the excess is attributed to goodwill, which produces capital gain for the seller. If, instead, the excess payment is attributed to a covenant not to compete, the related gain is classified as ordinary income rather than capital gain. Thus, the seller prefers the excess to be attributed to goodwill.

---

[30]§§ 707(c) and 1402.

[31]§§ 707(c) and 1402(a)(13).

Unless the legal protection provided by a covenant not to compete is needed, the buyer is neutral as to whether the excess is attributed to goodwill or a covenant. Both goodwill and a covenant are amortized over a 15-year statutory period.

Ethan, who is in the 32% Federal income tax bracket, sells his sole proprietorship to Tuan for $600,000. The identifiable assets are as follows.

	Adjusted Basis	Fair Market Value
Inventory	$ 20,000	$ 25,000
Accounts receivable	40,000	40,000
Machinery and equipment*	125,000	150,000
Buildings**	175,000	250,000
Land	40,000	100,000
	$400,000	$565,000

*Potential § 1245 recapture of $50,000.
**Potential § 1250 recapture of $20,000.

The sale produces the following results for Ethan.

	Gain (Loss)	Ordinary Income	§ 1231 Gain	Capital Gain
Inventory	$ 5,000	$ 5,000		
Accounts receivable	–0–			
Machinery and equipment	25,000	25,000		
Buildings	75,000	20,000	$ 55,000	
Land	60,000		60,000	
Goodwill	35,000			$35,000
	$200,000	$50,000	$115,000	$35,000

If the sale is structured this way, Tuan can amortize the $35,000 paid for goodwill over a 15-year period. If, instead, Tuan paid the $35,000 to Ethan for a covenant not to compete for a period of seven years, he still would amortize the $35,000 over a 15-year period. However, this would result in Ethan's $35,000 capital gain being classified as ordinary income. If the covenant bears no legal relevance to Tuan, in exchange for treating the payment as a goodwill payment, he should negotiate for a price reduction that reflects the benefit of the tax on capital gains to Ethan.

13-7b Partnership and Limited Liability Company

The sale of a partnership or an LLC can be structured as the sale of assets or as the sale of an ownership interest. If the transaction takes the form of an asset sale, it is treated the same as for a sole proprietorship (described previously). The sale of an ownership interest is treated as the sale of a capital asset, subject to ordinary income potential for unrealized receivables and substantially appreciated inventory. Thus, if capital gain treatment can produce beneficial results for the taxpayer, the sale of an ownership interest is preferable.

From the buyers' perspective, the form of the transaction does change the Federal income tax consequences. If the event is an asset purchase, the basis for the assets is the amount paid for them. Assuming that the buyers intend to continue to operate in the partnership or LLC form, the assets can be contributed to the entity tax-free, and the owners' basis for their entity interest is equal to the purchase price for the assets. Likewise, if ownership interests are purchased, the owners' basis is the purchase price and the entity's basis for the assets is the purchase price.[32]

---

[32]§§ 708(b)(1)(B), 721.

Inside and Outside Basis

Paul purchases Sandra's partnership interest for $100,000. He acquires both a 20% capital interest and a 20% interest in profits and losses. At the purchase date, the assets of the partnership include the following.

	Adjusted Basis	Fair Market Value
Cash	$ 10,000	$ 10,000
Inventory	30,000	35,000
Accounts receivable	15,000	15,000
Machinery and equipment	70,000	90,000
Buildings	100,000	150,000
Land	175,000	200,000
	$400,000	$500,000

In effect, Paul paid $100,000 for his 20% share of partnership assets ($500,000 × 20%). His basis for his partnership interest reflects the purchase price of $100,000. However, Paul's proportionate share of the partnership assets is based on the partnership's adjusted basis for the assets of $400,000 (i.e., $400,000 × 20% = $80,000).

In the prior example, Paul's basis in the entity (referred to as his "outside basis") is $100,000. However, his share of the partnership's adjusted basis of assets is only $80,000 (referred to as his "inside basis"). Because Paul's acquisition of his ownership interest from Sandra did not result in a termination of the partnership, the partnership's adjusted basis for the assets does not change. Therefore, if the partnership were to liquidate all of its assets immediately for $500,000, Paul's share of the recognized gain of $100,000 ($500,000 − $400,000) would be $20,000 ($100,000 × 20%). This result occurs even though Paul paid fair market value for his partnership interest.

The Code provides an opportunity to rectify this inequity to Paul. If the partnership elects the optional adjustment to basis under § 754, the operational provisions of § 743 will result in Paul having a special additional basis for each of the appreciated partnership assets.

The amount is the excess of the amount Paul effectively paid for each of the assets over his pro rata share of the partnership's basis for the assets.

	Amount Paid (20% Share)	Pro Rata Share of Adjusted Basis	Special Basis Adjustment
Cash	$ 2,000	$ 2,000	$ –0–
Inventory	7,000	6,000	1,000
Accounts receivable	3,000	3,000	–0–
Machinery and equipment	18,000	14,000	4,000
Buildings	30,000	20,000	10,000
Land	40,000	35,000	5,000
	$100,000	$80,000	$20,000

Therefore, if the partnership sells the inventory, Paul's share of the ordinary income is $1,000 ($5,000 × 20%). He then reduces this amount by his special additional basis of $1,000. Thus, the net effect, as it equitably should be, is $0 ($1,000 − $1,000).

13-7c C Corporation

The sale of the business held by a C corporation can be structured as either an asset sale or a stock sale. The stock sale has the dual advantage to the seller of being less complex both as a legal transaction and as a tax transaction. It also has the advantage of providing a way to avoid double taxation. Finally, the gain or loss on the sale of the stock usually is a tax-favored capital gain or loss to the shareholder.

EXAMPLE

28

> **The Big Picture**
>
> Return to the facts of *The Big Picture* on p. 13-1. Assume that Madison and Doug each own 50% of the stock of MD Corporation. Madison and Doug now have owned their interests in the business for 10 years. Assume that Madison's basis for her stock is $40,000 and Doug's basis for his stock is $60,000. The two shareholders agree to sell all of their stock to Rex for $200,000. Madison incurs a long-term capital gain of $60,000 ($100,000 − $40,000, while Doug records a long-term capital gain of $40,000 ($100,000 − $60,000). Rex takes a basis for his stock of $200,000. MD's basis for its assets does not change as a result of the stock sale.

Structuring the sale of the business as a stock sale may produce detrimental tax results for the purchaser. As Example 28 illustrates, the basis of the corporation's assets is not affected by the stock sale. If the fair market value of the stock exceeds the corporation's adjusted basis for its assets, the purchaser is denied the opportunity to step up the basis of the assets to reflect the amount in effect paid for them through the stock acquisition.[33]

For an asset sale, the seller of the business can be either the corporation or the shareholders. If the seller is the corporation, the corporation sells the business (the assets), pays any debts not transferred, and makes a liquidating distribution to the shareholders. If the sellers are the shareholders, the corporation pays any debts that will not be transferred and makes a liquidating distribution to the shareholders; then the shareholders sell the business.

Regardless of the approach used for an asset sale, double taxation will occur. The corporation is taxed on the actual sale of the assets and is taxed as if it had sold the assets when it makes the liquidating distribution of the assets to the shareholders who then sell the assets. The shareholders are taxed when they receive cash or assets distributed in kind by the corporation.

The asset sale resolves the purchaser's problem of not being able to step up the basis of the assets to their fair market value. The basis for each asset is the amount paid for it. To operate in corporate form (assuming that the purchaser is not a corporation), the purchaser then needs to transfer the property to a corporation in a § 351 transaction.

From the perspective of the seller, the ideal form of the transaction often is a stock sale. Conversely, from the purchaser's perspective, the ideal form is an asset purchase. Thus, a conflict exists between the buyer's and the seller's objectives regarding the form of the transaction. Therefore, the bargaining ability of the seller and the purchaser to structure the sale as a stock sale or an asset sale, respectively, is critical.

13-7d S Corporation

Because the S corporation is a corporation, it is subject to the provisions for a C corporation discussed previously. Either an asset sale at the corporate level or a liquidating distribution of assets produces recognition at the corporate level. However, under the conduit concept applicable to the S corporation, the recognized amount is taxed at the shareholder level. Therefore, double taxation is avoided directly (only the shareholder is involved) for a stock sale and indirectly (the conduit concept ignores the involvement of the corporation) for an asset sale.

---

[33]This result is similar to the problem at the partnership (or LLC) level if the § 754 election is not made.

13-8 CONVERTING TO OTHER ENTITY TYPES

Rather than disposing of a business, the owners may decide to convert the tax entity form to a different tax entity form. This raises three primary issues.

- Does the conversion result in the recognition of gain or loss?
- What is the basis for the ownership interest in the new entity form?
- What is the basis of the assets of the new entity form?

13-8a Sole Proprietorship

The conversion of a sole proprietorship into another entity form can be achieved without any recognition of gain or loss at the entity level or at the owner level. This occurs regardless of the new entity form.[34]

In these situations, the basis of an ownership interest (i.e., for the shareholder, partner, or LLC member) will be a carryover basis.[35] As to the entity, the basis for its assets also is a carryover basis.[36]

13-8b C Corporation

A C corporation can convert to any of the following entity forms.

- Sole proprietorship (if only one owner).
- Partnership (if more than one owner).
- LLC.
- S corporation.

Converting to the S corporation tax entity form merely requires the election of S status. An S election can be made only if all shareholders consent to the election and if the qualification requirements are satisfied.[37] Therefore, the election of S status produces the following tax consequences.

- No recognition of gain or loss.
- Carryover basis for the shareholders' stock.
- Carryover basis for the assets of the corporation.

A corporation also can convert to a partnership or LLC form. Unfortunately, to make this conversion, the corporation must be liquidated. This produces the following tax consequences.

- Recognition of gain or loss at the corporate level.[38]
- Recognition of gain or loss at the shareholder level.[39]
- Fair market value basis for the assets distributed in liquidation.[40]

After liquidation, it is necessary to contribute the assets to the new entity (i.e., the partnership or the LLC). The tax consequences to the owners and to the entity would be the same as those for a sole proprietorship that converts to a partnership or an LLC.

13-8c Partnership or LLC

A partnership or an LLC can convert to either of the following entity forms, which permit having multiple owners.

- C corporation.
- S corporation.

---

[34]§§ 721(a) and 351(a).
[35]§§ 722 and 358(a).
[36]§§ 723 and 362(a).
[37]§§ 1361(a), 1361(b), 1362(a), and 1362(a)(1).

[38]§ 336(a).
[39]§ 331(a).
[40]§ 334(a).

The partners can transfer their partnership interests to a corporation (either a C corporation or an S corporation) in exchange for the stock of the corporation. Because this will satisfy the control requirements, any realized gain or loss is not recognized.[41] If, however, the 80 percent control requirement is not satisfied, the realized gain or loss is recognized to the partners.[42]

Assuming that the § 351 requirements for nonrecognition are satisfied, the following occur.[43]

- The basis of the stock to the shareholders is a carryover basis.
- The basis of the assets to the corporation is a carryover basis.

Compare the key tax rules for the various forms of doing business.

13-9 OVERALL COMPARISON OF FORMS OF DOING BUSINESS

See Concept Summary 13.1 for a detailed comparison of the tax consequences of the following forms of doing business: sole proprietorship, partnership, limited liability company, S corporation, and C corporation.

Concept Summary 13.1

Tax Attributes of Different Forms of Business
(Assume That Partners and Shareholders Are All Individuals)

	Sole Proprietorship	Partnership/Limited Liability Company*	S Corporation**	Regular (C) Corporation***
Restrictions on type or number of owners	One owner. The owner must be an individual.	Must have at least two owners.	Only individuals, estates, certain trusts, and certain tax-exempt entities can be owners. Maximum number of shareholders limited to 100.****	None, except that some states require a minimum of two shareholders.
Incidence of tax	Sole proprietorship's income and deductions are reported on Schedule C of the individual's Form 1040. A separate Schedule C is prepared for each business.	Entity not subject to tax. Owners in their separate capacity subject to tax on their distributive share of income. Entity files Form 1065.	Except for certain built-in gains and passive investment income when earnings and profits are present from C corporation tax years, entity not subject to Federal income tax. S corporation files Form 1120S. Shareholders are subject to tax on income attributable to their stock ownership.	Income subject to double taxation. Entity subject to tax, and shareholder subject to tax on any corporate dividends received. Corporation files Form 1120.
Highest tax rate	37% at individual level.	37% at owner level.	37% at shareholder level.	21% at corporate level plus 0%/15%/20% on any corporate dividends at shareholder level (if qualified dividends; otherwise 37%). NIIT of 3.8% may apply to dividend income.

continued

continued

---

[41]§ 351(a).
[42]§ 368(c).

[43]§§ 358(a) and 362(a).

Tax Attributes of Different Forms of Business—(Continued)

	Sole Proprietorship	Partnership/Limited Liability Company*	S Corporation**	Regular (C) Corporation***
Qualified business income deduction (§ 199A)	Applicable.	Applicable. Eligible partners (noncorporate) need data from the entity to compute the deduction amount.	Applicable. Eligible shareholders need data from the entity to compute the deduction amount.	Deduction not applicable to C corporations.
Self-employment (SE) tax on owner	Schedule C income subject to SE tax. Owner not treated as employee.	Guaranteed payment for services and distributive share of net earnings of general partner subject to SE tax. Partners not treated as employees.	Not applicable. Payroll taxes owed on reasonable compensation paid to shareholder/employee; no SE tax on shareholder's distributive share of earnings.	Not applicable. Payroll taxes owed on wages of shareholder/employee.
Choice of tax year	Same tax year as owner.	Selection generally restricted to coincide with tax year of majority owners or principal owners or to tax year determined under the least aggregate deferral method.	Restricted to a calendar year unless IRS approves a different year for business purposes or other exceptions apply.	Unrestricted selection allowed at time of filing first tax return.
Return due date (normal and extended) for a calendar year entity	April 15 October 15	March 15 September 15	March 15 September 15	April 15 October 15
Timing of taxation	Based on owner's tax year.	Owners report their share of income in their tax year with or within which the entity's tax year ends. Owners in their separate capacities are subject to payment of estimated taxes.	Shareholders report their shares of income in their tax year with or within which the corporation's tax year ends. Shareholders may be subject to payment of estimated taxes.	Corporation subject to tax at close of its tax year. May be subject to payment of estimated taxes. Dividends will be subject to tax at the shareholder level in the tax year received.
Basis for allocating income to owners	Not applicable (only one owner).	Profit and loss sharing agreement. Cash basis items of cash basis entities are allocated on a daily basis. Other entity items are allocated after considering varying interests of owners.	Pro rata share based on stock ownership. Shareholder's pro rata share is determined on a daily basis, according to the number of shares of stock held on each day of the corporation's tax year.	Not applicable.
Contribution of property to the entity	Not a taxable transaction.	Generally not a taxable transaction.	Taxable transaction unless the § 351 requirements are satisfied.	Taxable transaction unless the § 351 requirements are satisfied.
Character of income taxed to owners	Retains source characteristics.	Conduit—retains source characteristics.	Conduit—retains source characteristics.	All source characteristics are lost when income is distributed to owners.
Basis for allocating a net operating loss to owners	Not applicable (only one owner).	Profit and loss sharing agreement. Cash basis items of cash basis entities are allocated on a daily basis. Other entity items are allocated after considering varying interests of owners.	Prorated among shareholders on a daily basis.	Not applicable.

continued

Tax Attributes of Different Forms of Business—(Continued)

	Sole Proprietorship	Partnership/Limited Liability Company*	S Corporation**	Regular (C) Corporation***
Limitation on losses deductible by owners	Investment plus liabilities.	Owner's investment plus share of liabilities.	Shareholder's investment plus loans made by shareholder to corporation.	Not applicable.
Subject to at-risk rules	Yes, at the owner level. Indefinite carryover of excess loss.	Yes, at the owner level. Indefinite carryover of excess loss.	Yes, at the shareholder level. Indefinite carryover of excess loss.	Yes, for closely held corporations. Indefinite carryover of excess loss.
Subject to passive activity loss rules	Yes, at the owner level. Indefinite carryover of excess loss.	Yes, at the owner level. Indefinite carryover of excess loss.	Yes, at the shareholder level. Indefinite carryover of excess loss.	Yes, for closely held corporations and personal service corporations. Indefinite carryover of excess loss.
Subject to limitation on excess business losses	Yes, at the owner level.	Yes, at the owner level (unless partner is a corporation).	Yes, at the shareholder level.	No. Limitation does not apply to corporate taxpayers.
Tax consequences of earnings retained by entity	Taxed to owner when earned and increases his or her investment in the sole proprietorship.	Taxed to owners when earned and increases their respective interests in the entity.	Taxed to shareholders when earned and increases their respective bases in stock.	Taxed to corporation as earned and may be subject to penalty tax if accumulated unreasonably.
Nonliquidating distributions to owners	Not taxable.	Not taxable unless money received exceeds recipient owner's basis in entity interest. Existence of § 751 assets may cause recognition of ordinary income.	Generally not taxable unless the distribution exceeds the shareholder's AAA or stock basis. Existence of accumulated earnings and profits could cause some distributions to be dividends.	Taxable in year of receipt to extent of earnings and profits or if exceeds basis in stock.
Capital gains	Taxed at owner level with opportunity to use alternative tax rate.	Conduit—owners must account for their respective shares.	Conduit, with certain exceptions (a possible penalty tax)—shareholders must account for their respective shares.	Taxed at corporate level with a maximum 21% rate. No other benefits.
Capital losses	Only $3,000 of capital losses can be offset each tax year against ordinary income. Indefinite carryover.	Conduit—owners must account for their respective shares.	Conduit—shareholders must account for their respective shares.	Carried back three years and carried forward five years. Deductible only to the extent of capital gains.
§ 1231 gains and losses	Taxable or deductible at owner level. Five-year lookback rule for § 1231 losses.	Conduit—owners must account for their respective shares.	Conduit—shareholders must account for their respective shares.	Taxable or deductible at corporate level only. Five-year lookback rule for § 1231 losses.
Foreign tax credits	Available at owner level.	Conduit—passed through to owners.	Generally conduit—passed through to shareholders.	Available at corporate level only.
§ 1244 treatment of loss on sale of interest	Not applicable.	Not applicable.	Available.	Available.
Basis treatment of entity liabilities	Includible in interest basis.	Includible in interest basis.	Not includible in stock basis.	Not includible in stock basis.
Built-in gains	Not applicable.	Not applicable.	Possible corporate tax.	Not applicable.
Special allocations to owners	Not applicable (only one owner).	Available if supported by substantial economic effect.	Not available.	Not applicable.

continued

Tax Attributes of Different Forms of Business—(Continued)

	Sole Proprietorship	Partnership/Limited Liability Company*	S Corporation**	Regular (C) Corporation***
Availability of fringe benefits to owners	None.	None.	None unless a 2%-or-less shareholder.	Available within antidiscrimination rules.
Effect of liquidation/ redemption/ reorganization on basis of entity assets	Not applicable.	Usually carried over from entity to owner unless a § 754 election is made, excessive cash is distributed, or more than 50% of the capital interests are transferred within 12 months.	Taxable step-up to fair market value.	Taxable step-up to fair market value.
Sale of ownership interest	Treated as the sale of individual assets. Classification of recognized gain or loss depends on the nature of the individual assets.	Treated as the sale of an entity interest. Recognized gain or loss is classified as capital under § 741, subject to ordinary income treatment under § 751.	Treated as the sale of corporate stock. Recognized gain is classified as capital gain. Recognized loss is classified as capital loss, subject to ordinary loss treatment under § 1244.	Treated as the sale of corporate stock. Recognized gain is classified as capital gain. Recognized loss is classified as capital loss, subject to ordinary loss treatment under § 1244. If stock qualifies as original issue qualified business stock under § 1202, gain is excluded if noncorporate owner held the stock over 5 years.
Distribution of appreciated property	Not taxable.	No recognition at the entity level.	Recognition at the corporate level to the extent of the appreciation. Conduit— amount of recognized gain is passed through to shareholders.	Taxable at the corporate level to the extent of the appreciation.
Splitting of income among family members	Not applicable (only one owner).	Difficult—IRS will not recognize a family member as an owner unless certain requirements are met.	Rather easy—gift of stock will transfer tax on a pro rata share of income to the donee. However, IRS can make adjustments to reflect adequate compensation for services.	Same as an S corporation, except that donees will be subject to tax only on earnings actually or constructively distributed to them. Other than unreasonable compensation, IRS generally cannot make adjustments to reflect adequate compensation for services and capital.
Organizational costs	Startup expenditures are eligible for $5,000 limited expensing (subject to phaseout) and amortizing balance over 180 months.	Organizational costs are eligible for $5,000 limited expensing (subject to phaseout) and amortizing balance over 180 months.	Same as partnership.	Same as partnership.
Charitable contributions	Limitations apply at owner level.	Conduit—owners are subject to deduction limitations in their own capacities.	Conduit—shareholders are subject to deduction limitations in their own capacities.	Limited to 10% of taxable income before certain deductions.

continued

Tax Attributes of Different Forms of Business—(Continued)

	Sole Proprietorship	Partnership/Limited Liability Company*	S Corporation**	Regular (C) Corporation***
Alternative minimum tax	Applies at owner level. AMT rates are 26% and 28%.	Applies at the owner level rather than at the entity level. AMT preferences and adjustments are passed through from the entity to the owners.	Applies at the shareholder level rather than at the corporate level. AMT preferences and adjustments are passed through from the S corporation to the shareholders.	C corporations are not subject to AMT.
Tax preference items	Apply at owner level in determining AMT.	Conduit—passed through to owners who must account for such items in their separate capacities.	Conduit—passed through to shareholders who must account for such items in their separate capacities.	C corporations are not subject to AMT.

*Refer to Chapters 10 and 11 for additional details on partnerships and limited liability companies.
**Refer to Chapter 12 for additional details on S corporations.
***Refer to Chapters 2 through 9 for additional details on regular (C) corporations.
****Spouses and family members are treated as one shareholder.

13-10 **TAX PLANNING**

The initial choice of legal or tax entity for a business, as well as subsequent considerations as to whether an entity should change its form, can present a number of Federal income tax planning opportunities. In selecting the right entity for conducting any business, tax consequences are important. Consideration should be given to the tax consequences of, among other items:

- Contribution of assets to the entity by the owners at the time the entity is created and at later dates.
- Taxation of the results of operations.
- Distributions to owners.
- Disposition of an ownership interest.
- Termination of the entity.

EXAMPLE 29

Eva is a tax practitioner in Kentwood, the Dairy Center of the South. Many of her clients are dairy farmers. She recently had tax planning discussions with two of them, Jesse, a Line Creek dairy farmer, and Larry, a Spring Creek dairy farmer. Jesse and Larry both have other sources of income.

Jesse recently purchased his dairy farm. He is 52 years old and just retired after 30 years of service as a chemical engineer at an oil refinery in Baton Rouge. Eva recommended that he incorporate his dairy farm and elect S corporation status for Federal income tax purposes.

Larry inherited his dairy farm from his father. At that time, Larry retired after 20 years of service in the U.S. Air Force. He has a master's degree in Agricultural Economics from LSU. His farm is incorporated, and shortly after the date of incorporation, Eva had advised him to elect S corporation status. She now advises him to revoke the S election.

Example 29 illustrates the relationship between tax planning and the choice of business form; it also raised a variety of questions about the advice given by the tax practitioner. By this time, you should be able to develop various scenarios supporting the tax advice given. The fact situations that produced the tax adviser's recommendations included the following.

- Jesse's experience in the dairy industry consists of raising a few heifers during the last five years he was employed. Eva anticipates that Jesse will be incurring tax losses for the indeterminate future. In choosing between the partnership and the S corporation forms, Jesse indicated that he and his wife must have limited liability associated with the dairy farm.

- Larry was born and raised on his father's dairy farm. Both his education and Air Force managerial experience provide him with useful tools for managing his business. However, Larry inherited his farm when milk prices were at a low for the modern era. Because none of her dairy farm clients were generating tax profits at that time, Eva anticipated that Larry would operate his dairy farm at a loss. Larry, like Jesse, thought that limited liability was imperative. Thus, he incorporated the dairy farm and made the S election.

- For the first two years, Larry's dairy farm produced tax losses. Since then, the dairy farm has produced tax profits large enough to absorb the losses. Larry anticipates that his profits will remain relatively stable in the $50,000 to $75,000 range. Because he is in the 24 percent marginal Federal income tax bracket and anticipates no dividend distributions to him from the corporation, his tax liability associated with the dairy farm may be less if he terminates the S election.

- Larry also needs to factor in the qualified business income deduction available to him when operating the farm as an S corporation. That is not available to a C corporation.

As Jesse and Larry's example illustrates, selection of the proper business form can result in both nontax and tax advantages. Both of these factors should be considered in making the selection decision. Furthermore, this choice should be reviewed periodically, because a proper business form at one point in time may not be the proper format at a different time.

REFOCUS ON THE BIG PICTURE

SELECTION OF A TAX ENTITY FORM

Even if Madison and Doug have narrowed their choice of tax entity to either a C corporation or a general partnership, the tax adviser should not be so limited in suggesting which of the various entities achieves the clients' objectives. As the tax expert, the adviser has a much clearer perspective and may point out factors the clients have overlooked.

Because Madison and Doug want limited liability so that their other assets will not be at risk, this likely eliminates the use of a general partnership. Likewise, the limited partnership option (which does provide limited liability for the limited partner) is not feasible because both Madison and Doug intend to be active in operating the business. Thus, the remaining choices to be reviewed are the following.

- C corporation.
- S corporation.
- LLC.

continued

SIMON POTTER/CULTURA/GETTY IMAGES

C Corporation

The C corporation satisfies the clients' limited liability objective. However, the C corporation is subject to the Federal income tax at the entity level. In addition, the shareholders are taxed (likely at a 15 percent rate) on the distributions of the after-tax earnings. Presuming taxable income of $200,000, the following takes place.

Tax at corporate level	$ 42,000
Tax at shareholder level	
Madison ($79,000 × 15%)	11,850
Doug ($79,000 × 15%)	11,850
Combined entity/owner tax liability	$ 65,700
After-tax cash flow ($200,000 − $65,700)	$134,300

S Corporation

The S corporation also satisfies the limited liability objective. Because the S corporation is not subject to Federal income taxation at the entity level, only the shareholders are taxed on the earnings of the corporation. Assume that these individual shareholders also obtain a qualified business income deduction equal to 20 percent of their share of S corporation income, resulting in net income of $80,000.

Tax at corporate level	$ –0–
Tax at shareholder level	
Madison ($80,000 × 22%)	17,600
Doug ($80,000 × 22%)	17,600
Combined entity/owner tax liability	$ 35,200
After-tax cash flow ($200,000 − $35,200)	$164,800

LLC

The LLC also generally satisfies the limited liability objective. Because the LLC is not subject to Federal income taxation at the entity level, only the owners are taxed on the earnings of the LLC. As with the S corporation form, assume that the individual shareholders claim a qualified business income deduction equal to 20 percent of their LLC income.

Tax at the LLC level	$ –0–
Tax at the owner level	
Madison ($80,000 × 22%)	17,600
Doug ($80,000 × 22%)	17,600
Combined entity/owner tax liability	$ 35,200
After-tax cash flow ($200,000 − $35,200)	$164,800

It appears that either the S corporation or the LLC meets Madison and Doug's objectives of having limited liability and minimizing their tax liability. The LLC offers an additional advantage in that an LLC does not include the numerous statutory qualification requirements that must be met to elect and maintain S status. Based on the facts in this situation, however, it is unlikely that satisfying these requirements would create any difficulty for Madison and Doug.

Key Terms

Conduit concept, 13-11

Entity concept, 13-11

Limited liability company (LLC), 13-2

Qualified business income deduction, 13-11

Thin capitalization, 13-9

Discussion Questions

1. **LO.1, 3** Compare C and S corporations as to the taxation of the entity and its owners.

2. **LO.1** What are the advantages of a limited liability company compared to an S corporation?

3. **LO.3** The corporate tax rate of 21% is lower than the top brackets for individuals. Consequently, C corporations will always owe less tax than most individual business owners. Do you agree? Why or why not?

4. **LO.2, 3** All of the Big 4 accounting firms changed their ownership form from a general partnership to a limited liability partnership. Discuss the legal and tax ramifications of this modification of ownership form.

5. **LO.2** Soong is considering opening a lawn-servicing business.   *Critical Thinking*
   a. What nontax factors should Soong consider in choosing a business entity?
   b. Are nontax factors more important than tax factors to Soong? Explain.

6. **LO.1, 2, 3** Sara is an entrepreneur who likes to be actively involved in her business   *Decision Making*
   ventures. She is going to invest $500,000 in a business that she projects will produce a tax loss of approximately $100,000 per year in the short run. However, once consumers become aware of the new product being sold by the business and the quality of the service it provides, she is confident the business will generate a profit of at least $125,000 per year.

   Sara earns substantial other income (from both business ventures and investment activities) each year. Advise Sara on the business form she should select for the short run. She will be the sole owner.

7. **LO.3, 4, 7** Sam is deciding whether he should operate his business as a C corporation   *Decision Making*
   or as an S corporation. Due to potential environmental hazard problems, it is imperative that the business have limited liability. Sam is leaning toward the S corporation form because it avoids double taxation. However, he is concerned that he may encounter difficulty several years in the future if he decides to issue some preferred stock to his son as a way of motivating him to remain active in the business.

   Sue, Sam's friend, says that he can maintain maximum flexibility by operating as a C corporation. According to her, Sam can avoid double taxation by paying himself a salary equal to the before-tax earnings. As Sam's tax adviser, what is your advice to him?

8. **LO.3** Paul, who is in the 24% tax bracket, is the sole shareholder of a corporation and receives a salary of $60,000 each year. To avoid double taxation, he makes an S election for the corporation. The corporation currently is earning $100,000, and he expects earnings to grow at a rate between 15% and 20% per year. The earnings are reinvested in the growth of the corporation, and no plans exist for distributions to Paul. What problem may Paul have created by making the S election?

9. **LO.3** Which of the following are subject either directly or indirectly to the AMT?

   • Sole proprietorship.
   • Partnership.
   • C corporation.
   • S corporation.

Decision Making   10. **LO.3** Mary and Richerd plan to establish a retail business that will have outlets in six cities in a southeastern state. Because the business probably will generate losses in at least the first three years, they want to use an entity that will pass the losses through to them for both Federal and state income tax purposes. They have narrowed their choices to an S corporation and a limited liability company. Advise Mary and Richerd on selecting an entity form.

Decision Making   11. **LO.6** Prior to the Tax Cuts and Jobs Act of 2017, bonus depreciation applied only to new assets. Under the TCJA, qualified property, whether new or used, qualifies for 100% bonus depreciation. How does this change affect Amy's decision on whether to buy the stock of Maple Corporation or its assets?

12. **LO.4** What techniques can the shareholders of a C corporation use to reduce its taxable income and thereby minimize or avoid double taxation? How can the IRS challenge these techniques?

Decision Making   13. **LO.4** Teresa is considering contributing $900,000 to the capital of Beige, Inc., a C corporation. A business acquaintance suggests that, instead, she should invest only $600,000 in capital and lend the $300,000 balance to the corporation. The interest rate on the loan would be the Federal rate that applies for the year. Are there any tax benefits to this advice? Any tax pitfalls? Explain.

14. **LO.4** Is it possible to permanently avoid double taxation of a C corporation by never making distributions to shareholders (because the stock will appreciate in value and the heirs will receive a step-up in basis on the death of the shareholder)? Explain.

Decision Making   15. **LO.4, 5** Arnold is going to conduct his business in the corporate form. What factors should he consider in deciding whether to operate as a C corporation or as an S corporation?

Critical Thinking   16. **LO.4** Tammy and Willy own 40% of the stock of Roadrunner, an S corporation. The other 60% is owned by 99 other shareholders (all are single and unrelated). Tammy and Willy have agreed to a divorce and are in the process of negotiating a property settlement.

   a.   Identify the relevant tax issues for Tammy and Willy.
   b.   The divorce resulted in the Roadrunner stock being distributed equally to Tammy and Willy. Do these developments change the S status of Roadrunner?

17. **LO.5** Tula is a general partner in the ABT Partnership. How might she be subject to the NIIT and additional Medicare tax?

18. **LO.5** Using the legend provided, indicate whether the following items cause the indicated tax to increase. The taxpayer already is subject to these taxes.

Legend
SE = Self-employment tax
M = Additional Medicare tax
N = NIIT
NE = No effect

   a.   Wage income.
   b.   Sole proprietorship income.
   c.   Dividend received from a C corporation.
   d.   Taxable distribution from a retirement plan.
   e.   General partner's distributive share of income from a partnership.
   f.   Return of capital from a C corporation.
   g.   Guaranteed payment from a partnership for services.

19. **LO.5** Why are special allocations either permitted or required for the partners in a partnership yet they are not permitted or required for the shareholders in a C or S corporation? *Critical Thinking*

20. **LO.5** Entity liabilities have an effect on a partner's basis in a partnership interest. Yet entity liabilities do not affect a corporate shareholder's stock basis (for either a C corporation or an S corporation). What is the reason for this difference?

21. **LO.5** Identify the effect of each of the following on a partner's basis for a partnership interest and a shareholder's (both C corporation and S corporation) basis for stock.
    - Profits.
    - Losses.
    - Liability increase.
    - Liability decrease.
    - Contribution of assets.
    - Distribution of assets.

22. **LO.5** Distributions of earnings by a C corporation are taxed at the shareholder level as dividend income. Why are the earnings of an S corporation that are distributed to shareholders not similarly treated?

23. **LO.6** Sandra and Renee each own 50% of the stock of Olive, an S corporation. They acquired their stock four years ago when Olive was formed. They have decided to dispose of their ownership interests in the corporation, and a substantial gain will result. Sandra thinks they should sell their stock, whereas Renee thinks they should first liquidate the corporation and then sell the assets. Advise them on the consequences of each approach. *Critical Thinking*

24. **LO.6** Vance owns all of the stock of Rose, Inc., a C corporation. The fair market value of the stock (and Rose's assets) is about six times Vance's adjusted basis for the stock. He is negotiating with an investor group for the sale of the corporation. Identify the relevant tax issues for Vance. *Critical Thinking*

25. **LO.2, 3, 4, 5, 6** Using the legend provided, indicate which form of business entity each of the following characteristics describes. Some of the characteristics may apply to more than one form of business entity.

Legend
SP = Applies to sole proprietorship
P = Applies to partnership
S = Applies to S corporation
C = Applies to C corporation
N = Applies to none

   a. Has limited liability.
   b. Greatest ability to raise capital.
   c. Subject to double taxation.
   d. Not subject to double taxation.
   e. Is directly subject to the NIIT if has high income and NII.
   f. Limit on types and number of shareholders.
   g. Has unlimited liability.
   h. Sale of the business can be subject to double taxation.

    i.   Profits and losses affect the basis for an ownership interest.

    j.   Entity liabilities affect the basis for an ownership interest.

    k.   Distributions of earnings are taxed as dividend income to the owners.

    l.   Total invested capital cannot exceed $1 million.

    m.   AAA is an account that relates to this entity.

    n.   Individual owners potentially can claim the 20% qualified business income deduction.

26. **LO.5** Using the legend provided, indicate which form of business entity each of the following characteristics describes. Some of the characteristics may apply to more than one form of business entity.

Legend

P = Applies to partnership
S = Applies to S corporation
C = Applies to C corporation

The basis for an ownership interest is:

    a.   Increased by an investment by the owner.

    b.   Decreased by a distribution to the owner.

    c.   Increased by entity profits.

    d.   Decreased by entity losses.

    e.   Increased as the entity's liabilities increase.

    f.   Decreased as the entity's liabilities decrease.

Computational Exercises

27. **LO.5** Henry is a 50% partner in HJ Partnership. This year, the tax form he receives from HJ (Schedule K–1 of Form 1065) shows business income of $40,000. During the year, Henry received a $10,000 distribution from HJ.

    a.   How much must Henry report on his Form 1040 from HJ for the tax year?

    b.   How would your answer change if HJ were instead an S corporation?

28. **LO.5** Roscoe contributes to a business entity a personal use asset with an adjusted basis of $15,000 and a fair market value of $28,000 on the contribution date. Determine whether Roscoe recognizes any gain or loss on the contribution, and determine the basis of the asset to the entity under each of the following circumstances.

    a.   Roscoe contributes the asset to a sole proprietorship.

    b.   Roscoe contributes the asset to a partnership for 10% interest.

    c.   Roscoe contributes the asset to a corporation for 25% interest. (Assume that the control requirement is satisfied.)

29. **LO.5** Mira and Lemma are equal owners of an entity. Each contributed $25,000 cash to the entity. In addition, the entity obtains a loan of $100,000. The profits for the year are $30,000. Determine Mira and Lemma's basis of the ownership interest at the end of the period assuming the entity is:

    a.   A partnership.

    b.   A C corporation.

    c.   An S corporation.

30. **LO.5** Castle and Dave formed an S corporation that is owned as follows: Castle 75% and Dave 25%. The corporation distributes an asset to each owner. The corporation has a basis of $45,000 for each asset. The fair market value of each of the assets is as follows: Castle $90,000 and Dave $50,000. The distribution results in:

    a. How much recognized gain for the corporation?

    b. How much gain to Dave?

    c. How much gain to Castle?

31. **LO.5** Basu owns 100% of an S corporation. This year, the corporation paid Basu a salary of $100,000. His share of S corporation income for the year was $42,000. Assuming that this is Basu's only income for the year, compute any resulting payroll and self-employment income taxes.

32. **LO.5** Andrea is an employee of Fern Corporation. She also has her own business working as a life coach. For 2019, Andrea's wages from Fern were $210,000. Her self-employment income was $30,000.

    a. Compute the payroll, self-employment, and additional Medicare taxes for Andrea for 2019.

    b. Assume the same facts except that Andrea's 2019 self-employment activities resulted in a loss of $15,000. Compute the payroll, self-employment, and additional Medicare taxes for Andrea for 2019.

    c. Compute Andrea's NIIT for 2019 using wages of $210,000, self-employment income of $30,000, and NII of $20,000.

Problems

33. **LO.2** Sea Green Enterprises reports the following assets and liabilities on its balance sheet.

	Net Book Value	Fair Market Value
Assets	$600,000	$925,000
Liabilities	200,000	200,000

    Sea Green has just lost a product liability lawsuit, with damages of $10,000,000 being awarded to the plaintiff. Although Sea Green will appeal the judgment, legal counsel indicates that the judgment is highly unlikely to be overturned by the appellate court. The product liability insurance carried by Sea Green has a policy ceiling of $6,000,000. What is the amount of liability of Sea Green Enterprises and its owners if the form of the business entity is:

    a. A sole proprietorship?

    b. A partnership?

    c. A C corporation?

    d. An S corporation?

34. **LO.1, 2, 3** Amy and Jeff Barnes are going to operate their florist shop as a partnership or as an S corporation. After paying salaries of $45,000 to each of the owners, the shop's earnings are projected to be about $60,000. The earnings are to be invested in the growth of the business. Write a letter to Amy and Jeff Barnes (5700 Redmont Highway, Washington, D.C. 20024) advising them as to which of the two entity forms they should select.

Decision Making

Communications

Decision Making   35.   **LO.2, 3** Mr. and Mrs. Coleman are going to establish a manufacturing business. They anticipate that the business will be profitable immediately due to a patent Mrs. Coleman holds. They predict that profits for the first year will be about $300,000 and will increase at a rate of about 20% per year for the foreseeable future. Advise the Colemans on the form of business entity they should select. Assume that they will be in the 37% Federal income tax bracket.

Critical Thinking   36.   **LO.3** Plum Corporation will begin operations on January 1. Earnings for the next five years are projected to be relatively stable at about $80,000 per year. The shareholders of Plum are in the 32% income tax bracket.

    a.   Assume that Plum will reinvest its after-tax earnings in the growth of the company. Should Plum operate as a C corporation or as an S corporation?

    b.   Assume that Plum will distribute its after-tax earnings each year to its shareholders. Should Plum operate as a C corporation or as an S corporation?

    37.   **LO.3** Mabel and Alan, who are in the 32% tax bracket, recently acquired a fast-food franchise. They both will work in the business and receive a salary of $175,000. They anticipate that the annual profits of the business, after deducting salaries, will be approximately $450,000. The entity will distribute enough cash each year to Mabel and Alan to cover their Federal income taxes associated with the franchise.

    a.   What amount will the entity distribute if the franchise operates as a C corporation?

    b.   What amount will the entity distribute if the franchise operates as an S corporation?

    c.   What will be the amount of the combined entity/owner tax liability in parts (a) and (b)?

    38.   **LO.3** Owl is a closely held corporation owned by eight shareholders (each owns 12.5% of the stock). Selected financial information provided by Owl shows taxable income of $6,250,000.

    a.   Calculate Owl's tax liability if Owl is a C corporation.

    b.   Calculate Owl's tax liability if Owl is an S corporation.

    c.   How would your answers in parts (a) and (b) change if Owl was not closely held (e.g., 5,000 shareholders with no shareholder owning more than 2% of the stock)?

    39.   **LO.4** A business entity's taxable income before the cost of certain fringe benefits paid to owners and other employees is $400,000. The amounts paid for these fringe benefits are reported as follows.

	Owners	Other Employees
Group term life insurance	$20,000	$40,000
Lodging incurred for the convenience of the employer	50,000	75,000
Qualified retirement plan	30,000	90,000

The business entity is equally owned by four owners.

    a.   Calculate the taxable income of the business entity if the entity is a partnership, a C corporation, and an S corporation.

    b.   Determine the effect on the owners for each of the three business forms.

    40.   **LO.4** Turtle, a C corporation, has taxable income of $300,000 before paying salaries to the three equal shareholder-employees, Britney, Shania, and Alan. Turtle follows a policy of distributing all after-tax earnings to the shareholders.

a.   Determine the tax consequences for Turtle, Britney, Shania, and Alan if the corporation pays salaries to Britney, Shania, and Alan as follows.

Option 1		Option 2	
Britney	$135,000	Britney	$67,500
Shania	90,000	Shania	45,000
Alan	75,000	Alan	37,500

b.   Is Turtle likely to encounter any Federal income tax problems associated with either option? Explain.

41. **LO.4** Parrott, Inc., a C corporation, is owned by Alfonso (60%) and Deanna (40%). Alfonso is the president, and Deanna is the vice president for sales. All three are cash basis taxpayers. Late in 2018, Parrott encounters working capital difficulties. Therefore, Alfonso loans the corporation $810,000, and Deanna loans the corporation $540,000. Each loan is supported by a 5% note that is due in five years, with interest payable annually. Determine the tax consequences to Parrott, Alfonso, and Deanna for 2019 if:

a.   The notes are classified as debt.

b.   The notes are classified as equity.

42. **LO.4** Marci and Jennifer each own 50% of the stock of Lavender, a C corporation. After each of them is paid a "reasonable" salary of $125,000, the taxable income of Lavender is normally around $600,000. The corporation is about to purchase a $2,000,000 shopping mall ($1,500,000 allocated to the building and $500,000 allocated to the land). The mall will be rented to tenants at a net rent income (i.e., includes rental commissions, depreciation, etc.) of $500,000 annually. Marci and Jennifer will contribute $1,000,000 each to the corporation to provide the cash required for the acquisition. [Decision Making]

Lavender's CPA has suggested that Marci and Jennifer purchase the shopping mall as individuals and lease it to Lavender for a fair rental of $300,000. Both Marci and Jennifer are in the 32% tax bracket. The acquisition will occur on January 2, 2020.

Determine whether the shopping mall should be acquired by Lavender, or by Marci and Jennifer, in accordance with their CPA's recommendation. Deductible depreciation on the shopping mall for the year is $37,000.

43. **LO.4** Since Garnet Corporation was formed five years ago, its stock has been held as follows: 525 shares by Frank and 175 shares by Grace. Their basis in the stock is $350,000 for Frank and $150,000 for Grace. As part of a stock redemption, Garnet redeems 125 of Frank's shares for $175,000 and 125 of Grace's shares for $175,000. [Decision Making]

a.   What are the tax consequences of the stock redemption to Frank and Grace?

b.   How would the tax consequences to Frank and Grace be different if, instead of the redemption, they each sold 125 shares to Chuck (an unrelated party)?

c.   What factors should influence their decision on whether to redeem or sell the 250 shares of stock?

44. **LO.4** Clay Corporation has been an S corporation since its incorporation 10 years ago. During the first three years of operations, it incurred total losses of $250,000. Since then, Clay has generated earnings of approximately $180,000 each year. None of the earnings have been distributed to the three equal shareholders, Claire, Lynn, and Tomás, because the corporation has been in an expansion mode. [Decision Making]

At the beginning of the current year, Claire sells her stock to Nell for $400,000. Nell has reservations about the utility of the S election. Therefore, Lynn, Tomás, and Nell are discussing whether the election should be continued. They expect the earnings to remain at approximately $180,000 each year. However, because they perceive that the expansion period is over and Clay has adequate working capital, they may start distributing the earnings to the shareholders.

All of the shareholders are in the 32% tax bracket. Advise the three shareholders on whether the S election should be maintained.

Decision Making   45. **LO.5** Phillip and Evans form a business entity with each contributing the following property.

	Phillip	**Evans**
Cash	$600,000	
Land		$600,000*

*Fair market value. Adjusted basis is $200,000.

Three months later, the land is sold for $652,000 because of unexpected zoning problems. The proceeds are to be applied toward the purchase of another parcel of land to be used for real estate development. Determine the tax consequences to the entity and to the owners upon formation and the later sale of the land if the entity is:

a.   A partnership.

b.   An S corporation.

c.   A C corporation.

46. **LO.5** Amy, Becky, and Chau form a business entity with each contributing the following.

	Adjusted Basis	**Fair Market Value**	**Ownership Percentage**
Amy: Cash	$100,000	$100,000	40%
Becky: Land	60,000	120,000	40%
Chau: Services		50,000	20%

Becky's land has a $20,000 mortgage that is assumed by the entity. Chau, an attorney, receives her ownership interest in exchange for legal services. Determine the recognized gain to the owners, the basis for their ownership interests, and the entity's basis for its assets if the entity is:

a.   A partnership.

b.   A C corporation.

c.   An S corporation.

47. **LO.5** Emmy contributes $40,000 to a business entity in exchange for a 30% ownership interest. During the first year of operations, the entity earns a profit of $200,000, and at the end of the year, it has liabilities of $75,000. Calculate Emmy's basis for her ownership interest if the entity is:

a.   A C corporation.

b.   An S corporation.

c.   A partnership.

48. **LO.5** An entity reports the following income for the current year.

Operations	$92,000
Tax-exempt interest income	19,000
Long-term capital gain	60,000

The entity holds earnings and profits (AAA for an S corporation) of $900,000 at the beginning of the year. A distribution of $200,000 is made to the owners.

a.   Calculate the taxable income if the entity is (1) a C corporation and (2) an S corporation.

b.   Determine the effect of the distribution on the shareholders if the entity is (1) a C corporation and (2) an S corporation.

49. **LO.5** Indigo, Inc., a closely held C corporation, records the following income and losses for the current tax year.

Active income	$325,000
Portfolio income	49,000
Passive activity loss	333,000

    a.   Calculate Indigo's taxable income for its current tax year.

    b.   Would the answer in part (a) change if the passive loss was only $320,000 rather than $333,000? Explain.

50. **LO.5** Jo and Velma are equal owners of the JV Partnership, with Jo investing $500,000 and Velma contributing land and a building (adjusted basis of $125,000; fair market value of $500,000). In addition, the entity borrows $250,000 using recourse financing and $100,000 using nonrecourse financing.

    a.   What are Jo's and Velma's bases for their partnership interests (i.e., outside bases)?

    b.   What are Jo's and Velma's at-risk bases?

51. **LO.5** Rosa contributes $50,000 to a business entity in exchange for a 10% ownership interest. Rosa materially participates in the entity. The entity incurs a loss of $900,000 for the current year and holds liabilities at the end of the year of $700,000. Of this amount, $150,000 is recourse debt and $550,000 is nonrecourse debt.

    a.   Assume that the business entity is a partnership. How much of the entity loss can Rosa deduct on her income tax return? What is her basis for the partnership interest at the end of the current tax year?

    b.   Assume that the business entity is a C corporation. How much can Rosa deduct on her income tax return? What is her basis for the stock at the end of the current tax year?

52. **LO.6** Emily and Frida are negotiating with George to purchase the business he operates as Pelican, Inc. The assets of Pelican, Inc., a C corporation, are as follows.

Asset	Basis	FMV
Cash	$ 20,000	$ 20,000
Accounts receivable	50,000	50,000
Inventory	100,000	110,000
Furniture and fixtures*	150,000	170,000
Building**	200,000	250,000
Land	40,000	150,000

*Potential depreciation recapture under § 1245 is $45,000.
**The straight-line method was used to depreciate the building. The balance in the accumulated depreciation account is $340,000.

George's basis for the stock of Pelican is $560,000. George is in the 32% tax bracket.

    a.   Assume that Emily and Frida purchase the stock of Pelican from George and that the purchase price is $908,000. Determine the tax consequences to Emily and Frida, Pelican, and George.

    b.   Assume that Emily and Frida purchase the assets from Pelican and that the purchase price is $908,000. Determine the tax consequences to Emily and Frida, Pelican, and George.

    c.   Assume that the purchase price is $550,000 because the fair market value of the building is $150,000 and the fair market value of the land is $50,000. A zero amount is assigned to goodwill. Emily and Frida purchase the stock of Pelican from George. Determine the Federal income tax consequences to Emily, Frida, Pelican, and George.

Critical Thinking   53.   **LO.6** Linda is the owner of a sole proprietorship. The entity holds assets as follows.

Asset	Basis	FMV
Cash	$10,000	$10,000
Accounts receivable	–0–	25,000
Office furniture and fixtures*	15,000	17,000
Building**	75,000	90,000
Land	60,000	80,000

*Potential depreciation recapture under § 1245 of $5,000.
**The straight-line method of depreciation has been used to depreciate the building.

Linda sells the business to Juan for $260,000.

a.   Determine the tax consequences to Linda, including the classification of any recognized gain or loss.

b.   Determine the tax consequences to Juan.

c.   Advise Juan on how the purchase agreement could be modified to provide him with a more beneficial tax result.

Critical Thinking   54.   **LO.6** Gail and Harry own the GH Partnership, which has conducted business for 10 years. The bases for their partnership interests are $100,000 for Gail and $150,000 for Harry. GH Partnership holds the following assets.

Asset	Basis	FMV
Cash	$ 10,000	$ 10,000
Accounts receivable	30,000	28,000
Inventory	25,000	26,000
Building*	100,000	150,000
Land	250,000	400,000

*The straight-line method has been used to depreciate the building.
 Accumulated depreciation is $70,000.

Gail and Harry sell their partnership interests to Keith and Liang for $307,000 each.

a.   Determine the tax consequences of the sale to Gail, Harry, and GH Partnership.

b.   From a tax perspective, would it matter to Keith and Liang whether they purchase Gail's and Harry's partnership interests or the partnership assets from GH Partnership?

Decision Making   55.   **LO.6** Miguel Allred will purchase either the stock or the assets of Jewel Corporation. All of the Jewel stock is owned by Charley. Miguel and Charley agree that Communications   Jewel is worth $700,000. The tax basis for Jewel's assets is $500,000. Write a letter to Miguel advising him on whether he should negotiate to purchase the stock or the assets. Then prepare a memo on these matters for the tax research files. Miguel's address is 100 Aspen Green, Chattanooga, TN 37403.

Research Problems

Note: Solutions to the Research Problems can be prepared by using the Thomson Reuters Checkpoint™ online tax research database, which accompanies this textbook. Solutions can also be prepared by using research materials found in a typical tax library.

Research Problem 1. Turnaround LLC was formed several years ago. It incurred losses for several years, reducing many of its members' bases in their interests to zero. However, the business has recently obtained some new and promising contracts, anticipating profits in the coming years if it can obtain some financing. It admitted new members who each made capital contributions for their interests. The owners anticipate it will be necessary to reinvest most of the profits back into the business for some time.

Because there will no longer be losses to pass through and the double taxation of profits will be delayed for some time, the owners of Turnaround are considering converting the business to a C corporation. The business holds the following assets. There is no § 754 election in effect.

	FMV	Adjusted Basis
Cash	$ 500,000	$500,000
Property, plant, equipment	500,000	500,000
Customer contracts	1,000,000	–0–

The original owners of Turnaround, who now have a 50% capital and profits interest, have come to you for advice regarding the potential tax consequences of the conversion for them as well as for the new corporation.

Partial list of research aids:
Rev.Rul. 84–111.
Rev.Rul. 2004–59.
Reg. § 301.7701–3(g)(i).

Research Problem 2. Dr. Sanders is a veterinarian who is the sole shareholder of Vet, Inc., an S corporation. The corporation offers Sanders's consulting and surgical services to other veterinarians. Sanders does not receive regular payments from the corporation, but she withdraws funds as the need arises. During the current year, she withdraws $118,000, and the net income of the corporation is $225,000. The corporation does not deduct the $118,000, nor does Sanders include it in gross income. Sanders does, however, report the $225,000 in gross income.

Because Dr. Sanders has recognized all of the corporation's income, she sees no need to pay herself a salary. She justifies the treatment by arguing that she is not an employee (i.e., she is the owner) of the corporation, and that the Federal income tax consequences are the same. Evaluate the approach taken by Dr. Sanders and Vet, Inc.

Use internet tax resources to address the following questions. Look for reliable websites and blogs of the IRS and other government agencies, media outlets, businesses, tax professionals, academics, think tanks, and political outlets.

Research Problem 3. How do C and S corporations, partnerships, and limited liability entities compare in terms of aggregate business receipts? Construct a pie chart indicating the aggregate business receipts of C corporations, S corporations, partnerships (separating limited liability entities from other partnership types), and non-farm sole proprietorships. Use the most recent data available at the IRS stats website. Also explain how this data compares to the data in Exhibit 13.1 on numbers of different entities.

Communications

Data Analytics

Research Problem 4. Find an article describing how a specific business put together its employee fringe benefit package in light of the limitations presented by the tax law and the business's form of operation.

Research Problem 5. Find a recent article written by a tax practitioner that discusses how the TCJA of 2017 changes choice of entity considerations for businesses. In a paper that you send to your instructor, summarize the article and explain how the changes are relevant to a retail clothing business and a CPA firm.

Communications

Research Problem 6. Bitcoin, and the blockchain technology that makes it work, has created new methods for commerce and investment. One of these new vehicles is initial coin offerings (ICOs). Find an example in the United States where an ICO was used to generate capital for an entity. Describe the offering process and the type of entity. Does this type of financing create any new tax issues? Explain.

Communications

Taxes on the Financial Statements

LEARNING OBJECTIVES: *After completing Chapter 14, you should be able to:*

LO.1 Determine the differences between book and tax methods of computing income tax expense.

LO.2 Compute a corporation's book income tax expense.

LO.3 Describe the purpose of the valuation allowance.

LO.4 Interpret the disclosure information contained in the financial statements.

LO.5 Identify the GAAP treatment concerning tax uncertainties and tax law changes.

LO.6 Use financial statement income tax information to benchmark a company's tax position.

CHAPTER OUTLINE

TAXES ON THE FINANCIAL STATEMENTS

Raymond Jones, the CEO of Arctic Corporation, would like some help reconciling the amount of income tax expense on Arctic's financial statements with the amount of income tax reported on the company's corporate income tax return for its first year of operations. Mr. Jones does not understand why he can't simply multiply the financial statement income by the company's combined Federal and state 25 percent marginal income tax rate to get the financial tax expense. Although the financial statements show book income before tax of $25 million, the reported income tax expense is only $5 million. In addition, the corporate tax return reports taxable income of $19 million and Federal income taxes payable of $3.99 million ($19 million × 21%).

Without knowing the specifics of the company's financial statements, does Arctic's situation look reasonable? Why is Arctic's financial accounting tax expense not equal to $6.25 million ($25 million × 25%)? What causes the $1.01 million difference between the taxes shown on the financial statements and the taxes due on the tax return?

Read the chapter and formulate your response.

The ultimate result of the many tax planning ideas, advice, and compliance efforts provided by tax professionals to their clients is captured in a simple summary number—income tax expense. A U.S. corporation's tax expense is reported in its annual Federal tax return, its financial statements, and other regulatory filings and is often the starting point for state and local tax returns. As it turns out, however, deriving a corporation's income tax expense (i.e., its "provision" for income taxes) is not so simple.

A corporation may report millions of dollars in tax expense in its financial statements and yet pay virtually nothing to the U.S., state, or foreign governments. Alternatively, a corporation may pay substantial amounts to the U.S., state, and foreign governments and report a very small income tax expense in its financial statements. Why do such differences exist? Which income tax expense is the "correct" number? How can data regarding a corporation's income tax provision provide valuable information for the corporation, its competitors, and tax professionals assisting in the planning function? This chapter addresses these questions, which are of great interest to those who want to develop as tax and financial specialists.

14-1 BOOK-TAX DIFFERENCES

LO.1

Determine the differences between book and tax methods of computing income tax expense.

A significant difference may exist between a corporation's Federal income tax liability as reported on its Form 1120 (tax) and the corporation's income tax expense as reported on its financial statements (book) prepared using generally accepted accounting principles (GAAP). This book-tax difference is caused by one or more of the following.

- Different reporting entities included in the calculation.
- Different definition of taxes included in the income tax expense amount.
- Different accounting methods.

A corporation's activities are captured in its accounting records, producing general ledger results. At the end of the year, these records are summarized to produce a trial balance. Adjustments to these accounting data may be necessary to produce both the corporation's financial statements and its corporate income tax return. These book and tax adjustments rarely match.

Different entities may be included in the reports, and the book and tax rules can be quite different. For instance, GAAP includes a materiality principle, under which some items can be ignored if they are insignificant in amount. The tax law includes no similar materiality threshold: all items are material in computing taxable income.

On a tax return, Schedule M–1 or M–3 reconciles the differences between an entity's book income and its taxable income (see text Section 3-3 and Exhibit 14.1).

14-1a Different Reporting Entities

Under GAAP, a corporate group must consolidate all U.S. and foreign subsidiaries within a single financial statement when the parent corporation controls more than 50 percent of the voting power of those subsidiaries.[1] In cases where the parent corporation owns between 20 and 50 percent of another corporation, the parent uses the equity method to account for the earnings of the subsidiary. Under the equity method, the parent currently records its share of the subsidiary's income or loss for the year.[2] Corporations that own less than 20 percent of other corporations typically use the *cost method* to account for income from these investments and include income only when actual dividends are received.

---

[1]*Consolidation*, ASC 810. Certain adjustments are made to reduce book income for the after-tax income related to minority shareholders.

[2]*Investments—Equity Method and Joint Ventures*, ASC 323.

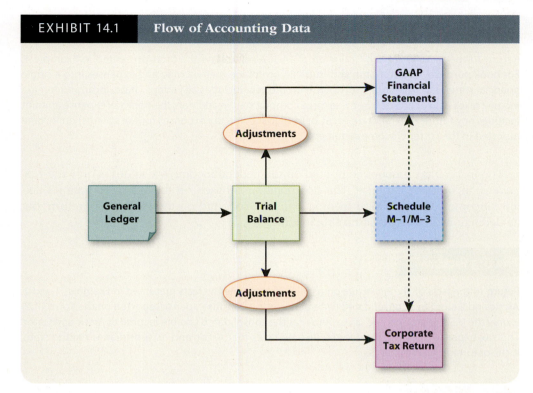

EXHIBIT 14.1 Flow of Accounting Data

The Big Picture

EXAMPLE 1

Return to the facts of *The Big Picture* on p. 14-1. Arctic Corporation owns 100% of Gator, Inc., a domestic corporation; 100% of Hurricane, Ltd., a foreign corporation; and 40% of Beach, Inc., a domestic corporation. Arctic's combined financial statement includes its own net income and the net income of both Gator and Hurricane. In addition, Arctic's financial statement includes its 40% share of Beach's net income. Arctic's financial statement includes the income of these subsidiaries regardless of whether Arctic receives any actual profit distributions from its subsidiaries.

For Federal income tax purposes, a U.S. corporation may elect to include in its consolidated tax return any *domestic* subsidiaries that are 80 percent or more owned.[3] On the other hand, the income of non-U.S. subsidiaries and less than 80 percent owned domestic subsidiaries is not included in the consolidated tax return.

The Big Picture

EXAMPLE 2

Return to the facts of *The Big Picture* on p. 14-1. Also assume the facts presented in Example 1. If Arctic elects to include Gator as part of its consolidated Federal income tax return, Arctic's return includes its own taxable income and the taxable income generated by Gator. Hurricane's taxable income is not included in the consolidated return because it is a non-U.S. corporation. Beach, although a domestic corporation, cannot be consolidated with Arctic because Arctic owns only 40% of the stock. Results related to Hurricane and Beach will be included in Arctic's U.S. taxable income only when Arctic receives actual or constructive dividends from those two companies.

14-1b Different Taxes

The income tax expense reported on a corporation's financial statement is the combination of the entity's Federal, state, local, and foreign income taxes. This number includes both current and deferred tax expense amounts. The distinction between current and deferred income taxes is discussed in text Section 14-2a.

---

[3]§§ 1501–1504. An existing election to consolidate an 80% or more owned subsidiary generally can be changed only with the permission of the IRS. See text Section 8-3d.

The Big Picture

EXAMPLE 3

Return to the facts of *The Big Picture* on p. 14-1. Also assume the facts presented in Example 1. For book purposes, Arctic, Gator, and Hurricane combine their income and expenses into a single financial statement. The book tax expense for the year includes all Federal, state, local, and foreign income taxes paid or accrued by these three corporations. In addition, the book tax expense amount includes any future Federal, state, local, or foreign income tax expenses (or tax savings) on income reported in the current income statement.

The income tax amount computed on the Federal income tax return is only the U.S. *Federal* income tax expense. This computation is based on the U.S. corporation's taxable income. State and local income taxes are reported on the Federal tax return, but as deductions in arriving at taxable income.

The Big Picture

EXAMPLE 4

Return to the facts of *The Big Picture* on p. 14-1. Also assume the facts presented in Examples 1 and 2. Arctic and Gator file a consolidated Federal tax return. The tax expense reported on the Form 1120 is only the U.S. Federal income tax expense for the consolidated taxable income of Arctic and Gator. This tax expense does not include the income taxes that Arctic and its subsidiaries paid to state, local, or foreign governments.

14-1c Different Methods

Many differences exist between book and tax accounting methods. Some are temporary differences, with income and expenses appearing in *both* the financial statement and the tax return, but in different reporting periods (i.e., a timing difference). Others are permanent differences, with items appearing in *either* the financial statement or the tax return, but not both.

Temporary differences include the following.

- *Depreciation on fixed assets.* An entity may use an accelerated depreciation method for tax purposes [e.g., the modified accelerated cost recovery system (MACRS)] but adopt the straight-line method for book purposes. Even if identical methods are used, the period over which the asset is depreciated is likely to differ between book and tax (with tax depreciable lives often shorter than book). As a result, tax rules can allow the acceleration of the deductions over the asset's life.

- *Compensation-related expenses.* Generally, the tax law does not allow the use of estimates or reserves, as is common under GAAP. For example, under GAAP, corporations accrue the future expenses related to providing postretirement benefits other than pensions (e.g., health insurance coverage). However, these expenses are deductible for tax purposes only when paid.[4]

- *Accrued income and expenses.* Although most income and expense items are recognized for tax and book purposes in the same period, a number of items potentially appear in different periods. For example, warranty expenses are accrued for book purposes but are not deductible for tax purposes until incurred. Inventory write-offs are accrued for book but are not deductible for tax until incurred. Similarly, different methods regarding the timing of income recognition may create temporary differences. For instance, GAAP does not follow any of the various income tax deferral methods allowed by the Code for transactions with customers.[5] Similarly, GAAP recognizes income and loss when the *fair value* of most investment assets changes during the year; tax rules recognize this realized gain or loss only upon a sale or other taxable disposition of the asset.

---

[4]Exceptions to this rule exist (e.g., concerning stock incentive plans and deferred compensation).

[5]ASC 606, *Revenue from Contracts with Customers*; c.f. Rev.Proc. 2004–34, 2004–1 C.B. 991.

- *Net operating losses.* Taxable income for the year cannot be less than zero; thus, operating losses from one tax year may be "carried over" (i.e., used to offset taxable income in another tax year). No such loss carryovers are used under GAAP; GAAP losses are reported as negative income amounts in the year incurred. As a result, the losses incurred in one year for book purposes may be used as a deduction for tax purposes in a different year.
- *Intangible assets.* Goodwill and some other intangibles are not amortizable for book purposes. However, GAAP requires an annual determination of whether the intangible asset has suffered a reduction in value (i.e., impairment).[6] If an intangible has suffered an impairment, a current expense is required to reduce the asset's book value to the lower level. For tax purposes, certain intangibles (including goodwill) can be amortized over 15 years.[7]

Permanent differences include the following.

- *Nontaxable income.* A common example is municipal bond interest, which is income for book purposes but is not taxable.
- *Nondeductible expenses.* A portion of business meals, all entertainment expenses, and certain penalties are not deductible for tax purposes, but they are fully expensed in arriving at book income.
- *Special tax deductions.* GAAP does not allow expenses for certain income tax deductions, such as the dividends received deduction.
- *Tax credits.* Credits such as the research activities credit reduce the Federal income tax liability but have no corresponding book treatment.

EXAMPLE 5

Wise, Inc., reported the following results for the current year.

Book income (before tax)	$685,000
Tax depreciation in excess of book	(125,000)
Nondeductible warranty expense	65,000
Municipal bond interest income	(35,000)
Taxable income (Form 1120)	$590,000

Wise reports net income before tax of $685,000 on its financial statement but must adjust this amount for differences between book and tax income.

Tax depreciation in excess of book is a tax deduction not currently expensed for book purposes, and warranty expense is deductible for book purposes but not yet deductible for tax. Both of these items are temporary differences because they eventually reverse (with book depreciation eventually exceeding tax depreciation and the warranty expense ultimately deducted for tax when incurred).

The municipal bond interest is a permanent difference because this income will never be subject to tax.

14-1d **Tax Return Disclosures**

Exhibit 14.2 contains the Schedule M–1 from Form 1120, the corporate income tax return. The purpose of Schedule M–1 is to reconcile book income to the taxable income as reported on the tax return. Line 1 is the net income or loss per books, and line 2 adds back the book tax expense to get back to book income before tax.[8] The remainder

---

[6]*Intangibles—Goodwill and Other,* ASC 350.

[7]§ 197.

[8]Line 1, "Net income (loss) per books," is not defined in the instructions to the form, and corporations can use various starting points in the Schedule M–1

(e.g., only the book income from U.S. members of the group). The Schedule M–3 is more specific in defining book income.

EXHIBIT 14.2 **Schedule M–1**

Schedule M–1 **Reconciliation of Income (Loss) per Books With Income per Return**
Note: The corporation may be required to file Schedule M-3. See instructions.

1	Net income (loss) per books		7	Income recorded on books this year not included on this return (itemize):
2	Federal income tax per books			Tax-exempt interest $ _____
3	Excess of capital losses over capital gains .			_____
4	Income subject to tax not recorded on books this year (itemize): _____			_____
			8	Deductions on this return not charged against book income this year (itemize):
	_____		a	Depreciation . . $ _____
5	Expenses recorded on books this year not deducted on this return (itemize):		b	Charitable contributions $ _____
a	Depreciation . . . . $ _____			_____
b	Charitable contributions . $ _____			_____
c	Travel and entertainment . $ _____		9	Add lines 7 and 8 . . . . . .
	_____		10	Income (page 1, line 28)—line 6 less line 9
6	Add lines 1 through 5			

---

of Schedule M–1 contains adjustments for both temporary and permanent differences, until arriving at taxable income (before the net operating loss and dividends received deductions) on line 10.

Schedule M–3 is required for a C corporation or consolidated tax group with total year-end assets of at least $10 million. The Schedule M–3 provides the IRS with more detailed information than is provided in the Schedule M–1. In addition, the Schedule M–3 requires identification of whether a book-tax difference is temporary or permanent.

Schedule M–1 or M–3 typically is the starting point for IRS audits of corporations. Identifying large differences between book and taxable income may offer the IRS auditor insights into tax saving strategies (some perhaps questionable) employed by the taxpayer. Concept Summary 14.1 summarizes the sources of typical corporate book-tax differences.

FINANCIAL DISCLOSURE INSIGHTS **Supersized Goodwill**

When a balance sheet includes an asset value for goodwill, the company's total valuation is seen to exceed the aggregate value of its physical assets, such as cash and equipment. Goodwill typically is created as the result of the takeover of a target entity in an acquisition transaction.

GAAP rules concerning goodwill and its impairment evolved in a context of stable market values and managed income. But when goodwill gets to be so large that it is a major asset in itself, are GAAP impairment write-downs sure to follow?

An impairment write-down often is an indication that an acquiror overpaid for the target entity in a takeover transaction. Thus, conglomerates that grow by a series of acquisitions may be doubly exposed to goodwill write-downs. Accordingly, goodwill and its impairment can become an outsized element of the financial statements for many companies.

In a recent year, the following data concerning recorded goodwill were reported.

Company	Goodwill as a Percentage of Balance Sheet Assets
Time Warner	42.1%
Kraft Heinz	36.6%
Frontier Communications	33.3%
Dr Pepper Snapple Group	30.6%
Starbucks	12.0%
Netflix	0.0%

Concept Summary 14.1

Income Amounts—Book versus Tax

Financial Statement	U.S. Federal Income Tax Return
Reporting entities	**Reporting entities**
• 50% or more owned domestic and foreign subsidiaries *must* be consolidated.	• 80% or more owned domestic subsidiaries *may* be consolidated.
• Share of income from 20%–50% owned domestic and foreign corporations included in current income.	• Share of income from other corporations reported only when actual or constructive dividends are received.
Income tax expense	**Income tax expense**
• Federal income taxes.	• Federal income taxes.
• State income taxes.	• Current only.
• Local income taxes.	
• Non-U.S. income taxes.	
• Current and deferred.	
Methods	**Methods**
• Temporary differences.	• Temporary differences.
• Permanent differences.	• Permanent differences.
• Income tax note reconciliation.	• Schedule M–1 or M–3 reconciliation.

Uncertain Tax Positions

The IRS requires that large corporations list the tax return positions they have taken that may not be fully supported by the law. Schedule UTP ("uncertain tax positions") is added to the Form 1120 for all corporations with assets of at least $10 million.[9]

Disclosures on the Schedule UTP include a list of tax return positions for the current and prior tax years where:

- The taxpayer or a related party recorded a reserve against the Federal income tax expense on its audited financial statements, or

- The taxpayer or a related party did *not* record a tax reserve based on its analysis of expected litigation with the IRS. This means that in the taxpayer's view, the issue will not be settled with the IRS and, instead, will be litigated. In addition, after analyzing relevant tax law, the taxpayer determines that, if it chooses to take the issue to court, it is *more likely than not* (a greater than 50 percent likelihood) to win the case.

Disclosures are not required for items that are immaterial under GAAP rules, or for items which the filing position is sufficiently certain that no financial accounting reserve is required.

The IRS maintains that it will limit releases of the Schedule UTP to other taxing jurisdictions, and that it will not use Schedule UTP data to usurp the attorney-client and tax practitioner privileges of confidentiality or the work-product doctrine. Taxpayers are not required to disclose the amounts of any reserves or the precise nature of the tax planning technique that led to the reserve for the filing position.

---

[9]Some tax professionals believe that the Schedule UTP alerts the IRS to specific items that will be most vulnerable to audit adjustments. The public and other Federal agencies do not have access to a corporation's Schedule UTP because tax returns are confidential documents.

For some taxpayers, tax filing positions reported on Schedules UTP are few in number because they are "less aggressive" in making filing decisions, or because they negotiate with the IRS before filing a return as to certain deductions and credits. The most commonly reported uncertain tax positions on a Schedule UTP involve the research credit and transfer pricing computations.

Compute a corporation's book income tax expense.

14-2 INCOME TAXES IN THE FINANCIAL STATEMENTS

14-2a GAAP Principles

A corporation's financial statements are prepared in accordance with GAAP. The purpose and objectives of these statements are quite different from the objective of the corporation's income tax return.

The **ASC 740** approach produces a total income tax expense (also called the **income tax provision**) for the income currently reported on a corporation's combined financial statement.[10] This approach follows the so-called *matching principle*, where all of the expenses related to earning income are reported in the same period in which the revenue is reported (no matter when the expenses are actually paid). If an entity fails to follow GAAP in reporting its tax provision and related accounts, the SEC could respond with a comment letter indicating a material weakness in the financial statements, or the agency might require a full restatement of the financial statements.

PanCo, Inc., earns $100,000 in book income before tax and is subject to a 21% marginal Federal income tax rate. PanCo records a single temporary difference. Tax depreciation exceeds book depreciation by $20,000. Accordingly, PanCo's taxable income is $80,000 ($100,000 − $20,000 additional tax deduction).

On its income tax return, PanCo reports a current Federal tax liability of $16,800 ($80,000 × 21%). On its financial statement, PanCo reports a total tax provision of $21,000 ($100,000 × 21%). This $4,200 book-tax difference relates to the difference between the book and tax basis of the depreciable asset times the current corporate tax rate ($4,200 = $20,000 × 21%).

Although PanCo did not actually pay the $4,200 Federal income tax this year, in future years when the book-tax depreciation difference reverses, the $4,200 eventually will be paid. As a result, the *future* income tax expense is matched to the related book income and is reported in the GAAP statements for the current year.

The total book tax expense under ASC 740 is made up of both current and deferred components. Theoretically, the **current tax expense** represents the taxes actually payable to (or refund receivable from) the governmental authorities for the current period.[11] You might think of this amount as the actual check the taxpayer writes to the government (or refund received) for the current year; some tax professionals refer to this as the "cash tax" amount. Exhibit 14.3 summarizes the computation of a corporation's current tax expense.

---

[10]*Income Taxes*, ASC 740.

[11]ASC 740-10-10-1(a).

EXHIBIT 14.3	**Current Tax Expense (Simplified)**

	Pretax book income
±	Schedule M–1/M–3 adjustments
	Taxable income before NOLs
−	NOL carryforwards
	Taxable income
×	Applicable tax rate
	Current tax expense (provision) before tax credits
−	Tax credits
	Current tax expense (provision)

The deferred component of the book tax expense is called the **deferred tax expense** or **deferred tax benefit**. This component represents the future tax cost (or savings) connected with income reported in the current-period financial statement.[12] Deferred tax expense or benefit is created as a result of temporary differences. More technically, ASC 740 adopts a **balance sheet approach** to measuring deferred taxes. Under this approach, the deferred tax expense or benefit can be seen as the change from one year to the next in the entity's net, cumulative **deferred tax liability** or **deferred tax asset**.

A *deferred tax liability* is the expected future tax liability related to current income (measured using enacted tax rates and rules).[13] A deferred tax liability is created in the following situations.

- An item is deductible for tax in the current period but is not expensed for book until some future period.
- Income is includible currently for book purposes but is not includible in taxable income until a future period.

In essence, a deferred tax liability is created when the book basis of an asset exceeds its tax basis. The opposite condition creates a deferred tax asset.

GLOBAL TAX ISSUES   Accounting for Income Taxes in International Standards

The FASB and the International Accounting Standards Board (IASB) have worked to move the GAAP and IFRS treatment of income taxes closer together in light of the proposed convergence of GAAP and IFRS. Both ASC 740 and IAS 12 (the IFRS guidance for income taxes) are based on a balance sheet approach.

Nevertheless, several significant differences exist between the two standards. These include the thresholds for recognition and approach to valuation allowances and the measurement of uncertain tax positions.[14] The IRS looks for comments from the public on the Federal tax aspects of these convergence projects.[15]

---

[12]ASC 740-10-10-1(b).

[13]ASC 740-10-30-2. Tax amounts are not reduced to their present values. If the tax rate will be different in future years, the *future* tax rate should be used in the computation.

[14]One can keep up with the FASB and the IASB's work on income tax reporting by visiting the FASB website at **fasb.org** and selecting the "Technical Agenda" section under "Projects," and then choosing "Presentation & Disclosure" or "Research."

[15]See, for example, Notice 2017–17, 2017–15 I.R.B. 1074, as to the joint FASB and IFRS revenue recognition projects.

FINANCIAL DISCLOSURE INSIGHTS The Book-Tax Income Gap

According to one study, 115 companies in the Standard and Poor's stock index incurred a Federal and state income tax rate of less than 20 percent. In fact, the rate for 39 of those companies was less than 10 percent.

At least 30 of the Fortune 500 companies paid zero or negative Federal corporate income taxes over a recent three-year period. These companies included General Electric, American Electric Power, FedEx, Honeywell, Pfizer, Verizon, Boeing, and PG&E. Pepco Holdings reported an effective Federal income tax rate of *negative* 57.6 percent!

The firms maintained that they had paid all of their required tax liabilities, and that effective income tax planning had resulted in their zero or negative effective tax rates.

Corporations further maintain that the large differences in book and tax income are a function of the different rules and objectives of GAAP for financial statements and the Internal Revenue Code for tax returns.

Low effective tax rates often are traceable to one or more of the following.

- use of NOL carryovers
- large investments in depreciable assets
- use of state, local, Federal, and international tax incentives (e.g., to encourage new companies and targeted industries such as high-tech, energy, and domestic manufacturing)
- use of temporary tax provisions (e.g., stimulus, anti-recession, or other targeted rules designed to stimulate the economy via tax cuts)
- negotiations and settlements with revenue agencies[16]
- application of acceptable tax planning techniques

Deferred Tax Expense

EXAMPLE 7

PJ Enterprises earns net income before depreciation of $500,000 in 2018 and $600,000 in 2019. PJ uses equipment acquired in 2018 for $80,000. For tax purposes, assume that PJ uses an accelerated method and deducts $60,000 in depreciation expense for the first year and $20,000 in depreciation expense for the second year. For book purposes, PJ depreciates the asset on a straight-line basis over two years ($40,000 in depreciation expense per year).

2018

	Beginning of Year			End of Year			Change in Basis Difference This Year	Federal and State Income Tax Rate	Change in Deferred Tax Liability
	Book Basis	Tax Basis	Basis Differences, Book to Tax	Book Basis	Tax Basis	Basis Differences, Book to Tax			
Equipment	$—	$—	$—	$40,000	$20,000	$20,000	$20,000	25%	$5,000

A $5,000 deferred tax liability is created in 2018, due to the timing difference for the equipment depreciation.

2019

	Beginning of Year			End of Year			Change in Basis Difference This Year	Federal and State Income Tax Rate	Change in Deferred Tax Liability
	Book Basis	Tax Basis	Basis Differences, Book to Tax	Book Basis	Tax Basis	Basis Differences, Book to Tax			
Equipment	$40,000	$20,000	$20,000	$—	$—	$—	($20,000)	25%	($5,000)

The book-tax difference in the asset basis reverses in 2019, with a resulting reduction of the deferred tax liability account.

EXAMPLE 8

Continue with the facts in Example 7. The following journal entries record the book tax expense (provision) for each year. The book total tax expense combines the current amount (income tax payable) and the future amount (deferred tax liability).

continued

---

[16]For instance, AstraZeneca reduced its effective tax rate after settling an audit with U.S. and U.K. tax authorities about its transfer pricing policies (see text Section 9-3d). The taxpayer's liability after the settlement was less than the tax reserve it had set aside on its GAAP statements with respect to the audit.

2018 Journal Entry

Income tax expense (provision)	$115,000*	
Income tax payable		$110,000**
Deferred tax liability		5,000

2019 Journal Entry

Income tax expense (provision)	$140,000*	
Deferred tax liability	5,000	
Income tax payable		$145,000**

At the end of 2018, the PJ balance sheet reflects a net deferred tax liability of $5,000. At the end of 2019, the PJ balance sheet contains a zero deferred tax liability; the temporary difference that created the deferred tax liability has reversed itself.

*2018: ($500,000 − $40,000) × 25%   ** 2018: ($500,000 − $60,000) × 25%
 2019: ($600,000 − $40,000) × 25%   2019: ($600,000 − $20,000) × 25%

A *deferred tax asset* is the expected future tax benefit related to current book income (measured using enacted tax rates and rules). A deferred tax asset is created in the following situations.

- An expense is deductible for book in the current period but is not deductible for tax until some future period.
- Income is includible in taxable income currently but is not includible in book income until a future period.

Deferred Tax Assets

EXAMPLE 9

MollCo, Inc., earns net income before warranty expense of $400,000 in 2018 and $450,000 in 2019. In 2018, MollCo records $30,000 in warranty expense for book purposes related to expected warranty repairs. This warranty expense is not deductible for tax purposes until actually incurred. Assume that the $30,000 warranty obligation is paid in 2019 and that this is MollCo's only temporary difference.

2018

	Beginning of Year			End of Year			Change in Basis Difference This Year	Federal and State Income Tax Rate	Change in Deferred Tax Liability
	Book Basis	Tax Basis	Basis Differences, Book to Tax	Book Basis	Tax Basis	Basis Differences, Book to Tax			
Warranty	$—	$—	$—	$—	$30,000	($30,000)	($30,000)	25%	($7,500)

A $7,500 deferred tax asset is created in 2018, due to the timing difference for the warranty obligations.

2019

	Beginning of Year			End of Year			Change in Basis Difference This Year	Federal and State Income Tax Rate	Change in Deferred Tax Asset
	Book Basis	Tax Basis	Basis Differences, Book to Tax	Book Basis	Tax Basis	Basis Differences, Book to Tax			
Warranty	$—	$30,000	($30,000)	$—	$—	$—	$30,000	25%	$7,500

The book-tax difference in the warranty expense payable reverses in 2019, with a resulting reduction of the deferred tax asset account.

EXAMPLE 10

Continue with the facts in Example 9. The following journal entries record the book tax expense (provision) for each year. The book total tax expense combines the current amount (income tax payable) and the future amount (deferred tax asset).

continued

2018 Journal Entry		
Income tax expense (provision)	$ 92,500	
Deferred tax asset	7,500	
Income tax payable		$100,000
2019 Journal Entry		
Income tax expense (provision)	$112,500	
Deferred tax asset		$ 7,500
Income tax payable		105,000

At the end of 2018, the MollCo balance sheet reflects a net deferred tax asset of $7,500. At the end of 2019, the MollCo balance sheet contains a zero deferred tax asset; the temporary difference that created the deferred tax asset has reversed itself.

Deferred tax assets and liabilities are reported on the balance sheet just like any other asset or liability. However, the interpretation of these assets and liabilities is quite different. Typically, an asset is "good" because it represents a claim on something of value, and a liability is "bad" because it represents a future claim against the corporation's assets. In the case of deferred tax assets and liabilities, the interpretation is reversed. Deferred tax liabilities are "good" because they represent an amount that may be paid to the government in the future.

In essence, deferred tax liabilities are like an interest-free loan to the taxpayer from the government with a due date perhaps many years in the future. Deferred tax assets, on the other hand, are future tax benefits, so they are similar to a receivable from the government that may not be received until many years in the future.

14-2b Valuation Allowance

LO.3

Describe the purpose of the valuation allowance.

Much of GAAP is based on the conservatism principle . That is, accounting rules are designed to provide assurance that assets are not overstated and liabilities are not understated. Current recognition of deferred tax liabilities does not require significant professional judgment because future tax liabilities always are expected to be settled in full. However, under ASC 740, deferred tax assets are recognized only when it is *more likely than not* (a greater than 50 percent likelihood) that the future tax benefits will be realized.

Using Future Tax Benefits

EXAMPLE 11

Warren, Inc., reported book income before tax of $2,000,000 in 2019. Warren's taxable income also is $2,000,000 (i.e., there are no temporary or permanent differences). Warren reports a current U.S. income tax liability for the year of $420,000 before tax credits ($2,000,000 × 21%). During the year, Warren earned $100,000 in general business credits that it is not able to use on its 2019 tax return.

Warren's auditors believe it is *more likely than not* that Warren will be able to use the $100,000 of tax credits within the next 20 years (i.e., in a period before they expire). Consequently, the future tax benefit of the tax credits is accounted for in the current-year book tax expense as a $100,000 future tax benefit.

The current and deferred tax expense are calculated as follows.

	Book	Tax
Income tax expense/payable	$320,000	$420,000
Current tax expense	$420,000	
Deferred tax expense (benefit)	($100,000)	

Using Future Tax Benefits

Continue with the facts of Example 11. Warren records the following journal entry for the book income tax expense and deferred tax asset related to the expected use of the FTCs.

Income tax expense (provision)	$320,000	
Deferred tax asset	100,000	
Income tax payable		$420,000

Because Warren can record the benefit of the future tax credits, its effective tax rate is 16% ($320,000 tax expense/$2,000,000 book income before tax).

EXAMPLE 12

When a deferred tax asset does not meet the *more likely than not* threshold for recognition, ASC 740 requires that a valuation allowance be created. The **valuation allowance** is a contra-asset account that offsets all or a portion of the deferred tax asset.

Valuation Allowance

Assume that the auditors in Example 11 believe that Warren will be able to use only $40,000 of the 2019 general business credits in any tax year, with the remaining $60,000 expiring unused. In this case, the future tax benefit recognized currently should be only $40,000 rather than the full $100,000. To implement this reduction in the deferred tax asset, Warren records a valuation allowance of $60,000, resulting in a book tax expense of $380,000.

	Book	Tax
Income tax expense/payable	$380,000	$420,000
Current tax expense	$420,000	
Deferred tax expense (benefit)	($ 40,000)	

EXAMPLE 13

Continue with the facts of Example 13. Warren records the following journal entry for the book income tax expense and deferred tax asset related to the expected use of the FTCs.

Income tax expense (provision)	$380,000	
Deferred tax asset	100,000	
Valuation allowance		$ 60,000
Income tax payable		420,000

Warren reduces the deferred tax asset by $60,000, which increases its effective tax rate to 19% ($380,000 tax expense/$2,000,000 book income before tax), compared with the 16% effective tax rate in Example 12.

EXAMPLE 14

GLOBAL TAX ISSUES Tax Losses and the Deferred Tax Asset

Although a current-year net operating loss (NOL) represents a failure of an entity's business model to some, others see it as an immediate tax refund. But when an NOL hits the balance sheet as a deferred tax asset, the story is not over. The NOL creates or increases a deferred tax asset that may or may not be used in future financial accounting reporting periods: the key question for a financial analyst is whether the entity will generate enough net revenue in future years to create a positive tax liability that can be offset by the NOL carryover amount.

IFRS rules do not allow for a valuation allowance. Under IAS 12, a deferred tax asset is recorded only when it is "probable" (a higher standard than GAAP's "more likely than not") that the deferred tax amount will be realized, and then only to the extent of that probable amount. Thus, no offsetting valuation allowance is needed.

To determine whether a valuation allowance is required, both positive and negative evidence must be evaluated. Negative evidence (i.e., evidence suggesting that the deferred tax asset will not be realized) includes the following.

- History of losses.
- Expected future losses.
- Short tax credit carryback/carryforward periods.
- Adverse tax and legal results (e.g., the expiration of a patent or trademark).
- History of tax credits expiring unused.

Positive evidence (i.e., support for realizing the current benefit of future tax savings) includes the following.

- Strong earnings history.
- Existing present or future contracts.
- Unrealized appreciation in assets.
- Sales backlog of profitable orders.

The valuation allowance is examined for appropriateness each year. The allowance may be increased or decreased in subsequent reporting periods if facts and circumstances change.

Interpret the disclosure information contained in the financial statements.

14-2c Tax Disclosures in the Financial Statements

As illustrated earlier, any temporary differences create deferred tax liabilities or deferred tax assets and these amounts appear in the corporation's balance sheet.

The Balance Sheet

Deferred tax accounts are treated as noncurrent items on the GAAP balance sheet.[17] A corporation may hold both deferred tax assets and liabilities. The corporation can keep these items separate or report the *net* noncurrent deferred tax assets or liabilities.[18]

The Income Statement

In its GAAP income statement, a corporation reports a total income tax expense that consists of both the current tax expense (or benefit) and the deferred tax expense (or benefit). The tax expense is allocated among income from continuing operations, discontinued operations, extraordinary items, prior-period adjustments, and the cumulative effect of accounting changes. Additional disclosures are required for the tax expense allocated to income from continuing operations (e.g., current versus deferred, benefits of NOL deductions, and changes in valuation allowances).

Financial Statement Footnotes

The income tax footnote contains a wealth of information, including the following.

- Breakdown of income between domestic and foreign.
- Analysis of the provision for income tax expense.
- Analysis of deferred tax assets and liabilities.
- Effective tax **rate reconciliation** (dollar amount or percentage).
- Discussion of significant tax matters.

---

[17]ASC 740-10-45-4.   [18]ASC 740-10-45-6.

The steps in determining a corporation's income tax expense for book purposes are summarized in Concept Summary 14.2.

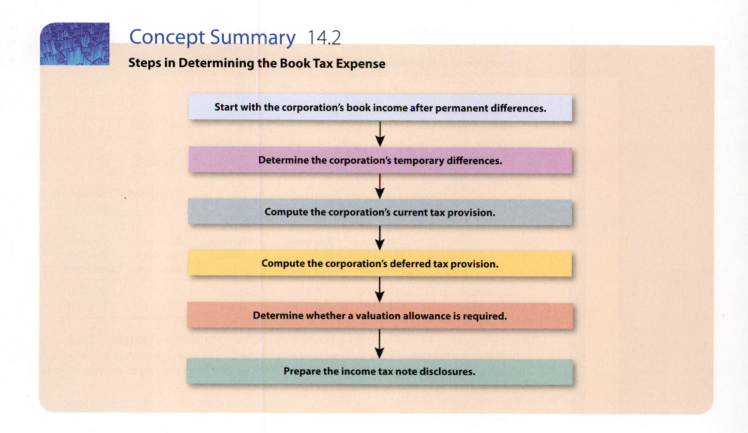

Concept Summary 14.2

Steps in Determining the Book Tax Expense

Start with the corporation's book income after permanent differences.

↓

Determine the corporation's temporary differences.

↓

Compute the corporation's current tax provision.

↓

Compute the corporation's deferred tax provision.

↓

Determine whether a valuation allowance is required.

↓

Prepare the income tax note disclosures.

Rate Reconciliation

The purpose of the rate reconciliation is to demonstrate how a corporation's actual book effective tax rate relates to its "hypothetical tax rate" (i.e., as if the book income were taxed fully at the top U.S. corporate rate of 21 percent).[19] Although similar to Schedule M–1 or M–3, the tax footnote rate reconciliation generally reports only differences triggered by permanent book-tax differences. An analysis of the rate reconciliation can provide substantial indicators as to the tax planning strategies adopted (or not adopted) by a company; see text Section 14-3: Benchmarking.

Rate Reconciliations

BoxCo, Inc., a domestic corporation, owns 100% of PaperCo, Ltd., an Erasmus corporation. BoxCo's U.S. corporate tax rate is 21%, and its Erasmus rate is 10%. Book income, permanent and temporary differences, and current tax expense are computed as follows.

EXAMPLE

15

continued

---

[19]ASC 740-10-50-12.

	BoxCo	PaperCo
Book income before tax	$300,000	$200,000
Permanent differences		
Business meals expense	20,000	—
Municipal bond interest income	(50,000)	—
Book income after permanent differences	$270,000	$200,000
Temporary differences		
Tax > book depreciation	(50,000)	—
Book > tax bad debt expense	10,000	—
Taxable income	$230,000	$200,000
Tax rate	× 21%	× 10%
Current tax expense	$ 48,300	$ 20,000

Specifically, basis amounts and current deductions for the two assets are reported as follows.

	Book Basis, Beginning of Year	Tax Basis, Beginning of Year	Basis Difference, Beginning of Year	Current-Year Book Expense	Current-Year Tax Deduction
Depreciable assets	$900,000	$750,000	$150,000	$40,000	$90,000
Receivables	800,000	850,000	(50,000)	15,000	5,000

Thus, the beginning-of-the-year deferred tax liability is $21,000 [($150,000 − $50,000) × 21%].

To determine the deferred tax expense (benefit) for the current year, the change in the balance sheet amounts for these temporary differences from the beginning to the end of the year must be determined and then multiplied by the appropriate tax rate.

	Beginning of Year			End of Year			Change in Basis Difference This Year	Tax Rate	Change in Deferred Tax Liability/ (Asset)
	Book Basis	Tax Basis	Basis Differences, Book to Tax	Book Basis	Tax Basis	Basis Differences, Book to Tax			
Depreciation	$900,000	$750,000	$150,000	$860,000	$660,000	$200,000	$ 50,000	21%	$10,500
Receivables	800,000	850,000	(50,000)	785,000	845,000	(60,000)	(10,000)	21	(2,100)

The deferred tax liability increased by $8,400 for the year. Consequently, BoxCo's total tax provision for book purposes is $76,700.

Current tax expense	
Domestic	$48,300
Foreign	20,000
Deferred tax expense	
Domestic	8,400
Foreign	—
Total tax expense	$76,700

The journal entry to record the book income tax expense is constructed as follows.

Income tax expense (provision)	$76,700	
Income tax payable		$68,300
Deferred tax liability		8,400

BoxCo's book income is $500,000 (the combined book income of both BoxCo and PaperCo). The effective tax rate reconciliation is based on this book income, with the dollar amounts in the table representing the tax expense (benefit) related to the item and the percentage representing the tax

continued

expense (benefit) as a percentage of book income. For example, the municipal bond interest of $50,000 reduces tax liability by $10,500 ($50,000 × 21%). This $10,500 as a percentage of the $500,000 book income equals 2.1%.

	Effective Tax Rate Reconciliation	
	$	%
Hypothetical tax at U.S. rate	$105,000	21.0%
Disallowed meals expense	4,200	0.8
Municipal bond interest	(10,500)	(2.1)
Foreign income taxed at less than U.S. rate	(22,000)*	(4.4)
Income tax expense (provision)	$ 76,700	15.3%

*$200,000 × (21% − 10%).

Only permanent differences appear in the rate reconciliation. Temporary differences do not affect the *total* book income tax expense; they simply affect the amount of the tax expense that is current versus deferred.

14-2d Special Issues

Financial Accounting for Tax Uncertainties

LO.5

Identify the GAAP treatment concerning tax uncertainties and tax law changes.

Companies take positions in their tax returns that may not ultimately survive the scrutiny of the IRS or other tax authorities. If a taxpayer loses the benefit of a favorable tax position after an audit, there may be an unfavorable effect on the company's financial statement tax expense in that year. The additional tax cost will become part of the current tax expense, yet the income to which this tax is related would have been reported in a previous year. This result can wreak havoc with a company's effective tax rate.

To avoid such an increase in effective tax rate, companies may record a book reserve (or "cushion") for the uncertain tax position in the year the position is taken. That is, rather than book the entire tax benefit (and thus reduce tax expense in the current year), the company may book only a portion (or none) of the tax benefit. If the company later loses the actual tax benefit upon audit, to the extent the additional tax imposed is charged against the reserve, the additional tax does not affect the future-year tax expense. If the company's tax position is not challenged in the future (or the company successfully defends any challenge), the reserve can be released. This release reduces the current tax expense in the future (release) year, and it lowers the company's effective tax rate in that year.

To add more structure to the accounting for tax reserves, the FASB released an interpretation, "Accounting for Uncertainty in Income Taxes" (ASC 740-10). The approach required under this interpretation results in significantly more disclosure about uncertain tax positions by companies.

When ASC 740-10 applies, uncertain tax positions are defined as those material items that the taxpayer believes, based on the technical merits, it might lose on audit. Such tax positions result in a permanent reduction of income taxes payable, a deferral of income taxes otherwise currently payable to future years, or a change in the expected realizability of deferred tax assets.

Application of the ASC 740-10 rules requires a two-step process—recognition and measurement (see Concept Summary 14.3).

Recognition First, a tax benefit from an uncertain tax position may be *recognized* in the financial statements only if it is *more likely than not* (a greater than 50 percent likelihood) that the position would be sustained on its technical merits.[20] In this regard, audit or detection risk cannot be considered.

---

[20]ASC 740-10-25-5 through -7.

Concept Summary 14.3

Disclosures Under ASC 740-10

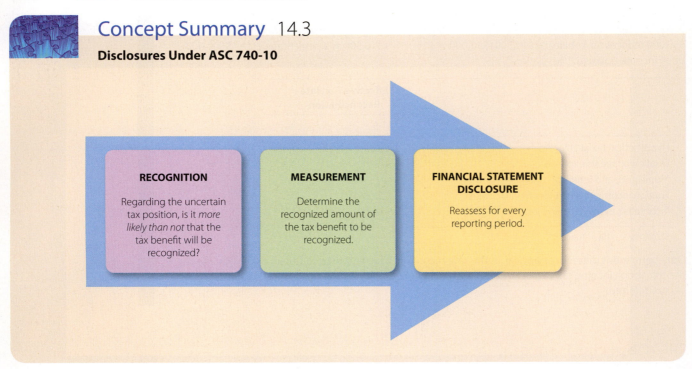

This first step determines whether any of the tax benefit is recognized. If the *more likely than not* standard is failed, the position requires no financial statement disclosure (i.e., the taxpayer cannot book any of the tax benefit related to the issue).

Measurement If the uncertain tax position meets the *more likely than not* threshold, the second step is to determine the amount of the tax benefit to report (the *measurement* process). This computation is based on the probabilities associated with the position not being challenged, or with it being challenged using a negotiated settlement or litigation.

A probability table is constructed, considering all of the possible post-audit and post-settlement outcomes for the tax benefit from the filing position. The filing position is recorded (i.e., the income or deduction amount is recognized for GAAP purposes) as the largest amount of the related tax benefit that is *more likely than not* (a greater than 50 percent probability) to be agreeable to the taxing authority, assuming that the taxing authority has full knowledge of all relevant information.[21]

EXAMPLE 16

StarksCo has adopted certain aggressive transfer pricing strategies with related parties overseas. StarksCo estimates that it will reduce its Federal income tax liability by $100,000 as a result of these strategies but that the IRS is likely to challenge the pricing structure in an audit. StarksCo estimates that, after an IRS audit and related negotiations, the tax benefit may be reduced (amounts as indicated with related probabilities); StarksCo constructs a table of these probabilities and results.

Resulting Estimated Tax Benefit	Probability of Agreement Between StarksCo and IRS	Cumulative Probability Computed
$100,000	40%	40%
80,000	35%	75%
45,000	20%	95%
–0–	5%	100%

continued

---

[21]ASC 740-10-30-7.

Assume that StarksCo recorded a book tax provision of $250,000, *including* the $100,000 tax benefit from this tax uncertainty. In light of the requirements of ASC 740-10, StarksCo instead should record an $80,000 tax benefit for this item. That amount is the estimated tax benefit that first exceeds a 50% cumulative probability of agreement with the IRS (here, a 75% chance of acceptance exists).

The journal entry that StarksCo records for this computation is constructed as follows, increasing the tax provision by $20,000, the amount dictated by ASC 740-10 = $100,000 − $80,000.

Current income tax expense (provision)	$20,000	
ASC 740-10 liability		$20,000

If the taxpayer prevails and the full $100,000 tax benefit is attained in a later year, a journal entry then will show the ASC 740-10 amount reversed, and the current income tax expense in that later year is reduced.

The recognition and measurement of uncertain tax positions must be reassessed at each reporting date. ASC 740-10 requires a reconciliation of the beginning and ending balances of the unrecognized tax benefits and a discussion of potential changes in these unrecognized tax benefits that might occur over the next 12 months.

ETHICS & EQUITY Disclosing Aggressive Tax Positions

In the current year, Dickinson, Inc., reports an effective tax rate of 36 percent, and Badger, Inc., reports an effective tax rate of 21 percent. Both companies are domestic and operate in the same industry. Your initial examination of the financial statements of the two companies indicates that Badger apparently is doing a better job with its tax planning, explaining the difference in effective tax rates. Consequently, all else being equal, you decide to invest in Badger.

In a subsequent year, it comes to light that Badger had used some very aggressive tax planning techniques to reduce its reported tax expense. After an examination by the IRS, Badger loses the tax benefits and reports a very large tax expense in that year. Over this multiple-year period, it turns out that Dickinson had the lower effective tax rate after all.

Do you believe Badger was ethical in not fully disclosing the aggressiveness of its tax positions in its current financial statements? How does ASC 740-10 affect Badger's disclosure requirement? Does ASC 740-10 still leave room for ethical decision making by management in determining how to report uncertain tax positions? Explain.

Effects of Statutory Tax Law Changes

Tax rules involving business transactions change only rarely in the Federal tax law; major changes to the taxation of C corporations are described as occurring perhaps only once in a generation. If there are tax policy reasons for this practice, they might involve the need for businesses to plan their tax and budget effects for many years into the future. If the corporate tax law changed almost annually, as do some of the statutory and administrative rules involving individuals, businesses would find it difficult to construct plans for compensation, asset acquisitions, mergers and takeovers, and similar transactions.

Additional reasons supporting the stability of the Federal corporate income tax rules over time include the following.

- State and local income tax rules often are linked to their Federal counterparts; see the discussion in text Section 16-1a. Federal tax law changes sometimes trigger automatic changes at the state and local level, but those jurisdictions have their own budgetary concerns, and a new Federal tax law rule (e.g., to increase the rate of acceleration for cost recovery deductions) might not be adopted (immediately or ever) by all of the states.

- A Federal tax law change may have significant effects on the financial statements of the entities affected, and Congress may be reluctant to make business tax law changes that could trigger changes in stock market valuations for publicly traded corporations.

The Tax Cuts and Jobs Act (TCJA) of 2017 was adopted by Congress late in 2017, and those provisions were significant in their scope. Most taxpayers living or doing business in the United States were affected by those changes, which generally were effective beginning in 2018. We will use a few of these revisions to illustrate how changes in the tax law affect GAAP financial statements and other book items that relate to the Federal tax law. Our discussion assumes that taxpayers use a calendar tax year; computations are different for fiscal-year corporations.

Decrease in C Corporation Tax Rate Congress cut the top income tax rate that applies to most C corporations as part of the TCJA of 2017. Previously, the top rate had been 34 or 35 percent, and those were among the highest marginal tax rates in the world as they applied to business income. For many reasons, including to encourage the global competitiveness of the U.S. economy and to provide increased after-tax cash flow for U.S.-based taxpayers, the C corporation tax rate was reduced to 21 percent beginning in 2018.

As a result, adjustments were made to the amounts of tax-deferred assets and liabilities that incorporate the enacted Federal income tax rate. For instance, if a GAAP deferred tax liability related to the acceleration of cost recovery deductions over those claimed for book purposes, the deferred tax liability was "worth less" after the lower tax rate was enacted. This resulted in an immediate book gain for the taxpayer; the deferral account is adjusted downward and financial accounting income increases. For many taxpayers, this initiated a significant amount of 2017 accounting income.

Opposite results occurred with respect to deferred tax assets. Because the reduced corporate tax rate is scheduled for all future years, many corporations took an immediate reduction in financial accounting income on their deferred tax assets, in exchange for significant future tax reductions. Financial accounting income for 2017 for these entities was adversely affected to a significant degree.

Effects of Change in Corporate Tax Rate

Alpha Corporation generated a temporary book-tax difference before 2018 when it accelerated its cost recovery deductions by $1,000,000 over GAAP amounts. Accordingly, its deferred tax liability account increased by $350,000 ($1,000,000 × 35%).

When the new tax law reduced the applicable Federal corporate income tax rate to 21%, the balance of the deferred tax liability account was adjusted to $210,000, book income tax expense was reduced by $140,000 ($350,000 prior balance − $210,000 new balance), and book income increased by that amount.

Beta Corporation generated a temporary book-tax difference before 2018 when it incurred a $1,000,000 operating loss for GAAP purposes that it could not deduct immediately under Federal tax law. Accordingly, its deferred tax asset account increased by $350,000.

When the new tax law reduced the applicable Federal corporate income tax rate to 21%, the balance of the deferred tax asset account was adjusted to $210,000, book tax expense increased by $140,000, and book income decreased by that amount.

Treatment of Net Operating Losses and Carryovers Several changes to the provisions concerning net operating losses (NOLs) can affect the related deferred tax asset account. Generally, NOLs generated after 2017 cannot be carried back, and they can offset only 80 percent of future-year taxable income. In addition, NOLs can be carried forward indefinitely, rather than expiring at a future date.

Among other effects, these new provisions may affect the corporation's valuation allowance balances for the losses. For some entities, the valuation allowance was reduced because future losses were available for deduction without expiring.

However, one cannot assume that the entire NOL now will be deductible in the future, even with the indefinite carryforward of NOLs; the corporation still must demonstrate that corresponding taxable income amounts will arise in the future.

Gamma Corporation holds a $1 million net operating loss carryforward going into 2018. Because of the new rules concerning NOL carryovers, it is more likely that the NOL will be deductible in future tax years. As a result, some (or all) of the valuation allowance related to the loss was released (see text Section 14-2b), and book income increased.

EXAMPLE 19

Repeal of C Corporation Alternative Minimum Tax Prior law applied an alternative minimum tax (AMT) to C corporations, an additional Federal income tax computation that computed a broader tax base and used a flat 20 percent tax rate. C corporations paid the regular tax liability or the AMT amount, whichever was larger. The corporate AMT was a mere prepayment of tax, though, because a minimum tax credit was available for AMT taxpayers to apply in a future tax year against regular tax liabilities, in the amount of any AMT paid. Only a few C corporations incurred an AMT liability, but the related credit amount was recorded as a deferred tax asset.

The corporate AMT does not exist after 2017, and any AMT credit amount is fully refundable against regular Federal corporate income taxes beginning in 2018. For most corporations, then, any valuation allowance against the AMT credit can be removed. However, this treatment precludes any conversion of the carryforward amount to a GAAP receivable.

Delta Corporation had been subject to the AMT in a few of its tax years prior to 2018. It had generated a $1,000,000 carryforward amount for its minimum tax credit, and it recorded a corresponding deferred tax asset for the credit. Delta placed a $100,000 valuation allowance against the credit, showing uncertainty that enough regular tax liability would be generated in future tax years, against which to apply the credit. For 2018, the valuation allowance can be released in full, and book income increases as a result.

EXAMPLE 20

One-Time Transition Tax for Unrepatriated Profits of U.S. Entities Before 2018, U.S. taxpayers with global income were subject to a Federal corporate income tax on their *worldwide* taxable income, with a foreign tax credit allowed against the U.S. tax when income was subject to taxation in more than one country; see text Section 9-1. For most U.S. taxpayers, this system put them at a competitive disadvantage, as other countries applied tax rates much lower than the U.S. top rate of 35 percent, and they applied a *territorial* approach to the tax base, subjecting to tax only that income generated within the borders of the country and not on worldwide income.

Prior tax rules allowed U.S. taxpayers to defer the taxation on certain overseas income, though, until the profits were repatriated (paid back as a dividend) to the United States. Effective tax planning then encouraged taxpayers to keep profits unrepatriated so as to reduce the present value of the related income tax liability, and U.S. entities held perhaps $3 trillion of cash profits overseas as a result.

To encourage the return of unrepatriated profits to the United States and to accomplish other tax goals, U.S. tax rules adopted a modified form of territorial taxation for tax years beginning in 2018; see text Section 9-1. For many U.S. taxpayers, this new approach to international taxation, combined with the new 21 percent corporate income tax rate, resulted in a projection of significantly lower future Federal income tax liabilities. But Congress accompanied this tax cut with a one-time tax cost: a tax on the balance of unrepatriated profits at a rate of 15.5 percent (if held as cash) or 8 percent (for nonliquid overseas assets).

The tax applied whether or not the profits actually were repatriated. By election, the tax liability could be deferred and paid over as many as eight tax years. The taxpayer could apply certain amounts of NOL and foreign tax credit carryforwards against the tax.

For GAAP purposes, the one-time transition tax was recorded as a 2017 income tax expense, because the TCJA was enacted in late 2017. Depending on elections made by the taxpayer, the expenses could be recorded as partly current and noncurrent, but they were not to be discounted to present values. Valuation allowances for the loss and credit carryforwards likely would be adjusted to reflect the higher probability that they now would be used.

EXAMPLE 21

U.S. taxpayer Epsilon Corporation held $1,000,000 cash in overseas accounts from its unrepatriated foreign profits, to defer the related U.S. corporate income tax liability. As of the end of 2017, it owed the one-time transition tax on these profits, even though it retained the cash balance overseas into 2018. After applying NOL carryforwards against the taxable amount, Epsilon owed a tax of $100,000, which it elected to pay over eight years. The valuation allowance against the NOL carryforward was released, increasing book income, and the transition tax liability was divided into its current and noncurrent elements.

14-2e Summary

The tax department of a business often is charged with shaping and implementing the entity's tax strategies (*tax planning*) and filing all required tax returns (*tax compliance*) while preparing for subsequent audit and litigation activity (*tax controversy*). Tax professionals often work closely with those who prepare the entity's financial statements, especially concerning the tax footnote, tax deferral accounts, and tax rate reconciliations. Professional tax and accounting research underlies all of this work.

The functions of a modern tax department are illustrated in Exhibit 14.4. Tax professionals must be proficient in all of the indicated areas to meet the demands of the entity and its shareholders, regulators, and taxing agencies.

Information related to tax expenses and balance sheet effects is required for SEC taxpayers long before the corporate income tax return is due. Tax professionals must work with those charged with completing financial reporting requirements so that these SEC deadlines are met (e.g., in filing a Form 10–K for a calendar-year corporation in February or March of the following year, even though the extended due date of the Form 1120 is not until mid-October).

If the tax professional grasps both the tax and financial statement effects of various tax planning and compliance activities, he or she brings great value to the entity through the tax department.

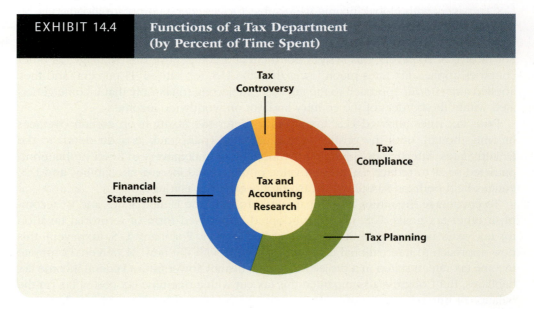

EXHIBIT 14.4   Functions of a Tax Department (by Percent of Time Spent)

14-3 BENCHMARKING

LO.6

Use financial statement income tax information to benchmark a company's tax position.

An entity's income tax expense amount may appear to be of little interest to anyone beyond the taxpayer that makes the payment and the government agencies that collect it. The tax year is over, the transactions are completed, and the final costs have been tallied. Still, this historical tax information may prove valuable. A company's income tax expense is one of the single largest expense items on its income statement, and understanding the components of this expense is a critical activity for the tax professional.

Consider a typical baseball game. Two teams meet; interact following a specific set of rules; and ultimately complete the game, generating a final score. Of course, the final score is of immediate interest to the teams and the fans, but once the game is over, the score and associated statistics (runs, hits, and errors) are relegated to the history books. Yet these statistics still can be quite useful. A team coach may use the game statistics to evaluate the strengths and weaknesses of the players to assist in improving performance. Other teams may use the data to develop strategies for upcoming games. Players can use this information to "benchmark" themselves against their own performance in prior games or against players on other teams. In short, there is a wealth of analytical possibilities in these historical data.

A taxpayer's reported income tax expense also is a valuable source of information for the company, its tax advisers, and its competitors. The reported information provides clues about a company's operational and tax planning strategies.

Companies may benchmark their tax situation to other years' results or to other companies in the same industry. The starting point for a <mark>benchmarking</mark> exercise usually is the data from the income tax note rate reconciliation.

14-3a **Refining the Analysis**

In addition to comparing effective tax rates, one can analyze entities' levels of deferred tax assets and liabilities.

EXAMPLE 22

Akiko Enterprises reports a net deferred tax liability of $280,000. Erde, Inc., a company in the same industry, reports a net deferred tax liability of $860,000. The presence of deferred tax liabilities on the balance sheet indicates that both companies are benefiting from deferring actual tax payments (essentially, an interest-free loan from the government).

At first glance, it may appear that Erde is doing better in this regard. However, what if Akiko holds total assets of $2,600,000 and Erde's assets total $19,200,000? This information indicates that Akiko has 10.8% ($280,000/$2,600,000) of its total assets "financed" with an interest-free loan from the government; Erde has only 4.5% ($860,000/$19,200,000) of its assets "financed" with its deferred tax liabilities.

One may do a more refined benchmarking analysis by examining each component of an entity's deferred tax assets and liabilities as a percentage of total assets. For example, an observer can examine how the deferred tax assets or liabilities related to property, plant, and equipment compare with those of its competitors. The nature of the components of deferred tax liabilities and deferred tax assets becomes important in a benchmarking analysis.

Benchmarking Financial Results

EXAMPLE 23

LinCo reports total book income before taxes of $10 million and a total tax provision of $1.6 million, producing a 16% effective tax rate. TuckCo also reports book income before taxes of $10 million. TuckCo's total tax expense is $1.5 million, producing an effective tax rate of 15%. At first glance, it appears that the entities are similar based on their effective tax rates. The total tax expense divided between current and deferred is as follows.

continued

	LinCo	TuckCo
Current tax expense	$2,500,000	$2,600,000
Deferred tax benefit	(900,000)	(1,100,000)
Total tax expense	$1,600,000	$1,500,000

Again, it appears that both companies have created deferred tax assets in the current year that are expected to produce tax savings in the future. Knowing the nature of the underlying deferred tax assets will add greatly to one's interpretation of the effective tax rates.

With additional investigation, though, you determine that the deferred tax asset generating LinCo's expected future tax savings is the use of an NOL carryover. The deferred tax asset generating TuckCo's expected future tax savings is generated by different book and tax methods in accounting for warranty expense. This additional information reveals that LinCo previously has incurred losses; to use the NOLs in the coming years, it will be critical for LinCo to generate future taxable income.

This is quite different from TuckCo's situation, which reveals only that common differences in accounting methods exist, and that the future deductions likely will be used fully. Although the tax positions of LinCo and TuckCo seem very similar on the surface, a closer look reveals a striking difference.

EXAMPLE 24

WageCo and SalaryCo operate in the same industry, and they report the same effective tax rate. Their book income and current, deferred, and total tax expense were reported as follows.

	WageCo	SalaryCo
Book income before tax	$1,500,000	$2,300,000
Current tax expense	$ 680,000	$ 24,000
Deferred tax expense (benefit)	(410,000)	390,000
Total tax expense	$ 270,000	$ 414,000
Effective tax rate	18%	18%

WageCo's total tax expense is highly dependent on the current recognition of future tax savings of $410,000. SalaryCo appears to be deferring a substantial portion of its tax expense to future years. Although both companies report the same effective tax rate, the details indicate that the two companies face very different tax situations. By looking more closely at the financial statements, an analyst should be able to determine why these differences exist.

14-3b Sustaining the Tax Rate

It is important in benchmarking exercises to remove the effect of one-time items in comparing sustainable effective tax rates across time or companies. Examples of one-time items include restructuring costs, legal settlements, and IRS or other tax liability settlements. A one-time item may seem beneficial or detrimental to a company's effective tax rate. But the very nature of this item implies that it has little to do with the company's *long-term* sustainable tax costs.

EXAMPLE 25

MetalCo and IronCo operate in the same industry, and they report the following tax rate reconciliations in their tax footnotes.

	MetalCo	IronCo
Hypothetical tax at U.S. rate	21.0%	21.0%
State and local taxes	2.2	2.1
Foreign income taxed at less than U.S. rate	(6.2)	(6.1)
Tax Court settlement on disputed tax issue	(18.6)	—
Effective tax rate	(1.6)%	17.0%

Although it appears that MetalCo has a significantly lower effective tax rate than Iron-Co's effective tax rate, removing MetalCo's one-time item related to the court settlement indicates that both companies may operate under a similar 17% effective tax rate [(1.6)% + 18.6% = 17%].

14-3c **Uses of Benchmarking Analysis**

Benchmarking is part science and part art. A useful analysis requires both an accountant's knowledge of how the underlying financial statements are constructed, including arriving at the appropriate tax expense, and a detective's sense of where to look and what questions to ask.

In addition to benchmarking, financial analysts perform an important function for the capital markets in their detailed analyses of companies. The analyst combs through both the financial reports and other information about a company to produce an informed opinion on how a company is performing. Analysts' earnings forecasts often constitute an important metric to examine when making decisions about investing in companies.

An experienced financial analyst typically will have a good handle on interpreting financial statement information. However, even experienced analysts will often "punt" when it comes to interpreting the tax information contained in a financial statement, preferring to look at net income before taxes (or even EBITDA, earnings before interest, taxes, depreciation, and amortization). A great deal of useful information about a business is contained in its tax footnote, and analysts might have an edge if they work at understanding the mysteries of taxes in the financial statements. Some typical uses of benchmarking in an analysis of an entity's financial results are summarized in Concept Summary 14.4.

Concept Summary 14.4

Benchmarking Analysis

A benchmarking analysis can be helpful in comparing the tax positions of two or more business entities. One might consider the following aspects of the taxpayers' financial disclosures in this regard. This list is not all-inclusive; benchmarking also includes the judgment and experience of the parties conducting the analysis.

- Compare the effective tax rates of the entities.

- Explain the differences in effective rates. Are these differences sustainable over time?

- Apply the analysis to both the tax dollars involved and the underlying net assets of the entities.

- Discount (but do not ignore) any one-time tax benefits/detriments that are observed.

- Include in your analysis any knowledge of the nontax, competitive strategy and tactics employed and planned by the entity.

14-4 **TAX PLANNING**

14-4a **Releasing Valuation Allowances**

When a corporation records a valuation allowance, it loses the ability to recognize the benefit of future tax savings in the current period. However, all is not lost if the taxpayer can demonstrate that facts and circumstances have changed. For example, if a taxpayer generates an NOL, it records a deferred tax asset for the future tax savings related to using the NOL. However, if the evidence suggests that it is *more likely than not* that all or a portion of the NOL never will be used, a valuation allowance must be recorded.

To reduce this valuation allowance and increase financial accounting income, the taxpayer must demonstrate that there will be enough future taxable income to absorb the NOL in the future. Sources of future taxable income include reversals of temporary differences that will produce future taxable income, demonstrated efficiencies that will reduce future expenses, documented expected increases in sales (and capacity), and any other sources of future profits.

Taxpayers also may demonstrate that the adoption of new tax planning strategies will allow the use of deferred tax assets. The proposed tax strategies must be prudent and feasible in their execution, and the taxpayer must be willing to execute the strategy in a manner that will use the deferred tax assets. Such strategies might include the following.

- Slow down cost recovery deductions (e.g., by using straight-line methods or electing to capitalize expenditures).
- Sell off appreciated assets.
- Convert tax-exempt investments into taxable holdings.
- Change tax accounting methods (e.g., moving from LIFO to FIFO for inventories).

The Big Picture

EXAMPLE 26

Return to the facts of *The Big Picture* on p. 14-1. Arctic Corporation's $3,000,000 deferred tax asset for an NOL carryforward has been offset by a $1,000,000 valuation allowance, due to doubts over the levels of future sales and profitability.

But this year Arctic completed improvements to its inventory management system that are likely to increase the contribution margin of every product that Arctic sells. In addition, two of Arctic's largest customers have secured financing that will relieve the financial difficulties that have restricted them. In fact, Arctic just received purchase orders from those customers that will increase unit sales by 20% over the next 18 months. As a result, Arctic's auditors now support a release of $200,000 of the valuation allowance in the current quarter.

EXAMPLE 27

Warren, Inc., from Example 13, adopts new planning strategies in 2020 that will allow it ultimately to use all $100,000 of its general business credit carryforward. Warren earns $2,300,000 in book income before tax and reports $2,300,000 in taxable income in 2020 (i.e., there are no permanent or temporary differences). The current Federal income tax expense is $483,000 ($2,300,000 × 21%).

Based on new evidence (implementation of tax planning strategies), the auditors determine that the entire $100,000 in credits will be used in the future before they expire. Accordingly, the $60,000 valuation allowance from 2019 is "released," and the tax benefit of this release affects the 2020 financial results as follows.

	Book	Tax
Income tax expense/payable	$423,000	$483,000
Current tax expense	$483,000	
Deferred tax expense	($ 60,000)	

Warren makes the following 2020 journal entry to record the book income tax expense and valuation allowance release related to the expected use of the credits.

Income tax expense (provision)	$423,000	
Valuation allowance	60,000	
Income tax payable		$483,000

Warren's effective tax rate for 2020 is 18.4% ($423,000/$2,300,000). Without the valuation allowance release, Warren's effective tax rate would have been 21% ($483,000/$2,300,000). This tax rate benefit is realized even though the $100,000 in credit carryforwards has yet to be used in Warren's tax return.

14-4b Comparing Tax Savings

Many different types of tax planning strategies can produce tax savings. Yet even when planning ideas produce identical current cash-flow effects, some ideas may have an edge. CEOs and CFOs of public companies are focused on the bottom line—the company's net income after tax and related earnings per share. A CFO is likely to be just as interested in an idea's effect on the company's bottom line income as on the cash tax savings.

For example, consider two tax planning ideas that each produce $420,000 of current Federal income tax savings. The first idea generates its $420,000 in tax savings by increasing tax depreciation relative to book depreciation by $2,000,000 ($420,000 = $2,000,000 × 21%). The second idea produces research activities tax credits of $420,000, thus reducing current-year tax by $420,000.

Idea 1 produces its current tax savings via a temporary difference. Accordingly, the book tax expense will not reflect the related tax savings. Instead, this $420,000 simply moves from the current tax category into the deferred tax category. Even if the book-tax difference is not expected to reverse in the next 30 years (effectively generating "permanent" savings), the book tax expense does not reflect this savings.

In contrast, idea 2 produces its current tax savings via a permanent difference. Thus, the book tax expense also declines by $420,000. This item appears in the income tax note rate reconciliation. The credit constitutes a very attractive book result of effective income tax planning.

TAXES ON THE FINANCIAL STATEMENTS

Raymond Jones should understand that the tax expense reported on the company's financial statements and the tax payable on the company's income tax returns often differ as a result of differences in the reporting entities used in the calculation and the different accounting methods used for book purposes and tax purposes. The use of different accounting methods may result in both temporary and permanent differences in financial statement income and taxable income. Examples of permanent differences include nontaxable income such as municipal bond interest and tax credits. Temporary differences include depreciation differences and other amounts that are affected by the timing of a deduction or an inclusion, but they ultimately result in the same amount being reflected in the financial statements and income tax returns.

Permanent differences such as municipal bond interest cause Arctic's book income to be greater than its taxable income. In calculating the tax provision shown on the financial statements, Arctic's book income must be adjusted for these permanent differences. This results in an effective tax rate for financial statement purposes (20 percent) that is below the U.S. statutory corporate income tax rate of 21 percent.

In this case, Arctic's income tax expense of $5 million is higher than the current Federal income tax payable. This results from timing differences and creates a $1.01 million deferred tax liability that is reported on the company's balance sheet. Unlike other liabilities, deferred tax liabilities are "good" in the sense that they represent an amount that may be paid to the government in the future rather than today.

What If?

Mr. Jones is concerned about a newspaper article that said that companies reporting less tax on their tax returns than on their financial statements were cheating the IRS. Is this an accurate assessment?

Although differences in income taxes payable to the IRS and financial tax expense can result from aggressive and illegal tax shelters, differences also result from different methods of accounting that are required for financial statement reporting using GAAP and tax laws enacted by Congress.

Key Terms

ASC 740, 14-8	Deferred tax benefit, 14-9	Permanent differences, 14-4
ASC 740-10, 14-17	Deferred tax expense, 14-9	Rate reconciliation, 14-14
Balance sheet approach, 14-9	Deferred tax liability, 14-9	Schedule M–1, 14-5
Benchmarking, 14-23	Equity method, 14-2	Schedule M–3, 14-6
Conservatism principle, 14-12	Generally accepted accounting	Temporary differences, 14-4
Current tax expense, 14-8	principles (GAAP), 14-2	Valuation allowance, 14-13
Deferred tax asset, 14-9	Income tax provision, 14-8	

Discussion Questions

1. **LO.1** Evaluate the following statement: For most business entities, book income differs from taxable income because "income" has different meanings for the users of the data in the income computation.

2. **LO.1** Parent, a domestic corporation, owns 100% of Block, a non-U.S. corporation, and Chip, a domestic corporation. Parent also owns 45% of Trial, a domestic corporation. Parent receives no distributions from any of these corporations. Which of these entities' net income is included in Parent's income statement for current-year financial reporting purposes?

3. **LO.1** Parent, a domestic corporation, owns 100% of Block, a non-U.S. corporation, and Chip, a domestic corporation. Parent also owns 45% of Trial, a domestic corporation. Parent receives no distributions from any of these corporations. Which of these entities' taxable income is included in Parent's current-year Form 1120, U.S. income tax return? Parent consolidates all eligible subsidiaries for Federal income tax purposes.

Communications 4. **LO.1** Marcellus Jackson, the CFO of Mac, Inc., notices that the tax liability reported on Mac's tax return is less than the tax expense reported on Mac's financial statements. Provide a letter to Jackson outlining why these two tax expense numbers differ. Mac's address is 482 Linden Road, Paris, KY 40362.

Critical Thinking 5. **LO.1** Define the terms *temporary difference* and *permanent difference* as they pertain to the financial reporting of income tax expenses. Describe how these two book-tax differences affect the gap between book and taxable income. How are permanent and temporary differences alike? How are they different?

Communications 6. **LO.1** In no more than three PowerPoint slides, list several commonly encountered temporary and permanent book-tax differences. The slides will be used in your presentation next week to your school's Future CPAs Club.

7. **LO.3** You saw on the online Business News Channel that YoungCo has "released one-third of its valuation allowances because of an upbeat forecast for sales of its tablet computers over the next 30 months." What effect does such a release likely have on YoungCo's current-year book effective tax rate? Be specific.

Decision Making 8. **LO.6** Jill is the CFO of Portech, Inc. Portech's tax advisers have recommended two tax planning ideas that each will provide $5 million of current-year cash tax savings. One idea is based on a timing difference and is expected to reverse in full 10 years in the future. The other idea creates a permanent difference that never will reverse.

Determine whether these ideas will allow Portech to reduce its reported book income tax expense for the current year. Illustrate in a table or timeline your preference for one planning strategy over the other. Which idea will you recommend to Jill?

9. **LO.5** Significant changes to U.S. corporate income tax law are made only on rare occasions. What tax policy principles might underlie this characterization?   Critical Thinking

10. **LO.5** U.S. corporate income tax law changed dramatically at the end of 2017 due to amendments to the Internal Revenue Code by Congress. List at least two specific changes to the law and their general effects on the presentation of tax items on GAAP financial statements.

11. **LO.6** RoofCo reports total book income before taxes of $20 million and a total tax expense of $8 million. FloorCo reports book income before taxes of $30 million and a total tax expense of $12 million. The companies' breakdown between current and deferred tax expense (benefit) is as follows.

	RoofCo	FloorCo
Current tax expense	$10.0	$13.0
Deferred tax benefit	(2.0)	(1.0)
Total tax expense	$ 8.0	$12.0

RoofCo's deferred tax benefit is from a deferred tax asset created because of differences in book and tax depreciation methods for equipment. FloorCo's deferred tax benefit is created by the expected future use of an NOL. Compare and contrast these two companies' effective tax rates. How are they similar? How are they different?

12. **LO.6** LawnCo and TreeCo operate in the same industry, and both report a 25% effective tax rate (combined Federal, state, and global). Their book income and current, deferred, and total tax expense are reported below.   Critical Thinking
Communications

	LawnCo	TreeCo
Book income before tax	$600,000	$780,000
Current tax expense	$200,000	$ 20,000
Deferred tax expense (benefit)	(50,000)	175,000
Total Federal, state, and global tax expense	$150,000	$195,000
Effective tax rate	25%	25%

ShrubCo is a competitor of both of these companies. Prepare a letter to Laura Collins, VP-Taxation of ShrubCo, outlining your analysis of the other two companies' effective tax rates, using only the preceding information. ShrubCo's address is 9979 West Third Street, Peru, IN 46970.

13. **LO.6** HippCo and HoppCo operate in the same industry and report the following tax rate reconciliations in their tax footnotes.

	HippCo	HoppCo
Hypothetical tax at U.S. rate	35.0%	35.0%
State and local taxes	2.7	3.9
Municipal bond interest	(12.5)	(7.8)
Tax Court settlement on disputed tax issue	6.0	—
Effective tax rate	31.2%	31.1%

Compare and contrast the effective tax rates of these two companies.

Computational Exercises

14. **LO.2** Prance, Inc., earns pretax book net income of $800,000 in 2018. Prance acquires a depreciable asset that year, and first-year tax depreciation exceeds book depreciation by $80,000. Prance reported no other temporary or permanent book-tax differences. The pertinent U.S. tax rate is 21%, and Prance earns an after-tax rate of return on capital of 8%. Compute Prance's total income tax expense, current income tax expense, and deferred income tax expense.

15. **LO.2** Using the facts of Problem 14, determine the 2018 end-of-year balance in Prance's deferred tax asset and deferred tax liability balance sheet accounts.

16. **LO.2** Prance reports $600,000 of pretax book net income in 2019. Prance's book depreciation exceeds tax depreciation that year by $20,000. Prance reports no other temporary or permanent book-tax differences. Assuming that the pertinent U.S. tax rate is 21%, compute Prance's total income tax expense, current income tax expense, and deferred income tax expense.

17. **LO.2** Using the facts of Problem 16, determine the 2019 end-of-year balance in Prance's deferred tax asset and deferred tax liability balance sheet accounts. In time value of money terms, what has been the value to Prance of the accelerated tax deduction for depreciation? Use text Appendix F to construct your answer.

18. **LO.2** Mini, Inc., earns pretax book net income of $750,000 in 2018. Mini deducted $20,000 in bad debt expense for book purposes. This expense is not yet deductible for tax purposes. Mini reports no other temporary or permanent differences. The applicable U.S. tax rate is 21%, and Mini earns an after-tax rate of return on capital of 8%. Compute Mini's total income tax expense, current income tax expense, and deferred income tax expense.

19. **LO.2** Using the facts of Problem 18, determine the 2018 end-of-year balance in Mini's deferred tax asset and deferred tax liability balance sheet accounts.

20. **LO.2** Mini, in Problem 18, reports $800,000 of pretax book net income in 2019. For that year, Mini did not deduct any bad debt expense for book purposes but did deduct $15,000 in bad debt expense for tax purposes. Mini reports no other temporary or permanent differences. Assuming that the U.S. tax rate is 21%, compute Mini's total income tax expense, current income tax expense, and deferred income tax expense.

21. **LO.2** Using the facts of Problem 20, determine the 2019 end-of-year balance in Mini's deferred tax asset and deferred tax liability balance sheet accounts. In time value of money terms, what has been the cost to Mini of the deferred tax deduction for bad debts? Use text Appendix F to construct your answer.

22. **LO.2** Ovate, Inc., earns $140,000 in book income before tax and is subject to a 21% marginal Federal income tax rate. Ovate records a single temporary difference; there have been no book-tax differences in prior tax years. Warranty expenses deducted for book purposes are $8,000, of which only $2,000 are deductible for tax purposes.
    a.   Determine the amount of Ovate's deferred tax asset or liability.
    b.   Express your computation as a Microsoft Excel formula.

23. **LO.3** Ion Corporation reports income tax expense/payable for book purposes of $200,000 and $250,000 for tax purposes. Assume that Ion only will be able to use $30,000 of any deferred tax asset, with the balance expiring unused. Determine the amount of Ion's deferred tax asset and valuation allowance, and construct the appropriate journal entry that Ion would record.

24. **LO.4** RadioCo, a domestic corporation, reports a deferred tax asset relating to receivables of $100,000 and a deferred tax liability relating to cost recovery of $165,000. How and where on the GAAP financial statement will RadioCo report these items?

Problems

25. **LO.2** Phillips, Inc., a cash basis C corporation, completes $100,000 in sales for year 1, but only $75,000 of this amount is collected during year 1. The remaining $25,000 from these sales is collected promptly during the first quarter of year 2. The applicable combined income tax rate for year 1 and thereafter is 30%. Compute Phillips's year 1 current and deferred income tax expense.

26. **LO.2** Continue with the results of Problem 25. Prepare the GAAP journal entries for Phillips's year 1 income tax expense.

27. **LO.2** Britton, Inc., an accrual basis C corporation, sells widgets on credit. Its book and taxable income for year 1 totals $60,000, before accounting for bad debts. Britton's book allowance for uncollectible accounts increased for year 1 by $10,000, but none of the entity's bad debts received a specific write-off for tax purposes. The applicable income tax rate (combined Federal, state, and global) for year 1 and thereafter is 30%. Compute Britton's year 1 current and deferred income tax expense.

28. **LO.2** Continue with the results of Problem 27. Prepare the GAAP journal entries for Britton's year 1 income tax expense.

29. **LO.2** Rubio, Inc., an accrual basis C corporation, reports the following amounts for the tax year. The applicable income tax rate is 30% (combined Federal, state, and global). Compute Rubio's taxable income.

Book income, including the items below	$80,000
Increase in book allowance for anticipated warranty costs	5,000
Interest income from City of Westerville bonds	10,000
Bribes paid to Federal inspectors	17,000

30. **LO.2** Continue with the results of Problem 29.
    a. Determine Rubio's income tax expense and GAAP income for the year.
    b. Express your computations as Microsoft Excel commands.

31. **LO.2** Willingham, Inc., an accrual basis C corporation, reports pretax book income of $1,600,000. At the beginning of the tax year, Willingham reported no deferred tax accounts on its balance sheet. It is subject to a 21% U.S. income tax rate in the current year and for the foreseeable future.

   Willingham's book-tax differences include the following. Compute the entity's current and deferred Federal income tax expense for the year.

Addition to the book reserve for uncollectible receivables (no specific write-offs occurred; therefore, no income tax deduction)	$4,000,000
Tax depreciation in excess of book	3,000,000
Book gain from installment sale of nonbusiness asset, deferred for tax	2,000,000
Interest income from school district bonds	200,000

32. **LO.2** Continue with the results of Problem 31. Prepare the GAAP journal entries for Willingham's income tax expense.

33. **LO.2** Relix, Inc., is a domestic corporation with the following balance sheet for book and tax purposes at the end of the year. Based on this information, determine Relix's Federal net deferred tax asset or net deferred tax liability at year-end. Assume a 21% Federal corporate tax rate and no valuation allowance.

	Tax Debit/ (Credit)	Book Debit/ (Credit)
Assets		
Cash	$ 500	$ 500
Accounts receivable	8,000	8,000
Buildings	750,000	750,000
Accumulated depreciation	(450,000)	(380,000)
Furniture & fixtures	70,000	70,000
Accumulated depreciation	(46,000)	(38,000)
Total assets	$332,500	$410,500

	Tax Debit/ (Credit)	Book Debit/ (Credit)
Liabilities		
Accrued litigation expense	$ —0—	($ 50,000)
Note payable	(78,000)	(78,000)
Total liabilities	($ 78,000)	($128,000)
Stockholders' Equity		
Paid-in capital	($ 10,000)	($ 10,000)
Retained earnings	(244,500)	(272,500)
Total liabilities and stockholders' equity	($332,500)	($410,500)

34. **LO.2** Based on the facts and results of Problem 33 and the beginning-of-the-year book-tax basis difference listed below, determine the change in Relix's deferred tax assets for the current year.

	Beginning of Year
Accrued litigation expense	$34,000
Subtotal	$34,000
Applicable tax rate	× 21%
Gross deferred tax asset	$ 7,140

35. **LO.2** Based on the facts and results of Problem 33 and the beginning-of-the-year book-tax basis differences listed below, determine the change in Relix's deferred tax liabilities for the current year.

	Beginning of Year
Building—accumulated depreciation	($57,000)
Furniture & fixtures—accumulated depreciation	(4,200)
Subtotal	($61,200)
Applicable tax rate	× 21%
Gross deferred tax liability	($12,852)

36. **LO.2** Based on the facts and results of Problems 33–35, determine Relix's change in net deferred tax asset or net deferred tax liability for the current year. Provide the journal entry to record this amount.

37. **LO.2** In addition to the temporary differences identified in Problems 33–36, Relix, Inc., reported two permanent differences between book and taxable income. It earned $2,375 in tax-exempt municipal bond interest, and it incurred $780 in nondeductible business meals expense. Relix's book income before tax is $4,800. With this additional information, calculate Relix's current tax expense.

38. **LO.2** Provide the journal entry to record Relix's current tax expense as determined in Problem 37.

39. **LO.2** Based on the facts and results of Problems 33–38, calculate Relix's total provision for income tax reported in its financial statements, and determine its book net income after tax.

40. **LO.2** Based on the facts and results of Problems 33–39, provide the income tax footnote rate reconciliation for Relix.

41. **LO.2** Kantner, Inc., is a domestic corporation with the following balance sheet for book and tax purposes at the end of the year. Based on this information, determine Kantner's net Federal deferred tax asset or net deferred tax liability at year-end. Assume a 21% Federal corporate tax rate and no valuation allowance.

	Tax Debit/ (Credit)	Book Debit/ (Credit)
Assets		
Cash	$ 1,000	$ 1,000
Accounts receivable	9,000	9,000
Buildings	850,000	850,000
Accumulated depreciation	(700,000)	(620,000)
Furniture & fixtures	40,000	40,000
Accumulated depreciation	(10,000)	(8,000)
Total assets	$190,000	$272,000
Liabilities		
Accrued warranty expense	$ –0–	($ 40,000)
Note payable	(16,000)	(16,000)
Total liabilities	($ 16,000)	($ 56,000)
Stockholders' Equity		
Paid-in capital	($ 50,000)	($ 50,000)
Retained earnings	(124,000)	(166,000)
Total liabilities and stockholders' equity	($190,000)	($272,000)

42. **LO.2** Based on the facts and results of Problem 41 and the beginning-of-the-year book-tax basis difference listed below, determine the change in Kantner's deferred tax assets for the current year.

	Beginning of Year
Accrued warranty expense	$30,000
Subtotal	$30,000
Applicable tax rate	× 21%
Gross deferred tax asset	$ 6,300

43. **LO.2** Based on the facts and results of Problem 41 and the beginning-of-the-year book-tax basis differences listed below, determine the change in Kantner's deferred tax liabilities for the current year.

	Beginning of Year
Building—accumulated depreciation	($62,000)
Furniture & fixtures—accumulated depreciation	(400)
Subtotal	($62,400)
Applicable tax rate	× 21%
Gross deferred tax liability	($13,104)

44. **LO.2** Based on the facts and results of Problems 41–43, determine Kantner's change in net deferred tax asset or net deferred tax liability for the current year. Provide the journal entry to record this amount.

45. **LO.2** In addition to the temporary differences identified in Problems 41–44, Kantner reported two permanent differences between book and taxable income. It earned $7,800 in tax-exempt municipal bond interest, and it reported $850 in non-deductible business meals expense. Kantner's book income before tax is $50,000. With this additional information, calculate Kantner's current tax expense.

46. **LO.2** Provide the journal entry to record Kantner's current tax expense as determined in Problem 45.

47. **LO.2** Based on the facts and results of Problems 41–46, calculate Kantner's total provision for income tax expense reported on its financial statement and its book net income after tax.

48. **LO.2** Based on the facts and results of Problems 41–47, provide the income tax footnote rate reconciliation for Kantner.

49. **LO.3** Does the taxpayer's effective tax rate increase or decrease when:

    a. It creates a valuation allowance against the deferred tax asset for a net operating loss?

    b. It releases a valuation allowance against the deferred tax asset for a net operating loss?

50. **LO.3** Identify whether each of the following items typically constitutes *positive* or *negative* evidence when a manufacturing entity assesses whether a valuation allowance is required or should be adjusted for its net operating losses.

    a. Product orders are increasing.

    b. Book income for the past three years totals to a negative amount.

    c. Investment assets held by the taxpayer show a realized gain.

    d. The industry in which the taxpayer operates is in a down cycle.

    e. The entity's tax plan includes a switch from MACRS accelerated depreciation to straight-line.

51. **LO.3** GinnyCo reports a $100,000 income tax payable in the current year. GinnyCo holds a general business tax credit of $40,000 that it cannot use this year, and its auditors maintain that one-fourth of the credit carryforward will expire unused.

    a. Compute GinnyCo's income tax provision for the year, expressed as a Microsoft Excel formula.

    b. Construct the journal entry to report these items.

52. **LO.4** KellerCo reports $5,000,000 of U.S. taxable income, the same as its book income, because there are no temporary book-tax differences this year. KellerCo is subject to a 21% Federal income tax rate. Its book-tax differences include the following.

Nondeductible business meals	$ 400,000
Tax depreciation in excess of book depreciation	1,500,000

    Construct KellerCo's tax rate reconciliation for its GAAP tax footnote. Use either dollars or percentages in your reconciliation.

53. **LO.5** LaceCo has adopted certain aggressive policies concerning its transfer pricing procedures. The entity estimates that it will reduce its Federal income tax liability by $400,000 as a result of these strategies, but that the IRS is likely to challenge the policies in an audit.

    LaceCo estimates that the tax benefit may be reduced after an IRS audit and related negotiations (amounts as indicated with related probabilities); LaceCo constructs a table of these probabilities and results.

Resulting Estimated Tax Benefit	Probability of Agreement Between LaceCo and IRS	Cumulative Probability Computed
$400,000	10%	10%
300,000	35%	45%
250,000	40%	85%
—0—	15%	100%

LaceCo recorded a book tax provision of $600,000, *including* the $400,000 tax benefit from this tax uncertainty.

a.   Determine the amount that LaceCo should record for the tax benefit from this item under GAAP rules and ASC 740-10.

b.   Construct the journal entry that LaceCo should record.

Research Problems

Use internet tax resources to address the following questions. Look for reliable websites and blogs of the IRS and other government agencies, media outlets, businesses, tax professionals, academics, think tanks, and political outlets.

Research Problem 1. Locate the most recent financial statements of two companies in the same industry using the companies' websites or the SEC's website (**sec.gov**). Perform a benchmarking analysis of the two companies' effective tax rates, components of the effective tax rate reconciliation, levels of deferred tax assets and liabilities, and other relevant data. Summarize this information in an e-mail to your instructor.

Communications

Research Problem 2. Metro builds and operates traditional shopping malls. It holds a $25 million deferred tax asset relating to credit carryforwards at the state, local, and Federal levels. No valuation allowances exist.

Critical Thinking

Communications

The shopping mall industry finds itself in hard times due to the loss of anchor stores and the increase in online shopping activity by consumers. Review various sources in the press that discuss how these problems arose and what some proposed solutions might be.

Metro's business plan for the next three years includes:

- The conversion of store space by new tenants (e.g., theaters, gyms, religious groups), none of which are likely to produce the profit levels lost from the stores they replace, and
- The sale of several malls at depressed prices.

In no more than three PowerPoint slides, summarize your thoughts as to the need for Metro to establish a valuation allowance against its deferred tax assets. Be specific in listing the indicators of future activity that support your conclusions.

Research Problem 3. Locate the financial statements of three different companies that report information in the income tax footnote regarding uncertain tax positions under ASC 740-10. Create a schedule that identifies the changes reported and then compares and contrasts the changes in uncertain tax positions reported by the three companies. E-mail the schedule to your instructor.

Communications

Research Problem 4. Locate the financial statements of three different companies. Review the income tax footnote information on deferred tax assets (DTAs) and deferred tax liabilities (DTLs). Create a schedule that compares the end-of-the-year amounts of DTAs and DTLs, including any valuation allowances. E-mail the schedule to your instructor.

Communications

Communications
Critical Thinking

Research Problem 5. Locate summary financial information for two companies in the same industry. Compare and contrast the following items across the two companies: debt-to-equity ratio, return on assets, shareholder yield, return on equity, inventory turnover ratio, and effective tax rate. In your comparison, include the Federal, state/local, and international effective rates for the entities. Summarize in one paragraph the key reasons that make you believe that the effective tax rates are so similar (or different).

Communications

Research Problem 6. Choose one of the so-called FAANG stocks (i.e., Facebook, Apple, Amazon, Netflix, Google/Alphabet). Using data that you find at EDGAR or the company website, provide the following information for the latest full reporting year, and indicate where in the financial statements you found this data. E-mail your findings to your instructor.

- Cash tax rate.
- Effective tax rate.
- Tax rate on international income.
- Total deferred tax assets.
- The largest single deferred tax asset.
- Total deferred tax liabilities.
- The largest single deferred tax liability.

Becker CPA Review Questions

1. Two independent situations are described below. Each situation has future deductible amounts and/or future taxable amounts produced by temporary differences.

Situation	1	2
Taxable income	$40,000	$80,000
Amounts at year-end:		
Future deductible amounts	5,000	10,000
Future taxable amounts	–0–	5,000
Balances at beginning of year:		
Deferred tax asset	1,000	4,000
Deferred tax liability	–0–	1,000

   The enacted state and Federal tax rate is 25% for both situations. Determine the income tax expense for the year.

	Situation 1	**Situation 2**
a.	$10,000	$20,000
b.	$9,000	$21,000
c.	$5,000	$17,000
d.	$0	$0

2. Two independent situations are described below. Each involves future deductible amounts and/or future taxable amounts produced by temporary differences.

Situation	1	2
Taxable income	$40,000	$80,000
Amounts at year-end:		
Future deductible amounts	5,000	10,000
Future taxable amounts	–0–	5,000
Balances at beginning of year:		
Deferred tax asset	1,000	4,000
Deferred tax liability	–0–	1,000

The enacted state and Federal tax rate is 25% for both situations. Determine the change in the deferred tax asset balance for the year.

	Situation 1	Situation 2
a.	$5,000	$10,000
b.	$1,250	$1,250
c.	$1,250	$2,500
d.	$0	$0

3. At the end of year 6, the tax effects of temporary differences reported in Tortoise Company's year-end financial statements were as follows.

	Deferred Tax Assets (Liabilites)
Accelerated tax depreciation	($120,000)
Warranty expense	80,000
NOL carryforward	200,000
Total	$160,000

A valuation allowance was not considered necessary. Tortoise anticipates that $40,000 of the deferred tax liability will reverse in year 7, that actual warranty costs will be incurred evenly in year 8 and year 9, and that the NOL carryforward will be used in year 7. On Tortoise's December 31, year 6 balance sheet, what amount should be reported as a deferred tax asset under U.S. GAAP?

a. $160,000

b. $200,000

c. $240,000

d. $280,000

4. Cavan Company prepared the following reconciliation between book income and taxable income for the current year ended December 31, year 1.

Pretax accounting income	$1,000,000
Taxable income	(600,000)
Difference	$ 400,000
Book-tax differences:	
Interest on municipal income	$ 100,000
Lower financial depreciation	300,000
Total	$ 400,000

Cavan's effective Federal and state income tax rate for year 1 is 30%. The depreciation difference will reverse equally over the next three years at enacted tax rates as follows.

Year	Tax Rate
Year 2	30%
Year 3	25%
Year 4	25%

In Cavan's year 1 income statement, the deferred portion of its provision for income taxes should be:

a. $120,000

b. $80,000

c. $100,000

d. $90,000

Exempt Entities

LEARNING OBJECTIVES: *After completing Chapter 15, you should be able to:*

LO.1 Identify the different types of exempt organizations.

LO.2 List additional requirements for exempt status.

LO.3 Apply the tax consequences of exempt status, including certain restrictions on public charities and private foundations.

LO.4 Determine which exempt organizations are classified as private foundations.

LO.5 Recognize the taxes imposed on private foundations and calculate the related initial tax and additional tax amounts.

LO.6 Determine when an exempt organization is subject to the unrelated business income tax and calculate the amount of the tax.

LO.7 List the reports that exempt organizations must file with the IRS and the related due dates.

LO.8 Identify tax planning opportunities for exempt organizations.

CHAPTER OUTLINE

EFFECT OF A FOR-PROFIT BUSINESS ON A TAX-EXEMPT ENTITY

Hopeful, Inc., is a tax-exempt organization under § 501(c)(3) that provides temporary lodging and psychological services for abused women. Its annual operating budget is $12 million. More than two decades ago, Betty Jones was a recipient of the services provided by Hopeful. Now Hopeful's administrator has been notified by the attorney for Betty's estate that her will transfers to Hopeful her share of the outstanding stock of Taste Good Ice Cream, a chain of 40 gourmet ice cream shops located in Virginia, North Carolina, and South Carolina. The business has been in existence for eight years and has produced substantially higher profits each year.

Hopeful's board is considering the following options regarding the bequest from Betty and has hired you to provide an analysis of the tax consequences of each option.

- Sell the stock of Taste Good Ice Cream and add the net proceeds to Hopeful's endowment.
- Continue to conduct the Taste Good Ice Cream business as a *division* of Hopeful.
- Continue to conduct the business as a *wholly owned subsidiary* of Hopeful.

With the second and the third options, the existing Taste Good management team will remain in place. After-tax profits not needed to expand the ice cream shop chain will be transferred to Hopeful, to be used in carrying out its exempt mission.

Read the chapter and formulate your response.

A s discussed so far in this text, the Federal income tax falls on most individuals and other entities. But entities classified as <mark>exempt organizations</mark> may be able to escape Federal income taxation. The House Report on the Revenue Act of 1938 explains:

> The exemption from taxation of money or property devoted to charitable and other purposes is based upon the theory that the Government is compensated for the loss of revenue by its relief from the financial burden which would otherwise have to be met by appropriations from public funds, and by the benefits resulting from the promotion of the general welfare.[1]

Subchapter F (Exempt Organizations) of the Code (§§ 501–530) provides the authority under which certain organizations are exempt from Federal income tax. Exempt status does not grant an absolute immunity from Federal taxation (e.g., Federal payroll taxes may apply to the entity). Two other broad categories of taxes can fall on otherwise exempt entities. First, the nature or scope of the organization may result in it being subjected to income tax on some of its activities.[2] Second, the organization may be subject to taxes that are designed to encourage or discourage certain of its activities.[3] Nonetheless, exemption from Federal income taxation is a valuable characteristic for an exempt entity.

Benefits of Exempt Status

Governments support exempt entities in ways that far exceed the mere exemption from Federal income taxation. For instance, consider the most important of Federal tax benefits that accrue to a university sports team, in addition to its basic exemption from income taxes.

- *Charitable Contributions*. Donors can claim charitable contribution deductions for gifts to support the team and (to a limited extent) for assessments associated with obtaining and keeping "good seats" at games.

- *Interest Income Exclusion*. Bondholders do not pay Federal income tax on interest earned from purchases of university- or state-level debt that is used to build stadiums, workout facilities, and other permanent sports structures.

- *Business Deductions*. Businesses can claim advertising deductions for costs incurred to promote goods and services at sports facilities and in websites and publications.

- *Payroll Tax Exemption*. College athletes are not employees of the university, so all parties are exempt from payroll taxes, unemployment insurance, workers' compensation benefits, contributions to retirement plans, and the like.

The Exempt Economy

The tax-exempt sector is an important component of the U.S. economy. At least 1.8 million entities hold Federal income tax exempt status. These entities employ almost 15 million workers, representing over 10 percent of the nongovernment U.S. workforce and wages paid. Public charities control about $3.7 trillion in assets and account for over 5 percent of annual GDP.

About 60 percent of public charities are "small" (i.e., they hold assets of less than $500,000). Only about 8 percent of tax-exempt entities hold more than $10 million of assets, but they account for 93 percent of the assets held and 88 percent of the revenue reported. About 3 percent of tax-exempt entities hold assets exceeding $50 million. The IRS audits fewer than 1 percent of these entities every tax year. The Federal government gives up about $100 billion per year in tax revenues by granting tax-exempt status to these entities.

A typical exempt organization uses a dual budgeting and reporting system.

- An *operating fund* is used to make expenditures in support of the entity's exempt purpose (e.g., providing hospital services or offering educational programs). Revenues are raised from donors, sales of goods and services, and contracts with governmental bodies or other exempt entities.

---

[1] See 1939–1 (Part 2) C.B. 742 for a reprint of H.R. No. 1860, 75th Congress, 3rd Session.

[2] See the subsequent discussion of Unrelated Business Income Tax (text Section 15-5).

[3] See the subsequent discussions of Prohibited Transactions (text Section 15-3a) and Taxes Imposed on Private Foundations (text Section 15-4b).

- An *endowment* holds long-term funds contributed by donors or accumulated from operating surpluses; these amounts are used to provide support for the organization's mission. Most endowments require that the principal of the endowment be invested for the entity's security and growth and that the operating budget can spend only the current income earned by the endowment fund.

In addition to being exempt from Federal income tax, an exempt organization may be eligible for other benefits, including the following.

- The organization may be exempt from state income tax, state franchise tax, sales tax, or property tax.
- The organization may receive discounts on postage rates.

Not all exempt organizations are "charities" (i.e., qualifying their donors for tax deductions). For instance, one can claim a charitable contribution deduction for a gift to the Dallas Museum of Art, but not for a gift to the LPGA, the Teachers' Retirement Fund, or the Tempe Chamber of Commerce.

15-1 TYPES OF EXEMPT ORGANIZATIONS

LO.1

Identify the different types of exempt organizations.

An organization qualifies for exempt status *only* if it fits into one of the categories provided in the Code. Examples of qualifying exempt organizations and the specific statutory authority for their exempt status are listed in Exhibit 15.1.[4]

15-2 REQUIREMENTS FOR EXEMPT STATUS

LO.2

List additional requirements for exempt status.

Exempt status frequently requires more than just fitting one of the exempt organization categories. Many of the organizations that qualify for exempt status share the following characteristics.

- The organization serves some type of *common good*.[5]
- The organization is *not a for-profit* entity.[6]
- *Net earnings* do not benefit the members of the organization.[7]
- The organization can *influence legislation* to only a limited extent.[8]

15-2a Serving the Common Good

The underlying rationale for all exempt organizations is that they serve some type of *common good*. However, depending on the type of exempt organization, the term *common good* may be interpreted broadly or narrowly. If the test is interpreted broadly, the group being served is the general public (or a large subgroup of that population). If it is interpreted narrowly, the group being served may be a specific neighborhood or interest group.

15-2b Not-for-Profit Entity

The organization may not be organized or operated for the purpose of making a profit. For some types of exempt organizations, the *for-profit prohibition* appears in the statutory language. For other types, the prohibition is implied.

15-2c Net Earnings and Members of the Organization

How can the net earnings of a tax-exempt organization be used? One might think that the earnings should be used for the organization's exempt purpose. However, if the organization exists to help a specific group of members, such an open-ended

---

[4]Section 501(a) provides for exempt status for organizations described in §§ 401 and 501. The orientation of this chapter is toward organizations that conduct business activities. Therefore, the exempt organizations described in § 401 (i.e., qualified pension, profit sharing, and stock bonus trusts) are outside the scope of the chapter and are not discussed.

[5]See, for example, §§ 501(c)(3) and (4).
[6]See, for example, §§ 501(c)(3), (4), (6), (13), and (14).
[7]See, for example, §§ 501(c)(3), (6), (7), (9), (10), (11), and (19).
[8]§ 501(h).

EXHIBIT 15.1	Types of Exempt Organizations

Statutory Authority	Brief Description	Examples or Comments
§ 501(c)(1)	Federal and related agencies.	Commodity Credit Corporation, Federal Deposit Insurance Corporation, Federal Land Bank.
§ 501(c)(2)	Corporations holding title to property for and paying income to exempt organizations.	Corporation holding title to college fraternity house.
§ 501(c)(3)	Religious, charitable, educational, scientific, literary, etc., organizations.	Boy Scouts of America, Red Cross, Salvation Army, Episcopal Church, PTA, United Fund, University of Richmond.
§ 501(c)(4)	Civic leagues and employee unions.	Garden club, tenants' association promoting tenants' legal rights in entire community, League of Women Voters.
§ 501(c)(5)	Labor, agricultural, and horticultural organizations.	Teachers' association, organization formed to promote effective agricultural pest control, organization formed to test soil and to educate community members in soil treatment, garden club.
§ 501(c)(6)	Business leagues, chambers of commerce, real estate boards, etc.	Chambers of Commerce, American Plywood Association, National Hockey League (NHL), Ladies Professional Golfers Association (LPGA) Tour, medical association peer review board, organization promoting acceptance of women in business and professions.
§ 501(c)(7)	Social clubs.	Country club, rodeo and riding club, press club, bowling club, college fraternities.
§ 501(c)(8)	Fraternal beneficiary societies.	Lodges. Must provide for the payment of life, sickness, accident, or other benefits to members or their dependents.
§ 501(c)(9)	Voluntary employees' beneficiary associations.	Provide for the payment of life, sickness, accident, or other benefits to members, their dependents, or their designated beneficiaries.
§ 501(c)(10)	Domestic fraternal societies.	Lodges. Must not provide for the payment of life, sickness, accident, or other benefits and must devote the net earnings exclusively to religious, charitable, scientific, literary, educational, and fraternal purposes.
§ 501(c)(11)	Local teachers' retirement fund associations.	Only permitted sources of income are amounts received from (1) public taxation, (2) assessments on teaching salaries of members, and (3) income from investments.
§ 501(c)(12)	Local benevolent life insurance associations, mutual or cooperative telephone companies, etc.	Local cooperative telephone company, local mutual water company, local mutual electric company.
§ 501(c)(13)	Cemetery companies.	Must be operated exclusively for the benefit of lot owners who hold the lots for burial purposes.
§ 501(c)(14)	Credit unions.	Other than credit unions exempt under § 501(c)(1).
§ 501(c)(15)	Mutual insurance companies.	Mutual fire insurance company, mutual automobile insurance company.
§ 501(c)(16)	Corporations organized by farmers' cooperatives for financing crop operations.	Related farmers' cooperative must be exempt from tax under § 521.
§ 501(c)(19)	Armed forces members' posts or organizations.	Veterans of Foreign Wars (VFW), Reserve Officers Association.
§ 501(c)(20)	Group legal service plans.	Provided by a corporation for its employees.
§ 501(d)	Religious and apostolic organizations.	Communal organization. Members must include pro rata share of the net income of the organization in their gross income as dividends.
§ 501(e)	Cooperative hospital service organizations.	Centralized purchasing organization for exempt hospitals.
§ 501(f)	Cooperative service organization of educational institutions.	Organization formed to manage universities' endowment funds.
§ 529	Qualified tuition programs.	Prepaid tuition and educational savings programs.
§ 530	Coverdell Education Savings Accounts.	Qualified education savings accounts.

interpretation could permit net earnings to benefit specific group members. As a result, the Code specifically prohibits certain types of exempt organizations from using their earnings in this way.

> . . . no part of the net earnings . . . inures to the benefit of any private shareholder or individual.[9]

In other instances, the definition of the exempt organization in the Code effectively prevents this kind of use.

> . . . the net earnings of which are devoted exclusively to religious, charitable, scientific, literary, educational, and fraternal purposes.[10]

15-3 TAXES ON EXEMPT ENTITIES

LO.3

Apply the tax consequences of exempt status, including certain restrictions on public charities and private foundations.

Some exempt organizations still can incur Federal taxes.

- An exempt organization that engages in a *prohibited transaction* or is a so-called *feeder organization* is subject to tax.
- If the organization is classified as a *private foundation*, it may be partially subject to tax.
- An exempt organization can be subject to tax on its *unrelated business taxable income*.

The first two exceptions are discussed in text Sections 15-3 and 15-4. The third exception is discussed in text Section 15-5.

15-3a Taxable Transactions

Effects of Lobbying

A *public charity* (religious, charitable, educational, etc., organization)[11] cannot, as a "substantial" part of its activities, attempt to influence legislation (lobbying activities).[12] Such an organization that makes lobbying expenditures is subject to a 5 percent tax on the expenditures for the taxable year, and the entity's exempt status is jeopardized. A separate 5 percent tax also may be levied on the organization's management. This tax does not apply to private foundations.[13]

Public charities can engage in lobbying activities on a limited basis by making an affirmative election, the terms of which determine whether the lobbying activity is substantial.[14] Eligible for the election are most § 501(c)(3) organizations, but not churches.

If the election is made, some of the entity's lobbying expenditures are subject to a 25 percent tax. If the lobbying expenditures are excessive (i.e., they exceed a computed ceiling amount), the organization's exempt status may be in jeopardy.

Computing the Ceiling Two terms are key to the calculation of the ceiling amount: **lobbying expenditures** and **grass roots expenditures**. The same entity can incur both types of expenditures in the same tax year.

Lobbying expenditures influence legislation by communicating with any legislator, government official, or staff member who may participate in developing legislation (e.g., by taking a legislator out for a meal and discussing the desired outcome of the proposed law change). *Grass roots expenditures* influence legislation by attempting to affect the opinions of the general public, or a segment of that population (e.g., by printing and distributing posters and fliers promoting a position on a proposed law change).

A ceiling is computed for both lobbying expenditures and grass roots expenditures. Those amounts are derived as follows.

- 150% × Lobbying nontaxable amount = Lobbying expenditures ceiling.
- 150% × Grass roots nontaxable amount = Grass roots expenditures ceiling.

---

[9]§ 501(c)(6).
[10]§ 501(c)(10).
[11]§ 501(c)(3). Public charities are discussed further in text Section 15-4a.

[12]§ 4912(a).
[13]§§ 4912(b), (c).
[14]§ 501(h).

EXHIBIT 15.2   Calculation of Lobbying Nontaxable Amount

Exempt Purpose Expenditures	Lobbying Nontaxable Amount Is
Not over $500,000	20% of exempt purpose expenditures*
Over $500,000 but not over $1 million	$100,000 + 15% of the excess of exempt purpose expenditures over $500,000
Over $1 million but not over $1.5 million	$175,000 + 10% of the excess of exempt purpose expenditures over $1 million
Over $1.5 million	$225,000 + 5% of the excess of exempt purpose expenditures over $1.5 million

*Exempt purpose expenditures generally are the amounts paid or incurred for the taxable year to accomplish the following purposes: religious, charitable, scientific, literary, educational, fostering of national or international amateur sports competition, or the prevention of cruelty to children or animals.

The *lobbying nontaxable amount* is the lesser of (1) $1 million or (2) the amount determined in Exhibit 15.2.[15] The *grass roots nontaxable amount* is 25 percent of the lobbying nontaxable amount.[16]

Determining the Tax   An electing public charity is assessed a 25 percent tax on its <mark>excess lobbying expenditures</mark>.[17] Excess lobbying expenditures are the *greater* of the following amounts.[18]

- The excess of the lobbying expenditures for the taxable year over the lobbying nontaxable amount, or
- The excess of the grass roots expenditures for the taxable year over the grass roots nontaxable amount.

EXAMPLE 1

Tan, Inc., a qualifying § 501(c)(3) organization, makes a § 501(h) election. Its exempt purpose expenditures for the taxable year are $5,000,000, and during the year, it incurs lobbying expenditures of $525,000 and grass roots expenditures of $0.

Applying the data in Exhibit 15.2, the lobbying nontaxable amount is $400,000 [$225,000 + 5% ($5,000,000 − $1,500,000)]. The ceiling on lobbying expenditures is $600,000 (150% × $400,000).

Tan's $525,000 of lobbying expenditures are under the ceiling of $600,000. However, the election results in a tax on the excess lobbying expenditures of $125,000 ($525,000 lobbying expenditures − $400,000 lobbying nontaxable amount). The resulting tax liability is $31,250 ($125,000 × 25%).

The entity computes its tax at the 25 percent rate even if the expenditures for the year exceed the ceiling, but the entity's exempt status is at risk if the ceiling amount is exceeded repeatedly. See Exhibit 15.3.

EXHIBIT 15.3   Taxes on Lobbying Expenditures by Public Charities

- **Without § 501(h) election:** A 5 percent tax is assessed on all lobbying expenditures; exempt status is jeopardized.

- **With § 501(h) election:** Exempt status is not jeopardized unless the lobbying or grass roots expenditures ceiling is exceeded repeatedly.

---

[15]§ 4911(c)(2).

[16]§ 4911(c)(4).

[17]§ 4911(a)(1).

[18]§ 4911(b).

Intermediate Sanctions on Excess Benefit Transactions

When an individual who is related to a public charity receives inappropriate benefits from the charity, the Code applies **intermediate sanctions**, rather than revoking the entity's exempt status.[19] The intermediate sanctions consist of excise taxes imposed on disqualified persons (individuals who can exercise substantial influence over the affairs of the organization) who engage in *excess benefit transactions*.

In this case, a disqualified person engages in a non-fair-market-value transaction with the exempt organization (e.g., the purchase of property from the exempt entity at a large discount) or receives unreasonable compensation. The tax also can be assessed on exempt organization managers who participate in such a transaction, knowing that it is improper.

The excise tax on the disqualified person is 25 percent of the excess benefit. For the exempt organization management, the excise tax is 10 percent of the excess benefit (with a maximum of $20,000 for each excess benefit transaction), unless the participation is not willful and is due to reasonable cause. These excise taxes are referred to as first-level taxes.

A second-level tax applies to the disqualified person if the excess benefit transaction is not corrected (e.g., if the excess amount is *not* paid back to the charity) before the first-level tax is due. This excise tax is 200 percent of the excess benefit.

Excess Benefit Transactions

The compensation committee of an exempt organization is deciding what to pay its new president. A member of the organization's board of directors is on the committee and knows that the fair market value of the president's services is no more than $150,000. However, the board member votes to approve setting the new president's compensation at $250,000.

The board member will be subject to an excise tax of $10,000 (10% × $100,000 excess benefit), since he is an organization manager. In addition, the president will be subject to an excise tax of $25,000 (25% × $100,000 excess benefit) and would be required to repay the $100,000 excess benefit, plus interest, to the organization. If the president does not repay this amount, a second-level tax of $200,000 could be applied (200% × $100,000 excess benefit).

EXAMPLE 2

An exempt organization rents office space to a member of its board of directors for $100,000 per year. It later is determined that fair rental value is $140,000 per year.

The board member is subject to a first-level tax of $10,000 (25% × $40,000 excess benefit), and she must repay the $40,000 excess benefit, plus interest, to the organization. Failure to repay may result in a second-level tax of $80,000 (200% × $40,000 excess benefit).

If the board member participated in the decision to enter into the lease, she could be liable for an additional tax of $4,000 (10% × $40,000 excess benefit) as an organization manager.

EXAMPLE 3

Other Taxes on Certain Exempt Entities

Certain large private colleges and universities are subject to a 1.4 percent excise tax on their net investment income for the tax year. The tax is meant to encourage these institutions to use "excessive" endowment funds to increase student financial aid and to decrease tuition levels. The tax applies if the fair market value of the school's endowment fund divided by the number of tuition-paying full-time equivalent students at the school exceeds $500,000.[20] Perhaps 75 schools appear to be liable for this tax.

In addition, a 21 percent excise tax is applied to compensation paid to certain highly paid employees of exempt organizations. In general, the tax applies to compensation in excess of $1 million for the tax year and can be assessed only on the five highest-paid employees of the organization.[21] This tax might apply to a hospital administrator, a symphony conductor, or a university president or an athletic department employee (e.g., the athletic director, football coach, or basketball coach).

---

[19] § 4958.

[20] § 4968.

[21] § 4960. Once an individual is a top-five paid employee, he or she is subject to the excise tax for the duration of employment with the organization. As a result, more than five individuals may be subject to the tax in a single year; § 4960(c)(2).

15-3b **Feeder Organizations**

A <mark>feeder organization</mark> carries on a trade or business for the benefit of an exempt organization and remits its profits to the exempt organization. Feeder organizations are *not* exempt from Federal income tax.[22] This treatment prevents an entity, whose primary purpose is to conduct a profitable trade or business, from escaping taxation merely because its profits are given to one or more exempt organizations.

The Big Picture

EXAMPLE 4

Return to the facts of *The Big Picture* on p. 15-1. Recall that Hopeful, Inc., an exempt organization under § 501(c)(3) that provides temporary lodging and psychological services to abused women, is trying to decide what it should do with Taste Good Ice Cream, a chain of gourmet ice cream shops it has received as a bequest.

Assume that Hopeful decides to operate Taste Good as a *subsidiary*, with the profits going to Hopeful to support its tax-exempt mission. The subsidiary is a feeder organization, and its profits will be subject to the Federal income tax on corporations.

Concept Summary 15.1 provides an overview of the consequences of tax-exempt status.

Concept Summary 15.1

Consequences of Exempt Status

General

Exempt from Federal income tax.

Exempt from most state and local income, franchise, sales, and property taxes.

Qualify for reductions in postage rates.

Gifts to the organization often can be deducted by donor.

Exceptions

May be subject to Federal income tax associated with other activities, including the following.

- Engaging in a taxable transaction (text Section 15-3a).
- Being a feeder organization (text Section 15-3b).
- Being a private foundation (text Section 15-4).
- Generating unrelated business taxable income (text Section 15-5).

15-4 **PRIVATE FOUNDATIONS**

LO.4

Determine which exempt organizations are classified as private foundations.

15-4a **Tax Consequences of Private Foundation Status**

Certain exempt organizations are classified as <mark>private foundations</mark>. This classification produces two negative consequences. First, the classification may have an adverse effect on the contributions it receives, because the tax consequences for donors may not be as favorable as those given to other exempt organizations.[23] Second, the private foundation may be subject to Federal taxation. The reason for this less beneficial tax treatment is that private foundations define *common good* more narrowly and are not seen as being supported by, and operated for the good of, the public.

Definition of a Private Foundation

All § 501(c)(3) organizations are private foundations by default, unless one of the statutory exceptions applies. The following entities are *not* private foundations.[24]

1. Churches; educational institutions; hospitals and medical research organizations; and governmental units (favored activities category).
2. Organizations that are broadly supported by the general public, by governmental units, or by organizations described in (1) above.
3. Entities organized and operated exclusively for the benefit of organizations described in (1) or (2) above (i.e., a supporting organization).

---

[22]§ 502(a).

[23]§ 170(e)(1)(B)(ii).

[24]§ 509(a).

Public Charities

A *public charity* is one that falls into the favored activities category in (1) above, or meets the "broadly supported" requirement in (2) above. To be a public charity and avoid private foundation status, *both* an *external support test* and an *internal support test* must be satisfied.[25]

The intent of the two tests is to grant the more favorable public charity status to those organizations that are responsive to the general public, rather than to the private interests of a limited number of donors or other persons.

Under the *external support test*, more than one-third of the organization's support each taxable year *normally* must come in the following forms.

- Gifts, grants, contributions, and membership fees.
- Gross receipts from admissions, sales of merchandise, performance of services, or the furnishing of facilities in an activity that is not an unrelated trade or business for purposes of the unrelated business income tax (discussed subsequently).
  - ➤ Gross receipts of this type from any person or governmental agency in excess of the greater of $5,000 or 1 percent of the organization's support for the taxable year are not counted in the numerator of the support fraction.

Amounts received from disqualified persons are not included in the numerator of the support fraction. For this purpose, disqualified persons include, among others:

- Substantial contributors whose cumulative gifts and bequests to the exempt entity exceed both 2 percent of aggregate contributions received by the entity and $5,000.
- Significant members of the governing body of the exempt entity, including officers, directors, trustees, and their families.

The *internal support test* limits the amount of support *normally* received from the sum of the following sources to one-third of the organization's support for the taxable year.

- Gross investment income (gross income from interest, dividends, rents, and royalties).
- Unrelated business taxable income (discussed subsequently) minus the related tax.

Support does not include *unusual grants* received or gain/loss from the sale of the entity's investment assets.

Lion, Inc., a § 501(c)(3) organization, received the following support during the taxable year. Lion wants to be classified as a public charity, not as a private foundation.

Governmental unit A for services rendered	$ 30,000
Governmental unit B for services rendered	20,000
General public for services rendered	20,000
Gross investment income	15,000
Contributions from individual substantial contributors (disqualified persons)	15,000
Total support	$100,000

In calculating the *internal support test*, only the gross investment income of $15,000 is included in the numerator. Thus, the test is satisfied ($15,000/$100,000 = 15%; cannot exceed 33.33%) for the taxable year.

continued

---

[25]§ 509(a)(2). An alternative means by which to qualify as a public charity, designed for organizations that operate largely using donations from third parties, is found at § 509(a)(1). The external and internal support tests generally must be met in each of the four preceding tax years. When these tests are met, public charity status is granted for the current year and for the subsequent year. Reg. §§ 1.509(a)–3(c) and 1.170A–9(e)(4)(i).

Internal Support Test	
Gross investment income	$15,000
Unrelated business taxable income	–0–
Total countable support	$15,000

$$\frac{\$15,000}{\$100,000} = 15\% \quad \textbf{Passes internal support test}$$

For purposes of the *external support test*, the support from A is counted only to the extent of $5,000 (greater of $5,000 or 1% of $100,000 support). Likewise, for B, only $5,000 is counted as support. The $15,000 received from disqualified persons is excluded from the numerator but is included in the denominator. As a result, the total countable support is $30,000 ($20,000 from the general public + $5,000 + $5,000), and Lion fails the test for the taxable year ($30,000/$100,000 = 30%; needs to exceed 33.33%).

External Support Test	
Governmental unit A for services rendered	$ 5,000
Governmental unit B for services rendered	5,000
General public for services rendered	20,000
Total countable support	$30,000

$$\frac{\$30,000}{\$100,000} = 30\% \quad \textbf{Fails external support test}$$

Because Lion did not satisfy both tests, it does not qualify as an organization that is broadly supported. Therefore, it is a private foundation.

Concept Summary 15.2 shows the classifications of exempt organizations and indicates the potential negative consequences of classification as a private foundation.

Concept Summary 15.2

Exempt Organizations: Classification

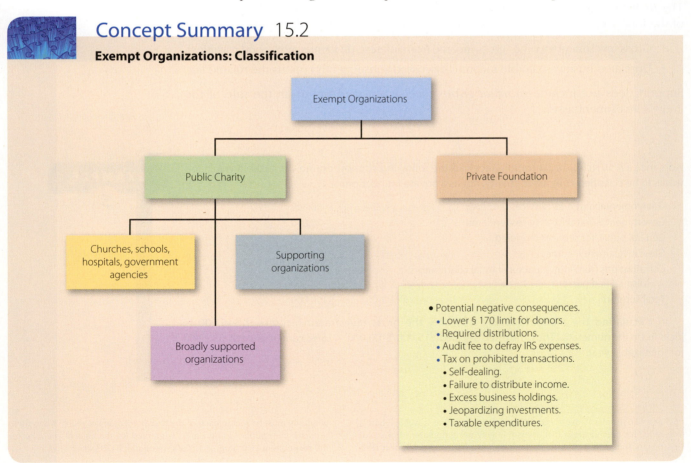

15-4b Taxes Imposed on Private Foundations

There are about 100,000 private foundations that file annually with the IRS. These entities largely hold investment assets and make annual grants to third parties. Private foundations control about $830 billion in assets, but most of them are family-controlled organizations that hold no more than $10 million of investable assets.

Distributions of almost $75 million are made each tax year by private foundations of all sizes. Most of these distributions are made to other charitable entities.

In general, a private foundation is exempt from Federal income tax. However, it may be subject to several Federal excise taxes.[26] Exhibit 15.4 includes additional information about these taxes.

These taxes restrict the permitted activities of private foundations. Two levels of tax may be imposed on the private foundation and the foundation manager: an initial tax and an additional tax. The initial taxes (first-level), with the exception of the tax based on investment income, are imposed because the private foundation engages in an undesirable activity (called a *prohibited transaction*). The additional taxes (second-level) are imposed only if these activities are not corrected within a statutory time period.[27]

Annually, about 1,700 private foundations incur an excise tax of this type. About $13 million in taxes are collected under these provisions; the largest amount of tax is collected for failing to distribute adequate amounts of the private foundation's income.

The tax on undistributed income will be used to illustrate how expensive these taxes can be (and why they should be avoided). Both an initial (first-level) tax and an additional (second-level) tax may be assessed. The initial (first-level) tax is 30 percent on the undistributed income for the taxable year that is not distributed by the end of the following taxable year. The tax applies on this undistributed income for each year until the tax is assessed by the IRS.

The additional (second-level) tax is 100 percent on the amount of the inadequate distribution. The additional tax is waived if the undistributed income is distributed within 90 days after the IRS mails a deficiency notice for the additional tax.

LO.5

Recognize the taxes imposed on private foundations and calculate the related initial tax and additional tax amounts.

| EXHIBIT 15.4 | Taxes Imposed on Private Foundations |

			Private Foundation		Foundation Manager	
Type of Tax	Code Section	Purpose	Initial Tax	Additional Tax	Initial Tax	Additional Tax
On investment income	§ 4940	Audit fee to defray IRS expenses.	2%*			
On self-dealing	§ 4941	Engaging in transactions with disqualified persons.	10%**	200%**	5%†	50%†
On failure to distribute income	§ 4942	Failing to distribute adequate amount of income for exempt purposes, usually 5% of asset value.	30%	100%		
On excess business holdings	§ 4943	Investments that enable the private foundation to control unrelated businesses (usually by owning >35% of outstanding shares).	10%	200%		
On jeopardizing investments	§ 4944	Speculative investments that put the private foundation's assets at risk.	10%	25%	10%‡	5%†

*May be possible to reduce the tax rate to 1% if adequate distributions are made during the year; § 4940(e). An exempt operating foundation [see §§ 4940(d)(2) and 4942(j)(3)] is not subject to the tax.

**Imposed on the disqualified person rather than the foundation.

†Subject to a statutory ceiling of $20,000.

‡Subject to a statutory ceiling of $10,000.

---

[26]§§ 4940–4945. [27]§ 4961.

Undistributed income is the excess of the amount that should have been distributed over qualifying distributions made by the entity. The tax applies if the entity did not distribute its minimum investment return (i.e., typically 5 percent of the fair market value of the foundation's assets, net of any outstanding debt).[28] The undistributed amount is reduced by related salaries and administrative expenses, so the actual required distribution usually is less than 5 percent of asset value. The 5 percent rule was designed to provide a minimum amount that private foundations would distribute every year, but it acts more as a ceiling amount; most private foundations make distributions of 6 percent of their assets or less per year.

Distributions can lead to one other favorable result for private foundations. If the entity increases its distributions for the tax year over its historical levels, the tax on investment income is reduced to 1 percent.

Gold, Inc., a private foundation, records undistributed income of $80,000 for the 2016 taxable year. It distributes $15,000 of this amount during 2017 and an additional $45,000 during 2018. An IRS deficiency notice is mailed to Gold on August 5, 2019. The initial tax is $25,500 [($65,000* × 30%) + ($20,000** × 30%)].

As of the date of the deficiency notice, Gold has made no additional distributions from the 2016 undistributed income. Therefore, because the remaining undistributed income of $20,000 has not been distributed by August 5, 2019, an additional tax of $20,000 ($20,000 × 100%) is imposed.

If Gold distributes the $20,000 of 2016 undistributed income within 90 days of the deficiency notice, the additional tax is waived. Without this distribution, however, the foundation will owe $45,500 in taxes ($25,500 + $20,000).

*$80,000 − $15,000.
**$80,000 − $15,000 − $45,000.

15-5 UNRELATED BUSINESS INCOME TAX

Determine when an exempt organization is subject to the unrelated business income tax and calculate the amount of the tax.

Some entities that hold a Federal income tax exemption still are subject to a Federal income tax. We discussed the excise taxes that apply to private foundations in the previous section. In addition, an income tax on the business operations of an exempt organization may be incurred. About 200,000 exempt entities file a tax return with the IRS every year, and about 10 percent of those report a tax liability on business income. Tax collections in a typical year equal about $600 million.

The **unrelated business income tax (UBIT)** is designed to treat charitable entities as if they were subject to the corporate income tax, chiefly because they compete with taxable enterprises. The corporate income tax rate is used for this purpose.[29]

In general, **unrelated business income (UBI)** is derived from activities not related to the exempt purpose of the exempt organization. The tax applies because the organization is engaging in substantial commercial activities.[30] Without this tax, taxable business entities would be at a competitive disadvantage. Thus, the UBIT is intended to neutralize the exempt entity's tax advantage.[31]

It is the source of the business profits that triggers the UBIT, not their use. UBI that is employed for the entity's exempt purpose still is subject to the tax.

The Big Picture

EXAMPLE 7

Return to the facts of *The Big Picture* on p. 15-1. Recall that Hopeful, Inc., an exempt organization under § 501(c)(3), has received Taste Good Ice Cream, a chain of gourmet ice cream shops, as a bequest.

Assume that Hopeful has decided to operate Taste Good as a *division*. Although the income from Taste Good's shops will be used to support Hopeful's exempt purpose, the net revenue constitutes unrelated business income; therefore, it is subject to the UBIT.

[28]§ 4940.
[29]§ 511(a)(1).
[30]§ 512(a)(1).
[31]Reg. § 1.513–1(b).

The UBIT applies to all organizations that are exempt from Federal income tax under § 501(c), except Federal agencies. In addition, the tax applies to state colleges and universities.[32]

A materiality exception generally exempts an entity from being subject to the UBIT if such income is insignificant. This $1,000 "standard deduction" generally available to all exempt organizations is discussed later.

15-5a **Unrelated Trade or Business**

An exempt organization will be subject to the UBIT when all of the following conditions are met.[33]

- The organization conducts a trade or business.
- The trade or business is *not* substantially related to the exempt purpose of the organization.
- The trade or business is regularly carried on by the organization.

However, the Code specifically excludes the following activities from classification as an unrelated trade or business.

- A trade or business where the individuals performing substantially all of its work do so without compensation (e.g., an orphanage operates a retail store for sales to the general public, and all of the work is done by volunteers).
- The trade or business consists of selling merchandise, and substantially all of the merchandise has been received as contributions (e.g., thrift shops).
- For § 501(c)(3) organizations and for state colleges or universities, the trade or business is conducted primarily for the convenience of the organization's members, students, patients, officers, or employees (e.g., a college bookstore and a laundry operated by the college for laundering dormitory linens and students' clothing).
- For most employee unions, the trade or business consists of selling to members, at their usual place of employment, work-related clothing and equipment and items normally sold through vending machines, snack bars, or food-dispensing facilities.

Conducting a Trade or Business

Trade or business, for this purpose, is broadly defined. It includes any activity conducted for the production of income through the sale of merchandise or the performance of services. An activity need not generate a profit to be treated as a trade or business.[34]

EXAMPLE 8

Health, Inc., is an exempt hospital that operates a pharmacy. The pharmacy provides medicines and supplies to the patients in the hospital (i.e., it contributes to the conduct of the hospital's exempt purpose). In addition, the pharmacy sells medicines and supplies to the general public.

The activity of selling to the general public constitutes a trade or business for purposes of the UBIT.

An organization that has more than one unrelated trade or business must compute unrelated business taxable income separately for each of the activities. Losses from one unrelated trade or business cannot be used to offset income derived from a different activity.[35]

Not Substantially Related to the Exempt Purpose

Exempt organizations frequently conduct unrelated trades or businesses to provide income to help defray their costs. If the activity is related to its exempt purpose, it will escape the UBIT. To be related to the accomplishment of the exempt purpose, the business activities must contribute importantly to the exempt purpose.[36]

---

[32]§ 511(a)(2) and Reg. § 1.511–2(a)(2).

[33]§ 513(a) and Reg. § 1.513–2(a).

[34]Reg. § 1.513–1(b).

[35]§ 512(a)(6). The first unrelated trade or business is reported on the Form 990–T, and each additional business is reported on its own Schedule M (Form 990–T).

[36]Reg. § 1.513–1(d).

Is It an Unrelated Trade or Business?

EXAMPLE 9

Art, Inc., an exempt organization, operates a school for training children in the performing arts. As an essential part of that training, the children perform for the general public once a month. The children are paid for their performances, and Art receives income by charging admission to the performances.

The income from admissions is *not* income from an unrelated trade or business. The performances by the children contribute importantly to the accomplishment of the exempt purpose of providing training in the performing arts.

EXAMPLE 10

Assume the same facts as in Example 9, except that four performances are conducted each weekend of the year; each child must appear in three of the performances every week. Further, assume that this number of performances far exceeds that required for training the children.

Here, the income derived from admissions for any *excess* performances is income from an unrelated trade or business.

The trade or business may sell merchandise that has been produced as part of the accomplishment of the exempt purpose.[37] Income derived by the organization from use of its property for a nonexempt purpose is UBI.[38]

Unrelated Business Income

EXAMPLE 11

Help-Self, Inc., an exempt organization, conducts programs for the rehabilitation of the handicapped. One of the programs includes training in radio and television repair. Help-Self derives gross income by selling the repaired items.

The income is substantially related to the accomplishment of the exempt purpose (and, therefore, is not UBI).

EXAMPLE 12

Civil, Inc., an exempt organization, operates a museum. As part of the exempt purpose of the museum, educational lectures are given in the museum's theater during the operating hours of the museum. In the evening, when the museum is closed, the theater is leased to an individual who sells tickets and shows current movies to the general public. The lease income is UBI.

Special Rule for Corporate Sponsorship Payments The term *unrelated trade or business* does not include the soliciting and receiving of qualified sponsorship payments.[39] A qualified sponsorship payment must meet all of the following requirements.

- The trade or business making the payment expects no substantial benefit other than the use or acknowledgment of its name, logo, or product lines in connection with the activities of the exempt organization.

- The exempt organization does not advertise or endorse the payor's products or services.

- The payment does not include any amount that is contingent on the degree of public exposure that results (e.g., the level of attendance at one or more events, the number of website hits, or broadcast ratings).

---

[37]Reg. § 1.513–1(d)(4)(ii). If the merchandise is not sold in substantially the same state it was in at the completion of the exempt purpose (e.g., it has been converted into another product), the gross income subsequently derived from the sale of the merchandise *is* unrelated business income (UBI).

[38]Reg. § 1.513–1(d)(4)(iii) addresses the allocation of expenses to exempt and nonexempt activities.

[39]§ 513(i).

Sponsorship Payments

Pets, Inc., a manufacturer of cat food, contributes $25,000 to Feline Care, Inc., an exempt organization that cares for abandoned cats. In return for the contribution, Feline agrees to put Pets' corporate logo in its monthly newsletter to donors. The $25,000 payment is a qualified sponsorship payment and is not subject to the UBIT.

Assume the same facts as in Example 13, except that Feline agrees to endorse Pets' cat food in its monthly newsletter by stating that it feeds only Pets' cat food to its cats. The $25,000 payment is not a qualified sponsorship payment and is subject to the UBIT.

Special Rule for Bingo Games A *qualified bingo game* is not an unrelated trade or business if both of the following requirements are met.[40]

- The bingo game is legal under both state and local law.
- Commercial bingo games (conducted for a profit motive) ordinarily are not allowed in the pertinent jurisdiction.

Play, Inc., an exempt organization, conducts weekly bingo games. The state and municipality in which Play conducts the games allow exempt organizations to conduct bingo games, but they do not permit profit-oriented entities to do so.

Because both of the requirements for bingo games are satisfied, the bingo games conducted by Play are not an unrelated trade or business.

Special Rule for Distribution of Low-Cost Articles When a donor receives a product, like a briefcase, in exchange for a gift to a charity, it appears that a sale has occurred, and the entity has generated UBI. But where an exempt organization distributes low-cost items as an incidental part of its solicitation for charitable contributions, the activity is not considered an unrelated trade or business.

A low-cost article is an item that costs $11.10 or less in 2019 (indexed annually). Examples of such items are pens, stamps, stickers, stationery, and address labels. If more than one item is distributed to a person during the calendar year, the costs of the items are combined.[41]

Special Rule for Rental or Exchange of Membership Lists If an exempt organization sells or rents its donor or membership list (i.e., its mailing list) to other exempt organizations, the activity is *not* an unrelated trade or business.[42]

Regularly Carried on by the Organization

Requiring the activity to be one that is regularly carried on by the exempt organization ensures that only activities that are actually competing with taxable organizations are subject to the UBIT. The factors considered in applying the *regularly carried on* test include the frequency of the activity, the continuity of the activity, and the manner in which the activity is pursued.[43]

---

[40]§ 513(f).
[41]§ 513(h)(1)(A).

[42]§ 513(h)(1)(B).
[43]§ 512(a)(1) and Reg. § 1.513–1(c).

Activity Regularly Carried On

EXAMPLE 16

Silver, Inc., an exempt organization, owns land that is located next to the state fairgrounds. During the 10 days of the state fair, Silver uses the land as a parking lot and charges individuals attending the state fair for parking there. The activity is not regularly carried on.

EXAMPLE 17

Black, Inc., an exempt organization, has its offices in the downtown area. It owns a parking lot adjacent to its offices on which its employees park during the week. On Saturdays, it rents the spaces in the parking lot to individuals shopping or working in the downtown area. Black is conducting a business activity on a year-round basis, even though it is only for one day per week. Thus, an activity is regularly being carried on.

15-5b Unrelated Business Taxable Income

General Tax Model

A template for computing unrelated business taxable income (UBTI) appears in Exhibit 15.5. In computing UBTI, several adjustments are made to the entity's net UBI for the year, including the following.[44]

Positive adjustments—Add to UBI

1. A deduction is allowed for gifts to another charity, but it is limited to 10 percent of UBTI (without regard to the charitable contribution deduction). Amounts in excess of this limit are added back to UBI as a positive adjustment.

EXAMPLE 18

Brown, Inc., an exempt organization, records UBTI of $100,000 (before considering any charitable contributions). Total charitable contributions equal $13,000.

If $13,000 is deducted in calculating net unrelated business income, then $3,000 [$13,000 − 10%($100,000)] is a positive adjustment (i.e., an "add back" to reduce the deduction) in calculating UBTI.

2. Unrelated debt-financed income net of the unrelated debt-financed deductions (see subsequent discussion).

Negative adjustments—Subtract from UBI

1. Income from dividends, interest, and annuities, net of all directly related deductions.
2. Royalty income, regardless of whether it is measured by production, gross income, or taxable income from the property, net of all directly related deductions.

EXHIBIT 15.5	Tax Formula for Unrelated Business Taxable Income

Gross unrelated business income

− Deductions related to the business income

= Net unrelated business income

± Adjustments (positive and negative)

− $1,000 "standard deduction"

= Unrelated business taxable income (UBTI)

[44]§ 512(b) and Reg. § 1.512(b)–1.

3. Rent income from real property and from certain personal property net of all directly related deductions.

- Personal property rents are included in the negative adjustment only if the personal property is leased with the real property. In addition, the personal property rent income must not exceed 10 percent of the gross rent income under the lease.
- None of rents are a negative adjustment if more than 50 percent of the rent income under the lease is derived from personal property.

Rentals as UBI

Beaver, Inc., an exempt organization, leases land and a building (realty) and computers (personalty) housed in the building. Under the lease, $46,000 of the rent is for the land and building and $4,000 is for the computers. Expenses incurred for the land and building are $10,000.

Here, the personal property rent ($4,000) does not exceed 10 percent of the gross rental income ($5,000; $50,000 × 10%). As a result, the net rent income from both the land and building of $36,000 ($46,000 − $10,000) and the income from the computers of $4,000 are negative adjustments in computing UBTI.

EXAMPLE 19

Assume the same facts as in Example 19, except that the rent income is $35,000 from the land and building and $15,000 from the computers.

Because the rent income from the computers exceeds $5,000 (10% × $50,000) and is not incidental, it is *not* a negative adjustment; it is a business activity and is included in UBTI. The $35,000 rent income from the real property remains a negative adjustment.

EXAMPLE 20

Assume the same facts as in Example 19, except that the rent income is $20,000 from the land and building and $30,000 from the computers.

Because more than 50% of the rent income under the lease is from the computers, neither the rent income from the land and building nor that from the computers is a negative adjustment.

EXAMPLE 21

4. Gains and losses from the sale, exchange, or other disposition of property *except for* inventory.

Beaver, the owner of the land, building, and computers in Example 19, sells these assets for $450,000. Their adjusted basis is $300,000.

Beaver's recognized gain of $150,000 is a negative adjustment.

EXAMPLE 22

In determining UBTI, a "standard deduction" of $1,000 is allowed.[45]

Petit Care, Inc., an exempt organization, reports net unrelated business income of $800. Because Petit claims a $1,000 "standard deduction," its UBTI is $0. Therefore, its income tax liability is $0.

EXAMPLE 23

After UBTI is determined, that amount is subject to tax using the Federal corporate income tax rate.[46]

Patient, Inc., an exempt organization, has UBTI of $500,000. Patient's income tax liability is $105,000 ($500,000 UBTI × 21% corporate tax rate).

EXAMPLE 24

Concept Summary 15.3 provides a summary of the UBIT rules.

[45]§ 512(b)(12).

[46]If the charity is organized as a trust, the rates under Subchapter J are used. See Exhibit 20.3 in Chapter 20.

Concept Summary 15.3

Unrelated Business Income Tax

Purpose	To tax the entity on unrelated business income as if it were subject to the corporate income tax.
Applicable tax rates	Corporate or trust tax rate.
Exempt organizations to which applicable	All organizations exempt under § 501(c), except Federal agencies.
Entities subject to the tax	The organization conducts a trade or business, the trade or business is not substantially related to the exempt purpose of the organization, and the trade or business is regularly carried on by the organization.
Exceptions to the tax	• Substantially all of the work is performed by volunteers.
	• Substantially all of the merchandise being sold has been received by gift.
	• For § 501(c)(3) organizations, the business is conducted primarily for the benefit of the organization's members, students, patients, officers, or employees.
	• For most employee unions, the trade or business consists of selling to members work-related clothing and equipment and items normally sold through vending machines, snack bars, or food-dispensing facilities.
	• Other items relating to bingo games, corporate sponsorships, list rentals, and the like.
$1,000 "standard deduction"	If gross income from an unrelated trade or business is less than $1,000, it is not necessary to file a return associated with the unrelated business income tax.

Unrelated Debt-Financed Income

In calculating UBTI (see Exhibit 15.5), unrelated debt-financed income is one of the positive adjustments. Examples of income from debt-financed property include rent income from real estate or tangible personal property (e.g., a church that owns and leases space in a leveraged office building), and gains from the disposition of debt-financed property.

Without this provision, a tax-exempt organization could use borrowed funds to acquire unrelated business or investment property and use the exempt earnings from the acquisition to pay for the property.

Definition of Debt-Financed Income **Debt-financed income** is the gross income generated from debt-financed property. *Debt-financed property* is all property of the exempt organization that is held to produce income and on which there is acquisition indebtedness, *except* for the following.[47]

- Property where substantially all (at least 85 percent) of the use is devoted to the organization's exempt purpose.[48]
- Property whose gross income otherwise is treated as unrelated business income.
- Property whose gross income is from the following sources and otherwise is not treated as unrelated business income.
  - ➤ Income from research performed for the United States or a Federal governmental agency, or a state or a political subdivision thereof.
  - ➤ Income from research activities performed by a college, university, or hospital.

If the 85 percent test is not satisfied, only the portion of the property that is *not* used for the exempt purpose is debt-financed property.

EXAMPLE 25

Deer, Inc., an exempt organization, owns a five-story office building on which there is acquisition indebtedness. Three of the floors are used for Deer's exempt purpose. The two other floors are leased to Purple Corporation. In this case, the *substantially all* test is not satisfied. Therefore, 40% of the office building is debt-financed property, and 60% is not.

continued

---

[47]§ 514(b).   [48]Reg. § 1.514(b)–1(b)(1)(ii).

What if Deer used all but one-half of one floor for its exempt purpose (with Purple leasing the half floor)? Now the "substantially all" test is met, and Deer does not need to include any of the rental income as a positive adjustment.

Certain land that is acquired by an exempt organization for later exempt use is excluded from debt-financed property if the following requirements are satisfied.[49]

- The principal purpose of acquiring the land is for use (substantially all) in achieving the organization's exempt purpose.
- This use will begin within 10 years of the acquisition date.
- At the date when the land is acquired, it is located in the *neighborhood* of other property of the organization for which substantially all of the use is for achieving the organization's exempt purpose.

If the exempt organization is a church, the 10-year period becomes a 15-year period and the neighborhood requirement is waived.

Definition of Acquisition Indebtedness   Acquisition indebtedness consists of amounts used to acquire or improve the debt-financed property.[50]

Red, Inc., an exempt organization, acquires land for $100,000. To finance the acquisition, Red mortgages the land and receives loan proceeds of $80,000. Red leases the land to Duck Corporation. The mortgage is acquisition indebtedness. Net profits from the leasing activities constitute UBTI for Red.

EXAMPLE
26

Rose, Inc., an exempt organization, makes improvements to an office building that it rents to Bird Corporation. Excess working capital funds are used to finance the improvements. Rose later is required to mortgage its own laboratory building, which it uses for its exempt purpose, to replenish working capital.

The mortgage on the laboratory building constitutes acquisition indebtedness; it indirectly provided funds to improve the office building.

EXAMPLE
27

15-6 REPORTING REQUIREMENTS

LO.7

List the reports that exempt organizations must file with the IRS and the related due dates.

15-6a Obtaining Exempt Organization Status

Not all exempt organizations are required to obtain IRS approval to ensure their exempt status. Churches, and entities with typical annual gross receipts of up to $5,000, need not apply for exempt status.[51] The IRS approves about 80,000 applications for exempt status every year.

Even when not required to obtain IRS approval, most exempt organizations do apply for exempt status. Typically, an organization does not want to assume that it qualifies for exempt status and describe itself in that way to the public, only to have the IRS rule later that it does not qualify.

Organizations exempt under § 501(c)(3) use Form 1023 [Application for Recognition of Exemption under Section 501(c)(3)]; small organizations file Form 1023-EZ, which requires a smaller application fee.[52] Form 1024 [Application for Recognition of Exemption under Section 501(a)] is used by most other types of exempt organizations.

---

[49]§ 514(b)(3).

[50]§ 514(c)(1). Educational organizations can exclude certain debt incurred for real property acquisitions from acquisition indebtedness.

[51]§ 508(c)(1).

[52]A small organization is defined as one that holds assets not in excess of $250,000, and its annual gross receipts for the last 3 years have not exceeded $50,000. More than one-half of all new applications for exempt status are received on Form 1023-EZ.

15-6b **Annual Filing Requirements**

Most exempt organizations are required to file an annual information return.[53] The return is filed on Form 990 (Return of Organization Exempt from Income Tax). Religious groups and Federal agencies are exempt from filing a Form 990.[54]

Small exempt organizations, whose annual gross receipts normally are $50,000 or less, must file a Form 990–N, an online form known as the e-Postcard.[55] The e-Postcard is designed to be a simpler version of the full Form 990. Supporting organizations and private foundations cannot use the Form 990–N.

The Form 990–EZ, another abbreviated version of the Form 990, can be used by exempt organizations with gross receipts of less than $200,000 and total assets of less than $500,000.

Private foundations must file Form 990–PF (Return of Private Foundation). Form 990–PF requires more information than does Form 990. Form 4720 (Return of Certain Excise Taxes on Charities and Other Persons) is used to compute any excise tax liabilities of the private foundation. The return is filed with the private foundation's Form 990–PF.

The due date for Form 990 or Form 990–PF is the fifteenth day of the fifth month after the end of the taxable year. An automatic six-month extension of the filing deadline is available.

EXAMPLE 28

Green, Inc., a § 501(c)(3) organization, has a fiscal year that ends June 30, 2020. The due date for the annual return is November 15, 2020.

If Green were a calendar year entity, the due date for its 2020 return would be May 15, 2021, with an extension available to November 15, 2021.

Exempt organizations generating UBI file Form 990–T (Exempt Organization Business Income Tax Return). The return must be filed if the organization records gross income of at least $1,000 from an unrelated trade or business.

EXAMPLE 29

Here are some illustrations of the annual filing requirements faced by exempt organizations.

- During the year, the First Church of Kentwood receives parishioner contributions of $450,000. Of this amount, $125,000 is designated for the church building fund. None of its receipts constitute unrelated business income. First Church is not required to file an annual return (Form 990) because churches are exempt from doing so. In addition, it is not required to file Form 990–T.

- Colonial, Inc., is a private foundation. Gross receipts for the year total $800,000, of which 40% is from admission fees paid by members of the general public who visit Colonial's museum of eighteenth-century life. The balance is endowment income and contributions from the founding donor. Because Colonial is a private foundation, it files Form 990–PF.

- Orange, Inc., is an exempt organization and is not a private foundation. Gross receipts for the year are $20,000. None of this amount is unrelated business income. Orange is not required to file Form 990 because its annual gross receipts do not exceed $50,000. However, it must file an e-Postcard (Form 990–N).

- Restoration, Inc., is an exempt organization. Gross receipts for the year are $100,000. None of this amount is unrelated business income. Restoration files Form 990–EZ because of its level of gross receipts.

- During the year, the Second Church of Port Allen receives parishioner contributions of $300,000. In addition, the church has unrelated business income of $5,000. Second Church is not required to file Form 990 because churches are exempt from doing so. Form 990–T must be filed, however, because churches are not exempt from the UBIT, and Second Church's earnings exceed the $1,000 "standard deduction."

---

[53] § 6033(a)(1). For public charities, the form includes the names and addresses of significant donors. Other exempt entities can omit this information from the form, but they must keep the names and addresses in their private records. This data can facilitate a later IRS audit. See Rev.Proc. 2018–38, 2018–31 I.R.B. 280.

[54] § 6033(a)(3).

[55] Rev.Proc. 2011–15, 2011–3 I.R.B. 322.

15-6c **Disclosure Requirements**

Exempt entities must make certain information readily available to the general public.[56] Copies of the following must be made available to anyone who asks.[57]

- Form 990.
- Form 1023 (or Form 1024).

Copies of the three most recent Forms 990 must be made available. Private foundations must make Form 990–PF available for public inspection.

If an individual requests the entity's tax form in person, the exempt entity must provide a copy immediately. If the request is received in writing or by e-mail, the copy must be provided within 30 days. The copy must be provided without charge, except for a reasonable fee for reproduction and mailing costs.

If the exempt entity has made the forms widely available to the general public, it is not required to fill individual requests.[58] Putting the forms on the organization's website meets this requirement. Individual requests can be disregarded if the exempt entity can show that the request is part of a harassment campaign.[59]

15-7 **TAX PLANNING**

LO.8

Identify tax planning opportunities for exempt organizations.

15-7a **General Considerations**

An organization is exempt from taxation only if it fits into one of the categories enumerated in the Code. Thus, particular attention must be given to the entity's qualification requirements. These requirements must continue to be satisfied to avoid termination of exempt status (in effect, they become maintenance requirements).

Organizations that want to engage in political activities beyond the elective lobbying limits cannot use the § 501(c)(3) classification. A § 501(c)(4) social welfare organization might be used instead. Such an entity can engage in partisan political work and promote specific candidates, as long as these activities do not reach 50 percent of its annual expenditures. Payments to a § 501(c)(4) entity are not deductible; the entity does not disclose the names of its donors.

15-7b **Maintaining Exempt Status**

To maintain exempt status, the organization must satisfy both an organizational test and an operational test. The organizational test requires that the entity satisfy the statutory requirements for exempt status based on its legal structure. The operational test ensures that the entity satisfies the statutory requirements for exempt status through its mission and operations.

King Shipping Consum., Inc. (Zion Coptic Church, Inc.) illustrates that it is usually much easier to satisfy the organizational test than the operational test.[60] Zion's stated purpose was to engage in activities usually and normally associated with churches. Based on this, the IRS approved Zion's exempt status as a § 501(c)(3) organization.

Zion's real intent, however, was to smuggle illegal drugs into the country and to distribute them for profit. The church's justification for the drugs was that it used marijuana in its sacraments. During a four-month period, however, the police confiscated 33 tons of marijuana from church members. The IRS calculated that even assuming the maximum alleged church membership of several thousand, each member would have had to consume over 33 pounds of marijuana during the four-month period.

The court concluded that Zion's real purpose was to hide a large commercial drug smuggling operation. Because this activity was inconsistent with the religious purpose for exempt status, the court upheld the IRS's revocation of Zion's exempt status and the related tax assessment of approximately $1.6 million.

---

[56]§ 6104(d), Reg. § 301.6104(d)–1, and T.D. 8818 (April 1999).

[57]An internet source of Forms 990 and 990–PF and other relevant materials concerning exempt entities is **guidestar.org**.

[58]Reg. § 301.6104(d)-2.

[59]§ 6104(d)(4).

[60]58 TCM 574, T.C.Memo. 1989–593.

15-7c Private Foundation Status

Exempt organizations that can qualify as public charities receive more beneficial tax treatment than do those that qualify as private foundations. If possible, the organization should be structured to qualify as a public charity.

EXAMPLE

30

David has undeveloped land ($25,000 adjusted basis, $100,000 fair market value) that he is going to contribute to one of the following exempt organizations: Blue, Inc., a public charity, or Teal, Inc., a private foundation. David has owned the land for five years.

David asks the manager of each organization to describe the tax benefits of contributing the land to that organization. He tells them that he is in the 35% marginal income tax bracket.

Based on the data provided by the managers, David decides to contribute the land to Blue, Inc. He calculates the amount of the charitable contribution under each option as follows.[61]

Donee	David's Contribution Deduction	David's Tax Rate	Contribution Borne by U.S. Government
Blue	$100,000	35%	$35,000
Teal	25,000 ($100,000 − $75,000)	35%	8,750

If the organization is a private foundation, care must be exercised to avoid the assessment of a tax liability on one of the prohibited transactions. This objective can best be achieved by establishing board-level and administrative controls that prevent the private foundation from engaging in transactions that trigger the imposition of the taxes. If an initial tax is assessed, corrective actions should be implemented to avoid the assessment of an additional tax.

15-7d Unrelated Business Income Tax

If the exempt organization conducts an unrelated trade or business, it may be subject to Federal income tax on the unrelated business income. Further, the unrelated trade or business could result in the loss of exempt status if the IRS determines that the activity is the primary purpose of the organization. In addition, land and buildings used to produce unrelated business income may be subject to state and local property taxes.

One approach that can be used to avoid the UBIT is for the organization to establish a taxable subsidiary to conduct the unrelated trade or business. With a subsidiary, the revenues and expenses of the exempt organization can be separated from those of the unrelated business. When the subsidiary remits its after-tax profits to the exempt organization in the form of dividends, the dividends will not be taxable to the exempt organization; dividends are eliminated from UBTI by a negative adjustment. In addition, having a taxable subsidiary conduct the unrelated trade or business avoids the possibility that the IRS will consider the unrelated business income to be an excessive percentage of the total revenues of the exempt organization.

Another approach to avoiding the UBIT is to fail the definition of an unrelated trade or business. This is accomplished by *not* satisfying at least one of the following requirements.

- The organization conducts a trade or business.
- The trade or business is not substantially related to the exempt purpose of the organization.
- The trade or business is regularly carried on by the organization.

---

[61]Contribution deductions for gifts of capital gain property made to private nonoperating foundations are limited to asset basis; § 170(e)(1)(B)(ii).

REFOCUS ON THE BIG PICTURE

EFFECT OF A FOR-PROFIT BUSINESS ON A TAX-EXEMPT ENTITY

A § 501(c)(3) entity is exempt from Federal income tax only on the conduct of its charitable activities. However, if an exempt entity generates income from the conduct of a trade or business that is not related to the organization's exempt purpose, this income generally is subject to Federal income tax. These principles can be used in analyzing Hopeful's options for the ice cream business it inherited.

- *Sell the stock of Taste Good Ice Cream.* A sale of the Taste Good Ice Cream stock is unlikely to result in much realized gain because the fair market value probably has not changed very much in the limited time between the date of Betty's death and the present. In any case, this amount is not relevant because any realized gain on the sale of the stock is tax-exempt under § 501(c)(3).

- *Conduct the ice cream business as a division of Hopeful.* Under this option, the taxable income of the ice cream chain is classified as unrelated business income. Because the ice cream division is competing with for-profit entities, it is subject to the Federal income tax that applies to corporate entities. In essence, the tax is levied because the exempt organization is engaging in substantial commercial activities.

- *Conduct the ice cream business as a wholly owned subsidiary of Hopeful.* Under this option, the ice cream chain subsidiary is classified as a feeder organization (i.e., carries on a trade or business for the benefit of an exempt organization and remits its profits to that entity). As a result, its profits will be subject to the Federal income tax on corporations.

What If?

Hopeful's board of directors must be careful that an acceptance of the Taste Good stock does not change the exempt status of the entity. If Hopeful owns "too much" of the Taste Good shares, Hopeful could lose its status as a § 501(c)(3) entity and be reclassified as a private foundation. Moreover, an excise tax could apply if Hopeful is found to have "excess business holdings" in the form of the stock.

The Hopeful board must determine how much of the total outstanding stock of Taste Good it will receive from the estate. Then it must determine the effects of a loss of the entity's public charity status, and of the UBIT on its share of Taste Good profits.

Key Terms

Debt-financed income, 15-18	Grass roots expenditures, 15-5	Unrelated business income (UBI), 15-12
Excess lobbying expenditures, 15-6	Intermediate sanctions, 15-7	
Exempt organizations, 15-2	Lobbying expenditures, 15-5	Unrelated business income tax (UBIT), 15-12
Feeder organization, 15-8	Private foundations, 15-8	

Discussion Questions

1. **LO.3** An exempt organization appropriately makes the § 501(h) election to lobby on a limited basis. The amount of its lobbying expenditures is less than its lobbying expenditures ceiling, yet it is subject to a tax at a 25% rate. Explain.

2. **LO.5** Although private foundations generally are exempt from Federal income tax, they may be subject to certain excise taxes. Identify these taxes, and discuss why they are imposed on private foundations.

3. **LO.5** Sunset, Inc., a § 501(c)(3) exempt organization that is classified as a private foundation, generates investment income of $500,000 for the current tax year. This amount represents 18% of Sunset's total income.

   a.   What type of tax imposed on Sunset is associated with its investment income?

   b.   Is the receipt of this investment income likely to result in Sunset losing its exempt status? Why or why not?

   c.   Would your answers in parts (a) and (b) change if the $500,000 represented greater than 50% of Sunset's total income? Explain.

Critical Thinking   4. **LO.4, 5** Really Welcome, Inc., a tax-exempt organization, receives 30% of its support from disqualified persons. Another disqualified person has agreed to match this support if Really Welcome will appoint him to the organization's board of directors. What tax issues are relevant to Really Welcome as it makes this decision?

5. **LO.6** Winston recently became the treasurer of Homeless, Inc., a § 501(c)(3) organization that feeds individuals who are in challenging circumstances. One of the entity's directors has proposed that Homeless purchase and operate a fast-food franchise to raise additional revenue (a projected annual increase of 45%) for its charitable mission. Because the earnings generated by the fast-food franchise would be tax-exempt, substantial additional net revenues would be provided. How should Winston respond?

6. **LO.6** An exempt hospital operates a pharmacy that is staffed by a pharmacist 24 hours per day. The pharmacy serves only hospital patients. Is the pharmacy likely an unrelated trade or business? Explain.

Critical Thinking   7. **LO.6** An exempt organization is considering conducting bingo games on Thursday nights as a way of generating additional revenue to support its exempt purpose. Before doing so, however, the president of the organization has come to you for advice regarding the effect on the organization's exempt status and whether the net income from the bingo games will be taxable. Identify the relevant tax issues.

8. **LO.6** Define the following with respect to unrelated business income computations.

   a.   Debt-financed income.

   b.   Debt-financed property.

   c.   Acquisition indebtedness.

9. **LO.1, 7** Tom is the treasurer of the Chestnut City Garden Club, a new entity in the community. A friend who is the treasurer of the garden club in a neighboring community tells Tom that it is not necessary for Chestnut to file a request for exempt status with the IRS. Has Tom received correct advice? Explain.

Critical Thinking   10. **LO.1, 7** Abby Wang recently became the treasurer of First Point Church. The church has existed for three years and never has filed any documents with the IRS.

   a.   Identify any Federal income tax reporting responsibilities that Abby might have as church treasurer.

   b.   Would your answer in part (a) change if First Point Church had existed for more than 10 years? Explain.

   c.   Would your answer in part (a) change if First Point Church had reported some unrelated business income? Explain.

11. **LO.7** Wren, Inc., a private foundation, generated $46,000 of gross receipts this year.

   a.   Must Wren file an annual information return? If so, what form should be used?

   b.   Assume instead that Wren is a § 501(c)(3) organization that is not classified as a private foundation. How would your answer in part (a) change?

12. **LO.7** Shane and Brittany both serve as treasurer for a § 501(c)(3) exempt organization. Neither exempt organization is a church. Each year Shane's exempt organization files a Form 990, while Brittany's exempt organization files a Form 990–PF. Discuss the public disclosure requirements for each exempt organization.

Computational Exercises

13. **LO.3** Helpers, Inc., a qualifying § 501(c)(3) organization, incurs lobbying expenditures of $250,000 for the taxable year and grass roots expenditures of $0. Exempt purpose expenditures for the taxable year are $1,200,000. Helpers elects to be eligible to make lobbying expenditures on a limited basis.

    a. What amount of lobbying expenditures is Helpers allowed to make tax-free under the terms of the election?

    b. What is its tax liability as a result of the election?

    c. Express your answer to part (b) as a Microsoft Excel formula.

14. **LO.3** Davis, an officer for a § 501(c)(3) organization, receives benefits in the form of an overly generous health insurance plan; these benefits are inappropriate in the context of a charitable entity of its type. The excess benefits are determined to be $35,000. Davis does not pay back the excess benefits to the organization before the first-level tax is due.

    a. Apply the rules for intermediate sanctions. What amount of first-level taxes are imposed on Davis? On the exempt organization management?

    b. What amount of second-level taxes are imposed on Davis?

15. **LO.5** Rejoice, Inc., a private foundation, has existed for 10 years. Rejoice held undistributed income of $160,000 at the end of its 2017 tax year. Of this amount, $90,000 was distributed in 2018, and $70,000 was distributed during the first quarter of 2019. The IRS mailed a deficiency notice to Rejoice on August 1, 2020, relating to the entity's undistributed income.

    a. What is Rejoice's initial tax on the 2017 undistributed taxable income for 2018? For 2019?

    b. Express the 2018 tax computation as a Microsoft Excel formula.

    c. What is Rejoice's additional tax for 2020?

Problems

16. **LO.1** Match the following exempt organizations with the statutory authority under which exempt status is granted. The statutory authority may apply to more than one exempt organization. Not all of the authority citations are used.

Exempt Organizations	Statutory Authority
Girl Scouts	§ 501(c)(1)
St. Mary Catholic Church	§ 501(c)(2)
American Red Cross	§ 501(c)(3)
Salvation Army	§ 501(c)(4)
United Fund	§ 501(c)(5)
Bill and Melinda Gates Foundation	§ 501(c)(6)
University of Richmond	§ 501(c)(7)
Underwriters Laboratories (UL)	§ 501(c)(8)
Ladies PGA Tour	§ 501(c)(9)
Veterans of Foreign Wars (VFW)	§ 501(c)(10)
Dallas Rodeo Club	§ 501(c)(11)
PTA	§ 501(c)(12)
Toano Cemetery Association	§ 501(c)(13)
Alpha Chi Omega Sorority	§ 501(c)(14)
Green, Inc., Legal Services Plan	§ 501(c)(15)
National Press Club	§ 501(c)(16)
Federal Deposit Insurance Corporation (FDIC)	§ 501(c)(19)
League of Women Voters	§ 501(c)(20)
	§ 501(d)

17. **LO.2, 3** Wellness, Inc., a § 501(c)(3) organization, makes lobbying expenditures of $340,000 this year. Charitable expenditures were $600,000 for the first six months of the year and $950,000 for the last six months of the year. Determine the Federal income tax consequences to Wellness if:

    a. It does not make the § 501(h) lobbying election.

    b. It does make the § 501(h) lobbying election.

18. **LO.3** Wish, Inc., a § 501(c)(3) organization, pays unreasonable compensation to Renata, the treasurer of Wish. Renata's compensation is $600,000. Assume that reasonable compensation would be $500,000.

    a. Apply the rules for intermediate sanctions. Determine any tax consequences for Wish, Inc.

    b. Determine any tax consequences for Renata.

Decision Making

Communications

19. **LO.3, 6, 8** Roadrunner, Inc., is an exempt medical organization. Quail, Inc., a sporting goods retailer, is a wholly owned subsidiary of Roadrunner. Roadrunner inherited the Quail stock last year from a major benefactor of the medical organization. Quail's taxable income is $550,000. Quail will remit all of its earnings, net of any taxes, to Roadrunner every year, to support the exempt purpose of the parent.

    a. Is Quail subject to Federal income tax? If so, calculate the liability.

    b. Arthur Morgan, the treasurer of Roadrunner, has contacted you regarding minimizing or eliminating Quail's Federal income tax liability. He would like to know if the tax consequences would be better if Quail were liquidated into Roadrunner. Write a letter to Arthur that contains your advice. Roadrunner's address is 500 Rouse Tower, Rochester, NY 14627.

20. **LO.3** Initiate, Inc., a § 501(c)(3) organization, receives the following revenues and incurs the following expenses.

Grant from Bill and Melinda Gates Foundation	$ 70,000
Charitable contributions received	625,000
Expenses in carrying out its exempt mission	500,000
Net income before taxes of Landscaping, Inc., a wholly owned for-profit subsidiary	400,000

Landscaping, Inc., remits all of its after-tax profits each year to Initiate. Calculate the amount of the Federal income tax, if any, for Initiate and for Landscaping.

Communications

21. **LO.4** Pigeon, Inc., a § 501(c)(3) organization, received support from the following sources.

Governmental unit A for services rendered	$ 6,300
Governmental unit B for services rendered	4,500
Fees from the general public for services rendered (Each payment was of $100)	75,000
Gross investment income	39,000
Contributions from disqualified persons	26,000
Contributions from other than disqualified persons (Each gift was of $50)	160,000
Total support	$310,800

    a. Does Pigeon satisfy the test for receiving broad public support? Why or why not?

    b. Is Pigeon a private foundation? Be specific in your answer.

    c. Elena Mariñez, Pigeon's treasurer, has asked you for advice on whether Pigeon is a private foundation. Write a letter to Elena in which you address the issue. Her address is 250 Bristol Road, Charlottesville, VA 22903.

22. **LO.5** Gray, Inc., a private foundation, reports the following items of income and deductions. Gray is not eligible for the 1% tax rate on net investment income.

Interest income	$ 29,000
Rent income	61,000
Dividend income	15,000
Royalty income	22,000
Unrelated business income	80,000
Rent expenses	(26,000)
Unrelated business expenses	(12,000)

a. Calculate Gray's net investment income.
b. Calculate Gray's tax on net investment income.

23. **LO.5, 8** Otis is the CEO of Rectify, Inc., a private foundation. Otis invests $500,000 **Critical Thinking** (80%) of the foundation's investment portfolio in high-risk derivatives. Previously, the $500,000 had been invested in corporate bonds with an AA rating that earned 4% per annum. If the derivatives investment works as Otis's investment adviser claims, the annual earnings could be as high as 20%.

a. Determine whether Rectify is subject to any of the taxes imposed on private foundations.
b. If so, calculate the amount of the initial tax.
c. If so, calculate the amount of the additional tax if the act causing the imposition of the tax is not addressed within the correction period.
d. Are Otis and the foundation better off financially if the prohibited transaction, if any, is addressed within the correction period? Explain.

24. **LO.5** The board of directors of White Pearl, Inc., a private foundation, consists of Charlyne, Beth, and Carlos. They vote unanimously to provide a $500,000 grant to Carlos. The grant is to be used for travel and education and does not qualify as a permitted grant to individuals (i.e., it is an act of self-dealing).

a. Calculate the initial tax imposed on White Pearl.
b. Calculate the initial tax imposed on the foundation manager (i.e., board of directors).
c. Express the computation in part (b) as a Microsoft Excel formula.

25. **LO.6** The Open Museum is an exempt organization that operates a gift shop. The **Communications** museum's annual operations budget is $3,200,000. Gift shop sales generate a profit of $900,000. Another $600,000 of investment income is generated by the museum's endowment fund.

Both the income from the gift shop and the endowment income are used to support the exempt purpose of the museum. The balance of $1,700,000 required for annual operations is provided through admission fees.

Wayne Hsu, a new board member, does not understand why the museum is subject to tax at all, particularly because all of the entity's profits are used in carrying out the mission of the museum. The museum's address is 250 Oak Avenue, Peoria, IL 61625.

a. Calculate the amount of unrelated business income.
b. Assume instead that the investment income is reinvested in the endowment fund, rather than used to support annual operations. Calculate the amount of unrelated business income.
c. As the museum treasurer, write a letter to Wayne explaining the reason for the tax consequences. Wayne's address is 45 Pine Avenue, Peoria, IL 61625.

26. **LO.6** Upward and Onward, Inc., a § 501(c)(3) organization that provides training programs for government assistance recipients, reports the following income and expenses from the sale of products associated with the training program. Calculate Upward and Onward's UBIT.

Gross income from sales	$425,000
Cost of goods sold	106,000
Advertising and selling expenses	26,000
Administrative expenses	112,500

a. Assume that the sale of the training program products is substantially related to Upward and Onward's exempt purpose.

b. Assume that the sale of the training program products is not substantially related to Upward and Onward's exempt purpose.

Communications   27. **LO.6** Perch, Inc., an exempt organization, records unrelated business taxable income of $4,000,000.

a. Calculate Perch's UBIT.

b. Prepare an outline of a presentation you are going to give to the new members of Perch's board on why Perch is subject to the UBIT even though it is an exempt organization.

28. **LO.6** For each of the following organizations, determine its UBTI and any related UBIT.

a. AIDS, Inc., an exempt charitable organization that provides support for individuals with AIDS, operates a retail medical supply store open to the general public. The net income of the store, before any Federal income taxes, is $305,000.

b. St. Andrew Episcopal Church operates a retail gift shop. The inventory consists of the typical items sold by commercial gift shops in the city. The director of the gift shop estimates that 80% of the gift shop sales are to tourists and 20% are to church members. The net income of the gift shop, before the salaries of the three gift shop employees and any Federal income taxes, is $300,000. The salaries of the employees total $80,000.

c. Education, Inc., a private university, has placed vending machines in the student dormitories and academic buildings on campus. In recognition of recent tuition increases, the university has adopted a policy of merely trying to recover its costs associated with the vending machine activity. For the current year, however, the net income of the activity, before any Federal income taxes, is $75,000.

29. **LO.6** For each of the following organizations, determine its UBTI and any related UBIT.

a. Worn, Inc., an exempt organization, provides food for the homeless. It operates a thrift store that sells used clothing to the general public. The thrift shop is staffed solely by four salaried employees. All of the clothes it sells are received as contributions. The $100,000 profit generated for the year by the thrift shop is used in Worn's mission of providing food to the homeless.

b. Small, Inc., an exempt organization, recorded gross unrelated business income of $900 and unrelated business expenses of $400.

c. In Care, Inc., is a § 501(c)(3) exempt organization. It owns a convenience store and gas pumps, which it received as a bequest from a patron. The store/gas pumps entity is operated as StopBy, a C corporation. Because StopBy is profitable, In Care hires a manager and several employees to run the entity. For the current year, StopBy's profit is $640,000. All of this amount is distributed by StopBy to In Care to use in carrying out its exempt mission.

30. **LO.6** Harmony, Inc., an exempt organization, reports unrelated business income of $7,500 and unrelated business expenses of $4,000. Calculate Harmony's UBIT.

31. **LO.6** Falcon Basketball League, an exempt organization, is a youth basketball   Communications
      league for children ages 12 through 14. The league has been in existence for
30 years. In the past, revenue for operations has been provided through community
fund-raising and the sale of snacks at the games by the parents. Due to a projected
revenue shortfall of approximately $5,000, the governing board has decided to
charge admission to the basketball games of $1.00 for adults and $0.50 for children.

   a.   Will the admission charge affect Falcon's exempt status? Explain.

   b.   What are the tax consequences to Falcon of the net income from snack sales
        and the new admission fee?

   c.   As the volunteer treasurer of the Falcon League, prepare a memo for the entity's
        board in which you explain the effect, if any, of the admission fee policy on
        Falcon's exempt status.

32. **LO.6** Forward, Inc., is an exempt organization that assists disabled individuals by
      training them in digital TV repair. Used digital TVs are donated to Forward,
Inc., by both organizations and individuals. Some of the donated digital TVs are
operational, but others are not. After being used in the training program, the digital
TVs, all of which are now operational, are sold to the general public. Forward's
revenues and expenses for the current period are reported as follows.

Contributions	$ 700,000
Revenues from digital TV sales	3,600,000
Administrative expenses	500,000
Materials and supplies for digital TV repairs	800,000
Utilities	25,000
Wages paid to disabled individuals in the training program	
(at minimum-wage rate)	1,200,000
Rent for building and equipment	250,000

   Any revenues not expended during the current period are deposited in a reserve
fund to finance future activities.

   a.   Is the digital TV repair and sales activity an unrelated trade or business?
        Explain.

   b.   Calculate the net income of Forward, Inc., and the related Federal income tax
        liability, if any.

33. **LO.6** Save the Squirrels, Inc., a § 501(c)(3) organization that feeds the squirrels in
      municipal parks, receives a $250,000 contribution from Animal Feed, Inc.,
a for-profit entity that sells animal feed. In exchange for the contribution, Save the
Squirrels will identify Animal Feed as a major supporter in its monthly newsletter.
Determine Save the Squirrels's UBTI and any related UBIT under the following
independent assumptions.

   a.   Save the Squirrels receives no other similar payments.

   b.   Save the Squirrels agrees to identify Animal Feed as a major supporter and
        to include a half-page advertisement for Animal Feed products in its monthly
        newsletter as a result of the contribution.

34. **LO.6** Faith Community Church is exempt from Federal income taxation under   Critical Thinking
      § 501(c)(3). To supplement its contribution revenue, it holds bingo games on
Saturday nights. It holds all of the licenses and permits required to do so.

   The net income from the bingo games is $90,000. Of these funds, $60,000 is used
to support the ministry of the church. The balance of $30,000 is invested in Faith's
endowment fund for church music.

   Faith Community Church is located in a resort city where bingo games can be
conducted by churches, charities, and for-profit entities.

   a.   Will conducting the bingo games affect the exempt status of Faith Community
        Church? Explain.

   b.   Calculate the Federal tax liability, if any, associated with the bingo games.

35. **LO.6** Fish, Inc., an exempt organization, reports unrelated business income of $500,000 (before any charitable contribution deduction). During the year, Fish makes charitable contributions of $54,000, of which $38,000 is associated with the unrelated trade or business.

    a.   Calculate Fish's unrelated business taxable income (UBTI).

    b.   Express your computation in part (a) as a Microsoft Excel formula.

    c.   Assume instead that the charitable contributions are $41,000, of which $38,000 is associated with the unrelated trade or business. Calculate the UBTI.

36. **LO.3, 6** Comfort, Inc., an exempt hospital, is going to operate a pharmacy that will be classified as an unrelated trade or business. Comfort establishes the pharmacy as a wholly owned subsidiary. During the current year, the subsidiary generates taxable income of $280,000 and pays dividends of $200,000 to Comfort.

    a.   What are the tax consequences to the subsidiary?

    b.   What are the tax consequences to Comfort?

37. **LO.6** Kind, Inc., an exempt organization, leases land, a building, and factory equipment to Shirts, Inc. Shirts is a taxable entity that manufactures shirts for distribution through its factory outlet stores. The rent income and the related expenses for Kind are as follows.

	Rent Income	Rent Expenses
Land and building	$100,000	$40,000
Factory equipment	125,000	25,000

    a.   Calculate the amount of Kind's unrelated business income.

    b.   Assume instead that Kind's rent income and expenses are recorded as follows. Compute Kind's unrelated business income.

	Rent Income	Rent Expenses
Land and building	$100,000	$20,000
Factory equipment	125,000	50,000

38. **LO.6** Save, Inc., an exempt organization, sells the following assets during the tax year. Determine the effect of these transactions on Save's unrelated business taxable income.

Asset	Gain (Loss)	Use
Land and building	$100,000	In exempt purpose
Land	25,000	In exempt purpose
Equipment	(12,000)	Leased to a taxable entity
Automobile	(9,000)	Leased to a taxable entity

39. **LO.7** Seagull, Inc., a § 501(c)(3) exempt organization, uses a tax year that ends on October 31. Seagull's gross receipts are $600,000, and related expenses are $580,000.

    a.   Is Seagull required to file an annual Form 990?

    b.   If so, what is the due date?

40. **LO.7** Wong, Inc., a § 501(c)(3) organization, is a private foundation with a tax year that ends on May 31. Gross receipts for the fiscal year are $180,000, and the related expenses are $160,000.

    a.   Is the entity required to file an annual information return?

    b.   If so, what form is used?

    c.   If so, what is the due date?

    d.   How would your answers in parts (a), (b), and (c) change if Wong were an exempt organization that was not a private foundation?

Research Problems

Note: Solutions to the Research Problems can be prepared by using the Thomson Reuters Checkpoint™ online tax research database, which accompanies this textbook. Solutions can also be prepared by using research materials found in a typical tax library.

THOMSON REUTERS
CHECKPOINT™

Research Problem 1. Wonderful Wilderness, Inc., is a tax-exempt organization. Its mission is to "make the world a greener place through education, research, exploration, and restoration."

Communications

Lloyd Morgan, the chief financial officer, presents you with the following information. Wonderful Wilderness raises funds to support its mission in a variety of ways, including contributions and membership fees. As part of this effort, Wonderful Wilderness develops and maintains mailing lists of its members, donors, catalog purchasers, and other supporters.

Wonderful Wilderness holds exclusive ownership rights to its mailing lists. To acquire the names of additional prospective members and supporters, Wonderful Wilderness occasionally exchanges membership lists with other organizations. In addition, Wonderful Wilderness permits other tax-exempt organizations and commercial entities to pay a fee, identified in an annually updated schedule, to use its mailing lists on a one-time basis per transaction.

Lloyd is aware that the Federal income tax law applies a UBIT. He is also aware of the § 512(b)(2) provision that excludes royalties from the UBIT. An IRS agent has raised the issue that the revenue from the use of the mailing lists by other entities may be taxable as unrelated business income. Lloyd wants you to research this issue.

Write a letter to Lloyd that contains your findings, and prepare a memo for the tax research files. Wonderful Wilderness's address is 100 Wilderness Way, Pocatello, ID 83209.

Research Problem 2. Your client, Rich N. Ready, has come to you for advice. Rich is interested in many social welfare issues (e.g., access to higher education, prison reform, and abortion rights). He wants to use his wealth to educate the general public on these issues, as well as to influence related legislation. Further, he wants to assist the financing of campaigns for political candidates who reflect his views.

Communications

Rich's friend Penny suggested that he organize a § 501(c)(4) organization, telling him not only that such organizations are tax-exempt but also that they need not disclose the names of their donors. Thus, Rich could participate in these activities anonymously. However, Rich read that such an organization must be operated exclusively for "the promotion of social welfare." This would seem to preclude the lobbying and political campaigning support that Rich desires.

Is a § 501(c)(4) organization appropriate for Rich's plans? Summarize your findings in an e-mail to your instructor; be specific in your answer(s).

Use internet tax resources to address the following questions. Look for reliable websites and blogs of the IRS and other government agencies, media outlets, businesses, tax professionals, academics, think tanks, and political outlets.

Research Problem 3. With respect to the constitutionality of a church to engage in political activities, submit to your instructor a two-page paper defining and tracing the history of the so-called *Johnson Amendment*.

Communications
Critical Thinking

Research Problem 4. Send your instructor a graph of the number of tax returns reporting UBI, and the UBIT collected from those returns, for the last 20 years. Use five-year intervals in your analysis.

Data Analytics

Communications   **Research Problem 5.** Verify the exempt status of the symphony orchestra that performs closest to your home. Who are its three highest-paid associates? Send an e-mail to your instructor summarizing your results and explaining how you found this information.

Data Analytics   **Research Problem 6.** Use **guidestar.org** to obtain the following information on the Jamestown Yorktown Foundation, Inc., which is located in Williamsburg, Virginia.

- Locate the foundation's website.
- Under what paragraph of § 501(c) do you believe is the organization exempt from Federal income tax?
- Use the organization's Form 990 to determine the entity's total budget and the amount of compensation paid to officers and directors.

Becker CPA Review Questions

1. Unrelated business income (UBI):
   a. includes unrelated income from an activity where all the work is performed by volunteers.
   b. is not created if the activity results in a loss.
   c. is 100% taxable on the exempt organization's tax return.
   d. specifically excludes income from the research of a college or hospital.

2. Which of the following is a false statement?
   a. An annual information return (Form 990) stating gross income, receipts, contributions, and disbursements is required of most exempt organizations that are exempt from tax.
   b. For organizations that normally have less than $50,000 in annual gross receipts, a Form 990 or 990–EZ is not required; however, an electronic postcard (Form 990–N) is filed with the IRS and provides only limited information.
   c. An organization operated primarily for the purposes of carrying on a trade or business for profit can claim exemption from tax if all of its profits are payable to exempt organizations.
   d. If an organization fails to file the required return for three consecutive years, the tax-exempt status of the organization will be revoked.

Multistate Corporate Taxation

LEARNING OBJECTIVES: *After completing Chapter 16, you should be able to:*

LO.1 Illustrate the computation of a multistate corporation's state income tax liability.

LO.2 Define nexus and explain its role in state income taxation.

LO.3 Distinguish between allocation and apportionment of a multistate corporation's taxable income.

LO.4 Describe the nature and treatment of business and nonbusiness income.

LO.5 Discuss the sales, payroll, and property apportionment factors.

LO.6 Apply the unitary method of state income taxation.

LO.7 Discuss the states' income tax treatment of S corporations, partnerships, and LLCs.

LO.8 Describe other commonly encountered state and local taxes on businesses.

LO.9 Recognize tax planning opportunities available to minimize a corporation's state and local tax liability.

CHAPTER OUTLINE

THE BIG PICTURE

MAKING A MULTISTATE LOCATION DECISION

LocalCo has customers in most U.S. states. It does not employ a traditional sales force. Instead, it sells its products exclusively through internet solicitations and its elaborate website.

LocalCo has two product lines: cell phone accessories, which it manufactures in Alabama, and various sports-themed apparel items, all of which are produced in California. LocalCo has been quite profitable in the past, and it holds a sizable investment portfolio, made up chiefly of U.S. Treasury securities. Banking, payroll, and other administrative operations are located in rural New York State, where the entity is incorporated. LocalCo's rank-and-file employees receive compensation packages that are below the national median, but its top 10 executives are highly paid.

In an effort to "go green," LocalCo wants to hold down its costs for shipping raw materials to its manufacturing facilities and for sending its sold goods to customers. Thus, it is considering the construction of a sizable new multifunction building. Ideally, the new facility would have access to both interstate highways and a reliable airport with excess capacity for freight operations.

How will LocalCo's expansion decision be affected by state and local tax considerations?

Read the chapter and formulate your response.

Although most of this text concentrates on the effects of the Federal income tax law upon the computation of a taxpayer's annual tax liability, a variety of tax bases apply to most business taxpayers. For instance, a multinational corporation may be subject to tax in a number of different countries (see Chapter 9). Furthermore, estimates are that at least 40 percent of the income tax dollars paid by business taxpayers go to state and local authorities.

U.S. state and local governments collect more than $2.3 trillion in taxes and fees each year; this comes to almost $5,000 per individual citizen. Individual income and sales/use taxes account for about one-fourth of state and local tax collections each. Local property taxes bring in about one-third of all revenues, and corporate income taxes bring in almost 5 percent.

State/Local Taxes in Context

Businesses operate in a multistate environment for a variety of reasons. For the most part, nontax motivations drive such location decisions as where to build new plants or distribution centers or whether to move communications and data processing facilities and corporate headquarters. For instance, a business typically wants to be close to its largest markets and to operate in a positive private- and public-sector business climate, where it has access to well-trained and reasonably priced labor, suppliers and support operations, sources of natural resources, communication facilities, and transportation networks.

Many location decisions, though, are motivated by multistate tax considerations, such as the following.

- Tax credits and other incentives that encourage businesses to relocate, expand, or retain jobs in the area. Some of the incentives include *clawback* provisions, under which the tax savings granted must be returned to the state by the business if new job targets are not met or construction projects not completed.

- The compliance burdens created by each new level of tax compliance. For instance, how many tax returns must be filed by a three-shareholder S corporation operating in 15 states?

- The extent to which a local political climate encourages tax burdens on visitors and others who have no direct say in the reelection of local politicians.

This chapter reviews the basic tax concepts that are predominant among most states that impose a tax based on net income,[1] and it discusses the major areas in which tax planning can reduce a corporation's overall state tax burden. The discussion concludes with a review of other types of taxes used by the U.S. states, with a special focus on sales and use taxes.

16-1 OVERVIEW OF CORPORATE STATE INCOME TAXATION

Forty-six states and the District of Columbia impose a tax based on a C corporation's taxable income. Because each state is free to create its own tax provisions, the taxpayer could be faced with 47 entirely different sets of state tax provisions.[2] None of the states, moreover, have piggybacked their tax collections with the IRS.

---

[1]Some states refer to their tax on corporate income as a franchise tax, a business tax, a license tax, or a business profits tax.

[2]The District of Columbia operates in much the same manner as a state and imposes a tax based on income. Four states impose no corporate income tax at all: Nevada, South Dakota, Washington, and Wyoming. Corporations, however, are subject to a business and occupation tax in Washington. Several states base the tax on the entity's gross receipts, not on net income.

16-1a **Computing State Income Tax**

LO.1

Illustrate the computation of a multistate corporation's state income tax liability.

In more than 40 of the states that impose a corporate income tax, the starting point in computing the tax base is taxable income as reflected on the Federal corporate income tax return (Form 1120). Those states whose computation of state taxable income is not coupled to the Federal tax return have their own state-specific definitions of gross and taxable income. Nonetheless, even these states typically adopt most Federal income and deduction provisions.

Although Federal tax law plays a significant role in the computation of state taxable income, there is a wide disparity in both the methods used to determine a state's taxable income and the tax rates imposed on that income. Only a few states apply more than one or two tax rates to taxable income, so there is little progressivity to these tax systems.

State tax credits typically are designed to encourage increased hiring and investment in local facilities. Cities and states often use targeted tax credits to entice businesses to expand within their borders. For instance, a state might offer a $50,000 credit for each new job created by the taxpayer or a 15 percent credit for taxpayers who purchase automobiles that were assembled in the state.

Generally, the accounting period and methods used by a corporation for state tax purposes must be consistent with those used on the Federal return. States often apply different rules, however, in identifying the members of a group filing a consolidated return and the income of each group member that is subject to tax.

Virtually all of the states that levy an income tax require notification of the final settlement of a Federal income tax audit. In addition, some states share their audit results with other states. State authorities then adjust the originally calculated state tax liability to account for these out-of-state audit changes.

The formula used by a multistate corporation to determine its tax liability in a typical state is illustrated in Exhibit 16.1.

16-1b **State Modifications**

Federal taxable income generally is used as the starting point in computing the state's income tax base, but state adjustments or modifications often are made to Federal taxable income to:

- Reflect differences between state and Federal tax statutes.
- Remove income that a state is constitutionally prohibited from taxing.

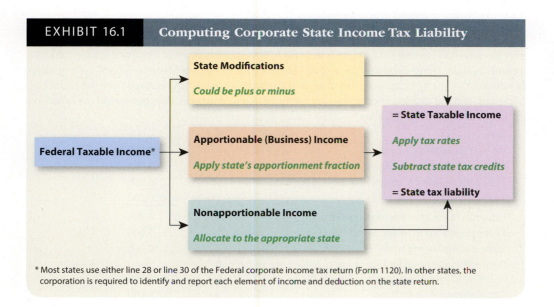

EXHIBIT 16.1   Computing Corporate State Income Tax Liability

* Most states use either line 28 or line 30 of the Federal corporate income tax return (Form 1120). In other states, the corporation is required to identify and report each element of income and deduction on the state return.

EXHIBIT 16.2	Common State Corporate Income Tax Modifications

Addition Modifications

Interest income received on state and municipal obligations and any other interest income that is exempt from Federal income tax. For this purpose, some states exempt interest earned on their own obligations.

Expenses deducted in computing Federal taxable income that are directly or indirectly related to U.S. obligations.

Income-based franchise and income taxes imposed by any state and the District of Columbia that were deducted in computing Federal taxable income.

The amount by which the Federal deductions for depreciation, amortization, or depletion exceed those permitted by the state.

The amount by which the state gain or loss from the disposal of assets differs from the Federal gain or loss. Due to the difference in permitted depreciation methods and other adjustments, a corporation's assets may have different Federal and state tax bases. This adjustment is not necessary if the state and Federal basis provisions are identical.

Adjustments required as a result of different elections being made for state and Federal purposes. Examples of such elections include the methods under which income from installment sales or long-term contracts is determined.

Federal net operating loss deduction, if the starting point in the computation of taxable income is Federal taxable income after special deductions.

Subtraction Modifications

Interest on U.S. obligations or obligations of Federal agencies to the extent included in Federal taxable income but exempt from state income taxes under U.S. law.

Expenses that are directly or indirectly related to the state and municipal interest that is taxable for state purposes.

Refunds of franchise and income taxes imposed by any state and the District of Columbia, to the extent included in Federal taxable income.

The amount by which the state deductions for depreciation, amortization, or depletion exceed the deductions permitted for Federal tax purposes.

Adjustments required as a result of different elections being made for state and Federal purposes, as above.

Dividends received from other U.S. corporations, to the extent included in Federal taxable income.

Net operating loss deduction as determined for state tax purposes.

The required modifications to Federal taxable income vary significantly among the states. Accordingly, this discussion is limited to the most common additions and subtractions the states require. Exhibit 16.2 lists the most frequently encountered modifications. In computing the taxable income for a given state, only a selected number of these modifications may be applicable.

Computing State Taxable Income

EXAMPLE 1

Blue Corporation is subject to tax only in State A. The starting point in computing Blue's taxable income in State A is Federal taxable income. Modifications then are made to reflect, among other provisions, the exempt status of interest on A obligations, all dividends received from other U.S. corporations, and the disallowance of a deduction for state income taxes. Blue generated the following income and deductions this year.

Sales	$1,500,000
Interest on Federal obligations	50,000
Interest on municipal obligations of State B	100,000
Dividends received from 30% owned U.S. corporations	200,000
Total income	$1,850,000
Expenses related to Federal obligations	$ 1,000
Expenses related to municipal obligations	5,000
State income tax expense	50,000
Depreciation allowed for Federal tax purposes (the deduction allowed for state purposes is $300,000)	400,000
Other allowable deductions	1,000,000
Total deductions	$1,456,000

continued

Blue's taxable income for Federal and state purposes is computed as follows.

Federal Taxable Income	
Sales	$1,500,000
Interest on Federal obligations	50,000
Dividends received from U.S. corporations	200,000
Total income	$1,750,000
Expenses related to Federal obligations	$ 1,000
State income tax expense	50,000
Depreciation	400,000
Other allowable deductions	1,000,000
Total deductions	$1,451,000
Taxable income before special deductions	$ 299,000
Less: Dividends received deduction (65% × $200,000)	(130,000)
Federal taxable income	$ 169,000

State A Taxable Income	
Federal taxable income	$169,000
Addition Modifications	
Interest on State B obligations	100,000
State income tax expense	50,000
Excess depreciation deduction allowed for Federal purposes ($400,000 − $300,000)	100,000
Expenses related to Federal obligations	1,000
Subtraction Modifications	
Expenses related to State B obligations	(5,000)
Dividends from other corporations, to extent included in Federal taxable income ($200,000 − $130,000)	(70,000)
Interest on Federal obligations	(50,000)
State A taxable income	$295,000

Continue with the facts of Example 1, except that the $100,000 of municipal bond interest (and related expenses) are associated with State A obligations. The computation of Federal taxable income is unaffected by this change. Because State A exempts interest on its own obligations from taxation, Blue's A taxable income now is $200,000.

EXAMPLE
2

State A Taxable Income	
Federal taxable income	$169,000
Addition Modifications	
State income tax expense	50,000
Excess depreciation deduction allowed for Federal purposes ($400,000 − $300,000)	100,000
Expenses related to Federal obligations	1,000
Subtraction Modifications	
Dividends from other U.S. corporations, to extent included in Federal taxable income ($200,000 − $130,000)	(70,000)
Interest on Federal obligations	(50,000)
State A taxable income	$200,000

16-1c The UDITPA and the Multistate Tax Commission

The Uniform Division of Income for Tax Purposes Act (**UDITPA**) is a model law relating to the assignment of income among the states for corporations that maintain operations in more than one state (multistate corporations). Many states have adopted the provisions of the UDITPA, either by joining the Multistate Tax Compact or by modeling their laws after the provisions of the UDITPA.

The **Multistate Tax Commission (MTC)** writes regulations and other rules that interpret the UDITPA. When a new MTC rule or regulation is created, the member states propose its adoption to their respective legislatures. The majority of member states adopt the regulations with no exceptions or only minor changes.[3]

Define nexus and explain its role in state income taxation.

16-1d Jurisdiction to Impose Tax: Nexus and Public Law 86–272

The state in which a business is incorporated (i.e., its state of *domicile*) has the jurisdiction to tax the corporation regardless of the volume of its business activity within the state. Whether a state can tax the income of a business that is incorporated in a different state (i.e., in a nondomicile state) usually depends on the level of activity of the taxpayer in the state and on state law and principles of the U.S. constitution.

The term **nexus** describes the degree of business activity that must be present before a taxing jurisdiction has the right to impose a tax on an out-of-state entity's income. Generally, each state defines nexus differently. Typically, sufficient nexus is present when a corporation derives income from sources within the state, owns or leases property in the state, employs personnel in the state, or has physical or financial capital there.

Public Law 86–272 (P.L. 86–272) limits the states' right to impose an income tax on certain interstate activities.[4] This Federal law prohibits a state from taxing a business whose only connection with the state is to solicit orders for sales of tangible personal property that is sent outside the state for approval or rejection. If approved, the orders must be filled and shipped by the business from a point outside the state.

Only the sales of tangible personal property are immune from taxation under this law, however. Leases, rentals, and other dispositions of tangible personal property are not protected activities. Moreover, dispositions of real property and intangible property, as well as sales of services, are not protected by P.L. 86–272.

Business activity that involves tangible personal property and consists merely of solicitation is immune from taxation. The statute does not define the term *solicitation*, but the Supreme Court has held that *solicitation of orders* includes any explicit verbal request for orders and any speech or conduct that implicitly invites an order.[5] The Court also created a *de minimis* rule, allowing immunity from nexus where a limited amount of solicitation occurs.

Exhibit 16.3 summarizes the activities the MTC has identified as being directly related to solicitation (protected activities) and activities unrelated to solicitation (which establish income tax nexus for the entity).

16-1e Nexus beyond P.L. 86–272

P.L. 86–272 was enacted by Congress in 1959. Along with providing an income tax nexus standard for businesses selling tangible personal property, it called for a congressional study of state taxes. The goal was to derive an appropriate solution for state taxation of multistate business income without impeding interstate commerce. No substantial changes came out of the study despite its detailed comments and recommendations.

---

[3]Many of the states that are not members of the Multistate Tax Compact still model their laws after the UDITPA and the MTC regulations.

[4]15 U.S.C. §§ 381–385.

[5]*Wisconsin Department of Revenue v. William Wrigley, Jr., Co.*, 505 U.S. 214 (1992).

EXHIBIT 16.3	Common Nexus Definitions under P.L. 86–272

General rule P.L. 86–272 immunity from income tax nexus applies for sales of tangible personal property, where the sales representative's activities are ancillary to the order-solicitation process.

Activities That Usually Do Not Create Nexus

- Advertising campaigns.
- Carrying free samples only for display or distribution.
- Owning or furnishing automobiles, phones, and computers to salespersons.
- Passing inquiries or complaints on to the home office.
- Maintaining a sample or display room for two weeks or less during the year.

Activities Usually Sufficient to Establish Nexus

- Approving or rejecting orders.
- Making repairs or providing maintenance.
- Collecting delinquent accounts; investigating creditworthiness.
- Conducting installation or supervising installation.
- Conducting training classes, seminars, or lectures for persons other than sales personnel.
- Picking up or replacing damaged or returned property.
- Hiring, training, or supervising personnel other than sales employees.
- Providing shipping information and coordinating deliveries.
- Owning, leasing, maintaining, or otherwise using any of the following facilities or property in the state.

  - ➤ Real estate.
  - ➤ Parts department.
  - ➤ Employment office.
  - ➤ Meeting place for directors, officers, or employees.

  - ➤ Purchasing office.
  - ➤ Warehouse.
  - ➤ Call center.
  - ➤ Mobile retailing (e.g., trucks with driver-salespersons).

States and the MTC have issued regulations and interpretations of P.L. 86–272, but the law is not robust enough to account for many of today's economic transactions (e.g., sales of realty and intangible assets, net income from services, and sales conducted using e-commerce). As a result, many states contend that a broader definition of income tax nexus is needed. This alternative approach often is referred to as *economic nexus* because it is triggered by business and other activities, and not by more traditional legal connections or physical presence.

Several states, following an MTC model statute, automatically assign nexus to a taxpayer that exceeds at least one of the following thresholds for the tax year. As more states take this approach, the "factor presence nexus" standard may provide additional uniformity among the states as to measuring the taxpayer's business activities.

- $50,000 of property.
- $50,000 of payroll.
- $500,000 of sales.

- 25% of total property.
- 25% of total payroll.
- 25% of total sales.

These nexus standards provide a measure of the sales or solicitation activity in the state that indicates a "sufficient" economic presence to trigger income taxation there, even if the business has little or no physical presence in the state.

Concept Summary 16.1 places in context the role of multistate income taxation for U.S. business entities.

Concept Summary 16.1

Multistate Taxation

1. For a profitable business entity that operates in multiple U.S. states, at least 40 percent of the total tax expense may be made up of levies by state and local governments.

2. State and local tax incentives might be used to accomplish political goals or to provide incentives for businesses to remain in, or relocate to, the taxing jurisdiction.

3. A U.S. state can apply an income tax only on a business that has a sufficient presence ("nexus") with the state.

4. Multistate income tax planning involves the reduction of the overall state and local tax burden. This may be the result of being subject to tax in the fewest number of states or of reducing the tax burden in a particular state.

LO.3

Distinguish between allocation and apportionment of a multistate corporation's taxable income.

16-2 ALLOCATION AND APPORTIONMENT OF INCOME

A corporation that conducts business activities in more than one state must determine the portion of its net income that is subject to tax by each state. A corporation that has established sufficient nexus with another state generally must both **allocate** and **apportion** its income.

Apportionment is a means by which a corporation's taxable income is divided among the states in which it conducts business. Under an apportionment procedure, a corporation determines allowable income and deductions for the company as a whole and then apportions its income among the states in which it has nexus, according to an approved formula.

Allocation is a method under which specific components of a corporation's income, net of related expenses, are directly assigned to a certain state. Allocable income is assigned to a single state, whereas apportionable income is divided among several states. Nonapportionable (nonbusiness) income generally includes:

- Income or losses derived from the sale of nonbusiness real or tangible property, or

- Income or losses in the form of rentals and royalties from nonbusiness real or tangible personal property. Rentals and royalties constituting a business are apportioned.

Nonapportionable income is allocated to the state where the property that generated the income or loss is located.

EXAMPLE 3

Green Corporation conducts business in States N, O, P, and Q. Green's $900,000 taxable income consists of $800,000 apportionable income and $100,000 allocable income generated from transactions conducted in State Q. Green's sales, property, and payroll are evenly divided among the four states, and the states all employ an identical apportionment formula. Accordingly, $200,000 of Green's income is taxable in each of States N, O, and P. Green is subject to income tax on $300,000 of income in State Q.

Apportionable income	$800,000
Apportionment percentage (apportionable income is divided equally among the four states)	× 25%
Income apportioned to each state	$200,000

	State N	State O	State P	State Q
Income apportioned	$200,000	$200,000	$200,000	$200,000
Income allocated	–0–	–0–	–0–	100,000
Taxable income	$200,000	$200,000	$200,000	$300,000

16-2a **The Apportionment Procedure**

Apportionment assumes that the production of the taxpayer's income is linked to business activity, and the laws of each state define one or more factors believed to indicate the amount of corporate activity conducted within the state. However, apportionment often does not provide a uniform division of an organization's income based on its business activity, because each state is free to choose the type and number of factors it believes are indicative of the business activity conducted within its borders. Therefore, a business may be subject to state income tax on more or less than 100 percent of its Federal taxable income.

An equally incongruous consequence of apportionment may occur when the operations in a state result in a loss.

EXAMPLE 4

Red Corporation's operations include two manufacturing facilities, one in State A and one in State B. The plant located in A generated $500,000 of income, and the plant located in B generated a loss of $200,000. Therefore, Red's total taxable income is $300,000.

Applying the statutes of each state, Red determines that its apportionment factors for A and B are 0.65 and 0.35, respectively. Accordingly, Red's income is apportioned to the states as follows.

$$\text{Income apportioned to State A:} \quad 0.65 \times \$300,000 = \$195,000$$
$$\text{Income apportioned to State B:} \quad 0.35 \times \$300,000 = \$105,000$$

Red is subject to tax in B on $105,000 of income, even though the operations conducted in that state resulted in a loss.

16-2b **Apportionable Income**

Apportionable income is assigned among the states by using an apportionment formula. In contrast, *nonapportionable income* is allocated to the state where the income-producing asset is located. For instance, income derived from the rental of nonbusiness real property generally is allocated to the state where the property is located.

LO.4

Describe the nature and treatment of business and nonbusiness income.

EXAMPLE 5

TNT Corporation, a manufacturer of explosive devices, is a multistate taxpayer that has nexus with States P and Q. During the taxable year, TNT's net sales of explosive devices were $900,000; $600,000 of these sales were made in P, and $300,000 were made in Q. The corporation also received $90,000 from the rental of nonbusiness real property located in P. TNT's Federal taxable income, thus, is $990,000.

Both states employ a three-factor apportionment formula under which sales, property, and payroll are equally weighted. Applying the statutes of each state, TNT determines that its apportionment factors for P and Q are 0.65 and 0.42, respectively. TNT's taxable income for each state is determined as follows.

Income apportioned to State P	0.65 × $900,000 =	$585,000
Income allocated to State P		90,000
P taxable income		$ 675,000
Income apportioned to State Q	0.42 × $900,000 = Q taxable income	378,000
Aggregate state taxable income		$1,053,000

TNT's aggregate state taxable income exceeds its Federal taxable income. Tax rules in the two states differed, such that the apportionment factors totaled to more than 100%.

Apportionable income arises from the taxpayer's regular course of business or constitutes an integral part of the taxpayer's regular business.[6] In determining whether an item of income is apportionable (business) income, state courts have developed

[6]MTC Reg. IV.1.(a).

a variety of approaches to determine what constitutes a taxpayer's "regular course of business."[7]

Nonapportionable income is "all income other than apportionable income."[8] Usually, nonapportionable income comprises passive and portfolio income, such as dividends, interest, rents, royalties, and certain capital gains. However, passive activity or portfolio income may be apportionable when the acquisition, management, and disposition of the underlying property constitute an integral part of the taxpayer's regular business operation.[9]

A few states fail to distinguish between apportionable and nonapportionable income. In these states, all of a corporation's income is deemed to be subject to apportionment.

Apportionable Income

EXAMPLE 6

Scarlet Corporation is subject to income tax in several states. Scarlet earned $2.5 million from the sales of its products and $1 million from the sale of assets that were unrelated to its regular business operations.

In the states that distinguish between business and nonbusiness income, $2.5 million of Scarlet's income is apportioned to the state according to the state's apportionment formula. The gain on the sale of the nonbusiness assets is allocated to the state where the assets were located. In the states that subject a corporation's entire income to apportionment, $3.5 million ($2,500,000 + $1,000,000) is apportioned to the states in which the taxpayer conducts business.

EXAMPLE 7

Gray Corporation owns and operates two manufacturing facilities, one in State A and the other in State B. Due to a temporary decline in sales, Gray has rented 10% of its A facility to an unaffiliated corporation. Gray generated $100,000 net rent income and $900,000 income from manufacturing.

Both A and B classify such rent income as allocable income. By applying the statutes of each state, as discussed in the next section, Gray determines that its apportionment factors are 0.40 for A and 0.60 for B.

Income Subject to Tax in State A	
Taxable income	$1,000,000
Less: Allocable income	(100,000)
Apportionable income	$ 900,000
Times: Apportionment factor	× 40%
Income apportioned to State A	$ 360,000
Plus: Income allocated to State A	100,000
Income subject to tax in State A	$ 460,000

Income Subject to Tax in State B	
Taxable income	$1,000,000
Less: Allocable income	(100,000)
Apportionable income	$ 900,000
Times: Apportionment factor	× 60%
Income apportioned to State B	$ 540,000
Plus: Income allocated to State B	–0–
Income subject to tax in State B	$ 540,000

---

[7]*Atlantic Richfield Co. v. State of Colorado and Joseph F. Dolan*, 601 P.2d 628 (Colo.S.Ct., 1979); *Appeal of A. Epstein and Sons, Inc*. (Cal.State Bd. of Equalization, 1984).

[8]UDITPA § 1(e).

[9]MTC Reg. IV.1(a)(5).

Apportionable Income

Continue with the facts of Example 7, but assume that B does not distinguish between apportionable and nonapportionable income. Thus, all of Gray's income is apportionable in State B.

Gray properly determines that its apportionment factors are 0.40 for A and 0.58 for B. In this situation, Gray's income that is subject to tax is greater than $1,000,000.

EXAMPLE 8

Income Subject to Tax in State A	$ 460,000
Income Subject to Tax in State B	
Apportionable income	$1,000,000
Times: Apportionment factor	× 58%
Income apportioned to State B	$ 580,000

16-2c **Apportionment Factors: Elements and Planning**

Apportionable income is divided among the states by determining the appropriate apportionment percentage for each state that has a right to tax the entity. To determine the apportionment percentage for each state, a ratio is established for each of the factors included in the state's apportionment formula. Each ratio is calculated by comparing the level of a specific business activity within a state to the total corporate activity of that type. The ratios then are summed, averaged, and appropriately weighted to determine the taxpayer's apportionment percentage for a specific state.

The traditional three-factor formula equally weights sales, property, and payroll.[10] However, fewer than 10 states use an equal three-factor formula; in all other states, the sales factor receives more than a one-third weight.

The use of a higher-weighted sales factor tends to pull a larger percentage of an out-of-state corporation's income into the taxing jurisdiction of the state, because the corporation's major activity within the state—the sales of its goods and services—is weighted more heavily than are its payroll and property activities. Overweighting the sales factor, however, provides income tax relief for corporations that are domiciled in the state. Those corporations generally own significantly more property and incur more payroll costs (factors that are given less weight in the apportionment formula) within the state than do out-of-state corporations.

LO.5
Discuss the sales, payroll, and property apportionment factors.

Musk Corporation realized $500,000 of taxable income from the sales of its products in States A and B. Musk's activities in both states establish nexus for income tax purposes. Musk's sales, payroll, and property in the states include the following.

EXAMPLE 9

	State A	State B	Total
Sales	$1,250,000	$750,000	$2,000,000
Property	2,500,000	–0–	2,500,000
Payroll	1,500,000	–0–	1,500,000

If State B uses an equally weighted three-factor apportionment formula, $62,500 of Musk's taxable income is apportioned to B.

continued

---

[10]Certain industries, such as financial services institutions, insurance companies, air and motor carriers, pipeline companies, and communications providers, typically are required to use special apportionment formulas.

Sales ($750,000/$2,000,000)	=	37.5%
Property ($0/$2,500,000)	=	–0–
Payroll ($0/$1,500,000)	=	–0–
Sum of apportionment factors		37.5%
Average	÷	3
Apportionment factor for State B		12.5%
Taxable income	×	$500,000
Income apportioned to State B		$ 62,500

If State B uses a double-weighted sales factor in its three-factor apportionment formula, $93,750 of Musk's taxable income is apportioned to B.

Sales ($750,000/$2,000,000)	=	37.5% × 2	=	75%
Property ($0/$2,500,000)	=			–0–
Payroll ($0/$1,500,000)	=			–0–
Sum of apportionment factors				75%
Average			÷	4
Apportionment factor for State B				18.75%
Taxable income			×	$500,000
Income apportioned to State B				$ 93,750

When a state uses a double-weighted sales factor, typically a larger percentage of an out-of-state corporation's income is subject to tax in the state. Here, an additional $31,250 ($93,750 − $62,500) of Musk's income is subject to tax in B.

A single-factor apportionment formula consisting solely of a sales factor is even more detrimental to an out-of-state corporation than an apportionment factor that double-weights the sales factor. About 25 states use or allow a sales-factor-only apportionment formula.

EXAMPLE
10

Continue with the facts of Example 9. If State B uses a sales-factor-only apportionment formula, Musk's income apportionable to B becomes $187,500.

Sales ($750,000/$2,000,000)	=	37.5%
Sum of apportionment factors		37.5%
Average	÷	1
Apportionment factor for State B		37.5%
Taxable income	×	$500,000
Income apportioned to State B		$187,500

Concept Summary 16.2 highlights the most important aspects of multistate income allocation and apportionment.

Concept Summary 16.2

Apportionable Income

1. In most states, an apportionment procedure is used to assign the income of a multistate taxpayer to the various states in which business is conducted. Generally, nonapportionable income is allocated, rather than apportioned, directly to the state in which the nonbusiness income-generating assets are located.

2. Variations in state apportionment factors and formulas offer planning opportunities for businesses, in that more or less than 100% of the taxpayer's income may be subjected to state income tax.

3. Some states employ an equally weighted three-factor apportionment formula. In some states, the sales factor is doubled, and in other states, only the sales factor is used in apportioning multistate taxable income. Generally, the greater the relative weight assigned to the sales factor, the greater the tax burden on out-of-state taxpayers.

16-2d The Sales Factor

The **sales factor** is a fraction whose numerator is the corporation's total receipts in the state during the tax period. The denominator is the corporation's total receipts generated everywhere during the tax period. Gross receipts for this purpose generally are determined net of returns, allowances, and discounts.

Because the sales factor is a component in the formula used to apportion a corporation's business income to a state, only receipts that generate apportionable income are includible in the fraction. The sales factor generally includes business income from the sale of inventory or services, interest, dividends, rentals, royalties, sales of assets, and other business income. Income on Federal obligations, however, is not included in the sales factor.

These rules work best when the object of the sale is tangible property. Different rules may be needed when the taxpayer sells services, conducting work in one state for a customer in another. UDITPA sources service transactions to the location where the taxpayer incurred costs in conducting its work. About 20 states, though, have adopted *market-sourcing* rules, where a sale of services is sourced to the customer's state (or states). The states do not apply uniform rules in this area, so aggregate state taxable income from service transactions may be greater or less than the corresponding Federal taxable income amount.

When the sale involves capital assets, some states require that the gross proceeds, rather than the net gain or loss, be included in the fraction. Most states allow incidental or occasional asset sales and sales of certain intangible assets to be excluded from gross receipts.[11]

In determining the numerator of the sales factor, most states follow the UDITPA's "ultimate destination concept," under which tangible asset sales are assumed to take place at the point of delivery, not at the location at which the shipment originates.

EXAMPLE 11

Olive Corporation, whose only manufacturing plant is located in State A, sells its products to residents of A through its local retail store. Olive also ships its products to customers in States B and C. The products that are sold to residents of A are assigned to A, and the products that are delivered to B and C are assigned to B and C, respectively, even though all goods are manufactured in and shipped from A.

Several exceptions exist concerning the ultimate destination concept. The most important of these exceptions include the following.

Sales to U.S. Government

Because the U.S. government is present in every state, the ultimate destination concept becomes difficult to use. Accordingly, sales to the Federal government are assigned to the sales factor numerator of the state from which the sale occurs.

Dock Sales

Dock sales occur where a purchaser uses its owned or rented vehicles, or a common carrier with which it has made arrangements, to take delivery of the product at the seller's shipping dock. Most states apply the destination test to dock sales in the same manner it is applied to other sales. Thus, if the seller makes dock sales to a purchaser that has an out-of-state location to which it returns with the product, the sale is assigned to the purchaser's state.

Throwback Rule

Out-of-state sales that are not subject to tax in the destination state are pulled back into the origination state if that state has adopted a **throwback rule**. About half of the states apply this exception to the destination test. States that adopt a throwback rule attempt to make sure that a sale does not escape income taxation because it is made

---

[11]MTC Reg. IV.18.(c).

to a customer in a state in which the seller is not taxable. Such a case would place the sale in neither state's sales factor numerator (i.e., it could be called a "nowhere sale").

The throwback rule provides that when a corporation is not subject to tax in the destination state, the sales are treated as in-state receipts of the origination state, and the actual destination of the product is disregarded. Consequently, when the seller is immune from tax in the destination state under P.L. 86–272, the sales are considered to be in-state receipts of the origination state if that state has a throwback provision.

EXAMPLE

12

Braun Corporation's entire operations are located in State A. Seventy percent ($700,000) of Braun's sales are made in State A, and the remaining 30% ($300,000) are made in State B. Braun's solicitation of sales in State B is limited to mailing a monthly catalog to its customers in that state. However, Braun employees do pick up and replace damaged merchandise in State B.

Under State A's rules, the pickup and replacement of damaged goods establishes nexus with State B. Braun's activities in State B are sufficient (as determined by State A's law) to subject Braun to a positive tax, based on its income. Therefore, Braun is permitted to apportion its income between States A and B (70% and 30%, respectively). However, State B's definition of activities necessary to create nexus is less strict than that imposed by State A; in State B, the mere pickup and replacement of damaged goods does not establish income tax nexus.

Braun's taxable income is $900,000. Both States A and B impose a 10% corporate income tax and include only the sales factor in their apportionment formulas. If State A has not adopted a throwback rule, Braun's effective state income tax rate is 7%.

	Apportionment Factors	Taxable Income	Tax Rate	Tax
State A	70%	$900,000	10%	$63,000
State B	*	900,000	10%	–0–
Total tax liability				$63,000
Effective state income tax rate: $63,000/$900,000 =				7%

*As determined under State B's laws, Braun's income is not apportionable to State B, because of insufficient nexus.

If State A has adopted a throwback rule, Braun does not benefit from its lack of nexus with State B, because the sales in State B are considered to be in-state receipts of State A. Thus, Braun's effective tax rate is 10%.

	Apportionment Factors	Taxable Income	Tax Rate	Tax
State A	100%	$900,000	10%	$90,000
State B	–0–	900,000	10%	–0–
Total tax liability				$90,000
Effective state income tax rate: $90,000/$900,000 =				10%
Tax increase due to throwback provision ($90,000 − $63,000)				$27,000

16-2e **The Payroll Factor**

The **payroll factor** is determined by comparing the compensation paid for services rendered within a state to the total compensation paid by the corporation. Generally, the payroll factor is a fraction whose numerator is the total amount a corporation paid or accrued for compensation in a state during the tax period. The denominator is the total amount paid or accrued by the corporation for compensation during the tax period.

For purposes of the payroll factor, compensation includes wages, salaries, commissions, and any other form of remuneration paid or accrued to employees for personal services. Compensation also may include the value of board, rent, housing, lodging, and other benefits or services furnished to employees by the taxpayer in return for personal services, if these amounts constitute Federal gross income.

Payments made to an independent contractor or any other person who is not properly classifiable as an employee generally are excluded from the numerator and denominator of the payroll factor. A few states, including Delaware, New York, and North Carolina, exclude from the payroll factor the compensation paid to corporate officers. Most states exclude from the payroll factor any compensation made to corporate directors.

More than half of the states provide that earnings paid to a cash or deferred compensation plan, excluded from Federal gross income under § 401(k), are to be included in the numerator and the denominator of the payroll factor. Accordingly, the total compensation that is included in the denominator of a corporation's payroll factor may vary among the states in which the corporation's income is apportioned.

Mice Corporation's sales office and manufacturing plant are located in State A. Mice also maintains a manufacturing plant and sales office in State C. For purposes of apportionment, A defines payroll as all compensation paid to employees, including contributions to § 401(k) deferred compensation plans. Under the statutes of C, neither compensation paid to officers nor contributions to § 401(k) plans are included in the payroll factor. Mice incurred the following personnel costs.

EXAMPLE 13

	State A	State C	Total
Wages and salaries for employees other than officers	$350,000	$250,000	$600,000
Salaries for officers	150,000	100,000	250,000
Contributions to § 401(k) plans	30,000	20,000	50,000
Total	$530,000	$370,000	$900,000

The payroll factor for State A is computed as follows.

$$\frac{\$530,000}{\$900,000} = 58.89\%$$

Because C excludes from the payroll factor any compensation paid to officers and contributions to § 401(k) plans, C's factor is computed as follows.

$$\frac{\$250,000}{\$600,000} = 41.67\%$$

The aggregate of Mice's payroll factors is 100.56% (58.89% + 41.67%).

Typically, the compensation of an employee is not split between two or more states during the year unless he or she is transferred or changes positions during the year. Instead, each employee's entire compensation is assigned to only one state. Under the UDITPA, compensation is treated as being paid in the state (i.e., it is included in the numerator of the payroll factor) in which the services primarily are performed.

When an employee's services are performed in more than one state, his or her entire compensation is attributed to the employee's base of operations or, if there is no base of operations in any state in which some part of the service is performed, to the place from which the services are directed or controlled. When no services are performed in the state that serves as the base of operations or the place from which the services are directed, the employee's compensation is attributed to his or her state of residency.[12]

Geese Corporation has its headquarters and a manufacturing plant in State A. Reggie, a resident of State Y, works at the A manufacturing plant. His compensation is included in the numerator of A's payroll factor, because the service is performed entirely in A. None of Reggie's compensation is included in the payroll factor of State Y, Reggie's "home" state.

EXAMPLE 14

Only compensation that is related to the production of apportionable income is included in the payroll factor.

---

[12]UDITPA § 14.

EXAMPLE 15

Dog Corporation, a manufacturer of automobile parts, is subject to tax in States X and Y. Dog incurred the following payroll costs.

	State X	State Y	Total
Wages and salaries for officers and personnel of manufacturing facilities	$450,000	$350,000	$800,000
Wages and salaries for personnel involved in nonapportionable rental activities	50,000	–0–	50,000

Dog's payroll factors are computed as follows.

Payroll factor for State X : $450,000/$800,000 = 56.25%

Payroll factor for State Y : $350,000/$800,000 = 43.75%

16-2f The Property Factor

The property factor generally is a fraction whose numerator is the average value of the corporation's real property and its tangible personal property owned and used or rented and used in the state during the taxable year. The denominator is the average value of all of the corporation's real property and its tangible personal property owned or rented and used during the taxable year, wherever it is located. In this manner, a state's property factor reflects the extent of total property usage by the taxpayer in the state.

For this purpose, property includes land, buildings, machinery, inventory, equipment, and other real and tangible personal property.[13] Other types of property that may be included in the factor are offshore property, outer space property (satellites), and partnership property.

In the case of property that is in transit between locations of the taxpayer or between a buyer and seller, the assets are included in the numerator of the destination state. With respect to mobile or movable property such as construction equipment, trucks, and leased equipment, which is both in- and outside the state during the tax period, the numerator of a state's property factor generally is determined on the basis of the total time the property was within the state.

Property owned by the corporation typically is valued at its average original or historical cost plus the cost of additions and improvements, but without adjusting for depreciation. Some states allow property to be included at net book value or adjusted tax basis. The value of the property usually is determined by averaging the values at the beginning and end of the tax period. Alternatively, some states allow or require the amount to be calculated on a monthly basis if annual computation results in substantial distortions.

EXAMPLE 16

Blond Corporation, a calendar year taxpayer, owns property in States A and B. Both A and B require that the average value of assets be included in the property factor. A requires that the property be valued at its historical cost, and B requires that the property be included in the property factor at its net book value.

Account Balances at January 1			
	State A	State B	Total
Inventories	$ 150,000	$100,000	$ 250,000
Building and machinery (cost)	200,000	400,000	600,000
Accumulated depreciation for building and machinery	(150,000)	(50,000)	(200,000)
Land	50,000	100,000	150,000
Total	$ 250,000	$550,000	$ 800,000

continued

---

[13]MTC Reg. IV.10.(a).

Account Balances at December 31			
	State A	**State B**	**Total**
Inventories	$ 250,000	$ 200,000	$ 450,000
Building and machinery (cost)	200,000	400,000	600,000
Accumulated depreciation for building and machinery	(175,000)	(100,000)	(275,000)
Land	50,000	100,000	150,000
Total	$ 325,000	$ 600,000	$ 925,000

State A Property Factor			
Historical Cost	**January 1**	**December 31**	**Average**
Property in State A	$ 400,000*	$ 500,000**	$ 450,000
Total property	1,000,000†	1,200,000‡	1,100,000

  *$150,000 + $200,000 + $50,000.
 **$250,000 + $200,000 + $50,000.
  †$250,000 + $600,000 + $150,000.
  ‡$450,000 + $600,000 + $150,000.

$$\text{Property factor for State A: } \frac{\$450,000}{\$1,100,000} = 40.91\%$$

State B Property Factor			
Net Book Value	**January 1**	**December 31**	**Average**
Property in State B	$550,000	$600,000	$575,000
Total property	800,000	925,000	862,500

$$\text{Property factor for State B: } \frac{\$575,000}{\$862,500} = 66.67\%$$

Due to the variations in the property factor rules, the aggregate of Blond's property factors equals 107.58% (40.91% + 66.67%).

Leased property, when included in the property factor, is valued at eight times its annual rental. Annual rentals may include payments such as real estate taxes and insurance made by the lessee in lieu of rent.

FINANCIAL DISCLOSURE INSIGHTS State/Local Taxes and the Tax Expense

In applying GAAP principles for a business entity, state and local tax expenses are found in several places in the taxpayer's financial reports. In the tax footnote, the state/local tax costs often are reported in dollar and/or percentage terms, in both current and deferred components. The following are examples of state/local tax expenses that were reported in a recent year.

	Current State/ Local Tax Expenses ($ million)	Deferred State/ Local Tax Expenses ($ million)
Eli Lilly	$ 4	$ 0.4
Wal-Mart	405	(12)
Amazon	211	(26)
Ford Motor	(9)	63

Jasper Corporation is subject to tax in States D and G. Both states require that leased or rented property be included in the property factor at eight times the annual rental costs and that the average historical cost be used for other assets. Information regarding Jasper's property and rental expenses follows.

Average Historical Cost	
Property located in State D	$ 750,000
Property located in State G	450,000
Total property	$1,200,000

Lease and Rental Expenses	
State D	$ 50,000
State G	150,000
Total	$200,000

Property factor for State D

$$\frac{\$750,000 + 8(\$50,000)}{\$1,200,000 + 8(\$200,000)} = \frac{\$1,150,000}{\$2,800,000} = 41.07\%$$

Property factor for State G

$$\frac{\$450,000 + 8(\$150,000)}{\$1,200,000 + 8(\$200,000)} = \frac{\$1,650,000}{\$2,800,000} = 58.93\%$$

Only property that is used in the production of apportionable income is includible in the numerator and denominator of the property factor. In this regard, idle property, property under construction, and property that is used in producing nonapportionable income generally are excluded. However, assets that are temporarily idle or currently unused generally remain in the property factor.

16-3 THE UNITARY THEORY

LO.6

Apply the unitary method of state income taxation.

When two affiliated corporations are subject to tax in different states, each entity must file a return and report its income in the state in which it conducts business. Each entity reports its income separately from that of its affiliated corporations. In an effort to minimize overall state income tax, multistate entities have attempted to separate the parts of the business that are carried on in the various states.

Arts Corporation owns a chain of retail stores located in several states. To enable each store to file and report the income earned only in that state, each store was organized as a separate subsidiary in the state in which it did business. In this manner, each store is separately subject to tax only in the state in which it is located.

Most states attempt to assign as much of an entity's income to in-state sources as possible, so the ==unitary theory== for computing state taxable income is attractive to them. Under this method, a corporation is required to file a ==combined return== that includes the results from all of the operations of the related corporations, not just from those that transacted business in the state. In this manner, the unitary method allows a state to apply the apportionment formula to a firm's nationwide or worldwide unitary income. To include the activities of the corporation's subsidiaries in the apportionment formula, the state must determine that the subsidiaries' activities are an integral part of a unitary business and, as a result, are subject to apportionment.

16-3a What Is a Unitary Business?

A unitary business operates as a unit and cannot be segregated into independently operating divisions. The operations are integrated, and each division depends on or contributes to the operation of the business as a whole. It is not necessary that each unit operating within a state contribute to the activities of all divisions outside the state.

The unitary theory ignores the separate legal existence of the entities and focuses instead on practical business realities. Accordingly, the separate entities are treated as a single business for state income tax purposes, and the apportionment formula is applied to the combined income of the unitary business.

What Is a Unitary Business?

EXAMPLE 19

Continue with the facts of Example 18. Arts manufactured no goods, but it housed the central management, purchasing, distribution, advertising, and administrative departments. Each of the subsidiaries carried on a purely intrastate business, and they paid for the goods and services received at the parent company's cost plus overhead.

Arts and the subsidiaries constitute a unitary business due to their unitary operations (purchasing, distribution, advertising, and administrative functions). Accordingly, in states that have adopted the unitary method, the income and apportionment factors of the entire unitary group are combined and apportioned to the states in which at least one member of the group has nexus.

EXAMPLE 20

Crafts Corporation organized its departments as separate corporations on the basis of function: mining copper ore, refining the ore, and fabricating the refined copper into consumer products. Even though the various steps in the process are operated substantially independently of each other with only general supervision from Crafts' executive offices, Crafts is engaged in a single unitary business. Its various divisions are part of a large, vertically structured enterprise in which each business segment needs the products or raw materials provided by another. The flow of products among the affiliates also provides evidence of functional integration, which generally requires some form of central decision or policy making, another characteristic of a unitary business.

More than half of the states require or allow unitary reporting. Notice that the application of the unitary theory is based on a series of subjective observations about the organization and operation of the taxpayer's businesses, whereas the availability of Federal controlled and affiliated group status (see text Section 8-3a) is based on objective, mechanical ownership tests.

16-3b Tax Effects of the Unitary Theory

Use of the unitary approach by a state eliminates several of the planning techniques that could be used to shift income between corporate segments to avoid or minimize state taxes. In addition, the unitary approach usually results in a larger portion of the corporation's income being taxable in states where the compensation, property values, and sales prices are high relative to other states. This occurs because the larger in-state costs (numerators in the apportionment formula) include in the tax base a larger portion of the taxable income within the state's taxing jurisdiction. This has an adverse effect on the corporation's overall state tax burden if the states in which the larger portions are allocated impose a high tax rate relative to the other states in which the business is conducted.

The presence of a unitary business is favorable when losses of unprofitable affiliates may be offset against the earnings of profitable affiliates. It also is favorable when income earned in a high-tax state may be shifted to low-tax states due to the use of combined apportionment factors.

Effects of Unitary Computations

EXAMPLE

21

Rita Corporation owns two subsidiaries, Brown and Tan. Brown, located in State K, generated taxable income of $700,000. During this same period, Tan, located in State M, generated a loss of $400,000. If the subsidiaries are independent corporations, Brown is required to pay K tax on $700,000 of income. However, if the corporations constitute a unitary business, the incomes, as well as the apportionment factors, of the two entities are combined. As a result, the combined income of $300,000 ($700,000 − $400,000) is apportioned to unitary states K and M.

EXAMPLE

22

Eve Corporation, a wholly owned subsidiary of Dan Corporation, generated $1,000,000 of taxable income. Eve's activities and sales are restricted to State P, which imposes a 10% income tax. Dan's income for the taxable period is $1,500,000. Dan's activities and sales are restricted to State Q, which imposes a 5% income tax. Both states use a three-factor apportionment formula that equally weights sales, payroll, and property. Sales, payroll, and average property for each of the corporations are as follows.

	Eve Corporation	Dan Corporation	Total
Sales	$3,000,000	$7,000,000	$10,000,000
Payroll	2,000,000	3,500,000	5,500,000
Property	2,500,000	4,500,000	7,000,000

If the corporations are independent entities, the overall state income tax liability is $175,000.

State P (10% × $1,000,000)	=	$100,000
State Q (5% × $1,500,000)	=	75,000
Total state income tax		$175,000

If the corporations are members of a unitary business, the income and apportionment factors are combined in determining the income tax liability in unitary States P and Q. As a result of the combined reporting, the overall state income tax liability is reduced.

State P Income Tax			
Total apportionable income			$2,500,000
Apportionment formula			
Sales ($3,000,000/$10,000,000)	=	30.00%	
Payroll ($2,000,000/$5,500,000)	=	36.36%	
Property ($2,500,000/$7,000,000)	=	35.71%	
Total		102.07%	
Average (102.07% ÷ 3)			× 34.02%
State P taxable income			$ 850,500
Tax rate			× 10%
State P tax liability			$85,050

State Q Income Tax			
Total apportionable income			$2,500,000
Apportionment formula			
Sales ($7,000,000/$10,000,000)	=	70.00%	
Payroll ($3,500,000/$5,500,000)	=	63.64%	
Property ($4,500,000/$7,000,000)	=	64.29%	
Total		197.93%	
Average (197.93% ÷ 3)			× 65.98%
State Q taxable income			$1,649,500
Tax rate			× 5%
State Q tax liability			$82,475

continued

Total State Income Tax

Total state income tax if nonunitary	$175,000
Total state income tax if unitary ($85,050 + $82,475)	(167,525)
Tax reduction from unitary combined reporting	$ 7,475

The results of unitary reporting would have been detrimental if Q had imposed a higher rate of tax than P, because a larger percentage of the corporation's income is attributable to Q when the apportionment factors are combined.

The principles underlying apportionment factors and the unitary theory are set forth in Concept Summary 16.3.

Concept Summary 16.3

Using Apportionment Formulas

1. The sales factor is based on the ultimate destination concept for sales of tangible personal property. Other rules apply when a sale of services is involved and when other exceptions are available.

2. The payroll factor generally includes compensation that is included in Federal gross income, but some states include excludible fringe benefits. An employee's compensation usually is not divided among states.

3. The property factor generally is derived using the average undepreciated historical costs for the assets and eight times the rental value of the assets.

4. The unitary theory may require the taxpayer to include worldwide activities and holdings in the apportionment factors. A *water's edge election* can limit these amounts to U.S. transactions.

5. When the unitary theory applies, a combined return is filed. This is different from the consolidated return that an affiliated group of corporations would file for Federal income tax purposes.

16-3c Consolidated and Combined Returns

As discussed in Chapter 8, an affiliated group of corporations may file a consolidated Federal return if all members of the group consent. Once such a return has been filed, the group must continue to file on a consolidated basis as long as it remains in existence, or until permission to file separate returns has been obtained. The consolidated return essentially treats the controlled corporations as a single taxable entity. Thus, the affiliated group pays only one tax, based on the combined income of its members after certain adjustments (e.g., net operating losses) and eliminations (e.g., intercompany dividends and inventory profits).

Several states permit affiliated corporations to file a consolidated return if such a return has been filed for Federal purposes. The filing of a consolidated return is mandatory in only a few states.

Usually, only corporations that are subject to tax in the state can be included in a consolidated return, unless specific requirements are met or the state permits the inclusion of corporations that do not have in-state nexus.

Do not confuse elective consolidated returns with required combined returns in unitary states. A combined return is filed in every unitary state in which one or more of the affiliates have nexus. A consolidated return often includes an election for affiliates to join in a return-filing group as initiated by the taxpayers; most states apply rules similar to those presented in text Section 8-3a.

GLOBAL TAX ISSUES   **Water's Edge Is Not a Day at the Beach**

As a result of pressure from the business community, the Federal government, and foreign countries, most of the states that impose an income tax on a unitary business's worldwide operations permit a multinational business to elect **water's edge** unitary reporting as an alternative to worldwide unitary filing.

The water's edge provision permits a multinational corporation to elect to limit the reach of the state's taxing jurisdiction over out-of-state affiliates to activities occurring within the boundaries of the United States. The decision to make a water's edge election may have a substantial effect on the apportionment computations and the tax liability of a multinational corporation. A water's edge election usually cannot be revoked for a number of years without permission from the appropriate tax authority.

Corporations making this election may be assessed an additional tax or fee for the privilege of excluding out-of-state entities from the combined report.

LO.7

Discuss the states' income tax treatment of S corporations, partnerships, and LLCs.

16-4 TAXATION OF S CORPORATIONS

The majority of the states that impose a corporate income tax apply special provisions, similar to the Federal law, that govern the taxation of S corporations. Only a few states—including New York and Tennessee—and the District of Columbia do not provide pass-through (no corporate-level tax) treatment for Federal S corporations.

In the non-S election states, a Federal S corporation generally is subject to tax in the same manner as a C corporation. Accordingly, if a multistate S corporation operates in any of these states, it is subject to state income tax and does not realize one of the primary benefits of S status—the avoidance of double taxation. Other potential tax-related benefits of the S election, such as the immediate deduction of net operating losses, may not be allowed.

EXAMPLE

23

Bryan, an S corporation, has established nexus in States A and B. A recognizes S status; B does not. Bryan generated $600,000 of ordinary business income and $100,000 of dividends that were received from corporations in which Bryan owns 5% of the stock. Bryan's State B apportionment percentage is 50%.

For B tax purposes, Bryan first computes its income as though it were a C corporation. It then apportions the resulting income to B. Assuming that B has adopted the Federal provisions governing the dividends received deduction, Bryan's income, determined as though it were a C corporation, is $650,000 {$600,000 + [(100% − 50%) × $100,000]}. Accordingly, Bryan may be subject to B corporate income tax on $325,000 ($650,000 × 50% apportionment percentage) of taxable income.

16-4a Eligibility

All of the states that recognize S status permit a corporation to be treated as an S corporation for state purposes only if the corporation has a valid Federal S election in place. Generally, the filing of a Federal S election is sufficient to render the corporation an S corporation for state tax purposes. In most states, an entity that is an S corporation for Federal tax purposes automatically is treated as an S corporation for state tax purposes. New Jersey requires a separate state-level S election, and Pennsylvania allows the entity to *elect out* of its S status for state purposes.

16-4b State Tax Filing Requirements

About half of the states require the corporation to withhold taxes on the nonresident shareholders' portions of the entity's income.

EXAMPLE

24

Maple, an S corporation, is subject to income tax only in Vermont. On the last day of its taxable year, 40% of Maple's stock is held by nonresident shareholders. Maple withholds Vermont income tax for its nonresident shareholders.

In an effort to decrease compliance burdens and simplify the filing process for nonresident shareholders of S corporations, several states allow an S corporation to file a single income tax return and pay the resulting tax on behalf of some or all of its nonresident shareholders. State requirements for the filing of a "block" or **composite return** vary substantially.

16-5 TAXATION OF PARTNERSHIPS AND LLCS

Most states apply income tax provisions to partnerships, limited liability companies (LLCs), and limited liability partnerships (LLPs) in a manner that parallels Federal treatment. For income tax purposes, the entity is a tax-reporting, not a taxpaying, entity. Income, loss, and credit items are allocated and apportioned among the partners according to the terms of the partnership agreement and state income tax law.

Some states require that the entity make estimated tax payments on behalf of out-of-state partners. This approach helps to ensure that nonresident partners file appropriate forms and pay any resulting tax to the state. As is the case with S corporations, some states allow composite returns to be filed relative to out-of-state partners.

16-6 OTHER STATE AND LOCAL TAXES

LO.8

Describe other commonly encountered state and local taxes on businesses.

16-6a State and Local Sales and Use Taxes

Forty-five states and the District of Columbia impose a sales tax on retail sales of tangible personal property for use or consumption. In many of these states, in-state localities, including cities, towns, school districts, and counties, also have the power to levy a sales tax. A sales tax is imposed directly on the purchaser who acquires the asset at retail; the tax is measured by the price of the sale. The vendor or retailer merely acts as a collection agent for the state.

A use tax is designed to complement the sales tax. The use tax has two purposes: to prevent consumers from evading sales tax by purchasing goods outside the state for instate use and to provide an equitable sales environment between in-state and out-of-state retailers.

Generally, sales of tangible personal property are subject to tax. In several states, selected services and digital goods also are subject to tax.

Each jurisdiction that applies a sales/use tax defines its own tax base (i.e., which items are taxable and to whom). For a multistate business, complying with the thousands of sets of sales/use tax statutes and regulations can be a difficult burden. In an effort to ease this confusion, state and local government officials in about half of the states developed the Streamlined Sales Tax Project (SSTP). Members working in conjunction with the SSTP wrote a model law for taxing jurisdictions to adopt, thereby allowing for a more uniform application of the rules and for a more efficient exchange of information among revenue agencies. However, little interest has been shown in having identical sales/use tax rates among the jurisdictions.

To date, the most commonly adopted SSTP rules are those defining which products and services are subject to sales/use tax. For instance, SSTP rules set out the items of clothing that would be subject to tax, but each jurisdiction decides on its own whether to include clothing in the tax base and whether to allow "back-to-school" clothing amnesties (or holidays) during specific weeks of the year.

Sales/Use Tax Exemptions

A majority of the states exempt sales of certain items from the sales/use tax base. The most common exemptions and exclusions include the following.

- *Sales for resale* are exempt because the purchaser is not the ultimate user of the sold property. For instance, meat purchased by a grocer and a garment purchased by a retailer are not subject to sales/use tax under the resale rule.

- *Casual or occasional sales* that occur infrequently are exempt from the sales/use tax base chiefly for administrative convenience. Most states exclude rummage sales, the transfer of an entire business, and the like under this rule.

- Most *purchases by exempt organizations* are excluded from taxable sales. Charities, governments and their agencies, and other organizations qualifying for Federal income tax exemption are relieved of sales/use tax liabilities in all of the states.

- *Sales of necessities* such as groceries and medical prescriptions and equipment. Restaurant and other prepared meals typically are subject to tax, though.

- *Sales of targeted items* can be exempt to improve the equity of the sales/use tax system or support particular industries. Special exemptions for sales of farm, industrial, and computing equipment are allowed by several states.

- *Economic development concerns* A state or local government might waive the tax for a period of time to encourage a business to move to or remain in the jurisdiction.

- Certain *sales to manufacturers, producers, and processors* may also be exempt. Exemptions usually include one or more of the following.

  - Containers and other packing, packaging, and shipping materials actually used to transfer merchandise to customers of the purchaser.

  - Machines and specific processing equipment and repair parts or replacements exclusively and directly used in manufacturing tangible personal property.

Sales/Use Tax Nexus

Rules governing nexus for sales/use taxes are different from those used for income taxes. The regular solicitation of sales by independent brokers establishes sufficient nexus to require a nonresident seller to register and collect the use tax, even though the seller does not have regular employees, agents, and an office or other place of business in the state.[14] As a result, a corporation may be required to collect sales and use taxes in a state even though it is immune from the imposition of an income tax.

The states have a great degree of freedom to define sales/use tax nexus in their jurisdictions.[15] Nexus definitions for this purpose range from having a physical presence in the state to having customers in the jurisdiction (e.g., where the seller's only contact with the jurisdiction is through online sales).[16]

Sales/Use Tax on Services

Some states have added specific service transactions to their sales/use tax base. The services most commonly subjected to tax include transactions involving hotels and restaurants, hair and beauty salons, entertainment events, cable and satellite television subscriptions, and lawn care. To date, taxation of legal/accounting, medical, education, and advertising services largely has been blocked in most legislatures by the providers of these services.

Revenue shortfalls at the state and local levels and shifts in the general economy to the sales of services and goods other than tangible personal property, however, have led some legislatures to expand the sales/use tax base to include a broader array of

---

[14] *Scripto, Inc., v. Carson*, 362 U.S. 207 (1960).

[15] These privileges were confirmed in *South Dakota v. Wayfair, Inc.*, 585 U.S. ___ (2018).

[16] The *Wayfair* decision seems to require that the taxing jurisdiction establish a *de minimis* rule, providing relief for sellers with only a limited amount of sales in the state.

consumption. For instance, some states tax the transfer of digital goods, such as downloads of songs, books, software, and games.

16-6b Local Property Taxes

Property taxes, a major source of revenue at the city and county levels, often are designated as *ad valorem* taxes because they are based on the value of property that is located in the state on a specific date. Generally, that date fixes taxable ownership, situs (location), and the valuation of the property. Nonetheless, to avoid tax evasion, personal property that is temporarily outside the state may be taxed at the domicile of the owner.

Property taxes can take the form of either real property taxes or personal property taxes. States apply different tax rates and means of assessment to the two classes of property. The methods of assessing the value of the real and tangible property also vary in different taxing jurisdictions.

Although a personal property tax may be imposed on both intangible and tangible property, most states limit the tax to tangible property. The distinction between the various items of personal property is important because special rates, computations, or exemptions may apply. For instance, inventory constitutes tangible personal property, but it is exempt from property taxation in most states.

16-6c Other Taxes

States may impose a variety of other state and local taxes on corporations, including incorporation or entrance fees or taxes, gross receipt taxes, stock transfer taxes, realty transfer and mortgage recording taxes, license taxes, and franchise taxes based on net worth or capital stock outstanding.

Administrative Taxes

An *incorporation tax* is an excise tax for the corporate privilege conferred on the business. At the time the business is incorporated, the state generally imposes a fee or tax for the privilege of conducting business as a corporation within the state. Similarly, an out-of-state corporation usually must pay an entrance fee or tax before it can transact business in a state other than its state of incorporation.

A *license tax* is an excise tax on the privilege of engaging in a certain business, occupation, or profession. A jurisdiction may impose business, occupational, or professional license taxes as a means of generating revenue or regulating the activities of the business, occupation, or profession for the public welfare.

Taxes on nonresident visitors to a state are common, since the one who pays the tax lives somewhere else and cannot vote against it. Examples are taxes on hotel rooms (such as a *transient occupancy tax*), rental cars, and other transient arrangements, like house sharing or swapping.

Stock and realty transfer and mortgage recording taxes are nonrecurring taxes that are imposed at the time of recording or transfer. *Stock transfer taxes* are imposed on the transfer of shares or certificates of stock of domestic and foreign corporations. The tax typically is based on the number of shares transferred and the par or market value of the stock.

The base of the *realty transfer tax* usually is measured by the consideration paid or to be paid for the realty. The *mortgage recording tax* may be based on the actual consideration given, the value of the property, or the debt to be secured by the instrument.

Collections of Unclaimed Property

All of the U.S. states enforce rules that allow them to take possession of certain unclaimed property. In essence, this procedure acts like a tax on businesses with large consumer operations.

Unclaimed property might take the form of an unused gift card or a paycheck the employee has not yet cashed. On the balance sheet, these amounts are reported as payables by the business. After a stated period of time passes (usually 7 to 15 years) and an effort is made to contact the holder of the business's obligation, the value of the property reverts to the state. These rights of the states often are referred to as *escheat* laws.

Because unclaimed property rules are not enacted as a taxing statute, the usual nexus and apportionment tests do not apply. Instead, the property is taken by the state in which the business is incorporated.[17]

Capital Stock and Franchise Taxes

Typically, a *capital stock tax* is an excise tax imposed on a domestic corporation for the privilege of existing as a corporation or imposed on an out-of-state corporation, either for the privilege of doing business or for the actual transaction of business within the state. This annual tax usually is based on the book value of the corporation's net worth, including capital, surplus, and retained earnings.

The majority of capital stock taxes are apportioned if the corporation does business or maintains an office in another state. In some states, however, the tax is levied on the entire authorized or issued capital stock of a domestic corporation, even though the corporation may be engaged in business in other states. For corporations based in other states, the tax is imposed only on the capital that is employed in the state as determined by an apportionment formula.

State Franchise Tax on Net Worth

EXAMPLE 25

The balance sheet of Bull, a domestic corporation of State A, at the end of its taxable year is as follows.

Cash	$100,000
Equipment (net of $50,000 accumulated depreciation)	150,000
Building (net of $75,000 accumulated depreciation)	225,000
Land	125,000
Total assets	$600,000

Accounts payable and other short-term liabilities	$100,000
Long-term liabilities	200,000
Capital stock	50,000
Paid-in capital in excess of par value	50,000
Retained earnings	200,000
Total liabilities and equity	$600,000

State A imposes a 2% franchise tax based on the entire net worth of a domestic corporation. Bull is subject to a franchise tax in A of $6,000 ($600,000 assets − $300,000 liabilities = $300,000 net worth × 2% rate).

EXAMPLE 26

Continue with the facts of Example 25, except that State A subjects a domestic corporation to tax only on the capital that is employed in the state. Bull properly determines that its A apportionment percentage is 20%. In this case, Bull's A franchise tax liability is $1,200 ($300,000 net worth × 20% apportionment percentage = $60,000 capital employed in A × 2% rate).

---

[17]*Texas v. New Jersey*, 379 U.S. 674 (1965).

16-7 **TAX PLANNING**

LO.9

Recognize tax planning opportunities available to minimize a corporation's state and local tax liability.

The inconsistencies in the tax laws and rates among the states not only complicate state tax planning but also provide the nucleus of pertinent planning opportunities. Although several income tax planning devices are available to a corporation that does business in only one state, most planning techniques are directed toward corporations that do business or maintain property in more than one state. All suggested tax planning strategies should be reviewed in light of practical business considerations and the additional administrative and other costs that may be incurred, because simply minimizing state taxes may not be prudent from a business perspective.

16-7a **Selecting the Optimal State in Which to Operate**

Because the states employ different definitions of the amount and type of activity necessary to establish nexus, a company has some latitude in selecting the states by which it will be taxed. When a corporation has only a limited connection with a high-tax state, it may abandon that activity by electing an alternative means of accomplishing the same result. For example, if providing a sales representative with a company-owned iPad constitutes nexus in an undesired state, the company could eliminate its connection with that state by reimbursing sales personnel for equipment expenses, instead of providing a company communications device. Similarly, when nexus is caused by conducting customer training sessions or seminars in the state, the corporation could conduct the meetings in another way. This can be done by sending the personnel to a nearby state in which nexus clearly has been established or in which the activity would not constitute nexus, or by meeting electronically.

In addition, when sufficient activity originates from the repair and maintenance of the corporation's products or the activities performed by the sales representatives within the state, the organization could incorporate the service or sales divisions. This would invalidate a nonunitary state's right to tax the parent corporation's income; only the income of the service or sales divisions would be subject to tax. However, this technique is successful only if the incorporated division is a *bona fide* business operation. Therefore, the pricing of any sales or services between the new subsidiary and the parent corporation must be at arm's length, and the operations of the new corporation preferably should result in a profit.

Although planning techniques often are employed to disconnect a corporation's activities from an undesirable state, they also can be utilized to create nexus in a desirable state. For example, when the presence of a company-owned computer creates nexus in a desirable state, the corporation could provide its sales representatives in that state with company-owned equipment, rather than reimbursing or providing increased compensation for equipment costs.

Establishing nexus in a state is advantageous, for instance, when that state has a lower tax rate than the state in which the income currently is taxed or when losses or credits become available to reduce tax liabilities in the state.

EXAMPLE 27

Bird Corporation generates $500,000 of taxable income from selling goods; specifically, 40% of its product is sold in State A and 60% in State B. Both states levy a corporate income tax and include only the sales factor in their apportionment formulas. The tax rate in A is 10%; B's rate is only 3%. Bird's manufacturing operation is located in A; therefore, the corporation's income is subject to tax in that state. Currently, Bird is immune from tax under P.L. 86–272 in B. Because A has adopted a throwback provision, Bird incurs $50,000 of state income taxes.

	Apportionment Formula	Net Income	Tax Rate	Tax
State A	100/100	$500,000	10%	$50,000
State B	0/100	500,000	3%	–0–
Total tax liability				$50,000

Because B imposes a lower tax rate than A does, Bird substantially reduces its state tax liability if sufficient nexus is created with B.

	Apportionment Formula	Net Income	Tax Rate	Tax
State A	40/100	$500,000	10%	$20,000
State B	60/100	500,000	3%	9,000
Total tax liability				$29,000

16-7b Restructuring Corporate Entities

One of the major objectives of state tax planning is to design the proper mix of corporate entities. An optimal mix of entities often generates the lowest combined state income tax for the corporation. The goal of designing a good corporate combination often is to situate the highly profitable entities in states that impose a low (or no) income tax.

Matching Tax Rates and Corporate Income

When the corporation must operate in a high-tax state, divisions that generate losses also should be located there. Alternatively, unprofitable or less profitable operations can be merged into profitable operations to reduce the overall income subject to tax in the state. An ideal candidate for this type of merger may be a research and development subsidiary that is only marginally profitable but is vital to the parent corporation's strategic goals, and that may attract research credits and incentives for the taxpayer. By using simulation models, a variety of different combinations can be tested to determine the optimal corporate structure.

Unitary Operations

By identifying the states that have adopted the unitary method and the criteria under which a particular state defines a unitary business, a taxpayer may reduce its overall state tax by restructuring its corporate relationships to create or guard against a unitary relationship. For instance, an independent business enterprise can be made unitary by exercising day-to-day operational control and by centralizing functions such as marketing, financing, accounting, and legal services.

The Big Picture

EXAMPLE 28

Return to the facts of *The Big Picture* on p. 16-1. Assume that LocalCo already operates in both unitary and nonunitary states. Application of unitary corporate income tax rules can make tax planning more difficult. Subjecting certain LocalCo activities to the unitary theory could either increase or decrease the combined corporate income tax liability of the affiliates, depending especially on the apportionment formulas applied in the unitary states.

LocalCo needs to make projections of the profitability of its operations in the new multifunction building. Then LocalCo should determine the income tax effects of expanding its operations into several target states, including both unitary and nonunitary jurisdictions, and compare how the unitary rules (and all associated compliance costs) affect its after-tax profits.

Passive Investment Companies

The creation of a passive investment company is another restructuring technique utilized to minimize a nonunitary corporation's state tax burden. Nonbusiness or passive/portfolio income generally is allocated to the state in which the income-producing asset is located, rather than being apportioned among the states in which the corporation does business. Therefore, significant tax savings may be realized when nonbusiness assets are located in a state that either does not levy an income tax or provides favorable tax treatment for passive/portfolio income.

The corporation need not be domiciled in the state to benefit from these favorable provisions. Instead, the tax savings can be realized by forming a passive investment subsidiary to hold the intangible assets and handle the corporation's investment activities.

The passive investment subsidiary technique usually produces the desired result in any no-tax state. Delaware, however, often is selected for this purpose due to its other corporate statutory provisions and favorable political, business, and legal climate.

Delaware does not impose an income tax upon a corporation whose only activity within the state is the maintenance and management of intangible investments and the collection and distribution of income from such investments or from tangible property physically located in another state. Consequently, trademarks, patents, stock, and other intangible property can be transferred to a Delaware corporation whose activity is limited to collecting such income. The assets can be transferred to the subsidiary without incurring a current Federal income tax on the exchange (see text Section 4-1).

However, to receive the desired preferential state tax treatment, the holding company's activities within the state must be sufficient to establish income tax nexus in the state. The passive investment company should avoid performing any activity outside the state that may result in establishing nexus with another state. In addition, the formation of the subsidiary must be properly implemented to ensure the legal substance of the operation. The passive investment company must have a physical office, and it must function as an independent operation.

Because the subsidiary's activities are confined to Delaware (or some other no- or low-tax state) and its operations generate only passive/portfolio income, its income will not be taxed in any nonunitary state. Moreover, most states exclude dividends from taxation or otherwise treat them favorably; therefore, the earnings of a passive investment subsidiary can be distributed as a dividend to the parent at a minimal tax cost. If the state in which the parent is located does not levy the full income tax on dividends received, the entire measure of passive/portfolio income may escape taxation.

EXAMPLE 29

Purple Corporation generates $800,000 of taxable income; $600,000 is income from its manufacturing operations, and $200,000 is dividend income from passive investments. All of Purple's sales are made and assets are kept in State A, which imposes a 10% corporate income tax and permits a 100% deduction for dividends received from subsidiaries. The corporation is not subject to tax in any other state. Consequently, Purple incurs $80,000 of income tax (tax base $800,000 × tax rate 10%).

If Purple creates a passive investment subsidiary in State B, which does not impose an income tax upon a corporation whose only activity within the state is the maintenance and management of passive investments, Purple's tax liability is reduced by $20,000 (a 25% decrease). Because such income is nonapportionable (allocated for state tax purposes to the state in which it is located), the income earned from its passive investments is not subject to tax in A.

	State A (Purple Corporation)	State B (Passive Investment Company)
Taxable income	$600,000	$200,000
Tax rate	× 10%	× –0–*
Tax liability	$ 60,000	$ –0–
Tax liability without restructuring		$ 80,000
Tax liability with restructuring		(60,000)
Tax reduction due to use of subsidiary		$ 20,000

*B does not impose an income tax on a passive investment corporation.

The income earned by the subsidiary from its passive investments can be distributed to Purple as a dividend without incurring a tax liability because A allows a 100% deduction for dividends that are received from subsidiary corporations.

These desired results, however, will not be fully available in states that view the entire corporate operation as being unitary. Because those states require combined reporting, the income earned by the passive investment subsidiary is included in the corporation's apportionable or allocable income. Other states may levy gross receipts taxes or restrict interest and dividend deductions, or legislatively include in the income tax base any income resulting from the use of intangible assets in the state,[18] to limit the effectiveness of the passive investment subsidiary.

16-7c Subjecting the Corporation's Income to Apportionment

When a multistate organization is domiciled in a high-tax state, some of its apportionable income is eliminated from the tax base in that state. In light of the high tax rate, this may result in significant tax savings. Apportioning income will be especially effective where the income that is attributed to the other states is not subject to income tax. The income removed from the taxing jurisdiction of the domicile state entirely escapes state income taxation when the state to which the income is attributed (1) does not levy a corporate income tax, (2) requires a higher level of activity necessary to subject an out-of-state company to taxation than that adopted by the state of domicile, or (3) is prohibited under P.L. 86–272 from taxing the income (assuming that the domicile state has not adopted a throwback provision). Thus, the right to apportion income may provide substantial benefits because the out-of-state sales are excluded from the numerator of the sales factor and may not be taxed in another state.

However, to acquire the right to apportion its income, the organization must have sufficient activities in or contacts with one or more other states. Whether the type and amount of activities and/or contacts are considered adequate is determined by the other state's nexus rules. Therefore, a corporation should analyze its current activities in and contacts with other states to determine which, if any, activities or contacts could be redirected so that the corporation gains the right to apportion its income.

---

[18]These laws often are rooted in *Geoffrey, Inc. v. South Carolina Tax Commission*, 437 SE2d 13 (SC S.Ct., 1993).

Return to the facts of *The Big Picture* on p. 16-1. Most corporate taxpayers consist of a parent corporation and perhaps one or more existing subsidiaries. Given its expansion plans, LocalCo has the opportunity to determine "from scratch" in which states it wants to create nexus for the operations in the multifunction building.

EXAMPLE
30

The tax professional needs to offer advice to LocalCo's board of directors as to where the building might be situated and how the operations of any related sales and administrative personnel might be structured in an effort to provide optimal tax consequences. Nexus issues to be considered include the following.

- Is income tax nexus created with the target state?
- Is sales/use tax nexus created with the target state?
- How are the income tax apportionment factors affected by the expansion plans (e.g., whether the target state uses a property factor in the apportionment formula and, if so, how it is weighted)?
- Would a building such as that planned by LocalCo receive any special computational treatment for the target state's property factor (e.g., in averaging the building's costs or applying accumulated depreciation)?

ETHICS & EQUITY Can You Be a Nowhere Adviser?

The intent of much of today's multistate income tax planning is to create so-called *nowhere sales*, such that the income from the transaction is not subject to tax in any state. Suppose, for instance, that a sale is made from Georgia (a state with no throwback rule) into Nevada (the place of ultimate destination, but a state with no income tax). No state-level income tax liability is generated.

Is it ethical for a tax adviser to suggest such a strategy? Could you ethically propose the establishment of a sales office in a nonthrowback state, thereby avoiding state income tax on a transaction that is fully taxable under Federal rules?

16-7d **Planning with Apportionment Factors**

Sales Factor

Working with the sales factor often yields the greatest planning opportunities for a multistate corporation. In-state receipts include sales to purchasers with a destination point in that state; sales delivered to out-of-state purchasers are included in the numerator of the sales factor of the destination state. However, to be permitted to exclude out-of-state sales from the sales factor of the origination state, the seller generally must substantiate the shipment of goods to an out-of-state location. Therefore, the destinations of sales that a corporation makes and the means by which the goods are shipped must be carefully reviewed.

The corporation's overall state tax possibly can be reduced by establishing a better record-keeping system or by affecting the numerator of the sales factor by changing the delivery location or method.

For example, a corporation may substantially reduce its state income tax if the delivery location of its sales is changed from a state in which the company is taxed to one in which it is not. This technique may not benefit the corporation if the state in which the sales originate has adopted the throwback rule.

Property Factor

Because most fixed assets are physically stationary in nature, the property factor is not so easily manipulated in the short term. Nonetheless, significant tax savings can be realized by establishing a leasing subsidiary in a low- or no-tax state. If the property is located in a state that does not include leased assets in the property factor, the establishment of a subsidiary from which to lease the property eliminates the assets from the property factor in the parent's state.

Permanently idle property generally is excluded from the property factor. Accordingly, a corporation should identify and remove such assets from the property factor to ensure that the factor is not distorted.

The property factor valuations of Quake Corporation's holdings are as follows.

	State A	Total
Equipment (average historical cost)	$1,200,000	$2,000,000
Accumulated depreciation (average)	800,000	1,000,000

Twenty percent of the equipment in State A is fully depreciated and is idle. Assuming that A includes property in the factor at historical cost, Quake's property factor is 54.55% [($1,200,000 − $240,000 idle property)/($2,000,000 − $240,000)]. If the idle property is not removed from the property factor, Quake's property factor in A is incorrectly computed as 60% ($1,200,000/$2,000,000).

Payroll Factor

The payroll factor provides income tax planning potential where several corporate employees spend substantial periods of time outside their state of employment or the corporation is able to relocate highly paid employees to low- or no-tax states.

Because the commissions paid to independent contractors are excluded from the payroll factor, the taxpayer may reduce its payroll factor in a high-tax state.

EXAMPLE 32

Yellow Corporation's total payroll costs are $1,400,000. Of this amount, $1,000,000 was attributable to State A, a high-tax state. Yellow's payroll factor in A is 71.43% ($1,000,000/$1,400,000).

Assuming that $200,000 of the A compensation had been paid to sales representatives and that Yellow replaced its sales force with independent contractors, Yellow's payroll factor in A would be reduced to 66.67% [($1,000,000 − $200,000)/($1,400,000 − $200,000)].

16-7e **Sales/Use Tax Compliance**

A seller conceivably must deal with thousands of different sales/use taxing jurisdictions, each with its own forms and filing deadlines, rates of applicable tax, and definitions of what is taxable or exempt. Examples of issues on which jurisdictions may disagree, presenting compliance problems for sellers, include the following.

- Are snack foods exempt groceries or taxable candy?
- Are therapeutic stockings exempt medical supplies or taxable clothing?
- Which types of software are subject to tax?

16-7f **Capital Stock Taxation**

Capital stock tax liabilities can be significant for capital-intensive taxpayers to the extent they reinvest a large portion of retained earnings (the tax base) in productive assets. If all nontax factors are equal, a taxpayer with sizable exposure to a capital stock tax should consider the following techniques.

- Funding expansion with debt rather than retained earnings.
- Funding subsidiary operations with debt rather than direct capital contributions.
- Regularly paying dividends to parent companies that are domiciled in tax-favored states such as Delaware and Nevada.

REFOCUS ON THE BIG PICTURE

MAKING A MULTISTATE LOCATION DECISION

LocalCo holds a competitive advantage with the states and localities in negotiating where its new facility should be located. Politicians like to attract new facilities to their jurisdictions as a way to create construction jobs and to expand the income and sales/use tax base. LocalCo's top management should work with the governors and development executives of the states that are final candidates for the location of the proposed new building.

LocalCo's agenda for these negotiations should include the following items.

- Many states offer targeted tax incentives to attract and retain "clean" businesses such as LocalCo. These incentives might include property tax abatements, research and investment credits, and tax waivers for the state and local income and payroll taxes on new jobs. The company should determine whether it qualifies for any existing incentives, and whether the incentives are attractive after considering their inclusion in the gross income of the business.

- Currently, LocalCo's manufacturing operations are split between a low-tax state (Alabama) and a high-tax state (California). Under a relocation plan that does not jeopardize LocalCo's customer base, nexus might be eliminated with California and shifted to a low-tax jurisdiction. Nevada is a good candidate, given its proximity to the current sportswear location. But economic nexus thresholds might prevent this technique from working effectively.

- California applies the unitary theory of income taxation. LocalCo should determine whether unitary rules increase or decrease its total tax burden.

- Corporate headquarters currently are located in New York, another high-tax jurisdiction. If the new facility is located in a corporation-favorable, low-tax state, the company should consider moving its headquarters there.

- Relocating the corporate headquarters also could benefit the entity's highly paid executives. The individual income and sales/use tax burden of employees should be a factor in LocalCo's decision.

- States often assess special taxes on trucking and airport functions and might apply different income tax apportionment formulas to these operations. LocalCo's tax department and its outside advisers should research these features of the various relevant tax systems to avoid any unexpected surprises.

What If?

If LocalCo did not have a history of strong profitability, some of these state and local tax recommendations might be different. In that case, the company would consider issues such as how a state allows loss and credit carryovers. In addition, if there is no state income tax liability to pay, income tax credits and deductions would be less attractive, so the negotiations might focus on property and payroll taxes instead.

LocalCo's tax plans might be exposed to tax law changes that will work to its detriment. Its locations include some of the most aggressive legislatures and taxing agencies in the country, so the taxpayer must watch for changes in those states' rules concerning nexus, income sourcing, apportionment, and incentives. Tax planning ideas that work currently might be undone by the adoption of gross receipts taxes, a unitary approach, market-based income sourcing, or economic nexus provisions.

Key Terms

Allocate, 16-8	Nexus, 16-6	Throwback rule, 16-13
Apportion, 16-8	Passive investment company, 16-29	UDITPA, 16-6
Combined return, 16-18	Payroll factor, 16-14	Unclaimed property, 16-26
Composite return, 16-23	Property factor, 16-16	Unitary theory, 16-18
Dock sales, 16-13 ·	Public Law 86–272, 16-6	Water's edge, 16-22
Multistate Tax Commission (MTC), 16-6	Sales factor, 16-13	

Discussion Questions

Critical Thinking

Communications

1. **LO.1** You are working with the top management of one of your clients in selecting the U.S. location for a new manufacturing operation. Craft a plan for the CEO to use in discussions with the economic development representatives of several candidate states. In no more than three PowerPoint slides, list some of the tax incentives the CEO should request from a particular state during the negotiations. Be both creative and aggressive in the requests.

2. **LO.1** Complete the following chart by indicating whether each item is true or false. Explain your answers by referencing the overlap of rules appearing in Federal and most state income tax laws.

Item	True or False
a. Most of the states start with Federal taxable income in computing state taxable income.	_____
b. The states use a wide variety of rules to compute corporate taxable income; thus, there is no "typical" state income tax computation.	_____
c. Aggregate state taxable incomes always equal Federal taxable income; tax rules merely split the income among the states.	_____
d. The corporate income tax systems of most states can be described as applying progressive rate structures.	_____
e. A typical state income tax credit would equal 10% of the costs incurred to purchase and install solar energy panels for an existing factory.	_____

Communications

3. **LO.2** In no more than three PowerPoint slides, list some general guidelines that a taxpayer can use to determine whether it has an obligation to file an income tax return with a particular state. (Include the terms *nexus* and *domicile* in your answer.)

4. **LO.2** Josie is a sales representative for Talk2Me, a communications retailer based in Fort Smith, Arkansas. Josie's sales territory is Oklahoma, and she regularly takes day trips to Tulsa to meet with customers.

   During a typical sales call, Josie takes the customers' current orders for phones, cases, and attachments and, using an app on her wireless phone, sends the orders to headquarters in Fort Smith for immediate action. Approved orders are shipped from the Little Rock warehouse.

   Are Josie's sales subject to the Oklahoma corporate income tax? Explain.

5. **LO.2** Continue with the facts of Question 4. CheapPhones, one of Josie's customers who is facing tight cash-flow problems, wants to return about 100 defective cell phones. Talk2Me tells Josie to bring the phones back to headquarters. Fearing that she will lose CheapPhones as a customer if she does not comply with the

request, Josie says, "Let me save you the time and cost of packing and shipping the defective phones. Put them in the trunk of my car, and I'll take them back." Does Josie's action change the answer to Question 4? Why or why not?

6. **LO.3** Indicate whether each of the following items should be *allocated* or *apportioned* by the taxpayer in computing state corporate taxable income. Assume that the state follows the general rules of UDITPA.

    a. Profits from sales activities.

    b. Profits from consulting and other service activities.

    c. Losses from sales activities.

    d. Profits from managing the stock portfolio of a client.

    e. Profits from managing one's own stock portfolio.

    f. Gain on the sale of a plot of land held by a real estate developer.

    g. Gain on the sale of a plot of land held by a manufacturer, on which it may expand its factory.

    h. Rent income received by a manufacturer from the leasing of space to a supplier.

7. **LO.3** Regarding the apportionment formula used to compute state taxable income,   **Critical Thinking** does each of the following independent characterizations describe a taxpayer that likely is based in state or out of state? Explain.

    a. The sales factor is positively correlated with the payroll, but not the property, factor.

    b. The sales factor is much higher than the property and payroll factors.

    c. The property and payroll factors are much higher than those for other nexus states.

    d. The sales and payroll factors are low, but the property factor is very high.

    e. The sales factor is remaining constant, but the payroll factor is decreasing.

8. **LO.5** The trend in state income taxation is to adopt an apportionment formula that   **Critical Thinking** places extra weight on the sales factor. Many states now use sales-factor-only apportionment. Explain why this development is attractive to the taxing states.

9. **LO.5** Megan is an accountant for KnoxCo. She is a telecommuter and works most days from her home in Tennessee. Twice a month, she travels to Georgia for a staff meeting at the employer's Atlanta headquarters. In which state's payroll factor should Megan's compensation be included if:

    a. Megan is an employee and is covered by the qualified retirement plan of her Atlanta employer?

    b. Megan works as an independent contractor for several clients, including the Atlanta-based firm?

    c. Megan is an employee, and for one day each month, she provides accounting services for KnoxCo's Memphis rental properties?

10. **LO.5** Keystone, your tax consulting client, is considering an expansion program   **Critical Thinking** that would entail the construction of a new logistics center in State Q. List at least five questions you should ask in determining whether an asset that is owned by Keystone is to be included in State Q's property factor numerator.

11. **LO.6** The trend in state income taxation is for states to adopt a version of the unitary theory of multijurisdictional taxation in their statutes and regulations.

    a. Explain why some states are attracted to the unitary theory and a combined reporting scheme of multistate income taxation.

    b. Is the application of the unitary theory a help or a detriment to the taxpayer? Why?

Critical Thinking

12. **LO.6** State A enjoys a prosperous economy, with high real estate values and compensation levels. State B's economy has seen better days—property values are depressed, and unemployment is higher than in other states. Most consumer goods are priced at about 10% less in B than in A. Both A and B apply unitary income taxation to businesses that operate within the state. Does unitary taxation distort the assignment of taxable income between A and B? Explain.

13. **LO.7** Evaluate this statement: An S corporation can facilitate the meeting of its state income tax filing obligations by developing a common spreadsheet that allocates and apportions income among the states with which it has nexus. This spreadsheet is attached to each of the state returns to be filed. (*Hint:* Use the term *composite return* in your answer.)

Communications

14. **LO.8** Create a PowerPoint outline describing the major exemptions and exclusions from the sales/use tax base of most states. Use your slides to discuss this topic with your accounting students' club.

Critical Thinking

15. **LO.8** Your client, HillTop, is a retailer of women's clothing. It has increased sales during the holiday season by advertising gift cards for in-store and online use. HillTop has found that gift card holders who come into the store tend to purchase goods that total more than the amount of the gift card. Further, about one-third of the gift cards never are redeemed, thereby yielding cash to the company without a reduction of inventory. What are the tax issues confronting HillTop related to the gift cards?

Communications

16. **LO.2, 9** Your client, Ecru Limited, uses a small sales force to solicit sales of its wholesale restaurant supplies. Ecru is based in State W, and the sales representatives are assigned territories in States X, Y, and Z. Ecru owns no property and employs no other personnel outside of W.

As Ecru's tax adviser, you are to write a policy manual listing various "do's and don'ts" for the sales personnel so that Ecru does not create income tax nexus with X, Y, and Z.

To prepare for your assignment, write a memo for the tax research file, summarizing the rules as to the ability of a corporation to terminate or create income tax nexus. Make certain that you discuss the *Wrigley* case in your analysis.

Communications

17. **LO.9** Your client, Royal Corporation, generates significant interest income from its working capital liquid investments. Write a memo for the tax research file, discussing the planning opportunities presented by establishing a passive investment company. Support your memo with a diagram of the resulting flow of assets and income.

18. **LO.2, 5, 9** As the director of the multistate tax planning department of a consulting firm, you are developing a brochure to highlight the services it can provide. Part of the brochure is a list of five or so key techniques that clients can use to reduce state income tax liabilities. Develop this list for the brochure. Consider only income tax consequences in your analysis.

Computational Exercises

19. **LO.3, 5** Castle Corporation conducts business in States 1, 2, and 3. Castle's $630,000 taxable income consists of $555,000 apportionable income and $75,000 allocable income generated from transactions conducted in State 3. Castle's sales, property, and payroll are evenly divided among the three states, and the states all employ a three-equal-factors apportionment formula. How much of Castle's income is taxable in:

a. State 1?

b. State 2?

c. State 3?

d. Express your computation as a Microsoft Excel formula that will provide the correct solution for all three states.

20. **LO.3** Fillon Corporation's operations include two manufacturing facilities, one in State A and one in State B. The plant located in A generated $200,000 of income, and the plant located in B generated a loss of $50,000. Therefore, Fillon's total taxable income is $150,000. By applying the statutes of each state, Fillon determines that its apportionment factors for A and B are 0.70 and 0.30, respectively.

How much of Fillon's income is apportioned to:

a. State A?
b. State B?

21. **LO.3, 4** Legends Corporation owns and operates two manufacturing facilities, one in State A and the other in State B. Due to a temporary decline in sales, Legend has rented 25% of its State A facility to an unaffiliated corporation. Legend generated $200,000 net rent income and $1,400,000 income from manufacturing. Both states classify the rent income as allocable (nonapportionable) income. By applying the statutes of each state, Legends determines that its apportionment factors are 0.70 for A and 0.30 for B.

How much income is subject to tax in:

a. State A?
b. State B?

22. **LO.5** Beckett Corporation realized $800,000 of taxable income from the sales of its products in States A and B. Beckett's activities establish nexus for income tax purposes in both states. Beckett's sales, payroll, and property in the states include the following.

	State A	State B	Total
Sales	$960,000	$640,000	$1,600,000
Property	180,000	–0–	180,000
Payroll	220,000	–0–	220,000

State B uses a double-weighted sales factor in its three-factor apportionment formula. How much of Beckett's taxable income is apportioned to State B?

23. **LO.5** Isle Corporation's entire operations are located in State A. Of Isle's $600,000 sales, 60% are made in State A and 40% are made in State B. Isle's solicitation of sales in State B is limited to mailing a monthly catalog to its customers in that state. However, Isle's employees pick up and replace damaged merchandise in State B. The pickup and replacement of damaged goods establish nexus with State A.

However, B's definition of activities necessary to create income-tax nexus is less strict than that imposed by A; in B, the mere pickup and replacement of damaged goods does not create nexus there. Isle's taxable income is $60,000. Both states impose a 10% corporate income tax and include only the sales factor in their apportionment formulas.

Determine Isle's effective state income tax rate if:

a. State A *has not* adopted a throwback rule.
b. State A *has* adopted a throwback rule.
c. Create a Microsoft Excel formula that will compute correctly the State A taxable income regardless of whether a throwback rule has been adopted.

24. **LO.5** Sante Fe Corporation's sales office and manufacturing plant are located in State A. Sante Fe also maintains a manufacturing plant and sales office in State B. For purposes of apportionment, State A defines payroll as all compensation paid to employees, including contributions to § 401(k) deferred compensation plans. Under the statutes of State B, neither compensation paid to officers nor contributions

to § 401(k) plans are included in the payroll factor. Sante Fe incurred the following personnel costs.

	State A	State B	Total
Wages and salaries for employees other than officers	$ 60,000	$40,000	$100,000
Salaries for officers	40,000	20,000	60,000
Contributions to § 401(k) plans	20,000	10,000	30,000
Total	$120,000	$70,000	$190,000

What is the payroll factor for:

a.   State A?

b.   State B?

25. **LO.6** Vogel Corporation owns two subsidiaries, Song and Bird. Song, located in State A, generated taxable income of $500,000. During this same period, Bird, located in State B, generated a loss of $100,000.

a.   Determine Song's taxable income in States A and B, assuming that the subsidiaries constitute independent corporations under the tax law.

b.   How does your answer change if the corporations constitute a unitary business?

Problems

26. **LO.1** Use Exhibit 16.1 to compute Balboa Corporation's State F taxable income for the year.

Addition modifications	$29,000
Allocated income (total)	25,000
Allocated income (State F)	3,000
Allocated income (State G)	22,000
Apportionment percentage	40%
Credits	800
Federal taxable income	90,000
Subtraction modifications	15,000
Tax rate	5%

27. **LO.1, 4** Use Exhibit 16.1 to provide the required information for Warbler Corporation, whose Federal taxable income totals $10 million.

Warbler apportions 70% of its manufacturing income to State C. Warbler generates $4 million of nonapportionable income each year, and 30% of that income is allocated to C. Applying the state income tax modifications, Warbler's total business income from the manufacturing operation this year is $12 million.

a.   How much of Warbler's manufacturing income does State C tax?

b.   How much of Warbler's allocable income does State C tax?

c.   Explain your results.

28. **LO.1** For each of the following items considered independently, indicate whether the circumstances call for an addition modification (*A*), a subtraction modification (*S*), or no modification (*N*) in computing state taxable income. Then indicate the amount of any modification. The starting point in computing State Q taxable income is the year's Federal taxable income before any deduction for net operating losses.

a.   Federal cost recovery = $10,000, and Q cost recovery = $15,000.

b.   Federal cost recovery = $15,000, and Q cost recovery = $10,000.

c.   Federal income taxes paid = $30,000.

d. Refund received from last year's Q income taxes = $3,000.

e. Local property taxes, deducted on the Federal return as a business expense = $80,000.

f. Interest income from holding U.S. Treasury bonds = $5,000.

g. Interest income from holding Q revenue anticipation bonds = $3,000.

h. Interest income from State P school district bonds = $10,000.

i. Change in the excess of FIFO inventory valuation over the Federal LIFO amount = $6,000. Q does not allow the LIFO method.

j. An asset was sold for $18,000; its purchase price was $20,000. Accumulated Federal cost recovery = $15,000, and accumulated Q cost recovery = $8,000.

k. Dividend income received from State R corporation = $30,000, subject to a Federal dividends received deduction of 70%.

29. **LO.1** Perk Corporation is subject to tax only in State A. Perk generated the following income and deductions.

Federal taxable income	$300,000
State A income tax expense	15,000
Refund of State A income tax	3,000
Depreciation allowed for Federal tax purposes	200,000
Depreciation allowed for state tax purposes	120,000

Federal taxable income is the starting point in computing A taxable income. State income taxes are not deductible for A tax purposes. Determine Perk's A taxable income.

30. **LO.1** Fallow Corporation is subject to tax only in State X. Fallow generated the following income and deductions. State income taxes are not deductible for X income tax purposes.

Sales	$4,000,000
Cost of sales	2,800,000
State X income tax expense	200,000
Depreciation allowed for Federal tax purposes	400,000
Depreciation allowed for state tax purposes	250,000
Interest income on Federal obligations	40,000
Interest income on X obligations	30,000
Expenses related to carrying X obligations	2,000

a. The starting point in computing the X income tax base is Federal taxable income. Derive this amount.

b. Determine Fallow's X taxable income assuming that interest on X obligations is exempt from X income tax.

c. Determine Fallow's X taxable income assuming that interest on X obligations is subject to X income tax.

31. **LO.5** Dillman Corporation has nexus in States A and B. Dillman's activities for the year are summarized below.

	State A	State B	Total
Sales	$1,200,000	$ 400,000	$1,600,000
Property			
Average historical cost	500,000	300,000	800,000
Average accumulated depreciation	(300,000)	(100,000)	(400,000)
Payroll	2,500,000	500,000	3,000,000
Rent expense	–0–	35,000	35,000

Determine the apportionment factors for A and B assuming that A uses a three-factor apportionment formula under which sales, property (net depreciated basis), and payroll are equally weighted and B employs a single-factor formula that consists solely of sales. State A has adopted the UDITPA with respect to the inclusion of rent payments in the property factor.

32. **LO.5** Assume the same facts as in Problem 31, except that A uses a single-factor apportionment formula that consists solely of sales and B uses a three-factor apportionment formula that equally weights sales, property (at historical cost), and payroll. State B does not include rent payments in the property factor.

33. **LO.5** Assume the same facts as in Problem 31, except that both states employ a three-factor formula, under which sales are double-weighted. The property factor in A is computed using historical cost; this factor in B is computed using the net depreciated basis. Neither A nor B includes rent payments in the property factor.

34. **LO.5** Roger Corporation operates in two states, as indicated below. This year's operations generated $400,000 of apportionable income.

	State A	State B	Total
Sales	$800,000	$200,000	$1,000,000
Property	300,000	300,000	600,000
Payroll	200,000	50,000	250,000

Compute Roger's State A taxable income assuming that State A apportions income based on a:

a. Three-factor formula, equally weighted.

b. Three-factor formula, with double-weighted sales factor.

c. Sales factor only.

35. **LO.5** Tootie Corporation operates in states A and B as indicated below. All goods are manufactured in State A. Determine the sales to be assigned to both states in computing Tootie's sales factor for the year. Both states follow the UDITPA and the MTC regulations in this regard.

Sales shipped to A locations	$300,000
Sales shipped to B locations	500,000
Interest income from Tootie's B business checking accounts	5,000
Rent income from excess space in A warehouse	40,000
Interest income from Treasury bills in Tootie's B brokerage account, holding only idle cash from operations	65,000
One-time sale of display equipment to B purchaser (tax basis $90,000)	75,000
Royalty received from holding patent, licensed to B user	90,000

Critical Thinking   36. **LO.5, 9** State E applies a throwback rule to sales, but State F does not. State G has not adopted an income tax to date. Clay Corporation, headquartered in E, reported the following sales for the year. All of the goods were shipped from Clay's E manufacturing facilities.

Customer	Customer's Location	This Year's Sales
ShellTell, Inc.	E	$ 75,000,000
Tourists, Ltd.	F	40,000,000
PageToo Corp.	G	100,000,000
Total		$215,000,000

a. Determine Clay's sales factor in those states.

b. Comment on Clay's location strategy using only your tax computations.

37. **LO.5, 9** Quinn Corporation is subject to tax in States G, H, and I. Quinn's compen- **Critical Thinking**
sation expense includes the following.

	State G	State H	State I	Total
Salaries and wages for nonofficers	$200,000	$400,000	$400,000	$1,000,000
Officers' salaries	–0–	–0–	500,000	500,000
Total				$1,500,000

Officers' salaries are included in the payroll factor for G and I, but not for H. Compute Quinn's payroll factors for G, H, and I. Comment on your results.

38. **LO.5** Fiona, a regional sales manager, works from her office in State U. Her region includes several states, as indicated in the sales report below. Fiona is compensated through straight commissions on the sales in her region and a fully excludible cafeteria plan conveying various fringe benefits to her. Determine how much of Fiona's $250,000 commissions and $75,000 fringe benefit package is assigned to the payroll factor of State U.

State	Sales Generated	Fiona's Time Spent There
U	$3,000,000	20%
V	4,000,000	50%
X	8,000,000	30%

39. **LO.5** Kim Corporation, a calendar year taxpayer, operates manufacturing facilities in States A and B. A summary of Kim's property holdings follows.

	Beginning of Year		
	State A	State B	Total
Inventory	$ 300,000	$ 200,000	$ 500,000
Plant and equipment	2,500,000	1,500,000	4,000,000
Accumulated depreciation: plant and equipment	(1,000,000)	(600,000)	(1,600,000)
Land	600,000	1,000,000	1,600,000
Rental property*	900,000	300,000	1,200,000
Accumulated depreciation: rental property	(200,000)	(90,000)	(290,000)

	End of Year		
	State A	State B	Total
Inventory	$ 400,000	$ 200,000	$ 600,000
Plant and equipment	2,800,000	1,200,000	4,000,000
Accumulated depreciation: plant and equipment	(1,200,000)	(650,000)	(1,850,000)
Land	600,000	1,200,000	1,800,000
Rental property*	1,000,000	300,000	1,300,000
Accumulated depreciation: rental property	(250,000)	(100,000)	(350,000)

*Unrelated to regular business operations.

Determine Kim's property factors for the two states. The statutes of both A and B provide that average historical cost of business property is to be included in the property factor.

Decision Making

Communications

40. **LO.6, 9** True Corporation, a wholly owned subsidiary of Trumaine Corporation, generated a $400,000 taxable loss in its first year of operations. True's activities and sales are restricted to State A, which imposes an 8% income tax.

In the same year, Trumaine's taxable income is $1,000,000. Trumaine's activities and sales are restricted to State B, which imposes an 11% income tax. Both states use a three-factor apportionment formula that equally weights sales, payroll, and property, and both require a unitary group to file on a combined basis. Sales, payroll, and average property for each corporation are as follows.

	True Corporation	**Trumaine Corporation**	**Total**
Sales	$2,500,000	$4,000,000	$6,500,000
Property	1,000,000	2,500,000	3,500,000
Payroll	500,000	1,500,000	2,000,000

True and Trumaine have been found to be members of a unitary business.

a. Determine the overall state income tax for the unitary group.

b. Determine aggregate state income tax for the entities as if they were nonunitary.

c. Compare your results, and comment on the desirability of True's arrangement. Incorporate this analysis in a letter to Trumaine's board of directors. Corporate offices are located at 1234 Mulberry Lane, Birmingham, AL 35298.

41. **LO.6** Chang Corporation is part of a three-corporation unitary business. The group has a water's edge election in effect with respect to unitary State Q. State B does not apply the unitary concept with respect to its corporate income tax laws. Nor does Despina, a European country to which Saldez paid a $7,000,000 value added tax this year.

Saldez was organized in Despina and conducts all of its business there. Given the summary of operations that follows, determine Chang's and Elena's sales factors in B and Q.

Corporation	**Customer's Location**	**Sales**
Chang	B	$20,000,000
	Q	60,000,000
Elena	Q	70,000,000
Saldez	Despina	50,000,000

42. **LO.8** Using the following information from the books and records of Grande Corporation, determine Grande's total sales that are subject to State C's sales tax. Grande operates a retail general store.

Sales to C consumers, general merchandise	$1,100,000
Sales to C consumers, crutches and other medical supplies	245,000
Sales to consumers in State D, via mail order	80,000
Purchases from suppliers	55,000

43. **LO.8** As a retailer, Zertan Corporation sells software programs manufactured and packaged by other parties. Zertan also purchases computer parts, assembles them as specified by a customer in a purchase order, and sells them as operating standalone computers. All of Zertan's operations take place in State F, which levies a 9% sales tax. Results for the current year are as follows.

Sales of software	$2,500,000
Purchases of computer parts	1,600,000
Sales of computer systems	8,500,000
Purchases of office supplies	60,000
Purchases of packaging materials for the computer systems	20,000
Purchases of tools used by computer assemblers	50,000

a. What is Zertan's own sales tax expense for the year?

b. How much F sales tax must Zertan collect and pay to the state on behalf of other taxpayers subject to the tax?

44. **LO.8** Indicate for each transaction whether a sales (*S*) or use (*U*) tax applies or whether the transaction is nontaxable (*N*). Assume that the most common definitional rules apply in both states. All taxpayers are individuals.

a. A resident of State A purchases an automobile in A.

b. A resident of State A purchases groceries in A.

c. A resident of State B purchases an automobile in A.

d. A charity purchases office supplies in A.

e. An A resident purchases in B an item that will be in the inventory of her business.

45. **LO.5, 8** Wayne Corporation is subject to State A's franchise tax. The tax is imposed at a rate of 1.2% of the corporation's net worth, as apportioned to the state by use of a two-factor formula (sales and property factors, equally weighted). The property factor includes real and tangible personal property valued at historical cost as of the end of the taxable year.

Forty percent of Wayne's sales are attributable to A, and $600,000 of the cost of Wayne's tangible personal property is located in A.

Determine the A franchise tax payable by Wayne this year given the following end-of-the-year balance sheet.

Cash		$ 200,000
Equipment	$1,000,000	
Accumulated depreciation	(300,000)	700,000
Furniture and fixtures	$ 800,000	
Accumulated depreciation	(50,000)	750,000
Intangible assets		450,000
Total assets		$2,100,000
Accounts and taxes payable		$ 600,000
Long-term debt		750,000
Common stock		1,000
Additional paid-in capital		249,000
Retained earnings		500,000
Total liabilities and equity		$2,100,000

46. **LO.5, 9** Dread Corporation operates in a high-tax state. The firm asks you for advice on a plan to outsource administrative work done in its home state to independent contractors. This work now costs the company $750,000 in wages and benefits. Dread's total payroll for the year is $8,000,000, of which $6,000,000 is for work currently done in the home state.   *Decision Making*

47. **LO.2, 5, 9** Prepare a PowerPoint presentation (maximum of six slides) entitled "Planning Principles for Our Multistate Clients." The slides will be used to lead a 20-minute discussion with colleagues in the corporate tax department. Keep the outline general, but assume that your colleagues have clients among them operating in at least 15 states. Address only income tax issues.   *Critical Thinking* *Communications*

Research Problems

Use internet tax resources to address the following questions. Look for reliable websites and blogs of the IRS and other government agencies, media outlets, businesses, tax professionals, academics, think tanks, and political outlets.

Critical Thinking

Communications

Research Problem 1. Pick two of the following provisions that currently do not exist in your state. If your state does not levy a sales/use tax or an income tax on corporations, review the rules of a neighboring state. Send an e-mail to your instructor, listing pro and con arguments for the state to adopt the provisions.

a. Exempt "green" technology from the apportionment weight for the property factor.

b. Subject song and movie downloads to the sales/use tax.

c. Allow an income tax credit for 20% of the cost of in-state construction projects that are substantially completed within the next 18 months.

d. Tax the income of vendors who do not have a physical presence in your state but sell to in-state customers online.

e. Add an income-tax "nexus team" to find the taxpayers operating in your state but based in Ohio, Illinois, or Arizona.

f. Adopt the definitions and other rules of the Streamlined Sales Tax Project.

g. Allow an income tax credit for 25% of the wages paid to newly hired employees and contractors who work in the tech and pharma industries.

h. Apply a tax on S corporations operating in the state equal to 2% of the entity's gross receipts.

i. Convert the corporate income tax to a tax on gross receipts, in an effort to tax the profits of passive investment companies owned by in-state parent entities.

j. Broaden the definition of sales/use tax nexus so as to force sellers or sales facilitators to remit the tax for online sales.

Communications

Research Problem 2. For your state and one of its neighbors, find the following income tax rules. Place your data in a chart, and e-mail your findings to your instructor.

a. To what extent does each state follow the rulings of the Multistate Tax Commission?

b. Does the state adopt pertinent changes to the Internal Revenue Code? If so, as of what date?

c. What is the highest income tax rate for corporations?

d. Is the tax effectiveness of a passive investment company limited in some way? Has the state adopted the *Geoffrey* approach to the taxation of income from intangibles? Explain.

e. Does the state apply entity-level income taxes for S corporations, partnerships, and LLCs? If so, what are the terms of those taxes?

Communications

Research Problem 3. For your state and one of its neighbors, find the following sales/use tax rules. Place your data in a chart, and e-mail your findings to your instructor.

a. What are the requirements for the occasional-sale rule as an exception to the sales/use tax? Who can use this rule?

b. Describe any exemptions from the sales/use tax base that are allowed for transactions involving groceries, school clothing and supplies, religious goods, and legal services.

c. What is the discount allowed, if any, when a vendor remits sales/use tax to the state in a timely manner?

d. Is manufacturing equipment exempt from the sales/use tax? Medical devices for a clinic? Medical devices for a consumer?

e. Can a vendor use an electronic funds transfer system to remit its sales/use tax collections? If so, when is it required to do so?

f. Has the state joined the Streamlined Sales Tax Project? If yes, what is the effective date?

Research Problem 4. Identify three states considered to be in the same economic region as your own. For each of the three states, answer the following questions. Answers to most can be found at **taxadmin.org**.

Data Analytics

Communications

- What is the overall tax burden per capita, and where does it rank among all states?
- What is the overall tax burden as a percentage of personal income, and where does it rank among all states?
- From what source(s) does it raise most of its revenues (e.g., sales/use tax, highway tolls)? In what proportions?
- What is the highest marginal tax rate on corporate income?
- What is its apportionment formula, including factors and weights?

Summarize your findings in a Microsoft Excel spreadsheet, and submit it to your instructor.

Research Problem 5. Read the "tax footnote" of five publicly traded U.S. corporations. Find the effective state/local income tax rates of each. Create a PowerPoint presentation (maximum of three slides) for your instructor, summarizing the search and reporting your findings.

Data Analytics

Communications

Becker CPA Review Questions

1. Olinto, Inc., has taxable income (before special deductions and the net operating loss deduction) of $92,000. Included in that amount is $12,000 of interest and dividend income. Forty percent of Olinto's property, payroll, and sales are in its home state. What amount of this taxable income will be taxed by Olinto, Inc.'s home state?

   a. $12,000
   b. $36,800

   c. $44,000
   d. $90,000

2. In which of the following cases will Federal law prohibit a state from imposing an income tax on net income?

   a. The business has a retail outlet store in the state.

   b. The business has its corporate headquarters in the state and generates sales from there.

   c. Orders are taken within the state and accepted at corporate headquarters outside of the state and shipped from a location outside of the state.

   d. Orders are taken within the state and accepted at corporate headquarters outside of the state and shipped from a location inside the state.

Tax Practice and Ethics

LEARNING OBJECTIVES: *After completing Chapter 17, you should be able to:*

LO.1 Illustrate the organization and structure of the IRS.

LO.2 Identify the various administrative pronouncements issued by the IRS and explain how they can be used in tax practice.

LO.3 Describe the audit process, including how tax returns are selected for audit and the various types of audits.

LO.4 Explain the taxpayer appeal process, including various settlement options available.

LO.5 Determine the amount of interest on a deficiency or a refund and when it is due.

LO.6 List and explain the various penalties that can be imposed on acts of noncompliance by taxpayers and return preparers.

LO.7 Recognize and apply the rules governing the statute of limitations on assessments and on refunds.

LO.8 Summarize the legal and ethical guidelines that apply to those engaged in tax practice.

CHAPTER OUTLINE

ID1974/Shutterstock.com

A TAX ADVISER'S DILEMMA

Campbell Corporation is preparing its Form 1120 for the tax year. The entity develops and manufactures a number of high-tech products, including a line of GPS applications that are downloaded onto tablets and phones. Campbell's research department needs to work with the U.S. government on this line of software because of the potential for security breaches when the software is used in sensitive parts of the world. Other efforts of the research department include traditional software architecture and development. Projections show that the GPS products will be highly profitable, with sales concentrated among various commercial and governmental communications providers around the world.

Some of the research department's work on the GPS products clearly qualifies for the Federal income tax credit for incremental research expenditures, but for some other items, the availability of the credit is not so certain. Because of the unclear language of the pertinent Regulations with regard to Campbell's setting or because of the innovative aspects of the products under development, the law is silent as to whether Campbell can claim the credit.

You are Campbell's tax adviser. This situation presents you with several levels of difficulty. How aggressive should you advise Campbell to be in reporting items on the Form 1120 that qualify for the research credit? Will an overly aggressive position on the credit trigger a tax preparer penalty for your tax consulting firm? What level of diligence should you exercise in advising Campbell as to whether specific expenditures qualify for the credit, given that your expertise with GPS software is limited to using the unit in your personal auto?

Read the chapter and formulate your response.

Few events arouse so much fear in the typical individual or corporate tax department as the receipt of a letter from the Internal Revenue Service (IRS) notifying the taxpayer that prior years' tax returns are the subject of an audit. Almost immediately, calls are made to the tax adviser. Advice is sought as to what to reveal (or not reveal) in the course of the audit, how to delay or avoid the audit, and how friendly one should be with the auditor when he or she ultimately arrives.

The tax professional can render valuable services to the taxpayer in an audit context, thereby ensuring that tax payments for the disputed years are neither under- nor overreported, as part of an ongoing tax practice. In this regard, the adviser must appreciate the following, each of which is addressed in this chapter.

- The elements of the Treasury's tax administration process and opportunities for appeal within the structure of the IRS.
- The extent of the negative sanctions that can be brought to bear against taxpayers whose returns are found to have been inaccurate.
- The ethical and professional constraints on the advice tax advisers can give and the actions they can take on behalf of their clients within the context of an adversarial relationship with the IRS.

17-1 **TAX ADMINISTRATION**

The Treasury has delegated the administration and enforcement of the tax laws to its subsidiary agency, the IRS. In this process, the IRS carries out duties concerning taxpayer service, tax compliance, and tax law enforcement. The IRS is responsible for providing adequate information, in the form of publications and forms with instructions, to taxpayers so that they can comply with the laws in an appropriate manner. The IRS collects current and delinquent tax payments. It carries out assessment and collection procedures under the restrictions of due process and other constitutional guarantees. The agency also is responsible for several taxes under the Affordable Care Act.

The IRS employs about 75,000 staff members, about two-thirds of whom are women; fewer than 3 percent of the staff is under age 30. The total agency budget is almost $12 billion. In meeting its responsibilities, the Service conducts audits of selected tax returns. About 0.6 percent of all individual tax returns are subjected to audit in a given tax year. However, certain types of both taxpayers and income—including, for instance, high-income individuals, cash-oriented businesses, real estate transactions, and estate- and gift-taxable transfers—are subject to much higher probabilities of audit, about 15 percent for individuals with $10 million or more of income.

The audit rate for corporations with at least $5 million in assets is about 27 percent, but only about 10 percent for businesses with less than $1 million in assets. In the past few years, the IRS has seen hiring freezes and personnel cuts in its audit and enforcement activities, and in the training of its staff, but it is targeting narrower issues that are projected to produce more revenue for the time spent. Thus, audit rates for large corporations have decreased, although the dollars collected from such audits continue to increase.

In recent years, Congress and the IRS have found ways to improve reporting by taxpayers, such as through information returns and document matching. For instance, when a taxpayer engages in a like-kind exchange or sells a personal residence, various parties to the transaction are required to report the nature and magnitude of the transaction to the IRS. Later, the Treasury's computers determine whether the transaction has been reported properly by comparing the information reported by the third parties with the events included on the relevant taxpayers' returns for the year.

In addition, the IRS has been placing increasing pressure on the community of tax advisers. Severe penalties may be assessed on those who have prepared the appropriate return when the Service's interpretation of applicable law conflicts with that of the preparer.

Taxes Collected and the Tax Gap

The IRS processes more than 150 million individual income tax returns every year, of which about 88 percent are filed electronically (i.e., known as **e-filing**). About 60 percent of e-filed returns are submitted by tax professionals, and 40 percent are prepared by the taxpayers themselves.

The agency collects more than $3.4 trillion in annual tax revenues and pays refunds to about 117 million individual taxpayers every year. The average Form 1040 refund is about $3,500.

As directed by Congress, the IRS estimates the size of the Federal income "tax gap"—the difference between how much tax *is* collected and how much *should be* collected.

According to the most recent analysis, the tax gap is a net amount of over $405 billion in income and employment taxes annually. More specifically, the underpayments total about $460 billion per year but are offset by $55 billion obtained through related IRS enforcement efforts (e.g., audits and collection procedures).

The IRS maintains that only 85 percent of taxpayers report the "correct" amount of tax under the existing system of voluntary compliance, after accounting for audits. The main sources of the tax gap are:

- Underreporting net taxable income (85 percent of the tax gap).
- Underpayment of tax (8 percent of the tax gap).
- Nonfiling (7 percent of the tax gap).

17-1a **Organizational Structure of the IRS**

The structure of the IRS is illustrated in Exhibit 17.1. The IRS Commissioner, a Presidential appointee who serves a five-year renewable term, has organized the day-to-day activities of the agency into four major operating divisions based on the type of tax returns to be processed. Administrative functions, such as those relating to personnel and computer issues, are organized on a shared-services model managed from the national office. Broader functions, such as litigation, investigations, and taxpayer relations, are managed at the national level as well.

LO.1

Illustrate the organization and structure of the IRS.

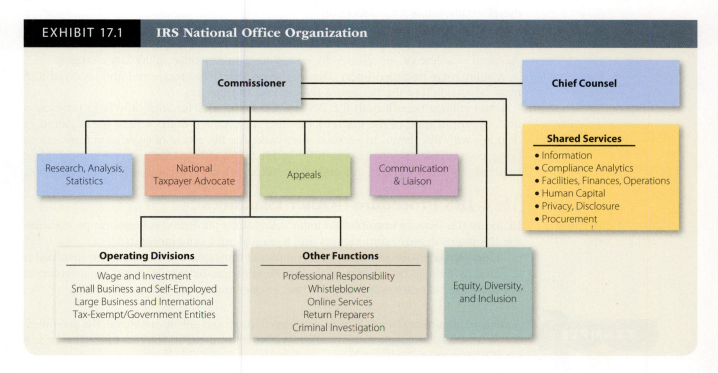

EXHIBIT 17.1   IRS National Office Organization

The Chief Counsel, another Presidential appointee, is the head legal officer of the IRS. The Chief Counsel's office provides legal advice to the IRS and guidance to the public on matters pertaining to the administration and enforcement of the tax laws. For instance, the Chief Counsel's duties include establishing uniform nationwide interpretive positions on the law, drafting tax guide material for taxpayers and IRS personnel, issuing technical rulings to taxpayers, and providing advice and technical assistance to IRS personnel. The Chief Counsel represents the IRS in all litigation before the Tax Court.

The National Taxpayer Advocate is appointed by the Secretary of the Treasury and reports to the IRS Commissioner.[1] The Advocate's office includes about 2,000 employees who work with taxpayers when normal IRS channels have not brought about a satisfactory result; the Advocate works to ensure the fair treatment of the taxpayer and the exercise of applicable taxpayer rights. This independent office represents taxpayers who have experienced a delay of more than 30 days in resolving a matter and have experienced economic harm as a result. The Advocate issues an annual report to Congress,[2] identifying structural problems in Federal tax administration and offering proposed legislative and other solutions for them.

17-1b IRS Procedure—Letter Rulings

LO.2

Identify the various administrative pronouncements issued by the IRS and explain how they can be used in tax practice.

When a tax issue is controversial or a transaction involves considerable tax dollars, the taxpayer often wants to obtain either assurance or direction from the IRS as to the treatment of the event. The **letter ruling** process is an effective means of dealing directly with the IRS while in the planning stages of a large or otherwise important transaction.

Rulings issued by the National Office provide a written statement of the position of the IRS concerning the tax consequences of a course of action contemplated by the taxpayer. Letter rulings do not have the force and effect of law, but they do provide guidance and support for taxpayers in similar transactions. The IRS issues rulings only on uncompleted, actual (rather than hypothetical) transactions or on transactions that have been completed before the filing of the tax return for the year in question.

In certain circumstances, the IRS will not issue a ruling. It ordinarily will not rule in cases that essentially involve a question of fact.[3] For example, no ruling will be issued to determine whether compensation paid to employees is reasonable in amount and therefore allowable as a deduction.

A letter ruling represents the current opinion of the IRS on the tax consequences of a transaction with a given set of facts. IRS rulings are not unchangeable. They can be declared obsolete or superseded by new rulings in response to tax law changes.

A ruling may be relied upon only by the taxpayer who requested and received it. It must be attached to the tax return for the year in question.

Letter rulings benefit both the IRS and the taxpayer. They not only help promote a uniform application of the tax laws but also may reduce the potential for litigation or disputes with IRS agents. In addition, they make the IRS aware of significant transactions being consummated by taxpayers. A fee of $30,000 is charged for processing most ruling requests; the fee is reduced to $2,800 if the taxpayer's gross income is less than $250,000.

17-1c IRS Procedure—Other Issuances

In addition to issuing unpublished letter rulings and published rulings and procedures, the IRS issues determination letters and technical advice memoranda.

A **determination letter** relates to a completed transaction when the issue involved is covered by judicial or statutory authority, Regulations, or rulings. Determination letters are issued for various estate, gift, income, excise, and employment tax matters.

EXAMPLE 1

A group of physicians plans to form an entity to construct and operate a hospital. The determination letter procedure is appropriate to ascertain whether the group is subject to the Federal income tax or is tax-exempt.

---

[1]§ 7803(c).

[2]See **irs.gov/advocate/reports-to-congress**.

[3]Rev.Proc. 2019–1, 2019–1 I.R.B. 1.

ETHICS & EQUITY Tax Compliance Costs

By one estimate, the cost of compliance with Federal tax laws exceeds *$400 billion* per year. Roughly, this means that compliance costs act as an additional tax of almost *40 cents* for every tax dollar collected. This amount exceeds the gross domestic product of 36 U.S. states.

In this estimate, the following items were counted as costs of tax compliance.[4]

- The value of taxpayers' time spent record keeping, filing, planning, and otherwise complying with the tax laws.

- Tax collection costs (chiefly wages and benefits) of IRS employees.

- Expenditures made to professional tax preparers, consultants, and other preparers.

Comment on the appropriateness of Congress and the Treasury passing along to taxpayers the costs of its revenue collection operation.

A **technical advice memorandum (TAM)** is issued by the National Office to IRS personnel in response to a specific request by an agent, Appellate Conferee, or IRS executive. The taxpayer may request a TAM if an issue in dispute is not treated by the law or precedent and/or published rulings or Regulations. Technical advice requests arise from the audit or appeals process, whereas letter ruling requests typically are issued as part of the filing of an original tax return (i.e., before any IRS audit).

17-1d Administrative Powers of the IRS

Examination of Records

The IRS can examine the taxpayer's books and records as part of the process of determining the correct amount of tax due. The IRS also can require the persons responsible for the return to appear and to produce any necessary books and records.[5] Taxpayers are required to maintain certain record-keeping procedures and retain the records necessary to facilitate the audit.

Burden of Proof

If the taxpayer meets the record-keeping requirement and substantiates income and deductions properly, the IRS bears the burden of proof in establishing a tax deficiency during litigation. The taxpayer must have cooperated with the IRS regarding reasonable requests for information, documents, meetings, and interviews. For individual taxpayers, the IRS's burden of proof extends to penalties and interest amounts that it assesses in a court proceeding with the taxpayer.[6]

Assessment and Demand

The Code permits the IRS to assess a deficiency and to demand payment for the tax. However, no assessment or effort to collect the tax may be made until 90 days after a statutory notice of a deficiency (a *90-day letter*) is issued. The taxpayer therefore has 90 days to file a petition to the U.S. Tax Court, effectively preventing the deficiency from being assessed or collected pending the outcome of the case.[7]

Following assessment of the tax, the IRS issues a notice and demand for payment. The taxpayer can be given as little as 10 days to pay the tax after the demand for payment is issued. If the IRS believes the assessment or collection of a deficiency is in jeopardy, it may assess the deficiency and demand immediate payment.[8]

---

[4]**taxfoundation.org/compliance-costs-irs-regulations**.

[5]§ 7602.

[6]§§ 7491(a)(1), (a)(2)(B), and (c).

[7]§§ 6212 and 6213.

[8]§ 6861. A jeopardy assessment is appropriate, for instance, when the IRS fears that the taxpayer will flee the country or destroy valuable property.

Collection

If the taxpayer neglects or refuses to pay the tax after receiving the demand for payment, a lien in favor of the IRS is placed on all property (realty and personalty, tangible and intangible) belonging to the taxpayer.

The levy power of the IRS is very broad. It allows the IRS to garnish (*attach*) wages and salary and to seize and sell all nonexempt property by any means. After a notice period, the IRS can make successive seizures on any property owned by the taxpayer until the levy is satisfied.[9] A taxpayer's principal residence is exempt from the levy process, unless the disputed tax, interest, and penalty exceed $5,000 and a U.S. District Court judge approves of the seizure.[10]

17-1e The Audit Process

LO.3

Describe the audit process, including how tax returns are selected for audit and the various types of audits.

Selection of Returns for Audit

The IRS utilizes mathematical formulas to select tax returns that are most likely to contain errors and yield substantial amounts of additional tax revenues upon audit. The IRS does not disclose all of its audit selection techniques. However, some observations can be made regarding the probability of a return's selection for audit.

- Certain groups of taxpayers are subject to audit more frequently than others. These groups include individuals with gross income in excess of $200,000, self-employed individuals with substantial business income and deductions, and cash businesses where the potential for tax evasion is high.

EXAMPLE 2

Tracey owns and operates a liquor store. Because nearly all of her sales are for cash, Tracey might be a prime candidate for an audit by the IRS. Cash transactions are easier to conceal from the tax authorities than are those made by credit card or by using a payment "app" where funds are transferred between accounts of the seller and customer.

- If a taxpayer has been audited in a past year and the audit led to the assessment of a substantial deficiency, the IRS often makes a return visit for a later tax year.
- An audit might materialize if information returns (e.g., Form W–2 and Form 1099) are not in substantial agreement with the income reported on the taxpayer's return. Obvious discrepancies do not necessitate formal audits and usually can be handled by correspondence with the taxpayer.

EXAMPLE 3

The IRS audits Phil's Form 1040 and finds that his dividend income increased sharply. The auditor wonders how Phil financed this stock purchase: there were no corresponding stock sales on his return that would create cash with which to make the acquisition.

Upon further inquiry, the auditor learns that the dividend yielding stock was a gift to Phil from his mother, Julie. Accordingly, the IRS investigates whether Julie filed a Federal gift tax return for the year of the stock transfer.

- If an individual's itemized deductions are in excess of norms established for various income levels, the probability of an audit increases. Certain deductions (e.g., casualty and theft losses, business use of the home, and tax-sheltered investments) are sensitive areas, because the IRS realizes that many taxpayers determine the amount of the deduction incorrectly or may not be entitled to the deduction at all.
- Information often is obtained by the IRS from outside sources, including other government agencies, news items, and informants.

---

[9]The taxpayer can keep certain personal and business property and a minimal amount of his or her income as a subsistence allowance, even if a lien is outstanding. § 6334(a).

[10]§§ 6334(a)(13)(A) and (e)(1).

After 15 years of employment, Betty is discharged by her employer, Dr. Franklin. Shortly thereafter, the IRS receives a letter from Betty stating that Franklin keeps two sets of books, one of which substantially understates his cash receipts.

EXAMPLE 4

The statistical models used by the IRS to select individual tax returns for audit come from random audits of a small number of taxpayers, who are required to document every entry they made on the Form 1040. The latest round of these National Research Program (NRP) audits resulted in the construction of new Discriminant Inventory Function (DIF) scores that project the amount of revenue the IRS will gain from pursuing tax returns with various statistical profiles. The higher the DIF score, the better the return to the IRS from pursuing the audit, and the higher the probability of selection for an examination.

These data-seeking audits are controversial and have led to taxpayer complaints to Congress about the stress they create.[11] The IRS believes that by constantly updating the NRP data through a diligent review of randomly selected tax returns, changes in tax avoidance behaviors will be detected and fewer routine audits will be required.

Many individual taxpayers mistakenly assume that if they do not hear from the IRS within a few weeks after filing their return or if they receive a refund check, no audit will be forthcoming. As a practical matter, most individual returns are examined about two years from the date of filing. If a return is not audited within this time period, it generally remains unaudited. All large corporations, however, are subject to annual audits.

About 10 percent of all completed audits of individual returns result in a "no change" recommendation for the taxpayer. A "no change" recommendation results for about one-half of all partnership/LLC and S corporation audits, and for about 40 percent of audits of large corporations.

ETHICS & EQUITY Can the IRS Pretend to Be Your Friend?

Should IRS agents be allowed to identify audit subjects by reading the society page of the newspaper, looking for indicators of wealth? What if the agency subscribes to Facebook and seeks comments from its "friends" as to income windfalls and stock market dealings? In the past, some state and local taxing agencies have used social networking sites for audit selection purposes. State and local revenue agents have used the sites to find self-employed individuals who advertise their business and report about upcoming income-producing events. The sites also have been used to determine whether a taxpayer who has requested an extension of time to pay a delinquent tax actually is strapped for cash.

Some state tax officials claim that looking for a taxpayer's self-declarations on a website is a much more efficient way to find income understatements than searching through most other sources of nonstatistical data. Should taxing agencies be using Google, Facebook, and other public-domain online sources of taxpayer information to help find non-filers and identify tax returns for audit?

Role of Informants

The IRS can pay awards to persons who provide information that leads to the detection and punishment of those who violate the tax laws. The awards are paid at the discretion of the IRS. Such a payment usually cannot exceed 15 percent of the taxes, fines, and penalties recovered as a result of such information.[12]

About 250 informant awards are paid in the typical year. For fiscal year 2017, the IRS collected about $200 million in underpaid taxes from the informants' program, and it paid awards of over $30 million (i.e., at approximately a 15 percent rate).

Another IRS office, through the so-called **Whistleblower Program**, offers special awards to informants who provide information concerning businesses or high-income (gross income exceeds $200,000) individuals when more than $2 million of tax, penalty, and

---

[11]On average, the total annual NRP audit sample consists of 13,000 returns. Some of these returns are analyzed without contacting the taxpayer, and other taxpayers are contacted only by mail with queries about one or two items. Only a few returns are subjected to "line-by-line" review. Most of the returns are reviewed for a period of three tax years.

[12]§ 7623 and Reg. § 301.7623–1.

interest is at stake. Some informants claim that hundreds of millions of dollars of tax, penalty, and interest are due from allegedly noncompliant taxpayers.

A whistleblower award can reach 30 percent of the amount collected by the Treasury and traceable to the whistleblower's information. The award can be reduced if the whistleblower participated in the original understatement of tax. About 12,000 claims are initiated every year, and the IRS annually pays awards to about 400 whistleblowers.

A final decision on a whistleblower case might not be made until five to seven years after the date the claim is filed. The award itself constitutes gross income when it is received. Legal fees for the whistleblower tend to be about 30 percent of the award; such fees may be deductible by the informant.

The whistleblower awards are paid out of the taxes recovered under the informant and whistleblower programs. To claim an award of this sort, an informant files Form 211 with the IRS. Federal income taxes are withheld from the whistleblower award. A whistleblower has 30 days to appeal to the IRS if his or her claim is denied or reduced from the original amount requested.

Verification and Audit Procedures

The filed tax return is reviewed for mathematical accuracy when the IRS receives it. A check is also made for deductions, exclusions, etc., that are clearly erroneous. One obvious error would be the failure to comply with the AGI limitation on the deduction for medical expenses.

About 2 percent of all paper-filed individual returns show a math error. The math error rate for e-filed returns is only 0.1 percent. When a math or clerical error occurs, the Service Center merely sends the taxpayer revised computations and a bill or refund as appropriate, usually within one year of the filing date.

Taxpayers usually are able to settle routine tax disputes (e.g., queries involving the documentation of deductions) through a by-mail-only *correspondence audit* with the IRS, without the necessity of a formal meeting. The taxpayer receives a letter from the IRS wherein the tax is recomputed upward (e.g., because the amount of reported wages does not match that on Form W–2). The taxpayer then complies by paying the additional tax or objects by providing information and documentation showing that the reported amount was correct. More than two-thirds of all Form 1040 audits are handled in this way.

Office audits are rare today; they are conducted in an office of the IRS. In most instances, the taxpayer is required merely to substantiate a deduction, a credit, or an item of income that appears on the return. The taxpayer presents documentation in the form of canceled checks, invoices, etc., for the items in question.

The *field audit* procedure commonly is used for corporate returns and for returns of individuals engaged in business or professional activities. This type of audit generally involves a more complete examination of a taxpayer's transactions.

A field audit is conducted by IRS agents at the office or home of the taxpayer or at the office of the taxpayer's representative. The agent's work may be facilitated by a review of certain tax workpapers and discussions with the taxpayer's representative about items appearing on the tax return.

Prior to or at the initial interview, the IRS must provide the taxpayer with an explanation of the audit process that is the subject of the interview and describe the taxpayer's rights under that process. If the taxpayer clearly states at any time during the interview the desire to consult with an attorney, a CPA, or an enrolled agent or any other person permitted to represent the taxpayer before the IRS, then the IRS representative must suspend the interview.[13]

Any officer or employee of the IRS must, upon advance request, allow a taxpayer to make an audio recording of any in-person interview with the officer or employee concerning the determination and collection of any tax.[14]

Settlement with the Revenue Agent

Following an audit, the IRS agent may either accept the return as filed or recommend certain adjustments. The **Revenue Agent's Report (RAR)** is reviewed within the IRS. In most instances, the agent's proposed adjustments are approved.

---

[13]§ 7521(b).   [14]§ 7521(a).

Agents must adhere strictly to IRS policy as reflected in published rulings, Regulations, and other releases. The agent cannot settle an unresolved issue based upon the probability of winning the case in court. Usually, issues involving factual questions can be settled at the agent level, and it may be advantageous for both the taxpayer and the IRS to reach agreement at the earliest point in the settlement process. For example, it may be to the taxpayer's advantage to reach agreement at the agent level and avoid any further opportunity for the IRS to raise new issues.

If agreement is reached upon the proposed deficiency, the taxpayer signs Form 870 (Waiver of Restrictions on Assessment and Collection of Deficiency in Tax). One advantage to the taxpayer of signing Form 870 at this point is that interest stops accumulating on the deficiency 30 days after the form is filed.[15] When this form is signed, the taxpayer effectively waives the right to receive a statutory notice of deficiency (90-day letter) and to subsequently petition the Tax Court. In addition, it is no longer possible for the taxpayer later to go to the IRS Appeals Division.

17-1f **The Taxpayer Appeal Process**

LO.4

Explain the taxpayer appeal process, including various settlement options available.

If agreement cannot be reached at the agent level, the taxpayer receives a copy of the Revenue Agent's Report and a 30-day letter. The taxpayer has 30 days to request an administrative appeal. If an appeal is not requested, a 90-day letter is issued. Exhibit 17.2 illustrates the taxpayer's alternatives when a disagreement with the IRS persists.

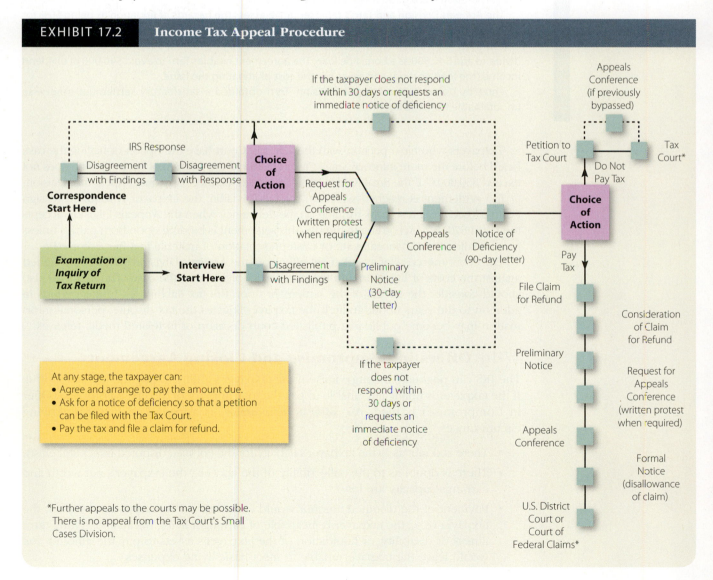

EXHIBIT 17.2   Income Tax Appeal Procedure

A taxpayer must make an appropriate request to the Appeals Division. The request must be accompanied by a written protest, except when:

- The proposed tax deficiency does not exceed $10,000 for any of the tax periods involved in the audit, and

- The deficiency resulted from a correspondence or office audit (i.e., not as a result of a field audit).

The Appeals Division is authorized to settle all tax disputes based on the hazards of litigation (the chances of winning in court). Because the Appeals Division has final settlement authority until a 90-day letter has been issued, the taxpayer may be able to negotiate a settlement. In addition, an overall favorable settlement may be reached by "trading" disputed issues.

EXAMPLE 5

At the time Terri is audited, the corporation that she controls had advances outstanding to her in the amount of $80,000. The IRS field agent held that these advances were constructive dividends to her (refer to the discussion in text Section 5-3d). Some facts point toward this result (e.g., the corporation is closely held, Terri has made no repayments, and the loan balance has increased over several years). Other facts, however, appear to indicate that these advances are bona fide loans (e.g., a written instrument provides for interest, Terri has the independent means of repayment, and the corporation has a good dividend-paying record).

The Appeals Division and Terri's representative assess the hazards of litigation as being 50% for each side. Thus, if Terri chooses to take the issue to court, she would have an even chance of winning or losing her case. Based on this assessment, both sides agree to treat $40,000 of the advance as a dividend and $40,000 as a bona fide loan. The agreement enables Terri to avoid $40,000 of dividend income (the loan portion) and saves her the cost of litigating the issue.

Thus, by going to the Appeals Division, Terri obtained a satisfactory settlement otherwise unobtainable from the agent.

Taxpayers who file a petition with the U.S. Tax Court have the option of having the case heard before the more informal Small Cases Division if the amount of tax in dispute does not exceed $50,000.[16] If the Small Cases Division is used, neither party may appeal the decision.

If a settlement is reached with the Appeals Division, the taxpayer is required to sign Form 870–AD. Interest stops running on the deficiency when the Appeals Division accepts the Form 870–AD. According to the IRS, this settlement is binding upon both parties unless fraud, malfeasance, concealment, or misrepresentation of material fact has occurred.

The economic costs of a settlement offer from the Appeals Division should be weighed against the costs of litigation and the probability of winning the case. The taxpayer also should consider the effects of the settlement upon the tax liability for future periods in addition to the years under audit. If the taxpayer litigates the tax dispute, personal information may become public in a published court decision or in related media releases.

17-1g Offers in Compromise and Closing Agreements

The IRS can negotiate a compromise if the taxpayer's ability to pay the tax is doubtful. If the taxpayer is financially unable to pay the total amount of the tax, a Form 656 (Offer in Compromise) is filed. An **offer in compromise** is appropriate in the following circumstances.[17]

- There is doubt as to the taxpayer's liability for the tax (i.e., disputed issues still exist).

- There is doubt as to the collectibility of the tax (i.e., the taxpayer's net worth and earnings capacity are low).

- Payment of the disputed amount would constitute an economic hardship for the taxpayer (e.g., the taxpayer is incapable of earning a living because of a long-term illness or disability, or liquidation of the taxpayer's assets to pay the amount due would leave the taxpayer unable to meet basic living expenses).

---

[16]§ 7463(a).   [17]§ 7122 and Reg. § 301.7122–1(b).

ETHICS & EQUITY Our Taxing System of Self-Assessment

The United States is a large country of diverse taxpayers and businesses. Perhaps the only way the massive dollar amounts of Federal income taxes can be collected on a timely basis is through a *self-assessment* process, whereby the taxpayer is charged with disclosing a full picture of the tax year's results and the corresponding computation of taxable income. But a system of self-assessment depends heavily on the honesty and integrity of the taxpayers and their ability to know and comply with the pertinent tax rules.

A recent survey of taxpayer attitudes by the IRS revealed the results shown to the right.

Given the results of this survey, do you think the current self-assessment system is satisfactory? If not, should Congress create additional enforcement procedures to ensure taxpayer compliance? What sort of new reporting rules might be useful?

Why Do You Report and Pay Your Taxes Honestly? (more than one answer allowed)

Taxpayer Responses	Taxpayers for Whom This Reason Is Key (Percent)
My own personal integrity	91%
A third party reported my information to the IRS (e.g., through a Form W–2 or Form 1099), so I must match that amount in my tax form	66%
Fear of an audit	61%
My neighbors report and pay their taxes honestly, so I will too	43%

What Is an Acceptable Amount by Which to Cheat on Your Income Taxes?

	Taxpayers Responding (Percent)
Not at all	88%
A little here and a little there	9%
As much as possible	3%
Other answers	<1%

Source: *2017 Taxpayer Attitude Survey* at **tinyurl.com/17-TP-Attitudes**.

The IRS investigates the offer by evaluating the taxpayer's financial ability to pay the tax. In some instances, the compromise settlement includes an agreement for final settlement of the tax through payments of a specified percentage of the taxpayer's future earnings. This settlement procedure usually entails lengthy negotiations with the IRS, but the presumption is that the agency will find terms upon which to enter into a compromise with the taxpayer.

A 20 percent nonrefundable current payment is required to set up the compromise offer paying the taxes in a lump sum, and a $186 filing fee is required. Low-income individuals can apply for a waiver of the fee and of the 20 percent down payment.[18]

Every year, the IRS accepts about 10,000 offers in compromise, involving about $250 million in unpaid taxes, interest, and penalties.

The IRS can agree to allow taxes to be paid on an installment basis if that arrangement facilitates the tax collection. An individual who has filed timely tax returns for five years is guaranteed the right to use an installment agreement when the amount in dispute does not exceed $10,000. The taxpayer uses Form 9465 to initiate an installment plan. If the tax owed does not exceed $50,000, a taxpayer can use an online application for an installment agreement.

A user fee is assessed with the application for the installment plan. The fee is between $31 and $225, depending on the taxpayer's income level and the form of payment (e.g., credit card, e-check, or funds transfer).

The IRS provides an annual statement accounting for the status of the agreement. The agreement may later be modified or terminated because of (1) inadequate

---

[18]Reg. § 300.3(b)(1)(ii). "Low-income" is defined as less than 250% of the Federal poverty level.

information, (2) subsequent change in financial condition, or (3) failure to pay an installment when due or to provide requested information.[19]

A **closing agreement** is binding on both the taxpayer and the IRS except upon a subsequent showing of fraud, malfeasance, or misrepresentation of a material fact.[20] The closing agreement may be used when disputed issues carry over to future years. It may also be employed to dispose of a dispute involving a specific issue for a prior year or a proposed transaction involving future years. If, for example, the IRS is willing to make substantial concessions in the valuation of assets for estate tax purposes, it may require a closing agreement from the recipient of the property to establish the income tax basis of the assets.

17-1h Interest

LO.5

Determine the amount of interest on a deficiency or a refund and when it is due.

Determination of the Interest Rate

Congress sets the interest rates applicable to Federal tax underpayments (deficiencies) and overpayments (refunds) close to the rates available in financial markets. The Code provides for the rates to be determined quarterly.[21] Thus, the rates that are determined during March are effective for the following April through June.

For tax purposes, interest is based on the Federal short-term rates published periodically by the IRS in Revenue Rulings. They are based on the average market yield on outstanding marketable obligations of the United States with remaining maturity of three years or less.

For noncorporate taxpayers, the interest rate applicable to *both* overpayments and underpayments is 6 percent for the first quarter of 2019. For most corporate taxpayers, the rate is 5 percent for overpayments and 6 percent for underpayments. Corporations with large overpayments or underpayments are subject to different rates. IRS interest is compounded daily. Tables for determining the daily compounded amount are available from the IRS and online.[22]

IRS Deficiency Assessments

Interest usually accrues from the unextended due date of the return until 30 days after the taxpayer agrees to the deficiency by signing Form 870. If the taxpayer does not pay the amount shown on the IRS's notice and demand (final tax bill) within 30 days, interest again accrues on the deficiency.

Refund of Taxpayer's Overpayments

If an overpayment is refunded to the taxpayer within 45 days after the date the return is filed or is due, no interest is allowed. When the taxpayer files an amended return or makes a claim for refund of a prior year's tax (e.g., when net operating loss carrybacks result in refunds of a prior year's tax payments), however, interest is authorized from the original due date of the return through the date when the amended return is filed. In general, taxpayers applying for refunds receive interest as follows.

- When a return is filed after the due date, interest on any overpayment accrues from the date of filing. However, no interest is due if the IRS makes the refund within 45 days of the date of filing.

IRS Interest Payments

EXAMPLE
6

Naomi, a calendar year taxpayer, files her 2018 return on December 1, 2019. The return reflects an overwithholding of $2,500. On June 8, 2020, Naomi receives a refund of her 2018 overpayment. Interest on the refund began to accrue on December 1, 2019 (not April 15, 2019).

---

[19]§ 6159.

[20]§7121(b).

[21]§ 6621.

[22]§ 6622. See, e.g., Rev.Rul. 2016–28, 2016–51 I.R.B. 805.

IRS Interest Payments

Assume the same facts as in Example 6, except that the refund is paid to Naomi on January 5, 2020 (rather than June 8, 2020). No interest is payable by the IRS, because the refund was made within 45 days of the filing of the return.

EXAMPLE 7

- In no event will interest accrue on an overpayment unless the return that is filed is in "processible form." Generally, this means that the return must be signed[23] and contain enough information in a readable format to enable the IRS to identify the taxpayer and to determine the tax (and overpayment) involved.

- In the case of a carryback (e.g., capital loss or tax credit), interest on any refund begins to accrue on the due date of the return (disregarding extensions) for the year in which the carryback arises. Even then, however, no interest accrues until a return is filed or, if the return has been filed, if the IRS pays the refund within 45 days.

Top Corporation, a calendar year taxpayer, incurs a net capital loss during 2019 that it can carry back to tax year 2017 and obtain a refund. On December 28, 2020, Top files a claim for refund. The earliest that interest begins to accrue in this situation is April 15, 2020, the due date of the Form 1120, but because the return was not filed until December 28, 2020, the later date controls. If the IRS pays the refund within 45 days of December 28, 2020, no interest need be paid.

EXAMPLE 8

Concept Summary 17.1

Working with the IRS

1. The Internal Revenue Service (IRS) enforces the tax laws of the United States. Its size and form of organization reflect its various responsibilities relative to taxpayer interaction, litigation, and collection, as well as its internal functions.

2. The IRS issues various pronouncements in communicating its position on certain tax issues. These pronouncements promote the uniform enforcement of the tax law among taxpayers and among the internal divisions of the IRS. Taxpayers should seek such rulings and memoranda when the nature or magnitude of a pending transaction requires a high degree of certainty in the planning process.

3. IRS audits can take several forms. Taxpayers are selected for audit based on the probable net dollar return to the Treasury

from the process. Offers in compromise and closing agreements can be a useful means of completing an audit without resorting to litigation.

4. Certain IRS personnel are empowered to consider the hazards of litigation in developing a settlement with the taxpayer during the audit process.

5. The IRS pays interest to taxpayers on overpaid taxes, starting essentially 45 days after the due date of the return, in amounts tied to the Federal short-term rate. Interest paid to the IRS on underpayments is similarly based on the Federal rate, starting essentially on the due date of the return. Interest for both purposes is compounded daily.

17-1i **Taxpayer Penalties**

Congress has enacted a comprehensive array of penalties for improper actions by taxpayers. In the typical year, about 40 million penalties are assessed, totaling almost $15 billion in payments.

Tax penalties may involve both criminal and civil offenses. Criminal tax penalties are imposed only after the usual criminal process in which the taxpayer is entitled to the same constitutional guarantees as nontax criminal defendants. Normally, a criminal penalty

LO.6

List and explain the various penalties that can be imposed on acts of noncompliance by taxpayers and return preparers.

---

[23]Both taxpayers must sign on a Form 1040 joint return. *Reifler*, 106 TCM 554, T.C.Memo. 2015–199.

provides for fines and imprisonment. Civil tax penalties are collected in the same manner as other taxes and usually provide only for monetary fines. Criminal and civil penalties are not mutually exclusive; both types of sanctions may be imposed on a taxpayer.

The Code characterizes tax penalties as additions to tax; thus, the taxpayer cannot subsequently deduct them.

Ad valorem penalties are additions to tax that are based upon a percentage of the owed tax. *Assessable penalties*, on the other hand, typically include a flat dollar amount. Assessable penalties are not subject to review by the Tax Court, but ad valorem penalties are subject to the same deficiency procedures that apply to the underlying tax.

Failure to File and Failure to Pay

For a *failure to file a tax return* by the due date (including extensions), a penalty of 5 percent per month (up to a maximum of 25 percent) is imposed on the amount of tax shown as due on the return, with a minimum penalty amount of $215.[24] If the failure to file is attributable to fraud, the penalty becomes 15 percent per month, to a maximum of 75 percent of the tax.[25]

For a *failure to pay the tax due* as shown on the return, a penalty of 0.5 percent per month (up to a maximum of 25 percent) is imposed on the amount of the tax. The penalty is doubled if the taxpayer fails to pay the tax after receiving a deficiency assessment.

In all of these cases, a fraction of a month counts as a full month. These penalties relate to the net amount of the tax due.

Obtaining an extension for filing a tax return does not by itself extend the date by which the taxes due must be paid. Thus, an application for an extended due date for a tax return almost always is accompanied by the taxpayer's payment of a good faith estimate of the taxes that will be owed with the return when it is filed by the extended due date. If the taxpayer does not make a good faith estimate and payment, the extension itself may be voided by the IRS (e.g., when the return is filed by the extended due date with a much larger amount due than had been estimated).

EXAMPLE 9

Conchita uses an automatic six-month extension for the filing of her Federal income tax return. Thus, the return is due on October 15, not on April 15. Conchita's application for the extension includes a $5,000 check, the amount that she estimates her return will show as owing for the year when she files it in October.

During any month in which both the failure to file penalty and the failure to pay penalty apply, the failure to file penalty is reduced by the amount of the failure to pay penalty.

EXAMPLE 10

Jason files his tax return 10 days after the due date. Along with the return, he remits a check for $5,000, which is the balance of the tax he owes. Disregarding any interest liabilities, Jason's total penalties are as follows.

Failure to pay penalty (0.5% × $5,000)		$ 25
Failure to file penalty (5% × $5,000)	$250	
Less: Failure to pay penalty for the same period	(25)	
Failure to file penalty		225
Total penalties		$250

The penalties for one full month are imposed even though Jason was delinquent by only 10 days. Unlike the method used to compute interest, any part of a month is treated as a whole month.

---

[24]§ 6651(a). The minimum penalty cannot exceed the amount of tax due on the return. Thus, if no tax is due, the penalty is zero. The penalty is waived if the tax is paid within 60 days of the due date of the return.

[25]§ 6651(f).

These penalties can be avoided if the taxpayer shows that the failure to file and/or failure to pay was due to reasonable cause and not due to willful neglect. The Code is silent as to what constitutes reasonable cause, and the Regulations do little to clarify this important concept.[26] Reasonable cause for failure to pay is presumed under the automatic six-month extension (Form 4868) when the additional tax due is not more than 10 percent of the tax liability shown on the return. In addition, the courts have ruled on some aspects of reasonable cause.

- Reasonable cause was found where the taxpayer worked with a competent tax adviser in good faith, the facts were fully disclosed to the adviser, and the taxpayer actually relied on the adviser's judgment in filing the return.[27] No reasonable cause was found, however, where the taxpayer delegated the filing task to another, even when that person was an accountant or an attorney.[28]
- Among the reasons not qualifying as reasonable cause were lack of information on the due date of the return,[29] illness that did not incapacitate a taxpayer from completing a return,[30] refusal of the taxpayer's spouse to cooperate for a joint return,[31] and ignorance or misunderstanding of the tax law.[32]

Accuracy-Related Penalties

Major civil penalties relating to the accuracy of tax return data, including misstatements stemming from taxpayer negligence and improper valuation of income and deductions, are coordinated under the umbrella term accuracy-related penalties.[33] This consolidation of related penalties into a single levy eliminates the possibility that multiple penalties will apply to a single understatement of tax.

The accuracy-related penalties each amount to 20 percent of the portion of the tax underpayment that is attributable to one or more of the following infractions.

- Negligence or disregard of rules and regulations.
- Substantial understatement of tax liability.
- Substantial valuation overstatement.
- Substantial valuation understatement.

The penalties apply only where the taxpayer fails to show a *reasonable basis* for the position taken on the return.[34]

Negligence

For purposes of this accuracy-related penalty, negligence includes any failure to make a reasonable attempt to comply with the provisions of the tax law. The penalty also applies to any disregard (whether careless, reckless, or intentional) of rules and Regulations.[35] The penalty can be avoided upon a showing of reasonable cause and the fact that the taxpayer acted in good faith.[36]

---

[26] Reg. § 301.6651–1(c)(1) likens reasonable cause to the exercise of "ordinary business care and prudence" on the part of the taxpayer.

[27] *Neonatology Assoc., PC*, 115 T.C. 43 (2000).

[28] *U.S. v. Boyle*, 85–1 USTC ¶13,602, 55 AFTR 2d 85–1535, 105 S.Ct. 687 (USSC, 1985). This rule appears to apply to electronic as well as paper-based return filings, to employment as well as income taxes, and to returns where the tax preparer himself or herself commits a fraudulent act. *Brandon R. Ballantyne*, 99 TCM 1523, T.C.Memo. 2010–125; *McNair Eye Center, Inc.*, 99 TCM 1345, T.C.Memo. 2010–81. Knowledgeable taxpayers such as a tax attorney are held to a higher standard in determining negligence. *Pelton & Gunther P.C.*, 78 TCM 578, T.C.Memo. 1999–339. A taxpayer might be negligent if, when a complicated tax issue is involved, a tax expert is *not* consulted. *Zmuda v. Comm.*, 84-1 USTC ¶9,442, 53 AFTR 2d 84–1269, 731 F.2d 1417 (CA–9, 1984).

[29] *Beck Chemical Equipment Co.*, 27 T.C. 840 (1957).

[30] *Alex and Tonya Oria*, 94 TCM 170, T.C.Memo. 2007–276, and *Babetta Schmidt*, 28 T.C. 367 (1957). Compare *Estate of Kirchner*, 46 B.T.A. 578 (1942).

[31] *Electric and Neon, Inc.*, 56 T.C. 1324 (1971).

[32] *Stevens Brothers Foundation, Inc.*, 39 T.C. 93 (1965).

[33] § 6662.

[34] Reg. § 1.6662–3(b)(3). Most tax professionals measure this standard as a 20% probability of prevailing in court.

[35] § 6662(c). There can be no intentional disregard of the rules where the underlying law is unclear, complex, or subject to disagreement. *Simonsen*, 150 TC No. 8 (2018), and *Lansdown v. Comm.*, 96–1 USTC ¶50,025, 77 AFTR 2d 96–491, 73 F.3d 373 (CA–10, 1996).

[36] § 6664(c)(1).

The negligence penalty applies to *all* taxes, except when fraud is involved. A negligence penalty may be assessed when the taxpayer fails to report gross income, overstates deductions, or fails to keep adequate records. When the taxpayer takes a nonnegligent position on the return that is contrary to a judicial precedent or published pronouncement of the IRS, the penalty is waived if the taxpayer has a reasonable basis for the interpretation and has disclosed the disputed position on Form 8275.

Substantial Understatement of Tax Liability

The understatement penalty is designed to strike at middle- and high-income taxpayers who fail to apply the law correctly or take overly aggressive tax return filing positions.[37] A substantial understatement of a tax liability transpires when the understatement exceeds the larger of 10 percent of the tax due or $5,000. For a C corporation, a substantial understatement is the lesser of the following.[38]

- 10 percent of the tax due, but at least $10,000.
- $10 million.

The understatement to which the penalty applies is the difference between the amount of tax required to be paid and the amount of tax actually shown on the return. The penalty is avoided under any of the following circumstances.[39]

- The taxpayer has **substantial authority** for the treatment. Substantial authority exists when it is perhaps 40 percent likely that a court would find in favor of the taxpayer's position. This conclusion might be reached with an examination of pertinent statutory, administrative, and judicial tax law.
- There is a *reasonable basis* for the tax return position, which is adequately disclosed in the return by attaching Form 8275 or as otherwise allowed by the IRS.[40]

Penalty for Overvaluation

The overvaluation penalty is meant to deter taxpayers from inflating values (or basis), usually of charitable contributions of property, to reduce income taxes.[41]

- The penalty is 20 percent of the additional tax that would have been paid had the correct valuation been used.
- The penalty is doubled if the valuation error is *gross* (overstated by 200 percent or more).
- The penalty applies only when the valuation used by the taxpayer is 150 percent or more of the correct valuation.
- The penalty applies only when the resulting income tax underpayment exceeds $5,000 ($10,000 for C corporations).

EXAMPLE 11

Gretchen (a calendar year taxpayer) purchased a painting for $10,000. When the painting is worth $18,000 (as later determined by the IRS), Gretchen donates it to an art museum. Based on the appraisal of a cousin who is an amateur artist, she deducts $40,000 for the donation. Because Gretchen was in the 32% tax bracket, overstating the deduction by $22,000 results in a tax underpayment of $7,040.

Gretchen's penalty for overvaluation is $2,816, or *double* the regular penalty of $1,408 (20% × $7,040 underpayment) because the $40,000 deduction constitutes a gross overvaluation.

---

[37]§ 6662(b)(2).

[38]§ 6662(d)(1). For noncorporate taxpayers claiming the qualified business income deduction of § 199A, 5% is substituted for 10%. § 6662(d)(1)(C).

[39]§ 6662(d)(2)(B). Substantial authority is measured as of either the last day of the tax year to which the return relates or the date the return was filed. Reg. § 1.6662–4(d)(3)(iv)(C).

[40]See, for example, Rev.Proc. 2016–13, 2016–4 I.R.B. 290 and Rev.Proc. 2018-11, 2018-5 I.R.B. 335.

[41]§§ 6662(b)(3), (e), and (h).

The substantial valuation overstatement penalty is avoided if the taxpayer can show reasonable cause and good faith. However, when the overvaluation involves *charitable deduction property*, the taxpayer must substantiate both of the following.

- The claimed value of the property is based on a qualified appraisal made by a qualified appraiser.
- The taxpayer made a good faith investigation of the value of the contributed property.[42]

Based on these criteria, Gretchen in Example 11 would find it difficult to avoid the penalty. A cousin who is an amateur artist does not meet the definition of a qualified appraiser. Likewise, Gretchen apparently has not made her own good faith investigation of the value of the contributed property.

Penalty for Undervaluation

When attempting to minimize the income tax, it is to the benefit of taxpayers to *over-value* deductions. When attempting to minimize transfer taxes (estate and gift taxes), however, executors and donors may be inclined to *undervalue* the assets transferred. A lower valuation reduces estate and gift taxes. An accuracy-related penalty is imposed for substantial estate or gift tax valuation understatements.[43] As with other accuracy-related penalties, reasonable cause and good faith on the part of the taxpayer can result in a waiver of the penalty.

- The penalty is 20 percent of the additional transfer tax that would have been due had the correct valuation been used on Form 706 (estate and generation-skipping tax return) or Form 709 (gift and generation-skipping tax return).
- The penalty applies only if the value of the property claimed on the return is 65 percent or less than the amount determined to be correct. The penalty is doubled if the reported valuation error is *gross* (reported value is 40 percent or less than the correct determination).
- The penalty applies only to an additional transfer tax liability in excess of $5,000.

Appraiser's Penalty

When a valuation penalty arises because of the taxpayer's reliance on an appraisal, a further penalty can apply.[44] If the appraiser knew or reasonably should have known that the appraisal would be used as part of a tax or refund computation and that the appraised value more likely than not was improper, then the appraiser pays a penalty equal to the lesser of:

- 10 percent of the tax understatement, but at least $1,000, or
- 125 percent of the gross income received by the appraiser from the engagement (e.g., the appraisal fee collected).

Penalty for Improper Refund Claim

Whenever a taxpayer files a claim for a tax refund and the refund claim later is found to exceed the final amount allowed by the IRS or a court, a penalty of 20 percent of the disallowed refund results.[45] The penalty is waived if the taxpayer can show a *reasonable cause* for the refund claim (i.e., probably a one-third chance that a court would allow the refund). This penalty is meant to discourage the taxpayer from overstating the amount of the refund requested from the IRS. It does not apply to claims for the earned income tax credit.

---

[42]§§ 6664(c)(2) and (3).
[43]§§ 6662(b)(5), (g), and (h).

[44]§ 6695A.
[45]§ 6676.

Civil Fraud Penalty

A 75 percent civil penalty is imposed on any underpayment resulting from <mark>fraud</mark> by the taxpayer who has filed a return.[46] For this penalty, the burden of proof *is on the IRS* to show that the taxpayer acted with a specific intent to evade a tax.

Once the IRS initially has established that fraud occurred, the taxpayer then bears the burden of proof to show by a preponderance of the evidence the portion of the underpayment that is not attributable to fraud.

Although the Code and Regulations do not provide any assistance in ascertaining what constitutes civil fraud, fraud can be described as actual, intentional wrongdoing, usually occurring over several tax years. Fraud has been found in cases of manipulations of the books, substantial omissions from income, and erroneous deductions.[47]

EXAMPLE 12

Frank underpaid his income tax by $90,000. The IRS can prove that $60,000 of the underpayment was due to fraud. The civil fraud penalty is $45,000 (75% × $60,000).

Failure to Pay Estimated Taxes

A penalty is imposed for a failure to pay estimated income taxes. The penalty applies to individuals and corporations and is based on the rate of interest in effect for deficiency assessments.[48] The penalty also applies to trusts and certain estates that are required to make estimated tax payments. The penalty is not imposed if the tax due for the year (less amounts withheld and credits) is less than $500 for corporations, $1,000 for all others. For employees, an equal part of withholding is deemed paid on each due date.

Quarterly payments are made on or before the fifteenth day of the fourth month (April 15 for a calendar year taxpayer), sixth month, ninth month, and the first month of the following year. Corporations must make the last quarterly payment by the twelfth month of the same year. Generally, the payment is one-fourth of the tax expected to be due.

ETHICS & EQUITY   First-Time Tax Violators Can Get Off with Just a Warning

Tax penalties can be a harsh wake-up call when a taxpayer understates a tax liability, and there appears to be "no mercy" when a penalty is applied. Often, a tax penalty arises when the taxpayer has undergone a change in life/business circumstances (e.g., as the consequence of a divorce, retirement, or merger). The taxpayer may not have prepared adequately for the resulting tax increase and a penalty results, but the taxpayer's legitimate response might be "I didn't mean to do it; I just didn't know the rules."

The Federal income tax law does allow a measure of mercy, though. A procedure exists under which the taxpayer can apply for an abatement (waiver) of a tax penalty if all of the following circumstances are met.

- The penalty relates to a single tax year.

- The taxpayer shows *reasonable cause* for the understatement of tax.

- The taxpayer otherwise is current as to tax filings and payment compliance.

- The taxpayer has not been assessed any other penalties of a significant amount on similar tax returns within the last three years.

An IRS oversight study estimates that only 10 percent of eligible taxpayers know about the first-time abatement (FTA) penalty waiver.[49] This likely is because guidelines for the program are difficult to find at **irs.gov**. Comment on how the IRS benefits from this penalty waiver.

---

[46]§ 6663. As noted later in the chapter, underpayments traceable to fraudulent acts are not subject to a statute of limitations.

[47]*Dogget v. Comm.*, 60–1 USTC ¶9342, 5 AFTR 2d 1034, 275 F.2d 823 (CA–4, 1960); *Harvey Brodsky*, 21 TCM 578, T.C.Memo. 1962–105; and *Lash v. Comm.*, 57–2 USTC ¶9725, 51 AFTR 492, 245 F.2d 20 (CA–1, 1957).

[48]§§ 6655 (corporations) and 6654 (other taxpayers). Other computations can avoid the penalty. See §§ 6654(d)(2) and (k), 6655(e) and (i).

[49]**tinyurl.com/first-time-abate**. The Service estimates that almost 2 million FTA waivers will occur every year, abating about $850 million in penalties.

An individual's underpayment of estimated tax is the difference between the estimates that were paid and the least of:

- 90 percent of the current-year tax,
- 100 percent of the prior-year tax (the tax year must have been a full 12 months, and a return must have been filed), and
- 90 percent of the tax that would be due on an annualized income computation for the period running through the end of the quarter.

If the taxpayer's prior-year AGI exceeds $150,000, the 100 percent requirement becomes 110 percent.

A corporation's underpayment of estimated tax is the difference between the estimates that were paid and the least of:

- The current-year tax,
- The prior-year tax, and
- The tax on an annualized income computation using one of three methods of computation sanctioned by the Code.

For the prior-year alternative, (1) the prior tax year must have been a full 12 months, (2) a nonzero tax amount must have been generated for that year, and (3) large corporations (taxable income of $1 million or more in any of the three immediately preceding tax years) can use the alternative only for the first installment of a year.

In computing the penalty, Form 2210 (Underpayment of Estimated Tax by Individuals) or Form 2220 (Underpayment of Estimated Tax by Corporations) is used.

False Information with Respect to Withholding

Withholding from wages is an important element of the Federal income tax system, which is based on a pay-as-you-go approach. One way employees might hope to avoid this withholding would be to falsify the information provided to the employer on Form W–4 (Employee Withholding Allowance Certificate). For example, by overstating the number of exemptions, income tax withholdings could be reduced or completely eliminated.

To encourage compliance, a civil penalty of $500 applies when a taxpayer claims withholding allowances based on false information. The criminal penalty for willfully failing to supply information or for willfully supplying false or fraudulent information in connection with wage withholding is an additional fine of up to $1,000 and/or up to one year of imprisonment.[50]

Failure to Make Deposits of Taxes and Overstatements of Deposits

When a business is not doing well or cash-flow problems develop, employers have a great temptation to "borrow" from Uncle Sam. One way this can be done is to fail to pay to the IRS the amounts that have been withheld from the wages of employees for FICA and income tax purposes. The IRS can apply a number of weapons to discourage the practice.

- It can impose a penalty of up to 15 percent of any underdeposited amount not paid, unless the employer can show that the failure is due to reasonable cause and not to willful neglect.[51]
- It can impose various criminal penalties.[52]
- It can impose a 100 percent penalty if the employer's actions are willful.[53] The penalty is based on the amount of the tax evaded (i.e., not collected or not accounted for or paid over). Because the penalty is assessable against the

---

[50]§§ 6682 and 7205.
[51]§ 6656.

[52]See, for example, § 7202 (willful failure to collect or pay over a tax).
[53]§ 6672.

"responsible person" of the business, more than one party may be vulnerable (e.g., the president and treasurer of a corporation, the third-party payroll service of the entity). Although the IRS may assess the penalty against several persons, it cannot collect more than 100 percent of the tax that is due.

- In addition to these penalties, the actual tax due must be remitted. For instance, an employer remains liable for the employees' income and payroll taxes that should have been paid.

Failure to Provide Information Regarding Tax Shelters

The IRS has identified over two dozen transactions that it regards as improper in determining one's tax liability, usually because the transaction lacks economic substance beyond the resulting tax reduction. These arrangements are termed "reportable transactions" or "tax shelters," and they often involve leveraged financing and accelerated interest and cost recovery deductions.

A tax shelter organizer must inform the IRS of the arrangement before any sales are made to investors.[54] A penalty of $50,000 is assessed if the required information is not filed with the Service, using Form 8886. The disclosure includes a description of the shelter and the tax benefits that are being used to attract investors.

Criminal Penalties

In addition to civil fraud penalties, the Code contains numerous criminal sanctions that carry various monetary fines and/or imprisonment. The IRS annually attains about 3,000 convictions. About 15 percent of the cases involve identity theft. About 80 percent of criminal tax convictions result in incarceration, home confinement, or electronic monitoring.

The difference between civil and criminal fraud often is one of degree. Thus, § 7201, dealing with attempts to evade or defeat a tax, contains the following language.

> Any person who *willfully* attempts in any manner to evade or defeat any tax imposed by this title or the payment thereof shall, in addition to other penalties provided by law, be guilty of a felony and, upon conviction thereof, shall be fined not more than $100,000 ($500,000 in the case of a corporation), or imprisoned not more than five years, or both, together with the costs of prosecution. [Emphasis added.]

As to the burden of proof, the IRS must show that the taxpayer was guilty of willful evasion "beyond the shadow of any reasonable doubt." Thus, to avoid a criminal tax penalty, the taxpayer needs to create a degree of reasonable doubt as to guilt. To do so, the taxpayer might assert that he or she was confused or ignorant about the application of the tax law or relied on the erroneous advice of a competent tax adviser. Another defense against a criminal tax penalty is the lack of capacity to plan and carry out tax evasion (e.g., mental limitations or other medical disorder).

Violations of the Federal criminal code in the context of filing tax returns also may arise from other crimes that are not provided for in the Internal Revenue Code. Examples include:

- Making a false claim against the Federal government.
- Participating in a conspiracy to evade Federal taxes (i.e., in addition to the tax understatement).
- Making a false statement to the Federal government or filing a false document (i.e., perjury).

---

[54]§ 6111. The penalty amount increases if the failure to disclose relates to a listed transaction or is intentional by the taxpayer.

17-1j **Statute of Limitations**

A **statute of limitations** defines the period of time during which one party may pursue against another party a cause of action or other suit allowed under the governing law. Failure to satisfy any requirement provides the other party with an absolute defense should the statute be invoked. Inequity would result if no limits were placed on such suits. Permitting an extended period of time to elapse between the initiation of a claim and its pursuit could place the defense at a serious disadvantage. Witnesses may have died or disappeared; records or other evidence may have been discarded or destroyed.

LO.7

Recognize and apply the rules governing the statute of limitations on assessments and on refunds.

Assessment and the Statute of Limitations

In general, any tax that is imposed must be assessed within three years of the later of (a) the filing date of the return or (b) the unextended due date of the return.[55] Some exceptions to this three-year limitation exist.

- If no return is filed or a fraudulent return is filed, assessments can be made at any time. The statute of limitations, in effect, never expires in these cases.

- If a taxpayer omits an amount of gross income in excess of 25 percent of the gross income stated on the return, the statute of limitations is increased to six years. The courts have interpreted this rule as including only items affecting income and not the omission of items affecting deductions, operating losses, or cost of sales.[56] *Gross income* here includes capital gains, but not reduced by capital losses. It also includes any gross income that results from an overstatement of tax basis (e.g., in an asset sale).[57]

During 2014, Jerry recorded the following income transactions (all of which were duly reported on his timely filed return).

Gross receipts	$ 480,000
Cost of sales	(400,000)
Net business income	$ 80,000
Capital gains and losses	
Capital gain	$ 36,000
Capital loss	(12,000) 24,000
Total income	$ 104,000

EXAMPLE

13

Jerry retains your services in 2019 as a tax consultant. It seems that he inadvertently omitted some income on his 2014 return, and he wants to know if he is "safe" under the statute of limitations. The three-year statute of limitations has expired, but the six-year statute of limitations still applies, putting Jerry in a vulnerable position only if he omitted more than $129,000 on his 2014 return [($480,000 + $36,000) × 25%].

- The statute of limitations may be extended for a fixed period of time by mutual consent of the IRS and the taxpayer. This extension covers a definite period and is made by signing Form 872 (Consent to Extend the Time to Assess Tax). The extension frequently is requested by the IRS when the lapse of the statutory period is imminent and the audit has not been completed. This practice often is applied to audits of corporate taxpayers and explains why many corporations have more than three "open years."

The statute also is suspended when the taxpayer is "financially disabled"; that is, the taxpayer has been rendered unable to manage his or her financial affairs by a physical or mental impairment that is likely to last for a year or more or to cause the taxpayer's death.[58]

---

[55]§§ 6501(a) and (b)(1).
[56]*The Colony, Inc. v. Comm.*, 58–2 USTC ¶9593, 1 AFTR 2d 1894, 78 S.Ct. 1033 (USSC, 1958).
[57]§ 6501(e)(1)(B)(ii).
[58]§§ 6501(c)(4) and 6511(h).

Refund Claims and the Statute of Limitations

To receive a tax refund, the taxpayer is required to file a valid refund claim. The official form for filing a claim is Form 1040X for individuals and Form 1120X for corporations. If the refund claim does not meet certain procedural requirements, the IRS may reject the claim with no consideration of its merit.

- A separate claim must be filed for each taxable period.
- The grounds for the claim must be stated in sufficient detail.
- The statement of facts must be sufficient to permit the IRS to evaluate the merits of the claim.

The refund claim must be filed within three years of the filing of the tax return or within two years following the payment of the tax if this period expires on a later date.[59]

EXAMPLE 14

On March 10, 2018, Louise filed her 2017 income tax return reflecting a tax of $10,500. On July 11, 2019, she filed an amended 2017 return showing an additional $3,000 of tax that was then paid. On May 19, 2021, she filed a claim for refund of $4,500.

Assuming that Louise is correct in claiming a refund, how much tax can she recover? The answer is only $3,000. Because the claim was not filed within the three-year statute of limitations period, Louise is limited to the amount she actually paid during the last two years.

Special rules are available for claims relating to bad debts and worthless securities. A seven-year period of limitations applies in lieu of the normal three-year rule.[60] The extended period is provided in recognition of the inherent difficulty of identifying the exact year in which a bad debt or security becomes worthless.

17-2 THE TAX PROFESSION AND TAX ETHICS

LO.8

Summarize the legal and ethical guidelines that apply to those engaged in tax practice.

Society and its governments expect taxpayers to comply with the letter and the spirit of the tax laws. Tax audits and penalties encourage a high degree of technical tax conformity, but the proper functioning of a voluntary tax compliance system also depends on the ethics of the taxpayer and the tax adviser.

The Treasury and various professional organizations have issued ethical guidelines that are relevant to the tax profession. Professional licensing agencies also are likely to require tax professionals to receive training in ethics to obtain initial certification and to remain in good standing over time.

17-2a The Tax Professional

Who is a tax professional? What services does a tax professional perform? A number of different groups apply constraints on the way a tax professional conducts his or her practice.

Generally, practice before the IRS is limited to CPAs, attorneys, and persons who have been enrolled to practice before the IRS [**enrolled agents (EAs)**]. In most cases, EAs are admitted to practice only if they pass an examination administered by the IRS. CPAs and attorneys are not required to take this examination and are automatically admitted to practice if they are in good standing with the appropriate licensing board regulating their profession.

Persons other than CPAs, attorneys, and EAs may be allowed to practice before the IRS in limited situations. **Circular 230** ("Regulations Governing Practice before the Internal Revenue Service") issued by the Treasury Department permits certain notable exceptions.

---

[59]§§ 6511(a) and 6513(a).   [60]§ 6511(d)(1).

- A taxpayer always may represent himself or herself. A person also may represent a member of the immediate family if no compensation is received for such services.

- Full-time employees may represent their employers.

- Corporations may be represented by any of their officers.

- Partnerships may be represented by any of the partners.

- Trusts, receiverships, guardianships, or estates may be represented by their trustees, receivers, guardians, or administrators or executors, respectively.

- A taxpayer may be represented by the individual or entity who prepared the return for the year in question. Preparers who are not a CPA, an EA, or an attorney can represent a taxpayer in an audit only if they prepared and signed the return and completed a voluntary IRS continuing education program.

All nonattorney tax professionals should avoid becoming engaged in activities that constitute the *unauthorized practice of law*. If they engage in this practice (e.g., by drafting legal documents for a third party), action could be instituted against them in the appropriate state court by the local or state bar association or state Attorney General's office. What actions constitute the unauthorized practice of law are often specified by state statute or case law.

17-2b Regulating Tax Preparers

There are no minimum education or experience requirements for those who are paid to file Federal tax returns for others. But the IRS does require that all paid tax return preparers, including CPAs and attorneys, obtain a Preparer Tax Identification Number (PTIN) before they assist taxpayers with returns for a new filing season.

The IRS may use PTIN data to identify preparers who commit a pattern of errors or who participate in fraudulent actions. With more than 700,000 paid preparers at work in any filing season,[61] the IRS uses an outside consultant to manage the registration process.

17-2c IRS Rules Governing Tax Practice

Circular 230 prescribes the rules governing practice before the IRS. Following are some of the most important rules imposed on CPAs, attorneys, EAs, and a few others specified in Circular 230.

- A requirement that the tax practitioner be competent in the matters involved in the engagement with the taxpayer (i.e., the practitioner can show appropriate levels of knowledge, skill, thoroughness, and preparation for the assigned tasks).

- A prohibition against willful or reckless behavior in signing a return that includes a position that could subject the practitioner to the preparer penalty such as because the position lacks a reasonable basis (see text Section 17-2d).

The Big Picture

Return to the facts of *The Big Picture* on p. 17-1. Campbell has developed a testing program to be used by its in-house engineers before a new GPS app is released to the public; Campbell wants to claim the research credit for that program. Based on their tax research on this issue, the members of your firm's tax department have severe doubts about taking the credit for this program. Your firm's position is that there is a one-in-six chance that the courts would allow Campbell's credit.

Claiming the credit fails the standard of Circular 230 because there is no reasonable basis (roughly 20% probability of prevailing if challenged by the government) for the position.

EXAMPLE

15

---

[61]Included in this number are about 210,000 CPAs, 55,000 EAs, and 30,000 attorneys.

- A requirement to inform clients of penalties likely to apply to return positions and of ways such penalties can be avoided.

- A requirement to make known to a client any error or omission the client may have made on any return or other document submitted to the IRS.

- A duty to submit, in a timely fashion, records or information lawfully requested by the IRS.

- An obligation to exercise *due diligence* and to use the *best practices* of the tax profession in preparing, reviewing, and filing tax returns accurately.

EXAMPLE 16

Your niece, Selma, plans to start a tax return preparation service. She seeks advice on what procedures and practices to establish in order to develop and maintain a successful business. As a starting point, Selma should set up a standardized procedure for receiving, processing, and reviewing client tax returns. A key to achieving a high-quality product would be an appropriate choice of tax accounting software. She should be sure that all client data are kept confidential and that the electronic files holding such data are secure and properly backed up.

Any employees who are hired should be technically competent and properly trained as to office procedure. All hires will be subject to a background check and be made aware that they are expected to participate in continuing education covering developments in tax law changes. In addition, Selma should formulate adequate disclaiming language so that e-mail and text recipients do not assume that the content represents technical advice upon which they can rely.

- A restriction against unreasonably delaying the prompt disposition of any matter before the IRS.

- A restriction against charging the client a contingent fee for preparing an original return. Such a fee can be charged when the tax professional deals with an audited return and when assisting the taxpayer in filing certain refund claims.

- A restriction against charging the client "an unconscionable fee" for representation before the IRS.

- A restriction against representing clients with conflicting interests.

In a firm that prepares tax returns for compensation, personnel supervisors must ensure that the work of staff members complies with Circular 230 rules. This usually entails education programs and other means by which the current Circular 230 rules are conveyed to all affected employees.

Circular 230 is administered by the IRS Office of Professional Responsibility (OPR). Among other duties, the OPR carries out disciplinary hearings and issues penalties, such as fines and licensing restrictions and retractions, relative to tax preparers. Information about Circular 230 violations is published in the Internal Revenue Bulletin. A Circular 230 violation could lead to the loss or suspension of a CPA's license at the state level as well.

17-2d **Preparer Penalties**

The Code provides penalties to discourage improper actions by tax professionals. **Tax preparer** penalties are assessed on any person who prepares for compensation, or engages employees to prepare, a substantial portion of any Federal tax return or refund claim.[62] The following individuals are exempt from the preparer penalties:[63]

- An IRS employee.

- A volunteer who prepares tax returns in a government assistance effort such as Tax Counseling for the Elderly (TCE) or the Volunteer Income Tax Assistance (VITA) program.

---

[62]§ 7701(a)(36); Reg. § 301.7701–15(a).

[63]Reg. § 301.7701–15(f).

- An employee preparing a return for the employer.
- A fiduciary preparing a return for a trust or an estate.
- An individual who provides only data processing, typing, reproduction, or other assistance in preparing a return.

The preparer penalties can compound quickly within a tax practice with many professionals. Some of the most important tax preparer penalties include the following.

1. A penalty for understatements due to taking an **unreasonable position** on a tax return.[64] The penalty is imposed if the tax position:

   - Is not disclosed on the return and there was no *substantial authority* (i.e., a greater than 40 percent chance) that the tax position would be sustained by its merits on a final court review, or

   - Is disclosed on the return and there was not a *reasonable basis* (i.e., probably a 20 percent chance) for the position.

   The penalty is computed as the greater of $1,000 or one-half of the income of the practitioner that is attributable to the return or claim that violated the conduct standard. The penalty can be avoided by showing reasonable cause and by showing that the preparer acted in good faith.

> **EXAMPLE 17**
>
> Josie is the tax return preparer for Hal's Form 1040. The return includes a deduction that has a 60% chance of being sustained on its merits even though it is contrary to an applicable tax Regulation. If a court denies the deduction, Josie is not assessed a penalty for taking an unreasonable position on the tax return.
>
> Now assume that Hal's deduction has a 30% chance of being sustained on its merits. If a court denies the deduction, Josie is assessed the penalty (unless the disputed position was disclosed on the return with a Form 8275–R). The amount of the penalty is the greater of $1,000 or one-half of Josie's fees for preparing Hal's Form 1040.
>
> What if Hal's deduction has a 15% chance of being sustained on its merits? If a court denies the deduction, Josie is assessed a penalty for taking an unreasonable tax return position (even if the disputed position was disclosed on the return with a Form 8275–R). The amount of the penalty is the greater of $1,000 or one-half of Josie's fees for preparing Hal's Form 1040.

2. A penalty for willful and reckless conduct.[65] The penalty applies if any part of the understatement of a taxpayer's liability on a return or claim for refund is due to:

   - The preparer's willful attempt to understate the taxpayer's tax liability in any manner.

   - Any reckless or intentional disregard of IRS rules or Regulations by the preparer.

   The penalty is computed as the greater of $5,000 or 75 percent of the income of the practitioner that is attributable to the return or claim that violated the conduct standard. Adequate disclosure can avoid the penalty. If both this penalty and the unreasonable position penalty (see item 1) apply to the same return, the reckless conduct penalty is reduced by the amount of the penalty for unreasonable positions.

3. A $1,000 ($10,000 for the tax returns of corporations) penalty per return or document is imposed against persons who aid in the preparation of returns or other documents they know (or have reason to believe) would result in an understatement of the tax liability of another person.[66] Thus, this penalty also applies to

---

[64]§ 6694(a). For the most part, these standards match those that apply to the taxpayer penalties of § 6662(d). Stricter disclosure standards apply for tax shelter items and reportable transactions. § 6662A.

[65]§ 6694(b).

[66]§ 6701.

those other than the preparer of the actual tax return (e.g., advisers, attorneys, corporate officers and executives, and tax shelter promoters). Clerical assistance in the return preparation process does not incur the penalty.

If this penalty applies, neither the unreasonable position penalty (item 1) nor the willful and reckless conduct penalty (item 2) is assessed.

4. A $250 penalty for each third-party disclosure or improper use of tax return data, up to a $10,000 annual maximum per practitioner.[67]

5. A $50 penalty is assessed against the preparer for failure to sign a return or furnish the preparer's PTIN.[68]

6. A $50 penalty is assessed if the preparer fails to furnish a copy of the return or claim for refund to the taxpayer, and if the preparer fails to keeps its own copy thereof.

7. A $530 penalty may be assessed if a preparer endorses or otherwise negotiates a check for refund of tax issued to the taxpayer.

8. A $530 penalty for each instance of failure to be diligent in determining the taxpayer's eligibility for the earned income tax credit, child tax credit, other dependent credit, American Opportunity tax credit, or head-of-household filing status.

Other parts of the Code provide additional constraints to govern all parties engaged in rendering tax returns for the general public.

• A person who holds himself or herself out to the general public as possessing tax expertise could be liable to the client if services are performed in a negligent manner. At a minimum, the practitioner is liable for any interest and penalties the client incurs because of the practitioner's failure to exercise due professional care.

• If a practitioner agrees to perform a service (e.g., prepare a tax return) and subsequently fails to do so, the aggrieved party may be in a position to obtain damages for breach of contract.

• All persons who prepare tax returns or refund claims for a fee must sign as preparer of the return.[69] Failure to comply with this requirement could result in a penalty assessment against the preparer.

• Various penalties apply concerning the deliberate filing of false or fraudulent returns. These felonies apply to a tax practitioner who either was aware of the situation or actually perpetrated the false information or the fraud.[70]

• Penalties are prescribed for tax practitioners who disclose to third parties information they have received from clients in connection with the preparation of tax returns or the rendering of tax advice.[71]

EXAMPLE 18

Sarah operates a tax return preparation service. Her brother-in-law, Butch, has just taken a job as a life insurance salesperson. To help Butch find contacts, Sarah furnishes him with a list of the names and addresses of all of her clients who report AGI of $50,000 or more. Sarah is subject to the disclosure penalty.

17-2e Privileged Communications

Communications between an attorney and a client long have been protected from disclosure to other parties (such as the IRS and the courts). A similar privilege of

---

[67]§ 6713.

[68]§ 6695. The penalty amounts for the rest of this list are adjusted annually for inflation. Items 5. and 6. cannot exceed $26,500 per year for the preparer or firm. See § 6695(h) and Rev.Proc. 2018–18, 2018–410 I.R.B. 392.

[69]Reg. § 1.6065–1(b)(1). Rev.Rul. 84–3, 1984–1 C.B. 264, contains a series of examples illustrating when a person is deemed to be a preparer of the return.

[70]§ 7206.

[71]§ 7216.

confidentiality extends to tax advice between a taxpayer and a Federally authorized tax practitioner (attorney, CPA, EA). The privilege is not available for matters involving criminal charges or questions brought by other agencies, such as the Securities and Exchange Commission. Nor is it allowed in matters involving promoting or participating in tax shelters.[72]

A taxpayer likely will want to protect documents such as the tax adviser's research memo detailing the strengths and weaknesses of a tax return position or a conversation about an appeals strategy. The confidentiality privilege should be interpreted in the following manner.

- The privilege for CPAs and EAs applies only to tax advice. Only attorneys can exercise the privilege concerning advice rendered as a business consultant, an estate/financial planner, etc.

- The privilege is not available for tax accrual workpapers prepared as part of an independent financial audit.

- Generally, there is no privilege as to taxpayer information that is intended to be disclosed on a tax return.

17-2f AICPA Statements on Standards for Tax Services

Tax practitioners who are CPAs, attorneys, or EAs must abide by the codes or canons of professional ethics applicable to their respective professions. The various codes and canons have much in common with and parallel the standards of conduct set forth in Circular 230.[73]

The AICPA has issued a series of Statements on Standards for Tax Services (SSTSs). The Statements are enforceable standards of professional practice for AICPA members working in state or Federal tax practice. The SSTSs comprise part of the AICPA's Code of Professional Conduct. Together with the provisions of Circular 230 and the penalty provisions of the Code, the SSTSs make up a set of guidelines for the conduct of the tax practitioner who is also a CPA. Other sources of professional ethics are issued by state bar associations and CPA societies, the American Bar Association, and the associations of enrolled agents.

Key provisions of the SSTSs are presented next.

Statement No. 1: Tax Return Positions

Under certain circumstances, a CPA may take a position that is contrary to that taken by the IRS. To do so, however, the CPA must have a good faith belief that the position has a realistic possibility (i.e., probably a one-in-three chance) of being sustained administratively or judicially on its merits if challenged. If the taxing authority (e.g., a state revenue statute) uses a lower standard than that of a *realistic possibility*, this higher standard still applies. But where the taxing authority applies a higher standard, such as one of *substantial authority*, that standard is in effect.

The client should be fully advised of the risks involved and the penalties that may result if the position taken on the tax return is not successful. The client also should be informed that disclosure on the return may avoid some or all of these penalties.

In no case, though, should the CPA exploit the audit lottery. That is, the CPA should not take a questionable position based on the probabilities that the client's return will not be chosen by the IRS for audit. Furthermore, the CPA should not "load" the return with questionable items in the hope that they might aid the client in a later settlement negotiation with the IRS.

---

[72]§ 7525.

[73]For an additional discussion of tax ethics, see Sawyers and Gill, *Federal Tax Research*, 11th ed. (Cengage Learning, 2018), especially Chapters 1 and 14.

The Big Picture

Return to the facts of *The Big Picture* on p. 17-1. Campbell's new marketing program solicits the opinions of a virtual focus group to test ideas for new products. Based on your tax research, you believe that because the program relies on innovative algorithms that use online contacts to carry out the focus group activities, the program might qualify for the Federal income tax research credit even though it involves marketing research that is excluded from the credit under § 41(d)(4). Still, you believe that there is only a 30% chance the courts would allow the credit.

You meet with Seung Watkins, Campbell's tax director, to convey the results of your research. Watkins agrees that the research credit would be turned down by an IRS auditor, but she says that Campbell never has been audited and that it is not likely to be audited as long as its legal structure and income levels do not significantly change. Watkins believes that Campbell's corporate officers will sign off on the credit, given both the firm's weak cash position and the low chances that the item will be discovered.

As a CPA, you must inform Campbell that claiming the credit for this activity is a position that lacks substantial authority. The 30% chance of being upheld indicates that it may have a reasonable basis, though. In that case, the position needs to be disclosed on the return to avoid a taxpayer penalty.

Whether the credit is claimed is the decision of your client, the taxpayer. But if Campbell wants to claim the credit without the required additional disclosures, you must terminate your engagement with Campbell, under the SSTS and other AICPA provisions.

Statement No. 2: Questions on Returns

A CPA should make a reasonable effort to obtain from the client and provide appropriate answers to all questions on a tax return before signing as preparer. Reasonable grounds may exist for omitting an answer.

- The information is not readily available, and the answer is not significant in amount in computing the tax.
- The meaning of the question as it applies to a particular situation is genuinely uncertain.
- The answer to the question is voluminous.

The fact that an answer to a question could prove disadvantageous to the client does not justify omitting the answer.

Statement No. 3: Procedural Aspects of Preparing Returns

In preparing a return, a CPA may in good faith rely without verification on information furnished by the client or by third parties. However, the CPA should make reasonable inquiries if the information appears to be incorrect, incomplete, or inconsistent. In this regard, the CPA should refer to the client's returns for prior years whenever appropriate.

While preparing Sunni's income tax return, you review her prior year's income tax return. In comparing the dividend income reported on the Schedule B for the two years, you note a significant decrease from last year's amounts. Further investigation reveals that the variation is due to a stock sale this year that was unknown to you until now. Thus, the review of the prior year's return has unearthed a transaction that should be reported on this year's return.

If the Code or Regulations require certain types of verification (as is the case with travel and entertainment expenditures), the CPA must advise the client of these rules. Further, inquiry must be made to ascertain whether the client has complied with the verification requirements.

Statement No. 4: Estimates

A CPA may prepare a tax return using estimates received from a taxpayer if it is impracticable to obtain exact data. The estimates must be reasonable under the facts and circumstances as known to the CPA. When estimates are used, they should avoid the impression of greater accuracy than exists.

Statement No. 5: Recognition of Administrative Proceeding or Court Decision

As facts may vary from year to year, so may the position taken by a CPA. In these situations, the CPA is not bound by an administrative or judicial proceeding for a prior year.

As part of a prior year's audit of Ramon Corporation's income tax return, the IRS disallowed $78,000 of the $600,000 salary paid to its president and sole shareholder on the grounds that it is unreasonable. You are the CPA who has been engaged to prepare Ramon's income tax return for the current year. Again, the corporation paid its president a salary of $600,000 and chose to deduct this amount. Because you are not bound for this year's return by what the IRS deemed reasonable for the prior tax year, the full $600,000 can be claimed as a salary deduction, assuming that you and Ramon both believe that the entire salary represents reasonable compensation.

EXAMPLE 21

Statement No. 6: Knowledge of Error

A CPA should advise a client promptly upon learning of an error in a previously filed return or upon learning of a client's failure to file a required return, where the error has a significant (material in amount) effect on the tax liability. The advice can be oral or written and should include a recommendation of the corrective measures, if any, to be taken. The error or other omission should not be disclosed to the IRS without the client's consent.

If the past error is material in amount and is not corrected by the client, the CPA may be unable to prepare the current year's tax return. The CPA must consider the cumulative effects of the error on the taxpayer's liabilities for all tax years, including those in the future.

In preparing a client's year 2 income tax return, you discover that final inventory for year 1 was materially understated. First, you should advise the client to file an amended return for year 1 reflecting the correct amount in final inventory. Second, if the client refuses to make this adjustment, you should consider whether the error will preclude you from preparing a substantially correct return for year 2. Because this will probably be the case (last year's closing inventory becomes this year's beginning inventory), you should withdraw from the engagement.

If the client corrects the error, you may proceed with the preparation of the year 2 tax return. You must assure yourself that the error is not repeated on the return that you are preparing.

EXAMPLE 22

Statement No. 7: Advice to Clients

In providing tax advice to a client, the CPA must use judgment to ensure that the advice reflects professional competence and appropriately serves the client's needs. No standard format or guidelines can be established to cover all situations and circumstances involving written or oral advice by the CPA.

The CPA may communicate with the client when subsequent developments affect previous advice on significant matters. However, the CPA is not expected to assume responsibility for initiating the communication unless he or she has agreed to do so in the engagement letter with the client.

The rules regarding professional standards and ethics in tax practice are summarized in Concept Summary 17.2.

Concept Summary 17.2

Tax Profession and Ethics

1. The Treasury assesses penalties when the taxpayer fails to file a required tax return or pay a tax. Penalties also are assessed when an inaccurate return is filed due to negligence or other disregard of tax rules. Tax preparers are subject to penalties for assisting a taxpayer in filing an inaccurate return, failing to follow IRS rules in an appropriate manner, or mishandling taxpayer data or funds.

2. Statutes of limitations place outer boundaries on the timing and amounts of proposed amendments to completed tax returns that can be made by the taxpayer or the IRS.

3. Tax practitioners must operate under constraints imposed on them by codes of ethics or pertinent professional societies and by Treasury Circular 230. These rules also define the parties who can represent others in an IRS proceeding.

4. A limited privilege of confidentiality exists between the taxpayer and tax preparer who also is a CPA, an EA, or a attorney.

17-3 TAX PLANNING

17-3a Strategies in Seeking a Letter Ruling

In some cases, it may not be necessary or desirable to request an advance ruling from the IRS. For example, it generally is not desirable to request a ruling if the tax results are doubtful and the company is committed to completing the transaction in any event. If a ruling is requested and negotiations with the IRS indicate that an adverse determination will be forthcoming, it usually is possible to have the ruling request withdrawn. In determining the advisability of a ruling request, the taxpayer should consider the potential exposure of other items in the tax returns of all "open years."

17-3b Considerations in Handling an IRS Audit

As a general rule, a taxpayer should attempt to settle disputes at the earliest possible stage of the administrative appeal process. It usually is possible to limit the scope of the examination by furnishing pertinent information requested by the agent. Extraneous information or fortuitous comments may result in the opening of new issues and should be avoided. Agents usually appreciate prompt and efficient responses to inquiries, because their performance may in part be judged by their ability to close or settle assigned cases.

To the extent possible, it is advisable to conduct the investigation of field audits in the practitioner's office, not the client's office. This permits greater control over the audit investigation and facilitates the agent's review and prompt closure of the case.

Many practitioners believe that it is generally not advisable to have clients present at the scheduled conferences with the agent, because the client may give emotional or gratuitous comments that impair prompt settlement. If the client is not present, however, he or she should be advised of the status of negotiations. The client makes the final decision on any proposed settlement.

Preparing for the Audit

The tax professional must prepare thoroughly for the audit or Appeals proceeding. Practitioners often cite the following steps as critical to such preparations. Carrying out a level of due diligence in preparing for the proceeding is part of the tax professional's responsibility in representing the client.

- Make certain that both sides agree on the issues to be resolved in the audit. The goal here is to limit the IRS agent's list of open issues.

- Identify all of the facts underlying the issues in dispute, including those favorable to the IRS. Gather evidence to support the taxpayer's position, and evaluate the evidence supporting the other side.

- Conduct research with current tax law authorities as they bear on the facts and open issues, within the parameters of the audit that you and the IRS have agreed to. Remember that the IRS agent is bound only by Supreme Court cases and IRS pronouncements. Determine the degree of discretion that the IRS is likely to have in disposing of the case.

- Prepare a list of points supporting and contradicting the taxpayer's case. Include both minor points bearing little weight and core principles. Short research memos also will be useful in the discussion with the agent. Points favoring the taxpayer should be mentioned during the discussion and "entered into the record."

- Prepare tax and interest computations showing the effects of points that are in dispute so that the consequences of closing or compromising an issue can be readily determined.

- Determine a "litigation point" (i.e., at which the taxpayer will withdraw from further audit negotiation and pursue the case in the courts). This position should be based on the dollars of tax, interest, and penalty involved; the chances of prevailing in various trial-level courts; and other strategies discussed with the taxpayer. One must have an "end game" strategy for the audit, and thorough tax research is critical in developing that position in this context.

Documentation Issues

The tax practitioner's workpapers should include all research memoranda, and a list of resolved and unresolved issues should be continually updated during the course of the IRS audit. Occasionally, agents request access to excessive amounts of accounting data to engage in a so-called fishing expedition. Providing blanket access to working papers should be avoided. Workpapers should be reviewed carefully to minimize opportunities for the agent to raise new issues not otherwise apparent. It generally is advisable to provide the agent with copies of specific workpapers upon request.

In unusual situations, a Special Agent may appear to gather evidence in the investigation of possible criminal fraud. When this occurs, the tax professional should be advised to seek legal counsel to determine the extent of his or her cooperation in providing information to the agent. If the taxpayer receives a Revenue Agent's Report, it generally indicates that the IRS has decided not to initiate criminal proceedings. The IRS usually does not take any action on a tax deficiency until the criminal matter has been resolved.

17-3c **Statute of Limitations**

The IRS requests an extension of the statute of limitations when it finds that there is insufficient time to complete an audit or appellate review. The taxpayer is not compelled to agree to the extension request and may be averse to giving the IRS more time. But adverse consequences can result if the taxpayer denies the IRS request.

Although the statute of limitations governing Thornton's tax return is scheduled to expire in 15 days, the IRS has requested an extension for another 60 days. It wants to complete a more thorough investigation into a disputed $500,000 deduction. If Thornton refuses to agree to the extension, the IRS likely will disallow the entire deduction and issue a 90-day letter. However, if Thornton agrees to the extension, all or part of the deduction may be salvaged.

EXAMPLE

23

A disadvantage of extending the statute is that the IRS sometimes can raise new issues during the extension period. Moreover, any extension of the statute further extends the period for which the return is subject to audit in subsequent years. However, the taxpayer can take the following protective measures as a condition to agreeing to the extension.

- Shorten the extension period requested before signing the Form 872. This will reduce the chance that the IRS will find and investigate new issues.
- Restrict the scope of the issues covered by the extension (e.g., extend the period only as to the computation of cost of goods sold).

17-3d **Litigation Considerations**

During the process of settlement with the IRS, the taxpayer must assess the economic consequences of possible litigation. Specifically, the probability of winning in court should be weighed against the costs of litigating the dispute (legal, support, and court costs). In some instances, taxpayers become overly emotional and do not adequately consider the economic and psychological costs of litigation, nor do they consider the public nature of documents and other materials involved in litigation.

In selecting a proper tax forum, consideration should be given to the decisions of the various courts in related cases. The Tax Court follows the decisions of U.S. Courts of Appeals if the court is one to which the taxpayer may appeal.[74] For example, if an individual is in the jurisdiction of the Fifth Circuit Court of Appeals and that court has issued a favorable opinion on the same issue that currently confronts the taxpayer, the Tax Court will follow this opinion in deciding the taxpayer's case, even if previous Tax Court decisions have been adverse.

If the issue involves a question in which some special consideration is needed, strategy may dictate the choice of the Court of Federal Claims, which is seen by some observers as on occasion giving greater weight to equity considerations than to strict legal precedent, or of a Federal District Court, where a jury trial is available.

17-3e **Penalties**

The failure to file and failure to pay penalties are not a threat for most individual taxpayers. Those penalties are computed as a percentage of the unpaid tax liability; because most taxpayers receive a refund on the Form 1040, the penalty as computed would be zero.

The penalty for failure to pay estimated taxes can become quite severe. Often trapped by the provision are employed taxpayers with outside income. They may forget about the outside income and assume that the amount withheld from wages and salaries is adequate to cover their liability, and a penalty may be triggered.

To avoid tax preparer penalties, the tax professional must carry out a number of quality control measures within the context of his or her firm.

- Adopt a "tone at the top" that stresses ethical tax practice, emphasizing at all times the importance of integrity and objectivity in the context of client advocacy. Stress the importance of all employees to stay current with the requirements of Circular 230 and the tax preparer penalty rules.
- Establish and follow ethical guidelines with respect to all forms of client communication and documentation, including tax returns and written, spoken, and electronic tax advice.
- Prepare an engagement letter to lay out the responsibilities of all parties in complying with the tax law when taking on a new client, or whenever the scope of the work to be performed for a client changes. The firm should use the engagement

---

[74]*Jack E. Golsen*, 54 T.C. 742 (1970). See text Sections 1-4c and 1-6c.

letter to make certain that the client provides all documents needed to avoid penalties and compute the tax liability correctly, and to establish the high levels of tax ethics that will be met in the engagement. The client should be aware of, and participate in, this dedication to ethical behavior.

- Conduct annual reviews to ascertain that all tax preparers in the firm are current as to their PTIN registration and CPA or other licenses and certifications held. Emphasize the importance of data security and confidentiality, and of other aspects of the firm's best practices to all who handle tax return data.

- Monitor the compliance of all members of the firm with its established ethical guidelines. Use a peer review process periodically to confirm that the system is working as designed and to bring third-party suggestions into the process.

17-3f **Privileged Communications**

The CPA needs to exercise care to ensure that the privilege of confidentiality will apply to his or her tax work. Taking the following steps can help.

- Segregate the time spent and documents produced in rendering services for tax compliance from that devoted to tax advice. Doing this will protect the privilege from being waived as to the tax advice.

- Explain the extent of the privilege to the client—specify what will and will not be protected from the IRS in a dispute.

- Do not inadvertently waive the privilege, for example, by telling "too much" to the IRS or to a third party who is not protected by the privilege.

REFOCUS ON THE BIG PICTURE

A Tax Adviser's Dilemma

Your work with Campbell Corporation and its incremental research credit may prove troublesome. To avoid the taxpayer and tax preparer penalties, substantial authority must exist for claiming the credit, but the tax cases and Regulations do not appear to provide much guidance with respect to research expenditures of this sort. How does one craft a tax return position when the tax law largely is silent as to the particulars of the facts of the taxpayer's situation? How much risk of incurring a tax penalty are the taxpayer and your firm willing to assume in deciding how and whether to report these expenditures?

Beyond the monetary effects of claiming the credit, you and the client must consider the publicity aspects of taking this issue to court: Does Campbell want to be the "test case" in the Tax Court on this matter? What would be the effects on your consulting firm if a preparer penalty or even loss of professional certification were to result? If the credit is to be claimed, what degree of "disclosure" does the law require?

At a minimum, your firm and Campbell's tax department must conduct thorough research of analogous situations in the law in which the incremental research credit was and was not allowed for the taxpayer. Due diligence in this regard would require that you examine how other software applications and similar technological innovations, probably having nothing to do with GPS software and national security concerns, were treated for tax credit purposes. Constrained only by the budget dollars that Campbell is willing to dedicate to this task, your research is likely to be both interesting and frustrating, as no "on point" resolution is likely to be found prior to a later audit of the Form 1120 and its disclosures.

continued

What If?

The risk profiles of the tax adviser and a client seldom are identical. What position should your firm take if Campbell's tax department decides to claim the full incremental research credit for an item on which the tax law is silent or unclear, but your firm recommends that a special disclosure be made on the return concerning the item? A disclosure of this sort would protect the parties from later assessment of tax penalties, but Campbell believes that drawing attention to the credit item would increase the likelihood of a targeted audit of the expenditures by the IRS.

Although you are certain that tax fraud is not a problem on the Campbell return, you are concerned about the ramifications of Campbell's desire to omit the recommended disclosure. Your firm might decide to leave the Campbell engagement altogether if it is especially sensitive to exposure to penalties, or if it is not certain that your tax research has established and documented that there is substantial authority or a reasonable basis for the tax return position. Charges of a lack of appropriate competence or due diligence by your firm might be brought by the IRS, the firm's professional ethics or certification bodies, or the issuer of its malpractice insurance. Clearly, none of these results is attractive to your firm.

Key Terms

30-day letter, 17-9	Enrolled agents (EAs), 17-22	Statute of limitations, 17-21
90-day letter, 17-9	Fraud, 17-18	Substantial authority, 17-16
Accuracy-related penalties, 17-15	Letter ruling, 17-4	Tax preparer, 17-24
Circular 230, 17-22	Negligence, 17-15	Technical advice memorandum
Closing agreement, 17-12	Offer in compromise, 17-10	(TAM), 17-5
Determination letter, 17-4	Reasonable cause, 17-15	Unreasonable position, 17-25
E-filing, 17-3	Revenue Agent's Report (RAR), 17-8	Whistleblower Program, 17-7

Discussion Questions

1. **LO.1** As a tax professional with a diverse group of clients and tax issues, why is it important that you understand how the IRS is organized and how its personnel are deployed?

2. **LO.1** Your tax client Chen asks whether it is likely that her Form 1040 will be audited this year. You suspect that Chen might modify the information she reports on her return based on your answer. Address Chen's question, and provide her with a justification to comply fully with the tax law's reporting requirements.

Critical Thinking 3. **LO.1** Recently, a politician was interviewed about fiscal policy, and she mentioned reducing the "tax gap." Explain what this term means. What are some of the pertinent political and economic issues relative to the tax gap?

4. **LO.1** Review Exhibit 17.1, and identify the following.
   a. The title of the IRS's chief executive officer.
   b. The title of the "IRS's attorney."
   c. The names of the four major operating divisions of the IRS.
   d. The placement in the IRS organization of the Appeals and Criminal Investigation functions.
   e. Initiatives of the IRS to become a more modern, well-managed organization.

5. **LO.3** During an interview with an IRS official on *Dateline*, the interviewer asks, "So how do you decide which Forms 1040 get audited and which do not?" How should the IRS official respond, taking into account that only some of the audit selection process is public information?

6. **LO.3** On June 10, Ming states, "I filed my Form 1040 on April 5 and haven't heard from the IRS since then, so I know I will not be audited!" Evaluate Ming's assumption.

7. **LO.3** You overhear Matheus say, "I am so glad to be divorced from my cheating wife Larissa. She keeps two sets of books in her design business, and I wish the IRS would find out about it." Is Matheus a candidate for the informant award program that is operated by the IRS? Explain how the program works and how an award might be paid to Matheus.

8. **LO.6** Define the following terms in the context of tax law enforcement.
   a. Civil penalty.
   b. Criminal penalty.
   c. *Ad valorem* penalty.
   d. *Assessable* penalty.
   e. Deductible penalty.

9. **LO.6** Which of the valuation penalties is likely to arise when an aggressive taxpayer reports:
   a. A charitable contribution?
   b. A business deduction?
   c. A decedent's taxable estate?

10. **LO.4, 5** Indicate whether each of the following statements is true or false.
    a. The government never pays a taxpayer interest on an overpayment of tax.
    b. The IRS can compromise on the amount of tax liability if there is doubt as to the taxpayer's ability to pay.
    c. The IRS is required to accept an application for an installment plan that delays the payment of the taxpayer's $6,000 outstanding tax liability.
    d. The offer in compromise program attempts to allow upper-income taxpayers additional time in which to pay delinquent tax amounts.

11. **LO.4, 6** In each of the following cases, distinguish between the terms.
    a. Offer in compromise and closing agreement.
    b. Failure to file and failure to pay.
    c. 90-day letter and 30-day letter.
    d. Negligence and fraud.
    e. Criminal and civil tax fraud.

12. **LO.7** Discuss the concept of statutes of limitations in the context of the Federal income tax law. **Critical Thinking**
    a. Who benefits when the statute applies—the government, the taxpayer, or both?
    b. What happens when the statute is scheduled to expire within two weeks but the IRS audit will not be completed by then?

13. **LO.8** Consider the ethical standards under which the tax profession operates. Who regulates the behavior of tax return preparers? What documents provide the major constraints on the conduct of the tax profession?

14. **LO.8** Give the Circular 230 position concerning each of the following situations sometimes encountered in the tax profession.
    a. Taking an aggressive pro-taxpayer position on a tax return.
    b. Not having a quality review process for a return completed by a partner of the tax firm.

c.   Purposely delaying compliance with a document request received from the IRS.

d.   Not keeping up with changes in the tax law.

e.   Charging $1,500 to complete a simple Form 1040 with no supporting schedules.

f.   When representing a taxpayer in a Federal income tax audit, charging a fee equal to one-third of the reduction of the tax proposed by the IRS agent.

g.   Representing both the husband and wife when negotiating tax matters pertinent to their divorce.

h.   Advertising on the Web for new tax clients and including *Se habla español* in the text of the ads.

15. **LO.8** Indicate whether each of the following parties could be subject to the tax preparer penalties.

a.   Tom prepared Sally's return for $250.

b.   Theresa prepared her grandmother's return for no charge.

c.   Georgia prepared her church's return for $500 (she would have charged an unrelated party $3,000 for the same work).

d.   Geoff prepared returns for low-income taxpayers under his college's VITA program.

e.   Hildy prepared the return of her corporate employer.

f.   Heejeo, an administrative assistant for an accounting firm, processed a client's return through TurboTax.

Communications   16. **LO.8** Using no more than five PowerPoint slides, create a presentation for your Advanced Accounting class, listing at least three of the Statements on Standards for Tax Services that apply to CPAs. For each standard you choose, provide a short explanation of its content.

Computational Exercises

17. **LO.6** Alexi files her tax return 20 days after the due date. Along with the return, she remits a check for $3,000, which is the balance of the tax she owes. Disregarding any interest liabilities, compute Alexi's total penalties for this period.

18. **LO.6** Marcella (a calendar year taxpayer) purchased a sculpture for $5,000. When the sculpture is worth $12,000 (as later determined by the IRS), Marcella donates it to the Peoria Museum of Art, a public charity. Based on the appraisal of a friend, Marcella deducts $38,000 for the donation. Because Marcella was in the 24% marginal Federal income tax bracket, overstating the deduction by $26,000 results in a tax underpayment of $6,240.

a.   Compute Marcella's overvaluation penalty.

b.   Construct a Microsoft Excel formula that will compute the penalty for all non-corporate taxpayers.

19. **LO.6** Rivera underpaid her income tax by $45,000. The IRS can prove that $40,000 of the underpayment was due to fraud.

a.   Determine Rivera's civil fraud penalty.

b.   Rivera pays the penalty five years after committing the fraudulent act. Her after-tax rate of return on available cash is 9%. What is the present value of Rivera's penalty?

20. **LO.7** On June 15, 2018, Sheridan filed his 2017 income tax return, paying a tax of $10,500. On October 5, 2019, he filed an amended 2017 return showing an additional $6,400 of tax, which he paid with the amended return. On August 22, 2021, he filed a claim for a refund of $7,000. How much Federal income tax can Sheridan recover on the amended return?

21. **LO.5** Gordon paid the $10,000 balance of his Federal income tax three months late. Ignore daily compounding of interest. Determine the interest rate that applies relative to this amount for the current period, assuming that:

    a. Gordon is an individual.

    b. Gordon is a C corporation.

    c. The $10,000 is not a tax that is due, but is a refund payable by the IRS to Gordon (an individual).

    d. The $10,000 is not a tax that is due, but is a refund payable by the IRS to Gordon (a C corporation).

22. **LO.6** Rita forgot to pay her Federal income tax on time. When she actually filed, she reported a balance due. Compute Rita's failure to file penalty in each of the following cases.

    a. Two months late, $1,000 additional tax due.

    b. Five months late, $3,000 additional tax due.

    c. Eight months late, $4,000 additional tax due.

    d. Two and a half months late, $3,000 additional tax due.

    e. Five months late due to fraud by Rita, $4,000 additional tax due.

    f. Ten months late due to fraud by Rita, $15,000 additional tax due.

23. **LO.6** Wade filed his Federal income tax return on time but did not remit the balance due. Compute Wade's failure to pay penalty in each of the following cases. The IRS has not issued a deficiency notice.

    a. Four months late, $3,000 additional tax due.

    b. Ten months late, $4,000 additional tax due.

    c. Five years late, $5,000 additional tax due.

24. **LO.6** Compute the failure to pay and failure to file penalties for John, who filed his 2019 income tax return on December 20, 2020, paying the $10,000 amount due at that time. On April 1, 2020, John received a six-month extension of time in which to file his return. He has no reasonable cause for failing to file his return by October 15 or for failing to pay the tax that was due on April 15. John's failure to comply with the tax laws was not fraudulent.

25. **LO.6** Olivia, a calendar year taxpayer, does not file her 2019 Form 1040 until December 12, 2020. At this point, she pays the $40,000 balance due on her 2019 tax liability of $70,000. Olivia did not apply for and obtain any extension of time for filing the 2019 return. When questioned by the IRS on her delinquency, Olivia asserts: "If I was too busy to file my regular tax return, I was too busy to request an extension."

    a. Is Olivia liable for any penalties for failure to file and for failure to pay?

    b. If so, compute the penalty amounts.

26. **LO.6** Blake, a cash basis, calendar year taxpayer, filed his Federal income tax return 48 days after the due date. Blake never extended his return, and he paid the taxes that were due when he filed the return. What penalty will Blake incur, and how much will he have to pay if his additional tax is $10,000? Disregard any interest he must pay.

27. **LO.6** Maureen, a calendar year individual taxpayer, files her 2018 return on November 4, 2020. She did not obtain an extension for filing her return, and the return reflects additional income tax due of $15,000.

    a. What are Maureen's penalties for failure to file and to pay?

    b. Would your answer to part (a) change if Maureen, before the due date of the return, had retained a CPA to prepare the return and it was the CPA's negligence that caused the delay? Explain.

28. **LO.6** Blair underpaid her taxes by $250,000. A portion of the underpayment was shown to be attributable to Blair's negligence ($100,000). A court found that the rest of the deficiency constituted civil fraud ($150,000).

    a. Compute the total fraud and negligence penalties incurred.

    b. Construct a Microsoft Excel formula that will compute the penalties incurred in part (a).

    c. Blair pays the penalties four years after committing the improper acts. Her after-tax rate of return on available cash is 7%. What is the present value of Blair's penalty obligations?

29. **LO.6** Compute the overvaluation penalty for each of the following independent cases involving the fair market value of charitable contribution property.

	Taxpayer	Corrected IRS Value	Reported Valuation	Applicable Tax Rate
a.	Individual	$ 40,000	$ 50,000	35%
b.	C corporation	30,000	50,000	21
c.	S corporation	40,000	50,000	35
d.	Individual	150,000	200,000	35
e.	Individual	150,000	250,000	35
f.	C corporation	150,000	750,000	21

30. **LO.6** Compute the undervaluation penalty for each of the following independent cases involving the value of a closely held business in the decedent's gross estate. In each case, assume a marginal Federal estate tax rate of 40%.

	Reported Value	Corrected IRS Valuation
a.	$ 20,000	$ 25,000
b.	100,000	150,000
c.	150,000	250,000
d.	150,000	500,000

31. **LO.6** Singh, a qualified appraiser of fine art and other collectibles, was advising Colleen when she was determining the amount of the charitable contribution deduction for a gift of a sculpture to a museum. Singh sanctioned a $900,000 appraisal, even though he knew the market value of the piece was only $300,000. Colleen assured Singh that she had never been audited by the IRS and that the risk of the government questioning his appraisal was negligible.

    But Colleen was wrong, and her return was audited. The IRS used its own appraisers to set the value of the sculpture at $400,000. Colleen is in the 32% Federal income tax bracket. Singh's fee for preparing the appraisal was $20,000.

    a. Compute the penalty the IRS can assess against Singh. (Do not consider the valuation penalty as to Colleen's return.)

    b. What is the penalty if Singh's appraisal fee was $7,500 (not $20,000)?

    c. Construct a Microsoft Excel formula that would generate the correct answer for parts (a) and (b).

32. **LO.6** Eggers Corporation filed an amended Form 1120, claiming an additional $400,000 deduction for payments to a contractor for a prior tax year. The amended return was based on the entity's interpretation of a Regulation that defined deductible advance payment expenditures. The nature of Eggers's activity with the contractor did not exactly fit the language of the Regulation. Nevertheless, because so much tax was at stake, Eggers's tax department decided to claim the deduction.

    Eggers's tax department estimated that there was only a 15% chance that Eggers's interpretation would stand up to a Tax Court review.

a. What is the amount of tax penalty that Eggers is risking by taking this position?

b. What would be the result if there was a 45% chance that Eggers's interpretation of the Regulation was correct?

c. Construct a Microsoft Excel formula that would generate the correct answer for parts (a) and (b).

33. **LO.6** Kaitlin donated a painting to the local art museum. Because she is subject to a 35% marginal tax rate, she needs a large charitable contribution deduction for the year. She engaged Vargas (who was referred to her by the staff of the museum) to provide an appraisal of the painting before she filed her Form 1040 for the year. Kaitlin told Vargas, "Be kind to me on this appraisal, and I'll send several more clients to you in the future." Kaitlin paid Vargas a $45,000 fee for his services.

Vargas completed his appraisal and determined that the painting was worth $500,000 under current market conditions. Still, in light of Kaitlin's promise of future business, Vargas sent Kaitlin an official appraisal reporting a $900,000 value for the artwork. Vargas had never compromised his integrity, but this time the temptation was too much.

Kaitlin used the appraisal to claim a $900,000 deduction for her charitable gift. Kaitlin will incur a valuation penalty now that her Form 1040 has been audited and the IRS has determined that the correct amount of the deduction is $500,000.

a. Compute any appraiser's penalty to which Vargas might be exposed.

b. Express the computation of this penalty as a Microsoft Excel formula.

34. **LO.6** Trudy's AGI last year was $200,000. Her Federal income tax came to $65,000, paid through both withholding and estimated payments. This year, her AGI will be $300,000, with a projected tax liability of $50,000, all to be paid through estimates. Trudy wants to pay the least amount of tax that does not incur a penalty.

a. Ignore the annualized income method. Compute Trudy's quarterly estimated tax payment schedule for this year.

b. Assume instead that Trudy's AGI last year was $100,000 and resulted in a Federal income tax of $20,000. Determine her quarterly estimated tax payment schedule for this year.

35. **LO.6** Kold Services Corporation estimates that its 2019 taxable income will be $500,000. Thus, it is subject to a 21% income tax rate and incurs a $105,000 liability. For each of the following independent cases, compute Kold's 2019 minimum quarterly estimated tax payments that will avoid an underpayment penalty.

a. For 2018, taxable income was ($200,000). Thus, Kold generated a zero 2018 liability.

b. For 2018, taxable income was $450,000, and tax liability was $94,500.

c. For 2017, taxable income was $2,000,000, and tax liability was $680,000. For 2018, taxable income was $400,000, and tax liability was $84,000.

36. **LO.6** Leake Company, owned equally by Jacquie (chair of the board of directors) and Jeff (company president), is in very difficult financial straits. Last month, Jeff used the $300,000 withheld from employee paychecks for Federal payroll and income taxes to pay a creditor who threatened to cut off all supplies. To keep the company afloat, Jeff used these government funds willfully for the operations of the business, but even that effort was not enough. The company missed the next two payrolls, and today other creditors took action to shut down Leake altogether.

Critical Thinking

Communications

How much will the IRS assess in taxes and penalties in this matter and from whom? How can you as a tax professional best offer service to Jacquie, Jeff, and Leake? Address these matters in a memo for the tax research file.

37. **LO.7** Jane filed her 2018 Form 1040 on April 4, 2019. What is the date on which the applicable statute of limitations expires in each of the following independent situations?

a. Jane incurred a bad debt loss that she failed to claim.

b. Jane inadvertently omitted one-third of the correct gross income.

    c.   Same as part (b), except that the omission was deliberate.

    d.   Jane innocently overstated her deductions by a large amount.

    e.   No return was filed by Jane.

38. **LO.7** Loraine (a calendar year taxpayer) reported the following transactions, all of which were properly included in a timely filed return.

Gross receipts		$ 975,000
Cost of sales		(850,000)
Gross profit		$ 125,000
Capital gain	$ 40,000	
Capital loss	(25,000)	15,000
Total income		$ 140,000

    a.   Presuming the absence of fraud, how much of an omission from gross income would trigger the six-year statute of limitations?

    b.   Would it matter if cost of sales had been inadvertently overstated by $150,000?

    c.   How does the situation change in the context of fraud by Loraine?

Critical Thinking   39. **LO.5, 7** On April 3, 2017, Luis filed his 2016 income tax return, which showed a tax due of $75,000. On June 1, 2019, he filed an amended return for 2016 that showed an additional tax of $10,000. Luis paid the additional amount. On May 18, 2020, Luis filed a claim for a 2016 refund of $25,000.

    a.   If Luis's claim for a refund is correct in amount, how much tax will he recover?

    b.   What is the period that government-paid interest runs with respect to Luis's claim for a refund?

    c.   How would you have advised him differently?

40. **LO.8** Rod's Federal income tax returns (Form 1040) for the indicated years were prepared by the following persons.

Year	Preparer
1	Rod
2	Ann
3	Cheryl

    Ann is Rod's next-door neighbor and owns and operates a pharmacy. Cheryl is a licensed CPA and is engaged in private practice. In the event Rod is audited and all three returns are examined, who may represent him before the IRS at the agent level? Who may represent Rod before the Appeals Division?

41. **LO.8** Christie is the preparer of the Form 1120 for Yostern Corporation. On the return, Yostern claimed a deduction that the IRS later disallowed on audit. Compute the tax preparer penalty that could be assessed against Christie in each of the following independent situations.

	Form 8275 Disclosure on the Return of the Disputed Deduction?	Tax Reduction Resulting from the Deduction	Probability That the Courts Would Approve the Deduction	Christie's Fee to Complete Yostern's Return
a.	No	$40,000	65%	$7,000
b.	No	40,000	35	7,000
c.	No	40,000	35	1,500
d.	Yes	40,000	35	7,000
e.	Yes	40,000	15	4,000

42. **LO.8** Discuss which penalties, if any, might be imposed on the tax adviser in each of the following independent circumstances. In this regard, assume that the tax adviser:

   a.   Suggested to the client various means by which to generate excludible income.

   b.   Suggested to the client various means by which to conceal cash receipts from gross income.

   c.   Suggested to the client means by which to improve her cash flow by delaying for six months or more the deposit of the employees' share of Federal employment taxes.

   d.   Failed, because of pressing time conflicts, to conduct the usual review of the client's tax return. The IRS later discovered that the return included fraudulent data.

   e.   Failed, because of pressing time conflicts, to conduct the usual review of the client's tax return. The IRS later discovered a math error in the computation of the personal exemption.

43. **LO.8** Compute the preparer penalty the IRS could assess on Gerry in each of the following independent cases.

   a.   On March 21, the copy machine was not working, so Gerry gave original returns to her 20 clients that day without providing any duplicates for them. Copies for Gerry's files and for use in preparing state tax returns had been made on March 20.

   b.   Because Gerry extended her vacation a few days, she missed the Annual Tax Update seminar that she usually attends. As a result, she was unaware that Congress had changed a law affecting limited partnerships. The change affected the transactions of 25 of Gerry's clients, all of whom understated their tax as a result.

   c.   Gerry heard that the IRS was increasing its audits of corporations that hold assets in a foreign trust. As a result, Gerry instructed Hulan, the intern who prepared the initial drafts of the returns for five corporate clients, to leave blank the question about such trusts. Not wanting to lose her position, Hulan, a senior accounting major at State University, complied with Gerry's instructions.

44. **LO.8** You are the chair of the Ethics Committee of your state's CPA Licensing Commission. Interpret controlling AICPA authority in addressing the following assertions by your membership.   **Decision Making**

   a.   When a CPA has reasonable grounds for not answering an applicable question on a client's return, a brief explanation of the reason for the omission should not be provided, because it would flag the return for audit by the IRS.

   b.   If a CPA discovers during an IRS audit that the client has a material error in the return under examination, he should immediately withdraw from the engagement.

   c.   If the client tells you that she paid $500 for office supplies but has lost the receipts, you should deduct an odd amount on her return (e.g., $499), because an even amount ($500) would indicate to the IRS that her deduction was based on an estimate.

   d.   If a CPA knows that the client has a material error in a prior year's return, he should not, without the client's consent, disclose the error to the IRS.

   e.   If a CPA's client will not correct a material error in a prior year's return, the CPA should not prepare the current year's return for the client.

Research Problems

THOMSON REUTERS
CHECKPOINT™

Note: Solutions to the Research Problems can be prepared by using the Thomson Reuters Checkpoint™ online tax research database, which accompanies this textbook. Solutions can also be prepared by using research materials found in a typical tax library.

Communications

Critical Thinking

Research Problem 1. Lopez always had taken his Form 1040 data to the franchise tax preparers in a local mall, but this year, his friend Cheryl asked to prepare his return. Cheryl quoted a reasonable fee, and Lopez reasoned that, with finances especially tight in Cheryl's household, she could use the money.

Lopez delivered his Forms W–2, 1099, and other documentation and said, "I'll pick up the finished return from you on Monday." Cheryl completed the return by that deadline, and without signing and reviewing the forms, Lopez allowed Cheryl to e-file it that day. The arrangement was that Cheryl would receive the refund through a special bank account and write Lopez a check for that amount, minus her fee. When the refund came through about three weeks later, Cheryl wrote Lopez a check for $2,400, and all parties were satisfied. Lopez gladly used Cheryl to e-file the next year's return using the same procedures.

To his surprise, Lopez received a letter from the IRS about 18 months later. The auditor had found that the return Cheryl had e-filed vastly overstated deductions and wrongly calculated the earned income tax credit. According to the audit report, the refund issued was $4,500—Cheryl had pocketed the difference. Thus, the corrected tax liability meant that Lopez now owed $7,000 in tax, before considering interest and penalties.

Lopez contends that he relied on Cheryl's expertise in the tax law and e-filing procedures. Consequently, there was reasonable cause for the underpayment of tax, and the IRS should waive the understatement and negligence penalties. The IRS has expressed sympathy for Lopez's position, but it maintains that the penalty should stand. What do you think? Summarize your findings in a memo for the tax research file.

Communications

Research Problem 2. Blanche Creek (111 Elm Avenue, Plymouth, IN 46563) has engaged your firm because she has been charged with failure to file her 2017 Federal Form 1040. Blanche maintains that the "reasonable cause" exception should apply. During the entire tax filing season in 2018, she was under a great deal of stress at work and in her personal life. As a result, Blanche developed a sleep disorder, which was treated through a combination of pills and counseling.

Your firm ultimately prepared the 2017 tax return for Blanche, but it was filed far beyond the due date. Blanche is willing to pay the delinquent tax and related interest. However, she believes that the failure to pay penalty is unfair, because she was ill. Consequently, she could not be expected to keep to the usual deadlines for filing.

Write a letter to Blanche concerning these matters.

Use internet tax resources to address the following questions. Look for reliable websites and blogs of the IRS and other government agencies, media outlets, businesses, tax professionals, academics, think tanks, and political outlets.

Communications

Research Problem 3. Make a list of the individuals currently serving in the following tax-related positions. Give the website address where you found this information. Send this list to your instructor.

   a.   IRS Commissioner.
   b.   IRS Chief Counsel.
   c.   Heads of the four major operating divisions of the IRS.
   d.   Heads of the IRS Appeals and Criminal Investigation divisions.
   e.   Chair of the House Ways and Means Committee.

    f.   Chair of the Senate Finance Committee.

    g.   President of the Tax Foundation.

    h.   Chair of the AICPA Tax Executive Committee.

Research Problem 4. Taxpayers generally "go to jail" on tax charges only when criminal activities have been involved. Find information about the criminal tax prosecutions the Treasury undertakes. Compare data for the last year of information available from the IRS and for five years prior to that.

    How many criminal tax charges are initiated in a year? How much time does a criminal tax case take from the filing of charges to disposition by the IRS or a court? What issues tend to be the focus of a criminal tax prosecution? How much additional tax, interest, and penalty revenue does the Treasury collect due to its criminal prosecutions? Summarize your findings for your classmates in no more than four PowerPoint slides.

Data Analytics
Communications

Research Problem 5. Corporations with large estimated tax overpayments and underpayments are subject to special interest rates.

    a.   Find in the Code how these rates are determined.

    b.   List the rates that have been in effect for the last six calendar quarters.

    c.   Find and subscribe to a feed that will alert you automatically when the interest rate changes.

Research Problem 6. Every year toward the end of the Form 1040 filing season, suggestions are offered to taxpayers about how to pay their taxes if they lack the funds to do so. The discussions address filing extensions, installment plans, and credit card payments. Find two online videos of this sort. Summarize the videoclips, and develop a speech outline and no more than four PowerPoint slides for a presentation you will make to your town's Young Executives Club.

Communications

Research Problem 7. Find a website that lists suggestions on how to deal with an IRS auditor during the first meeting with him or her. You might start at **irs.gov** by reading Publication 556. Then find at least three sites offered by tax professionals with different credentials and certifications. Summarize and evaluate each of the key points in an e-mail to your instructor.

Communications

Research Problem 8. Find a report issued by the Treasury Inspector General for Tax Administration, an IRS oversight group. Using information from this report, construct a chart for a specific tax year, showing the audit rate for high-income tax returns, broken down by income ranges such as $200,000 to $400,000 of total positive income, $400,000 to $600,000, and so on. Indicate in your chart how many Forms 1040 were filed in each income range for the tax year and how many of those were audited by the IRS.

Data Analytics
Communications

Research Problem 9. Your client Ellie, a single U.S. individual, owes the IRS $84,000 in income taxes that relate to her tax year 2010. This year, Ellie submits a renewal request for her U.S. passport. In a research memo to your instructor, explain what is likely to happen concerning Ellie's passport. *Hint*: Search using the phrase "seriously delinquent tax debt."

Communications

Becker CPA Review Questions

1. A taxpayer presented her tax return preparer, Dev Powell, with documentation supporting income she had earned as an independent contractor. Although Powell knew that the taxpayer's income should be reported on the taxpayer's Form 1040 (U.S. individual income tax return), he intentionally did not report the income on the taxpayer's tax return. Powell understated the taxpayer's liability because he believed keeping the tax liability low would help retain the taxpayer as a client. In this situation, Powell may be subject to which of the following penalties?

    a. Understatement of taxpayer's liability due to failure to follow substantial authority by the tax return preparer

    b. Failure to file correct information returns by a tax return preparer

    c. Wrongful disclosure or use of tax return information by the tax return preparer

    d. Understatement of taxpayer's liability due to willful or reckless conduct of the tax return preparer

2. Treasury Department Circular 230 provides guidance for doing which of the following activities?

    a. Practicing before the IRS

    b. Practicing before the U.S. Tax Court

    c. Presenting before state boards of accountancy

    d. Reporting income taxes in financial statements

3. Which of the following is *not* required conduct for a preparer of an income tax return?

    a. Abide by the tax Code and legally minimize the taxpayer's tax liability.

    b. Verify that the information the client provides is correct.

    c. Notify the client if the preparer becomes aware of an error in a tax return.

    d. Inform the taxpayer about how to correct the situation of the taxpayer's failure to file an income tax return.

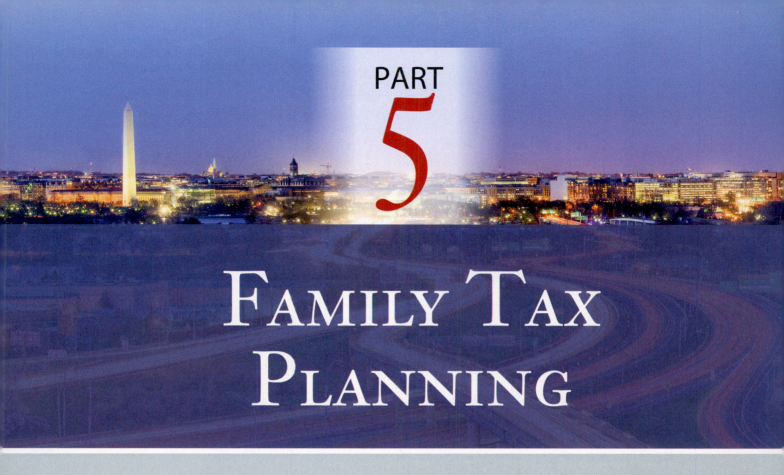

PART 5

FAMILY TAX PLANNING

Family tax planning has as its objective the minimization of the present value of income and transfer taxes imposed on the family unit. Carrying out this objective requires a familiarity with the rules applicable to transfers by gift and at death. Entities often created as a result of these transfers (trusts and estates) are subject to unique income tax rules, as discussed in this part of the text.

The Federal Gift and Estate Taxes

LEARNING OBJECTIVES: *After completing Chapter 18, you should be able to:*

LO.1 Explain the nature of the Federal asset transfer taxes.

LO.2 Describe and analyze the Federal gift tax formula.

LO.3 Describe and analyze the Federal estate tax formula.

LO.4 Illustrate the operation of the Federal gift tax.

LO.5 Calculate the Federal gift tax.

LO.6 Identify the components of the gross estate.

LO.7 Describe the components of the taxable estate.

LO.8 Calculate the Federal estate tax liability.

LO.9 Review and demonstrate the role of the generation-skipping transfer tax.

CHAPTER OUTLINE

THE BIG PICTURE

AN EVENTFUL AND FINAL YEAR

Over his lifetime, Peter Hood started and purchased numerous automobile dealerships that he eventually transferred to a newly formed entity, Hood Corporation. Upon his death in a previous year, the stock in Hood Corporation passed in equal shares to Peter's surviving spouse, Martha, and their adult children, John and Helen.

For John Hood, 2019 proved to be an eventful and final tax year. Among the major happenings were the following.

- In January, John's divorce from his first wife, Hannah, became final.
- In February, he married Ashley, the manager of one of the Hood car dealerships.
- He made various gifts to family members.
- In July, John's mother Martha died of a heart condition, and John served as executor of her estate.
- In late November, he was seriously injured in a car accident (caused by another motorist).
- In early December, John carried out some pre-death tax and estate planning.
- John died of his injuries in mid-December.

What are some of the tax problems (i.e., income, gift, and estate taxes) that might be encountered as a result of these events?

Read the chapter and formulate your response.

U ntil now, this text has dealt primarily with various applications of the Federal income tax. We now add to the discussion the Federal excise taxes on an individual's right to transfer property to another party. The Federal estate, gift, and generation-skipping taxes constitute the central focus of Chapters 18 and 19.

18-1 TRANSFER TAXES—IN GENERAL

LO.1

Explain the nature of the Federal asset transfer taxes.

For about 100 years, Congress has applied a gift and estate tax on the right of individuals (rather than the government) to determine who will receive their assets as the result of a legal transfer of title during life or at death. The chief purposes of these taxes are to keep wealthy families from retaining "too much" over the generations such that competition in the marketplace would become unfair, and to increase the chances that wealthy individuals pay a "fair share" of taxes to the government to support annual Federal expenditures.

In the typical year, fewer than 3 million U.S. individuals die. At the same time, only about 5,000 estates file a Federal estate tax return showing an estate tax liability. About half of these returns are filed for residents of New York, Florida, Illinois, and California. Likewise, about 4,000 Federal gift tax returns are filed each year showing a gift tax liability. Total collections of Federal estate and gift tax revenues amount to $25 to $30 billion per year.

18-1a Nature of the Taxes

The Code imposes a tax on the gratuitous transfer of property. If the transfer occurs during the owner's life (e.g., by a cash transfer or the use of a trust), it is subject to the Federal gift tax. If the property passes by virtue of the death of the owner (e.g., under the terms of a will or life insurance policy), the Federal estate tax applies. If the recipient (i.e., the donee, heir, or beneficiary) of the transfer is two or more generations younger than the person making the transfer, the separate generation-skipping transfer tax also applies.[1]

A **unified transfer tax** applies to all gratuitous transfers of assets by an individual, regardless of how or when the transfers are made.

The gift, estate, and generation-skipping transfer taxes operate as a single, cumulative tax over the course of one's lifetime. In general, planning techniques relative to transfer taxes attempt to avoid or defer the payment of any gift tax liabilities during lifetime; such payments essentially act as a prepayment of the estate tax on a given asset, and to avoid the payment of the tax on generation-skipping transfers, which acts as a tax penalty on aggressive family wealth transfers.

Persons Subject to the Tax

The Federal gift tax is imposed on the right to transfer property by one person (the donor) to another (the donee) for less than full and adequate consideration. The tax is payable by the donor.[2] If the donor fails to pay the tax when due, the donee may be held liable for the tax to the extent of the value of the property received.[3]

Upon the death of an individual, the Federal estate tax is imposed on the taxable estate.[4] The executor (or administrator) of the estate pays any estate tax that may be due.

The Federal gift, estate, and generation-skipping taxes apply to a resident or citizen of the United States, regardless of where the transferred property is located. Someone who is not a U.S. citizen or resident is subject to the taxes only if the transferred property is located in the United States.[5]

---

[1]The estate tax was enacted in 1916. Because the estate tax could be avoided by making transfers just prior to dying (i.e., "deathbed gifts"), a gift tax was added in 1932.

[2]§ 2502(c).

[3]§ 6324(b). Known as the doctrine of transferee liability, this rule also operates to enable the IRS to enforce the collection of other taxes (e.g., income tax and estate tax).

[4]§ 2001(a). Subchapter A (§§ 2001 through 2058) covers the estate tax treatment of those who are either residents or citizens. Subchapter B (§§ 2101 through 2108) covers the estate tax applicable to NRAs; in those cases, different exemption and exclusion amounts apply.

[5]§§ 2001(a), 2511(a), 2801

GLOBAL TAX ISSUES   U.S. Transfer Taxes and NRAs

For individuals who are neither residents nor citizens of the United States (i.e., nonresident aliens, or NRAs), the Federal gift tax applies only to gifts of property situated within the United States. Exempted, however, are gifts of intangibles, such as stocks and bonds.

For decedents who are NRAs, the Federal estate tax is imposed on the value of property located within the United States. Unlike the gift tax, however, the estate tax applies to stock in U.S. corporations.

Types of Tax at Death

Taxes payable by virtue of a person's death fall into two categories: estate and inheritance. The U.S. government, some states, and several other countries impose estate taxes. Inheritance taxes are imposed by some states and other countries. Some states and countries use both types of taxes.

The Federal estate tax differs in several respects from the typical *inheritance tax*. First, the Federal estate tax is levied on the decedent's taxable estate. It is a tax on the right to pass property at death. Inheritance taxes apply to the right to receive property at death and are therefore levied on the heirs. Second, the relationship of the heirs to the decedent usually has a direct bearing on the amount of the inheritance tax. In general, the more closely related the parties, the larger the exemptions and the lower the applicable rates. Except for transfers to surviving spouses that may result in a marital deduction, the relationship of the heirs to the decedent has no effect on the Federal estate tax.

Formula for the Gift Tax

The Federal gift tax is reported annually on Form 709. Like the income tax, which uses taxable income (not gross income) as a tax base, the gift tax usually does not apply to the full amount of the gift. Deductions and the annual exclusion may be allowed to arrive at the **taxable gift**.[6] Concept Summary 18.1 outlines the formula for the gift tax and its chief deductions and exclusions. For this purpose, we assume that the gift tax is applied at a flat 40 percent rate on the taxable gifts for the year.[7]

Because Congress did not intend for the gift tax to apply to smaller transfers, it provided for an annual exclusion, which reduces the taxable gift to zero when a small amount is involved. The exclusion amount periodically is adjusted for *significant* inflation. For 2018 and 2019, the exclusion is $15,000.[8]

Describe and analyze the Federal gift tax formula.

Formula for the Federal Estate Tax

When a decedent transfers property as a result of death, the Federal estate tax can apply. As a simplifying assumption, a flat 40 percent tax rate applies to the taxable estate—the fair market value of property owned or controlled by the decedent at the date of death, minus various deductions. The unified transfer tax credit applies against this tax. There are more deductions allowed against the estate tax than can be used in computing the gift tax, as illustrated in Concept Summary 18.2.

The tax on generation-skipping transfers (GSTT)[9] acts as a penalty for passing assets to certain younger individuals. It applies to both lifetime and deathtime transfers, and the GSTT is added to the gift or estate tax that is computed above. Such a transfer thus can become quite expensive from a Federal transfer tax standpoint.

Describe and analyze the Federal estate tax formula.

---

[6] § 2503(a).

[7] The flat rate assumption is made throughout Chapters 18 through 20 to simplify the tax computations. The § 2001 tax rate schedule for gifts and estates is reproduced on the inside front cover of this text. It shows some progressivity for taxable amounts under $1 million.

[8] § 2503(b)(2).

[9] § 2601.

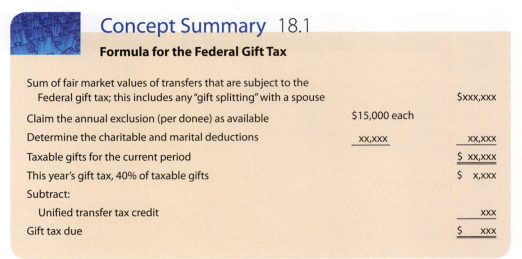

Concept Summary 18.1

Formula for the Federal Gift Tax

Sum of fair market values of transfers that are subject to the Federal gift tax; this includes any "gift splitting" with a spouse		$xxx,xxx
Claim the annual exclusion (per donee) as available	$15,000 each	
Determine the charitable and marital deductions	xx,xxx	xx,xxx
Taxable gifts for the current period		$ xx,xxx
This year's gift tax, 40% of taxable gifts		$ x,xxx
Subtract:		
Unified transfer tax credit		xxx
Gift tax due		$ xxx

Concept Summary 18.2

Formula for the Federal Estate Tax

Gross estate, sum of fair market values of property owned and controlled on the date of death		$xxx,xxx
Subtract:		
Expenses, indebtedness, and taxes	$xx	
Losses	xx	
Charitable bequests	xx	
Marital deduction	xx	
State-level estate or inheritance taxes	xx	x,xxx
Taxable estate		$ xx,xxx
Estate tax, 40% of taxable estate		$ xx,xxx
Subtract:		
Unified transfer tax credit, minus amount used against lifetime gifts	$xx	
Other tax credits (e.g., for non-U.S. taxes paid at death)	xx	x,xxx
Estate tax due		$ xxx

The chief purpose of the GSTT is to prevent families from transferring assets to much younger members, so as to reduce the present value of the transfer tax on the older generation's asset accumulations. The GSTT aims to apply a transfer tax to the family assets at least once every other generation.

The Unified Transfer Tax Credit

The purpose of the **unified transfer tax credit** is to allow donors and decedents to transfer specified amounts of wealth without being subject to current gift, estate, and GST taxes. The unified credit offsets tax, computed using the applicable estate and gift tax rates, on a specified amount of transfers, referred to as the applicable exclusion amount.

Exhibit 18.1 shows the exclusion amount applicable to taxable asset transfers for the past several years. The exclusion amount is subject to annual indexation from its statutory amount of $10 million.[10]

---

[10]§ 2010.

EXHIBIT 18.1	Unified Transfer Tax Exclusion Amount

Year of Transfer	Exclusion Amount
2016	$ 5,450,000
2017	5,490,000
2018	11,180,000
2019	11,400,000

The **exclusion amount** (also termed the **exemption equivalent** and the **bypass amount**) is the amount of the transfer that will pass free of the gift or estate tax by virtue of the credit. Because the Federal transfer taxes are unified and cumulative in effect, these amounts are available to an individual only once during his or her lifetime.

Unified Transfer Tax Credit

In 2019, Janet makes a taxable gift of $6 million, the first taxable gift that she ever has made. Janet does not owe any Federal gift tax for the year.[11]

EXAMPLE 1

In 2019, Sanjay makes a taxable gift of $2,000,000. In prior years, Sanjay's taxable gifts totaled $10,000,000. The exclusion amount applies to Sanjay in a cumulative manner, such that his lifetime taxable gifts amount to $12,000,000, and a Federal gift tax is due for 2019 on $600,000 ($12,000,000 − $11,400,000).

EXAMPLE 2

In 2019, Dulcea dies reporting a taxable estate of $2,000,000. In prior years, Dulcea's taxable gifts totaled $10,000,000. The exclusion amount applies to Dulcea in a cumulative manner, such that her lifetime and at-death taxable asset transfers amount to $12,000,000, and a Federal estate tax is due on $600,000 ($12,000,000 − $11,400,000).

EXAMPLE 3

18-1b **Valuation for Federal Transfer Tax Purposes**

The value of the property on the date of its transfer generally determines the amount that is subject to the Federal gift, GST, or estate tax. For this purpose, fair market value is used; matters of asset valuation are discussed further in text Section 19-1. Under certain conditions, however, an executor can elect to value estate assets on the **alternate valuation date**. The election is made by the executor of the estate and is irrevocable. There is no alternate valuation date election available for the gift tax.

The alternate valuation date election was designed as a relief provision to ease the economic hardship that could result when estate assets decline in value between the date of death and the payment of the estate tax liability. If the election is made, all assets of the estate are valued six months after death *or* on the date of disposition if this occurs earlier.[12] The election covers *all* assets in the gross estate and cannot be applied to only a portion of the property.

Robert's gross estate consists of the following property.

EXAMPLE 4

	Value on Date of Death	Value Six Months Later
Land	$14,800,000	$14,840,000
Stock in Brown Corporation	900,000	700,000
Stock in Green Corporation	500,000	460,000
Total	$16,200,000	$16,000,000

continued

---

[11]§ 2001(c).   [12]§ 2032(a)(1).

> If Robert's executor elects the alternate valuation date, the estate must be valued at $16,000,000. It is not permissible to value the land at its date of death value ($14,800,000) and choose the alternate valuation date for the rest of the gross estate, so as to reduce the tax base.

To be allowed, the election of the alternate valuation date must decrease the value of the gross estate *and* decrease the estate tax liability. The reason for this last requirement is that the income tax basis of property acquired from a decedent will be the value used for estate tax purposes (discussed further in text Section 19-2b). Without a special limitation, the alternate valuation date could be elected solely to add to income tax basis, at a zero estate tax cost.

EXAMPLE 5

> Al's gross estate consists of assets with a date of death value of $16 million and an alternate valuation date value of $16.1 million. Under Al's will, all of his property passes outright to Jean (Al's wife). Because of the marital deduction, no estate tax results regardless of which value is used. But if the alternate valuation date could be elected (which it cannot, because the tax liability is zero with and without the election), Jean would take a stepped-up income tax basis of $16.1 million in the property acquired from Al, without incurring any Federal transfer tax liability.

18-1c **Key Property Concepts**

Separate and Joint Asset Ownership

Most property is owned by one individual, who holds title to the asset and perhaps to a liability associated with it. When that individual passes the title to the asset to another party, during lifetime or at death, a gift or bequest may occur, and a Federal transfer tax may apply.

Now assume that Dan and Vicky jointly own equal interests in a tract of land. Such ownership can fall into any of four categories, originating in common law statutes of the states: joint tenancy, tenancy by the entirety, tenancy in common, or community property. Estate tax consequences that arise when jointly owned property like this transfers on account of death are discussed in text Section 18-3a. During lifetime, one of the joint owners can make a gift of his or her "share" of the property, and a gift tax may apply at that time.

If Dan and Vicky hold ownership as **joint tenants** or **tenants by the entirety**, the right of survivorship exists. This means that the tenant(s) who survive receive full ownership of the property. Thus, if Dan predeceases Vicky, the land belongs entirely to Vicky. None of the land will pass to Dan's heirs or will be subject to administration by Dan's executor. A tenancy by the entirety is a joint tenancy between only a married couple.[13]

If Dan and Vicky hold ownership as **tenants in common** or as community property, death does not defeat an owner's interest. Thus, if Dan predeceases Vicky, Dan's one-half interest in the land will pass to his estate or heirs, as determined under his will or other arrangements. Vicky continues to own her share outright.

Community property interests arise from the marital relationship. Under this system, all property acquired after marriage, except by gift or inheritance, by spouses residing in a community property state becomes part of the community assets. The following states operate under the community property system: Louisiana, Texas, New Mexico, Arizona, California, Washington, Idaho, Nevada, Wisconsin, and (by election of the spouses) Alaska. All other states follow the common law system of ascertaining a spouse's rights to property acquired after marriage.

---

[13]Some state laws do not use the term *tenancy by the entirety* but, nevertheless, recognize a joint tenancy between spouses.

Marisol owns a building in an equal joint tenancy with Jada. While both individuals are living, Marisol can make a gift of her half of the property to Willie. But if Marisol dies and Jada survives, Marisol's one-half interest in the building passes to Jada automatically under state law, in the form of the survivorship feature of the joint tenancy. At that point, Marisol no longer can pass her half of the building to Willie, and a clause in Marisol's will that transfers a half interest to Willie is invalid.

If Marisol and Jada own the building as tenants in common or as community property, Marisol can pass her half of the asset to Willie as a lifetime gift or as a bequest at death. No right of survivorship exists under state property law.

18-2 THE FEDERAL GIFT TAX

18-2a General Considerations

LO.4

Illustrate the operation of the Federal gift tax.

In working with the gift tax, one first determines whether a gift has in fact taken place. In the typical situation, a gift occurs when one party takes ownership of an asset without providing full and adequate consideration to the other party.

Motivated by respect and admiration, Julie transfers some shares of stock to Pattie and receives nothing in return. Julie has made a gift to Pattie in the amount of the fair market value of the stock. Julie is the *donor*, and Pattie is the *donee*.

Similarly, if the stock is worth $50,000 and Pattie pays Julie $12,000 to take ownership of it, Julie has made a $38,000 gift to Pattie.

Requirements for a Gift

For a gift to be complete under state law, the following elements typically must be present.

- A donor competent to make the gift.
- A donee capable of receiving and possessing the property.
- Donative intent on behalf of the donor.
- Actual or constructive delivery of the property to the donee or the donee's representative.
- Acceptance of the gift by the donee.

Incomplete Transfers

The Federal gift tax does not apply to transfers that are incomplete. Thus, if the transferor retains the right to reclaim the property or has not really parted with the possession of the property, a taxable event has not taken place.

Business versus Personal Setting

In a business setting, full and adequate consideration for an exchange is apt to exist; thus, gifts in a business setting are rare. If the parties are acting in a personal setting, however, a gift usually is the result.

Grace loans money to Debby in connection with a business venture. About a year later, Grace forgives part of the loan. Grace probably has not made a gift to Debby if she and Debby are unrelated parties.

Valuable consideration (such as would preclude a gift result) does not include a payment or transfer based on "love and affection … promise of marriage, etc."[14] Consequently, property settlements in consideration of marriage (i.e., pre- or antenuptial agreements) are regarded as gifts.

---

[14] Reg. § 25.2512–8.

Joe (age 86) and Nicole (age 22) are married. Two days later, they exchange wedding gifts. Joe's gift to Nicole is stock in IBM (valued at $2 million), and Nicole's gift to Joe is a bottle of cologne (value of $32). What tax goals are they trying to accomplish? Will their plan work?

Do not conclude that the presence of *some* consideration is enough to preclude Federal gift tax consequences. Again, the answer may rest on whether the transfer occurred in a business setting.

Peter sells Bob some real estate for $40,000. Unknown to Peter, the property contains valuable mineral deposits and is really worth $200,000. Peter may have made a bad business deal, but he has not made a gift of $160,000 to Bob.

Excluded Transfers

Transfers to political organizations are exempt from the application of the Federal gift tax.[15] This provision includes gifts to political parties, candidates, committees, and the like.

The Federal gift tax does not apply to tuition payments made to an educational organization (e.g., a college) on another's behalf. Nor does it apply to amounts paid on another's behalf for medical care.[16] In this regard, the law is realistic because it is unlikely that most donors would make such transfers when motivated solely by tax planning concerns. The payments, however, must be made directly to the provider (e.g., physician, hospital, or college). There is no requirement that the patient or student qualify as a relative or dependent of the person making the payment.

The Big Picture

EXAMPLE 10

Return to the facts of *The Big Picture* on p. 18-1. After Peter died, his widow, Martha, continued to live in the family home and refused to move in with either of her children (John or Helen). As Martha's health and mental condition deteriorated, her children did everything possible to keep the family housekeeper from quitting. In fact, Helen paid for the housekeeper's gallbladder operation, and John paid the college tuition of her oldest son.

Neither Helen nor John has made gifts to the housekeeper or her son that are subject to taxation. Gifts would have occurred, however, if Helen and John had reimbursed the housekeeper for the amounts involved, instead of paying the providers (i.e., physician, hospital, and college) directly.

Satisfying an obligation of support is not subject to the gift tax. Thus, no gift takes place when parents pay for their children's education, because one of the state-level obligations of parents is to educate their children. What constitutes an obligation of support is determined by applicable state law. In many states, for example, adult children may have an obligation of support with respect to providing for indigent parents, or a wealthy parent may have an obligation to support the law school tuition of a child. Similarly, payment of alimony or child support to an ex-spouse satisfies a legal obligation and does not constitute a gift to the recipient.

Lifetime versus Death Transfers

One must distinguish between lifetime *(inter vivos)* and deathtime (testamentary) transfers.

[15]§ 2501(a)(5).   [16]§ 2503(e).

EXAMPLE 11

Dudley buys a 12-month certificate of deposit (CD) from State Bank and lists ownership as follows: "Dudley, payable on proof of death to Faye." Nine months later, Dudley dies. When the CD matures, Faye collects the proceeds from State Bank. No gift takes place when Dudley invests in the CD; Faye has received a mere expectancy (i.e., to obtain ownership of the CD upon Dudley's death). At any time before his death, Dudley may withdraw the funds or delete Faye's name from the account, thereby cutting off her expectancy. Furthermore, no gift occurs upon Dudley's death; the CD passes to Faye as "payable on death."

A payable on death (POD) designation is a form of ownership frequently used in a family setting when investments are involved (e.g., stocks and bonds and savings accounts). The POD designation is simpler to use than a will or trust arrangement in the case of bank accounts and securities.

18-2b **Transfers Subject to the Gift Tax**

Property Settlements in Divorce

Transfers of property interests made under the terms of a written agreement between spouses in settlement of their marital or property rights are deemed to be for adequate consideration.[17] These transfers are exempt from the Federal gift tax if a final decree of divorce is obtained within the three-year period beginning on the date one year before the parties entered into the agreement. Likewise excluded are child support arrangements. Such an agreement need not be approved by the divorce decree.

The Big Picture

EXAMPLE 12

Return to the facts of *The Big Picture* on p. 18-1. Recall that John and Hannah's divorce became final in January. After extended but amicable negotiations, in September John and Hannah agreed on a property settlement. In return for the receipt of $200,000 and title to their home, Hannah released all of her marital rights. Shortly thereafter, John made the transfer. The property settlement resulted in no gift tax consequences to John.

Disclaimers

A **disclaimer** is a refusal by a person to accept property that is designated to pass to him or her. The effect of the disclaimer is to pass the property to someone else, for instance, under the terms of the will. Assume that Julio dies and passes an asset to Maria. Maria does not want the asset, so she disclaims it back to Julio's estate, and the will directs that the asset now passes to Eva. If the disclaimer is executed properly, Maria *has not* made a gift of her own to Eva, and no gift tax is due from Maria.

The Big Picture

EXAMPLE 13

Return to the facts of *The Big Picture* on p. 18-1. Recall that Martha died of a heart condition in July. Under her will, her estate passes in equal parts to her son and daughter or, if they disclaim, to their children. Helen disclaims her share of the inheritance, and the assets pass to her children.

Why might Helen disclaim her inheritance and have the property pass directly from Martha to the children? By doing so, an extra transfer tax may be avoided. If the disclaimer does not take place (i.e., Helen accepts the inheritance) and the property eventually passes to the children (either by gift or by death), the later transfer is subject to the application of either the gift tax or the estate tax.

The Federal gift tax can also be avoided in cases of a partial disclaimer of assets.

---

[17]§ 2516.

The Big Picture

EXAMPLE 14

Assume the same facts as in Example 13. John's share of his inheritance from Martha also includes the family hunting lodge. Except for the hunting lodge, John disclaims his share of the inheritance, and the remaining assets pass to his children.

To be effective, the disclaimer must be in writing and timely made. Generally, this means that a statement must be executed no later than nine months after the right to the property arose. Furthermore, the person making the disclaimer must not have accepted any benefits or interest in the property during the nine-month period.

Other Transfers Subject to Gift Tax

Other transfers that may carry gift tax consequences (e.g., the creation of joint ownership) are discussed and illustrated in connection with the Federal estate tax.

Income Tax Considerations

Generally, a donor incurs no Federal income tax consequences on making a gift.[18] A donee recognizes no income on the receipt of a gift.[19] A donee's income tax basis in the property received depends on a number of factors (e.g., donor's basis, fair market value of the asset on the transfer date).[20]

18-2c **Annual Gift Tax Exclusion**

In General

The first $15,000 of gifts made to any one person during any calendar year is excluded in determining the total amount of taxable gifts for the year.[21] The **annual exclusion** applies to all gifts of a *present interest* made during the calendar year, in the order in which they are made until the amount of the exclusion per donee is exhausted. For a gift in trust, each beneficiary of the trust is treated as a separate person for purposes of the exclusion.

EXAMPLE 15

Laura makes the following cash gifts: $8,000 to Rita and $18,000 to Maureen. Laura may claim an annual exclusion of $8,000 with respect to Rita and $15,000 with respect to Maureen.

A **future interest** is defined as an interest that will come into being (as to use, possession, or enjoyment) at some future date. Examples of future interests include rights such as remainder interests that are commonly encountered when property is transferred to a trust. A *present interest* is an unrestricted right to the immediate use, possession, or enjoyment of property or of the income.

EXAMPLE 16

By a lifetime gift, Ron transfers property to a trust with a life estate (with income payable annually) to June and remainder upon June's death to Albert. Ron has made two gifts when the trust was created: one to June of a life estate and one to Albert of a remainder interest. (The valuation of each of these gifts is discussed in text Section 19-1b.) The life estate is a present interest and qualifies for the annual exclusion. Albert's remainder is a future interest and does not qualify for the exclusion.

---

[18]For situations where recognition can occur, see text Section 19-3c.

[19]Both gifts and inheritances are excluded from the recipient's gross income under § 103.

[20]See text Section 19-2.

[21]§ 2503(b).

If a possibility exists that the income beneficiary may not receive the immediate enjoyment of the property, the transfer is of a future interest.

Assume the same facts as in Example 16, except that the income from the trust need not be payable annually to June. It may, at the trustee's discretion, be accumulated and added to the principal. Because June's right to receive the income from the trust is conditioned on the trustee's discretion, it is not a present interest. No annual exclusion is allowed.

The mere possibility of diversion is enough. It would not matter if the trustee never exercised the discretion to accumulate and did, in fact, distribute the trust income to June annually.

Contributions to Qualified Tuition Programs

For income tax purposes, § 529 plans possess attributes that reflect the best of all possible worlds. Although no up-front Federal income tax deduction is allowed,[22] income earned by the fund accumulates free of income tax and distributions are not taxed if they are used for educational purposes. A special provision allows a donor to enjoy a gift tax advantage by using five years of annual exclusions, but only once in a five-year period. Moreover, these college plans are not included in the gross estate of the transferor.[23]

Trevor and Audrey would like to start building a college education fund for their 10-year-old granddaughter Loni. Trevor contributes $150,000 to the designated carrier of their state's § 529 plan. By electing to split the gift and using five annual exclusions [2 (number of donors) × $15,000 (annual exclusion) × 5 years = $150,000], no taxable gift results. (The gift-splitting election is discussed in detail in text Section 18-2e.) Making the five-year election precludes Trevor and Audrey from using an annual exclusion on gifts to Loni for the next four years.

18-2d **Deductions**

In arriving at taxable gifts, a deduction is allowed for transfers to certain qualified charitable organizations. On transfers between spouses, a marital deduction may be available. Because both the charitable and marital deductions also apply in determining the Federal estate tax, these deductions are discussed later in the chapter.

18-2e **Computing the Federal Gift Tax**

The Unified Transfer Tax

The unified transfer tax rate is a flat 40 percent for most U.S. citizens and residents.[24]

The Election to Split Gifts by Married Persons

To understand the reason for the gift-splitting election of § 2513, consider the following situations.

---

[22]Depending on the taxpayer's home state, some (or all) of the deduction may be allowed for *state* income tax purposes.

[23]§ 529(c)(4).

[24]§ 2001(c)(2)(B). Cf. footnote 7.

Effect of Splitting Gifts

EXAMPLE 19

Kong and Margaret are husband and wife who reside in Michigan, a common law property state. Kong has been the only breadwinner in the family, and Margaret has no significant property of her own. Neither has made any prior taxable gifts. Kong makes a gift to Gita of $16,015,000. Presuming that the election to split gifts did not exist, Kong's gift tax is computed as follows.

Amount of gift	$16,015,000
Subtract: Annual exclusion	(15,000)
Taxable gift	$16,000,000
Taxable gift after exemption equivalent ($16,000,000 − $11,400,000)	$ 4,600,000
Gift tax due at 40% rate	$ 1,840,000

EXAMPLE 20

Assume the same facts as in Example 19, except that Kong and Margaret always have resided in California (a community property state). Even though Kong is the sole breadwinner, income from personal services generally is community property. Consequently, the gift to Gita probably involves community property. If this is the case, the gift tax is computed as follows.

	Kong	Margaret
Amount of gift	$8,007,500	$8,007,500
Subtract: Annual exclusion	(15,000)	(15,000)
Taxable gift	$7,992,500	$7,992,500
Taxable gift after exemption equivalent	$ –0–	$ –0–
Gift tax due	$ –0–	$ –0–

As the results of Examples 19 and 20 indicate, married donors residing in community property jurisdictions could possess a significant Federal gift tax advantage over those residing in common law states. To rectify this inequity, when a gift-splitting election is made, a gift made by a person to someone other than his or her spouse may be considered as having been made one-half by each spouse.[25]

Returning to Example 19, Kong and Margaret could treat the gift passing to Gita as being made one-half by each of them. They may do this even though all of the cash belonged to Kong. As a result, the parties are able to achieve the same tax consequence as in Example 20. There is no such thing as a "joint return" for Federal gift tax purposes, but the gift-splitting election achieves the same result; both spouses must file a gift tax return making the election and assigning the "two halves" of the gift separately.

To split gifts, the spouses must be legally married to each other at the time of the gift. A gift-splitting election means that all gifts made in that calendar year are split between them. In addition, both must be citizens or residents of the United States on the date of the gift.

18-2f Procedural Matters

The Federal Gift Tax Return

For transfers by gift, a Form 709 (U.S. Gift Tax Return) must be filed whenever the gifts for any one calendar year exceed the annual exclusion or involve a gift of a future

---

[25]§ 2513.

interest. The Form 709 also must be filed when the election to split gifts is made by the nonowner spouse (see Example 22). A Form 709 need not be filed, however, for transfers between spouses that are offset by the unlimited marital deduction, regardless of the amount of the transfer.[26]

When Must a Form 709 Be Filed?

This year, Larry makes five gifts, each in the amount of $15,000, to his five children. If the gifts do not involve future interests, a Form 709 need not be filed to report the transfers.

EXAMPLE 21

Esther makes a gift of $30,000 cash of her separate property to her daughter. To double the amount of the annual exclusion allowed, Jerry (Esther's husband) is willing to split the gift. To make the gift-splitting election, a Form 709 must be filed, even though no gift tax will be due as a result of the transfer.

EXAMPLE 22

Presuming that a gift tax return is due, it must be filed on or before the fifteenth day of April following the year of the gift.[27] As is the case with other Federal taxes, when the due date falls on Saturday, Sunday, or a legal holiday, the date for filing the return is the next business day. If sufficient reason is shown, the IRS is authorized to grant reasonable extensions of time for filing the return.[28]

Concept Summary 18.3

Federal Gift Tax Provisions

1. The Federal gift tax applies to all gratuitous transfers of property made by U.S. citizens or residents. In this regard, it does not matter where the property is located.

2. A gratuitous transfer is one not supported by full and adequate consideration. If the parties are acting in a business setting, such consideration usually exists. If, however, purported sales are between family members, a gift element may be suspected.

3. Property settlements can escape the gift tax if a divorce occurs within a prescribed period of time.

4. A disclaimer is a refusal by a person to accept property designated to pass to that person. The effect of a disclaimer is to pass the property to someone else. If certain conditions are satisfied, the issuance of a

disclaimer will not subject to the Federal gift tax the party making the disclaimer.

5. The donor is allowed an annual exclusion for a gift of a present interest to a donee.

6. The election to split a gift enables a married couple to be treated as two donors. The election doubles the annual exclusion and makes the nonowner spouse's exemption equivalent available to the owner spouse.

7. The Federal gift tax generally applies at a flat 40% rate on cumulative taxable gifts in excess of the exemption equivalent amount.

8. Taxable gifts are reported on Form 709. The return is due on April 15 following the year of the gift.

18-3 THE FEDERAL ESTATE TAX

The following discussion of the estate tax applies the formula that appeared earlier in the chapter in Concept Summary 18.2. The key components in the formula are the gross estate, the taxable estate, and the credits allowed against the tentative tax. This formula can be summarized as follows.

---

[26]§ 6019(a)(2).

[27]§ 6075(b)(1).

[28]§ 6081. Under § 6075(b)(2), an extension of time granted to a calendar year taxpayer for filing an income tax return automatically extends the due date of a gift tax return.

Gross estate − Deductions allowed = Taxable estate − Exemption equivalent × 40% tax rate − Tax credits* = Estate tax due

* Other than unified transfer tax credit

LO.6

Identify the components of the gross estate.

18-3a Gross Estate

Simply stated, the **gross estate** includes all property subject to the Federal estate tax. This includes the net assets owned and controlled by the decedent as of the date of death.

In contrast to the gross estate, one's **probate estate** is determined by state (rather than Federal) law. The probate estate consists of all of a decedent's property subject to disposition by the executor or administrator of the estate under the terms of the will. The administration is supervised by a local court (usually designated as a probate court). An executor is the decedent's personal representative appointed under the decedent's will. When a decedent dies without a will or fails to name an executor in the will (or that person refuses to serve), the local probate court appoints an administrator.

The probate estate frequently is smaller than the gross estate. It contains only property owned by the decedent at the time of death and passing to heirs under a will or under state law. Certain items like the proceeds of many life insurance policies and distributions from retirement plans become part of the gross estate but are not included in the probate estate.

All states provide for an order of distribution in the event someone dies *intestate* (i.e., without a will). After the surviving spouse, who receives some or all of the estate, the preference is usually in the following order: down to lineal descendants (e.g., children and grandchildren), up to lineal ascendants (e.g., parents and grandparents), and out to collateral relations (e.g., brothers, sisters, aunts, and uncles).

Property Owned by the Decedent

Property owned by the decedent at the time of death is included in the gross estate. The nature of the property or the use to which it was put during the decedent-owner's lifetime has no significance as far as the estate tax is concerned. Thus, personal effects (such as clothing), stocks, bonds, mutual funds, furniture, jewelry, bank accounts, and certificates of deposit are included in the deceased owner's gross estate. No distinction is made between tangible and intangible, depreciable and nondepreciable, or business and personal assets.

Property Owned at Death

EXAMPLE 23

Rani dies owning some City of Denver bonds. The fair market value of the bonds plus any interest accrued to the date of Rani's death is included in her gross estate. Although interest on municipal bonds usually is not taxable under the Federal income tax, it is property owned by Rani at the time of death and is subject to the estate tax. Any interest accrued after death is not part of the gross estate.

EXAMPLE 24

Sharon dies on April 7, when she owns stock in Robin Corporation and Wren Corporation. On March 2, both corporations authorized a cash dividend payable on May 4. Robin's dividend is payable to shareholders of record as of April 2. Wren's date of record is April 9. Sharon's gross estate includes the following: the stock in Robin, the stock in Wren, and the dividend on the Robin stock. It does not include the dividend on the Wren stock.

EXAMPLE 25

Ray dies holding some promissory notes issued to him by his son. In his will, Ray forgives these notes, relieving the son of the obligation to make any payments. The fair market value of these notes is included in Ray's gross estate.

> **The Big Picture**
>
> **EXAMPLE 26**
>
> Return to the facts of *The Big Picture* on p. 18-1. At the time of his death, John was the president of Hood Corporation. John's estate receives a distribution from Hood's qualified pension plan of $1,100,000 consisting of the following.
>
> | | |
> |---|---|
> | Hood's contributions | $450,000 |
> | John's after-tax contributions | 350,000 |
> | Income earned by the plan | 300,000 |
>
> John's estate also receives $150,000 from Hawk Insurance Company. The payment represents the maturity value of term life insurance from a group plan that Hood maintains for its employees. As to these amounts, John's gross estate includes $1,250,000 ($1,100,000 + $150,000). For income tax purposes, however, $750,000 ($450,000 + $300,000) is subject to tax and $500,000 ($350,000 + $150,000) is not.

In most cases, retirement plan benefits are subject to estate tax. Besides the conventional qualified pension and profit sharing plans involved in Example 26, retirement plans include those under § 401(k), § 403(b) for employees of tax-exempt organizations, § 457 for government employees, Keogh (H.R. 10) for self-employed persons, and IRAs—both traditional and Roth.

In addition to the items noted previously, the gross estate includes many other assets that can be of significant value. Examples include:

- Real estate holdings.
- Present value of future royalty rights (e.g., patents, copyrights, and mineral interests).
- Interests in a business (e.g., sole proprietorship and partnership).
- Collectibles (e.g., works of art and coin collections).
- Unmatured insurance policies on the lives of others.
- Present value of pending and potential lawsuits or past judgments rendered.
- Certain transfers that occur in the three years before death, or are made during lifetime but are effective only at death.[29]

Revocable Transfers

The gross estate includes the value of property interests transferred by the decedent (except to the extent that the transfer was made for full consideration) if the enjoyment of the property transferred was subject, at the date of the decedent's death, to any power of the decedent to *alter, amend, revoke, or terminate* the transfer. Transfers of this sort typically occur because the donor is not able or ready to part with the asset without qualifications (e.g., due to reservations about future events or about how the donee will use the transferred asset).

Joint Interests

Recall that joint tenancies and tenancies by the entirety are characterized by the right of survivorship. Thus, upon the death of a joint tenant, title to the property passes to the surviving tenant. None of the property is included in the *probate* estate of the deceased tenant. In the case of tenancies in common and community property, death does not defeat the decedent's ownership interest; thus, the deceased owner's interest is part of the probate estate.

The Federal *estate tax treatment* of tenancies in common or of community property follows the logical approach of taxing only the portion of the property included in the deceased owner's probate estate.

---

[29]§§ 2035–2037, 2041.

EXAMPLE 27

Homer, Wilma, and Thelma acquire a tract of land, ownership listed as tenants in common, each party furnishing $200,000 of the $600,000 purchase price. When the property is worth $900,000, Homer dies. If Homer's undivided interest in the property is 33⅓%, the gross estate *and* probate estate each include $300,000. This one-third interest is also the same amount that passes to Homer's heirs.

Unless the parties have provided otherwise, each tenant is deemed to own an interest equal to the portion of the original consideration he or she furnished. The parties in Example 27 could have provided that Homer would receive an undivided half interest in the property although he contributed only one-third of the purchase price. In that case, Wilma and Thelma have made a gift to Homer when the tenancy was created, and Homer's gross estate and probate estate each include $450,000.

For certain joint tenancies, the tax consequences are different. All of the property is included in the deceased co-owner's gross estate unless it can be proved that the surviving co-owners contributed to the cost of the property.[30] If a contribution can be shown, the amount to be *excluded* is calculated by the following formula.

$$\frac{\text{Surviving co-owner's initial contribution}}{\text{Total initial cost of the property}} \quad \times \quad \text{Fair market value of the property at death}$$

In computing a survivor's contribution, any funds received as a gift *from the deceased co-owner* and applied to the cost of the property are counted as zero. However, recognized income or gain from gift assets are attributed to the survivor.

EXAMPLE 28

Keith and Steve (father and son) acquire a tract of land, ownership listed as joint tenancy with right of survivorship. Keith furnished $400,000 and Steve $200,000 of the $600,000 purchase price. Of the $200,000 provided by Steve, $100,000 had previously been received as a gift from Keith. When the property is worth $900,000, Keith dies. Because only $100,000 of Steve's contribution can be counted (the other $100,000 was received as a gift from Keith), Steve has furnished only one-sixth ($100,000/$600,000) of the cost. Thus, Keith's gross estate must include five-sixths of $900,000, or $750,000.

This result presumes that Steve can prove that he did in fact make the $100,000 contribution. In the absence of such proof, the full value of the property is included in Keith's gross estate. Keith's death makes Steve the immediate owner of the property by virtue of the right of survivorship. None of the property is part of Keith's probate estate.

If the co-owners receive the property as a gift or bequest *from another*, each owner is deemed to have contributed to the cost (or value on date of death) of his or her own interest.

The Big Picture

EXAMPLE 29

Return to the facts of *The Big Picture* on p. 18-1. During his lifetime, Peter Hood purchased timberland listing title as follows: "John and Helen Hood as equal tenants in common." John's basis in the property is one-half of Peter's cost. Upon John's death, one-half of the value of the timberland is included in his gross estate.

The Big Picture

EXAMPLE 30

Return to the facts of *The Big Picture* on p. 18-1. In her will, Martha leaves the Hood family residence to her children (John and Helen) as joint tenants with right of survivorship. John's income tax basis in the residence is one-half of the value on Martha's death. On John's later death, one-half of the value at that time will be included in his gross estate. Under the right of survivorship, outright ownership of the residence goes to Helen and none of the property passes to John's heirs.

---

[30]§ 2040(a).

To simplify the joint ownership rules for *married persons*, § 2040(b) provides for an automatic inclusion rule upon the death of the first joint-owner spouse to die. Regardless of the amount contributed by each spouse, one-half of the value of the property is included in the gross estate of the spouse who dies first. The special rule eliminates the need to trace the source of contributions and recognizes that any inclusion in the gross estate is neutralized by the marital deduction.

The Big Picture

EXAMPLE 31

Return to the facts of *The Big Picture* on p. 18-1. Recall that after his divorce from Hannah, John married Ashley. Because Hannah kept John's prior home as part of the property settlement (see Example 12), he purchased a new residence. He listed title to the property as "John and Ashley Hood, tenancy by the entirety with right of survivorship." Upon John's death, only one-half of the value of the property is included in his gross estate.

If Ashley had died first, one-half of the value of the residence would have been included in her gross estate, even though she made no contribution to its cost.

Whether a *gift* results when property is transferred into some form of joint ownership depends on the consideration furnished by each of the contributing parties for the ownership interest acquired.

Joint Ownership and the Gift Tax

EXAMPLE 32

Brenda and Sarah purchase real estate as tenants in common. Of the $800,000 purchase price, Brenda furnishes $600,000, and Sarah furnishes $200,000. If each is an equal owner in the property, Brenda has made a gift to Sarah of $200,000.

EXAMPLE 33

Martha purchases real estate for $900,000, the title to the property being listed as follows: "Martha, Sylvia, and Dan as joint tenants with the right of survivorship." If under state law the mother (Martha), the daughter (Sylvia), and the son (Dan) are deemed to be equal owners in the property, Martha is treated as having made gifts of $300,000 to Sylvia and $300,000 to Dan.

Several important exceptions exist to the general rule that gift treatment is triggered by the creation of a joint ownership with disproportionate interests resulting from unequal consideration. First, if the transfer involves a joint bank account, there is no gift at the time of the contribution. If a gift occurs, it is when the noncontributing party withdraws the funds provided by the other joint tenant. Second, the same rule applies to the purchase of U.S. savings bonds.[31] Again, any gift tax consequences are postponed until the noncontributing party appropriates some or all of the proceeds for his or her individual use.

When a Gift Occurs

EXAMPLE 34

Cynthia deposits $400,000 in a bank account under the names of Cynthia and Carla as joint tenants. Both Cynthia and Carla have the right to withdraw funds from the account without the other's consent. Cynthia has not made a gift to Carla when the account is established.

EXAMPLE 35

Assume the same facts as in Example 34. At some later date, Carla withdraws $100,000 from the account for her own use. At this point, Cynthia has made a gift to Carla of $100,000.

---

[31]Reg. § 25.2511–1(h)(4).

When a Gift Occurs

EXAMPLE 36

Wesley purchases a U.S. savings bond that he registers in the names of Wesley and Harriet. After Wesley dies, Harriet redeems the bond. No gift takes place when Wesley buys the bond. However, the fair market value of the bond is included in Wesley's gross estate.

Life Insurance

The gross estate includes life insurance on the decedent's life if:

- The policy's proceeds are receivable by the estate,
- The proceeds are receivable by another for the benefit of the estate, or
- The decedent possessed any of the incidents of ownership in the policy.

Life insurance on the life of another owned by a decedent at the time of death is included in the gross estate as an asset owned by the decedent. The amount includible is the replacement value of the policy.[32] Under these circumstances, inclusion of the face amount of the policy is inappropriate, as the policy has not yet matured.

EXAMPLE 37

At the time of his death, Luigi owned a life insurance policy on the life of Benito, face amount of $500,000 and replacement value of $50,000, with Sofia as the designated beneficiary. Because the policy has not matured at Luigi's death, only $50,000 (the policy's replacement value) is included in Luigi's gross estate.

Life insurance includes whole life policies, term insurance, group life insurance, and travel and accident insurance.[33]

Proceeds of insurance on the life of the decedent not receivable by or for the benefit of the estate are includible if the decedent at death possessed any of the incidents of ownership in the policy. In this connection, the term *incidents of ownership* means not only the ownership of the policy but also the right of the insured or his or her estate to the economic benefits of the policy. Thus, it includes the power to change beneficiaries, pledge the policy for a loan, or surrender or cancel the policy.[34]

EXAMPLE 38

At the time of death, Broderick was the insured under a policy (face amount of $1 million) owned by Gregory with Demi as the designated beneficiary. Broderick took out the policy five years ago and immediately transferred it as a gift to Gregory. Under the assignment, Broderick transferred all rights in the policy except the right to change beneficiaries.

Broderick died without having exercised this right, and the policy proceeds are paid to Demi. Broderick's retention of an incident of ownership in the policy (i.e., the right to change beneficiaries) causes $1 million to be included in his gross estate, even though he never exercised the right.

Merely purchasing a life insurance contract with someone else designated as the beneficiary does not constitute a *gift*. As long as the purchaser still owns the policy, nothing yet has passed to the beneficiary, and the beneficiary can be changed. Even on the death of the insured-owner, no gift takes place. The proceeds paid to the beneficiary constitute a testamentary and not a lifetime transfer. But consider the following possibility.

---

[32]Reg. § 20.2031–8(a)(1).

[33]Reg. § 20.2042–1(a)(1). As to travel and accident insurance, see *Comm. v. Estate of Noel*, 65–1 USTC ¶12,311, 15 AFTR 2d 1397, 85 S.Ct. 1238 (USSC, 1965). As to employer-sponsored group term life insurance, see Example 26.

[34]Reg. § 20.2042–1(c)(2).

Kurt purchases an insurance policy on his own life that he transfers to Olga. Kurt retains no interest in the policy (such as the power to change beneficiaries). In these circumstances, Kurt has made a gift to Olga. Furthermore, if Kurt continues to pay the premiums on the transferred policy, each payment constitutes a separate gift.

Under certain conditions, the death of the insured may constitute a gift to the beneficiary of part or all of the proceeds. This occurs when the owner of the policy is not the insured.

Randolph owns an insurance policy on the life of Frank, with Tracy as the designated beneficiary. Up until the time of Frank's death, Randolph retained the right to change the beneficiary of the policy. The proceeds paid to Tracy by the insurance company by reason of Frank's death constitute a gift from Randolph to Tracy.[35]

Concept Summary 18.4

Federal Estate Tax Provisions—Gross Estate

1. The starting point for applying the Federal estate tax is to determine which assets are subject to tax. Such assets comprise a decedent's gross estate.

2. The gross estate includes all assets owned by the decedent, regardless of where they are located.

3. Upon the death of a joint tenant, the full value of the property is included in the gross estate unless the survivor(s) made a contribution toward the cost of the property. Spouses employ a special rule that calls for automatic inclusion of half of the value of the property in the gross estate of the first tenant to die.

4. The creation of joint ownership is subject to the gift tax when a tenant receives a lesser interest in the property than is warranted by the consideration furnished.

5. If the decedent is the insured, life insurance proceeds are included in the gross estate if either of two conditions is satisfied. First, the proceeds are paid to the estate or for the benefit of the estate. Second, the decedent possessed incidents of ownership (e.g., the right to change beneficiaries) over the policy.

18-3b Taxable Estate

LO.7
Describe the components of the taxable estate.

After the gross estate has been determined, the next step is to compute the taxable estate. The **taxable estate** is the gross estate minus a number of important deductions.

Expenses, Indebtedness, and Taxes

A deduction is allowed for funeral expenses; expenses incurred in administering property; claims against the estate; and unpaid mortgages and other charges against property, whose value is included in the gross estate (without reduction for the mortgage or other indebtedness).

Expenses incurred in administering community property are deductible only in proportion to the deceased spouse's interest in the community.[36] Administration expenses include commissions of the executor or administrator, attorney's fees of the estate, accountant's fees, court costs, and certain selling expenses for disposition of estate property.

---

[35]*Goodman v. Comm.*, 46–1 USTC ¶10,275, 34 AFTR 1534, 156 F.2d 218 (CA–2, 1946).

[36]*U.S. v. Stapf*, 63–2 USTC ¶12,192, 12 AFTR 2d 6326, 84 S.Ct. 248 (USSC, 1963).

Claims against the estate include property taxes accrued before the decedent's death, unpaid income taxes on income received by the decedent before he or she died, and unpaid gift taxes on gifts made by the decedent before death.

The decedent's unpaid pledge or subscription in favor of a public, charitable, religious, or educational organization is deductible to the extent that it would have constituted an allowable deduction had it been a bequest.[37]

Deductible funeral expenses include the cost of interment or inurnment, the burial plot or vault, a gravestone, perpetual care of the grave site, and the transportation expense of the person bringing the body to the place of burial. No deduction is allowed for cemetery lots the decedent acquired before death, but the lots are not included in the decedent's gross estate as an asset of the decedent.

Losses

An estate tax deduction is allowed for losses from a casualty or theft incurred during the period when the estate is being settled. As is true with casualty or theft losses for income tax purposes, any anticipated insurance recovery must be taken into account in arriving at the amount of the deductible loss. Unlike the income tax, however, the deduction is not limited by a floor ($100) or a percentage amount (the excess of 10 percent of adjusted gross income).

As is true of certain administration expenses, a casualty or theft loss of estate property can be claimed as an income tax deduction on the fiduciary return of the estate (Form 1041; see text Sections 20-3c and 20-3d). But a double deduction prohibition applies, and claiming the income tax deduction requires a waiver of the estate tax deduction.[38]

Transfers to Charity

A transfer tax deduction is allowed for the value of property in the decedent's gross estate that is transferred by the decedent through testamentary disposition to (or for the use of) any of the following.

- Federal, state, and local governments and agencies.
- Any corporation or association organized and operated exclusively for religious, charitable, scientific, literary, or educational purposes.
- Various veterans' organizations.

The organizations just described are identical to those that qualify for the Federal gift tax deduction. With the following exceptions, they are also the same organizations that qualify a donor for an income tax deduction.[39]

- Certain nonprofit cemetery associations qualify for income tax but not estate and gift tax purposes.
- Non-U.S. charities may qualify under the estate and gift tax but not under the income tax.

No deduction is allowed unless the charitable bequest is specified by a provision in the decedent's will or the transfer was made before death and the property is subsequently included in the gross estate. Generally, a deduction does not materialize when an individual dies intestate (without a will).

The amount of the bequest to charity must be mandatory and cannot be left to someone else's discretion. It is, however, permissible to allow another person—such as the executor of the estate—to choose which charity will receive the specified donation.

---

[37]§ 2053(c)(1)(A) and Reg. § 20.2053–5.
[38]§§ 642(g), 2054.
[39]§§ 170, 2055, 2522.

The Big Picture

EXAMPLE 41

Return to the facts of *The Big Picture* on p. 18-1. After John's accident, he was in the intensive care unit at a local hospital. Although physically incapacitated, he was mentally alert. In early December, he reviewed his financial affairs with his attorney and CPA and executed a new will. His prior will, drawn up several years ago, contained a bequest to the Hood Scholarship Foundation (HSF), an organization created by Peter (John's father) to provide financial assistance to community college students. HSF's qualified status never had been evaluated by the IRS, so the attorney agreed to apply for a determination letter.

John's new will kept the bequest, but only if the IRS approved HSF's qualified status. John's CPA arranged to have all of John's medical expenses (e.g., hospital and physicians) paid as incurred. He also advised John to make a substantial payment on his property taxes and state income taxes.

Marital Deduction

The marital deduction allows spouses to arrange their financial affairs without Federal gift or estate tax consequences. Assets can pass between them without any immediate gift or estate tax liability, with a deduction allowed to offset an otherwise taxable gift or estate amount. Used well, the marital deduction can be seen as a means by which to reduce the present value of the couple's transfer tax liability: the gift or bequest places the asset into the hands of (perhaps) a younger or healthier spouse, such that the Federal transfer tax on the asset is deferred until a later date.

The marital deduction is available to same-sex married couples. Registered domestic partnerships, civil unions, and similar formal relationships *are not* marriages, so no marital deduction can be claimed.

Passing Requirement The marital deduction is allowed only for property that is included in the deceased spouse's gross estate *and* that passes or has passed to the surviving spouse.[40]

The Big Picture

EXAMPLE 42

Return to the facts of *The Big Picture* on p. 18-1 and Example 41. In reviewing John's prior will, the parties discovered that one of the main beneficiaries was Hannah, John's first wife. The new will substituted Ashley (John's present wife) for Hannah, thereby preserving the marital deduction.

Property that *passes* from the decedent to the surviving spouse includes any interest received as (1) the decedent's heir or donee, (2) the decedent's surviving tenant by the entirety or joint tenant, or (3) the beneficiary of insurance on the life of the decedent.

EXAMPLE 43

At the time of his death in the current year, Tao owned an insurance policy on his own life (face amount of $500,000) with Ella (his wife) as the designated beneficiary. Tao and Ella also owned real estate (worth $600,000) as tenants by the entirety (Tao had furnished all of the purchase price). As to these transfers, $800,000 ($500,000 + $300,000) is included in Tao's gross estate, and this amount represents the property that passes to Ella for purposes of the marital deduction, under the terms of the insurance contract and the state law survivorship feature.

---

[40]§§ 2056, 2523.

Disclaimers can affect the amount passing to the surviving spouse. If, for example, the surviving spouse receives the remainder of the estate after all other obligations have been met, a disclaimer by another heir increases the amount passing to the surviving spouse. This, in turn, increases the amount of the marital deduction allowed.

When a property interest passing to the surviving spouse is subject to a mortgage or other debt, only the net value of the interest after reduction by the amount of the debt qualifies for the marital deduction.

EXAMPLE 44

In his will, Jacob leaves real estate (fair market value of $500,000) to Rachel, his wife. If the real estate is subject to a mortgage of $100,000 (upon which Jacob was personally liable), the marital deduction is limited to $400,000 ($500,000 − $100,000). The $100,000 mortgage is deductible as an obligation of the decedent (Jacob).

Terminable Interest Limitation Certain interests in property passing from the deceased spouse to the surviving spouse are referred to as **terminable interests**. Such an interest will terminate or fail after the passage of time, upon the happening of some contingency, or upon the failure of some event to occur. Examples are life estates, annuities, receivables for terms of years, and patents. A terminable interest does not qualify for the marital deduction.[41]

The marital deduction should not be available in situations where the surviving spouse can enjoy the property and still pass it to another with zero Federal estate tax consequences. The marital deduction merely postpones the transfer tax upon the death of the first spouse, and it operates to shift any such tax to the surviving spouse.

EXAMPLE 45

Olivia's gross estate includes an installment note receivable with payments scheduled to occur for 5 more years, as of the date of her death. Under Olivia's will, the note passes to her husband Josh, whose life expectancy is 17 years. The note is a terminable interest, and no marital deduction is allowed in computing Olivia's taxable estate. Because no asset will be placed in Josh's gross estate as to the note, the marital deduction for Olivia's estate is disallowed.

Consistent with the objective of the terminable interest rule, the marital deduction is allowed for transfers of **qualified terminable interest property (QTIP)**. This is defined as property that passes from one spouse to another by gift or at death and for which the transferee-spouse has a qualifying income interest for life.

- The person is entitled for life to all of the income from the property (or a specific portion of it), payable at annual or more frequent intervals.
- No person has a power to appoint any part of the property to any person other than the surviving spouse during his or her life.[42]

If these conditions are met, an election can be made to claim a marital deduction as to the QTIP. The election is irrevocable.

If the election is made, a transfer tax is imposed on the QTIP when the surviving spouse disposes of it by gift or upon death. If the later transfer occurs during the surviving spouse's life, the gift tax applies, measured by the fair market value of the property as of that time.[43] If no lifetime disposition takes place, the fair market value of the property on the date of death (or alternate valuation date) is included in the gross estate of the second spouse to die.[44]

In this manner, the QTIP election "plays fair" with the transferred income interest: a marital deduction is claimed on the first death, and the asset is included in the gross estate of the second death.

---

[41]§§ 2056(b)(1) and 2523(b)(1).

[42]§§ 2523(f) and 2056(b)(7).

[43]§ 2519.

[44]§ 2044.

Clyde dies and provides in his will that certain assets (fair market value of $2.1 million) are to be transferred to a trust under which Lily (Clyde's wife) receives the income of the trust for her life, with the remainder passing to their children upon Lily's death. Presuming that all of the preceding requirements are satisfied and Clyde's executor so elects, his estate receives a marital deduction of $2.1 million.

Lily dies when the trust assets are worth $6.4 million. This amount is included in her gross estate.

Because the estate tax is imposed on assets not physically included in the probate estate when a QTIP election is used, the liability for any Federal transfer tax on those assets is shifted to the heirs. The amount to be shifted is determined by comparing the estate tax liability both with and without the inclusion of the QTIP. This right of recovery can be canceled by a provision in the deceased spouse's will.[45]

Citizenship and Residency of Spouses Property passing to a surviving spouse who is not a U.S. citizen is not eligible for the estate tax marital deduction.[46] Similarly, no gift tax marital deduction is allowed where the spouse is not a U.S. citizen.[47] However, the annual exclusion for these gift transfers is $155,000 for 2019.[48]

State Taxes at Death

About a dozen states, and a number of cities, counties, and similar jurisdictions, levy taxes when property passes to another party because of the death of a decedent. These taxes can be assessed at marginal rates of almost 20 percent, and the applicable exemption amounts typically are less than that for the Federal estate tax. A deduction is allowed against the taxable estate for estate and inheritance taxes paid to such jurisdictions.[49]

The deduction for taxes paid to a state at death mitigates the effect of subjecting property to multiple taxes payable because of a death.

18-3c **Estate Tax Credits**

Several other credits are allowed in computing the Federal estate tax liability.

LO.8

Calculate the Federal estate tax liability.

Credit for Tax on Prior Transfers

Suppose that Nancy owns some property that she passes at death to Lisa. Shortly thereafter, Lisa dies and passes the property to Rita. Assuming that both estates are subject to the Federal estate tax, the successive deaths result in an expensive and undesirable double taxation of the same asset.

To mitigate the multiple taxation that might result from successive unanticipated deaths, a credit is allowed for Federal estate tax paid on prior, overlapping transfers.[50] Here, Lisa's estate may be able to claim as a credit some of the taxes paid by Nancy's estate.

The credit is limited to the lesser of the following amounts.

1. The amount of the Federal estate tax attributable to the transferred property in the transferor's estate.
2. The amount of the Federal estate tax attributable to the transferred property in the decedent's estate.

The credit is allowed when the property is subjected to Federal estate taxation "too soon" after it was taxed at the first death. Exhibit 18.2 shows the relationship between the credit allowed and the time interval between the two deaths.

---

[45]§ 2207A(a).
[46]§ 2056(d)(1).
[47]§ 2523(i)(2).

[48]§ 2523(i).
[49]§ 2058.
[50]§ 2013.

EXHIBIT 18.2	Credit for Tax on Prior Transfers	
Interval between Deaths		**Credit Allowed**
Within 2 years		100%
Within 3 to 4 years		80%
Within 5 to 6 years		60%
Within 7 to 8 years		40%
Within 9 to 10 years		20%

Time Interval between Successive Deaths

Under Nancy's will, Lisa inherits property. One year later, Lisa dies. Assume that the estate tax attributable to the inclusion of the property in Nancy's gross estate was $160,000 and that the estate tax attributable to the inclusion of the property in Lisa's gross estate is $120,000. Under these circumstances, Lisa's estate claims a credit against the estate tax of $120,000 (refer to limitation 2).

EXAMPLE 48

Assume the same facts as in Example 47, except that Lisa dies three years after Nancy. The credit now is 80% of $120,000, or $96,000 (see Exhibit 18.2).

Credit for Foreign Taxes Paid at Death

A credit is allowed against the estate tax for any estate, inheritance, legacy, or succession tax actually paid to another country.[51] The credit is allowed for taxes paid not only to countries in the international sense but also to possessions or political subdivisions of foreign countries, and to U.S. possessions (e.g., Puerto Rico and Guam).

The credit is allowed for taxes paid on account of a death with respect to:

- Property situated in the country to which the tax is paid,
- Property included in the decedent's gross estate, and
- The decedent's taxable estate.

The credit is limited to the lesser of the following amounts.

- The amount of the foreign tax paid at death, attributable to the property situated in the country imposing the tax and included in the decedent's gross estate for Federal estate tax purposes.
- The amount of the Federal estate tax attributable to particular property situated in the other country, subject to estate or inheritance tax in that country, and included in the decedent's gross estate for Federal estate tax purposes.

Similar credits are allowable under estate/gift tax treaties with a number of countries. If a credit is allowed under either the provisions of the Code or the provisions of a treaty, the credit that is most beneficial to the estate should be claimed.[52]

---

[51]§ 2014.

[52]Reg. § 20.2014–4 illustrates the selection process when both the § 2014 credit and an estate tax treaty are involved.

18-3d Procedural Matters

A Federal estate tax return, if required, is due nine months after the date of the decedent's death.[53] The time limit applies to all estates regardless of the nationality or residence of the decedent. Not infrequently, an executor will request and obtain from the IRS an extension of time for filing Form 706 (estate tax return).[54] Also available is an *automatic* six-month extension of time to file the estate tax return.

Concept Summary 18.5

Federal Estate Tax Provisions—Taxable Estate and Procedural Matters

1. In computing the taxable estate, certain deductions are allowed.

2. Deductions are permitted for various administration expenses (e.g., executor's commissions), professional fees (appraisal, accounting, and legal), debts of the decedent, certain unpaid taxes, and funeral expenses.

3. Casualty and theft losses occurring during the settlement of the estate and not compensated for by insurance can be deducted.

4. Charitable transfers are deductible if the designated organization holds qualified status with the IRS at the time of death.

5. Transfers to a surviving spouse yield a marital deduction if they do not violate the terminable interest rule. The terminable interest rule can be avoided by the use of a general power of appointment or by making a QTIP election.

6. A deduction is allowed for certain state and local taxes paid on account of a death.

7. If required, a Federal estate tax return (Form 706) must be filed within nine months of the date of the decedent's death. An extension for filing beyond this date is available.

18-4 THE GENERATION-SKIPPING TRANSFER TAX

LO.9

Review and demonstrate the role of the generation-skipping transfer tax.

As a penalty to discourage families from deferring Federal gift and estate taxes by transferring assets to very young beneficiaries, the tax law imposes an additional generation-skipping transfer tax (GSTT). The tax is added to any gift or estate tax that may be due. The GSTT attempts to collect a Federal transfer tax from a family at least once *every other* generation, by blood or marriage.

18-4a Inter-Generational Transfers

Previously, by structuring the transaction carefully, it was possible to bypass a generation or more of Federal gift and estate taxes.

---

[53]§ 6075(a).   [54]§ 6081.

Types of Generation-Skipping Transfers

EXAMPLE 49

Under his will, Edward creates a trust, life estate to Stephen (Edward's son) and remainder to Ava (Edward's granddaughter) upon Stephen's death. Edward is subject to the Federal estate tax, but no tax results upon Stephen's death. The result is that the property in trust skips a generation of transfer taxes.

EXAMPLE 50

Amy gives assets to Eric (her grandson). The gift would circumvent any transfer taxes that would have resulted had the assets been channeled through Eric's parents.

18-4b The Tax on Generation-Skipping Transfers

The GSTT is designed to preclude the avoidance of either the estate tax or the gift tax by making transfers that bypass the next lower generation. In the typical family setting, this involves transfers from grandparents to grandchildren.

The GSTT is triggered by any of these three events: a taxable *termination* occurs, a taxable *distribution* takes place, or a *direct skip* is made.[55] Example 49 illustrates a termination event. Upon Stephen's death, the fair market value of the trust property that passes to Ava is subject to the GSTT (imposed on the trust). The GSTT will have the effect of reducing the amount Ava receives from the trust.

Example 50 illustrates a lifetime version of the direct skip event.[56] In this situation, the GSTT is imposed upon Amy when the gift is made to Eric, because the gift skips over the generation of Eric's parents.

The GSTT rate is the highest rate under the gift and estate tax schedules (i.e., 40 percent). The GSTT base is reduced by the same exemption equivalent amount that is available against the Federal estate and gift tax (see Exhibit 18.1).[57] For a donor who is married, the election to split the gift (under § 2513) can double the amount of the exemption.[58]

The tax base also is reduced by the annual gift tax exclusion and the charitable and marital deductions. The GSTT does not apply to gifts made for political, medical, and educational purposes, if the corresponding gift tax exemption applies. A credit is allowed for certain state-level GST taxes paid.

Generations are assigned by birth or marriage. For other parties, a generation is 25 years long. The GSTT computation is made on a schedule that is part of Form 706 or 709 (i.e., the gift or estate tax return to which it relates).

EXAMPLE 51

Mother Anna (age 60) and son Barry (age 40) are in two successive GSTT generations. Father Carl (age 60) and daughter Denny (age 15) are in two successive generations.

Spouses E'Toin (age 60) and Fantasia (age 58) are in the same generation. Spouses Gerardo (age 60) and Hermosa (age 20) are in the same generation.

Unrelated individuals Ishu (age 60) and Jiva (age 50) are in the same generation. Unrelated individuals Kong (age 60) and Lian (age 12) are two generations apart.

18-5 TAX PLANNING

Tax planning techniques for the Federal gift, estate, and generation-skipping transfer taxes are discussed in Chapter 19 in connection with family tax planning matters.

---

[55]§ 2611.

[56]§ 2612(c)(1).

[57]§ 2631(c).

[58]§ 2652(a)(2).

REFOCUS ON THE BIG PICTURE

AN EVENTFUL AND FINAL YEAR

By making use of § 2516, John was able to carry out a property settlement with Hannah without incurring any gift tax consequences (see Example 12). Both Helen and John acted wisely when they chose to disclaim most of their inheritance from their mother. By making the disclaimers, they were able to pass the property to their children without a transfer tax being imposed (see Examples 13 and 14).

John's retirement plan benefits and any proceeds paid under his life insurance policy are included in his gross estate (see Example 26).

John's pre-death planning was highly advantageous in several respects.

- By drawing up a new will, the charitable and marital deductions were retained (see Examples 41 and 42).

- By prepaying state and local property and income taxes and staying current on medical expenses, John improved his Federal income tax position (see Example 41). He also avoided any estate taxes on the amounts used to pay these expenses.

WILL SANDERS/STONE/GETTY IMAGES

Key Terms

Alternate valuation date, 18-5	Future interest, 18-10	Taxable estate, 18-19
Annual exclusion, 18-10	Gross estate, 18-14	Taxable gift, 18-3
Bypass amount, 18-5	Joint tenants, 18-6	Tenants by the entirety, 18-6
Community property, 18-6	Marital deduction, 18-21	Tenants in common, 18-6
Disclaimer, 18-9	Probate estate, 18-14	Terminable interests, 18-22
Exclusion amount, 18-5	Qualified terminable interest property (QTIP), 18-22	Unified transfer tax, 18-2
Exemption equivalent, 18-5		Unified transfer tax credit, 18-4

Discussion Questions

1. **LO.1** How does the Federal unified transfer tax differ from an income tax?

2. **LO.1** Kim, a wealthy Korean national, is advised by his physicians to have an operation performed at the Mayo Clinic. Kim is hesitant to come to the United States because of the possible tax consequences. If the procedure is not successful, Kim does not want his wealth to be subject to the Federal estate tax. Are Kim's concerns justified? Explain.

   Critical Thinking

3. **LO.1** Felipe will incur a $1 million Federal transfer tax when he passes a plot of land to Barbara, an unrelated friend. Felipe's after-tax rate of return on his real estate investments is 3%. Compute the present value of the transfer tax if:

   a. Felipe transfers the land to Barbara as a lifetime taxable gift today.

   b. Felipe transfers the land to Barbara through his will after his death 20 years from now, as a gross estate asset.

Communications   4. **LO.1, 2, 3, 4** In no more than three PowerPoint slides, indicate how the time value of money affects the application of the Federal unified transfer taxes. Prepare your slides for a 45-minute presentation at your school's homecoming seminar, primarily attended by wealthy alumni.

Critical Thinking   5. **LO.2, 4, 5** Regarding the formula for the Federal gift tax (see Concept Summary 18.1 in the text), comment on the following observations.

    a.   The annual exclusion is adjusted each year for inflation.

    b.   The charitable and marital deductions play an important role.

    c.   Some gratuitous transfers might not be subject to the gift tax.

6. **LO.3** Regarding the formula for the Federal estate tax (see Concept Summary 18.2 in the text), comment on the following.

    a.   The gross estate includes only property interests owned by the decedent at the time of death.

    b.   The gross estate is not the same as the probate estate.

    c.   Taxable estate × Applicable unified transfer tax rate = Estate tax due.

7. **LO.3** As to the alternate valuation date for asset transfers at death, comment on the following.

    a.   The justification for the election.

    b.   The main heir prefers the date of death value.

    c.   An estate asset is sold seven months after the decedent's death.

    d.   Effect of the election on income tax basis.

Critical Thinking   8. **LO.4, 6** At a local bank, Jack purchases for $100,000 a five-year CD listing title as follows: "Meredith, payable on death to Briana." Four years later, Meredith dies. Briana, Meredith's daughter, then redeems the CD when it matures. Discuss the transfer tax consequences if Meredith is:

    a.   Jack's wife.

    b.   Jack's ex-wife.

    c.   Jack's girlfriend.

Critical Thinking   9. **LO.4** Derek dies intestate (i.e., without a will) and is survived by a daughter, Ruth, and a grandson, Ted (Ruth's son). Derek's assets include a large portfolio of stocks and bonds and a beach house. Ruth has considerable wealth of her own; Ted just finished college and is unemployed. Under applicable state law, children have first priority as to bequests, and then grandchildren.

    a.   To minimize future transfer taxes, what action might Ruth take? *Hint:* Use the term *disclaimer* in your answer, and consider the time value of money in your analysis.

    b.   What if Ruth wants only the beach house?

10. **LO.4** Qualified tuition programs under § 529 enjoy significant tax advantages. Describe these advantages with regard to the Federal:

    a.   Income tax.

    b.   Gift tax.

    c.   Estate tax.

11. **LO.5** Regarding the gift-splitting election, comment on the following.

    a.   What it is designed to accomplish.

    b.   How the election is made.

12. **LO.5** In connection with the filing of a Federal gift tax return, comment on the following.
    a. No Federal gift tax is due.
    b. The gift is between spouses.
    c. The donor obtained from the IRS an extension of time for filing his or her Federal income tax return.

13. **LO.4** In each of the following independent situations, indicate whether the transfer is subject to the Federal gift tax.
    a. Asa contributes to his mayor's reelection campaign fund. The mayor has promised to try to get some of Asa's property rezoned from residential to commercial use.
    b. Mary Ann inherits her father's collection of guns and mounted animals. Five months later, she disclaims any interest in the mounted animals.
    c. Same as part (b). Ten months later, Mary Ann disclaims any interest in the guns.
    d. Haydon pays an orthodontist for the dental work performed on Michele, his cousin.
    e. Florence purchases a U.S. savings bond listing herself and Taylor (her daughter) as joint owners.
    f. Same as part (e). One year later, Taylor predeceases Florence.
    g. Same as part (e). One year later, Florence predeceases Taylor.

14. **LO.6** At the time of Emile's death, he was a joint tenant with Colette in a parcel of real estate. With regard to the inclusion of the realty in Emile's gross estate, comment on the following independent assumptions.
    a. Emile and Colette received the property as a gift from Douglas.
    b. Colette provided the entire purchase price of the property.
    c. Colette's contribution was received as a gift from Emile.
    d. Emile's contribution was derived from income generated by property he received as a gift from Colette.

15. **LO.6** With regard to "life insurance" in the context of the Federal estate tax, comment on the following.
    a. What the term includes (i.e., types of policies).
    b. The meaning of "incidents of ownership."
    c. When a gift occurs upon maturity of the policy.
    d. The tax consequences when the owner of the policy predeceases the insured and the beneficiary.

16. **LO.7** Troy predeceases his wife, Nell. Under his will, his estate is placed in trust, income for her life to Nell, remainder to his children. Regarding any marital deduction allowed to Troy's estate, comment on the effect of the following independent cases.
    Critical Thinking
    a. Troy's executor makes a QTIP election.
    b. Nell issues a timely disclaimer that rejects her income interest.

17. **LO.7** Bernice dies and, under a valid will, passes real estate to her surviving husband. The real estate is subject to a mortgage. For estate tax purposes, how is any marital deduction determined? Can Bernice's estate deduct the mortgage in computing the taxable estate? Explain.

18. **LO.8** Three unmarried and childless sisters live together. All are of advanced age and in poor health, and each owns a significant amount of wealth. Each has a will that passes her property to her surviving sister(s) or, if no survivor, to their church. Within a period of two years and on different dates, all three sisters die. Discuss the Federal estate tax consequences of these deaths.
    Critical Thinking

Computational Exercises

19. **LO.2** Elizabeth made taxable gifts of $3 million in 2019 and $14 million in 2020. She paid no gift tax on the 2019 transfer. On what amount is the Federal gift tax computed for the 2020 gift?

20. **LO.3** Included in Mary's gross estate are the following assets.

	Fair Market Value	
	Date of Death	**Six Months Later**
Stock in Orange Corporation	$13,000,000	$13,100,000
Stock in Crimson Corporation	6,100,000	5,900,000

   a. How much is included in her gross estate if the alternate valuation date is elected?

   b. Instead, what if all of Mary's assets pass to her surviving husband?

   c. Express your answer in part (a) as a Microsoft Excel formula.

21. **LO.4** During the year, Rajeev makes the following transfers.

   • $1,000 to his mayor's reelection campaign.

   • $21,000 to his aunt, Ava, to reimburse her for what she paid the hospital for her gallbladder operation.

   • $18,000 paid directly to the surgeon who performed Ava's gallbladder operation.

   • $22,000 to purchase a used car for his son to use at college.

   Which of these transfers are subject to the Federal gift tax? (Include the total amount, and disregard the annual exclusion.)

22. **LO.4** In 2013 and with $200,000, Alice purchases a CD at State Bank listing title as follows: "Alice, payable on proof of death to Clark." Alice dies in 2020, and Clark (Alice's nephew) redeems the CD (now worth $205,000). Disregarding the annual exclusion, what is Alice's gift to Clark in:

   a. 2013?

   b. 2020?

Critical Thinking

23. **LO.5** Christian wants to transfer as much as possible to his four adult married children (including spouses) and eight minor grandchildren without using any unified transfer tax credit.

   a. How much can Christian give, so as to accomplish his tax goal?

   b. What if Christian's wife, Mia, joins in the gifts?

   c. Express your computations for parts (a) and (b) as Microsoft Excel commands.

24. **LO.5** Noah and Sophia want to make a maximum contribution to their state's qualified tuition program (§ 529 plan) on behalf of their minor granddaughter, Amanda, without exceeding the annual Federal gift tax exclusion.

   a. How much can they transfer to the plan for Amanda without incurring a current Federal gift tax?

   b. Express your answer as a Microsoft Excel command.

25. **LO.6** At his death, Andrew was a participant in his employer's contributory qualified pension plan. His account reflects the following.

Employer's contribution	$1,000,000
Andrew's contribution	800,000
Income earned	500,000

   a.   As to this plan, how much is included in Andrew's gross estate?

   b.   If the account balance is paid to Andrew's surviving wife, how much qualifies for the marital deduction?

   c.   How much is subject to the Federal income tax?

26. **LO.6** Mason buys real estate for $1.5 million and lists ownership as follows: "Mason and Dana, joint tenants with the right of survivorship." Mason dies first, when the real estate is valued at $2 million. How much is included in Mason's gross estate if Mason and Dana are:

   a.   Brother and sister.

   b.   Husband and wife.

27. **LO.6** Matthew owns an insurance policy (face amount of $500,000) on the life of Emily with Uma listed as the designated beneficiary. If Emily dies first and the $500,000 is paid to Uma, how much as to this policy is included in:

   a.   Matthew's gross estate?

   b.   Emily's gross estate?

28. **LO.7** Donald dies this year, and under his will, a trust is created in the amount of $6 million with the following provisions: life estate to Cindy (Donald's wife) and remainder to their children. His will also passes land (cost basis of $1 million and fair market value of $3 million) to the Salvation Army for the site of a new homeless housing project.

   a.   If a QTIP election is made, how much will these transactions reduce Donald's gross estate to arrive at the taxable estate?

   b.   If a QTIP election is not made?

29. **LO.8** Under Emma's will, Addison inherits property that generates an estate tax of $800,000. Three years later, Addison dies and the property generates an estate tax of $700,000. How much of a credit for estate tax on prior transfers is Addison's estate entitled to?

30. **LO.9** With $5 million, Paul's will creates a trust with the following provisions: life estate to Jacob (Paul's son) and remainder to Anastasia (Paul's granddaughter and Jacob's daughter). Jacob dies when the value of the trust is $8 million.

   a.   Does a generation-skipping transfer result?

   b.   If so, when and in what amount?

Problems

31. **LO.3** In each of the following independent situations, indicate whether the alternate valuation date can be elected. Explain why or why not.

Decedent	Value of Gross Estate		Estate Tax Liability	
	Date of Death	Six Months Later	Date of Death	Six Months Later
Jayden	$16,000,000	$15,900,000	$5,040,000	$5,039,000
Isabella	16,100,000	16,000,000	5,065,000	5,060,000
Liam	16,100,000	16,000,000	5,000,000	5,010,000
Lily	16,500,000	16,400,000	5,005,000	5,004,000

32. **LO.4** Carl made the following transfers during the current year. What are Carl's taxable gifts for the current year?

- Transferred $900,000 in cash and securities to a revocable trust, life estate to himself and remainder interest to his three adult children by a former wife.
- In consideration of their upcoming marriage, gave Lindsey a $90,000 convertible.
- Purchased a $100,000 certificate of deposit listing title as "Carl, payable on proof of death to Lindsey."
- Established a joint checking account with his now-wife, Lindsey, in December of the current year with $30,000 of funds he inherited from his parents. In January of the following year, Lindsey withdrew $18,000 of the funds.
- Purchased for $80,000 a paid-up insurance policy on his life (maturity value of $500,000). Carl designated Lindsey as the beneficiary.
- Paid $23,400 to a college for his niece Mindy's tuition and $11,000 for her room and board. Mindy is not Carl's dependent.
- Gave his aunt Betty $52,000 for her heart bypass operation. Betty is not Carl's dependent.

Critical Thinking

33. **LO.4, 7** In May 2019, Dudley and Eva enter into a property settlement preparatory to the dissolution of their marriage. Under the agreement, Dudley is to pay Eva $6 million in full satisfaction of her marital rights. Of this amount, Dudley pays $2.5 million immediately, and the balance is due one year later. The parties are divorced in July. Dudley dies in December, and his estate pays Eva the remaining $3.5 million in May 2020. Discuss the Federal estate and gift tax ramifications of these transactions to the parties involved.

Critical Thinking

34. **LO.4** Jesse dies intestate (i.e., without a will) in May year 1. Jesse's major asset is a tract of land. Under applicable state law, Jesse's property will pass to Lorena, who is his only child. In December year 1, Lorena disclaims one-half of the property. In June year 2, Lorena disclaims the other half interest. Under state law, Lorena's disclaimer results in the property passing to Arnold (Lorena's only child).

The value of the land (in its entirety) is as follows: $2 million in May year 1, $2.1 million in December year 1, and $2.2 million in June year 2. Discuss the transfer tax ramifications of these transactions.

35. **LO.5** Using property she inherited, Myrna makes a gift of $16.2 million to her adult daughter, Doris. Neither Myrna nor her husband, Greg, have made any prior taxable gifts. Assuming that a flat 40% tax rate applies, determine the Federal gift tax liability if:

a. The election to split gifts is not made.

b. The election to split gifts is made.

c. What are the tax savings from making the election?

36. **LO.6** At the time of his death this year on September 4, Kenneth owned the following assets, among others.

	Fair Market Value
City of Boston bonds	$2,500,000
Stock in Brown Corporation	900,000
Promissory note issued by Brad (Kenneth's son)	600,000

In October, the executor of Kenneth's estate received the following: $120,000 interest on the City of Boston bonds ($10,000 accrued since September 4) and a $7,000 cash dividend on the Brown stock (date of record was September 5). The declaration date on the dividend was August 12.

The $600,000 loan was made to Brad in late 2015, and he used the money to create a very successful business. The note was forgiven by Kenneth in his will. What are the estate tax consequences of these transactions?

37. **LO.6** Assume the same facts as in Problem 36 with the following modifications.

- The bonds were issued by the Houston (TX) Independent School District.
- The dividend record date was September 3 (not September 5).
- Kenneth's will does not forgive Brad's note. The business that Brad started with the loan funds was not successful and is near receivership.

What amount is included in Kenneth's gross estate?

38. **LO.6** At the time of her death on September 4, Alicia held the following assets.

	Fair Market Value
Bonds of Emerald Tool Corporation	$ 900,000
Stock in Drab Corporation	1,100,000
Insurance policy (face amount of $400,000) on the life of her father, Mitch	80,000*
Traditional IRAs	300,000

*Cash surrender value.

Alicia was also the life tenant of a trust (fair market value of $2,000,000) created by her late husband Bert. (The executor of Bert's estate had made a QTIP election.)

In October, Alicia's estate received an interest payment of $11,500 ($6,000 accrued before September 4) paid by Emerald and a cash dividend of $9,000 from Drab. The Drab dividend was declared on August 19 and was payable to date of record shareholders on September 3.

Although Mitch survives Alicia, she is the designated beneficiary of the policy. The IRAs are distributed to Alicia's children.

What amount is included in Alicia's gross estate for these items?

39. **LO.6** Assume the same facts as in Problem 38 with the following modifications. What amount is included in Alicia's gross estate for these items?

- Mitch is killed by a rock slide while mountain climbing in November, and the insurer pays Alicia's estate $400,000 before the end of the year.
- Bert's executor did not make a QTIP election.
- Alicia's IRAs were the Roth type (not traditional).
- The record date for the Drab Corporation dividend is September 5 (not September 3).
- On November 7, Alicia's estate receives from the IRS an $8,000 income tax refund on the taxes she paid for the preceding calendar year.

40. **LO.6, 7** At the time of Matthew's death, he was involved in the transactions described below.

- Matthew was a participant in his employer's contributory qualified pension plan. The plan balance of $2,000,000 is paid to Olivia, Matthew's daughter and beneficiary. The distribution consists of the following.

Employer contributions	$900,000
Matthew's after-tax contributions	600,000
Income earned by the plan	500,000

- Matthew was covered by his employer's group term life insurance plan for employees. The $200,000 proceeds are paid to Olivia, the designated beneficiary.

    a.   What are the Federal estate tax consequences of these events?

    b.   The income tax consequences?

    c.   Would the answer to part (a) change if Olivia was Matthew's surviving spouse (not his daughter)? Explain.

41. **LO.6** At the time of his death on July 9, Aiden held rights in the following real estate.

	Fair Market Value (on July 9)
Apartment building	$2,100,000
Tree farm	1,500,000
Pastureland	750,000
Residence	900,000

The apartment building was purchased by Chloe, Aiden's mother, and is owned in a joint tenancy with her. The tree farm and pastureland were gifts from Chloe to Aiden and his two sisters. The tree farm is held in joint tenancy, and the pastureland is owned as tenants in common. Aiden purchased the residence and owns it with his wife as tenants by the entirety. How much is included in Aiden's gross estate based on the following assumptions?

    a.   Aiden dies first and is survived by Chloe, his sisters, and his wife.

    b.   Aiden dies after Chloe, but before his sisters and his wife.

    c.   Aiden dies after Chloe and his sisters, but before his wife.

    d.   Aiden dies last (i.e., he survives Chloe, his sisters, and his wife).

42. **LO.4, 6, 7** Gordon purchased real estate for $900,000 and listed title to the property as "Gordon and Fawn, joint tenants with right of survivorship." Gordon predeceases Fawn when the real estate is worth $2,900,000. Gordon and Fawn are brother and sister.

    a.   Did a gift occur when the real estate was purchased? Explain.

    b.   What, if any, are the estate tax consequences upon Gordon's death?

    c.   Under part (b), would your answer change if it was Fawn (not Gordon) who died? Explain.

43. **LO.4, 6, 7** Assume the same facts as in Problem 42, except that Gordon and Fawn are husband and wife (not brother and sister).

    a.   What are the gift tax consequences when the real estate was purchased?

    b.   What are the estate tax consequences upon Gordon's death?

    c.   Under part (b), would your answer change if it was Fawn (not Gordon) who died? Explain.

44. **LO.5, 6, 7** In each of the independent situations below, determine the Federal estate and gift tax consequences of what has occurred. (In all cases, assume that Gene and Mary are married and that Ashley is their daughter.)

    a.   Mary purchases an insurance policy on Gene's life and designates Ashley as the beneficiary. Mary dies first, and under her will, the policy passes to Gene.

    b.   Gene purchases an insurance policy on Mary's life and designates Ashley as the beneficiary. Ashley dies first one year later.

    c.   Assume the same facts as in part (b). Two years later, Mary dies. Because Gene has not designated a new beneficiary, the insurance proceeds are paid to him.

    d.   Gene purchases an insurance policy on his life and designates Mary as the beneficiary. Gene dies first, and the policy proceeds are paid to Mary.

45. **LO.7** While vacationing in Florida in November, Sally was seriously injured in an automobile accident. Sally died several days later. Apply the Federal estate tax rules to each of these items.

    a. Bruce, Sally's son and executor, incurred $6,200 in travel expenses in flying to Florida, retrieving the body, and returning it to Frankfort, Kentucky, for burial.

    b. Sally had pledged $50,000 to the building fund of her church. Bruce paid this pledge from the assets of the estate.

    c. Prior to her death, Sally had promised to give her nephew, Gary, $20,000 when he passed the bar exam. Gary passed the exam late in the year, and Bruce kept Sally's promise by paying him $20,000 from estate assets.

    d. At the scene of the accident and before the ambulance arrived, someone took Sally's jewelry (i.e., Rolex watch and wedding ring) and money. The property (valued at $33,000) was not insured and was never recovered.

    e. As a result of the accident, Sally's auto was totally destroyed. The auto had a basis of $52,000 and a fair market value of $28,000. In January of the next year, the insurance company pays Sally's estate $27,000.

46. **LO.7** Roy dies and is survived by his wife, Marge. Under Roy's will, all of his otherwise uncommitted assets pass to Marge. For each of the property interests listed below, determine the marital deduction allowed to Roy's estate.

    a. Timberland worth $1,200,000 owned by Roy, Marge, and Amber (Marge's sister) as equal tenants in common. Amber furnished the original purchase price.

    b. Residence of Roy and Marge worth $900,000 owned by them as tenants by the entirety with right of survivorship. Roy provided the original purchase price.

    c. Insurance policy on Roy's life (maturity value of $1,000,000) owned by Marge and payable to her as the beneficiary.

    d. Insurance policy on Roy's life (maturity value of $500,000) owned by Roy with Marge as the designated beneficiary.

    e. Distribution from a qualified pension plan of $1,600,000 (Roy matched his employer's contribution of $500,000) with Marge as the designated beneficiary.

47. **LO.8** Under Rowena's will, Mandy (Rowena's sister) inherits her property. One year later, Mandy dies. Based on the following independent assumptions, what is Mandy's credit for the tax on prior transfers?

    a. The estate tax attributable to the inclusion of the property in Rowena's gross estate is $700,000, and the estate tax attributable to the inclusion of the property in Mandy's gross estate is $800,000.

    b. The estate tax attributable to the inclusion of the property in Rowena's gross estate is $1,200,000, and the estate tax attributable to the inclusion of the property in Mandy's gross estate is $1,100,000.

    c. Express your computations for parts (a) and (b) as Microsoft Excel commands.

    d. Would your answers to parts (a) and (b) change if Mandy died seven years (rather than one year) after Rowena?

Tax Return Problems

1. James A. and Ella R. Polk, ages 70 and 65, respectively, are retired physicians who live at 3319 Taylorcrest Street, Houston, Texas 77079. Their three adult children (Benjamin Polk, Michael Polk, and Olivia Turner) are mature and responsible persons.

    The Polks have heard that some in Congress have proposed lowering the Federal gift tax exclusion to $3 million. Although this change likely will not occur, the Polks believe that they should take advantage of the more generous exclusion available under existing law. Thus, the Polks make transfers of many of their high-value investments. These and other gifts made during the year are summarized below.

	Donor	
Asset Transfer	**James**	**Ella**
Condominium located in Conroe (TX) acquired in 2009, cost $1,200,000, to Benjamin, Michael, and Olivia as equal tenants in common.	$1,900,000	$1,900,000
Office building, located in Round Rock (TX) built in 2011, cost $1,800,000, to Benjamin, Michael, and Olivia as equal tenants in common.	2,300,000	2,300,000
Vacation ranch in Bandera (TX) inherited by James from his father in 2006, value then $900,000, to Benjamin, Michael, and Olivia as equal joint tenants with right of survivorship.	2,600,000	–0–
Ella used her separate property to reimburse her father (Alan Roberts) for his heart bypass operation.	–0–	82,000
Paid for daughter's (Olivia's) wedding to John Turner, a state-law obligation of support	20,000	20,000
James used his separate property to purchase a new automobile (BMW) as a graduation present (from medical school) for his favorite niece (Carol Polk)	42,000	–0–

    Prepare 2018 gift tax returns (Form 709) for both of the Polks to compute the total taxable gifts (line 3) for James and Ella; stop with line 3 of page 1, but complete pages 2 and 3 of the return.

    An election to split gifts is made. The Polks have made no taxable gifts in prior years. Relevant Social Security numbers are 123-45-6789 (James) and 123-45-6788 (Ella).

2. Natalie Bryan, a widow who lives at 425 Flathead Way, Kalispell, Montana 59901, has three adult children (Daniel Bryan, Amanda Green, and Samantha Cruz). During the year, Natalie makes the following gifts to the children.

    - **To Daniel.** Office building in Helena acquired in 2011 at a cost of $900,000, current value $1,900,000.

    - **To Amanda.** Rental cabins in Whitefish inherited in 2009 (value $1,000,000) from her father, current value $1,800,000.

    - **To Samantha.** Vacation lodge on Flathead Lake acquired in 2005 at a cost of $800,000, current value $1,900,000.

    Prepare a 2018 gift tax return (Form 709) for Natalie (Social Security number 123-45-6787) to compute the total taxable gifts (line 3) for her; stop with line 3 of page 1, but complete pages 2 and 3 of the return. Natalie made no taxable gifts in prior years.

Research Problems

Note: Solutions to the Research Problems can be prepared by using the Thomson Reuters Checkpoint™ online tax research database, which accompanies this textbook. Solutions can also be prepared by using research materials found in a typical tax library.

Research Problem 1. Grace Lang was employed as a waitress at the Pancake House in Grand Bay, Alabama. While working the morning shift on March 7, 2012, one of Grace's customers left her a Florida lottery ticket as a tip. When Grace discovered that the ticket had won part of the Florida Lotto jackpot, the following steps were taken.

- Upon advice of her father and legal counsel, the Lang Corporation was formed and immediately made an S election.
- Grace received 49% of the stock in Lang, and the 51% balance was distributed to family members.
- Grace had the Florida gaming authorities designate the Lang Corporation as the recipient of the prize money—approximately $10 million payable over 30 years.
- Grace's coworkers at the Pancake House filed suit against Grace based on an agreement they had to share any lottery winnings equally. The Alabama courts eventually decided that such an agreement did exist but that it was not enforceable. (Alabama law does not permit enforcement of contracts involving illegal activities—gambling is illegal in Alabama.)

In 2020, the IRS determined that Grace had made taxable gifts in 2012 when she shifted some of the lottery winnings to family members. She made the gifts by having 51% of the Lang Corporation stock issued to them. (Because Lang is an S corporation, gross income from the lottery passes through to the shareholders.)

Grace disputed the gift tax assessment by contending that her actions were required by the Lang family agreement. Under this agreement, it was understood that each member would take care of the others in the event he or she came into a "substantial amount" of money. Because Grace was bound by the Lang family agreement, she was compelled to relinquish any right to 51% of the Lang stock. Thus, the satisfaction of an obligation is not a gift. As no gift occurred, the imposition of the gift tax is not appropriate.

Who should prevail?

Partial list of research aids:
Estate of Emerson Winkler, 36 TCM 1657, T.C.Memo. 1997–4.
Tonda Lynn Dickerson, 103 TCM 1280, T.C.Memo. 2012–60.

Research Problem 2. Before her death, Lucy entered into the following transactions. Discuss the estate and income tax ramifications of each of these transactions.

a. Lucy borrowed $600,000 from her brother, Irwin, so that Lucy could start a business. The loan was on open account, and no interest or due date was provided for. Under applicable state law, collection on the loan was barred by the statute of limitations before Lucy died. Because the family thought that Irwin should recover his funds, the executor of the estate paid him $600,000.

b. Lucy promised her sister, Ida, a bequest of $500,000 if Ida would move in with her and care for her during an illness (which eventually proved to be terminal). Lucy never kept her promise; her will was silent on any bequest to Ida. After Lucy's death, Ida sued the estate and eventually recovered $600,000 for breach of contract.

Partial list of research aids:
§ 2053.
Reg. §§ 20.2053–4(d)(4) and (7).
Estate of Allie W. Pittard, 69 T.C. 391 (1977).
Joseph F. Kenefic, 36 TCM 1226, T.C.Memo. 1977–310.
Hibernia Bank v. U.S., 78–2 USTC ¶13,261, 42 AFTR 2d 78–6510, 581 F.2d 741 (CA–9, 1978).

Use internet tax resources to address the following questions. Look for reliable websites and blogs of the IRS and other government agencies, media outlets, businesses, tax professionals, academics, think tanks, and political outlets.

Communications

Research Problem 3. What type of transfer tax, if any, does your home state impose? What about the state(s) contiguous to your home state? (For Alaska, use Washington; for Hawaii, use California.) Make a chart relating your findings, and send it to your instructor.

Data Analytics
Communications

Research Problem 4. Make a graph showing the number of Forms 706 and 709 that have been filed for every third year starting with 2005. On the same graph, indicate the revenue collected by the Treasury from these taxes for each year.

Communications

Research Problem 5. Find two articles that address tax policy reasons supporting a repeal of the Federal estate tax. Prepare two PowerPoint slides summarizing these arguments for a presentation to your school's accounting fraternity as part of its Tax Night.

Becker CPA Review Questions

1. Fred and Amy Kehl, both U.S. citizens, are married. All of their real and personal property is owned by them as tenants by the entirety or as joint tenants with right of survivorship. The gross estate of the first spouse to die:

   a. Includes 50% of the value of all property owned by the couple, regardless of which spouse furnished the original consideration

   b. Includes only the property that had been acquired with the funds of the deceased spouse

   c. Does not include any of the value of the property held as joint tenancy with right of survivorship (or tenancy by the entirety) because of the unlimited marital deduction

   d. Includes one-third of the value of all real estate owned by the Kehls as the dower right in the case of the wife or courtesy right in the case of the husband

2. Which of the following requires filing a gift tax return if the transfer exceeds the available annual gift tax exclusion?

   a. Medical expenses paid directly to a physician on behalf of an individual unrelated to the donor

   b. Tuition paid directly to an accredited university on behalf of an individual unrelated to the donor

   c. Payments for college books, supplies, and dormitory fees on behalf of an individual unrelated to the donor

   d. Campaign expenses paid to a political organization

3. Steve and Kay Briar, U.S. citizens, were married for the entire calendar year. During the year, Steve gave a $32,000 cash gift to his sister. The Briars made no other gifts in the year. They each signed a timely election to treat the $32,000 gift as made one-half by each spouse. Disregarding the applicable credit and estate tax consequences, what amount of the current-year gift is taxable to the Briars?

   a. $32,000   c. $2,000
   b. $30,000   d. $0

4. Larry plans to gift his daughter $25,000 during the current taxable year. Further, provided she graduates from a four-year accredited college, he will also gift her $100,000. Which of the following is correct with regard to these gifts during the current year, assuming the cash is given to his daughter in the current year and she does not graduate from a four-year accredited college in the current year?

$25,000	**$100,000**
a. Completed Gift	Incomplete Gift
b. Completed Gift	Completed Gift
c. Incomplete Gift	Incomplete Gift
d. Incomplete Gift	Completed Gift

5. Which of the following statements about the estate tax is *not* correct?

   a. The estate tax return, Form 706, is due nine months after the date of death.

   b. The alternate valuation date for an estate, if elected, is six months after the date of death.

   c. The estate may not deduct outstanding debts of the decedent.

   d. An estate is allowed an unlimited marital deduction.

6. Bob died in year 3. His gross estate consisted of assets with a fair market value of $13,500,000. In his will, Bob leaves $1,000,000 to his wife, $500,000 to his only daughter, and $250,000 to his favorite charity. Prior to Bob's death, he was involved in a lawsuit when one of his tenants slipped and fell at one of the rental properties owned by Bob. After his death, the personal representative settled the lawsuit for $750,000. The expenses to close Bob's estate were $50,000. In year 3, the Federal estate exclusion amount is $11,000,000. What amount, if any, does Bob's estate exceed the $11,000,000 exclusion amount?

   a. $450,000

   b. $500,000

   c. $1,200,000

   d. $0

7. David Collins died during the current year. The personal representative of David's estate reviewed the following assets.

Stocks in David's name only	$ 2,000,000
Investment property in a trust that David has the right to revoke	1,500,000
Primary home owned jointly with his wife (wife did not contribute to the purchase)	1,000,000
Insurance policy owned by and insuring David with the proceeds payable to his daughter	800,000
Vacation home owned jointly with his son (son did not contribute to the purchase)	500,000
Cash placed in an irrevocable trust by David eight years ago with David's friend as trustee	600,000

   What is the value of David's gross estate for estate tax purposes?

   a. $3,500,000

   b. $4,250,000

   c. $5,300,000

   d. $6,400,000

Family Tax Planning

LEARNING OBJECTIVES: *After completing Chapter 19, you should be able to:*

LO.1 Describe various established concepts used in carrying out the valuation process.

LO.2 Apply the special use valuation method in appropriate situations.

LO.3 Identify problems involved in valuing an interest in a closely held business.

LO.4 Compare the income tax basis rules applying to property received by gift and by death.

LO.5 Explain how gifts can minimize gift taxes and avoid estate taxes.

LO.6 Recognize when gifts trigger income taxes for the donor.

LO.7 Illustrate how to reduce probate costs in the administration of an estate.

LO.8 Apply procedures that reduce estate tax liabilities.

LO.9 List and review procedures to increase the liquidity of an estate.

CHAPTER OUTLINE

LIFETIME GIVING—THE GOOD AND THE BAD

Martin, age 75, is a wealthy widower who is considering making a lifetime gift of $500,000 to his only daughter, Francine. Among the assets Martin can choose from, *each* worth $500,000, are the following.

- Partial interest in a closely held partnership.
- Insurance policy on Martin's life with a maturity value of $3 million.
- Marketable securities (adjusted basis to Martin of $900,000).
- Unimproved residential city lot (adjusted basis to Martin of $100,000).
- Ten annual installment notes from the sale of land (basis of $200,000) with a maturity value of $700,000.

Martin's other Federal gross estate assets are valued at $20 million. In terms of present and future Federal tax consequences, evaluate each choice.

Read the chapter and formulate your response.

Broadly speaking, *family tax planning* involves the use of various procedures that manage the tax and nontax consequences of transferring income and assets within the family unit. In this regard, one must consider not only transfer taxes (i.e., gift and estate) but also the income tax ramifications to both the transferor (i.e., donor, decedent, estate, or trust) and the transferees (i.e., donees, heirs, or beneficiaries). In fact, with a large transfer tax exemption equivalent, the income tax consequences of estate and gift tax planning are especially important for most taxpayers.

The valuation of the transferred property also is an essential element of family tax planning. The gift tax is based on the fair market value of the property on the date of the transfer. For Federal estate taxes, the fair market value on the date of the owner's death or the alternate valuation date (if available and elected) controls, and that value becomes the income tax basis of the asset going forward.

LO.1

Describe various established concepts used in carrying out the valuation process.

19-1 **VALUATION CONCEPTS**

19-1a **Valuation in General**

The Internal Revenue Code refers to "value" and "fair market value," but does not discuss these terms at length.[1] Section 2031(b) comes closest to a definition when it treats the problem of stocks and securities for which no sales price information (the usual case with closely held corporations) is available. In such situations, "the value thereof shall be determined by taking into consideration, in addition to all other factors, the value of stock or securities of corporations engaged in the same or similar line of business which are listed on an exchange."

Regulation § 20.2031–1(b) is more specific in defining fair market value as "the price at which property would change hands between a willing buyer and a willing seller, neither being under any compulsion to buy or to sell and both having reasonable knowledge of relevant facts." The same Regulation makes clear that the fair market value of an item of property is not determined by a forced sale price. Nor is the fair market value determined by the sale price of the item in a market other than the market where the item is most commonly sold to the public.

Sentiment should not play a part in the determination of value. Suppose, for example, the decedent's daughter is willing to pay $5,000 for a portrait of her mother. If the painting is really worth $2,000 (i.e., what the general public would pay), then $2,000 should be its value for Federal transfer tax purposes.

The market placement of the item also must be considered. So if there is a public market for an item, its fair market value in that market should be used; this would be its retail price.

EXAMPLE 1

At the time of his death, Don owned three automobiles. The vehicles are included in Don's gross estate at their fair market value on the date of his death or on the alternate valuation date (if elected). The fair market value of the automobiles is determined by looking at the price a member of the general public would pay for vehicles of approximately the same description, make, model, age, condition, etc. The price a dealer in used cars would pay for these automobiles is inappropriate for this purpose.

If a tangible asset other than real estate is sold as a result of a posting on Craigslist, and the property is of a type often sold in this manner or if the property is sold at a public auction, the price for which it is sold is presumed to be the retail sales price

---

[1]See, for example, §§ 1001(b), 2031(a), and 2512(a). Sections 2032A(e)(7) and (8) set forth certain procedures for valuing farms and interests in closely held businesses.

of the item at the time of the sale. The retail sales price also is used if the sale is made within a reasonable period following the valuation date, and market conditions have not changed substantially.[2]

19-1b **Valuation of Specific Assets**

Stocks and Bonds

If there is a market for stocks and bonds on a stock exchange, in an over-the-counter market or otherwise, the average between the highest and lowest quoted selling prices on the valuation date is the fair market value per unit. A special rule applies if no sales occurred on the valuation date but did occur on dates within a reasonable period before and after the valuation date. Here, the fair market value is the weighted average of the means between the highest and lowest sales prices on the nearest date before and the nearest date after the valuation date. The average is weighted *inversely* by the respective number of trading days between the selling dates and the valuation date.[3]

Carla makes a gift to Antonio of shares of stock in Green Corporation. The transactions involving this stock that occurred closest to the date of the gift took place two trading days before the date of the gift at a mean selling price of $10 and three trading days after the gift at a mean selling price of $15. The $12 fair market value of each share of Green stock is determined as follows.

$$\frac{(3 \times \$10) + (2 \times \$15)}{5} = \$12$$

If no transactions occurred within a reasonable period before and after the valuation date, the fair market value is determined by taking a weighted average of the means between the bona fide bid and asked prices on the nearest trading dates before and after the valuation date.

In many instances, there are no established market prices for securities. This lack of information is typical with stock in closely held corporations. Problems unique to valuing interests in closely held businesses are discussed later in this chapter.

Notes Receivable

The fair market value of notes, secured or unsecured, is the amount of unpaid principal plus interest accrued to the valuation date, unless the parties (e.g., executor or donor) establish a lower value or prove the notes are worthless. Crucial elements in proving that a note is entirely or partially worthless are the financial condition of the borrower and the absence of any value for the property pledged or mortgaged as security for the obligation.[4]

At the time of his death, Ira held a note (face amount of $50,000) issued by his son, Kevin. Although Kevin is solvent, he is relieved of the obligation because Ira forgives the note in his will. Presuming that the note is payable on demand, it is included in Ira's gross estate at $50,000 plus accrued interest.

If the note is not due immediately and/or the interest provided for is under the current rate, a discount may be in order, and the fair market value of the note would be less than $50,000. The burden of proof in supporting a discount for the note is on the executor.

---

[2]Rev.Proc. 65–19, 1965–2 C.B. 1002.
[3]Reg. §§ 20.2031–2(b) and 25.2512–2(b).

[4]Reg. §§ 20.2031–4 and 25.2512–4.

At the time of his death, Tim Landry held a note, payable on demand, in the amount of $40,000. The note had been issued by Roy Briggs, Tim's former brother-in-law, 10 years earlier. Roy used the funds to help pay the wedding and honeymoon expenses when he married Colleen Landry, Tim's sister. The couple have since separated, and Roy disappeared for parts unknown in 2016.

The executor of Tim's estate handled this matter as follows.

- He filed an amended income tax return for 2016 claiming a bad debt deduction.

- He made no mention of the note on the Form 706 filed for Tim Landry's estate.

What, if any, could be the justification for the executor's actions? If an audit results, what position(s) might the IRS take?

Insurance Policies and Annuity Contracts

The value of a life insurance policy on the life of a person other than the decedent, or the value of an annuity contract issued by a company regularly engaged in selling annuities, is the cost of a comparable contract.[5]

Valuing Insurance and Annuity Policies

EXAMPLE 4

Paul purchased a joint and survivor annuity contract from an insurance company. Under the contract's terms, Paul is to receive payments of $120,000 per year for his life. Upon Paul's death, his wife (Kate) is to receive $90,000 annually for her life. Ten years after purchasing the annuity, when Kate is 40 years old, Paul dies.

The value of the annuity contract on the date of Paul's death (and the amount includible in Paul's gross estate) is the amount the insurance company would charge in the year of Paul's death for an annuity that would pay $90,000 annually for the life of a 40-year-old female.

EXAMPLE 5

At the time of her death, Lana owns an insurance policy (face amount of $500,000) on the life of her son, Sam. No further payments need be made on the policy (e.g., it is a single premium policy or a paid-up policy).

The value of the policy on the date of Lana's death (and the amount includible in her gross estate) is the amount the insurance company would charge in the year of her death for a single premium contract (face amount of $500,000) on the life of someone Sam's age.

Life Estates, Terms for Years, Reversions, and Remainders

As with noncommercial annuities, the valuation of life estates, income interests for a term of years, reversions, and remainders involves the use of tables.[6]

Because life expectancies change, the IRS is required to issue new tables at least every 10 years.[7] The current tables were issued in 2009 and are effective, as indexed monthly, for transfers beginning in May of that year.[8]

The tables provide only the remainder factor. If the income interest (life estate) has also been transferred, the factor to be used is one minus the remainder factor.

---

[5]Reg. §§ 20.2031–8(a)(1) and 25.2512–6(a). The valuation of annuities issued by parties *not regularly engaged in the sale of annuities* (i.e., noncommercial contracts) requires the use of special tables issued by the IRS.

[6]A portion of such tables is reproduced in text Appendix A. The full tables are available at **irs.gov**.

[7]§ 7520.

[8]The valuation factors in the tables represent 120% of the Federal midterm rate for the month of the valuation date.

Matt transfers $1,000,000 in trust, specifying a life estate to Rita, and a remainder interest to Rick on Rita's death. The gift took place when Rita was age 35. Assume that the appropriate rate for the month of the gift is 4.4%.

Using the table extract in Appendix A (Table S on p. A-6) for a person age 35 under the 4.4% column, the value of the remainder interest is $184,230 (0.18423 × $1,000,000). The life estate factor is 0.81577 (1.00000 − 0.18423). So, Matt has made a gift to Rita of $815,770 and a gift to Rick of $184,230.

In computing the value of an *income interest* for a term of years, a different table is used. Again, the table furnishes the remainder factor. To compute the factor for the income interest, subtract the remainder factor from 1.

Julia transfers $400,000 by gift to a trust. Under the terms of the trust, income is payable to Paul for eight years. After the eight-year period, the trust terminates, and the trust principal passes to Sara. For the month in which the trust was created, the appropriate rate was 4.6%.

The valuation of $1 due at the end of eight years is 0.697825 (Table B on p. A-7). As a result, Julia has made a gift to Sara of $279,130 (0.697825 × $400,000). The factor for the income interest becomes 0.302175 (1.000000 − 0.697825), so the gift to Paul is $120,870 (0.302175 × $400,000).

What is the significance of dividing a gift into several distinct parts? This is important in determining the applicability of the annual gift tax exclusion (see text Section 18-2c). Under the facts of Example 6, an annual exclusion probably would be allowed for the gift to Rita but not for the interest passing to Rick (because of the future interest limitation).

Why might a trust be arranged so that the income interest is limited to a term of years rather than the life of a beneficiary? Suppose in Example 7 that Paul is the 13-year-old son of Sara, a single parent. Julia, the grandmother, establishes the trust to ensure that Paul's support needs (e.g., medical and educational) will be provided for until he reaches the age of majority. Then, the trust income will help meet Sara's financial needs.

ETHICS & EQUITY **Can IRS Valuation Tables Be Disregarded?**

Ted Lucas (age 48) is killed in an automobile accident. One of the provisions of Ted's will establishes a trust with $3 million in assets. Under the terms of the trust, a life estate is granted to Mel (age 69) with the remainder interest passing to Faye (age 45) upon Mel's death. Mel is Ted's widower father, who is suffering from pancreatic cancer. Faye is Ted's wife, who is in good health. Under the applicable valuation tables, the life estate value in $3 million for a person age 69 is $1,709,280 (based on an interest rate of 4.2 percent).

If the Lucas estate valued Mel's estate in accordance with the IRS tables, this would reduce the marital deduction allowed for Faye's remainder interest to $1,290,720 ($3,000,000 − $1,709,280). Because Mel has aggressive terminal cancer, however, life estate is disregarded, and the full $3 million is claimed as a marital deduction.

Is the estate correct in disregarding the valuation factor for a life estate in light of Mel's medical condition?

19-1c **Real Estate and the Special Use Valuation Method**

LO.2
Apply the special use valuation method in appropriate situations.

Proper valuation principles usually require that real estate be valued at its most suitable (i.e., "best" or "highest") use. Section 2032A, however, permits an executor to elect to value certain classes of real estate used in farming or a closely held business at its "current" use, rather than the most suitable use, for Federal estate (not gift) tax purposes. The major objective of the special use value election is to provide limited relief to protect the heirs against the possibility of having to sell a portion of the family farm or business to pay estate taxes.

EXAMPLE 8

At the time of his death, Rex owned a dairy farm on the outskirts of a large city. For farming purposes, the property's value is $1.5 million (the current use value).[9] As a potential site for a data center, however, the property is worth $2.2 million (the most suitable use value). The executor of Rex's estate can elect to include only $1.5 million in the gross estate.

The special use valuation procedure, however, permits a reduction of no more than $1,160,000 in estate tax valuation in 2019 ($1,140,000 in 2018). This amount is subject to annual indexation.

EXAMPLE 9

At the time of her death in 2019, Wanda owned a farm with a most suitable use value of $3.5 million but a current use value of $2 million. Assuming that the property qualifies under § 2032A and the special use valuation election is made, Wanda's gross estate includes $2.34 million, not $2 million. The farm's most suitable use value can be reduced by no more than $1.16 million.

The special use valuation election is available if *all* of the following conditions are satisfied.

- At least 50 percent of the adjusted value of the gross estate consists of *real* or *personal* property devoted to a qualifying use (used for farming or in a closely held business) at the time of the owner's death.[10] For purposes of satisfying the percentage requirement, the assets involved are considered at their most suitable use value.

- Ownership and material participation by the decedent for a specified period prior to death is required.[11]

- The qualifying heir must be a family member.[12]

Any estate tax savings derived from the special use valuation method are recaptured from the heir if he or she disposes of the property, or if the property ceases to be qualifying use property, within a period of 10 years from the date of the decedent's death.

EXAMPLE 10

Assume the same facts as in Example 9. Further assume that by electing § 2032A, Wanda's estate tax liability was reduced by $464,000. Three years after Wanda's death, Otis (the qualifying heir) leases the farm to an unrelated party. At this point, Otis must pay back to the U.S. Treasury the $464,000 additional estate tax liability that would have been imposed had § 2032A not been used.

LO.3

Identify problems involved in valuing an interest in a closely held business.

19-1d **Valuation Problems with a Closely Held Business**

The IRS establishes the approach, methods, and factors to be considered in valuing the shares of closely held corporations for gift and estate tax purposes.[13] The following factors, although not all-inclusive, are fundamental and require careful analysis in each case.

- The nature of the business and the history of the enterprise from its inception.

- The economic outlook in general and the condition and outlook of the specific industry in particular.

- The book value of the stock and the financial condition of the business.

- The earning capacity of the company.

- The company's dividend-paying capacity.

- Whether the enterprise has goodwill or other intangible value.

---

[9]Sections 2032A(e)(7) and (8) set forth various methods of valuation to be applied in arriving at current use value.

[10]§§ 2032A(b)(1)(A) and (b)(2). For a definition of *farm* and *farming*, see §§ 2032A(e)(4) and (5).

[11]§ 2032A(b)(1)(C)(ii). Material participation is defined in § 2032A(e)(6).

[12]§ 2032A(e)(2). Other requirements are found in § 2032A and the instructions to Form 706.

[13]Rev.Rul. 59–60, 1959–1 C.B. 237. See also Reg. § 20.2031–2(f).

- The prices and number of shares of the stock sold previously and the size of the block of stock to be valued.
- The market price of stocks issued by corporations in the same or a similar line of business and actively traded in a free and open market, either on an exchange or over the counter.

Goodwill Aspects

If a closely held corporation's record of past earnings is higher than usual for the industry, the IRS is likely to claim that corporate goodwill should be included in the valuation of the business.

Adam owned 70% of the stock of White Corporation, with the remaining 30% held by various family members. Over the past five years, White Corporation has generated average net profits of $200,000, and on the date of Adam's death, the book value of the corporation's stock was $500,000. If the IRS identifies 8% as an appropriate after-tax rate of return for White, one approach to the valuation of White stock would yield the following result.

Average net profit for the past five years	$ 200,000
8% of the $500,000 book value	40,000
Excess earnings over 8%	$ 160,000
Value of goodwill (5 years × $160,000)	$ 800,000
Book value	500,000
Total value of the White stock	$1,300,000

As a result, the IRS might contend that the stock should be included in Adam's gross estate at $910,000 (70 percent of $1,300,000). If the estate wants to argue for a lower valuation (i.e., to reduce the estate tax liability), relevant factors might include any of the following.

- The average net profit figure for the past five years ($200,000) may be overstated. Perhaps it includes some extraordinary gains that normally do not occur or are extraneous to the business conducted by the corporation. Or, the figure may fail to take into account certain expenses that normally would be incurred but for some justifiable reason have been deferred. In a family business during periods of expansion and development, it is not uncommon to find an unusually low salary structure. Profits might be considerably less if the owner-employees of the business were being paid the true worth of their services.
- The appropriate after-tax rate of return for this type of business may not be 8 percent. If it is higher, there would be less goodwill because the business is not as profitable as it seems.[14]
- If Adam was a key person in the operation of White Corporation, could some or all of any goodwill developed by the business be attributed to his efforts? If so, is it not reasonable to assume that the goodwill might be seriously impaired by Adam's death?

Other Factors

Aside from the issue of goodwill, the valuation of closely held stock must take other factors into account. For example, consider the percentage of ownership involved. If the percentage represents a *minority interest* and the corporation has a poor dividend-paying record, a substantial discount is in order.[15] The justification for the discount is the general inability of the holder of the minority interest to affect corporate policy, particularly with respect to the distribution of dividends. At the other extreme is an interest

---

[14]Industry surveys or data sets can be used to establish a more common rate of return.

[15]See, for example, *Jack D. Carr*, 49 TCM 507, T.C.Memo. 1985–19.

large enough to represent control, either actual or effective. Considered alone, a controlling interest calls for valuation at a premium.[16]

A controlling interest may be so large, however, that the disposition of the stock within a reasonable period of time after the valuation date could have a negative effect on the market for these shares. The **blockage rule** recognizes what may happen to per-unit value when a large block of shares is marketed at one time.[17] Most often, the rule is applied to stock that trades in a recognized market. The rule permits a discount from the amount at which smaller lots are selling on or about the valuation date.[18] Although the blockage rule may have a bearing on the valuation of other assets, it more frequently is applied to stocks and securities.[19]

Because most stock in closely held corporations does not trade in a recognized market, a discount for *lack of marketability* may be in order. The discount recognizes the costs that would be incurred in creating a market for such shares to effect their orderly disposition.[20] The discount could be significant considering typical underwriting expenses and other costs involved in going public.

Closely related to the reasons that an asset's marketability might be impaired is the possibility of built-in income tax consequences. In one case, the value of stock in a holding company was significantly discounted because of the income tax that would result if the holding company distributed its major asset to its shareholders.[21]

Resolving the Valuation Problem for Stock in Closely Held Corporations

Because the valuation of closely held stock is subject to so many variables, planning should be directed toward bringing about some measure of certainty.

EXAMPLE 12

Polly wants to transfer some of her stock in Brown Corporation to a trust formed for her children. She would also like to make a substantial contribution to her alma mater, State University. At present, the Brown stock is owned entirely by Polly and has never been traded on any market or otherwise sold or exchanged. Brown's past operations have proved profitable, and Brown has established a respectable record of dividend distributions. Based on the best available information and taking into account various adjustments (e.g., discount for lack of marketability), Polly believes each share of Brown stock possesses a fair market value of $120.

If Polly makes a gift of some of the stock to the trust set up for the children and uses the $120 per-share valuation, what assurance is there that the IRS will accept this figure? If the IRS is successful in increasing the fair market value per share, Polly could end up with additional gift tax liability. Here, a buy-sell agreement might be in order.

The Buy-Sell Agreement and Valuation

The main objective of a **buy-sell agreement** is to effect the orderly disposition of a closely held business interest without the risk of the interest falling into the hands of outsiders. Moreover, a buy-sell agreement can ease the problems of estate liquidity and valuation.

Two types of buy-sell agreements frequently are encountered: **entity** and **cross-purchase** arrangements. Under the entity type, the business itself (partnership or corporation) agrees

---

[16]*Helvering v. Safe Deposit and Trust Co. of Baltimore, Exr. (Estate of H. Walters)*, 38–1 USTC ¶9240, 21 AFTR 12, 95 F.2d 806 (CA–4, 1938), *aff'g* 35 B.T.A. 259 (1937).

[17]Reg. § 20.2031–2(e).

[18]See, for example, *Estate of Robert Damon*, 49 T.C. 108 (1967).

[19]In *Estate of David Smith*, 57 T.C. 650 (1972), the estate of a now-famous sculptor successfully argued for the application of the blockage rule to 425 sculptures included in the gross estate. See also *Estate of Georgia T. O'Keeffe*, 63 TCM 2699, T.C.Memo. 1992–210.

[20]See, for example, *Estate of Mark S. Gallo*, 50 TCM 470, T.C.Memo. 1985–363. In this case, the taxpayer also argued that a bad product image (i.e., the Thunderbird, Ripple, and Boone's Farm brands) would depress the value of the stock. Because the trend was toward better wines, association with cheaper products had a negative consumer impact. Not emphasized were the enormous profits that the sale of the cheap wines generated.

[21]*Estate of Artemus D. Davis*, 110 T.C. 530 (1998). The major asset held by the holding company was a considerable block of substantially appreciated stock in the Winn-Dixie supermarket chain.

to buy out the interest of the withdrawing owner (partner or shareholder). Under a cross-purchase agreement, the surviving owners (partners or shareholders) agree to buy out the withdrawing owner. The structures of the most typical buy-sell agreements are illustrated in Exhibit 19.1.

Buy-Sell Agreements Compared

Iris, Ned, and Hal are equal and unrelated shareholders in Blue Corporation, and all three share in Blue's management. All agree to turn in their stock to the corporation for redemption at $100 per share if any one of them withdraws (by death or otherwise) from the business. Shortly thereafter, Hal dies, and Blue Corporation redeems the stock from Hal's estate at the agreed-upon price of $100 per share.

EXAMPLE 13

Assume the same facts as in Example 13, except that the agreement is the cross-purchase type under which each shareholder promises to buy a portion of the withdrawing shareholder's interest. When Hal dies, the estate sells the Blue stock to Iris and Ned for $100 per share.

EXAMPLE 14

| **EXHIBIT 19.1** | **Structures of Typical Buy-Sell Agreements** |

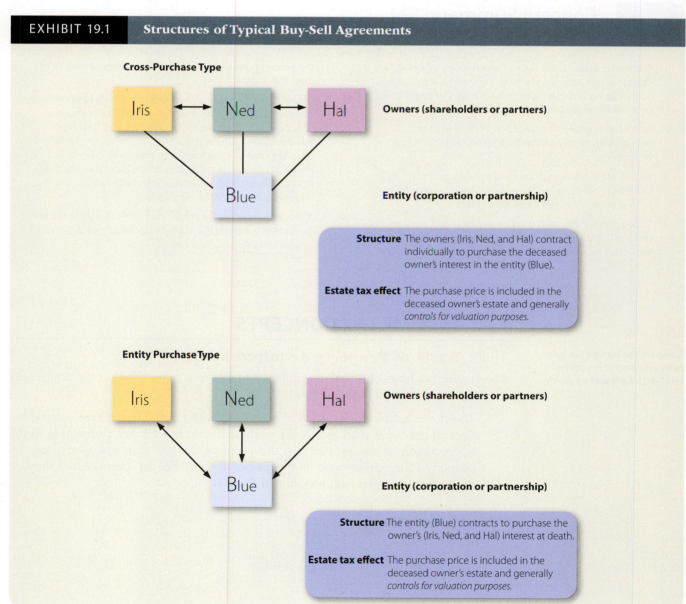

Cross-Purchase Type

Iris ↔ Ned ↔ Hal — Owners (shareholders or partners)

Blue — Entity (corporation or partnership)

Structure The owners (Iris, Ned, and Hal) contract individually to purchase the deceased owner's interest in the entity (Blue).

Estate tax effect The purchase price is included in the deceased owner's estate and generally *controls for valuation purposes.*

Entity Purchase Type

Iris   Ned   Hal — Owners (shareholders or partners)

Blue — Entity (corporation or partnership)

Structure The entity (Blue) contracts to purchase the owner's (Iris, Ned, and Hal) interest at death.

Estate tax effect The purchase price is included in the deceased owner's estate and generally *controls for valuation purposes.*

Will the $100 per share paid to Hal's estate determine the amount to be included in his gross estate? In general, the answer is *yes*, and this provides certainty as to the estate tax valuation of the business. However, this result is subject to the following conditions.

- The price is the result of a bona fide business agreement.
- The agreement is not a device to transfer property to family members.
- The agreement is comparable to other arrangements entered into by persons dealing at arm's length.[22]

Life insurance often is used to provide some or all of the financing needed to carry out buy-sell agreements. If insurance is used in the entity type of agreement, the corporation (or partnership) takes out a policy on the life of each owner. With the cross-purchase type, however, each owner must insure the life of every other owner, so more policies will be needed.

Valuation concepts are reviewed in Concept Summary 19.1.

Concept Summary 19.1

Valuation Concepts

1. Fair market value is "the price at which property would change hands between a willing buyer and a willing seller, neither being under any compulsion to buy or to sell and both having reasonable knowledge of relevant facts."

2. Special rules govern the valuation of life insurance policies and annuity contracts. IRS valuation tables may be required.

3. IRS valuation tables must be used to value multiple interests in property. Such interests include income for a term of years, life estates, and remainders.

4. Code provides valuation relief for the estates of persons who hold real estate used in farming or a closely held business. If the Code's requirements are met and if the executor elects, the property can be valued at its *current use* rather than its *most suitable use*.

5. Determining the value of the stock in a closely held corporation presents unique problems. The presence or absence of *goodwill* at the corporate level has a direct bearing on the stock being valued. A discount may be desired by the taxpayer for any of the following: a minority interest, lack of marketability, or the application of the blockage rule. The IRS will contend that a premium attaches to an interest that represents control of the corporation.

6. A properly structured and executed buy-sell agreement will control the value to be assigned a deceased owner's interest in a partnership or a corporation.

LO.4

Compare the income tax basis rules applying to property received by gift and by death.

19-2 INCOME TAX CONCEPTS

19-2a Basis of Property Acquired by Gift

The income tax basis of property acquired by gift depends on whether the donee sells the property for a gain or for a loss.

- The donee's *basis for gain* is the donor's adjusted basis. In the rare case where Federal gift tax is paid as a result of the gift, add the gift tax attributable to the appreciation of the property to the point of the gift (but not to exceed the property's fair market value on the date of the gift). For this purpose, use the *taxable gift* amount (i.e., gift less annual exclusion).[23]

---

[22]§ 2703.

[23]§§ 1015(a) and (d).

Norm receives stock as a gift from Lana. Lana paid $20,000 for the stock, and it was worth $100,000 on the date of the gift. As a result of the transfer, Lana paid a gift tax of $10,000. In arriving at Norm's basis for gain, first compute the gift tax adjustment. Only the portion of the gift tax that is attributable to the appreciation is considered. This portion is determined using the following percentage.

$$\frac{\$80,000 \text{ (appreciation)}}{\$85,000 \text{ (taxable gift; } \$100,000 \text{ less } \$15,000 \text{ annual exclusion)}} = 94\% \text{ (rounded)}$$

Consequently, Norm's income tax basis for gain is $29,400.

Lana's basis	$20,000
Allowable gift tax adjustment (94% × $10,000)	9,400
Basis for gain	$29,400

- The donee's *basis for loss* is the *lesser of* the basis for gain or the fair market value of the property on the date of the gift.

Connie receives stock as a gift from Trevor. The stock cost Trevor $100,000 and had a value of $20,000 on the date of the gift. No gift tax resulted from the transfer. Connie's basis for loss is $20,000—the lesser of $100,000 or $20,000. Her basis for gain is $100,000 (Trevor's cost basis).[24]

When the donee assumes the donor's basis in the property, the donee's holding period includes that of the donor.

19-2b Basis of Property Acquired by Death

Except as otherwise noted in the following sections, the income tax basis of property acquired from a decedent is the fair market value on the date of death or, if elected, on the alternate valuation date. When property has appreciated in value between acquisition and the date of death, the estate or heirs receive a <mark>step-up in basis</mark> for income tax purposes. In other words, the appreciation existing on the date of death escapes the Federal income tax. If, however, the property has declined in value, a <mark>step-down in basis</mark> occurs and built-in losses disappear.

The Big Picture

Return to the facts of *The Big Picture* on p. 19-1. Suppose Martin is considering only the city lot and the marketable securities. A gift of either asset would make $500,000 subject to the Federal gift tax. Under § 1015, Francine's income tax basis would be $100,000 for the city lot. For the securities, however, she would have a dual basis of $900,000 for gain and $500,000 for loss purposes.

If, instead, these assets pass to Francine by Martin's death, she would receive a step-up in basis in the city lot (i.e., from $100,000 to $500,000) but a step-down in basis as to the marketable securities (from $900,000 to $500,000). As a result, Martin should sell the securities while he is alive, so as to take the tax benefit from the $400,000 built-in loss.

The holding period for property acquired from a decedent automatically is treated as long-term.[25]

For property acquired from an estate, where the transferred asset increased the decedent's Federal estate tax after credits, the executor files Form 8971, reporting the estate tax valuation to the IRS and to the recipients of the property. This disclosure helps to ensure that the resulting basis amount matches that of the asset's valuation in the gross estate.[26]

---

[24]If the donee later sells the gift property for less than the donee's basis and for more than its fair market value on date of gift, no gain or loss is recognized. As a result, if Connie in Example 16 sells the gift for less than $100,000 and more than $20,000, there is no recognized gain or loss.

[25]The holding period rules for gift tax purposes are in § 1223(2), while those addressing property acquired by death are in § 1223(11).

[26]§§ 1014(f), 6035.

Jointly Owned Property

If the property does not pass through a decedent's estate, there is no step-up (or step-down) in income tax basis.[27]

EXAMPLE 18

Several years ago, Aaron and Sandra (brother and sister) purchased land for $200,000, listing title as "joint tenants with the right of survivorship." Each furnished one-half of the purchase price. This year, when the land is worth $1,600,000, Aaron dies.

Aaron's estate includes $800,000 as to the land. Sandra's income tax basis in the land is $900,000: [$100,000 (Sandra's original cost basis) + $800,000 (amount passing through Aaron's estate)].

Community Property

A different rule applies when the gross estate includes community property. In this case, the surviving spouse's half of the community takes the same basis as the half included in the deceased spouse's gross estate. This can be a valuable feature of the Federal income tax law.

Community Property and Basis

EXAMPLE 19

Leif and Rosa were husband and wife and lived in a *common law* state. At the time of Leif's death, he owned land (worth $3 million with a basis to him of $1.4 million), which he bequeathed to Rosa. As the property passes through Leif's estate, Rosa receives a step-up in basis to $3 million.

EXAMPLE 20

Assume the same facts as in Example 19, except that Leif and Rosa had always lived in California (a *community property* state). If the $3 million in land is community property, only one-half of this value is included in Leif's gross estate. Because the other half does not pass through Leif's estate (it already belongs to Rosa), is it fair to deny Rosa a new basis in it? By assigning Rosa an income tax basis of $3 million ($1.5 million for Leif's half passing to her plus $1.5 million for her half) and including only $1.5 million in Leif's gross estate, the tax outcome is the same as in Example 19.

Step-Up in Basis and the One-Year Rule

Consider the following situation.

EXAMPLE 21

Gary and Hazel are husband and wife who reside in a common law state. When the couple learns that Hazel has a terminal illness, Gary transfers property (basis of $100,000 and fair market value of $900,000) to her as a gift. Hazel dies within a month, and under the provisions of her will, the property returns to Gary.

What have the parties attempted to accomplish? No gift tax occurs on the transfer from Gary to Hazel because of the application of the marital deduction. Upon Hazel's death, her bequest to Gary does not generate any estate tax because the inclusion of the property in her gross estate is offset by the marital deduction. Under the general basis rules, Gary ends up with the same property, with its basis stepped up to $900,000. As a result, the procedure enables Gary to get a "free" increase in income tax basis of $800,000.

---

[27]For most decedents who died in 2010, no Federal estate tax was imposed. Special rules may apply in determining the income tax basis of such property passing to the heirs.

Instead, a special one-year rule forces Gary (the original donor) to assume the property with the same basis it had to Hazel immediately before her death.[28] Specifically, if an asset is acquired within one year of the decedent's death as a gift, the decedent's basis is assigned to the recipient, and the step-up in basis rules do not apply. So in this case, the property returns to Gary with a basis of $100,000.

Income in Respect of a Decedent

Income in respect of a decedent (IRD) is income earned by a decedent to the point of his or her death but not reportable on the final income tax return under the method of tax accounting used. IRD most frequently arises for decedents using the cash basis of accounting. IRD also occurs, for example, when a taxpayer at the time of death held installment notes receivable on which the gain has been deferred. For both cash and accrual taxpayers, IRD often includes postdeath distributions from retirement plans [e.g., traditional IRA, § 401(k), and other qualified plans]. Distributions from Roth IRAs, though, typically do not constitute IRD.

IRD is included in the gross estate at its fair market value on the appropriate valuation date. However, the income tax basis of the decedent transfers to the estate or heirs. Neither a step-up nor a step-down in basis is available.[29] In addition, the recipient of IRD must classify the resulting gross income in the same manner (e.g., ordinary income or capital gain) as the decedent would have.[30]

The various income tax ramifications of property transferred by gift and by death are reviewed in Concept Summary 19.2.

Concept Summary 19.2

Income Tax Concepts

1. The income tax basis of property acquired by gift is the donor's basis with appropriate adjustment for any gift tax paid. With built-in loss situations, the income tax basis is the fair market value of the property on the date of the gift.

2. The income tax basis of property acquired through the death of the owner is its fair market value on the appropriate estate tax valuation date.

3. No step-up in basis is allowed if the property returns to the donor or donor's spouse within one year.

4. Items of income in respect of a decedent do not undergo a step-up or step-down in basis.

19-3 GIFT PLANNING

LO.5

Explain how gifts can minimize gift taxes and avoid estate taxes.

One of the ways to carry out family tax planning is to start a program of lifetime giving. The objectives of such a program are to minimize transfer taxes while keeping income tax consequences in mind. In general, gift and estate tax planning also is motivated by the following.

- Reduce the present value of any tax liability that is to be incurred. This is accomplished by deferring the tax liability within the family by:
  - Using the marital deduction to move tax liabilities from the death of the first spouse to the death of the second.
  - Using lifetime gifts and asset sales to move assets into younger generations at no or little immediate income or gift tax cost.

---

[28] § 1014(e).
[29] § 1014(c).

[30] § 691(a)(3). See text Section 20-3b for a further discussion of IRD.

- Increase the present value of the transfer tax deductions, exemptions, and exclusions. This is accomplished by:
  - ➤ Making lifetime gifts as early in the donor's life as possible, to maximize and increase the time value of money of the annual gift tax exclusion and the lifetime transfer tax exemption equivalent.
  - ➤ Making certain that the exemption equivalents of both spouses are used in full.
- Maximize the use of valuation and liquidity provisions provided by the Code that benefit the estate and any survivors of the decedent.

19-3a **Minimizing Gift Taxes**

The Federal gift tax can be avoided through proper use of the annual exclusion. Because a new annual exclusion is available each year, spacing gifts over multiple years increases the amount that can be transferred free of gift tax.

Starting in 2013, Cora makes gifts in the amount of the annual exclusion to each of her five grandchildren. Taking into account the changes in the amount of the annual exclusion allowed, Cora will have transferred $500,000 through 2019 with no Federal gift tax consequences.

Years		Amount of Exclusion
2018–2019	$15,000 (annual exclusion) × 5 (number of donees) × 2 (number of years)	$150,000
2013–2017	$14,000 (annual exclusion) × 5 (number of donees) × 5 (number of years)	350,000

For married donors, the election to split gifts can double the amount of a tax-free transfer. Referring to Example 22, if Cora is married and her husband Julio makes the gift-splitting election for each year, $1 million [$500,000 (amount allowed Cora) × 2 (number of donors)] can be transferred with no gift tax consequences.

From a practical standpoint, many donors who want to take advantage of the annual exclusion do *not* want to give cash or near-cash assets (e.g., marketable securities); they may be their chief source of income. Where the value of the gift property substantially exceeds the amount of the annual exclusion, as often is the case with real estate, gifts of a partial interest are an attractive option.

Ajit and Kate want to give a parcel of unimproved land to their three adult children and five grandchildren as equal owners. The land has an adjusted basis of $100,000, is held by Ajit and Kate as community property, and has an appraised value of $475,000 as of December 19, 2018.

On December 23, 2018, Ajit and Kate convey a one-half undivided interest in the land to their children and grandchildren as tenants in common. This is followed by a transfer of the remaining one-half interest on January 3, 2019. Neither transfer causes gift tax; for 2018, the annual exclusion is $240,000 [$30,000 (annual exclusion for two donors) × 8 (number of donees)], and the same amount is used for 2019. So, in a period of two weeks, Ajit and Kate can transfer $480,000 in value, and the land passes to the children free of any Federal tax consequences.

No current income tax consequences result from the couple's gifts. However, had Ajit and Kate first sold the land and then made a gift of the cash proceeds, recognized gain of $375,000 [$475,000 (selling price) − $100,000 (adjusted basis)] would have resulted, with the related tax reducing the cash available for the gifts.

19-3b **Minimizing Estate Taxes**

Future estate taxes are reduced by the making of gifts to the extent that annual exclusions are applied in the current year. But many taxpayers hesitate to make gifts during their lifetime, finding it difficult to part with property "too soon." From a tax planning standpoint, do lifetime gifts offer any tax advantages over transfers at death? A lifetime gift can offer advantages for both the Federal transfer and income taxes.

Avoiding a Transfer Tax on Future Appreciation

If property is expected to appreciate in value, a gift removes the appreciation from the donor's gross estate.

The Big Picture

**EXAMPLE
24**

Return to the facts of *The Big Picture* on p. 19-1. One of the assets Martin is considering giving to Francine is an insurance policy on his life. Although the policy has a current value of only $500,000, it has a maturity value of $3,000,000. By making a gift of $500,000, Martin would save a future inclusion in his gross estate of $3,000,000.

Besides life insurance, other assets that often appreciate in value include real estate, art objects, and special collections (e.g., rare books, coins, and stamps). Assets that will decline in value (e.g., most personal assets, patents, and trademarks) typically are not good candidates for lifetime gifts, as holding such assets over time tends to reduce future estate and gift tax liabilities.

In making these gifts, one needs to consider the financial status of the donee. Will receiving the property create an economic hardship for him or her? The recipient of the family vacation home will have upkeep expenses and property taxes to pay. The donee of an art collection can anticipate maintenance costs including storage fees and provision for security of the property (e.g., insurance against fire and theft).

Unfortunately, the properties most likely to appreciate often are "dry assets" (i.e., those that do not generate income). It may be necessary, therefore, for a donor to plan to make follow-up gifts of cash to mitigate any financial strain placed on the donee by the transfer taxes and other costs that arise from the original gift. Returning to the facts of Example 24, if Martin decides to give Francine the insurance policy, he may need to make annual gifts to her so that she can pay the premiums required to keep the policy from lapsing.

19-3c Income Tax Considerations

LO.6

Recognize when gifts trigger income taxes for the donor.

Income Shifting

One way to lower the overall tax burden on the family unit is to shift capital gain income from high-bracket taxpayers to lower-bracket family members. The maximum rates on dividends and net capital gain provide an excellent opportunity to take advantage of the zero percent rate that normally would apply to certain younger donees. The shifting is accomplished by giving capital assets (frequently securities) to others who then will make the sale and recognize the gain.

**EXAMPLE
25**

The Millers are subject to a 24% marginal Federal income tax rate. They have four daughters who are in graduate school. As each child reaches age 24, they give her appreciated stock with a $30,000 realized gain and a long-term holding period. Then each daughter sells the stock and uses the proceeds to pay off some student loans. The realized gain is recognized and results in a $30,000 net capital gain. If this is the only item of taxable income, the net capital gain will be taxed at a zero percent rate, resulting in no Federal income tax.

Had the Millers sold the stock on their own instead of using it for family gifts, the income tax on each sale would have been $4,500 (15% × $30,000). As a result, the Millers have saved $4,500 in Federal income taxes by making each transfer. Taking into account all four Miller daughters, the total savings amounts to $18,000 ($4,500 × 4).

This process can be repeated with more stock for each daughter in a later year with the same tax effect.

If a gift of property is to shift income to the donee, the transfer must be *complete*.

EXAMPLE 26

Gloria, subject to a 35% marginal income tax rate, owns all of the stock in Orange, an S corporation. Gloria transfers by gift 60% of the Orange stock to her three married children. The children range in age from 24 to 28 and are all in the 12% Federal income tax bracket. After the transfer, Gloria continues to operate the business. No shareholder meetings are held. Except for reporting 60% of the pass-through of Orange's profits, Gloria's children have no contact with the business. Aside from the salary paid to Gloria, Orange makes no cash distributions to its shareholders.

The situation posed in Example 26 occurs frequently and may bring undesirable tax results. If the purported gift by Gloria lacks economic reality and Gloria is the true economic owner of all of Orange's stock, the pass-through to the children is disregarded.[31] The profits are taxed to Gloria at her 35 percent rate rather than to the children at their 12 percent rates. Consequently, the transfer has not accomplished the intended shifting of income.

What can be done to make the transfer in Example 26 tax-effective? First, a distribution of dividends would provide some economic benefit to the children. As the transfer currently is constituted, the children have received an economic detriment, because they must pay income taxes on their share of Orange's pass-through of profits. Second, some steps should be taken to recognize and protect the interests of the children as donees. Shareholder meetings should be held and attendance encouraged.

Income Tax Consequences to the Donor

Generally, a gift of property results in no immediate income tax consequences to the donor. However, a gift of an installment note receivable is a taxable disposition, and the donor is treated as if the note had been sold for its fair market value.[32] As a result, the donor recognizes the deferred profit. In addition:

- Proceeds from installment notes receivable are taxed to whoever collects the notes (the estate or heirs).[33] If the notes are forgiven or canceled by the decedent's will, the income is taxed to the estate.
- Deferred interest income on U.S. savings bonds is taxed to whoever redeems the bonds (the estate or heirs).
- Recapture potential disappears at death.[34] The estate or heirs take the property free of any deduction or credit recapture potential existing at the time of the owner's death.

The Big Picture

EXAMPLE 27

Return to the facts of *The Big Picture* on p. 19-1. Recall that another asset that Martin is considering giving Francine is installment notes receivable. Although the notes have a face amount of $700,000, due to the extended payout period and possibly other factors (e.g., a low interest rate), their current value is only $500,000. Martin's basis in the notes is $200,000. Since the gift is treated as a sale, Martin would incur a taxable gain of $300,000 ($500,000 − $200,000).

Carryover Basis Situations

When considering the income tax effect of a transfer on the donee or heir, the basis rules discussed in text Section 19-2 must be considered. If *appreciated* property is involved, receiving the property at death is preferred to a gift during the donor's lifetime.

---

[31]*Donald O. Kirkpatrick*, 36 TCM 1122, T.C.Memo. 1977–281; *Michael F. Beirne*, 52 T.C. 210 (1969) and 61 T.C. 268 (1973).

[32]§ 453B(a).

[33]The deferred gain element of an installment note is income in respect of a decedent (see the discussions in text Sections 19-2b and 20-3b) and does not receive a step-up in basis at death. § 453B(c).

[34]Contrast this result with what happens when § 1245 or § 1250 property is transferred by gift. There, the recapture potential carries over to the donee. §§ 1245(b)(1) and 1250(d)(1).

The situation may be different, however, when the property to be transferred has *depreciated* in value. Presuming that the transferor cannot take advantage of the built-in loss (e.g., no existing or potential offsetting gains), should the transfer be made by gift or at death?

The Big Picture

EXAMPLE

28

Return to the facts of *The Big Picture* on p. 19-1. Assume that Martin is terminally ill and cannot take advantage of newly incurred capital losses (e.g., he holds excess capital loss carryovers from prior years). Is it preferable for Martin to give the marketable securities to Francine or for them to pass to her at his death?

If Martin *gives* the stock to Francine, she takes the securities with a basis for gain of $900,000 and a basis for loss of $500,000. If Francine receives the property as a result of Martin's death, however, her basis for *both* gain and loss steps down to $500,000. As a result, the gift result might protect Francine from later *gain* on the disposition of the securities.

Effect of Valuation Elections

Because the election of either special use valuation or the alternative valuation date (see text Section 18-1b) reduces the value of the property for estate tax purposes, a lower income tax basis results for the recipient of this property. As a result, any estate tax savings from the valuation election should be contrasted with the income tax consequences (i.e., higher gain or lower loss) when the property is sold. This analysis should be conducted using the present values of the taxes to be incurred.

19-4 ESTATE PLANNING

Estate planning considers the nontax and tax aspects of death. The nontax area identifies steps that can be taken to reduce the costs of probating an estate. The tax area focuses on controlling the amount of the gross estate and maximizing estate tax deductions.

19-4a Probate Costs

LO.7

Illustrate how to reduce probate costs in the administration of an estate.

The probate estate consists of all properties subject to administration by an executor. The administration is conducted under the supervision of a local court, usually called a probate court. In certain states, probate functions are performed by county courts, surrogate courts, or orphan's courts.

Probate costs include attorney fees, accountant fees, appraisal and inventory fees, court costs, expenses incident to the disposition of assets and satisfaction of liabilities, litigation costs needed to resolve will contests, and charges for the preparation of tax returns. Related fees often total 3 to 10 percent of the probate assets of the estate.

A variety of techniques can reduce the probate estate and save probate costs, including:

- Owning property as joint tenants (or tenants by the entirety) with right of survivorship.
- Making life insurance payable to a beneficiary other than the estate.
- Using *payable on death* arrangements with banks or brokers that designate specific beneficiaries to receive assets when an account holder dies.

19-4b Proper Handling of Estate Tax Deductions

LO.8

Apply procedures that reduce estate tax liabilities.

Estate taxes can be reduced either by decreasing the size of the gross estate or by increasing the total allowable deductions. The lower the taxable estate, the less estate tax is generated. Planning with deductions includes:

- Making proper use of the marital deduction.
- Working effectively with the charitable deduction.
- Taking advantage of the bypass amount.
- Optimizing other deductions and losses allowed (discussed in text Section 18-3b).

The Marital Deduction

When planning for the estate tax marital deduction, both tax and nontax factors are taken into account. Taking into account the present value of taxes deferred, taxpayers should try to postpone estate taxation as long as possible. Usually, by maximizing the marital deduction on the death of the first spouse to die, taxes are saved and the surviving spouse can trim his or her future estate by entering into a program of lifetime gifts. By making optimum use of the annual gift tax exclusion, considerable amounts can be shifted without incurring *any* transfer tax.

The Charitable Deduction

As a general guide to obtaining overall tax savings, contributions to charities during a taxpayer's life are preferred over a charitable bequest (a transfer via a will). For example, an individual who gives $200,000 to a qualified charity during his or her life secures an income tax deduction, uses the gift tax deduction to avoid any gift tax, and reduces the gross estate by the amount of the gift. On the other hand, if the $200,000 is transferred by will after the donor's death to the charity, no individual income tax deduction is available, and the amount of the gift is includible in the decedent's gross estate (although later deducted for estate tax purposes). In short, the lifetime contribution provides a double tax benefit (income tax deduction plus reduced estate taxes) at no gift tax cost.

On occasion, a charitable bequest depends on the issuance of a disclaimer by a noncharitable heir.[35] Usually this involves special types of property or collections where the decedent allows a noncharitable heir to choose whether to receive the property or allow it to transfer to the charity.

Use of Disclaimers in Charitable Bequests

 **EXAMPLE 29**

Megan specified in her will that her valuable art collection is to pass to her son Teddy. If Teddy refuses the gift, the collection passes to the local art museum. At the time the will was drawn, Megan knew that Teddy was not interested in owning the collection. If, after Megan's death, Teddy issues a timely disclaimer, the collection passes to the museum, and Megan's estate takes a charitable deduction for its estate tax value.

EXAMPLE 30

Paresh's will specifies that one-half of his disposable estate is to pass to his wife, Amanda. The remainder of his property passes to a specified qualified charitable organization. If Amanda issues a timely disclaimer after Paresh's death, all of the property passes to the charity and qualifies for the charitable deduction.

Has Teddy in Example 29 acted wisely if he issues the disclaimer in favor of the museum? Although the disclaimer will provide Megan's estate with a deduction for the value of the art collection, consider the income tax deduction alternative. If Teddy accepts the bequest, he still can dispose of the collection (and fulfill his mother's philanthropic objectives) through a donation to the museum. As a result, he obtains an income tax deduction of his own. Whether this plan reduces taxes for the family depends on a comparison of the mother's estate tax bracket with the estimated income tax bracket of the son.

The use of a disclaimer in Example 30 would be sheer folly. It would not reduce Paresh's estate tax; it would merely substitute a charitable deduction for the marital deduction. Whether or not Amanda issues a disclaimer, no estate taxes will be due. Amanda should accept her bequest and, if she is so inclined, make lifetime gifts of it to a qualified charity. In so doing, she could generate an income tax deduction for herself.

---

[35]As noted in text Section 18-2b, a disclaimer is a refusal to accept the property. If the disclaimer is timely made, the property is not treated as having passed through the person issuing the disclaimer, and a gift tax is avoided.

Taking Advantage of the Bypass Amount

The **bypass amount**, also known as the exclusion amount or the exemption equivalent, is the amount that can pass free of a transfer tax due to the unified credit. Generally, this amount of property should be transferred to children or other parties for whom the transfer does not produce an estate or gift tax deduction. The bypass amount increased significantly as a result of 2017 tax law changes.

Year	Bypass Amount
2015	$ 5,430,000
2016	5,450,000
2017	5,490,000
2018	11,180,000
2019	11,400,000

Spousal Transfers In the past, a bypass amount frequently was wasted when the first spouse died. Human nature often compels a spouse to leave all of his or her assets to the survivor.

Ethan and Hope are married, and each has a net worth of $3.5 million. Upon Ethan's prior death in 2009, his will passed his entire net worth to Hope; this often is called an "I Love You will." Although Ethan avoided any Federal estate tax due to the marital deduction, he wasted his bypass amount and concentrated additional assets in Hope's potential estate.

Under current Federal estate tax law, the bypass amount is "portable," meaning that a **deceased spouse's unused exclusion (DSUE)** amount is available to the surviving spouse.[36] This provision effectively treats a married couple as a single unit for estate tax purposes; lifetime transfers between spouses are not necessary to make use of the combined bypass amounts. Portability is not allowed for the exemption in computing the tax on generation-skipping transfers.

Assume the same facts as in Example 31, except that Ethan dies in 2017 with a net worth of $5.49 million, all of which he passes to Hope. Presuming a proper election was made on his return, Ethan's DSUE amount transfers to his wife. Should Hope die in 2019, her exclusion amount would be $16.89 million [$5.49 million (Ethan's DSUE amount) + $11.4 million (her own exclusion amount)].

If a surviving spouse is predeceased by more than one spouse, the DSUE amount that is available for the surviving spouse is limited to the unused exclusion of the *last* surviving spouse.

Use of Disclaimers to Maximize the Benefits of the Bypass Amount In some cases, it may be possible to control the bypass amount by the careful use of disclaimers.

Using Disclaimers

Deepak dies in 2019 leaving an estate of $15 million. He is survived by his wife, Emma, and an adult daughter, Riya. Deepak's will passes $6 million to Emma and the remainder ($9 million) to Riya. Emma disclaims $2.4 million of her inheritance, increasing the amount passing to Riya at no Federal estate tax cost.

Assume the same facts as in Example 33, except that Deepak's will passes $12,000,000 to Riya and the remainder to Emma. Riya disclaims $600,000 of her inheritance, thereby reducing the Federal estate tax to zero, as the disclaimed amount passes to the surviving spouse.

---

[36] § 2010(c). Portability is available for those who die after 2010.

Both examples reflect the wise use of disclaimers. In Example 33, Emma's disclaimer has the effect of increasing Riya's inheritance from Deepak to $11.4 million, and optimizing the allowable bypass amount for the year. If the disclaimer is not desired and only $9 million passes to Riya, the $2.4 million unused bypass amount will not be wasted if it passes to Emma as a DSUE.

In Example 34, Riya eliminates any estate tax on $600,000 (the excess over the $11.4 million bypass amount) by shifting it to Emma, the remainder beneficiary. Because that party is the surviving spouse, the $600,000 is sheltered from current estate tax by the marital deduction.

Proper Handling of Other Deductions and Losses under §§ 2053 and 2054

Many estate-related deductions and losses may be claimed either as estate tax deductions or as income tax deductions by the estate on the fiduciary return (Form 1041), but not both.[37] The income tax deduction is not allowed unless the estate tax deduction is waived. It is possible for these deductions to be apportioned between the two returns.

In situations where the taxpayer has a terminal illness (i.e., death is imminent), it may be possible to shift some upcoming expenses to obtain a lifetime income tax benefit. For example, accrued medical expenses can be paid prior to death if they will be deductible on the decedent's final income tax return. The funds used to pay these expenses are not part of the gross estate, so the taxable estate is correspondingly reduced, and the estate tax savings still exist. Rate differentials and a present value analysis should be considered before these techniques are carried out.

LO.9

List and review procedures to increase the liquidity of an estate.

19-4c **Providing Estate Liquidity**

Recognizing the Problem

Even with effective predeath family tax planning directed toward a minimization of transfer taxes, the smooth administration of an estate requires a certain degree of liquidity. After all, probate costs will be incurred, and most important of all, estate tax liabilities must be paid. In the meantime, the surviving spouse and dependent beneficiaries may need financial support. Without funds to satisfy these claims, estate assets may need to be sold at sacrifice prices, and most likely, the decedent's estate tax planning is compromised.

EXAMPLE 35

At the time of Ruth's death, her estate was made up almost entirely of a large ranch currently being operated by Jim, one of Ruth's two sons. Because the ranch had been in the family for several generations and was a successful business, Ruth hoped that Jim would continue its operation and share the profits with Bob, her other son.

Unfortunately, Bob, upon learning that his mother had died without a will, forced a split of the property and sold his share. Additional land was sold to pay for administration expenses and estate taxes. After all of the sales had taken place, the ranch land that remained for Jim could not be operated profitably, and he was forced to give up the family business.

What type of predeath planning might have avoided the result reached in Example 35? Certainly, Ruth made a serious error in dying without a will. A carefully crafted will could have precluded Bob's actions, and perhaps kept more of the ranch property intact. The ranch could have been placed in trust, life estate to Jim and Bob, remainder to their children.[38] With this arrangement, Bob would have been unable to sell the trust principal (the ranch).

In addition, Ruth should have recognized and provided for the cash needs of the estate. Life insurance payable to her estate, although increasing the gross estate, could have eased or solved the problem. This assumes that she was insurable and that the cost of the insurance would not be prohibitive.

---

[37]§ 642(g) and Reg. § 20.2053–1(d).

[38]These terms are defined and illustrated in text Section 20-1.

Being able to defer the payment of estate taxes may be an invaluable option for an estate that lacks cash or near-cash assets (e.g., marketable securities). Two major possibilities exist.

- A discretionary extension of time (§ 6161).
- An extension of time when the estate consists largely of an interest in a closely held business (§ 6166).

Discretionary Extension of Time to Pay Estate Taxes—§ 6161

An executor or administrator may request an extension of time for paying the estate tax for a period not to exceed 10 years from the date fixed for the payment. The IRS grants these requests when there is "reasonable cause." Reasonable cause is not limited to a showing of undue hardship. It includes cases where the executor or administrator is unable to easily collect liquid assets because they are located in several jurisdictions. It also includes situations where the estate is largely made up of assets generating payments in the future (e.g., annuities, copyright royalties, contingent fees, or accounts receivable), or where the assets that must be liquidated to pay the estate tax need to be sold at a sacrifice or in a depressed market.

Extension of Time When the Estate Consists Largely of an Interest in a Closely Held Business—§ 6166

Congress always has been sympathetic to the plight of an estate that consists of an interest in a closely held business, as was seen in text Section 19-1c regarding special use estate tax valuation. The immediate imposition of the estate tax on a continuing business may force its liquidation at distress prices or cause the interest to be sold to outside parties.

A possible resolution of the problem is to use § 6166, which requires the IRS to accept a deferred payment process for the estate tax related to the business (5 interest-only payments, followed by no more than 10 installment payments of the estate tax). This delay can enable the business to generate enough income to buy out the deceased owner's interest without disruption of operations or other financial sacrifice.

In order to use this payment deferral, the decedent's interest in a farm or other closely held business must *exceed* 35 percent of the decedent's **adjusted gross estate**.[39] The adjusted gross estate is the gross estate less the sum allowable as deductions for expenses, indebtedness, and taxes, and for any casualty and theft losses that occur during the administration of an estate.

For this purpose, an interest in a closely held business includes:[40]

- Any sole proprietorship.
- An interest in a partnership carrying on a trade or business, if 20 percent of the capital interest in the partnership is included in the gross estate *or* the partnership has 45 or fewer partners.
- Stock in a corporation carrying on a trade or business, if 20 percent or more of the value of the voting stock of the corporation is included in the gross estate *or* the corporation has 45 or fewer shareholders.

In meeting these requirements, a decedent and his or her surviving spouse are treated as one owner (shareholder or partner) if the interest is held as community property, tenants in common, joint tenants, or tenants by the entirety. Attribution from family members is allowed.[41]

---

[39]§ 6166(a)(1).
[40]§ 6166(b)(1).

[41]As described in § 267(c)(4).

Decedent Lina held a 15% capital interest in the Wren Partnership. Her son Parag holds another 10%. Wren had 46 partners including Lina and Parag. Because Parag's interest is attributed to Lina, the estate is deemed to hold a 25% interest, and Wren (for this purpose) has only 45 partners; as a result, the deferral election is available.

In satisfying the more-than-35-percent test, interests in more than one closely held business are aggregated when the decedent's gross estate includes 20 percent or more of the value of each business.[42]

Henry's estate includes stock in Green Corporation and Brown Corporation, each of which qualifies as a closely held business. If the stock held in each entity represents 20% or more of the total value outstanding, these interests can be combined for purposes of the more-than-35% test.

When the election to defer estate tax payments is made, interest at the rate of 2 percent is paid.[43] The 2 percent interest rate applies only to the first $1 million of estate tax value, as indexed for 2019 to $1.55 million. Finally, when considering this option, taxpayers should examine estate assets to ensure that the 35 percent test will be met. Lifetime gifts of marketable securities and life insurance should be considered.

Concept Summary 19.3

Estate and Gift Tax Planning

1. In reducing the present value of any estate or gift taxes, one should take advantage of the annual exclusion and the election to split gifts. In the case of a single asset with high value (e.g., land), annual gifts of partial interests should be considered.

2. Gifts can reduce later estate taxes. This is accomplished by giving away assets that will appreciate in value (e.g., life insurance policies, artwork, and rare collections).

3. Gifts can relieve the income tax burden on the family unit. This objective is accomplished by shifting the income from the gift property to family members who are in a lower income tax bracket. In this regard, make sure the gift is *complete* and circumvents kiddie tax treatment.

4. Avoid gifts of property that result in income tax consequences to the donor.

5. Potential *probate costs* can be an important consideration in meaningful estate planning. Some procedures that reduce these costs include joint tenancies with the right of survivorship, living trusts, and predeath dispositions of out-of-state real estate.

6. A program of lifetime gifts and proper use of valuation techniques will reduce a decedent's *gross* estate. Further planning can reduce the *taxable* estate by proper handling of estate tax deductions.

7. For a married decedent, the most important deduction is the *marital deduction*. The major tax objective of the marital deduction is to defer estate taxes.

8. Lifetime charitable contributions are preferable to transfers by death. The lifetime contributions provide the donor with an income tax deduction, and the amount donated is not included in the gross estate.

9. The *disclaimer* procedure can be used to control (either lower or raise) the amount of the marital deduction and to increase the amount of the charitable deduction. Disclaimers can also be effective in taking full advantage of the available bypass amount.

10. Portability provisions allow both spouses to make full use of their bypass (exclusion) amounts. After the death of one spouse, for example, the surviving spouse can add to the basic exclusion amount the deceased spouse's unused exclusion (DSUE) amount.

11. Gift planning can help ease potential *estate liquidity* problems. After death, the executor of a closely held business owner can elect to make installment payments of deferred estate taxes over an extended period of time.

---

[42]§ 6166(c).

[43]§ 6601(j)(1).

LIFETIME GIVING—THE GOOD AND THE BAD

Martin is considering several tax-effective ideas.

The gift of the life insurance policy is very attractive. By making a gift of $500,000, Martin avoids $3 million being subject to the Federal estate tax (see Example 24).

The marketable securities might better be sold to enable Martin to recognize an income tax loss of $400,000. However, a gift could preserve some of the built-in loss for the donee (see Example 28). Otherwise, there will be a step-down in income tax basis if Martin dies with these securities.

Under the circumstances, the gift of the city lot shifts to the donee a built-in gain of $400,000. Moreover, if this property passes by death, it receives a step-up in basis (see Example 17), and the gain component disappears. In either case (i.e., gift or inheritance), the amount subject to a transfer tax is $500,000.

The installment notes receivable present a no-win situation. If Martin transfers them by gift, he must recognize income on the transfer (see Example 27). If they pass by death, however, either the estate or the heirs will recognize the deferred gain. As the gain constitutes income in respect of a decedent, there is no step-up in basis due to Martin's death.

JUPITERIMAGES/GETTY IMAGES

Key Terms

Adjusted gross estate, 19-21

Blockage rule, 19-8

Buy-sell agreement, 19-8

Bypass amount, 19-19

Cross-purchase buy-sell agreement, 19-8

Deceased spouse's unused exclusion (DSUE), 19-19

Entity buy-sell agreement, 19-8

Probate costs, 19-17

Special use value, 19-5

Step-down in basis, 19-11

Step-up in basis, 19-11

Discussion Questions

1. **LO.1** Discuss the relevance of the following in defining "fair market value" for Federal gift and estate tax purposes.

   a. Code § 2031(b).

   b. The definition contained in Reg. § 20.2031–1(b).

   c. The sentimental value of the property being valued.

   d. Tangible personalty sold as a result of a Craigslist offer.

   e. Sporadic sales (occurring on other than the valuation date) of stocks traded in an over-the-counter stock exchange.

2. **LO.1** Six years ago, Alvin loaned his prospective brother-in-law, Bruno, $20,000.   *Critical Thinking*
   The money was used to help Bruno pay for the wedding to Alvin's sister Kitty. Shortly after the wedding, it was discovered that Bruno already was married to someone else. Before Bruno could be indicted for bigamy, he disappeared and has not been heard from since. In the current year, Alvin dies still holding Bruno's note. For tax purposes, what do you suggest as to the handling of Bruno's note?

3.   **LO.1** Brian creates a trust, life estate to Freda, remainder on Freda's death to Daniel.

   a.   Presuming that the trust is irrevocable, how is the value of each gift determined?

   b.   Which gift, if any, qualifies for the annual exclusion?

   c.   If Freda is Brian's wife, does this transfer qualify Brian for a marital deduction? Why or why not?

4.   **LO.3** In determining the value of goodwill attributable to stock in a closely held corporation, comment on the following factors.

   a.   The corporation's average profit figure includes large gains from the sale of assets not related to the business conducted.

   b.   The salary structure of the owner-employees is low when compared to comparable businesses.

   c.   The rate of return used by the IRS for this type of business is too high.

   d.   The deceased owner was not active in the operation of the business.

5.   **LO.3** The blockage rule most often is applied to estates that own large amounts of stocks or securities.

   a.   What is the justification for applying a blockage discount?

   b.   Could the blockage rule be applied when other assets are involved? Explain.

Critical Thinking   6.   **LO.3** One of the major assets in John's estate is stock in Falcon Corporation, a closely held investment company. Falcon has a large portfolio of ExxonMobil stock, acquired when crude oil was selling for under $20 a barrel. In valuing the Falcon stock for estate tax purposes, what considerations should you address?

7.   **LO.3** The Sullivan family has developed a profitable business in which all adult members participate. They would like to make sure that the business stays in the family in the event of any future negative event (e.g., death, divorce, or other discord). What do you suggest?

Critical Thinking   8.   **LO.4** Katelyn receives stock in Kite Corporation as a gift from her father, which she sells four months later. Although Katelyn sold the stock for more than it was worth when she received it as a gift, her accountant tells her that no recognized gain results.

   a.   Under what circumstances is her accountant correct?

   b.   Suppose Katelyn had received the Kite stock by inheritance, not by gift. Now what should her accountant advise?

Critical Thinking   9.   **LO.4** When Mason learns that he has a terminal illness, his financial adviser recommends that he sell all of his investments that have a realized loss. Is this good advice? Explain.

Critical Thinking   10.   **LO.4** Christopher has told the beneficiaries of his Roth and traditional IRAs that they will receive the distributions from these plans free of any tax. Christopher bases his advice on the "step-up" in basis that takes place when appreciated property is passed by death. Comment on the accuracy of this advice.

11.   **LO.5** April is considering making gifts to her granddaughter, Paige, who just graduated from college. Among the assets April has in mind are an insurance policy on her own life and the family beach house. Could gifts of these items create a problem for Paige? Explain.

12.   **LO.4, 6** For income tax purposes, what difference does it make to the parties (i.e., transferor and transferee) whether the following assets are transferred by gift or by death?

   a.   Installment notes receivable.

   b.   Property with depreciation recapture potential.

13. **LO.6** Charles Horn wants his daughter Sharon to receive stock that he owns in Crimson Corporation. He acquired the stock two years ago at a cost of $800,000, and it currently has a fair market value of $650,000. Charles has made prior taxable gifts and is in poor health. He seeks your advice as to whether he should gift the stock to Sharon or pass it to her under his will. Charles has a large capital loss carryforward and has no prospect for any capital gains.

Critical Thinking

Communications

   a. Write a letter to Charles regarding the tax implications of the alternatives he has suggested. His address is 648 Scenic Drive, Chattanooga, TN 37403.

   b. Prepare a memo for your firm's tax research files on this matter.

14. **LO.8** What is the *bypass amount*? How can it be utilized effectively through the use of disclaimers in the case of:

   a. A surviving spouse?

   b. The estate of the predeceased spouse (i.e., electing the DSUE)?

   c. Nonspousal heirs?

Computational Exercises

15. **LO.1** When Rama died in the current year, he owned shares of Orange Corporation which are traded in the over-the-counter market. The market trades before and after Rama's date of death occurred as follows.

	Per-Share Mean Selling Price
Six days before death	$400
Four days after death	450

   What value per share should be included in Rama's gross estate?

16. **LO.1** Jim creates an irrevocable trust with $1 million in securities. Under the trust terms, Alice (age 40) receives a life estate and Bernice (age 10) receives the remainder interest. The appropriate IRS valuation table reflects a remainder factor of 0.05347 for age 10 and 0.18619 for age 40.

   a. What is Jim's gift to Bernice?

   b. Is the annual exclusion available for the gift to Bernice?

   c. If Alice is Jim's wife, does Jim's gift to her qualify for the marital deduction?

17. **LO.1** Fred creates an irrevocable trust with $1 million in cash, income payable to Terri (age 13) for 10 years, remainder to Madison (age 30). The appropriate IRS Table B for a term certain remainder factor is 0.613913 (for 10 years) and 0.231377 (for 30 years).

   a. What is Fred's gift to Terri?

   b. Does the gift qualify for the annual exclusion?

   c. If Madison is Fred's wife, does the gift to her generate a marital deduction?

18. **LO.2** At the time of his death in 2019, Donald owned a farm (a qualified, closely held business) with a most suitable use value of $5 million and a current use value of $3.5 million.

   a. If the special-use valuation election is made, Donald's gross estate must include how much as to the farm?

   b. What if the farm had a current use value of $4 million (not $3.5 million)?

19. **LO.3** At the time of her death, Betty owned 60% of the stock of Crane Corporation. Over the past five years, Crane reported an average net profit of $150,000, and the book value of its stock is $500,000. Assume that 6% is an appropriate after-tax rate of return for Crane's type of business.

a.   What is the amount of Crane's goodwill?

b.   How much as to the Crane stock is included in Betty's gross estate?

20. **LO.4** Merle gives stock to her son Marvin. The stock has a basis to Merle of $200,000 and a value of $180,000 on the date of the gift. No gift tax was incurred on the transfer. What are Marvin's income tax consequences if he later sells the stock for:

a. $170,000?

b. $190,000?

c. $210,000?

21. **LO.4** Tom and Elizabeth purchase land for $1,000,000—Tom furnishes $400,000 and Elizabeth $600,000 of the purchase price. Title to the property is held as joint tenants with right of survivorship. Elizabeth dies first ten years later when the land is worth $2,000,000.

a.   How much of the property is included in Elizabeth's gross estate?

b.   What is Tom's income tax basis in the property?

22. **LO.5** During 2019, Vasu wants to take advantage of the annual exclusion and make gifts to his 6 married children (including their spouses) and his 12 minor grandchildren.

a.   How much property can Vasu give away in 2019 without creating a taxable gift?

b.   How does your answer change if Vasu's wife, Coleen, elects to join in making the gifts?

23. **LO.4, 6** Just prior to a major medical procedure, Cody gives his son, Martin, stock in Robin Corporation (fair market value of $500,000 and basis of $700,000). At the time of the gift, Cody held some unused capital losses. The surgery is unsuccessful, and after Cody's death, Martin sells the stock for $800,000.

a.   What is the income tax result for Martin?

b.   What if the gift had not been made and the stock passed to Martin as a bequest from Cody?

24. **LO.8** Right before his death from a terminal affliction, Ed makes a gift of $500,000 cash that he had planned to bequeath to the church anyway. Presuming Ed had a marginal Federal income tax rate of 35% and his Federal estate tax bracket is 40%, describe the tax effect of his lifetime transfer.

Problems

25. **LO.1** Barry creates a trust with property valued at $7 million. Under the terms of the trust instrument, Michelle (age 48) receives a life estate, while Terry (age 24) receives the remainder interest. In the month the trust is created, the interest rate is 4.4%. Determine the value of Barry's gifts.

26. **LO.1** Arlene creates a trust with assets worth $1 million. Under the terms of the trust, Tracy (age 15) receives the income for eight years, remainder to Dawn (age 34). In the month the trust is created, the interest rate is 4.2%. Determine the value of Arlene's gifts.

27. **LO.1** Dale (age 68) creates a trust with assets worth $5 million. Under the terms of the trust, Dale retains a life estate with the remainder passing to Nicole (age 34) upon his death. In the month the trust is created, the interest rate is 4.8%.

a.   Determine the amount of Dale's gift. Of his taxable gift.

b.   Does the answer in part (a) change if Nicole is Dale's wife? (Refer to text Section 18-3b, if necessary.)

28. **LO.2** In each of the following independent situations, determine the valuation to be used for estate tax purposes if § 2032A is elected. All deaths occurred in 2019.

Decedent	Most Suitable Use Value	Special Use Value
Perry	$3,000,000	$3,500,000
Hopkins	3,000,000	1,500,000
Morris	5,000,000	2,000,000
Allen	5,000,000	4,200,000

29. **LO.3** At her death, Abigail owned 55% of the stock in Finch Corporation, with the balance held by family members. In the past five years, Finch has earned average net profits of $1.6 million, and on the date of Abigail's death, the book value of its stock is $3.8 million. An appropriate rate of return for the type of business Finch is in is 8%.

    a. Assuming that goodwill exists, what is the value of the Finch stock?

    b. What factors could be present to reduce the value of such goodwill?

30. **LO.4** Clinton makes a gift of stock (basis of $600,000 and fair market value of $500,000) to Morgan. Compute Morgan's gain or loss if she later sells the stock for:

    a. $650,000.

    b. $550,000.

    c. $480,000.

31. **LO.4, 5, 6** Ted and Marge Dean are married and always have lived in a community property state. Ted (age 92) suffers from numerous disorders and is frequently ill, while Marge (age 70) is in good health. The Deans currently need $500,000 to meet living expenses, make debt payments, and pay Ted's backlog of medical expenses. They are willing to sell any one of the following assets.

    Decision Making

    Communications

	Adjusted Basis	Fair Market Value
Wren Corporation stock	$200,000	$500,000
Gull Corporation stock	600,000	500,000
Unimproved land	650,000	500,000

    The stock investments are part of the Deans' community property, while the land is Ted's separate property that he inherited from his mother. If the land is not sold, Ted is considering making a gift of it to Marge.

    a. Write a letter to the Deans advising them on these matters. Their address is 290 Cedar Road, Carson, CA 90747.

    b. Prepare a memo on this matter for your firm's tax research files.

32. **LO.4** In July, Lily gives Larry a house (basis of $200,000; fair market value of $650,000) to be used as his personal residence. Before his death 11 months later, Larry installs a tennis court in the backyard at a cost of $25,000. The residence is worth $670,000 when Larry dies. Determine the income tax basis of the property to Lily, who received the house back under terms of Larry's will.

33. **LO.5** Bill and Ellen are husband and wife with five married children and eight grandchildren. Commencing in December 2019, they would like to transfer a tract of land (worth $1.2 million) equally to their children (including spouses) and grandchildren as quickly as possible without making a taxable gift. What do you suggest?

    Critical Thinking

34. **LO.2, 5** At the time of her death in 2019, Wanda has an adjusted gross estate of $6.5 million. Her estate includes the family farm, with a most suitable use value of $3.3 million and a current use value of $2.3 million. The farm is inherited

by Jim, Wanda's son, who has worked it for her since 2005. Jim plans to continue farming there indefinitely.

    a.   Based on the information given, is the § 2032A election available to Wanda's estate?

    b.   If so, what estate tax value is used for the farm if the election is made?

    c.   Express your solution to part (b) as a Microsoft Excel command.

35. **LO.4, 6** Last year Salvador sold a tract of land (basis of $1 million) to Kate (an unrelated party) for $4 million, with a cash down payment of $1 million and notes for the balance. The notes carry a 3.5% rate of interest and mature annually at $1 million each over three years.

    Salvador did not elect out of the installment method. Before any of the notes mature and when they have a fair market value of $2.8 million, Salvador dies and the notes pass to his estate. The executor sells the notes for their fair market value. What is the Federal estate and income tax result?

36. **LO.7** At the time of her death, Ariana held the following assets.

	Fair Market Value
Personal residence (title listed as "Ariana and Peter, tenants by the entirety with right of survivorship")	$900,000
Savings account (listed as "Ariana and Rex, joint tenants with right of survivorship") with funds provided by Rex	40,000
Certificate of deposit (listed as "Ariana, payable on proof of death to Rex") with funds provided by Ariana	100,000
Unimproved real estate (title listed as "Ariana and Rex, equal tenants in common")	500,000
Insurance policy on Ariana's life, issued by Lavender Company (Ariana's estate is the designated beneficiary)	300,000
Insurance policy on Ariana's life, issued by Crimson Company (Rex is the designated beneficiary, but Ariana can change beneficiaries)	400,000

Assuming that Peter and Rex survive Ariana, how much is included in Ariana's *probate estate*? Ariana's *gross estate*? (Refer to text Section 18-3a as needed.)

37. **LO.8** In terms of the Federal income and transfer taxes, comment on what is accomplished in the following disclaimer situations occurring in 2019.

    a.   Lester dies without a will and is survived by a daughter, Nora, and a grandson, Nick. The major asset in Lester's estate is stock worth $3.5 million. As Nora is already well-off and in ill health, she disclaims Lester's property.

    b.   Under her will, Audrey's estate is to pass $16 million to her son, Raymond, and the $3 million remainder to her husband, George. Raymond disclaims $4.6 million of his inheritance.

    c.   Under Isaac's will, $4 million is to pass to his wife Brenda, and the $9 million remainder to his daughter Sybil. Brenda disclaims $2.4 million of her inheritance.

    d.   Under Tricia's will, her $3 million cubist art collection is to pass to her husband, Leroy. If Leroy disclaims the collection, it passes to the San Francisco Museum of Modern Art. Leroy neither understands nor admires this type of art.

38. **LO.8** In each of the following *independent situations*, what bypass (exclusion) amount is available to Ava's estate when she dies in 2019? Assume that any appropriate procedures are followed and that elections are made to transfer to Ava any DSUE amount of Al, her deceased husband.

a.   Al died in 2015 and did not use any of his bypass amount.

b.   Continue with part (a). Ava remarried in 2016, and Andy, her second husband, had used $1 million of his bypass amount on prior Federal gift tax returns. Andy predeceases Ava in June 2017.

c.   Construct a Microsoft Excel command that will produce the correct answer for both parts (a) and (b).

39. **LO.9** At the time of his death, Clint recorded an adjusted gross estate of $6.2 million. Included in the estate is a 15% capital interest in a partnership. Clint's interest is valued at $2.6 million. Except for Clint's daughter Phoebe, none of the other 48 partners are related to him. Phoebe holds a 10% capital interest. Does Clint's estate qualify for the § 6166 election? Explain.

40. **LO.9** At the time of her death, June had an adjusted gross estate of $16,000,000. Included in the estate were the following business interests.

	Fair Market Value
A 30% capital interest in the JZ Partnership	$5,700,000
A 25% interest (i.e., 250 shares out of 1,000) in Silver Corporation	500,000
A catering service operated as a sole proprietorship	950,000

The JZ Partnership has 32 partners, while Silver Corporation has a total of 30 shareholders. None of the other partners or shareholders are related to June. Can June's estate qualify for an election under § 6166? Explain.

Research Problems

Note: Solutions to the Research Problems can be prepared by using the Thomson Reuters Checkpoint™ online tax research database, which accompanies this textbook. Solutions can also be prepared by using research materials found in a typical tax library.

THOMSON REUTERS
CHECKPOINT™

Research Problem 1. On June 1, Mario entered into a contract to sell real estate for $1,000,000 (adjusted basis $200,000). The sale was conditioned on a rezoning of the property for commercial use. A $50,000 deposit placed in escrow by the purchaser was refundable in the event the rezoning was not accomplished.

Critical Thinking

Mario died unexpectedly on November 1. After considerable controversy, the rezoning application was approved on November 10, and two days later, $950,000 was paid to Mario's estate in full satisfaction of the purchase price. Discuss the estate and income tax consequences of this scenario, assuming that the sale of the real estate occurred:

a. After Mario's death.

b. Before Mario's death.

When do you think the sale occurred? Why?

Partial list of research aids:
§§ 691 and 1014.
George W. Keck, 49 T.C. 313 (1968), *rev'd* 69–2 USTC ¶9626, 24 AFTR 2d 69–5554, 415 F.2d 531 (CA–6, 1969).
Trust Company of Georgia v. Ross, 68–1 USTC ¶9133, 21 AFTR 2d 311, 392 F.2d 694 (CA–5, 1967).

Use internet tax resources to address the following questions. Look for reliable websites and blogs of the IRS and other government agencies, media outlets, businesses, tax professionals, academics, think tanks, and political outlets.

Data Analytics

Communications

Research Problem 2. Consider the Deceased Spouse Unused Exclusion amount. For the last three years, on one graph, show the number of returns that included such an amount, and the dollar amount of such exclusions claimed. Comment on the size of the estate that tends to use the DSUE provision. Send your results to your instructor.

Communications

Research Problem 3. For your jurisdiction, find the name of the court that handles bequests and inheritances, the maximum fee that can be charged against the probate estate, and the deadlines for filing various documents with the court. *Hint:* Look at the web pages of several probate attorneys in your area. Summarize your comments in an e-mail to your instructor.

Becker CPA Review Questions

1. During the current year, Diane Stevens made two gifts to her son Greg. The first gift was ABC stock with a value at the date of the gift of $5,000. Diane's basis in ABC was $2,000. The second gift, in the same year, was XYZ stock with a value of $3,000 at the date of the gift and a basis to Diane of $4,000. For gift tax purposes, what is the value of the gifts made by Diane to Greg?

	Value of ABC Stock	Value of XYZ Stock
a.	$5,000	$4,000
b.	$5,000	$3,000
c.	$3,000	$0
d.	$2,000	$0

CHAPTER

20

Income Taxation of Trusts and Estates

LEARNING OBJECTIVES: *After completing Chapter 20, you should be able to:*

LO.1 Use working definitions with respect to trusts, estates, beneficiaries, and other parties.

LO.2 Identify the steps in determining the accounting and taxable income of a trust or an estate and the related taxable income of the beneficiaries.

LO.3 Illustrate the uses and implications of distributable net income.

LO.4 Use the special rules that apply to trusts where the creator (grantor) of the trust retains certain rights.

LO.5 Apply the fiduciary income tax rules in a manner that minimizes the income taxation of trusts and estates and still accomplishes the intended objectives of the grantor or decedent.

CHAPTER OUTLINE

DAVE & LES JACOBS/BLEND IMAGES/GETTY IMAGES

SETTING UP A TRUST TO PROTECT A FAMILY

Anna Jiang is the main breadwinner in her family, which includes her husband Tom, a social worker, and two children, Bobby, age 6, and Sally, age 8. Anna has accumulated about $2 million in after-tax investment accounts, largely made up of growth stocks that do not regularly pay dividends; she inherited most of these securities when her grandmother died about five years ago. Anna has addressed the problem of probate costs through joint property ownership, life insurance policies, and beneficiary arrangements for her retirement plans. She and Tom update their wills every five years or so.

Because there is a history of Alzheimer's disease in her family, Anna Jiang wants to make certain that, if she becomes unable to work and cannot manage her financial assets, Tom and the children will have adequate cash flow from the investment assets. In addition, one of Anna's colleagues at the office suggests that Anna should set up a trust to take care of her family in case a medical problem ever arises.

Read the chapter and formulate your response.

axpayers create trusts for a variety of reasons. Some trusts are established primarily for tax purposes, but most are designed to accomplish a specific financial goal or to provide for the orderly management of assets in case of an emergency. Because a trust is a separate tax entity, its gross income and deductions must be measured and an annual tax return must be filed. Similarly, when an individual dies, a legal entity is created in the form of his or her estate. This chapter examines the rules related to the income taxation of trusts and estates.

20-1 AN OVERVIEW OF FIDUCIARY TAXATION

When a trust or estate is involved, a taxpayer has put a third party into a **fiduciary** relationship, where the third party (i.e., the trustee or executor) is required to act on the behalf (and for the benefit) of the taxpayer who assigned the fiduciary power to them. The fiduciary essentially acts in the place of the decedent or the creator of the trust, for instance, in making investment decisions and meeting financial obligations.

The income taxation of trusts and estates is governed by Subchapter J of Chapter 1 of the Internal Revenue Code, §§ 641 through 692. Certain similarities are apparent between Subchapter J and the income taxation of individuals (e.g., the definitions of gross income and deductible expenditures), partnerships and limited liability entities (e.g., the pass-through principle), and S corporations (e.g., the pass-through principle and the trust or estate as a separate taxable entity). Trusts also involve several important new concepts, however, including the determination of *distributable net income* and the *tier system* of distributions to beneficiaries.

Exhibit 20.1 lists some of the more common reasons that might prompt an individual to create a trust, and Exhibit 20.2 illustrates the structure of a typical trust and estate.

20-1a What Is a Trust?

The Code does not contain a definition of a trust; instead, trusts are defined and governed by state law. However, the term usually refers to an arrangement created by a will or by an *inter vivos* (lifetime) declaration through which trustees take title to property for the purpose of protecting or conserving it for the beneficiaries.[1] Usually, trust operations are controlled by the trust document and by the fiduciary laws of the state in which the trust documents are executed.

LO.1

Use working definitions with respect to trusts, estates, beneficiaries, and other parties.

EXHIBIT 20.1	Common Motivations for Creating a Trust
Type of Trust	**Financial and Other Goals**
Life insurance trust	Holds life insurance policies on the insured, removes the proceeds of the policies from the gross estate (if an irrevocable trust), and safeguards against receipt of the proceeds by a young or inexperienced beneficiary.
"Living" (revocable) trust	Manages assets, reduces probate costs, provides privacy for asset disposition, protects against medical or other emergencies, and provides relief from the necessity of day-to-day management of the underlying assets. No estate tax savings.
Trust for minors	Provides funds for a college education or other needs of the minor and transfers accumulated income without permanently parting with the underlying assets.
Divorce trust	Manages the assets of an ex-spouse and ensures that they are distributed in a timely fashion to specified beneficiaries (e.g., as alimony or child support).

---

[1]Reg. § 301.7701–4(a).

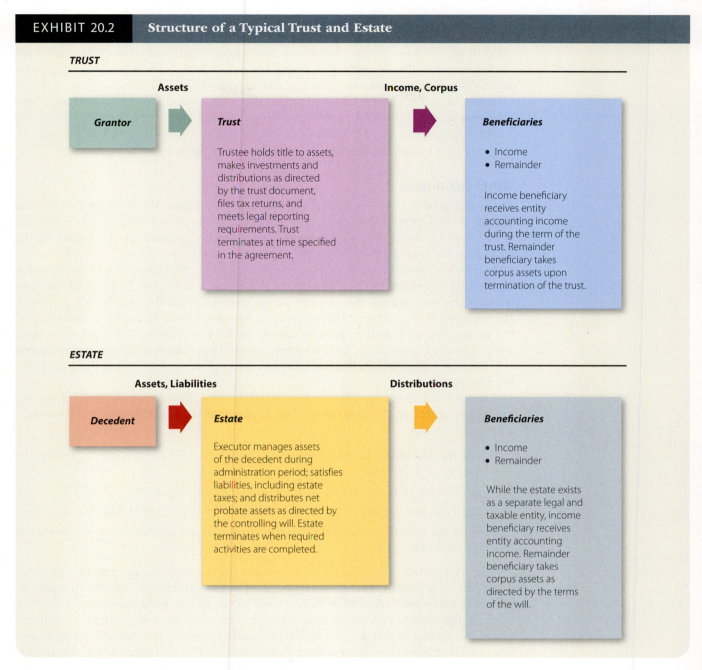

EXHIBIT 20.2   **Structure of a Typical Trust and Estate**

TRUST

Assets   Income, Corpus

Grantor

Trust

Trustee holds title to assets, makes investments and distributions as directed by the trust document, files tax returns, and meets legal reporting requirements. Trust terminates at time specified in the agreement.

Beneficiaries

- Income
- Remainder

Income beneficiary receives entity accounting income during the term of the trust. Remainder beneficiary takes corpus assets upon termination of the trust.

ESTATE

Assets, Liabilities   Distributions

Decedent

Estate

Executor manages assets of the decedent during administration period; satisfies liabilities, including estate taxes; and distributes net probate assets as directed by the controlling will. Estate terminates when required activities are completed.

Beneficiaries

- Income
- Remainder

While the estate exists as a separate legal and taxable entity, income beneficiary receives entity accounting income. Remainder beneficiary takes corpus assets as directed by the terms of the will.

Typically, the creation of a trust involves at least three parties.

1. The **grantor** (sometimes referred to as the settlor or donor) transfers selected assets to the trust entity.
2. The trustee, who usually is either an individual or a corporation, is charged with the fiduciary duties associated with the trust.
3. The beneficiary is designated to receive income or property from the trust.

In some situations, fewer than three persons may be involved, as specified by the trust agreement. For instance, an elderly individual who no longer can manage his or her own property (e.g., because of ill health) may create a trust under which he or she is both the grantor and the beneficiary. In this case, a family member or corporate trustee is charged with the management of the grantor's assets.

In another situation, the grantor might designate himself or herself as the trustee of the trust assets. For example, someone who wants to transfer selected assets to a minor child or elderly parent could use a trust entity to ensure that the beneficiary does not misuse or waste the property. By naming himself or herself as the trustee, the grantor retains virtual control over the property that is transferred.

When only one party is involved (when the same individual is grantor, trustee, and sole beneficiary of the trust), Subchapter J rules do not apply and the entity is ignored for Federal income tax purposes. This might occur, for instance, when the grantor desires protection of the assets and/or income from creditors or an ex-spouse.

Other Definitions

When the grantor transfers title of selected assets to a trust, those assets become the **corpus** (body), or principal, of the trust. Trust corpus, in most situations, earns *income*, which may be distributed to the beneficiaries or accumulated for the future by the trustee, as the trust instrument directs.

In a typical trust, the grantor creates two types of beneficiaries: one who receives the accounting income of the trust (a concept defined in text Section 20-3a), and one who receives the trust corpus that remains at the termination of the trust as a legal entity. Beneficiaries in the former category hold an *income interest* in the trust, and those in the latter category hold a *remainder interest* in the trust's assets. If the grantor retains the remainder interest (e.g., for a trust for a minor beneficiary's education), the interest is known as a **reversionary interest** (corpus reverts to the grantor when the trust entity terminates).

The trust document establishes the term of the trust. The term may be for a specific number of years (*term certain*) or until the occurrence of a specified event. For instance, a trust might exist:

- For the life of the income beneficiary, in which case the income beneficiary is known as a *life tenant* in the trust corpus;
- For the life of some other individual (e.g., one's spouse);
- Until the income or remainder beneficiary reaches the age of majority; or
- Until the beneficiary, or another individual, marries, graduates, or reaches some specified age.

The trustee may be required to distribute the accounting income of the entity according to a distribution schedule specified in the agreement. Usually, though, the trustee is given more discretion with respect to the timing and nature of the distributions. If the trustee can determine, within guidelines found in the trust document, either the timing of the income or corpus distributions or the specific beneficiaries who will receive them (from among those identified in the agreement), the trust is called a discretionary or **sprinkling trust**. Here, the trustee can "sprinkle" the distributions among the various beneficiaries. As discussed in Chapters 18 and 19, family-wide income taxes can be reduced by directing income to those who are subject to lower marginal tax rates. Thus, by giving the trustee a sprinkling power, the income tax liability of the family unit can be manipulated by applying the terms of the trust agreement.

For purposes of certain provisions of Subchapter J, a trust is classified as either a **simple trust** or a **complex trust**. A simple trust:

- Is required to distribute its entire accounting income to designated beneficiaries every year,
- Has no beneficiaries that are qualifying charitable organizations, and
- Makes no distributions of trust corpus during the year.

A complex trust is any trust that is not a simple trust.[2] These criteria are applied to the trust every year. Thus, every trust is classified as a complex trust in the year in which it terminates (because it distributes all of its corpus during that year).

20-1b What Is an Estate?

An estate is created upon the death of every individual. The entity is charged with collecting and conserving all of the individual's assets, satisfying all liabilities, and distributing the remaining assets to the heirs identified by state law or the will.

Typically, the creation of an estate involves at least three parties: the decedent, all of whose probate assets are transferred to the estate for disposition; the executor, who is appointed under the decedent's valid will (or the administrator, if no valid will exists); and the beneficiaries of the estate, who are to receive assets or income from the entity, as the decedent has indicated in the will. Refer to Exhibit 20.2 for an illustration of these relationships.

An estate's operations are controlled by the probate laws of the decedent's state of residence and by the terms of the will as interpreted by the probate court. If the decedent did not execute a valid will, state law dictates who will carry out the executor's duties and which beneficiaries will receive which of the decedent's net assets.

An estate is a separate legal and taxable entity. The termination date of the estate is somewhat discretionary, as it occurs when all of the assets and income of the decedent have been distributed, all estate and decedent liabilities have been satisfied, and all other business of the entity is completed. Thus, there may be an incentive to use the estate as part of an income-shifting strategy (e.g., where the income beneficiaries are subject to low marginal tax rates).

Maria dies, and her estate holds a high-yield investment portfolio. Paulo, the income beneficiary, is subject to a 15% marginal state and Federal income tax rate, and Julia, the remainder beneficiary, is subject to a 30% marginal rate. The tax adviser might suggest that Maria's estate delay its final distribution of assets by a year or more to take advantage of the income tax reduction that is available from Paulo's low rates, before the entity terminates.

EXAMPLE 1

If an estate's existence is unduly prolonged, however, the IRS can terminate it for Federal income tax purposes after the expiration of a reasonable period for completing the duties of administration.[3]

20-2 NATURE OF TRUST AND ESTATE TAXATION

Subchapter J produces a significant amount of income tax revenue. More than 3 million Forms 1041 are filed every year, and these returns reflect the following approximate aggregate amounts.

- Gross income of over $140 billion.
- Taxable income of about $70 billion.
- Tax liability of almost $25 billion.

For most fiduciaries, almost 75 percent of income is in the form of capital gains and dividends. The remaining income tends to be interest, rents, and royalties, in addition to pass-through amounts from partnerships and other fiduciaries.

In general, the taxable income of a trust or an estate is taxed to the entity or to its beneficiaries to the extent that each has received the accounting income of the entity. Thus, the Federal income tax law creates a modified pass-through principle relative to the income taxation of trusts, estates, and their beneficiaries. Whoever receives the accounting income of the entity, or some portion of it, is liable for the income tax that results.

---

[2]Reg. § 1.651(a)–1. [3]Reg. § 1.641(b)–3(a).

EXAMPLE 2

Adam receives 80% of the accounting income of the Zero Trust. The trustee accumulated the other 20% of the income at her discretion under the trust agreement and added it to trust corpus. Adam is liable for income tax only on the amount of the distribution, and Zero is liable for the income tax on the accumulated portion of the income.

Concept Summary 20.1 summarizes the major similarities and differences between the taxation of trusts and estates and that of other **pass-through entities**—partnerships, limited liability entities, and S corporations.

Concept Summary 20.1

Tax Characteristics of Major Pass-Through Entities

Tax Treatment	Subchapter K (Partnerships, LLCs)	Subchapter S (S Corporations)	Subchapter J (Trusts, Estates)
Controlling documents	Partnership agreement, LLC operating agreement.	Corporate charter and bylaws.	Trust document or will, state fiduciary or probate law.
Taxing structure	Pure pass-through, only one level of Federal income tax.	Chiefly pass-through, usually one level of Federal income tax.	Modified pass-through, Federal income tax falls on the recipient(s) of entity accounting income.
Entity-level Federal income tax?	Never.	Rarely. See text Sections 12-3h and 12-3i.	Yes, if the entity retains any net taxable income amounts.
Form for reporting income and expense pass-through	Schedules K and K–1, Form 1065.	Schedules K and K–1, Form 1120S.	Schedules K and K–1, Form 1041.
Subject to entity-level AMT?	No, but preferences and adjustments pass through to owners.	No, but preferences and adjustments pass through to owners.	Yes, if the entity retains any AMT-related accounting income amounts.
Subject to entity-level NIIT?	No, but amounts and types of income are reported to owners.	No, but amounts and types of income are reported to shareholders.	Yes, on income items retained by the entity (i.e., not distributed to beneficiaries).

20-2a Tax Accounting Periods and Methods

An estate or a trust may use many of the tax accounting methods available to individuals. The method of accounting used by the grantor of a trust or the decedent of an estate need not carry over to the entity.

An estate has the same options for choosing a tax year as any new taxpayer. Thus, the estate of a calendar year decedent dying on March 3 can select any fiscal year or report on a calendar year basis. To eliminate the possibility of deferring the taxation of fiduciary-source income simply by using a fiscal tax year, virtually all trusts (other than tax-exempt trusts) are required to use a calendar tax year.[4]

20-2b Tax Rates and Personal Exemption

Congress's desire to stop trusts from being used as income-shifting devices has made the fiduciary entity the highest-taxed taxpayer in the Code. The entity reaches the 37 percent marginal Federal income tax rate in 2019 once taxable income exceeds $12,750, so the grantor's ability to shift income in a tax-effective manner is nearly eliminated. Exhibit 20.3, which lists the 2019 Federal income taxes paid by various entities on taxable income of $50,000, shows how expensive the taxes on an accumulation of

---

[4]§ 645.

EXHIBIT 20.3	Comparative Tax Liabilities		
Filing Status/Entity	**Taxable Income**	**Marginal Income Tax Rate (%)**	**2019 Federal Income Tax Liability**
Single	$50,000	22	$ 6,859
Married, filing jointly	50,000	12	5,612
C corporation	50,000	21	10,500
Trust or estate	50,000	37	16,858

income within an estate or a trust can be. Given the current tax rates for individuals, proper income shifting usually will move assets *out of* the estate or trust and into the hands of the lower-bracket grantor or beneficiary.

A fiduciary's dividend income and net long-term capital gain are taxed at a nominal rate of no more than 20 percent. In addition to the regular income tax, an estate or a trust may be subject to the alternative minimum tax and the additional tax on net investment income (discussed in text Sections 20-2c and 20-2d). Estimated tax payments must take into account any liabilities for these taxes.[5]

Both trusts and estates are allowed a personal exemption in computing the fiduciary tax liability. All estates are allowed a personal exemption of $600. The exemption available to a trust depends upon the type of trust involved. A trust that is required to distribute all of its income currently is allowed an exemption of $300. All other trusts are allowed an exemption of $100 per year.[6]

The classification of trusts as to the appropriate personal exemption is similar but not identical to the distinction between simple and complex trusts. The classification as a simple trust is more stringent.

EXAMPLE 3

Three trusts appear to operate in a similar fashion, but they are subject to different Subchapter J classifications and exemptions.

Trust Alpha is required to distribute all of its current accounting income to Susan. Thus, it is allowed a $300 personal exemption. No corpus distributions or charitable contributions are made during the year. Accordingly, Alpha is a simple trust.

Trust Beta is required to distribute all of its current accounting income; it is allowed a $300 personal exemption. The beneficiaries of these distributions are specified in the trust instrument: one-half of accounting income is to be distributed to Tyrone, and one-half is to be distributed to State University, a qualifying charitable organization. Because Beta has made a charitable distribution for the tax year, it is a complex trust.

The trustee of Trust Gamma can, at her discretion, distribute the current-year accounting income or corpus of the trust to Dr. Chapman. Because the trustee is not required to distribute current accounting income, only a $100 personal exemption is allowed. During the current year, the trustee distributed all of the accounting income of the entity to Dr. Chapman, but made no corpus or charitable distributions. Nonetheless, because it lacks the current-year income distribution requirement, Gamma is a complex trust.

20-2c Alternative Minimum Tax

The alternative minimum tax (AMT) may apply to a trust or an estate in any tax year. Given the nature and magnitude of the tax preferences, adjustments, and exemptions that determine alternative minimum taxable income (AMTI), however, most trusts and estates are unlikely to incur the tax.

---

[5]§§ 55 and 1411.

[6]§ 642(b). Fiduciary exemption amounts are not indexed for inflation.

In general, derivation of AMTI for the entity follows the rules that apply to individual taxpayers. AMTI may be created through the application of most of the AMT preference and adjustment items.

The fiduciary's AMT is computed using Schedule I of Form 1041. Two full pages of the Form 1041 are dedicated to the computation of taxable income and other items when the AMT applies to the trust or estate. A minimum tax credit might be available in future years through these computations.

The entity claims a $25,000 annual AMT exemption. The exemption phases out at a rate of one-fourth of the amount by which AMTI exceeds $83,500. These amounts are indexed annually.

A 26 percent AMT rate is applied to AMTI, increasing to 28 percent when AMTI in excess of the exemption reaches $194,800.

20-2d Additional Tax on Net Investment Income

Trusts and estates that are subject to the highest Federal income tax rate for the tax year must pay an additional tax to support the Medicare system, using Form 8960. Thus, a 3.8 percent additional tax applies to the entity's undistributed net investment income (NII) that exceeds $12,750 for 2019 (indexed annually).

NII includes gross income (less deductions) from interest, dividends, royalties, rents, and passive activities. NII also includes net recognized gains from the disposition of assets producing such income (e.g., capital gains). NII items make up about 90 percent of income items for many investment-oriented fiduciary entities. The NII tax (NIIT) is in addition to the entity's ordinary income tax (maximum rate 37 percent) and net capital gains tax (maximum rate 20 percent).

EXAMPLE 4

The Zeta Trust reports $20,000 of net investment income and $30,000 in net profits from an active business operation for 2019. Zeta retains all of the business profits but, under the terms of the trust agreement, distributes $5,000 cash from the NII to its sole beneficiary Victoria. Zeta's liability under the additional tax on NII is $86 [3.8% tax × ($15,000 undistributed portfolio income − $12,750 income amount at which the top tax rate applies)].

20-3 TAXABLE INCOME OF TRUSTS AND ESTATES

LO.2

Identify the steps in determining the accounting and taxable income of a trust or an estate and the related taxable income of the beneficiaries.

Generally, the taxable income of an estate or a trust is computed similarly to that for an individual. Fiduciary income tax rules, however, include several important exceptions and provisions that make it necessary to use a systematic approach to calculate the taxable income of these entities. Exhibit 20.4 illustrates the procedure implied by the Code, and Exhibit 20.5 presents a systematic computation method followed in this chapter.

20-3a Entity Accounting Income

Step 1 in determining the taxable income of a trust or an estate is to compute the entity's accounting income for the period. Although this prerequisite is not apparent from a cursory reading of Subchapter J, a closer look at the Code reveals a number of references to the *income* of the entity.[7] Wherever the term *income* is used in this part of the Code without some modifier (e.g., *gross* income or *taxable* income), the statute is referring to the accounting income of the trust or estate for the tax year.

A definition of **entity accounting income** is critical to understanding the computation of fiduciary taxable income. Usually, entity accounting income is the amount the income beneficiary of the trust or estate is eligible to receive from the entity. More importantly, the calculation of accounting income is virtually under the control of the grantor or decedent (through a properly drafted trust agreement or will). If the document has been drafted at arm's length, a court will enforce a fiduciary's good faith efforts to carry out the specified computation of accounting income.

---

[7]For example, see §§ 651(a)(1), 652(a), and 661(a)(1).

EXHIBIT 20.4	**Accounting Income, Distributable Net Income, and Taxable Income of the Entity and Its Beneficiaries—The Five-Step Procedure**

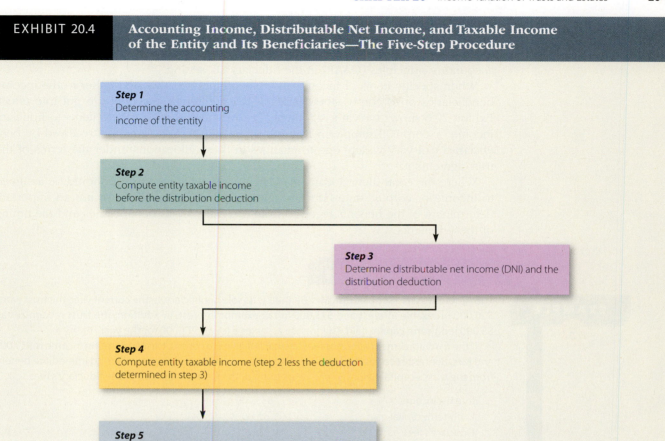

Step 1
Determine the accounting income of the entity

Step 2
Compute entity taxable income before the distribution deduction

Step 3
Determine distributable net income (DNI) and the distribution deduction

Step 4
Compute entity taxable income (step 2 less the deduction determined in step 3)

Step 5
Allocate DNI and its character to the beneficiaries. Use the tier system, if necessary.

EXHIBIT 20.5	**Computational Template Applying the Five-Step Procedure**

Item	Totals	Accounting Income	Taxable Income	Distributable Net Income/Distribution Deduction
Income	_____	_____	_____	
Income	_____	_____	_____	
Expense	_____	_____	_____	
Expense	_____	_____	_____	
Personal exemption			_____	
Accounting income/taxable income before the distribution deduction		_____ *Step 1*	_____ *Step 2*	_____
Personal exemption				_____
Corpus capital gain/loss				_____
Net tax-exempt income				_____
Distributable net income				_____
Distribution deduction			_____ *Step 3*	
Entity taxable income			_____ *Step 4*	

Beneficiary taxable income is addressed in *step 5*.

Entity accounting income generally is defined by state laws that are derived from the Uniform Principal and Income Act (latest major revision, 1997). Most states have adopted some form of the Uniform Act, which essentially constitutes generally accepted accounting principles (GAAP) in the fiduciary tax setting.

When specific items of income and expenditure are allocated either to the income beneficiaries or to corpus, the desires of the grantor or decedent are put into effect. Exhibit 20.6 shows typical assignments of revenue and expenditure items to fiduciary income or corpus. Examples 5 through 7 illustrate that the amounts received by beneficiaries can vary widely due to changes in these allocations under the terms of the trust agreement.

Where the controlling document is silent as to whether an item should be assigned to income or corpus, state fiduciary law prevails. These allocations are an important determinant of the benefits received from the entity by its beneficiaries and the timing of those benefits.

Entity Accounting Income

EXAMPLE 5

The Arnold Trust is a simple trust. Mrs. Bennett is its sole beneficiary. In the current year, the trust earns $20,000 in taxable interest and $15,000 in tax-exempt interest. In addition, the trust recognizes an $8,000 long-term capital gain. The trustee assesses a fee of $11,000 for the year.

If the trust agreement allocates fees and capital gains to corpus, trust accounting income is $35,000 and Mrs. Bennett receives that amount. Thus, the income beneficiary receives no immediate benefit from the trust's capital gain, and she bears none of the financial burden of the fiduciary's fees.

Interest income	$35,000
Long-term capital gain	± –0–*
Fiduciary's fees	± –0–*
Trust accounting income	$35,000

*Allocable to corpus.

EXAMPLE 6

Assume the same facts as in Example 5, except that the trust agreement allocates the fiduciary's fees to income. The trust accounting income is $24,000, and Mrs. Bennett receives that amount.

Interest income	$35,000
Long-term capital gain	± –0–*
Fiduciary's fees	–11,000
Trust accounting income	$24,000

*Allocable to corpus.

EXAMPLE 7

Assume the same facts as in Example 5, except that the trust agreement allocates to income all capital gains and losses and one-half of the trustee's commissions. The trust accounting income is $37,500, and Mrs. Bennett receives that amount.

Interest income	$35,000
Long-term capital gain	+8,000
Fiduciary's fees	–5,500*
Trust accounting income	$37,500

*One-half allocable to corpus.

EXHIBIT 20.6	Common Allocations of Items to Income or Corpus

Allocable to Income	Allocable to Corpus
Ordinary and operating net income from trust assets	Depreciation on business assets
	Casualty gain/loss on income-producing assets
Interest, dividend, rent, and royalty income	Insurance recoveries on income-producing assets
Stock dividends	Capital gain/loss on investment assets
One-half of fiduciary fees/commissions	Adjustments due to stock splits
	One-half of fiduciary fees/commissions

20-3b Gross Income

The gross income of an estate or a trust is similar to that of an individual. In determining the gain or loss to be recognized by an estate or a trust upon the sale or other taxable disposition of assets, the rules for basis determination are similar to those applicable to other taxpayers. Thus, an estate's basis for property received from a decedent is stepped up or stepped down to the gross estate valuation (refer to text Section 19-2b for a more detailed discussion). Property received as a gift during the donor's lifetime (e.g., in irrevocable trust arrangements) usually takes the donor's basis. Property purchased by the trust from a third party is assigned a basis equal to the purchase price.

Noncash Property Distributions

In general, the fiduciary entity does not recognize gain or loss upon its distribution of property to a beneficiary under the provisions of the will or trust document. The distributed property has the same basis to the beneficiary of the distribution as it did to the estate or trust. Moreover, the distribution absorbs distributable net income (DNI) and qualifies for a distribution deduction (both of which are explained later in this chapter) to the extent of the lesser of the distributed asset's basis to the beneficiary or the asset's fair market value as of the distribution date.[8]

The Big Picture

EXAMPLE 8

Return to the facts of *The Big Picture* on p. 20-1. Assume that Anna has established the Jiang Family Trust. The trust distributes a painting (basis of $40,000 and fair market value of $90,000) to beneficiary Sally. Sally's basis in the painting is $40,000. The distribution absorbs $40,000 of the Jiang Family Trust's DNI, and the trust claims a $40,000 distribution deduction relative to the transaction.

A trustee or an executor can elect for the entity to recognize gain or loss with respect to all of its in-kind property distributions for the year. If the election is made, the beneficiary's basis in the asset is equal to the asset's fair market value as of the distribution date. The distribution absorbs DNI and qualifies for a distribution deduction to the extent of the asset's fair market value. However, the related-party rules can restrict an estate's or trust's deduction for such losses. Generally, related parties include a trust, its trustee, its grantor, and its beneficiaries, as well as an estate, its executor, and its beneficiaries.

Distributing Property

EXAMPLE 9

The Green Estate distributes an antique piano, basis to Green of $10,000 and fair market value of $15,000, to beneficiary Kyle. The executor elects that Green recognize the related $5,000 gain on the distribution. Accordingly, Kyle's basis in the piano is $15,000 ($10,000 basis to Green + $5,000 gain recognized). The election likely increased the Federal income tax paid related to the gain: Green almost certainly is subject to a higher marginal income tax rate than is Kyle. Without the election, Green would not recognize any gain, and Kyle's basis in the piano would be $10,000.

---

[8]§ 643(e).

<table>
<tr><td>**EXAMPLE**
10</td><td>**Distributing Property**

Assume the same facts as in Example 9, except that Green's basis in the piano is $18,000. The executor elects that Green be assigned the related $3,000 loss on the distribution. Accordingly, Kyle's basis in the piano is $15,000 ($18,000 − $3,000). Without the election, Kyle's basis in the piano would be $18,000.

The estate cannot deduct this loss, however. Because an estate and its beneficiaries are related parties, realized losses cannot be recognized immediately.[9] Instead, the disallowed loss can be recognized if Kyle later sells the piano to an unrelated party.</td></tr>
</table>

Income in Respect of a Decedent

The gross income of a trust or an estate includes ==income in respect of a decedent (IRD)== that the entity received.[10] For a cash basis decedent, IRD includes accrued salary, interest, rent, and other income items that were not constructively received before death. For both cash and accrual basis decedents, IRD includes, for instance, death benefits from qualified retirement plans and deferred compensation contracts.

The tax consequences of IRD can be summarized as follows.

- The fair market value of the right to IRD on the appropriate valuation date is included in the decedent's gross estate. Thus, it is subject to the Federal estate tax.[11]

- The decedent's basis in the property carries over to the recipient (the estate or heirs). There is no step-up or step-down in the basis of IRD items.

- The recipient of the income recognizes gain or loss, measured by the difference between the amount realized and the adjusted basis of the IRD in the hands of the decedent. The character of the gain or loss matches the treatment that it would have received had it been realized by the decedent before death. Thus, if the decedent would have realized capital gain, the recipient must do likewise.

- Expenses related to the IRD (such as interest, taxes, and depletion) that were not deducted on the final income tax return of the decedent may be claimed by the recipient. These items are known as ==deductions in respect of a decedent==. Typically, such deductions also include fiduciary fees, commissions paid to dispose of estate assets, and state income taxes payable. They are deductible for both Federal estate and income tax purposes, *for* or *from* adjusted gross income (AGI) as would have been the case for the decedent.

<table>
<tr><td>**EXAMPLE**
11</td><td>**Working with IRD**

Amanda died on July 13 of the current year. On August 2, the estate received a check (before deductions) for $1,200 from Amanda's former employer; this was Amanda's compensation for the last pay period of her life. On November 23, the estate received a $45,000 distribution from the qualified profit sharing plan of Amanda's employer, the full amount to which Amanda was entitled under the plan. Both Amanda and the estate are calendar year, cash basis taxpayers.

The last salary payment and the profit sharing plan distribution constitute IRD to the estate. Amanda had earned these items during her lifetime, and the estate was to receive each of them after Amanda's death. Consequently, the gross estate includes $46,200 with respect to these two items. However, the income tax basis to the estate for these items is not stepped up (from zero to $1,200 and $45,000, respectively) upon distribution to the estate.

In addition, the estate must report gross income of $46,200 for the current tax year with respect to the IRD items [$1,200 + $45,000 (amounts realized) − $0 (adjusted bases)].</td></tr>
</table>

---

[9]§ 267(b)(13).

[10]See § 691 and the Regulations thereunder. The concept of IRD was introduced in text Section 19-2b.

[11]To mitigate the effect of double taxation (imposition of both the estate tax and the income tax), § 691(c) allows the recipient an income tax deduction for the incremental estate tax attributable to the net IRD.

Working with IRD

Assume the same facts as in Example 11. Amanda's last paycheck was reduced by $165 for state income taxes that were withheld by the employer. The $165 tax payment is a deduction in respect of a decedent and is allowed as a deduction on *both* Amanda's estate tax return *and* the estate's income tax return.

EXAMPLE 12

Including the IRD in both the taxpayer's gross estate and the gross income of the estate may seem harsh. Nevertheless, the tax consequences of IRD are similar to the treatment that applies to all of a taxpayer's earned income. The item is subject to income tax upon receipt, and to the extent it is not consumed by the taxpayer before death, it is included in the gross estate.

ETHICS & EQUITY To Whom Can I Trust My Pet?

Humane societies encourage the general public to care for their own pets and to adopt those who need owners. It is not uncommon to find provisions in a will to establish a trust or an endowment to care for the pets that the deceased leaves behind. After all, over 60 percent of all individuals live with a pet and about $70 billion is spent each year in caring for these companions.

Boilerplate legal language is available to establish a pet-assistance trust. The trust should provide a guaranteed distribution for pet care, including the costs of pet sitters, kennels, and veterinary fees. A few states (e.g., Kentucky and Minnesota) do not recognize such trusts, however.

When decedents establish permanent funds to provide for a favorite pet, the surviving (human) family members may not be so enthused. In a few cases, the survivors challenge the terms of the will or trust, often requesting that a judge downsize the principal amount involved or reduce the specified annual distributions. In this way, the human heirs benefit from any adjustment that is made.

How would you advise a client who wants to establish a well-funded trust to care for Fifi when the family members have income and asset needs of their own?

20-3c **Ordinary Deductions**

As a general rule, the taxable income of an estate or a trust is similar to that of an individual.[12] Deductions are allowed for ordinary and necessary expenses paid or incurred in carrying on a trade or business; for the production or collection of income; for the management, conservation, or maintenance of property; and in connection with the determination, collection, or refund of any tax.[13] Reasonable administration expenses, including fiduciary fees and litigation costs in connection with the duties of administration, also can be deductible.

Expenses attributable to the production or collection of tax-exempt income are not deductible.[14] The amount of the disallowed deduction is found by using a formula based on the composition of the income elements of entity accounting income for the year of the deduction. The deductibility of the fees is determined strictly by the usual Federal income tax rules, and the allocation of expenditures to income and to corpus is controlled by the trust agreement or will or by state law.

The Silver Trust operates a business and invests idle cash in marketable securities. Its sales proceeds for the current year are $180,000. Expenses for wages, cost of sales, and office administration are $80,000. Interest income recognized is $20,000 from taxable bonds and $50,000 from tax-exempt bonds. The trustee claims a $35,000 fee for its activities. According to the trust agreement, $30,000 of this amount is allocated to the income beneficiaries, and $5,000 is allocated to corpus.

continued

EXAMPLE 13

---

[12]§ 641(b).

[13]§§ 162 and 212.

[14]§ 265.

Sales proceeds	$180,000
Deductible expenses	−80,000
Interest income ($50,000 is tax-exempt)	+70,000
Fiduciary's fees, as allocated	−30,000
Trust accounting income	$140,000

The sales proceeds are included in the gross income of the trust under § 61. The costs associated with the business are deductible in full under § 162. The taxable interest income is included in Silver's gross income under § 61, but the tax-exempt interest is excluded under § 103. The fiduciary's fees are deductible by Silver under § 212, but a portion of the deduction is lost because § 265 prohibits deductions for expenses incurred in the generation of tax-exempt income.

As shown below, 50/250 of the fees of $35,000 can be traced to tax-exempt income, so $7,000 of the fees is nondeductible. For purposes of the computation, only the income elements of the year's trust accounting income are included in the denominator. Moreover, the allocation of portions of the fees to income and to corpus is irrelevant in the calculation. The disallowed deduction for fiduciary's fees is computed in the following manner.

$$\$35{,}000^{*}\text{(total fees paid)} \times \frac{\$50{,}000^{**}\ (\textit{tax-exempt}\ \text{income elements of trust accounting income})}{\$250{,}000^{**}\ (\textit{all}\ \text{income elements of trust accounting income})}$$

$$= \$7{,}000\ (\text{amount disallowed})$$

*All fees, and not just those that are allocated to income, are deductible by the trust under § 212.
**The numerator and denominator of this fraction are *not* reduced by expense items allocable to income (e.g., cost of sales).

Amounts deductible as administration expenses or losses for estate tax purposes cannot be claimed by the estate for income tax purposes unless the estate waives the estate tax deduction. Although these expenses cannot be deducted twice, they may be allocated as the fiduciary sees fit between Forms 706 and 1041; they need not be claimed in their entirety on either return.[15]

Trusts and estates are allowed cost recovery deductions. Such deductions are assigned proportionately among the recipients of the entity accounting income.[16]

Cost Recovery Deductions

EXAMPLE 14

Lisa and Martin are the equal income beneficiaries of the Needle Trust. Under the terms of the trust agreement, the trustee has complete discretion as to the timing of the distributions from Needle's current accounting income. The trust agreement allocates all depreciation expense to income. In the current year, the trustee distributes 40% of the current trust accounting income to Lisa and 40% to Martin; thus, 20% of the income is accumulated. The depreciation deduction allowable to Needle is $100,000. This deduction is allocated among the trust and its beneficiaries on the basis of the distribution of current accounting income: Lisa and Martin each claim a $40,000 deduction, and the trust can deduct $20,000.

EXAMPLE 15

Assume the same facts as in Example 14, except that the trust agreement allocates all depreciation expense to corpus. There is no change in the tax result; Lisa and Martin both still claim a $40,000 depreciation deduction, and Needle retains its $20,000 deduction. The Code assigns the depreciation deduction proportionately to the recipients of entity accounting income. Allocation of depreciation to income or to corpus is irrelevant in determining which party can properly claim the deduction.

---

[15]Reg. § 1.642(g)–2.

[16]§§ 167(h) and 611(b)(3) and (4).

If the entity operates a trade or business, the income beneficiaries of a fiduciary entity may qualify for the 20 percent deduction for qualified business income (QBI); see text Section 2-3k. The trust or estate will report to the beneficiaries all information necessary for those parties to compute the deduction, such as QBI and W–2 wages. Such items are allocated to the beneficiaries proportionate to the amount of distributable net income (see text Section 20-3f) that they receive.[17] This means that the entity will claim its own QBI deduction if it retains some of the DNI for the tax year.

20-3d Deductions for Losses

An estate or a trust is allowed a deduction for casualty or theft losses that are not reimbursed by insurance or other arrangements. Such losses may also be deductible by an estate for Federal tax purposes.[18] An estate is not allowed an income tax deduction unless the estate tax deduction is waived.

The net operating loss (NOL) deduction is available for estates and trusts (i.e., where trade or business income is generated). No more than 80 percent of entity taxable income can be offset by the NOL; see text Section 3-1j. The net capital losses of an estate or a trust can be claimed by the fiduciary. The tax treatment of these losses is the same as for individual taxpayers.

Fiduciary entities are subject to the passive activity loss limitations; passive activity losses can be deducted by the trust or estate only against income from passive activities.

20-3e Charitable Contributions

An estate or a complex trust is allowed a deduction for contributions from the gross income of the current tax year to charitable organizations under certain conditions.[19]

- The contribution is made pursuant to the will or trust instrument, and its amount is determinable using the language of that document.

- The recipient is a qualified organization. For this purpose, qualified organizations include the same charities for which individual and corporate donors are allowed deductions, except that estates and trusts also are permitted a deduction for contributions to certain foreign charitable organizations.

- Generally, the contribution is claimed in the tax year it is paid, but a fiduciary can treat amounts paid in the year immediately following as a deduction for the preceding year. Under this rule, estates and complex trusts may receive more favorable treatment than do individuals or C corporations.

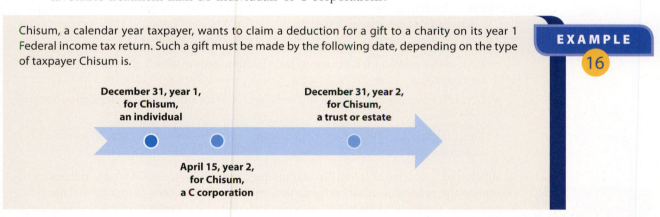

EXAMPLE 16

Chisum, a calendar year taxpayer, wants to claim a deduction for a gift to a charity on its year 1 Federal income tax return. Such a gift must be made by the following date, depending on the type of taxpayer Chisum is.

December 31, year 1, for Chisum, an individual

December 31, year 2, for Chisum, a trust or estate

April 15, year 2, for Chisum, a C corporation

Unlike the charitable contribution deductions of individuals and corporations, the deductions of estates and complex trusts are not limited in amount (e.g., to a percentage of taxable or adjusted gross income). Nonetheless, the deduction is limited to amounts that have been included in the gross income of the entity.

---

[17]Prop.Reg. §1.199A–6(d).

[18]§ 2054.

[19]§ 642(c)(1) and Reg. §§ 1.642(c)−1 and −3. But see *Green v. U.S.*,121 AFTR 2d 2018–427, 2018–1 USTC ¶50,126, 880 F.3d 519 (CA–10).

The deduction for a gift of a noncash asset is limited to that asset's basis to the fiduciary. A contribution is deemed to be made proportionately from each of the income elements of entity accounting income. However, if the will or trust agreement requires that the contribution be made from a specific type of income, or from income from a specified asset, the allocation of the contribution to taxable and tax-exempt income is not required.

The Big Picture

EXAMPLE 17

Return to the facts of *The Big Picture* on p. 20-1. Again assume that Anna has established the Jiang Family Trust. The trust reports gross rent income of $80,000, expenses attributable to the rents of $60,000, and tax-exempt interest from state bonds of $20,000. Under the trust agreement, the trustee is to pay 30% of the annual trust accounting income to the United Way, a qualifying organization. Accordingly, the trustee pays $12,000 to the charity (i.e., 30% × $40,000). The charitable contribution deduction allowed is $9,600 [($80,000/$100,000) × $12,000], even if the payment to the charity is not made until the following tax year.

The Big Picture

EXAMPLE 18

Assume the same facts as in Example 17, except that the trust instrument also requires that the contribution be paid from the net rent income. The agreement controls, and the allocation formula need not be applied. The entire $12,000 is allowed as a charitable deduction.

LO.3

Illustrate the uses and implications of distributable net income.

20-3f Deduction for Distributions to Beneficiaries

The modified pass-through approach of Subchapter J is embodied in the deduction allowed to trusts and estates for the distributions made to beneficiaries during the year. Some portion of any distribution that a beneficiary receives from a trust may be subject to income tax on the beneficiary's own return. At the same time, the distributing entity is allowed a deduction for some or all of the distribution.

A good analogy is to the taxability of corporate profits distributed to employees as taxable wages. The corporation is allowed a deduction for the payment, but the employee receives gross income in the form of compensation.

Distributable Net Income

A critical value that is used in computing the amount of the entity's distribution deduction is **distributable net income (DNI)**. As it is defined in Subchapter J, DNI serves several functions. Concept Summary 20.2 illustrates these critical roles of DNI.

- DNI is the maximum amount of the distribution on which the beneficiaries can be taxed.[20]

- DNI is the maximum amount the entity can use as a distribution deduction for the year.[21]

- The makeup of DNI carries over to the beneficiaries (the items of income and expenses retain their DNI character in the hands of the distributees).[22]

Subchapter J defines DNI in a circular manner, however. The DNI value is necessary to determine the entity's distribution deduction and therefore its taxable income for the year. Nonetheless, the Code defines DNI as a modification of the entity's taxable income itself. Using the systematic approach to determining the taxable income of the entity and its beneficiaries, as shown earlier in Exhibit 20.4, compute *taxable income before the distribution deduction*, modify that amount to determine DNI and the distribution deduction, return to the calculation of *taxable income*, and apply the deduction that has resulted.

---

[20]§§ 652(a) and 662(a).

[21]§§ 651(b) and 661(c).

[22]§§ 652(b) and 662(b).

Concept Summary 20.2

Uses of the DNI Amount

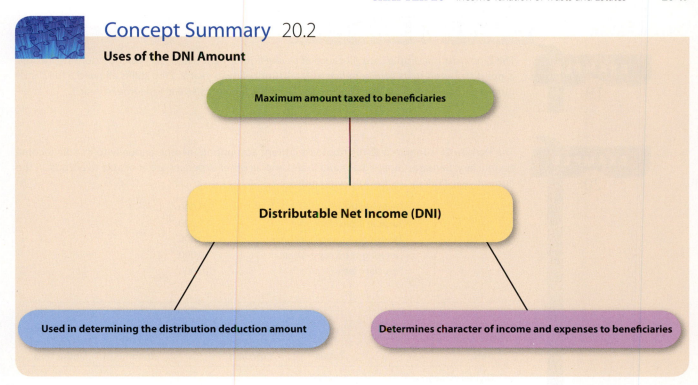

Maximum amount taxed to beneficiaries

Distributable Net Income (DNI)

Used in determining the distribution deduction amount

Determines character of income and expenses to beneficiaries

Taxable income before the distribution deduction (step 2) includes all of the entity's items of gross income, deductions, gains, losses, and exemptions for the year.

Therefore, to compute this amount, (1) determine the appropriate personal exemption for the year and (2) account for all of the other gross income and deductions of the entity.

Step 3 in Exhibit 20.4 is the determination of *distributable net income*, computed by making the following adjustments to the entity's *taxable income before the distribution deduction*.[23]

- Add back the entity's personal exemption.
- Add back *net* tax-exempt interest; reduce the total tax-exempt interest by charitable contributions and by related expenses that are not deductible.
- Add back the entity's net capital losses.
- Subtract any net capital gains allocable to corpus. The only net capital gains included in DNI are those attributable to income beneficiaries or to charitable contributions.[24]

Distribution Deduction

DNI includes the net tax-exempt interest income of the entity, so that amount must be removed from DNI in computing the distribution deduction. Moreover, for estates and complex trusts, DNI and the distribution amount may not be the same; the amount actually distributed during the year may include discretionary distributions of income and distributions of corpus permissible under the will or trust instrument.

The distribution deduction for estates and complex trusts is computed as the lesser of (1) the deductible portion of DNI or (2) the taxable amount actually distributed to the beneficiaries during the year. For a simple trust, however, full distribution is always assumed, relative to both the entity and its beneficiaries, in a manner similar to the pass-through entities.

DNI and the distribution deduction are computed on the entity's Form 1041. The beneficiaries' Schedules K–1 report the allocations of income, deduction, and credit items to them.

---

[23]These and other (less common) adjustments are detailed in § 643.   [24]§ 643(a)(3).

DNI and Distribution Deduction

EXAMPLE 19

The Zinc Trust is a simple trust. Because of severe liquidity problems, its year 1 accounting income is not distributed to its sole beneficiary, Mark, until early in year 2. Zinc still is allowed a full distribution deduction for, and Mark still is taxable upon, the entity's year 1 income in year 1.

EXAMPLE 20

The Pork Trust is required to distribute its current accounting income annually to its sole income beneficiary, Barbara. Capital gains and losses and all other expenses are allocable to corpus. In the current year, Pork incurs the following items.

Dividend income	$25,000
Taxable interest income	15,000
Tax-exempt interest income	20,000
Net long-term capital gain	10,000
Fiduciary fees	6,000

Item	Totals	Accounting Income	Taxable Income	Distributable Net Income/ Distribution Deduction
Dividend income	$25,000	$25,000	$ 25,000	
Taxable interest income	15,000	15,000	15,000	
Tax-exempt interest income	20,000	20,000		
Net long-term capital gain	10,000		10,000	
Fiduciary fees	6,000		(4,000)	
Personal exemption			(300)	
Accounting income/taxable income before the distribution deduction		$60,000	$ 45,700	$ 45,700
		Step 1	*Step 2*	
Personal exemption				300
Corpus capital gain/loss				(10,000)
Net tax-exempt income				18,000
Distributable net income				$ 54,000
Distribution deduction			*Step 3* (36,000)	
Entity taxable income			*Step 4* $ 9,700	

Step 1. Trust accounting income is $60,000; this includes the tax-exempt interest income, but not the fees or the capital gains, pursuant to the trust document. Barbara receives $60,000 from the trust for the current year.

Step 2. Taxable income before the distribution deduction is computed as directed by the Code. The tax-exempt interest is excluded under § 103. Only a portion of the fees is deductible {[($60,000 − $20,000)/$60,000] × $6,000 = $4,000} because some of the fees ($6,000 − $4,000) are traceable to the tax-exempt income. The trust claims a $300 personal exemption, because it is required to distribute its annual trust accounting income.

Step 3. DNI and the distribution deduction reflect the required adjustments. The distribution deduction is the lesser of the distributed amount ($60,000) or the deductible portion of DNI [$54,000 − $18,000 (net tax-exempt income)].

Step 4. Finally, return to the computation of the taxable income of the Pork Trust. A simple test should be applied at this point to ensure that the proper figure for the trust's taxable income has been determined. On what is Pork to be taxed? Pork has distributed to Barbara $60,000, which is all of its gross income except the $10,000 net long-term capital gain. The $300 personal exemption reduces Pork's taxable income to $9,700.

DNI and Distribution Deduction

> **EXAMPLE 21**

The Quick Trust is required to distribute all of its current accounting income equally to its two beneficiaries, Faith and the Universal Church, a qualifying charitable organization. Capital gains and losses and depreciation expenses are allocable to income. Fiduciary fees are allocable to corpus. In the current year, Quick incurs various items as indicated.

Item	Totals	Accounting Income	Taxable Income	Distributable Net Income/ Distribution Deduction
Rent income	$100,000	$100,000	$100,000	
Expenses—rent income	30,000	(30,000)	(30,000)	
Depreciation—rent income	15,000	(15,000)		
Net long-term capital gain	20,000	20,000	20,000	
Charitable contribution			(37,500)	
Fiduciary fees	18,000		(18,000)	
Personal exemption			(300)	
Accounting income/taxable income before the distribution deduction		$ 75,000	$ 34,200	$34,200
		Step 1	Step 2	
Personal exemption				300
Corpus capital gain/loss				
Net tax-exempt income				
Distributable net income				$34,500
Distribution deduction		Step 3	(34,500)	
Entity taxable income		Step 4	($ 300)	

Step 1. Trust accounting income of $75,000 reflects the indicated allocations of items to income and to corpus. Each income beneficiary receives $37,500.

Step 2. In the absence of tax-exempt income, a deduction is allowed for the full amount of the fiduciary's fees. Quick is a complex trust, but because it is required to distribute its full accounting income annually, a $300 exemption is allowed. Properly, the trust does not deduct any depreciation for the rental property. The depreciation deduction is available only to the recipients of the entity's accounting income for the period. Thus, the deduction is split equally between Faith and the church. The deduction probably is of no direct value to the church, a tax-exempt organization. The trust's charitable contribution deduction is based on the $37,500 the charity actually received (one-half of trust accounting income).

Step 3. Because there is no tax-exempt income, the only adjustment needed to compute DNI is to add back the trust's personal exemption. Subchapter J requires no adjustment for the charitable contribution. DNI is computed only from the perspective of Faith, who also received $37,500 from the trust.

Step 4. Perform the simple test (referred to in the previous example) to ensure that the proper taxable income for the Quick Trust has been computed. All of the trust's gross income has been distributed to Faith and the charity. As is the case with most trusts that distribute all of their accounting income, the Quick Trust "wastes" the personal exemption.

20-3g Tax Credits

Available tax credits are apportioned between the estate or trust and the beneficiaries on the basis of the entity accounting income allocable to each.

Concept Summary 20.3 outlines the principles underlying the Federal taxation of estates and trusts.

Concept Summary 20.3

Principles of Fiduciary Income Taxation

1. Estates and trusts are temporary entities created to locate, maintain, and distribute assets and to satisfy liabilities according to the wishes of the decedent or grantor as expressed in the will or trust document.

2. Generally, the estate or trust acts as a conduit of the taxable income that it receives. To the extent the income is distributed by the entity, it is taxed to the beneficiary. Taxable income retained by the entity is taxed to the entity itself.

3. The entity's accounting income first must be determined. Accounting conventions that are stated in the controlling document or, lacking such provisions, in state law allocate specific items of receipt and expenditure either to income or to corpus. Income beneficiaries typically receive payments

   from the entity that are equal to the accounting income.

4. The taxable income of the entity is computed using the scheme in Exhibit 20.4. The entity usually recognizes income in respect of a decedent.

5. Deductions for fiduciary's fees and for charitable contributions may be reduced if the entity received any tax-exempt income during the year. Business deductions are allowed, including the QBI and NOL deductions, if the entity operates a trade or business. Cost recovery deductions are assigned proportionately to the recipients of accounting income.

6. Upon election, realized gain or loss on assets that are properly distributed in kind can be recognized by the entity.

20-4 TAXATION OF BENEFICIARIES

The beneficiaries of an estate or a trust receive taxable income from the entity under the modified pass-through principle of fiduciary income taxation. Distributable net income determines the maximum amount that can be taxed to the beneficiaries for any tax year. The constitution of DNI also carries over to the beneficiaries (e.g., net long-term capital gains and dividends retain their character when they are distributed from the entity to the beneficiary).

A beneficiary includes in gross income an amount based upon the DNI of the trust for any taxable year or years of the entity ending with or within his or her taxable year.[25] These amounts are reported to the beneficiary on the Form 1041, Schedule K–1.

20-4a Distributions by Simple Trusts

The amount taxable to the beneficiaries of a trust is limited by the trust's DNI. However, because DNI includes net tax-exempt income, the amount included in the gross income of the beneficiaries could be less than DNI. When there is more than one income beneficiary, the elements of DNI are apportioned ratably according to the amount required to be distributed currently to each.

EXAMPLE 22

A simple trust has ordinary income of $40,000, a long-term capital gain of $15,000 (allocable to corpus), and a trustee commission expense of $4,000 (payable from corpus). The two income beneficiaries, Allie and Bart, are entitled to the trust's annual accounting income, based on shares of 75% and 25%, respectively.

Although Allie receives $30,000 as her share (75% × trust accounting income of $40,000), she is allocated DNI of only $27,000 (75% × $36,000). Likewise, Bart is entitled to receive $10,000 (25% × $40,000), but he is allocated DNI of only $9,000 (25% × $36,000). The $15,000 capital gain is taxed to the trust.

20-4b Distributions by Estates and Complex Trusts

Typically, an estate or a complex trust makes only discretionary distributions. In those cases, the DNI is apportioned ratably according to the distributed amounts as seen in Example 23.

A computational problem arises with estates and complex trusts when more than one beneficiary receives a distribution from the entity and the controlling document does not require a distribution of the entire accounting income of the entity.

---

[25]§§ 652(c) and 662(c).

The trustee of the Wilson Trust has the discretion to distribute the income or corpus of the trust in any proportion between the two beneficiaries of the trust, Wong and Washington. Under the trust instrument, Wong must receive $15,000 from the trust every year. In the current year, the trust's accounting income is $50,000, and its DNI is $40,000. The trustee pays $15,000 to Wong and $25,000 to Washington.

How is Wilson's DNI to be divided between Wong and Washington? Several arbitrary methods of allocating DNI between the beneficiaries could be devised. Subchapter J resolves the problem by creating a two-tier system to govern the taxation of beneficiaries in such situations.[26] The tier system determines which distributions will be included in the gross income of the beneficiaries in full, which will be included in part, and which will not be included at all.

First and Second Tiers

Income that is required to be distributed currently, whether or not it is distributed, is categorized as a *first-tier distribution*. All other discretionary amounts paid, credited, or distributed are *second-tier distributions*.[27] A formula is used to allocate DNI among the appropriate beneficiaries when only first-tier distributions are made and those amounts exceed DNI.

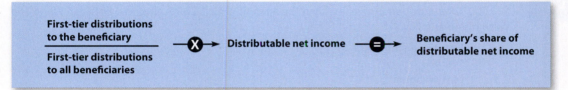

When both first-tier and second-tier distributions are made and the first-tier distributions exceed DNI, the above formula is applied to the first-tier distributions. In this case, none of the second-tier distributions are taxed, because all of the DNI has been allocated to the first-tier beneficiaries.

If both first-tier and second-tier distributions are made and the first-tier distributions do not exceed DNI, but the total of both first-tier and second-tier distributions does exceed DNI, the second-tier beneficiaries recognize income as shown below.

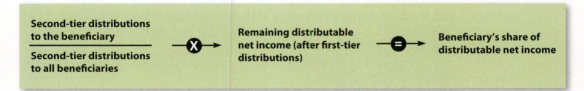

The trustee of the Gray Trust is required annually to distribute $10,000 each to Harriet and Wally, the two beneficiaries of the entity. In addition, the trustee can distribute other amounts of trust income or corpus at his sole discretion. In the current year, the trust reports accounting income of $60,000 and DNI of $50,000. However, the trustee distributes only the required $10,000 each to Harriet and to Wally. The balance of the income is accumulated and added to trust corpus.

In this case, only first-tier distributions have been made, but the total amount of the distributions does not exceed DNI for the year. Although DNI is the maximum amount included by the beneficiaries for the year, they can include no more in gross income than is distributed by the entity. Thus, both Harriet and Wally may be subject to tax on $10,000 as their proportionate shares of DNI.

---

[26]§§ 662(a)(1) and (2).   [27]Reg. §§ 1.662(a)−2 and −3.

Distributing DNI

EXAMPLE 25

Assume the same facts as in Example 24, except that DNI is $12,000. Harriet and Wally each receive $10,000, but they cannot be taxed in total on more than DNI. Each is taxed on $6,000 [DNI $12,000 × ($10,000/$20,000 of the first-tier distributions)].

EXAMPLE 26

Return to the facts in Example 23. Wong receives a first-tier distribution of $15,000. Now assume that second-tier distributions include $20,000 to Wong and $25,000 to Washington. Wilson's DNI is $40,000. Total distributions exceed the amount of DNI. The DNI is allocated between Wong and Washington as follows.

(1)	**First-tier distributions**	
	To Wong	$15,000 DNI
	To Washington	–0–
	Remaining DNI = $25,000	
(2)	**Second-tier distributions**	
	To Wong	$11,111 DNI [(20/45) × $25,000]
	To Washington	$13,889 DNI [(25/45) × $25,000]

EXAMPLE 27

Assume the same facts as in Example 26, except that accounting income is $80,000 and DNI is $70,000. Total distributions are less than the amount of DNI. DNI is allocated between Wong and Washington as follows.

(1)	**First-tier distributions**	
	To Wong	$15,000 DNI
	To Washington	–0–
	Remaining DNI = $55,000	
(2)	**Second-tier distributions**	
	To Wong	$20,000 DNI
	To Washington	$25,000 DNI

20-4c **Character of Income**

Consistent with the modified pass-through principle of Subchapter J, various classes of income (e.g., dividends, passive activity or portfolio gain and loss, AMT adjustments and preferences, tax-exempt interest) retain the same character for the beneficiaries that they had when they were received by the entity. If there are multiple beneficiaries *and* if all of the DNI is distributed, a problem arises in allocating the various classes of income among the beneficiaries.

Distributions are treated as consisting of the same proportion as the items that enter into the computation of DNI.

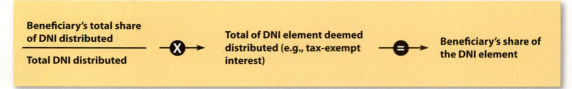

If the entity distributes only a part of its DNI, the amount of a specific class of DNI that is deemed distributed first must be determined.[28]

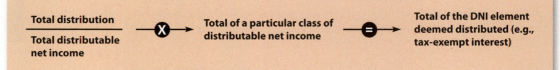

[28]Reg. § 1.662(b)–1.

DNI Flow-Throughs

The Baron Trust has DNI of $40,000, including the following: $10,000 of taxable interest, $10,000 of tax-exempt interest, and $20,000 of passive activity income. The trustee distributes, at her discretion, $8,000 to Mai and $12,000 to Nancy.

Beneficiary	Amount Received	Income Type		
		Taxable Interest	Tax-Exempt Interest	Passive Activity Income
Mai	$ 8,000	$2,000*	$2,000	$4,000
Nancy	12,000	3,000	3,000	6,000

*$8,000 distribution/$40,000 total DNI × $10,000 taxable interest in DNI.

EXAMPLE 28

Continue with the facts of Example 28. The character of the income that flows through to Mai and Nancy is effective for all other tax purposes. For instance, the $4,000 passive activity income that is allocated to Mai is available for offset against passive activity losses that she incurred from limited partnerships and rental activities for the year. Similarly, the $3,000 taxable interest income allocated to Nancy can be used to increase the amount of investment interest expense deductible by her in the year of the flow-through, and it may be subject to the net investment income tax. The interest is treated as if it had been received directly by the taxpayer.

EXAMPLE 29

Special Allocations

Under limited circumstances, the parties may modify the character-of-income allocation method set forth above. A modification is permitted only to the extent the allocation is required in the trust instrument and only to the extent it has an economic effect independent of the cash-flow and income tax consequences of the allocation.[29]

Return to the facts in Example 28. Assume that the beneficiaries are elderly individuals who have pooled their investment portfolios to avail themselves of the trustee's professional asset management skills. Suppose the trustee has the discretion to allocate different classes of income to different beneficiaries and she designates $10,000 of Nancy's $12,000 distribution as being from the tax-exempt income. Such a designation *would not be recognized* for tax purposes, and the allocation method of Example 28 must be used.

Suppose, however, the trust instrument stipulated that Nancy was to receive all of the income from the tax-exempt securities because Nancy alone contributed the exempt securities to trust corpus. Under this provision, the $10,000 of the nontaxable interest is paid to Nancy. This allocation *is recognized*, and $10,000 of Nancy's distribution is tax-exempt.

EXAMPLE 30

20-5 GRANTOR TRUSTS

A series of special provisions applies when the grantor of the trust retains beneficial enjoyment or substantial control over the trust property or income.[30] In that event, the grantor is taxed on the trust income, and the trust is disregarded for income tax purposes. Such an entity is known as a **grantor trust**.

The person who is taxed on the income is allowed to claim, on his or her own return, any deductions or credits attributable to the income. Such taxes restrict the grantor's ability to redirect the income recognized from trust corpus to the trust or its beneficiaries. The trustee still files a Form 1041, but no dollar amounts are included on the mostly "blank" return. All income and deduction items are reported on the grantor's Form 1040.[31]

LO.4

Use the special rules that apply to trusts where the creator (grantor) of the trust retains certain rights.

---

[29]Reg. § 1.652(b)–2(b). This is similar to the § 704(b)(2) requirement for partnerships.

[30]§§ 671–679.
[31]Reg § 1.671–4(a).

The grantor is taxed on the income if he or she retains (1) control of the corpus or (2) the power to dispose of the trust income without the approval or consent of any adverse party. An *adverse party* is any person having a substantial beneficial interest in the trust who could be affected adversely by the power the grantor possesses over the trust assets.[32]

A number of important powers, including the following, will *not* cause such income to be taxed to the grantor.[33]

- To apply the income toward the support of the grantor's dependents.[34]
- To allocate trust income or corpus among charitable beneficiaries.
- To invade corpus on behalf of a designated beneficiary.
- To withhold income from a beneficiary during his or her minority or disability.
- To allocate receipts and disbursements between income and corpus.

The retention by the grantor of certain administrative powers over the trust causes the income to be taxed to the grantor. Such powers include those to deal with trust income or corpus for less than full and adequate consideration, and to borrow from the trust without providing adequate interest or security.[35]

The grantor of a trust is taxed on the trust's income if he or she can revoke the trust.[36] In addition, a grantor is taxed on all or part of the income of a trust when, without the consent of any adverse party, the income may be:

- Distributed to the grantor or the grantor's spouse.
- Held or accumulated for future distribution to the grantor or the grantor's spouse.
- Applied to the payment of premiums on insurance policies on the life of the grantor or the grantor's spouse.[37]

EXAMPLE 31

Frank creates an irrevocable trust for his children with a transfer of income-producing property and an insurance policy on the life of Marion, his wife. During the year, the trustee uses $3,000 of the trust income to pay the premiums on the policy covering Marion's life. Frank is taxed on $3,000 of the trust's income.

Moreover, trust income accumulated for the benefit of someone whom the grantor is *legally obligated* to support is taxed to the grantor, but only to the extent it is applied for that purpose.[38] In these cases, the beneficiary often is a child or an ex-spouse.

EXAMPLE 32

Melanie creates an irrevocable accumulation trust. Her son, Sean, is the life beneficiary, and the remainder goes to any grandchildren. During the year, the trust income of $8,000 is applied as follows: $5,000 toward Sean's college tuition and other related educational expenses and $3,000 accumulated on Sean's behalf. If under state law Melanie has an obligation to support Sean and if this obligation includes providing a college education, Melanie is taxed on the $5,000 that is so applied.

---

[32] §§ 672(a), (b), and 674. See Reg. § 1.672(a)–1 for examples of adverse party situations.

[33] 674(b).

[34] § 677(b). However, when the income actually is applied for this purpose, the grantor is subject to income tax on that amount.

[35] See Reg. § 1.675–1(b) for a further discussion of this matter.

[36] § 676.

[37] § 677(a).

[38] § 677(b). The taxpayer's legal obligations vary according to state law, financial resources, and family expectations. See *Frederick C. Braun, Jr.*, 48 TCM 210, T.C.Memo. 1984–285, and *Cristopher Stone*, 54 TCM 462, T.C.Memo. 1987–454.

20-6 PROCEDURAL MATTERS

The fiduciary is required to file a Form 1041 (U.S. Income Tax Return for Estates and Trusts) in the following situations.[39]

- For an estate that has gross income of $600 or more for the year.
- For a trust that either has any taxable income or, if there is no taxable income, has gross income of $600 or more.

The fiduciary return (and any related tax liability) is due no later than the fifteenth day of the fourth month following the close of the entity's taxable year. A filing extension is available to the last day of the ninth month after the end of the tax year. For calendar year entities, these dates are April 15 and September 30.

Many fiduciary entities recognize capital gains during the year, through sales of assets that are part of corpus. In that event, a Schedule D is filed with the Form 1041, and the fiduciary entity or its beneficiaries can qualify for the lower tax rates on long-term capital gains.

The pass-through of income and deduction items to the beneficiary is accomplished through Schedule K–1 to Form 1041. This form is similar in format and function to the Schedule K–1 for partners and S corporation shareholders (see Chapters 10 and 12). Because the typical fiduciary entity records only a few transactions during the year, the Schedule K–1 for Form 1041 is less detailed than those for Forms 1065 and 1120S.

Trusts and estates must make estimated Federal income tax payments using the same quarterly schedule that applies to individual taxpayers. This requirement applies to estates and grantor trusts only for tax years that end two or more years after the date of the decedent's death.[40]

Fiduciary entities also must determine filing requirements that must be met for each of the U.S. states. These matters may turn on the location of the entity, the trustee/executor, and the beneficiaries.

20-7 TAX PLANNING

LO.5

Apply the fiduciary income tax rules in a manner that minimizes the income taxation of trusts and estates and still accomplishes the intended objectives of the grantor or decedent.

Many of the tax planning possibilities for estates and trusts were discussed in Chapter 19. However, several specific tax planning possibilities are available to help minimize the present value of any income tax liabilities on estates and trusts and their beneficiaries.

20-7a A Trust or an Estate as an Income-Shifting Device

Opportunities to use fiduciary entities for effective income shifting from one individual to another are limited, because the kiddie tax might apply to the amounts received by the beneficiary, and the fiduciary is likely to be subject to a marginal tax rate that is equal to or higher than that of the grantor/decedent. Other strategies still should be considered by the parties.

- Trust corpus should be invested in growth assets that are low on yield but high on appreciation, so that the trustee can determine the timing of the gain and somewhat control the effective tax rate that applies.
- Trust corpus should be invested in tax-exempt securities such as municipal bonds and mutual funds that invest in them to eliminate the tax costs associated with the investment. If this approach is taken, a trust might be unnecessary—the parent should simply retain full control over the assets and invest in the tax-exempt securities in his or her own account.

---

[39]§§ 6012(a)(3) and (4).

[40]§ 6654(l)(2)(A).

- The grantor should retain high-yield assets, rather than contribute them to a fiduciary entity (i.e., where the tax cost is too high).

- Use of trust vehicles should be reserved for cases where professional management of the assets is necessary for portfolio growth and the additional tax costs can be justified.

20-7b Income Tax Planning for Estates

As a separate taxable entity, an estate can select its own tax year and accounting methods. The executor of an estate should consider selecting a fiscal year because this will determine when beneficiaries must include income distributions from the estate in their own tax returns. Beneficiaries must include the income for their tax year with or within which the estate's tax year ends. Proper selection of the estate's tax year can result in a smoothing out of income and a reduction of the income taxes for all parties involved.

The timing and amounts of income distributions to the beneficiaries present important tax planning opportunities. If the executor can make discretionary income distributions, he or she should evaluate the relative marginal income tax rates of the estate and its beneficiaries. By timing the distributions properly, the overall income tax liability can be minimized. Care should be taken, however, to time the distributions in light of the estate's DNI.

Distribution Strategies

EXAMPLE 33

For several years before his death on March 7, Don had entered into annual deferred compensation agreements with his employer. These agreements collectively called for the payment of $200,000 six months after Don's retirement or death. To provide a maximum 12-month period within which to generate deductions to offset this large item of income in respect of a decedent, the executor or administrator of the estate should elect a fiscal year ending August 31. The election is made simply by filing the estate's first tax return for the short period of March 7 to August 31.

EXAMPLE 34

Carol, the sole beneficiary of an estate, is a calendar year, cash basis taxpayer. If the estate elects a fiscal year ending January 31, all distributions during the period of February 1 to December 31, 2018, are reported on Carol's tax return for calendar year 2019 (due April 15, 2020). Thus, assuming that estimated tax requirements otherwise have been met, any income taxes that result from a $50,000 distribution made by the estate on February 20, 2018, may be deferred until April 15, 2020.

EXAMPLE 35

Assume the same facts as in Example 34. If the estate is closed on December 15, 2019, the DNI for both the fiscal year ending January 31, 2019, and the final tax year ending December 15, 2019, is included in Carol's tax return for the same calendar year. To avoid the effect of this bunching of income, the estate should not be closed until early in calendar year 2020.

In general, those beneficiaries who are subject to high income tax rates should be made beneficiaries of second-tier (but not IRD) distributions of the estate. Most likely, these individuals will have less need for an additional steady stream of (taxable) income while their income tax savings can be relatively large. Moreover, a special allocation of tax-favored types of income and expenses should be considered. For example, tax-exempt income can be directed more easily to beneficiaries in higher income tax brackets.

EXAMPLE 36

Review Examples 26 and 27 carefully. Note, for instance, the flexibility that is available to the executor or administrator in timing the second-tier distributions of income and corpus of the estate. To illustrate, if Washington is subject to a high tax rate, distributions to him should be minimized except in years when DNI is low. In this manner, Washington's exposure to gross income from the distributions can be controlled so that most of the distributions he receives will be free of income tax.

20-7c Distributions of In-Kind Property

The ability of the trustee or executor to elect to recognize the realized gain or loss relative to a distributed noncash asset allows the gain or loss to be allocated to the optimal taxpayer.

EXAMPLE 37

The Yorba Linda Estate distributed some inventory, basis of $40,000 and fair market value of $41,500, to beneficiary Larry. Yorba Linda is subject to a 24% marginal income tax rate, and Larry is subject to a 35% marginal rate. The executor of Yorba Linda should elect that the entity recognize the related $1,500 realized gain, thereby subjecting the gain to the estate's lower marginal tax rate.

Tax without election, at Larry's 35% rate	$525
Tax with election, at estate's 24% rate	360

ETHICS & EQUITY Who Should Be a Trustee?

Often, grantors choose a family member to be the trustee of the family savings, the children's education fund, or whatever other assets are placed into management by the trust. The relative chosen is often the most trusted but not always the one with the business skills. However, as the financial world has become more complex, with wild stock market fluctuations, increased fiduciary standards, and potential conflicts of interest, some are questioning the wisdom of using a family member as the trustee.

Using a trust company or other financial institution as a trustee usually results in more stable (if lower) investment returns, eliminating both the highs and the lows of the stock market cycle. Institutions also can bring other advantages.

- They do not die, run away, become mentally or physically incapacitated, or otherwise unexpectedly become unqualified for the position.
- They are not easily swayed by emotional appeals; nor do they react to family jealousies.

- They are prohibited by law from acting under a conflict of interest, such as might exist between family members when the related trustee is also a trust beneficiary.

On the negative side, human trustees often waive or discount their fiduciary fee, but institutions do not. Especially for trusts with a small corpus, institutional trustees can be prohibitively expensive. And the trust company most often is oriented toward expanding its customer base rather than offering individual attention to existing clients.

How would you advise a client to address this delicate issue? Compromise solutions might be to:

- Appoint co-trustees. Aunt Grace or Uncle Roberto can provide the personal touch and ensure that trust decisions recognize family needs, and the trust company maximizes investment returns and furnishes professional management.
- Keep the family trustee but hire professionals at an hourly rate, to provide advice only when needed. This approach avoids the fees based on asset values that trust companies usually charge.

20-7d Deductibility of Fiduciary Expenses

Some deductions and losses may be claimed either on the estate tax return or as income tax deductions of the estate on the fiduciary return, at the taxpayer's choice.[41] In such a case, the deduction for income tax purposes is not allowed unless the estate tax deduction is waived. These deductions can be apportioned between the two returns.

---

[41]§ 642(g) and Reg. § 20.2053–1(d).

EXAMPLE 38

Don's will named his surviving spouse, Donna, as the executor of his estate. The estate's assets total $10,000,000. The will includes bequests to pay various debts, make gifts to certain charities, and provide for the grandchildren through trusts. The will also allows for the payment of an executor's fee equal to 5% of the assets ($500,000).

Should Donna pay herself an executor's fee? If Donna is the estate's remainder beneficiary, a common occurrence, payment of the fee would result in the following.

- A deduction by the estate on the Form 706 (e.g., at the 40% marginal rate) or the estate's Form 1041 (at the 37% marginal rate).

- Gross income for services to Donna (e.g., at her individual 32% marginal tax rate).

If Donna waives the executor's fee, she will receive the $500,000 as the remainder beneficiary of the estate. Then the results would be:

- An increased marital deduction on the Form 706 (deductible at the 40% tax rate).

- No gross income to Donna, because the receipt of a bequest is nontaxable.

Almost certainly, a remainder beneficiary who is a surviving spouse would waive the fee.

An expense deductible for estate tax purposes may not qualify as an income tax deduction. Interest expense incurred to carry tax-exempt bonds is disallowed for income tax purposes. The expenses likely should be claimed for estate tax purposes; otherwise, they will be completely lost.

EXAMPLE 39

The executor of Dana's estate pays $5,000 in burial expenses (authorized under local law and approved by the probate court) from estate assets. The $5,000 expense should be claimed on the estate tax return, as it is not deductible at all for income tax purposes.

20-7e Duties of an Executor

One of the duties of an estate's executor is to file the last income tax return of the decedent.[42] That Form 1040 is due on April 15 of the year following the date of death, regardless of when during the year death occurs.[43] Several planning considerations are apparent in this regard.

The executor must be aware that the decedent's tax year ends on the date of death, but any personal and dependency exemptions, and standard deduction, are not reduced even though a short tax year results.

The final Form 1040 may be filed simply to claim a refund of the decedent's estimated tax payments or withholdings. However, it includes gross income and deductions to the point of death and can result in income tax being due. If the decedent was married on the date of death, a joint return can be filed with signatures of both the executor and the surviving spouse.[44]

Medical expenses incurred by the decedent but unpaid at the time of the decedent's death are treated with a special rule. If paid by the estate during a one-year period beginning with the day after death, the expenses may be claimed as an income tax deduction in the year incurred or as an estate tax deduction, but not both.[45] The executor may divide such expenses in any way between the decedent's Form 1040 and his or her estate tax return.

---

[42]§ 6012(b)(1).

[43]Reg. § 1.6072–1(b).

[44]§ 6013(a). This also might occur for the prior year (when the spouse was alive) if the return for that year has not yet been filed.

[45]§ 213(c).

20-7f Additional Taxes on Capital Gains and Net Investment Income

Aggressive income shifting among a fiduciary entity and its beneficiaries may be prompted by the fiduciary's exposure to the liabilities for additional Federal income taxes on capital gains and net investment income (NII). These additional taxes apply only to "high-income" taxpayers, but the income level at which the tax applies is much lower for fiduciaries than it is for individuals.

Thus, investment income and capital gains might best be distributed to individual beneficiaries, removing the items from the NII of the fiduciary, perhaps without creating an additional tax liability for the beneficiary.

The tax also can be reduced if the fiduciary invests in securities that produce tax-exempt or tax-deferred income or meets the material participation requirement for otherwise passive activities. In addition, the tax liability can be minimized if the entity invests in assets that produce a low yield (like growth stocks or funds) and if it arranges its portfolio to produce a low turnover rate.

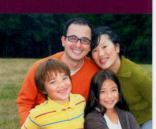

REFOCUS ON THE BIG PICTURE

SETTING UP A TRUST TO PROTECT A FAMILY

Anna Jiang and her family should consider the creation of one or more trusts to provide security in case Anna is incapacitated by medical problems and unable to manage the family's finances. Some suggestions for the family might be:

- Anna transfers some or all of the $2 million assets to the Jiang Family Trust, with quarterly income payable to Tom and the children. Recipients would be designated by the trustee, but all of the entity's accounting income must be distributed. In this way, the income could be directed to the beneficiary most in need (e.g., to pay for education expenses or to start a new business). The children could be named first-tier beneficiaries, with Tom as a second-tier income beneficiary.

- While Anna is still healthy and earning a regular salary, the trustee could accumulate the accounting income and allow the corpus to grow. Alternatively, the trustee could make gifts to charity or fund education plans for Bobby and Sally.

- Anna should provide clear instructions to the trustee as to her preferences on how the trust corpus should be invested and specify which of Tom's and the children's expenses should and should not be covered.

- The children should be named as remainder beneficiaries of the Jiang Family Trust. In case the trust corpus exceeds the estate tax bypass amount, other remainder beneficiaries could be named to avoid any generation-skipping tax (see Chapters 18 and 19).

- Amendments to the trust document should be considered whenever Tom and Anna update their wills.

What If?

If Anna remains healthy, the Jiang Family Trust might be terminated when the children reach the age of majority, as the need for financial support will have diminished. However, if Tom is unable or unwilling to take over management of the assets, the trust should continue. In this event, the trustee should be chosen from family members or business associates who know Anna and Tom well and are familiar with the couple's objectives. Then the trustee might shift the focus to funding long-term care for the couple, making charitable gifts, or financing the education needs of grandchildren.

Key Terms

Complex trust, 20-4

Corpus, 20-4

Deductions in respect of a
decedent, 20-12

Distributable net income (DNI), 20-16

Entity accounting income, 20-8

Fiduciary, 20-2

Grantor, 20-3

Grantor trust, 20-23

Income in respect of a decedent (IRD),
20-12

Pass-through entities, 20-6

Reversionary interest, 20-4

Simple trust, 20-4

Sprinkling trust, 20-4

Discussion Questions

Communications   1.   **LO.1** A local bank has asked you to speak at its Building Personal Wealth Conference on the topic of "What Should Your Trust Do for You?" Develop at least four PowerPoint slides, each one listing a function that a trust might be able to accomplish for an individual who has more than a modest level of financial resources.

2.   **LO.1** In general terms, describe how the following entities are subject to the Federal income tax. (Answer only for the entity, not for its owners, beneficiaries, etc.)

   a.   C corporations (Subchapter C).

   b.   Partnerships (Subchapter K).

   c.   S corporations (Subchapter S).

   d.   Trusts and estates (Subchapter J).

3.   **LO.1** Create a fact pattern that illustrates each of the following tax situations. Be specific.

   a.   A simple trust.

   b.   A complex trust with a $300 personal exemption.

   c.   A complex trust with a $100 personal exemption.

Communications   4.   **LO.2** Your college's accounting group has asked you to give a 10-minute speech titled "Trusts, Estates, and the QBI Deduction." The audience will be students who have completed at least one course concerning Federal income taxation. Develop a brief outline for your remarks, and e-mail it to your instructor.

5.   **LO.2** Using Exhibit 20.4 as a guide, describe the computation of a fiduciary entity's accounting income, taxable income, and distributable net income.

6.   **LO.2** The Liu Trust is short of cash. It is required to distribute $100,000 to Yang every year, and that payment is due in six weeks. In its asset corpus, Liu holds a number of investments that are valued at $100,000. One of them is a plot of land with a tax basis to the trust of $80,000. Assuming that the trust agreement allows, what are the Federal income tax consequences if Liu distributes this land to Yang?

Critical Thinking   7.   **LO.2** In its first tax year, the Vasquez Estate generated $50,000 of taxable interest income and $30,000 of tax-exempt interest income. It paid fiduciary fees of $8,000. The estate is subject to a 40% marginal estate tax rate and a 37% marginal income tax rate.

   a.   How much should the executor assign as a Form 706 deduction for the payment of the fees?

   b.   Express this computation as a Microsoft Excel command.

8.   **LO.2** The Sterling Trust owns a business and generated $100,000 in depreciation deductions for the tax year. Mona is one of the income beneficiaries of the entity.

   a.   Given the following information, compute Mona's deduction, if any, for the Sterling depreciation.

   b.   Express your solution as a Microsoft Excel command.

Sterling's taxable income from the business	$ 800,000
Sterling's gross income from the business	4,000,000
Mona's share of trust accounting income	500,000
Total trust accounting income	2,500,000
Mona's share of distributable net income	1,200,000
Total distributable net income	1,600,000

9. **LO.2** In year 1, the Helpful Trust agreed to make a $50,000 cash contribution to Local Soup Kitchen, a charitable organization. Helpful's board agreed to the gift at a November year 1 meeting, but the check was not issued until February 20, year 2 (i.e., during the next tax year).

    a. Can the trust claim a charitable contribution deduction? If so, describe how Helpful should treat its gift.

    b. Would the answer to part (a) change if the check was issued on May 1, year 2? If so, how?

10. **LO.3** One of the key concepts in fiduciary income taxation is that of *distributable net income* (DNI). List the major functions of DNI on one PowerPoint slide, with no more than five bullets, to present to your classmates as part of the discussion of this chapter of the text. Just review the uses of DNI in Subchapter J, and do not discuss its computation.

    Communications

11. **LO.4** Jada wants to transfer some assets to a trust this year; the income beneficiaries will be her two grandchildren. The trust income and assets will be used to pay the grandchildren's tuition to private high schools and universities. Upon the younger grandchild's graduation, the trust assets will return to Jada's ownership. Identify tax issues related to Jada's plan to use a temporary fiduciary entity.

    Critical Thinking

12. **LO.4** Carol has been promoted several times, and she may be named a partner in her consulting firm next year. Thus, she will be subject to higher marginal income tax rates than in the past. Carol's colleague Isaiah has told her about a "college education trust" from which he pays tuition and fees for his children. He has implied that there are sizable tax advantages to setting up a trust for this purpose.

    Decision Making

    Communications

    Carol is considering establishing a similar trust to pay tuition for her own children. She believes that the trust will be able to deduct the tuition payments, something that she cannot currently do on her Form 1040. Write a memo for the tax research file addressing Carol's ideas and recommending a tax-effective course of action.

13. **LO.5** Comment on the following items relative to tax planning strategies of a fiduciary entity.

    Decision Making

    a. To reduce taxes for a typical family, should income be shifted *to* a trust or *from* a trust? Why?

    b. From a tax planning standpoint, who should invest in tax-exempt bonds, the trust or its beneficiaries?

    c. To reduce overall taxes, should a high-income, wealthy beneficiary be assigned to the first or second tier of trust distributions? Why?

    d. To minimize taxes, how should a trust treat the distribution of an in-kind asset? Why?

Computational Exercises

14. **LO.1** Compute the Federal income tax liability for the Valerio Trust. The entity reports the following transactions for the 2019 tax year. The trustee accumulates all accounting income for the year.

Operating income from a business	$ 500,000
Dividend income, all from U.S. corporations	30,000
Interest income, City of San Antonio bonds	40,000
Fiduciary fees, deductible portion	(15,000)
Net rental losses, passive activity	(100,000)

15. **LO.1** The Wes Trust reports $100,000 of AMT income before the annual exemption. The entity's AMT for 2019 is:

    a. $19,604.

    b. $20,573.

    c. $26,000.

    d. $28,000.

16. **LO.1** For 2019, the Guess Trust retains all of its income items, which include only $100,000 of net investment income and $40,000 of profits from an active business operation. Guess incurs an additional tax on net investment income (NIIT) of:

    a. $4,837.

    b. $3,800.

    c. $3,316.

    d. $0.

17. **LO.2** The Biltmore Trust is a simple trust. Crawford is its sole beneficiary. In the current year, the trust earns $3,200 in taxable interest and $8,000 in tax-exempt interest. In addition, the trust recognizes a $2,500 long-term capital gain. The trustee assesses a fee of $1,800 for the year.

    a.   Compute trust accounting income, where the trust agreement allocates fees and capital gains to corpus.

    b.   Same as part (a), except that fees are allocated to income.

    c.   Construct a Microsoft Excel formula that will generate the correct answer to both parts (a) and (b).

18. **LO.2** The Hosta Trust reports gross rent income of $72,000, expenses attributable to the rents of $55,000, and tax-exempt interest from state bonds of $18,000. Under the trust agreement, the trustee is to pay 20% of the annual trust accounting income to the American Red Cross, a qualifying charitable organization.

    a.   Compute Hosta's charitable contribution deduction.

    b.   Express the solution as a Microsoft Excel command.

Problems

19. **LO.1** Complete the following chart, indicating the comparative attributes of the typical simple trust and complex trust by answering yes/no or explaining the differences between the entities where appropriate.

Attribute	Simple Trust	Complex Trust
Trust could incur its own tax liability for the year		
Trust generally distributes all of the DNI		
Trust can deduct its charitable contributions in the year of, or the year after, payment		
Maximum tax rate on net long-term capital gains = 20%		
Trust can adopt the FIFO method for its inventory assets; the grantor had been using lower of cost or market		
Trust can use a tax year other than the calendar year		
Amount of personal exemption		

20. **LO.2** The Polozzi Trust will incur the following items in the next tax year, its first   **Decision Making**
    year of existence.

Interest income	$ 25,000
Rent income	100,000
Cost recovery deductions for the rental activity	35,000
Capital gain income	40,000
Fiduciary and tax preparation fees	7,000

Betty, the grantor of the trust, is working with you on the language in the trust instrument relative to the derivation of annual accounting income for the entity. She will name Shirley as the sole income beneficiary and Benny as the remainder beneficiary.

a. Suggest language to Betty that will maximize the annual income distribution to Shirley.

b. Suggest language to Betty that will minimize the annual distribution to Shirley and maximize the accumulation on Benny's behalf.

21. **LO.2** Complete the chart below, indicating the Calvet Trust's entity accounting income for each of the alternatives. For this purpose, use the following information.

Interest income, taxable	$300,000 ✓
Interest income, tax-exempt	30,000
Interest income, tax-exempt but AMT preference item	20,000
Long-term capital gain	40,000
Trustee fee	10,000

Trust Agreement Provisions	Trust Accounting Income
Fees and capital gains allocable to corpus	
Capital gains allocable to corpus, one-half of fees allocable to income	
Capital gains allocable to income, silent concerning allocation of fees	
Fees and exempt income allocable to corpus, silent concerning allocation of capital gain/loss	

22. **LO.1, 2, 3** Complete the following chart, indicating the comparative attributes of the typical trust and estate by answering yes/no or explaining the differences between the entities where appropriate.

Attribute	Estate	Trust
Separate income tax entity		
Controlling document		
Can have both income and remainder beneficiaries		
Computes entity accounting income before determining entity taxable income		
Termination date is determinable from controlling document		
Document identifies both income and remainder beneficiaries		
Generally must use calendar tax year		

23. **LO.2** Roberto is one of the income beneficiaries of the Carol LeMans Estate. This year, as directed by the will, Roberto received all of the sales commissions that were earned and payable to Carol (cash basis) at her death, as well as one of three

remaining installment payments. Compute Roberto's gross income attributable to Carol's activities for the current year, given the following financial data.

Sales commissions receivable	$40,000
Ordinary gain, $60,000, on installment sale; first of three payments received this year	20,000

24. **LO.2** Sanchez incurred the following items.

Business income, exclusive of the following items	$80,000
Tax-exempt interest income	40,000
Payment to charity from 2020 Sanchez gross income, paid 3/1/21	20,000

Complete the following chart, indicating the charitable contributions deduction under the various assumptions.

Assumption	2020 Deduction for Contribution
Sanchez is a cash basis individual.	
Sanchez is an accrual basis corporation.	
Sanchez is a trust.	

25. **LO.2** The Twist Trust has generated $60,000 in depreciation deductions for the year. Its accounting income is $75,000. In computing this amount, pursuant to the trust document, depreciation was allocated to corpus. Accounting income was distributed at the trustee's discretion: $25,000 to Hernandez and $50,000 to Jackson.

   a.   Compute the depreciation deductions that Hernandez, Jackson, and Twist may claim.

   b.   Same as part (a), except that depreciation was allocated to income.

   c.   Same as part (a), except that the trustee distributed $15,000 each to Hernandez and to Jackson and retained the remaining accounting income.

   d.   Same as part (a), except that Twist is an estate (and not a trust).

26. **LO.2, 3** The Allwardt Trust is a simple trust that correctly uses the calendar year for tax purposes. Its income beneficiaries (Lucy and Ethel) are entitled to the trust's annual accounting income in shares of one-half each.

For the current tax year, Allwardt reports the following.

Ordinary income	$100,000
Long-term capital gains, allocable to corpus	30,000
Trustee commission expense, allocable to corpus	5,000

Use the format of Exhibit 20.5 to address the following items.

   a.   How much income is each beneficiary entitled to receive?

   b.   What is the trust's DNI?

   c.   What is the trust's taxable income?

   d.   How much gross income is reported by each of the beneficiaries?

27. **LO.2, 3** The Allwardt Trust is a simple trust that correctly uses the calendar year for tax purposes. Its income beneficiaries (Lucy and Ethel) are entitled to the trust's annual accounting income in shares of one-half each.

For the current tax year, Allwardt reports the following.

Ordinary income	$100,000
Long-term capital gains, allocable to income	30,000
Trustee commission expense, allocable to corpus	5,000

   a.   How much income is each beneficiary entitled to receive?

   b.   What is the trust's DNI?

   c.   What is the trust's taxable income?

   d.   How much gross income is reported by each of the beneficiaries?

28. **LO.3** The Kilp Sisters Trust is required to distribute $60,000 annually equally to its two income beneficiaries, Clare and Renee. If trust income is not sufficient to pay these amounts, the trustee can invade corpus to the extent necessary.

    During the current year, the trust generates only taxable interest income and records DNI of $160,000; the trustee distributes $30,000 to Clare and $150,000 to Renee.

    a. How much of the $150,000 distributed to Renee is included in her gross income?

    b. How much of the $30,000 distributed to Clare is included in her gross income?

    c. Are these distributions first-tier or second-tier distributions?

29. **LO.3** The Dolce Estate reports the following items for the current tax year.

Dividend income	$ 50,000
Taxable interest income	8,000
Passive activity income	30,000
Tax-exempt interest income	12,000
Distributable net income	$100,000

    Dolce's two noncharitable income beneficiaries, Brenda and Dev, receive cash distributions of $20,000 each. How much of each class of income is deemed to have been distributed to Brenda? To Dev?

30. **LO.2, 3** The trustee of the Pieper Trust can distribute any amount of accounting income and corpus to the trust's beneficiaries, Lydia and Avi. This year, the trust incurred the following.

Taxable interest income	$40,000
Tax-exempt interest income	20,000
Long-term capital gains—allocable to corpus	80,000
Fiduciary's fees—allocable to corpus	9,000

    The trustee distributed $26,000 to Lydia and $13,000 to Avi.

    a. What is Pieper's trust accounting income?

    b. What is Pieper's DNI?

    c. What is Pieper's taxable income?

    d. What amounts are taxed to each of the beneficiaries?

31. **LO.2** Each of the following items was incurred by José, the cash basis, calendar year decedent. Under the terms of the will, Dora took immediate ownership in all of José's assets, except the dividend-paying stock. The estate received José's final paycheck.

    Applying the rules for income and deductions in respect of a decedent, indicate on which return each item should be reported: Dora's income tax return (Form 1040), the estate's first income tax return (Form 1041), or the estate's estate tax return (Form 706). More than one alternative may apply in some cases.

Item Incurred	Form(s) Reported on
a. Wages, last paycheck	
b. State income tax withheld on last paycheck	
c. Capital gain portion of installment payment received	
d. Ordinary income portion of installment payment received	
e. Dividend income, record date was two days prior to José's death	
f. Unrealized appreciation on a mutual fund investment	
g. Apartment building, rents accrued but not collected as of death	
h. Apartment building, property tax accrued and assessed but not paid as of death	

Decision Making

Communications

32. **LO.4** In each of the following independent cases, write a memo for the tax research file in preparation for a meeting with Gary. In each memo, explain whether the proposed plan meets his objective of shifting income and avoiding the grantor trust rules.

a. Gary transfers property in trust, income payable to Winnie (his wife) for life, remainder to his grandson. Gary's son is designated as the trustee.

b. Gary transfers income-producing assets and a life insurance policy to a trust, life estate to his children, remainder to his grandchildren. The policy is on Winnie's life, and the trustee (an independent trust company) is instructed to pay the premiums with income from the income-producing assets. The trust is designated as the beneficiary of the policy.

c. Gary transfers property in trust, income payable to Winnie (Gary's ex-wife), remainder to Gary or his estate upon Winnie's death. The transfer was made in satisfaction of Gary's alimony obligation to Winnie. An independent trust company is designated as the trustee.

Decision Making

33. **LO.4** Woody wants to transfer some of the income from his investment portfolio to his daughter Wendy, age 10. Woody wants the trust to be able to accumulate income on Wendy's behalf and to meet any excessive expenses associated with her chronic medical conditions. Furthermore, Woody wants the trust to protect Wendy against his premature death without increasing his Federal gross estate. Thus, Woody provides the trustee with the powers to purchase insurance on his life and to meet any medical expenses that Wendy incurs.

The trust is created in 2008. A whole life insurance policy with five annual premium payments is purchased during that year. The trustee spends $30,000 for Wendy's medical expenses in 2018 (but in no other year). Woody dies in 2019. Has the trust been tax-effective? Explain.

Decision Making

Communications

34. **LO.2, 3** Your client, Annie O'Toole (22 Beneficiary Lane, Wellington, KS 67152), has come to you for some advice regarding gifts of property. She has just learned that she must undergo major surgery, and she would like to make certain gifts before entering the hospital. On your earlier advice, Annie had established a plan of lifetime giving for four prior years.

Build a table summarizing your findings, supplemented by a list of your assumptions, and write a cover letter to Annie, discussing each of the following assets that she is considering using as gifts to family and friends. In doing so, evaluate the income tax consequences of having such property pass through her estate to the designated heir. Be sure to consider the time value of money in your analysis.

a. Annie plans to give a cottage to her son Nico to fulfill a promise made many years ago. She has owned the cottage for the past 15 years and has a basis in it of $30,000 (fair market value of $20,000).

b. Annie has $100,000 of long-term capital losses that she has been carrying forward for the past few years. Now she is considering making a gift of $200,000 in installment notes to her daughter Nyah. Annie's basis in the notes is $100,000, and the notes' current fair market value is $190,000.

Tax Return Problems

1. Compute the 2018 fiduciary income and Federal income tax for the Blue Trust. Prepare a spreadsheet solution to make your computations, and complete a Form 1041 for the entity.

    In addition, determine the amount and character of the income and expense items that each beneficiary must report for the year. Omit any alternative minimum tax computations. The year's activities of the trust include the following.

Dividend income, all U.S. stocks	$50,000
Taxable interest income	10,000
Tax-exempt interest income	15,000
Fiduciary's fees	4,000

    The trust and Betty both use the calendar tax year. Under the terms of the trust instrument, fiduciary's fees are allocated to income. The trustee must distribute all of the entity's accounting income to Betty Blue by February 15 of the following year. The trustee followed this charge and made no other distributions during the year. Fiduciary's fees properly were assigned as an offset to taxable interest income.

    The trust was created on July 8, 2000. There are no tax credits for the year, and none of the entity's income was derived from a personal services contract. The trust has no economic interest in any foreign trust. Its Federal identification number is 11-1111111.

    The trustee, Hoover State Federal Bank, is located at 4959 Cold Harbor Boulevard, Mountain Brook, AL 35223. Its employer identification number is 98-7654321. Betty lives at 67671 Crestline Road, Birmingham, AL 35212. Her Social Security number is 123-45-6788.

2. Compute the 2018 fiduciary income tax return (Form 1041) and Federal income tax for the Green Trust. Prepare a spreadsheet solution to make your computations, and complete a Form 1041 for the entity and a Schedule K–1 for beneficiary Marcus. In addition, determine the amount and character of the income and expense items that each beneficiary must report for the year. Omit the Form 8960 for the entity's NIIT; the trust is not subject to the AMT. The year's activities of the trust include the following.

Dividend income, all qualified U.S. stocks	$10,000
Taxable interest income	50,000
Tax-exempt interest income	20,000
Net long-term capital gain, incurred 11/1	25,000
Fiduciary's fees	6,000

    Under the terms of the trust instrument, cost recovery, net capital gains and losses, and fiduciary fees are allocable to corpus. The trustee is required to distribute $25,000 to Marcus every year. For the year, the trustee distributed $40,000 to Marcus and $40,000 to Marcus's sister, Ellen Hayes. No other distributions were made.

    In computing DNI, the trustee properly assigned all of the deductible fiduciary's fees to the taxable interest income.

    The trustee paid $4,000 in estimated taxes for the year on behalf of the trust. Any resulting refund is to be credited to the next tax year. The exempt income was not derived from private activity bonds.

    The trust was created on December 14, 1953. It is not subject to any recapture taxes, nor does it have any tax credits. None of its income was derived under a personal services contract. The trust has no economic interest in any foreign trust. Its Federal identification number is 11-1111111.

    The trustee, Wisconsin State National Bank, is located at 3100 East Wisconsin Avenue, Milwaukee, WI 53201. Its employer identification number is 11-1111111. Marcus lives at 9880 East North Avenue, Shorewood, WI 53211. His Social Security number is 123-45-6788. Ellen lives at 6772 East Oklahoma Avenue, Milwaukee, WI 53204. Her Social Security number is 987-65-4321.

Research Problems

THOMSON REUTERS
CHECKPOINT™

Note: Solutions to the Research Problems can be prepared by using the Thomson Reuters Checkpoint™ online tax research database, which accompanies this textbook. Solutions can also be prepared by using research materials found in a typical tax library.

Critical Thinking

Communications

Research Problem 1. Winder Ltd. is an S corporation that is wholly owned by Juan Plowright. Because several of Juan's ancestors have had Alzheimer's disease, Juan is transferring many of his assets to trusts, and he is funding living wills in anticipation of future medical issues.

Juan wants to transfer his Winder stock to a trust, but he wants to keep control over its operations for as long as possible. Thus, he wants to retain a right to revoke the trust, until such time as the trustee (a Winder executive who is on good terms with Juan) and a medical professional determine that Juan no longer is competent. You have explained to Juan that this entity is a grantor trust and that there are no income-shifting or transfer-tax-saving aspects in using such a trust.

The pertinent tax issues to be addressed are summarized below.

- Does the grantor trust terminate Winder's status as an S corporation?
- Will Winder's S election survive Juan's death? Under the terms of Juan's will, the S shares will be held by his estate and not be distributed to his niece Beatriz until she reaches age 25.

All parties are residents of New Mexico. Cite and summarize your findings in an outline for a talk that you will deliver next week to your school's Accounting Club. Assume that Club members are knowledgeable about the taxation of S corporations and their shareholders (e.g., from Chapter 12).

Research Problem 2. For three generations, the Dexter family has sent its children to Private University, preparing them for successful professional careers. The Edna Dexter Trust was established in the 1950s by LaKeisha's late grandmother and has accumulated a sizable corpus. It makes distributions to Edna's descendants rarely, and then only when they need large capital amounts. For example, two years ago, the trust distributed $500,000 to DuJuan Dexter to aid him in starting a practice in retirement and elder law. In most years, the trust's income is donated to a single charity.

Under the terms of the trust, Bigby Dexter, LaKeisha's uncle and legal guardian, can specify the trust beneficiaries and the amounts to be distributed to them. He also can replace the trustee and designate the charity that will receive the year's contribution. Accordingly, the trust falls under the grantor trust rules, and Bigby reports the trust's transactions on his own Form 1040.

LaKeisha wants to attend the prestigious local Academy High School, which will require a four-year expenditure for tuition and fees of $150,000, payable in advance. She approaches the Dexter trustee and requests a current-year distribution of this amount, payable directly to the Academy. Under the laws of the state, the parent or guardian must provide a child with a public school education (no tuition charge) until age 16.

If the payment to the Academy is made, how is it treated under the Subchapter J rules: as a charitable contribution to the Academy, as a corpus distribution to LaKeisha, or in some other manner? Be specific.

Use internet tax resources to address the following questions. Look for reliable websites and blogs of the IRS and other government agencies, media outlets, businesses, tax professionals, academics, think tanks, and political outlets.

Research Problem 3. How many estates filed a Form 1041 last year? Simple trusts? Complex trusts? Grantor trusts? How much Federal income tax has been collected on Forms 1041 over the last three tax years? Summarize your findings in a series of graphs to share with your classmates.

Data Analytics

Communications

Research Problem 4. Under the income tax laws of your state applicable to fiduciaries, how are the following items allocated among the entity and the beneficiaries? Put your findings in a PowerPoint presentation for your classmates. *Hint:* Use the CCH, RIA, or other online tax research service to find this information.

Communications

- Capital gain.
- Cost recovery.
- Fiduciary fees.
- Exempt interest income.
- QBI deduction.
- General business credits.

Research Problem 5. Find the website of a law firm that seems to specialize in fiduciary entities, preferably a firm located in your state. Ask the firm to quote you a fee for (1) establishing a simple trust and (2) filing the annual Form 1041. Summarize your findings and your communications with the firm in an e-mail to your instructor.

Communications

Becker CPA Review Questions

1. On January 1, year 1, Olinto created a $650,000 trust that provided his mother with a lifetime income interest starting on January 1, year 1, with the remainder interest to go to his son. Olinto expressly retained the power to revoke both the income interest and the remainder interest at any time. Who is taxed on the trust's year 1 income?

   a. Olinto's mother
   b. Olinto's son
   c. Olinto
   d. The trust

2. A distribution from estate income *currently* required was made to the estate's sole beneficiary during its calendar year. The maximum amount of the distribution to be included in the beneficiary's gross income is limited to the estate's:

   a. Capital gain income.
   b. Ordinary gross income.
   c. Distributable net income.
   d. Net investment income.

3. Lyon, a cash basis taxpayer, died on January 15 of the current year. During the current year, the estate executor made the required periodic distribution of $9,000 from estate income to Lyon's sole heir. The following information pertains to the estate's income and disbursements for the year. For the current calendar year, what was the estate's distributable net income (DNI)?

Estate Income	
Taxable interest	$20,000
Net long-term capital gains allocable to corpus	10,000

Estate Disbursements	
Administrative expenses attributable to taxable income	$5,000

   a. $15,000
   b. $20,000
   c. $25,000
   d. $30,000

4. Reinus, a cash basis taxpayer, died on February 3. During the year, the estate's executor made a distribution of $12,000 from estate income to Reinus's sole heir and adopted a calendar year to determine the estate's taxable income. The following additional information pertains to the estate's income and disbursements for the year. For the calendar year, what was the estate's distributable net income (DNI)?

Estate Income	
Taxable interest	$85,000
Net long-term capital gains allocable to corpus	10,000

Estate Disbursements	
Administrative expenses attributable to taxable income	$24,000
Charitable contributions from gross income to a public charity, made under the terms of the will	19,000

   a. $39,000   c. $58,000

   b. $42,000   d. $65,000

5. A distribution to an estate's sole beneficiary for the calendar year equaled $15,000, the amount currently required to be distributed by the will. The estate's records showed the following. What amount of the distribution was taxable to the beneficiary?

Estate Income	
Taxable interest	$40,000

Estate Disbursements	
Expenses attributable to taxable interest	$34,000

   a. $40,000   c. $6,000

   b. $15,000   d. $0

6. Peyton Trust, which is a simple trust, distributed $45,000 to its sole beneficiary, Brooke, in the current year. Further, it had the following items of income and expense for the current year.

Interest income from municipal bonds	$10,000
Gross income from rental properties	30,000
Operating expenses for the rental properties	5,000
Trust fees allocable to the rental properties	2,000

    What is Peyton's income distribution deduction for the current year?

   a. $23,000   c. $40,000

   b. $33,000   d. $45,000

Appendix A

Tax Rate Schedules and Tables

2018 Tax Rate Schedules

Single—Schedule X

If taxable income is: Over—	But not over—	The tax is:	of the amount over—
$ 0	$ 9,525	.........10%	$ 0
9,525	38,700	$ 952.50 + 12%	9,525
38,700	82,500	4,453.50 + 22%	38,700
82,500	157,500	14,089.50 + 24%	82,500
157,500	200,000	32,089.50 + 32%	157,500
200,000	500,000	45,689.50 + 35%	200,000
500,000	....	150,689.50 + 37%	500,000

Head of household—Schedule Z

If taxable income is: Over—	But not over—	The tax is:	of the amount over—
$ 0	$ 13,600	.........10%	$ 0
13,600	51,800	$ 1,360.00 + 12%	13,600
51,800	82,500	5,944.00 + 22%	51,800
82,500	157,500	12,698.00 + 24%	82,500
157,500	200,000	30,698.00 + 32%	157,500
200,000	500,000	44,298.00 + 35%	200,000
500,000	....	149,298.00 + 37%	500,000

Married filing jointly or Qualifying widow(er)—Schedule Y–1

If taxable income is: Over—	But not over—	The tax is:	of the amount over—
$ 0	$ 19,050	.........10%	$ 0
19,050	77,400	$ 1,905.00 + 12%	19,050
77,400	165,000	8,907.00 + 22%	77,400
165,000	315,000	28,179.00 + 24%	165,000
315,000	400,000	64,179.00 + 32%	315,000
400,000	600,000	91,379.00 + 35%	400,000
600,000	....	161,379.00 + 37%	600,000

Married filing separately—Schedule Y–2

If taxable income is: Over—	But not over—	The tax is:	of the amount over—
$ 0	$ 9,525	.........10%	$ 0
9,525	38,700	$ 952.50 + 12%	9,525
38,700	82,500	4,453.50 + 22%	38,700
82,500	157,500	14,089.50 + 24%	82,500
157,500	200,000	32,089.50 + 32%	157,500
200,000	300,000	45,689.50 + 35%	200,000
300,000	....	80,689.50 + 37%	300,000

2019 Tax Rate Schedules

Single—Schedule X

If taxable income is: Over—	But not over—	The tax is:	of the amount over—
$ 0	$ 9,700	.........10%	$ 0
9,700	39,475	$ 970.00 + 12%	9,700
39,475	84,200	4,543.00 + 22%	39,475
84,200	160,725	14,382.50 + 24%	84,200
160,725	204,100	32,748.50 + 32%	160,725
204,100	510,300	46,628.50 + 35%	204,100
510,300	....	153,798.50 + 37%	510,300

Head of household—Schedule Z

If taxable income is: Over—	But not over—	The tax is:	of the amount over—
$ 0	$ 13,850	.........10%	$ 0
13,850	52,850	$ 1,385.00 + 12%	13,850
52,850	84,200	6,065.00 + 22%	52,850
84,200	160,700	12,962.00 + 24%	84,200
160,700	204,100	31,322.00 + 32%	160,700
204,100	510,300	45,210.00 + 35%	204,100
510,300	....	152,380.00 + 37%	510,300

Married filing jointly or Qualifying widow(er)—Schedule Y–1

If taxable income is: Over—	But not over—	The tax is:	of the amount over—
$ 0	$ 19,400	.........10%	$ 0
19,400	78,950	$ 1,940.00 + 12%	19,400
78,950	168,400	9,086.00 + 22%	78,950
168,400	321,450	28,765.00 + 24%	168,400
321,450	408,200	65,497.00 + 32%	321,450
408,200	612,350	93,257.00 + 35%	408,200
612,350	....	164,709.50 + 37%	612,350

Married filing separately—Schedule Y–2

If taxable income is: Over—	But not over—	The tax is:	of the amount over—
$ 0	$ 9,700	.........10%	$ 0
9,700	39,475	$ 970.00 + 12%	9,700
39,475	84,200	4,543.00 + 22%	39,475
84,200	160,725	14,382.50 + 24%	84,200
160,725	204,100	32,748.50 + 32%	160,725
204,100	306,175	46,628.50 + 35%	204,100
306,175	....	82,354.75 + 37%	306,175

Income Tax Rates—Estates and Trusts

Tax Year 2019

Taxable Income		The Tax Is:	Of the Amount
Over—	But not Over—		Over—
$ 0	$ 2,600	10%	$ 0
2,600	9,300	$ 260.00 + 24%	2,600
9,300	12,750	1,868.00 + 35%	9,300
12,750	....	3,075.50 + 37%	12,750

Tax Year 2018

Taxable Income		The Tax Is:	Of the Amount
Over—	But not Over—		Over—
$ 0	$ 2,550	10%	$ 0
2,550	9,150	$ 255.00 + 24%	2,550
9,150	12,500	1,839.00 + 35%	9,150
12,500	....	3,011.50 + 37%	12,500

Income Tax Rates—C Corporations, 2018 and after

For all income levels, the tax rate is 21%.

Unified Transfer Tax Rates

For Gifts Made and for Deaths after 2012

If the Amount with Respect to Which the Tentative Tax to Be Computed Is:	The Tentative Tax Is:
Not over $10,000	18 percent of such amount.
Over $10,000 but not over $20,000	$1,800, plus 20 percent of the excess of such amount over $10,000.
Over $20,000 but not over $40,000	$3,800, plus 22 percent of the excess of such amount over $20,000.
Over $40,000 but not over $60,000	$8,200, plus 24 percent of the excess of such amount over $40,000.
Over $60,000 but not over $80,000	$13,000, plus 26 percent of the excess of such amount over $60,000.
Over $80,000 but not over $100,000	$18,200, plus 28 percent of the excess of such amount over $80,000.
Over $100,000 but not over $150,000	$23,800, plus 30 percent of the excess of such amount over $100,000.
Over $150,000 but not over $250,000	$38,800, plus 32 percent of the excess of such amount over $150,000.
Over $250,000 but not over $500,000	$70,800, plus 34 percent of the excess of such amount over $250,000.
Over $500,000 but not over $750,000	$155,800, plus 37 percent of the excess of such amount over $500,000.
Over $750,000 but not over $1,000,000	$248,300, plus 39 percent of the excess of such amount over $750,000.
Over $1,000,000	$345,800, plus 40 percent of the excess of such amount over $1,000,000.

Valuation Tables, Excerpts

Table S Single Life Remainder Factors Interest Rate

AGE	4.2%	4.4%	4.6%	4.8%	5.0%	5.2%	5.4%	5.6%
0	.06083	.05483	.04959	.04501	.04101	.03749	.03441	.03170
1	.05668	.05049	.04507	.04034	.03618	.03254	.02934	.02652
2	.05858	.05222	.04665	.04178	.03750	.03373	.03042	.02750
3	.06072	.05420	.04848	.04346	.03904	.03516	.03173	.02871
4	.06303	.05634	.05046	.04530	.04075	.03674	.03319	.03006
5	.06547	.05861	.05258	.04726	.04258	.03844	.03478	.03153
6	.06805	.06102	.05482	.04935	.04453	.04026	.03647	.03312
7	.07074	.06353	.05717	.05155	.04658	.04217	.03826	.03479
8	.07356	.06617	.05964	.05386	.04875	.04421	.04017	.03658
9	.07651	.06895	.06225	.05631	.05105	.04637	.04220	.03849
10	.07960	.07185	.06499	.05889	.05347	.04865	.04435	.04052
11	.08283	.07490	.06786	.06160	.05603	.05106	.04663	.04267
12	.08620	.07808	.07087	.06444	.05871	.05360	.04903	.04494
13	.08967	.08137	.07397	.06738	.06149	.05623	.05152	.04729
14	.09321	.08472	.07715	.07038	.06433	.05892	.05406	.04971
15	.09680	.08812	.08036	.07342	.06721	.06164	.05664	.05214
16	.10041	.09154	.08360	.07649	.07011	.06438	.05923	.05459
17	.10409	.09502	.08689	.07960	.07305	.06716	.06185	.05707
18	.10782	.09855	.09024	.08276	.07604	.06998	.06452	.05959
19	.11164	.10217	.09366	.08600	.07910	.07288	.06726	.06218
20	.11559	.10592	.09721	.08937	.08228	.07589	.07010	.06487
21	.11965	.10977	.10087	.09283	.08557	.07900	.07305	.06765
22	.12383	.11376	.10465	.09642	.08897	.08223	.07610	.07055
23	.12817	.11789	.10859	.10016	.09252	.08559	.07930	.07358
24	.13270	.12221	.11270	.10408	.09625	.08914	.08267	.07678
25	.13744	.12674	.11703	.10821	.10019	.09289	.08625	.08018
26	.14239	.13149	.12158	.11256	.10435	.09686	.09003	.08380
27	.14758	.13647	.12636	.11714	.10873	.10106	.09405	.08764
28	.15300	.14169	.13137	.12195	.11335	.10549	.09829	.09171
29	.15864	.14712	.13660	.12698	.11819	.11013	.10275	.09598
30	.16448	.15275	.14203	.13222	.12323	.11498	.10742	.10047
31	.17053	.15861	.14769	.13768	.12849	.12006	.11230	.10517
32	.17680	.16468	.15357	.14336	.13398	.12535	.11741	.11009
33	.18330	.17099	.15968	.14927	.13970	.13088	.12275	.11525
34	.19000	.17750	.16599	.15539	.14562	.13661	.12829	.12061

continued

Valuation Tables, Excerpts

Table S Single Life Remainder Factors Interest Rate

AGE	4.2%	4.4%	4.6%	4.8%	5.0%	5.2%	5.4%	5.6%
35	.19692	.18423	.17253	.16174	.15178	.14258	.13408	.12621
36	.20407	.19119	.17931	.16833	.15818	.14879	.14009	.13204
37	.21144	.19838	.18631	.17515	.16481	.15523	.14635	.13811
38	.21904	.20582	.19357	.18222	.17170	.16193	.15287	.14444
39	.22687	.21348	.20105	.18952	.17882	.16887	.15962	.15102
40	.23493	.22137	.20878	.19707	.18619	.17606	.16663	.15784
41	.24322	.22950	.21674	.20487	.19381	.18350	.17390	.16493
42	.25173	.23786	.22494	.21290	.20168	.19120	.18141	.17227
43	.26049	.24648	.23342	.22122	.20982	.19918	.18922	.17990
44	.26950	.25535	.24214	.22979	.21824	.20742	.19730	.18781
45	.27874	.26447	.25112	.23862	.22692	.21595	.20566	.19600
46	.28824	.27385	.26038	.24774	.23589	.22476	.21431	.20450
47	.29798	.28349	.26989	.25712	.24513	.23386	.22326	.21328
48	.30797	.29338	.27967	.26678	.25466	.24325	.23250	.22238
49	.31822	.30355	.28974	.27674	.26449	.25294	.24206	.23179
50	.32876	.31401	.30011	.28701	.27465	.26298	.25196	.24156
51	.33958	.32477	.31079	.29759	.28513	.27335	.26221	.25168
52	.35068	.33582	.32178	.30851	.29595	.28407	.27282	.26216
53	.36206	.34717	.33308	.31974	.30710	.29513	.28378	.27301
54	.37371	.35880	.34467	.33127	.31857	.30651	.29507	.28420
55	.38559	.37067	.35652	.34308	.33032	.31820	.30668	.29572
56	.39765	.38275	.36859	.35512	.34232	.33014	.31855	.30751
57	.40990	.39502	.38086	.36739	.35455	.34233	.33068	.31957
58	.42231	.40747	.39333	.37985	.36700	.35474	.34304	.33188
59	.43490	.42011	.40600	.39253	.37968	.36740	.35567	.34446
60	.44768	.43296	.41890	.40546	.39261	.38033	.36858	.35733
61	.46064	.44600	.43200	.41860	.40578	.39351	.38175	.37048
62	.47373	.45920	.44527	.43194	.41915	.40690	.39514	.38387
63	.48696	.47253	.45870	.44544	.43271	.42049	.40876	.39749
64	.50030	.48601	.47229	.45911	.44645	.43428	.42258	.41133
65	.51377	.49963	.48603	.47295	.46037	.44827	.43662	.42540
66	.52750	.51352	.50007	.48711	.47464	.46262	.45103	.43987
67	.54144	.52765	.51436	.50154	.48919	.47727	.46578	.45468
68	.55554	.54196	.52885	.51619	.50398	.49218	.48079	.46978
69	.56976	.55640	.54349	.53102	.51896	.50731	.49603	.48513

Valuation Tables, Excerpts

Table B Term Certain Remainder Factors Interest Rate

YEARS	4.2%	4.4%	4.6%	4.8%	5.0%	5.2%	5.4%	5.6%
1	.959693	.957854	.956023	.954198	.952381	.950570	.948767	.946970
2	.921010	.917485	.913980	.910495	.907029	.903584	.900158	.896752
3	.883887	.878817	.873786	.868793	.863838	.858920	.854040	.849197
4	.848260	.841779	.835359	.829001	.822702	.816464	.810285	.804163
5	.814069	.806302	.798623	.791031	.783526	.776106	.768771	.761518
6	.781257	.772320	.763501	.754801	.746215	.737744	.729384	.721135
7	.749766	.739770	.729925	.720230	.710681	.701277	.692015	.682893
8	.719545	.708592	.697825	.687242	.676839	.666613	.656561	.646679
9	.690543	.678728	.667137	.655765	.644609	.633663	.622923	.612385
10	.662709	.650122	.637798	.625730	.613913	.602341	.591009	.579910
11	.635997	.622722	.609750	.597071	.584679	.572568	.560729	.549157
12	.610362	.596477	.582935	.569724	.556837	.544266	.532001	.520035
13	.585760	.571339	.557299	.543630	.530321	.517363	.504745	.492458
14	.562150	.547259	.532790	.518731	.505068	.491790	.478885	.466343
15	.539491	.524195	.509360	.494972	.481017	.467481	.454350	.441612
16	.517746	.502102	.486960	.472302	.458112	.444374	.431072	.418194
17	.496877	.480941	.465545	.450670	.436297	.422408	.408987	.396017
18	.476849	.460671	.445071	.430028	.415521	.401529	.388033	.375016
19	.457629	.441256	.425498	.410332	.395734	.381681	.368153	.355129
20	.439183	.422659	.406786	.391538	.376889	.362815	.349291	.336296
21	.421481	.404846	.388897	.373605	.358942	.344881	.331396	.318462
22	.404492	.387783	.371794	.356494	.341850	.327834	.314417	.301574
23	.388188	.371440	.355444	.340166	.325571	.311629	.298309	.285581
24	.372542	.355785	.339813	.324586	.310068	.296225	.283025	.270437
25	.357526	.340791	.324869	.309719	.295303	.281583	.268525	.256096
26	.343115	.326428	.310582	.295533	.281241	.267664	.254768	.242515
27	.329285	.312670	.296923	.281998	.267848	.254434	.241715	.229654
28	.316012	.299493	.283866	.269082	.255094	.241857	.229331	.217475
29	.303275	.286870	.271382	.256757	.242946	.229902	.217582	.205943
30	.291051	.274780	.259447	.244997	.231377	.218538	.206434	.195021
31	.279319	.263199	.248038	.233776	.220359	.207736	.195858	.184679
32	.268061	.252106	.237130	.223069	.209866	.197468	.185823	.174886
33	.257256	.241481	.226702	.212852	.199873	.187707	.176303	.165612
34	.246887	.231304	.216732	.203103	.190355	.178429	.167270	.156829
35	.236935	.221556	.207201	.193801	.181290	.169609	.158701	.148512

Appendix B

Tax Forms

(These forms were current as of 3/1/2019. Up-to-date forms are available at **irs.gov/forms-instructions**)

Form **709**

Department of the Treasury
Internal Revenue Service

United States Gift (and Generation-Skipping Transfer) Tax Return

▶ Go to *www.irs.gov/Form709* for instructions and the latest information.

(For gifts made during calendar year 2018)
▶ **See instructions.**

OMB No. 1545-0020

2018

Part 1—General Information

1 Donor's first name and middle initial	2 Donor's last name	3 Donor's social security number

4 Address (number, street, and apartment number)	5 Legal residence (domicile)

6 City or town, state or province, country, and ZIP or foreign postal code	7 Citizenship (see instructions)

		Yes	No
8	If the donor died during the year, check here ▶ ☐ and enter date of death _____ , _____		
9	If you extended the time to file this Form 709, check here ▶ ☐		
10	Enter the total number of donees listed on Schedule A. Count each person only once ▶		
11a	Have you (the donor) previously filed a Form 709 (or 709-A) for any other year? If "No," skip line 11b		
b	Has your address changed since you last filed Form 709 (or 709-A)?		
12	**Gifts by husband or wife to third parties.** Do you consent to have the gifts (including generation-skipping transfers) made by you and by your spouse to third parties during the calendar year considered as made one-half by each of you? (See instructions.) (If the answer is "Yes," the following information must be furnished and your spouse must sign the consent shown below. **If the answer is "No," skip lines 13–18.**)		

13 Name of consenting spouse	14 SSN		

		Yes	No
15	Were you married to one another during the entire calendar year? See instructions		
16	If line 15 is "No," check whether ☐ married ☐ divorced or ☐ widowed/deceased, and give date. See instructions ▶		
17	Will a gift tax return for this year be filed by your spouse? If "Yes," mail both returns in the same envelope		
18	**Consent of Spouse.** I consent to have the gifts (and generation-skipping transfers) made by me and by my spouse to third parties during the calendar year considered as made one-half by each of us. We are both aware of the joint and several liability for tax created by the execution of this consent.		

Consenting spouse's signature ▶   Date ▶

19	Have you applied a DSUE amount received from a predeceased spouse to a gift or gifts reported on this or a previous Form 709? If "Yes," complete Schedule C		

Part 2—Tax Computation

1	Enter the amount from Schedule A, Part 4, line 11	1	
2	Enter the amount from Schedule B, line 3	2	
3	Total taxable gifts. Add lines 1 and 2	3	
4	Tax computed on amount on line 3 (see *Table for Computing Gift Tax* in instructions)	4	
5	Tax computed on amount on line 2 (see *Table for Computing Gift Tax* in instructions)	5	
6	Balance. Subtract line 5 from line 4	6	
7	Applicable credit amount. If donor has DSUE amount from predeceased spouse(s) or Restored Exclusion Amount, enter amount from Schedule C, line 5; otherwise, see instructions	7	
8	Enter the applicable credit against tax allowable for all prior periods (from Sch. B, line 1, col. C) .	8	
9	Balance. Subtract line 8 from line 7. Do not enter less than zero	9	
10	Enter 20% (0.20) of the amount allowed as a specific exemption for gifts made after September 8, 1976, and before January 1, 1977. See instructions	10	
11	Balance. Subtract line 10 from line 9. Do not enter less than zero	11	
12	Applicable credit. Enter the smaller of line 6 or line 11	12	
13	Credit for foreign gift taxes (see instructions)	13	
14	Total credits. Add lines 12 and 13	14	
15	Balance. Subtract line 14 from line 6. Do not enter less than zero	15	
16	Generation-skipping transfer taxes (from Schedule D, Part 3, col. H, total)	16	
17	Total tax. Add lines 15 and 16	17	
18	Gift and generation-skipping transfer taxes prepaid with extension of time to file	18	
19	If line 18 is less than line 17, enter **balance due.** See instructions	19	
20	If line 18 is greater than line 17, enter **amount to be refunded**	20	

Under penalties of perjury, I declare that I have examined this return, including any accompanying schedules and statements, and to the best of my knowledge and belief, it is true, correct, and complete. Declaration of preparer (other than donor) is based on all information of which preparer has any knowledge.

Sign Here

May the IRS discuss this return with the preparer shown below? See instructions. ☐ Yes ☐ No

▶

Signature of donor   Date

Attach check or money order here.

Paid Preparer Use Only

Print/Type preparer's name	Preparer's signature	Date	Check ☐ if self-employed	PTIN
Firm's name ▶			Firm's EIN ▶	
Firm's address ▶			Phone no.	

For Disclosure, Privacy Act, and Paperwork Reduction Act Notice, see the instructions for this form.   Cat. No. 16783M   Form **709** (2018)

Form 709 (2018) Page **2**

SCHEDULE A   Computation of Taxable Gifts (Including transfers in trust) (see instructions)

A   Does the value of any item listed on Schedule A reflect any valuation discount? If "Yes," attach explanation . . . .   Yes ☐   No ☐

B   ☐ ◄ Check here if you elect under section 529(c)(2)(B) to treat any transfers made this year to a qualified tuition program as made ratably over a 5-year period beginning this year. See instructions. Attach explanation.

Part 1—Gifts Subject Only to Gift Tax. Gifts less political organization, medical, and educational exclusions. See instructions.

A Item number	B • Donee's name and address • Relationship to donor (if any) • Description of gift • If the gift was of securities, give CUSIP no. • If closely held entity, give EIN	C	D Donor's adjusted basis of gift	E Date of gift	F Value at date of gift	G For split gifts, enter 1/2 of column F	H Net transfer (subtract col. G from col. F)
1							

Gifts made by spouse—complete **only** if you are splitting gifts with your spouse and he/she also made gifts.

Total of Part 1. Add amounts from Part 1, column H . . . . ►

Part 2—Direct Skips. Gifts that are direct skips and are subject to both gift tax and generation-skipping transfer tax. You must list the gifts in chronological order.

A Item number	B • Donee's name and address • Relationship to donor (if any) • Description of gift • If the gift was of securities, give CUSIP no. • If closely held entity, give EIN	C 2632(b) election out	D Donor's adjusted basis of gift	E Date of gift	F Value at date of gift	G For split gifts, enter 1/2 of column F	H Net transfer (subtract col. G from col. F)
1							

Gifts made by spouse—complete **only** if you are splitting gifts with your spouse and he/she also made gifts.

Total of Part 2. Add amounts from Part 2, column H . . . . ►

Part 3—Indirect Skips. Gifts to trusts that are currently subject to gift tax and may later be subject to generation-skipping transfer tax. You must list these gifts in chronological order.

A Item number	B • Donee's name and address • Relationship to donor (if any) • Description of gift • If the gift was of securities, give CUSIP no. • If closely held entity, give EIN	C 2632(c) election	D Donor's adjusted basis of gift	E Date of gift	F Value at date of gift	G For split gifts, enter 1/2 of column F	H Net transfer (subtract col. G from col. F)
1							

Gifts made by spouse—complete **only** if you are splitting gifts with your spouse and he/she also made gifts.

Total of Part 3. Add amounts from Part 3, column H . . . . ►

(If more space is needed, attach additional statements.)   Form **709** (2018)

Form 709 (2018)   Page **3**

Part 4—Taxable Gift Reconciliation

1	Total value of gifts of donor. Add totals from column H of Parts 1, 2, and 3	**1**	
2	Total annual exclusions for gifts listed on line 1 (see instructions)	**2**	
3	Total included amount of gifts. Subtract line 2 from line 1	**3**	

Deductions (see instructions)

4	Gifts of interests to spouse for which a marital deduction will be claimed, based on item numbers _____ of Schedule A . .	**4**		
5	Exclusions attributable to gifts on line 4	**5**		
6	Marital deduction. Subtract line 5 from line 4	**6**		
7	Charitable deduction, based on item nos. _____ less exclusions .	**7**		
8	Total deductions. Add lines 6 and 7		**8**	
9	Subtract line 8 from line 3		**9**	
10	Generation-skipping transfer taxes payable with this Form 709 (from Schedule D, Part 3, col. H, total) . .		**10**	
11	**Taxable gifts.** Add lines 9 and 10. Enter here and on page 1, Part 2—Tax Computation, line 1		**11**	

Terminable Interest (QTIP) Marital Deduction. (See instructions for Schedule A, Part 4, line 4.)

If a trust (or other property) meets the requirements of qualified terminable interest property under section 2523(f), and:

   a. The trust (or other property) is listed on Schedule A; and

   b. The value of the trust (or other property) is entered in whole or in part as a deduction on Schedule A, Part 4, line 4,
then the donor shall be deemed to have made an election to have such trust (or other property) treated as qualified terminable interest property under section 2523(f).

If less than the entire value of the trust (or other property) that the donor has included in Parts 1 and 3 of Schedule A is entered as a deduction on line 4, the donor shall be considered to have made an election only as to a fraction of the trust (or other property). The numerator of this fraction is equal to the amount of the trust (or other property) deducted on Schedule A, Part 4, line 6. The denominator is equal to the total value of the trust (or other property) listed in Parts 1 and 3 of Schedule A.

If you make the QTIP election, the terminable interest property involved will be included in your spouse's gross estate upon his or her death (section 2044). See instructions for line 4 of Schedule A. If your spouse disposes (by gift or otherwise) of all or part of the qualifying life income interest, he or she will be considered to have made a transfer of the entire property that is subject to the gift tax. See *Transfer of Certain Life Estates Received From Spouse* in the instructions.

12   Election Out of QTIP Treatment of Annuities

  ☐ ◄ Check here if you elect under section 2523(f)(6) **not** to treat as qualified terminable interest property any joint and survivor annuities that are reported on Schedule A and would otherwise be treated as qualified terminable interest property under section 2523(f). See instructions. Enter the item numbers from Schedule A for the annuities for which you are making this election ► _____

SCHEDULE B   Gifts From Prior Periods

If you answered "Yes" on line 11a of page 1, Part 1, see the instructions for completing Schedule B. If you answered "No," skip to the Tax Computation on page 1 (or Schedule C or D, if applicable). Complete Schedule A before beginning Schedule B. See instructions for recalculation of the column C amounts. Attach calculations.

A Calendar year or calendar quarter (see instructions)	B Internal Revenue office where prior return was filed	C Amount of applicable credit (unified credit) against gift tax for periods after December 31, 1976	D Amount of specific exemption for prior periods ending before January 1, 1977	E Amount of taxable gifts

1	Totals for prior periods	**1**		
2	Amount, if any, by which total specific exemption, line 1, column D, is more than $30,000	**2**		
3	Total amount of taxable gifts for prior periods. Add amount on line 1, column E, and amount, if any, on line 2. Enter here and on page 1, Part 2—Tax Computation, line 2	**3**		

(If more space is needed, attach additional statements.)   Form **709** (2018)

SCHEDULE C Deceased Spousal Unused Exclusion (DSUE) Amount and Restored Exclusion

Provide the following information to determine the DSUE amount and applicable credit received from prior spouses. Complete Schedule A before beginning Schedule C.

A	B	C		D	E	F
Name of Deceased Spouse (dates of death after December 31, 2010, only)	Date of Death	Portability Election Made?		If "Yes," DSUE Amount Received From Spouse	DSUE Amount Applied by Donor to Lifetime Gifts (list current and prior gifts)	Date of Gift(s) (enter as mm/dd/yy for Part 1 and as yyyy for Part 2)
		Yes	No			

Part 1—DSUE RECEIVED FROM LAST DECEASED SPOUSE

Part 2—DSUE RECEIVED FROM PREDECEASED SPOUSE(S)

TOTAL (for all DSUE amounts applied from column E for Part 1 and Part 2)

1	Donor's basic exclusion amount (see instructions)	**1**	
2	Total from column E, Parts 1 and 2	**2**	
3	Restored Exclusion Amount (see instructions)	**3**	
4	Add lines 1, 2, and 3	**4**	
5	Applicable credit on amount in line 4 (see *Table for Computing Gift Tax* in the instructions). Enter here and on line 7, Part 2—Tax Computation	**5**	

SCHEDULE D Computation of Generation-Skipping Transfer Tax

Note: Inter vivos direct skips that are completely excluded by the GST exemption must still be fully reported (including value and exemptions claimed) on Schedule D.

Part 1—Generation-Skipping Transfers

A Item No. (from Schedule A, Part 2, col. A)	B Value (from Schedule A, Part 2, col. H)	C Nontaxable Portion of Transfer	D Net Transfer (subtract col. C from col. B)
1			

Gifts made by spouse (for gift splitting only)

(If more space is needed, attach additional statements.)   Form **709** (2018)

Form **990-EZ**

Short Form
Return of Organization Exempt From Income Tax

Under section 501(c), 527, or 4947(a)(1) of the Internal Revenue Code (except private foundations)

▶ **Do not enter social security numbers on this form as it may be made public.**

▶ **Go to** *www.irs.gov/Form990EZ* **for instructions and the latest information.**

OMB No. 1545-1150

2018

Open to Public Inspection

Department of the Treasury
Internal Revenue Service

A For the 2018 calendar year, or tax year beginning _____ , 2018, and ending _____ , 20 _____

B Check if applicable:	**C** Name of organization		**D** Employer identification number
☐ Address change			
☐ Name change	Number and street (or P.O. box, if mail is not delivered to street address)	Room/suite	**E** Telephone number
☐ Initial return			
☐ Final return/terminated	City or town, state or province, country, and ZIP or foreign postal code		**F** Group Exemption
☐ Amended return			Number ▶
☐ Application pending			

G Accounting Method: ☐ Cash ☐ Accrual Other (specify) ▶ _____

I Website: ▶ _____

J Tax-exempt status (check only one) — ☐ 501(c)(3) ☐ 501(c) ( ) ◀ (insert no.) ☐ 4947(a)(1) or ☐ 527

K Form of organization: ☐ Corporation ☐ Trust ☐ Association ☐ Other _____

H Check ▶ ☐ if the organization is **not** required to attach Schedule B (Form 990, 990-EZ, or 990-PF).

L Add lines 5b, 6c, and 7b to line 9 to determine gross receipts. If gross receipts are $200,000 or more, or if total assets (Part II, column (B)) are $500,000 or more, file Form 990 instead of Form 990-EZ . . . . ▶ $ _____

Part I	**Revenue, Expenses, and Changes in Net Assets or Fund Balances** (see the instructions for Part I)		
	Check if the organization used Schedule O to respond to any question in this Part I . . . . ☐		

1	Contributions, gifts, grants, and similar amounts received	**1**	
2	Program service revenue including government fees and contracts	**2**	
3	Membership dues and assessments	**3**	
4	Investment income	**4**	
5a	Gross amount from sale of assets other than inventory	**5a**	
b	Less: cost or other basis and sales expenses	**5b**	
c	Gain or (loss) from sale of assets other than inventory (Subtract line 5b from line 5a)	**5c**	
6	Gaming and fundraising events:		
a	Gross income from gaming (attach Schedule G if greater than $15,000)	**6a**	
b	Gross income from fundraising events (not including $ _____ of contributions from fundraising events reported on line 1) (attach Schedule G if the sum of such gross income and contributions exceeds $15,000) . .	**6b**	
c	Less: direct expenses from gaming and fundraising events . . .	**6c**	
d	Net income or (loss) from gaming and fundraising events (add lines 6a and 6b and subtract line 6c)	**6d**	
7a	Gross sales of inventory, less returns and allowances	**7a**	
b	Less: cost of goods sold	**7b**	
c	Gross profit or (loss) from sales of inventory (Subtract line 7b from line 7a)	**7c**	
8	Other revenue (describe in Schedule O)	**8**	
9	**Total revenue.** Add lines 1, 2, 3, 4, 5c, 6d, 7c, and 8 . . . . ▶	**9**	
10	Grants and similar amounts paid (list in Schedule O)	**10**	
11	Benefits paid to or for members	**11**	
12	Salaries, other compensation, and employee benefits	**12**	
13	Professional fees and other payments to independent contractors	**13**	
14	Occupancy, rent, utilities, and maintenance	**14**	
15	Printing, publications, postage, and shipping	**15**	
16	Other expenses (describe in Schedule O)	**16**	
17	**Total expenses.** Add lines 10 through 16 . . . . ▶	**17**	
18	Excess or (deficit) for the year (Subtract line 17 from line 9)	**18**	
19	Net assets or fund balances at beginning of year (from line 27, column (A)) (must agree with end-of-year figure reported on prior year's return)	**19**	
20	Other changes in net assets or fund balances (explain in Schedule O)	**20**	
21	Net assets or fund balances at end of year. Combine lines 18 through 20 . . . . . ▶	**21**	

Revenue — lines 1–9
Expenses — lines 10–17
Net Assets — lines 18–21

For Paperwork Reduction Act Notice, see the separate instructions.   Cat. No. 10642I   Form **990-EZ** (2018)

Form 990-EZ (2018)   Page **2**

Part II   Balance Sheets (see the instructions for Part II)

Check if the organization used Schedule O to respond to any question in this Part II . . . . ☐

		(A) Beginning of year		(B) End of year
22	Cash, savings, and investments		22	
23	Land and buildings		23	
24	Other assets (describe in Schedule O)		24	
25	**Total assets**		25	
26	**Total liabilities** (describe in Schedule O)		26	
27	**Net assets or fund balances** (line 27 of column (B) **must** agree with line 21) . .		27	

Part III   Statement of Program Service Accomplishments (see the instructions for Part III)

Check if the organization used Schedule O to respond to any question in this Part III . . ☐

What is the organization's primary exempt purpose? _____

Describe the organization's program service accomplishments for each of its three largest program services, as measured by expenses. In a clear and concise manner, describe the services provided, the number of persons benefited, and other relevant information for each program title.

Expenses
(Required for section 501(c)(3) and 501(c)(4) organizations; optional for others.)

28 _____

(Grants $ _____) If this amount includes foreign grants, check here . . . . ▶ ☐ | 28a |

29 _____

(Grants $ _____) If this amount includes foreign grants, check here . . . . ▶ ☐ | 29a |

30 _____

(Grants $ _____) If this amount includes foreign grants, check here . . . . ▶ ☐ | 30a |

31 Other program services (describe in Schedule O) . . . .

(Grants $ _____) If this amount includes foreign grants, check here . . . . ▶ ☐ | 31a |

32 **Total program service expenses** (add lines 28a through 31a) . . . . ▶ | 32 |

Part IV   List of Officers, Directors, Trustees, and Key Employees (list each one even if not compensated—see the instructions for Part IV)

Check if the organization used Schedule O to respond to any question in this Part IV . . . . ☐

(a) Name and title	(b) Average hours per week devoted to position	(c) Reportable compensation (Forms W-2/1099-MISC) (if not paid, enter -0-)	(d) Health benefits, contributions to employee benefit plans, and deferred compensation	(e) Estimated amount of other compensation
_____				
_____				
_____				
_____				
_____				
_____				
_____				
_____				
_____				
_____				
_____				
_____				

Form **990-EZ** (2018)

Form 990-EZ (2018)   Page **3**

Part V	**Other Information** (Note the Schedule A and personal benefit contract statement requirements in the instructions for Part V.) Check if the organization used Schedule O to respond to any question in this Part V . ☐		

		Yes	No
33	Did the organization engage in any significant activity not previously reported to the IRS? If "Yes," provide a detailed description of each activity in Schedule O **33**		
34	Were any significant changes made to the organizing or governing documents? If "Yes," attach a conformed copy of the amended documents if they reflect a change to the organization's name. Otherwise, explain the change on Schedule O. See instructions **34**		
35a	Did the organization have unrelated business gross income of $1,000 or more during the year from business activities (such as those reported on lines 2, 6a, and 7a, among others)? **35a**		
b	If "Yes" to line 35a, has the organization filed a Form 990-T for the year? If "No," provide an explanation in Schedule O **35b**		
c	Was the organization a section 501(c)(4), 501(c)(5), or 501(c)(6) organization subject to section 6033(e) notice, reporting, and proxy tax requirements during the year? If "Yes," complete Schedule C, Part III **35c**		
36	Did the organization undergo a liquidation, dissolution, termination, or significant disposition of net assets during the year? If "Yes," complete applicable parts of Schedule N **36**		
37a	Enter amount of political expenditures, direct or indirect, as described in the instructions ▶	**37a**			
b	Did the organization file **Form 1120-POL** for this year? **37b**		
38a	Did the organization borrow from, or make any loans to, any officer, director, trustee, or key employee **or** were any such loans made in a prior year and still outstanding at the end of the tax year covered by this return? . **38a**		
b	If "Yes," complete Schedule L, Part II and enter the total amount involved	**38b**			
39	Section 501(c)(7) organizations. Enter:			
a	Initiation fees and capital contributions included on line 9	**39a**			
b	Gross receipts, included on line 9, for public use of club facilities	**39b**			
40a	Section 501(c)(3) organizations. Enter amount of tax imposed on the organization during the year under: section 4911 ▶ _____ ; section 4912 ▶ _____ ; section 4955 ▶ _____			
b	Section 501(c)(3), 501(c)(4), and 501(c)(29) organizations. Did the organization engage in any section 4958 excess benefit transaction during the year, or did it engage in an excess benefit transaction in a prior year that has not been reported on any of its prior Forms 990 or 990-EZ? If "Yes," complete Schedule L, Part I **40b**		
c	Section 501(c)(3), 501(c)(4), and 501(c)(29) organizations. Enter amount of tax imposed on organization managers or disqualified persons during the year under sections 4912, 4955, and 4958 . . . . ▶ _____			
d	Section 501(c)(3), 501(c)(4), and 501(c)(29) organizations. Enter amount of tax on line 40c reimbursed by the organization . . . . ▶ _____			
e	All organizations. At any time during the tax year, was the organization a party to a prohibited tax shelter transaction? If "Yes," complete Form 8886-T **40e**		
41	List the states with which a copy of this return is filed ▶ _____			
42a	The organization's books are in care of ▶ _____ Telephone no. ▶ _____ Located at ▶ _____ ZIP + 4 ▶ _____			

		Yes	No
b	At any time during the calendar year, did the organization have an interest in or a signature or other authority over a financial account in a foreign country (such as a bank account, securities account, or other financial account)? **42b**		
	If "Yes," enter the name of the foreign country ▶ _____ See the instructions for exceptions and filing requirements for FinCEN Form 114, Report of Foreign Bank and Financial Accounts (FBAR).			
c	At any time during the calendar year, did the organization maintain an office outside the United States? . **42c**		
	If "Yes," enter the name of the foreign country ▶ _____			
43	Section 4947(a)(1) nonexempt charitable trusts filing Form 990-EZ in lieu of **Form 1041**—Check here . . . . ▶ ☐ and enter the amount of tax-exempt interest received or accrued during the tax year . . . . . ▶	**43**			

		Yes	No
44a	Did the organization maintain any donor advised funds during the year? If "Yes," Form 990 must be completed instead of Form 990-EZ **44a**		
b	Did the organization operate one or more hospital facilities during the year? If "Yes," Form 990 must be completed instead of Form 990-EZ **44b**		
c	Did the organization receive any payments for indoor tanning services during the year? **44c**		
d	If "Yes" to line 44c, has the organization filed a Form 720 to report these payments? If "No," provide an explanation in Schedule O **44d**		
45a	Did the organization have a controlled entity within the meaning of section 512(b)(13)? **45a**		
b	Did the organization receive any payment from or engage in any transaction with a controlled entity within the meaning of section 512(b)(13)? If "Yes," Form 990 and Schedule R may need to be completed instead of Form 990-EZ. See instructions **45b**		

Form **990-EZ** (2018)

Form 990-EZ (2018)   Page **4**

			Yes	No
46	Did the organization engage, directly or indirectly, in political campaign activities on behalf of or in opposition to candidates for public office? If "Yes," complete Schedule C, Part I	**46**		

Part VI   **Section 501(c)(3) Organizations Only**

All section 501(c)(3) organizations must answer questions 47–49b and 52, and complete the tables for lines 50 and 51.

Check if the organization used Schedule O to respond to any question in this Part VI   . . . . ☐

			Yes	No
47	Did the organization engage in lobbying activities or have a section 501(h) election in effect during the tax year? If "Yes," complete Schedule C, Part II	**47**		
48	Is the organization a school as described in section 170(b)(1)(A)(ii)? If "Yes," complete Schedule E	**48**		
49a	Did the organization make any transfers to an exempt non-charitable related organization?	**49a**		
b	If "Yes," was the related organization a section 527 organization?	**49b**		

50 Complete this table for the organization's five highest compensated employees (other than officers, directors, trustees, and key employees) who each received more than $100,000 of compensation from the organization. If there is none, enter "None."

(a) Name and title of each employee	**(b)** Average hours per week devoted to position	**(c)** Reportable compensation (Forms W-2/1099-MISC)	**(d)** Health benefits, contributions to employee benefit plans, and deferred compensation	**(e)** Estimated amount of other compensation

f Total number of other employees paid over $100,000   . . . . ▶ _____

51 Complete this table for the organization's five highest compensated independent contractors who each received more than $100,000 of compensation from the organization. If there is none, enter "None."

(a) Name and business address of each independent contractor	**(b)** Type of service	**(c)** Compensation

d Total number of other independent contractors each receiving over $100,000   . . ▶ _____

52 Did the organization complete Schedule A? **Note:** All section 501(c)(3) organizations must attach a completed Schedule A   . . . . ▶ ☐ Yes ☐ No

Under penalties of perjury, I declare that I have examined this return, including accompanying schedules and statements, and to the best of my knowledge and belief, it is true, correct, and complete. Declaration of preparer (other than officer) is based on all information of which preparer has any knowledge.

Sign Here	▶ Signature of officer		Date		
	▶ Type or print name and title				

Paid Preparer Use Only	Print/Type preparer's name	Preparer's signature	Date	Check ☐ if self-employed	PTIN
	Firm's name ▶			Firm's EIN ▶	
	Firm's address ▶			Phone no.	

May the IRS discuss this return with the preparer shown above? See instructions   . . . . ▶ ☐ Yes ☐ No

Form **990-EZ** (2018)

Form 990-T

Exempt Organization Business Income Tax Return
(and proxy tax under section 6033(e))

OMB No. 1545-0687

2018

For calendar year 2018 or other tax year beginning _____, 2018, and ending _____, 20 _____.

▶ Go to *www.irs.gov/Form990T* for instructions and the latest information.

▶ Do not enter SSN numbers on this form as it may be made public if your organization is a 501(c)(3).

Department of the Treasury
Internal Revenue Service

Open to Public Inspection for 501(c)(3) Organizations Only

A ☐ Check box if address changed	**Print or Type**	Name of organization (☐ Check box if name changed and see instructions.)	**D Employer identification number** (Employees' trust, see instructions.)
B Exempt under section ☐ 501( )( ) ☐ 408(e) ☐ 220(e) ☐ 408A ☐ 530(a) ☐ 529(a)		Number, street, and room or suite no. If a P.O. box, see instructions.	**E Unrelated business activity code** (See instructions.)
C Book value of all assets at end of year		City or town, state or province, country, and ZIP or foreign postal code	

F Group exemption number (See instructions.) ▶

G Check organization type ▶ ☐ 501(c) corporation ☐ 501(c) trust ☐ 401(a) trust ☐ Other trust

H Enter the number of the organization's unrelated trades or businesses. ▶ _____ Describe the only (or first) unrelated trade or business here ▶ _____. If only one, complete Parts I–V. If more than one, describe the first in the blank space at the end of the previous sentence, complete Parts I and II, complete a Schedule M for each additional trade or business, then complete Parts III–V.

I During the tax year, was the corporation a subsidiary in an affiliated group or a parent-subsidiary controlled group? . . ▶ ☐ Yes ☐ No
If "Yes," enter the name and identifying number of the parent corporation. ▶

J The books are in care of ▶ _____   Telephone number ▶ _____

Part I   Unrelated Trade or Business Income

			(A) Income	(B) Expenses	(C) Net
1a	Gross receipts or sales				
b	Less returns and allowances _____ **c** Balance ▶	**1c**			
2	Cost of goods sold (Schedule A, line 7)	**2**			
3	Gross profit. Subtract line 2 from line 1c	**3**			
4a	Capital gain net income (attach Schedule D)	**4a**			
b	Net gain (loss) (Form 4797, Part II, line 17) (attach Form 4797)	**4b**			
c	Capital loss deduction for trusts	**4c**			
5	Income (loss) from a partnership or an S corporation (attach statement)	**5**			
6	Rent income (Schedule C)	**6**			
7	Unrelated debt-financed income (Schedule E)	**7**			
8	Interest, annuities, royalties, and rents from a controlled organization (Schedule F)	**8**			
9	Investment income of a section 501(c)(7), (9), or (17) organization (Schedule G)	**9**			
10	Exploited exempt activity income (Schedule I)	**10**			
11	Advertising income (Schedule J)	**11**			
12	Other income (See instructions; attach schedule)	**12**			
13	**Total.** Combine lines 3 through 12	**13**			

Part II   Deductions Not Taken Elsewhere (See instructions for limitations on deductions.) (Except for contributions, deductions must be directly connected with the unrelated business income.)

14	Compensation of officers, directors, and trustees (Schedule K)	**14**	
15	Salaries and wages	**15**	
16	Repairs and maintenance	**16**	
17	Bad debts	**17**	
18	Interest (attach schedule) (see instructions)	**18**	
19	Taxes and licenses	**19**	
20	Charitable contributions (See instructions for limitation rules)	**20**	
21	Depreciation (attach Form 4562) **21**		
22	Less depreciation claimed on Schedule A and elsewhere on return . . **22a**	**22b**	
23	Depletion	**23**	
24	Contributions to deferred compensation plans	**24**	
25	Employee benefit programs	**25**	
26	Excess exempt expenses (Schedule I)	**26**	
27	Excess readership costs (Schedule J)	**27**	
28	Other deductions (attach schedule)	**28**	
29	**Total deductions.** Add lines 14 through 28	**29**	
30	Unrelated business taxable income before net operating loss deduction. Subtract line 29 from line 13	**30**	
31	Deduction for net operating loss arising in tax years beginning on or after January 1, 2018 (see instructions)	**31**	
32	Unrelated business taxable income. Subtract line 31 from line 30	**32**	

For Paperwork Reduction Act Notice, see instructions.   Cat. No. 11291J   Form **990-T** (2018)

Form 990-T (2018)   Page **2**

Part III		Total Unrelated Business Taxable Income		
33		Total of unrelated business taxable income computed from all unrelated trades or businesses (see instructions)	**33**	
34		Amounts paid for disallowed fringes	**34**	
35		Deduction for net operating loss arising in tax years beginning before January 1, 2018 (see instructions)	**35**	
36		Total of unrelated business taxable income before specific deduction. Subtract line 35 from the sum of lines 33 and 34	**36**	
37		Specific deduction (Generally $1,000, but see line 37 instructions for exceptions)	**37**	
38		**Unrelated business taxable income.** Subtract line 37 from line 36. If line 37 is greater than line 36, enter the smaller of zero or line 36	**38**	

Part IV		Tax Computation		
39		**Organizations Taxable as Corporations.** Multiply line 38 by 21% (0.21) . . . . ▶	**39**	
40		**Trusts Taxable at Trust Rates.** See instructions for tax computation. Income tax on the amount on line 38 from: ☐ Tax rate schedule or ☐ Schedule D (Form 1041) . . . . . ▶	**40**	
41		**Proxy tax.** See instructions . . . . ▶	**41**	
42		Alternative minimum tax (trusts only)	**42**	
43		**Tax on Noncompliant Facility Income.** See instructions	**43**	
44		**Total.** Add lines 41, 42, and 43 to line 39 or 40, whichever applies	**44**	

Part V		Tax and Payments				
45a		Foreign tax credit (corporations attach Form 1118; trusts attach Form 1116) .	**45a**			
b		Other credits (see instructions)	**45b**			
c		General business credit. Attach Form 3800 (see instructions)	**45c**			
d		Credit for prior year minimum tax (attach Form 8801 or 8827)	**45d**			
e		**Total credits.** Add lines 45a through 45d		**45e**	
46		Subtract line 45e from line 44		**46**	
47		Other taxes. Check if from: ☐ Form 4255 ☐ Form 8611 ☐ Form 8697 ☐ Form 8866 ☐ Other (attach schedule) .		**47**	
48		**Total tax.** Add lines 46 and 47 (see instructions)		**48**	
49		2018 net 965 tax liability paid from Form 965-A or Form 965-B, Part II, column (k), line 2		**49**	
50a		Payments: A 2017 overpayment credited to 2018	**50a**			
b		2018 estimated tax payments	**50b**			
c		Tax deposited with Form 8868	**50c**			
d		Foreign organizations: Tax paid or withheld at source (see instructions) .	**50d**			
e		Backup withholding (see instructions)	**50e**			
f		Credit for small employer health insurance premiums (attach Form 8941) .	**50f**			
g		Other credits, adjustments, and payments: ☐ Form 2439 _____ ☐ Form 4136 _____ ☐ Other _____ Total ▶	**50g**			
51		**Total payments.** Add lines 50a through 50g		**51**	
52		Estimated tax penalty (see instructions). Check if Form 2220 is attached . . . . ▶ ☐		**52**	
53		**Tax due.** If line 51 is less than the total of lines 48, 49, and 52, enter amount owed . . . ▶		**53**	
54		**Overpayment.** If line 51 is larger than the total of lines 48, 49, and 52, enter amount overpaid . ▶		**54**	
55		Enter the amount of line 54 you want: **Credited to 2019 estimated tax** ▶ _____ Refunded ▶		**55**	

Part VI		Statements Regarding Certain Activities and Other Information (see instructions)		Yes	No
56		At any time during the 2018 calendar year, did the organization have an interest in or a signature or other authority over a financial account (bank, securities, or other) in a foreign country? If "Yes," the organization may have to file FinCEN Form 114, Report of Foreign Bank and Financial Accounts. If "Yes," enter the name of the foreign country here ▶ _____			
57		During the tax year, did the organization receive a distribution from, or was it the grantor of, or transferor to, a foreign trust? . If "Yes," see instructions for other forms the organization may have to file.			
58		Enter the amount of tax-exempt interest received or accrued during the tax year ▶ $			

Sign Here ▶

Under penalties of perjury, I declare that I have examined this return, including accompanying schedules and statements, and to the best of my knowledge and belief, it is true, correct, and complete. Declaration of preparer (other than taxpayer) is based on all information of which preparer has any knowledge.

▶ _____	_____	▶ _____	May the IRS discuss this return with the preparer shown below (see instructions)? ☐ Yes ☐ No
Signature of officer	Date	Title	

Paid Preparer Use Only	Print/Type preparer's name	Preparer's signature	Date	Check ☐ if self-employed	PTIN
	Firm's name ▶			Firm's EIN ▶	
	Firm's address ▶			Phone no.	

Form **990-T** (2018)

Form 990-T (2018)   Page **3**

Schedule A—Cost of Goods Sold. Enter method of inventory valuation ▶

1	Inventory at beginning of year	**1**		6	Inventory at end of year . . .	**6**
2	Purchases	**2**		7	**Cost of goods sold.** Subtract line 6 from line 5. Enter here and in Part I, line 2	**7**
3	Cost of labor	**3**				
4a	Additional section 263A costs (attach schedule)	**4a**		8	Do the rules of section 263A (with respect to property produced or acquired for resale) apply to the organization?	Yes / No
b	Other costs (attach schedule)	**4b**				
5	**Total.** Add lines 1 through 4b	**5**				

Schedule C—Rent Income (From Real Property and Personal Property Leased With Real Property)

(see instructions)

1. Description of property

(1)
(2)
(3)
(4)

2. Rent received or accrued		3(a) Deductions directly connected with the income in columns 2(a) and 2(b) (attach schedule)
(a) From personal property (if the percentage of rent for personal property is more than 10% but not more than 50%)	**(b)** From real and personal property (if the percentage of rent for personal property exceeds 50% or if the rent is based on profit or income)	
(1)		
(2)		
(3)		
(4)		
Total	Total	

(c) Total income. Add totals of columns 2(a) and 2(b). Enter here and on page 1, Part I, line 6, column (A) . . . ▶

(b) Total deductions. Enter here and on page 1, Part I, line 6, column (B) ▶

Schedule E—Unrelated Debt-Financed Income (see instructions)

1. Description of debt-financed property	2. Gross income from or allocable to debt-financed property	3. Deductions directly connected with or allocable to debt-financed property	
		(a) Straight line depreciation (attach schedule)	**(b)** Other deductions (attach schedule)
(1)			
(2)			
(3)			
(4)			

4. Amount of average acquisition debt on or allocable to debt-financed property (attach schedule)	5. Average adjusted basis of or allocable to debt-financed property (attach schedule)	6. Column 4 divided by column 5	7. Gross income reportable (column 2 × column 6)	8. Allocable deductions (column 6 × total of columns 3(a) and 3(b))
(1)		%		
(2)		%		
(3)		%		
(4)		%		
			Enter here and on page 1, Part I, line 7, column (A).	Enter here and on page 1, Part I, line 7, column (B).

Totals . . . . ▶

Total dividends-received deductions included in column 8 . . . . ▶

Form **990-T** (2018)

Form **1041**

Department of the Treasury—Internal Revenue Service

U.S. Income Tax Return for Estates and Trusts

2018

OMB No. 1545-0092

A Check all that apply:

- ☐ Decedent's estate
- ☐ Simple trust
- ☐ Complex trust
- ☐ Qualified disability trust
- ☐ ESBT (S portion only)
- ☐ Grantor type trust
- ☐ Bankruptcy estate-Ch. 7
- ☐ Bankruptcy estate-Ch. 11
- ☐ Pooled income fund

For calendar year 2018 or fiscal year beginning _____ , 2018, and ending _____ , 20 ____

Name of estate or trust (If a grantor type trust, see the instructions.)

Name and title of fiduciary

Number, street, and room or suite no. (If a P.O. box, see the instructions.)

City or town, state or province, country, and ZIP or foreign postal code

C Employer identification number

D Date entity created

E Nonexempt charitable and split-interest trusts, check applicable box(es), see instructions.
- ☐ Described in sec. 4947(a)(1). Check here if not a private foundation . . . ▶ ☐
- ☐ Described in sec. 4947(a)(2)

B Number of Schedules K-1 attached (see instructions) ▶

F Check applicable boxes:
- ☐ Initial return
- ☐ Final return
- ☐ Amended return
- ☐ Change in trust's name
- ☐ Change in fiduciary
- ☐ Change in fiduciary's name
- ☐ Net operating loss carryback
- ☐ Change in fiduciary's address

G Check here if the estate or filing trust made a section 645 election . . . . . . ▶ ☐   Trust TIN ▶

Income		
1 Interest income	**1**	
2a Total ordinary dividends	**2a**	
b Qualified dividends allocable to: **(1)** Beneficiaries _____ **(2)** Estate or trust _____		
3 Business income or (loss). Attach Schedule C or C-EZ (Form 1040)	**3**	
4 Capital gain or (loss). Attach Schedule D (Form 1041)	**4**	
5 Rents, royalties, partnerships, other estates and trusts, etc. Attach Schedule E (Form 1040) .	**5**	
6 Farm income or (loss). Attach Schedule F (Form 1040)	**6**	
7 Ordinary gain or (loss). Attach Form 4797	**7**	
8 Other income. List type and amount _____	**8**	
9 **Total income.** Combine lines 1, 2a, and 3 through 8 . . . . ▶	**9**	

Deductions		
10 Interest. Check if Form 4952 is attached ▶ ☐	**10**	
11 Taxes	**11**	
12 Fiduciary fees. If only a portion is deductible under section 67(e), see instructions	**12**	
13 Charitable deduction (from Schedule A, line 7)	**13**	
14 Attorney, accountant, and return preparer fees. If only a portion is deductible under section 67(e), see instructions	**14**	
15a Other deductions (attach schedule). See instructions for deductions allowable under section 67(e) .	**15a**	
b Net operating loss deduction. See instructions	**15b**	
16 Add lines 10 through 15b . . . . ▶	**16**	
17 Adjusted total income or (loss). Subtract line 16 from line 9 . . . **17**		
18 Income distribution deduction (from Schedule B, line 15). Attach Schedules K-1 (Form 1041)	**18**	
19 Estate tax deduction including certain generation-skipping taxes (attach computation) . . .	**19**	
20 Exemption	**20**	
21 Add lines 18 through 20 . . . . ▶	**21**	

Tax and Payments		
22 Taxable income. Subtract line 21 from line 17. If a loss, see instructions	**22**	
23 **Total tax** (from Schedule G, line 7)	**23**	
24 2018 net 965 tax liability paid from Form 965-A, Part II, column (k), line 2	**24**	
25 **Payments: a** 2018 estimated tax payments and amount applied from 2017 return . . .	**25a**	
b Estimated tax payments allocated to beneficiaries (from Form 1041-T)	**25b**	
c Subtract line 25b from line 25a	**25c**	
d Tax paid with Form 7004. See instructions	**25d**	
e Federal income tax withheld. If any is from Form(s) 1099, check ▶ ☐	**25e**	
f 2018 net 965 tax liability from Form 965-A, Part I, column (f), line 2	**25f**	
Other payments: **g** Form 2439 _____ ; **h** Form 4136 _____ ; Total ▶	**25i**	
26 **Total payments.** Add lines 25c through 25f, and 25i . . . . ▶	**26**	
27 Estimated tax penalty. See instructions	**27**	
28 **Tax due.** If line 26 is smaller than the total of lines 23, 24, and 27, enter amount owed . .	**28**	
29 **Overpayment.** If line 26 is larger than the total of lines 23, 24, and 27, enter amount overpaid .	**29**	
30 Amount of line 29 to be: **a Credited to 2019** ▶ _____ ; **b Refunded** ▶	**30**	

Sign Here

Under penalties of perjury, I declare that I have examined this return, including accompanying schedules and statements, and to the best of my knowledge and belief, it is true, correct, and complete. Declaration of preparer (other than taxpayer) is based on all information of which preparer has any knowledge.

▶ _____ Signature of fiduciary or officer representing fiduciary   Date   ▶ _____   EIN of fiduciary if a financial institution

May the IRS discuss this return with the preparer shown below (see instr.)? ☐ Yes ☐ No

Paid Preparer Use Only

Print/Type preparer's name	Preparer's signature	Date	Check ☐ if self-employed	PTIN
Firm's name ▶			Firm's EIN ▶	
Firm's address ▶			Phone no.	

For Paperwork Reduction Act Notice, see the separate instructions.   **www.IRS.gov/Form1041**   Cat. No. 11370H   Form **1041** (2018)

Form 1041 (2018)   Page **2**

Schedule A   Charitable Deduction. Don't complete for a simple trust or a pooled income fund.

1	Amounts paid or permanently set aside for charitable purposes from gross income. See instructions	1	
2	Tax-exempt income allocable to charitable contributions. See instructions	2	
3	Subtract line 2 from line 1	3	
4	Capital gains for the tax year allocated to corpus and paid or permanently set aside for charitable purposes	4	
5	Add lines 3 and 4	5	
6	Section 1202 exclusion allocable to capital gains paid or permanently set aside for charitable purposes. See instructions	6	
7	**Charitable deduction.** Subtract line 6 from line 5. Enter here and on page 1, line 13	7	

Schedule B   Income Distribution Deduction

1	Adjusted total income. See instructions	1	
2	Adjusted tax-exempt interest	2	
3	Total net gain from Schedule D (Form 1041), line 19, column (1). See instructions	3	
4	Enter amount from Schedule A, line 4 (minus any allocable section 1202 exclusion)	4	
5	Capital gains for the tax year included on Schedule A, line 1. See instructions	5	
6	Enter any gain from page 1, line 4, as a negative number. If page 1, line 4, is a loss, enter the loss as a positive number	6	
7	**Distributable net income.** Combine lines 1 through 6. If zero or less, enter -0-	7	
8	If a complex trust, enter accounting income for the tax year as determined under the governing instrument and applicable local law 8		
9	Income required to be distributed currently	9	
10	Other amounts paid, credited, or otherwise required to be distributed	10	
11	Total distributions. Add lines 9 and 10. If greater than line 8, see instructions	11	
12	Enter the amount of tax-exempt income included on line 11	12	
13	Tentative income distribution deduction. Subtract line 12 from line 11	13	
14	Tentative income distribution deduction. Subtract line 2 from line 7. If zero or less, enter -0-	14	
15	**Income distribution deduction.** Enter the smaller of line 13 or line 14 here and on page 1, line 18	15	

Schedule G   Tax Computation (see instructions)

1	**Tax: a**	Tax on taxable income. See instructions	1a	
	b	Tax on lump-sum distributions. Attach Form 4972	1b	
	c	Alternative minimum tax (from Schedule I (Form 1041), line 56)	1c	
	d	**Total.** Add lines 1a through 1c	1d	
2a		Foreign tax credit. Attach Form 1116	2a	
b		General business credit. Attach Form 3800	2b	
c		Credit for prior year minimum tax. Attach Form 8801	2c	
d		Bond credits. Attach Form 8912	2d	
e		**Total credits.** Add lines 2a through 2d	2e	
3		Subtract line 2e from line 1d. If zero or less, enter -0-	3	
4		Net investment income tax from Form 8960, line 21	4	
5		Recapture taxes. Check if from: ☐ Form 4255 ☐ Form 8611	5	
6		Household employment taxes. Attach Schedule H (Form 1040)	6	
7		**Total tax.** Add lines 3 through 6. Enter here and on page 1, line 23	7	

Other Information

		Yes	No
1	Did the estate or trust receive tax-exempt income? If "Yes," attach a computation of the allocation of expenses. Enter the amount of tax-exempt interest income and exempt-interest dividends ▶ $ _____		
2	Did the estate or trust receive all or any part of the earnings (salary, wages, and other compensation) of any individual by reason of a contract assignment or similar arrangement?		
3	At any time during calendar year 2018, did the estate or trust have an interest in or a signature or other authority over a bank, securities, or other financial account in a foreign country?		
	See the instructions for exceptions and filing requirements for FinCEN Form 114. If "Yes," enter the name of the foreign country ▶ _____		
4	During the tax year, did the estate or trust receive a distribution from, or was it the grantor of, or transferor to, a foreign trust? If "Yes," the estate or trust may have to file Form 3520. See instructions		
5	Did the estate or trust receive, or pay, any qualified residence interest on seller-provided financing? If "Yes," see the instructions for required attachment		
6	If this is an estate or a complex trust making the section 663(b) election, check here. See instructions ▶ ☐		
7	To make a section 643(e)(3) election, attach Schedule D (Form 1041), and check here. See instructions ▶ ☐		
8	If the decedent's estate has been open for more than 2 years, attach an explanation for the delay in closing the estate, and check here ▶ ☐		
9	Are any present or future trust beneficiaries skip persons? See instructions		
10	Was the trust a specified domestic entity required to file Form 8938 for the tax year (see the Instructions for Form 8938)?		

Form **1041** (2018)

661117

| | Final K-1 | | Amended K-1 | OMB No. 1545-0092 |

**Schedule K-1
(Form 1041)**

Department of the Treasury
Internal Revenue Service

2018

For calendar year 2018, or tax year

beginning ___ / ___ / 2018   ending ___ / ___ / ___

Beneficiary's Share of Income, Deductions, Credits, etc.

▶ **See back of form and instructions.**

| Part I | Information About the Estate or Trust |

A Estate's or trust's employer identification number

B Estate's or trust's name

C Fiduciary's name, address, city, state, and ZIP code

D ☐ Check if Form 1041-T was filed and enter the date it was filed

_____

E ☐ Check if this is the final Form 1041 for the estate or trust

| Part II | Information About the Beneficiary |

F Beneficiary's identifying number

G Beneficiary's name, address, city, state, and ZIP code

H ☐ Domestic beneficiary   ☐ Foreign beneficiary

Part III	Beneficiary's Share of Current Year Income, Deductions, Credits, and Other Items

No.	Item	No.	Item
1	Interest income	11	Final year deductions
2a	Ordinary dividends		
2b	Qualified dividends		
3	Net short-term capital gain		
4a	Net long-term capital gain		
4b	28% rate gain	12	Alternative minimum tax adjustment
4c	Unrecaptured section 1250 gain		
5	Other portfolio and nonbusiness income		
6	Ordinary business income		
7	Net rental real estate income	13	Credits and credit recapture
8	Other rental income		
9	Directly apportioned deductions		
		14	Other information
10	Estate tax deduction		

*See attached statement for additional information.

Note: A statement must be attached showing the beneficiary's share of income and directly apportioned deductions from each business, rental real estate, and other rental activity.

For IRS Use Only

For Paperwork Reduction Act Notice, see the Instructions for Form 1041.   *www.irs.gov/Form1041*   Cat. No. 11380D   **Schedule K-1 (Form 1041) 2018**

This list identifies the codes used on Schedule K-1 for beneficiaries and provides summarized reporting information for beneficiaries who file Form 1040. For detailed reporting and filing information, see the Instructions for Schedule K-1 (Form 1041) for a Beneficiary Filing Form 1040 and the instructions for your income tax return.

		Report on
1.	Interest income	Form 1040, line 2b
2a.	Ordinary dividends	Form 1040, line 3b
2b.	Qualified dividends	Form 1040, line 3a
3.	Net short-term capital gain	Schedule D, line 5
4a.	Net long-term capital gain	Schedule D, line 12
4b.	28% rate gain	28% Rate Gain Worksheet, line 4 (Schedule D Instructions)
4c.	Unrecaptured section 1250 gain	Unrecaptured Section 1250 Gain Worksheet, line 11 (Schedule D Instructions)
5.	Other portfolio and nonbusiness income	Schedule E, line 33, column (f)
6.	Ordinary business income	Schedule E, line 33, column (d) or (f)
7.	Net rental real estate income	Schedule E, line 33, column (d) or (f)
8.	Other rental income	Schedule E, line 33, column (d) or (f)
9.	Directly apportioned deductions	
	Code	
	A Depreciation	Form 8582 or Schedule E, line 33, column (c) or (e)
	B Depletion	Form 8582 or Schedule E, line 33, column (c) or (e)
	C Amortization	Form 8582 or Schedule E, line 33, column (c) or (e)
10.	Estate tax deduction	Schedule A, line 16
11.	Final year deductions	
	A Excess deductions	See the beneficiary's instructions
	B Short-term capital loss carryover	Schedule D, line 5
	C Long-term capital loss carryover	Schedule D, line 12; line 5 of the wksht. for Sch. D, line 18; and line 16 of the wksht. for Sch. D, line 19
	D Net operating loss carryover — regular tax	Form 1040, Schedule 1, line 21
	E Net operating loss carryover — minimum tax	Form 6251, line 2f
12.	Alternative minimum tax (AMT) items	
	A Adjustment for minimum tax purposes	Form 6251, line 2j
	B AMT adjustment attributable to qualified dividends	
	C AMT adjustment attributable to net short-term capital gain	
	D AMT adjustment attributable to net long-term capital gain	
	E AMT adjustment attributable to unrecaptured section 1250 gain	See the beneficiary's instructions and the Instructions for Form 6251
	F AMT adjustment attributable to 28% rate gain	
	G Accelerated depreciation	
	H Depletion	
	I Amortization	
	J Exclusion items	2019 Form 8801

13.	Credits and credit recapture	
	Code	*Report on*
	A Credit for estimated taxes	Form 1040, Schedule 5, line 66
	B Credit for backup withholding	Form 1040, line 16
	C Low-income housing credit	
	D Rehabilitation credit and energy credit	
	E Other qualifying investment credit	
	F Work opportunity credit	
	G Credit for small employer health insurance premiums	
	H Biofuel producer credit	
	I Credit for increasing research activities	
	J Renewable electricity, refined coal, and Indian coal production credit	
	K Empowerment zone employment credit	See the beneficiary's instructions
	L Indian employment credit	
	M Orphan drug credit	
	N Credit for employer-provided child care and facilities	
	O Biodiesel and renewable diesel fuels credit	
	P Credit to holders of tax credit bonds	
	Q Credit for employer differential wage payments	
	R Recapture of credits	
	Z Other credits	
14.	Other information	
	A Tax-exempt interest	Form 1040, line 2a
	B Foreign taxes	Form 1040, Schedule 3, line 48 or Sch. A, line 6
	C Reserved	
	D Reserved	
	E Net investment income	Form 4952, line 4a
	F Gross farm and fishing income	Schedule E, line 42
	G Foreign trading gross receipts (IRC 942(a))	See the Instructions for Form 8873
	H Adjustment for section 1411 net investment income or deductions	Form 8960, line 7 (also see the beneficiary's instructions)
	I Qualified business income, section 199A	See the beneficiary's instructions
	Z Other information	See the beneficiary's instructions

Note: If you are a beneficiary who does not file a Form 1040, see instructions for the type of income tax return you are filing.

Form **8960**

Department of the Treasury
Internal Revenue Service (99)

Net Investment Income Tax—
Individuals, Estates, and Trusts

▶ **Attach to your tax return.**
▶ **Go to www.irs.gov/Form8960 for instructions and the latest information.**

OMB No. 1545-2227

2018

Attachment
Sequence No. **72**

Name(s) shown on your tax return

Your social security number or EIN

Part I   Investment Income

☐ Section 6013(g) election (see instructions)
☐ Section 6013(h) election (see instructions)
☐ Regulations section 1.1411-10(g) election (see instructions)

1	Taxable interest (see instructions)	**1**	
2	Ordinary dividends (see instructions)	**2**	
3	Annuities (see instructions)	**3**	
4a	Rental real estate, royalties, partnerships, S corporations, trusts, etc. (see instructions)	**4a**	
b	Adjustment for net income or loss derived in the ordinary course of a non-section 1411 trade or business (see instructions)	**4b**	
c	Combine lines 4a and 4b	**4c**	
5a	Net gain or loss from disposition of property (see instructions)	**5a**	
b	Net gain or loss from disposition of property that is not subject to net investment income tax (see instructions)	**5b**	
c	Adjustment from disposition of partnership interest or S corporation stock (see instructions)	**5c**	
d	Combine lines 5a through 5c	**5d**	
6	Adjustments to investment income for certain CFCs and PFICs (see instructions)	**6**	
7	Other modifications to investment income (see instructions)	**7**	
8	Total investment income. Combine lines 1, 2, 3, 4c, 5d, 6, and 7	**8**	

Part II   Investment Expenses Allocable to Investment Income and Modifications

9a	Investment interest expenses (see instructions)	**9a**	
b	State, local, and foreign income tax (see instructions)	**9b**	
c	Miscellaneous investment expenses (see instructions)	**9c**	
d	Add lines 9a, 9b, and 9c	**9d**	
10	Additional modifications (see instructions)	**10**	
11	Total deductions and modifications. Add lines 9d and 10	**11**	

Part III   Tax Computation

12	Net investment income. Subtract Part II, line 11, from Part I, line 8. Individuals, complete lines 13–17. Estates and trusts, complete lines 18a–21. If zero or less, enter -0-	**12**	

Individuals:

13	Modified adjusted gross income (see instructions)	**13**	
14	Threshold based on filing status (see instructions)	**14**	
15	Subtract line 14 from line 13. If zero or less, enter -0-	**15**	
16	Enter the smaller of line 12 or line 15	**16**	
17	Net investment income tax for individuals. Multiply line 16 by 3.8% (0.038). **Enter here and include on your tax return** (see instructions)	**17**	

Estates and Trusts:

18a	Net investment income (line 12 above)	**18a**	
b	Deductions for distributions of net investment income and deductions under section 642(c) (see instructions)	**18b**	
c	Undistributed net investment income. Subtract line 18b from 18a (see instructions). If zero or less, enter -0-	**18c**	
19a	Adjusted gross income (see instructions)	**19a**	
b	Highest tax bracket for estates and trusts for the year (see instructions)	**19b**	
c	Subtract line 19b from line 19a. If zero or less, enter -0-	**19c**	
20	Enter the smaller of line 18c or line 19c	**20**	
21	Net investment income tax for estates and trusts. Multiply line 20 by 3.8% (0.038). **Enter here and include on your tax return** (see instructions)	**21**	

For Paperwork Reduction Act Notice, see your tax return instructions.   Cat. No. 59474M   Form **8960** (2018)

Form **1065**

Department of the Treasury
Internal Revenue Service

U.S. Return of Partnership Income

For calendar year 2018, or tax year beginning _____ , 2018, ending _____ , 20 _____ .

▶ Go to *www.irs.gov/Form1065* for instructions and the latest information.

OMB No. 1545-0123

2018

A Principal business activity	**Type or Print**	Name of partnership	**D** Employer identification number
B Principal product or service		Number, street, and room or suite no. If a P.O. box, see instructions.	**E** Date business started
C Business code number		City or town, state or province, country, and ZIP or foreign postal code	**F** Total assets (see instructions) $

G Check applicable boxes: **(1)** ☐ Initial return **(2)** ☐ Final return **(3)** ☐ Name change **(4)** ☐ Address change **(5)** ☐ Amended return

H Check accounting method: **(1)** ☐ Cash **(2)** ☐ Accrual **(3)** ☐ Other (specify) ▶ _____

I Number of Schedules K-1. Attach one for each person who was a partner at any time during the tax year. ▶ _____

J Check if Schedules C and M-3 are attached . . . . ▶ ☐

Caution: Include **only** trade or business income and expenses on lines 1a through 22 below. See instructions for more information.

Income

1a	Gross receipts or sales	**1a**	
b	Returns and allowances	**1b**	
c	Balance. Subtract line 1b from line 1a	**1c**	
2	Cost of goods sold (attach Form 1125-A)	**2**	
3	Gross profit. Subtract line 2 from line 1c	**3**	
4	Ordinary income (loss) from other partnerships, estates, and trusts (attach statement) . .	**4**	
5	Net farm profit (loss) (attach Schedule F (Form 1040))	**5**	
6	Net gain (loss) from Form 4797, Part II, line 17 (attach Form 4797)	**6**	
7	Other income (loss) (attach statement)	**7**	
8	**Total income (loss).** Combine lines 3 through 7	**8**	

Deductions (see instructions for limitations)

9	Salaries and wages (other than to partners) (less employment credits)	**9**	
10	Guaranteed payments to partners	**10**	
11	Repairs and maintenance	**11**	
12	Bad debts	**12**	
13	Rent	**13**	
14	Taxes and licenses	**14**	
15	Interest (see instructions)	**15**	
16a	Depreciation (if required, attach Form 4562)	**16a**	
b	Less depreciation reported on Form 1125-A and elsewhere on return	**16b**	**16c**
17	Depletion **(Do not deduct oil and gas depletion.)**	**17**	
18	Retirement plans, etc.	**18**	
19	Employee benefit programs	**19**	
20	Other deductions (attach statement)	**20**	
21	**Total deductions.** Add the amounts shown in the far right column for lines 9 through 20 .	**21**	
22	**Ordinary business income (loss).** Subtract line 21 from line 8	**22**	

Tax and Payment

23	Interest due under the look-back method—completed long-term contracts (attach Form 8697)	**23**	
24	Interest due under the look-back method—income forecast method (attach Form 8866) .	**24**	
25	BBA AAR imputed underpayment (see instructions)	**25**	
26	Other taxes (see instructions)	**26**	
27	**Total balance due.** Add lines 23 through 27	**27**	
28	Payment (see instructions)	**28**	
29	**Amount owed.** If line 28 is smaller than line 27, enter amount owed	**29**	
30	**Overpayment.** If line 28 is larger than line 27, enter overpayment	**30**	

Sign Here

Under penalties of perjury, I declare that I have examined this return, including accompanying schedules and statements, and to the best of my knowledge and belief, it is true, correct, and complete. Declaration of preparer (other than partner or limited liability company member) is based on all information of which preparer has any knowledge.

May the IRS discuss this return with the preparer shown below? See instructions. ☐ **Yes** ☐ **No**

▶ _____ Signature of partner or limited liability company member

▶ _____ Date

Paid Preparer Use Only

Print/Type preparer's name	Preparer's signature	Date	Check ☐ if self-employed	PTIN
Firm's name ▶			Firm's EIN ▶	
Firm's address ▶			Phone no.	

For Paperwork Reduction Act Notice, see separate instructions.   Cat. No. 11390Z   Form **1065** (2018)

Form 1065 (2018)   Page **2**

Schedule B	**Other Information**		

		Yes	No
1	What type of entity is filing this return? Check the applicable box:		

a	☐ Domestic general partnership	**b**	☐ Domestic limited partnership	
c	☐ Domestic limited liability company	**d**	☐ Domestic limited liability partnership	
e	☐ Foreign partnership	**f**	☐ Other ▶	

2 At the end of the tax year:

a Did any foreign or domestic corporation, partnership (including any entity treated as a partnership), trust, or tax-exempt organization, or any foreign government own, directly or indirectly, an interest of 50% or more in the profit, loss, or capital of the partnership? For rules of constructive ownership, see instructions. If "Yes," attach Schedule B-1, Information on Partners Owning 50% or More of the Partnership . . . .

b Did any individual or estate own, directly or indirectly, an interest of 50% or more in the profit, loss, or capital of the partnership? For rules of constructive ownership, see instructions. If "Yes," attach Schedule B-1, Information on Partners Owning 50% or More of the Partnership . . . .

3 At the end of the tax year, did the partnership:

a Own directly 20% or more, or own, directly or indirectly, 50% or more of the total voting power of all classes of stock entitled to vote of any foreign or domestic corporation? For rules of constructive ownership, see instructions. If "Yes," complete (i) through (iv) below . . . .

(i) Name of Corporation	**(ii)** Employer Identification Number (if any)	**(iii)** Country of Incorporation	**(iv)** Percentage Owned in Voting Stock

b Own directly an interest of 20% or more, or own, directly or indirectly, an interest of 50% or more in the profit, loss, or capital in any foreign or domestic partnership (including an entity treated as a partnership) or in the beneficial interest of a trust? For rules of constructive ownership, see instructions. If "Yes," complete (i) through (v) below . .

(i) Name of Entity	**(ii)** Employer Identification Number (if any)	**(iii)** Type of Entity	**(iv)** Country of Organization	**(v)** Maximum Percentage Owned in Profit, Loss, or Capital

		Yes	No
4	Does the partnership satisfy **all four** of the following conditions?		
a	The partnership's total receipts for the tax year were less than $250,000.		
b	The partnership's total assets at the end of the tax year were less than $1 million.		
c	Schedules K-1 are filed with the return and furnished to the partners on or before the due date (including extensions) for the partnership return.		
d	The partnership is not filing and is not required to file Schedule M-3		

If "Yes," the partnership is not required to complete Schedules L, M-1, and M-2; item F on page 1 of Form 1065; or item L on Schedule K-1.

5 Is this partnership a publicly traded partnership, as defined in section 469(k)(2)? . . . .

6 During the tax year, did the partnership have any debt that was canceled, was forgiven, or had the terms modified so as to reduce the principal amount of the debt? . . . .

7 Has this partnership filed, or is it required to file, Form 8918, Material Advisor Disclosure Statement, to provide information on any reportable transaction? . . . .

8 At any time during calendar year 2018, did the partnership have an interest in or a signature or other authority over a financial account in a foreign country (such as a bank account, securities account, or other financial account)? See instructions for exceptions and filing requirements for FinCEN Form 114, Report of Foreign Bank and Financial Accounts (FBAR). If "Yes," enter the name of the foreign country. ▶

9 At any time during the tax year, did the partnership receive a distribution from, or was it the grantor of, or transferor to, a foreign trust? If "Yes," the partnership may have to file Form 3520, Annual Return To Report Transactions With Foreign Trusts and Receipt of Certain Foreign Gifts. See instructions . . . .

10a Is the partnership making, or had it previously made (and not revoked), a section 754 election? . . . . . . See instructions for details regarding a section 754 election.

b Did the partnership make for this tax year an optional basis adjustment under section 743(b) or 734(b)? If "Yes," attach a statement showing the computation and allocation of the basis adjustment. See instructions . . . .

Form **1065** (2018)

Form 1065 (2018)   Page **3**

Schedule B	**Other Information** (continued)	Yes	No

		Yes	No
c	Is the partnership required to adjust the basis of partnership assets under section 743(b) or 734(b) because of a substantial built-in loss (as defined under section 743(d)) or substantial basis reduction (as defined under section 734(d))? If "Yes," attach a statement showing the computation and allocation of the basis adjustment. See instructions		
11	Check this box if, during the current or prior tax year, the partnership distributed any property received in a like-kind exchange or contributed such property to another entity (other than disregarded entities wholly owned by the partnership throughout the tax year) . . . . ▶ ☐		
12	At any time during the tax year, did the partnership distribute to any partner a tenancy-in-common or other undivided interest in partnership property?		
13	If the partnership is required to file Form 8858, Information Return of U.S. Persons With Respect To Foreign Disregarded Entities (FDEs) and Foreign Branches (FBs), enter the number of Forms 8858 attached. See instructions . . . . ▶		
14	Does the partnership have any foreign partners? If "Yes," enter the number of Forms 8805, Foreign Partner's Information Statement of Section 1446 Withholding Tax, filed for this partnership. ▶		
15	Enter the number of Forms 8865, Return of U.S. Persons With Respect to Certain Foreign Partnerships, attached to this return. ▶		
16a	Did you make any payments in 2018 that would require you to file Form(s) 1099? See instructions		
b	If "Yes," did you or will you file required Form(s) 1099?		
17	Enter the number of Form(s) 5471, Information Return of U.S. Persons With Respect To Certain Foreign Corporations, attached to this return. ▶		
18	Enter the number of partners that are foreign governments under section 892. ▶		
19	During the partnership's tax year, did the partnership make any payments that would require it to file Form 1042 and 1042-S under chapter 3 (sections 1441 through 1464) or chapter 4 (sections 1471 through 1474)?		
20	Was the partnership a specified domestic entity required to file Form 8938 for the tax year? See the Instructions for Form 8938		
21	Is the partnership a section 721(c) partnership, as defined in Treasury Regulations section 1.721(c)-1T(b)(14)? .		
22	During the tax year, did the partnership pay or accrue any interest or royalty for which the deduction is not allowed under section 267A? See instructions. If "Yes," enter the total amount of the disallowed deductions. ▶ $		
23	Did the partnership have an election under section 163(j) for any real property trade or business or any farming business in effect during the tax year? See instructions		
24	Does the partnership satisfy one of the following conditions and the partnership does not own a pass-through entity with current year, or prior year, carryover excess business interest expense? See instructions		
a	The partnership's aggregate average annual gross receipts (determined under section 448(c)) for the 3 tax years preceding the current tax year do not exceed $25 million, and the partnership is not a tax shelter, or		
b	The partnership only has business interest expense from (1) an electing real property trade or business, (2) an electing farming business, or (3) certain utility businesses under section 163(j)(7).		
	If "No," complete and attach Form 8990.		
25	Is the partnership electing out of the centralized partnership audit regime under section 6221(b)? See instructions. If "Yes," the partnership must complete Schedule B-2 (Form 1065). Enter the total from Schedule B-2, Part III, line 3. ▶ _____		
	If "No," complete Designation of Partnership Representative below.		

Designation of Partnership Representative (see instructions)

Enter below the information for the partnership representative (PR) for the tax year covered by this return.

Name of PR ▶		U.S. taxpayer identification number of PR ▶
U.S. address of PR ▶		U.S. phone number of PR ▶
If the PR is an entity, name of the designated individual for the PR ▶		U.S. taxpayer identification number of the designated individual ▶
U.S. address of designated individual ▶		U.S. phone number of designated individual ▶

		Yes	No
26	Is the partnership attaching Form 8996 to certify as a Qualified Opportunity Fund? . . . . If "Yes," enter the amount from Form 8996, line 13. ▶ $		

Form **1065** (2018)

Form 1065 (2018) Page **4**

Schedule K		Partners' Distributive Share Items		Total amount
	1	Ordinary business income (loss) (page 1, line 22)	**1**	
	2	Net rental real estate income (loss) (attach Form 8825)	**2**	
	3a	Other gross rental income (loss)	**3a**	
	b	Expenses from other rental activities (attach statement)	**3b**	
	c	Other net rental income (loss). Subtract line 3b from line 3a . . .	**3c**	
	4	Guaranteed payments	**4**	
	5	Interest income	**5**	
	6	Dividends and dividend equivalents: **a** Ordinary dividends . . .	**6a**	
		b Qualified dividends	**6b**	
		c Dividend equivalents	**6c**	
	7	Royalties	**7**	
	8	Net short-term capital gain (loss) (attach Schedule D (Form 1065)) . .	**8**	
	9a	Net long-term capital gain (loss) (attach Schedule D (Form 1065)) . .	**9a**	
	b	Collectibles (28%) gain (loss)	**9b**	
	c	Unrecaptured section 1250 gain (attach statement) . .	**9c**	
	10	Net section 1231 gain (loss) (attach Form 4797)	**10**	
	11	Other income (loss) (see instructions) Type ▶	**11**	
	12	Section 179 deduction (attach Form 4562)	**12**	
	13a	Contributions	**13a**	
	b	Investment interest expense	**13b**	
	c	Section 59(e)(2) expenditures: **(1)** Type ▶ _____ **(2)** Amount ▶	**13c(2)**	
	d	Other deductions (see instructions) Type ▶	**13d**	
	14a	Net earnings (loss) from self-employment	**14a**	
	b	Gross farming or fishing income	**14b**	
	c	Gross nonfarm income	**14c**	
	15a	Low-income housing credit (section 42(j)(5))	**15a**	
	b	Low-income housing credit (other)	**15b**	
	c	Qualified rehabilitation expenditures (rental real estate) (attach Form 3468, if applicable)	**15c**	
	d	Other rental real estate credits (see instructions) Type ▶	**15d**	
	e	Other rental credits (see instructions) Type ▶	**15e**	
	f	Other credits (see instructions) Type ▶	**15f**	
	16a	Name of country or U.S. possession ▶		
	b	Gross income from all sources	**16b**	
	c	Gross income sourced at partner level	**16c**	
		Foreign gross income sourced at partnership level		
	d	Section 951A category ▶ _____ **e** Foreign branch category ▶ _____	**16e**	
	f	Passive category ▶ _____ **g** General category ▶ _____ **h** Other (attach statement) . ▶	**16h**	
		Deductions allocated and apportioned at partner level		
	i	Interest expense ▶ _____ **j** Other . . . . ▶	**16j**	
		Deductions allocated and apportioned at partnership level to foreign source income		
	k	Section 951A category ▶ _____ **l** Foreign branch category ▶ _____	**16l**	
	m	Passive category ▶ _____ **n** General category ▶ _____ **o** Other (attach statement) ▶	**16o**	
	p	Total foreign taxes (check one): ▶ Paid ☐ Accrued ☐	**16p**	
	q	Reduction in taxes available for credit (attach statement)	**16q**	
	r	Other foreign tax information (attach statement)		
	17a	Post-1986 depreciation adjustment	**17a**	
	b	Adjusted gain or loss	**17b**	
	c	Depletion (other than oil and gas)	**17c**	
	d	Oil, gas, and geothermal properties—gross income	**17d**	
	e	Oil, gas, and geothermal properties—deductions	**17e**	
	f	Other AMT items (attach statement)	**17f**	
	18a	Tax-exempt interest income	**18a**	
	b	Other tax-exempt income	**18b**	
	c	Nondeductible expenses	**18c**	
	19a	Distributions of cash and marketable securities	**19a**	
	b	Distributions of other property	**19b**	
	20a	Investment income	**20a**	
	b	Investment expenses	**20b**	
	c	Other items and amounts (attach statement)		

Row labels (left margin, vertical): Income (Loss) — Deductions — Self-Employment — Credits — Foreign Transactions — Alternative Minimum Tax (AMT) Items — Other Information

Form **1065** (2018)

Analysis of Net Income (Loss)

1 Net income (loss). Combine Schedule K, lines 1 through 11. From the result, subtract the sum of Schedule K, lines 12 through 13d, and 16p **1**

2 Analysis by partner type:

	(i) Corporate	(ii) Individual (active)	(iii) Individual (passive)	(iv) Partnership	(v) Exempt Organization	(vi) Nominee/Other
a General partners						
b Limited partners						

Schedule L   Balance Sheets per Books

Assets	Beginning of tax year (a)	(b)	End of tax year (c)	(d)
1 Cash				
2a Trade notes and accounts receivable . . .				
b Less allowance for bad debts				
3 Inventories				
4 U.S. government obligations				
5 Tax-exempt securities				
6 Other current assets (attach statement) . .				
7a Loans to partners (or persons related to partners)				
b Mortgage and real estate loans				
8 Other investments (attach statement) . . .				
9a Buildings and other depreciable assets . .				
b Less accumulated depreciation				
10a Depletable assets				
b Less accumulated depletion				
11 Land (net of any amortization)				
12a Intangible assets (amortizable only) . . .				
b Less accumulated amortization				
13 Other assets (attach statement)				
14 Total assets				
Liabilities and Capital				
15 Accounts payable				
16 Mortgages, notes, bonds payable in less than 1 year				
17 Other current liabilities (attach statement) .				
18 All nonrecourse loans				
19a Loans from partners (or persons related to partners)				
b Mortgages, notes, bonds payable in 1 year or more				
20 Other liabilities (attach statement)				
21 Partners' capital accounts				
22 Total liabilities and capital				

Schedule M-1   Reconciliation of Income (Loss) per Books With Income (Loss) per Return
Note: The partnership may be required to file Schedule M-3. See instructions.

1 Net income (loss) per books . . . .

2 Income included on Schedule K, lines 1, 2, 3c, 5, 6a, 7, 8, 9a, 10, and 11, not recorded on books this year (itemize): _____

3 Guaranteed payments (other than health insurance) . . . .

4 Expenses recorded on books this year not included on Schedule K, lines 1 through 13d, and 16p (itemize):

a Depreciation $ _____

b Travel and entertainment $ _____

5 Add lines 1 through 4 . . . . . .

6 Income recorded on books this year not included on Schedule K, lines 1 through 11 (itemize):

a Tax-exempt interest $ _____

7 Deductions included on Schedule K, lines 1 through 13d, and 16p, not charged against book income this year (itemize):

a Depreciation $ _____

8 Add lines 6 and 7 . . . .

9 Income (loss) (Analysis of Net Income (Loss), line 1). Subtract line 8 from line 5 .

Schedule M-2   Analysis of Partners' Capital Accounts

1 Balance at beginning of year . . .

2 Capital contributed: **a** Cash . . .
                              b Property . .

3 Net income (loss) per books . . . .

4 Other increases (itemize): _____

5 Add lines 1 through 4 . . . . . .

6 Distributions: **a** Cash . . . . . .
                          b Property . . . . .

7 Other decreases (itemize): _____

8 Add lines 6 and 7 . . . .

9 Balance at end of year. Subtract line 8 from line 5

651118

☐ Final K-1   ☐ Amended K-1   OMB No. 1545-0123

Schedule K-1
(Form 1065)

Department of the Treasury
Internal Revenue Service

2018

For calendar year 2018, or tax year

beginning / / 2018 ending / /

Partner's Share of Income, Deductions, Credits, etc.
► **See back of form and separate instructions.**

Part III	Partner's Share of Current Year Income, Deductions, Credits, and Other Items

1	Ordinary business income (loss)	15	Credits
2	Net rental real estate income (loss)		
3	Other net rental income (loss)	16	Foreign transactions
4	Guaranteed payments		
5	Interest income		
6a	Ordinary dividends		
6b	Qualified dividends		
6c	Dividend equivalents		
7	Royalties		
8	Net short-term capital gain (loss)	17	Alternative minimum tax (AMT) items
9a	Net long-term capital gain (loss)		
9b	Collectibles (28%) gain (loss)		
9c	Unrecaptured section 1250 gain	18	Tax-exempt income and nondeductible expenses
10	Net section 1231 gain (loss)		
11	Other income (loss)		
		19	Distributions
12	Section 179 deduction		
		20	Other information
13	Other deductions		
14	Self-employment earnings (loss)		

See attached statement for additional information.

Part I   Information About the Partnership

A Partnership's employer identification number

B Partnership's name, address, city, state, and ZIP code

C IRS Center where partnership filed return

D ☐ Check if this is a publicly traded partnership (PTP)

Part II   Information About the Partner

E Partner's identifying number

F Partner's name, address, city, state, and ZIP code

G ☐ General partner or LLC member-manager   ☐ Limited partner or other LLC member

H ☐ Domestic partner   ☐ Foreign partner

I1 What type of entity is this partner? _____

I2 If this partner is a retirement plan (IRA/SEP/Keogh/etc.), check here ☐

J Partner's share of profit, loss, and capital (see instructions):

	Beginning	Ending
Profit	%	%
Loss	%	%
Capital	%	%

K Partner's share of liabilities:

	Beginning	Ending
Nonrecourse	$	$
Qualified nonrecourse financing	$	$
Recourse	$	$

L Partner's capital account analysis:

Beginning capital account . . . . . $

Capital contributed during the year . $

Current year increase (decrease) . . $

Withdrawals & distributions . . . $ ( )

Ending capital account . . . . . $

☐ Tax basis   ☐ GAAP   ☐ Section 704(b) book
☐ Other (explain)

M Did the partner contribute property with a built-in gain or loss?
☐ Yes   ☐ No
If "Yes," attach statement (see instructions)

For IRS Use Only

For Paperwork Reduction Act Notice, see Instructions for Form 1065.   www.irs.gov/Form1065   Cat. No. 11394R   **Schedule K-1 (Form 1065) 2018**

This list identifies the codes used on Schedule K-1 for all partners and provides summarized reporting information for partners who file Form 1040. For detailed reporting and filing information, see the separate Partner's Instructions for Schedule K-1 and the instructions for your income tax return.

1. Ordinary business income (loss). Determine whether the income (loss) is passive or nonpassive and enter on your return as follows.

	Report on
Passive loss	See the Partner's Instructions
Passive income	Schedule E, line 28, column (h)
Nonpassive loss	See the Partner's Instructions
Nonpassive income	Schedule E, line 28, column (k)

2. Net rental real estate income (loss) — See the Partner's Instructions

3. Other net rental income (loss)
Net income	Schedule E, line 28, column (h)
Net loss	See the Partner's Instructions

4. Guaranteed payments — Schedule E, line 28, column (k)
5. Interest income — Form 1040, line 2b
6a. Ordinary dividends — Form 1040, line 3b
6b. Qualified dividends — Form 1040, line 3a
6c. Dividend equivalents — See the Partner's Instructions
7. Royalties — Schedule E, line 4
8. Net short-term capital gain (loss) — Schedule D, line 5
9a. Net long-term capital gain (loss) — Schedule D, line 12
9b. Collectibles (28%) gain (loss) — 28% Rate Gain Worksheet, line 4 (Schedule D instructions)
9c. Unrecaptured section 1250 gain — See the Partner's Instructions
10. Net section 1231 gain (loss) — See the Partner's Instructions
11. Other income (loss)
Code

A	Other portfolio income (loss)	See the Partner's Instructions
B	Involuntary conversions	See the Partner's Instructions
C	Sec. 1256 contracts & straddles	Form 6781, line 1
D	Mining exploration costs recapture	See Pub. 535
E	Cancellation of debt	Schedule 1 (Form 1040), line 21 or Form 982
F	Section 951A income	
G	Section 965(a) inclusion	
H	Subpart F income other than sections 951A and 965 inclusion	See the Partner's Instructions
I	Other income (loss)	

12. Section 179 deduction — See the Partner's Instructions
13. Other deductions

A	Cash contributions (60%)	
B	Cash contributions (30%)	
C	Noncash contributions (50%)	
D	Noncash contributions (30%)	See the Partner's Instructions
E	Capital gain property to a 50% organization (30%)	
F	Capital gain property (20%)	
G	Contributions (100%)	
H	Investment interest expense	Form 4952, line 1
I	Deductions—royalty income	Schedule E, line 19
J	Section 59(e)(2) expenditures	See the Partner's Instructions
K	Excess business interest expense	See the Partner's Instructions
L	Deductions—portfolio (other)	Schedule A, line 16
M	Amounts paid for medical insurance	Schedule A, line 1 or Schedule 1 (Form 1040), line 29
N	Educational assistance benefits	See the Partner's Instructions
O	Dependent care benefits	Form 2441, line 12
P	Preproductive period expenses	See the Partner's Instructions
Q	Commercial revitalization deduction from rental real estate activities	See Form 8582 instructions
R	Pensions and IRAs	See the Partner's Instructions
S	Reforestation expense deduction	See the Partner's Instructions
T	through **V**	Reserved for future use
W	Other deductions	See the Partner's Instructions
X	Section 965(c) deduction	See the Partner's Instructions

14. Self-employment earnings (loss)
Note: If you have a section 179 deduction or any partner-level deductions, see the Partner's Instructions before completing Schedule SE.

A	Net earnings (loss) from self-employment	Schedule SE, Section A or B
B	Gross farming or fishing income	See the Partner's Instructions
C	Gross non-farm income	See the Partner's Instructions

15. Credits

A	Low-income housing credit (section 42(j)(5)) from pre-2008 buildings	
B	Low-income housing credit (other) from pre-2008 buildings	
C	Low-income housing credit (section 42(j)(5)) from post-2007 buildings	
D	Low-income housing credit (other) from post-2007 buildings	See the Partner's Instructions
E	Qualified rehabilitation expenditures (rental real estate)	
F	Other rental real estate credits	
G	Other rental credits	
H	Undistributed capital gains credit	Schedule 5 (Form 1040), line 74, box a
I	Biofuel producer credit	See the Partner's Instructions

Code — Report on

J	Work opportunity credit	
K	Disabled access credit	
L	Empowerment zone employment credit	
M	Credit for increasing research activities	See the Partner's Instructions
N	Credit for employer social security and Medicare taxes	
O	Backup withholding	
P	Other credits	

16. Foreign transactions

A	Name of country or U.S. possession	
B	Gross income from all sources	Form 1116, Part I
C	Gross income sourced at partner level	

Foreign gross income sourced at partnership level

D	Section 951A category	
E	Foreign branch category	
F	Passive category	Form 1116, Part I
G	General category	
H	Other	

Deductions allocated and apportioned at partner level

I	Interest expense	Form 1116, Part I
J	Other	Form 1116, Part I

Deductions allocated and apportioned at partnership level to foreign source income

K	Section 951A category	
L	Foreign branch category	
M	Passive category	Form 1116, Part I
N	General category	
O	Other	

Other information

P	Total foreign taxes paid	Form 1116, Part II
Q	Total foreign taxes accrued	Form 1116, Part II
R	Reduction in taxes available for credit	Form 1116, line 12
S	Foreign trading gross receipts	Form 8873
T	Extraterritorial income exclusion	Form 8873
U	Section 951A(c)(1)(A) tested income	
V	Tested foreign income tax	
W	Section 965 information	See the Partner's Instructions
X	Other foreign transactions	

17. Alternative minimum tax (AMT) items

A	Post-1986 depreciation adjustment	
B	Adjusted gain or loss	See the Partner's Instructions and the Instructions for Form 6251
C	Depletion (other than oil & gas)	
D	Oil, gas, & geothermal—gross income	
E	Oil, gas, & geothermal—deductions	
F	Other AMT items	

18. Tax-exempt income and nondeductible expenses

A	Tax-exempt interest income	Form 1040, line 2a
B	Other tax-exempt income	See the Partner's Instructions
C	Nondeductible expenses	See the Partner's Instructions

19. Distributions

A	Cash and marketable securities	
B	Distribution subject to section 737	See the Partner's Instructions
C	Other property	

20. Other information

A	Investment income	Form 4952, line 4a
B	Investment expenses	Form 4952, line 5
C	Fuel tax credit information	Form 4136
D	Qualified rehabilitation expenditures (other than rental real estate)	See the Partner's Instructions
E	Basis of energy property	See the Partner's Instructions
F	Recapture of low-income housing credit (section 42(j)(5))	Form 8611, line 8
G	Recapture of low-income housing credit (other)	Form 8611, line 8
H	Recapture of investment credit	See Form 4255
I	Recapture of other credits	See the Partner's Instructions
J	Look-back interest—completed long-term contracts	See Form 8697
K	Look-back interest—income forecast method	See Form 8866
L	Dispositions of property with section 179 deductions	
M	Recapture of section 179 deduction	
N	Interest expense for corporate partners	
O	through **Y**	
Z	Section 199A income	
AA	Section 199A W-2 wages	See the Partner's Instructions
AB	Section 199A unadjusted basis	
AC	Section 199A REIT dividends	
AD	Section 199A PTP income	
AE	Excess taxable income	
AF	Excess business interest income	
AG	Gross receipts for section 59A(e)	
AH	Other information	

Form **1120**
Department of the Treasury
Internal Revenue Service

U.S. Corporation Income Tax Return

For calendar year 2018 or tax year beginning _____ , 2018, ending _____ , 20 _____

▶ Go to *www.irs.gov/Form1120* for instructions and the latest information.

OMB No. 1545-0123

2018

A Check if:
1a Consolidated return (attach Form 851) ☐
b Life/nonlife consolidated return . . ☐
2 Personal holding co. (attach Sch. PH) . ☐
3 Personal service corp. (see instructions) . ☐
4 Schedule M-3 attached ☐

TYPE OR PRINT

Name

Number, street, and room or suite no. If a P.O. box, see instructions.

City or town, state or province, country, and ZIP or foreign postal code

B Employer identification number

C Date incorporated

D Total assets (see instructions)
$

E Check if: **(1)** ☐ Initial return **(2)** ☐ Final return **(3)** ☐ Name change **(4)** ☐ Address change

Income	**1a** Gross receipts or sales	**1a**	
	b Returns and allowances	**1b**	
	c Balance. Subtract line 1b from line 1a	**1c**	
	2 Cost of goods sold (attach Form 1125-A)	**2**	
	3 Gross profit. Subtract line 2 from line 1c	**3**	
	4 Dividends and inclusions (Schedule C, line 23, column (a))	**4**	
	5 Interest	**5**	
	6 Gross rents	**6**	
	7 Gross royalties	**7**	
	8 Capital gain net income (attach Schedule D (Form 1120))	**8**	
	9 Net gain or (loss) from Form 4797, Part II, line 17 (attach Form 4797) . . .	**9**	
	10 Other income (see instructions—attach statement)	**10**	
	11 **Total income.** Add lines 3 through 10 . . . . ▶	**11**	

Deductions (See instructions for limitations on deductions.)	**12** Compensation of officers (see instructions—attach Form 1125-E) . . . . . . ▶	**12**	
	13 Salaries and wages (less employment credits)	**13**	
	14 Repairs and maintenance	**14**	
	15 Bad debts	**15**	
	16 Rents	**16**	
	17 Taxes and licenses	**17**	
	18 Interest (see instructions)	**18**	
	19 Charitable contributions	**19**	
	20 Depreciation from Form 4562 not claimed on Form 1125-A or elsewhere on return (attach Form 4562) . .	**20**	
	21 Depletion	**21**	
	22 Advertising	**22**	
	23 Pension, profit-sharing, etc., plans	**23**	
	24 Employee benefit programs	**24**	
	25 Reserved for future use	**25**	
	26 Other deductions (attach statement)	**26**	
	27 **Total deductions.** Add lines 12 through 26 . . . . ▶	**27**	
	28 Taxable income before net operating loss deduction and special deductions. Subtract line 27 from line 11.	**28**	
	29a Net operating loss deduction (see instructions)	**29a**	
	b Special deductions (Schedule C, line 24, column (c))	**29b**	
	c Add lines 29a and 29b	**29c**	

Tax, Refundable Credits, and Payments	**30** **Taxable income.** Subtract line 29c from line 28. See instructions	**30**	
	31 Total tax (Schedule J, Part I, line 11)	**31**	
	32 2018 net 965 tax liability paid (Schedule J, Part II, line 12)	**32**	
	33 Total payments, credits, and section 965 net tax liability (Schedule J, Part III, line 23)	**33**	
	34 Estimated tax penalty. See instructions. Check if Form 2220 is attached . . . . . ▶ ☐	**34**	
	35 **Amount owed.** If line 33 is smaller than the total of lines 31, 32, and 34, enter amount owed	**35**	
	36 **Overpayment.** If line 33 is larger than the total of lines 31, 32, and 34, enter amount overpaid	**36**	
	37 Enter amount from line 36 you want: **Credited to 2019 estimated tax** ▶	**Refunded** ▶ **37**	

Sign Here

Under penalties of perjury, I declare that I have examined this return, including accompanying schedules and statements, and to the best of my knowledge and belief, it is true, correct, and complete. Declaration of preparer (other than taxpayer) is based on all information of which preparer has any knowledge.

▶ _____   _____
Signature of officer   Date

▶ _____
Title

May the IRS discuss this return with the preparer shown below? See instructions. ☐ **Yes** ☐ **No**

Paid Preparer Use Only

Print/Type preparer's name	Preparer's signature	Date	Check ☐ if self-employed	PTIN
Firm's name ▶			Firm's EIN ▶	
Firm's address ▶			Phone no.	

For Paperwork Reduction Act Notice, see separate instructions.   Cat. No. 11450Q   Form **1120** (2018)

Form 1120 (2018)   Page **2**

Schedule C	Dividends, Inclusions, and Special Deductions (see instructions)	(a) Dividends and inclusions	(b) %	(c) Special deductions (a) × (b)
1	Dividends from less-than-20%-owned domestic corporations (other than debt-financed stock)		50	
2	Dividends from 20%-or-more-owned domestic corporations (other than debt-financed stock)		65	
3	Dividends on certain debt-financed stock of domestic and foreign corporations . .		See Instructions	
4	Dividends on certain preferred stock of less-than-20%-owned public utilities . . .		23.3	
5	Dividends on certain preferred stock of 20%-or-more-owned public utilities		26.7	
6	Dividends from less-than-20%-owned foreign corporations and certain FSCs . . .		50	
7	Dividends from 20%-or-more-owned foreign corporations and certain FSCs . . .		65	
8	Dividends from wholly owned foreign subsidiaries		100	
9	**Subtotal.** Add lines 1 through 8. See instructions for limitations		See Instructions	
10	Dividends from domestic corporations received by a small business investment company operating under the Small Business Investment Act of 1958		100	
11	Dividends from affiliated group members		100	
12	Dividends from certain FSCs		100	
13	Foreign-source portion of dividends received from a specified 10%-owned foreign corporation (excluding hybrid dividends) (see instructions)		100	
14	Dividends from foreign corporations not included on line 3, 6, 7, 8, 11, 12, or 13 (including any hybrid dividends)			
15	Section 965(a) inclusion		See Instructions	
16a	Subpart F inclusions derived from the sale by a controlled foreign corporation (CFC) of the stock of a lower-tier foreign corporation treated as a dividend (attach Form(s) 5471) (see instructions)		100	
b	Subpart F inclusions derived from hybrid dividends of tiered corporations (attach Form(s) 5471) (see instructions)			
c	Other inclusions from CFCs under subpart F not included on line 15, 16a, 16b, or 17 (attach Form(s) 5471) (see instructions).			
17	Global Intangible Low-Taxed Income (GILTI) (attach Form(s) 5471 and Form 8992) . .			
18	Gross-up for foreign taxes deemed paid			
19	IC-DISC and former DISC dividends not included on line 1, 2, or 3			
20	Other dividends			
21	Deduction for dividends paid on certain preferred stock of public utilities			
22	Section 250 deduction (attach Form 8993)			
23	**Total dividends and inclusions.** Add lines 9 through 20. Enter here and on page 1, line 4			
24	**Total special deductions.** Add lines 9 through 22, column (c). Enter here and on page 1, line 29b			

Form **1120** (2018)

Form 1120 (2018) Page **3**

Schedule J Tax Computation and Payment (see instructions)

Part I—Tax Computation

1	Check if the corporation is a member of a controlled group (attach Schedule O (Form 1120)). See instructions ▶ ☐			
2	Income tax. See instructions		**2**	
3	Base erosion minimum tax (attach Form 8991)		**3**	
4	Add lines 2 and 3		**4**	
5a	Foreign tax credit (attach Form 1118)	**5a**		
b	Credit from Form 8834 (see instructions)	**5b**		
c	General business credit (attach Form 3800)	**5c**		
d	Credit for prior year minimum tax (attach Form 8827)	**5d**		
e	Bond credits from Form 8912	**5e**		
6	**Total credits.** Add lines 5a through 5e		**6**	
7	Subtract line 6 from line 4		**7**	
8	Personal holding company tax (attach Schedule PH (Form 1120))		**8**	
9a	Recapture of investment credit (attach Form 4255)	**9a**		
b	Recapture of low-income housing credit (attach Form 8611)	**9b**		
c	Interest due under the look-back method—completed long-term contracts (attach Form 8697)	**9c**		
d	Interest due under the look-back method—income forecast method (attach Form 8866)	**9d**		
e	Alternative tax on qualifying shipping activities (attach Form 8902)	**9e**		
f	Other (see instructions—attach statement)	**9f**		
10	**Total.** Add lines 9a through 9f		**10**	
11	**Total tax.** Add lines 7, 8, and 10. Enter here and on page 1, line 31		**11**	

Part II—Section 965 Payments (see instructions)

12	2018 net 965 tax liability paid from Form 965-B, Part II, column (k), line 2. Enter here and on page 1, line 32	**12**	

Part III—Payments, Refundable Credits, and Section 965 Net Tax Liability

13	2017 overpayment credited to 2018		**13**	
14	2018 estimated tax payments		**14**	
15	2018 refund applied for on Form 4466		**15**	( )
16	Combine lines 13, 14, and 15		**16**	
17	Tax deposited with Form 7004		**17**	
18	Withholding (see instructions)		**18**	
19	**Total payments.** Add lines 16, 17, and 18		**19**	
20	Refundable credits from:			
a	Form 2439	**20a**		
b	Form 4136	**20b**		
c	Form 8827, line 8c	**20c**		
d	Other (attach statement—see instructions)	**20d**		
21	**Total credits.** Add lines 20a through 20d		**21**	
22	2018 net 965 tax liability from Form 965-B, Part I, column (d), line 2. See instructions		**22**	
23	**Total payments, credits, and section 965 net tax liability.** Add lines 19, 21, and 22. Enter here and on page 1, line 33		**23**	

Form **1120** (2018)

Form 1120 (2018)   Page **4**

Schedule K	**Other Information** (see instructions)		Yes	No

1 Check accounting method: **a** ☐ Cash   **b** ☐ Accrual   **c** ☐ Other (specify) ▶ _____

2 See the instructions and enter the:

a Business activity code no. ▶ _____

b Business activity ▶ _____

c Product or service ▶ _____

3 Is the corporation a subsidiary in an affiliated group or a parent-subsidiary controlled group? . . . .

If "Yes," enter name and EIN of the parent corporation ▶ _____

_____

4 At the end of the tax year:

a Did any foreign or domestic corporation, partnership (including any entity treated as a partnership), trust, or tax-exempt organization own directly 20% or more, or own, directly or indirectly, 50% or more of the total voting power of all classes of the corporation's stock entitled to vote? If "Yes," complete Part I of Schedule G (Form 1120) (attach Schedule G) . . . . . .

b Did any individual or estate own directly 20% or more, or own, directly or indirectly, 50% or more of the total voting power of all classes of the corporation's stock entitled to vote? If "Yes," complete Part II of Schedule G (Form 1120) (attach Schedule G) .

5 At the end of the tax year, did the corporation:

a Own directly 20% or more, or own, directly or indirectly, 50% or more of the total voting power of all classes of stock entitled to vote of any foreign or domestic corporation not included on **Form 851,** Affiliations Schedule? For rules of constructive ownership, see instructions. If "Yes," complete (i) through (iv) below.

(i) Name of Corporation	**(ii)** Employer Identification Number (if any)	**(iii)** Country of Incorporation	**(iv)** Percentage Owned in Voting Stock

b Own directly an interest of 20% or more, or own, directly or indirectly, an interest of 50% or more in any foreign or domestic partnership (including an entity treated as a partnership) or in the beneficial interest of a trust? For rules of constructive ownership, see instructions. If "Yes," complete (i) through (iv) below.

(i) Name of Entity	**(ii)** Employer Identification Number (if any)	**(iii)** Country of Organization	**(iv)** Maximum Percentage Owned in Profit, Loss, or Capital

6 During this tax year, did the corporation pay dividends (other than stock dividends and distributions in exchange for stock) in excess of the corporation's current and accumulated earnings and profits? See sections 301 and 316 . . . .

If "Yes," file **Form 5452,** Corporate Report of Nondividend Distributions. See the instructions for Form 5452.

If this is a consolidated return, answer here for the parent corporation and on Form 851 for each subsidiary.

7 At any time during the tax year, did one foreign person own, directly or indirectly, at least 25% of the total voting power of all classes of the corporation's stock entitled to vote or at least 25% of the total value of all classes of the corporation's stock? .

For rules of attribution, see section 318. If "Yes," enter:

(a) Percentage owned ▶ _____ and **(b)** Owner's country ▶ _____

(c) The corporation may have to file **Form 5472,** Information Return of a 25% Foreign-Owned U.S. Corporation or a Foreign Corporation Engaged in a U.S. Trade or Business. Enter the number of Forms 5472 attached ▶ _____

8 Check this box if the corporation issued publicly offered debt instruments with original issue discount . . . . ▶ ☐

If checked, the corporation may have to file **Form 8281,** Information Return for Publicly Offered Original Issue Discount Instruments.

9 Enter the amount of tax-exempt interest received or accrued during the tax year ▶ $ _____

10 Enter the number of shareholders at the end of the tax year (if 100 or fewer) ▶ _____

11 If the corporation has an NOL for the tax year and is electing to forego the carryback period, check here (see instructions) ▶ ☐

If the corporation is filing a consolidated return, the statement required by Regulations section 1.1502-21(b)(3) must be attached or the election will not be valid.

12 Enter the available NOL carryover from prior tax years (do not reduce it by any deduction reported on page 1, line 29a.) . . . . ▶ $ _____

Form **1120** (2018)

Form 1120 (2018) Page **5**

Schedule K	Other Information *(continued from page 4)*		

		Yes	No
13	Are the corporation's total receipts (page 1, line 1a, plus lines 4 through 10) for the tax year **and** its total assets at the end of the tax year less than $250,000?		
	If "Yes," the corporation is not required to complete Schedules L, M-1, and M-2. Instead, enter the total amount of cash distributions and the book value of property distributions (other than cash) made during the tax year ▶ $ _____		
14	Is the corporation required to file Schedule UTP (Form 1120), Uncertain Tax Position Statement? See instructions		
	If "Yes," complete and attach Schedule UTP.		
15a	Did the corporation make any payments in 2018 that would require it to file Form(s) 1099?		
b	If "Yes," did or will the corporation file required Forms 1099?		
16	During this tax year, did the corporation have an 80% or more change in ownership, including a change due to redemption of its own stock?		
17	During or subsequent to this tax year, but before the filing of this return, did the corporation dispose of more than 65% (by value) of its assets in a taxable, non-taxable, or tax deferred transaction?		
18	Did the corporation receive assets in a section 351 transfer in which any of the transferred assets had a fair market basis or fair market value of more than $1 million?		
19	During the corporation's tax year, did the corporation make any payments that would require it to file Forms 1042 and 1042-S under chapter 3 (sections 1441 through 1464) or chapter 4 (sections 1471 through 1474) of the Code?		
20	Is the corporation operating on a cooperative basis?.		
21	During the tax year, did the corporation pay or accrue any interest or royalty for which the deduction is not allowed under section 267A? See instructions		
	If "Yes," enter the total amount of the disallowed deductions ▶ $ _____		
22	Does the corporation have gross receipts of at least $500 million in any of the 3 preceding tax years? (See sections 59A(e)(2) and (3))		
	If "Yes," complete and attach Form 8991.		
23	Did the corporation have an election under section 163(j) for any real property trade or business or any farming business in effect during the tax year? See instructions		
24	Does the corporation satisfy **one** of the following conditions and the corporation does not own a pass-through entity with current year, or prior year carryover, excess business interest expense? See instructions		
a	The corporation's aggregate average annual gross receipts (determined under section 448(c)) for the 3 tax years preceding the current tax year do not exceed $25 million, and the corporation is not a tax shelter, or		
b	The corporation only has business interest expense from (1) an electing real property trade or business, (2) an electing farming business, or (3) certain utility businesses under section 163(j)(7).		
	If "No," complete and attach Form 8990.		
25	Is the corporation attaching Form 8996 to certify as a Qualified Opportunity Fund?		
	If "Yes," enter amount from Form 8996, line 13 . . . . . ▶ $		

Form **1120** (2018)

Form 1120 (2018)   Page **6**

Schedule L	**Balance Sheets per Books**	Beginning of tax year		End of tax year	
	Assets	(a)	(b)	(c)	(d)
1	Cash				
2a	Trade notes and accounts receivable				
b	Less allowance for bad debts	( )		( )	
3	Inventories				
4	U.S. government obligations				
5	Tax-exempt securities (see instructions)				
6	Other current assets (attach statement)				
7	Loans to shareholders				
8	Mortgage and real estate loans				
9	Other investments (attach statement)				
10a	Buildings and other depreciable assets				
b	Less accumulated depreciation	( )		( )	
11a	Depletable assets				
b	Less accumulated depletion	( )		( )	
12	Land (net of any amortization)				
13a	Intangible assets (amortizable only)				
b	Less accumulated amortization	( )		( )	
14	Other assets (attach statement)				
15	Total assets				
	Liabilities and Shareholders' Equity				
16	Accounts payable				
17	Mortgages, notes, bonds payable in less than 1 year				
18	Other current liabilities (attach statement)				
19	Loans from shareholders				
20	Mortgages, notes, bonds payable in 1 year or more				
21	Other liabilities (attach statement)				
22	Capital stock: **a** Preferred stock				
	b Common stock				
23	Additional paid-in capital				
24	Retained earnings—Appropriated (attach statement)				
25	Retained earnings—Unappropriated				
26	Adjustments to shareholders' equity (attach statement)				
27	Less cost of treasury stock		( )		( )
28	Total liabilities and shareholders' equity				

Schedule M-1	**Reconciliation of Income (Loss) per Books With Income per Return**

Note: The corporation may be required to file Schedule M-3. See instructions.

1	Net income (loss) per books		7	Income recorded on books this year not included on this return (itemize): Tax-exempt interest $ _____	
2	Federal income tax per books				
3	Excess of capital losses over capital gains				
4	Income subject to tax not recorded on books this year (itemize): _____		8	Deductions on this return not charged against book income this year (itemize):	
			a	Depreciation $ _____	
5	Expenses recorded on books this year not deducted on this return (itemize):		b	Charitable contributions $ _____	
a	Depreciation $ _____				
b	Charitable contributions $ _____		9	Add lines 7 and 8	
c	Travel and entertainment $ _____		10	Income (page 1, line 28)—line 6 less line 9	
6	Add lines 1 through 5				

Schedule M-2	**Analysis of Unappropriated Retained Earnings per Books (Line 25, Schedule L)**

1	Balance at beginning of year		5	Distributions: **a** Cash	
2	Net income (loss) per books			**b** Stock	
3	Other increases (itemize): _____			**c** Property	
			6	Other decreases (itemize): _____	
			7	Add lines 5 and 6	
4	Add lines 1, 2, and 3		8	Balance at end of year (line 4 less line 7)	

Form **1120** (2018)

SCHEDULE M-3	Net Income (Loss) Reconciliation for Corporations	OMB No. 1545-0123
(Form 1120)	With Total Assets of \$10 Million or More	
Department of the Treasury Internal Revenue Service	▶ Attach to Form 1120 or 1120-C. ▶ Go to *www.irs.gov/Form1120* for instructions and the latest information.	2018

Name of corporation (common parent, if consolidated return)	Employer identification number

Check applicable box(es): (1) ☐ Non-consolidated return (2) ☐ Consolidated return (Form 1120 only)

(3) ☐ Mixed 1120/L/PC group (4) ☐ Dormant subsidiaries schedule attached

Part I Financial Information and Net Income (Loss) Reconciliation (see instructions)

1a Did the corporation file SEC Form 10-K for its income statement period ending with or within this tax year?
  ☐ **Yes.** Skip lines 1b and 1c and complete lines 2a through 11 with respect to that SEC Form 10-K.
  ☐ **No.** Go to line 1b. See instructions if multiple non-tax-basis income statements are prepared.

  b Did the corporation prepare a certified audited non-tax-basis income statement for that period?
  ☐ **Yes.** Skip line 1c and complete lines 2a through 11 with respect to that income statement.
  ☐ **No.** Go to line 1c.

  c Did the corporation prepare a non-tax-basis income statement for that period?
  ☐ **Yes.** Complete lines 2a through 11 with respect to that income statement.
  ☐ **No.** Skip lines 2a through 3c and enter the corporation's net income (loss) per its books and records on line 4a.

2a Enter the income statement period: Beginning   MM/DD/YYYY   Ending   MM/DD/YYYY

  b Has the corporation's income statement been restated for the income statement period on line 2a?
  ☐ **Yes.** (If "Yes," attach an explanation and the amount of each item restated.)
  ☐ **No.**

  c Has the corporation's income statement been restated for any of the five income statement periods immediately preceding the period on line 2a?
  ☐ **Yes.** (If "Yes," attach an explanation and the amount of each item restated.)
  ☐ **No.**

3a Is any of the corporation's voting common stock publicly traded?
  ☐ **Yes.**
  ☐ **No.** If "No," go to line 4a.

  b Enter the symbol of the corporation's primary U.S. publicly traded voting common stock . . . .

  c Enter the nine-digit CUSIP number of the corporation's primary publicly traded voting common stock . . . .

4a	Worldwide consolidated net income (loss) from income statement source identified in Part I, line 1 .	**4a**
b	Indicate accounting standard used for line 4a (see instructions): (1) ☐ GAAP (2) ☐ IFRS (3) ☐ Statutory (4) ☐ Tax-basis (5) ☐ Other (specify) _____	
5a	Net income from nonincludible foreign entities (attach statement)	**5a** ( )
b	Net loss from nonincludible foreign entities (attach statement and enter as a positive amount) . . .	**5b**
6a	Net income from nonincludible U.S. entities (attach statement)	**6a** ( )
b	Net loss from nonincludible U.S. entities (attach statement and enter as a positive amount)	**6b**
7a	Net income (loss) of other includible foreign disregarded entities (attach statement)	**7a**
b	Net income (loss) of other includible U.S. disregarded entities (attach statement)	**7b**
c	Net income (loss) of other includible entities (attach statement)	**7c**
8	Adjustment to eliminations of transactions between includible entities and nonincludible entities (attach statement)	**8**
9	Adjustment to reconcile income statement period to tax year (attach statement)	**9**
10a	Intercompany dividend adjustments to reconcile to line 11 (attach statement)	**10a**
b	Other statutory accounting adjustments to reconcile to line 11 (attach statement)	**10b**
c	Other adjustments to reconcile to amount on line 11 (attach statement)	**10c**
11	**Net income (loss) per income statement of includible corporations.** Combine lines 4 through 10 .	**11**

  Note: Part I, line 11, must equal Part II, line 30, column (a), or Schedule M-1, line 1 (see instructions).

12 Enter the total amount (not just the corporation's share) of the assets and liabilities of all entities included or removed on the following lines.

		Total Assets	Total Liabilities
a	Included on Part I, line 4 . . . . ▶		
b	Removed on Part I, line 5 . . . . ▶		
c	Removed on Part I, line 6 . . . . ▶		
d	Included on Part I, line 7 . . . . ▶		

For Paperwork Reduction Act Notice, see the Instructions for Form 1120.	Cat. No. 37961C	Schedule M-3 (Form 1120) 2018

Schedule M-3 (Form 1120) 2018   Page **2**

Name of corporation (common parent, if consolidated return)	Employer identification number

Check applicable box(es): **(1)** ☐ Consolidated group   **(2)** ☐ Parent corp   **(3)** ☐ Consolidated eliminations   **(4)** ☐ Subsidiary corp   **(5)** ☐ Mixed 1120/L/PC group

Check if a sub-consolidated: **(6)** ☐ 1120 group   **(7)** ☐ 1120 eliminations

Name of subsidiary (if consolidated return)	Employer identification number

Part II	Reconciliation of Net Income (Loss) per Income Statement of Includible Corporations With Taxable Income per Return (see instructions)

Income (Loss) Items (Attach statements for lines 1 through 12)	(a) Income (Loss) per Income Statement	(b) Temporary Difference	(c) Permanent Difference	(d) Income (Loss) per Tax Return
1 Income (loss) from equity method foreign corporations				
2 Gross foreign dividends not previously taxed				
3 Subpart F, QEF, and similar income inclusions				
4 Gross-up for foreign taxes deemed paid				
5 Gross foreign distributions previously taxed				
6 Income (loss) from equity method U.S. corporations				
7 U.S. dividends not eliminated in tax consolidation				
8 Minority interest for includible corporations				
9 Income (loss) from U.S. partnerships				
10 Income (loss) from foreign partnerships				
11 Income (loss) from other pass-through entities				
12 Items relating to reportable transactions				
13 Interest income (see instructions)				
14 Total accrual to cash adjustment				
15 Hedging transactions				
16 Mark-to-market income (loss)				
17 Cost of goods sold (see instructions)	( )			( )
18 Sale versus lease (for sellers and/or lessors)				
19 Section 481(a) adjustments				
20 Unearned/deferred revenue				
21 Income recognition from long-term contracts				
22 Original issue discount and other imputed interest				
23a Income statement gain/loss on sale, exchange, abandonment, worthlessness, or other disposition of assets other than inventory and pass-through entities				
b Gross capital gains from Schedule D, excluding amounts from pass-through entities				
c Gross capital losses from Schedule D, excluding amounts from pass-through entities, abandonment losses, and worthless stock losses				
d Net gain/loss reported on Form 4797, line 17, excluding amounts from pass-through entities, abandonment losses, and worthless stock losses				
e Abandonment losses				
f Worthless stock losses (attach statement)				
g Other gain/loss on disposition of assets other than inventory				
24 Capital loss limitation and carryforward used				
25 Other income (loss) items with differences (attach statement)				
26 **Total income (loss) items.** Combine lines 1 through 25				
27 **Total expense/deduction items** (from Part III, line 39)				
28 Other items with no differences				
29a Mixed groups, see instructions. All others, combine lines 26 through 28				
b PC insurance subgroup reconciliation totals				
c Life insurance subgroup reconciliation totals				
30 **Reconciliation totals.** Combine lines 29a through 29c				

Note: Line 30, column (a), must equal Part I, line 11, and column (d) must equal Form 1120, page 1, line 28.

Schedule M-3 (Form 1120) 2018

Schedule M-3 (Form 1120) 2018   Page **3**

Name of corporation (common parent, if consolidated return)	Employer identification number

Check applicable box(es): **(1)** ☐ Consolidated group   **(2)** ☐ Parent corp   **(3)** ☐ Consolidated eliminations   **(4)** ☐ Subsidiary corp   **(5)** ☐ Mixed 1120/L/PC group

Check if a sub-consolidated: **(6)** ☐ 1120 group   **(7)** ☐ 1120 eliminations

Name of subsidiary (if consolidated return)	Employer identification number

Part III Reconciliation of Net Income (Loss) per Income Statement of Includible Corporations With Taxable Income per Return—Expense/Deduction Items (see instructions)

Expense/Deduction Items	(a) Expense per Income Statement	(b) Temporary Difference	(c) Permanent Difference	(d) Deduction per Tax Return
1 U.S. current income tax expense				
2 U.S. deferred income tax expense				
3 State and local current income tax expense . . .				
4 State and local deferred income tax expense . . .				
5 Foreign current income tax expense (other than foreign withholding taxes)				
6 Foreign deferred income tax expense				
7 Foreign withholding taxes				
8 Interest expense (see instructions)				
9 Stock option expense				
10 Other equity-based compensation				
11 Meals and entertainment				
12 Fines and penalties				
13 Judgments, damages, awards, and similar costs .				
14 Parachute payments				
15 Compensation with section 162(m) limitation . . .				
16 Pension and profit-sharing				
17 Other post-retirement benefits				
18 Deferred compensation				
19 Charitable contribution of cash and tangible property				
20 Charitable contribution of intangible property . .				
21 Charitable contribution limitation/carryforward . .				
22 Domestic production activities deduction (see instructions)				
23 Current year acquisition or reorganization investment banking fees				
24 Current year acquisition or reorganization legal and accounting fees				
25 Current year acquisition/reorganization other costs .				
26 Amortization/impairment of goodwill				
27 Amortization of acquisition, reorganization, and start-up costs				
28 Other amortization or impairment write-offs . . .				
29 Reserved				
30 Depletion				
31 Depreciation				
32 Bad debt expense				
33 Corporate owned life insurance premiums . . .				
34 Purchase versus lease (for purchasers and/or lessees) .				
35 Research and development costs				
36 Section 118 exclusion (attach statement)				
37 Section 162(r)—FDIC premiums paid by certain large financial institutions (see instructions) . . .				
38 Other expense/deduction items with differences (attach statement)				
39 **Total expense/deduction items.** Combine lines 1 through 38. Enter here and on Part II, line 27, reporting positive amounts as negative and negative amounts as positive				

Schedule M-3 (Form 1120) 2018

Form **1120S**

Department of the Treasury
Internal Revenue Service

U.S. Income Tax Return for an S Corporation

▶ Do not file this form unless the corporation has filed or is attaching Form 2553 to elect to be an S corporation.
▶ Go to *www.irs.gov/Form1120S* for instructions and the latest information.

OMB No. 1545-0123

2018

For calendar year 2018 or tax year beginning _____ , 2018, ending _____ , 20 ____

A S election effective date		Name	D Employer identification number
B Business activity code number (see instructions)	**TYPE OR PRINT**	Number, street, and room or suite no. If a P.O. box, see instructions.	E Date incorporated
C Check if Sch. M-3 attached ☐		City or town, state or province, country, and ZIP or foreign postal code	F Total assets (see instructions) $

G Is the corporation electing to be an S corporation beginning with this tax year? ☐ Yes ☐ No   If "Yes," attach Form 2553 if not already filed
H Check if: **(1)** ☐ Final return **(2)** ☐ Name change **(3)** ☐ Address change **(4)** ☐ Amended return **(5)** ☐ S election termination or revocation
I Enter the number of shareholders who were shareholders during any part of the tax year . . . . ▶

Caution: Include **only** trade or business income and expenses on lines 1a through 21. See the instructions for more information.

Income

1a	Gross receipts or sales	**1a**		
b	Returns and allowances	**1b**		
c	Balance. Subtract line 1b from line 1a		**1c**	
2	Cost of goods sold (attach Form 1125-A)		**2**	
3	Gross profit. Subtract line 2 from line 1c		**3**	
4	Net gain (loss) from Form 4797, line 17 (attach Form 4797)		**4**	
5	Other income (loss) (see instructions—attach statement)		**5**	
6	**Total income (loss).** Add lines 3 through 5 . . . . ▶		**6**	

Deductions (see instructions for limitations)

7	Compensation of officers (see instructions—attach Form 1125-E)	**7**	
8	Salaries and wages (less employment credits)	**8**	
9	Repairs and maintenance	**9**	
10	Bad debts	**10**	
11	Rents	**11**	
12	Taxes and licenses	**12**	
13	Interest (see instructions)	**13**	
14	Depreciation not claimed on Form 1125-A or elsewhere on return (attach Form 4562)	**14**	
15	Depletion **(Do not deduct oil and gas depletion.)**	**15**	
16	Advertising	**16**	
17	Pension, profit-sharing, etc., plans	**17**	
18	Employee benefit programs	**18**	
19	Other deductions (attach statement)	**19**	
20	**Total deductions.** Add lines 7 through 19 . . . . ▶	**20**	
21	**Ordinary business income (loss).** Subtract line 20 from line 6	**21**	

Tax and Payments

22a	Excess net passive income or LIFO recapture tax (see instructions) .	**22a**		
b	Tax from Schedule D (Form 1120S)	**22b**		
c	Add lines 22a and 22b (see instructions for additional taxes) . . .		**22c**	
23a	2018 estimated tax payments and 2017 overpayment credited to 2018	**23a**		
b	Tax deposited with Form 7004	**23b**		
c	Credit for federal tax paid on fuels (attach Form 4136)	**23c**		
d	Refundable credit from Form 8827, line 8c	**23d**		
e	Add lines 23a through 23d		**23e**	
24	Estimated tax penalty (see instructions). Check if Form 2220 is attached . . . . . . ▶ ☐		**24**	
25	**Amount owed.** If line 23e is smaller than the total of lines 22c and 24, enter amount owed . .		**25**	
26	**Overpayment.** If line 23e is larger than the total of lines 22c and 24, enter amount overpaid . .		**26**	
27	Enter amount from line 26: **Credited to 2019 estimated tax** ▶ ____ **Refunded** ▶		**27**	

Sign Here

Under penalties of perjury, I declare that I have examined this return, including accompanying schedules and statements, and to the best of my knowledge and belief, it is true, correct, and complete. Declaration of preparer (other than taxpayer) is based on all information of which preparer has any knowledge.

▶ _____ _____ ▶ _____
Signature of officer   Date   Title

May the IRS discuss this return with the preparer shown below (see instructions)? ☐ Yes ☐ No

Paid Preparer Use Only

Print/Type preparer's name	Preparer's signature	Date	Check ☐ if self-employed	PTIN
Firm's name ▶			Firm's EIN ▶	
Firm's address ▶			Phone no.	

For Paperwork Reduction Act Notice, see separate instructions.   Cat. No. 11510H   Form **1120S** (2018)

Form 1120S (2018)   Page **2**

Schedule B	**Other Information** (see instructions)	Yes	No

1 Check accounting method: **a** ☐ Cash   **b** ☐ Accrual
   c ☐ Other (specify) ▶ _____

2 See the instructions and enter the:
   a Business activity ▶ _____   **b** Product or service ▶ _____

3 At any time during the tax year, was any shareholder of the corporation a disregarded entity, a trust, an estate, or a nominee or similar person? If "Yes," attach Schedule B-1, Information on Certain Shareholders of an S Corporation . .

4 At the end of the tax year, did the corporation:

a Own directly 20% or more, or own, directly or indirectly, 50% or more of the total stock issued and outstanding of any foreign or domestic corporation? For rules of constructive ownership, see instructions. If "Yes," complete (i) through (v) below . . . .

(i) Name of Corporation	(ii) Employer Identification Number (if any)	(iii) Country of Incorporation	(iv) Percentage of Stock Owned	(v) If Percentage in (iv) is 100%, Enter the Date (if any) a Qualified Subchapter S Subsidiary Election Was Made

b Own directly an interest of 20% or more, or own, directly or indirectly, an interest of 50% or more in the profit, loss, or capital in any foreign or domestic partnership (including an entity treated as a partnership) or in the beneficial interest of a trust? For rules of constructive ownership, see instructions. If "Yes," complete (i) through (v) below . . . .

(i) Name of Entity	(ii) Employer Identification Number (if any)	(iii) Type of Entity	(iv) Country of Organization	(v) Maximum Percentage Owned in Profit, Loss, or Capital

5a At the end of the tax year, did the corporation have any outstanding shares of restricted stock? . . . .
   If "Yes," complete lines (i) and (ii) below.
   (i) Total shares of restricted stock . . . . ▶ _____
   (ii) Total shares of non-restricted stock . . . . ▶ _____

b At the end of the tax year, did the corporation have any outstanding stock options, warrants, or similar instruments? .
   If "Yes," complete lines (i) and (ii) below.
   (i) Total shares of stock outstanding at the end of the tax year ▶ _____
   (ii) Total shares of stock outstanding if all instruments were executed ▶ _____

6 Has this corporation filed, or is it required to file, **Form 8918,** Material Advisor Disclosure Statement, to provide information on any reportable transaction? . . . .

7 Check this box if the corporation issued publicly offered debt instruments with original issue discount . . . . ▶ ☐
   If checked, the corporation may have to file **Form 8281,** Information Return for Publicly Offered Original Issue Discount Instruments.

8 If the corporation **(a)** was a C corporation before it elected to be an S corporation **or** the corporation acquired an asset with a basis determined by reference to the basis of the asset (or the basis of any other property) in the hands of a C corporation **and (b)** has net unrealized built-in gain in excess of the net recognized built-in gain from prior years, enter the net unrealized built-in gain reduced by net recognized built-in gain from prior years (see instructions) ▶ $ _____

9 Did the corporation have an election under section 163(j) for any real property trade or business or any farming business in effect during the tax year? See instructions . . . .

10 Does the corporation satisfy one of the following conditions and the corporation doesn't own a pass-through entity with current year, or prior year carryover, excess business interest expense? See instructions . . . .

a The corporation's aggregate average annual gross receipts (determined under section 448(c)) for the 3 tax years preceding the current tax year don't exceed $25 million, and the corporation isn't a tax shelter; or

b The corporation only has business interest expense from (1) an electing real property trade or business, (2) an electing farming business, or (3) certain utility businesses under section 163(j)(7).
   If "No," complete and attach Form 8990.

11 Does the corporation satisfy **both** of the following conditions?

a The corporation's total receipts (see instructions) for the tax year were less than $250,000 . . . .

b The corporation's total assets at the end of the tax year were less than $250,000 . . . .
   If "Yes," the corporation is not required to complete Schedules L and M-1.

Form 1120S (2018)   Page **3**

Schedule B	Other Information (see instructions) (continued)	Yes	No
12	During the tax year, did the corporation have any non-shareholder debt that was canceled, was forgiven, or had the terms modified so as to reduce the principal amount of the debt?		
	If "Yes," enter the amount of principal reduction . . . . ▶ $ _____		
13	During the tax year, was a qualified subchapter S subsidiary election terminated or revoked? If "Yes," see instructions .		
14a	Did the corporation make any payments in 2018 that would require it to file Form(s) 1099?		
b	If "Yes," did the corporation file or will it file required Forms 1099?		
15	Is the corporation attaching Form 8996 to certify as a Qualified Opportunity Fund?		
	If "Yes," enter the amount from Form 8996, line 13 . . . . ▶ $		

Schedule K	Shareholders' Pro Rata Share Items		Total amount	
Income (Loss)	**1** Ordinary business income (loss) (page 1, line 21)	**1**		
	2 Net rental real estate income (loss) (attach Form 8825)	**2**		
	3a Other gross rental income (loss) **3a**			
	b Expenses from other rental activities (attach statement) . . **3b**			
	c Other net rental income (loss). Subtract line 3b from line 3a	**3c**		
	4 Interest income	**4**		
	5 Dividends: **a** Ordinary dividends	**5a**		
	b Qualified dividends **5b**			
	6 Royalties	**6**		
	7 Net short-term capital gain (loss) (attach Schedule D (Form 1120S))	**7**		
	8a Net long-term capital gain (loss) (attach Schedule D (Form 1120S))	**8a**		
	b Collectibles (28%) gain (loss) **8b**			
	c Unrecaptured section 1250 gain (attach statement) **8c**			
	9 Net section 1231 gain (loss) (attach Form 4797)	**9**		
	10 Other income (loss) (see instructions) . . Type ▶	**10**		
Deductions	**11** Section 179 deduction (attach Form 4562)	**11**		
	12a Charitable contributions	**12a**		
	b Investment interest expense	**12b**		
	c Section 59(e)(2) expenditures **(1)** Type ▶ _____ **(2)** Amount ▶	**12c(2)**		
	d Other deductions (see instructions) . . . Type ▶	**12d**		
Credits	**13a** Low-income housing credit (section 42(j)(5))	**13a**		
	b Low-income housing credit (other)	**13b**		
	c Qualified rehabilitation expenditures (rental real estate) (attach Form 3468, if applicable) .	**13c**		
	d Other rental real estate credits (see instructions) Type ▶	**13d**		
	e Other rental credits (see instructions) . . . Type ▶	**13e**		
	f Biofuel producer credit (attach Form 6478)	**13f**		
	g Other credits (see instructions) . . . . . Type ▶	**13g**		
Foreign Transactions	**14a** Name of country or U.S. possession ▶			
	b Gross income from all sources	**14b**		
	c Gross income sourced at shareholder level	**14c**		
	Foreign gross income sourced at corporate level			
	d Section 951A category	**14d**		
	e Foreign branch category	**14e**		
	f Passive category	**14f**		
	g General category	**14g**		
	h Other (attach statement)	**14h**		
	Deductions allocated and apportioned at shareholder level			
	i Interest expense	**14i**		
	j Other	**14j**		
	Deductions allocated and apportioned at corporate level to foreign source income			
	k Section 951A category	**14k**		
	l Foreign branch category	**14l**		
	m Passive category	**14m**		
	n General category	**14n**		
	o Other (attach statement)	**14o**		
	Other information			
	p Total foreign taxes (check one): ▶ ☐ Paid ☐ Accrued	**14p**		
	q Reduction in taxes available for credit (attach statement)	**14q**		
	r Other foreign tax information (attach statement)			

Form **1120S** (2018)

Form 1120S (2018)   Page **4**

Schedule K		Shareholders' Pro Rata Share Items *(continued)*		Total amount	
Alternative Minimum Tax (AMT) Items	15a	Post-1986 depreciation adjustment	15a		
	b	Adjusted gain or loss	15b		
	c	Depletion (other than oil and gas)	15c		
	d	Oil, gas, and geothermal properties—gross income	15d		
	e	Oil, gas, and geothermal properties—deductions	15e		
	f	Other AMT items (attach statement)	15f		
Items Affecting Shareholder Basis	16a	Tax-exempt interest income	16a		
	b	Other tax-exempt income	16b		
	c	Nondeductible expenses	16c		
	d	Distributions (attach statement if required) (see instructions)	16d		
	e	Repayment of loans from shareholders	16e		
Other Information	17a	Investment income	17a		
	b	Investment expenses	17b		
	c	Dividend distributions paid from accumulated earnings and profits	17c		
	d	Other items and amounts (attach statement)			
Recon- ciliation	18	**Income/loss reconciliation.** Combine the amounts on lines 1 through 10 in the far right column. From the result, subtract the sum of the amounts on lines 11 through 12d and 14p	18		

Schedule L		Balance Sheets per Books	Beginning of tax year		End of tax year	
		Assets	**(a)**	**(b)**	**(c)**	**(d)**
1		Cash				
2a		Trade notes and accounts receivable				
	b	Less allowance for bad debts	( )		( )	
3		Inventories				
4		U.S. government obligations				
5		Tax-exempt securities (see instructions)				
6		Other current assets (attach statement)				
7		Loans to shareholders				
8		Mortgage and real estate loans				
9		Other investments (attach statement)				
10a		Buildings and other depreciable assets				
	b	Less accumulated depreciation	( )		( )	
11a		Depletable assets				
	b	Less accumulated depletion	( )		( )	
12		Land (net of any amortization)				
13a		Intangible assets (amortizable only)				
	b	Less accumulated amortization	( )		( )	
14		Other assets (attach statement)				
15		Total assets				
		Liabilities and Shareholders' Equity				
16		Accounts payable				
17		Mortgages, notes, bonds payable in less than 1 year				
18		Other current liabilities (attach statement)				
19		Loans from shareholders				
20		Mortgages, notes, bonds payable in 1 year or more				
21		Other liabilities (attach statement)				
22		Capital stock				
23		Additional paid-in capital				
24		Retained earnings				
25		Adjustments to shareholders' equity (attach statement)				
26		Less cost of treasury stock		( )		( )
27		Total liabilities and shareholders' equity				

Form **1120S** (2018)

Form 1120S (2018)   Page **5**

Schedule M-1	Reconciliation of Income (Loss) per Books With Income (Loss) per Return

Note: The corporation may be required to file Schedule M-3 (see instructions)

1	Net income (loss) per books		5	Income recorded on books this year not included on Schedule K, lines 1 through 10 (itemize):
2	Income included on Schedule K, lines 1, 2, 3c, 4, 5a, 6, 7, 8a, 9, and 10, not recorded on books this year (itemize) _____			**a** Tax-exempt interest $ _____
	_____			
3	Expenses recorded on books this year not included on Schedule K, lines 1 through 12 and 14p (itemize):		6	Deductions included on Schedule K, lines 1 through 12 and 14p, not charged against book income this year (itemize):
	a Depreciation $ _____			**a** Depreciation $ _____
	_____			
	b Travel and entertainment $ _____		7	Add lines 5 and 6 . . . .
	_____		8	Income (loss) (Schedule K, line 18). Line 4 less line 7 . . . .
4	Add lines 1 through 3			

Schedule M-2	Analysis of Accumulated Adjustments Account, Shareholders' Undistributed Taxable Income Previously Taxed, Accumulated Earnings and Profits, and Other Adjustments Account

(see instructions)

		(a) Accumulated adjustments account	(b) Shareholders' undistributed taxable income previously taxed	(c) Accumulated earnings and profits	(d) Other adjustments account
1	Balance at beginning of tax year				
2	Ordinary income from page 1, line 21				
3	Other additions				
4	Loss from page 1, line 21	( )			
5	Other reductions	( )			( )
6	Combine lines 1 through 5				
7	Distributions				
8	Balance at end of tax year. Subtract line 7 from line 6				

Form **1120S** (2018)

671117

☐ Final K-1   ☐ Amended K-1   OMB No. 1545-0123

Schedule K-1
(Form 1120S)

Department of the Treasury
Internal Revenue Service

2018

For calendar year 2018, or tax year

beginning ___ / ___ / 2018   ending ___ / ___ / ___

Shareholder's Share of Income, Deductions, Credits, etc.

▶ See back of form and separate instructions.

Part I   Information About the Corporation

A Corporation's employer identification number

B Corporation's name, address, city, state, and ZIP code

C IRS Center where corporation filed return

Part II   Information About the Shareholder

D Shareholder's identifying number

E Shareholder's name, address, city, state, and ZIP code

F Shareholder's percentage of stock ownership for tax year . . . . _____ %

For IRS Use Only

Part III   Shareholder's Share of Current Year Income, Deductions, Credits, and Other Items

1	Ordinary business income (loss)	13	Credits
2	Net rental real estate income (loss)		
3	Other net rental income (loss)		
4	Interest income		
5a	Ordinary dividends		
5b	Qualified dividends	14	Foreign transactions
6	Royalties		
7	Net short-term capital gain (loss)		
8a	Net long-term capital gain (loss)		
8b	Collectibles (28%) gain (loss)		
8c	Unrecaptured section 1250 gain		
9	Net section 1231 gain (loss)		
10	Other income (loss)	15	Alternative minimum tax (AMT) items
11	Section 179 deduction	16	Items affecting shareholder basis
12	Other deductions		
		17	Other information

* See attached statement for additional information.

For Paperwork Reduction Act Notice, see the Instructions for Form 1120S.   www.irs.gov/Form1120S   Cat. No. 11520D   **Schedule K-1 (Form 1120S) 2018**

This list identifies the codes used on Schedule K-1 for all shareholders and provides summarized reporting information for shareholders who file Form 1040. For detailed reporting and filing information, see the separate Shareholder's Instructions for Schedule K-1 and the instructions for your income tax return.

1. **Ordinary business income (loss).** Determine whether the income (loss) is passive or nonpassive and enter on your return as follows:

	Report on
Passive loss	See the Shareholder's Instructions
Passive income	Schedule E, line 28, column (h)
Nonpassive loss	See the Shareholder's Instructions
Nonpassive income	Schedule E, line 28, column (k)

2. **Net rental real estate income (loss)**   See the Shareholder's Instructions
3. **Other net rental income (loss)**

Net income	Schedule E, line 28, column (h)
Net loss	See the Shareholder's Instructions

4. **Interest income**   Form 1040, line 2b
5a. **Ordinary dividends**   Form 1040, line 3b
5b. **Qualified dividends**   Form 1040, line 3a
6. **Royalties**   Schedule E, line 4
7. **Net short-term capital gain (loss)**   Schedule D, line 5
8a. **Net long-term capital gain (loss)**   Schedule D, line 12
8b. **Collectibles (28%) gain (loss)**   28% Rate Gain Worksheet, line 4 (Schedule D instructions)
8c. **Unrecaptured section 1250 gain**   See the Shareholder's Instructions
9. **Net section 1231 gain (loss)**   See the Shareholder's Instructions
10. **Other income (loss)**

Code

A	Other portfolio income (loss)	See the Shareholder's Instructions
B	Involuntary conversions	See the Shareholder's Instructions
C	Sec. 1256 contracts & straddles	Form 6781, line 1
D	Mining exploration costs recapture	See Pub. 535
E	Section 951A income	
F	Section 965(a) inclusion	
G	Subpart F income other than sections 951A and 965 inclusion	See the Shareholder's Instructions
H	Other income (loss)	

11. **Section 179 deduction**   See the Shareholder's Instructions
12. **Other deductions**

A	Cash contributions (60%)	
B	Cash contributions (30%)	
C	Noncash contributions (50%)	
D	Noncash contributions (30%)	See the Shareholder's Instructions
E	Capital gain property to a 50% organization (30%)	
F	Capital gain property (20%)	
G	Contributions (100%)	
H	Investment interest expense	Form 4952, line 1
I	Deductions—royalty income	Schedule E, line 19
J	Section 59(e)(2) expenditures	See the Shareholder's Instructions
K	Section 965(c) deduction	See the Shareholder's Instructions
L	Deductions—portfolio (other)	Schedule A, line 16
M	Preproductive period expenses	See the Shareholder's Instructions
N	Commercial revitalization deduction from rental real estate activities	See Form 8582 instructions
O	Reforestation expense deduction	See the Shareholder's Instructions
P	through **R**	Reserved for future use
S	Other deductions	See the Shareholder's Instructions

13. **Credits**

A	Low-income housing credit (section 42(j)(5)) from pre-2008 buildings	
B	Low-income housing credit (other) from pre-2008 buildings	
C	Low-income housing credit (section 42(j)(5)) from post-2007 buildings	See the Shareholder's Instructions
D	Low-income housing credit (other) from post-2007 buildings	
E	Qualified rehabilitation expenditures (rental real estate)	
F	Other rental real estate credits	
G	Other rental credits	
H	Undistributed capital gains credit	Schedule 5 (Form 1040), line 74, box a
I	Biofuel producer credit	
J	Work opportunity credit	
K	Disabled access credit	
L	Empowerment zone employment credit	See the Shareholder's Instructions
M	Credit for increasing research activities	
N	Credit for employer social security and Medicare taxes	

Code		Report on
O	Backup withholding	See the Shareholder's Instructions
P	Other credits	See the Shareholder's Instructions

14. **Foreign transactions**

A	Name of country or U.S. possession	
B	Gross income from all sources	Form 1116, Part I
C	Gross income sourced at shareholder level	

Foreign gross income sourced at corporate level

D	Section 951A category	
E	Foreign branch category	
F	Passive category	Form 1116, Part I
G	General category	
H	Other	

Deductions allocated and apportioned at shareholder level

I	Interest expense	Form 1116, Part I
J	Other	Form 1116, Part I

Deductions allocated and apportioned at corporate level to foreign source income

K	Section 951A category	
L	Foreign branch category	
M	Passive category	Form 1116, Part I
N	General category	
O	Other	

Other information

P	Total foreign taxes paid	Form 1116, Part II
Q	Total foreign taxes accrued	Form 1116, Part II
R	Reduction in taxes available for credit	Form 1116, line 12
S	Foreign trading gross receipts	Form 8873
T	Extraterritorial income exclusion	Form 8873
U	Section 965 information	See the Shareholder's Instructions
V	Other foreign transactions	See the Shareholder's Instructions

15. **Alternative minimum tax (AMT) items**

A	Post-1986 depreciation adjustment	
B	Adjusted gain or loss	
C	Depletion (other than oil & gas)	See the Shareholder's Instructions and the Instructions for Form 6251
D	Oil, gas, & geothermal—gross income	
E	Oil, gas, & geothermal—deductions	
F	Other AMT items	

16. **Items affecting shareholder basis**

A	Tax-exempt interest income	Form 1040, line 2a
B	Other tax-exempt income	
C	Nondeductible expenses	
D	Distributions	See the Shareholder's Instructions
E	Repayment of loans from shareholders	

17. **Other information**

A	Investment income	Form 4952, line 4a
B	Investment expenses	Form 4952, line 5
C	Qualified rehabilitation expenditures (other than rental real estate)	See the Shareholder's Instructions
D	Basis of energy property	See the Shareholder's Instructions
E	Recapture of low-income housing credit (section 42(j)(5))	Form 8611, line 8
F	Recapture of low-income housing credit (other)	Form 8611, line 8
G	Recapture of investment credit	See Form 4255
H	Recapture of other credits	See the Shareholder's Instructions
I	Look-back interest—completed long-term contracts	See Form 8697
J	Look-back interest—income forecast method	See Form 8866
K	Dispositions of property with section 179 deductions	
L	Recapture of section 179 deduction	
M	through **U**	
V	Section 199A income	
W	Section 199A W-2 wages	
X	Section 199A unadjusted basis	See the Shareholder's Instructions
Y	Section 199A REIT dividends	
Z	Section 199A PTP income	
AA	Excess taxable income	
AB	Excess business interest income	
AC	Other information	

Appendix C

Glossary

The key terms in this glossary have been defined to reflect their conventional use in the field of taxation. The definitions may therefore be incomplete for other purposes.

A

AAA bypass election. In the context of a distribution by an S corporation, an election made by the entity to designate that the distribution is first from accumulated earnings and profits (AEP) and only then from the accumulated adjustments account (AAA).

Abandoned spouse. The abandoned spouse provision enables a married taxpayer with a dependent child whose spouse did not live in the taxpayer's home during the last six months of the tax year to file as a head of household rather than as married filing separately.

Accelerated cost recovery system (ACRS). A method in which the cost of tangible property is recovered (depreciated) over a prescribed period of time. This depreciation approach disregards salvage value, imposes a period of cost recovery that depends upon the classification of the asset into one of various recovery periods, and prescribes the applicable percentage of cost that can be deducted each year. A modified system is currently the default cost recovery method; it is referred to as MACRS. § 168.

Accelerated death benefits. The amount received from a life insurance policy by the insured who is terminally ill or chronically ill. Any realized gain may be excluded from the gross income of the insured if the policy is surrendered to the insurer or is sold to a licensed viatical settlement provider. § 101(g).

Acceleration rule. Treatment of an intercompany transaction on a consolidated return, when a sold asset leaves the group.

Accident and health benefits. Employee fringe benefits provided by employers through the payment of health and accident insurance premiums or the establishment of employer-funded medical reimbursement plans. Employers generally are entitled to a deduction for such payments, whereas employees generally exclude such fringe benefits from gross income. §§ 105 and 106.

Accident and health insurance benefits. See *accident and health benefits.*

Accountable plan. A type of expense reimbursement plan that requires an employee to render an adequate accounting to the employer and return any excess reimbursement or allowance. If the expense qualifies, it will be treated as a deduction *for* AGI.

Accounting income. The accountant's concept of income is generally based upon the realization principle. Financial accounting income may differ from taxable income (e.g., accelerated depreciation might be used for Federal income tax and straight-line depreciation for financial accounting purposes). Differences are included in a reconciliation of taxable and accounting income on Schedule M–1 or Schedule M–3 of Form 1120 for corporations.

Accounting method. The method under which income and expenses are determined for tax purposes. Important accounting methods include the cash basis and the accrual basis. Special methods are available for the reporting of gain on installment sales, recognition of income on construction projects (the completed contract and percentage of completion methods), and the valuation of inventories (last-in, first-out and first-in, first-out). §§ 446–474.

Accounting period. The period of time, usually a year, used by a taxpayer for the determination of tax liability. Unless a fiscal year is chosen, taxpayers must determine and pay their income tax liability by using the calendar year (January 1 through December 31) as the period of measurement. An example of a fiscal year is July 1 through June 30. A change in accounting period (e.g., from a calendar year to a fiscal year) generally requires the consent of the IRS. Usually, taxpayers are free to select either an initial calendar or a fiscal year without the consent of the IRS. §§ 441–444.

Accrual method. A method of accounting that recognizes expenses as incurred and income as earned. In contrast to the cash basis of accounting, expenses need not be paid to be deductible, nor need income be received to be taxable. § 446(c)(2).

Accumulated adjustments account (AAA). An account that aggregates an S corporation's post-1982 income, loss, and deductions for the tax year (including nontaxable income and nondeductible losses and expenses). After the year-end income and expense adjustments are made, the account is reduced by distributions made during the tax year.

Accumulated E & P. See *accumulated earnings and profits (AEP)*.

Accumulated earnings and profits (AEP). Net undistributed tax-basis earnings of a corporation aggregated from March 1, 1913, to the end of the prior tax year. Used to determine the amount of dividend income associated with a distribution to shareholders. § 316 and Reg. § 1.316–2.

Accumulated earnings tax. A special 20 percent tax imposed on C corporations that accumulate (rather than distribute) their earnings beyond the reasonable needs of the business. The accumulated earnings tax and related interest are imposed on accumulated taxable income in addition to the corporate income tax. §§ 531–537.

Accuracy-related penalties. Major civil taxpayer penalties relating to the accuracy of tax return data, including misstatements stemming from taxpayer negligence and improper valuation of income and deductions, are coordinated under this umbrella term. The penalty usually equals 20 percent of the understated tax liability.

Acquiescence. Agreement by the IRS on the results reached in certain judicial decisions; sometimes abbreviated *Acq.* or *A*.

Acquisition indebtedness. Debt incurred in acquiring, constructing, or substantially improving a qualified residence of the taxpayer. The interest on such loans is deductible as qualified residence interest. However, interest on such debt is deductible only on the portion of the indebtedness that does not exceed $750,000 ($1,000,000 for debt incurred before December 15, 2017). § 163(h)(3).

Active income. Wages, salary, commissions, bonuses, profits from a trade or business in which the taxpayer is a material participant, gain on the sale or other disposition of assets used in an active trade or business, and income from intangible property if the taxpayer's personal efforts significantly contributed to the creation of the property. The passive activity loss rules require classification of income and losses into three categories with active income being one of them.

Ad valorem taxes. A tax imposed on the value of property. The most common ad valorem tax is that imposed by states, counties, and cities on real estate. Ad valorem taxes can be imposed on personal property as well.

Additional first-year depreciation. In general, this provision provides for an additional cost recovery deduction of 100 percent for qualified property acquired and placed in service after September 27, 2017, and before January 1, 2027. (The bonus depreciation percentage is reduced by 20 percent for each tax year after 2022.) Qualified property includes most types of new and used property other than buildings. The taxpayer can elect to forgo this bonus depreciation. Different rules applied between 2008 and September 28, 2017.

Adjusted basis. The cost or other basis of property reduced by depreciation allowed or allowable and increased by capital improvements. Other special adjustments are provided in § 1016 and the related Regulations.

Adjusted gross estate. The gross estate less the sum allowable as deductions under § 2053 (expenses, indebtedness, and taxes) and § 2054 (casualty and theft losses during the administration of the estate). § 6166(b)(6).

Adjustments. In calculating AMTI, certain adjustments are added to or deducted from taxable income. These adjustments generally reflect timing differences. § 56.

Adoption expenses credit. A provision intended to assist taxpayers who incur nonrecurring costs directly associated with the adoption process, such as legal costs, social service review costs, and transportation costs. Up to $14,080 of costs incurred to adopt an eligible child qualify for the credit (unique rules apply when adopting a special needs child). A taxpayer may claim the credit in the year qualifying expenses are paid or incurred if the expenses are paid during or after the year in which the adoption is finalized. For qualifying expenses paid or incurred in a tax year prior to the year the adoption is finalized, the credit must be claimed in the tax year following the tax year during which the expenses are paid or incurred. § 23.

Affiliated group. A parent-subsidiary group of corporations that is eligible to elect to file on a consolidated basis. Eighty percent ownership of the voting power and value of all of the corporations must be achieved every day of the tax year, and an identifiable parent corporation must exist (i.e., it must own at least 80 percent of another group member without applying attribution rules).

Aggregate (or conduit) concept. A perspective taken towards a venture that regards the venture as an aggregation of its owners joined together in an agency relationship rather than as a separate entity. For tax purposes, this results in the income of the venture being taxable directly to its owners. For example, items of income and expense, capital gains and losses, tax credits, etc., realized by a partnership pass through the partnership (a conduit) and are subject to taxation at the partner level. Also, in an S corporation, certain items pass through and are reported on the returns of the shareholders. See also *entity concept*.

Alimony and separate maintenance payments. Alimony deductions result from the payment of a legal obligation arising from the termination of a marital relationship. Payments designated as alimony generally are included in the gross income of the recipient and are deductible *for* AGI by the payor. For divorce or separation instruments executed after December 31, 2018, alimony is neither gross income for the recipient nor deductible by the payor.

Alimony recapture. The amount of alimony that previously has been included in the gross income of the recipient and deducted by the payor that now is deducted by the recipient and included in the gross income of the payor as the result of front-loading. Alimony recapture is applicable for divorce or separation agreements executed before 2019. § 71(f).

All events test. As applied to the recognition of income, the all events test requires that income of an accrual basis taxpayer be recognized when (1) all events have occurred that fix the taxpayer's right to receive the income and (2) the amount can be determined with reasonable accuracy. The TCJA of 2017 added a rule at § 451(b) requiring an accrual method taxpayer to include amounts in income no later than for financial reporting purposes other than for special rules such as the installment method. As applied to the recognition of expenses, the all events test prevents the recognition of a deduction by an accrual basis taxpayer until all the events have occurred that fix the taxpayer's related obligation. This can be contrasted with GAAP under which a fixed or legal obligation is not required before an expense is recognized. Reg. §§ 1.446–1(c)(1)(ii) and 1.461–1(a)(2).

Allocate. The assignment of income for various tax purposes. A multistate corporation's nonbusiness income usually is allocated to the state where the nonbusiness assets are located; it is not apportioned with the rest of the entity's income. The income and expense items of an estate or a trust are allocated between income and corpus components. Specific items of income, expense, gain, loss, and credit can be allocated to specific partners if a substantial economic nontax purpose for the allocation is established.

Alternate valuation date. Property passing from a decedent by death may be valued for estate tax purposes as of the date of death or the alternate valuation date. The alternate valuation date is six months after the date of death or the date the property is disposed of by the estate, whichever comes first. To use the alternate valuation date, the executor or administrator of the estate must make an affirmative election. Election of the alternate valuation date is not available unless it decreases the amount of the gross estate and reduces the estate tax liability.

Alternative depreciation system (ADS). A cost recovery system in which the cost or other initial basis of an asset is recovered using the straight-line method over recovery periods similar to those used in MACRS. The alternative system must be used in certain instances and can be elected in other instances. § 168(g).

Alternative minimum tax (AMT). The AMT is a surtax, calculated as a percentage of alternative minimum taxable income (AMTI). AMTI generally starts with the taxpayer's taxable income, prior to any standard deduction taken. To this amount, the taxpayer (1) adds designated preference items (e.g., tax-exempt interest income on private activity bonds), (2) makes other specified adjustments (e.g., to reflect a slower cost recovery method), (3) adjusts certain AMT itemized deductions for individuals (e.g., interest incurred on housing), and (4) subtracts an exemption amount. The taxpayer must pay the greater of the resulting AMT or the regular income tax (reduced by all allowable tax credits). AMT preferences and adjustments are assigned to partners, LLC members, and S corporation shareholders. The AMT does not apply to C corporations for tax years beginning after 2017.

Alternative minimum tax credit. AMT liability can result from timing differences that give rise to positive adjustments in calculating AMTI. To provide equity for the taxpayer when these timing differences reverse, the regular tax liability may be reduced by a tax credit for a prior year's minimum tax liability attributable to timing differences. § 53.

Alternative minimum taxable income (AMTI). The base (prior to deducting the exemption amount) for computing a taxpayer's alternative minimum tax. This consists of the taxable income for the year modified for AMT adjustments and AMT preferences. § 55(b)(2).

Alternative tax. An option that is allowed in computing the tax on net capital gain. For noncorporate taxpayers, the rate is usually 15 percent (but is 25 percent for unrecaptured § 1250 gain and 28 percent for collectibles). However, the alternative tax rate is 0 percent (rather than 15 percent) for lower-income taxpayers (e.g., taxable income of $78,750 or less for married persons filing jointly). Certain high-income taxpayers (e.g., taxable income of more than $488,850 for married persons filing jointly) have an alternative tax rate of 20 percent. § 1(h).

Alternative tax NOL deduction (ATNOLD). In calculating the AMT, the taxpayer is allowed to deduct NOL carryovers following the regular tax NOL carryover provisions. The AMT NOL amount is referred to as the ATNOLD. The regular income tax NOL is modified for AMT adjustments and preferences to produce the ATNOLD. § 56(d).

American Opportunity credit. This credit applies for qualifying expenses for the first four years of postsecondary education. Qualified expenses include tuition and related expenses and books and other course materials. Room and board are ineligible for the credit. The maximum credit available per student is $2,500 (100 percent of the first $2,000 of qualified expenses and 25 percent of the next $2,000 of qualified expenses). Eligible students include the taxpayer, taxpayer's spouse, and taxpayer's dependents. To qualify for the credit, a student must take at least one-half of the full-time course load for at least one academic term at a qualifying educational institution. The credit is phased out for higher-income taxpayers. § 25A.

Amortization. The tax deduction for the cost or other basis of an intangible asset over the asset's estimated useful life. Examples of amortizable intangibles include patents, copyrights, and leasehold interests. Most purchased intangible assets (e.g., goodwill) can be amortized for income tax purposes over a 15-year period.

Amount realized. The amount received by a taxpayer upon the sale or exchange of property. Amount realized is the sum of the cash and the fair market value of any property or services received by the taxpayer plus any related debt assumed by the buyer. Determining the amount realized is the starting point for arriving at realized gain or loss. § 1001(b).

Annual exclusion. In computing the taxable gifts for the year, each donor excludes the first $15,000 (for 2019) of a gift to each donee. Usually, the annual exclusion is not available for gifts of future interests. § 2503(b).

Annuity. A fixed sum of money payable to a person at specified times for a specified period of time or for life. If the party making the payment (i.e., the obligor) is regularly engaged in this type of business (e.g., an insurance company), the arrangement is classified as a commercial annuity. A so-called private annuity involves an obligor that is not regularly engaged in selling annuities (e.g., a charity or family member).

Apportion. The assignment of the business income of a multistate corporation to specific states for income taxation. Usually, the apportionment procedure accounts for the property, payroll, and sales activity levels of the various states, and a proportionate assignment of the entity's total income is made using a three-factor apportionment formula. These activities indicate the commercial domicile of the corporation relative to that income. Some states exclude nonbusiness income from the apportionment procedure; they allocate nonbusiness income to the states where the nonbusiness assets are located.

Appreciated inventory. In partnership taxation, appreciated inventory is a hot asset, and a partner's share of its ordinary income potential must be allocated. If a partner sells an interest in the partnership, ordinary income is recognized to the extent of the partner's share in the partnership's inventory and unrealized receivables. The definition of "inventory" here is broad enough to include any accounts receivable, including unrealized receivables.

Arm's length. See *arm's length price*.

Arm's length price. The standard under which unrelated parties would determine an exchange price for a transaction. Suppose, for example, Cardinal Corporation sells property to its sole shareholder for $10,000. In testing whether the $10,000 is an "arm's length" price, one would ascertain the price that would have been negotiated between the corporation and an unrelated party in a bargained exchange.

ASC 740. Under Generally Accepted Accounting Principles, the rules for the financial reporting of the tax expense of an enterprise. Permanent differences affect the enterprise's effective tax rate. Temporary differences create a deferred tax asset or a deferred tax liability on the balance sheet.

ASC 740-10. An interpretation by the Financial Accounting Standards Board. When an uncertain tax return position exists, this interpretation is used to determine the financial reporting treatment, if any, for the taxpayer. If it is more likely than not (i.e., a greater than 50 percent probability) that the uncertain return position will be sustained (e.g., by the courts) on its technical merits, it must be reported on the financial statements. The amount to be reported then is computed based on the probabilities of the outcome of the technical review and the amounts at which the dispute would be resolved. If the more-likely-than-not test is failed, no current financial disclosure of the results of the return position is required.

Asset Depreciation Range (ADR) system. A system of estimated useful lives for categories of tangible assets prescribed by the IRS. The system provides a range for each category that extends from 20 percent above to 20 percent below the guideline class lives prescribed by the IRS.

Asset use test. In the context of a corporate reorganization, a means by which to determine if the continuity of business enterprise requirement is met. The acquiring corporation must continue to use the target entity's assets in the acquiror's business going forward; if this is not the case, the requirement is failed.

Assignment of income. A taxpayer attempts to avoid the recognition of income by assigning to another the property that generates the income. Such a procedure will not avoid income recognition by the taxpayer making the assignment if the income was earned at the point of the transfer. In this case, the income is taxed to the person who earns it.

At-risk limitation. Generally, a taxpayer can deduct losses related to a trade or business, S corporation, partnership, or investment asset only to the extent of the at-risk amount. The taxpayer has an amount at risk in a business or investment venture to the extent that personal assets have been subjected to the risks of the business. Typically, the taxpayer's at-risk amount includes (1) the amount of money or other property that the investor contributed to the venture for the investment, (2) the amount of any of the entity's liabilities for which the taxpayer personally is liable and that relate to the investment, and (3) an allocable share of nonrecourse debts incurred by the venture from third parties in arm's length transactions for real estate investments.

Attribution. Under certain circumstances, the tax law applies attribution (constructive ownership) rules to assign to one taxpayer the ownership interest of another taxpayer. If, for example, the stock of Gold Corporation is held 60 percent by Marsha and 40 percent by Sidney, Marsha may be deemed to own 100 percent of Gold Corporation if Marsha and Sidney are mother and child. In that case, the stock owned by Sidney is attributed to Marsha. Stated differently, Marsha has a 60 percent direct and a 40 percent indirect interest in Gold Corporation. It can also be said that Marsha is the constructive owner of Sidney's interest.

Automatic mileage method. Automobile expenses are generally deductible only to the extent the automobile is used in business or for the production of income. Personal commuting expenses are not deductible. The taxpayer may deduct actual expenses (including depreciation and insurance), or the standard (automatic) mileage rate may be used (58 cents per mile for 2019 and 54.5 cents per mile for 2018). Automobile expenses incurred for medical purposes are deductible to the extent of actual out-of-pocket expenses or at the rate of 20 cents per mile for 2019 and 18 cents per mile for 2018. For charitable activities, the rate is 14 cents per mile.

B

Bad debt. A deduction is permitted if a business account receivable subsequently becomes partially or completely worthless, providing the income arising from the debt previously was included in income. Available methods are the specific charge-off method and the reserve method. However, except for certain financial institutions, TRA of 1986 repealed the use of the reserve method for 1987 and thereafter. If the reserve method is used, partially or totally worthless accounts are charged to the reserve. A nonbusiness bad debt deduction is allowed as a short-term capital loss if the loan did not arise in connection with the creditor's trade or business activities. Loans between related parties (family members) generally are classified as nonbusiness. § 166.

Balance sheet approach. The process under ASC 740 (SFAS 109) by which an entity's deferred tax expense or deferred tax benefit is determined as a result of the reporting period's changes in the balance sheet's deferred tax asset and deferred tax liability accounts.

Basis in partnership interest. The acquisition cost of the partner's ownership interest in the partnership. Includes purchase price and associated debt acquired from other partners and in the course of the entity's trade or business.

Benchmarking. The tax professional's use of two or more entities' effective tax rates and deferred tax balance sheet accounts. Used chiefly to compare the effectiveness of the entities' tax planning techniques and to suggest future tax-motivated courses of action.

Blockage rule. A factor to be considered in valuing a large block of corporate stock. Application of this rule generally justifies a discount in the asset's fair market value, because the disposition of a large amount of stock at any one time may depress the value of the shares in the marketplace.

Boot. Cash or property of a type not included in the definition of a tax-deferred exchange. The receipt of boot causes an otherwise tax-deferred transfer to become immediately taxable to the extent of the lesser of the fair market value of the boot or the realized gain on the transfer. For example, see transfers to controlled corporations under § 351(b), reorganizations under § 368, and like-kind exchanges under § 1031(b).

Built-in gains tax. A penalty tax designed to discourage a shift of the incidence of taxation on unrealized gains from a C corporation to its shareholders, via an S election. Under this provision, any recognized gain during the first 10 (or 7 or 5) years of S status generates a corporate-level tax on a base not to exceed the aggregate untaxed built-in gains brought into the S corporation upon its election from C corporation taxable years.

Built-in loss property. Property contributed to a corporation under § 351 or as a contribution to capital that has a basis in excess of its fair market value. An adjustment is necessary to step down the basis of the property to its fair market value. The adjustment prevents the corporation and the contributing shareholder from obtaining a double tax benefit. The corporation allocates the adjustment proportionately among the assets with the built-in loss. As an alternative to the corporate adjustment, the shareholder may elect to reduce the basis in the stock.

Business bad debt. A tax deduction allowed for obligations obtained in connection with a trade or business that have become either partially or completely worthless. In contrast to nonbusiness bad debts, business bad debts are deductible as business expenses. § 166.

Business purpose. A justifiable business reason for carrying out a transaction. Mere tax avoidance is not an acceptable business purpose. The presence of a business purpose is crucial in the area of corporate reorganizations and certain liquidations.

Buy-sell agreement. An arrangement, particularly appropriate in the case of a closely held corporation or a partnership, whereby the surviving owners (shareholders or partners) or the entity agrees to purchase the interest of a withdrawing owner. The buy-sell agreement provides for an orderly disposition of an interest in a business and may aid in setting the value of the interest for estate tax purposes.

Bypass amount. The amount that can be transferred by gift or at death free of any unified transfer tax. For 2019, the bypass amount is $11.4 million for estate tax and 11.4 million for gift tax.

Bypass election. In the context of a distribution by an S corporation, an election made by the entity to designate that the distribution is first from accumulated earnings and profits and only then from the accumulated adjustments account (AAA).

C

C corporation. A separate taxable entity subject to the rules of Subchapter C of the Code. This business form may create a double taxation effect relative to its shareholders. The entity is subject to the regular corporate tax and a number of penalty taxes at the Federal level.

Cafeteria benefit plans. See *cafeteria plan.*

Cafeteria plan. An employee benefit plan under which an employee is allowed to select from among a variety of employer-provided fringe benefits. Some of the benefits may be taxable, and some may be statutory nontaxable benefits (e.g., health and accident insurance and group term life insurance). The employee is taxed only on the taxable benefits selected. A cafeteria benefit plan is also referred to as a flexible benefit plan. § 125.

Capital account. The financial accounting analog of a partner's tax basis in the entity.

Capital account maintenance. Under the § 704(b) Regulations, partnership allocations will be respected only if capital accounts are maintained in accordance with those regulations. These so-called "§ 704(b) book capital accounts" are properly maintained if they reflect the partner's contributions and distributions of cash; increases and decreases for the fair market value of contributed/distributed property; and adjustments for the partner's share of income, gains, losses, and deductions. Certain other adjustments are also required. See also *economic effect test* and *Section 704(b) book capital accounts.*

Capital asset. Broadly speaking, all assets are capital except those specifically excluded from that definition by the Code. Major categories of noncapital assets include property held for resale in the normal course of business (inventory), trade accounts and notes receivable, and depreciable property and real estate used in a trade or business (§ 1231 assets). § 1221.

Capital contribution. Various means by which a shareholder makes additional funds available to the corporation (placed at the risk of the business), sometimes without the receipt of additional stock. If no stock is received, the contributions are added to the basis of the shareholder's existing stock investment and do not generate gross income to the corporation. § 118.

Capital gains. The gain from the sale or exchange of a capital asset.

Capital gain property. Property contributed to a charitable organization that if sold rather than contributed, would have resulted in long-term capital gain to the donor.

Capital interest. Usually, the percentage of the entity's net assets that a partner would receive on liquidation. Typically determined by the partner's capital sharing ratio.

Capital losses. The loss from the sale or exchange of a capital asset.

Capital sharing ratio. A partner's percentage ownership of the entity's capital.

Carbon tax. A tax on fossil fuels to help reduce greenhouse gas emissions.

Carried interest. A "partnership interest held in connection with performance of services," as defined under § 1061. Long-term capital gains from such an interest are reclassified as short-term capital gains (with potential ordinary income treatment) unless the underlying asset that triggered the gain had more than a three-year holding period. This provision only applies to income and gains arising from managing portfolio investments on behalf of third-party investors, including publicly traded securities, commodities, certain real estate, or options to buy/sell such assets. Section 1061 was enacted in the TCJA of 2017 in an effort to curtail an industry practice that resulted in fund managers receiving partnership profits interests in exchange for services: these "profits partners" received long-term capital gain allocations from the fund, rather than ordinary income for the services provided in managing the fund's assets. In addition to § 1061, the IRS has, from time to time, announced that it might issue regulations (under its general "anti-abuse" authority) to expand the scope of the carried interest rules.

Cash balance plan. A hybrid form of pension plan similar in some aspects to a defined benefit plan. Such a plan is funded by the employer, and the employer bears the investment risks and rewards. But like defined contribution plans, a cash balance plan establishes allocations to individual employee accounts, and the payout for an employee depends on investment performance.

Cash method. See *cash receipts method*.

Cash receipts method. A method of accounting that reflects deductions as paid and income as received in any one tax year. However, deductions for prepaid expenses that benefit more than one tax year (e.g., prepaid rent and prepaid interest) usually are spread over the period benefited rather than deducted in the year paid. § 446(c)(1).

Casualty loss. A casualty is defined as "the complete or partial destruction of property resulting from an identifiable event of a sudden, unexpected or unusual nature" (e.g., floods, storms, fires, auto accidents). Individuals may deduct a casualty loss only if the loss is incurred in a trade or business or in a transaction entered into for profit or arises from fire, storm, shipwreck, or other casualty or from theft. Individuals usually deduct personal casualty losses as itemized deductions subject to a $100 nondeductible amount and to an annual floor equal to 10 percent of adjusted gross income that applies after the $100 per casualty floor has been applied. Special rules are provided for the netting of certain casualty gains and losses. For tax years beginning after 2017 (and before 2026), personal casualty losses are limited to those sustained in an area designated as a disaster area by the President of the United States.

Charitable contribution. Contributions made to qualified nonprofit organizations. Taxpayers, regardless of their accounting method, are generally allowed to deduct (subject to various restrictions and limitations) contributions in the year of payment. Accrual basis corporations may accrue contributions at year-end if payment is properly authorized before the end of the year and payment is made within three and one-half months after the end of the year. § 170.

Check-the-box Regulations. By using the check-the-box rules prudently, an entity can select the most attractive tax results offered by the Code, without being bound by legal forms. By default, an unincorporated entity with more than one owner is taxed as a partnership; an unincorporated entity with one owner is a disregarded entity, taxed as a sole proprietorship or corporate division. No action is necessary by the taxpayer if the legal form or default status is desired. Form 8832 is used to "check a box" and change the tax status. Not available if the entity is incorporated under state law.

Child tax credit. A tax credit based solely on the number of qualifying children under age 17. The maximum credit available is $2,000 per qualifying child. (In addition, a $500 nonrefundable credit is available for qualifying dependents other than qualifying children.) A qualifying child must be claimed as a dependent on a parent's tax return and have a Social Security number to qualify for the credit. Taxpayers who qualify for the child tax credit may also qualify for a supplemental credit. The supplemental credit is treated as a component of the earned income credit and is therefore refundable. The credit is phased out for higher-income taxpayers. § 24. See also *dependent tax credit*.

Circuit Court of Appeals. Any of 13 Federal courts that consider tax matters appealed from the U.S. Tax Court, a U.S. District Court, or the U.S. Court of Federal Claims. Appeal from a U.S. Court of Appeals is to the U.S. Supreme Court by Certiorari.

Circular 230. A portion of the Federal tax Regulations that describes the levels of conduct at which a tax preparer must operate. Circular 230 dictates, for instance, that a tax preparer may not charge an unconscionable fee or delay the execution of a tax audit with inappropriate delays. Circular 230 requires that there be a reasonable basis for a tax return position and that no frivolous returns be filed.

Citator. A tax research resource that presents the judicial history of a court case and traces the subsequent references to the case. When these references include the citing cases' evaluations of the cited case's precedents, the research can obtain some measure of the efficacy and reliability of the original holding.

Claim of right doctrine. A judicially imposed doctrine applicable to both cash and accrual basis taxpayers that holds that an amount is includible in income upon actual or constructive receipt if the taxpayer has an unrestricted claim to the payment. For the tax treatment of amounts repaid when previously included in income under the claim of right doctrine, see § 1341.

Closely held C corporation. A regular corporation (i.e., the S election is not in effect) for which more than 50 percent of the value of its outstanding stock is owned, directly or indirectly, by five or fewer individuals at any time during the tax year. The term is relevant in identifying C corporations that are subject to the passive activity loss provisions. § 469.

Closely held corporation. A corporation where stock ownership is not widely dispersed. Rather, a few shareholders are in control of corporate policy and are in a position to benefit personally from that policy.

Closing agreement. In a tax dispute, the parties sign a closing agreement to spell out the terms under which the matters are settled. The agreement is binding on both the Service and the taxpayer.

Collectibles. A special type of capital asset, the gain from which is taxed at a maximum rate of 28 percent if the holding period is more than one year. Examples include art, rugs, antiques, gems, metals, stamps, some coins and bullion, and alcoholic beverages held for investment.

Combined return. In multistate taxation, a group of unitary corporations may elect or be required to file an income tax return that includes operating results for all of the affiliates, not just those with nexus in the state. Thus, apportionment data is reported for the group's worldwide or water's-edge operations.

Community property. Louisiana, Texas, New Mexico, Arizona, California, Washington, Idaho, Nevada, and Wisconsin have community property systems. Alaska residents can elect community property status for assets. The rest of the states are common law property jurisdictions. The difference between common law and community property systems centers around the property rights possessed by married persons. In a common law system, each spouse owns whatever he or she earns. Under a community property system, one-half of the earnings of each spouse is considered owned by the other spouse. Assume, for example, that Jeff and Alice are husband and wife and that their only income is the $50,000 annual salary Jeff receives. If they live in New York (a common law state), the $50,000 salary belongs to Jeff. If, however, they live in Texas (a community property state), the $50,000 salary is owned one-half each by Jeff and Alice.

Compensatory damages. Damages received or paid by the taxpayer can be classified as compensatory damages or as punitive damages. Compensatory damages are paid to compensate one for harm caused by another. Compensatory damages received on account of physical injuries are excludible from the recipient's gross income.

Complete termination redemption. Sale or exchange treatment is available relative to this type of redemption. The shareholder must retire all of his or her outstanding shares in the corporation (ignoring family attribution rules) and cannot hold an interest, other than that of a creditor, for the 10 years following the redemption. § 302(b)(3).

Completed contract method. A method of reporting gain or loss on certain long-term contracts. Under this method of accounting, all gross income and expenses are recognized in the tax year in which the contract is completed. Reg. § 1.451–3.

Complex trust. Not a simple trust. Such trusts may have charitable beneficiaries, accumulate income, and distribute corpus. §§ 661–663.

Composite return. In multistate taxation, an S corporation may be allowed to file a single income tax return that assigns pass-through items to resident and nonresident shareholders. The composite or "block" return allows the entity to remit any tax that is attributable to the nonresident shareholders.

Conduit concept. A perspective taken toward a venture that regards the venture as an aggregation of its owners joined together in an agency relationship rather than as a separate entity. For tax purposes, this results in the income of the venture being taxable directly to its owners. For example, items of income and expense, capital gains and losses, tax credits, etc., realized by a partnership pass through the partnership (a conduit) and are subject to taxation at the partner level. Also, in an S corporation, certain items pass through and are reported on the returns of the shareholders.

Conduit perspective. See *conduit concept.*

Conservatism principle. The theory behind much of Generally Accepted Accounting Principles, under which assurance is provided that an entity's balance sheet assets are not overstated, nor liabilities understated. For instance, under ASC 740 (SFAS 109), a deferred tax asset is not recorded until it is more likely than not that the future tax benefit will be realized.

Consolidated returns. A procedure whereby certain affiliated corporations may file a single return, combine the tax transactions of each corporation, and arrive at a single income tax liability for the group. The election to file a consolidated return usually is binding on future years. §§ 1501–1505 and related Regulations.

Consolidation. The combination of two or more corporations into a newly created corporation. Thus, Black Corporation and White Corporation combine to form Gray Corporation. A consolidation may qualify as a nontaxable reorganization if certain conditions are satisfied. §§ 354 and 368(a)(1)(A).

Constructive dividends. A taxable benefit derived by a shareholder from his or her corporation that is not actually initiated by the board of directors as a dividend. Examples include unreasonable compensation, excessive rent payments, bargain purchases of corporate property, and shareholder use of corporate property. Constructive dividends generally are found in closely held corporations.

Constructive liquidation scenario. The means by which recourse debt is shared among partners in basis determination.

Constructive receipt. If income is unqualifiedly available although not physically in the taxpayer's possession, it still is subject to the income tax. An example is accrued interest on a savings account. Under the constructive receipt concept, the interest is taxed to a depositor in the year available, rather than the year actually withdrawn. The fact that the depositor uses the cash basis of accounting for tax purposes is irrelevant. See Reg. § 1.451–2.

Continuity of business enterprise. In a tax-favored reorganization, the acquiring corporation must continue the historic business of the target or use a significant portion of the target's assets in the new business.

Continuity of interest. In a tax-favored reorganization, a shareholder or corporation that has substantially the same investment after an exchange as before should not be taxed on the transaction. Specifically, the target shareholders must acquire an equity interest in the acquiring corporation equal in value to at least 40 percent of all the outstanding stock of the target entity.

Control. Holding a specified level of stock ownership in a corporation. For § 351, the new shareholder(s) must hold at least 80 percent of the total combined voting power of all voting classes of stock and at least 80 percent of the shares of all nonvoting classes. Other tax provisions require different levels of control to bring about desired effects, such as 50 or 100 percent.

Controlled foreign corporation (CFC). A non-U.S. corporation in which more than 50 percent of the total combined voting power of all classes of stock entitled to vote or the total value of the stock of the corporation is owned by U.S. shareholders on any day during the taxable year of the foreign corporation. For purposes of this definition, a U.S. shareholder is any U.S. person who owns, or is considered to own, 10 percent or more of the total combined voting power of all classes of voting stock of the foreign corporation. Stock owned directly, indirectly, and constructively is used in this measure. See *U.S. shareholder.*

Controlled group. Controlled groups include parent-subsidiary groups, brother-sister groups, combined groups, and certain insurance companies. Controlled groups are required to share certain elements of tax calculations (e.g., $250,000 accumulated earnings credit) or tax credits (e.g., research credit). In addition, some transactions between a controlled group might be treated differently. §§ 1561 and 1563.

Corporate liquidation. Occurs when a corporation distributes its net assets to its shareholders and ceases to be a going concern. Generally, a shareholder recognizes capital gain or loss upon the liquidation of the entity, regardless of the corporation's balance in its earnings and profits account. The liquidating corporation recognizes gain and loss on assets that it sells during the liquidation period and on assets that it distributes to shareholders in kind.

Corpus. The body or principal of a trust. Suppose, for example, Grant transfers an apartment building into a trust, income payable to Ruth for life, remainder to Shawn upon Ruth's death. Corpus of the trust is the apartment building.

Correspondence audit. An audit conducted by the IRS by the U.S. mail. Typically, the IRS writes to the taxpayer requesting the verification of a particular deduction or exemption. The remittance of copies of records or other support is requested of the taxpayer.

Cost depletion. Depletion that is calculated based on the adjusted basis of the asset. The adjusted basis is divided by the expected recoverable units to determine the depletion per unit. The depletion per unit is multiplied by the units sold during the tax year to calculate cost depletion.

Cost recovery. The system by which taxpayers are allowed to recover their investment in an asset by reducing their taxable income by the asset's cost or initial basis. Cost recovery methods include MACRS, § 179 expense, additional first-year deprecation, amortization, and depletion. §§ 168, 179, and 613.

Court of original jurisdiction. The Federal courts are divided into courts of original jurisdiction and appellate courts. A dispute between a taxpayer and the IRS is first considered by a court of original jurisdiction (i.e., a trial court). The four Federal courts of original jurisdiction are the U.S. Tax Court, the U.S. District Court, the Court of Federal Claims, and the Small Cases Division of the U.S. Tax Court.

Coverdell education savings account (§ 530 plan). Coverdell education savings account exempts from tax the earnings on amounts placed in a qualified account for the education expenses of a named beneficiary. Contributions are limited to $2,000 per year per beneficiary, and the proceeds can be withdrawn without tax provided the funds are used to pay qualified educational expenses for primary, secondary, or higher education. (There is an annual $10,000 per student limitation on distributions for tuition expenses for primary and secondary education.) Qualified educational expenses also include certain homeschooling expenses. The account is named for the late Senator Paul Coverdell (R-GA), who sponsored the legislation in Congress. § 530.

Credit for certain retirement plan contributions. A nonrefundable credit is available based on eligible contributions of up to $2,000 to certain qualified retirement plans, such as traditional and Roth IRAs and § 401(k) plans. The benefit provided by this credit is in addition to any deduction or exclusion that otherwise is available resulting from the qualifying contribution. The amount of the credit depends on the taxpayer's AGI and filing status. § 25B.

Credit for child and dependent care expenses. A tax credit ranging from 20 percent to 35 percent of employment-related expenses (child and dependent care expenses) for amounts of up to $6,000 is available to individuals who are employed (or deemed to be employed) and maintain a household for a dependent child under age 13, disabled spouse, or disabled dependent. § 21.

Credit for employer-provided child care. A nonrefundable credit is available to employers who provide child care facilities to their employees during normal working hours. The credit, limited to $150,000, is comprised of two components. The portion of the credit for qualified child care expenses is equal to 25 percent of these expenses, while the portion of the credit for qualified child care resource and referral services is equal to 10 percent of these expenses. Any qualifying expenses otherwise deductible by the taxpayer must be reduced by the amount of the credit. In addition, the taxpayer's basis for any property used for qualifying purposes is reduced by the amount of the credit. § 45F.

Credit for employer-provided family and medical leave. A nonrefundable credit is available to employers who pay wages to employees while they are on family and medical leave. The credit is equal to 12.5% of wages paid to qualifying employees (limited to 12 weeks per employee per year). Employers must pay a minimum of 50% of the wages normally paid; if wages paid during the leave *exceed* 50% of normal wages, the credit is increased by 0.25% for each percentage point above 50% to a maximum of 25% of wages paid. § 45S.

Credit for small employer pension plan startup costs. A nonrefundable credit available to small businesses based on administrative costs associated with establishing and maintaining certain qualified plans. While such qualifying costs generally are deductible as ordinary and necessary business expenses, the availability of the credit is intended to lower the costs of starting a qualified retirement program and therefore encourage qualifying businesses to establish retirement plans for their employees. The credit is available for eligible employers at the rate of 50 percent of qualified startup costs. The maximum credit is $500 (based on a maximum $1,000 of qualifying expenses). § 45E.

Crop insurance proceeds. The proceeds received when an insured crop is destroyed. Section 451(d) permits the farmer to defer reporting the income from the insurance proceeds until the tax year following the taxable year of the destruction.

Crop method. A method of accounting for agricultural crops that are planted in one year but harvested in a subsequent year. Under this method, the costs of raising the crop are accumulated as inventory and are deducted when the income from the crop is realized.

Cross-purchase buy-sell agreement. Under this arrangement, the surviving owners of the business agree to buy out the withdrawing owner. Assume, for example, Ron and Sara are equal shareholders in Tip Corporation. Under a cross-purchase buy-sell agreement, Ron and Sara would contract to purchase the other's interest, should that person decide to withdraw from the business.

Current distribution. A payment made by a partnership to a partner when the partnership's legal existence does not cease thereafter. The partner usually assigns a basis in the distributed property that is equal to the lesser of the partner's basis in the partnership interest or the basis of the distributed asset to the partnership. The partner first assigns basis to any cash that he or she receives in the distribution. A cash distribution in excess of the partner's basis triggers a gain. The partner's remaining basis, if any, is assigned to the noncash assets according to their relative bases to the partnership.

Current E & P. Net tax-basis earnings of a corporation aggregated during the current tax year. A corporate distribution is deemed to be first from the entity's current earnings and profits and then from accumulated earnings and profits. Shareholders recognize dividend income to the extent of the earnings and profits of the corporation. A dividend results to the extent of current earnings and profits, even if there is a larger negative balance in accumulated earnings and profits.

Current tax expense. Under ASC 740 (SFAS 109), the book tax expense that relates to the current reporting period's net income and is actually payable (or creditable) to the appropriate governmental agencies for the current period. Also known as "cash tax" or "tax payable."

D

De minimis fringe. Benefits provided to employees that are too insignificant to warrant the time and effort required to account for the benefits received by each employee and the value of those benefits. Such amounts are excludible from the employee's gross income. § 132.

De minimis fringe benefits. See *de minimis fringe*.

Death benefits. A payment made by an employer to the beneficiary or beneficiaries of a deceased employee on account of the death of the employee.

Debt-financed income. Included in computations of the unrelated business income of an exempt organization, the gross income generated from debt-financed property.

Deceased spouse's unused exclusion (DSUE). In computing the Federal estate tax, the decedent uses the exclusion amount to shelter an amount of the gross estate from taxation. When the first spouse to die fails to use a portion of his/her exclusion amount, the unused portion is "portable" and becomes available to the surviving spouse. The surviving spouse can use the DSUE only of his/her last spouse to predecease.

Deduction for qualified business income. A deduction allowed for noncorporate taxpayers based on the qualified business income of a qualified trade or business. In general, the deduction is limited to the lesser of 20 percent of qualified business income, or 20 percent of taxable income before the qualified business income deduction less any net capital gain. There are *three limitations* on the deduction—an overall limitation (based on modified taxable income), another that applies to high-income taxpayers, and a third that applies to certain types of services businesses. § 199A.

Deduction for qualified tuition and related expenses. Taxpayers are allowed a deduction of up to $4,000 for higher education expenses. Certain taxpayers are not eligible for the deduction: those whose gross AGI exceeds a specified amount and those who can be claimed as a dependent by another taxpayer. These expenses are classified as a deduction *for* AGI, and they need not be employment-related. The deduction expired for tax years after 2017. § 222.

Deductions *for* adjusted gross income. The Federal income tax is not imposed upon gross income. Rather, it is imposed upon taxable income. Congressionally identified deductions for individual taxpayers are subtracted either from gross income to arrive at adjusted gross income or from adjusted gross income to arrive at the tax base, taxable income.

Deductions *from* adjusted gross income. See *deductions for adjusted gross income*.

Deductions in respect of a decedent. Deductions accrued at the moment of death but not recognizable on the final income tax return of a decedent because of the method of accounting used. Such items are allowed as deductions on the estate tax return and on the income tax return of the estate (Form 1041) or the heir (Form 1040). An example of a deduction in respect of a decedent is interest expense accrued to the date of death by a cash basis debtor.

Deferred compensation. Compensation that will be taxed when received or upon the removal of certain restrictions on receipt and not when earned. Contributions by an employer to a qualified pension or profit sharing plan on behalf of an employee are an example. The contributions will not be taxed to the employee until the funds are made available or distributed to the employee (e.g., upon retirement).

Deferred tax asset. Under ASC 740, an asset recorded on the balance sheet to reflect the future tax benefits related to a transaction or activity which has already been reflected in the financial statements. A deferred tax asset is often the result of the deferral of a deduction or the acceleration of income for tax purposes relative to Generally Accepted Accounting Principles.

Deferred tax benefit. Under ASC 740, a reduction in the book tax expense that relates to the current reporting period's net income but will not be realized until a future reporting period. Creates or adds to the entity's deferred tax asset balance sheet account. For instance, the carryforward of a net operating loss is a deferred tax benefit.

Deferred tax expense. Under ASC 740, a book tax expense that relates to the current reporting period's net income but will not be realized until a future reporting period. Creates or adds to the entity's deferred tax liability balance sheet account. For instance, a deferred tax expense is created when tax depreciation deductions for the period are "accelerated" and exceed the corresponding book depreciation expense.

Deferred tax liability. Under ASC 740, a liability recorded on the balance sheet to reflect the future tax costs of a transaction or activity which has already been reflected in the financial statements. A deferred tax liability is often the result of the deferral of the recognition of income or the acceleration of a deduction for tax purposes relative to Generally Accepted Accounting Principles.

Defined benefit plan. Qualified plans can be dichotomized into defined benefit plans and defined contribution plans. Under a defined benefit plan, a formula defines the benefits employees are to receive. The formula usually includes years of service, employee compensation, and some stated percentage. The employer must make annual contributions based on actuarial computations that will be sufficient to pay the vested retirement benefits.

Defined contribution pension plan. Qualified plans can be dichotomized into defined benefit plans and defined contribution plans. Under a defined contribution plan, a separate account is maintained for each covered employee. The employee's benefits under the plan are based solely on (1) the amount contributed and (2) income from the fund that accrues to the employee's account. The plan defines the amount the employer is required to contribute (e.g., a flat dollar amount, an amount based on a special formula, or an amount equal to a certain percentage of compensation).

Dependency exemptions. See *personal and dependency exemptions.*

Dependent tax credit. For 2018 through 2025, the TCJA of 2017 replaced the dependency exemption with a $500 non-refundable credit. This credit can be claimed for dependents who are not a qualifying child or under the age of 17. The dependent must be a citizen or resident of the United States.

Depletion. The process by which the cost or other basis of a natural resource (e.g., an oil or gas interest) is recovered upon extraction and sale of the resource. The two ways to determine the depletion allowance are the cost and percentage (or statutory) methods. Under cost depletion, each unit of production sold is assigned a portion of the cost or other basis of the interest. This is determined by dividing the cost or other basis by the total units expected to be recovered. Under percentage (or statutory) depletion, the tax law provides a special percentage factor for different types of minerals and other natural resources. This percentage is multiplied by the gross income from the interest to arrive at the depletion allowance. §§ 613 and 613A.

Depreciation. The system by which a taxpayer allocates for financial reporting purposes the cost of an asset to periods benefited by the asset.

Determination letter. Upon the request of a taxpayer, the IRS will comment on the tax status of a completed transaction. Determination letters frequently are used to determine whether a retirement or profit sharing plan qualifies under the Code and to determine the tax-exempt status of certain nonprofit organizations.

Disabled access credit. A tax credit designed to encourage small businesses to make their facilities more accessible to disabled individuals. The credit is equal to 50 percent of the eligible expenditures that exceed $250 but do not exceed $10,250. Thus, the maximum amount for the credit is $5,000. The adjusted basis for depreciation is reduced by the amount of the credit. To qualify, the facility must have been placed in service before November 6, 1990. § 44.

Disaster area losses. A casualty sustained in an area designated as a disaster area by the President of the United States. In such an event, the disaster loss may be treated as having occurred in the taxable year immediately preceding the year in which the disaster actually occurred. Thus, immediate tax benefits are provided to victims of a disaster. § 165(i).

Disclaimer. Rejections, refusals, or renunciations of claims, powers, or property. Section 2518 sets forth the conditions required to avoid gift tax consequences as the result of a disclaimer.

Disguised sale. When a partner contributes property to the entity and soon thereafter receives a distribution from the partnership, the transactions are collapsed and the distribution is seen as a purchase of the asset by the partnership. § 707(a)(2)(B).

Disproportionate distribution. A distribution from a partnership to one or more of its partners in which at least one partner's interest in partnership hot assets is increased or decreased. For example, a distribution of cash to one partner and hot assets to another changes both partners' interest in hot assets and is disproportionate. The intent of rules for taxation of disproportionate distributions is to ensure that each partner eventually recognizes his or her proportionate share of partnership ordinary income.

Disproportionate redemption. Sale or exchange treatment is available relative to this type of redemption. After the exchange, the shareholder owns less than 80 percent of his or her pre-redemption interest in the corporation and only a minority interest in the entity. § 302(b)(2).

Disregarded entity. The Federal income tax treatment of business income usually follows the legal form of the taxpayer (i.e., an individual's sole proprietorship is reported on the Form 1040); a C corporation's taxable income is computed on Form 1120. The check-the-box Regulations are used if the unincorporated taxpayer wants to use a different tax regime. Under these rules, a disregarded entity is taxed as an individual or a corporate division; other tax regimes are not available. For instance, a one-member limited liability company is a disregarded entity.

Distributable net income (DNI). The measure that determines the nature and amount of the distributions from estates and trusts that the beneficiaries must include in income. DNI also limits the amount that estates and trusts can claim as a deduction for such distributions. § 643(a).

Dividend. A nondeductible distribution to the shareholders of a corporation. A dividend constitutes gross income to the recipient if it is paid from the current or accumulated earnings and profits of the corporation.

Dividends received deduction. A deduction allowed a shareholder that is a corporation for dividends received from a domestic corporation. The deduction usually is 50 percent of the dividends received, but it could be 65 or 100 percent depending upon the ownership percentage held by the recipient corporation. §§ 243–246.

Divisive reorganization. A "Type D" spin-off, split-off, or split-up reorganization in which the original corporation divides its active business (in existence for at least five years) assets among two or more corporations. The stock received by the original corporation shareholders must be at least 80 percent of the other corporations.

Dock sales. A purchaser uses its owned or rented vehicles to take possession of the product at the seller's shipping dock. In most states, the sale is apportioned to the operating state of the purchaser, rather than the seller. See also *apportion* and *sales factor.*

Dollar-value LIFO. An inventory technique that focuses on the dollars invested in the inventory rather than the particular items on hand each period. Each inventory item is assigned to a pool. A pool is a collection of similar items and is treated as a separate inventory. At the end of the period, each pool is valued in terms of prices at the time LIFO was adopted (base period prices), whether or not the particular items were actually on hand in the year LIFO was adopted, to compare with current prices to determine if there has been an increase or decrease in inventories.

E

Earned income credit. A tax credit designed to provide assistance to certain low-income individuals who generally have a qualifying child. This is a refundable credit. To receive the most beneficial treatment, the taxpayer must have qualifying children. However, it is possible to qualify for the credit without having a child. See the text chapter on credits for the computation procedure required in order to determine the amount of the credit allowed.

Earnings and profits (E & P). Measures the economic capacity of a corporation to make a distribution to shareholders that is not a return of capital. Such a distribution results in dividend income to the shareholders to the extent of the corporation's current and accumulated earnings and profits.

Economic effect test. Requirements that must be met before a special allocation may be used by a partnership. The premise behind the test is that each partner who receives an allocation of income or loss from a partnership bears the economic benefit or burden of the allocation.

Economic income. The change in the taxpayer's net worth, as measured in terms of market values, plus the value of the assets the taxpayer consumed during the year. Because of the impracticality of this income model, it is not used for tax purposes.

Economic performance test. One of the requirements that must be satisfied for an accrual basis taxpayer to deduct an expense. Economic performance occurs when property or services are provided to the taxpayer, or in the case in which the taxpayer is required to provide property or services, whenever the property or services are actually provided by the taxpayer.

Education expenses. Employees may deduct education expenses that are incurred either (1) to maintain or improve existing job-related skills or (2) to meet the express requirements of the employer or the requirements imposed by law to retain employment status. The expenses are not deductible if the education is required to meet the minimum educational standards for the taxpayer's job or if the education qualifies the individual for a new trade or business. Reg. § 1.162–5.

Educational savings bonds. U.S. Series EE bonds whose proceeds are used for qualified higher educational expenses for the taxpayer, the taxpayer's spouse, or a dependent. The interest may be excluded from gross income, provided the taxpayer's adjusted gross income does not exceed certain amounts. § 135.

Effective tax rate. The financial statements for an entity include several footnotes, one of which reconciles the expected (statutory) income tax rate (e.g., 21 percent for a C corporation) with the effective tax rate (i.e., total tax expense as a percentage of book income). The reconciliation often is done in dollar and/or percentage terms.

Effectively connected income. Income of a nonresident alien or foreign corporation that is attributable to the operation of a U.S. trade or business under either the asset-use or the business-activities test.

E-file. The electronic filing of a tax return. The filing is either direct or indirect. As to direct, the taxpayer goes online using a computer and tax return preparation software. Indirect filing occurs when a taxpayer utilizes an authorized IRS e-file provider. The provider often is the tax return preparer.

E-filing. See *e-file*.

Employment taxes. Taxes that an employer must pay on account of its employees. Employment taxes include FICA (Federal Insurance Contributions Act) and FUTA (Federal Unemployment Tax Act) taxes. Employment taxes are paid to the IRS in addition to income tax withholdings at specified intervals. Such taxes can be levied on the employees, the employer, or both.

Energy credits. See *energy tax credits*.

Energy tax credits. Various tax credits are available to those who invest in certain energy property. The purpose of the credit is to create incentives for conservation and to develop alternative energy sources.

Enrolled agents (EAs). A tax practitioner who has gained admission to practice before the IRS by passing an IRS examination and maintaining a required level of continuing professional education.

Entertainment expenses. Expenses that are deductible only if they are directly related to or associated with a trade or business. Various restrictions and documentation requirements have been imposed upon the deductibility of entertainment expenses to prevent abuses by taxpayers. The TCJA of 2017 repealed the deduction for entertainment expenses paid or incurred after 2017. § 274.

Entity accounting income. Entity accounting income is not identical to the taxable income of a trust or estate, nor is it determined in the same manner as the entity's financial accounting income would be. The trust document or will determines whether certain income, expenses, gains, or losses are allocated to the corpus of the entity or to the entity's income beneficiaries. Only the items that are allocated to the income beneficiaries are included in entity accounting income.

Entity buy-sell agreement. An arrangement whereby the entity is to purchase a withdrawing owner's interest. When the entity is a corporation, the agreement generally involves a stock redemption on the part of the withdrawing shareholder. See also *buy-sell agreement* and *cross-purchase buy-sell agreement*.

Entity concept. A perspective taken toward a venture that regards the venture as an entity separate and distinct from its owners. For tax purposes, this results in the venture being directly responsible for the tax on the income it generates. The entity perspective taken toward C corporations results in the double taxation of income distributed to the corporation's owners.

Entity perspective. See *entity concept*.

Equity method. Under Generally Accepted Accounting Principles, the method of financial reporting for the operations of a subsidiary when the parent corporation owns between 20 and 50 percent of the subsidiary's stock. Creates a book-tax difference, as the two entities' operating results are combined for book purposes, but a Federal income tax consolidated return cannot be filed.

Estate tax. A tax imposed on the right to transfer property by death. Thus, an estate tax is levied on the decedent's estate and not on the heir receiving the property.

Estimated tax. The amount of tax (including alternative minimum tax and self-employment tax) a taxpayer expects to owe for the year after subtracting tax credits and income tax withheld. The estimated tax must be paid in installments at designated intervals (e.g., for the individual taxpayer, by April 15, June 15, September 15, and January 15 of the following year).

Excess business loss. The excess of aggregate deductions of the taxpayer attributable to trades or businesses of the taxpayer over the sum of aggregate gross income or gain of the taxpayer plus a threshold amount. In 2019, the threshold amount is $255,000 ($510,000 in the case of a married taxpayer filing a joint return). The threshold amount is adjusted for inflation each year. This loss limitation applies to taxpayers other than C corporations and applies after the passive activity loss limitation of § 469. § 461(l).

Excess lobbying expenditures. An excise tax is applied on otherwise tax-exempt organizations with respect to the excess of total lobbying expenditures over grass roots lobbying expenditures for the year.

Excess loss account. When a subsidiary has generated more historical losses than its parent has invested in the entity, the parent's basis in the subsidiary is zero, and the parent records additional losses in an excess loss account. This treatment allows the parent to continue to deduct losses of the subsidiary, even where no basis reduction is possible, while avoiding the need to show a negative stock basis on various financial records. If the subsidiary stock is sold while an excess loss account exists, capital gain income usually is recognized to the extent of the balance in the account.

Excise taxes. A tax on the manufacture, sale, or use of goods; on the carrying on of an occupation or activity; or on the transfer of property. Thus, the Federal estate and gift taxes are, theoretically, excise taxes.

Exclusion amount. The value of assets that is exempt from transfer tax due to the credit allowed for gifts or transfers by death. For gifts and deaths in 2019, the exclusion amount is $11.4 million. An exclusion amount unused by a deceased spouse may be used by the surviving spouse. See also *exemption equivalent amount.*

Exempt organizations. An organization that is either partially or completely exempt from Federal income taxation. § 501.

Exemption amount. An amount deducted from alternative minimum taxable income (AMTI) to determine the alternative minimum tax base. The exemption amount is phased out when AMTI exceeds specified threshold amounts. § 55(d).

Exemption equivalent. The maximum value of assets that can be transferred to another party without incurring any Federal gift or estate tax because of the application of the unified tax credit. See also *exemption equivalent amount.*

Exemption equivalent amount. The nontaxable amount (in 2019, $11.4 million for gift tax and estate tax) that is the equivalent of the unified transfer tax credit allowed.

F

Fair market value. The amount at which property would change hands between a willing buyer and a willing seller, neither being under any compulsion to buy or to sell and both having reasonable knowledge of the relevant facts. Reg. §§ 1.1001–1(a) and 20.2031–1(b).

Farm price method. A method of accounting for agricultural crops. The inventory of crops is valued at its market price less the estimated cost of disposition (e.g., freight and selling expense).

Feeder organization. An entity that carries on a trade or business for the benefit of an exempt organization. However, such a relationship does not result in the feeder organization itself being tax-exempt. § 502.

FICA tax. An abbreviation that stands for Federal Insurance Contributions Act, commonly referred to as the Social Security tax. The FICA tax is comprised of the Social Security tax (old age, survivors, and disability insurance) and the Medicare tax (hospital insurance) and is imposed on both employers and employees. The employer is responsible for withholding from the employee's wages the Social Security tax at a rate of 6.2 percent on a maximum wage base and the Medicare tax at a rate of 1.45 percent (no maximum wage base). The maximum Social Security wage base for 2019 is $132,900 and for 2018 is $128,400.

Fiduciary. One who holds a legal obligation to act on another's behalf. A *trustee* and an *executor* take fiduciary relationships relative to the *grantor* and the *decedent*, respectively. The fiduciary is assigned specific duties by the principal party (e.g., to file tax returns, manage assets, satisfy debt and other obligations, and to make investment decisions). The fiduciary often possesses specialized knowledge and experience. A fiduciary must avoid conflicts of interest in which the principal's goals are compromised in some way.

Field audit. An audit conducted by the IRS on the business premises of the taxpayer or in the office of the tax practitioner representing the taxpayer.

Filing status. Individual taxpayers are placed in one of five filing statuses each year (single, married filing jointly, married filing separately, surviving spouse, or head of household). Marital status and household support are key determinants. Filing status is used to determine the taxpayer's filing requirements, standard deduction, eligibility for certain deductions and credits, and tax liability.

Final Regulations. The U.S. Treasury Department Regulations (abbreviated Reg.) represent the position of the IRS as to how the Internal Revenue Code is to be interpreted. Their purpose is to provide taxpayers and IRS personnel with rules of general and specific application to the various provisions of the tax law. Regulations are published in the *Federal Register* and in all tax services.

Financial Accounting Standards Board (FASB). See *Generally Accepted Accounting Principles (GAAP).*

Financial transaction tax. A tax imposed on some type of financial transaction, such as stock sales.

Fiscal year. A 12-month period ending on the last day of a month other than December. In certain circumstances, a taxpayer is permitted to elect a fiscal year instead of being required to use a calendar year.

Flat tax. A form of consumption tax designed to alleviate the regressivity of a value added tax (VAT). It is imposed on individuals and businesses at the same single (flat) rate.

Flexible spending plans. An employee benefit plan that allows the employee to take a reduction in salary in exchange for the employer paying benefits that can be provided by the employer without the employee being required to recognize income (e.g., medical and child care benefits). Contributions to a flexible spending plan are limited to $2,700 for 2019. § 125(i).

Flow-through entity. The entity is a tax reporter rather than a taxpayer. The owners are subject to tax. Examples are partnerships, S corporations, and limited liability companies.

Foreign earned income exclusion. The Code allows exclusions for earned income generated outside the United States to alleviate any tax base and rate disparities among countries. In addition, the exclusion is allowed for housing expenditures incurred by the taxpayer's employer with respect to the non-U.S. assignment, and self-employed individuals can deduct foreign housing expenses incurred in a trade or business. The exclusion is limited to $105,900 per year for 2019 ($103,900 in 2018). § 911.

Foreign Investment in Real Property Tax Act (FIRPTA). Under the Foreign Investment in Real Property Tax Act, gains or losses realized by nonresident aliens and non-U.S. corporations on the disposition of U.S. real estate creates U.S. source income and are subject to U.S. income tax.

Foreign tax credit (FTC). A U.S. citizen or resident who incurs or pays income taxes to a foreign country on income subject to U.S. tax may be able to claim some of these taxes as a credit against the U.S. income tax. §§ 27 and 901–905.

Franchise. An agreement that gives the transferee the right to distribute, sell, or provide goods, services, or facilities within a specified area. The cost of obtaining a franchise may be amortized over a statutory period of 15 years. In general, the franchisor's gain on the sale of franchise rights is an ordinary gain because the franchisor retains a significant power, right, or continuing interest in the subject of the franchise. §§ 197 and 1253.

Franchise tax. A tax levied on the right to do business in a state as a corporation. Although income considerations may come into play, the tax usually is based on the capitalization of the corporation.

Fraud. Tax fraud falls into two categories: civil and criminal. Under civil fraud, the IRS may impose as a penalty an amount equal to as much as 75 percent of the underpayment [§ 6651(f)]. Fines and/or imprisonment are prescribed for conviction of various types of criminal tax fraud (§§ 7201–7207). Both civil and criminal fraud involve a specific intent on the part of the taxpayer to evade the tax; mere negligence is not enough. Criminal fraud requires the additional element of willfulness (i.e., done deliberately and with evil purpose). In practice, it becomes difficult to distinguish between the degree of intent necessary to support criminal, rather than civil, fraud. In either situation, the IRS has the burden of proof to show the taxpayer committed fraud.

Fringe benefits. Compensation or other benefit received by an employee that is not in the form of cash. Some fringe benefits (e.g., accident and health plans, group term life insurance) may be excluded from the employee's gross income and therefore are not subject to the Federal income tax.

Fruit and tree metaphor. The courts have held that an individual who earns income from property or services cannot assign that income to another. For example, a father cannot assign his earnings from commissions to his child and escape income tax on those amounts.

Functional currency. The currency of the economic environment in which the taxpayer carries on most of its activities and in which the taxpayer transacts most of its business.

FUTA tax. An employment tax levied on employers. Jointly administered by the Federal and state governments, the tax provides funding for unemployment benefits. FUTA applies at a rate of 6.0 percent on the first $7,000 of covered wages paid during the year for each employee in 2019. The Federal government allows a credit for FUTA paid (or allowed under a merit rating system) to the state. The credit cannot exceed 5.4 percent of the covered wages.

Future interest. An interest that will come into being at some future time. It is distinguished from a present interest, which already exists. Assume that Dan transfers securities to a newly created trust. Under the terms of the trust instrument, income from the securities is to be paid each year to Wilma for her life, with the securities passing to Sam upon Wilma's death. Wilma has a present interest in the trust because she is entitled to current income distributions. Sam has a future interest because he must wait for Wilma's death to benefit from the trust. The annual exclusion of $15,000 (in 2019) is not allowed for a gift of a future interest. § 2503(b).

G

General business credit. The summation of various nonrefundable business credits, including the tax credit for rehabilitation expenditures, business energy credit, work opportunity credit, research activities credit, low-income housing credit, and disabled access credit. The amount of general business credit that can be used to reduce the tax liability is limited to the taxpayer's net income tax reduced by the greater of (1) the tentative minimum tax or (2) 25 percent of the net regular tax liability that exceeds $25,000. Unused general business credits can be carried back one year and forward 20 years. § 38.

General partners. A partner who is fully liable in an individual capacity for the debts owed by the partnership to third parties. A general partner's liability is not limited to the investment in the partnership. See also *limited partners.*

General partnership (GP). A partnership that is owned by general partners (only). Creditors of a general partnership can collect amounts owed them from both the partnership assets and the assets of the partners individually.

Generally Accepted Accounting Principles (GAAP). Guidelines relating to how to construct the financial statements of enterprises doing business in the United States. Promulgated chiefly by the Financial Accounting Standards Board (FASB).

Gift tax. A tax imposed on the transfer of property by gift. The tax is imposed upon the donor of a gift and is based on the fair market value of the property on the date of the gift.

Golden parachute payments. A severance payment to employees that meets the following requirements: (1) the payment is contingent on a change of ownership of a corporation through a stock or asset acquisition and (2) the aggregate present value of the payment equals or exceeds three times the employee's average annual compensation. To the extent the severance payment meets these conditions, a deduction is disallowed to the employer for the excess of the payment over a statutory base amount (a five-year average of compensation if the taxpayer was an employee for the entire five-year period). In addition, a 20 percent excise tax is imposed on the employee who receives the excess severance pay. §§ 280G and 4999.

Goodwill. The reputation and other unidentifiable intangible assets of a company. For accounting purposes, goodwill has no basis unless it is purchased. In the purchase of a business, goodwill generally is the difference between the purchase price and the fair market value of the assets acquired. The intangible asset goodwill can be amortized for tax purposes over a 15-year period. § 197 and Reg. § 1.167(a)–3.

Grantor. A transferor of property. The creator of a trust is usually referred to as the grantor of the entity.

Grantor trust. A trust under which the grantor retains control over the income or corpus (or both) to such an extent that he or she is treated as the owner of the property and its income for income tax purposes. Income from a grantor trust is taxable to the grantor and not to the beneficiary who receives it. §§ 671–679.

Grass roots expenditures. Exempt organizations are prohibited from engaging in political activities, but spending incurred to influence the opinions of the general public relative to specific legislation is permitted by the law.

Gross estate. The property owned or previously transferred by a decedent that is subject to the Federal estate tax. The gross estate can be distinguished from the probate estate, which is property actually subject to administration by the administrator or executor of an estate. §§ 2031–2046.

Gross income. Income subject to the Federal income tax. Gross income does not include all economic income. That is, certain exclusions are allowed (e.g., interest on municipal bonds). For a manufacturing or merchandising business, gross income usually means gross profit (gross sales or gross receipts less cost of goods sold). § 61 and Reg. § 1.61–3(a).

Group term life insurance. Life insurance coverage provided by an employer for a group of employees. Such insurance is renewable on a year-to-year basis, and typically no cash surrender value is built up. The premiums paid by the employer on the insurance are not taxed to the employees on coverage of up to $50,000 per person. § 79 and Reg. § 1.79–1(b).

Guaranteed payments. Payments made by a partnership to a partner for services rendered or for the use of capital to the extent the payments are determined without regard to the income of the partnership. The payments are treated as though they were made to a nonpartner and thus are deducted by the entity. A guaranteed payment might be subject to self-employment tax (guaranteed payment for services) or net-investment income tax (guaranteed payment for capital). Guaranteed payments are not eligible for the qualified business income deduction.

H

H.R. 10 (Keogh) plans. See *Keogh plans*.

Half-year convention. A cost recovery convention that assumes that property is placed in service at mid-year and thus provides for a half-year's cost recovery for that year.

Head of household. An unmarried individual who maintains a household for another and satisfies certain conditions set forth in § 2(b). This status enables the taxpayer to use a set of income tax rates that are lower than those applicable to other unmarried individuals but higher than those applicable to surviving spouses and married persons filing a joint return.

Health Savings Account (HSA). A medical savings account created in legislation enacted in December 2003 that is designed to replace and expand Archer Medical Savings Accounts.

Highly compensated employee. The employee group is generally divided into two categories for fringe benefit (including pension and profit sharing plans) purposes. These are (1) highly compensated employees and (2) non-highly compensated employees. For most fringe benefits, if the fringe benefit plan discriminates in favor of highly compensated employees, it will not be a qualified plan with respect, at a minimum, to the highly compensated employees.

Historic business test. In a corporate reorganization, a means by which to determine if the continuity of business enterprise requirement is met. The acquiring corporation must continue to operate the target entity's existing business(es) going forward; if this is not the case, the requirement is failed.

Hobby losses. Losses from an activity not engaged in for profit. The Code restricts the amount of losses that an individual can deduct for hobby activities so that these transactions cannot be used to offset income from other sources. The TCJA of 2017 suspended the deduction of hobby expenses for tax years after 2017 (and through 2025). § 183.

Holding period. The period of time during which property has been held for income tax purposes. The holding period is significant in determining whether gain or loss from the sale or exchange of a capital asset is long or short term. § 1223.

Home equity loans. Loans that utilize the personal residence of the taxpayer as security. The interest on such loans is deductible as qualified residence interest. However, interest is deductible only on the portion of the loan that does not exceed the lesser of (1) the fair market value of the residence, reduced by the acquisition indebtedness, or (2) $100,000 ($50,000 for married persons filing separate returns). A major benefit of a home equity loan is that there are no tracing rules regarding the use of the loan proceeds. The TCJA of 2017 suspended the deduction of interest on home equity indebtedness for tax years after 2017 (and through 2025). § 163(h)(3).

Hot assets. Unrealized receivables and substantially appreciated inventory under § 751. When hot assets are present, the sale of a partnership interest or the disproportionate distribution of the assets can cause ordinary income to be recognized.

Hybrid method. A combination of the accrual and cash methods of accounting. That is, the taxpayer may account for some items of income on the accrual method (e.g., sales and cost of goods sold) and other items (e.g., interest income) on the cash method.

I

Imputed interest. For certain long-term sales of property, under §§ 483 and 1274 the IRS can convert some of the gain from the sale into interest income if the contract does not provide for a minimum rate of interest to be paid by the purchaser. The seller recognizes less long-term capital gain and more ordinary income (interest income). Imputed interest rules also apply on certain below-market loans under § 7872.

Inbound taxation. U.S. tax effects when a non-U.S. person begins an investment or business activity in the United States.

Incentive stock options (ISOs). A type of stock option that receives favorable tax treatment. If various qualification requirements can be satisfied, stock option grants do not create taxable income for the recipient. However, the spread (the excess of the fair market value at the date of exercise over the option price) is a tax preference item for purposes of the alternative minimum tax (AMT). The gain on disposition of the stock resulting from the exercise of the stock option will be classified as long-term capital gain if certain holding period requirements are met (the employee must not dispose of the stock within two years after the option is granted or within one year after acquiring the stock). § 422.

Income. For tax purposes, an increase in wealth that has been realized.

Income in respect of a decedent (IRD). Income earned by a decedent at the time of death but not reportable on the final income tax return because of the method of accounting that appropriately is utilized. Such income is included in the gross estate and is taxed to the eventual recipient (either the estate or heirs). The recipient is, however, allowed an income tax deduction for the estate tax attributable to the income. § 691.

Income tax provision. Under ASC 740, a synonym for the book tax expense of an entity for the financial reporting period. Following the "matching principle," all book tax expense that relates to the net income for the reporting period is reported on that period's financial statements, including not only the current tax expense but also any deferred tax expense and deferred tax benefit.

Income tax treaties. See *tax treaties*.

Independent contractor. A self-employed person as distinguished from one who is employed as an employee.

Indexation. A procedure whereby adjustments are made by the IRS to key tax components (e.g., standard deduction, tax brackets, personal and dependency exemptions) to reflect inflation. The adjustments usually are made annually and are based on the change in the consumer price index.

Individual Retirement Account (IRA). A type of retirement plan to which an individual with earned income can contribute a statutory maximum of $6,000 in 2019. IRAs can be classified as traditional IRAs or Roth IRAs. With a traditional IRA, an individual can contribute and deduct a maximum of $6,000 per tax year in 2019. The deduction is a deduction *for* AGI. However, if the individual is an active participant in another qualified retirement plan, the deduction is phased out proportionally between certain AGI ranges (note that the phaseout limits the amount of the deduction and not the amount of the contribution). With a Roth IRA, an individual can contribute a maximum of $6,000 per tax year in 2019. No deduction is permitted. However, if a five-year holding period requirement is satisfied and if the distribution is a qualified distribution, the taxpayer can make tax-free withdrawals from a Roth IRA. The maximum annual contribution is phased out proportionally between certain AGI ranges. §§ 219 and 408A.

Individual Shared Responsibility Payment (ISRP). A mandate or penalty tax that individuals owe starting in 2014 for any month in which they do not have health coverage and do not qualify for an exemption. This mandate was created as part of the Affordable Care Act to encourage individuals to obtain health care coverage. If owed, the penalty is the greater of a "flat dollar amount" or a percentage of household income less the filing threshold. For 2018, the flat dollar amount is $695 and the percent applied to household income is 2.5 percent. For a family, the flat dollar amount cannot exceed three times the flat dollar amount. The overall cap on the penalty is the national average cost of a bronze level plan (this amount is published by the IRS). Worksheets for computing the penalty are included in the instructions to Form 8965 (Health Coverage Exemptions). For months beginning after 2018, the penalty is zero. § 5000A.

Inheritance tax. A tax imposed on the right to receive property from a decedent. Thus, theoretically, an inheritance tax is imposed on the heir. The Federal estate tax is imposed on the estate.

Inside basis. A partnership's basis in the assets it owns.

Installment method. A method of accounting enabling certain taxpayers to spread the recognition of gain on the sale of property over the collection period. Under this procedure, the seller arrives at the gain to be recognized by computing the gross profit percentage from the sale (the gain divided by the contract price) and applying it to each payment received. § 453.

Intangible drilling and development costs (IDCs). Taxpayers may elect to expense or capitalize (subject to amortization) intangible drilling and development costs. However, ordinary income recapture provisions apply to oil and gas properties on a sale or other disposition if the expense method is elected. §§ 263(c) and 1254(a).

Intermediate sanctions. The IRS can assess excise taxes on disqualified persons and organization management associated with so-called public charities engaging in excess benefit transactions. An excess benefit transaction is one in which a disqualified person engages in a non-fair market value transaction with the exempt organization or receives unreasonable compensation. Prior to the idea of intermediate sanctions, the only option available to the IRS was to revoke the organization's exempt status.

International Accounting Standards Board (IASB). The body that promulgates International Financial Reporting Standards (IFRS). Based in London, representing accounting standard setting bodies in over 100 countries, the IASB develops accounting standards that can serve as the basis for harmonizing conflicting reporting standards among nations.

International Financial Reporting Standards (IFRS). Produced by the International Accounting Standards Board (IASB), guidelines developed since 2001 as to revenue recognition, accounting for business combinations, and a conceptual framework for financial reporting. IFRS provisions are designed so that they can be used by all entities, regardless of where they are based or conduct business. IFRS have gained widespread acceptance throughout the world, and the SEC is considering how to require U.S. entities to use IFRS in addition to, or in lieu of, the accounting rules of the Financial Accounting Standards Board.

Interpretive Regulations. A Regulation issued by the Treasury Department that purports to explain the meaning of a particular Code Section. An interpretive Regulation is given less deference than a legislative Regulation.

Inventory. Under § 1221(a)(1), a taxpayer's stock in trade or property held for resale. For partnership tax purposes, inventory is defined in § 751(d) as inventory (per the above definition) or any partnership asset other than capital or § 1231 assets. See also *appreciated inventory*.

Investment income. Consisting of virtually the same elements as portfolio income, a measure by which to justify a deduction for interest on investment indebtedness.

Investment interest. Payment for the use of funds used to acquire assets that produce investment income. The deduction for investment interest is limited to net investment income for the tax year.

Investor loss. Losses on stock and securities. If stocks and bonds are capital assets in the hands of the holder, a capital loss materializes as of the last day of the taxable year in which the stocks or bonds become worthless. Under certain circumstances involving stocks and bonds of affiliated corporations, an ordinary loss is permitted upon worthlessness.

Involuntary conversion. The loss or destruction of property through theft, casualty, or condemnation. Gain realized on an involuntary conversion can, at the taxpayer's election, be deferred for Federal income tax purposes if the owner reinvests the proceeds within a prescribed period of time in property that is similar or related in service or use. § 1033.

Itemized deductions. Personal expenditures allowed by the Code as deductions from adjusted gross income. Examples include certain medical expenses, interest on home mortgages, state income taxes, and charitable contributions. Itemized deductions are reported on Schedule A of Form 1040.

J

Joint tenants. Two or more persons having undivided ownership of property with the right of survivorship. Right of survivorship gives the surviving owner full ownership of the property. Suppose Bob and Tami are joint tenants of a tract of land. Upon Bob's death, Tami becomes the sole owner of the property. For the estate tax consequences upon the death of a joint tenant, see § 2040.

K

Keogh plans. Retirement plans available to self-employed taxpayers. They are also referred to as H.R. 10 plans. Under such plans, a taxpayer may deduct each year up to 100 percent of net earnings from self-employment or $56,000 for 2019, whichever is less. If the plan is a profit sharing plan, the percentage is 25 percent.

Kiddie tax. Passive income, such as interest and dividends, that is recognized by a child under age 19 (or under age 24 if a full-time student) is taxed according to the brackets applicable to estates and trusts, generally to the extent the income exceeds $2,200 for 2019. The additional tax is assessed regardless of the source of the income or the income's underlying property. § 1(g).

L

Least aggregate deferral method. An algorithm set forth in the Regulations to determine the tax year for a partnership or an S corporation with owners whose tax years differ. The tax year selected is the one that produces the least aggregate deferral of income for the owners.

Least aggregate deferral rule. See *least aggregate deferral method.*

Legislative Regulations. Some Code Sections give the Secretary of the Treasury or his delegate the authority to prescribe Regulations to carry out the details of administration or to otherwise complete the operating rules. Regulations issued pursuant to this type of authority truly possess the force and effect of law. In effect, Congress is almost delegating its legislative powers to the Treasury Department.

Lessee. One who rents property from another. In the case of real estate, the lessee is also known as the tenant.

Lessor. One who rents property to another. In the case of real estate, the lessor is also known as the landlord.

Letter ruling. The written response of the IRS to a taxpayer's request for interpretation of the revenue laws with respect to a proposed transaction (e.g., concerning the tax-free status of a reorganization). Not to be relied on as precedent by other than the party who requested the ruling.

Liabilities in excess of basis. On the contribution of capital to a corporation, an investor recognizes gain on the exchange to the extent contributed assets carry liabilities with a face amount in excess of the tax basis of the contributed assets. This rule keeps the investor from holding the investment asset received with a negative basis. § 357(c).

Life insurance proceeds. A specified sum (the face value or maturity value of the policy) paid to the designated beneficiary of the policy by the life insurance company upon the death of the insured.

Lifetime learning credit. A tax credit for qualifying expenses for taxpayers pursuing education beyond the first two years of postsecondary education. Individuals who are completing their last two years of undergraduate studies, pursuing graduate or professional degrees, or otherwise seeking new job skills or maintaining existing job skills are all eligible for the credit. Eligible individuals include the taxpayer, taxpayer's spouse, and taxpayer's dependents. The maximum credit is 20 percent of the first $10,000 of qualifying expenses and is computed per taxpayer. The credit is phased out for higher-income taxpayers. § 25A.

Like-kind exchanges. An exchange of real property held for productive use in a trade or business or for investment for other investment or trade or business real property. Unless non-like-kind property (boot) is received, the exchange is fully tax-deferred. § 1031.

Limited liability company (LLC). A legal entity in which all owners are protected from the entity's debts but which may lack other characteristics of a corporation (i.e., centralized management, unlimited life, free transferability of interests). LLCs generally are treated as partnerships (or disregarded entities if they have only one owner) for tax purposes.

Limited liability partnership (LLP). A legal entity allowed by many of the states, where a general partnership registers with the state as an LLP. All partners are at risk with respect to any contractual liabilities of the entity as well as any liabilities arising from their own malpractice or torts or those of their subordinates. However, all partners are protected from any liabilities resulting from the malpractice or torts of other partners.

Limited partners. A partner whose liability to third-party creditors of the partnership is limited to the amounts invested in the partnership. See also *general partners* and *limited partnership (LP)*.

Limited partnership (LP). A partnership in which some of the partners are limited partners. At least one of the partners in a limited partnership must be a general partner.

Liquidating distribution. A distribution by a partnership that is in complete liquidation of the entity's trade or business activities or in complete liquidation of a partner's interest in the partnership. A liquidating distribution is generally a tax-deferred transaction if it is proportionate with respect to the partnership's hot assets. In a proportionate liquidating distribution, the partnership recognizes no gain or loss. The partner only recognizes gain if the distributed cash (and cash equivalents, such as debt relief or certain marketable securities) exceeds the partner's basis in the partnership. The partner recognizes a loss if *only* cash and hot assets are distributed and their combined inside (partnership) basis is less than the partner's basis in the partnership interest. In any case where no gain or loss is recognized, the partner's basis in the partnership interest is fully assigned to the basis of the assets received in the distribution.

Listed property. Property that includes (1) any passenger automobile; (2) any other property used as a means of transportation; (3) any property of a type generally used for purposes of entertainment, recreation, or amusement; and (4) any other property of a type specified in the Regulations. If listed property is predominantly used for business, the taxpayer is allowed to use the statutory percentage method of cost recovery. Otherwise, the straight-line cost recovery method must be used. § 280F.

Lobbying expenditures. An expenditure made for the purpose of influencing legislation. Such payments can result in the loss of the exempt status of, and the imposition of Federal income tax on, an exempt organization. Lobby expenditures are not deductible.

Long-term care insurance. Insurance that helps pay the cost of care when the insured is unable to care for himself or herself. Such insurance is generally thought of as insurance against the cost of an aged person entering a nursing home. The employer can provide the insurance, and the premiums may be excluded from the employee's gross income. § 7702B.

Long-term contract. A building, installation, construction, or manufacturing contract that is entered into but not completed within the same tax year. A manufacturing contract is a long-term contract only if the contract is to manufacture (1) a unique item not normally carried in finished goods inventory or (2) items that normally require more than 12 calendar months to complete. The two available methods to account for long-term contracts are the percentage of completion method and the completed contract method. The completed contract method can be used only in limited circumstances. § 460.

Long-term nonpersonal use capital assets. Includes investment property with a long-term holding period. Such property disposed of by casualty or theft may receive § 1231 treatment.

Long-term tax-exempt rate. Used in deriving the yearly limitation on net operating loss and other tax benefits that carry over from the target to the acquiring when there is a more than 50-percentage-point ownership change (by value). The highest of the Federal long-term interest rates in effect for any of the last three months. § 382.

Lower of cost or market (replacement cost). An elective inventory method, whereby the taxpayer may value inventories at the lower of the taxpayer's actual cost or the current replacement cost of the goods. This method cannot be used in conjunction with the LIFO inventory method.

Low-income housing credit. Beneficial treatment to owners of low-income housing is provided in the form of a tax credit. The calculated credit is claimed in the year the building is placed in service and in the following nine years. § 42.

Lump-sum distribution. Payment of the entire amount due at one time rather than in installments. Such distributions often occur from qualified pension or profit sharing plans upon the retirement or death of a covered employee. The recipient of a lump-sum distribution may recognize both long-term capital gain and ordinary income upon the receipt of the distribution. The ordinary income portion may be subject to a special 10-year income averaging provision. § 402(e).

M

Majority interest partners. Partners who have more than a 50 percent interest in partnership profits and capital, counting only those partners who have the same taxable year. The term is of significance in determining the appropriate taxable year of a partnership. § 706(b).

Marital deduction. A deduction allowed against the taxable estate or taxable gifts upon the transfer of property from one spouse to another.

Marriage penalty. The additional tax liability that results for a married couple when compared with what their tax liability would be if they were not married and filed separate returns.

Matching rule. Treatment of an intercompany transaction on a consolidated return, when a sold asset remains within the group.

Material participation. If an individual taxpayer materially participates in a nonrental trade or business activity, any loss from that activity is treated as an active loss that can be offset against active income. Material participation is achieved by meeting any one of seven tests provided in the Regulations. § 469(h).

Meaningful reduction test. A decrease in the shareholder's voting control. Used to determine whether a stock redemption qualifies for sale or exchange treatment.

Medical expenses. Medical expenses of an individual, a spouse, and dependents are allowed as an itemized deduction to the extent such amounts (less insurance reimbursements) exceed 10 percent (7.5 percent for 2018) of adjusted gross income. § 213.

Merger. The absorption of one corporation by another with the corporation being absorbed losing its legal identity. Flow Corporation is merged into Jobs Corporation, and the shareholders of Flow receive stock in Jobs in exchange for their stock in Flow. After the merger, Flow ceases to exist as a separate legal entity. If a merger meets certain conditions, it is not currently taxable to the parties involved. § 368(a)(1).

Mid-month convention. A cost recovery convention that assumes that property is placed in service in the middle of the month that it is actually placed in service.

Mid-quarter convention. A cost recovery convention that assumes that property placed in service during the year is placed in service at the middle of the quarter in which it is actually placed in service. The mid-quarter convention applies if more than 40 percent of the value of property (other than eligible real estate) is placed in service during the last quarter of the year.

Miscellaneous itemized deductions. A special category of itemized deductions that includes expenses such as professional dues, tax return preparation fees, job-hunting costs, unreimbursed employee business expenses, and certain investment expenses. Such expenses are deductible only to the extent they exceed 2 percent of adjusted gross income. The TCJA of 2017 suspended the deduction for these items for 2018 through 2025. § 67.

Modified accelerated cost recovery system (MACRS). A method in which the cost of tangible property is recovered over a prescribed period of time. Enacted by the Economic Recovery Tax Act (ERTA) of 1981 and substantially modified by the Tax Reform Act (TRA) of 1986, the method disregards salvage value, imposes a period of cost recovery that depends upon the classification of the asset into one of various recovery periods, and prescribes the applicable percentage of cost that can be deducted each year. § 168.

Multiple support agreement. To qualify for a dependency exemption, the support test must be satisfied. This requires that over 50 percent of the support of the potential dependent be provided by the taxpayer. Where no one person provides more than 50 percent of the support, a multiple support agreement enables a taxpayer to still qualify for the dependency exemption. Any person who contributed more than 10 percent of the support is entitled to claim the exemption if each person in the group who contributed more than 10 percent files a written consent (Form 2120). Each person who is a party to the multiple support agreement must meet all of the other requirements for claiming the dependency exemption. § 152(c).

Multistate Tax Commission (MTC). A regulatory body of the states that develops operating rules and regulations for the implementation of the UDITPA and other provisions that assign the total taxable income of a multistate corporation to specific states.

N

National sales tax. Intended as a replacement for the current Federal income tax. Unlike a value added tax (VAT), which is levied on the manufacturer, it would be imposed on the consumer upon the final sale of goods and services. To reduce regressivity, individuals would receive a rebate to offset a portion of the tax.

Negligence. Failure to exercise the reasonable or ordinary degree of care of a prudent person in a situation that results in harm or damage to another. A penalty is assessed on taxpayers who exhibit negligence or intentional disregard of rules and Regulations with respect to the underpayment of certain taxes.

Net capital gain (NCG). The excess of the net long-term capital gain for the tax year over the net short-term capital loss. The net capital gain of an individual taxpayer is eligible for the alternative tax. § 1222(11).

Net capital loss (NCL). The excess of the losses from sales or exchanges of capital assets over the gains from sales or exchanges of such assets. Up to $3,000 per year of the net capital loss may be deductible by noncorporate taxpayers against ordinary income. The excess net capital loss carries over to future tax years. For corporate taxpayers, the net capital loss cannot be offset against ordinary income, but it can be carried back three years and forward five years to offset net capital gains. §§ 1211, 1212, and 1221(10).

Net investment income. The excess of investment income over investment expenses. Investment expenses are those deductible expenses directly connected with the production of investment income. Investment expenses do not include investment interest. The deduction for investment interest for the tax year is limited to net investment income. § 163(d).

Net operating loss (NOL). To mitigate the effect of the annual accounting period concept, § 172 allows taxpayers to use an excess loss of one year as a deduction for certain past or future years. In this regard, a carryback period of two (or more) years and a carryforward period of 20 years are allowed for NOLs generated before 2018. There is no carryback period and an indefinite carryforward period for NOLs arising in tax years beginning after 2017, and such NOLs are subject to an 80 percent of taxable income limitation in any carryforward year.

Nexus. The degree of activity that must be present before a taxing jurisdiction has the right to impose a tax on an out-of-state entity. The rules for income tax nexus are not the same as for sales tax nexus.

Ninety-day (90-day) letter. This notice is sent to a taxpayer upon request, upon the expiration of the 30-day letter, or upon exhaustion by the taxpayer of his or her administrative remedies before the IRS. The notice gives the taxpayer 90 days in which to file a petition with the U.S. Tax Court.

If a petition is not filed, the IRS will demand payment of the assessed deficiency. §§ 6211–6216.

No-additional-cost service. Services the employer may provide the employee at no additional cost to the employer. Generally, the benefit is the ability to utilize the employer's excess capacity (e.g., vacant seats on an airliner). Such amounts are excludible from the recipient's gross income.

Nonaccountable plan. An expense reimbursement plan that does not have an accountability feature. The result is that employee expenses are not deductible.

Nonacquiescence. Disagreement by the IRS on the result reached in certain judicial decisions. *Nonacq.* or *NA*.

Nonbusiness bad debt. A bad debt loss that is not incurred in connection with a creditor's trade or business. The loss is classified as a short-term capital loss and is allowed only in the year the debt becomes entirely worthless. In addition to family loans, many investor losses are nonbusiness bad debts. § 166(d).

Nonqualified deferred compensation (NQDC). Compensation arrangements that are frequently offered to executives. Such plans may include stock options and restricted stock, for example. Often, an executive may defer the recognition of taxable income. The employer, however, does not receive a tax deduction until the employee is required to include the compensation in income.

Nonqualified stock option (NQSO). A type of stock option that does not satisfy the statutory requirements of an incentive stock option. If the NQSO has a readily ascertainable fair market value (e.g., the option is traded on an established exchange), the value of the option must be included in the employee's gross income at the date of the grant. Otherwise, the employee does not recognize income at the grant date. Instead, ordinary income is recognized in the year of exercise of the option.

Nonrecourse debt. Debt secured by the property that it is used to purchase. The purchaser of the property is not personally liable for the debt upon default. Rather, the creditor's recourse is to repossess the related property. Nonrecourse debt generally does not increase the purchaser's at-risk amount.

Nonrefundable credits. A credit that is not paid if it exceeds the taxpayer's tax liability. Some nonrefundable credits qualify for carryback and carryover treatment.

Nonresident alien (NRA). An individual who is neither a citizen nor a resident of the United States. Citizenship is determined under the immigration and naturalization laws of the United States. Residency is determined under § 7701(b) of the Internal Revenue Code.

Nontaxable exchange. A transaction in which realized gains or losses are not recognized. The recognition of gain or loss is postponed (deferred) until the property received in the nontaxable exchange is subsequently disposed of in a taxable transaction. Examples are § 1031 like-kind exchanges and § 1033 involuntary conversions.

Not essentially equivalent redemption. Sale or exchange treatment is given to this type of redemption. Although various safe-harbor tests are failed, the nature of the redemption is such that dividend treatment is avoided, because it represents a meaningful reduction in the shareholder's interest in the corporation. § 302(b)(1).

O

Occupational fee. A tax imposed on various trades or businesses. A license fee that enables a taxpayer to engage in a particular occupation.

Occupational taxes. See *occupational fee*.

Offer in compromise. A settlement agreement offered by the IRS in a tax dispute, especially where there is doubt as to the collectibility of the full deficiency. Offers in compromise can include installment payment schedules as well as reductions in the tax and penalties owed by the taxpayer.

Office audit. An audit conducted by the IRS in the agent's office.

Office in the home expenses. Employment and business-related expenses attributable to the use of a residence (e.g., den or office) are allowed only if the portion of the residence is exclusively used on a regular basis as a principal place of business of the taxpayer or as a place of business that is used by patients, clients, or customers. In computing the office in the home expenses, a taxpayer can use either the regular method or simplified method. As a general rule, the regular method requires more effort and recordkeeping but results in a larger deduction. Office in home expenses incurred by an employee are not deductible. § 280A.

One-year rule for prepaid expenses. Taxpayers who use the cash method are required to use the accrual method for deducting certain prepaid expenses (i.e., must capitalize the item and can deduct only when used). If a prepayment will not be consumed or expire by the end of the tax year following the year of payment, the prepayment must be capitalized and prorated over the benefit period. Conversely, if the prepayment will be consumed by the end of the tax year following the year of payment, it can be expensed when paid. To obtain the current deduction under the one-year rule, the payment must be a required payment rather than a voluntary payment.

Operating agreement. The governing document of a limited liability company. This document is similar in structure, function, and purpose to a partnership agreement.

Optional adjustment election. See *Section 754 election*.

Options. The sale or exchange of an option to buy or sell property results in capital gain or loss if the property is a capital asset. Generally, the closing of an option transaction results in short-term capital gain or loss to the writer of the call and the purchaser of the call option. § 1234.

Ordinary and necessary. Two tests for the deductibility of expenses incurred or paid in connection with a trade or business; for the production or collection of income; for the management, conservation, or maintenance of property held for the production of income; or in connection with the determination, collection, or refund of any tax. An expense is ordinary if it is common and accepted in the general industry or type of activity in which the taxpayer is engaged. An expense is necessary if it is appropriate and helpful in furthering the taxpayer's business or income-producing activity. §§ 162(a) and 212.

Ordinary income property. Property contributed to a charitable organization that, if sold rather than contributed, would have resulted in other than long-term capital gain to the donor (i.e., ordinary income property and short-term capital gain property). Examples are inventory and capital assets held for less than the long-term holding period. A contribution of ordinary income property must generally be valued at its fair market value less the gain, if any, that would have been realized if sold.

Organizational costs. See *organizational expenditures.*

Organizational expenditures. Expenditures related to the creation of a corporation or partnership. Common organizational expenditures include legal and accounting fees and state incorporation payments. Organizational expenditures exclude those incurred to obtain capital (underwriting fees) or assets (subject to cost recovery). Such expenditures incurred by the end of the entity's first year are eligible for a $5,000 limited expensing (subject to phaseout) and an amortization of the balance over 180 months. §§ 248 and 709(b).

Original issue discount (OID). The difference between the issue price of a debt obligation (e.g., a corporate bond) and the maturity value of the obligation when the issue price is less than the maturity value. OID represents interest and must be amortized over the life of the debt obligation using the effective interest method. The difference is not considered to be original issue discount for tax purposes when it is less than one-fourth of 1 percent of the redemption price at maturity multiplied by the number of years to maturity. §§ 1272 and 1273(a)(3).

Other adjustments account (OAA). Used in the context of a distribution from an S corporation. The net accumulation of the entity's exempt income (e.g., municipal bond interest).

Other property. In a corporate reorganization, any property in the exchange that is not stock or securities, such as cash or land. This amount constitutes boot. This treatment is similar to that in a like-kind exchange.

Outbound taxation. U.S. tax effects when a U.S. person begins an investment or business activity outside the United States.

Outside basis. A partner's basis in his or her partnership interest.

Ownership change. An event that triggers a § 382 limitation for the acquiring corporation.

P

Parent-subsidiary controlled group. A controlled or affiliated group of corporations where at least one corporation is at least 80 percent owned by one or more of the others. The affiliated group definition is more difficult to meet.

Partial liquidation. A stock redemption where noncorporate shareholders are permitted sale or exchange treatment. In certain cases, an active business must have existed for at least five years. Only a portion of the outstanding stock in the entity is retired. §§ 302(b)(4) and (e).

Partnership. For income tax purposes, a partnership includes a syndicate, group, pool, or joint venture as well as ordinary partnerships. In an ordinary partnership, two or more parties combine capital and/or services to carry on a business for profit as co-owners. § 7701(a)(2).

Partnership agreement. The governing document of a partnership. A partnership agreement should describe the rights and obligations of the partners; the allocation of entity income, deductions, and cash flows; initial and future capital contribution requirements; conditions for terminating the partnership; and other matters.

Passive activity loss. Any loss from (1) activities in which the taxpayer does not materially participate or (2) rental activities (subject to certain exceptions). Net passive losses cannot be used to offset income from nonpassive sources. Rather, they are suspended until the taxpayer either generates net passive income (and a deduction of such losses is allowed) or disposes of the underlying property (at which time the loss deductions are allowed in full). One relief provision allows landlords who actively participate in the rental activities to deduct up to $25,000 of passive losses annually. However, a phaseout of the $25,000 amount commences when the landlord's AGI exceeds $100,000. Another relief provision applies for material participation in a real estate trade or business.

Passive investment company. A means by which a multistate corporation can reduce the overall effective tax rate by isolating investment income in a low- or no-tax state.

Passive investment income (PII). Gross receipts from royalties, certain rents, dividends, interest, annuities, and gains from the sale or exchange of stock and securities. When earnings and profits (E & P) also exists, if the passive investment income of an S corporation exceeds 25 percent of the corporation's gross receipts for three consecutive years, S status is lost.

Pass-through entities. A form of business structure for which the income and other tax items are attributed directly to the owners and generally no separate tax is levied upon the entity itself. Examples include sole proprietorships, partnerships, and S corporations. Also referred to as a flow-through entity.

Patent. An intangible asset that may be amortized over a statutory 15-year period as a § 197 intangible. The sale of a patent usually results in favorable long-term capital gain treatment. §§ 197 and 1235.

Payroll factor. The proportion of a multistate corporation's total payroll that is traceable to a specific state. Used in determining the taxable income that is to be apportioned to that state.

Pension plan. A type of deferred compensation arrangement that provides for systematic payments of definitely determinable retirement benefits to employees who meet the requirements set forth in the plan.

Percentage depletion. Depletion based on a statutory percentage applied to the gross income from the property. The taxpayer deducts the greater of cost depletion or percentage depletion. § 613.

Percentage of completion method. A method of reporting gain or loss on certain long-term contracts. Under this method of accounting, the gross contract price is included in income as the contract is completed. Reg. § 1.451–3.

Permanent differences. Under ASC 740, tax-related items that appear in the entity's financial statements or its tax return but not both. For instance, interest income from a municipal bond is a permanent book-tax difference.

Permanent establishment (PE). A level of business activity, as defined under an income tax treaty, that subjects the taxpayer to taxation in a country other than that in which the taxpayer is based. Often evidenced by the presence of a plant, an office, or other fixed place of business. Inventory storage and temporary activities do not rise to the level of a PE. PE is the treaty's equivalent to nexus.

Personal and dependency exemptions. The tax law provides an exemption for each individual taxpayer and an additional exemption for the taxpayer's spouse if a joint return is filed. An individual may also claim a dependency exemption for each dependent, provided certain tests are met. Beginning in 2018, however, the TCJA of 2017 suspended the deduction for exemptions through 2025.

Personal exemptions. See *personal and dependency exemptions.*

Personal holding company (PHC) tax. A penalty tax imposed on certain closely held corporations with excessive investment income. Assessed at a 20 percent tax rate on personal holding company income, reduced by dividends paid and other adjustments. § 541.

Personal residence. If a residence has been owned and used by the taxpayer as the principal residence for at least two years during the five-year period ending on the date of sale, up to $250,000 of realized gain is excluded from gross income. For a married couple filing a joint return, the $250,000 is increased to $500,000 if either spouse satisfies the ownership requirement and both spouses satisfy the use requirement. § 121.

Personal service corporation (PSC). A corporation whose principal activity is the performance of personal services (e.g., health, law, engineering, architecture, accounting, actuarial science, performing arts, or consulting) and where such services are substantially performed by the employee-owners.

Personalty. All property that is not attached to real estate (realty) and is movable. Examples of personalty are machinery, automobiles, clothing, household furnishings, and personal effects.

Points. Loan origination fees that may be deductible as interest by a buyer of property. A seller of property who pays points reduces the selling price by the amount of the points paid for the buyer. While the seller is not permitted to deduct this amount as interest, the buyer may do so.

Portfolio income. Income from interest, dividends, rentals, royalties, capital gains, or other investment sources. Net passive losses cannot be used to offset net portfolio income.

Precedents. A previously decided court decision that is recognized as authority for the disposition of future decisions.

Precontribution gain or loss. Partnerships allow for a variety of special allocations of gain or loss among the partners, but gain or loss that is "built in" on an asset contributed to the partnership is assigned specifically to the contributing partner. § 704(c)(1)(A).

Preferences. In calculating alternative minimum taxable income (AMTI), preference items are added to the taxable income starting point of the AMT calculation. AMT preferences are amounts allowed in the calculation of regular taxable income but not allowed in the calculation of AMTI. For instance, interest income from certain state and local bonds (i.e., private activity bonds) is an AMT preference item.

Preferred stock bailout. A process where a shareholder used the issuance and sale, or later redemption, of a preferred stock dividend to obtain long-term capital gains, without any loss of voting control over the corporation. In effect, the shareholder received corporate profits without suffering the consequences of dividend income treatment. This procedure led Congress to enact § 306, which, if applicable, converts the prior long-term capital gain on the sale or redemption of the tainted stock to dividend income.

Premium Tax Credit (PTC). A tax credit that is refundable and available in advance of filing a return for the year. The PTC serves to reduce the cost of health coverage obtained on the Marketplace (Exchange). A PTC is available to individuals who purchase coverage on the Exchange and have household income equal to or greater than 100 percent of the Federal poverty line (FPL) and no greater than 400 percent of the FPL. Also, an individual must not have been able to obtain affordable coverage from his or her employer. If obtained in advance, the PTC is given to the insurance provider to lower the monthly premium cost to the individual. The PTC is reconciled on Form 8962 (Premium Tax Credit) filed with Form 1040 or 1040-A (not Form 1040-EZ). Individuals who obtain insurance through the Marketplace receive Form 1095-A (Health Insurance Marketplace Statement) by January 31 of the following year. This form provides information necessary to claim or reconcile the PTC, including the monthly cost of premiums and the amount of PTC received in advance each month. § 36B.

Previously taxed income (PTI). Under prior law, the undistributed taxable income of an S corporation was taxed to the shareholders as of the last day of the corporation's tax year and usually could be withdrawn by the shareholders without tax consequences at some later point in time. The role of PTI has been taken over by the accumulated adjustments account. See also *accumulated adjustments account (AAA).*

Principal partner. A partner with a 5 percent or greater interest in partnership capital or profits. § 706(b)(3).

Private activity bonds. Interest on state and local bonds is excludible from gross income. Certain such bonds are labeled private activity bonds. Although the interest on such bonds is excludible for regular income tax purposes, it is treated as a tax preference in calculating the AMT. §§ 57(a)(5) and 103.

Private foundations. An exempt organization that is subject to additional statutory restrictions on its activities and on contributions made to it. Excise taxes may be levied on certain prohibited transactions, and the Code places more stringent restrictions on the deductibility of contributions to private foundations. § 509.

Probate costs. The costs incurred in administering a decedent's estate.

Probate estate. The property of a decedent that is subject to administration by the executor or administrator of an estate.

Procedural Regulations. A Regulation issued by the Treasury Department that is a housekeeping-type instruction indicating information that taxpayers should provide the IRS as well as information about the internal management and conduct of the IRS itself.

Profit and loss sharing ratios. Specified in the partnership agreement and used to determine each partner's allocation of ordinary taxable income and separately stated items. Profits and losses can be shared in different ratios. The ratios can be changed by amending the partnership agreement or by using a special allocation. § 704(a).

Profit sharing plan. A deferred compensation plan established and maintained by an employer to provide for employee participation in the company's profits. Contributions are paid from the employer's current or accumulated profits to a trustee. Separate accounts are maintained for each participant employee. The plan must provide a definite, predetermined formula for allocating the contributions among the participants. It also must include a definite, predetermined formula for distributing the accumulated funds after a fixed number of years, on the attainment of a stated age, or on the occurrence of certain events such as illness, layoff, or retirement.

Profits (loss) interest. The extent of a partner's entitlement to an allocation of the partnership's operating results. This interest is measured by the profit and loss sharing ratios.

Property. Assets defined in the broadest legal sense. Property includes the unrealized receivables of a cash basis taxpayer, but not services rendered. § 351.

Property dividend. Generally treated in the same manner as a cash distribution, measured by the fair market value of the property on the date of distribution. Distribution of appreciated property causes the distributing C or S corporation to recognize gain. The distributing corporation does not recognize loss on property that has depreciated in value.

Property factor. The proportion of a multistate corporation's total property that is traceable to a specific state. Used in determining the taxable income that is to be apportioned to that state.

Proportionate distribution. A distribution in which the partners' interests in hot assets does not change. This can happen, for instance, when no hot assets are distributed (e.g., a proportionate cash distribution) or when each partner in a partnership receives a pro rata share of hot assets being distributed. For example, a distribution of $10,000 of hot assets equally to two 50 percent partners is a proportionate distribution.

Proposed Regulations. A Regulation issued by the Treasury Department in proposed, rather than final, form. The interval between the proposal of a Regulation and its finalization permits taxpayers and other interested parties to comment on the propriety of the proposal.

Proprietorship. A business entity for which there is a single owner. The net profit of the entity is reported on the owner's Federal income tax return (Schedule C of Form 1040).

Public Law 86–272. A congressional limit on the ability of the state to force a multistate corporation to assign taxable income to that state. Under P.L. 86–272, where orders for tangible personal property are both filled and delivered outside the state, the entity must establish more than the mere solicitation of such orders before any income can be apportioned to the state.

Punitive damages. Damages received or paid by the taxpayer can be classified as compensatory damages or as punitive damages. Punitive damages are those awarded to punish the defendant for gross negligence or the intentional infliction of harm. Such damages are includible in gross income. § 104.

Q

QBI deduction. See *deduction for qualified business income*.

Qualified ABLE program. A state program that allows funds to be set aside for the benefit of an individual who became disabled or blind before age 26. Cash may be put into the fund annually up to the annual gift tax exclusion amount. Distributions to the designated beneficiary are not taxable provided they do not exceed qualified disability expenses for the year. § 529A.

Qualified business income (QBI). For purposes of the qualified business income deduction, it is the ordinary income less ordinary deductions a taxpayer earns from a qualified trade or business conducted in the United States by the taxpayer. It also includes the distributive share of these amounts from each partnership or S corporation interest held by the taxpayer. It does not include certain types of investment income (e.g., capital gains or losses and dividends), "reasonable compensation" paid to a taxpayer with respect to any qualified trade or business, or guaranteed payments made to a partner for services rendered. § 199A(c).

Qualified business income deduction (QBID). See *deduction for qualified business income*.

Qualified business unit (QBU). A subsidiary, branch, or other business entity that conducts business using a currency other than the U.S. dollar.

Qualified dividend income (QDI). See *qualified dividends*.

Qualified dividends. Distributions made by domestic (and certain non-U.S.) corporations to noncorporate shareholders that are subject to tax at the same rates as those applicable to net long-term capital gains (i.e., 0 percent, 15 percent, or 20 percent). The 20 percent rate applies to certain high-income taxpayers. The dividend must be paid out of earnings and profits, and the shareholders must meet certain holding period requirements as to the stock. §§ 1(h)(1) and (11).

Qualified employee discount. Discounts offered employees on merchandise or services that the employer ordinarily sells or provides to customers. The discounts must be generally available to all employees. In the case of property, the discount cannot exceed the employer's gross profit (the sales price cannot be less than the employer's cost). In the case of services, the discounts cannot exceed 20 percent of the normal sales price. § 132.

Qualified improvement property. Any improvement to an interior portion of nonresidential real property made after the property is placed in service, including leasehold improvements.

Qualified joint venture. At the election of the taxpayers, certain joint ventures between spouses can avoid partnership classification. Known as a qualified joint venture, the spouses generally report their share of the business activities from the venture as sole proprietors (using two

Schedule C forms). This would be reported on Schedule E if the venture relates to a rental property. § 761(f).

Qualified nonrecourse financing. Debt issued on realty by a bank, retirement plan, or governmental agency. Included in the at-risk amount by the investor. § 465(b)(6).

Qualified real property business indebtedness. Indebtedness that was incurred or assumed by the taxpayer in connection with real property used in a trade or business and is secured by such real property. The taxpayer must not be a C corporation. For qualified real property business indebtedness, the taxpayer may elect to exclude some or all of the income realized from cancellation of debt on qualified real property. If the election is made, the basis of the property must be reduced by the amount excluded. The amount excluded cannot be greater than the excess of the principal amount of the outstanding debt over the fair market value (net of any other debt outstanding on the property) of the property securing the debt. § 108(c).

Qualified residence interest. A term relevant in determining the amount of interest expense the individual taxpayer may deduct as an itemized deduction for what otherwise would be disallowed as a component of personal interest (consumer interest). Qualified residence interest consists of interest paid on qualified residences (principal residence and one other residence) of the taxpayer. Debt that qualifies as qualified residence interest is limited to $1,000,000 of debt to acquire, construct, or substantially improve qualified residences (acquisition indebtedness). For acquisition indebtedness incurred after December 15, 2017, the limit is reduced to $750,000. § 163(h)(3).

Qualified small business corporation. For purposes of computing an exclusion upon the sale of qualified small business stock, a C corporation that has aggregate gross assets not exceeding $50 million and that is conducting an active trade or business. § 1202.

Qualified small business stock. Stock in a qualified small business corporation, purchased as part of an original issue after August 10, 1993. The shareholder may exclude from gross income 100 (or 50 or 75) percent of the realized gain on the sale of the stock if he or she held the stock for more than five years. The exclusion percentage depends on when the stock was acquired. § 1202.

Qualified terminable interest property (QTIP). Generally, the marital deduction (for gift and estate tax purposes) is not available if the interest transferred will terminate upon the death of the transferee spouse and pass to someone else. Thus, if Jim (the husband) places property in trust, life estate to Mary (the wife), and remainder to their children upon Mary's death, this is a terminable interest that will not provide Jim (or Jim's estate) with a marital deduction. If, however, the transfer in trust is treated as qualified terminable interest property (the QTIP election is made), the terminable interest restriction is waived and the marital deduction becomes available. In exchange for this deduction, the surviving spouse's gross estate must include the value of the QTIP election assets, even though he or she has no control over the ultimate disposition of the asset. Terminable interest property qualifies for this election if the donee (or heir) is the only beneficiary of the asset during his or her lifetime and receives income distributions relative to the property at least annually. For gifts, the donor spouse is the one who makes the QTIP election. For property transferred by death, the executor of the estate of the deceased spouse makes the election. §§ 2056(b)(7) and 2523(f).

Qualified trade or business. Used in determining the deduction for qualified business income (§ 199A). In general, it includes any trade or business other than providing services as an employee. In addition, a "specified services trade or business" is not a qualified trade or business. § 199A(d)(1)(B).

Qualified transportation fringes. Transportation benefits provided by the employer to the employee. If these benefits are reimbursed by the employer, they are excludible from gross income by the employee, but not deductible by the employer after 2017. Such benefits include (1) transportation in a commuter highway vehicle between the employee's residence and the place of employment, (2) a transit pass, and (3) qualified parking. Qualified transportation fringes are excludible from the employee's gross income to the extent categories (1) and (2) above do not exceed $265 per month in 2019 and category (3) does not exceed $265 per month in 2019. These amounts are indexed annually for inflation. § 132.

Qualified tuition program (§ 529 plan). A program that allows college tuition to be prepaid for a beneficiary. When amounts in the plan are used, nothing is included in gross income provided they are used for qualified higher education expenses. § 529.

Qualifying child. An individual who, as to the taxpayer, satisfies the relationship, abode, and age tests. To be claimed as a dependent, such individual must also meet the citizenship and joint return tests and not be self-supporting. §§ 152(a)(1) and (c).

Qualifying relative. An individual who, as to the taxpayer, satisfies the relationship, gross income, support, citizenship, and joint return tests. Such an individual can be claimed as a dependent of the taxpayer. §§ 152(a)(2) and (d).

R

Rate reconciliation. Under Generally Accepted Accounting Principles, a footnote to the financial statements often includes a table that accounts for differences in the statutory income tax rate that applies to the entity (e.g., 21 percent) and the higher or lower effective tax rate that the entity realized for the reporting period. The rate reconciliation includes only permanent differences between the book tax expense and the entity's income tax provision. The rate reconciliation table often is expressed in dollar and/or percentage terms.

Realized gain. See *realized gain or loss*.

Realized gain or loss. The difference between the amount realized upon the sale or other disposition of property and the adjusted basis of the property. § 1001.

Realized loss. See *realized gain or loss*.

Realty. Real estate.

Reasonable cause. Relief from taxpayer and preparer penalties often is allowed where reasonable cause is found for the taxpayer's actions. For example, reasonable cause for the late filing of a tax return might be a flood that damaged the taxpayer's record-keeping systems and made a timely completion of the return difficult.

Reasonable needs of the business. A means of avoiding the penalty tax on an unreasonable accumulation of earnings. In determining the base for this tax (accumulated taxable income), § 535 allows a deduction for "such part of earnings and profits for the taxable year as are retained for the reasonable needs of the business." § 537.

Reasonableness. See *reasonableness requirement*.

Reasonableness requirement. The Code includes a reasonableness requirement with respect to the deduction of salaries and other compensation for services. The courts have expanded this requirement to all business expenses, ruling that an expense must be reasonable in order to be ordinary and necessary. What constitutes reasonableness is a question of fact. If an expense is unreasonable, the amount that is classified as unreasonable is not allowed as a deduction. The question of reasonableness generally arises with respect to closely held corporations where there is no separation of ownership and management. § 162(a)(1).

Recapitalization. A "Type E" reorganization, constituting a major change in the character and amount of outstanding equity of a corporation. Tax-free exchanges are stock for stock, bonds for bonds, and bonds for stock. For example, common stock exchanged for preferred stock can qualify as a tax-free "Type E" reorganization.

Recognized gain. See *recognized gain or loss*.

Recognized gain or loss. The portion of realized gain or loss subject to income taxation.

Recognized loss. See *recognized gain or loss*.

Recourse debt. Debt for which the lender may both foreclose on the property and assess a guarantor for any payments due under the loan. A lender also may make a claim against the assets of any general partner in a partnership to which debt is issued, without regard to whether the partner has guaranteed the debt.

Recovery of capital doctrine. When a taxable sale or exchange occurs, the seller may be permitted to recover his or her investment (or other adjusted basis) in the property before gain or loss is recognized.

Redemption to pay death taxes. Sale or exchange treatment is available relative to this type of stock redemption, to the extent of the proceeds up to the total amount paid by the estate or heir for estate/inheritance taxes and administration expenses. The stock value must exceed 35 percent of the value of the decedent's adjusted gross estate. In meeting this test, shareholdings in corporations where the decedent held at least 20 percent of the outstanding shares are combined. § 303.

Refundable credits. A credit that is paid to the taxpayer even if the amount of the credit (or credits) exceeds the taxpayer's tax liability.

Regular corporations. See *C corporation*.

Rehabilitation expenditures credit. A credit that is based on expenditures incurred to rehabilitate industrial and commercial buildings and certified historic structures. The credit is intended to discourage businesses from moving from older, economically distressed areas to newer locations and to encourage the preservation of historic structures. § 47.

Related party. Various Code Sections define related parties and often include a variety of persons within this (usually detrimental) category. Generally, related parties are accorded different tax treatment from that applicable to other taxpayers who enter into similar transactions. For instance, realized losses that are generated between related parties are not recognized in the year of the loss. However, these deferred losses can be used to offset recognized gains that occur upon the subsequent sale of the asset to a nonrelated party. Other uses of a related-party definition include the conversion of gain upon the sale of a depreciable asset into all ordinary income (§ 1239) and the identification of constructive ownership of stock relative to corporate distributions, redemptions, liquidations, reorganizations, and compensation.

Related-party transactions. The tax law places restrictions upon the recognition of gains and losses between related parties because of the potential for abuse. For example, restrictions are placed on the deduction of losses from the sale or exchange of property between related parties. In addition, under certain circumstances, related-party gains that would otherwise be classified as capital gain are classified as ordinary income. §§ 267, 707(b), and 1239.

Rental activity. Any activity where payments are received principally for the use of tangible property is a rental activity. Temporary Regulations provide that in certain circumstances, activities involving rentals of real and personal property are not to be treated as rental activities. The Temporary Regulations list six exceptions.

Reorganization. Any corporate restructuring, including when one corporation acquires another, a single corporation divides into two or more entities, a corporation makes a substantial change in its capital structure, a corporation undertakes a change in its legal name or domicile, or a corporation goes through a bankruptcy proceeding and continues to exist. The exchange of stock and other securities in a corporate reorganization can be effected favorably for tax purposes if certain statutory requirements are followed strictly. Tax consequences include the nonrecognition of any gain that is realized by the shareholders except to the extent of boot received. § 368.

Report of Foreign Bank and Financial Accounts (FBAR). FinCEN Form 114, Report of Foreign Bank and Financial Accounts (FBAR), must be filed by individuals and some businesses if they have foreign bank, brokerage or similar accounts where at any time during the calendar year the aggregate balance exceeds $10,000. The form is filed electronically with the U.S. Department of the Treasury and is due by April 15 with an automatic extension to October 15. Significant penalties apply for failure to file the FBAR. The form is not attached to the income tax return (it is separately filed), but any interest earned by the foreign accounts is generally included in the account holder's U.S. taxable income.

Required taxable year. A partnership or limited liability company must use a required tax year as its tax accounting period, or one of three allowable alternative tax year-ends. If there is a common tax year used by owners holding a majority of the entity's capital or profits interests or if the same year end is used by all "principal partners" (partners who hold 5 percent or more of the capital or profits interests), then that tax year-end is used by the entity. If neither of the first tests results in an allowable year-end (e.g., because there is no majority partner or because the principal partners do not have the same tax year), then the partnership uses the least aggregate deferral method to determine its tax year.

Research activities credit. A tax credit whose purpose is to encourage research and development. It consists of three components: the incremental research activities credit, the basic research credit, and the energy credit. The incremental research activities credit is equal to 20 percent of the excess qualified research expenditures over the base amount. The basic research credit is equal to 20 percent of the excess of basic research payments over the base amount. § 41.

Research and experimental expenditures. Costs incurred to develop a product or process for which there exists uncertainty regarding its viability. The Code provides three alternatives for the tax treatment of research and experimentation expenditures. They may be expensed in the year paid or incurred, deferred subject to amortization, or capitalized. If the taxpayer does not elect to expense such costs or to defer them subject to amortization (over 60 months), the expenditures must be capitalized. § 174. In general, research and experimentation expenditures paid or incurred after 2021 must be capitalized and amortized over a five-year period. Some of these expenditures may also qualify the taxpayer for the credit for increasing research activities. § 41.

Reserve method. A method of accounting whereby an allowance is permitted for estimated uncollectible accounts. Actual write-offs are charged to the reserve, and recoveries of amounts previously written off are credited to the reserve. The Code permits only certain financial institutions to use the reserve method. § 166.

Residential rental real estate. Buildings for which at least 80 percent of the gross rents are from dwelling units (e.g., an apartment building). This type of building is distinguished from nonresidential (commercial or industrial) buildings in applying the recapture of depreciation provisions. The term also is relevant in distinguishing between buildings that are eligible for a 27.5-year life versus a 39-year life for MACRS purposes. Generally, residential buildings receive preferential treatment.

Restricted property plan. An arrangement whereby an employer transfers property (usually stock) to an employee at a bargain price (for less than the fair market value). If the transfer is accompanied by a substantial risk of forfeiture and the property is not transferable, no compensation results to the employee until the restrictions disappear. An example of a substantial risk of forfeiture would be a requirement that the employee return the property if his or her employment is terminated within a specified period of time. § 83.

Revenue Agent's Report (RAR). A Revenue Agent's Report (RAR) reflects any adjustments made by the agent as a result of an audit of the taxpayer. The RAR is mailed to the taxpayer along with the 30-day letter, which outlines the appellate procedures available to the taxpayer.

Revenue neutrality. A description that characterizes tax legislation when it neither increases nor decreases the total revenue collected by the taxing jurisdiction. Thus, any tax revenue losses are offset by tax revenue gains.

Revenue Procedures. A matter of procedural importance to both taxpayers and the IRS concerning the administration of the tax laws is issued as a Revenue Procedure (abbreviated Rev.Proc.). A Revenue Procedure is published in an *Internal Revenue Bulletin* (I.R.B.).

Revenue Rulings. A Revenue Ruling (abbreviated Rev.Rul.) is issued by the National Office of the IRS to express an official interpretation of the tax law as applied to specific transactions. It is more limited in application than a Regulation. A Revenue Ruling is published in an *Internal Revenue Bulletin* (I.R.B.).

Reversionary interest. The trust property that reverts to the grantor after the expiration of an intervening income interest. Assume that Phil places real estate in trust with income to Junior for 11 years and that upon the expiration of this term, the property returns to Phil. Under these circumstances, Phil holds a reversionary interest in the property. A reversionary interest is the same as a remainder interest, except that, in the latter case, the property passes to someone other than the original owner (e.g., the grantor of a trust) upon the expiration of the intervening interest.

Roth IRA. See *Individual Retirement Account (IRA)*.

S

S corporation. The designation for a corporation that elects to be taxed similarly to a partnership. See also *Subchapter S*.

Sale or exchange. A requirement for the recognition of capital gain or loss. Generally, the seller of property must receive money or relief from debt to have sold the property. An exchange involves the transfer of property for other property. Thus, collection of a debt is neither a sale nor an exchange. The term *sale or exchange* is not defined by the Code.

Sales factor. The proportion of a multistate corporation's total sales that is traceable to a specific state. Used in determining the taxable income that is to be apportioned to that state.

Sales tax. A state- or local-level tax on the retail sale of specified property. Generally, the purchaser pays the tax, but the seller collects it, as an agent for the government. Various taxing jurisdictions allow exemptions for purchases of specific items, including certain food, services, and manufacturing equipment. If the purchaser and seller are in different states, a use tax usually applies.

Salvage value. The estimated amount a taxpayer will receive upon the disposition of an asset used in the taxpayer's trade or business. Salvage value is relevant in calculating depreciation under § 167, but is not relevant in calculating cost recovery under § 168.

Schedule K–1. A tax information form prepared for each partner in a partnership, each shareholder of an S corporation, and some beneficiaries of certain trusts. The Schedule K–1 reports the owner's share of the entity's ordinary income or loss from operations as well as the owner's share of separately stated items.

Schedule M–1. On the Form 1120, a reconciliation of book net income with Federal taxable income. Accounts for temporary and permanent differences in the two computations, such as depreciation differences, exempt income, and nondeductible items. On Forms 1120S and 1065, the Schedule M–1 reconciles book income with the owners' aggregate taxable income.

Schedule M–3. An *expanded* reconciliation of book net income with Federal taxable income (see *Schedule M–1*). Required of C and S corporations and partnerships/LLCs with total assets of $10 million or more.

Scholarship. Scholarships are generally excluded from the gross income of the recipient unless the payments are a disguised form of compensation for services rendered. However, the Code imposes restrictions on the exclusion. The recipient must be a degree candidate. The excluded amount is limited to amounts used for tuition, fees, books, supplies, and equipment required for courses of instruction. Amounts received for room and board are not eligible for the exclusion. § 117.

Section 121 exclusion. If a residence has been owned and used by the taxpayer as the principal residence for at least two years during the five-year period ending on the date of sale, up to $250,000 of realized gain is excluded from gross income. For a married couple filing a joint return, the $250,000 is increased to $500,000 if either spouse satisfies the ownership requirement and both spouses satisfy the use requirement.

Section 179 expensing. The ability to deduct the cost of qualified property in the year the property is placed in service rather than over the asset's useful life or cost recovery period. The annual ceiling on the deduction is $1,020,000 in 2019 ($1,000,000 in 2018). However, the deduction is reduced dollar for dollar when § 179 property placed in service during the taxable year exceeds $2,550,000 ($2,500,000 in 2018). In addition, the amount expensed under § 179 cannot exceed the aggregate amount of taxable income derived from the conduct of any trade or business by the taxpayer.

Section 179 expensing election. See *Section 179 expensing*.

Section 338 election. When a corporation acquires at least 80 percent of a subsidiary within a 12-month period, it can elect to treat the acquisition of such stock as an asset purchase. The acquiring corporation's basis in the subsidiary's assets then is the cost of the stock. The subsidiary is deemed to have sold its assets for an amount equal to the grossed-up basis in its stock.

Section 382 limitation. When one corporation acquires another, the acquiring corporation's ability to use the loss and credit carryovers of the target may be limited by this anti-abuse provision. For instance, the maximum NOL deduction available to the acquiring is the value of the target when acquired times the long-term tax-exempt interest rate on that date.

Section 401(k) plan. A cash or deferred arrangement plan that allows participants to elect to receive up to $19,000 in 2019 in cash (taxed currently) or to have a contribution made on their behalf to a profit sharing or stock bonus plan (excludible from gross income). The plan may also be in the form of a salary reduction agreement between the participant and the employer.

Section 704(b) book capital accounts. Capital accounts calculated as described under Reg. § 1.704–1(b)(2)(iv). All partnerships must maintain § 704(b) book capital accounts for the partners with the intent that final liquidating distributions are in accordance with these capital account balances. Partnership allocations will not be accepted unless they are properly reflected in the partners' § 704(b) book capital accounts. These capital accounts are a hybrid of book and tax accounting methods. They reflect contributions and distributions of property at their fair market values, but the capital accounts are otherwise generally increased by the partnership's tax-basis income and decreased by tax-basis deductions (as reported on the partner's Schedule K–1). Liabilities are only reflected in these capital accounts to the extent the partnership assumes a partner's liability [reduces that partner's § 704(b) book capital account] or a partner assumes a partnership liability [increases that partner's § 704(b) book capital account]. See also *capital account maintenance* and *economic effect test*.

Section 754 election. An election that may be made by a partnership to adjust the basis of partnership assets to reflect a purchasing partner's outside basis in interest or to reflect a gain, loss, or basis adjustment of a partner receiving a distribution from a partnership. The intent of the election is to maintain the equivalence between outside and inside basis for that partner. Once the election is made, the partnership must make basis adjustments for all future transactions, unless the IRS consents to revoke the election.

Section 1231 gains and losses. If the combined gains and losses from the taxable dispositions of § 1231 assets plus the net gain from business involuntary conversions (of both § 1231 assets and long-term capital assets) is a gain, the gains and losses are treated as long-term capital gains and losses. In arriving at § 1231 gains, however, the depreciation recapture provisions (e.g., § 1245) are applied first to produce ordinary income. If the net result of the combination is a loss, the gains and losses from § 1231 assets are treated as ordinary gains and losses. § 1231(a).

Section 1231 lookback. For gain to be classified as § 1231 gain, the gain must survive the § 1231 lookback. To the extent of nonrecaptured § 1231 losses for the five prior tax years, the gain is classified as ordinary income. § 1231(c).

Section 1231 property. Depreciable assets and real estate used in trade or business and held for the required long-term holding period. § 1231(b).

Section 1244 stock. Stock issued under § 1244 by qualifying small business corporations. If § 1244 stock becomes worthless, the shareholders may claim an ordinary loss rather than the usual capital loss, within statutory limitations.

Section 1245 property. Property that is subject to the recapture of depreciation under § 1245. For a definition of § 1245 property, see § 1245(a)(3).

Section 1245 recapture. Upon a taxable disposition of § 1245 property, all depreciation claimed on the property is recaptured as ordinary income (but not to exceed any recognized gain from the disposition).

Section 1250 property. Real estate that is subject to the recapture of depreciation under § 1250. For a definition of § 1250 property, see § 1250(c).

Section 1250 recapture. Upon a taxable disposition of § 1250 property, accelerated depreciation or cost recovery claimed on the property may be recaptured as ordinary income.

Securities. Stock, debt, and other financial assets. To the extent securities other than the stock of the transferee corporation are received in a § 351 exchange, the new shareholder recognizes a gain. For purposes of corporate reorganizations, securities are generally debt with terms longer than 10 years. To the extent stock and securities are transferred in a corporate reorganization under § 368, no gain or loss is recognized.

Self-employment tax. A tax of 12.4 percent is levied on individuals with net earnings from self-employment (up to $132,900 in 2019) to provide Social Security benefits (i.e., the old age, survivors, and disability insurance portion) for such individuals. In addition, a tax of 2.9 percent is levied on individuals with net earnings from self-employment (with no statutory ceiling) to provide Medicare benefits (i.e., the hospital insurance portion) for such individuals. If a self-employed individual also receives wages from an employer that are subject to FICA, the self-employment tax will be reduced. A partial deduction is allowed in calculating the self-employment tax. Individuals with net earnings of $400 or more from self-employment are subject to this tax. §§ 1401 and 1402.

Separate foreign tax credit income categories. The foreign tax credit of a taxpayer is computed for each of several types of income sources, as specified by the Code to limit the results of tax planning. FTC income "baskets" include general and passive. The FTC for the year is the sum of the credits as computed within all of the taxpayer's separate FTC baskets used for the tax year.

Separate return limitation year (SRLY). A series of rules limits the amount of an acquired corporation's net operating loss carryforwards that can be used by the acquiror. Generally, a consolidated return can include the acquiree's net operating loss carryforward only to the extent of the lesser of the subsidiary's (1) current-year or (2) cumulative positive contribution to consolidated taxable income.

Separately stated items. Any item of a partnership or an S corporation that might be taxed differently to any two owners of the entity. These amounts are not included in the ordinary income of the entity, but are instead reported separately to the owners; tax consequences are determined at the owner level.

Severance taxes. A tax imposed upon the extraction of natural resources.

Short period. See *short taxable year*.

Short sale. A sale that occurs when a taxpayer sells borrowed property (usually stock) and repays the lender with substantially identical property either held on the date of the short sale or purchased after the sale. No gain or loss is recognized until the short sale is closed, and such gain or loss is generally short term. § 1233.

Short taxable year. A tax year that is less than 12 months. A short taxable year may occur in the initial reporting period, in the final tax year, or when the taxpayer changes tax years.

Significant participation activity. Seven tests determine whether an individual has achieved material participation in an activity, one of which is based on more than 500 hours of participation in significant participation activities. A significant participation activity is one in which the individual's participation exceeds 100 hours during the year. Temp.Reg. § 1.469–5T.

Simple trust. Trusts that are not complex trusts. Such trusts may not have a charitable beneficiary, accumulate income, or distribute corpus.

Simplified employee pension (SEP) plans. An employer may make contributions to an employee's IRA in amounts not exceeding the lesser of 15 percent of compensation or $56,000 per individual in 2019. These employer-sponsored simplified employee pensions are permitted only if the contributions are nondiscriminatory and are made on behalf of all employees who have attained age 21 and have worked for the employer during at least three of the five preceding calendar years. § 219(b).

Small business corporation. A corporation that satisfies the definition of § 1361(b), § 1244(c), or both. Satisfaction of § 1361(b) permits an S election, and satisfaction of § 1244 enables the shareholders of the corporation to claim an ordinary loss on the worthlessness of stock.

Small business stock (§ 1244 stock). See *Section 1244 stock*.

Small Cases Division. A division within the U.S. Tax Court where jurisdiction is limited to claims of $50,000 or less. There is no appeal from this court.

Solicitation. A level of activity brought about by the taxpayer within a specific state. Under Public Law 86–272, certain types of solicitation activities do not create nexus with the state. Exceeding mere solicitation, though, creates nexus.

Special allocation. Any amount for which an agreement exists among the partners of a partnership outlining the method used for spreading the item among the partners.

Special use value. Permits the executor of an estate to value, for estate tax purposes, real estate used in a farming activity or in connection with a closely held business at its current use value rather than at its most suitable or optimal use value. Under this option, a farm is valued for farming purposes even though, for example, the property might have a higher potential value as a shopping center. For the executor of an estate to elect special use valuation, the conditions of § 2032A must be satisfied.

Specific charge-off method. A method of accounting for bad debts in which a deduction is permitted only when an account becomes partially or completely worthless.

Specified service trade or business. For purposes of the deduction for qualified business income, a specified service trade or business includes those involving the performance of services in certain fields, including health, law, accounting, actuarial science, performing arts, consulting, athletics, financial services, and brokerage services; services consisting of investing and investment management, trading or dealing in securities, partnership interests, or commodities; and any trade or business where the business's principal asset is the reputation of one or more of its employees or owners. § 199A(d)(2).

Spin-off. A type of reorganization where, for example, Apple Corporation transfers some assets to Core Corporation in exchange for Core stock representing control. Apple then distributes the Core stock to its shareholders.

Split-off. A type of reorganization where, for example, Apple Corporation transfers some assets to Core Corporation in exchange for Core stock representing control. Apple then distributes the Core stock to its shareholders in exchange for some of their Apple stock. Not all shareholders need to exchange stock.

Split-up. A type of reorganization where, for example, Firefly Corporation transfers some assets to Fire Corporation and the remainder to Fly Corporation. In return, Firefly receives enough Fire and Fly stock representing control of each corporation. Firefly then distributes the Fire and Fly stock to its shareholders in return for all of their Firefly stock. Firefly then liquidates, and its shareholders now have control of Fire and Fly.

Sprinkling trust. When a trustee has the discretion to either distribute or accumulate the entity accounting income of the trust and to distribute it among the trust's income beneficiaries in varying magnitudes. The trustee can "sprinkle" the income of the trust.

Standard deduction. The individual taxpayer can either itemize deductions or take the standard deduction. The amount of the standard deduction depends on the taxpayer's filing status (single, head of household, married filing jointly, surviving spouse, or married filing separately). For 2019, the amount of the standard deduction ranges from $12,200 (for single) to $24,400 (for married, filing jointly). Additional standard deductions of either $1,300 (for married taxpayers) or $1,650 (for single taxpayers) are available if the taxpayer is blind or age 65 or over. Limitations exist on the amount of the standard deduction of a taxpayer who is another taxpayer's dependent. The standard deduction amounts are adjusted for inflation each year. § 63(c).

Startup expenditures. Expenditures paid or incurred prior to the beginning of the business that would have been deductible as an ordinary and necessary business expense if business operations had begun. Examples of such expenditures include advertising; salaries and wages; travel and other expenses incurred in lining up prospective distributors, suppliers, or customers; and salaries and fees to executives, consultants, and professional service providers. A taxpayer will immediately expense the first $5,000 (subject to phaseout) of startup expenditures and amortize the balance over a period of 180 months, unless the taxpayer elects not to do so.

Statute of limitations. Provisions of the law that specify the maximum period of time in which action may be taken concerning a past event. Code §§ 6501–6504 contain the limitation periods applicable to the IRS for additional assessments, and §§ 6511–6515 relate to refund claims by taxpayers.

Statutory employees. Statutory employees are considered self-employed independent contractors for purposes of reporting income and expenses on their tax returns. Generally, a statutory employee must meet three tests:

- It is understood from a service contract that the services will be performed by the person.
- The person does not have a substantial investment in facilities (other than transportation used to perform the services).
- The services involve a continuing relationship with the person for whom they are performed.

For further information on statutory employees, see Circular E, *Employer's Tax Guide* (IRS Publication 15).

Step down. See *step-down in basis.*

Step transaction. Disregarding one or more transactions to arrive at the final result. Assume, for example, Beta Corporation creates Alpha Corporation by transferring assets desired by Beta's sole shareholder, Carl. Carl then causes Alpha to liquidate to obtain the assets. Under these circumstances, the IRS may contend that the creation and liquidation of Alpha be disregarded. What really happened was a dividend distribution from Beta to Carl.

Step up. See *step-up in basis.*

Step-down in basis. A reduction in the tax basis of property. See also *step-up in basis.*

Step-up in basis. An increase in the income tax basis of property. In an estate context, a step-up in basis occurs when a decedent dies owning appreciated property. Since the estate or heir acquires a basis in the property equal to the property's fair market value on the date of death (or alternate valuation date if available and elected), any appreciation is not subject to the income tax. Thus, a step-up in basis is the result, with no immediate income tax consequences. In the partnership context, a step-up arises when a § 754 election is in effect and when one of several transactions arises: (1) a partner purchases a partnership interest for an amount that exceeds the partner's share of the partnership's inside basis, (2) the partner recognizes a gain on a distribution of cash from the partnership, or (3) the partnership takes a basis in a partnership property that is less than the partnership's basis in that asset. In the opposite situations (e.g., loss recognition), a step-down can arise. See also *step-down in basis.*

Stock bonus plan. A type of deferred compensation plan in which the employer establishes and maintains the plan and contributes employer stock to the plan for the benefit of employees. The contributions need not be dependent on the employer's profits. Any benefits of the plan are distributable in the form of employer stock, except that distributable fractional shares may be paid in cash.

Stock dividend. Not taxable if pro rata distributions of stock or stock rights on common stock. Section 305 governs the taxability of stock dividends and sets out five exceptions to the general rule that stock dividends are nontaxable.

Stock option. The right to purchase a stated number of shares of stock from a corporation at a certain price within a specified period of time. §§ 421 and 422.

Stock redemption. A corporation buys back its own stock from a specified shareholder. Typically, the corporation recognizes any realized gain on the noncash assets that it uses to effect a redemption, and the shareholder obtains a capital gain or loss upon receipt of the purchase price.

Stock rights. Assets that convey to the holder the power to purchase corporate stock at a specified price, often for a limited period of time. Stock rights received may be taxed as a distribution of earnings and profits. After the right is exercised, the basis of the acquired share includes the investor's purchase price or gross income, if any, to obtain the right. Disposition of the right also can be taxable.

Subchapter S. Sections 1361–1379 of the Internal Revenue Code. An elective provision permitting certain small business corporations (§ 1361) and their shareholders (§ 1362) to elect to be treated for income tax purposes in accordance with the operating rules of §§ 1363–1379. However, some S corporations usually avoid the corporate income tax, and corporate losses can be claimed by the shareholders.

Subpart F income. Certain types of income earned by a controlled foreign corporation that are included in U.S. gross income by U.S. shareholders of such an entity as they are generated, not when they are repatriated.

Substance over form. A standard used when one must ascertain the true reality of what has occurred. Suppose, for example, a father sells stock to his daughter for $1,000. If the stock is really worth $50,000 at the time of the transfer, the substance of the transaction is probably a gift to her of $49,000.

Substantial authority. Taxpayer and tax preparer understatement penalties are waived where substantial authority existed for the disputed position taken on the return.

Substantial basis reduction. Arises when the partnership makes a distribution to a partner and the distributee partner recognizes a loss (or has a basis increase for the distributed assets) of at least $250,000. (The second situation would arise when the basis of the assets the partner receives must be stepped up to absorb all remaining partnership interest basis.) If there is a substantial basis reduction, the partnership is required to make a downward adjustment to the basis of its assets, even if the partnership does not have a § 754 election in effect. This adjustment is treated as a § 754 adjustment related to a distribution and so is allocated to the basis of all remaining partnership assets (except for cash). See also *substantial built-in loss* and *§ 754 election.*

Substantial built-in loss. Arises when a partner sells a partnership interest and the selling partner recognizes a loss on the sale of at least $250,000. In addition, a substantial built-in loss arises if the selling partner would be allocated more than a $250,000 loss if all partnership assets were sold (after considering special allocations). If there is a substantial built-in loss, the partnership is required to make a downward adjustment in the basis of its assets, even if the partnership does not have a § 754 election in effect. This adjustment is treated as a § 754 adjustment related to a sale of a partnership interest and so is allocated to the purchasing partner. See also *substantial basis reduction* and *§ 754 election.*

Substantial risk of forfeiture (SRF). A term that is associated with a restricted property plan. Generally, an employee who receives property (e.g., stock of the employer-corporation)

from the employer at a bargain price or at no cost must include the bargain element in gross income. However, the employee currently does not have to do so if there is a substantial risk of forfeiture. A substantial risk of forfeiture exists if a person's rights to full enjoyment of property are conditioned upon the future performance, or the refraining from the performance, of substantial services by the individual. § 83.

Sunset provision. A provision attached to new tax legislation that will cause such legislation to expire at a specified date. Sunset provisions are attached to tax cut bills for long-term budgetary reasons to make their effect temporary. Once the sunset provision comes into play, the tax cut is rescinded and former law is reinstated. An example of a sunset provision is contained in the Tax Relief Reconciliation Act of 2001 that related to the estate tax. After the estate tax was phased out in 2010, a sunset provision called for the reinstatement of the estate tax as of January 1, 2011.

Surviving spouse. When a husband or wife predeceases the other spouse, the survivor is known as a surviving spouse. Under certain conditions, a surviving spouse may be entitled to use the income tax rates in § 1(a) (those applicable to married persons filing a joint return) for the two years after the year of death of his or her spouse. § 2(a).

Syndication costs. Incurred in promoting and marketing partnership interests for sale to investors. Examples include legal and accounting fees, printing costs for prospectus and placement documents, and state registration fees. These items are capitalized by the partnership as incurred, with no amortization thereof allowed.

T

Tax avoidance. The minimization of one's tax liability by taking advantage of legally available tax planning opportunities. Tax avoidance can be contrasted with tax evasion, which entails the reduction of tax liability by illegal means.

Tax benefit rule. A provision that limits the recognition of income from the recovery of an expense or a loss properly deducted in a prior tax year to the amount of the deduction that generated a tax saving. Assume that last year Gary had medical expenses of $4,000 and adjusted gross income of $30,000. Because of the AGI limitation, Gary could deduct only $1,000 of these expenses [$4,000 − (10% × $30,000)]. If this year Gary is reimbursed in full by his insurance company for the $4,000 of expenses, the tax benefit rule limits the amount of income from the reimbursement to $1,000 (the amount previously deducted with a tax saving).

Tax credits. Amounts that directly reduce a taxpayer's tax liability. The tax benefit received from a tax credit is not dependent on the taxpayer's marginal tax rate, whereas the benefit of a tax deduction or exclusion is dependent on the taxpayer's tax bracket.

Tax evasion. The reduction of taxes by the use of subterfuge or fraud or other nonlegal means. For example, a cash basis taxpayer tries to increase his or her charitable contribution deduction by prepaying next year's church pledge with a pre-dated check issued in the following year.

Tax haven. A country in which either locally sourced income or residents of the country are subject to a low rate of taxation.

Tax preparer. One who prepares tax returns for compensation. A tax preparer must register with the IRS and receive a special ID number to practice before the IRS and represent taxpayers before the agency in tax audit actions. The conduct of a tax preparer is regulated under Circular 230. Tax preparers also are subject to penalties for inappropriate conduct when working in the tax profession.

Tax Rate Schedules. Rate schedules that are used by upper-income taxpayers and those not permitted to use the tax table. Separate rate schedules are provided for married individuals filing jointly, heads of households, single taxpayers, estates and trusts, and married individuals filing separate returns. § 1.

Tax research. The method used to determine the best available solution to a situation that possesses tax consequences. Both tax and nontax factors are considered.

Tax shelters. The typical tax shelter generated large losses in the early years of the activity. Investors would offset these losses against other types of income and therefore avoid paying income taxes on this income. These tax shelter investments could then be sold after a few years and produce capital gain income, which is taxed at a lower rate compared to ordinary income. The passive activity loss rules and the at-risk rules now limit tax shelter deductions.

Tax Table. A table that is provided for taxpayers with less than $100,000 of taxable income. Separate columns are provided for single taxpayers, married taxpayers filing jointly, heads of households, and married taxpayers filing separately. § 3.

Tax treaties. An agreement between the U.S. Department of State and another country designed to alleviate double taxation of income and asset transfers and to share administrative information useful to tax agencies in both countries. The United States has income tax treaties with almost 70 countries and transfer tax treaties with about 20.

Taxable estate. The taxable estate is the gross estate of a decedent reduced by the deductions allowed by §§ 2053–2057 (e.g., administration expenses, marital and charitable deductions). The taxable estate is subject to the unified transfer tax at death. § 2051.

Taxable gift. The amount of a gift that is subject to the unified transfer tax. Thus, a taxable gift has been adjusted by the annual exclusion and other appropriate deductions (e.g., marital and charitable). § 2053.

Taxable year. The annual period over which income is measured for income tax purposes. Most individuals use a calendar year, but many businesses use a fiscal year based on the natural business year. Certain entities, including S corporations, have a required taxable year. §§ 441, 706, and 1378.

Technical Advice Memoranda (TAM). TAMs are issued by the IRS in response to questions raised by IRS field personnel during audits. They deal with completed rather than proposed transactions and are often requested for questions related to exempt organizations and employee plans.

Temporary differences. Under ASC 740 (SFAS 109), tax-related items that appear in the entity's financial statements and its tax return, but in different time periods. For instance, doubtful accounts receivable often create a temporary book-tax difference, as a bad debt reserve is used to compute an expense for financial reporting purposes, but a bad debt often is deductible only under the specific write-off rule for tax purposes, and the difference observed for the current period creates a temporary difference.

Temporary Regulations. A Regulation issued by the Treasury Department in temporary form. When speed is critical, the Treasury Department issues Temporary Regulations that take effect immediately. These Regulations have the same authoritative value as Final Regulations and may be cited as precedent for three years. Temporary Regulations are also issued as proposed Regulations.

Tenants by the entirety. Essentially, a joint tenancy between husband and wife.

Tenants in common. A form of ownership where each tenant (owner) holds an undivided interest in property. Unlike a joint tenancy or a tenancy by the entirety, the interest of a tenant in common does not terminate upon that individual's death (there is no right of survivorship). Assume that Tim and Cindy acquire real estate as equal tenants in common. Upon Tim's death, his one-half interest in the property passes to his estate or heirs, not automatically to Cindy.

Terminable interests. An interest in property that terminates upon the death of the holder or upon the occurrence of some other specified event. The transfer of a terminable interest by one spouse to the other may not qualify for the marital deduction. §§ 2056(b) and 2523(b).

Theft losses. A loss from larceny, embezzlement, or robbery. It does not include misplacement of items.

Thin capitalization. When debt owed by a corporation to the shareholders becomes too large in relation to the corporation's capital structure (i.e., stock and shareholder equity), the IRS may contend that the corporation is thinly capitalized. In effect, some or all of the debt is reclassified as equity. The immediate result is to disallow any interest deduction to the corporation on the reclassified debt. To the extent of the corporation's earnings and profits, interest payments and loan repayments on the reclassified debt are treated as dividends to the shareholders.

Thirty-day (30-day) letter. A letter that accompanies an RAR (Revenue Agent's Report) issued as a result of an IRS audit of a taxpayer (or the rejection of a taxpayer's claim for refund). The letter outlines the taxpayer's appeal procedure before the IRS. If the taxpayer does not request any such procedures within the 30-day period, the IRS issues a statutory notice of deficiency (the 90-day letter).

Throwback rule. If there is no income tax in the state to which a sale otherwise would be apportioned, the sale essentially is exempt from state income tax, even though the seller is domiciled in a state that levies an income tax. Nonetheless, if the seller's state has adopted a throwback rule, the sale is attributed to the seller's state and the transaction is subjected to a state-level tax.

Traditional IRA. See *Individual Retirement Account (IRA)*.

Transfer pricing. The process of setting internal prices for transfers of goods and services among related taxpayers. For example, what price should be used when Subsidiary purchases management services from Parent? The IRS can adjust transfer prices when it can show that the taxpayers were attempting to avoid tax by, for example, shifting losses, deductions, or credits from low-tax to high-tax entities or jurisdictions.

Transportation expenses. Expenses that include the cost of transporting the self-employed taxpayer (or employee) from one place to another in the course of business when the taxpayer is not in travel status. For tax years beginning after 2017 and before 2026, only reimbursed transportation expenses are deductible by employees. Commuting expenses are not deductible.

Travel expenses. Expenses that include meals (generally subject to a 50 percent disallowance) and lodging and transportation expenses while away from home in the pursuit of a trade or business (including that of an employee). For tax years beginning after 2017 and before 2026, only reimbursed travel expenses are deductible by employees.

Treaty shopping. An international investor attempts to use the favorable aspects of a tax treaty to his or her advantage, often elevating the form of the transaction over its substance (e.g., by establishing only a nominal presence in the country offering the favorable treaty terms).

U

UDITPA. The Uniform Division of Income for Tax Purposes Act has been adopted in some form by many of the states. The Act develops criteria by which the total taxable income of a multistate corporation can be assigned to specific states.

Unclaimed property. A U.S. state may have the right to acquire property that has been made available to an individual or legal entity for a fixed period of time, where the claimant has not taken possession of the property after a notice period. Examples of such property that a state could acquire are an uncashed payroll check or an unused gift card.

Unearned income. Income received but not yet earned. Normally, such income is taxed when received, even for accrual basis taxpayers.

Unified transfer tax. Rates applicable to transfers by gift and death made after 1976. § 2001(c).

Unified transfer tax credit. A credit allowed against any unified transfer tax. §§ 2010 and 2505.

Uniform capitalization (UNICAP) rules. Under § 263A, the Regulations provide a set of rules that all taxpayers (regardless of the particular industry) can use to determine the items of cost (and means of allocating those costs) that must be capitalized with respect to the production of tangible property. Small businesses, defined as those with average annual gross receipts in the prior three-year period of $25 million or less, that are not a tax shelter, are not required to use the UNICAP rules.

Unitary approach. See *unitary theory*.

Unitary theory. Sales, property, and payroll of related corporations are combined for nexus and apportionment purposes, and the worldwide income of the unitary entity is apportioned to the state. Subsidiaries and other affiliated corporations found to be part of the corporation's unitary business (because they are subject to overlapping ownership, operation, or management) are included in the apportionment procedure. This approach can be limited if a water's-edge election is in effect.

Unit-livestock-price method. A method of accounting for the cost of livestock. The livestock are valued using a standard cost of raising an animal with the characteristics of the animals on hand to the same age as those animals.

Unrealized receivables. Amounts earned by a cash basis taxpayer but not yet received. Because of the method of accounting used by the taxpayer, these amounts have a zero income tax basis. When unrealized receivables are distributed to a partner, they generally convert a transaction from nontaxable to taxable or an otherwise capital gain to ordinary income (i.e., as a "hot asset").

Unreasonable compensation. A deduction is allowed for "reasonable" salaries or other compensation for personal services actually rendered. The issue of unreasonable compensation usually is limited to closely held corporations, where the motivation is to pay out profits in some form that is deductible to the corporation. To the extent compensation is "excessive" ("unreasonable"), the distribution could be treated as a dividend, such that no deduction is allowed.

Unreasonable position. A tax preparer penalty is assessed regarding the understatement of a client's tax liability due to a tax return position that is found to be too aggressive. The penalty is avoided if there is substantial authority for the position or if the position is disclosed adequately on the tax return. The penalty equals the greater of $1,000 or one-half of the tax preparer's fee that is traceable to the aggressive position.

Unrecaptured § 1250 gain. Gain from the sale of depreciable real estate held more than one year. The gain is equal to or less than the depreciation taken on such property and is reduced by § 1245 and § 1250 gain.

Unrelated business income (UBI). Income recognized by an exempt organization that is generated from activities not related to the exempt purpose of the entity. For instance, the gift shop located in a hospital may generate unrelated business income. §§ 511 and 512.

Unrelated business income tax (UBIT). Levied on the unrelated business income of an exempt organization.

U.S. Court of Federal Claims. A trial court (court of original jurisdiction) that decides litigation involving Federal tax matters. Appeal from this court is to the Court of Appeals for the Federal Circuit.

U.S. District Court. A trial court for purposes of litigating Federal tax matters. It is the only trial court in which a jury trial can be obtained.

U.S. shareholder. For purposes of classification of an entity as a controlled foreign corporation, a U.S. person who owns, or is considered to own, 10 percent or more of the total combined voting power of all classes of voting stock of a foreign corporation. Stock owned directly, indirectly, and constructively is counted for this purpose.

U.S. Supreme Court. The highest appellate court or the court of last resort in the Federal court system and in most states. Only a small number of tax decisions of the U.S. Courts of Appeal are reviewed by the U.S. Supreme Court under its certiorari procedure. The Supreme Court usually grants certiorari to resolve a conflict among the Courts of Appeal (e.g., two or more appellate courts have assumed opposing positions on a particular issue) or when the tax issue is extremely important (e.g., size of the revenue loss to the Federal government).

U.S. Tax Court. One of four trial courts of original jurisdiction that decides litigation involving Federal income, death, or gift taxes. It is the only trial court where the taxpayer must not first pay the deficiency assessed by the IRS. The Tax Court will not have jurisdiction over a case unless a statutory notice of deficiency (90-day letter) has been issued by the IRS and the taxpayer files the petition for hearing within the time prescribed.

U.S. trade or business. A set of activities that is carried on in a regular, continuous, and substantial manner. A non-U.S. taxpayer is subject to U.S. tax on the taxable income that is effectively connected with a U.S. trade or business.

Use tax. A use tax is designed to complement the sales tax. The use tax has two purposes: to prevent consumers from evading sales tax by purchasing goods outside the state for instate use and to provide an equitable sales environment between in-state and out-of-state retailers. Purchasers of taxable goods or services who were not charged sales tax because the seller did not have a physical presence in the state, owe use tax on the purchase.

V

Vacation homes. The Code places restrictions upon taxpayers who rent their residences or vacation homes for part of the tax year. The restrictions may result in a scaling down of expense deductions for the taxpayers. § 280A.

Valuation allowance. Under ASC 740 (SFAS 109), a tax-related item is reported for book purposes only when it is more likely than not that the item actually will be realized. When the "more likely than not" test is failed, a contra-asset account is created to offset some or all of the related deferred tax asset. For instance, if the entity projects that it will not be able to use all of its net operating loss carryforward due to a lack of future taxable income, a valuation allowance is created to reduce the net deferred tax asset that corresponds to the carryforward. If income projections later change and it appears that the carryforward will be used, the valuation allowance is reversed or "released." Creation of a valuation allowance usually increases the current tax expense and thereby reduces current book income, and its release often increases book income in the later reporting period.

Value added tax (VAT). A national sales tax that taxes the increment in value as goods move through the production process. A VAT is much used in the majority of countries but has not yet been incorporated as part of the U.S. Federal tax structure.

Vesting requirements. A qualified deferred compensation arrangement must satisfy a vesting requirement. Under this provision, an employee's right to accrued plan benefits derived from employer contributions must be nonforfeitable in accordance with one of two vesting time period schedules (or two required alternate vesting schedules for certain employer matching contributions).

Voluntary revocation. The owners of a majority of shares in an S corporation elect to terminate the S status of the entity as of a specified date. The day on which the revocation is effective is the first day of the corporation's C tax year.

W

W–2 Wages/Capital Investment Limit. A limitation on the deduction for qualified business income that caps the deduction at the greater of (1) 50 percent of the wages paid by a qualified trade or business or (2) 25 percent of the wages paid by the qualified trade or business plus 2.5 percent of the taxpayer's share of the unadjusted basis of property used in the business that has not been fully depreciated prior to the close of the taxable year. § 199A(b)(2)(B).

Wash sale. A loss from the sale of stock or securities that is disallowed because the taxpayer, within 30 days before or after the sale, has acquired stock or securities substantially identical to those sold. § 1091.

Waters' edge. A limitation on the worldwide scope of the unitary theory. If a corporate waters'-edge election is in effect, the state can consider in the apportionment procedure only the activities that occur within the boundaries of the United States.

Waters'-edge election. See *waters' edge.*

Wherewithal to pay. This concept recognizes the inequity of taxing a transaction when the taxpayer lacks the means with which to pay the tax. Under it, there is a correlation between the imposition of the tax and the ability to pay the tax. It is particularly suited to situations in which the taxpayer's economic position has not changed significantly as a result of the transaction.

Whistleblower Program. An IRS initiative that offers special rewards to informants who provide evidence regarding tax evasion activities of businesses or high-income individuals. More than $2 million of tax, interest, and penalty must be at stake. The reward can reach 30 percent of the tax recovery that is attributable to the whistleblower's information.

Withholding allowances. The number of withholding allowances serves as the basis for determining the amount of income taxes withheld from an employee's salary or wages. The more withholding allowances claimed, the less income tax withheld by an employer. An employee may claim withholding allowances for personal exemptions for self and spouse (unless claimed as a dependent of another person), dependency exemptions, and special withholding allowances.

Work opportunity tax credit. Employers are allowed a tax credit equal to 40 percent of the first $6,000 of wages (per eligible employee) for the first year of employment. Eligible employees include certain hard-to-employ individuals (e.g., qualified ex-felons, high-risk youth, food stamp recipients, and veterans). The employer's deduction for wages is reduced by the amount of the credit taken. For qualified summer youth employees, the 40 percent rate is applied to the first $3,000 of qualified wages.

Working condition fringes. A type of fringe benefit received by the employee that is excludible from the employee's gross income. It consists of property or services provided (paid or reimbursed) by the employer for which the employee could take a tax deduction if the employee had paid for them. § 132.

Worthless securities. A loss (usually capital) is allowed for a security that becomes worthless during the year. The loss is deemed to have occurred on the last day of the year. Special rules apply to securities of affiliated companies and small business stock. § 165.

Writ of Certiorari. Appeal from a U.S. Court of Appeals to the U.S. Supreme Court is by Writ of Certiorari. The Supreme Court need not accept the appeal, and it usually does not (*cert. den.*) unless a conflict exists among the lower courts that must be resolved or a constitutional issue is involved.

Appendix D-1

Table of Code Sections Cited

Appendix D-2

Table of Regulations Cited

Treasury Regulations

Treasury Regulations

Appendix D-3

Table of Revenue Procedures and Revenue Rulings Cited

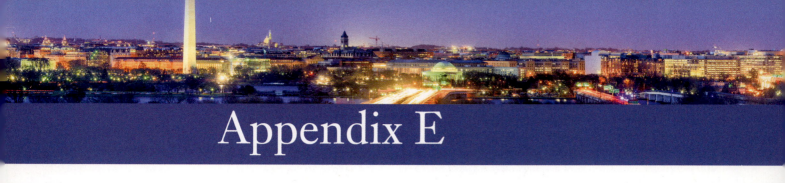

Appendix E

Table of Cases Cited

Appendix F

Present Value and Future Value Tables

Present Value of $1

N/R	1%	2%	3%	4%	5%	6%	7%	8%	9%	10%	11%	12%
1	0.9901	0.9804	0.9709	0.9615	0.9524	0.9434	0.9346	0.9259	0.9174	0.9091	0.9009	0.8929
2	0.9803	0.9612	0.9426	0.9246	0.9070	0.8900	0.8734	0.8573	0.8417	0.8264	0.8116	0.7972
3	0.9706	0.9423	0.9151	0.8890	0.8638	0.8396	0.8163	0.7938	0.7722	0.7513	0.7312	0.7118
4	0.9610	0.9238	0.8885	0.8548	0.8227	0.7921	0.7629	0.7350	0.7084	0.6830	0.6587	0.6355
5	0.9515	0.9057	0.8626	0.8219	0.7835	0.7473	0.7130	0.6806	0.6499	0.6209	0.5935	0.5674
6	0.9420	0.8880	0.8375	0.7903	0.7462	0.7050	0.6663	0.6302	0.5963	0.5645	0.5346	0.5066
7	0.9327	0.8706	0.8131	0.7599	0.7107	0.6651	0.6227	0.5835	0.5470	0.5132	0.4817	0.4523
8	0.9235	0.8535	0.7894	0.7307	0.6768	0.6274	0.5820	0.5403	0.5019	0.4665	0.4339	0.4039
9	0.9143	0.8368	0.7664	0.7026	0.6446	0.5919	0.5439	0.5002	0.4604	0.4241	0.3909	0.3606
10	0.9053	0.8203	0.7441	0.6756	0.6139	0.5584	0.5083	0.4632	0.4224	0.3855	0.3522	0.3220
11	0.8963	0.8043	0.7224	0.6496	0.5847	0.5268	0.4751	0.4289	0.3875	0.3505	0.3173	0.2875
12	0.8874	0.7885	0.7014	0.6246	0.5568	0.4970	0.4440	0.3971	0.3555	0.3186	0.2858	0.2567
13	0.8787	0.7730	0.6810	0.6006	0.5303	0.4688	0.4150	0.3677	0.3262	0.2897	0.2575	0.2292
14	0.8700	0.7579	0.6611	0.5775	0.5051	0.4423	0.3878	0.3405	0.2992	0.2633	0.2320	0.2046
15	0.8613	0.7430	0.6419	0.5553	0.4810	0.4173	0.3624	0.3152	0.2745	0.2394	0.2090	0.1827
16	0.8528	0.7284	0.6232	0.5339	0.4581	0.3936	0.3387	0.2919	0.2519	0.2176	0.1883	0.1631
17	0.8444	0.7142	0.6050	0.5134	0.4363	0.3714	0.3166	0.2703	0.2311	0.1978	0.1696	0.1456
18	0.8360	0.7002	0.5874	0.4936	0.4155	0.3503	0.2959	0.2502	0.2120	0.1799	0.1528	0.1300
19	0.8277	0.6864	0.5703	0.4746	0.3957	0.3305	0.2765	0.2317	0.1945	0.1635	0.1377	0.1161
20	0.8195	0.6730	0.5537	0.4564	0.3769	0.3118	0.2584	0.2145	0.1784	0.1486	0.1240	0.1037

Present Value of an Ordinary Annuity of $1

N/R	1%	2%	3%	4%	5%	6%	7%	8%	9%	10%	11%	12%
1	0.9901	0.9804	0.9709	0.9615	0.9524	0.9434	0.9346	0.9259	0.9174	0.9091	0.9009	0.8929
2	1.9704	1.9416	1.9135	1.8861	1.8594	1.8334	1.8080	1.7833	1.7591	1.7355	1.7125	1.6901
3	2.9410	2.8839	2.8286	2.7751	2.7232	2.6730	2.6243	2.5771	2.5313	2.4869	2.4437	2.4018
4	3.9020	3.8077	3.7171	3.6299	3.5460	3.4651	3.3872	3.3121	3.2397	3.1699	3.1024	3.0373
5	4.8534	4.7135	4.5797	4.4518	4.3295	4.2124	4.1002	3.9927	3.8897	3.7908	3.6959	3.6048
6	5.7955	5.6014	5.4172	5.2421	5.0757	4.9173	4.7665	4.6229	4.4859	4.3553	4.2305	4.1114
7	6.7282	6.4720	6.2303	6.0021	5.7864	5.5824	5.3893	5.2064	5.0330	4.8684	4.7122	4.5638
8	7.6517	7.3255	7.0197	6.7327	6.4632	6.2098	5.9713	5.7466	5.5348	5.3349	5.1461	4.9676
9	8.5660	8.1622	7.7861	7.4353	7.1078	6.8017	6.5152	6.2469	5.9952	5.7590	5.5370	5.3282
10	9.4713	8.9826	8.5302	8.1109	7.7217	7.3601	7.0236	6.7101	6.4177	6.1446	5.8892	5.6502
11	10.3676	9.7868	9.2526	8.7605	8.3064	7.8869	7.4987	7.1390	6.8052	6.4951	6.2065	5.9377
12	11.2551	10.5753	9.9540	9.3851	8.8633	8.3838	7.9427	7.5361	7.1607	6.8137	6.4924	6.1944
13	12.1337	11.3484	10.6350	9.9856	9.3936	8.8527	8.3577	7.9038	7.4869	7.1034	6.7499	6.4235
14	13.0037	12.1062	11.2961	10.5631	9.8986	9.2950	8.7455	8.2442	7.7862	7.3667	6.9819	6.6282
15	13.8651	12.8493	11.9379	11.1184	10.3797	9.7122	9.1079	8.5595	8.0607	7.6061	7.1909	6.8109
16	14.7179	13.5777	12.5611	11.6523	10.8378	10.1059	9.4466	8.8514	8.3126	7.8237	7.3792	6.9740
17	15.5623	14.2919	13.1661	12.1657	11.2741	10.4773	9.7632	9.1216	8.5436	8.0216	7.5488	7.1196
18	16.3983	14.9920	13.7535	12.6593	11.6896	10.8276	10.0591	9.3719	8.7556	8.2014	7.7016	7.2497
19	17.2260	15.6785	14.3238	13.1339	12.0853	11.1581	10.3356	9.6036	8.9501	8.3649	7.8393	7.3658
20	18.0456	16.3514	14.8775	13.5903	12.4622	11.4699	10.5940	9.8181	9.1285	8.5136	7.9633	7.4694

Future Value of $1

N/R	1%	2%	3%	4%	5%	6%	7%	8%	9%	10%	11%	12%
1	1.0100	1.0200	1.0300	1.0400	1.0500	1.0600	1.0700	1.0800	1.0900	1.1000	1.1100	1.1200
2	1.0201	1.0404	1.0609	1.0816	1.1025	1.1236	1.1449	1.1664	1.1881	1.2100	1.2321	1.2544
3	1.0303	1.0612	1.0927	1.1249	1.1576	1.1910	1.2250	1.2597	1.2950	1.3310	1.3676	1.4049
4	1.0406	1.0824	1.1255	1.1699	1.2155	1.2625	1.3108	1.3605	1.4116	1.4641	1.5181	1.5735
5	1.0510	1.1041	1.1593	1.2167	1.2763	1.3382	1.4026	1.4693	1.5386	1.6105	1.6851	1.7623
6	1.0615	1.1262	1.1941	1.2653	1.3401	1.4185	1.5007	1.5869	1.6771	1.7716	1.8704	1.9738
7	1.0721	1.1487	1.2299	1.3159	1.4071	1.5036	1.6058	1.7138	1.8280	1.9487	2.0762	2.2107
8	1.0829	1.1717	1.2668	1.3686	1.4775	1.5938	1.7182	1.8509	1.9926	2.1436	2.3045	2.4760
9	1.0937	1.1951	1.3048	1.4233	1.5513	1.6895	1.8385	1.9990	2.1719	2.3579	2.5580	2.7731
10	1.1046	1.2190	1.3439	1.4802	1.6289	1.7908	1.9672	2.1589	2.3674	2.5937	2.8394	3.1058
11	1.1157	1.2434	1.3842	1.5395	1.7103	1.8983	2.1049	2.3316	2.5804	2.8531	3.1518	3.4785
12	1.1268	1.2682	1.4258	1.6010	1.7959	2.0122	2.2522	2.5182	2.8127	3.1384	3.4985	3.8960
13	1.1381	1.2936	1.4685	1.6651	1.8856	2.1329	2.4098	2.7196	3.0658	3.4523	3.8833	4.3635
14	1.1495	1.3195	1.5126	1.7317	1.9799	2.2609	2.5785	2.9372	3.3417	3.7975	4.3104	4.8871
15	1.1610	1.3459	1.5580	1.8009	2.0789	2.3966	2.7590	3.1722	3.6425	4.1772	4.7846	5.4736
16	1.1726	1.3728	1.6047	1.8730	2.1829	2.5404	2.9522	3.4259	3.9703	4.5950	5.3109	6.1304
17	1.1843	1.4002	1.6528	1.9479	2.2920	2.6928	3.1588	3.7000	4.3276	5.0545	5.8951	6.8660
18	1.1961	1.4282	1.7024	2.0258	2.4066	2.8543	3.3799	3.9960	4.7171	5.5599	6.5436	7.6900
19	1.2081	1.4568	1.7535	2.1068	2.5270	3.0256	3.6165	4.3157	5.1417	6.1159	7.2633	8.6128
20	1.2202	1.4859	1.8061	2.1911	2.6533	3.2071	3.8697	4.6610	5.6044	6.7275	8.0623	9.6463

Future Value of an Ordinary Annuity of $1

N/R	1%	2%	3%	4%	5%	6%	7%	8%	9%	10%	11%	12%
1	1.0000	1.0000	1.0000	1.0000	1.0000	1.0000	1.0000	1.0000	1.0000	1.0000	1.0000	1.0000
2	2.0100	2.0200	2.0300	2.0400	2.0500	2.0600	2.0700	2.0800	2.0900	2.1000	2.1100	2.1200
3	3.0301	3.0604	3.0909	3.1216	3.1525	3.1836	3.2149	3.2464	3.2781	3.3100	3.3421	3.3744
4	4.0604	4.1216	4.1836	4.2465	4.3101	4.3746	4.4399	4.5061	4.5731	4.6410	4.7097	4.7793
5	5.1010	5.2040	5.3091	5.4163	5.5256	5.6371	5.7507	5.8666	5.9847	6.1051	6.2278	6.3528
6	6.1520	6.3081	6.4684	6.6330	6.8019	6.9753	7.1533	7.3359	7.5233	7.7156	7.9129	8.1152
7	7.2135	7.4343	7.6625	7.8983	8.1420	8.3938	8.6540	8.9228	9.2004	9.4872	9.7833	10.0890
8	8.2857	8.5830	8.8923	9.2142	9.5491	9.8975	10.2598	10.6366	11.0285	11.4359	11.8594	12.2997
9	9.3685	9.7546	10.1591	10.5828	11.0266	11.4913	11.9780	12.4876	13.0210	13.5795	14.1640	14.7757
10	10.4622	10.9497	11.4639	12.0061	12.5779	13.1808	13.8164	14.4866	15.1929	15.9374	16.7220	17.5487
11	11.5668	12.1687	12.8078	13.4864	14.2068	14.9716	15.7836	16.6455	17.5603	18.5312	19.5614	20.6546
12	12.6825	13.4121	14.1920	15.0258	15.9171	16.8699	17.8885	18.9771	20.1407	21.3843	22.7132	24.1331
13	13.8093	14.6803	15.6178	16.6268	17.7130	18.8821	20.1406	21.4953	22.9534	24.5227	26.2116	28.0291
14	14.9474	15.9739	17.0863	18.2919	19.5986	21.0151	22.5505	24.2149	26.0192	27.9750	30.0949	32.3926
15	16.0969	17.2934	18.5989	20.0236	21.5786	23.2760	25.1290	27.1521	29.3609	31.7725	34.4054	37.2797
16	17.2579	18.6393	20.1569	21.8245	23.6575	25.6725	27.8881	30.3243	33.0034	35.9497	39.1899	42.7533
17	18.4304	20.0121	21.7616	23.6975	25.8404	28.2129	30.8402	33.7502	36.9737	40.5447	44.5008	48.8837
18	19.6147	21.4123	23.4144	25.6454	28.1324	30.9057	33.9990	37.4502	41.3013	45.5992	50.3959	55.7497
19	20.8109	22.8406	25.1169	27.6712	30.5390	33.7600	37.3790	41.4463	46.0185	51.1591	56.9395	63.4397
20	22.0190	24.2974	26.8704	29.7781	33.0660	36.7856	40.9955	45.7620	51.1601	57.2750	64.2028	72.0524

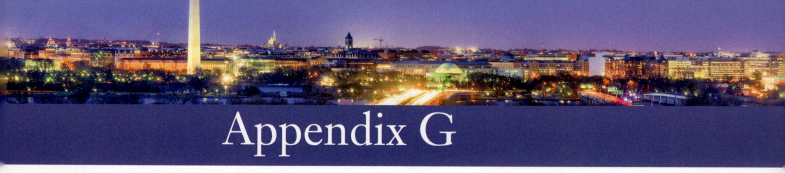

Appendix G

Tax Formulas

Income Tax Rates—Estates and Trusts

Tax Year 2019

Taxable Income		The Tax Is:	Of the Amount
Over—	But not Over—		Over—
$ 0	$ 2,600	10%	$ 0
2,600	9,300	$ 260.00 + 24%	2,600
9,300	12,750	1868.00 + 35%	9,300
12,750	....	3,075.50 + 37%	12,750

Income Tax Rates—C Corporations, 2018 and after

For all income levels, the tax rate is 21%.

Tax Formula for Corporate Taxpayers

Income *(from whatever source)*...............................	$ xxx,xxx
Less: Exclusions from gross income........................	− xx,xxx
Gross Income...	$ xxx,xxx
Less: Deductions...	− xx,xxx
Taxable Income...	$ xxx,xxx
Applicable tax rates......................................	× xx%
Gross Tax..	$ xx,xxx
Less: Tax credits and prepayments.........................	− x,xxx
Tax Due *(or refund)*.......................................	$ xx,xxx

Unified Transfer Tax Rates

For Gifts Made and for Deaths after 2012

If the Amount with Respect to Which the Tentative Tax to Be Computed Is:	The Tentative Tax Is:
Not over $10,000	18 percent of such amount.
Over $10,000 but not over $20,000	$1,800, plus 20 percent of the excess of such amount over $10,000.
Over $20,000 but not over $40,000	$3,800, plus 22 percent of the excess of such amount over $20,000.
Over $40,000 but not over $60,000	$8,200, plus 24 percent of the excess of such amount over $40,000.
Over $60,000 but not over $80,000	$13,000, plus 26 percent of the excess of such amount over $60,000.
Over $80,000 but not over $100,000	$18,200, plus 28 percent of the excess of such amount over $80,000.
Over $100,000 but not over $150,000	$23,800, plus 30 percent of the excess of such amount over $100,000.
Over $150,000 but not over $250,000	$38,800, plus 32 percent of the excess of such amount over $150,000.
Over $250,000 but not over $500,000	$70,800, plus 34 percent of the excess of such amount over $250,000.
Over $500,000 but not over $750,000	$155,800, plus 37 percent of the excess of such amount over $500,000.
Over $750,000 but not over $1,000,000	$248,300, plus 39 percent of the excess of such amount over $750,000.
Over $1,000,000	$345,800, plus 40 percent of the excess of such amount over $1,000,000.

Index

A

AAA. *See* Accumulated adjustments account
Accelerated depreciation method, **14**:4
Acceleration rule, **8**:25
Accounting concepts, reconciling of, **1**:13
Accounting data, flow of, **14**:3
Accounting methods
  book-tax differences, **14**:4–5
  consolidated tax returns, **8**:13
  corporations, **3**:4–5
  for trusts and estates, **20**:6
  partnership, **10**:13–14
Accounting periods
  consolidated tax returns, **8**:13
  corporations, **3**:4
  for trusts and estates, **20**:6
Accrual basis corporations, charitable
    contributions, **3**:10
Accrual basis taxpayer, **3**:5
Accrual method of accounting,
    corporations, **3**:5
Accrued income and expenses, book-tax
    differences, **14**:4
Accumulated adjustments account (AAA),
    12:14–16, **12**:27, **13**:14
  adjustments to corporate, **12**:15
  bypass election, **12**:16
Accumulated E & P, **5**:8, **12**:14
  allocating to distributions in
    chronological order, **5**:9
Accumulated earnings and profit (AEP). *See*
    Accumulated E & P
Accumulated earnings tax, **3**:20, **3**:39
  rate, closely held C corporations and,
    13:10
Accuracy-related penalties, **9**:12, **17**:15
  for substantial estate or gift tax valuation
    understatements, **17**:17
  in § 6662, **1**:36
Acquiescence (A or Acq.), **1**:26
Acquisition
  prescription to lower taxes has expired,
    global tax issues, **7**:19
  when it fails, **7**:20
Acquisition indebtedness, definition of,
    15:19
Acquisitive, summary of advantages and
    disadvantages, **7**:16
Action on Decision, **1**:26, **1**:35
Ad valorem penalties, **17**:14
Ad valorem (property) taxes, other state
    and local taxes of a multistate
    corporation, **16**:25
Additional tax on net investment income,
    20:8, **20**:29
Adjusted gross estate, **19**:21

Adjusted taxable income, business interest
    expense limitation and, **3**:8
Administration and anti-abuse, partnerships,
    11:30
Administrative proceeding or court
    decision, recognition of, SSTS No. 5,
    17:29
Administrative sources of tax law, **1**:17–20
  assessing the validity of other, **1**:35
  other administrative pronouncements,
    1:19–20
  Revenue Rulings and Revenue
    Procedures, **1**:18–19
  Treasury Department Regulations,
    1:17–18
Administrative taxes, **16**:25
Advance Pricing Agreement (APA) program,
    9:12
Adverse party, grantor trust, **20**:24
Affiliated group, **8**:6, **8**:7
  comparison of tax effects available
    to, **8**:8
  vs. controlled group, **8**:7–9
Affiliations Schedule, Form 851, **8**:11
Affordable Care Act, **17**:2
  tax rules included in, **13**:18
Aggregate (or conduit) concept, **10**:4–5
Aggregate net built-in gain, **12**:23
AICPA
  Code of Professional Conduct, **17**:27
  statements on standards for tax services,
    17:27–29
Allocate, **16**:8
Allocation, **16**:8
  conduit vs. entity treatment effect of
    special, **13**:16
  of items to income or corpus, **20**:11
  related to contributed property, **10**:11
Allocation and apportionment of
    deductions, **9**:9–10
Allocation and apportionment of
    income of multistate corporations,
    16:8–18
  apportionment procedure, **16**:9
  apportionable income, **16**:9–11
  apportionment factors: elements and
    planning, **16**:11–12
  sales factor, **16**:13–14
  payroll factor, **16**:14–16
  property factor, **16**:16–18
Allocation of income and loss in
    S corporations, **12**:13–14
Alternate valuation date, **18**:5
Alternative depreciation system (ADS),
    computing E & P, **5**:5
Alternative minimum tax
  business entities, **13**:6
  C corporation repeal of, **14**:21

corporate income tax liability, **3**:19
  income taxation of individuals and
    corporations compared, **3**:18
  tax planning for individual, **5**:23
  trusts and estates, **20**:7–8
Alternative minimum taxable income
    (AMTI), **20**:7–8
  QBI and, **2**:30
American Federal Tax Reports (AFTR),
    1:26–27
Amortization of organizational expenditures
    under Section 248, **3**:16
Analysis of Net Income (Loss), **10**:23
Analysis of unappropriated retained
    earnings per books, Schedule M-2,
    3:23
Annotated, **1**:28
Annual accounting period concept,
    mitigating the effect of, **1**:6–8
Annual exclusion, **18**:10–11
  minimizing gift taxes, **19**:14
Annual gift tax exclusion, GSTT, **18**:26
Annuity contracts, family tax planning
    valuation of, **19**:4
Anti-loss duplication rule, **4**:15
Antistuffing loss disallowance rules,
    summary of, **6**:19
Antistuffing rules, **6**:16–20
  built-in loss limitation, **6**:18–20
  related-party loss limitation, **6**:17–18
Appeals, **1**:22
Appellate courts, **1**:22–24, **1**:35–36
Apportion, **16**:8
Apportionable income, **16**:9–11, **16**:12
Apportionment, **16**:8
  factors, elements and planning, **16**:11–12,
    16:31–32
  formulas, using, **16**:21
  of income of a multistate corporation, tax
    planning for, **16**:30–31
  procedure, **16**:9
Appraiser's penalty, **17**:17
Appreciated inventory, **11**:11
Arm's length, **1**:11
ASC 740, **14**:8, **14**:9, **14**:12–13
  balance sheet approach to deferred taxes,
    14:9
ASC 740-10, Accounting for Uncertainty in
    Income Taxes, **14**:17–19
  disclosures under, **14**:18
Assessable penalties, **17**:14
Assessment and the statute of limitations,
    17:21
Asset Depreciation Range (ADR), **5**:5
Asset ownership, separate and joint, transfer
    taxes, **18**:6–7
Asset purchase vs. stock purchase, tax
    planning for, **6**:27